Lecture Notes in Computer Science 11727

More information about this series at http://www.springer.com/series/7407

Igor V. Tetko · Věra Kůrková ·
Pavel Karpov · Fabian Theis (Eds.)

Artificial Neural Networks and Machine Learning – ICANN 2019

Theoretical Neural Computation

28th International Conference on Artificial Neural Networks
Munich, Germany, September 17–19, 2019
Proceedings, Part I

Springer

Editors
Igor V. Tetko
Helmholtz Zentrum München - Deutsches Forschungszentrum für Gesundheit und Umwelt (GmbH)
Neuherberg, Germany

Pavel Karpov
Helmholtz Zentrum München - Deutsches Forschungszentrum für Gesundheit und Umwelt (GmbH)
Neuherberg, Germany

Věra Kůrková
Institute of Computer Science
Czech Academy of Sciences
Prague 8, Czech Republic

Fabian Theis
Helmholtz Zentrum München - Deutsches Forschungszentrum für Gesundheit und Umwelt (GmbH)
Neuherberg, Germany

ISSN 0302-9743 ISSN 1611-3349 (electronic)
Lecture Notes in Computer Science
ISBN 978-3-030-30486-7 ISBN 978-3-030-30487-4 (eBook)
https://doi.org/10.1007/978-3-030-30487-4

LNCS Sublibrary: SL1 – Theoretical Computer Science and General Issues

This Springer imprint is published by the registered company Springer Nature Switzerland AG
The registered company address is: Gewerbestrasse 11, 6330 Cham, Switzerland

Preface

The fast development of machine learning methods is influencing all aspects of our life and reaching new horizons of what we have previously considered being Artificial Intelligence (AI). Examples include autonomous car driving, virtual assistants, automated customer support, clinical decision support, healthcare data analytics, financial forecast, and smart devices in the home, to name a few, which contribute to the dramatic improvement in the quality of our lives. These developments, however, also bring risks for significant hazards, which were not imaginable previously, e.g., falsification of voice, videos, or even manipulation of people's opinions during elections. Many such developments become possible due to the appearance of large volumes of data ("Big Data"). These proceedings include the theory and applications of algorithms behind these developments, many of which were inspired by the functioning of the brain.

The International Conference on Artificial Neural Networks (ICANN) is the annual flagship conference of the European Neural Network Society (ENNS). The 28th International Conference on Artificial Neural Networks (ICANN 2019) was co-organized with the final conference of the Marie Skłodowska-Curie Innovative Training Network European Industrial Doctorate "Big Data in Chemistry" (http://bigchem.eu) project coordinated by Helmholtz Zentrum München (GmbH) to promote the use of machine learning in Chemistry. The conference featured the main tracks "Brain-Inspired Computing" and "Machine Learning Research." Within the conference the First International Workshop on Reservoir Computing as well as five special sessions were organized, namely:

Artificial Intelligence in Medicine
Informed and Explainable Methods for Machine Learning
Deep Learning in Image Reconstruction
Machine Learning with Graphs: Algorithms and Applications
BIGCHEM: Big Data and AI in chemistry

A Challenge for Automatic Dog Age Estimation (DogAge) also took place as part of the conference. The conference covered all main research fields dealing with neural networks. ICANN 2019 was held during September 17–19, 2019, at Klinikum rechts der Isar der Technische Universität München, Munich, Germany.

Following a long-standing tradition, the proceedings of the conference were published as Springer volumes belonging to the *Lecture Notes in Computer Science* series. The conference had a historical record of 494 article submissions. The papers went through a two-step peer-review process by at least two and in majority of cases by three or four independent referees. In total, 503 Program Committee (PC) members and reviewers participated in this process. The majority of PC members had Doctoral degrees (88%) and 52% of them were also Professors. These reviewers were assigned 46 articles. The others were PhD students in the last years of their studies, who reviewed one to two articles each. In total, for the 323 accepted articles, 975 and 985 reports were submitted for the first and the second revision sessions. Thus, on average, each accepted article received 6.1 reports. A list of reviewers/PC Members, who agreed to publish their names, are included in these proceedings.

Based on the reviewers' comments, 202 articles were accepted and more than 100 articles were rejected after the first review. The remaining articles received an undecided status. The authors of the accepted articles as well as of those with undecided status were requested to address the reviewers' comments within two weeks. On the basis of second reviewers' feedback, another 121 articles were accepted and the authors were requested to include reviewers' remarks into the final upload. Based on these evaluations, diversity of topics, as well as recommendations of reviewers, special session organizers, and PC Chairs, 120 articles were selected for oral presentations. Out of the total number of 323 accepted articles (65% of initially submitted), 46 manuscripts were short articles with a length of five pages each, while the others were full articles with an average length of 13 pages.

The accepted papers of the 28th ICANN conference were published as five volumes:

Volume I Theoretical Neural Computation
Volume II Deep Learning
Volume III Image Processing
Volume IV Text and Time series analysis
Volume V Workshop and Special Sessions

The authors of accepted articles came from 50 different countries. While the majority of the articles were from academic researchers, the conference also attracted contributions from manifold industries including automobile (Volkswagen, BMW, Honda, Toyota), multinational conglomerates (Hitachi, Mitsubishi), electronics (Philips), electrical systems (Thales), mobile (Samsung, Huawei, Nokia, Orange), software (Microsoft), multinational (Amazon) and global travel technology (Expedia), information (IBM), large (AstraZeneca, Boehringer Ingelheim) and medium (Idorsia Pharmaceuticals Ltd.) pharma companies, fragrance and flavor (Firmenich), architectural (Shimizu), weather forecast (Beijing Giant Weather Co.), robotics (UBTECH Robotics Corp., SoftBank Robotics Group Corp.), contract research organization (Lead Discovery Center GmbH), private credit bureau (Schufa), as well as multiple startups. This wide involvement of companies reflects the increasing use of artificial neural networks by the industry. Five keynote speakers were invited to give lectures on the timely aspects of intelligent robot design (gentle robots), nonlinear dynamical analysis of brain activity, deep learning in biology and biomedicine, explainable AI, artificial curiosity, and meta-learning machines.

These proceedings provide a comprehensive and up-to-date coverage of the dynamically developing field of Artificial Neural Networks. They are of major interest both for theoreticians as well as for applied scientists who are looking for new innovative approaches to solve their practical problems. We sincerely thank the Program and Steering Committee and the reviewers for their invaluable work.

September 2019

Igor V. Tetko
Fabian Theis
Pavel Karpov
Věra Kůrková

Organization

General Chairs

Igor V. Tetko	Helmholtz Zentrum München (GmbH), Germany
Fabian Theis	Helmholtz Zentrum München (GmbH), Germany

Honorary Chair

Věra Kůrková (ENNS President)	Czech Academy of Sciences, Czech Republic

Publication Chair

Pavel Karpov	Helmholtz Zentrum München (GmbH), Germany

Local Organizing Committee Chairs

Monica Campillos	Helmholtz Zentrum München (GmbH), Germany
Alessandra Lintas	University of Lausanne, Switzerland

Communication Chair

Paolo Masulli	Technical University of Denmark, Denmark

Steering Committee

Erkki Oja	Aalto University, Finland
Wlodzislaw Duch	Nicolaus Copernicus University, Poland
Alessandro Villa	University of Lausanne, Switzerland
Cesare Alippi	Politecnico di Milano, Italy, and Università della Svizzera italiana, Switzerland
Jérémie Cabessa	Université Paris 2 Panthéon-Assas, France
Maxim Fedorov	Skoltech, Russia
Barbara Hammer	Bielefeld University, Germany
Lazaros Iliadis	Democritus University of Thrace, Greece
Petia Koprinkova-Hristova	Bulgarian Academy of Sciences, Bulgaria
Antonis Papaleonidas	Democritus University of Thrace, Greece
Jaakko Peltonen	University of Tampere, Finland
Antonio Javier Pons Rivero	Universitat Politècnica de Catalunya, Spain
Yifat Prut	The Hebrew University Jerusalem, Israel
Paul F. M. J. Verschure	Catalan Institute of Advanced Studies, Spain
Francisco Zamora-Martínez	Veridas Digital Authentication Solutions SL, Spain

Program Committee

Nesreen Ahmed	Intel Labs, USA
Narges Ahmidi	Helmholtz Zentrum München (GmbH), Germany
Tetiana Aksenova	Commissariat à l'énergie atomique et aux énergies alternatives, France
Elie Aljalbout	Technical University Munich, Germany
Piotr Antonik	CentraleSupélec, France
Juan Manuel Moreno-Arostegui	Universitat Politècnica de Catalunya, Spain
Michael Aupetit	Qatar Computing Research Institute, Qatar
Cristian Axenie	Huawei German Research Center Munich, Germany
Davide Bacciu	University of Pisa, Italy
Noa Barbiro	Booking.com, Israel
Igor Baskin	Moscow State University, Russia
Christian Bauckhage	Fraunhofer IAIS, Germany
Costas Bekas	IBM Research, Switzerland
Barry Bentley	The Open University, UK
Daniel Berrar	Tokyo Institute of Technology, Japan
Soma Bhattacharya	Expedia, USA
Monica Bianchini	Università degli Studi di Siena, Italy
François Blayo	NeoInstinct, Switzerland
Sander Bohte	Centrum Wiskunde & Informatica, The Netherlands
András P. Borosy	QualySense AG, Switzerland
Giosuè Lo Bosco	Universita' di Palermo, Italy
Farah Bouakrif	University of Jijel, Algeria
Larbi Boubchir	University Paris 8, France
Maria Paula Brito	University of Porto, Portugal
Evgeny Burnaev	Skoltech, Russia
Mikhail Burtsev	Moscow Institute of Physics and Technology, Russia
Jérémie Cabessa	Université Panthéon Assas (Paris II), France
Francisco de Assis Tenório de Carvalho	Universidade Federal de Pernambuco, Brazil
Wolfgang Graf zu Castell-Ruedenhausen	Helmholtz Zentrum München (GmbH), Germany
Stephan Chalup	University of Newcastle, Australia
Hongming Chen	AstraZeneca, Sweden
Artem Cherkasov	University of British Columbia, Canada
Sylvain Chevallier	Université de Versailles, France
Vladimir Chupakhin	Janssen Pharmaceutical Companies, USA
Djork-Arné Clevert	Bayer, Germany
Paulo Cortez	University of Minho, Portugal
Gennady Cymbalyuk	Georgia State University, USA
Maximilien Danisch	Pierre and Marie Curie University, France
Tirtharaj Dash	Birla Institute of Technology and Science Pilani, India
Tyler Derr	Michigan State University, USA

Sergey Dolenko	Moscow State University, Russia
Shirin Dora	University of Amsterdam, The Netherlands
Werner Dubitzky	Helmholtz Zentrum München (GmbH), Germany
Wlodzislaw Duch	Nicolaus Copernicus University, Poland
Ujjal Kr Dutta	Indian Institute of Technology Madras, India
Mohamed El-Sharkawy	Purdue School of Engineering and Technology, USA
Mohamed Elati	Université de Lille, France
Reda Elbasiony	Tanta University, Egypt
Mark Embrechts	Rensselaer Polytechnic Institute, USA
Sebastian Engelke	University of Geneva, Switzerland
Ola Engkvist	AstraZeneca, Sweden
Manfred Eppe	University of Hamburg, Germany
Peter Erdi	Kalamazoo College, USA
Peter Ertl	Novartis Institutes for BioMedical Research, Switzerland
Igor Farkaš	Comenius University in Bratislava, Slovakia
Maxim Fedorov	Skoltech, Russia
Maurizio Fiasché	F-engineering Consulting, Italy
Marco Frasca	University of Milan, Italy
Benoît Frénay	Université de Namur, Belgium
Claudio Gallicchio	Università di Pisa, Italy
Udayan Ganguly	Indian Institute of Technology at Bombay, India
Tiantian Gao	Stony Brook University, USA
Juantomás García	Sngular, Spain
José García-Rodríguez	University of Alicante, Spain
Erol Gelenbe	Institute of Theoretical and Applied Informatics, Poland
Petia Georgieva	University of Aveiro, Portugal
Sajjad Gharaghani	University of Tehran, Iran
Evgin Goceri	Akdeniz University, Turkey
Alexander Gorban	University of Leicester, UK
Marco Gori	Università degli Studi di Siena, Italy
Denise Gorse	University College London, UK
Lyudmila Grigoryeva	University of Konstanz, Germany
Xiaodong Gu	Fudan University, China
Michael Guckert	Technische Hochschule Mittelhessen, Germany
Benjamin Guedj	Inria, France, and UCL, UK
Tatiana Valentine Guy	Institute of Information Theory and Automation, Czech Republic
Fabian Hadiji	Goedle.io, Germany
Abir Hadriche	University of Sfax, Tunisia
Barbara Hammer	Bielefeld University, Germany
Stefan Haufe	ERC Research Group Leader at Charité, Germany
Dominik Heider	Philipps-University of Marburg, Germany
Matthias Heinig	Helmholtz Zentrum München (GmbH), Germany
Christoph Henkelmann	DIVISIO GmbH, Germany

Jean Benoit Héroux	IBM Research, Japan
Christian Hidber	bSquare AG, Switzerland
Martin Holeňa	Institute of Computer Science, Czech Republic
Adrian Horzyk	AGH University of Science and Technology, Poland
Jian Hou	Bohai University, China
Lynn Houthuys	Thomas More, Belgium
Brian Hyland	University of Otago, New Zealand
Nicolangelo Iannella	University of Oslo, Norway
Lazaros Iliadis	Democritus University of Thrace, Greece
Francesco Iorio	Wellcome Trust Sanger Institute, UK
Olexandr Isayev	University of North Carolina at Chapel Hill, USA
Keiichi Ito	Helmholtz Zentrum München (GmbH), Germany
Nils Jansen	Radboud University Nijmegen, The Netherlands
Noman Javed	Université d'Orléans, France
Wenbin Jiang	Huazhong University of Science and Technology, China
Jan Kalina	Institute of Computer Science, Czech Republic
Argyris Kalogeratos	Université Paris-Saclay, France
Michael Kamp	Fraunhofer IAIS, Germany
Dmitry Karlov	Skoltech, Russia
Pavel Karpov	Helmholtz Zentrum München (GmbH), Germany
John Kelleher	Technological University Dublin, Ireland
Adil Mehmood Khan	Innopolis, Russia
Rainer Kiko	GEOMAR Helmholtz-Zentrum für Ozeanforschung, Germany
Christina Klüver	Universität Duisburg-Essen, Germany
Taisuke Kobayashi	Nara Institute of Science and Technology, Japan
Ekaterina Komendantskaya	University of Dundee, UK
Petia Koprinkova-Hristova	Bulgarian Academy of Sciences, Bulgaria
Irena Koprinska	University of Sydney, Australia
Constantine Kotropoulos	Aristotle University of Thessaloniki, Greece
Ilias Kotsireas	Wilfrid Laurier University, Canada
Athanasios Koutras	University of Peloponnese, Greece
Piotr Kowalski	AGH University of Science and Technology, Poland
Valentin Kozlov	Karlsruher Institut für Technologie, Germany
Dean J. Krusienski	Virginia Commonwealth University, USA
Adam Krzyzak	Concordia University, Canada
Hanna Kujawska	University of Bergen, Norway
Věra Kůrková	Institute of Computer Science, Czech Republic
Sumit Kushwaha	Kamla Nehru Institute of Technology, India
Anna Ladi	Fraunhofer IAIS, Germany
Ward Van Laer	Ixor, Belgium
Oliver Lange	Google Inc., USA
Jiyi Li	University of Yamanashi, Japan
Lei Li	Beijing University of Posts and Telecommunications, China

Spiros Likothanassis	University of Patras, Greece
Christian Limberg	Universität Bielefeld, Germany
Alessandra Lintas	University of Lausanne, Switzerland
Viktor Liviniuk	MIT, USA, and Skoltech, Russia
Doina Logofatu	Frankfurt University of Applied Sciences, Germany
Vincenzo Lomonaco	Università di Bologna, Italy
Sock Ching Low	Institute for Bioengineering of Catalonia, Spain
Abhijit Mahalunkar	Technological University Dublin, Ireland
Mufti Mahmud	Nottingham Trent University, UK
Alexander Makarenko	National Technical University of Ukraine - Kiev Polytechnic Institute, Ukraine
Kleanthis Malialis	University of Cyprus, Cyprus
Fragkiskos Malliaros	University of Paris-Saclay, France
Gilles Marcou	University of Strasbourg, France
Urszula Markowska-Kaczmar	Wroclaw University of Technology, Poland
Carsten Marr	Helmholtz Zentrum München (GmbH), Germany
Giuseppe Marra	University of Firenze, Italy
Paolo Masulli	Technical University of Denmark, Denmark
Siamak Mehrkanoon	Maastricht University, The Netherlands
Stefano Melacci	Università degli Studi di Siena, Italy
Michael Menden	Helmholtz Zentrum München (GmbH), Germany
Sebastian Mika	Comtravo, Germany
Nikolaos Mitianoudis	Democritus University of Thrace, Greece
Valeri Mladenov	Technical University of Sofia, Bulgaria
Hebatallah Mohamed	Università degli Studi Roma, Italy
Figlu Mohanty	International Institute of Information Technology at Bhubaneswar, India
Francesco Carlo Morabito	University of Reggio Calabria, Italy
Jerzy Mościński	Silesian University of Technology, Poland
Henning Müller	University of Applied Sciences Western Switzerland, Switzerland
Maria-Viorela Muntean	University of Alba-Iulia, Romania
Phivos Mylonas	Ionian University, Greece
Shinichi Nakajima	Technische Universität Berlin, Germany
Kohei Nakajima	University of Tokyo, Japan
Chi Nhan Nguyen	Itemis, Germany
Florian Nigsch	Novartis Institutes for BioMedical Research, Switzerland
Giannis Nikolentzos	École Polytechnique, France
Ikuko Nishikawa	Ritsumeikan University, Japan
Harri Niska	University of Eastern Finland
Hasna Njah	ISIM-Sfax, Tunisia
Dimitri Nowicki	Institute of Cybernetics of NASU, Ukraine
Alessandro Di Nuovo	Sheffield Hallam University, UK
Stefan Oehmcke	University of Copenhagen, Denmark

Erkki Oja	Aalto University, Finland
Luca Oneto	Università di Pisa, Italy
Silvia Ortin	Institute of Neurosciences (IN) Alicante, Spain
Ivan Oseledets	Skoltech, Russia
Dmitry Osolodkin	Chumakov FSC R&D IBP RAS, Russia
Sebastian Otte	University of Tübingen, Germany
Latifa Oukhellou	The French Institute of Science and Technology for Transport, France
Vladimir Palyulin	Moscow State University, Russia
George Panagopoulos	École Polytechnique, France
Massimo Panella	Università degli Studi di Roma La Sapienza, Italy
Antonis Papaleonidas	Democritus University of Thrace, Greece
Evangelos Papalexakis	University of California Riverside, USA
Daniel Paurat	Fraunhofer IAIS, Germany
Jaakko Peltonen	Tampere University, Finland
Tingying Peng	Technische Universität München, Germany
Alberto Guillén Perales	Universidad de Granada, Spain
Carlos Garcia Perez	Helmholtz Zentrum München (GmbH), Germany
Isabelle Perseil	INSERM, France
Vincenzo Piuri	University of Milan, Italy
Kathrin Plankensteiner	Fachhochschule Vorarlberg, Austria
Isabella Pozzi	Centrum Wiskunde & Informatica, The Netherlands
Mike Preuss	Leiden University, The Netherlands
Yifat Prut	The Hebrew University of Jerusalem, Israel
Eugene Radchenko	Moscow State University, Russia
Rajkumar Ramamurthy	Fraunhofer IAIS, Germany
Srikanth Ramaswamy	Swiss Federal Institute of Technology (EPFL), Switzerland
Beatriz Remeseiro	Universidad de Oviedo, Spain
Xingzhang Ren	Alibaba Group, China
Jean-Louis Reymond	University of Bern, Switzerland
Cristian Rodriguez Rivero	University of California, USA
Antonio Javier Pons Rivero	Universitat Politècnica de Catalunya, Spain
Andrea Emilio Rizzoli	IDSIA, SUPSI, Switzerland
Florian Röhrbein	Technical University Munich, Germany
Ryan Rossi	PARC - a Xerox Company, USA
Manuel Roveri	Politecnico di Milano, Italy
Vladimir Rybakov	WaveAccess, Russia
Maryam Sabzevari	Aalto University School of Science and Technology, Finland
Julio Saez-Rodriguez	Medizinische Fakultät Heidelberg, Germany
Yulia Sandamirskaya	NEUROTECH: Neuromorphic Computer Technology, Switzerland
Carlo Sansone	University of Naples Federico II, Italy
Sreela Sasi	Gannon University, USA
Burak Satar	Uludag University, Turkey

Axel Sauer	Munich School of Robotics and Machine Intelligence, Germany
Konstantin Savenkov	Intento, Inc., USA
Hanno Scharr	Forschungszentrum Jülich, Germany
Tjeerd olde Scheper	Oxford Brookes University, UK
Rafal Scherer	Czestochowa University of Technology, Poland
Maria Secrier	University College London, UK
Thomas Seidl	Ludwig-Maximilians-Universität München, Germany
Rafet Sifa	Fraunhofer IAIS, Germany
Pekka Siirtola	University of Oulu, Finland
Prashant Singh	Uppsala University, Sweden
Patrick van der Smagt	Volkswagen AG, Germany
Maximilian Soelch	Volkswagen Machine Learning Research Lab, Germany
Miguel Cornelles Soriano	Campus Universitat de les Illes Balears, Spain
Miguel Angelo Abreu Sousa	Institute of Education Science and Technology, Brazil
Michael Stiber	University of Washington Bothell, USA
Alessandro Sperduti	Università degli Studi di Padova, Italy
Ruxandra Stoean	University of Craiova, Romania
Nicola Strisciuglio	University of Groningen, The Netherlands
Irene Sturm	Deutsche Bahn AG, Germany
Jérémie Sublime	ISEP, France
Martin Swain	Aberystwyth University, UK
Zoltan Szabo	Ecole Polytechnique, France
Kazuhiko Takahashi	Doshisha University, Japan
Fabian Theis	Helmholtz Zentrum München (GmbH), Germany
Philippe Thomas	Universite de Lorraine, France
Matteo Tiezzi	University of Siena, Italy
Ruben Tikidji-Hamburyan	Louisiana State University, USA
Yancho Todorov	VTT, Finland
Andrei Tolstikov	Merck Group, Germany
Matthias Treder	Cardiff University, UK
Anton Tsitsulin	Rheinische Friedrich-Wilhelms-Universität Bonn, Germany
Yury Tsoy	Solidware Co. Ltd., South Korea
Antoni Valencia	Independent Consultant, Spain
Carlos Magno Valle	Technical University Munich, Germany
Marley Vellasco	Pontifícia Universidade Católica do Rio de Janeiro, Brazil
Sagar Verma	Université Paris-Saclay, France
Paul Verschure	Institute for Bioengineering of Catalonia, Spain
Varvara Vetrova	University of Canterbury, New Zealand
Ricardo Vigário	University Nova's School of Science and Technology, Portugal
Alessandro Villa	University of Lausanne, Switzerland
Bruno Villoutreix	Molecular informatics for Health, France

Paolo Viviani	Università degli Studi di Torino, Italy
George Vouros	University of Piraeus, Greece
Christian Wallraven	Korea University, South Korea
Tinghuai Wang	Nokia, Finland
Yu Wang	Leibniz Supercomputing Centre (LRZ), Germany
Roseli S. Wedemann	Universidade do Estado do Rio de Janeiro, Brazil
Thomas Wennekers	University of Plymouth, UK
Stefan Wermter	University of Hamburg, Germany
Heiko Wersing	Honda Research Institute and Bielefeld University, Germany
Tadeusz Wieczorek	Silesian University of Technology, Poland
Christoph Windheuser	ThoughtWorks Inc., Germany
Borys Wróbel	Adam Mickiewicz University in Poznan, Poland
Jianhong Wu	York University, Canada
Xia Xiao	University of Connecticut, USA
Takaharu Yaguchi	Kobe University, Japan
Seul-Ki Yeom	Technische Universität Berlin, Germany
Hujun Yin	University of Manchester, UK
Junichiro Yoshimoto	Nara Institute of Science and Technology, Japan
Qiang Yu	Tianjin University, China
Shigang Yue	University of Lincoln, UK
Wlodek Zadrozny	University of North Carolina Charlotte, USA
Danuta Zakrzewska	Technical University of Lodz, Poland
Francisco Zamora-Martínez	Veridas Digital Authentication Solutions SL, Spain
Gerson Zaverucha	Federal University of Rio de Janeiro, Brazil
Junge Zhang	Institute of Automation, China
Zhongnan Zhang	Xiamen University, China
Pengsheng Zheng	Daimler AG, Germany
Samson Zhou	Indiana University, USA
Riccardo Zucca	Institute for Bioengineering of Catalonia, Spain
Dietlind Zühlke	Horn & Company Data Analytics GmbH, Germany

Exclusive Platinum Sponsor for the Automotive Branch

ARGMAX.ai

VOLKSWAGEN GROUP ML RESEARCH

Keynote Talks

Recurrent Patterns of Brain Activity Associated with Cognitive Tasks and Attractor Dynamics (John Taylor Memorial Lecture)

Alessandro E. P. Villa

NeuroHeuristic Research Group, University of Lausanne,
Quartier UNIL-Chamberonne, 1015 Lausanne, Switzerland
alessandro.villa@unil.ch
http://www.neuroheuristic.org

The simultaneous recording of the time series formed by the sequences of neuronal discharges reveals important features of the dynamics of information processing in the brain. Experimental evidence of firing sequences with a precision of a few milliseconds have been observed in the brain of behaving animals. We review some critical findings showing that this activity is likely to be associated with higher order neural (mental) processes, such as predictive guesses of a coming stimulus in a complex sensorimotor discrimination task, in primates as well as in rats. We discuss some models of evolvable neural networks and their nonlinear deterministic dynamics and how such complex spatiotemporal patterns of firing may emerge. The attractors of such networks correspond precisely to the cycles in the graphs of their corresponding automata, and can thus be computed explicitly and exhaustively. We investigate further the effects of network topology on the dynamical activity of hierarchically organized networks of simulated spiking neurons. We describe how the activation and the biologically-inspired processes of plasticity on the network shape its topology using invariants based on algebro-topological constructions. General features of a brain theory based on these results is presented for discussion.

Unsupervised Learning: Passive and Active

Jürgen Schmidhuber

Co-founder and Chief Scientist, NNAISENSE, Scientific Director,
Swiss AI Lab IDSIA and Professor of AI, USI & SUPSI, Lugano, Switzerland

I'll start with a concept of 1990 that has become popular: unsupervised learning without a teacher through two adversarial neural networks (NNs) that duel in a mini-max game, where one NN minimizes the objective function maximized by the other. The first NN generates data through its output actions while the second NN predicts the data. The second NN minimizes its error, thus becoming a better predictor. But it is a zero sum game: the first NN tries to find actions that maximize the error of the second NN. The system exhibits what I called "artificial curiosity" because the first NN is motivated to invent actions that yield data that the second NN still finds surprising, until the data becomes familiar and eventually boring. A similar adversarial zero sum game was used for another unsupervised method called "predictability minimization," where two NNs fight each other to discover a disentangled code of the incoming data (since 1991), remarkably similar to codes found in biological brains. I'll also discuss passive unsupervised learning through predictive coding of an agent's observation stream (since 1991) to overcome the fundamental deep learning problem through data compression. I'll offer thoughts as to why most current commercial applications don't use unsupervised learning, and whether that will change in the future.

Machine Learning and AI for the Sciences—Towards Understanding

Klaus-Robert Müller

Machine Learning Group, Technical University of Berlin, Germany

In recent years machine learning (ML) and Artificial Intelligence (AI) methods have begun to play a more and more enabling role in the sciences and in industry. In particular, the advent of large and/or complex data corpora has given rise to new technological challenges and possibilities.

The talk will connect two topics (1) explainable AI (XAI) and (2) ML applications in sciences (e.g. Medicine and Quantum Chemistry) for gaining new insight. Specifically I will first introduce XAI methods (such as LRP) that are now readily available and allow for an understanding of the inner workings of nonlinear ML methods ranging from kernel methods to deep learning methods including LSTMs. In particular XAI allows unmasking clever Hans predictors. Then, ML for Quantum Chemistry is discussed, showing that ML methods can lead to highly useful predictors of quantum mechanical properties of molecules (and materials) reaching quantum chemical accuracies both across chemical compound space and in molecular dynamics simulations. Notably, these ML models do not only speed up computation by several orders of magnitude but can give rise to novel chemical insight. Finally, I will analyze morphological and molecular data for cancer diagnosis, also here highly interesting novel insights can be obtained.

Note that while XAI is used for gaining a better understanding in the sciences, the introduced XAI techniques are readily useful in other application domains and industry as well.

Large-Scale Lineage and Latent-Space Learning in Single-Cell Genomic

Fabian Theis

Institute of Computational Biology, Helmholtz Zentrum München (GmbH), Germany
http://comp.bio

Accurately modeling single cell state changes e.g. during differentiation or in response to perturbations is a central goal of computational biology. Single-cell technologies now give us easy and large-scale access to state observations on the transcriptomic and more recently also epigenomic level, separately for each single cell. In particular they allow resolving potential heterogeneities due to asynchronicity of differentiating or responding cells, and profiles across multiple conditions such as time points and replicates are being generated.

Typical questions asked to such data are how cells develop over time and after perturbation such as disease. The statistical tools to address these questions are techniques from pseudo-temporal ordering and lineage estimation, or more broadly latent space learning. In this talk I will give a short review of such approaches, in particular focusing on recent extensions towards large-scale data integration using single-cell graph mapping or neural networks, and finish with a perspective towards learning perturbations using variational autoencoders.

The Gentle Robot

Sami Haddadin

Technical University of Munich, Germany

Enabling robots for interaction with humans and unknown environments has been one of the primary goals of robotics research over decades. I will outline how human-centered robot design, nonlinear soft-robotics control inspired by human neuromechanics and physics grounded learning algorithms will let robots become a commodity in our near-future society. In particular, compliant and energy-controlled ultra-lightweight systems capable of complex collision handling enable high-performance human assistance over a wide variety of application domains. Together with novel methods for dynamics and skill learning, flexible and easy-to-use robotic power tools and systems can be designed. Recently, our work has led to the first next generation robot Franka Emika that has recently become commercially available. The system is able to safely interact with humans, execute and even learn sensitive manipulation skills, is affordable and designed as a distributed interconnected system.

Contents – Part I

Capsule Networks

Embedding Systems

Explainable Methods

New Architectures

Reinforcement Learning

Robots

Spiking Networks

Theoretical Neural Computation

Associative Memory

Bidirectional Associative Memory with Block Coding: A Comparison of Iterative Retrieval Methods

Andreas Knoblauch[1](✉) and Günther Palm[2]

[1] KEIM Institute, Albstadt-Sigmaringen University, Albstadt, Germany
knoblauch@hs-albsig.de

[2] Institute of Neural Information Processing, Ulm University, Ulm, Germany
guenther.palm@uni-ulm.de

Abstract. Recently, Gripon and Berrou (2011) have investigated a recurrently connected Willshaw-type auto-associative memory with block coding, a particular sparse coding method, reporting a significant increase in storage capacity compared to earlier approaches. In this study we verify and generalize their results by implementing bidirectional hetero-associative networks and comparing the performance of various retrieval methods both with block coding and without block coding. For iterative retrieval in networks of size $n = 4096$ our data confirms that block-coding with the so-called "sum-of-max" strategy performs best in terms of output noise (which is the normalized Hamming distance between stored and retrieved patterns), whereas the information storage capacity of the classical models cannot be exceeded because of the reduced Shannon information of block patterns. Our simulation experiments also provide accurate estimates of the maximum pattern number that can be stored at a tolerated noise level of 1%. It is revealed that block coding is most beneficial for sparse activity where each pattern has only $k \sim \log n$ active units.

Keywords: Associative networks · Willshaw model · Block coding · Potts model · Clique networks · GBNN · Biclique networks · Cell assembly

1 Introduction

Neural associative memories (NAM) are simple perceptron-type artificial neural networks that work as an associative memory and learning by simple, often "one-shot", synaptic plasticity (for a review see [47]). The retrieval of information from such a memory is typically not achieved by looking up a content under a final address, but rather by associating a meaningful output pattern

The authors acknowledge support by the state of Baden-Württemberg through bwHPC.

I. V. Tetko et al. (Eds.): ICANN 2019, LNCS 11727, pp. 3–19, 2019.
https://doi.org/10.1007/978-3-030-30487-4_1

to a meaningful input pattern. During the learning phase, pattern associations are stored or learned by a form of local Hebbian-type synaptic plasticity [22]. In classical associative memory, one distinguishes between hetero- and auto-association concerning the identity of the output patterns to the input patterns [44,59]. Hetero-association is more similar to the technical address $\rightarrow$ content scheme, but it is different because also the input patterns are considered to be meaningful and therefore their similarity (in terms of some vector distance, e.g., the Hamming-distance or overlap for binary patterns) should reflect similarity of content and should be roughly preserved by the association mapping (similar inputs to similar outputs). Auto-association is typically used for pattern completion or pattern correction. NAMs have various applications, e.g., for cluster analysis, speech and object recognition, robot control, or information retrieval in large databases [3,12,13,17,21,25,35,43,50,52,54,58]. Moreover, NAMs have been used as model of neural computation for various brain structures including neocortex, hippocampus, cerebellum, and mushroom body [1,4,5,14,16,22–24,26,27,37,40–42,45,51,53].

For practical applications the binary Willshaw model [44,57,59] is particularly relevant because learning and retrieval employing binary synaptic weights $w_{ij} \in \{0, 1\}$ is very simple and can be implemented in a very space-, time-, and energy-efficient way [28,33]. Despite its simplicity, this model has a very high information storage capacity, e.g., up to $\ln 2 \approx 0.69$ bit per binary synapse for hetero-association and still $\ln 2/4 \approx 0.173$ for auto-association in the limit of large networks $n \rightarrow \infty$ and sparse pattern activity $k \sim \ln n$ [44,59]. Interestingly, for auto-association it is even possible to exceed the asymptotic values by iterative retrieval where the output of the previous retrieval iteration is used as input for the next iteration until convergence. Alternative learning models employing continuous synapses have slightly higher asymptotic values [11,15,29,49] but are much more expensive to implement.

To achieve these high storage capacities, NAMs typically require uncorrelated *random patterns* with a fixed number k of active units that have maximal information content [33]. More recently, Gripon and Berrou [18] have rediscovered another coding strategy that employs *block patterns* where the n neurons of the network are divided into k equal sized "one hot" blocks, each having exactly one active neuron per pattern [36,60]. More interestingly, Gripon and Berrou have introduced a number of new iterative retrieval methods for block coding yielding comparatively high information capacity and retrieval efficiency [13,19,21,61].

In this exploratory study we compare the performance of various retrieval methods both for block coding and without block coding. Here we focus on bidirectional retrieval in hetero-associative networks [56] and generalize several of the previously suggested retrieval methods for auto-associative retrieval such as "LK+" [55] or "sum-of-max" [19,61]. Section 2 describes the learning model, the different retrieval algorithms, and different measures to evaluate "output noise" and "information storage capacity". Section 3 presents data from the simulation experiments for networks of size $n = 4096$ storing random patterns and block patterns. Finally, Sect. 4 discusses the results.

2 Modeling

2.1 Learning

The general hetero-associative learning task is to store M associations between binary memory patterns u^μ and v^μ (where $\mu = 1, 2, ..., M$) in a completely connected synaptic network W linking neuron population u to v. Here the input patterns u^μ are used to activate the associated output patterns v^μ. After learning according to the clipped Willshaw model [57, 59] the synaptic weights are

$$w_{ij} = \max_{\mu=1}^{M} u_i^\mu v_j^\mu = \begin{cases} 1, & \sum_{\mu=1}^{M} u_i^\mu v_j^\mu > 0 \\ 0, & \text{otherwise} \end{cases} \in \{0, 1\} . \tag{1}$$

For bidirectional retrieval we assume bidirectional synapses corresponding to a second symmetric transposed network W^{T} linking neuron population v to u such that both synapses between neurons i and j have the identical weight w_{ij}. For the special case of auto-association the two neuron populations $u = v$ as well as the corresponding patterns $u^\mu = v^\mu$ are assumed to be identical, implying a symmetric network with $w_{ij} = w_{ji}$.

We further assume that neuron populations consist of n neurons and each pattern u^μ and v^μ has exactly k active (and $n-k$ silent) neurons. Thus patterns are binary vectors of length n with k one-entries and $n - k$ zero-entries. We also identify patterns with the sets of their active neurons, e.g., when writing $u^\mu \subset \{u_1, \ldots, u_n\}$ or $|u^\mu| = k$.

2.2 Retrieval Task and Algorithms

Given a disrupted input pattern $\tilde{u}$ resembling one of the stored inputs u^μ, the memory task is to retrieve the corresponding content pattern v^μ and to reconstruct the correct input u^μ. The following defines various retrieval strategies for general hetero-associative networks, but they can easily be adapted for auto-association assuming $u = v$.

For **general patterns without block structure** we have implemented and tested the following retrieval algorithms:

- **One-Step-Retrieval (R1)** [59]: An output unit v_j gets activated iff it is connected to at least Θ active input units u_i with $\tilde{u}_i = 1$, that is,

$$\hat{v}_j = \begin{cases} 1, & x_j := \sum_{i=1}^{n} w_{ij} \tilde{u}_i \geq \Theta \\ 0, & \text{otherwise} \end{cases} \tag{2}$$

  where Θ is the firing threshold. In general, we assume that the input $\tilde{u}$ contains λk active units of one of the original address patterns u^μ, where $0 < \lambda \leq 1$, and possibly κk additional spurious units ($\kappa \geq 0$). Then choosing a firing threshold $\Theta = \lambda k$ results in the output $\hat{v} := \mathrm{R1}(\tilde{u})$ having all active units of v^μ and possibly additional spurious units, i.e., $\hat{v} \supseteq v^\mu$.

- **R1-KWTA:** This is a k-winners-take-all variant of R1 that chooses a maximal firing threshold Θ such that at least k output units get activated.
- **Iterative retrieval (IR-LK):** We can use the output $\hat{v}^{(1)} := \text{R1}(\tilde{u})$ of R1 as input pattern for the transposed network W^{T} yielding $\hat{u}^{(2)} := \text{R1}^{\text{T}}(\hat{v}^{(1)})$ with the transposed R1-operation. Iterating this procedure over time t yields further output patterns $\hat{v}^{(t+1)} := \text{R1}(\hat{u}^{(t)})$ and $\hat{u}^{(t+1)} := \text{R1}^{\text{T}}(\hat{v}^{(t)})$. By using firing thresholds $\Theta = \lambda k$ in the first iteration and $\Theta = k$ in all further iterations we obviously maintain that the outputs are supersets of the original patterns, that is, $\hat{u}^{(t)} \supseteq u^{\mu}$ and $\hat{v}^{(t)} \supseteq v^{\mu}$ for $t \geq 1$. In all our experiments we stop after $t_{\max} = 20$ iterations which is usually sufficient to finally get stable outputs $\hat{u} := \hat{u}^{(20)}$ and $\hat{v} := \hat{v}^{(19)}$.
- **IR-LK+** is the same as IR-LK except performing an AND-ing with the previous patterns in each iteration step, $\hat{v}^{(t+1)} := \hat{v}^{(t-1)} \wedge \text{R1}(\hat{u}^{(t)})$ and $\hat{u}^{(t+1)} := \hat{u}^{(t-1)} \wedge \text{R1}^{\text{T}}(\hat{v}^{(t)})$. As all outputs are supersets of the original patterns, this holds as well after AND-ing with the previous outputs. IR-LK and IR-LK+ have been introduced in [55] for auto-association, showing that, due to the AND-ing operation, IR-LK+ can greatly reduce output noise compared to IR-LK. Here we use them to investigate the performance of hetero-associative networks.
- **IR-KWTA:** Similar to IR-LK, but using R1-KWTA and R1-KWTA^{T} in each retrieval step.
- **IR-CBR:** This is a variant of the crosswise bidirectional retrieval (CBR) algorithm of [56] using a k-winners-take-all threshold control in each step. The basic idea of CBR is that an activation pattern in one neuron population implicitly induces conditional recurrent synaptic weights in the opposite population that can be used for auto-association. These auto-associative synaptic weights can be obtained by counting overlaps between the hetero-associative inputs to the two neurons of the synapse. For example, $w_{ik}^{v^{(t)}} := \sum_{j \in v^{(t)}} w_{ij} w_{kj} v_j^{(t)}$ is the auto-associative weight between neurons i and k in population u gated by pattern $v^{(t)}$. Similarly $w_{jl}^{u^{(t)}} := \sum_{i \in u^{(t)}} w_{ij} w_{il} u_i^{(t)}$ is the auto-associative weight between neurons j and l in population v gated by $u^{(t)}$. Note that the corresponding weight matrices $W^{v^{(t)}}$ and $W^{u^{(t)}}$ are symmetric. Therefore, given the previous patterns $u^{(t-2)}$ and $v^{(t-1)}$, the dendritic sums $x^{(t)}$ and $y^{(t+1)}$ in populations u and v after an auto-association step write

$$x_i^{(t)} := [u^{(t-2),\text{T}} W^{v^{(t-1)}}]_i = \sum_k w_{ik}^{v^{(t-1)}} u_k^{(t-2)} = \sum_{j \in v^{(t-1)}} w_{ij} [u^{(t-2),\text{T}} W]_j$$

$$y_j^{(t+1)} := [v^{(t-1),\text{T}} W^{u^{(t)}}]_j = \sum_l w_{jl}^{u^{(t)}} v_l^{(t-1)} = \sum_{i \in u^{(t)}} w_{ij} [v^{(t-1),\text{T}} W^{\text{T}}]_i$$

where the corresponding patterns are obtained from k-Winners-Take-All operations $u^{(t)} := \text{KWTA}(x^{(t)})$ and $v^{(t+1)} := \text{KWTA}(y^{(t+1)})$, similar as described above, with firing thresholds Θ being selected minimal to activate at least k neurons. By iterating this scheme we obtain the algorithm IR-CBR in pseudo-code:

1. $\hat{u}^{(0)} := \tilde{u}$; $\hat{v}^{(1)} := \text{R1}(\tilde{u})$; $x = (0...0)$; $y = (0...0)$; $t := 0$;
2. $t := t + 2$;
3. FOR each neuron i in population u DO $x[i] := \sum_{j \in \hat{v}^{(t-1)}} w_{ij} [\hat{u}^{(t-2),\text{T}} W]_j$
4. $\hat{u}^{(t)} := \text{KWTA}(x)$
5. FOR each neuron j in population v DO $y[j] := \sum_{i \in \hat{u}^{(t)}} w_{ij} [\hat{v}^{(t-1),\text{T}} W^{\text{T}}]_i$
6. $\hat{v}^{(t+1)} := \text{KWTA}(y)$
7. IF $\hat{u}^{(t)} \neq \hat{u}^{(t-2)}$ or $\hat{v}^{(t+1)} \neq \hat{v}^{(t-1)}$ and $t \leq t_{\max}$ THEN goto step 2.

Note that our algorithm does only a single hetero-association (implicit in the computation of the auto-associative weights) and a single auto-association step per iteration. We also tested several other variants of CBR-retrieval as described in [56] that have been optimized for decomposing superpositions of many original memory patterns and, therefore, avoid the KWTA-operation. However, as in our experiments the queries $\tilde{u}$ are parts of *individual* patterns, the described algorithm outperformed those variants (data not shown).

For **block patterns** consisting of k blocks of n/k neurons, each block having a single active unit, we have implemented and tested the following retrieval algorithms:

- **One-Step-Retrieval with Block-Constraint (R1B):** This is R1 followed by an elimination of all units of blocks having more than one active unit. The resulting output will be a subset of an original pattern, $\hat{v} \subseteq v^{\mu}$, thereby reducing output noise.
- **sIRB:** Simple iterative retrieval exploiting the block-constraint that only one unit per block can be activated [18], iterating R1B in a similar way as IR-LK iterates R1. For each R1B-step we use firing thresholds Θ equal to the number of active units in the output of the previous iteration. Then all outputs will be subsets of the corresponding original pattern, $\hat{u}^{(t)} \subseteq u^{\mu}$ and $\hat{v}^{(t)} \subseteq v^{\mu}$ for $t \geq 1$.
- **IRB:** This is the same as sIRB, but including an OR-operation (in analogy to the AND-ing of IR-LK+). Similar variants for auto-association have been introduced by [2,18].
- **eIRB** is an extended non-linear variant of IRB taking into account the constraint that any correctly active unit must receive synaptic inputs from each block. This is implemented by means of two ternary arrays c_u and c_v of length n keeping track of those neurons in populations u and v that still may be part of the pattern to be retrieved. Initialized with zeros, neurons that violate the block-constraint after a retrieval iteration step are marked by a negative array entry and, thereby, excluded from the further steps. For clarity we present the algorithm in pseudo-code:
  1. $\hat{u}^{(0)} := \tilde{u}$; $\hat{v}^{(-1)} := (0...0)$; $t := 0$; $c_u := (0...0)$; $c_v := (0...0)$.
  2. $t := t + 1$; $\hat{v}^{(t)} := \hat{v}^{(t-2)} \cup \text{R1B}(\hat{u}^{(t-1)})$.
  3. FOR each *unresolved block* b of c_v DO

     FOR each *unresolved neuron* j in b with $c_v[j] == 0$ DO

       IF $\hat{v}_j^{(t)} = 1$ THEN resolved$(j, b, c_v, \hat{v}^{(t)})$.

       ELSIF j misses *valid links* to at least one block of c_u THEN $c_v[j] := -1$.

     IF $|\{j \in b : c_v[j] \geq 0\}| = 1$ THEN resolved$(\text{argmax}_{j \in b} c_v[j], b, c_v, \hat{v}^{(t)})$.

4. $t := t+1$; $\hat{u}^{(t)} := \hat{u}^{(t-2)} \cup \mathrm{R1B}^{\mathrm{T}}(\hat{v}^{(t-1)})$
5. FOR each *unresolved block* b of c_u DO
   FOR each *unresolved neuron* i in b with $c_u[i] == 0$ DO
   IF $\hat{u}_i^{(t)} = 1$ THEN resolved$(i, b, c_u, \hat{u}^{(t)})$.
   ELSIF i misses *valid links* to at least one block of c_v THEN $c_u[i] := -1$.
   IF $|\{i \in b : c_u[i] \geq 0\}| = 1$ THEN resolved$(\mathrm{argmax}_{i \in b} c_u[i], b, c_u, \hat{u}^{(t)})$.
6. IF $\hat{v}^{(t)}$, $\hat{u}^{(t)}$, c_u, or c_v has changed and $t < t_{\max}$ THEN goto step 2.

For example, $c_u[i] = 1$ means that neuron u_i belongs with certainty to the correct pattern, $c_u[i] = -1$ means that u_i has been excluded, and $c_u[i] = 0$ means that the status of u_i is still uncertain, i.e., u_i is an *unresolved neuron.* Similarly, an *unresolved block* b is a block where the single correctly active neuron has not yet been found. For brevity the algorithm uses a subroutine to mark a neuron i as resolved,

7. DEF resolved(i,b,c,u):
   $c[i] := 1$; $c[i'] := -1$ for all $i' \neq i$ in block b; $u[i] := 1$.

Finally, we say that a neuron j misses a *valid link* to a block b if all of the neuron's non-zero synapses $w_{ij} > 0$ from that block connect to excluded neurons, e.g., if $\sum_{i \in b} w_{ij}(c_u[i] + 1) = 0$.

- **R1B-SMX:** Similar to R1, but each neuron can receive at most one active input from each block b,

$$\hat{v}_j = \begin{cases} 1, & x_j := \sum_{b=1}^{i} \max_{i \in b} w_{ij}\tilde{u}_i \geq \Theta \\ 0, & \text{otherwise} \end{cases} . \tag{3}$$

  If the input pattern $\tilde{u}$ is a super-set of one of the stored pattern u^μ then maximal threshold $\Theta = k$ yields again a superset of the associated pattern v^μ.
- **IRB-SMX:** Another non-linear variant of IRB using R1B-SMX instead of R1B is the *sum-of-max* strategy that has been introduced by [19,61] for auto-association. Our more general implementation starts with an R1-step to retrieve a super-set of the original pattern v^μ, whereas all subsequent iteration steps gate synaptic inputs by R1B-SMX such that each neuron receives at most one input from each block. As all outputs are super-sets of the originally stored pattern, we can use again $\Theta = k$.

If the number of correct one-entries λk in the noisy input $\tilde{u}$ is known, imposing the firing threshold in R1 to that same value $\Theta = \lambda k$ implies that, by definition, the retrieval strategies R1, IR-LK, IR-LK+, R1B-SMX, and IRB-SMX yield supersets (so-called "halos") of the original patterns, whereas R1B, sIRB, IRB, eIRB yield subsets (so-called "cores") of the original patterns [32]. The "core"-strategies have the advantage of limiting Hamming distances between retrieval outputs and original patterns to a maximum k, whereas the "halo"-strategies produce outputs that contain typically more (Shannon) information on the original patterns. For maximizing retrieved information we therefore investigated some additional variants **IRB-R1** and **eIRB-R1** of IRB and eIRB that include a final R1-step in order to produce halo patterns. Similarly, to reduce output noise, the variant **IRB-cSMX** of IRB-SMX produces core patterns by a final step eliminating activity in blocks with multiple active units.

As some of the models have a propensity towards activity explosion (in particular the "halo"-strategies IR-LK and IR-LK+), we have included a mechanism to limit the number of active neurons to a maximum of 1000 in each iteration step. If this value is exceeded, the retrieval procedure is terminated and the last pattern with fewer than 1000 active units is returned as retrieval result.

2.3 Evaluation Measures

An important measure to evaluate the performance of associative memory is **output noise** $\hat{\epsilon}$ defined as the expected Hamming distance between retrieval outputs and the original patterns. For example, for hetero-association we define output noise in population v as

$$\hat{\epsilon}_v := \mathrm{E}(\epsilon_v^\mu) \qquad \text{for} \quad \epsilon_v^\mu := \frac{||\hat{v} - v^\mu||_1}{||v^\mu||_1} = \frac{\sum_j |\hat{v}_j - v_j^\mu|}{k} \tag{4}$$

where $||.||_1$ is the L_1-norm. A similar definition applies for auto-association ($v = u$) and iterative retrieval. If the task is bidirectional retrieval of both u^μ and v^μ we average output noise $\hat{\epsilon} := \frac{\epsilon_u + \epsilon_v}{2}$ over both populations u and v. As parts of the retrieval result $\hat{u}$ are already given by the input $\tilde{u}$, we sometimes use also the weighted average $\epsilon := \frac{(1-\lambda)\epsilon_u + \epsilon_v}{2-\lambda}$ which is a fairer measure, in particular for block patterns (see Table 1).

Another measure is the critical pattern capacity M_ϵ at noise level ϵ,

$$M_\epsilon := \max\{M : \hat{\epsilon}(M) \leq \epsilon\}, \tag{5}$$

defined as the maximal pattern number M such that output noise $\hat{\epsilon}$ does not exceed ϵ. From this and the transinformation between original and retrieved patterns we can derive various measures of "storage capacity" based on Shannon information [10,44,46,48]. For example, for hetero-association we use the *mapping capacity* C_v defined as the transinformation between all stored and retrieved outputs v^μ and $\hat{v}^\mu$ normalized to the synapse number. Similarly, for auto-association we define the *completion capacity* C_u defined as the transinformation between the patterns u^μ and $\hat{u}^\mu$ minus the transinformation between u^μ and $\tilde{u}^\mu$. Finally, for hetero-association with iterative retrieval a meaningful measure is the *bidirectional capacity* $C_{uv} := C_u + C_v$. We sometimes index these measures by the tolerated output noise level ϵ similar as described for M_ϵ. For more details on how to compute these information-theoretic measures see [10,32,33].

2.4 Data and Experimental Set up

As in many previous works [7,18,55,56] we have stored randomly generated memory patterns u^μ and v^μ in all our simulation experiments. Specifically, the **patterns without block structure** are binary random vectors of length $n = 4096$ each having exactly k active components selected at random independently of other patterns. For **block patterns** we have divided each pattern vector into k aligned block vectors, each of length $N := n/k$. For example, for a pattern u block 1 corresponds to neurons $u_1, ..., u_N$, block 2 corresponds to neurons $u_{N+1}, ..., u_{2N}$, and so on. In each block we have randomly selected exactly one active unit independently of other blocks. Alternatively, block patterns may be interpreted as "one-hot"-coded integer vectors of length k where each component is drawn independently and uniformly from $\{1, ..., N\}$. In most simulation experiments (except those of Table 1) we have used close-to-optimal $k = 16$ corresponding to a block size of $N = 256$.

To test retrieval we have constructed a set of corrupted input patterns $\tilde{u}^\mu \subseteq u^\mu$ having half of the one-entries of the original pattern ($\lambda = 0.5$), but no additional false one-entries ($\kappa = 0$). In a more general setup we define λ and κ as fractions of the correct and false one-entries in a corrupted input query, respectively, when normalizing to the correct activity k.

Each of the following data values is estimated from averaging over at least 100000 retrievals in 20 different networks. In each simulated retrieval we count the number of component retrieval errors and, by averaging, we can compute the mean output noise ϵ_u and ϵ_v in the two populations. Thus, testing output noise for different pattern numbers M, we can estimate also the critical capacity M_ϵ at a certain noise level ϵ and the different information-theoretic capacity measures C_u, C_v and C_{uv} defined above.

3 Results

Figure 1 illustrates how output noise decreases with the number of iteration steps during retrieval. It can be seen that iterative retrieval can strongly reduce output noise compared to one-step retrieval (R1; see right panels). For low memory load ($M = 30000$; top panels) retrieval outputs converge quickly after a few steps, whereas convergence requires significantly more steps for a high memory load ($M = 50000$; bottom panels). It can also be seen that the block coding model variants reach significant lower noise levels compared to random patterns. Best performances are achieved by the "core"-retrieval strategies IRB, eIRB, and IRB-cSMX, whereas the "halo"-strategies IRB-R1, eIRB-R1, and IRB-SMX perform significantly worse. For the non-block coding models crosswise bidirectional retrieval (IR-CBR) performs best, closely followed by IR-KWTA, whereas the LK-strategies perform relatively poor.

Our data also reveals clear asymmetries between input and output populations u and v during bidirectional iterative retrieval. At high memory loads noise levels are typically higher in the output population v compared to input population u (whereas the reverse behavior can sometimes be observed at a low memory load, e.g., for IR-LK+). The reason seems to be that certain information on the initial input query $\tilde{u}$ can persist through the AND-ing and OR-ing operations in population u thereby suppressing the output noise.

For the non-monotonic behavior of the curves there are two reasons: First, the "core"-strategies with a final R1-step (IRB-R1, eIRB-R1) typically strongly increase output noise level in their final step. This upswing occurs earlier for IRB-R1 because IRB converges more quickly than eIRB. In fact, a closer look at the data indicates that, although convergence is clearly visible from their curves, eIRB and also IRB-SMX often do not convergence within the maximum iteration step number (19 or 20) under high memory load.

Next we investigated output noise ϵ as a function of stored memory number after the maximal number of iteration steps. Figure 2 shows the corresponding curves for the various model variants. Again, noise in the input population (top panel) can significantly differ from the noise in the output population (bottom panel). For low memory load all iterative retrieval variants perform much better than one-step-retrieval (R1). For high memory loads the retrieval variants group into three clusters: First, the "halo"-strategies (IR-LK(+), IRB-R1, eIRB-R1, IRB-SMX) converge towards the R1 curve with $\epsilon \to \infty$ as more and more neurons get activated. Second, the "core" strategies (IRB, eIRB, IRB-cSMX) converge towards noise level $\epsilon = 1$ as activity dies out. Third, the curves for the k-winner-take-all strategies (IR-KWTA, IR-CBR) are between the latter two. For the most relevant range of low noise levels (around $\epsilon = 0.01$) eIRB(-R1) and IRB-(c)SMX perform best. While the "softmax"-strategies IRB-(c)-SMX show the overall best performance at noise levels relevant for applications, eIRB(-R1) performs best at low memory loads and noise levels, in particular, within the input population u.

For non-block coding, IR-CBR performs best, again closely followed by IR-KWTA, whereas IR-LK(+) perform significantly worse. The non-monotonic behavior of IR-LK and IR-LK+ is due to a vulnerability of those retrieval strategies for an explosion of neural activity at higher memory loads, which terminates retrieval and freezes the patterns of the previous step. For IR-LK+ this explosion occurs only in population u due to the AND-ing with the R1-result in population v.

Figure 3 shows the different types of information storage capacities as a function of M corresponding to Fig. 2. All iterative retrieval strategies perform significant better than one-step-retrieval (R1). The networks storing random patterns achieve their maximum capacity for a lower memory number M than the block coding strategies. The best overall (bidirectional) capacity values are achieved by the two k-winners-take-all-strategies: IR-CBR achieves $C_{uv} \approx 0.529$ for $M = 39000$ and output noise $\epsilon_u \approx \epsilon_v \approx 0.018$, closely followed by IR-KWTA with $C_{uv} \approx 0.522$ for $M = 39000$ and $\epsilon_u \approx \epsilon_v \approx 0.032$. Note that this value exceeds the asymptotic limit $C_{uv} \leq (2-\lambda)\lambda \ln 2 = \frac{3}{4} \ln 2 \approx 0.51986$ for $\lambda = 0.5$ [32] and is not far from the overall asymptotic limit $C_{uv}, C_v \leq \ln 2 \approx 0.69$ bit/synapse [44, 56]. By contrast, the best block coding strategy IR-SMX achieves only $C_{uv} = 0.513$ for $M = 46000$ at $\epsilon_u = 0.55$ and $\epsilon_v = 0.12$, remaining slightly below the asymptotic capacity limit.

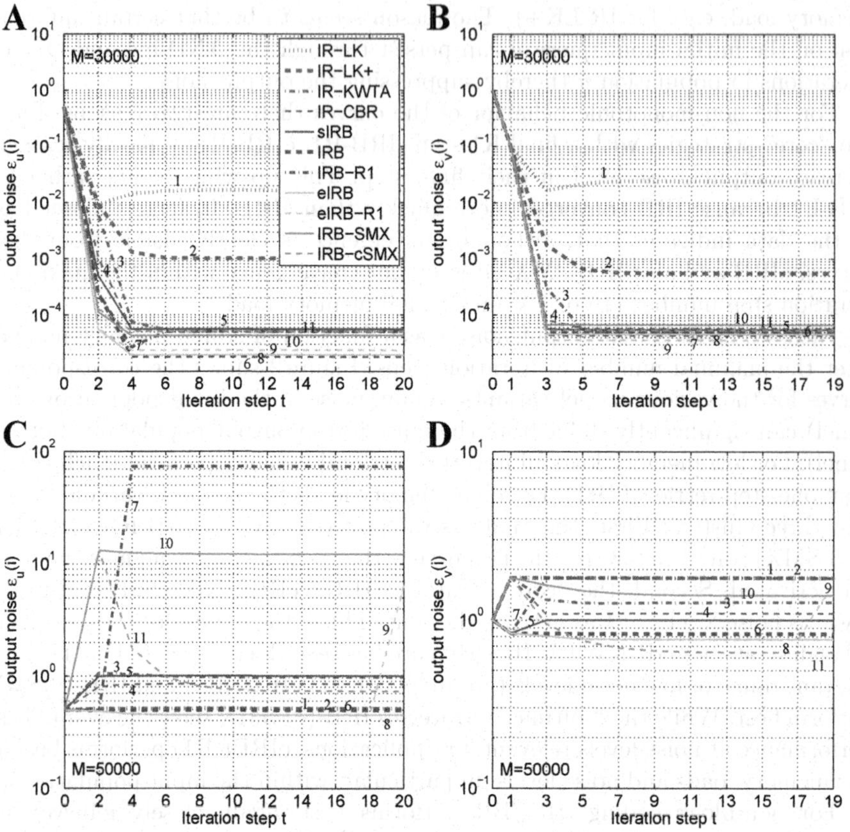

Fig. 1. Output noise ϵ as function of iteration step t for hetero-associative networks of size $n = 4096$ and activity $k = 16$ when addressing with half input patterns $\tilde{u}$ with $\lambda = 0.5$ and $\kappa = 0$. Top panels (A, B) show noise for $M = 30000$ patterns, bottom panels (C, D) for $M = 50000$. Left panels (A, C) show noise ϵ_u in the input population, right panels (B, D) show noise ϵ_v in the output population. Numbers indicate legends for black/white printing (e.g., 5 = sIRB).

Our data reveals further that the high bidirectional capacity of IR-CBR/KWTA is mostly due to the high completion capacity, namely $C_u \approx 0.186$ for IR-CBR and $C_u \approx 0.182$ for IR-KWTA, both significantly exceeding the asymptotic limit $C_u \leq \ln 2/4 \approx 0.173$ of auto-association [44,48,49,59]. By contrast the best block coding strategy IRB-SMX achieves only $C_u \approx 0.166$ again below the asymptotic limit. Mapping capacity is almost identical between the best strategies: $C_v \approx 0.343$ for IRB-CBR, $C_v \approx 0.340$ for IRB-KWTA, and $C_v \approx 0.347$ for IRB-SMX.

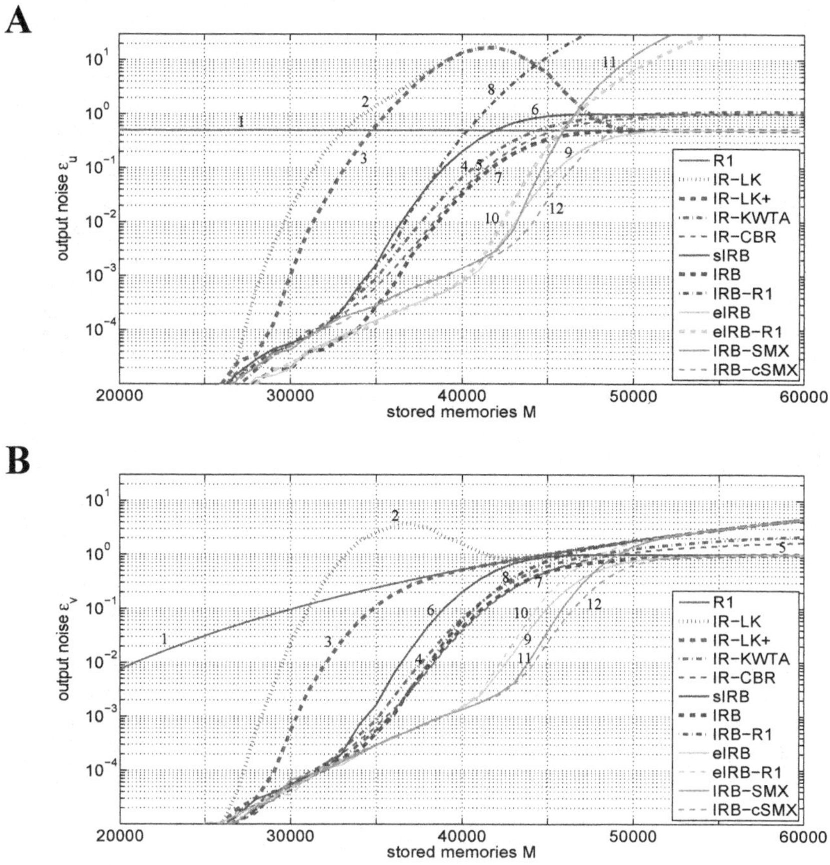

Fig. 2. Output noise ϵ after 20 iteration steps as function of stored memory number M for hetero-associative networks of size $n = 4096$ and activity $k = 16$ when addressing with half input patterns $\tilde{u}$ with $\lambda = 0.5$ and $\kappa = 0$. Top panel (A) shows noise ϵ_u in the input population u. Bottom panel (B) shows noise ϵ_v in the output population. Numbers indicate legends.

Note that the block coding strategies can store less information although they can store a larger absolute number of memory patterns: The reason for this phenomenon is that each block pattern contains less Shannon information than the random patterns used for the non-block-coding models (for further details see [32]).

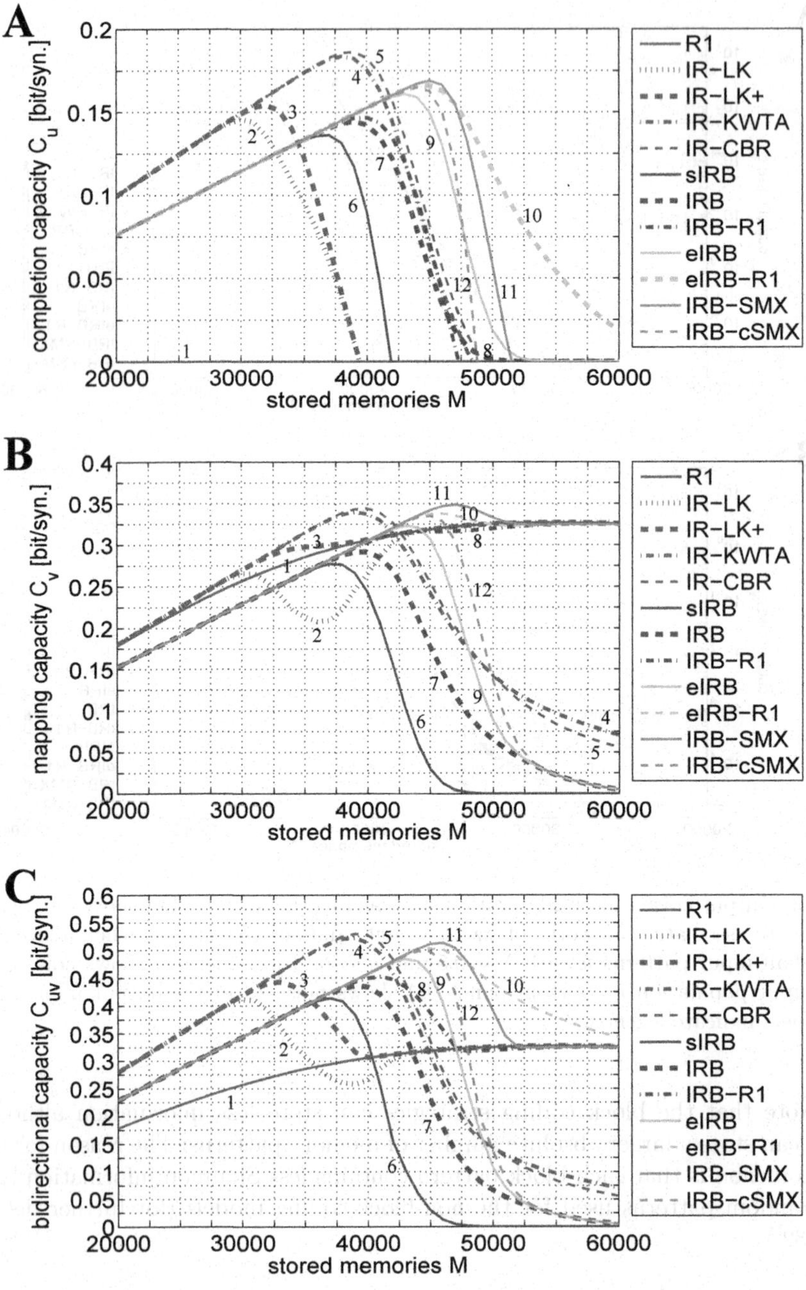

Fig. 3. Information storage capacity C after 20 iteration steps as function of stored memory number M for hetero-associative networks of size $n = 4096$ and activity $k = 16$ when addressing with half input patterns $\tilde{u}$ with $\lambda = 0.5$ and $\kappa = 0$. A: completion capacity C_u in the input population u. B: mapping capacity C_v for the patterns in the output population v. C: bidirectional capacity $C_{uv} := C_u + C_v$. Numbers indicate legends (e.g., 7 = IRB).

Table 1. Maximal pattern number M_ϵ that can be stored in hetero-associative networks ($n = 4096$) for half input patterns ($\lambda = 0.5, \kappa = 0$) at a maximum tolerated output noise level $\epsilon = 0.01$. Results are shown for averaged (avrgd) output noise by $\epsilon := \frac{\epsilon_u + \epsilon_v}{2}$ and weighted output noise (wghtd) by $\epsilon := \frac{(1-\lambda)\epsilon_u + \epsilon_v}{2-\lambda}$.

$n = 4096$	HETERO; $\lambda = 0.5$; $\kappa = 0$; $\epsilon = 1\%$									
k	4	8	16	32	64	128	256	512	1024	2048
R1 (from BRB)	2939	17283	20977	12657	5449	1942	609	175	46	12
± error	± 60	± 283	± 477	± 342	± 150	± 42	± 10	± 4	± 1	± 0
IR-KWTA (avrgd)	19152	49822	37625	18218	6916	2276	677	186	48	12
± error	± 2152	± 822	± 625	± 281	± 116	± 26	± 17	± 3	± 1	± 0
IR-KWTA (wghtd)	17264	49785	37628	18219	6917	2276	677	186	48	12
± error	± 1764	± 785	± 628	± 280	± 117	± 26	± 17	± 3	± 1	± 0
IR-LK+ (avrgd)	18390	45155	31454	15240	5928	2004	603	166	42	10
± error	± 390	± 844	± 545	± 259	± 128	± 45	± 16	± 3	± 1	± 0
IR-LK+ (wghtd)	16416	45258	31584	15319	5969	2009	605	166	42	10
± error	± 416	± 741	± 584	± 319	± 169	± 40	± 14	± 3	± 1	± 0
IR-CBR (avrgd)	18500	51426	38254	18502	7001	2305	679	190	48	12
± error	± 1000	± 573	± 745	± 497	± 198	± 44	± 29	± 4	± 3	± 0
IR-CBR (wghtd)	16274	51377	38259	18504	7004	2307	681	190	48	12
± error	± 274	± 622	± 740	± 495	± 195	± 42	± 31	± 4	± 3	± 0
IRB (avrgd)	10177	42558	38291	19825	7854	2589	768	212	55	12
± error	± 577	± 558	± 708	± 325	± 145	± 39	± 11	± 2	± 1	± 0
IRB (wghtd)	9224	42448	38242	19797	7839	2574	764	210	54	12
± error	± 175	± 551	± 757	± 297	± 160	± 25	± 15	± 4	± 1	± 0
eIRB (avrgd)	14074	61053	42774	20530	7937	2589	768	212	55	12
± error	± 425	± 946	± 774	± 469	± 137	± 39	± 11	± 2	± 1	± 0
eIRB (wghtd)	12531	60809	42665	20516	7900	2574	763	211	55	12
± error	± 468	± 809	± 665	± 483	± 100	± 25	± 16	± 3	± 1	± 0

4 Conclusions

We have tested several different strategies for iterative retrieval in hetero-associative Willshaw networks with and without block coding. For networks of size $n = 4096$ and activity $k = 16$ (that is optimal for fully connected networks and input noise with $\lambda = 0.5$ and $\kappa = 0$), our data indicates that the classical iterative retrieval strategies for random patterns, such as IR-KWTA and IR-CBR, achieve maximum information capacity $C \approx 0.52$ bit per synapse. Interestingly, this result exceeds the asymptotic limits of the Willshaw model, and is achieved for a pattern number $M \approx 39000$ where iterative retrieval works at a low output noise level $\epsilon \approx 0.032$ (compared to the high output noise-levels for one-step retrieval [7]).

By contrast, the best block-coding strategy IRB-SMX ("sum of max") minimizes output noise in most relevant parameter ranges, whereas the maximum information storage capacity is slightly lower ($C \approx 0.51$), and is achieved only for relatively high noise levels at a larger memory load ($M = 46000$ at $\epsilon_u = 0.55$ and $\epsilon_v = 0.12$). The reason for this discrepancy is that finite block patterns contain considerably less information than random patterns [32]. At least asymptotically, block patterns achieve the same information content and storage capacity as random patterns [20,32]. For larger finite networks it may be possible that block coding (most likely for the "sum-of-max" strategy) may surpass the performance of IR-CBR and IR-KWTA for random patterns, which will be investigated in a forthcoming paper.

The phenomenon that finite networks exceed the asymptotic limit has been described earlier for auto-association [55]. It is due to the fact that iterative retrieval and one-step retrieval have identical capacity limits, e.g., $C = (2 - \lambda)\lambda \ln 2$ for large hetero-associative networks ($n \to \infty$) and noisy inputs ($\lambda < 1$), whereas for finite n iterative retrieval can significantly improve retrieval results. An interesting question for future research is to find the absolute maximum value and the corresponding optimal network size by simulating very large networks. Some preliminary data [32] indicate that the optimal network size is in the range of $n \approx 10^5$, coinciding well with the size of a cortical macrocolumn [6].

Furthermore, we have presented data also for non-optimal pattern activity $k \not\sim \ln n$ that renders (at an acceptable output noise level) the network compressible due to an unbalanced distribution of potentiated and unpotentiated synapses [33]. We have found that for larger $k >> \ln n$, where the fraction $p_1 = 1 - (1 - \frac{k^2}{n^2})^M \to 1$ of potentiated synapses approaches one ("dense potentiation"), the improvements of block coding become rather negligible (Table 1). Still, as even minor changes in the number of stored patterns may significantly change the network compressibility in this regime, future work should investigate the capacity and efficiency gains of block coding for compressed networks [8,28,33,54] or structural plasticity [9,31,34]. It may also be interesting to investigate the effect of block coding for improved types of associative networks, such as zip nets [30] or Bayesian associative memory [11,29,38,39].

Acknowledgments. The authors are grateful to Friedhelm Schwenker and Fritz Sommer for valuable discussions. The authors acknowledge support by the state of Baden-Württemberg through bwHPC.

References

1. Albus, J.: A theory of cerebellar function. Math. Biosci. **10**, 25–61 (1971)
2. Aliabadi, B.K., Berrou, C., Gripon, V., Jiang, X.: Storing sparse messages in networks of neural cliques. IEEE Trans. Neural Netw. Learn. Syst. **25**, 980–989 (2014)
3. Bentz, H., Hagstroem, M., Palm, G.: Information storage and effective data retrieval in sparse matrices. Neural Netw. **2**, 289–293 (1989)
4. Bogacz, R., Brown, M., Giraud-Carrier, C.: Model of familiarity discrimination in the perirhinal cortex. J. Comput. Neurosci. **10**, 5–23 (2001)
5. Braitenberg, V.: Cell assemblies in the cerebral cortex. In: Heim, R., Palm, G. (eds.) Theoretical Approaches to Complex Systems. Lecture Notes in Biomathematics, vol. 21, pp. 171–188. Springer, Heidelberg (1978). https://doi.org/10.1007/978-3-642-93083-6_9
6. Braitenberg, V., Schüz, A.: Anatomy of the Cortex: Statistics and Geometry. Springer, Berlin (1991). https://doi.org/10.1007/978-3-662-02728-8
7. Buckingham, J., Willshaw, D.: Performance characteristics of the associative net. Netw.: Comput. Neural Syst. **3**, 407–414 (1992)

8. Chechik, G., Meilijson, I., Ruppin, E.: Synaptic pruning in development: a computational account. Neural Comput. **10**(7), 1759–1777 (1998)
9. Chklovskii, D., Mel, B., Svoboda, K.: Cortical rewiring and information storage. Nature **431**, 782–788 (2004)
10. Cover, T., Thomas, J.: Elements of Information Theory. Wiley, New York (1991)
11. Dayan, P., Willshaw, D.: Optimising synaptic learning rules in linear associative memory. Biol. Cybern. **65**, 253–265 (1991)
12. Fay, R., Kaufmann, U., Knoblauch, A., Markert, H., Palm, G.: Combining visual attention, object recognition and associative information processing in a neurobotic system. In: Wermter, S., Palm, G., Elshaw, M. (eds.) Biomimetic Neural Learning for Intelligent Robots. LNCS (LNAI), vol. 3575, pp. 118–143. Springer, Heidelberg (2005). https://doi.org/10.1007/11521082_8
13. Ferro, D., Gripon, V., Jiang, X.: Nearest neighbour search using binary neural networks. In: Proceedings of the International Joint Conference on Neural Networks (IJCNN), July 2016
14. Fransen, E., Lansner, A.: A model of cortical associative memory based on a horizontal network of connected columns. Netw. Comput. Neural Syst. **9**, 235–264 (1998)
15. Gardner, E.: Maximum storage capacity in neural networks. Europhys. Lett. **4**, 481–485 (1987)
16. Gardner-Medwin, A.: The recall of events through the learning of associations between their parts. Proc. Roy. Soc. London Ser. B **194**, 375–402 (1976)
17. Greene, D., Parnas, M., Yao, F.: Multi-index hashing for information retrieval. In: Proceedings of the 35th Annual Symposium on Foundations of Computer Science, pp. 722–731 (1994)
18. Gripon, V., Berrou, C.: Sparse neural networks with large learning diversity. IEEE Trans. Neural Netw. **22**(7), 1087–1096 (2011)
19. Gripon, V., Berrou, C.: Nearly-optimal associative memories based on distributed constant weight codes. In: Proceedings of the IEEE Information Theory and Applications Workshop (ITA), pp. 269–273 (2012)
20. Gripon, V., Heusel, J., Löwe, M., Vermet, F.: A comparative study of sparse associative memories. J. Stat. Phys. **164**(1), 105–129 (2016)
21. Gripon, V., Löwe, M., Vermet, F.: Associative memories to accelerate approximate nearest neighbor search. Appl. Sci. **8**(9), 1676 (2018)
22. Hebb, D.: The Organization of Behavior: A Neuropsychological Theory. Wiley, New York (1949)
23. Honegger, K., Campbell, R., Turner, G.: Cellular-resolution population imaging reveals robust sparse coding in the Drosophila mushroom body. J. Neurosci. **31**(33), 11772–11785 (2011)
24. Hopfield, J.: Neural networks and physical systems with emergent collective computational abilities. Proc. Natl. Acad. Sci. USA **79**, 2554–2558 (1982)
25. Huyck, C., Orengo, V.: Information retrieval and categorization using a cell assembly network. Neural Comput. Appl. **14**(4), 282–289 (2005)
26. Johansson, C., Lansner, A.: Imposing biological constraints onto an abstract neocortical attractor network model. Neural Comput. **19**(7), 1871–1896 (2007)
27. Kanerva, P.: Sparse Distributed Memory. MIT Press, Cambridge (1988)
28. Knoblauch, A.: Optimal matrix compression yields storage capacity 1 for binary willshaw associative memory. In: Kaynak, O., Alpaydin, E., Oja, E., Xu, L. (eds.) ICANN/ICONIP - 2003. LNCS, vol. 2714, pp. 325–332. Springer, Heidelberg (2003). https://doi.org/10.1007/3-540-44989-2_39

29. Knoblauch, A.: Neural associative memory with optimal Bayesian learning. Neural Comput. **23**(6), 1393–1451 (2011)
30. Knoblauch, A.: Efficient associative computation with discrete synapses. Neural Comput. **28**(1), 118–186 (2016)
31. Knoblauch, A., Körner, E., Körner, U., Sommer, F.: Structural plasticity has high memory capacity and can explain graded amnesia, catastrophic forgetting, and the spacing effect. PLoS One **9**(5), e96485 (2014). 1–19
32. Knoblauch, A., Palm, G.: Iterative retrieval and block coding in auto- and hetero-associative memory. Submitted to Neural Computation (2019)
33. Knoblauch, A., Palm, G., Sommer, F.: Memory capacities for synaptic and structural plasticity. Neural Comput. **22**(2), 289–341 (2010)
34. Knoblauch, A., Sommer, F.: Structural plasticity, effectual connectivity, and memory in cortex. Front. Neuroanat. **10**(63), 1–20 (2016)
35. Kohonen, T.: Associative Memory: A System Theoretic Approach. Springer, Heidelberg (1977). https://doi.org/10.1007/978-3-642-96384-1
36. Kryzhanovsky, B., Litinskii, L., Mikaelian, A.: Vector-neuron models of associative memory. In: 2004 IEEE International Joint Conference on Neural Networks (IEEE Cat. No.04CH37541; IJCNN-04), vol. 2, pp. 909–914 (2004)
37. Lansner, A.: Associative memory models: from the cell-assembly theory to biophysically detailed cortex simulations. Trends Neurosci. **32**(3), 178–186 (2009)
38. Lansner, A., Ekeberg, O.: A one-layer feedback artificial neural network with a Bayesian learning rule. Int. J. Neural Syst. **1**(1), 77–87 (1989)
39. Lansner, A., Holst, A.: A higher order Bayesian neural network with spiking units. Int. J. Neural Syst. **7**(2), 115–128 (1996)
40. Laurent, G.: Olfactory network dynamics and the coding of multidimensional signals. Nat. Rev. Neurosci. **3**, 884–895 (2002)
41. Marr, D.: A theory of cerebellar cortex. J. Physiol. **202**(2), 437–470 (1969)
42. Marr, D.: Simple memory: a theory for archicortex. Philos. Trans. Roy. Soc. London Ser. B **262**, 24–81 (1971)
43. Mu, X., Artiklar, M., Watta, P., Hassoun, M.: An RCE-based associative memory with application to human face recognition. Neural Process. Let. **23**, 257–271 (2006)
44. Palm, G.: On associative memories. Biol. Cybern. **36**, 19–31 (1980)
45. Palm, G.: Neural Assemblies: An Alternative Approach to Artificial Intelligence. Springer, Berlin (1982). https://doi.org/10.1007/978-3-642-81792-2
46. Palm, G.: Novelty: Information and Surprise. Springer, Heidelberg (2012). https://doi.org/10.1007/978-3-642-29075-6
47. Palm, G.: Neural associative memories and sparse coding. Neural Netw. **37**, 165–171 (2013)
48. Palm, G., Sommer, F.: Information capacity in recurrent McCulloch-Pitts networks with sparsely coded memory states. Network **3**, 177–186 (1992)
49. Palm, G., Sommer, F.: Associative data storage and retrieval in neural nets. In: Domany, E., van Hemmen, J., Schulten, K. (eds.) Models of Neural Networks III, pp. 79–118. Springer, New York (1996). https://doi.org/10.1007/978-1-4612-0723-8_3
50. Prager, R., Fallside, F.: The modified Kanerva model for automatic speech recognition. Comput. Speech Lang. **3**, 61–81 (1989)
51. Pulvermüller, F.: The Neuroscience of Language: On Brain Circuits of Words and Serial Order. Cambridge University Press, Cambridge (2003)
52. Rehn, M., Sommer, F.: Storing and restoring visual input with collaborative rank coding and associative memory. Neurocomputing **69**, 1219–1223 (2006)

53. Rolls, E.: A theory of hippocampal function in memory. Hippocampus **6**, 601–620 (1996)
54. Sacramento, J., Burnay, F., Wichert, A.: Regarding the temporal requirements of a hierarchical Willshaw network. Neural Netw. **25**, 84–93 (2012)
55. Schwenker, F., Sommer, F., Palm, G.: Iterative retrieval of sparsely coded associative memory patterns. Neural Netw. **9**, 445–455 (1996)
56. Sommer, F., Palm, G.: Improved bidirectional retrieval of sparse patterns stored by Hebbian learning. Neural Netw. **12**, 281–297 (1999)
57. Steinbuch, K.: Die Lernmatrix. Kybernetik **1**, 36–45 (1961)
58. Wichert, A.: Cell assemblies for diagnostic problem-solving. Neurocomputing **69**, 810–824 (2006)
59. Willshaw, D., Buneman, O., Longuet-Higgins, H.: Non-holographic associative memory. Nature **222**, 960–962 (1969)
60. Wu, F.: The potts model. Rev. Mod. Phys. **54**, 235–268 (1982)
61. Yao, Z., Gripon, V., Rabbat, M.: A GPU-based associative memory using sparse neural networks. In: Proceedings of the IEEE International Conference on High-Performance-Computing and Simulation (HPCS), pp. 688–692 (2014)

Stability Analysis of a Generalized Class of BAM Neural Networks with Mixed Delays

Chaouki Aouiti[1(✉)], Farouk Chérif[2], and Anis Zeglaoui[3]

[1] Faculty of Sciences of Bizerta, Department of Mathematics, Research Units of Mathematics and Applications UR13ES47, University of Carthage, BP W, 7021 Zarzouna, Bizerta, Tunisia
chaouki.aouiti@fsb.rnu.tn
[2] Laboratory of Math Physics; Specials Functions and Applications LR11ES35, ESSTHS, ISSAT, University of Sousse, 4002 Sousse, Tunisia
faroukcheriff@yahoo.fr
[3] Mathematics Department, King Khaled University-KSA, Abha, Saudi Arabia
anis.zeglaoui@gmail.com

Abstract. In this paper, we shall establish the existence and the uniqueness of the unique equilibrium point of a class of generalized BAM neural networks. We will construct a new and suitable Lyapunov function to derive the sufficient conditions which ensure that the equilibrium point exist and it is globally exponentially stable. A numerical example is given in order to confirm the theoretical developments of this paper.

Keywords: Bidirectional associative memory networks · Equilibria · Mixed delays · Exponential stability

1 Introduction

Dynamical behavior and oscillations of neural networks are fundamental to network designs. Due to these, stability analysis of various types neural networks has received, during the last two decades, specific attention from a lot of scholars so far [2,3,6,7,9]. Hence, the studies on neural networks not only involve discussions of stability property of equilibrium point, but also involve investigations of other dynamics behaviors such as oscillations, bifurcation and chaos. In particular, the bi-directional associative memory (BAM) neural networks have been paid much attention recently due to its applicability in many fields such as image and signal processing, pattern recognition, optimization and automatic control. Kosko [4] and [5] studied the stability of BAM neural networks described by a system of ordinary differential equations. Roughly speaking, the BAM neural network is composed of neurons arranged in two layers, the $X-$layer and $Y-$layer. The neurons in one layer are fully interconnected to the neurons in

I. V. Tetko et al. (Eds.): ICANN 2019, LNCS 11727, pp. 20–31, 2019.
https://doi.org/10.1007/978-3-030-30487-4_2

the other layer. Through iterations of forward and backward information flows between the two layer, it performs a two-way associative search for stored bipolar vector pairs and generalize the single-layer auto-associative Hebbian correlation to a two-layer pattern-matched hetero-associative circuits. Therefore, this class of networks possesses good applications prospects in the areas of pattern recognition, signal and image process, robotics. For instance we refer the reader to [7,8,10,11].

Hence, in a recent paper [1], the authors studied a new class of BAM neural networks with time-varying weights and continuously distributed delays. Without assuming boundedness, monotonicity or differentiability of the activation functions, sufficient new conditions are given in order to demonstrate the existence and uniqueness of weighted pseudo almost-periodic solution of the following model.

$$\begin{aligned}
\dot{x}_i(t) &= -a_i x_i(t) + I_i \\
&+ \sum_{j=1}^{m} \left[c_{ij} f_j(y_j(t-\tau_{ji})) + d_{ij} \int_{-\infty}^{t} k_{ij}(t-s) f_j(y_j(s)) ds \right] \\
\dot{y}_j(t) &= -b_j y_j(t) + J_j \\
&+ \sum_{i=1}^{n} \left[w_{ji} g_i(x_i(t-\sigma_{ji})) + \alpha_{ji} \int_{-\infty}^{t} N_{ji}(t-s) g_i(x_i(s)) ds \right]
\end{aligned} \tag{1}$$

where $i = 1, ..., n, j = 1, ..., m$, corresponds to the number of neurons in X-layer

and Y-layer, respectively, $x_i(\cdot)$, $y_j(\cdot)$, are the activation of the i-th and j-th neurons respectively $c_{ij}, d_{ij}, \alpha_{ji}$ and w_{ji} are connection weights and I_i and J_j denote the external inputs. $a_i \ (i \in \{1, \cdots, n\}), b_j \ (j \in \{1, \cdots, m\})$ represent the rate with which the ith neuron and jth neuron will reset its potential to the resting state in isolation when disconnected from the network and external inputs at the time t, respectively. $K_{ij}(\cdot), N_{ji}(\cdot)$ denoted the refractoriness of the $i-$th neuron and $j-$th neuron after they have fired or responded. $I_i \ (i \in \{1, \cdots, n\}), J_j \ (j \in \{1, \cdots, m\})$ are the external inputs. Pose $\tau = \max_{1 \le i \le n 1 \le j \le n} (\tau_{ji}, \sigma_{ij})$, let the initial conditions associated with (1) be of the form

$$\begin{cases} x_i(t) = \varphi_i(t) & t \in (-\infty, 0] \\ y_j(t) = \psi_j(t) & t \in (-\infty, 0] \end{cases}$$

where $\varphi_i(\cdot)$ and $\psi_j(\cdot)$ are assumed to be a continuous functions on $\mathbf{R}$. For an arbitrary vector:

$$(x(t), y(t)) := (x_1(t), \cdots, x_n(t), y_1(t), \cdots, y_m(t))^T \in \mathbf{R}^{n+m}$$

define the norm: $\|(x, y)\| = \|x\| + \|y\|$ where,

$$\|x\| = \sup_{t \in \mathbf{R}} \max_{1 \le i \le n} \{|x_i(t)|\}$$

and

$$\|y\| = \sup_{t\in\mathbf{R}} \max_{1\le j\le m} \left\{|y_j(t)|\right\}.$$

This paper can be seen as a natural continuation of the recent paper [1] and has as main purpose to establish the existence and uniqueness of the equilibria by using an adequate contraction principle. Also the global exponential stability of the equilibria is established by constructing a new and suitable Lyapunov function. The organization of this paper is as follows. In Sect. 2, the existence and global exponential stability of the unique equilibrium point is obtained. An example is given in Sect. 3 to illustrate the effectiveness of our theoretical results. It should be mentioned that the main results include Theorems 1 and 2. Let us consider the following assumptions

(H_1) For all $1 \le i \le n$, $a_i > 0$ and for all $1 \le j \le n$, $b_j > 0$.
(H_2) For all $1 \le i \le n$, $1 \le j \le m$ there exist constant numbers $L_j^f,\ L_i^g > 0$ such that for all $x, y \in \mathbf{R}$

$$|f_j(x) - f_j(y)| < L_j^f\,|x-y|\,,\quad |g_i(x) - g_i(y)| < L_i^g\,|x-y|\,.$$

Furthermore, we suppose that $f_j(0) = g_i\,(0) = 0$ for all for all $1 \le j \le m$, and for all $1 \le i \le n$.
(H_3) For all $1 \le i \le n, 1 \le j \le m$, the delay kernels $K_{ij} : [0,+\infty[\longrightarrow [0,+\infty[$ and $N_{ji} : [0,+\infty[\longrightarrow [0.+\infty[$ are continuous, integrable and there exist non negative constants k_{ij}, n_{ji} such that

$$\int_0^{+\infty} K_{ij}\,(s)\,ds \le k_{ij};\ \int_0^{+\infty} N_{ji}\,(s)\,ds \le n_{ji}.$$

2 Existence and Exponential Stability of Equilibria

In this section, we prove first the existence and uniqueness of the non trivial equilibrium point. Next *we* shall construct a suitable Lyapunov functions to derive the sufficient conditions which ensure that the equilibrium of (1) is globally exponentially stable.

Definition 1. *A constant vector* $(x_1^*, x_2^*, \cdots, x_n^*, y_1^*, y_2^*, \cdots, y_m^*) \in \mathbf{R}^{n+m}$ *is said to be an equilibrium solution to the model (1) if it satisfies the system of equations*

$$\begin{cases} a_i x_i^* = \sum\limits_{j=1}^{m} c_{ij}(t) f_j(y_j^*) + d_{ij}(t) f_j(y_j^*)) + I_i, \\ b_j y_j^* = \sum\limits_{i=1}^{n} w_{ji}\,(t)\,g_i(x_i^*) + \alpha_{ji}(t) g_i(x_i^*) + J_j, \end{cases} \tag{2}$$

Theorem 1. *Let the conditions* $(H_1) - (H_3)$ *hold. Suppose that*

$$(H_4)\quad \begin{aligned} &\kappa = \max(e, f) < 1 \\ &\text{where } e = \max_{1\le j\le m}\left(\sum_{i=1}^{n}\frac{L_j^f}{b_j}\left(|c_{ij}|+|d_{ij}|\right)\right) \\ &\text{and } f = \max_{1\le i\le n}\left(\sum_{j=1}^{m}\frac{L_i^g}{a_i}\left(|w_{ji}|+|\alpha_{ji}|\right)\right) \end{aligned}$$

Then the Eq. (1) possesses a non trivial equilibrium point $(x_1^*, x_2^*, \cdots, x_n^*, y_1^*, y_2^*, \cdots, y_m^*) \in \mathbf{R}^{n+m}$.

Proof. First, let us prove the existence and uniqueness of the equilibrium (x^*, y^*) of the Eq. (1). For all $i \in \{1, \cdots, n\}$ and for all $j \in \{1, \cdots, m\}$, pose $u_i^* = a_i x_i^*$ and $v_j^* = b_j y_j^*$. Immediately we obtain the following equations

$$\begin{cases} u_i^* = \sum_{j=1}^{m} c_{ij}(t) f_j(\frac{v_j^*}{b_j}) + d_{ij}(t) f_j(\frac{v_j^*}{b_j})) + I_i, \\ v_j^* = \sum_{i=1}^{n} w_{ji}(t)\, g_i(\frac{u_i^*}{a_i}) + \alpha_{ji}(t) g_i(\frac{u_i^*}{a_i}) + J_j. \end{cases}$$

Now, consider a mapping Λ: $\mathbf{R}^{n+m} \longrightarrow \mathbf{R}^{n+m}$ defined by

$$\Lambda(u_1, \cdots, u_n, v_1, \cdots, v_m) = \begin{pmatrix} \sum_{j=1}^{m} c_{1j} f_j(\frac{v_j}{b_j}) + d_{1j} f_j(\frac{v_j}{b_j})) + I_1 \\ \vdots \\ \sum_{j=1}^{m} c_{nj} f_j(\frac{v_j}{b_j}) + d_{nj} f_j(\frac{v_j}{b_j})) + I_n \\ \sum_{i=1}^{n} w_{1i} g_i(\frac{u_i}{a_i}) + \alpha_{1i} g_i(\frac{u_i}{a_i}) + J_1 \\ \vdots \\ \sum_{i=1}^{n} w_{mi} g_i(\frac{u_i}{a_i}) + \alpha_{mi} g_i(\frac{u_i}{a_i}) + J_m \end{pmatrix}$$

We shall prove that the operator Λ is a contraction mapping on $\mathbf{R}^{n+m}$. Here we will use the following norm on $\mathbf{R}^{n+m}$

$$\|z\| = <z, sign(z)>$$

where $<\xi, \zeta>$ denotes the standard inner product of vectors ξ and ζ in $\mathbf{R}^{n+m}$, and $sign(z) = (sign(z_1), sign(z_2), ..., sign(z_{n+m})))^T$ is the sign vector of z.

For $u = (u_1, \cdots, u_n, v_1, \cdots, v_m) \in \mathbf{R}^{n+m}, \overline{u} = (\overline{u}_1, \cdots, \overline{u}_n, \overline{v}_1, \cdots, \overline{v}_m) \in \mathbf{R}^{n+m}$, one has

$$
\begin{aligned}
&\left\|\Lambda\left(\overline{u}\right)-\Lambda\left(u\right)\right\| \\
&=\left\|\Lambda\left(\overline{u}_1,\cdots,\overline{u}_n,\overline{v}_1,\cdots,\overline{v}_m\right)-\Lambda\left(u_1,\cdots,u_n,v_1,\cdots,v_m\right)\right\| \\
&=\left\|\sum_{i=1}^{n}\sum_{j=1}^{m}c_{ij}f_j(\frac{\overline{v_j}}{b_j})+d_{ij}f_j(\frac{\overline{v_j}}{b_j}))+\sum_{j=1}^{m}\sum_{i=1}^{n}w_{ji}g_i(\frac{\overline{u_i}}{a_i})+\alpha_{ji}g_i(\frac{\overline{u_i}}{a_i})\right. \\
&\left.-\sum_{i=1}^{n}\sum_{j=1}^{m}c_{ij}f_j(\frac{v_j}{b_j})+d_{ij}f_j(\frac{v_j}{b_j})+\sum_{j=1}^{m}\sum_{i=1}^{n}w_{ji}g_i(\frac{u_i}{a_i})+\alpha_{ji}g_i(\frac{u_i}{a_i})\right\| \\
&=\sum_{i=1}^{n}\left|\sum_{j=1}^{n}c_{ij}\left(f_j(\frac{\overline{v_j}}{b_j})-f_j(\frac{v_j}{b_j})\right)\right|+\sum_{i=1}^{n}\left|\sum_{j=1}^{n}d_{ij}\left(f_j(\frac{\overline{v_j}}{b_j})-f_j(\frac{v_j}{b_j})\right)\right| \\
&+\sum_{j=1}^{m}\left|\sum_{i=1}^{n}w_{ji}\left(g_i(\frac{\overline{u_j}}{a_i})-g_i(\frac{u_i}{a_i})\right)\right|+\sum_{j=1}^{m}\left|\sum_{i=1}^{n}\alpha_{ji}\left(g_i(\frac{\overline{u_i}}{a_i})-g_i(\frac{u_i}{a_i})\right)\right| \\
&\leq\sum_{i=1}^{n}\sum_{j=1}^{m}\left|c_{ij}\right|L_j^f\left|\frac{\overline{v_j}}{b_j}-\frac{v_j}{b_j}\right|+\sum_{i=1}^{n}\sum_{j=1}^{m}\left|d_{ij}\right|L_j^f\left|\frac{\overline{v_j}}{b_j}-\frac{v_j}{b_j}\right| \\
&+\sum_{j=1}^{m}\sum_{i=1}^{n}\left|w_{ji}\right|L_j^g\left|\frac{\overline{u_j}}{a_i}-\frac{u_i}{a_i}\right|+\sum_{j=1}^{m}\sum_{i=1}^{n}\left|\alpha_{ji}\right|L_j^g\left|\frac{\overline{u_i}}{a_i}-\frac{u_i}{a_i}\right| \\
&\leq\left[\max_{1\leq j\leq m}\left(\sum_{i=1}^{n}\left(\left|c_{ij}\right|+\left|d_{ij}\right|\right)\frac{L_j^f}{b_j}\right)\right]\sum_{j=1}^{m}\left|\overline{v_j}-v_j\right| \\
&+\left[\max_{1\leq i\leq n}\left(\sum_{j=1}^{m}\left(\left|w_{ji}\right|+\left|\alpha_{ji}\right|\right)\frac{L_i^g}{a_i}\right)\right]\sum_{i=1}^{n}\left|\overline{u_i}-u_i\right| \\
&\leq\kappa\left(\sum_{i=1}^{n}\left|\overline{u_i}-u_i\right|+\sum_{j=1}^{m}\left|\overline{v_j}-v_j\right|\right)=\kappa\left\|\overline{u}-u\right\|.
\end{aligned}
$$

By the hypothesis $\kappa < 1$ which implies that the operator Λ: $\mathbf{R}^{n+m} \longrightarrow \mathbf{R}^{n+m}$ is a contraction on $\mathbf{R}^{n+m}$. Hence by the contraction mapping principle, there exists a unique fixed point of the map Λ which is a solution of the system (2) from which the existence of a unique solution of (1) will follow. The proof is completed.

Theorem 2. *Let the conditions* $(H_1)-(H_3)$ *hold. Suppose that*

$$
a_i-\sum_{j=1}^{m}\left(\left|d_{ij}\right|k_{ij}+\left|c_{ij}\right|\right)L_j^f\geq 0\ ,\ 1\leq i\leq n
$$

$$
b_j-\sum_{i=1}^{n}\left(\left|\alpha_{ji}\right|n_{ji}+\left|w_{ji}\right|\right)L_i^g\geq 0\,,\,1\leq j\leq m
$$

Then there exist constants $M \geq 1$ and $\mu > 0$ such that

$$\sum_{i=1}^{n} |x_i(t) - x_i^*| + \sum_{j=1}^{m} |y_j(t) - y_j^*| \leq M e^{-\mu t}$$
$$\times \left[\sum_{i=1}^{n} \sup_{s\in[-\tau,0]} |x_i(s) - x_i^*| + \sum_{j=1}^{m} \sup_{s\in[-\tau,0]} |y_j(s) - y_j^*| \right]$$

where $(x_1^*, x_2^*, \cdots, x_n^*, y_1^*, y_2^*, \cdots, y_m^*) \in \mathbf{R}^{n+m}$ is the equilibrium point of Theorem 1 and $(x_1, x_2, \cdots, x_n, y_1, y_2, \cdots, y_m)$ is an arbitrary bounded solution of (1) *and*

$$\tau = \max_{1\leq i\leq n,\ 1\leq j\leq m} (\tau_{ij}, \sigma_{ji})$$

Proof. First, note that for all $1 \leq i \leq n$,

$$\frac{d^+}{dt} |x_i(t) - x_i^*| \leq -a_i |x_i(t) - x_i^*| + \sum_{j=1}^{m} \left(|c_{ij}| L_j^f |y_j(t - \tau_j) - y_j^*| \right.$$
$$\left. + \sum_{j=1}^{n} |d_{ij}| L_j^f \int_{-\infty}^{t} K_{ij}(t-s) |y_j(s) - x_j^*| \, ds \right)$$

and for all $1 \leq j \leq m$,

$$\frac{d^+}{dt} |y_j(t) - y_j^*| \leq -b_j |y_i(t) - y_j^*| + \sum_{i=1}^{n} \left(|w_{ji}| L_i^g |x_i(t - \sigma_j) - x_i^*| \right.$$
$$\left. + \sum_{i=1}^{n} |\alpha_{ji}| L_i^g \int_{-\infty}^{t} N_{ji}(t-s) |x_i(s) - x_i^*| \, ds \right).$$

Let F_i and G_j the numerical functions defined by

$$F_i(\varepsilon_i) = (a_i - \varepsilon_i) - \sum_{j=1}^{m} |d_{ij}| k_{ij} L_j^f - \sum_{j=1}^{m} |c_{ij}| L_j^f e^{\varepsilon_i \tau_{ij}},$$
$$1 \leq i \leq n$$
$$G_j(\theta_j) = (b_j - \theta_j) - \sum_{i=1}^{n} |\alpha_{ji}| n_{ji} L_i^g - \sum_{i=1}^{n} |w_{ji}| L_i^g e^{\theta_j \sigma_{ij}},$$
$$1 \leq j \leq m,$$

where ε_i and $\theta_j \in [0, +\infty[$. Clearly, by hypothesis

$$F_i(0) = a_i - \sum_{j=1}^{m} |d_{ij}| k_{ij} L_j^f - \sum_{j=1}^{m} |c_{ij}| L_j^f \geq 0, 1 \leq i \leq n$$
$$G_j(0) = b_j - \sum_{i=1}^{n} |\alpha_{ji}| n_{ji} L_i^g - \sum_{i=1}^{n} |w_{ji}| L_i^g \geq 0, 1 \leq j \leq m$$

Since the functions F_i and G_j are continuous, there exist a sufficiently small constants $\mu_1, \cdots, \mu_n, \rho_1, \cdots, \rho_m > 0$ such that

$$F_i(\mu_i) = (a_i - \mu_i) - \sum_{j=1}^{m} |d_{ij}|\, k_{ij} L_j^f - \sum_{j=1}^{m} |c_{ij}|\, L_j^f e^{\mu_i \tau_{ij}},$$
$$1 \leq i \leq n$$
$$G_j(\rho_j) = (b_j - \rho_j) - \sum_{i=1}^{n} |\alpha_{ji}|\, n_{ji} L_i^g - \sum_{j=1}^{m} |w_{ji}|\, L_i^g e^{\rho_j \sigma_{ij}},$$
$$1 \leq j \leq m.$$

Let us take $\mu = \min(\mu_1, \cdots, \mu_n, \rho_1, \cdots, \rho_m)$, then for all $1 \leq i \leq n$ and for all $1 \leq j \leq m$, one has:

$$\begin{cases} F_i(\mu) = (a_i - \mu) - \sum_{j=1}^{m} |d_{ij}|\, L_j^f - \sum_{j=1}^{m} |c_{ij}|\, L_j^f e^{\mu \tau_{ij}} \geq 0 \\ G_j(\mu) = (b_j - \mu) - \sum_{i=1}^{n} |\alpha_{ji}|\, L_i^g - \sum_{j=1}^{m} |w_{ji}|\, L_i^g e^{\mu \sigma_{ij}} \geq 0. \end{cases}$$

Consider the Lyapunov function defined by

$$\begin{aligned} V(t) = \sum_{i=1}^{n} \Big\{ & e^{\mu t} |x_i(t) - x^*| \\ & + \sum_{j=1}^{m} |c_{ij}|\, L_j^f e^{\mu \tau_{ij}} \int_{t-\tau_{ij}}^{t} e^{\mu s} |y_j(s) - y_j^*|\, ds \\ & + \sum_{j=1}^{m} |d_{ij}|\, L_j^f \int_{0}^{+\infty} K_{ij}(s) \left(\int_{t-s}^{t} |y_j(\rho) - y_j^*|\, e^{\mu \rho} d\rho \right) ds \Big\} \\ & + \sum_{j=1}^{m} \Big\{ e^{\mu t} |y_j(t) - x^*| \\ & + \sum_{i=1}^{n} |w_{ji}|\, L_i^g e^{\mu \sigma_{ij}} \int_{t-\sigma_{ij}}^{t} e^{\mu s} |x_i(s) - x_i^*|\, ds \\ & + \sum_{i=1}^{n} |\alpha_{ji}|\, L_i^g \int_{0}^{+\infty} N_{ji}(s) \left(\int_{t-s}^{t} |x_i(\rho) - x_i^*|\, e^{\mu \rho} d\rho \right) ds \Big\} \end{aligned}$$

for all $t > 0$. In order to finish the proof, it is sufficient to calculate the upper Dini derivatives of V along the solutions of (3). One has

$$
\begin{aligned}
&\frac{d^+V(t)}{dt} \\
&\leq \sum_{i=1}^{n}\left\{ -(a_i-\mu)e^{\mu t}\left|x_i(t)-x_i^*\right| + \sum_{j=1}^{m}\left|c_{ij}\right| L_j^f e^{\mu t}\left|y_j(t-\tau_{ij})-y_j^*\right| \right. \\
&+\sum_{j=1}^{m}\left|d_{ij}\right| L_j^f \int_0^{+\infty} K_{ij}(s)\,e^{\mu(t-s)}\left|y_j(t-s)-y_j^*\right| ds \\
&+\sum_{j=1}^{m}\left|c_{ij}\right| L_j^f e^{\mu\tau_{ij}}\left|y_j(t)-y_j^*\right| e^{\mu t} - \sum_{j=1}^{m}\left|c_{ij}\right| L_j^f e^{\mu\tau_{ij}}\left|y_j(t-\tau_{ij})-y_j^*\right| e^{\mu(t-\tau_{ij})} \\
&+\sum_{j=1}^{m}\left|d_{ij}\right| L_j^f \left|y_j(t)-y_j^*\right| \int_0^{+\infty} K_{ij}(s)\,e^{\mu t} ds \\
&\left. -\sum_{j=1}^{m}\left|d_{ij}\right| L_j^f \int_0^{+\infty} K_{ij}(s)\,e^{\mu(t-s)}\left|y_j(t-s)-y_j^*\right| ds \right\} \\
&+\sum_{j=1}^{m}\left\{ -(b_j-\mu)e^{\mu t}\left|y_j(t)-y_j^*\right| + \sum_{i=1}^{n}\left|w_{ji}\right| L_i^g e^{\mu t}\left|x_i(t-\sigma_{ij})-y_i^*\right| \right. \\
&+\sum_{i=1}^{n}\left|\alpha_{ji}\right| L_j^g \int_0^{+\infty} N_{ji}(s)\,e^{\mu(t-s)}\left|x_i(t-s)-x_i^*\right| ds \\
&+\sum_{i=1}^{n}\left|w_{ji}\right| L_i^g e^{\mu\sigma_{ij}}\left|x_i(t)-x_i^*\right| e^{\mu t} - \sum_{i=1}^{n}\left|w_{ji}\right| L_i^g \left|x_i(t-\sigma_{ij})-x_i^*\right| e^{\mu(t)} \\
&+\sum_{i=1}^{n}\left|\alpha_{ji}\right| L_i^g \left|x_i(t)-x_i^*\right| \int_0^{+\infty} N_{ji}(s)\,e^{\mu t} ds \\
&\left. -\sum_{i=1}^{n}\left|\alpha_{ji}\right| L_i^g \int_0^{+\infty} N_{ji}(s)\,e^{\mu(t-s)}\left|x_i(t-s)-x_i^*\right| ds \right\}.
\end{aligned}
$$

Let us denote by

$$K = \sup_{t>0}\max_{1\leq i\leq n}\left|u_i(t)\right| \quad and \quad K' = \sup_{t>0}\max_{1\leq j\leq m}\left|v_j(t)\right|.$$

So we obtain

$$\begin{aligned}
&\frac{d^+V(t)}{dt} \\
&\leq \sum_{i=1}^{n} e^{\mu t}\left\{-(a_i-\mu)\left|x_i(t)-x^*\right|+\sum_{j=1}^{m}\left|c_{ij}\right| L_j^f e^{\mu\tau_{ij}}\left|y_j(t)-y_j^*\right|\right. \\
&\left.+\sum_{j=1}^{m}\left|d_{ij}\right| L_j^f\left|y_j(t)-y_j^*\right| \int_0^{+\infty} K_{ij}(s)\,ds\right\} \\
&+\sum_{j=1}^{m} e^{\mu t}\left\{-(b_j-\mu)\left|y_j(t)-x^*\right|+\sum_{i=1}^{n}\left|w_{ji}\right| L_i^g e^{\mu\sigma_{ij}}\left|x_i(t)-x_i^*\right|\right. \\
&\left.+\sum_{i=1}^{n}\left|\alpha_{ji}\right| L_i^g\left|x_i(t)-x_i^*\right| \int_0^{+\infty} N_{ji}(s)\,ds\right\} \\
&\leq -\sum_{i=1}^{n} e^{\mu t}\left((a_i-\mu)-\sum_{j=1}^{m}\left|d_{ij}\right| k_{ij} L_j^f-\sum_{j=1}^{m}\left|c_{ij}\right| L_f^j e^{\mu\tau_{ij}}\right) K \\
&-\sum_{j=1}^{m} e^{\mu t}\left((b_j-\mu)-\sum_{i=1}^{n}\left|\alpha_{ji}\right| n_{ji} L_i^g-\sum_{j=1}^{m}\left|w_{ji}\right| L_i^g e^{\mu\tau_{ij}}\right) K' \\
&\leq -e^{\mu t}\sum_{i=1}^{n} F_i(\mu) K-e^{\mu t}\sum_{j=1}^{m} G_j(\mu) K' \leq 0.
\end{aligned}$$

It follows that for all $t \in \mathbf{R}_+^*$, $V(t) \leq V(0)$. Consequently, one can write

$$\begin{aligned}
&e^{\mu t}\left[\sum_{i=1}^{n}\left|x_i(t)-x^*\right|+\sum_{j=1}^{m}\left|y_j(t)-y^*\right|\right] \\
&\leq e^{-\mu t}\sum_{i=1}^{n}\left(\sum_{i=1}^{n} u_i(0)+\sum_{j=1}^{m}\left|c_{ij}\right| L_j^f e^{\mu\tau_{ij}} \int_{-\tau_{ij}}^{0} e^{\mu s}\left|y_j(s)-y_j^*\right| ds\right. \\
&\left.+\sum_{j=1}^{m}\left|d_{ij}\right| L_j^f \int_0^{+\infty} N_{ji}(s)\left(\int_{-s}^{0}\left|y_j(\rho)-y_j^*\right| e^{\mu\rho} d\rho\right) ds\right)+e^{-\mu t}\sum_{j=1}^{m}\left(v_j(0)\right. \\
&+\sum_{i=1}^{n}\left|w_{ji}\right| L_i^g e^{\mu\sigma_{ij}} \int_{-\sigma_{ij}}^{0} e^{\mu s}\left|x_i(s)-x_i^*\right| ds \\
&\left.+\sum_{i=1}^{n}\left|\alpha_{ji}\right| L_g^j \int_0^{+\infty} K_{ij}(s)\left(\int_{-s}^{0}\left|x_i(\rho)-x_i^*\right| e^{\mu\rho} d\rho\right) ds\right)
\end{aligned}$$

$$\leq e^{-\mu t}\sum_{i=1}^{n}\left(1+\sum_{j=1}^{m}|w_{ji}|\,L_i^g\left(e^{\mu\sigma_{ij}}-1\right)+\sum_{j=1}^{m}|\alpha_{ji}|\,L_g^j\right)\times\sup_{s\in[-\tau,0]}|x_i(s)-x_i^*|$$
$$+e^{-\mu t}\sum_{j=1}^{m}\left(1+\sum_{i=1}^{n}|c_{ij}|\,L_j^f\left(e^{\mu\sigma_{ij}}-1\right)+\sum_{i=1}^{n}|\alpha_{ji}|\,L_j^f\right)\times\sup_{s\in[-\tau,0]}\left|y_j(s)-x_j^*\right|$$

In other words,

$$\sum_{i=1}^{n}|x_i(t)-x^*|+\sum_{j=1}^{m}|y_j(t)-y^*|\leq Me^{-\mu t}\times$$
$$\left[\sum_{i=1}^{n}\sup_{s\in[-\tau,0]}|x_i(s)-x_i^*|+\sum_{j=1}^{m}\sup_{s\in[-\tau,0]}\left|y_j(s)-y_j^*\right|\right]$$

where

$M=\max(M_1,M_2)$ with $M_1=\max\limits_{1\leq i\leq n}\left(1+\sum\limits_{j=1}^{m}L_i^g\left(|w_{ji}|\left(e^{\mu\sigma_{ij}}-1\right)+|\alpha_{ji}|\right)\right)$

and $M_2=\max\limits_{1\leq i\leq n}\left(1+\sum\limits_{i=1}^{n}\left(|c_{ij}|\left(e^{\mu\sigma_{ij}}-1\right)+|\alpha_{ji}|\right)L_j^f\right)$.

3 Numerical Example

Let us consider the following model

$$\begin{aligned}\dot{x}_i(t)&=-a_ix_i(t)+\sum_{j=1}^{3}c_{ij}f_j(y_j(t-\tau_{ij}))+d_{ij}\int_{-\infty}^{t}K_{ij}(t-s)\,f_j(y_j(s))ds+I_i,\\ \dot{y}_j(t)&=-b_jy_j(t)+\sum_{i=1}^{3}w_{ji}g_i(x_i(t-\sigma_{ij}))+\alpha_{ji}\int_{-\infty}^{t}N_{ji}(t-s)\,g_i(x_i(s))ds+J_j\end{aligned}\qquad(3)$$

where $\tau_{ij}=\sigma_{ij}=0.3,\ K_{ij}(s)=N_{ji}(s)=e^{-s},\ I_i=J_j=0,$
$(a_1,a_2,a_3)^T=(2,5,4),\ (b_1,b_2,b_3)^T=(7,3,5).$

$$(c_{ij})_{1\leq i,j\leq 3}=\begin{pmatrix}0.1\ 0.1\ 0.1\\0.2\ 0.2\ 0.1\\0.3\ 0.2\ 0.1\end{pmatrix},\ (d_{ij})_{1\leq i,j\leq 3}=\begin{pmatrix}0.1\ 0.1\ 0.1\\0.3\ 0.1\ 0.3\\0.1\ 0.3\ 0.2\end{pmatrix},$$
$$(w_{ji})_{1\leq i,j\leq 3}=\begin{pmatrix}0.3\ 0.1\ 0.2\\0.2\ 0.3\ 0.2\\0.5\ 0.2\ 0.2\end{pmatrix},\ (\alpha_{ji})_{1\leq i,j\leq 3}=\begin{pmatrix}0.3\ 0.1\ 0.5\\0.3\ 0.3\ 0.2\\0.2\ 0.2\ 0.5\end{pmatrix}$$

and for all $x\in\mathbf{R}$,

$$f_j(x)=g_i(x)=\frac{|x+1|-|x-1|}{2},$$

Clearly the conditions

$$a_i-2\sum_{j=1}^{3}\left(|d_{ij}|+|c_{ij}|\right)L_j^f\geq 0,\ b_j-2\sum_{i=1}^{3}\left(|c_{ij}|+|d_{ij}|\right)L_i^g\geq 0$$

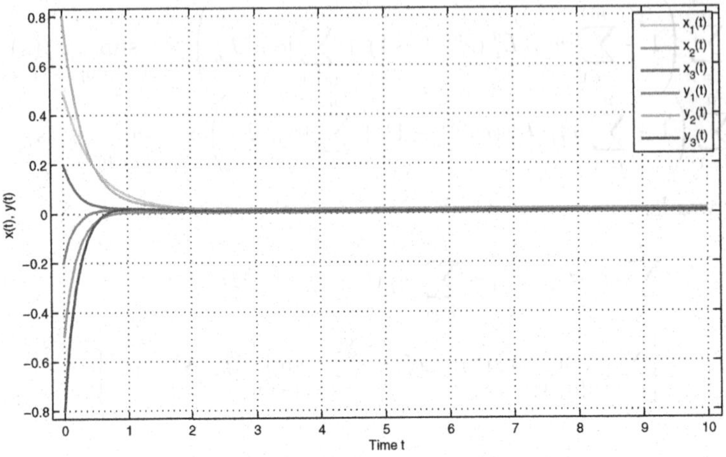

Fig. 1. The time responds trajectories of x(t) and y(t) in (3)

are satisfied for all $1 \leq i \leq n$. Then $\max(e, f) = 0.8 < 1$, where

$$e = \max_{1\leq j\leq m}\left(\sum_{i=1}^{3}\frac{L_j^f}{b_j}\left(|c_{ij}| + |d_{ij}|\right)\right), \quad f = \max_{1\leq i\leq n}\left(\sum_{j=1}^{3}|w_{ji}|\frac{L_i^g}{b_i}\left(|w_{ji}| + |\alpha_{ji}|\right)\right)$$

Thus, it follows from Theorems 1 and 2 that the unique equilibrium of system (3) is globally exponentially stable (Fig. 1).

4 Conclusion

A generalized model of bi-directional associative memory (BAM) neural networks with mixed delays has been presented. The existence of the equilibrium point as well as the global stablity are established. Note that, in our study, we just require that activation function is globally Lipschitz continuous, which is less conservative and less restrictive than the monotonic assumption in previous results. The method is very concise and the obtained results are new and they complement previously known results. Finally, two examples are given to illustrate our theory.

Future works aim at exploiting the described model to a BAM neural networks as a learning system in robotics and application to handicapped persons.

References

1. Ammar, B., Brahmi, H., Cherif, F.: On the weighted pseudo-almost periodic solution for BAM networks with delays. Neural Process. Lett. **48**(2), 849–862 (2018). https://doi.org/10.1007/s11063-017-9725-0

2. Ammar, B., Chérif, F., Alimi, A.M.: Existence and uniqueness of pseudo almost-periodic solutions of recurrent neural networks with time-varying coefficients and mixed delays. IEEE Trans. Neural Netw. Learn. Syst. **23**(1), 109–118 (2011). https://doi.org/10.1109/TNNLS.2011.2178444
3. Chérif, F.: Existence and global exponential stability of pseudo almost periodic solution for SICNNs with mixed delays. J. Appl. Math. Comput. **39**(1–2), 235–251 (2012). https://doi.org/10.1007/s12190-011-0520-1
4. Kosko, B.: Adaptive bidirectional associative memories. Appl. Opt. **26**(23), 4947–4960 (1987). https://doi.org/10.1364/AO.26.004947
5. Kosko, B.: Neural networks and fuzzy systems: a dynamical systems approach to machine intelligence. No. QA76. 76. E95 K86 (1992)
6. Liu, Z., Chen, A., Cao, J., Huang, L.: Existence and global exponential stability of almost periodic solutions of BAM neural networks with continuously distributed delays. Phys. Lett. A **319**(3–4), 305–316 (2003). https://doi.org/10.1016/j.physleta.2003.10.020
7. Lou, X., Cui, B.: On the global robust asymptotic stability of BAM neural networks with time-varying delays. Neurocomputing **70**(1–3), 273–279 (2006). https://doi.org/10.1016/j.neucom.2006.02.020
8. Park, J.H., Kwon, O.: On improved delay-dependent criterion for global stability of bidirectional associative memory neural networks with time-varying delays. Appl. Math. Comput. **199**(2), 435–446 (2008). https://doi.org/10.1016/j.amc.2007.10.001
9. Song, Q., Cao, J.: Global exponential stability of bidirectional associative memory neural networks with distributed delays. J. Comput. Appl. Math. **202**(2), 266–279 (2007). https://doi.org/10.1016/j.cam.2006.02.031
10. Wang, Z., Liu, Y., Li, M., Liu, X.: Stability analysis for stochastic cohen-grossberg neural networks with mixed time delays. IEEE Trans. Neural Netw. **17**(3), 814–820 (2006). https://doi.org/10.1109/TNN.2006.872355
11. Zhao, H.: Global stability of bidirectional associative memory neural networks with distributed delays. Phys. Lett. A **297**(3–4), 182–190 (2002). https://doi.org/10.1016/S0375-9601(02)00434-6

Dissipativity Analysis of a Class of Competitive Neural Networks with Proportional Delays

Chaouki Aouiti[1(✉)], Farouk Chérif[2], and Farid Touati[1]

[1] Faculty of Sciences of Bizerta, Department of Mathematics, Research Units of Mathematics and Applications UR13ES47, University of Carthage, BP W, 7021 Zarzouna, Bizerta, Tunisia
{chaouki.aouiti,farid.touati}@fsb.rnu.tn

[2] Laboratory of Math Physics; Specials Functions and Applications LR11ES35 ESSTHS ISSAT, University of Sousse, 4002 Sousse, Tunisia
faroukcheriff@yahoo.fr

Abstract. This paper dealt with the dissipativity problem for a class of competitive neural networks with proportional delays. Based on Lyapunov functionals approach, new sufficient conditions are derived to ensuring the strictly $(Q,\ S^*,\ R)-$dissipative of the model. The conditions are presented in terms of linear matrix inequalities (LMIs) and can be easily numerically checked by the MATLAB LMI toolbox. At last, a numerical example with simulation is given to illustrate the validity of the obtained theoretical results.

Keywords: Competitive Neural Networks · Proportional delays · Dissipativity · Lyapunov functionals · Linear matrix inequality

1 Introduction

During the last years, several researchers paid attention to the study of Artificial Neural Networks (ANNs) as an important branch of mathematics. Competitive Neural Networks (CNNs) are one of the largest class of ANNs. In CNNs, there are two types of state variables: the shortterm memory variables (STM) describing the fast neural activity and the long-term memory (LTM) variables describing the slow unsupervised synaptic modifications.

It is well known that time delays exist in ANNs because of the finite switching speed of neurons and amplifiers. Based on the Hopfield neural network model, Marcus and Westervelt proposed the first ANNs model with delay. Time delay is one of the main sources of instability or bad performances. Then, it has become necessary to consider ANNs with a time delay (see [1–7]). One of important types of delays is the proportional delay which is recently the subject of several studies (see [18–20]) due to its biological and physical reality.

I. V. Tetko et al. (Eds.): ICANN 2019, LNCS 11727, pp. 32–42, 2019.
https://doi.org/10.1007/978-3-030-30487-4_3

In 1972, Willems [14,15] introduced the theory of dissipativity. Therefore, the subject of dissipativity has received much attention because it is an important property in synchronization theory, stability theory, chaos, and robust control (see [8,11–13,17]).

Motivated by the above, in this paper, we try to establish the dissipativity of the following model:

$$\begin{cases} STM : \varepsilon \dot{x}_i(t) = -a_i x_i(t) + \sum_{j=1}^{n} b_{ij} f_j(x_j(t)) + \sum_{j=1}^{n} d_{ij} f_j(x_j(qt))) \\ \qquad + E_i \sum_{l=1}^{p} m_{il}(t) y_l + \omega(t), \qquad (s_1) \\ LTM : \dot{m}_{il}(t) = -c_i m_{il}(t) + y_l f_i(x_i(t)). \qquad (s_2) \end{cases} \tag{1}$$

where $x(\cdot) = [x_1(\cdot),\ x_2(\cdot), \cdots, x_n(\cdot)]^T \in \mathbf{R}^n$ is the state vector, $A = diag\{a_1,\ a_2, \cdots, a_n\} > 0$ is a diagonal positive matrix, $B = (b_{ij})_{n\times n}$, $D = (d_{ij})_{n\times n}$ are the connection weight matrix and the delayed connection weight matrix respectively; E is the strength of the external stimulus, $m_{il}(\cdot) = [m_{i1}(\cdot),\ m_{i2}(\cdot), \cdots, m_{ip}(\cdot)]^T$ is the synaptic efficiency, y_l is the constant external stimulus, $C = diag\{c_1,\ c_2, \cdots, c_n\}$ denote disposable scaling constants with $C > 0$, $\omega(\cdot)$ denote external inputs to the neurons from outside the network which belongs to $L^2[0,\ +\infty)$; $f(\cdot) = [f_1(\cdot),\ f_2(\cdot), \cdots, f_n(\cdot)]^T$ denote the activation function; q is the proportional delay factors. The initial function of system (1) is continuous defined as follows:

$$x_i(s) = \varphi_i(s), \quad s \in [qt_0,\ t_0], \quad i = 1, 2, \ldots, n, \tag{2}$$

Remark 1. The proportional delay factors satisfy $0 < q < 1$ and $qt = t-(1-q)t$, where $(1-q)t$ is the continuous time-varying functions satisfying $(1-q)t \to +\infty$ as $t \to +\infty$.

Remark 2. The proportional delay $\tau(t) = (1-q)t$ ($\to +\infty$ as $t \to +\infty, 0 < q < 1$) is among the delay exist in the dynamic of CNNs models is fewer conservative and more widely used in recent years. He is unlimited contrary to: distributed delay, constant delay and the limited delay.

The principal contributions of our paper are summarized as follows;

- As a first attempt, in this paper we consider the dissipativity analysis of the CNNs models with proportional delay.
- We introduce a necessary definition, which are employed in the derivation of the main results.
- New set of sufficient conditions in terms of LMIs is derived for ensuring the dissipativity results.
- Finally, a numerical example with simulation is provided to illustrate the effectiveness of the obtained theoretical results.

The main contents of the paper are outlined as follows:

In Sect. 2, we establish some assumptions and definitions which will be used later. New sufficient conditions on the dissipativity are discussed in Sect. 3. An example is given in Sect. 4 to illustrate the effectiveness of our results. At last, in Sect. 5 we close with conclusions.

2 Assumptions, Definitions and Notations

In this section, we introduce some assumptions, definitions and notations.

All along this paper, for the sake of simplicity, we adapt the following notations:

- **R**, $\mathbf{R}^n$, $\mathbf{R}^{n\times n}$ stand the set of real numbers, the set of all n-dimensional real vectors and the set of $n \times n$ real matrices respectively.
  Let $M \in \mathbf{R}^{n\times n}$,
- $M > 0$, $M \geq 0$, M^{-1}, M^T means that M is a positive defined matrix, positive semi-defined matrix, inverse matrix, transpose matrix respectively.
- $\star$ means a symmetric matrix block for the symmetric block.

Introducing the following dynamic variables to simplify system (1)

$$S_i(t) = \sum_{l=1}^{p} m_{il}(t) y_l = m_i^T(t) y,$$

where $y = (y_1,\ y_2, \cdots, y_p)^T$, $m_i(t) = (m_{i1}(t),\ m_{i2}(t), \cdots, m_{ip}(t))^T$, and summing up the LTM (s_2) over l, the neural networks (s_1) and (s_2) can be rewritten as the state-space form:

$$\begin{cases} STM: \varepsilon \dot{x}_i(t) = -a_i x_i(t) + \sum_{j=1}^{n} b_{ij} f_j(x_j(t)) + \sum_{j=1}^{n} d_{ij} f_j(x_j(qt)) \\ \qquad\qquad + E_i S_i(t) + \omega_i(t), \\ LTM: \dot{S}_i(t) = -c_i S_i(t) + |y|^2 f_i(x_i(t)) \end{cases} \tag{3}$$

where $|y|^2 = y_1^2 + y_2^2 + \cdots + y_p^2$ is a constant. Without loss of generality, the input stimulus vector is assumed to be normalized with unit magnitude $|y|^2 = 1$, Then system (3) can be rewritten as follows:

$$\begin{cases} STM: \varepsilon \dot{x}(t) = -Ax(t) + Bf(x(t)) + Df(x(qt)) + ES(t) + \omega(t), \\ LTM: \dot{S}(t) = -CS(t) + f(x(t)) \end{cases} \tag{4}$$

Throughout this paper, the following assumption will be adopted:

Assumption 1. For a given positive parameter b the external disturbance input $\omega(\cdot)$ satisfies:

$$\int_0^{T^*} \omega^T(t)\omega(t)dt \leq b,\ T^* > 0\ b \geq 0. \tag{5}$$

The quadratic energy supply function E associated with system (4) is defined as follows:

$$E(\omega, y, T^*) = \prec y,\ Qy \succ_{T^*} + 2 \prec y,\ S^*\beta \succ_{T^*} + \prec \omega,\ R\omega \succ_{T^*} \tag{6}$$

where,

$$\prec \varpi_1,\ \varpi_2 \succ_{T^*} = \int_0^T \varpi_1^T \varpi_2 dt,\ \ T^* \geq 0.$$

Definition 1 [17]. *The system in Eq. (1) is said to be strictly $(Q,\ S^*,\ R)-$dissipative if there exist a scalar $\gamma > 0$ such that for any $T^* \geq 0$ and under zero initial state, the following condition is satisfied*

$$E(\omega, y, T^*) \geq \gamma \prec \omega, \omega \succ_{T^*}.$$

3 Main Results

In this section, we will introduce some new criteria to guarantee the dissipativity for system (4).

Theorem 1. *If there exists a scalar $\beta > 0$ and a positive diagonal matrices $P = diag\{p_1,\ p_2, \cdots, p_n\}$, P_1 and $Q_1 > 0$, such that the following LMI holds:*

$$\Xi = \begin{pmatrix} \Omega_{1,1} & PB - A^T P & PD & PE & P \\ \star & \Omega_{2,2} & PB & PE + P_1 & P - S^T \\ \star & \star & -qQ_1 & 0 & 0 \\ \star & \star & \star & -P_1 C - C^T P_1 & 0 \\ \star & \star & \star & \star & \beta I - R \end{pmatrix} < 0, \tag{7}$$

where

$$\Omega_{1,1} = -PA - A^T P, \Omega_{2,2} = PA + A^T P + Q_1 - Q.$$

Then, system (4) is strictly $(Q,\ S^*,\ R)-$dissipative.

Proof. Consider the following Lyapunov function:

$$V(x(t)) = \sum_{i=1}^{3} V_i(x(t)), \tag{8}$$

where

$$V_1(x(t)) = x^T(t)Px(t) + S^T(t)P_1S(t),$$

$$V_2(x(t)) = 2\sum_{i=1}^{n} p_i \int_0^{x_i(t)} f_i(s)ds,$$

$$V_3(x(t)) = \int_{qt}^{t} f^T x(s))Q_1 f(x(s))ds.$$

Calculating the time-derivative of $V(x(\cdot))$ along the solution of system in equation (4), one has:

$$\dot{V}(x(t)) = \sum_{i=1}^{3} \dot{V}_i(x(t)), \tag{9}$$

$$\begin{aligned}
\dot{V}_1(x(t)) &= 2x^T(t)P[-Ax(t) + Bf(x(t)) + Df(x(qt)) + ES(t) + \omega(t)] \\
&+ 2S^T(t)P_1[-CS(t) + f(x(t))] \\
&= -2x^T(t)PAx(t) + 2x^T(t)PBf(x(t)) + 2x^T(t)PDf(x(qt)) \\
&+ 2x^T(t)PES(t) + 2x^T(t)P\omega(t) \\
&- 2S^T(t)P_1CS(t) + 2S^Tt)P_1f(x(t))
\end{aligned}$$

$$\begin{aligned}
\dot{V}_2(x(t)) &= 2f^T(x(t))P\dot{x}(t) \\
&= 2f^T(x(t))P[-Ax(t) + Bf(x(t)) + Df(x(qt)) + ES(t) + \omega(t)] \\
&= -2f^T(x(t))PAx(t) + 2f^T(x(t))PBf(x(t)) + 2f^T(x(t))PDf(x(qt)) \\
&+ 2f^T(x(t))PES(t) + 2f^T(x(t))P\omega(t)
\end{aligned}$$

$$\dot{V}_3(x(t)) = f^T(x(t))Q_1x(t) - qf^T(x(t-\tau(t)))Q_1f(x(qt)).$$

Then, we have

$$\begin{aligned}
&\dot{V}(x(t)) + \beta\omega^T(t)\omega(t) - [y^T(t)Qy(t) + 2y^T(t)S\omega(t) + \omega^T(t)R\omega(t)] \\
&= x^T(t)(-PA - A^TP)x(t) + 2x^T(t)(PB - A^TP)f(x(t)) + 2x^T(t)PDf(x(qt)) \\
&+ x^T(t)PES(t) + 2x^T(t)P\omega(t) + f^T(x(t))(PA + A^TP + Q_1 - Q)f(x(t)) \\
&+ 2f^T(x(t))PBf(x(qt)) + 2f^T(x(t))(PE + P_1)S(t) \\
&+ 2f^T(x(t))(P - S^T)\omega(t) - qf^T(x(qt))Q_1f(x(qt)) \\
&+ S^T(t)(-P_1C + C^TP_1^T) + \omega^T(t)(\beta I - R)\omega(t).
\end{aligned}$$

Then, we obtain:

$$\dot{V}(x(t)) + \beta\omega^T(t)\omega(t) - y^T(t)Qy(t) - 2y^T(t)S\omega(t) - \omega^T(t)R\omega(t) \le \xi^T(t)\Xi\xi(t) < 0, \quad (10)$$

where,

$$\xi(t) = [x^T(t)\ f^T(x(t))\ f^T(x(qt))\ S^T(t)\ \omega^T(t)]^T$$

and Ξ is shown in (7).

Since, $\Xi < 0$, it is easy to get

$$\dot{V}(x(t)) + \beta\omega^T(t)\omega(t) \le y^T(t)Qy(t) + 2y^T(t)S^*\omega(t) + \omega^T(t)R\omega(t) \quad (11)$$

Integrating from 0 to T^*, under zero initial conditions we obtain:

$$E(y, w, T^*) \ge \beta \prec \omega, \omega \succ_{T^*} + V(x(T^*)) - V(x(0)).$$

For $x_0 = 0$, we have $V(x(0)) = 0$. Then,

$$E(y, \omega, T^*) \ge \beta \prec \omega, \omega \succ_{T^*}, \text{ for all } T^* \ge 0.$$

According to Definition 1, when the condition (5) is satisfied, the CNNs is strictly $(Q,\ S^*,\ R)-$dissipative.

Now, when $S(t) = 0$ and $\varepsilon = 1$, system (4) turns into

$$\dot{x}(t) = -Ax(t) + Bf(x(t)) + Df(x(qt)) + \omega(t). \quad (12)$$

Then, we have the following result:

Theorem 2. *If there exists a scalar $\beta > 0$ and a positive diagonal matrix $R_1 = diag\{r_{11},\ r_{12}, \cdots, r_{1n}\}$ and a positive definite matrix $R_2 > 0$, such that the following LMI holds:*

$$\Upsilon = \begin{pmatrix} \Upsilon_{1,1} & R_1B - A^TR_1 & R_1D & R_1 \\ \star & \Upsilon_{2,2} & R_1B & R_1 - S^T \\ \star & \star & -qR_2 & 0 \\ \star & \star & \star & \alpha I - R \end{pmatrix} < 0, \quad (13)$$

where

$$\Upsilon_{1,1} = -R_1A - A^TR_1,$$
$$\Upsilon_{2,2} = R_1A + A^TR_1 + R_2 - Q.$$

Then, system (12) is strictly $(Q,\ S^*,\ R)-$dissipative.

Proof. The proof of Theorem 2 is similar to the one that of Theorem 1. We consider the Lyapunov functional:

$$V_1(x(t)) = x^T(t)R_1x(t),$$
$$V_2(x(t)) = 2\sum_{i=1}^{n} r_{1i}\int_0^{x_i(t)} f_i(s)ds,$$
$$V_3(x(t)) = \int_{qt}^{t} f^T x(s))R_2f(x(s))ds.$$

Then, by doing the same steps, we get:

$$\dot{V}(x(t)) + \beta\omega^T(t)\omega(t) - y^T(t)Qy(t) - 2y^T(t)S^*\omega(t) - \omega^T(t)R\omega(t) \leq \xi_1^T(t)\Upsilon\xi_1(t) < 0. \quad (14)$$

where,

$$\xi_1(t) = [\,x^T(t)\ f^T(x(t))\ f^T(x(qt))\ \omega^T(t)\,]^T$$

and Υ is shown in (13).

Since, $\Upsilon < 0$, it is easy to get

$$\dot{V}(x(t)) + \beta\omega^T(t)\omega(t) \leq y^T(t)Qy(t) + 2y^T(t)S^*\omega(t) + \omega^T(t)R\omega(t). \quad (15)$$

Integrating from 0 to T^*, under zero initial conditions, we obtain:

$$E(y, w, T^*) \geq \beta \prec \omega, \omega \succ_{T^*} + V(x(T^*)) - V(x(0)).$$

For $x_0 = 0$, we have $V(x(0)) = 0$. Then,

$$E(y, \omega, T^*) \geq \beta \prec \omega, \omega \succ_{T^*}, \quad \text{for all } T^* \geq 0.$$

According to Definition 1, when the condition (5) is satisfied, the system in Eq. (12) is strictly $(Q,\ S^*,\ R)-$dissipative.

Remark 3. In paper [17], Zeng *et al.*, investigated the problem of delay-dependent dissipativity analysis for a class of neural networks subject to time-varying delays. In article [13] Sun and Cui studied the dissipativity for delayed neural networks with or without time-varying parametric uncertainteis and the integro-differential neural networks in the presence of time-varying delays. In [16], Wu *et al.*, focused on the problem of robust dissipativity analysis for uncertain neural networks with time-varying delay. To the best of our knowledge, the dissipativity analysis of CNNs with proportional delays has not been considered before. This implies that the results of this paper are new.

Remark 4. Proportional delays are theoretically interesting. Then, it is important to investigate the dissipativity analysis of neural networks with proportional delays. In articles [13,16,17], the authors investigated the dissipativity analysis of neural networks with time-varying delays. While, our manuscript dealt with the problem of the dissipativity analysis of the neural networks with proportional delays. Then, the obtained results in this paper are more interesting than the previous results.

Remark 5. In articles [11,12,16,17,19], the activation function must be satisfied the condition of Lipschitz or should be bounded and differentiable. However, in this work we do not need the above conditions. Our results can be applied to any type of activation function.

4 Numerical Example

In this section, we will present an example to illustrate the feasibility of our main results.

Example 1. we consider a two-neuron competitive neural network as follows:

$$\begin{cases} STM: \dot{x}_1(t) = -\frac{1}{\varepsilon}a_1x(t) + \frac{1}{\varepsilon}\sum_{j=1}^{2} b_{1j}f_j(x_j(t)) + \frac{1}{\varepsilon}\sum_{j=1}^{2} d_{1j}f_j(x_j(qt)) \\ \quad + \frac{1}{\varepsilon}E_1S_1(t) + \frac{1}{\varepsilon}\omega_1(t), \\ STM: \dot{x}_2(t) = -\frac{1}{\varepsilon}a_2x_2(t) + \frac{1}{\varepsilon}\sum_{j=1}^{2} b_{2j}f_j(x_j(t)) + \frac{1}{\varepsilon}\sum_{j=1}^{2} d_{2j}f_j(x_j(qt)) \\ \quad + \frac{1}{\varepsilon}E_2S_2(t) + \frac{1}{\varepsilon}\omega_2(t), \\ LTM: \dot{S}_1(t) = -c_1S_1(t) + f_1(x_1(t)), \\ LTM: \dot{S}_2(t) = -c_2S_2(t) + f_2(x_2(t)) \end{cases} \tag{16}$$

where, $q = \frac{1}{10}$, $\varepsilon = 1$, $\alpha = 0.1$, $f_j(x_j(t)) = \tanh(x(t))$, $j = 1,\ 2$,

$\omega_1(t) = \omega_2(t) = e^{-0.1t}$,

$$A = \begin{pmatrix} 0.5 & 0 \\ 0 & 0.8 \end{pmatrix},\ B = \begin{pmatrix} 0.1 & 0 \\ 0.1 & 0.1 \end{pmatrix},\ D = \begin{pmatrix} -0.1 & 0 \\ 0.1 & -0.2 \end{pmatrix},$$

$$E = \begin{pmatrix} -0.1 & 0 \\ 0 & -0.1 \end{pmatrix},\ C = \begin{pmatrix} 0.1 & 0 \\ 0 & 0.25 \end{pmatrix},$$

and the parameters:

$$Q = \begin{pmatrix} 2 & 0 \\ 0 & 2 \end{pmatrix},\ S^* = \begin{pmatrix} 0.1 & -0.1 \\ -0.1 & 0.5 \end{pmatrix},\ R = \begin{pmatrix} 2.5 & 0 \\ 0 & 2.5 \end{pmatrix}.$$

Then, by using the Matlab LMI control toolbox to solve the LMIs in (7), we can obtain the feasible solution as follows:

$$P = \begin{pmatrix} 1.0080 & 0 \\ 0 & 1.1008 \end{pmatrix},\ P_1 = \begin{pmatrix} 0.2033 & 0 \\ 0 & 0.3426 \end{pmatrix},$$

$$Q_1 = \begin{pmatrix} 0.8144 & -0.0834 \\ -0.0834 & 0.7381 \end{pmatrix}.$$

According to Theorem 1, the competitive neural networks with proportional delay in (16) is (Q, S^*, R)−dissipative system. Figure 1 represents the state behaviors of the competitive neural networks with proportional delay of (16).

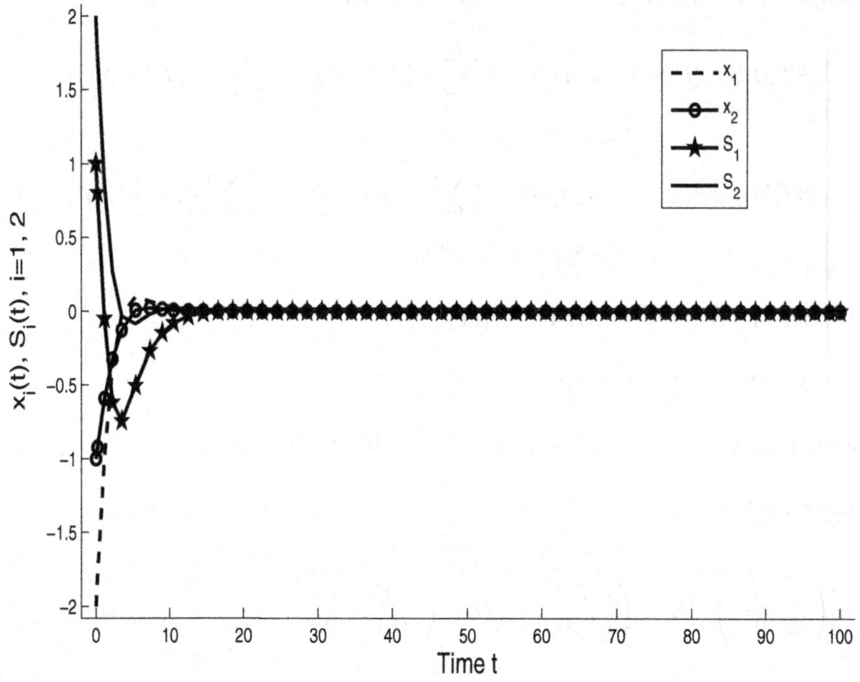

Fig. 1. The time responds trajectories of system (16).

5 Conclusions

It is well known that competitive neural networks are extensions of Hopfield neural networks [9,10]. First, we studied the dissipativity of CNNs with proportional delay. Second, we investigated the dissipativity of Hopfield neural networks with proportional delay. By utilizing Lyapunov functional method and collecting it with linear matrix inequality approach, new sufficient conditions have been developed to guarantee the dissipativity of the proposed model. The results are presented in terms of LMIs, which can be solved easily by using MATLAB LMI toolbox. At last, numerical example is given to demonstrate the effectiveness of our obtained results. To the best of our knowledge, this is the first studying of the dissipativity analysis for CNNs with proportional delays.

References

1. Alimi, A.M., Aouiti, C., Chérif, F., Dridi, F., M'hamdi, M.S.: Dynamics and oscillations of generalized high-order hopfield neural networks with mixed delays. Neurocomputing **321**, 274–295 (2018). https://doi.org/10.1016/j.neucom.2018.01.061
2. Aouiti, C., Assali, E.A., Cao, J., Alsaedi, A.: Global exponential convergence of neutral-type competitive neural networks with multi-proportional delays, distributed delays and time-varying delay in leakage delays. Int. J. Syst. Sci. **49**(10), 2202–2214 (2018). https://doi.org/10.1080/00207721.2018.1496297
3. Aouiti, C., Assali, E.A.: Stability analysis for a class of impulsive bidirectional associative memory (BAM) neural networks with distributed delays and leakage time-varying delays. Neural Process. Lett. 1–35 (2018). https://doi.org/10.1007/s11063-018-9937-y
4. Aouiti, C., Gharbia, I.B., Cao, J., Alsaedi, A.: Dynamics of impulsive neutral-type BAM neural networks. J. Franklin Inst. **356**(4), 2294–2324 (2019). https://doi.org/10.1016/j.jfranklin.2019.01.028
5. Aouiti, C., Gharbia, I.B., Cao, J., Mhamdi, M.S., Alsaedi, A.: Existence and global exponential stability of pseudo almost periodic solution for neutral delay BAM neural networks with time-varying delay in leakage terms. Chaos Solit. Fract. **107**, 111–127 (2018). https://doi.org/10.1016/j.chaos.2017.12.022
6. Aouiti, C., Miaadi, F.: Finite-time stabilization of neutral hopfield neural networks with mixed delays. Neural Process. Lett. **48**(3), 1645–1669 (2018). https://doi.org/10.1007/s11063-018-9791-y
7. Aouiti, C., Miaadi, F.: Pullback attractor for neutral hopfield neural networks with time delay in the leakage term and mixed time delays. Neural Comput. Appl. 1–10 (2018). https://doi.org/10.1007/s00521-017-3314-z
8. Aravindh, D., Sakthivel, R., Marshal Anthoni, S.: Extended dissipativity-based non-fragile control for multi-area power systems with actuator fault. Int. J. Syst. Sci. **50**(2), 256–272 (2019). https://doi.org/10.1080/00207721.2018.1551971
9. Hopfield, J.J.: Neural networks and physical systems with emergent collective computational abilities. Proc. Natl. Acad. Sci. **79**(8), 2554–2558 (1982). https://doi.org/10.1073/pnas.79.8.2554
10. Hopfield, J.J.: Neurons with graded response have collective computational properties like those of two-state neurons. Proc. Natl. Acad. Sci. **81**(10), 3088–3092 (1984). https://doi.org/10.1073/pnas.81.10.3088
11. Manivannan, R., Mahendrakumar, G., Samidurai, R., Cao, J., Alsaedi, A.: Exponential stability and extended dissipativity criteria for generalized neural networks with interval time-varying delay signals. J. Franklin Inst. **354**(11), 4353–4376 (2017). https://doi.org/10.1016/j.jfranklin.2017.04.007
12. Manivannan, R., Samidurai, R., Cao, J., Alsaedi, A., Alsaadi, F.E.: Design of extended dissipativity state estimation for generalized neural networks with mixed time-varying delay signals. Inform. Sci. **424**, 175–203 (2018). https://doi.org/10.1016/j.ins.2017.10.007
13. Sun, Y., Cui, B.T.: Dissipativity analysis of neural networks with time-varying delays. Int. J. Autom. Comput. **5**(3), 290–295 (2008). https://doi.org/10.1007/s11633-008-0290-x
14. Willems, J.C.: Dissipative dynamical systems part I: general theory. Arch. Ration. Mech. Anal. **45**(5), 321–351 (1972). https://doi.org/10.1007/BF00276493
15. Willems, J.C.: Dissipative dynamical systems part II: linear systems with quadratic supply rates. Arch. Ration. Mech. Anal. **45**(5), 352–393 (1972). https://doi.org/10.1007/BF00276494

16. Wu, Z.G., Park, J.H., Su, H., Chu, J.: Robust dissipativity analysis of neural networks with time-varying delay and randomly occurring uncertainties. Nonlinear Dyn. **69**(3), 1323–1332 (2012). https://doi.org/10.1007/s11071-012-0350-1
17. Zeng, H.B., He, Y., Shi, P., Wu, M., Xiao, S.P.: Dissipativity analysis of neural networks with time-varying delays. Neurocomputing **168**, 741–746 (2015). https://doi.org/10.1016/j.neucom.2015.05.050
18. Zhou, L.: Delay-dependent exponential stability of cellular neural networks with multi-proportional delays. Neural Process. Lett. **38**(3), 347–359 (2013). https://doi.org/10.1007/s11063-012-9271-8
19. Zhou, L.: Dissipativity of a class of cellular neural networks with proportional delays. Nonlinear Dyn. **73**(3), 1895–1903 (2013). https://doi.org/10.1007/s11071-013-0912-x
20. Zhou, L., Chen, X., Yang, Y.: Asymptotic stability of cellular neural networks with multiple proportional delays. Appl. Math. Comput. **229**, 457–466 (2014). https://doi.org/10.1016/j.amc.2013.12.061

A Nonlinear Fokker-Planck Description of Continuous Neural Network Dynamics

Roseli S. Wedemann[1(✉)] and Angel R. Plastino[2]

[1] Instituto de Matemática e Estatística, Universidade do Estado do Rio de Janeiro, Rua São Francisco Xavier 524, Rio de Janeiro, RJ 20550-900, Brazil
roseli@ime.uerj.br

[2] CeBio y Departamento de Ciencias Básicas, Universidad Nacional del Noroeste de la Provincia de Buenos Aires, UNNOBA, Conicet, Roque Saenz Peña 456, Junin, Argentina
arplastino@unnoba.edu.ar

Abstract. The nonextensive thermostatistical formalism has been increasingly applied to the description of many complex systems in physics, biology, psychology, economics, and other fields. The q-Maximum Entropy (q-MaxEnt) distributions, which optimize the S_q, power-law entropic functionals, are central to this formalism. We have done previous work regarding computational neural models of associative memory functioning, for mental phenomena such as neurosis, creativity, and the interplay between consciousness and unconsciousness, which suggest that q-MaxEnt distributions may be relevant for the development of neural models for these processes. Power-law behavior has also been experimentally observed in brain functioning. We propose here a nonlinear Fokker-Planck model, associated with the continuous-time evolution equations for interconnected neurons of the Hopfield model. The equation which characterizes the model has stationary solutions of the q-MaxEnt type and is associated with a free energy like quantity that decreases during the time-evolution of the system. This framework elucidates a possible dynamical mechanism which can generate q-MaxEnt distributions in Hopfield memory neural networks. It also provides a theoretical framework that supports the choice of different entropic measures for modelling and simulating complex networks such as the brain, as well as other artificial neural networks.

Keywords: Continuous neural networks · Fokker-Planck dynamics · Nonextensive thermostatistics · Associative memory · Attractors

1 Introduction

The McCulloch-Pitts discrete neural network model has been used as a powerful computational device, to model important cognitive functions, such as associative memory in the Hopfield model [1–3]. In recent years there has been

I. V. Tetko et al. (Eds.): ICANN 2019, LNCS 11727, pp. 43–56, 2019.
https://doi.org/10.1007/978-3-030-30487-4_4

intense *interdisciplinary* activity directed towards computational and neuroscientific modelling of both conscious and unconscious mental processes [3–14]. In these efforts, many conceptual and theoretical ideas from statistical mechanics and computer science have been employed by neuroscientists [9,11–16]. Human memory is central to several normal and pathological complex mental processes studied by psychiatry, psychoanalysis and neuroscience [3–10,17–19]. A standard assumption in neuroscience is that (associative) memory is encoded in the architecture of the brain's neural network. We have developed a line of research in recent years [3,10,17–19], regarding the development of neuronal network models, aimed at investigating an associative memory approach to describe aspects of mental processes such as neurosis, creativity, and the interaction between consciousness and unconsciousness. Both the standard Boltzmann Machine (BM) [2] and the Tsallis-Stariolo Generalized Simulated Annealing (GSA) [20] have been used, to simulate memory retrieval in these works.

A statistical analysis of the avalanches occuring during the retrieval process, while employing the Tsallis-Stariolo GSA, indicated the presence of q-Maximum Entropy (q-MaxEnt), power-law distributions, typical of scenarios where the nonextensive thermostatistics applies [19]. Interestingly, some of the results obtained through our theoretical models and simulations are consistent with recent experimental data, on the distribution of the time duration and spatial reach of signal propagation (captured by fMRI images), during brain stimulation [16,19]. We have also found power-law and q-MaxEnt behavior in other aspects of our models [3,17]. These findings have motivated us to discuss, in recent work and in the present one, possible dynamical mechanisms which can generate q-MaxEnt distributions in memory neural networks [19,21–24].

It is possible to generalize the McCulloch-Pitts model by considering neurons with continuous valued state variables [1,25]. This approach is biologically more realistic and can also be useful to describe the propagation (diffusion) of information through a network with noisy dynamics. In this context, we have previously discussed possible dynamical scenarios based on the Fokker-Planck description [23], and also used the nonlinear Fokker-Planck formalism to approach the problem of modelling biological asymmetric synapses, in real networks formed by different types of neurons [21,22,24].

In previous efforts [3,10,17–19], where we have studied mental processes related to memory, we have simulated memory access by using the BM [2], and its q-statistical generalization, the GSA algorithm [20]. These schemes for simulating pattern retrieval are based on two different implementations of the simulated annealing (SA) procedure. In both mechanisms, the probabilities of state transitions of the network depend on a temperature parameter T, that is gradually lowered according to an annealing schedule. We considered a network with N nodes, where each node i has a discrete state S_i in $\{-1, 1\}$. We assumed that synaptic weights ω_{ij} between nodes i and j were symmetric: $\omega_{ij} = \omega_{ji}$. This symmetry guarantees the existence of an energy function, $E(\{S_i\}) = -(1/2)\sum_{ij} \omega_{ij} S_i S_j$, such that the attractors of the memory retrieval mechanism (the SA scheme) are given by the minima of the (multidimensional) energy landscape determined by

$E(\{S_i\})$, and correspond to the stored memory patterns. The transition probabilities of the GSA mechanism [20], which concern us here because they lead to q-exponential distributions, are

$$P_{GSA}(S_i \to -S_i) = [1 + (q-1)(E(\{-S_i\}) - E(\{S_i\}))/T]^{\frac{1}{1-q}} \ . \quad (1)$$

In the case that $q \to 1$, the BM rule is recovered. When transitions between states follow the SA scheme, for both the BM and GSA, the system tends to evolve from the current state to a later state of lower energy, although energy may increase at some intermediate steps, allowing the escape from local minima. For neural networks described by discrete state variables [3,19], the GSA procedure constitutes a natural dynamics, which leads to q-exponential distributions, and this is consistent with many power-law distributions observed experimentally (see [15,16,19] and references therein). These previous results have stimulated us to continue exploring the use of concepts from the generalized thermostatistics formalism to study and develop neural network models, and the present work can be understood and contextualized within this framework.

In this paper, we present a nonlinear Fokker-Planck model, associated with the continuous-time evolution equations [1,2,25] for interconnected neurons of the Hopfield model. The state (output) of each neuron is then represented by a continuous variable. The nonlinear Fokker-Planck equation (NLFPE) which characterizes the model has stationary solutions of the q-MaxEnt type, and admits a free energy like quantity that decreases, during the time-evolution of the system. These developments provide possible dynamical mechanisms leading to the q-MaxEnt power-law distributions observed in systems that, as happens with brain networks, are characterized by long-range interactions and/or spatial disorder [26–30]. In this sense, the nonlinear Fokker-Planck dynamics explored here can be regarded as a generalization of the linear Fokker-Planck dynamics studied by other authors [31]. This generalization encompasses the nonextensive thermostatistical scenarios based on the power-law nonadditive S_q entropies. It also includes, as a particular instance, the Boltzmann-Gibbs scenario (given by the entropic parameter $q = 1$) associated with a linear Fokker-Planck dynamics.

This contribution deals with a theme into which we have already made some forays in recent years [21–24]. Here we generalize and extend in various directions the analysis done in those previous works. In contrast with the models discussed by us in [21,22,24], the model advanced here is fully nonlinear, both at the level of the Fokker-Planck equation itself, and at the level of the intrinsic deterministic noise-free dynamics of the neural network, which in this paper is assumed to precisely comply with the strictures of the Hopfield equations of motion. Moreover, we don't here assume, as we did in [23], that the deterministic contribution to the Fokker-Planck dynamics arises from a gradient flow in phase space. Instead, for this deterministic contribution (given by the drift term in the Fokker-Planck equation), we use a drift field explicitly incorporating the non-gradient aspects of the Hopfield dynamics [1,2,25]. Due to the appealing features of the Fokker-Planck dynamics advanced here, we are confident that the present developments may constitute a theoretical step forward, towards explaining the origin of the

q-MaxEnt, power-law distributions, observed in studies of brain neural network dynamics [15,16,19,29]. This theoretical understanding may also help to elucidate the applicability of different neural network models based on entropic measures, such as the noisy attractor dynamics of the Boltzmann Machine or GSA [20] and the perceptron [32], to solve artificial intelligence problems.

2 Nonextensive Thermostatistics

Nonextensive thermostatistics is a flourishing research field, which is currently being applied to a wide and diverse spread of applications [28,30,33,34]. This theoretical framework is based on the nonadditive, power-law entropy measure [30]

$$S_q[\mathcal{P}] = \frac{1}{q-1}\int \mathcal{P}\left(1-\left(\frac{\mathcal{P}}{\mathcal{P}_0}\right)^{q-1}\right) d^N\boldsymbol{x}, \tag{2}$$

evaluated on a time-dependent probability density $\mathcal{P}(\boldsymbol{x},t)$ (with $\boldsymbol{x} \in \Re^N$) and characterized by the real, entropic index q. $\mathcal{P}_0$ is a constant with the same dimensions as $\mathcal{P}(\boldsymbol{x},t)$. When one takes the limit $q \to 1$, the logarithmic Boltzmann-Gibss (BG) entropy, $S_{BG} = S_1 = -\int \mathcal{P}\ln(\mathcal{P}/\mathcal{P}_0)d^N\boldsymbol{x}$, is obtained. At the core of nonextensive thermostatistics is the q-exponential function defined by

$$\exp_q(x) = \begin{cases} [1+(1-q)x]^{\frac{1}{1-q}}, & \text{for } 1+(1-q)x > 0, \\ 0, & \text{for } 1+(1-q)x \leq 0. \end{cases} \tag{3}$$

This function arises naturally in constrained optimization problems based on the entropic functional S_q [30], and asymptomatically it behaves as a power-law. It is often found that complex systems which present power-law behavior can actually be described by q-exponentials. We will use here the alternative notation $\exp_q(x) = [1+(1-q)x]_+^{1/(1-q)}$.

Current work on applications of nonextensive thermostatistics involves scientists from a wide range of fields, such as physics, biology, computer science, machine learning, cognition, biomedicine, psychology and economics. Among the most studied applications are those that treat non-equilibrium (or meta-equilibrium) states of systems endowed with long-range interactions [28,33], nonlinear dynamical systems with weak chaos [34], and systems described by power-law, nonlinear Fokker-Planck equations [22,27,35–37]. q-MaxEnt distributions fit experimental data in diverse areas very well, and they have also been observed in data generated by many numerical simulations of complex systems [3,19,28,30,34]. Systems described by NLFPEs have gained much attention, because they constitute the area of application of nonextensive thermostatistics which is most developed from the analytical point of view, and where the dynamical origin of the q-MaxEnt distributions is better understood [36,37].

3 Dynamics of Continuous Neural Networks

In the basic framework for the study of continuous neural networks [1,2,25], these are formed by N neurons where, for a neuron i, its net input signal, u_i, is given by

$$u_i = \sum_j \omega_{ij} V_j \,, \tag{4}$$

and its output signal is represented by the state variable V_i, so that both u_i and V_i assume continuous values. As in the discrete case, discussed in the Introduction, the synaptic weights ω_{ij} between nodes i and j are here assumed to be symmetric, so that $\omega_{ij} = \omega_{ji}$. We consider the case where, for neuron i, its output V_i is, **in equilibrium**, a continuous function of its net input

$$V_i = g(u_i) = g(\sum_j \omega_{ij} V_j) \,, \tag{5}$$

and $g(u)$ is an appropriate activation function that saturates for large values of $|u|$, such as a sigmoid or $\tanh(u)$. From (5), we also have the inverse function

$$u_i = g^{-1}(V_i). \tag{6}$$

In the absence of noise (random perturbations), the continuous neural network can be regarded as a continuous deterministic dynamical system, whose dynamical state at a given time is described by a set of N phase space variables $\{x_1, x_2, \cdots, x_N\}$, where x_i represents either u_i or V_i. These state variables evolve in time according to a set of coupled ordinary differential equations,

$$dx_i/dt = G_i(x_1, x_2, \cdots, x_N) \,, \quad i = 1, \ldots, N, \tag{7}$$

which in vector notation can be written as $\frac{d\boldsymbol{x}}{dt} = \boldsymbol{G}(\boldsymbol{x})$, where $\boldsymbol{x}, \boldsymbol{G} \in \Re^N$. This means that the evolution of the system's state, which is represented by the vector $\boldsymbol{x}$, is given by the phase space flux associated with the vectorial field $\boldsymbol{G}$.

We will base our study on the continuous analogue of the McCulloch-Pitts neural model, where the time evolution of the continuous state variables u_i, given by a set of coupled, ordinary differential equations of the type (7), are expressed by the following updating rule [1,2]

$$\tau_i \frac{du_i}{dt} = -u_i + \sum_j \omega_{ij} V_j = -u_i + \sum_j \omega_{ij} g(u_j) = \tau_i G_i(u_1, u_2, \ldots, u_N), \tag{8}$$

where the τ_i are suitable time constants. These are thus the equations of motion for the u_i.

In the continuous Hopfield model with symmetric weights $\omega_{ij} = \omega_{ji}$, as we have assumed in this work, it is possible to define an appropriate *energy function* (the potential function), given by [2]

$$H = -\frac{1}{2} \sum_{ij} \omega_{ij} V_i V_j + \sum_i \int_0^{V_i} g^{(-1)}(V) dV. \tag{9}$$

If we take the partial derivative of H as defined in (9) with respect to u_i and use Eqs. (6) and (8), we obtain another expression for the equations of motion for the u_i, with a dependence on H and $dg/du_i = g'(u_i)$,

$$\frac{du_i}{dt} = -\left(\frac{1}{\tau_i * g'(u_i)}\right)\frac{\partial H}{\partial u_i} = G_i(\boldsymbol{u}). \tag{10}$$

4 Fokker-Planck Equations for Continuous Valued Neural Networks

In order to introduce some basic ideas, and also to fix notation, we first consider the simpler case of linear Fokker-Planck equations. The equations of motion (7), (8) and (10) govern the motion of one individual realization of a dynamical system, in particular a neural network, that evolves from one given set of initial conditions. When dealing with complex dynamical systems of high dimensionality, it is often more instructive to study the evolution of a statistical ensemble of copies of the system, each one starting from a different initial condition, instead of focussing on one instance of the system's evolution. This is indeed one of the main strategies of statistical mechanics. An interesting example of the application of the ensemble approach to the dynamics of continuous neural networks has been discussed in [31].

When applying the ensemble procedure to the study of the dynamical evolution of neural networks, instead of following the evolution of one realization of the system, governed by the Eqs. (7), (8) or (10), one studies the behavior of a time-dependent probability density $\mathcal{P}(u_1, \cdots, u_N, t)$ that describes the evolution of the statistical ensemble of networks. The time evolution of $\mathcal{P}$ is described by the Liouville equation $(\partial \mathcal{P}/\partial t) + \boldsymbol{\nabla} \cdot (\mathcal{P}\boldsymbol{G}) = 0$, which is a continuity equation in phase space, where $\boldsymbol{\nabla} = (\partial/\partial u_1, \ldots, \partial/\partial u_N)$ is the N-dimensional $\boldsymbol{\nabla}$-operator. If the networks under consideration present noisy behavior, the evolution is non-deterministic and the effects of noise can be represented by an extra diffusion-like term in the Liouville continuity equation, leading to the Fokker-Planck equation (FPE)

$$(\partial \mathcal{P}/\partial t) - D\nabla^2 \mathcal{P} + \boldsymbol{\nabla} \cdot (\mathcal{P}\boldsymbol{G}) = 0, \tag{11}$$

where D is the diffusion coefficient. The last term on the left hand side of Eq. (11) is usually called the *drift* term and we thus refer to $\boldsymbol{G}$ as the *drift* field. If $\boldsymbol{G} = -\boldsymbol{\nabla} H$, for some potential function $H(\boldsymbol{u})$, then the phase space flow $\boldsymbol{G}$ always drives the phase space variables to configurations that move "downhill" in the landscape given by H. The phase space flow of the continuous neural networks considered here has this downhill behavior for an appropriate energy function H. But, strictly speaking, the flow is not in the direction of $-\boldsymbol{\nabla} H$. It always has, however, a positive projection along that direction. Indeed, the components of the vector flow $\boldsymbol{G}$ are not $\left(\frac{\partial H}{\partial u_1}, \ldots, \frac{\partial H}{\partial u_N}\right)$ but, instead,

$$\left(\frac{1}{\tau_1 g'(u_1)}\frac{\partial H}{\partial u_1}, \ldots, \frac{1}{\tau_N g'(u_N)}\frac{\partial H}{\partial u_N}\right). \tag{12}$$

This departure from a gradient form, exhibited by the continuous Hopfield network dynamics, will play an important role in this work. In previous works [21,22,24], we have begun to explore situations where the drift field does not derive exclusively from a potential ($\boldsymbol{G} \neq -\boldsymbol{\nabla} H$). However, the non-gradient features which were the focus of those works, were different from the ones in (12). They were related to asymmetries in synaptic connections, which we shall not consider in the present work.

When the drift field has the gradient form $\boldsymbol{G} = -\boldsymbol{\nabla} H$, the FPE (11) admits BG types of stationary solutions,

$$\mathcal{P}_{BG} = Z^{-1} \exp\left[-H(\boldsymbol{u})/D\right], \tag{13}$$

where the partition function $Z = \int \exp\left[-\frac{1}{D}H(\boldsymbol{u})\right] d^N\boldsymbol{u}$ is a normalization constant. We assume here, as is usually done, that the shape of the potential function $H(\boldsymbol{u})$ is such that the integral which defines Z converges. The probability density $\mathcal{P}_{BG}$ maximizes the entropy S_{BG}, under the constraints corresponding to the norm of $\mathcal{P}_{BG}$ and to the mean value of the potential (energy) function H, given by $\langle H \rangle = \int H\mathcal{P}\, d^N\boldsymbol{u}$.

4.1 The NLFPE and q-Statistics in Memory Neural Networks

The nonlinear Fokker-Planck equation [27] is a powerful tool which can be used for the study of many phenomena in complex systems. In [38], Ribeiro, Nobre and Curado explain that "The linear differential equations in physics are, in many cases, valid for media characterized by specific conditions, like homogeneity, isotropy, and translational invariance, with particles interacting through short-range forces and with a dynamical behavior characterized by short-time memories.". The presence of a nonlinear diffusion term in the FPE may be used to describe a physical ensemble of interacting particles, and the nonlinearity is then an effective description of the interactions [22,27,30,38–40]. Physical systems which present spatial disorder and/or long-range interactions seem to be natural candidates for this formalism, which has recently attracted considerable attention from the complex systems, research community. Nonlinear evolution equations, governing the behavior of time-dependent probability densities, can also arise as approximate descriptions of a more fundamental underlying linear dynamics. To explore this possibility within the context of neural networks would be an enquiry worth pursuing, although beyond the scope of the present contribution. In this work, we propose a nonlinear Fokker-Planck dynamics for continuous Hopfield memory neural networks, as a phenomenological possible dynamical mechanism leading to the q-MaxEnt power-law distributions, which have been observed in some studies of brain neural network dynamics [15,16,19].

We here propose a NLFPE associated with the dynamics of neural networks, whose state variables assume continuous values and whose dynamics is governed by Eq. (8), as presented in Sect. 3. The appropriate form for such an equation which we propose here is

$$\frac{\partial \mathcal{P}}{\partial t} = D \sum_i \frac{\partial}{\partial u_i} \left\{ \left(\frac{2-q}{1-q} \right) \frac{\mathcal{P}}{\tau_i g'(u_i)} \frac{\partial}{\partial u_i} \left[\left(\frac{\mathcal{P}}{\mathcal{P}_0} \right)^{1-q} \right] \right\}$$
$$+ \sum_i \frac{\partial}{\partial u_i} \left[\frac{\mathcal{P}}{\tau_i g'(u_i)} \frac{\partial H}{\partial u_i} \right] . \quad (14)$$

Notice that in the above equation, the quantities

$$D_i = D \left(\frac{2-q}{1-q} \right) \frac{1}{\tau_i g'(u_i)}, \quad (15)$$

can be regarded as state-dependent diffusion coefficients.

We want to model stable properties of complex systems and, in the case of Hopfield neural networks, these stationary states correspond to the stored memories. We will seek for stationary (attractor) solutions to the NLFPE (14) (which satisfy $\partial \mathcal{P}/\partial t = 0$), of the q-exponential form (3),

$$\mathcal{P}_q = \mathcal{P}_0 A [1 - (1-q)\beta H(\boldsymbol{u})]_+^{\frac{1}{1-q}}, \quad (16)$$

where A and β are constants to be determined and $\mathcal{P}_0$ is a constant with the same dimensions as $\mathcal{P}$, as in Eq. (2). In [23], we have shown illustrations of this stationary probability density for a two-neuron circuit where, as expected, as the connection strength becomes stronger, the two neurons tend to have simultaneous firing or non-firing states.

The stationary NLFPE (14) may be written as

$$\sum_i \frac{\partial}{\partial u_i} \left[\frac{\mathcal{P}}{\tau_i g'(u_i)} \left(D \frac{2-q}{1-q} \frac{\partial}{\partial u_i} \left[\left(\frac{\mathcal{P}}{\mathcal{P}_0} \right)^{1-q} \right] + \frac{\partial H}{\partial u_i} \right) \right] = 0. \quad (17)$$

With a bit of algebra, it is possible to show that the q-exponential ansatz (16) is a stationary solution of

$$\frac{\mathcal{P}}{\tau_i g'(u_i)} \left(D \frac{2-q}{1-q} \frac{\partial}{\partial u_i} \left[\left(\frac{\mathcal{P}}{\mathcal{P}_0} \right)^{1-q} \right] + \frac{\partial H}{\partial u_i} \right) = 0, \quad (18)$$

and, therefore, it is also a solution of (17), provided that A and β follow the dependence

$$A = [(2-q)\beta D]^{1/(q-1)}. \quad (19)$$

5 H-Theorem

We shall now prove that the nonlinear Fokker-Planck dynamics admits an H-theorem, in terms of the free-energy like functional

$$\begin{aligned} F &= \langle H \rangle - DS_{q^*}[\mathcal{P}] \\ &= \int H(\boldsymbol{u})P(\boldsymbol{u})d^N\boldsymbol{u} - \frac{D}{q^*-1}\int \mathcal{P}\left(1-\left(\frac{\mathcal{P}}{\mathcal{P}_0}\right)^{q^*-1}\right)d^N\boldsymbol{u}, \end{aligned} \tag{20}$$

where $q^* = 2 - q$. The time derivative of F is given by,

$$\begin{aligned} \frac{dF}{dt} &= \int \left[H - \frac{D}{q^*-1}\left(1 - q^*\left(\frac{\mathcal{P}}{\mathcal{P}_0}\right)^{q^*-1}\right)\right]\frac{\partial \mathcal{P}}{\partial t}d^N\boldsymbol{u} \\ &= \int \left[H - \frac{D}{1-q}\left(1-(2-q)\left(\frac{\mathcal{P}}{\mathcal{P}_0}\right)^{1-q}\right)\right]\frac{\partial \mathcal{P}}{\partial t}d^N\boldsymbol{u}. \end{aligned} \tag{21}$$

As $\int \mathcal{P}d^N\boldsymbol{u}$ has a finite constant value, Eq. (21) can be written as

$$\frac{dF}{dt} = \int \left[H + D\frac{2-q}{1-q}\left(\frac{\mathcal{P}}{\mathcal{P}_0}\right)^{1-q}\right]\frac{\partial \mathcal{P}}{\partial t}d^N\boldsymbol{u}. \tag{22}$$

After some algebra, it can be shown that

$$\frac{dF}{dt} = \int -\mathcal{P}\sum_{i=1}^{N}\frac{1}{\tau_i g'(u_i)}\left\{\frac{\partial H}{\partial u_i} + D\frac{2-q}{1-q}\frac{\partial}{\partial u_i}\left[\left(\frac{\mathcal{P}}{\mathcal{P}_0}\right)^{1-q}\right]\right\}^2 d^N\boldsymbol{u}. \tag{23}$$

One of the steps leading to the above result involves an integration by parts, where one assumes that the density $\mathcal{P}$ goes to zero fast enough when $|\boldsymbol{u}| \to \infty$, so that the resulting surface terms vanish. As τ_i, $g'(u_i)$ and $\mathcal{P}(\boldsymbol{u}, t)$ are positive for all values of $\boldsymbol{u}$,

$$\frac{dF}{dt} \leq 0. \tag{24}$$

The power-law NLFPE thus complies with the H-theorem,

$$\frac{d}{dt}\left(\langle H \rangle - DS_{q^*}[\mathcal{P}]\right) \leq 0, \tag{25}$$

with equality corresponding to the stationary density. This means that the stationary solution can be obtained by minimizing the functional F, which is tantamount to maximizing the S_{q^*} entropy, under the constraints of normalization and the mean value of the network potential $H(\boldsymbol{u})$.

It is worth now to compare our present developments with those reported in our previous works [21,23,24]. In [21,24] we addressed the problem of neural synaptic asymmetry, obtaining some analytical results for Hopfield-like systems of few neurons interacting linearly. That is, we implemented a nonlinear Fokker-Planck dynamics, for systems where the intrinsic noise-free dynamics was linear. This linear limitation allowed us to investigate analytically some essential features of the symmetry-asymmetry issue. In the present work, we lift the linearity restriction affecting the examples investigated in [21,24]. Indeed, the model studied here is fully nonlinear. It is nonlinear at the level of the FPE, whose diffusion term depends on a power of the probability density. And it is also nonlinear at the level of the interactions between the neurons, which is now strictly described by the Hopfield prescription (in its continuous version). In addition, here we do not assume (as we did in [23]) that the drift term in the FPE corresponds to a gradient flow in the network's phase space. In other words, we now take into account that the phase flow in a continuous Hopfield model (see Eqs. (10) and (12)) is not given by minus the gradient of the network's energy H (although it always has a positive projection in $-\boldsymbol{\nabla} H$). In this regard, our present work represents a substantial improvement over the one reported in [23].

It is instructive to elaborate in some detail the last point mentioned in the previous paragraph. The gradient assumption made in [23] generates a Fokker-Planck evolution that describes, at least qualitatively, a reasonable behavior for a noisy Hopfield network. The dynamics proposed in [23] satisfies an H-theorem and leads to a stationary density of the generalized q-MaxEnt form. The Fokker-Planck dynamics investigated in this work, while still exhibiting these good features, also provides a more accurate description of the non-stationary properties of the behavior of a noisy Hopfield memory network. This can be clearly illustrated by considering the limit case of vanishing diffusion. In this extreme case, our present FPE reproduces exactly the Liouville equation associated with a continuous Hopfield network [1,2,25], while the FPE considered in [23] reproduces the alluded Liouville equation only approximately. Finally, another important difference between the Fokker-Planck dynamics advanced here, and the ones discussed in [21,23,24], is that the present one involves state-dependent local diffusion coefficients in the FPE, while in [21,23,24] we only considered constant (global) diffusion coefficients. These new features are, of course, closely intertwined with each other. For instance, in order to have an H-theorem, a non-gradient drift field of the form (12) has to be accompanied by a diffusion term with the state-dependent diffusion coefficients given by (15).

6 Conclusions

In the present work, we advanced a fully nonlinear Fokker-Planck dynamics for the continuous version of the Hopfield memory neural network. The dynamics explored here is governed by a nonlinear, power-law Fokker-Planck equation endowed with a drift term that is in strict accord with the Hopfield flow in the network's phase space. In particular, the drift term includes the nonlinear features exhibited by the continuous Hopfield equations of motion. The NLFPE proposed here also incorporates the non-gradient aspects of the Hopfield dynamics. That is, it takes into account that, in spite of always having a positive projection into $-\boldsymbol{\nabla} H$ and consequently always being downhill in the network's energy landscape $H(\boldsymbol{u})$, the Hopfield flow is not given by $-\boldsymbol{\nabla} H$. In these respects, our present model goes beyond the issues we have explored in previous contributions (see [21,23,24]).

We proved that our model satisfies an H-theorem in terms of a free energy-like functional F, which is a linear combination of a power-law nonadditive entropic measure S_{q^*} and of the mean value of the energy function H. The stationary solutions (the attractors) of the NLFPE, for which $dF/dt = 0$, are given by q-MaxEnt probability densities. These densities maximize a Tsallis q-entropy under the constraint imposed by the mean value $\langle H \rangle$ of the energy.

The theoretical framework proposed here elucidates a possible dynamical mechanism which can generate q-MaxEnt distributions in Hopfield memory neural networks. In this way, it helps to explain power-law behavior previously found in simulation models [3, 19] and experimental data [15, 16], regarding the brain and mental processes. It thus provides a theoretical framework that supports the choice of different entropic measures for modelling and simulating complex networks such as the brain, as well as other neural network models in artificial intelligence [32]. We note that the classical Bolztmann-Gibbs approach produces the exponential distributions (13) and does not account for observed power laws. We hope that our present results will contribute to establish the thermostatistical foundations for the application of q-MaxEnt probability densities in the neurosciences [11–16]. Any further developments along these or related lines will certainly be very welcome.

Acknowledgments. We acknowledge financial support from the Brazilian National Research Council (CNPq), the Brazilian agency which funds graduate studies (CAPES) and from the Rio de Janeiro State Research Foundation (FAPERJ).

References

1. Hopfield, J.J.: Neurons with graded responses have collective computational properties like those of two-state neurons. Proc. Natl. Acad. Sci. **81**, 3088–3092 (1984). https://doi.org/10.1073/pnas.81.10.3088
2. Hertz, J.A., Krogh, A., Palmer, R.G. (eds.): Introduction to the Theory of Neural Computation. Lecture Notes, vol. 1. Perseus Books, Cambridge (1991)
3. Wedemann, R.S., Donangelo, R., Carvalho, L.A.V.: Generalized memory associativity in a network model for the neuroses. Chaos **19**, 015116 (2009). https://doi.org/10.1063/1.3099608
4. Kandel, E.: Psychiatry, Psychoanalysis, and the New Biology of Mind. American Psychiatric Publishing Inc., Washington (2005)
5. Cleeremans, A., Timmermans, B., Pasquali, A.: Consciousness and metarepresentation: a computational sketch. Neural Netw. **20**, 1032–1039 (2007). https://doi.org/10.1016/j.neunet.2007.09.011
6. Taylor, J.G.: A neural model of the loss of self in schizophrenia. Schizophr. Bull. **37**(6), 1229–1247 (2011). https://doi.org/10.1093/schbul/sbq033
7. Edalat, A., Mancinelli, F.: Strong attractors of Hopfield neural networks to model attachment types and behavioural patterns. In: Angelov, P., Levine, D., Apolloni, B. (eds.) Proceedings of the 2013 International Joint Conference on Neural Networks (IJCNN), pp. 14027190–1-10. IEEE, Red Hook (2013). https://doi.org/10.1109/IJCNN.2013.6706924

8. Edalat, A.: Self-attachment: a holistic approach to computational psychiatry. In: Érdi, P., Sen Bhattacharya, B., Cochran, A.L. (eds.) Computational Neurology and Psychiatry. SSB, vol. 6, pp. 273–314. Springer, Cham (2017). https://doi.org/10.1007/978-3-319-49959-8_10
9. Taylor, J.G., Villa, A.E.P.: The "Conscious I": a neuroheuristic approach to the mind. In: Baltimore, D., Dulbecco, R., Francois, J., Levi-Montalcini, R. (eds.) Frontiers of Life, vol. 3, pp. 349–368. Academic Press, Cambridge (2001)
10. de Carvalho, L.A.V., Mendes, D.Q., Wedemann, R.S.: Creativity and delusions: the dopaminergic modulation of cortical maps. In: Sloot, P.M.A., Abramson, D., Bogdanov, A.V., Dongarra, J.J., Zomaya, A.Y., Gorbachev, Y.E. (eds.) ICCS 2003. LNCS, vol. 2657, pp. 511–520. Springer, Heidelberg (2003). https://doi.org/10.1007/3-540-44860-8_53
11. Carhart-Harris, R.L., Friston, K.J.: Free-energy and Freud: an update. In: Fotopoulou, A., Pfaff, D., Conway, M.A. (eds.) From the Couch to the Lab: Trends in Psychodynamic Neuroscience, pp. 219–229. Oxford University Press, Oxford (2012). https://doi.org/10.1093/med/9780199600526.003.0013
12. Carhart-Harris, R.L., Friston, K.J.: The default-mode, ego-functions and free-energy: a neurobiological account of Freudian ideas. Brain **133**(4), 1265–1283 (2010). https://doi.org/10.1093/brain/awq010
13. Carhart-Harris, R., et al.: The entropic brain: a theory of conscious states informed by neuroimaging research with psychedelic drugs. Front. Hum. Neurosci. **8**, 20 (2014). https://doi.org/10.3389/fnhum.2014.00020
14. Badcock, P.B., Friston, K.J., Ramstead, M.J.D.: The hierarchically mechanistic mind: a free-energy formulation of the human psyche. Phys. Life Rev. (2019, in Press). https://doi.org/10.1016/j.plrev.2018.10.002
15. Beggs, J.M., Plenz, D.: Neuronal avalanches in neocortical circuits. J. Neurosci. **23**, 11167–11177 (2003). https://doi.org/10.1523/JNEUROSCI.23-35-11167.2003
16. Tagliazucchi, E., Balenzuela, P., Fraiman, D., Chialvo, D.R.: Criticality in large-scale brain fMRI dynamics unveiled by a novel point process analysis. Front. Physiol.—Fract. Physiol. **3**, 15 (2012). https://doi.org/10.3389/fphys.2012.00015
17. Wedemann, R.S., Carvalho, L.A.V., Donangelo, R.: Access to symbolization and associativity mechanisms in a model of conscious and unconscious processes. In: Samsonovich, A.V., Jóhannsdóttir, K.R. (eds.) Biologically Inspired Cognitive Architectures 2011. Frontiers in Artificial Intelligence and Applications, vol. 233, pp. 444–449. IOS Press, Amsterdam (2011). https://doi.org/10.3233/978-1-60750-959-2-444
18. Wedemann, R.S., de Carvalho, L.A.V.: Some things psychopathologies can tell us about consciousness. In: Villa, A.E.P., Duch, W., Érdi, P., Masulli, F., Palm, G. (eds.) ICANN 2012. LNCS, vol. 7552, pp. 379–386. Springer, Heidelberg (2012). https://doi.org/10.1007/978-3-642-33269-2_48
19. Siddiqui, M., Wedemann, R.S., Jensen, H.J.: Avalanches and generalized memory associativity in a network model for conscious and unconscious mental functioning. Phys. A **490**, 127–138 (2018). https://doi.org/10.1016/j.physa.2017.08.011
20. Tsallis, C., Stariolo, D.A.: Generalized simulated annealing. Phys. A **233**, 395–406 (1996). https://doi.org/10.1016/S0378-4371(96)00271-3
21. Wedemann, R.S., Plastino, A.R.: Asymmetries in synaptic connections and the nonlinear Fokker-Planck formalism. In: Villa, A.E.P., Masulli, P., Pons Rivero, A.J. (eds.) ICANN 2016. LNCS, vol. 9886, pp. 19–27. Springer, Cham (2016). https://doi.org/10.1007/978-3-319-44778-0_3

22. Wedemann, R.S., Plastino, A.R., Tsallis, C.: Curl forces and the nonlinear Fokker-Planck equation. Phys. Rev. E **94**(6), 062105 (2016). https://doi.org/10.1103/PhysRevE.94.062105
23. Wedemann, R.S., Plastino, A.R.: q-maximum entropy distributions and memory neural networks. In: Lintas, A., Rovetta, S., Verschure, P.F.M.J., Villa, A.E.P. (eds.) ICANN 2017. LNCS, vol. 10613, pp. 300–308. Springer, Cham (2017). https://doi.org/10.1007/978-3-319-68600-4_35
24. de Luca, V.T.F., Wedemann, R.S., Plastino, A.R.: Neuronal asymmetries and Fokker-Planck dynamics. In: Kůrková, V., Manolopoulos, Y., Hammer, B., Iliadis, L., Maglogiannis, I. (eds.) ICANN 2018. LNCS, vol. 11141, pp. 703–713. Springer, Cham (2018). https://doi.org/10.1007/978-3-030-01424-7_69
25. Cohen, M.A., Grossberg, S.: Absolute stability of global pattern formation and parallel memory storage by competitive neural networks. IEEE Trans. Syst. Man Cybern. **13**, 815–826 (1983). https://doi.org/10.1109/TSMC.1983.6313075
26. Martinez, S., Plastino, A.R., Plastino, A.: Nonlinear Fokker-Planck equations and generalized entropies. Phys. A **259**(1–2), 183–192 (1998). https://doi.org/10.1016/S0378-4371(98)00277-5
27. Franck, T.D.: Nonlinear Fokker-Planck Equations: Fundamentals and Applications. Springer, Heidelberg (2005). https://doi.org/10.1007/b137680
28. Tsallis, C.: The nonadditive entropy S_q and its applications in physics and elsewhere: some remarks. Entropy **13**, 1765–1804 (2011). https://doi.org/10.3390/e13101765
29. Papa, A.R.R., da Silva, L.: Earthquakes in the brain. Theory Biosci. **116**, 321–327 (1997)
30. Tsallis, C.: Introduction to Nonextensive Statistical Mechanics, Approaching a Complex World. Springer, New York (2009). https://doi.org/10.1007/978-0-387-85359-8
31. Yan, H., Zhao, L., Hu, L., Wang, X., Wang, E., Wang, J.: Nonequilibrium landscape theory of neural networks. Proc. Natl. Acad. Sci. **110**(45), E4185–E4194 (2013). https://doi.org/10.1073/pnas.1310692110
32. Gajowniczek, K., Orłowski, A., Ząbkowski, T.: Simulation study on the application of the generalized entropy concept in artificial neural networks. Entropy **20**(4), 1–17 (2018). https://doi.org/10.3390/e20040249
33. Brito, S., da Silva, L.R., Tsallis, C.: Role of dimensionality in complex networks. Nature Sci. Rep. **6**, 27992 (2016). https://doi.org/10.1038/srep27992
34. Tirnakli, U., Borges, E.P.: The standard map: from Boltzmann-Gibbs statistics to Tsallis statistics. Nature Sci. Rep. **6**, 23644 (2016). https://doi.org/10.1038/srep23644
35. Malacarne, L.C., Mendes, R.S., Pedron, I.T., Lenzi, E.K.: N-dimensional nonlinear Fokker-Planck equation with time-dependent coefficients. Phys. Rev. E **65**(5), 052101 (2002). https://doi.org/10.1103/PhysRevE.65.052101
36. Schwämmle, V., Nobre, F.D., Curado, E.M.F.: Consequences of the H theorem from nonlinear Fokker-Planck equations. Phys. Rev. E **76**(4), 041123 (2007). https://doi.org/10.1103/PhysRevE.76.041123
37. Andrade, J.S., da Silva, G.F.T., Moreira, A.A., Nobre, F., Curado, E.M.F.: Thermostatistics of overdamped motion of interacting particles. Phys. Rev. Lett. **105**(26), 260601 (2010). https://doi.org/10.1103/PhysRevLett.105.260601
38. Ribeiro, M.S., Nobre, F.D., Curado, E.M.F.: Classes of N-dimensional nonlinear Fokker-Planck equations associated to Tsallis entropy. Entropy **13**(11), 1928–1944 (2011). https://doi.org/10.3390/e13111928

39. Plastino, A.R., Plastino, A.: Non-extensive statistical mechanics and generalized Fokker-Planck equation. Phys. A **222**(1), 347–354 (1995). https://doi.org/10.1016/0378-4371(95)00211-1
40. Tsallis, C., Bukman, D.J.: Anomalous diffusion in the presence of external forces: exact time-dependent solutions and their thermostatistical basis. Phys. Rev. E **54**(3), R2197–R2200 (1996). https://doi.org/10.1103/PhysRevE.54.R2197

Multi-modal Associative Storage and Retrieval Using Hopfield Auto-associative Memory Network

Rachna Shriwas, Prasun Joshi, Vandana M. Ladwani, and V. Ramasubramanian(✉)

International Institute of Information Technology - Bangalore (IIIT-B), Bangalore, India
{rachna.shriwas,prasun.joshi,vandana.ladwani}@iiitb.org, v.ramasubramanian@iiitb.ac.in

Abstract. Recently we presented text storage and retrieval in an auto-associative memory framework using the Hopfield neural-network. This realized the ideal functionality of Hopfield network as a content-addressable information retrieval system. In this paper, we extend this result to multi-modal patterns, namely, images with text captions and show that the Hopfield network indeed can store and retrieve such multi-modal patterns even in an auto-associative setting. Within this framework, we examine two central issues such as (i) performance characterization to show that the $O(N)$ capacity of the Hopfield network for a network of size N neurons under the Pseudo-inverse learning rule is still retained in the multi-modal case, and (ii) the retrieval dynamics of the multi-modal pattern (i.e., image and caption together) under various types of queries such as image+caption, image only and caption only, in line with a typical multi-modal retrieval system where the entire multi-modal pattern is expected to be retrieved even with a partial query pattern from any of the modalities. We present results related to these two issues on a large database of 7000+ captioned-images and establish the practical scalability of both the storage capacity and the retrieval robustness of the Hopfield network for content-addressable retrieval of multi-modal patterns. We point to the potential of this work to extend to a more wider definition of multi-modality as in multi-media content, with various modalities such as video (image sequence) synchronized with sub-title text, speech, music and non-speech.

Keywords: Hopfield network · Auto-associative memory · Multi-modal storage · Multi-modal retrieval · Captioned images · Content-addressable retrieval

1 Introduction

We consider an auto-associative memory framework, namely the Hopfield network, and examine how its content-addressable retrieval property can be adapted

I. V. Tetko et al. (Eds.): ICANN 2019, LNCS 11727, pp. 57–75, 2019.
https://doi.org/10.1007/978-3-030-30487-4_5

for 'multi-modal' associative storage and retrieval. The Hopfield network [6] was originally proposed as an associative memory formulation, allowing binary patterns to be stored and retrieved, typically from partial or corrupted patterns, particularly in the auto-associative realization, which is an ideal form of 'content-addressable memory', but which has not been explored for scalable storage/retrieval of real-world patterns such as text, image, speech, audio etc. or more generally complex multi-modal patterns such as multi-media content (e.g. movie content, video sequences etc.).

We define the most general form of multi-modal retrieval as illustrated in Fig. 1, in the context of a multi-media scenario (e.g. movie content) showing a multi-media clip, typically from a longer sequence (e.g. a full-length movie) or a larger corpus (or database), being searched. We could thus have a large number of such clips that needs to be stored, with each clip made of a sequence of image frames, synchornized sub-title text, speech, music and non-speech foley sounds. The clip could be viewed as a sequence of single-frame multi-modal data of a captioned-image, a single-frame of speech signal and music, foley sound signals and each movie/multi-media clip can therefore be stored as a sequence of such single-frame multi-modal data.

In our present work, we define the multi-modal storage and retrieval problem as being given a partial-query pattern from any of the modalities (e.g. sub-title text) and being required to retrive a complete video clip (comprising all the modalities) of some duration associated with that query pattern.

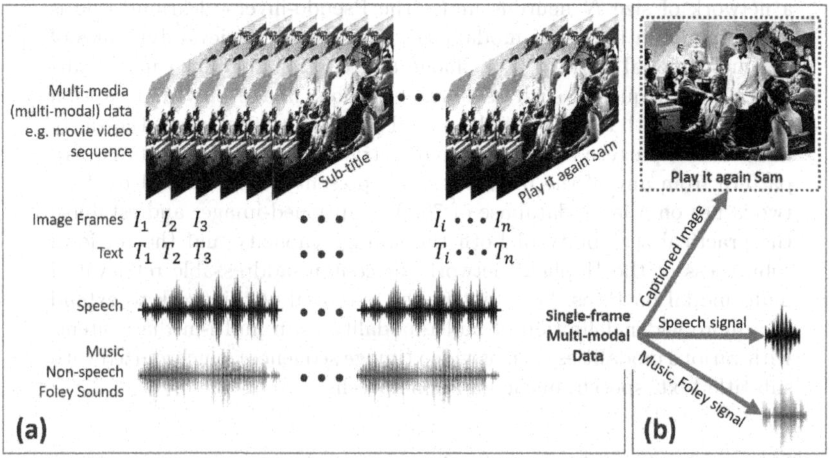

Fig. 1. Typical multi-modal data in a multi-media scenario (e.g. movie content): (a) Image frames, and synchornized sub-title text, speech, music and non-speech foley sounds and (b) viewed as made of single-frame multi-modal data of a captioned-image, a single-frame of speech signal and music, foley sound signals

In this paper, our main contribution is in adapting the Hopfield network for such a multi-modal storage and retrieval, by considering a sub-set of the problem, in terms of bi-modal 'captioned-images', i.e., a video sequence with sub-titles, or a collection of images each with a caption. Earlier, we have proposed and demonstrated the efficiacy of content-addressable memory based storage and retrieval for speech (termed audio-search) [13] and text-retrieval [12] (e.g for scalable text storage of 10000 sentences in networks with up to 100 million interconnections) and in this paper, we take up the more general and broader case of multi-modal data as heteroenous patterns and perhaps for the first time in literature address the problem of how such heterogenous patterns can be stored and retrieved in an auto-associative formulation of the Hopfield network.

In the following two sub-sections (Sects. 1.1 and 1.2), we provide a short but rather comprehensive outline of related work in the context of multi-modal information retrieval (and the closely defined cross-modal retrieval problem). In the first sub-section, we provide an overview of what can be considered traditional (non-associative) formulations and in the second sub-section, we touch upon (a much smaller) body of work within the 'associative' memory formulations. In doing so, our aim is to note, in the subsequent section (Sect. 1.3), that (i) our work here uniquely falls within the neural information retrieval framework - specifically in the Hopfield neural associative memory formulation to store and retrieve multi-modal patterns to perform cross-modal retrieval, which is one of the closest mechanisms of human memory with a strong biological realism as evidenced by the congitive functionality of the hippocampus (region CA3) to bind multi-modal information via the collateral effect or pattern completion as modeled by Hopfield networks and that (ii) this has not been attempted before, despite several closely related work of associative memory based approaches as outlined in the sub-section Sect. 1.2 below.

1.1 Related Work - Cross-Modal Retrieval

We first note here the definition of cross-modal retrieval as 'taking one type of data as the query to retrieve relevant data of another type', implicitly calling for a possibly specialized mechanism of jointly representing and storing multi-modal patterns in the first place and a retrieval mechanism for cross-modal queries from such multi-modal representations and storage.

We note the existence of a wide class of techniques and algorithms for cross-modal retrieval under classic paradigms such as sub-space learning methods, topic models, pair-wise based methods, rank based methods the more recently emerging deep-learning methods [14,26]. Even more traditionally, binary representation learning mainly used unimodal hashing, multi-view hashing and cross-modal hashing techniques [26]. We further highlight here the range of such techniques and algorithms available within each of these broad paradigms [14,26].

Sub-space learning methods typically include canonical correlation analysis (CCA), partial least squares (PLS), bilinear model (BLM), cross-modal factor analysis (CFA), maximum covariance unfolding (MCU), collective component analysis (CoCA), generalized multiview analysis (GMA), generalized multiview LDA (GMLDA), generalized multiview MFA (GMMFA), cluster canonical correlation analysis (cluster-CCA), intra-view and interview supervised correlation analysis (I2SCA), common discriminant feature extraction (CDFE), parallel field alignment retrieval (PFAR), joint representation learning (JRL), learning coupled feature spaces (LCFS)) and joint feature selection and subspace learning (JFSSL).

Topic models comprise latent dirichlet allocation (LDA), correspondence LDA (Corr-LDA), topic-regression multi-modal LDA (Tr-mm LDA), multimodal document random field (MDRF), document neural autoregressive distribution estimator (DocNADE) and its supervised extensions, nonparametric Bayesian upstream supervised (NPBUS), multi-modal topic model, supervised multi-modal mutual topic reinforce modeling (M3R) etc.

Pairwise based methods include multi-view neighborhood preserving projection (Multi-NPP), multiview metric learning with global consistency and local smoothness (MVML-GL), joint graph regularized heterogeneous metric learning (JGRHML) algorithm etc.

Rank based methods typically include supervised semantic indexing (SSI), aggressive model for image retrieval (PAMIR), latent semantic cross-modal ranking (LSCMR), ranking canonical correlation analysis (RCCA) etc.

Deep-learning methods range across restricted Boltzmann machine, deep canonical correlation analysis (DCCA), end-to-end DCCA, correspondence autoencoder (Corr-AE) for cross-modal retrieval, regularized deep neural network (RE-DNN) for semantic mapping across modalities, supervised multi-modal deep neural network (MDNN), relational generative deep belief nets (RGDBN), modality - specific deep structure (MSDS), dependency tree recursive neural networks (DT-RNNs), deep visual-semantic embedding model (DeViSE), deep compositional cross-modal learning to rank (C2MLR), cross-modal correlation learning with deep convolutional architecture (CMCDCA) etc.

Typical datasets on which multi-modal and cross-modal retrieval work has been conducted include MSCOCO, Wiki image-text dataset, INRIA-Websearch, Flickr30K, Pascal VOC, and NUS-WIDE [26]. In our work here, we use a Flickr subset of the Flickr30K dataset.

1.2 Related Work - Associative Memory Approaches

In this section, we provide a brief overview of approaches in multi-modal modeling, storage and retrieval essentially designed on principles of cognitively plausible ways of building representations that are consistent with the inherently re-constructive and associative nature of human memory. This is in contrast to the algorithmic techniques and frameworks outlined in the previous sub-section in the sense that techniques reviewed here are motivated and inspired by the re-constructive and associative nature of human memory (in integrating multi-sensory perceptual inputs), and in creating neural constructs and basis that support and realize such human memory functionality as close as possible. Even within such a cognitive modeling based approach, we note a dichotomy of formalisms – one comprising techniques that are not necessarily directly based on a 'biological realism', i.e., architectures that are at best functional equivalent of the said associative memory property (e.g. bi-directional associative memory, deep belief networks or the auto-encoder formulations) and the other that model the biological structure and function as closely as possible (e.g. auto-associative and hetero-associative memory formulations). We note that our work on the auto-associative mechanism of Hopfield networks falls in the latter category, and also that it seems a direction not attempted so far for multi-modal and cross-modal retrieval within the class of neural information retrieval algorithms.

Reynaud and Moisy [19] and Reynaud [18] proposed a dynamic neural network (a bidirectional associative memory (BAM)) that works as a memory for multiple associations (e.g. multiple BAM or the 'triple BAM'). Here, the aim was to associate heterogeneous pairs of patterns, tied together through learning within the BAM memory in such a way to facilitate easy recall. This work was further extended by Boniface and Reghis [1] with the aim of integrating different sensory inputs in order to memorize a unified and distributed representation. This work presented an experimental evaluation of the model with focus on its limitations in terms of noise robustness and learning capacities. In all of this work, the multi-modality was represented by pairs of images of letters and images of numbers. A further extension to this multiple-BAM architecture is the spiking BAM variant of Meunier and Moisy [16] which proposes a new implementation of the central module performing a multimodal associative memory, and in which the BAM is emulated in temporal coding with spiking neurons and set in the context of modeling 'intermodal priming'—where under temporal conditions, the presentation of a first stimulus, the primer is hypothesized to make easier the processing of a similar second stimulus, the target and where the primer and target are typically from two different perceptive modalities.

In the work of Chaminade et al. [2], an associative network links a 16 degrees of freedom robotic hand and a simple visual system. By this, they construct a minimal visuomotor association and show that this is sufficient to bootstrap basic imitation, particularly those involving generalization to new actions shown as possible to emerge from a connectionist associative network.

Deep-learning approaches to multi-modality include the recent work of Srivastava and Salakhutdinov [23,24] and Ngiam et al. [17] and those particularly focusing on multimodal systems that use images and text (Socher et al. [22], Karpathy and Fei-Fei [10] and Kiros et al. [11]). A work that uses a similar deep architecture and uses a form of hetero-associative framework is that of Iqbal [8] and Iqbal [9] where each sensory channel or modality is a generative deep belief network (DBN) composed of stacked restricted Boltzman machine (RBM) layers, with the top level features of each DBN further combined as input to another RBM layer (associative memory); here, the associative memory layer connects the features of one channel with all others, allowing it to reconstruct the values at the visible nodes of a channel, if they are missing—this comes closest to a hetero-associative formalism for multi-modal association, though differing considerably from our more biologically-realistic direct realization of the Hopfield neural network.

Collell et al. [3] aim to provide a cognitively plausible way of building representations, consistent with the inherently re-constructive and associative nature of human memory and towards this, they explore how to build multimodal representations by learning a language-to-vision mapping and using its output to build multimodal embeddings.

In a similar motivation and inspired by the re-constructive and associative nature of human memory (in integrating multi-sensory perceptual inputs), Wang et al. [27] address the problem of learning multimodal word representations by integrating textual, visual and auditory inputs using an associative multichannel autoencoder (AMA), which learns the associations between textual and perceptual modalities so as to predict the missing perceptual information of concepts.

1.3 Associative Memory Framework - Biological Realism

In contrast to these different associative memory formulations, the auto - associative memory formulation of Hopfield network for learning and storing such multi-modal patterns and retrieve them in a cross-modal manner is highly biologically inspired and pleasing, given the now well acknowledged neuroscience basis of human memory. Particularly, we refer to some of the studies that implicate hippocampus as an associative memory "convergence zone", binding together the multimodal elements of an experienced event into a single engram [7], where Horner and Burgess, 2013 point to how the relatively high proportion of recurrent collaterals in region CA3 of the hippocampus has been associated with the ability to bind multimodal information, via the collateral effect [15] or pattern completion as exactly modeled by Hopfield networks [6], further concluding that both the anatomical situation of the hippocampus (at the top of a hierarchy of inputs from neocortical regions) and the architecture of CA3 provide an ideal platform for rapidly binding elements of an event into a coherent representation. This is consistent with similar treatment of the CA3 (see for e.g. [21]) that it operates effectively as a single auto-association network to allow arbitrary associations between inputs originating from very different parts of the cerebral cortex to be formed, and later for the whole memory to be recalled from any part in the process termed completion. This is also consistent with other similar studies (see for e.g. [4]) that support the widely held view that the hippocampus contributes to the formation of associations between different components of an event ("memory binding").

In keeping with the well-defined notions (see for e.g. [20]), that auto-associative information supports the processes of recognition and pattern completion whereas hetero-associative information supports the processes of paired-associate learning and sequence generation, it is clearly plausible to model human memory mechanisms particularly for the task of multi-modal association either in the auto-associative framework (e.g. in line with the hippocampus and CA3 being auto-associative multi-sensory integration centers) as well in the hetero-associative framework. In general, such a view provides a strong 'biological realism' in realizing multi-modal storage and cross-modal retrieval using the Hopfield auto-associative network, in comparison to associative memory formulations referred to in Sect. 1.2 or the more conventional cross-modal retrieval frameworks and algorithms outlined in Sect. 1.1.

1.4 Proposed Work and Contributions

With regard to storing and retrieving multi-modal patterns such as captioned - images, comprising an image and an associated text, our emphasis is on showing that the auto-associative framework of Hopfield neural network can indeed store such heterogenous patterns, particularly given that though the two modalities are semantically related from human-centric view, they are essentially uncorrelated and constitute only a 'paired' data whose association has to be learnt in being presented together. While we seek a general solution of a (partial) query in any of the modalities (here, only the image or only the caption, and in a more unconstrained setting a partial pattern of both the image and the caption) to retrieve the entire captioned image, the kind of errors that could result in a poorly learnt auto-association (by the Hopfield network) would include retrieving a wrong captioned-image, a poorly formed spurious captioned-image (the image and caption with errors), or a correct image with the wrong caption or vice-versa. Such erroneous retrieval points to the non-trivial nature of the problem of Hopfield network to learn the multi-modal associativity across modalities as presented only in a paired kind of manner. While hetero-associative memory formulations can be viewed as more suited for such paired data learning, we expect the auto-associative memory formulation to be more appropriate given the range of learning rules that have been explored with high capacity, and the possibility of extending the multi-modality to several modalities seamlessly in an auto-associative framework, without having to explicity specify the multi-modal partitioning of the network on such data.

In this paper, our contributions primarily involve extending the auto-associative framework to multi-modal data (captioned-images) and in examining

- whether the Hopfield network can be adapted to store and retrieve such multi-modal associative patterns in the first place, i.e. whether it offers a storage-retrieval capacity under any of the specific learning rule (e.g. Pseudo-inverse rule, as studied here) as it would for uni-modal data for which it was originally formulated for,
- whether the Hopfield network can retrieve a particular modality pattern (or the entire multi-modal pattern as a consequence) when presented with a query from the 'other' modality, e.g. retrieving the entire captioned-image when the query is only the image or only the caption, thereby completing the query pattern in one modality with the originally paired other modality.

1.5 Experimental Scenarios

With regard to the different scenarios that present themselves in considering multi-modal patten storage and retrieval (e.g. bi-modal captioned-images here), Fig. 2 shows the potential combinations of query patterns vs retrieved patterns, when the stored patterns are complete captioned-images. Circles represent cases considered here:

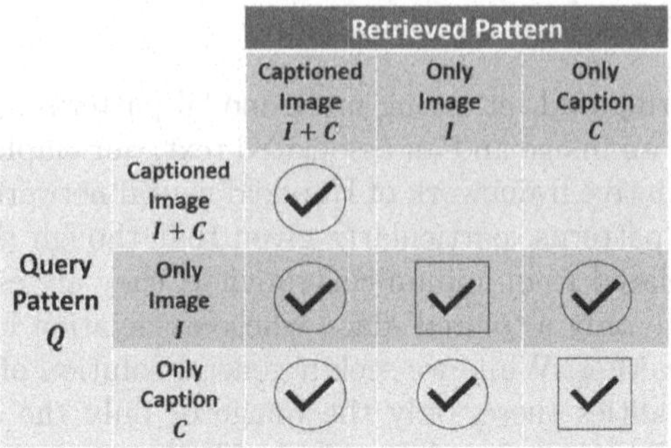

Fig. 2. Scenrios experimented with for captioned-image storage and retrieval: Circles represent multi-modal cases considered and reported here, Squares are uni-modal cases reported elsewhere, e.g. for text-retrieval, see [12]

- Query Q being a captioned-image ($Q = I+C$), retrieving the captioned-image $I+C$, representing the scenario that has not been attempted before, in showing Hopfield network can indeed handle heterogenous patterns and extends it learning to such patterns and allowing retrieval performances similar to well understood uni-modal behavior (e.g. the $O(N)$ capacity of pseudo-inverse learning rule).
- Query Q being 'only' the image ($Q = I$), retrieving the complete captioned image $I + C$, allowing reading off only the image I or caption C from the complete pattern thus retrieved. This represents the case when a partial query, from one of the modalities - image, here - retrieves the full captioned-image or the image or the caption. Showing that the Hopfield network's $O(N)$ pseudo-inverse rule capacity holds for such a cross-modal behavior is important here, and hitherto not attempted.
- Query Q being 'only' the caption ($Q = C$), retrieving the complete captioned image $I + C$ or allowing reading off only the image I or caption C from the complete pattern thus retrieved. This represents the case when a partial query, from one of the modalities - caption, here - retrieves the full captioned-image or the image or the caption.

These scenarios are practically of high interest, given the low information content in a text-caption, and showing its potential to retrieve across modality - i.e., to retrieve a more information bearing image or the captioned-image itself, representing a typical multi-media information retrieval scenario of a user presenting a text-query (e.g. of sub-titles of a movie) and being able to retrieve an appropriate movie-clip of some desired duration, bearing the sub-title.

In principle, extending the mechanism further, such a multi-modal association would allow retrieval of the full multi-modal pattern (or other cross-modal elements of the original pattern), even when presented a partial query pattern (in any of the modalities) that is a statistically or syntactically related variant of the original unimodal element, in such a way to take advantage of the attractor basin of the associative network to map the query pattern (variant pattern) to the original storage element or the multi-modal pattern, thereby capable of performing captioning of new images, retrieval of video from poorly formed (semantically related but linguistically different) text queries etc.

These scenarios are further taken up in Sect. 5 in terms of specific experiments and corresponding results of storage capacity and retrieval dynamics to illustrate the feasibility of these scenarios.

2 Hopfield Network and Multi-modal Pattern Retrieval

The Hopfield network was first proposed by Hopfield in 1982 [6] as an 'associative memory' formalism and belongs to the class of neurodynamical systems [5] which possesses 'attractors' representing stable states of the network, whose complete functioning can be encapsulated into two phases:

1. **Storage phase:** consisting of how a set of N-dimensional vectors, also termed the fundamental memories, are 'memorized' by the network and,
2. **Retrieval phase:** consisting of presenting an N-dimensional vector called a 'probe' is input to the Hopfield network trained as above, where the probe typically represents an incomplete (partial) or noisy version of a 'fundamental memory' in the network; the network evolves to this fundamental memory which then becomes the retrieved pattern in response to the input probe.

Such a mechanism represents a content-addressable memory, being able to retrieve a stored pattern, given a reasonable subset of the information content of that pattern. This primary property of the Hopfield model as a 'content addressable memory' makes it ideally suited for 'content addressable/based information retrieval', a functionality best exemplified by verbatim quote from Hopfield's original paper [6] in Fig. 3. However, despite this clearly enunciated property of the Hopfield network, this formulation has received little attention for realistic problems of 'information retrieval' as is currently of significant interest in multimedia retrieval which spans data domains such text, speech, audio, music, images, video and multi-modal combinations of these; recent examples of adapting the Hopfield network framework for speech recognition, audio-search and text-retrieval are [12,13,25].

> *Suppose that an item stored in memory is "H. A. Kramers & G. H. Wannier Physi Rev. 60, 252 (1941)". A general content-addressable memory would be capable of retrieving this entire memory item on the basis of sufficient partial information. The input "& Wannier (1941)" might suffice. An ideal memory could deal with errors and retrieve this reference even from the input "Vannier, (1941)".*

Fig. 3. Primary property of the Hopfield network as a 'content addressable memory': verbatim quote from Hopfield's original paper [6]

The main contributions in this paper are in the form of considering the following issues that present itself in adapting the generic Hopfield network as an efficient content-addressable retrieval framework for multi-modal (captioned-image) retrieval:

- **Heterogenous fused binarized pattern representation:** Using a binarized representation of the captioned-image for use in the discrete Hopfield network.
- **Multi-modal capacity:** Studying the capacity of the Hopfield network for the Pseudo-inverse learning rule, for the multi-modal patterns as a whole, in the process examining whether the Hopfield network can be adapted to store and retrieve such multi-modal associative patterns in the first place, i.e. whether it offers the capacity of $O(N)$ under the Pseudo-inverse rule, as it would for uni-modal data for which it was originally formulated for,
- **Cross-modal retrieval viability, performance and capacity:** Whether the Hopfield network can retrieve a particular modality pattern (or the entire multi-modal pattern as a consequence) when presented with a query from the 'other' modality, e.g. retrieving the entire captioned-image when the query is only the image or only the caption, thereby completing the query pattern in one modality with the originally paired other modality. This is done using a large captioned-image corpus, 'flickr' data, with 7396 images with captions of lengths up to 100 characters, making up heterogenous vectors of dimension 8196 and over 67 million interconnect weights.

3 Basics of Hopfield Network

The Hopfield network consists of N neurons, $i = 1, \ldots, N$, with neuron i connected to neuron j through synaptic weights $w_{ij}, j = 1, \ldots, N$, as in Fig. 4.

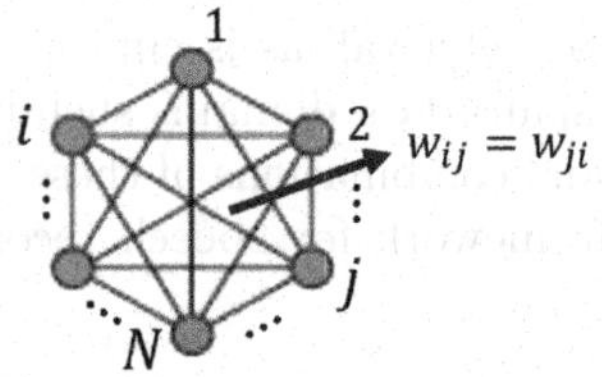

Fig. 4. Generic structure of a Hopfield network

The discrete Hopfield network, as is in focus here, is based on the McCulloch-Pitts model, where each neuron j can have two states: $x_j = +1$ (or the 'on' or 'firing' state) or $x_j = -1$ (or the 'off' or 'quiescent' state), with a 'state' of the network (made of N neurons) being represented by the vector, $\mathbf{x} = [x_1, x_2, \ldots, x_N]^T$. The state x_j of an individual neuron j is determined by the level of the induced local field v_j acting on it, which is determined by the collective influence of all neurons $i = 1, \ldots, N$ connected to it through respective synaptic weights w_{ij}, and is given by,

$$v_j = \sum_{i=1}^{N} w_{ij} x_i + b_j \tag{1}$$

where b_j is a fixed bias applied externally to neuron j. Neuron j changes its state x_j according to the deterministic rule,

$$x_j = sgn[v_j]$$

which is equivalent to

$$x_j = \begin{cases} +1 & \text{if } v_j > 0 \\ -1 & \text{if } v_j < 0 \end{cases} \tag{2}$$

with the neuron left in its previous state if v_j is exactly 0.

The two phases of the Hopfield network – the storage phase and the retrieval phase (as outlined in Sect. 2) are described below in some detail to specify the operation of the Hopfield network as a 'content addressable memory'.

3.1 Storage Phase (or Learning or Memorizing)

Let $\xi_1, \xi_2, \ldots, \xi_\mu, \ \ldots, \xi_M$ denote a set of N-dimensional fundamental memories. In our earlier work, the Pseudo-inverse (PI) learning rule, a generalization of the Hebbian rule (in the sense that Hebbian is a special case of Pseudo-inverse (PI) rule, for training vectors that are not orthogonal), was consistenly found to offer $O(N)$ storage for practical data (as against the lower $0.14N$ capacity of Hebbian rule). We consider this PI rule here. The learning (or 'training' or 'storage phase') of the Hopfield network comprises computing the synaptic weights $\{w_{ij}\}, i, j = 1, \ldots, N$ from $\xi_1, \xi_2, \ldots, \xi_\mu, \ \ldots, \xi_M$ to store them. The Pseudo-inverse (PI) learning rule is given by

$$w_{ij} = \frac{1}{N} \sum_{k,l} \xi_{ki} \left(C^{-1}\right) \xi_{lj} \tag{3}$$

where C is the co-variance matrix of the training vectors $\xi_1, \xi_2, \ldots, \xi_\mu, \ldots, \xi_M$ and $w_{ij}i = w_{ij}$ is the symmetric weight connecting neuron i to neuron j. Once the weights are computed from the input patterns $\{\xi_\mu | \mu = 1, 2, \ldots, M\}$ they are kept fixed, and the Hopfield network can now be used for retrieval.

3.2 Retrieval Phase

The retrieval phase is an iterative algorithm that can be described as follows: Given the probe pattern ξ_{probe} (an unknown N-dimensional vector), the retrieval algorithm is initialized by setting

$$x_j(0) = \xi_{j,probe} \qquad j = 1, \ldots, N \tag{4}$$

where $x_j(0)$ is the state of neuron j at time $n = 0$ and $\xi_{j,probe}$ is the jth element of the probe vector ξ_{probe}. This is followed by an 'iteration until convergence' which updates the elements of state vector $x(n)$ 'asynchronously' (i.e., randomly and one at a time) according to the rule,

$$x_j(n+1) = sgn\left[\sum_{i=1}^{N} w_{ji}x_i(n)\right], \qquad j = 1, \ldots, N \tag{5}$$

until the state vector $\mathbf{x}$ remains unchanged as $\mathbf{x}_{final}$, with the output vector $\mathbf{y}$ of the network set as $\mathbf{y} = \mathbf{x}_{final}$.

4 Hopfield Network for Captioned-Image Retrieval

The Hopfield network, once trained, possesses an energy landscape $E(\mathbf{x})$ as a function of the state vector $\mathbf{x}$ given by

$$E(\mathbf{x}) = -\frac{1}{2} \sum_{1 \leq i \leq N, i \neq j} \sum_{j=1}^{N} w_{ij}x_i x_j \tag{6}$$

The fundamental memories corresponding to the input patterns $\xi_1, \xi_2, \ldots, \xi_\mu, \ldots, \xi_M$ correspond to energy minimas in the energy landscape, and each such energy minima in itself is the minima in a energy well constituting the attractor basin in the neurodynamics of the network. Such a energy landscape with multiple energy wells or attractor basins, each with one stable minimum energy state is schematically shown in Fig. 5(Left-panel).

When a probe vector ξ_{probe} is presented to the network, the update step (Eq. (5) corresponds to the behavior shown in Fig. 5(Right-panel), where the state vector $\mathbf{x}(n)$ progressively changes in the direction of 'reducing' energy $E(\mathbf{x})$, 'rolling down' an energy well (or attractor basin), it is proximally located in, and finally settling into the energy state at the minimum energy of that particular basin, yielding the final state as the retrieved pattern – thereby completing the process of retrieving a 'complete' pattern corresponding to an incomplete/partial or noisy input probe pattern, and performing a 'content addressable retrieval'.

5 Captioned-Image Storage and Retrieval

In this section, we present results of using Hopfield network for storage and retrieval of captioned-images representing a bi-modal case of multi-modal data, i.e., images with text captions, in the form of paired data, the images being gray-scale images and the captions being text-sentences made of sequence of letters from the English alphabet and special characters.

We have used 7396 gray-scale captioned-images from the 'flickr' image - captioning dataset[1], where each image has a default caption of up to 72 characters

[1] https://www.kaggle.com/hsankesara/flickr-image-dataset.

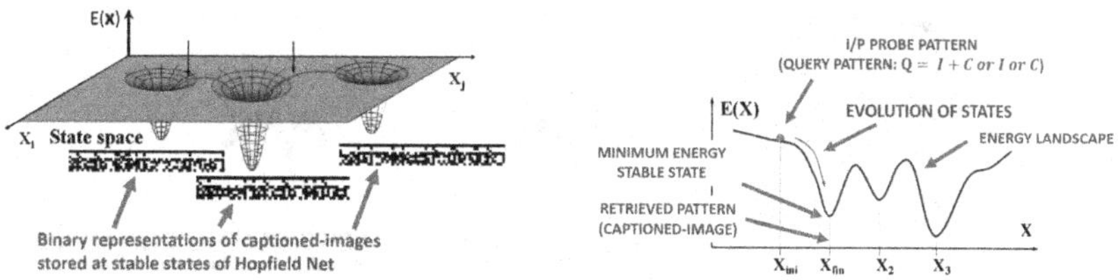

Fig. 5. **Left-panel:** energy landscape of a Hopfield network: stable states correspond to captioned-image patterns of the database being searched; **Right panel:** retrieval mechanism for an input probe (query vector which could be a captioned-image or only an image or only the caption or a partial caption): rolling down on the energy landscape to the nearest attractor basin and its minimum energy stable state, retrieving a complete original captioned-image

long (e.g. 'A dog leaps across the grass', as shown in Fig. 6). Each image is resized to $86 \times 86 = 7396$ pixels. For these 7396 images, we derived 2 data-sets: (a) **Data-set-1** - In this data-set, each default caption is represented by an encoding of 7 bits/char and 6 bits/space leading to a binarized vector of maximum length of 489 bits/caption for the default captions, (b) **Data-set-2** - In this data-set, we used 'generated captions' for each image, with a fixed length of 100 characters (to allow for more controlled and reliable representations with constant length captions, not requiring bit-paddings as was needed for the variable-length default captions) and applied a uniform ASCII encoding of 8 bits/char for the generated captions, leading to a constant length binarized vector of 800 bits/caption.

As shown in Fig. 6, the captioned-images were subject to (i) binarization of the images and captions, (ii) rasterization of the binarized image and the caption and, (iii) fusion of the rasterized vector of the image (of length 7396 bits) and caption (of length 489 bits (for default captions) or of length 800 bits (for generated captions)) to yield a final binary vector of dimension 7885 or 8196, respectively. This fused vector is an heterogenous representation of the captioned-image and is presented to the Hopfield network of size $N = 7885$ neurons or $N = 8196$ neurons as in the two cases of default captions and generated captions, and over 67 million interconnects.

We first show the "capacity performance" of the Hopfield network for heterogenous data, i.e. in being able to store and retrieve captioned-images as a bi-modal data. We use Data-set-1 for this, i.e. images with default captions.

- **Retrieving captioned-images with Query** $= I + C$: Figure 7(Left-panel) shows the capacity performance in terms of the number of captioned-images retrieved (in the y-axis) from the Hopfield storage (on being presented with the complete captioned-image ($I + C$) as a query (or probe) pattern), plotted against the number of captioned-images stored (in the x-axis), ranging up to 7885 (as defined above). It can be noted that the capacity of Pseudo-inverse rule yields close to the theoretical capacity of $N - 1$ or $O(N)$ i.e., up to 7885 captioned-images even with 0% error tolerance.

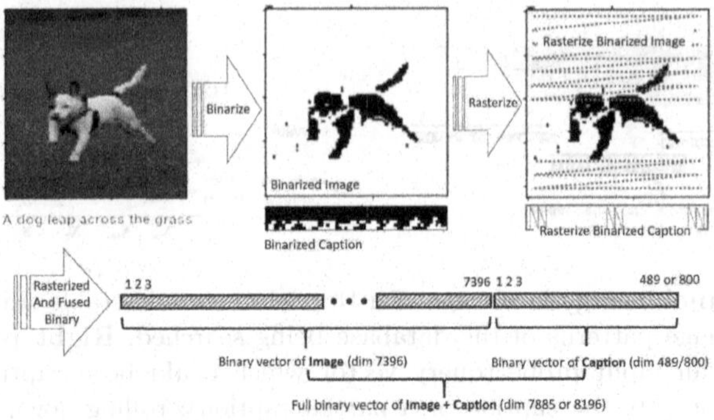

Fig. 6. Captioned-image representation: heterogenous binarized vectors of a captioned-image by binarization, rasterizing and fusion

- **Retrieving captioned-images with Query** = I**:** Figure 7(Right-panel) shows the capacity performance in terms of the number of captioned-images retrieved (in the y-axis) from the Hopfield storage (on being presented with only an image as a query (or probe) pattern (i.e., Query = I), plotted against the number of captioned-images stored (in the x-axis), ranging up to 7885 (as defined above). Note that we use a specified error-tolerance measured as the Hamming distance between the retrieved captioned-image and the original captioned-image (of which the query is the image-part), yielding a family of curves (as indexed and shown in the Legend). It can be noted that for 0% tolerance, the network has to operate at below $O(N)$ capacity, e.g. a maximum of 5000 images are retrieved without error, and this capacity drops with increase in number of images stored. In contrast, by allowing for a specific error-tolerance (e.g. 2 to 10%), the network is able to retrieve progressively more captioned-images 'correctly' (within the error-tolerance), reaching a $O(N)$ capacity, as in the case of matched $Q = I + C$ scenario of the Left-Panel.
- **Retrieving captioned-images with Query** = C**:** Figure 8 shows the summary of the capacity performance of Hopfield network for the above 2 cases (under a full loading of 100%) and for $Q = C$ under a loading of $\approx$10% (i.e., 800 captioned-images stored for $N = 8196$), allowing retrieval of all 800 images (i.e., $O(N)$ capacity with an error tolerance of 10%. Note that with the query progressing from $I + C$ to I to C, the capacity of Hopfield network decreases, indicating the difficulty of the task of retriving the more information bearing $I + C$ for progressively partial query patterns.

These results substantiate the feasibility of auto-associative Hopfield storage/retrieval mechanism to handle multi-modal data (bi-modal captioned-images here), allowing retrieval of up to $O(N)$ captioned-images stored with 0% error (for a Hopfield network of size N neurons). Specifically, with query as only image $Q = I$, the capacity lowers, but retains the full capacity of $O(N)$ within a 6% error tolerance. This is understandable, as the query being a partial pattern of

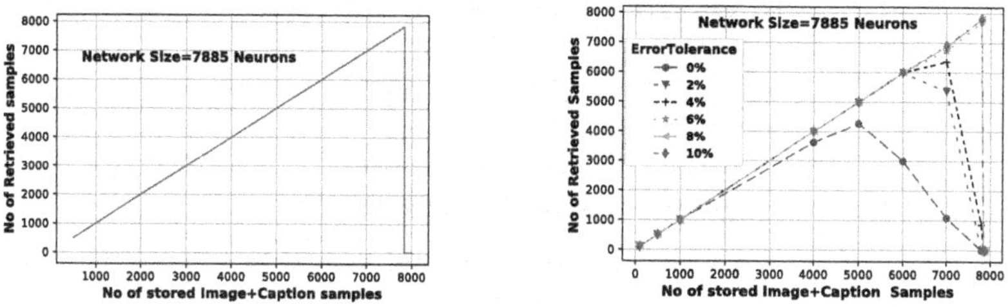

Fig. 7. Left-panel: Hopfield capacity plots for Captioned-Image (Image+Caption) storage and retrieval for Pseudo-inverse learning rule; **Right-panel:** Hopfield capacity for query as 'Image-only' and retrieval of corresponding full captioned-image under different error-tolerances

Captioned-Image Retrieval Performance	Query Pattern Q		
	Captioned Image $I + C$	Only Image I	Only Caption C
Capacity	$O(N)$	$O(N)$	$O(N)$
Error-Tolerance	0%	6%	10%

Fig. 8. Summary of Hopfield network performance for retrieval of captioned-images with different query patterns ($Q = I + C, Q = I, Q = C$)

the captioned-image is faced with the task of associatively retriving the complete captioned-image, with the correct caption. We believe this is a significant result, particularly on actual bi-modal captioned-images, hitherto neither attempted nor reported in literature.

This represents an interesting scenario of 'image-captioning' too, though considerable further work is required before substantiating the performance of such a captioning retrieval by the Hopfield network formulation under variations in the query pattern (with respect to the original image stored) in terms of illuminance, pose, scale, translation and statistical and semantic variations.

We now show the retrieval dynamics of retrieving the complete captioned-image from the following 3 cases of query (or probe) patterns, of focus in this paper: (i) 'Image and Caption' query, i.e., Query $= I + C$ - the 1st row in the table in Fig. 2, (ii) 'Only Image' query, i.e., Query $= I$ - the 2nd row in the table in Fig. 2 and (iii) 'Only Caption' query, i.e., Query $= C$ - the 3rd row in the table in Fig. 2. These are further detailed below. The Right-panel in all 3 figures shows the energy profile of the neurodynamic behavior of the retrieval (the network rolling down the energy landscape), as outlined in Sect. 4.

Query $= I + C$: Figure 9 shows the retrieval dynamics of Fig. 7(Left-panel), i.e., captioned-image retrieved with query $Q = I + C$. Note the Left-panel shows the sequence in which the query is iteratively refined into the retrieved pattern (at Iteration 2).

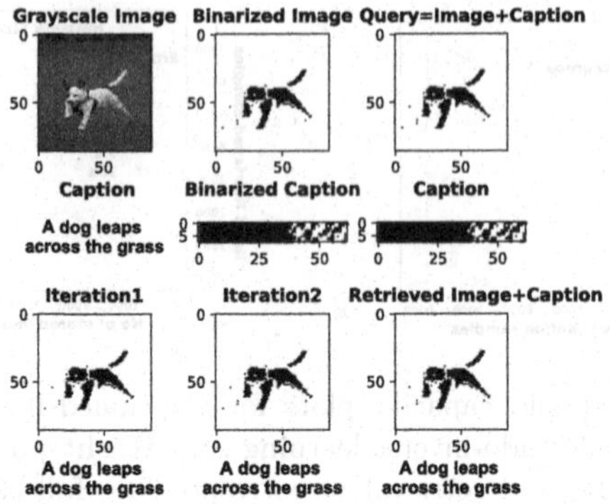

Fig. 9. Retrieval dynamics for query $Q = I + C$; Captioned-image sequence retrieval

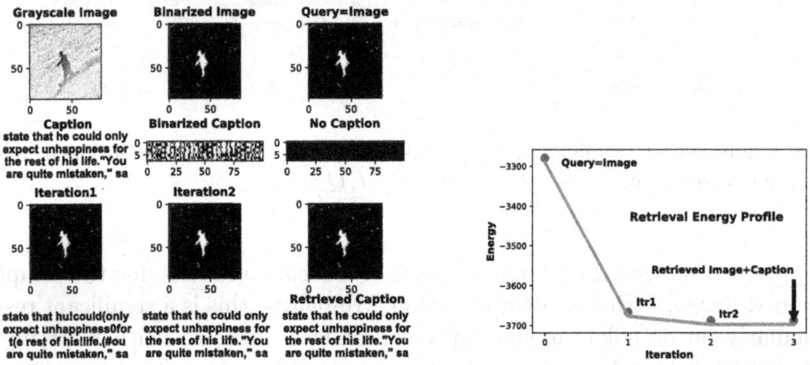

Fig. 10. Retrieval dynamics for query $Q = I$; **Left-panel:** Captioned-image sequence during retrieval **Right-panel:** Energy profile

Query $= I$: Figure 10 shows the retrieval dynamics of Fig. 7(Right-panel), i.e., captioned-image retrieved with query $Q = I$. Note the Left-panel shows the sequence in which the query is iteratively refined into the retrieved pattern (at Iteration 2); note the kind of errors in the retrieved caption at Iter 1.

Query $= C$: Figure 11 shows the most interesting of the 3 cases, namely, the retrieval dynamics of captioned-image retrieved with query $Q = C$. Note that in the Left-panel, which shows the sequence in which the query is iteratively refined into the retrieved pattern, the number of iterations (9) is far more than for the above 2 cases, given that the query now is a very partial, across-modality pattern.

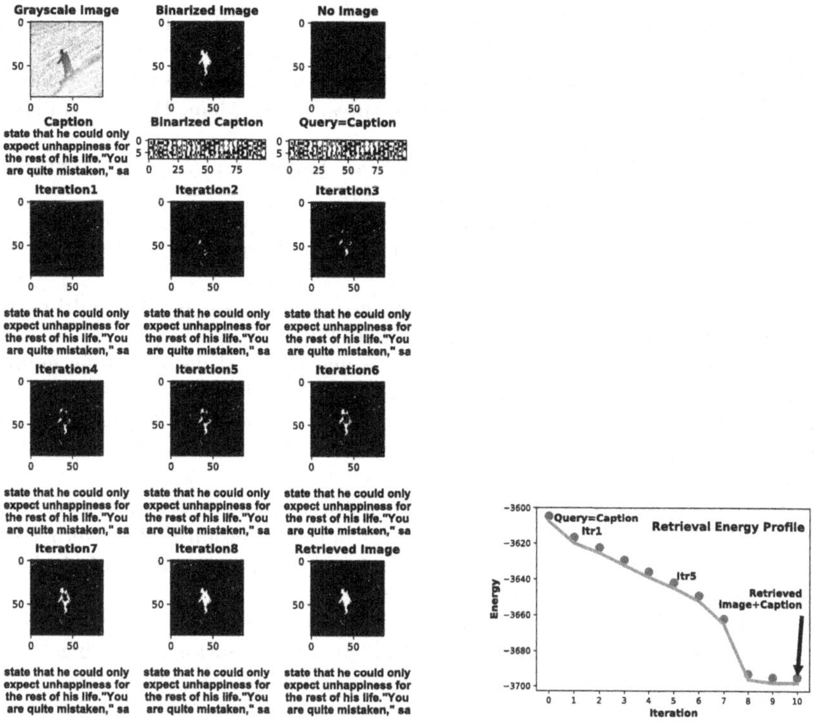

Fig. 11. Retrieval dynamics for query $Q = C$; **Left-panel:** Captioned-image sequence during retrieval **Right-panel:** Energy profile

6 Conclusions

We have examined and established the associative storage and retrieval of multi-modal patterns, namely, captioned-images represented as heterogenous fused binary vector in the auto-associative formulation of discrete Hopfield neural network. We have shown that the uni-modal $O(N)$ capacity under the Pseudo-inverse learning rule is retained in the multi-modal case too and presented the retrieval dynamics of captioned-image retrieval, under various types of queries such as image+caption, image only and caption only, in line with a cross-modal retrieval system where the entire multi-modal pattern is expected to be retrieved even with a partial query pattern from any of the modalities.

References

1. Boniface, Y., Reghis, A.: Some experiments around a neural network for multi-modal associations. In: IASTED The IASTED International Conference on Artificial Intelligence and Applications - AIA 2006, Innsbruck/Austria (2006)
2. Chaminade, T., Oztop, E., Chenga, G., Kawato, M.: From self-observation to imitation: visuomotor association on a robotic hand. Brain Res. Bull. **75**, 775–784 (2008). https://doi.org/10.1016/j.brainresbull.2008.01.016

3. Collell, G., Zhang, T., Moens, M.F.: Learning to predict: a fast re-constructive method to generate multimodal embeddings, March 2017. arXiv:1703.08737v1
4. Gottlieb, L.J., Wong, J., de Chastelaine, M., Rugg, M.D.: Neural correlates of the encoding of multimodal contextual features. Learn. Mem. **19**, 605–614 (2012). https://doi.org/10.1101/lm.027631.112
5. Haykin, S.: Neural Networks: A Comprehensive Foundation, 2nd edn. Prentice Hall International Inc., Upper Saddle River (1999)
6. Hopfield, J.J.: Neural networks and physical systems with emergent collective computational capabilities. Proc. Natl. Acad. Sci. **79**, 2554–2558 (1982). https://doi.org/10.1073/pnas.79.8.2554
7. Horner, A.J., Burgess, N.: The associative structure of memory for multi-element events. J. Exp. Psychol. Gener. **142**(4), 1370–1383 (2013)
8. Iqbal, M.S.: Mulit-modal learning using an unsupervised deep learning architecture, M.S. thesis, Acadia University, Canada
9. Iqbal, M.S., Silver, D.L.: A scalable unsupervised deep multimodal learning system. In: Proceedings of the 29th International Florida Artificial Intelligence Research Society Conference (2016)
10. Karpathy, A., Fei-Fei, L.: Deep visual-semantic alignments for generating image description. In: The IEEE Conference on Computer Vision and Pattern Recognition (CVPR) (2015). IEEE Trans. Pattern Anal. Mach. Intell. **39**(4) (2017). https://doi.org/10.1109/TPAMI.2016.2598339
11. Kiros, R., Salakhutdinov, R., Zemel, R.: Multimodal neural language models. In: Proceedings of the 31st International Conference on Machine Learning (ICML-2014), pp. 595–603 (2014). http://proceedings.mlr.press/v32/kiros14.html
12. Ladwani, V.M., Vaishnavi, Y., Ramasubramanian, V.: Hopfield auto-associative memory network for content-based text-retrieval. In: Proceedings of the ICANN-2017 26th International Conference on Artificial Neural Networks, September 2017. https://doi.org/10.1007/978-3-319-68612-7
13. Ladwani, V.M., et al.: Hopfield net framework for audio search. In: Proceedings NCC-2017 (2017). https://doi.org/10.1109/NCC.2017.8077074
14. Liu, J., Xu, C., Lu, H.: Cross-media retrieval: state-of-the-art and open issues. Int. J. Multimed. Intell. Secur. **1**(1), 33–52 (2010). https://doi.org/10.1504/IJMIS.2010.035970
15. Marr, D.: Simple memory: a theory for archicortex. Philos. Trans. Roy. Soc. London B Biol. Sci. **262**, 23–81 (1971). https://doi.org/10.1098/rstb.1971.0078
16. Meunier, D., Paugam-Moisy, H.: A spiking bidirectional associative memory for modeling intermodal priming. In: Proceedings of the 2nd IASTED International Conference Neural Network and Computational Intelligence, pp. 25–30 (2005). https://hal.archives-ouvertes.fr/hal-00001222
17. Ngiam, J., Khosla, A., Kim, M., Nam, J., Lee, H., Ng, A.Y.: Multimodal deep learning. In: Proceedings of the 28th International Conference on Machine Learning, ICML 2011, pp. 689–696 (2011)
18. Reynaud, E.: Modelisation connexionniste dune memoire associative multimodale. Ph.D. thesis, Institut National Polytechnique Grenoble (2002)
19. Reynaud, E., Paugam-Moisy, H.: A multiple BAM for hetero-association and multisensory integration modelling. In: Proceedings of the 2005 IEEE International Joint Conference on Neural Networks. IEEE (2005). https://doi.org/10.1109/IJCNN.2005.1556227
20. Rizzuto, D.S., Kahana, M.J.: An autoassociative neural network model of paired-associate learning. Neural Comput. **13**, 2075–2092 (2001). https://doi.org/10.1162/089976601750399317

21. Rolls, E.T.: The connected hippocampus. Prog. Brain Res. **219**, 21–43 (2015)
22. Socher, R., Karpathy, A., Le, Q.V., Manning, C.D., Ng, A.Y.: Grounded compositional semantics for finding and describing images with sentences. Trans. Assoc. Comput. Linguist. **2**, 207–218 (2014). https://doi.org/10.1162/tacl_a_00177
23. Srivastava, N., Salakhutdinov, R.: Multimodal learning with deep Boltzmann machines. In: Advances in Neural Information Processing Systems, pp. 2222–2230 (2012). http://dl.acm.org/citation.cfm?id=2999325.2999383
24. Srivastava, N., Salakhutdinov, R.: Multimodal learning with deep boltzmann machines. J. Mach. Learn. Res. **15**, 2949–2980 (2014). https://dl.acm.org/citation.cfm?id=2627435.2697059
25. Vaishnavi, Y., Shreyas, R., Suhas, S., Surya, U.N., Ladwani, V.M., Ramasubramanian, V.: Associative memory framework for speech recognition: adaptation of hopfield network. In: Proceedings of the IEEE INDICON (2016). https://doi.org/10.1109/INDICON.2016.7839105
26. Wang, K., Yin, Q., Wang, W., Wu, S., Wang, L.: A comprehensive survey on cross-modal retrieval. CoRR abs/1607.06215 (2016)
27. Wang, S., Zhang, J., Zong, C.: Associative multichannel autoencoder for multimodal word representation. In: Proceedings of the 2018 Conference on Empirical Methods in Natural Language Processing (Association of Computational Linguistics), pp. 115–124 (2018). https://www.aclweb.org/anthology/D18-1011

Chaotic Complex-Valued Associative Memory with Adaptive Scaling Factor Independent of Multi-values

Hiroaki Goto and Yuko Osana(✉)

Tokyo University of Technology, 1404-1, Katakura, Hachioji, Tokyo 192-0982, Japan
osana@stf.teu.ac.jp

Abstract. In this paper, we propose a chaotic complex-valued associative memory with adaptive scaling factor independent from multi-values. This model is based on the conventional chaotic complex-valued associative memory with adaptive scaling factor that can realize dynamic associations of multi-valued patterns. In the conventional chaotic complex-valued associative memory with adaptive scaling factor, parameters of the chaotic complex-valued neuron model are automatically adjusted according to the internal state of neurons. In the conventional model, a multi-value pattern is expressed by assigning points at positions obtained by equally dividing a unit circle of the complex plane into S multiple values. It has been confirmed that almost same recall ability can be obtained as in the case of performing manual adjustment in the model for $S = 4,\ 6,\ 8$, but no study has been conducted for other cases. In addition, it is known that the optimum method of automatically adjusting parameters also differs depending on the value of S. In this study, we also conduct experiments at $S = 10,\ 12,\ 14$ and 16, and propose a method to automatically adjust the parameters of the chaotic complex-valued neuron model independently from the value of S. Computer experiments were carried out and it was confirmed that automatic adjustment of parameters can be performed in the proposed model without depending on multi-values.

Keywords: Chaotic complex-valued neuron · Associative memory · Adaptive scaling factor

1 Introduction

Various researches on neural networks are actively conducted as a method for processing ambiguous information such as that found in the brain of living organisms. Many associative memory models have been proposed focusing on human associative memory ability. However, these models can only handle binary pattern associations and can not handle multi-valued pattern associations. On the other hand, complex-valued neural networks [1] have been proposed as models capable of handling multi-valued patterns. The complex-valued neural network

I. V. Tetko et al. (Eds.): ICANN 2019, LNCS 11727, pp. 76–86, 2019.
https://doi.org/10.1007/978-3-030-30487-4_6

consists of the complex neuron model, and multi-valued patterns are expressed by assigning points at positions obtained by equally dividing a unit circle of the complex plane into S into multiple values in this model.

On the other hand, chaos observed in the brain and nervous system of a living thing has attracted attention. Chaos is a phenomenon that can not be predicted long-term in a nonlinear system with deterministic time evolution, and it is said that chaos plays an important role in memory and learning in the brain. Also in research on neural networks, chaotic neuron models [2] that introduce chaos by taking into account spatio-temporal summation, refractoriness, and continuous-value output found in actual neurons have been proposed. In associative memory composed of chaotic neuron models, it is known that dynamic associations of stored patterns can be realized [2,3].

The complex-valued neuron model and the chaotic neuron model [2] are combined, a chaotic complex-valued neuron model [4] has been proposed. A chaotic complex-valued associative memory [4], which is a auto associative memory model composed of chaotic complex-valued neuron models, can realize dynamic associations of multi-valued patterns. However, in an associative memory composed of chaotic neuron models or chaotic neuron model-based models such as chaotic complex-valued neuron models, the recall ability depends on the parameters of the chaotic neuron model. Therefore, appropriate parameter values must be determined by trial and error because the appropriate parameter values differ depending on the size of the network, such as the number of neurons and the number of layers.

On the other hand, as the model which can choose appropriate parameters automatically, a chaotic complex-valued associative memory with adaptive scaling factor [5] has been proposed. In this model, automatic adjustment is realized by changing the parameter of the scaling factor of the refractoriness of the chaotic neuron model according to the value of the internal state. It has been confirmed that almost same recall ability can be obtained as in the case of performing manual adjustment in the model for $S = 4, 6, 8$ In addition, regardless of the number of neurons, it has also been confirmed that automatic adjustment of parameters is possible, but the automatic adjustment method is only considered for cases where specific multi-valued patterns ($S = 4, 6, 8$) are stored.

In this paper, we propose a chaotic complex-valued associative memory with adaptive scaling factor independent from multi-values.

2 Chaotic Complex-Valued Associative Memory with Adaptive Scaling Factor

Here, we explain the proposed chaotic complex-valued associative memory with adaptive scaling factor independent multi-values. This model is an auto-associative memory composed of chaotic complex-valued neuron models which have a scaling factor of refractoriness that varies with time, value of S (multi-values) and internal states of neurons. It can realize dynamic association of multi-valued stored patterns by internal state change by chaos.

2.1 Expression of Multi-valued Patterns

In the proposed model, multi-value patterns are expressed by assigning points at positions obtained by equally dividing a unit circle of the complex plane into S into multiple values, similarly to the conventional chaotic complex-valued associative memory with adaptive scaling factor [5].

A value corresponding to the points at positions obtained by equally dividing a unit circle of the complex plane into S, $\omega^s (s = 0, 1, \cdots, S-1)$ is given by

$$\omega^s = \left(\exp\left(i\frac{2\pi}{S}\right)\right)^s \tag{1}$$

where i is an imaginary unit.

Figure 1 shows an example of expression of multi-valued patterns in the case where $S = 10$.

2.2 Structure

The proposed model has the similar structure as the Hopfield network [6] and the conventional model [5] as shown in Fig. 2. This model is composed of N chaotic complex-valued neuron models with a scaling factor of refractoriness that varies with time value of S and internal states of neurons, and all neurons are coupled to each other.

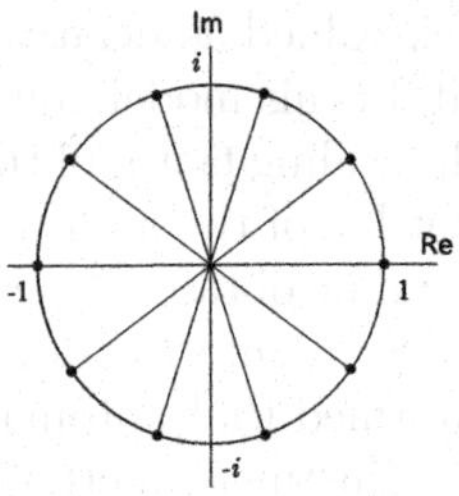

Fig. 1. Expression of multi-valued patterns ($S = 10$)

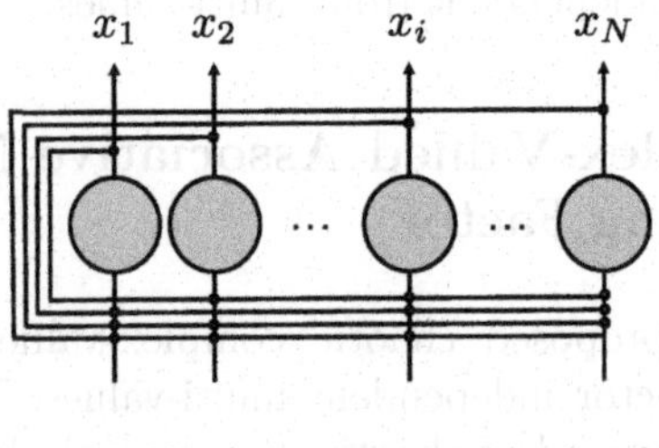

Fig. 2. Structure of proposed model.

2.3 Learning Process

In the learning process of the proposed model, the connection weights are determined based on the correlation learning similarly to the conventional model [5]. When P patterns are memorized into the network consisting of N neurons, the weight matrix $\boldsymbol{w}$ is given by

$$\boldsymbol{w} = \frac{10}{6.6326N + 2.0995} \sum_{p=1}^{P} \boldsymbol{X}^{(p)} \boldsymbol{X}^{(p)*} - P\boldsymbol{I}_N \tag{2}$$

where $\boldsymbol{X}^{(p)}$ is the p-th stored complex-valued pattern vector, $\boldsymbol{I}_N$ is a unit matrix ($N \times N$), and $*$ represents conjugate transposition. $10/6.6326N + 2.0995$ is the normalization parameter, so that the absolute value of the internal state of the neuron is approximately 10 in the proposed system.

2.4 Recall Process

The recall process of the proposed model has following four steps.

Step 1: Pattern Input

A pattern is given to the network.

Step 2: Calculation of Internal States

The internal states of the neuron i at the time $t+1$, $u_i(t+1)$ is calculated by

$$u_i(t+1) = \sum_{j=1}^{N} w_{ij} \sum_{d=0}^{t} k_m^d x_j(t-d) - \alpha(t, I(t)_{max}, S) \sum_{d=0}^{t} k_r^d x_i(t-d) \tag{3}$$

$$(u_i(t), x_i(t), w_{ij} \in \mathbb{C}, \quad k_m, k_r, \alpha(t, I(t)_{max}) \in \mathbb{R})$$

where N is the number of neurons, k_m is the damping factor of the mutual coupling term, k_r is the damping factor of the refractoriness term, w_{ij} is the connection weight between the neuron i and the neuron j, and $x_j(t)$ is the output of the neuron j at the time t. $\alpha(t, I(t)_{max}, S)$ is the scaling factor of refractoriness at the time t when the maximum absolute value of the internal state up to the time t is $I(t)_{max}$ and S-valued patterns are memorized. It is given by

$$\alpha(t, I(t)_{max}, S) = a(I(t)_{max}, S) + b(a(I(t)_{max}, S)) \cdot \sin\left(c \cdot \frac{\pi}{12} \cdot t\right) \tag{4}$$

where $I(t)_{max}$ is the maximum absolute value of the internal state up to the time t, and it is given by

$$I(t)_{max} = \max\{I(t), I(t-1)_{max}\} \quad (5)$$

where, $I(t)$ is the average of the absolute values of internal states excluding the refractoriness term at time t, and it is given by

$$I(t) = \frac{1}{N}\left|\sum_{j=1}^{N} w_{ij} \sum_{d=0}^{t} k_m^d x_j(t-d)\right|. \quad (6)$$

$a(I(t)_{max}, S)$, $b(a(I(t)_{max}, S))$, c are parameters that determine how to change the scaling factor of refractoriness. $a(I(t)_{max}, S)$ is the average value when the maximum absolute value of the internal state up to the time t is $I(t)_{max}$, $b(a(I(t)_{max}), S)$ is the amplitude when the maximum absolute value of the internal state up to the time t is $I(t)_{max}$, and c affects the cycle. Since the value of c at which a high recall rate is obtained in the preliminary experiment was not dependent on S, it was set to 2.0, which is the value at which a high recall rate was obtained.

$a(I(t)_{max}, S)$ is given by

$$a(I(t)_{max}, S) = \begin{cases} 8.6107 I(t)_{max} - 39.436 \\ \qquad (I(t)_{max} \leq 0.0076S + 0.9085) \\ -0.2786S + 48.971 \\ \qquad (S \leq 10 \text{ and } 0.0076S + 0.9085 < I(t)_{max}) \\ -0.5S + 23.6667 \\ \qquad (11 \leq S \text{ and } 0.0076S + 0.9085 < I(t)_{max}) \end{cases} \quad (7)$$

$b(a(I(t)_{max}), S)$ is given by

$$b(a(I(t)_{max}), S) = a(I(t)_{max}, S). \quad (8)$$

These equations are determined based on the relationship between the internal state and the parameters a and b in the parameter in which the high dynamic association ability is obtained in the chaotic complex-valued associative memory with variable scaling factor composed of 300 to 600 neurons which memorize multi-valued patterns ($S = 4, 6, 8, 10, 12, 14, 16$).

Step 3: Calculation of Output

The output of the neuron i at the time $t+1$, $x_i(t+1)$ is given by

$$x_i(t+1) = f(u_i(t+1)) \quad (9)$$

where $f(\cdot)$ is output function. Here, we use the following function:

$$f(u) = \frac{\eta u}{\eta - 1.0 + |u|} \tag{10}$$

where, η is a positive constant. The value of η was determined to be 1.00001 by examining the value at which the value of the internal state of the chaotic complex-valued neuron model is likely to change due to chaos in the preliminary experiment.

Step 4: Repeat
Steps 2 and **3** are repeated.

3 Computer Experiment Results

Here, we show the computer experiment results to demonstrate the effectiveness of the proposed model under the condition shown in Table 1. The following experiments are the average of 10 trials.

3.1 Comparison of Dynamic Association Ability Between Proposed Model and Conventional Model Tuned Manually

Here, we compare the recall rate of the proposed model with the well-tuned conventional chaotic complex-valued associative memory with variable scaling factor. The coefficients a, b and the damping factors k_m and k_r of the conventional model use values obtained when the highest recall rate is obtained. Figure 3 shows the recall rate when 1 to 20 10-valued patterns are memorized in each model. As shown in Fig. 3, we can see that the proposed model has almost same dynamic association ability as the well-tuned conventional chaotic complex-valued associative memory with variable scaling factor. An experiment was conducted also in the case where the patterns of $S = 4, 6, 8, 12, 14, 16$ were stored, and it was confirmed that similar results were obtained.

3.2 Dynamic Association Ability of Proposed Model Composed of More Neurons

Here, we conducted an experiment to investigate the dynamic recall ability in the proposed model with more neurons than the network used in the preliminary experiment. Figure 4 shows the recall rate when 1 to 20 patterns ($S = 10$) are memorized in each model. From this figure, it can be seen that the proposed model also has recall capability similar to that of the conventional model, even for the number of neurons not used for automatic adjustment of parameters. An experiment was conducted also in the case where the patterns of $S = 4, 6, 8, 12, 14, 16$ were stored, and it was confirmed that similar results were obtained.

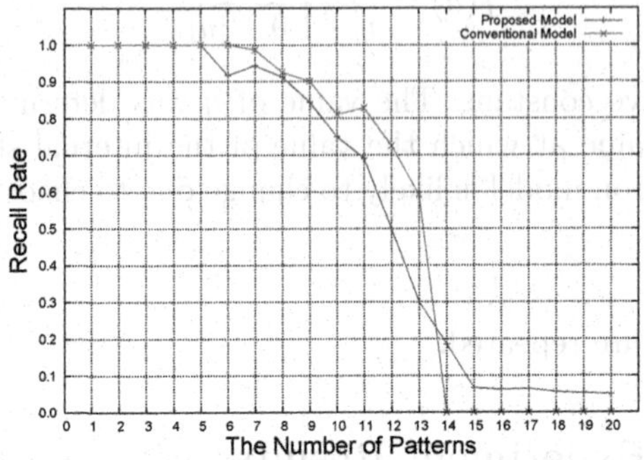

(a) $N400$

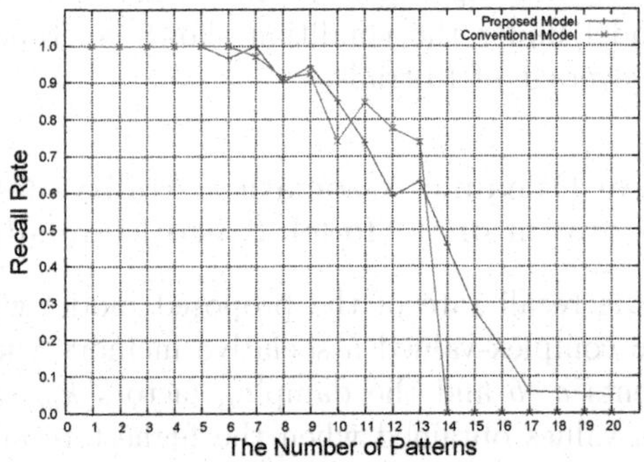

(b) $N500$

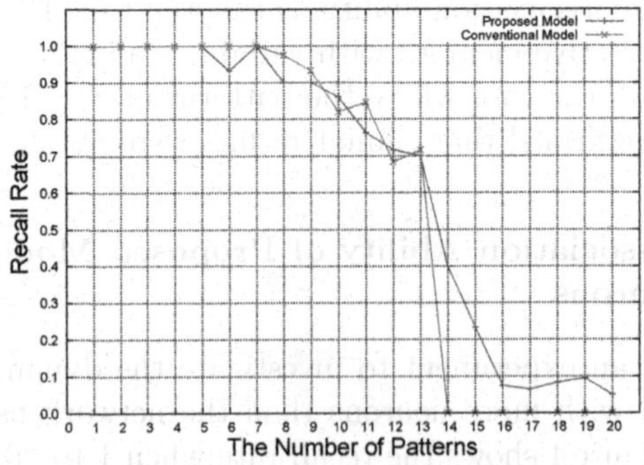

(c) $N600$

Fig. 3. Comparison of dynamic association ability between proposed model and conventional model tuned manually.

Table 1. Experimental conditions

The number of neurons	N	100–2000
The number of patterns	P	1–20
S-valued pattern	S	4–16
Damping factor	k_m	0.87
Damping factor	k_r	0.81
Parameter in output function	η	1.00001
Coefficient in scaling factor of refractoriness	c	2.0

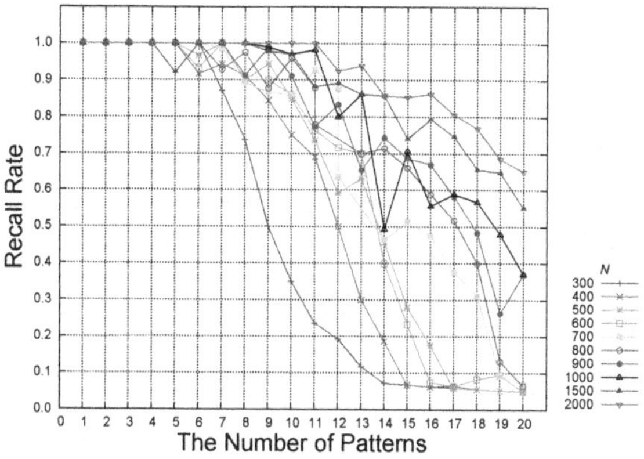

Fig. 4. Dynamic association ability of proposed model composed of more neurons.

3.3 Dynamic Association Ability for S-valued Patterns Which Are Not Used for Automatic Adjustment Method Decision

Here, an experiment was conducted to investigate the dynamic association ability of the proposed model for S-valued patterns which are not used for the determination of the automatic adjustment method of parameters. Figure 5 shows the recall rate when 1 to 20 patterns are memorized in the proposed model which has 300–2000 neurons. From this figure, even when S-value patterns which are not used in determining the automatic adjustment method of parameters are stored, the proposed model is able to obtain a relatively high recall rate.

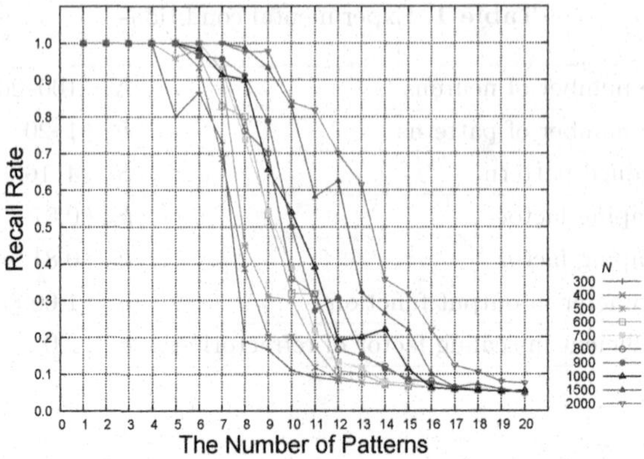

(a) $S7$

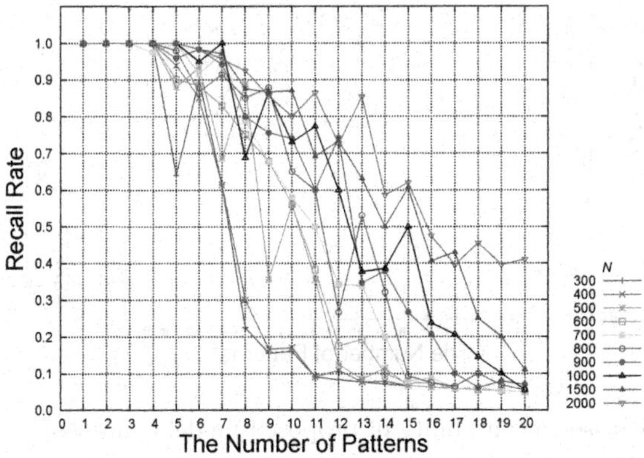

(b) $S9$

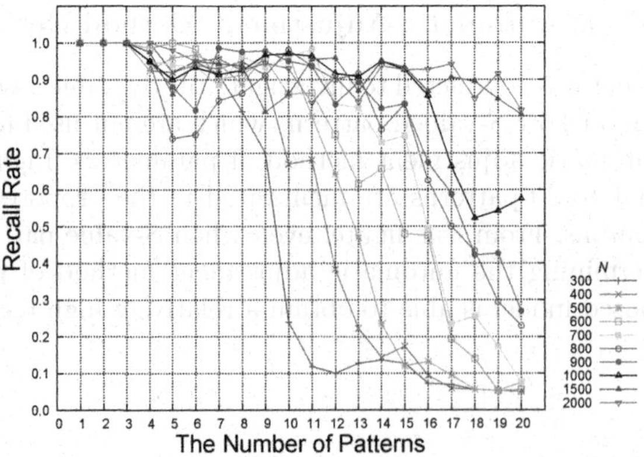

(c) $S11$

Fig. 5. Dynamic association ability for S-valued patterns which are not used for automatic adjustment method decision.

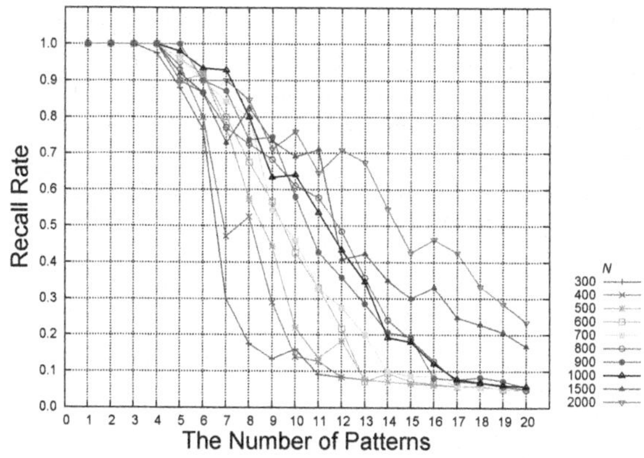

(d) $S13$

Fig. 5. (*continued*)

4 Conclusions

In this paper, we have proposed the chaotic complex-valued associative memory with adaptive scaling factor independent from multi-values. In the proposed model, the scaling factor of refractoriness is adjusted according to the maximum absolute value of the internal state up to that time. Computer experiments are carried out and we confirmed that the proposed model has the almost same dynamic association ability as the well-tuned conventional model. Moreover, we confirmed that the proposed model also has recall capability similar to that of the well-tuned conventional model, even for the number of neurons not used for automatic adjustment of parameters.

References

1. Jankowski, S., Lozowski, A., Zurada, J.M.: Complex-valued multistate neural associative memory. IEEE Trans. Neural Netw. **7**(6), 1491–1496 (1996)
2. Aihara, K., Takabe, T., Toyoda, M.: Chaotic neural networks. Phys. Lett. A **144**(6–7), 333–340 (1990)
3. Osana, Y., Hagiwara, M.: Separation of superimposed pattern and many-to-many associations by chaotic neural networks. In: Proceedings of IEEE and INNS International Joint Conference on Neural Networks, Anchorage, vol. 1, pp. 514–519 (1998)
4. Nakada, M., Osana,Y.: Chaotic complex-valued associative memory. In: Proceedings of International Symposium on Nonlinear Theory and its Applications, Vancouver (2007)

5. Karakama, D., Katamura, N., Nakano, C., Osana, Y.: Chaotic complex-valued associative memory with adaptive scaling factor. In: Kůrková, V., Manolopoulos, Y., Hammer, B., Iliadis, L., Maglogiannis, I. (eds.) ICANN 2018. LNCS, vol. 11140, pp. 523–531. Springer, Cham (2018). https://doi.org/10.1007/978-3-030-01421-6_50
6. Hopfield, J.J.: Neural networks and physical systems with emergent collective computational abilities. In: Proceedings of the National Academy of Sciences of the USA, vol. 79, pp. 2554–2558 (1982)

Brain Activity Analysis and Inspired Computing

A Comparative Analysis of Preprocessing Methods for Single-Trial Event Related Potential Detection

Wajid Mumtaz[1,2(✉)], Lukáš Vařeka[1], and Roman Mouček[1]

[1] Faculty of Applied Sciences,
NTIS - New Technologies for the Information Society,
University of West Bohemia,
Univerzitní 8, 306 14 Pilsen, Czech Republic
wajidmumtaz@gmail.com, {lvareka,moucek}@kiv.zcu.cz
[2] Department of Electrical Engineering,
School of Electrical Engineering and Computer Science,
National University of Sciences and Technology, H-12, Islamabad, Pakistan

Abstract. The choice of a suitable preprocessing method for single-trial event-related potential (ERP) data has fundamental importance because it may improve the efficiency of a brain-computer interface (BCI) system. However, the selection of an appropriate method can be challenging and may depend on the type of data as well. In order to elaborate on this point, this manuscript investigates the impact of preprocessing on single-trial ERP detection.

Method: This manuscript has investigated three scenarios for preprocessing ERP data: (1) ERP analysis without any preprocessing; (2) ERP analysis involving the amplitude-based artifact rejection method; (3) ERP analysis based on a combination of the amplitude-based artifact rejection and wavelet-enhanced independent component analysis (wICA) methods. In particular, the comparison of these preprocessing methods was based on a common machine learning (ML) framework. Therefore, the three different preprocessing methods could be compared. Also, three different classifiers (i.e., logistic regression (LR), k-nearest neighbors (kNN) and support vector machine (SVM)) were compared as well. In addition, the performance metrics utilized for this purpose were the single-trials classification recognition, precision and recall. The proposed ML framework involved the general sub-blocks of feature extraction, feature selection, classification and validation (10-fold cross-validation). The proposed ML framework was aimed to classify the single trials event-related potentials (ERPs) such as P300 (target) vs non-P300 (non-target).

Results: The maximum classification accuracy was achieved for scenario 3 as described above, i.e., the combination of amplitude-based artifact rejection and wICA methods. More specifically, the classification results were as follows: recognition = 0.77, recall = 0.77, and precision = 0.99.

Conclusion: The choice of an EEG preprocessing method has a significant impact on the subsequent analysis.

Keywords: Machine learning for biomedical systems · Time series analysis · Event-related potentials · Single-trial ERP detection · P300-based brain-computer interfaces

I. V. Tetko et al. (Eds.): ICANN 2019, LNCS 11727, pp. 89–101, 2019.
https://doi.org/10.1007/978-3-030-30487-4_7

1 Introduction

The development of brain-computer interface (BCI) systems has been significant because of their potential applications in the commercial industry such as developing controls for smart games and neuroergonomics applications [1]. There is a need for an efficient and online BCI system that may increase the chance of developing such robust systems. The successful identification of a single-trial P300 component could become the core of developing a BCI system. Also, the selection of an appropriate preprocessing method could improve the classification of the P300 component ultimately improving the performance of a BCI system [2, 3].

It is evident from the literature that the identification of P300 components based on single-trial ERPs has significant importance for BCIs. However, the detection of the P300 component involving the single-trial ERP analysis often confounded with the low signal-to-noise ratios. Hence, the P300 classification involving single-trial analysis is challenging because of the low classification accuracies [4]. Among many other techniques, the issue of low signal-to-noise ratio (SNR) may be addressed at the preprocessing level because reducing noise may improve the SNR. There could be many different methods for preprocessing; a scientific way is to perform a comparison involving various methods to investigate their impact on the classification of the P300 component.

In the literature, various linear and non-linear artifact reduction methods have been proposed [5, 6]. In general, the methods could be categorized as manual, semi-automatic and fully automatic methods. The manual methods are mainly based on visual inspection of long traces of EEG recordings and followed by the deletion or rejection of the segments confounded with artifacts. However, manual methods are inefficient because the rejection of noisy data segments can lead to a loss of useful neuronal information as well. On the other hand, semi-automatic methods are based on machine-based correction assisted by manual input, for example, an independent component analysis (ICA) [7] analysis and canonical correlation analysis (CCA) [8] where the independent component (IC) are computed by machine and the artifact-related components are selected manually. Consequently, the clean EEG data were reconstructed without using the artifact related component. The ICA method assumes that the IC only represents independent sources inside the brain. However, it is a weak assumption and an identification of a noisy component could be an iterative process. Moreover, an example of a fully automated method could be a method involving ICA with an objective selection criterion that can objectively select an artifact-related component such as the wavelet-enhanced ICA (wICA) [9]. In fully automatic methods, the artifact reduction or correction is performed without any human intervention. An automatic method may compute a threshold for each IC and compares it with a preset value to classify it either as artifact or clean data.

The objective of this paper is to investigate the impacts of performing different preprocessing methods on the classification of P300 components. The paper presents a machine learning (ML) framework for evaluation of single-trial P300 detection while investigating three scenarios such as no preprocessing, amplitude-based artifact rejection, and a combination of amplitude-based artifact rejection and wICA [9].

The results section provides the tables for the calculated efficiency of classification. In addition, the amplitude-based artifact rejection method is the most common method whereas the wICA has been claimed as an efficient online method for EEG analysis [9]. However, this manuscript has tested the wICA method on ERP data.

2 Methodology

Figure 1 presents a comprehensive block level representation of the proposed ERP experimental setup and analysis. A detailed description of the experimental setup is provided in Sects. 2.1 and 2.2. The recorded ERP data were further processed by the proposed ML methodology including the ERP segmentation, and online noise removal, features extraction and classification. In particular, the paper aims to develop an efficient and online method for binary classification including single trial P300 and non-P300 sweeps. The efficiency of the system is quantified by the classification recognition, precision and recall.

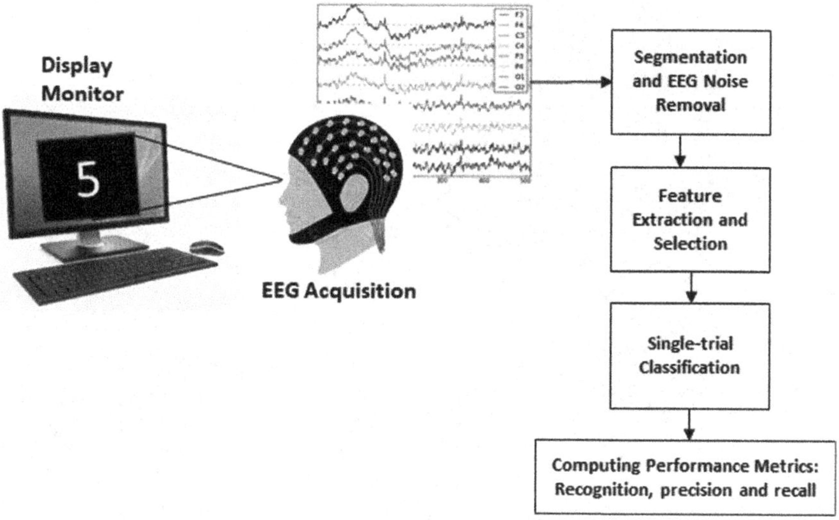

Fig. 1. The proposed automated method for ERP single-trial classification. The display randomly shows numbers between one and nine and the related EEG/ERP signal is acquired using a 10/20 EEG cap. After preprocessing and feature extraction, single-trial binary (target vs non-target) classification and its evaluation follows.

2.1 ERP Experimental Setup

In this study, the event-related potential (ERP) data were acquired from study participants including 250 children between ages 4 to 7 years, referred to as the study participants. The study participants were performing the guess the number experiment (a detailed description is provided in Sects. 2.2 and 2.3) [10]. The study participants and their parents have signed the informed consent and agreed for voluntary participation. The experimental procedure was explained to the study participant before commencing the EEG data recording.

2.2 Guess the Number Experiment

Figure 2 shows the experimental setup for guess the number experiment [10]. The experiment was designed to record the P300 responses generated by the brain. At the start of the recording session, the study participants were asked to remember a digit that can be any digit between 1 to 9. Then the participant was exposed to a computer screen with a random display of a sequence of the digits between 1 to 9. During this activity, the ERP responses were recorded and averaged so that the P300 could be observed. It was hypothesized that the elicitation of P300 corresponded to the digit thought by the participant at the start of the EPR recording session.

Fig. 2. The guess the number experiment [10]. The measured participant in the background is exposed to random visual stimuli sequence from one to nine while the experimenters can control both stimulation (on the right) and observe event-related potentials as they keep averaging in real time. Once they reach conclusion about the target stimulus, the experiment is stopped.

2.3 Data Acquisition

The EEG data acquisition was performed with a mobile EEG laboratory, a more comprehensive detail is provided in the reference [10]. In brief, the following hardware devices were used: the BrainVision standard V-Amp amplifier, standard small or medium 10/20 EEG cap, standard reference, ground and EOG electrodes, and monitor for presenting the numbers and two notebooks necessary to run stimulation and recording software applications. Only three electrodes named as the Fz, Cz and Pz, were used. The stimulation protocol was developed and run using the Presentation software tool produced by Neurobehavioral Systems, Inc. In addition, the Brain Vision Recorder was used for recording and storing raw EEG data, metadata describing the raw data, and stimuli data.

2.4 Segmentation of ERP Data

In this study, the preprocessing of the EEG data was followed by the segmentation of the EEG data according to the timing information of each stimulus. The segmentation has resulted in two types of ERP epochs: (1) the single trials representing the P300 responses (targets) and (2) the single trials that represented the non-P300 epochs (non-targets). The prestimulus interval was 200 ms and the post-stimulus interval was 1000 ms. The prestimulus interval was used to perform the baseline-correction for further ERP analysis. For illustration and validation purposes, Fig. 3 shows the grand averages of the ERP data acquired against the target and non-target stimuli. There is a clear P300 component following the target stimuli.

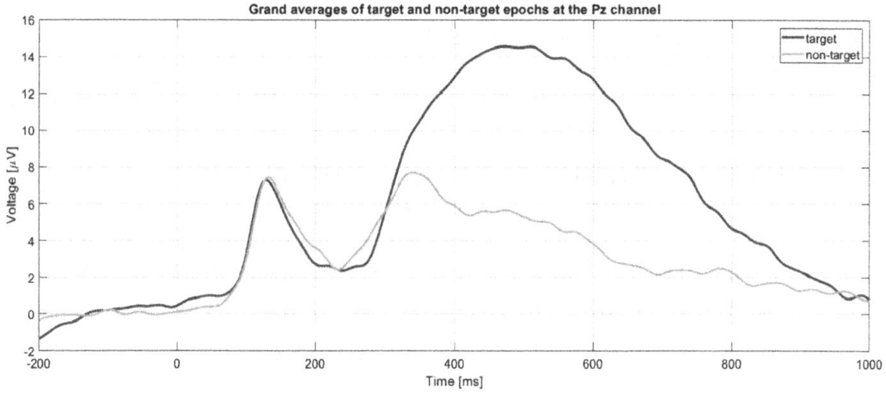

Fig. 3. The grand average involving the study participants; the two ERPs correspond to the target and non-targets

2.5 Preprocessing Scenarios

Figure 4 shows the preprocessing scenarios named as 'no preprocessing', 'amplitude-based artifact rejection', and 'combination of artifact rejection and wICA'. The results section shows the impact of the three scenarios on the classification performances. In this study, the purpose of the EEG data recording was to record quality data. Therefore, the study participants were asked to reduce the eye blinks and head movements during the recording. However, the eye movements are unavoidable and often seen during in the recorded data. Hence, preprocessing the EEG data is a requirement in order to achieve clean EEG data.

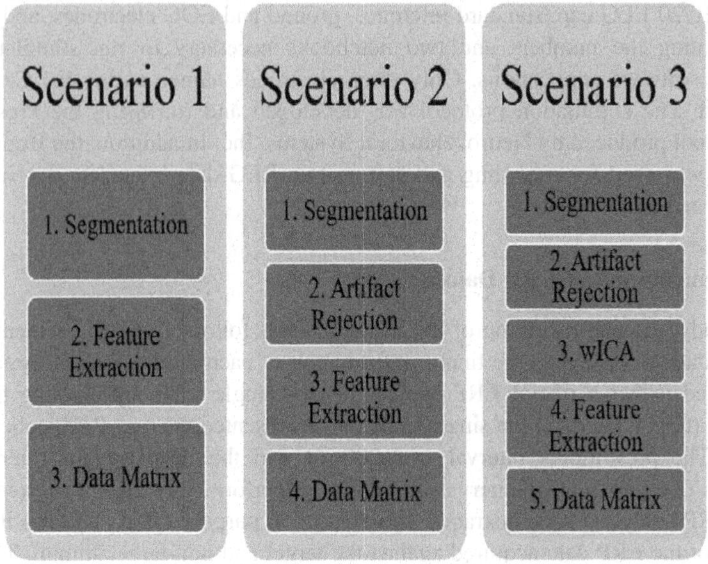

Fig. 4. Preprocessing scenarios and computation of data matrices

Scenario 1: Data with No Preprocessing (No-Prep)
These data were used without any artifact (epoch) rejection, served as the baseline data and were used for comparison purposes with the two other methods employed in this study.

Scenario 2: Amplitude-Based Artifact Rejection Method
During this scenario, the ERP epochs containing artifacts were rejected based on their amplitude. This can be performed by finding the maximum amplitude of the data and comparing it with a threshold value. In general, an ERP amplitude can go up to 20 to 30 microvolts. Any ERP epoch with an amplitude of 50 microvolt or more could be confounded with an ocular artifact [11]. Hence, in order to get rid of the artifactual epochs, these kinds of ERPs are eliminated from the analysis.

Scenario 3: Combining Amplitude-Based Artifact Rejection Method and wICA
In the original paper [9], the wICA method was applied on the resting-state EEG data and proved as effective. In addition, the paper has provided a complete description of the method. In the present study, the Daubechies wavelet function was used with decomposition level i.e., $j = 10$. (The decomposition level was set equal to the log of the length of the ICA component, in our case the ICA component length was 1200; therefore, $j = floor(log2(1200))$, and it is equal to $j = 10$). In particular, the selection of the Daubechies wavelet function was motivated by its near-optimal time-frequency location properties for EEG signals [12]. Moreover, the wavelet scale was calculated mathematically as $d = 2^j$. In this study, 'j' was equal to 10; therefore, $d = 2^{10} = 1024$.

2.6 Feature Extraction

Complexity Features

In this manuscript, the composite permutation entropy index (CPEI) [13] was used for extracting the complexity of the single sweep ERP segments. Also, the fractal dimension (FD) [14] was employed as well. Both measures were utilized to compute the complexity features for the underlying ERP segments.

Morphological Features

Morphological features provide time-based information including the shape of the individual ERP epochs. In [15], the corresponding mathematical formulas are provided. In this manuscript, the morphological features included the computation of eleven different features: latency, maximum signal value, latency and amplitude ratio, absolute amplitude, absolute amplitude and latency ratio, positive area, negative area, total area, absolute total area, and peak-to-peak difference.

Integration of Features

The classification performance was computed on the combined or integrated features. The integration of features followed the concatenation of CPEI, FD and the morphological feature into a single vector. Finally, the data matrix represented the number of epochs x features. The dimensions for different simulation scenarios are presented in the results section.

2.7 Classification, Validation, and Performance Evaluation

In this paper, three classification models were trained and tested involving the k-nearest neighbor (KNN), support vector machine (SVM) and the logistic regression (LR). A detailed description on these classification models is out-of-scope regarding this paper and can be found elsewhere: kNN [16], SVM [17], and LR [18]. Many studies in the literature have evidenced the significance of choosing linear SVM because it has been considered as a stable and standard classification method [19]. In this study, the Matlab-based 'Classification Learner App' was utilized to train and test the SVM. In particular, the type of regularization was selected as 'lasso'. In addition, the overfitting was effectively reduced by employing the 10-fold cross-validation (10-CV).

Figure 5 shows the scheme for 10-CV. According to the 10-CV, the observations in the EEG data matrix were randomly divided into test and train subgroups. The random division provides equal opportunity for the observations to be used both as test and train sequences. This method in part prevents over-fitting of the classifiers.

The classifiers performance was evaluated by computing the classification precision, recall, and recognition. The confusion matrix was constructed with values such as true positives (TP), true negatives (TN), false positives (FP), and false negatives (FN). Based on these values, the following performance metrics were computed and presented in Eqs. 1, 2, and 3 below:

$$Precision = \frac{TP}{TP + FP} \tag{1}$$

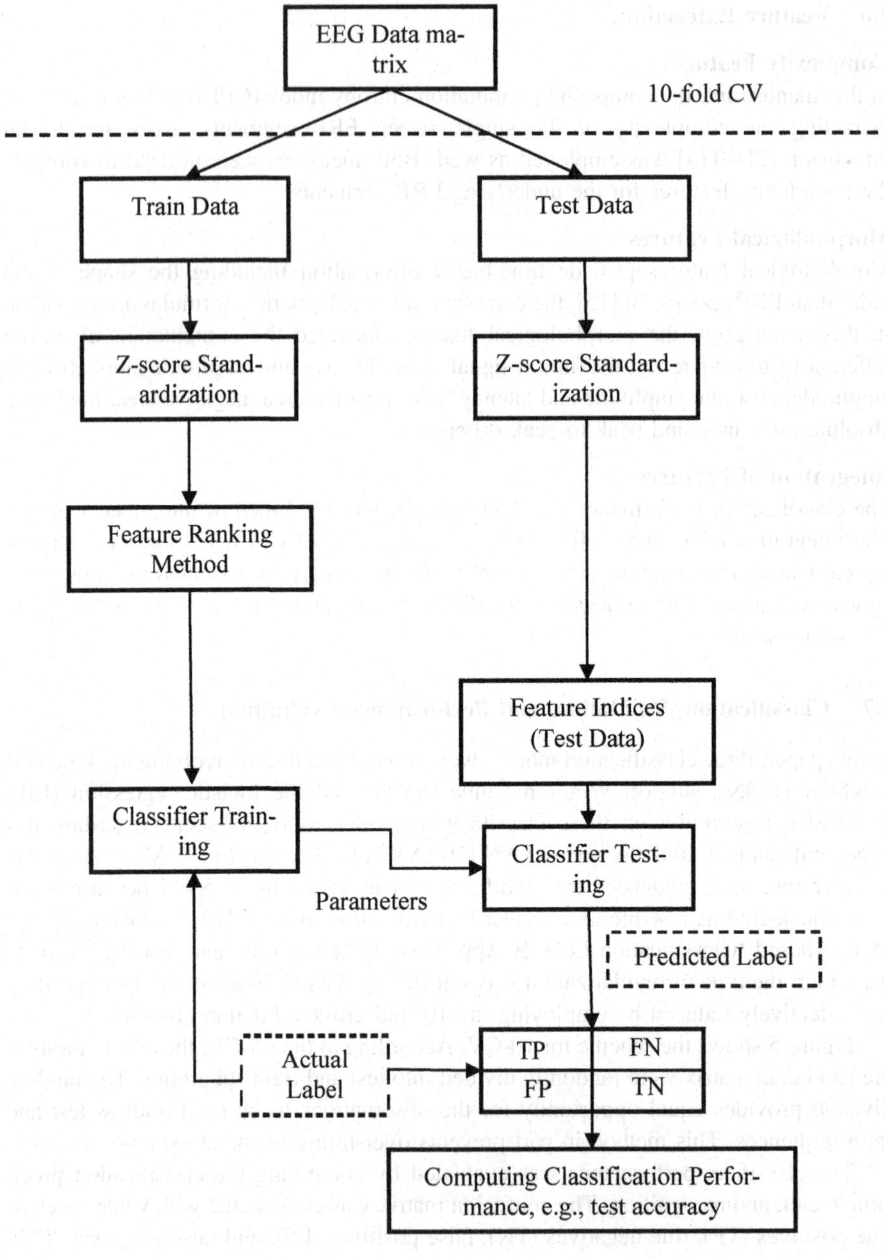

Fig. 5. The classification scheme for validating the proposed method

$$Recall = \frac{TP}{TP + FN} \tag{2}$$

$$Recognition = \frac{TP + TN}{TP + TN + FP + FN} \tag{3}$$

3 Results

Table 1 provides the model types and parameter values of the classifiers so that the study can be replicated for common datasets. In brief, the parameters were selected because of the classifier structure and underlying classification problem. In this study, only two classes were available; therefore, it was a binary classification problem. In the case of logistic regression, the preset value should be logit (because the LR classifier utilized a logistic function), and a binomial distribution suited the binary classification. Moreover, the k-NN was initialized with the nearest neighbor value as 1 to keep it simple, the distance measure has utilized a commonly known distance metric, i.e., Euclidean with equal weights. The classification method was one-vs-one that suits the binary classification with data standardization. In the case of SVM, a simple structure was investigated that led to the selection of a linear kernel with automatic scale. Like the kNN classifier, the SVM parameters 'multiclass method' was set to one-vs-one that suits the binary classification and 'standardize data' was set to true to remove any biases or outlier effects in the data. In this study, there was no optimization method utilized for optimizing the hyperparameters.

Table 1. Classification model types and parameters

Classification models	Model type
Logistic Regression (LR)	Preset: Logistic regression (logit) offset: 1 Distribution: binomial
k-Nearest Neighbour (kNN)	Preset: Linear fine KNN Number of neighbours: 1 Distance metric: Euclidean Distance weight: Equal Multiclass method: one-vs-one Standardize data: True
Support Vector Machine (SVM)	Preset: Linear SVM Kernel function: Linear Kernel Scale: Automatic Box constraint level: 1 Multiclass method: one-vs-one Standardize data: True

Table 2 provides an overall picture of classification performance during the three preprocessing scenarios. The classification recognition provides information on the classification accuracies. The maximum classification accuracy was observed during scenario 3. The SVM and KNN provide the maximum accuracy 76.3%. There was a little difference (slight improvement) between scenarios 1 and 2. It shows that the amplitude-based artifact rejection method has removed artifacts and slightly improved the SNR. It helped during the classification of the P300 vs non-P300.

Table 2. Classification efficiency for the three scenarios

Scenarios	Classification	Recognition	Recall	Precision
1st	LR	0.55	0.55	0.49
	KNN	0.50	0.50	0.44
	SVM	0.54	0.55	0.37
2nd	LR	0.56	0.56	0.43
	KNN	0.51	0.51	0.45
	SVM	0.55	0.55	0.34
3rd	LR	**0.77**	**0.77**	**0.99**
	KNN	**0.76**	**0.76**	**1**
	SVM	**0.76**	**0.76**	**1**

This is because the performance of classifiers can be explained with the given data. In the case of the first scenario, the noise in the data was not removed; it renders the decrease in the signal-to-noise ratio (SNR), overall. Therefore, the classifier was not able to separate the single trials of the P300 epochs from the non-P300 epochs. On the other hand, the performance of the classifier got better with a rejection of artifact epochs. This behavior was expected and proved that the SNR of the data got better because of the removal of the artifact epochs. Lastly, these noise-free epochs were subjected to the further removal of noise with the wICA method. In this scenario, the classifiers have performed much better than in scenarios 1 and 2. These results have signified the importance of preprocessing ERP data before making any further analysis.

In this study, it was observed that there was a limit to set the threshold for artifact rejection, i.e., 20 mV. A decrease less than this threshold value had resulted into decreased classification performance. One possible reason could be a rejection of many artifactual epochs that may provide useful information. Hence, information decreased due to rejection could not train the classifiers well.

Lastly, the wICA method was based on computing the ICA components; therefore, it inherently involved the limitations associated with the ICA. In this study, the application of wICA on the raw ERP segments decreased the classification accuracy because ICA could not perform in the presence of so many components. Therefore, the application of wICA should follow the rejection of artifactual components.

4 Discussion

The data used for this study were obtained on 250 school-age children, and are publicly available [10]. They were collected during a simple BCI experiment, involving P300-based guessing a number 1–9 following visual stimulation with corresponding numbers. Such a big number of participants is unique among publicly available P300 datasets and gives us opportunities to compare signal processing and machine learning methods with sufficient statistical significance. In [20] and [21], deep learning techniques were compared with state-of-the-art classifiers as parts of an off-line BCI system. This manuscript is focused on single-trial classification.

As shown in Table 2, the wICA method provided better classification results than the amplitude-based artifact rejection method on the raw ERP data. There could be few possible reasons for these results. For example, many studies have evidenced that the ICA method has been considered as a successful method for separating the sources of artifacts in the EEG data. The wICA method employed in this study is the enhancement of the ICA method that further helps improve the detection of artifactual components. Because it can successfully reduce the "leak" of cerebral activity of interest into ICA components [9]. In addition, the wICA method, based on its thresholding criterion, emphasized on correction of EEG data without any deletion. This strategy helps in preserving useful neuronal information as compared with the methods that employ deleting the whole ERP segment based on amplitude maximum values.

Besides methods mentioned in the manuscript, there are other ways how to improve classification accuracy. However, they have their limitations, too. For example, the conventional and straightforward method for P300 extraction is the averaging method. The averaging method reduces the random noise and hence significantly improves the signal to noise ratio of the P300 component. The improvement in the signal to noise ratio is directly proportional to the number of epochs to be averaged. There is a minimum limit (i.e., at least 20 trials) to the number of epochs to be averaged [22]. However, the number of ERP epochs may reduce the speed of a BCI system. On the contrary, the development of methods for extracting the parameters of the P300 component such as its amplitude and latency from single-trials ERP epochs faced the challenge of low accuracy of character detection. However, this method has significantly improved the speed of the BCI system.

By directly addressing the identification of single-trial P300 components, the speed and accuracy of a BCI speller can be improved. An online EEG ML-based framework normally included the online preprocessing, features extraction, feature selection, classification and validation. This allows the researchers to improve the P300-based system at multiple levels such as at the preprocessing stage by incorporating the best preprocessing method. Moreover, the EEG data recorded with one reference can be converted to a different EEG reference such as the REST in order to achieve a better signal to noise ratio [23]. In addition, the improvement can be observed at feature extraction, and classification stages as well.

However, there are also some limitations of this study. First, by rejecting epochs contaminated by artifacts, we decrease the number of epochs available for classification. In on-line BCIs, this would translate into lower transfer bit-rates. Therefore, more research on how to set the amplitude threshold optimally needs to be performed. Second, although ICA and related methods can be applied even to three-channel EEG data [24], separation of artifact-related independent component gets much easier with more channels. Therefore, more analysis into why wICA can increase class separability with low number of EEG channels would shed light on the achieved results. Finally, although large number of datasets and 10-fold cross-validation limit overfitting, it is still not clear if the results can be reproduced for adults or people with disabilities.

5 Conclusion

The paper has investigated the single-trial ERP extraction while comparing the effects of pre-processing on the identification of the P300 component. Moreover, the paper has presented an efficient classification scheme for this purpose. The comparison results have presented that the wICA method shows the best results for ERP single trial extraction as compared with the amplitude-based artifact rejection method. Hence, based on the results it can be concluded that the wICA method can be utilized for the development of BCI systems.

Acknowledgement. This publication was supported by the project LO1506 of the Czech Ministry of Education, Youth and Sports under the program NPU I. The authors would like to dedicate this work to their teachers and parents.

References

1. Lotte, F., Roy, R.N.: Brain–computer interface contributions to neuroergonomics. In: Neuroergonomics, p. 43–48. Elsevier (2019). https://doi.org/10.1016/b978-0-12-811926-6.00007-5
2. Tal, O., Friedman, D.: Recurrent neural networks for P300-based BCI. arXiv preprint arXiv:1901.10798 (2019)
3. Blankertz, B., et al.: Single-trial analysis and classification of ERP components—a tutorial. NeuroImage **56**(2), 814–825 (2011). https://doi.org/10.1016/j.neuroimage.2010.06.048
4. Joshi, R., Goel, P., Sur, M., Murthy, H.A.: Single trial P300 classification using convolutional LSTM and deep learning ensembles method. In: Tiwary, U.S. (ed.) IHCI 2018. LNCS, vol. 11278, pp. 3–15. Springer, Cham (2018). https://doi.org/10.1007/978-3-030-04021-5_1
5. Croft, R.J., Barry, R.J.: Removal of ocular artifact from the EEG: a review. Neurophys. Clin./Clin. Neurophys. **30**(1), 5–19 (2000). https://doi.org/10.1016/s0987-7053(00)00055-1
6. Fatourechi, M., et al.: EMG and EOG artifacts in brain computer interface systems: a survey. Clin. Neurophys. **118**(3), 480–494 (2007). https://doi.org/10.1016/j.clinph.2006.10.019
7. Makeig, S., et al.: Independent component analysis of electroencephalographic data. In: Advances in Neural Information Processing Systems (1996)
8. Gao, J., Zheng, C., Wang, P.: Online removal of muscle artifact from electroencephalogram signals based on canonical correlation analysis. Clin. EEG Neurosci. **41**(1), 53–59 (2010). https://doi.org/10.1177/155005941004100111

9. Castellanos, N.P., Makarov, V.A.: Recovering EEG brain signals: artifact suppression with wavelet enhanced independent component analysis. J. Neurosci. Methods **158**(2), 300–312 (2006). https://doi.org/10.1016/j.jneumeth.2006.05.033
10. Mouček, R., et al.: Event-related potential data from a guess the number brain-computer interface experiment on school children. Sci. Data **4**, 160121 (2017). https://doi.org/10.1038/sdata.2016.121
11. Luck, S.J.: An Introduction to the Event-Related Potential Technique. MIT Press, Cambridge (2014)
12. Subasi, A.: EEG signal classification using wavelet feature extraction and a mixture of expert model. Expert Syst. Appl. **32**(4), 1084–1093 (2007). https://doi.org/10.1016/j.eswa.2006.02.005
13. Bandt, C., Pompe, B.: Permutation entropy: a natural complexity measure for time series. Phys. Rev. Lett. **88**(17), 174102 (2002). https://doi.org/10.1103/physrevlett.88.174102
14. Accardo, A., et al.: Use of the fractal dimension for the analysis of electroencephalographic time series. Biol. Cybern. **77**(5), 339–350 (1997). https://doi.org/10.1007/s004220050394
15. Abootalebi, V., Moradi, M.H., Khalilzadeh, M.A.: A new approach for EEG feature extraction in P300-based lie detection. Comput. Methods Program. Biomed. **94**(1), 48–57 (2009). https://doi.org/10.1016/j.cmpb.2008.10.001
16. Denoeux, T.: A k-nearest neighbor classification rule based on Dempster-Shafer theory. IEEE Trans. Syst. Man Cybern. **25**(5), 804–813 (1995). https://doi.org/10.1109/21.376493
17. Vapnik, V.: The Nature of Statistical Learning Theory. Springer, Heidelberg (2013)
18. Hosmer Jr., D.W., Lemeshow, S., Sturdivant, R.X.: Applied Logistic Regression, vol. 398. Wiley, Hoboken (2013)
19. Burges, C.J.: A tutorial on support vector machines for pattern recognition. Data Min. Knowl. Discov. **2**(2), 121–167 (1998). https://doi.org/10.1023/a:1009715923555
20. Vařeka, L., Prokop, T., Mouček, R., Mautner, P., Štěbeták, J.: Application of stacked autoencoders to P300 experimental data. In: Rutkowski, L., Korytkowski, M., Scherer, R., Tadeusiewicz, R., Zadeh, L.A., Zurada, J.M. (eds.) ICAISC 2017. LNCS (LNAI), vol. 10245, pp. 187–198. Springer, Cham (2017). https://doi.org/10.1007/978-3-319-59063-9_17
21. Vaněk, J., Mouček, R.: Deep learning techniques for classification of P300 component. In: 11th International Joint Conference on Biomedical Engineering Systems and Technologies (BIOSTEC 2018), pp. 446–453 (2018). https://doi.org/10.5220/0006594104460453
22. Cohen, J., Polich, J.: On the number of trials needed for P300. Int. J. Psychophys. **25**(3), 249–255 (1997). https://doi.org/10.1016/s0167-8760(96)00743-x
23. Mumtaz, W., Malik, A.S.: A comparative study of different EEG reference choices for diagnosing unipolar depression. Brain Topogr. **31**(5), 875–885 (2018). https://doi.org/10.1007/s10548-018-0651-x
24. Rejer, I., Górski, P.: Benefits of ICA in the case of a few channel EEG. In: 2015 37th Annual International Conference of the IEEE Engineering in Medicine and Biology Society (EMBC). IEEE (2015). https://doi.org/10.1109/embc.2015.7320110

Sleep State Analysis Using Calcium Imaging Data by Non-negative Matrix Factorization

Mizuo Nagayama[1](✉), Toshimitsu Aritake[1], Hideitsu Hino[2,3], Takeshi Kanda[4], Takehiro Miyazaki[4], Masashi Yanagisawa[4], Shotaro Akaho[3,5], and Noboru Murata[1,3]

[1] Waseda University, Shinjuku, Tokyo 169-0072, Japan
mizuo.n@asagi.waseda.jp
[2] The Institute of Statistical Mathematics, Tachikawa, Tokyo 190-8562, Japan
[3] RIKEN Center for Advanced Intelligence Project, Chuo, Tokyo 103-0027, Japan
[4] University of Tsukuba, Tsukuba, Ibaraki 305-8573, Japan
[5] National Institute of Advanced Industrial Science and Technology, Tsukuba, Ibaraki 305-8568, Japan

Abstract. Sleep is an essential process for the survival of animals. However, its phenomenon is poorly understood. To understand the phenomenon of sleep, the analysis should be made from the activities of a large number of cortical neurons. Calcium imaging is a recently developed technique that can record a large number of neurons simultaneously, however, it has a disadvantage of low time resolution. In this paper, we aim to discover phenomena which characterize sleep/wake states from calcium imaging data. We made an assumption that groups of neurons become active simultaneously and the neuronal activities of groups differ between sleep and wake states. We used non-negative matrix factorization (NMF) to identify those groups and their neuronal activities in time from calcium imaging data. NMF was used because neural activity can be expressed by the sum of individual neuronal activity and fluorescence intensity data are always positive values. We found that there are certain groups of neurons that behave differently between sleep and wake states.

Keywords: Sleep state analysis · Calcium imaging · Non-negative matrix factorization

1 Introduction

Sleep is controlled by the brain [9] and is essential not only for the brain to function normally but also for the survival of animals. However, the phenomenon itself is not well understood [10]. Currently, only electroencephalography (EEG), an objective method, can detect sleep/wake states (wakefulness, non-rapid-eye-movement (NREM) sleep, and rapid-eye-movement (REM) sleep), whereas behavioral methods, which record animals' posture or movement, cannot [6].

I. V. Tetko et al. (Eds.): ICANN 2019, LNCS 11727, pp. 102–113, 2019.
https://doi.org/10.1007/978-3-030-30487-4_8

EEG recordings—signals from electrodes placed on the head—reflect extracellular electrical events across the cerebral cortex (the brain surface). Therefore, the neurophysiological behavior of cortical neuronal populations are assumed to differ across sleep/wake states. Nevertheless, it is still unclear how cortical neural ensembles behave during sleep/wake states owing to the lack of measurement and analysis technology. For example, EEG recordings reflect sleep/wake states; however, individual neural activity cannot be observed using EEG. It is possible to record neural activities at the cellular level with sufficient temporal resolution using electrophysiological techniques such as patch-clamp, intracellular, and extracellular unit recordings. However, it is difficult to record a large number of neurons or identify the recorded cell types using these techniques.

To overcome the technical limitations of electrophysiological methods, we use calcium imaging techniques to observe the cortical neural activity during sleep/wake states. Calcium imaging is a technique recently developed to record neural activities at the cellular level. The fluorescence intensity of calcium indicators such as GCaMP depends on the concentration of calcium ions. It reflects the neural activity because action potential generation (spike) increases the intracellular concentration of calcium. Another characteristic of GCaMP is that it is genetically encodable and can be delivered into the target cells using virus vectors and a Cre-LoxP system. Calcium imaging in the brain can be performed in vivo with two-photon laser scanning microscopy. Calcium imaging has the disadvantage of a low time resolution (e.g., individual spikes cannot easily be captured owing to the slow kinetics and low sampling rates.); however, it has the considerable advantages of (1) high spatial resolution, (2) large recording field, and (3) ease of combination with genetic methods, where the activity of various identified neurons can be obtained simultaneously.

In this study, we aim to understand sleep/wake-dependent neural ensembles in the cerebral cortex, which hopefully increase the understanding of sleep. Calcium imaging data were acquired from identified excitatory and inhibitory neurons in layer 2/3 of the primary motor cortex (M1)—a part of the cerebral cortex—of a sleeping/waking mouse at 8 Hz. It is well known that individual neurons in the M1 exhibit sleep/wake state-dependent activity patterns [8] and the M1 contributes to memory consolidation of acquired motor skills during sleep [5]. Their population behavior during sleep/wake states, however, is still unexplored, despite its close involvement in learning and memory.

Two approaches can be considered to analyze neural ensembles; estimation of correlation and causality of neurons. We take the first approach, estimating the correlation of observed cortical neurons. To estimate causality, we need to distinguish whether a presynaptic or postsynaptic cell is fired from the data. There are studies of inference on spikes [16] and neuronal connectivity [13] from calcium imaging data. However, it is claimed in [13] that the calcium imaging data sampled with a frequency lower than 30 Hz do not provide meaningful results. Therefore, we can estimate only correlation from the calcium imaging data sampled with low frequency.

There are few reports on the statistical analysis of calcium imaging data in the brain during sleep. One example of the sleep research using calcium imaging is an analysis of neural activity in and near the lateral dorsal tegmental nucleus (LDT) of the brainstem that is a component of the REM-regulatory circuits [4]. Neuronal activity in the LDT for 20 s before and after the state transition was analyzed by a principal component analysis (PCA). Then, k-means clustering was performed for the 2D plot of the first and second principal components. A few LDT neurons were observed to be more active in the wake state than the REM state and vice versa, and all LDT neurons were less active in the NREM state than in the REM or wake states. This research indicates that neurons can be divided into a few groups and the behavior of each group differs across sleep/wake states. This study focuses on the state transition and extracted the principal components of the fluorescence intensity during state transition. However, neuronal groups throughout sleep/wake states should be analyzed for our aim.

To better understand sleep/wake-dependent neural ensembles in the cerebral cortex, we assume that groups of cortical neurons become active simultaneously and the activated groups change over time. We used non-negative matrix factorization (NMF [11]) to estimate those groups and how they are activated in time. NMF was not performed to extract the fluorescence intensity like Cox [4] did, but for the neuronal groups. We used NMF because neural activity can be expressed by the sum of individual neuronal activity; further, fluorescence intensity data are always positive values. We found that there are certain groups of neurons that behave differently between sleep and wake states.

We proposed a protocol to analyze the calcium imaging data with a low sampling rate. We showed that the well-known NMF algorithm could effectively analyze such data by comparing its performance with those of PCA and independent component analysis (ICA).

2 Methodology

We acquire calcium imaging data of neurons in layer 2/3 from the primary motor cortex (M1) of a sleeping/waking mouse. The imaging lasted for 15 min at 8 Hz. A total of 154 neurons were observed. The fluorescence signal in each frame for each neuron was extracted by evaluating the mean intensity of the pixels within each region of interest (ROI) after subtracting the background signal. EEG and EMG signals were also recorded during the experiments, and NREM, REM, and wake states were scored.

We made an assumption regarding the generative model of the data, which is that there are K groups of observed neurons that are activated simultaneously, and the fluorescence intensity of observed neurons is generated by the combined activities of those groups. Groups can overlap and neurons can belong to multiple groups. We assume that the behavior of the groups vary over time and the activities of those groups differ between NREM, REM, and wake states. The schematic is shown in Fig. 1.

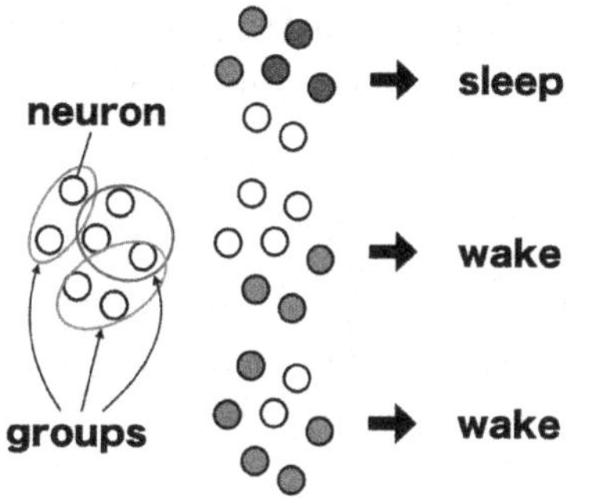

Fig. 1. Observed neurons are assumed to form K-grouped and the recorded fluorescence intensity is generated by the combined activities of those groups. In this figure, $K = 3$ groups are assumed and the activated neurons are colored.

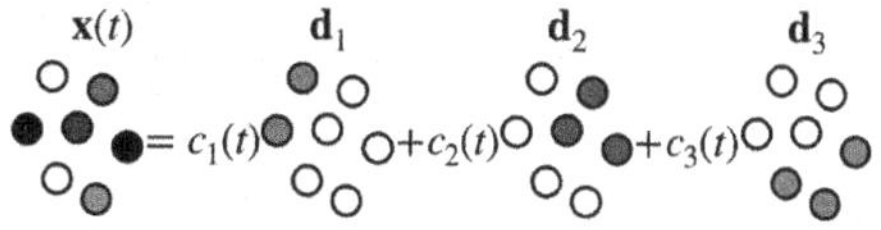

Fig. 2. Mathematical model designed based on the assumption Fig. 1. The fluorescence intensity of the observed neurons at time t, $\mathbf{x}(t)$, is represented as a weighted sum of K groups $\mathbf{d}_k$. The figure shows a schematic of the model when $K = 3$.

Based on the assumption above, we designed a mathematical model for the calcium imaging data. Let $\mathbb{R}_+$ be a set of non-negative real numbers. Let $\mathbf{x}(t) \in \mathbb{R}_+^N$, $(t = 1, 2, \cdots, T)$ be the fluorescence intensity of the observed neurons at time t and $\mathbf{d}_k \in \mathbb{R}_+^N$, $(k = 1, 2, \cdots, K)$ be K groups of neuronal activities where N is the number of observed neurons and T is the observation time. Fluorescence intensity data are all positive values; therefore, $\mathbf{x}(t)$ is a positive vector. Then, $\mathbf{x}(t)$ can be modeled by the weighted sum of the groups $\{\mathbf{d}_k; k = 1, \cdots, K\}$ as follows:

$$\mathbf{x}(t) = \sum_{k=1}^{K} c_k(t)\mathbf{d}_k + \boldsymbol{\eta}(t), \tag{1}$$

where $c_k(t)$ is a positive coefficient of $\mathbf{d}_k$ and $\boldsymbol{\eta}(t) \in \mathbb{R}^N$ is a noise vector at time t. The schematic of the model is shown in Fig. 2. We note that the groups $\mathbf{d}_k$ are constant over time and time dependency of the observed data $\mathbf{x}(t)$ is represented by the coefficient $c_k(t)$ and noise $\boldsymbol{\eta}(t)$. The noise of calcium imaging is mostly photon shot noise, which obeys a Poisson distribution. For high photon counts, shot noise can be approximated by a Gaussian distribution [15]; therefore, $\boldsymbol{\eta}(t)$ can be represented as

$$\boldsymbol{\eta}(t) \sim \mathcal{N}(0, \sigma^2), \tag{2}$$

where σ^2 is the variance.

Equation (1) can be written in a matrix form as follows:

$$\mathbf{X} = \mathbf{DC} + \mathbf{H}, \tag{3}$$

where $\mathbf{X} \in \mathbb{R}_+^{N \times T}$, $\mathbf{D} \in \mathbb{R}_+^{N \times K}$, $\mathbf{C} \in \mathbb{R}_+^{K \times T}$, and $\mathbf{H} \in \mathbb{R}^{N \times T}$. The columns of $\mathbf{X}$ are the observation $\mathbf{x}(t)$, columns of matrix $\mathbf{D}$ are the groups $\mathbf{d}_k$, (k, t)-element of matrix **C** are the coefficients $c_k(t)$, and the columns of **H** are noise vectors $\eta(t)$. The correspondence between Eqs. (1) and (3) is shown in Fig. 3.

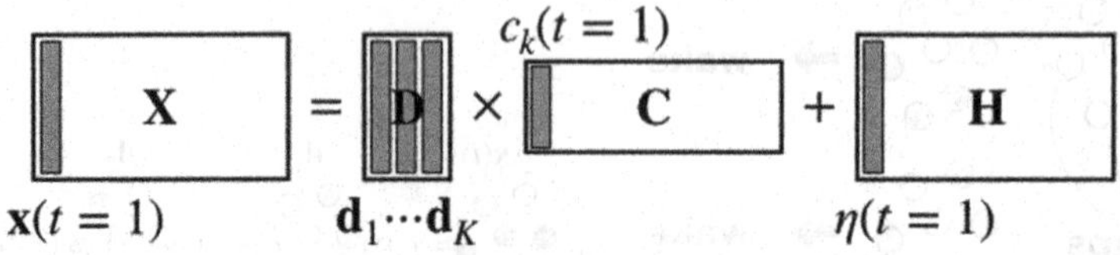

Fig. 3. Matrix form of Eq. (1).

We estimate the matrices **D** and **C** from the data matrix **X** by using NMF [11], which is an unsupervised learning method similar to PCA and ICA, as one of the approaches in the linear generalized component analysis [3]. NMF decomposes a non-negative matrix **X** into a product of non-negative matrices **D** and **C**. By decomposing the data matrix **X** by NMF, frequent signals will be obtained as the columns of **D**. The matrix **D** is called a *dictionary* in the literature of signal processing and machine learning. The columns of the dictionary **D** are interpreted as basis vectors or also called atoms. The columns of the matrix **C** are coefficients of atoms and we call **C** a coefficient matrix henceforth. Because of the non-negativity of the coefficient matrix **C**, **X** is represented by a non-negative weighted sum of atoms of **D**. The restriction of non-negativity also induces sparsity of **C**. The number of groups $K \in \mathbb{N}$ should be given a priori for decomposition.

From Eqs. (1) to (3), $\mathbf{X}_{ij}$ is i.i.d. Gaussian random variable with mean $[\mathbf{DC}]_{ij}$ and variance σ^2:

$$p(\mathbf{X}_{ij}; [\mathbf{DC}]_{ij}) = \mathcal{N}([\mathbf{DC}]_{ij}, \sigma^2). \tag{4}$$

The dictionary **D** and coefficient matrix **C** is estimated by the following maximum log-likelihood problem under the non-negative constraints on **D** and **C**:

$$\underset{\mathbf{D}\geq 0, \mathbf{C}\geq 0}{\text{maximize}} \sum_{i,j} \log p(\mathbf{X}_{ij} | [\mathbf{DC}]_{ij}). \tag{5}$$

By calculating Eq. (5), we can see that Eq. (5) is equivalent to minimizing the Frobenius norm of the difference between **X** and **DC** under the non-negative constraints on **D** and **C**:

$$\underset{\mathbf{D}\geq 0, \mathbf{C}\geq 0}{\text{minimize}} \, ||\mathbf{X} - \mathbf{DC}||_F, \tag{6}$$

where the Frobenius norm of matrix $\mathbf{A} \in \mathbb{R}^{m\times n}$ is defined as follows:

$$||\mathbf{A}||_F = \sqrt{\sum_{i=1}^{m}\sum_{j=1}^{n} a_{ij}^2}, \quad a_{ij} \text{ is the } (i,j)\text{-element of } \mathbf{A}. \tag{7}$$

3 Results

We used two-photon calcium imaging data of a transgenic mouse during sleep and wakefulness. To distinguish between excitatory (glutamatergic) and inhibitory (GABAergic) neurons, Vgat-tdTomato mice were generated. Red fluorescence protein tdTomato was expressed particularly in inhibitory neurons in layer 2/3 of the M1 of Vgat-tdTomato mice, which were histologically confirmed. A genetically encoded green fluorescence calcium indicator GCaMP6s was used to monitor neural activity. GCaMP6s was delivered to M1 neurons using adeno-associated virus vectors under the control of a neuron-specific human synapsin 1 promoter. Thus, we defined GCaMP6s-positive/tdTomato-negative and GCaMP6s-positive/tdTomato-positive neurons as excitatory and inhibitory neurons, respectively. Fluorescence imaging was performed with a custom-designed upright two-photon microscope (based on Axio Examiner Z1/LSM780) and a trackball-treadmill system [10]. The mice were acclimated to sleeping on the trackball-treadmill prior to imaging experiments. GCaMP6s and tdTomato were two-photon excited at 910 and 1040 nm, respectively, using a tunable Ti:Sa laser (Maitai DeepSee, Spectra-Physics). Fluorescence of GCaMP6s and tdTomato was detected with a non-descanned GaAsP detector in the range of 500–550 nm and >555 nm, respectively (BiG, Zeiss). A 1040-nm excitation was used only to identify inhibitory neurons prior to time-lapse calcium imaging. Two-photon time-lapse images were intermittently acquired six times between 12:00 and 17:00 (the rest time for mice) at 8 frames/s with 128×256 pixels of 16-bit depth. Each imaging lasted for 15 min and we refer to each 15 min data as a dataset. EEG and EMG signals were also recorded during imaging experiments. EEG signals were amplified 40,000x and filtered with a pass-band of 0.5–500 Hz, and EMG signals were amplified 4000x and filtered with a pass-band of 1.5–1000 Hz using an analog amplifier (MEG-5200, NIHON KOHDEN). EEG/EMG signals were digitized at 2000 Hz using a 16-bit analog-to-digital converter (Digidata 1440A, Molecular Devices), and they were acquired with Clampex 10.3 software (molecular devices). Scan timing signals for two-photon imaging were also digitized with the same systems to temporally match the EEG/EMG data to the two-photon images. EEG and EMG signals were downsampled at 250 Hz, divided into 4 s epochs, and analyzed for scoring NREM/REM/wake states using a homemade Matlab program. The fluorescence signal in each frame for each neuron was extracted by evaluating the mean intensity across the pixels within each region of interest (ROI) after subtracting the background signal using Fiji/ImageJ. ROIs were set such that the neuropil signals were not included.

We calculated $\Delta F/F$ from each dataset and the data matrix $\mathbf{X}$ was created by concatenating six datasets. Then, the data matrix $\mathbf{X}$ was normalized such that the sum of each column was one. By minimizing Frobenius norm cost function, the dictionary $\mathbf{D}$ and coefficient matrix $\mathbf{C}$ were obtained. We tried 29 different values for the number of atoms K, increasing 10 to 150 in increments of 5, because the appropriate value for K is unknown. Larger K can reconstruct $\mathbf{X}$ with small error; however, the atoms would have small information. We want atoms that have rich information; thus, we assumed a smaller K than the number of neurons. We also used PCA and ICA to validate the performance of NMF.

We used random forest [1] to solve the state classification problem to compare three methods and different K. The input of random forest are columns of the coefficient matrix $\mathbf{C}$ for NMF. For PCA and ICA, matrices equivalent to $\mathbf{C}$ were used for the input of random forest. High accuracy in random forest means that the extracted features of the corresponding method can distinguish states. We are comparing three methods and K by the accuracy of random forest. Three states, NREM, REM, and wake, were classified using 3-fold cross-validation. Train and test data were prepared after dividing the input data into 15 s blocks. The results are shown in Fig. 4. The accuracy of each validation is shown by markers, and the average of the three validations is shown by lines.

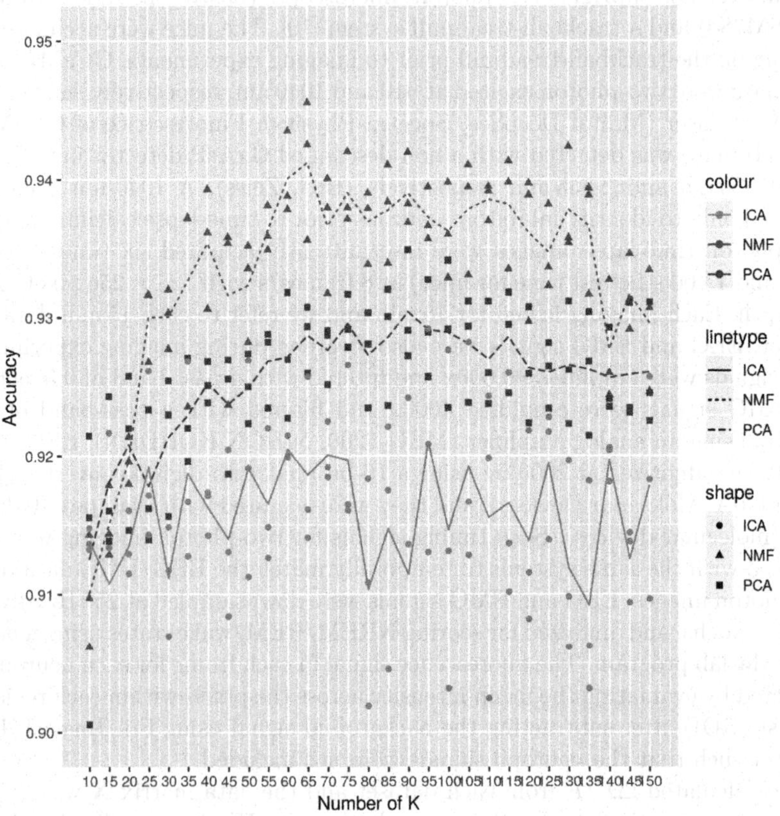

Fig. 4. Accuracies of state classification by the random forest with three methods and different numbers of atoms. Features used in the random forest are columns of the coefficient matrix $\mathbf{C}$ and matrices correspond to that. Three states, NREM, REM, and wake, were classified and the classification accuracy is calculated using 3-fold cross-validation. The accuracy of each validation is shown with markers and the average of three validations is shown with lines.

The result shows that NMF exhibits better performance than PCA and ICA. This suggests that NMF is more suitable for the generative process of the data with its non-negativity. The result also shows that $K = 65$ had the highest accuracy for NMF, suggesting that this is the best K that extracts atoms that differ across sleep/wake states.

We then analyzed the atoms of $K = 65$. To evaluate the atoms used differently between sleep and wake states, we used the importance of random forest and Jensen–Shannon divergence [12] (JSD). We used JSD because analyzing the importance of random forest might not be sufficient. The k-th row of $\mathbf{C}$, $\mathbf{c}_k(t)$, is a time series of the coefficient of the atom $\mathbf{d}_k$. When values of $\mathbf{c}_k(t)$ differ between states, the corresponding atom $\mathbf{d}_k$ is considered to be used differently between states. To measure how differently an atom was used in each state, we calculated the JSD of the coefficient of each atom between NREM and wake states. REM state was not used because it rarely appears in our dataset.

The importance from random forest and the JSD of each atom are presented in Figs. 5 and 6 respectively. Top 12 atoms that had high importance and the JSD is shown in Table 1. The 58th atom is the highest and the 18th atom is the second highest in both importance and the JSD. However, the order of atoms after third place differed in importance and the JSD. This difference should be carefully considered; however, we could not determine the same, and thus, we would leave it for our future work.

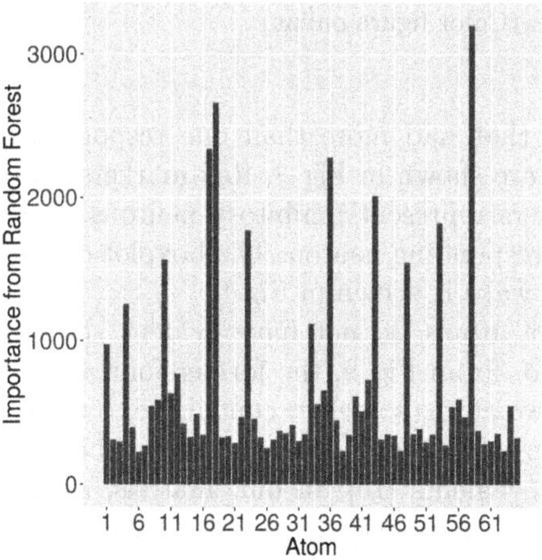

Fig. 5. The importance of $K = 65$ atoms from random forest.

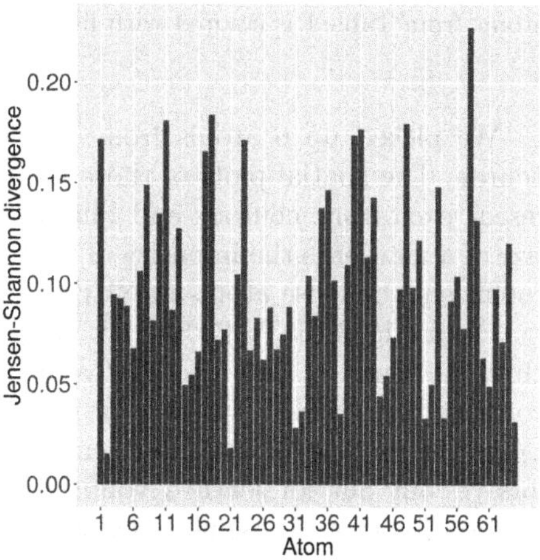

Fig. 6. JSD calculated from coefficients of $K = 65$ atoms.

Our aim is to analyze sleep/wake-dependent neural ensembles. Therefore, we used Otsu's method to obtain the number of neurons responsible in each atom. The result is shown in Fig. 7. Top 12 atoms from Table 1 is colored with light blue. 58th and 23rd atoms had more than 60 responsible neurons. Both atoms had high importance and the JSD.

Table 1. Top 12 atoms that had high importance and the JSD.

Method	Atom											
The importance	58	18	17	36	43	53	23	10	48	4	33	1
JSD	58	18	11	48	41	40	1	23	17	8	53	36

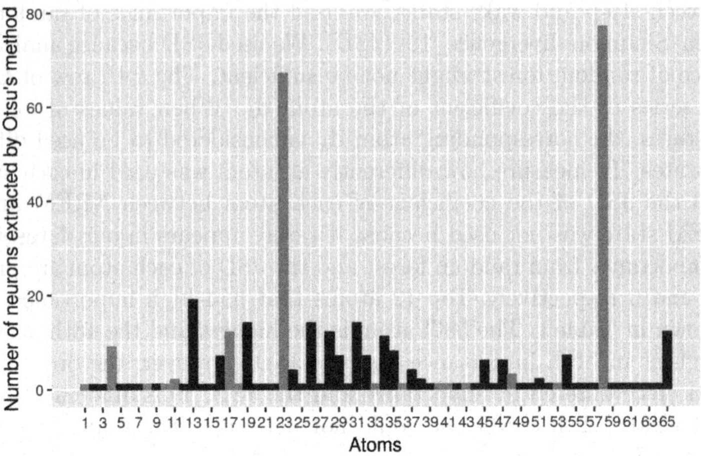

Fig. 7. Number of neurons responsible in each atom using Otsu's method. Top 12 atoms from Table 1 is colored with light blue. (Color figure online)

We picked up 6 atoms from Table 1 that had more than one responsible neuron. The spatial plots of those atoms are shown in Fig. 8. Red markers represent excitatory neurons and blue markers represent inhibitory neurons. The size of a marker is the intensity of the corresponding neuron. The boxplot of the coefficients of those atoms in NREM and wake is shown in Fig. 9.

From Fig. 8, 58th, 23rd, 17th, and 4th atoms do not have evident spatial clusters; however, 48th and 11th atoms do. From Fig. 9, the former four atoms contribute to NREM, whereas the latter two atoms somehow contribute to wake. Co-activation of nearby neurons emerges in the M1 for stereotyped simple behaviors [7] but not for learned voluntary movements [14]. In our analysis, sleep-preferred neuronal ensembles exhibited no evident spatial clustering, suggesting that the M1 is devoted to higher-order information processing for acquiring complex behaviors during sleep.

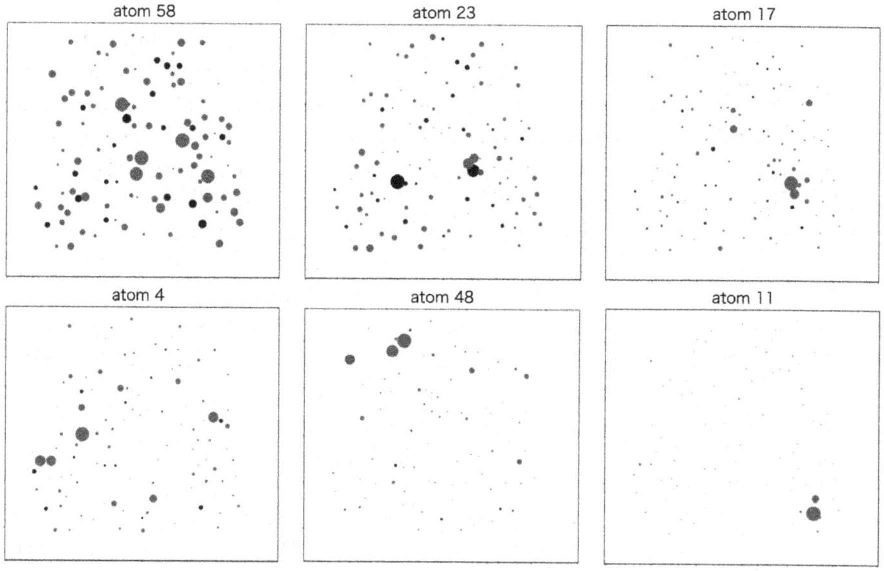

Fig. 8. The spatial plot of atoms. Each marker represents a neuron. The size of a marker is the intensity of the corresponding neuron.

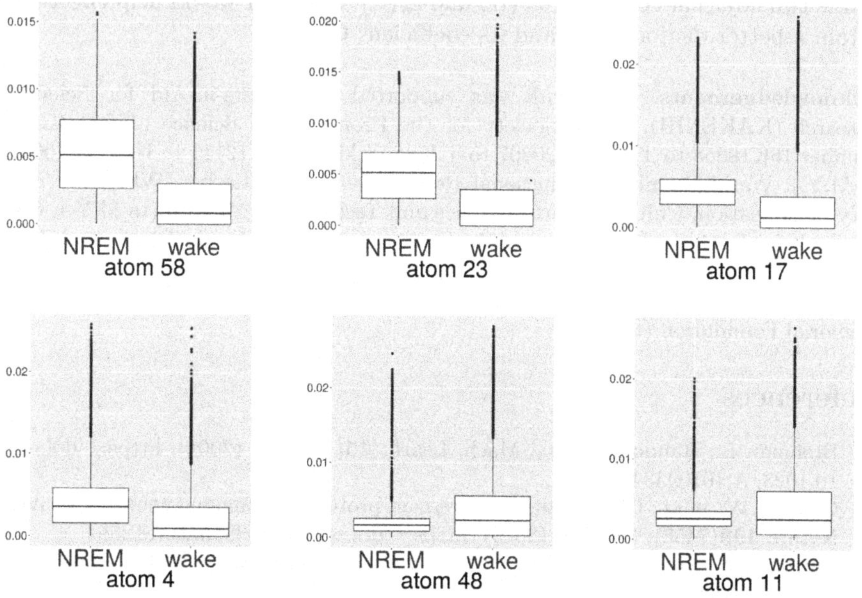

Fig. 9. The boxplot of the coefficients of the atoms in NREM and wake.

4 Conclusion

In this paper, we proposed a protocol to analyze the calcium imaging data with a low sampling rate. We decomposed the data matrix $\mathbf{X}$ with NMF and validated its performance by comparing the results obtained with those of PCA and ICA. The results showed that NMF performed better than PCA and ICA by extracting atoms whose activities differ between states. This suggests that NMF is more suitable for the generative process of the data with its non-negativity. Results also showed that there are groups of neuronal activities that become active simultaneously and some groups are related to sleep/wake states. This is a notable result because NMF does not use state information to decompose the data matrix $\mathbf{X}$. Furthermore, atoms contributing to NREM had no evident spatial clusters, which suggests that the M1 is devoted to high-order information processing for acquiring complex behavior during sleep.

For further investigation, two things should be considered. First, a method to determine the number of atoms K should be developed. NMF requires that the number of atoms K be determined beforehand. In this paper, we used a random forest to determine the number of atoms K; however, further consideration should be made from a biological perspective. Second, the characteristic of calcium imaging should be considered. Calcium imaging has a slow response to neuronal activities. The decay halftime of the calcium indicator GCaMP6s is approximately 0.5s [2], which is much higher than the sampling rate of the data we use. Therefore, we can expect better results if this property is incorporated into the decomposition model of NMF. For example, adding a constraint that makes two adjacent coefficients $c_k(t)$ and $c_k(t+1)$ similar would help effectively obtain a better dictionary $\mathbf{D}$ and its coefficient $\mathbf{C}$.

Acknowledgements. This work was supported by Grants-in-Aid for Scientific Research (KAKENHI), Japan Society for the Promotion of Science (JSPS) (Grant Number 16K18358 to T.K.; 26220207 to T.K. and M.Y.; 19K12111 to H.H; 17H06095 to M.Y.); World Premier International Research Center Initiative (WPI), the Ministry of Education, Culture, Sports, Science and Technology (MEXT) (to M.Y.); Core Research for Evolutional Science and Technology (CREST), Japan Science and Technology Agency (JST) (Grant Number JPMJCR1761 to H.H.; JPMJCR1655 to M.Y.); Yamada Research Grant (to T.K.), Takeda Science Foundation (to M.Y.), and Uehara Memorial Foundation (to M.Y.).

References

1. Breiman, L.: Random forests. Mach. Learn. **45**(1), 5–32 (2001). https://doi.org/10.1023/A:1010933404324
2. Chen, T.W., et al.: Ultrasensitive fluorescent proteins for imaging neuronal activity. Nature **499**(7458), 295–300 (2013). https://doi.org/10.1038/nature12354
3. Cichocki, A., Zdunek, R., Phan, A.H., Amari, S.: Nonnegative Matrix and Tensor Factorizations. Wiley, Chichester (2009)
4. Cox, J., Pinto, L., Dan, Y.: Calcium imaging of sleep-wake related neuronal activity in the dorsal pons. Nat. Commun. **7**(1), 10763 (2016). https://doi.org/10.1038/ncomms10763

5. Dayan, E., Cohen, L.G.: Neuroplasticity subserving motor skill learning. Neuron **72**(3), 443–54 (2011). https://doi.org/10.1016/j.neuron.2011.10.008
6. Deboer, T.: Technologies of sleep research. Cell. Mol. Life Sci. **64**(10), 1227 (2007). https://doi.org/10.1007/s00018-007-6533-0
7. Dombeck, D.A., Graziano, M.S., Tank, D.W.: Functional clustering of neurons in motor cortex determined by cellular resolution imaging in awake behaving mice. J. Neurosci. **29**(44), 13751–13760 (2009). https://doi.org/10.1523/JNEUROSCI.2985-09.2009
8. Evarts, E.V.: Temporal patterns of discharge of pyramidal tract neurons during sleep and waking in the monkey. J. Neurophys. **27**, 152–71 (1964). https://doi.org/10.1152/jn.1964.27.2.152
9. Hobson, J.A.: Sleep is of the brain, by the brain and for the brain. Nature **437**(7063), 1254–1256 (2005). https://doi.org/10.1038/nature04283
10. Kanda, T., et al.: Sleep as a biological problem: an overview of frontiers in sleep research. J. Physiol. Sci. **66**(1), 1–13 (2016). https://doi.org/10.1007/s12576-015-0414-3
11. Lee, D.D., Seung, H.S.: Learning the parts of objects by non-negative matrix factorization. Nature **401**(6755), 788–791 (1999). https://doi.org/10.1038/44565
12. Lin, J.: Divergence measures based on the Shannon entropy. IEEE Trans. Inform. Theory **37**(1), 145–151 (1991). https://doi.org/10.1109/18.61115
13. Mishchencko, Y., Vogelstein, J.T., Paninski, L.: A Bayesian approach for inferring neuronal connectivity from calcium fluorescent imaging data. Ann. Appl. Stat. **5**(2B), 1229–1261 (2011). https://doi.org/10.1214/09-AOAS303
14. Peters, A.J., Chen, S.X., Komiyama, T.: Emergence of reproducible spatiotemporal activity during motor learning. Nature **510**(7504), 263–267 (2014). https://doi.org/10.1038/nature13235
15. Sjulson, L., Miesenböck, G.: Optical recording of action potentials and other discrete physiological events: a perspective from signal detection theory. Physiology **22**(1), 47–55 (2007). https://doi.org/10.1152/physiol.00036.2006
16. Vogelstein, J.T., Watson, B.O., Packer, A.M., Yuste, R., Jedynak, B., Paninski, L.: Spike inference from calcium imaging using sequential Monte Carlo methods. Biophys. J. **97**(2), 636–655 (2009). https://doi.org/10.1016/J.BPJ.2008.08.005

Detection of Directional Information Flow Induced by TMS Based on Symbolic Transfer Entropy

Song Ye[1], Keiichi Kitajo[2,3,4], and Katsunori Kitano[5](✉)

[1] Graduate School of Information Science and Engineering, Ritsumeikan University, Kusatsu, Japan
is0390hf@ed.ritsumei.ac.jp

[2] CBS-TOYOTA Collaboration Center, RIKEN Center for Brain Science, Wako, Japan

[3] National Institutes for Physiological Sciences, National Institutes of Natural Sciences, Okazaki, Japan
kkitajo@nips.ac.jp

[4] Department of Physiological Sciences, School of Life Science, The Graduate University for Advanced Studies (SOKENDAI), Okazaki, Japan

[5] Department of Information Science and Engineering, Ritsumeikan University, 1-1-1 Nojihigashi, Kusatsu, Shiga 5258577, Japan
kitano@ci.ritsumei.ac.jp

1 Introduction

Inter-regional interactions of the brain activity obtained by non-invasive recording such as fMRI or EEG are drawing more attention in the whole brain-level studies. Most of previous studies have derived functional or effective connectivity or changes in such connectivity during the resting states or cognitive tasks. However, it is difficult to see how such connectivity derived from "passively" recorded data represent actual neural interactions. On the other hand, transcranial magnetic stimulation (TMS) enables us to evaluate the causal relation between the controllable direct perturbation and modulated neural activity. It is essential to see if functional or effective connectivity analysis can detect the neural activity modulated by TMS. In the present study, we investigated how TMS for subjects in the resting state influenced neural activities in each brain region and information flow between the regions using a method of effective connectivity analyses.

2 Methods

We analyzed TMS-EEG data using permutation entropy (PE) and symbolic transfer entropy (STE) as known as noise-tolerant methods. The EEG data were obtained by delivering TMS at the visual cortex (Oz electrode) of subjects ($n = 4$) for real TMS trials or sham TMS trials [3]. A session of each type of experiments consisted of 40 to 50 trials and two sessions were investigated.

I. V. Tetko et al. (Eds.): ICANN 2019, LNCS 11727, pp. 114–118, 2019.
https://doi.org/10.1007/978-3-030-30487-4_9

PE is the information-theoretic measure of complexity of time-series data that utilize ordinal patterns, but not measured values, in a time-series "motif" [1], which was used to detect EEG channels showing changes before and after TMS application. STE is the extended version of transfer entropy [4], which derives information flow between sequences of "symbols" defined by the ordinal patterns of time-series motifs [5]. We applied STE to TMS-EEG data in order to extract directional information flow between EEG channels with or without TMS application.

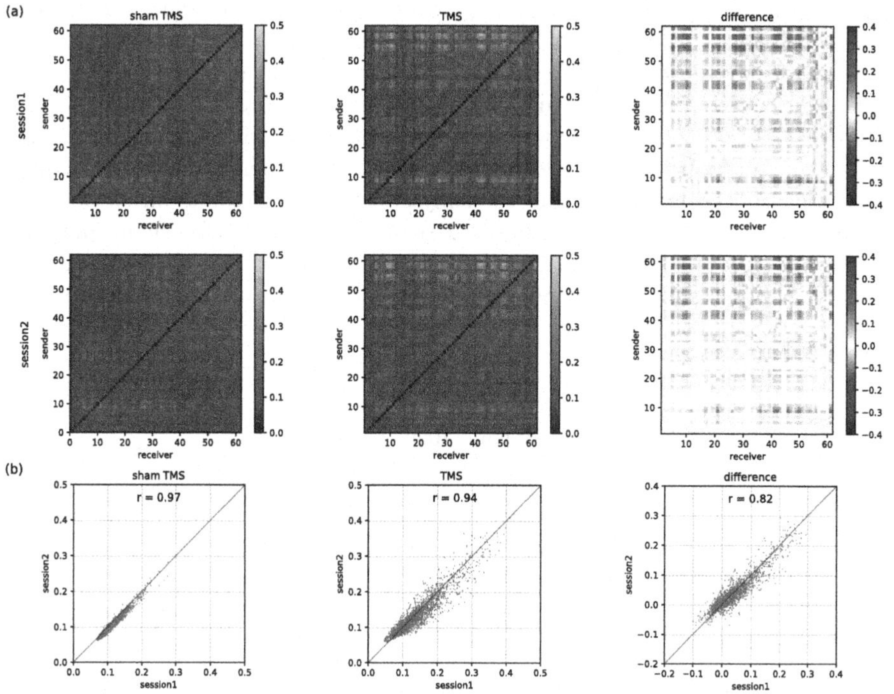

Fig. 1. STE analysis for sham and real TMS trials of a subject. (a) STE values of all directions in the form of matrices. The row and column indicate senders and receivers, respectively. The channel index was aligned from posterior (smaller) to anterior (larger). Sham TMS, real TMS, and differences between them ("real" - "sham") of each session are arranged in a row. (b) Scatter plots of STE values to see correlation between the two sessions. Each dot indicates values from the two sessions for a direction, i.e., if we denote the STE value from channel j to i in the session n by c_{ij}^n, (c_{ij}^1, c_{ij}^2) is plotted. A value in the plot is the Spearman correlation coefficient.

3 Results

Firstly, we applied PE analysis to EEG data of 62 channels for real and sham TMS trials. The result showed that PE of most of the channels decreased for real

TMS trials from sham TMS trials. The channels showing a marked change in PE were found not only in visual areas but also in the motor and frontal areas, suggesting that TMS had an impact on neural activity even at distant regions from the TMS-targeted area (Oz) (data not shown).

Next, we applied STE analysis to the same data. In order to see if the analysis yields robust results, we examined the similarity between the results of 2 sessions. Figure 1(a) shows STE values of all directions for a subject. The figure displayed results of sham and real TMS trials, and the changes between them by subtracting values of sham trials from those of real trials for 2 sessions. For any experimental conditions, the differences between the 2 sessions seem subtle, indicating that STE analysis was capable of stably detecting directional information flow across sessions. To confirm the degree of the similarity, we plotted STE values of all directions in the form of session 1 vs 2 (Fig. 1(b)). As Spearman rank-correlation coefficient shows, the correlation between them was high, suggesting the analysis should yield robust results for an identical subject. Indeed the correlation coefficients for all the subjects shown in Table 1 varied between subjects, but the results between the 2 sessions, especially for sham and real TMS trials could be regarded as similar. Although the pattern of the matrix was different between subjects, it had a similar structure within an identical subject.

Table 1. Correlations between session 1 and 2 for all subjects.

Subject	Sham	Real	Difference
1	0.97	0.94	0.82
2	0.90	0.65	0.51
3	0.72	0.83	0.47
4	0.94	0.91	0.60

Furthermore, we investigated information flow enhanced by TMS. We chose 1% ($62 \times 61 \times 0.01 \approx 38$) largest directions from the "real" - "sham" matrix of each session. We then adopted only the directions that were commonly chosen within these two sets (session 1 and 2). As shown in Fig. 2, the directions markedly enhanced by TMS highly depended on subjects, but they are likely to be classified into two types. In a type of subjects (subject 1), an effect of TMS was directly observed, namely, pathways from the TMS-targeted area (Oz in the visual area) were largely increased. In the other type (subject 2 to 4), an indirect effect of TMS was observed. In these subjects, pathways from non-TMS-targeted area, especially from frontal areas, were enhanced. In any case, this result suggested that TMS should have a considerable impact on neural activity in the frontal areas whether it was direct or indirect.

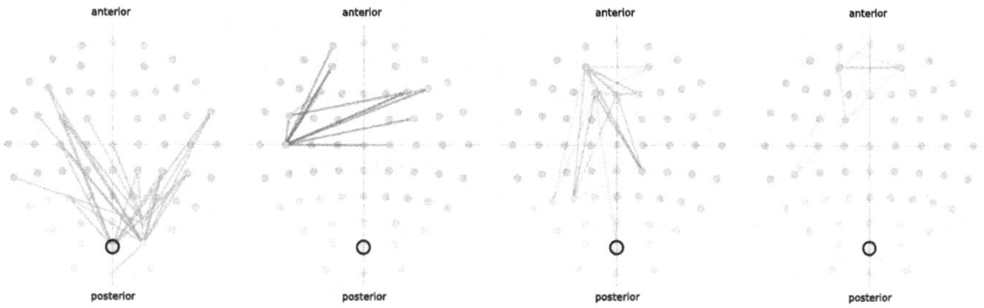

Fig. 2. Directional information flow enhanced by TMS. For each subject, 1% largest directions from each of the difference ("real" - "sham") matrix were chosen. Among the obtained two sets, common directions were illustrated. From the left, the maps of subject 1 to 4 are illustrated. The colors of arrows represent areas of arrows' starting points (i.e., "sender" channels). The stronger color indicates a larger STE value. Black circles display the TMS-targeted location (Oz).

4 Conclusions

Based on the high correlation between STE matrices for different sessions, STE analysis would yield robust results across sessions, especially for sham TMS trials. To obtain stable results on sham TMS trials is advantageous because they are the baselines to extract an effect of TMS from EEG signals modulated by TMS. In comparison with the results on sham TMS trials, those on real TMS trials slightly deteriorated, but the correlation across sessions was still high depending on subjects. Also changes from sham TMS trials to real TMS trials, which represents enhanced amount of information flows by TMS, correlated across sessions, suggesting that STE analysis could detect modulated information flow induced by TMS. Thus, although the number of subjects was limited here, we could conclude that STE analysis is useful for effective connectivity analysis for TMS-EEG and presumably for EEG during resting states and cognitive tasks.

Although the brain state during sham TMS trials is not necessarily the same as the so-called resting state, the matrices for the sham TMS trials might represent resting state networks. We confirmed that applying TMS at a visual area had an impact on neural activity in the frontal areas, suggesting that there would exist information pathways from posterior to frontal regions. Given that some studies report that information flow of frontal feedback is observed in a conscious state [2], our results implied that there would exist bi-directional information transfer between these regions in fact and TMS and STE could visualize an effect of the posterior-to-frontal pathway.

References

1. Bandt, C., Pompe, B.: Permutation entropy: a natural complexity measure for time series. Phys. Rev. Lett. **88**, 174102 (2002). https://doi.org/10.1103/PhysRevLett.88.174102

2. Jordan, D., et al.: Simultaneous electroencephalographic and functional magnetic resonance imaging indicate impaired cortical top-down processing in association with anesthetic-induced unconsciousness. Anesthesiology **119**, 1031–1042 (2013). https://doi.org/10.1097/ALN.0b013e3182a7ca92
3. Kawasaki, M., Uno, Y., Mori, J., Kobata, K., Kitajo, K.: Transcranial magnetic stimulation-induced global propagation of transient phase resetting associated with directional information flow. Front. Hum. Neurosci. **8**, 173 (2014). https://doi.org/10.3389/fnhum.2014.00173
4. Schreiber, T.: Measuring information transfer. Phys. Rev. Lett. **85**, 461–465 (2000). https://doi.org/10.1103/PhysRevLett.85.461
5. Staniek, M., Lehnertz, K.: Symbolic transfer entropy. Phys. Rev. Lett. **100**, 158101 (2008). https://doi.org/10.1103/PhysRevLett.100.158101

Brain-Inspired Hardware for Artificial Intelligence: Accelerated Learning in a Physical-Model Spiking Neural Network

Timo Wunderlich[1(✉)], Akos F. Kungl[1(✉)], Eric Müller[1], Johannes Schemmel[1], and Mihai Petrovici[1,2]

[1] Kirchhoff Institute for Physics, Heidelberg University, Heidelberg, Germany
{timo.wunderlich,fkungl}@kip.uni-heidelberg.de
[2] Department of Physiology, University of Bern, Bern, Switzerland

Abstract. Future developments in artificial intelligence will profit from the existence of novel, non-traditional substrates for brain-inspired computing. Neuromorphic computers aim to provide such a substrate that reproduces the brain's capabilities in terms of adaptive, low-power information processing. We present results from a prototype chip of the BrainScaleS-2 mixed-signal neuromorphic system that adopts a physical-model approach with a 1000-fold acceleration of spiking neural network dynamics relative to biological real time. Using the embedded plasticity processor, we both simulate the Pong arcade video game and implement a local plasticity rule that enables reinforcement learning, allowing the on-chip neural network to learn to play the game. The experiment demonstrates key aspects of the employed approach, such as accelerated and flexible learning, high energy efficiency and resilience to noise.

Keywords: Neuromorphic computing · Spiking networks · Plasticity

1 Introduction

Many breakthrough advances in artificial intelligence incorporate methods and algorithms that are inspired by the brain. For instance, the artificial neural networks employed in deep learning are inspired by the architecture of biological neural networks [1]. Very often, however, these brain-inspired algorithms are run on classical von Neumann devices that instantiate a computational architecture remarkably different from the one of the brain. It is therefore a widely held view that the future of artificial intelligence will depend critically on the deployment of novel computational substrates [2]. Neuromorphic computers represent an attempt to move beyond brain-inspired software by building hardware that structurally and functionally mimics the brain [3].

In this work, we use a prototype of the BrainScaleS-2 (BSS2) neuromorphic system [4]. The employed physical-model approach enables the accelerated (1000-fold with respect to biology) and energy-efficient emulation of spiking neural networks (SNNs). Beyond SNN emulation, the system contains an embedded

I. V. Tetko et al. (Eds.): ICANN 2019, LNCS 11727, pp. 119–122, 2019.
https://doi.org/10.1007/978-3-030-30487-4_10

plasticity processing unit (PPU) that provides facilities for the flexible implementation of learning rules. Our prototype chip (see Fig. 1A) contains 32 physical-model neurons with 32 synapses each, totalling 1024 synapses. The neurons are an electronic circuit implementation of the leaky integrate-and-fire neuron model. We use this prototype to demonstrate key advantages of our employed approach, such as the 1000-fold speed-up of neuronal dynamics, on-chip learning, high energy-efficiency and robustness to noise in a closed-loop reinforcement learning experiment.

2 Experiment

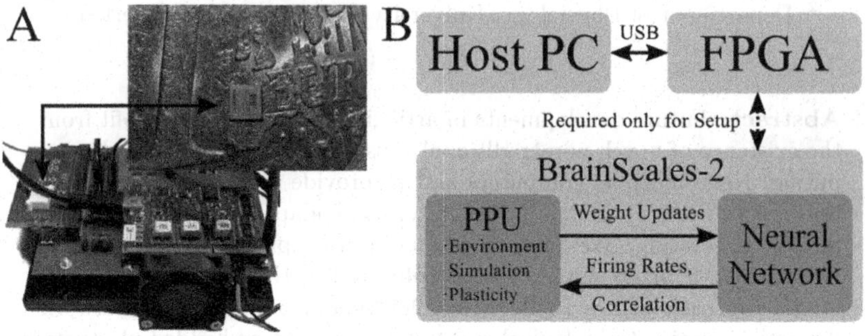

Fig. 1. A: prototype chip and evaluation board. B: schematic of experimental setup. The chip runs the experiment fully autonomously, with the PPU simulating the virtual environment (Pong) and calculating reward-based weight updates that are applied to the on-chip analog neural network. The neural network receives the discretized ball position as input and outputs the target paddle position. B taken from [5].

The experiment represents the first demonstration of on-chip closed-loop learning in an accelerated physical-model neuromorphic system [5]. It takes place on the chip fully autonomously, with external communication only required for initial configuration (see Fig. 1B). We use the embedded plasticity processor both to simulate a simplified version of the Pong video game (opponent is a solid wall) and to implement a reward-modulated spike-timing-dependent plasticity (R-STDP) learning rule [6] of the form $\Delta w_{ij} \propto (R - \bar{R})e_{ij}$, where R is the reward, $\bar{R}$ is a running average of the reward and e_{ij} is an STDP-like eligibility trace. Each synapse locally records the STDP-like eligibility trace and stores it as an analog value (a voltage), to be digitized and used by the plasticity processor [4].

The two-layer neural network receives the ball position along one axis as input and dictates the target paddle position, to which the paddle moves with constant velocity, using the neuronal firing rates. It receives reward depending on its aiming accuracy (i.e., how close it aims the paddle to the center of the ball), with $R = 1$ for perfect aiming, $R = 0$ for not aiming under the ball and graded steps in between. By correlating reward and synaptic activity via the given learning rule, the SNN on the chip learns to trace the ball with high fidelity.

3 Results

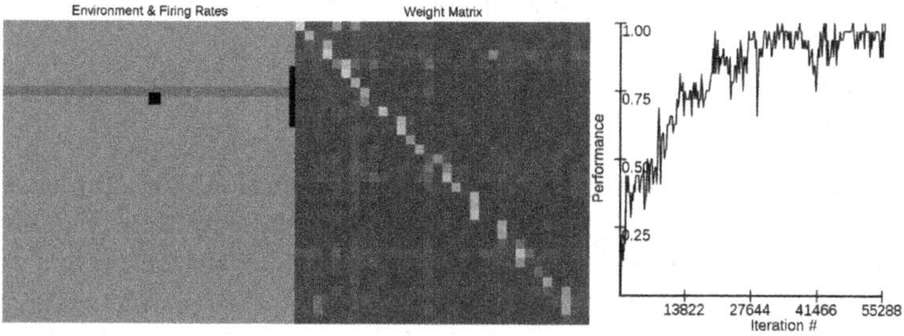

Fig. 2. Screenshot of experiment interface for live demonstration. Left: playing field and color-coded neuronal firing rates. Middle: color-coded synaptic weight matrix. Right: performance in playing Pong.

A screen recording of a live demonstration of the experiment (see Fig. 2) is available at https://www.youtube.com/watch?v=LW0Y5SSIQU4. The recording allows the viewer to follow the game dynamics, neuronal firing rates, synaptic weight dynamics and learning progress. The learning progress is quantified by measuring the relative number of ball positions for which the paddle is able to catch the ball. The learned weight matrix is diagonally dominant: this expresses a correct mapping of states to actions in the reinforcement learning paradigm.

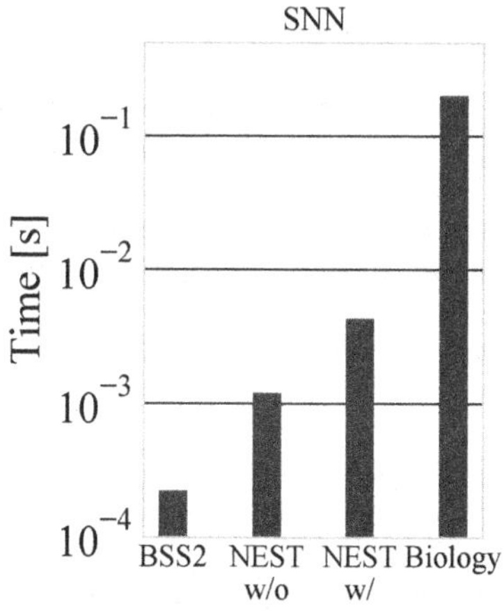

Fig. 3. Comparison of experiment durations. w/o: without. w/: with. Adapted from [5].

Importantly, neuronal firing rates vary from trial to trial due to noise in the analog chip components. Used appropriately, this can become an asset rather than a nuisance: in our reinforcement learning scenario, such variability endows the neural network with the ability to explore the action space and thereby with a necessary prerequisite for trial-and-error learning. We also found that neuronal parameter variability due to fixed-pattern noise, which is inevitable in analog neuromorphic hardware, is implicitly compensated by the chosen learning paradigm, leading to a correlation of learned weights and neuronal properties [4].

The accelerated nature of our substrate represents a key advantage. We found that a software simulation (NEST v2.14.0) on an Intel processor (i7-4771), when considering only the numerical state propagation, is at least an order of magnitude slower than our neuromorphic emulation (see Fig. 3 and [5]). Besides this, the emulation on our prototype is at least 1000 times more energy-efficient than the software simulation

(23 μJ vs. 106 mJ per iteration). This evinces the considerable benefit of using the BSS2 platform for emulating spiking networks and hints towards its decisive advantages when scaling the emulated networks to larger sizes.

4 Conclusions

These experiments demonstrate, for the first time, functional on-chip closed-loop learning on an accelerated physical-model neuromorphic system. The employed approach carries the potential to both enable researchers with the ability to investigate learning processes with a 1000-fold speed-up and to enable novel, energy-efficient and fast solutions for brain-inspired edge computing. While digital neuromorphic solutions and supercomputers generally achieve at most real-time simulation speed in large-scale neural networks [7–9], the speed-up of BrainScaleS-2 is independent of network size and will become a critical asset in future work on the full-scale BrainScaleS-2 system.

References

1. Hassabis, D., et al.: Neuroscience-inspired artificial intelligence. Neuron **95**, 245–258 (2017). https://doi.org/10.1016/j.neuron.2017.06.011
2. Dean, J., et al.: A new golden age in computer architecture: empowering the machine-learning revolution. IEEE Micro **38**(2), 21–29 (2018). https://doi.org/10.1109/MM.2018.112130030. ISSN 0272-1732
3. Schuman, C.D., et al.: A survey of neuromorphic computing and neural networks in hardware. CoRR abs/1705.06963 (2017)
4. Friedmann, S., et al.: Demonstrating hybrid learning in a flexible neuromorphic hardware system. IEEE Trans. Biomed. Circ. Syst. **11**(1), 128–142 (2017). https://doi.org/10.1109/TBCAS.2016.2579164
5. Wunderlich, T., et al.: Demonstrating advantages of neuromorphic computation: a pilot study. Front. Neurosci. **13**, 260 (2019). https://doi.org/10.3389/fnins.2019.00260
6. Frémaux, N., et al.: Neuromodulated spike-timing-dependent plasticity, and theory of three-factor learning rules. Front. Neural Circ. **9**, 85 (2015). https://doi.org/10.3389/fncir.2015.00085. ISSN 1662-5110
7. Jordan, J., et al.: Extremely scalable spiking neuronal network simulation code: from laptops to exascale computers. Front. Neu roinform. **12**, 2 (2018). https://doi.org/10.3389/fninf.2018.00002. ISSN 1662-5196
8. van Albada, S.J., et al.: Performance comparison of the digital neuromorphic hardware SpiNNaker and the neural network simulation software NEST for a full-scale cortical microcircuit model. Front. Neurosci. **12**, 291 (2018). https://doi.org/10.3389/fnins.2018.00291. ISSN 1662-453X
9. Mikaitis, M., et al.: Neuromodulated synaptic plasticity on the SpiNNaker neuromorphic system. Front. Neurosci. **12**, 105 (2018). https://doi.org/10.3389/fnins.2018.00105. ISSN 1662-453X

Distinguishing Violinists and Pianists Based on Their Brain Signals

Gianpaolo Coro[1(✉)], Giulio Masetti[1], Philipp Bonhoeffer[2], and Michael Betcher[2]

[1] Istituto di Scienza e Tecnologie dell'Informazione A. Faedo, Pisa, Italy
{gianpaolo.coro,giulio.masetti}@isti.cnr.it
[2] Auditorium della Compagnia Montecastelli, Castelnuovo di Val di Cecina, Pisa, Italy
bonhop1705@googlemail.com, m.betcher@gmx.de

Abstract. Many studies in neuropsychology have highlighted that expert musicians, who started learning music in childhood, present structural differences in their brains with respect to non-musicians. This indicates that early music learning affects the development of the brain. Also, musicians' neuronal activity is different depending on the played instrument and on the expertise. This difference can be analysed by processing electroencephalographic (EEG) signals through Artificial Intelligence models. This paper explores the feasibility to build an automatic model that distinguishes violinists from pianists based only on their brain signals. To this aim, EEG signals of violinists and pianists are recorded while they play classical music pieces and an Artificial Neural Network is trained through a cloud computing platform to build a binary classifier of segments of these signals. Our model has the best classification performance on 20 seconds EEG segments, but this performance depends on the involved musicians' expertise. Also, the brain signals of a cellist are demonstrated to be more similar to violinists' signals than to pianists' signals. In summary, this paper demonstrates that distinctive information is present in the two types of musicians' brain signals, and that this information can be detected even by an automatic model working with a basic EEG equipment.

Keywords: Artificial neural networks · Brain signals · Music

1 Introduction

Music influences the development of the brain from childhood to adulthood [11]. The pattern of brain architecture, brain's plasticity, and behaviour development are affected by early music learning, and music-specific neural networks have been also hypothesised [43]. Further, structural differences have been highlighted between the brains of adult musicians and non-musicians [24,55]. Nevertheless, the development and the nature of these structural differences are not

I. V. Tetko et al. (Eds.): ICANN 2019, LNCS 11727, pp. 123–137, 2019.
https://doi.org/10.1007/978-3-030-30487-4_11

clear, but generally they affect complex motor, auditory, and multi-modal skills [48]. Indeed, musicians' neural activity changes depending on the played instrument because playing music with different instruments usually involves different sensory-motor activities, different components of the nervous system, and hierarchically organized gross and fine movements [58]. Moreover, during a musical performance the sound is also processed by the musician's auditory circuitry, and the brain adjusts the movements based on the processed information. Also, the brain visually processes and interprets symbols if the musician is reading music [17].

These aspects can be studied by processing electrical brain activity, especially through computational models. To this aim, biosensors can be used to record brain signals that allow direct communication between neural activity and an external device [57]. The human brain contains billions of inter-connected neurons across different areas of the brain and the interactions between neurons create very small electrical discharges. Although each of these currents is very difficult to measure from outside the skull, the overall current created by thousands of neurons can be measured by external detectors and reported as electroencephalographic (EEG) signals [40]. Emotional states, thoughts, and music-related brain activity are somehow related to the signals produced by different concurrent neuronal aggregations from several areas of the brain. Using arrays of sensors on the skull, the signals of these aggregative regions can be recorded. Processing these signals through computational models helps finding patterns correlated to the thoughts, the actions, and the emotional states produced by a certain situation [50].

EEG signals have been used in research on human cognitive and sensory-motor functions [23,26], and applications to music have recently focussed on music perception and composition [22,34]. For example, music has been deduced from brain signals in neurotherapy [54], stress control [52], brain activity monitoring [4], and music generation [45]. Several studies have modelled the correlation between music and brain waves patterns to understand brain changes due to long-term music training using neurophysiological analytical frameworks [39,41,51]. The drawbacks of these approaches are that (i) they require complex and expensive equipment, (ii) aim at explicitly modelling very complex and unknown phenomena, and (iii) typically their answers are generic. For example, they can distinguish a musician from a non-musician but they cannot identify the type of musician.

In this paper, EEG signals and Artificial Neural Networks (ANNs) are used to automatically distinguish between piano and violin players based on their brain signals recorded while playing different classical music pieces. Results are presented based on a 40 min collection of recordings, and show that a high-performance automatic classifier can be built even using one biosensor placed at the frontal-pole position of the cerebral cortex (Fp1 in the International 10–20 electroencephalogram system [28]). Cloud computing is used to identify the highest accuracy ANN among a huge set of possible parametrisations. Overall, the aim of this paper is to demonstrate that it is possible to automatically detect the presence of similarities in the brain signals of professional musicians without using either complex equipment or neurophysiological analytical models.

Expert musicians who learned music in childhood (5–8 years old) were involved in the experiment, in order to include factors related to early modifications of the brain besides the played instrument. Also, a good (non-expert) violin player who started playing at adult age (18 years old) and a basic piano player were involved to test the model's performance when basic expertise is introduced in the training set. Finally, an expert cello player was introduced to test if his brain signals were better classified as belonging to a violinist or a pianist.

2 Equipment and Method

2.1 EEG Device

Electroencephalography (EEG) has applications in several domains, including health, education, and entertainment [9,27]. Although complex EEG systems may cost thousands of dollars, cheaper solutions exist that use biosensors collecting electrical signals from the surface of the scalp that originate from sources in the cerebral cortex. These systems can be quite accurate, portable, and may come with embedded noise filtering and signal processing functions [2,25].

For the experiment presented in this paper, the NeuroSky EEG biosensor embedded in the NeuroSky MindWave toolkit was used. This toolkit is a wearable headphone-like tool that uses one dry NeuroSky biosensor to be placed at the frontal-pole (Fp1) position of the cerebral cortex. This biosensor digitizes and amplifies raw analog brain signals, with a 512 Hz sampling frequency, and produces a one-dimensional signal. The NeuroSky product has been used as a development platform in other scientific experiments as well as in professional and entertainment products due to its fair precision and low cost [36,37]. The biosensor embedded in the NeuroSky products has been evaluated to be at 96% as accurate as state-of-the art EEG sensors [32,38,56].

The NeuroSky MindWave toolkit includes a built-in noise reduction filter and a signal processing module that calculates the power spectrum of the signal every 1s. The signal spectrum was band-pass filtered (between 0.5 Hz and 100 Hz) and classified according to common subdivision ranges of brain signals frequency bands [19]: Gamma (40–100 Hz), Beta (12–40 Hz), Alpha (8–12 Hz), Theta (4–8 Hz), and Delta (0.5–4 Hz) waves. Usually, these frequency bands are correlated with different brain states, for example Beta waves are correlated with logical-rational processing, whereas Alpha waves are associated with intuitive processes involving internal focus of attention and with top-down sensory inhibition [21]. The power spectrum of these five bands was used as numeric vector of features in our model.

One advantage of the NeuroSky MindWave toolkit is that it is sufficiently lightweight and portable to not obstruct musicians' movements. However, one problem in our recording sessions was that the biosensor was subject to shifts and disconnections. Thus, the collected signals included noise and gaps that our model had to manage. Generally, motion artefacts are a common source of noise when using dry sensors, although most of the artefact energy is concentrated in the frequencies under 5 Hz [42]. These artefacts can be reduced by using a high-pass filter (over 0.5 Hz) and a filter based on contact impedance variations [6]. In our experiment, the band-pass and the built-in noise reduction filters were used for this purpose.

One criticism in using the NeuroSky toolkit is that it uses one channel only at the Fp1 position, whose activity is correlated also to other movements (e.g. eyes' ones) and only indirectly to music [7,33]. However, one of the aims of this paper is to demonstrate that a machine learning approach can manage a musicians' classification task even using this equipment, because it can recognize the indirect effects of playing different instruments on the EEG signals in Fp1.

2.2 Classification Model

An Artificial Neural Network (ANN) can be used to build an automatic classifier that associates an input vector to one category among several [8]. In particular, a multi-layer Feed-Forward ANN was the best suited model for the dichotomic classification problem managed in this paper, i.e. classifying a segment of brain signal as belonging either to a violinist or a pianist (Sect. 3). Indeed, Feed-Forward ANNs are suited for classification tasks where a numeric vector represents a mono-dimensional time series spectrum like it was a picture, and have proven to gain comparable or higher performance than other techniques (e.g. Support Vector Machines and Naive Bayes classifiers) in several domains [16,18]. Further, our purpose was to assess the possibility to use brain signals for musicians classification more than reaching the highest possible classification performance, thus deep-learning convolution steps were not necessary [49].

Although ANNs are powerful models, the main disadvantage of using them is that it is not possible to reconstruct the analytical form of the simulated function. In fact, despite the model can recognize that similarities exist in vectors belonging to the same class, the related patterns remain unknown. Nevertheless, learning quality measurements can reveal if the model has been able to detect the presence of distinctive information in the training set [5].

2.3 Cloud Computing Platform

Our method required testing a large number of ANNs in order to find the length of the EEG signal portion and the best topology that optimised the classification. These tests were performed using a cloud computing platform that trained alternative ANNs concurrently and allowed exploring a large space of parameters in a reasonable amount of time. In particular, an open-source computational system was used (DataMiner [14,15]) that is part of a distributed e-Infrastructure for Open Science (D4Science [10]).

The ANN implementation used for this paper, is open-source and part of the DataMiner framework and is published as a free to use Web service [12,13] under the Web Processing Service standard (WPS [1]). WPS standardises the representation of the input and output and makes the service usable by a number of clients and by external software. DataMiner saves the history of all trained and tested models using a standard and exportable format [30]. Every executed process can be re-executed and parametrised multiple times by other users, thanks to collaborative experimentation spaces [35]. In this view, this platform allowed making the presented experiment compliant with Open Science directives of repeatability, reproducibility and re-usability of data and processes.

DataMiner is made up of 15 machines with Ubuntu 16.04.4 LTS x86 64 operating system, 16 virtual cores, 32 GB of RAM and 100 GB of disk space. As for our experiment, each machine concurrently trained and tested different ANN topologies.

3 Experiment and Results

3.1 Experimental Setup and Model Training

Using the technology presented in the previous section, an automatic classifier of nine male musicians was built (schematised in Fig. 2), which distinguished pianists from violinists based on the power spectra of their brain signals. The characteristics of these players are reported in Table 1 and a visual comparison of brain signals is displayed in Fig. 1. The musicians were all volunteers, and all expert musicians started their music training during childhood.

Table 1. Characteristics of the musicians involved in the presented experiment.

ID	Instrument	Age	Begin age	Expertise
Pianist 1	Piano	16	7	Expert
Pianist 2	Piano	19	5	Expert-Professional
Pianist 3	Piano	50	6	Expert
Violinist 1	Violin	16	6	Expert-Professional
Violinist 2	Violin	53	7	Expert
Violinist 3	Violin	19	7	Expert-Professional
Cellist	Cello	19	8	Expert-Professional
Non-expert 1	Violin	29	18	Good
Non-expert 2	Piano	30	18	Basic

Each player was asked to play two pieces without reading a score: the first was a piece the player knew well and that was not demanding (*easy-familiar* piece); the second was a more difficult piece requiring higher concentration (*challenging-unfamiliar* piece). All pieces were different from each other, because this maximised the players' comfort and allowed for better concentration on the music. The musicians played one after the other, and wore the NeuroSky MindWave toolkit while playing. The recording sessions were done in the Montecastelli Music Hall, a chamber concert hall that hosts both scientific venues and concerts [3].

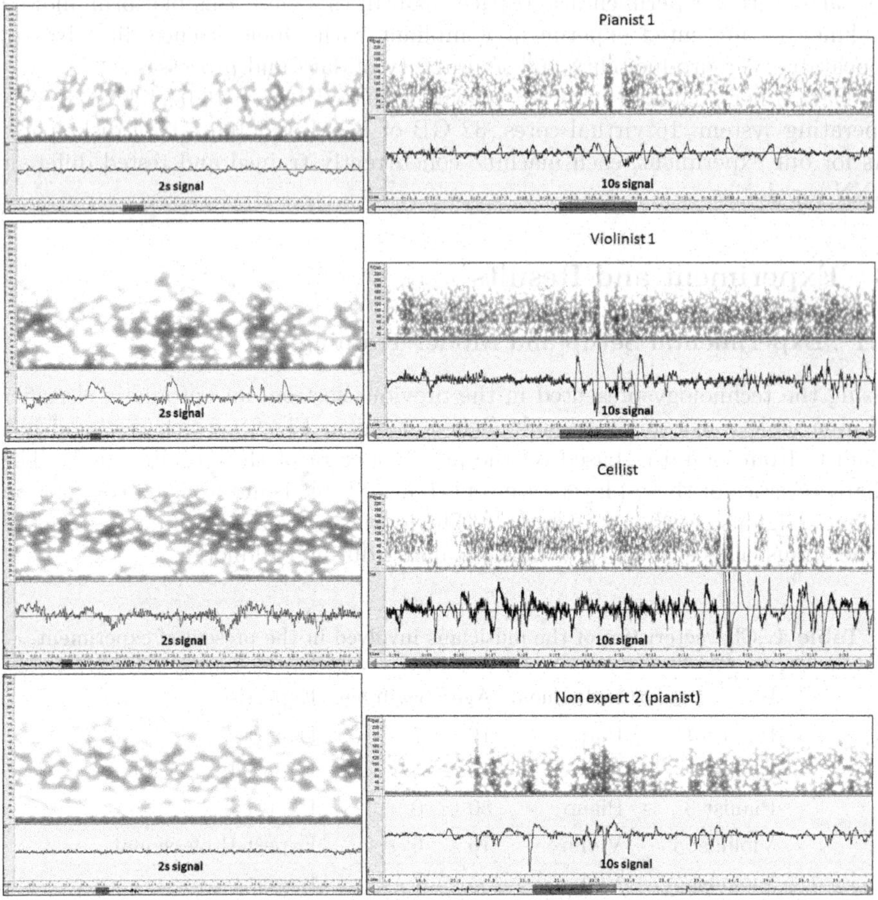

Fig. 1. Visual comparison of brain signals of the involved musicians. For each musician, signals of 2 s and 10 s are reported, which were selected from high-concentration moments in the execution of a piece.

The music hall was reserved for this experiment and the musicians were isolated from distractions. At the end of the recording sessions, 40 min of audio and brain signals had been recorded in total, with equal distribution of time per musician. The power spectra in the Gamma-Delta bands were extracted (5 features at 1s rate). Although the number of musicians was not high, a large number of brain signals and spectral features were collected.

Segments of EEG signals with several lengths were cut and treated as different signals for models training and testing. Training and test sets involved also signals belonging to the same musician, i.e. they included a potential intra-subject correlation. However, a time series cross-correlation analysis revealed an average 0.2 correlation score (with maximum 0.4 and minimum 0.008) across all training sets. This means that there was poor intra-subject correlation, possibly because the played pieces were articulated and did not contain repeated musical sequences. To further decrease this effect, completely disjoint training and test sets were also prepared though a *leave-one-out* procedure, where the tested musician's signals were not involved in the training set, i.e. for every musician, an ANN was tested for the classification of the EEG segments of the musician, after being trained on the EEG segments of the other musicians.

An Artificial Neural Network classifier was built to automatically classify a musician's signal segment as belonging to either a piano or a violin player (Fig. 2). The segment length containing the maximum discriminant information was one parameter to identify, other than the ANN topology maximising the classification performance. Segment lengths between 1 s and 30 s were explored (which maintained the size of the training and test sets statistically significant), and the optimal ANN topology was searched between 2 and 5 layers. The ANN used a logistic sigmoid activation function in the neurons and a standard backpropagation algorithm implementation for network training [47], with 1000 maximum iterations, 0.9 learning rate, and a 0.001 threshold on the mean squared error. A total number of ~700,000 combinations of segment lengths and topologies were tested, which explains the necessity of using a cloud computing platform. For each fixed-length segment, DataMiner used a *growing* strategy to search for the best (i) number of layers, (ii) number of neurons in each layer, and (iii) a dichotomic classification threshold on the output. This strategy basically consists in adding neurons and layers as far as the error with respect to the training set decreases down to a certain threshold [8].

As input to the ANN, power spectrum features vectors from the brain signal segments were used. Features associated to a segment larger than 1 s were built by concatenating the 1s power spectrum vectors completely included in the segment. For example, a 20 s segment was represented as the concatenation of 5 spectral features (one for each second), i.e. as a 100 features vector ($= 20 \cdot 5$). Features in all bands were used because the EEG reported instrument-specific activity in all of them, sometimes with long time span. The ANNs were trained to output 0 for pianists and 1 for violinists and a 10-fold cross-validation test (using each EEG segment as one instance) was used to assess the performance of each step of the growing process, i.e. the EEG segments were assigned to 10 clusters and one cluster was used to test the model trained with all the other clusters. For each cluster, the accuracy of the classification was calculated as $\frac{n.\ of\ test\ segments\ correctly\ classified}{overall\ n.\ of\ test\ segments}$ and an overall accuracy on all clusters was calculated as the average of the single-cluster accuracies. In order to reduce overfitting issues and dependency between the training vectors, consecutive signal segments were never assigned to the same cluster.

The schematic flow of our method for model building can be summarised as follows:

```
For each musician m ∈ [1,9]:
    Record brain signals while playing an easy-familiar piece
    Record brain signals while playing a challenging-unfamiliar
    piece

For each musician's brain signal:
    Prepare sets of segments containing signals from length 1s
    to 30s: {S1}m ··· {S30}m

For each union of all the sets of segments of length k seconds
(with k ∈ [1,30]), i.e Gk = {Sk}1 ∪ {Sk}2 ∪ ··· ∪ {Sk}9:
    Distribute all     Gk      segments onto 10 groups, with the
    constraint that one group should not contain consecutive
    segments from one brain signal
    Find the ANN topology with the highest performance, using a
    growing strategy while performing a 10-fold cross-validation
    test using the previously defined 10 groups
    Use the best found ANN topology to
    perform a cross-validation test based on the nine {Sk}m sets
    constituting Gk (leave-one-out process)

Record the ANN topology with the highest performance in the
10-fold cross-validation test, which thus identifies the
optimal segment length k*
```

By using this flow, the optimal segment length k^* was found to be 20 s (i.e. the ANN had 120 input neurons). The best topology was made up of 2 hidden layers with 100 neurons in the first hidden layer and 20 neurons in the second, and one output neuron (Fig. 2). Further, our flow reported an optimal classification threshold of 0.7 for this topology in the 10-fold cross-validation test.

3.2 Performance

The variation of the performance of our model was calculated at the variation of the musicians and of the pieces involved in the training process (Table 2). In particular, involving the cellist increased the performance when he was classified as a violinist in the training set (from 72.5% to 80%). On the contrary, indicating his brain signals as pianists' signals decreased the overall model's performance to 59.9%. This scenario indicates that the cellist's signals resemble more the violinists' ones. This observation may seem intuitive, but is not trivial because playing a cello involves completely different movements with respect to playing a violin, although these are both arc instruments. However, other studies have reported this same scenario from a neurophysiological perspective by observing that cellists and violinists have larger and similar cortical activation patterns in the right hemisphere, whereas pianists have larger activity in the left hemisphere [20,29].

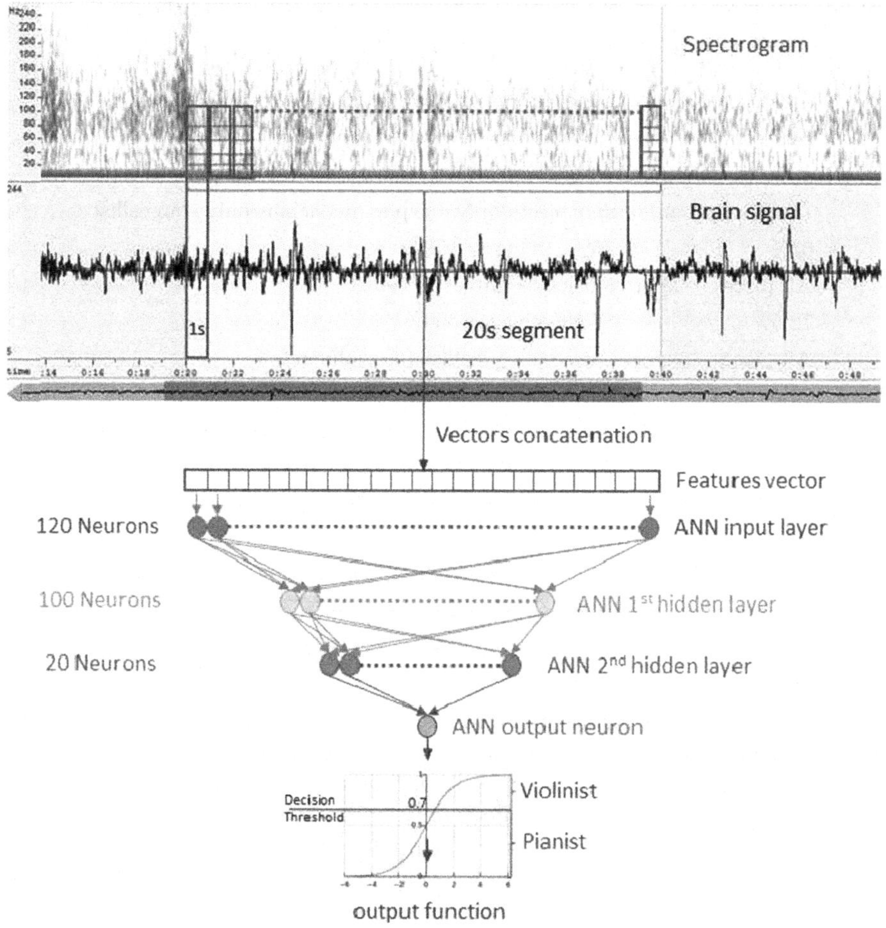

Fig. 2. Schema of our automatic classifier. The power spectrum is extracted from the spectrogram at 1s rate as a vector of numeric features; the vectors in a 20 s signal segment are concatenated and used as input to a multi-layer Artificial Neural Network; the output of the model is a continuous function on which a threshold is used to classify the input vector as either belonging to a violinist or a pianist.

Including a non-expert player in the model's training, improved the performance (from 80% to 81.6%) only if he had some experience. In fact, including a player with basic expertise strongly decreased the performance (down to 74.3%), i.e. the ANN was confounded by his brain signals. Overall, the model with the highest performance was the one involving both expert and good players and all pieces (81.6% with a peak of 91.7%). With these pieces and musicians, an average accuracy of 79.5% was calculated by using a *leave-one-out* approach, where all the signals of the tested musician were excluded from the training set and

Table 2. Performance of our automatic classifier at the variation of the pieces, of the involved musicians, and of their expertise.

Average accuracy	Max. accuracy	Min. accuracy
Easy-familiar pieces only - expert musicians only - no cellist		
65%	70%	50%
Challenging-unfamiliar pieces only - expert musicians only - no cellist		
65%	75%	50%
All pieces - expert musicians only - no cellist		
72.5%	87.5%	50%
All pieces - expert musicians + cellist (as violinist)		
80%	90%	70%
All pieces - expert and good musicians + cellist (as violinist)		
81.6%	**91.7%**	**75%**
All pieces - expert and good musicians + cellist (as pianist)		
59.9%	75%	50%
All pieces - expert, good, and basic musicians + cellist (as violinist)		
74.3%	85.7%	64.3%

were used only for testing the performance. This low decrease of performance indicates that the model is poorly affected by intra-subject correlation.

The performance of our model likely depends on other factors than motion artefacts, because these mostly affect only one of the involved features (the Delta) and were partially mitigated by the used filters. Thus, our model is indeed capturing distinctive information that exists in the brain signals recorder by the Fp1 EEG sensor.

4 Conclusions

In this paper, an automatic classifier of violinists and pianists has been presented, based on features extracted from EEG signals in the Fp1 cortex position. Existence of distinctive information, probably related to common patterns in the brain signal spectra of the players, has been identified especially in 20 s signal segments by a four-layer Artificial Neural Network. This model was built after testing a large parameters space through a cloud computing platform, which was able to overcome the use of a non-optimal equipment and the absence of neurophysiological *a priori* assumptions.

Our study is a preliminary investigation and enforcement of the very complex hypothesis that musicians' brain signals similarities depend on the played instrument and on musical expertise. The main drawback of our model is that it does not report explicit patterns, because it is not possible to extract an analytical form of the classification function associated to the ANN. Nevertheless, it reveals that distinctive information exists and should be further explored, e.g. with more powerful equipment or by embedding neurophysiological information in the model or by using deep-learning techniques. Also, our results suggest to investigate musicians' brain signals similarities in terms of their correlation with the way sound is produced [44]. For example, the highlighted similarity between the cellist and the violinists may be due to their constant interaction with a continuous sound, whereas pianists interact with digital-like sounds. This difference could be explored starting from the evaluation of how music reading and listening would change the performance of our classifier. Indeed, the effect of music on EEG activity has been already highlighted by other studies [53], some of which have also classified and categorized musicians based on their EEG response to music listening [31,46]. Our computational approach is suited for these further explorations especially because of its Open Science compliance, since it allows (i) repeating the experiment with a larger corpus, (ii) involving other musicians and instruments, and (iii) reusing the ANN model thanks to its publication a standardized Web service.

Acknowledgements. The authors wish to thank the Auditorium della Compagnia association for hosting the experiment, in particular Alessandro Lipari for the technical help, and the musicians for accepting their involvement in the experiment.

Compliance with Ethical Standards. The authors declare no conflict of interest. This research has been conducted in compliance with the Helsinki Declaration for Ethical Principles for Medical Research Involving Human Subjects, under the responsibility of the authors and of the Auditorium della Compagnia Montecastelli association. Consent was provided by the participants and, in the case of minors, by their parents who were present during the experiments. Since this is not a medical research and it is not an invasive experiment, we did not ask an official ethics committee to formally approve the experiment.

Supplementary Material

A sample of the collected corpus is downloadable through the D4Science e-Infrastructure at https://data.d4science.org/shub/E_dE9JVUw4Z1dFeWtIUG9xMnk0R09PVlNzU28rdnlvYTBEMDlnNkczNWlxdXRtNjA4YWl3b2RPZHNxdTlVN3BxZg==

The services used for this research are freely usable after registration on the D4Science cloud computing platform at the following links:

https://services.d4science.org/group/scalabledatamining/data-miner?OperatorId=org.gcube.dataanalysis.wps.statisticalmanager.synchserver.mappedclasses.transducerers.FEED_FORWARD_NEURAL_NETWORK_REGRESSOR

https://services.d4science.org/group/scalabledatamining/data-miner?OperatorId=org.gcube.dataanalysis.wps.statisticalmanager.synchserver.mappedclasses.transducerers.FEED_FORWARD_NEURAL_NETWORK_TRAINER

The source code is available at http://svn.research-infrastructures.eu/public/d4science/gcube/trunk/data-analysis/EcologicalEngine/src/main/java/org/gcube/dataanalysis/ecoengine/models/

References

1. 52North: The 52north WPS service (2016). http://52north.org/communities/geoprocessing/wps/
2. An, K.O., Kim, J.B., Song, W.K., Lee, I.H.: Development of an emergency call system using a brain computer interface (BCI). In: 2010 3rd IEEE RAS and EMBS International Conference on Biomedical Robotics and Biomechatronics (BioRob), pp. 918–923. IEEE (2010). https://doi.org/10.1109/BIOROB.2010.5626331
3. Auditorium della Compagnia: Auditorium della Compagnia Montecastelli - A project of Science and Music (2017). http://www.ilpoggiomontecastelli.com/en/
4. Baier, G., Hermann, T., Stephani, U.: Event-based sonification of eeg rhythms in real time. Clin. Neurophys. **118**(6), 1377–1386 (2007). https://doi.org/10.1016/j.clinph.2007.01.025
5. Bengio, Y., Boulanger-Lewandowski, N., Pascanu, R.: Advances in optimizing recurrent networks. In: 2013 IEEE International Conference on Acoustics, Speech and Signal Processing (ICASSP), pp. 8624–8628. IEEE (2013). https://doi.org/10.1109/ICASSP.2013.6639349
6. Bertrand, A., Mihajlovic, V., Grundlehner, B., Van Hoof, C., Moonen, M.: Motion artifact reduction in EEG recordings using multi-channel contact impedance measurements. In: 2013 IEEE Biomedical Circuits and Systems Conference (BioCAS), pp. 258–261. IEEE (2013). https://doi.org/10.1109/BioCAS.2013.6679688
7. Bigliassi, M., León-Domínguez, U., Altimari, L.R.: How does the prefrontal cortex "listen" to classical and techno music? A functional near-infrared spectroscopy (fNIRS) study. Psychol. Neurosci. **8**(2), 246 (2015). https://doi.org/10.1037/h0101064
8. Bishop, C.M.: Neural Networks for Pattern Recognition. Oxford University Press, Oxford (1995). ISBN 0198538642
9. Britton, J., et al.: Electroencephalography (EEG): an introductory text and atlas of normal and abnormal findings in adults, children, and infants. American Epilepsy Society (2016). ISBN 9780997975604
10. Candela, L., Castelli, D., Pagano, P.: D4Science: an e-infrastructure for supporting virtual research environments. In: IRCDL 2009 post-proceedings, pp. 166–169 (2009). ISBN 978-88-903541-7-5
11. Chen-Hafteck, L., Mang, E.: Music and language in early childhood development and learning. Music Learn. Teach. Infancy Child. Adolesc. Oxford Handb. Music Educ. **2**, 40 (2018). https://doi.org/10.1093/oxfordhb/9780199730810.013.0016
12. Coro, G.: Dataminer service for testing artificial neural networks in D4Science (2018). https://services.d4science.org/group/scalabledatamining/dataminer?OperatorId=org.gcube.dataanalysis.wps.statisticalmanager.synchserver.mappedclasses.transducerers.FEED_FORWARD_NEURAL_NETWORK_REGRESSOR
13. Coro, G.: Dataminer service for training artificial neural networks in D4Science (2018). https://services.d4science.org/group/scalabledatamining/dataminer?OperatorId=org.gcube.dataanalysis.wps.statisticalmanager.synchserver.mappedclasses.transducerers.FEED_FORWARD_NEURAL_NETWORK_TRAINER
14. Coro, G., Candela, L., Pagano, P., Italiano, A., Liccardo, L.: Parallelizing the execution of native data mining algorithms for computational biology. Concurr. Comput.: Pract. Exp. **27**(17), 4630–4644 (2015). https://doi.org/10.1002/cpe.3435

15. Coro, G., Panichi, G., Scarponi, P., Pagano, P.: Cloud computing in a distributed e-infrastructure using the web processing service standard. Concurr. Comput.: Pract. Exp **29**(18), e4219 (2017). https://doi.org/10.1002/cpe.4219
16. Coro, G., Vilas, L.G., Magliozzi, C., Ellenbroek, A., Scarponi, P., Pagano, P.: Forecasting the ongoing invasion of Lagocephalus sceleratus in the Mediterranean sea. Ecol. Modell. **371**, 37–49 (2018). https://doi.org/10.1016/j.ecolmodel.2018.01.007
17. Critchley, M., Henson, R.A.: Music and the Brain: Studies in the Neurology of Music. Butterworth-Heinemann, Oxford (2014). ISBN 9781483192796
18. Cutugno, F., Coro, G., Petrillo, M.: Multigranular scale speech recognizers: technological and cognitive view. In: Bandini, S., Manzoni, S. (eds.) AI*IA 2005. LNCS (LNAI), vol. 3673, pp. 327–330. Springer, Heidelberg (2005). https://doi.org/10.1007/11558590_33
19. Deuschl, G., Eisen, A.: Recommendations for the practice of clinical neurophysiology (guidelines of the international federation of clinical neurophysiology). Electroencephalography and Clinical Neurophysiology, Supplement (1999)
20. Elbert, T., Pantev, C., Wienbruch, C., Rockstroh, B., Taub, E.: Increased cortical representation of the fingers of the left hand in string players. Science **270**(5234), 305–307 (1995). https://doi.org/10.1126/science.270.5234.305
21. Fink, A., Benedek, M.: Eeg alpha power and creative ideation. Neurosci. Biobehav. Rev. **44**, 111–123 (2014). https://doi.org/10.1016/j.neubiorev.2012.12.002
22. Forcucci, L.: Music for brainwaves: embodiment of sound, space and EEG data. Body Space Technol. **17**(1) (2018). https://doi.org/10.16995/bst.297
23. Frisoli, A., Loconsole, C., Leonardis, D., Banno, F., Barsotti, M., Chisari, C., Bergamasco, M.: A new gaze-BCI-driven control of an upper limb exoskeleton for rehabilitation in real-world tasks. IEEE Trans. Syst. Man Cybern. Part C (Appl. Rev.) **42**(6), 1169–1179 (2012). https://doi.org/10.1109/TSMCC.2012.2226444
24. Gaser, C., Schlaug, G.: Brain structures differ between musicians and non-musicians. J. Neurosci. **23**(27), 9240–9245 (2003). https://doi.org/10.1523/JNEUROSCI.23-27-09240.2003
25. Genuth, I.: Brain computer interfaces bring neuroscience to the masses (2015). https://eandt.theiet.org/content/articles/2015/05/brain-computer-interfaces-bring-neuroscience-to-the-masses/
26. Herrmann, C.S., Strüber, D., Helfrich, R.F., Engel, A.K.: EEG oscillations: from correlation to causality. Int. J. Psychophys. **103**, 12–21 (2016). https://doi.org/10.1016/j.ijpsycho.2015.02.003
27. Hirata, Y., Hirata, Y.: Application of EEG in technology-enhanced language learning environments. In: Enhancing Learning Through Technology: Research on Emerging Technologies and Pedagogies, p. 115 (2008). https://doi.org/10.1142/97898127994560008
28. Homan, R.W., Herman, J., Purdy, P.: Cerebral location of international 10–20 system electrode placement. Electroencephal. Clin. Neurophys. **66**(4), 376–382 (1987). https://doi.org/10.1016/0013-4694(87)90206-9
29. Langheim, F.J., Callicott, J.H., Mattay, V.S., Duyn, J.H., Weinberger, D.R.: Cortical systems associated with covert music rehearsal. Neuroimage **16**(4), 901–908 (2002). https://doi.org/10.1006/nimg.2002.1144
30. Lebo, T., et al.: PROV-O: the PROV ontology. W3C Recommendation (2013). http://www.w3.org/TR/prov-o/
31. Liang, S.F., Hsieh, T.H., Chen, W.H., Lin, K.J.: Classification of EEG signals from musicians and non-musicians by neural networks. In: 2011 9th World Congress on Intelligent Control and Automation, pp. 865–869. IEEE (2011)

32. Lin, C.J., Ding, C.H., Liu, C.C., Liu, Y.L.: Development of a real-time drowsiness warning system based on an embedded system. In: 2015 International Conference on Advanced Robotics and Intelligent Systems (ARIS), pp. 1–4. IEEE (2015). https://doi.org/10.1109/ARIS.2015.7158365
33. Mansouri, F.A., Acevedo, N., Illipparampil, R., Fehring, D.J., Fitzgerald, P.B., Jaberzadeh, S.: Interactive effects of music and prefrontal cortex stimulation in modulating response inhibition. Sci. Rep. **7**(1), 18096 (2017). https://doi.org/10.1038/s41598-017-18119-x
34. Miranda, E.R.: Brain-computer music interface for composition and performance. Int. J. Disabil. Hum. Dev. **5**(2), 119 (2006). https://doi.org/10.1515/IJDHD.2006.5.2.119
35. National Research Council of Italy: The D4Science online workspace (2016). https://wiki.gcube-system.org/gcube/Workspace
36. Navalyal, G.U., Gavas, R.D.: A dynamic attention assessment and enhancement tool using computer graphics. Hum. Cent. Comput. Inform. Sci. **4**(1), 11 (2014). https://doi.org/10.1186/s13673-014-0011-0
37. NeuroSky: Ultimate guide to EEG (2017). http://neurosky.com/biosensors/eeg-sensor/ultimate-guide-to-eeg/
38. Nguyen, T., Chuang, C.l., Lee, K.H., Jin, L.J.: Conductive eartip assembly. US Patent US20090112077A1 (2004)
39. Oechslin, M.S., Imfeld, A., Loenneker, T., Meyer, M., Jäncke, L.: The plasticity of the superior longitudinal fasciculus as a function of musical expertise: a diffusion tensor imaging study. Front. Hum. Neurosci. **3**, 76 (2010). https://doi.org/10.3389/neuro.09.076.2009
40. O'Hare, D.: Biosensors and sensor systems. In: Yang, G.-Z. (ed.) Body Sensor Networks, pp. 55–115. Springer, London (2014). https://doi.org/10.1007/978-1-4471-6374-9_2
41. Paraskevopoulos, E., Kraneburg, A., Herholz, S.C., Bamidis, P.D., Pantev, C.: Musical expertise is related to altered functional connectivity during audiovisual integration. Proc. Natl. Acad. Sci. **112**(40), 12522–12527 (2015). https://doi.org/10.1073/pnas.1510662112
42. Patki, S., et al.: Wireless EEG system with real time impedance monitoring and active electrodes. In: 2012 IEEE Biomedical Circuits and Systems Conference (BioCAS), pp. 108–111. IEEE (2012). https://doi.org/10.1109/BioCAS.2012.6418408
43. Peretz, I., Zatorre, R.J.: Brain organization for music processing. Annu. Rev. Psychol. **56**, 89–114 (2005). https://doi.org/10.1146/annurev.psych.56.091103.070225
44. Petsche, H., von Stein, A., Filz, O.: Eeg aspects of mentally playing an instrument. Cogn. Brain Res. **3**(2), 115–123 (1996). https://doi.org/10.1016/0926-6410(95)00036-4
45. Potard, G., Schiemer, G.: Listening to the mind listening: sonification of the coherence matrix and power spectrum of EEG signals. In: ICAD Post-Proceedings, pp. 1–4 (2004). ISBN: 1-74108-048-7
46. Ribeiro, E., Thomaz, C.E.: A multivariate statistical analysis of EEG signals for differentiation of musicians and non-musicians. In: Anais do XV Encontro Nacional de Inteligência Artificial e Computacional, pp. 497–505. SBC (2018). https://doi.org/10.5753/eniac.2018.4442
47. Rumelhart, D.E., Hinton, G.E., Williams, R.J., et al.: Learning representations by back-propagating errors. Nature **323**(6088), 533–536 (1986). https://doi.org/10.1038/323533a0

48. Schlaug, G., Norton, A., Overy, K., Winner, E.: Effects of music training on the child's brain and cognitive development. Ann. New York Acad. Sci. **1060**(1), 219–230 (2005). https://doi.org/10.1196/annals.1360.015
49. Schmidhuber, J.: Deep learning in neural networks: an overview. Neural Netw. **61**, 85–117 (2015). https://doi.org/10.1016/j.neunet.2014.09.003
50. Smith, K.: Reading minds. Nature **502**(7472), 428 (2013). https://doi.org/10.1038/502428a
51. Stewart, L., Henson, R., Kampe, K., Walsh, V., Turner, R., Frith, U.: Brain changes after learning to read and play music. Neuroimage **20**(1), 71–83 (2003). https://doi.org/10.1016/S1053-8119(03)00248-9
52. Subhani, A.R., Kamel, N., Saad, M.N.M., Nandagopal, N., Kang, K., Malik, A.S.: Mitigation of stress: new treatment alternatives. Cogn. Neurodyn. **12**(1), 1–20 (2018). https://doi.org/10.1007/s11571-017-9460-2
53. Sun, C., et al.: The effects of different types of music on electroencephalogram. In: 2013 IEEE International Conference on Bioinformatics and Biomedicine, pp. 31–37. IEEE (2013). https://doi.org/10.1109/WCICA.2011.5970639
54. Trevisan, A.A., Jones, L.: Brain music system: brain music therapy based on real-time sonified brain signals. In: Proceedings of the IET Seminar on Assisted Living, pp. 1–8 (2011). https://doi.org/10.1016/j.neulet.2011.05.159
55. Vaquero, L., et al.: Structural neuroplasticity in expert pianists depends on the age of musical training onset. Neuroimage **126**, 106–119 (2016). https://doi.org/10.1016/j.neuroimage.2015.11.008
56. Wang, A., Andreas Larsen, E.: Using brain-computer interfaces in an interactive multimedia application. In: Proceedings of the IASTED International Conference on Software Engineering and Applications, SEA 2012 (2012).(2012). https://doi.org/10.2316/P.2012.790-046
57. Wolpaw, J.R., Birbaumer, N., McFarland, D.J., Pfurtscheller, G., Vaughan, T.M.: Brain-computer interfaces for communication and control. Clin. Neurophys. **113**(6), 767–791 (2002). https://doi.org/10.1016/S1388-24570200057-3
58. Zatorre, R.J., Chen, J.L., Penhune, V.B.: When the brain plays music: auditory-motor interactions in music perception and production. Nat. Rev. Neurosci. **8**(7), 547–558 (2007). https://doi.org/10.1038/nrn2152

Capsule Networks

Research on Image-to-Image Translation with Capsule Network

Jian Ye, Qing Chang(✉), and Xiaotian Jia

School of Information Science and Engineering, East China University of Science and Technology, Shanghai 200030, China
changqing@ecust.edu.cn

Abstract. Deep learning technologies provide a unified translation framework for image-to-image translation. In particular, Convolution Neural Network (CNN) plays a decisive role because of its remarkable flexibility and performance. Recently, a new architecture called Capsule Network (CapsNet) was proposed to improve CNN. Capsule Network is able to preserve more input's information, especially location information by it's unique capsule structure and dynamic routing algorithm. In this paper, we propose Capsule conditional Generative Adversarial Network (CapscGAN) for performing image-to-image translation tasks. The proposed model utilizes CapsNet to encode image into one capsule called PixelCapsule and combines it with Markovian discriminator (PatchGAN) as discriminator. For suiting to translation tasks, we modify CapsNet's structure and activation function. Through a series of experiments, we analyze effect of CapsNet's activation function, dimension and application in discriminator. Multiple datasets' results demonstrate that our model has higher translation quality than convolutional image translation framework.

Keywords: Capsule Network · Conditional Generative Adversarial Network · Image-to-image translation

1 Introduction

In the field of computer vision and image processing, numerous tasks can be formalized as image-to-image translation tasks, such as image colorization [1], image synthesis [10] and super-resolution [2]. These tasks try to "translate" the input image into another domain without changing inherent information. Traditionally, different kinds of tasks are solved by corresponding specific models or methods whereas this makes it inefficient to complete multiple different tasks. Therefore, it is necessary to develop a general framework for these tasks. Recently, Pix2Pix [5] which uses conditional Generative Adversarial Networks (cGAN) [15] to generate different styles of images tackled this problem. By utilizing ability of adversarial network to learn loss function, Pix2Pix is capable of obtaining appropriate loss function and minimize it, automatically.

I. V. Tetko et al. (Eds.): ICANN 2019, LNCS 11727, pp. 141–151, 2019.
https://doi.org/10.1007/978-3-030-30487-4_12

Convolution Neural Network (CNN) [13] has been the most popular framework in computer vision tasks, due to its remarkable flexibility and performance. However, it does not take into account the spatial hierarchy and rotation invariance between features [17,19]. People usually make up for these two shortcomings by deepening network structure or using data enhancement techniques, but these make computation more intensive. For attempting to overcome limits and drawbacks of CNN, Sabour et al. [17] introduces the idea of Capsule Network (CapsNet), where information at neuron level is stored as vectors, rather than scalars. In CapsNet, capsule is made up of several neurons and the active one's neurons represent particular entity's various properties. Via dynamic routing algorithm which is aimed at taking place of backpropagation, capsule is "routing" to another form of capsule in next layer, thus forming a meaningful part to the overall relationship.

In this paper, we propose Capsule conditional Generative Adversarial Network (CapscGAN) for performing image-to-image translation task. Different from convolutional encoder, we encode image into one capsule called PixelCapsule and use "U-net" structure [16] for passing low-level information from input to output in generator. Inspired by [6], we combine CapsNet with Markovian discriminator (PatchGAN) to produce a discriminative capsule in discriminator. We modify CapsNet's activation function and capsule parameters to suit our goal. We analyze influence of CapNet's different form on Cityscapes in 256×256 resolution and experiment on multiple datasets.

2 Related Work

Conditional Generation Adversarial Network adds conditional extensions to the conditional model based on Generation Adversarial Network (GAN). The generator and discriminator are applicable to additional conditions which are added to input layer to guide data generation process. cGAN has been applied and extended in multiple fields, especially in computer vision. It learns a structured loss that penalizes joint configuration of the output. This makes it suitable for different tasks and datasets. Lots of methods use GAN in computer vision unconditionally with traditional loss to associate input and output conditionally. In [3,11,14], cGAN has been applied to work on specific tasks. Isola et al. [5] uses cGAN with a regression loss forming a unified image translation framework. Michel et al. [14] combines encoder with cGAN to enhance mapping ability and re-generate real images with deterministic complex modifications.

CapsNet uses activity vector's length and orientation to represent probability of entity existence and instantiation parameters, respectively. It adopts iterative routing-by-agreement mechanism to improve network's performance [17]. A typical CapsNet is composed of convolutional layers, PrimaryCapsule and DigitCapsule layers. Convolutional layers extract the input's information and takes it as PrimaryCapsule layer's input. PrimaryCapsule and DigitCapsule layers contact by dynamic routing. CapsNet's outputs are computed by the squashing function:

$$v_j = \frac{||s_j^2||}{1 + ||s_j^2||} \frac{s_j}{||s_j||} \tag{1}$$

where v_j is the capsule j's output and s_j is its input. The squashing function compresses input vector's length between zero and one while preserving input vector's direction. The input vector can be divided into two phases:

$$s_j = \sum_j c_{ij} \hat{u}_{j|i} \qquad \hat{u}_{j|i} = \mathbf{W_{ij}} u_i \tag{2}$$

where $\hat{u}_{j|i}$ is obtained by multiplying lower layer's output capsule u_j and weight matrix $\mathbf{W_{ij}}$ which represents prediction vector's weighted sum in higher layers. c_{ij} is coupling coefficient in process of dynamic routing. It is decided by two coupled capsule's prior probabilities b_{ij}, b_{ik}:

$$c_{ij} = \frac{\exp(b_{ij})}{\sum_k \exp(b_{ik})} \tag{3}$$

Since CapsNet is a novel deep learning architecture, only a few researches have applied and explored it. A generative version of the capsule has been proposed in [4], named variational capsule. Each variational capsule produces a latent variable for a specific entity, making it possible to integrate image analysis and image synthesis into a unified framework. LaLonde et al. [8] expands CapsNet in several significant way, and proposes convolutional-deconvolutional capsule network for object segmentation. This network shows promising accuracy in pathological lung segmentation from CT scans. Generative Adversarial Capsule Network (CapsuleGAN) [6] uses CapsNet as discriminator that output just contains one capsule and performs better than convolutional GAN in image modeling on CIFAR-10 and MNIST datasets.

Our work is based on Pix2Pix framework. Inspired by the idea of [14,19], we enhance translation ability by using capsule rather than scalar to represent a specific entity. We use CapsuleGAN's strategy in our model's discriminator. In order to achieve satisfactory translation quality, we have made a series of changes in CapsNet.

3 Method

We introduce Capsule conditional Generative Adversarial Network in this section. Its translation model is composed of CapsNet encoder and deep convolutional decoder with "U-net". The discriminator consists of PatchGAN and CapsNet. Although the use of encoder-decoder in GAN framework is common, we are the first to use one capsule as encoder's result for image-to-image translation.

3.1 The Modification and Application of CapsNet in Generator

Encoder-decoder network is a common framework in the field of image processing. For the generator of proposed model, we use such network as a benchmark.

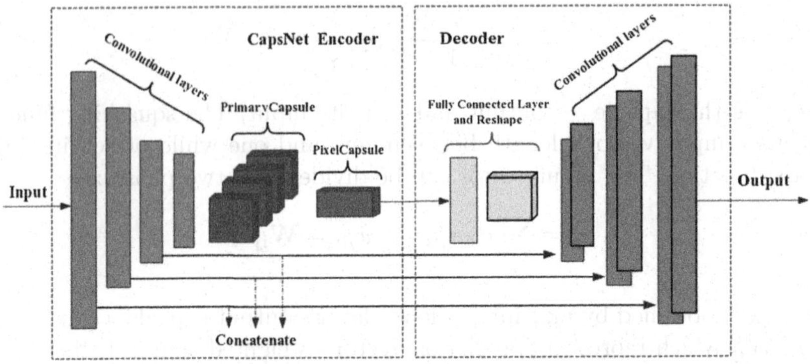

Fig. 1. Architecture of our model's generator.

Because of the capsule nature that information is contained in the vector, CapsNet is used as the encoder to save spatial orientation and other attributes of the extracted feature. This operation enables the encoder to obtain richer and more representative entity information than deep CNN. But it reduces the ability of encoder to capture input's low-level information, which has adverse effects on the results. To solve this problem, we use a method similar to [5], which adds skip connections between convolution layers of encoder and decoder to share low-level information. The generator model is diagrammed in Fig. 1.

For the generator, because the task and input size are different from original CapsNet which input size is less than 32×32, there are three main differences:

1. We use multiple convolution layers with small kernel size instead of convolution layers with large kernel in CapsNet. This enables us to store image information which is prepared for skipping connections at different depths and getting much latent information.
2. The capsule's number and dimension in PrimaryCapsule and DigitCapsule layers are modified. Especially, in DigitCapsule layer, the output has only one capsule that contains input latent information. In the meantime, it also keeps parameter's number low and reduces computation. We renamed it PixelCapsule layer on account of its special function in our model. We discuss the effect with different PixelCapsule's dimensions on experimental results (Sect. 4.5).
3. Since the number of output capsule is one, it represents entire entity of the input. In this situation, the squashing function change ratio of entity's information and this makes the translation model fail. We choose Leaky ReLU as the activation function in routing part. This change maintains the entity's inherent information while routing. In experiments, we compare the results with different activation functions (Sect. 4.4).

3.2 CapsNet in Discriminator

In image generation problems, L1 and L2 loss produce blurry results [9], because they're more focused on the low frequencies of image. To address this question, Pix2Pix uses PatchGAN that penalizes structure at patch scale and tries to determine the authenticity of image's each patch. But this operation reduces the integrity of image.

Inspired by [6], we add a CapsNet after PatchGAN and use combination of the two as our model's discriminator. The discriminator focuses on the local image patches first, and then take them as a whole to CapsNet. In our model, PatchGAN is used to get high-level information about each patch of image and classify it. Then CapsNet identifies the input's authenticity by this information. The CapsNet in discriminator is modified in the same way as the one in generator. Discriminator model is shown in Fig. 2. We analyze the role of CapsNet in discriminator in Sect. 4.6.

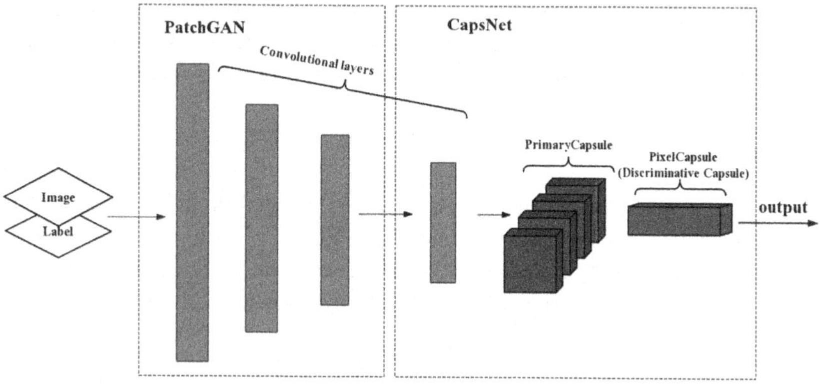

Fig. 2. Discriminator's architecture made up of PatchGAN and CapsNet.

3.3 Objective

Following [1], the loss function of Conditional GAN is given by the equation:

$$\mathcal{L}_{cGAN}(G, D) = \mathbb{E}_{x,y}[\log D(x, y)] + \mathbb{E}_{x,z}[\log 1 - D(x, G(x, z))] \tag{4}$$

where x is input, y is correct label and z is output. And L1 loss is added to this loss function for encouraging less burring. L1 loss is given by:

$$\mathcal{L}_{L1}(G) = \mathbb{E}_{x,y,z}[||y - G(x, z)||_1] \tag{5}$$

Thus, Eq. 6 is the final object. Discriminator D aims to maximize this object and adversarial G tries to minimize it. Both G and D are optimized by it.

$$G^* = \arg\min_{\mathrm{G}}\max_{\mathrm{D}}\mathcal{L}_{\mathrm{cGAN}}(\mathrm{G}, \mathrm{D}) + \lambda\mathcal{L}_{\mathrm{L1}} \tag{6}$$

where λ is the regularization constant, used to adjust the role of L1 loss.

4 Experiment

4.1 Network Architecture and Training Details

Our model is compared with Pix2Pix in multiple datasets. In order to ensure effectiveness of experiment, we keep the setting and parameters of our model same with Pix2Pix except CapsNet and fully connected layer.

For the CapsNet encoder, it has four stride-2 convolutions of 64, 64, 128, 256 channels. PrimaryCapsule layer has $32 \times 32 \times 4$ capsule outputs (each output is a 64D vector) and PixelCapsule layer has one capsule of 256 dimensions. In Decoder, fully connected layer's size is 2048. Then, its output is reshaped to $4 \times 4 \times 128$. CapsNet in discriminator has one stride-2 convolution of 128 channels. And PrimaryCapsule layer's output shape is $16 \times 16 \times 8 \times 4$. The dimension of PixelCapsule layer's capsule is 512. All convolutions have 4×4 kernels and Leaky ReLU activation function.

As suggested in original GAN paper, we train to maximize $logD(x, G(x, z))$ ranter than training G to minimize $log(1 - D(x, G(x, z)))$. We set batch size to one, $\lambda = 100$, epochs = 200 and dynamic routing iterations = 3 in all experiments. And we use Adam [7] to optimize network. Learning rate is 0.0002.

4.2 Datasets

To demonstrate and assess our proposed model's capability, we first do experiment on the Cityscapes dateset. Analysis of model's form and the activation function are based on it. In addition to this, we select Map↔Aerial task and Facades↔Labels task from [20]. We compare our model and Pix2Pix from different perspectives in these tasks.

4.3 Evaluation Metrics

Segmentation Score and FCN Score. We use FCN score [5] as evaluation metrics for Labels→ Photo task on Cityscapes dataset. FCN Score assesses the translation ability of the network by using a ready-made FCN Segmentation network. Segmentation Score is used in corresponding Photo→Labels task. It has three segmentation metrics(i.e., per-pixel accuracy, per-class accuracy, mean class accuracy) defined in [12] to evaluate the classification quality of results.

PSNR and SSIM. Instead of FCN Score and Segmentaion Score, PSNR and SSIM [18] are also calculated as quantitative evaluation to measure similarity of color and structural between the generated image and ground truth. We apply these metrics on the Map↔Aerial task and Facades↔Labels task.

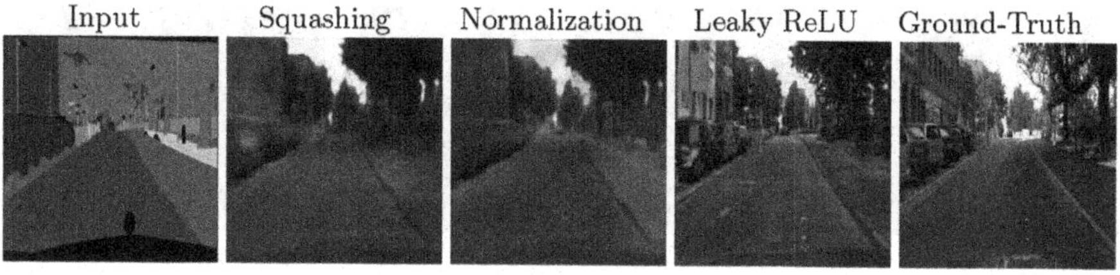

Fig. 3. Different activation functions' results in CapscGAN.

Table 1. Labels→Photo task's FCN Score on the Cityscapes with different dimension. The number in method's name represents dimension of generator's PixelCapsule.

Method	Pixel acc.	Class acc.	Class IoU.
CapscGAN-256	**0.79**	**0.25**	**0.20**
CapscGAN-384	0.62	0.23	0.19
CapscGAN-512	0.66	0.22	0.17
CapscGAN-1024	0.56	0.18	0.14

4.4 Analysis of the Activation Function

The activation function used in the dynamic routing algorithm compresses and normalizes the input. Thus, active capsule representing the entity can be found. But such an operation does not meet our goals. Our model has only one output capsule. The activation function should only filter the image information or extract advanced features through the dynamic routing algorithm, and do not change their distribution ratio. We use Squashing, Normalization ($f(x) = \frac{x}{||x||}$) and Leaky ReLU as activation function for experiments, respectively.

Figure 3 shows results of different activation functions. Squashing function and normalization function do not work in our model. Leaky ReLU has the best effect in our experiments. Note that it is not necessarily the most suitable. We believe that other functions which do not change state of information distribution are likely to achieve better results.

4.5 Effect of PixelCapsule's Dimension

For our model, capsule's dimension in PixelCapsule layer determines capacity of encoding information. We do a series of experiments on this. As shown in the Table 1, in our experiments, the model with 256 dimensions is the most suitable one. And the model with longer dimension make translation quality worse. In particular, we find some special case in the 1024 dimension experiment that "red" color appears too often. CapscGAN-1024's partial results are shown in Fig. 4. The framed cars in figure are a bit red and it means that the capsule contain extra special information. Thus, generalization ability of translation has reduced.

Fig. 4. Examples of CapcGAN-1024 in Labels→Photo task. (Color figure online)

Fig. 5. Result of PatchGAN and PatchGAN with CapsNet in Labels→Photo task.

4.6 Role of CapsNet in Discriminator

Translation ability has been promoted to some extent on account of CapsNet's use in generator. We have explored the role of CapsNet in discriminator. Figure 5 shows examples of PatchGAN and PatchGAN with CapsNet. We can see that PatchGAN do not well in such generator. PatchGAN fail to adapt the change in generator's translation capability and could only translate simple figure outline. But CapsNet used in discriminator and generator makes the two more compatible.

4.7 Comparisons

Labels↔Photo. Table 2 shows the comparison of CapscGAN-256 and Pix2Pix on Segmentation score and FCN score in the Cityscapes Labels↔Photo tasks. Due to the use of CapsNet, our model has significantly improved over Pix2Pix in FCN scores' all metrics. And for Segmentation score, our model improves slightly on both pixel accuracy and class accuracy.

Map↔Aerial and Facades↔Labels. As shown in Table 3, our model is superior to Pix2Pix in PSNR and SSIM metrics. This indicates that our translation results are closer to ground truth in terms of color parts and overall structure. Figure 6 compares our model and Pix2Pix's results in these tasks. Our model shows better performance in some details.

Table 2. Segmentation scores of Photo→Labels task and FCN scores of Labels→Photo task on Cityscapse dataset.

Method	Photo↔Labels			Labels↔Photo		
	Pixel acc.	Class acc.	Class IoU.	Pixel acc.	Class acc.	Class IoU.
Pix2Pix	0.80	0.32	0.27	0.72	0.24	0.18
CapscGAN-256	**0.82**	**0.33**	0.27	**0.79**	**0.25**	**0.20**
Ground truth	0.94	0.83	0.66	0.80	0.26	0.21

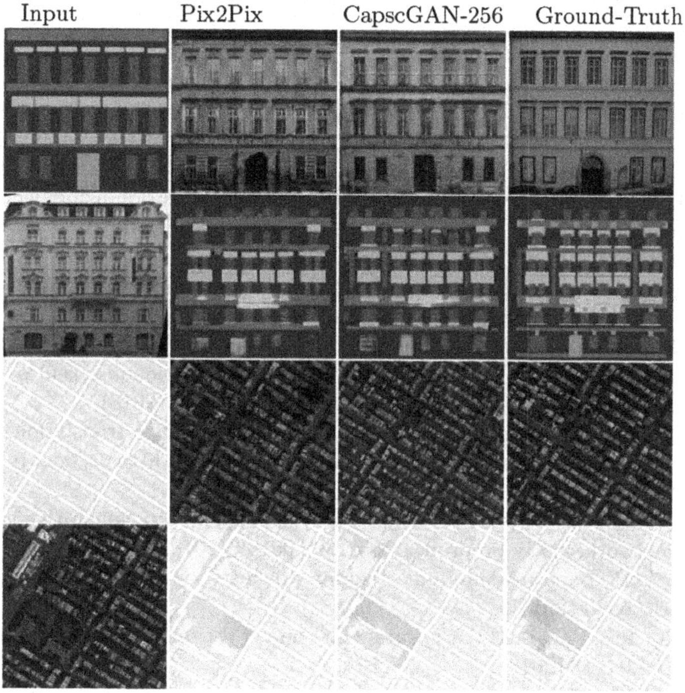

Fig. 6. Translation results in the Labels↔Facades task and Aerial↔Map task on Pix2Pix and CapscGAN-256.

Table 3. Values of PSNR and SSIM in the Aerial↔Map and Facades↔Labels task.

Method	Aerial → Map		Map → Aerial		Facades → Labels		Labels → Facades	
	PSNR	SSIM	PSNR	SSIM	PSNR	SSIM	PSNR	SSIM
Pix2Pix	26.10	0.67	15.30	0.22	10.76	0.43	12.60	0.25
CapcGAN-256	**26.61**	**0.70**	**15.82**	**0.24**	**10.94**	**0.45**	**13.04**	**0.26**

5 Conclusion

In this paper, we propose Capsule conditional Generation Adversarial Network to build a general framework for image to image translation. The Capsule conditional Generation Adversarial Network exploit CapsNet to encode images as capsules. By combing PatchGAN and CapsNet, the corresponding capabilities of the discriminator and generator are adaptive to each other. We modify part of CapsNet's structure and analyze the impact of these changes through experiments. A series of experiments on multiple datasets show that the images produced by our model are more precise and our model has higher translation ability than convolutional image translation framework.

References

1. AbdulHalim, M.F., Mejbil, Z.A.: Automatic colorization without human intervention. In: 2008 International Conference on Computer and Communication Engineering, pp. 62–65. IEEE (2008). https://doi.org/10.1109/ICCCE.2008.4580569
2. Dong, C., Loy, C.C., He, K., Tang, X.: Image super-resolution using deep convolutional networks. IEEE Trans. Pattern Anal. Mach. Intell. **38**(2), 295–307 (2016). https://doi.org/10.1109/TPAMI.2015.2439281
3. Gauthier, J.: Conditional generative adversarial nets for convolutional face generation. Class Project for Stanford CS231N: Convolutional Neural Networks for Visual Recognition, Winter semester 2014(5), 2 (2014)
4. Huang, H., Song, L., He, R., Sun, Z., Tan, T.: Variational capsules for image analysis and synthesis. arXiv preprint arXiv:1807.04099 (2018)
5. Isola, P., Zhu, J.Y., Zhou, T., Efros, A.A.: Image-to-image translation with conditional adversarial networks. arXiv preprint (2017). https://doi.org/10.1109/CVPR.2017.632
6. Jaiswal, A., AbdAlmageed, W., Natarajan, P.: Capsulegan: generative adversarial capsule network. arXiv preprint arXiv:1802.06167 (2018)
7. Kingma, D.P., Ba, J.: Adam: a method for stochastic optimization. arXiv preprint arXiv:1412.6980 (2014)
8. LaLonde, R., Bagci, U.: Capsules for object segmentation. arXiv preprint arXiv:1804.04241 (2018)
9. Larsen, A.B.L., Sønderby, S.K., Larochelle, H., Winther, O.: Autoencoding beyond pixels using a learned similarity metric. arXiv preprint arXiv:1512.09300 (2015)
10. Li, C., Wand, M.: Combining markov random fields and convolutional neural networks for image synthesis. In: Proceedings of the IEEE Conference on Computer Vision and Pattern Recognition, pp. 2479–2486 (2016). https://doi.org/10.1109/CVPR.2016.272
11. Li, C., Wand, M.: Precomputed real-time texture synthesis with Markovian generative adversarial networks. In: Leibe, B., Matas, J., Sebe, N., Welling, M. (eds.) ECCV 2016. LNCS, vol. 9907, pp. 702–716. Springer, Cham (2016). https://doi.org/10.1007/978-3-319-46487-9_43
12. Long, J., Shelhamer, E., Darrell, T.: Fully convolutional networks for semantic segmentation. In: Proceedings of the IEEE Conference on Computer Vision and Pattern Recognition, pp. 3431–3440 (2015). https://doi.org/10.1109/CVPR.2015.7298965

13. Makantasis, K., Karantzalos, K., Doulamis, A., Doulamis, N.: Deep supervised learning for hyperspectral data classification through convolutional neural networks. In: 2015 IEEE International Geoscience and Remote Sensing Symposium (IGARSS), pp. 4959–4962. IEEE (2015). https://doi.org/10.1109/IGARSS.2015.7326945
14. Michelsanti, D., Tan, Z.H.: Conditional generative adversarial networks for speech enhancement and noise-robust speaker verification. arXiv preprint arXiv:1709.01703 (2017)
15. Mirza, M., Osindero, S.: Conditional generative adversarial nets. arXiv preprint arXiv:1411.1784 (2014)
16. Ronneberger, O., Fischer, P., Brox, T.: U-Net: convolutional networks for biomedical image segmentation. In: Navab, N., Hornegger, J., Wells, W.M., Frangi, A.F. (eds.) MICCAI 2015. LNCS, vol. 9351, pp. 234–241. Springer, Cham (2015). https://doi.org/10.1007/978-3-319-24574-4_28
17. Sabour, S., Frosst, N., Hinton, G.E.: Dynamic routing between capsules. In: Advances in Neural Information Processing Systems, pp. 3856–3866 (2017). http://papers.nips.cc/paper/6975-dynamic-routing-between-capsules
18. Wang, Z., Bovik, A.C., Sheikh, H.R., Simoncelli, E.P., et al.: Image quality assessment: from error visibility to structural similarity. IEEE Trans. Image Process. **13**(4), 600–612 (2004). https://doi.org/10.1109/TIP.2003.819861
19. Xi, E., Bing, S., Jin, Y.: Capsule network performance on complex data. arXiv preprint arXiv:1712.03480 (2017)
20. Zhu, J.Y., Park, T., Isola, P., Efros, A.A.: Unpaired image-to-image translation using cycle-consistent adversarial networks, pp. 2242–2251 (2017). https://doi.org/10.1109/ICCV.2017.244

Multi-View Capsule Network

Jian-wei Liu[1(✉)], Xi-hao Ding[1], Run-kun Lu[1], Yuan-feng Lian[2], Dian-zhong Wang[3], and Xiong-lin Luo[1]

[1] Department of Automation, China University of Petroleum, Beijing Campus (CUP), Beijing, China
{liujw,luoxl}@cup.edu.cn, 964465871@qq.com, 983194327@qq.com

[2] Department of Computer, China University of Petroleum, Beijing Campus (CUP), Beijing, China
lianyuanfeng@cup.edu.cn

[3] Beijing Institute of Space Mechanics and Electricity, Beijing, China
wangdz_bisme@spacechina.com

Abstract. Multi-view learning attempts to generate a model with a better performance by exploiting information among multi-view data. Most existing approaches only focus on either consistency or complementarity principle, and learn representations (or features) of the multi-view data. In this paper, to utilize both complementarity and consistency simultaneously, and explore the potential of deep learning in multi-view learning, we propose a novel supervised multi-view learning algorithm, called multi-view capsule network (MVCapsNet), which extracts a feature matrix of all views by a group of encoders, and obtains a classification matrix fusing common and special information of multiple views. Extensive experiments conducted on eight real-world datasets have demonstrated the effectiveness of our proposed method, and show its superiority over several state-of-the-art baseline methods.

Keywords: CapsNet · Multi-view learning · Complementarity and consistency · Representation learning

1 Introduction

In the real world, multi-view data and its applications are widespread, such as web pages [1], multi-lingual news [2], and neuroimaging [3]. Aiming to make good use of the information from multi-view data and improve the generalization performance [4–7]. And until now, nearly all relevant literatures of multi-view learning assume that consistency and complementarity, which separately represents the common and specific information of multiple views, are two main underlying properties of the multi-view data. What's more, researchers mainly exploit either the consistency or the complementary principle to ensure the efficiency of multi-view learning. However, many advanced multi-view learning algorithms has two common limitations: (1) only focus on consistency or complementarity to improve the performance of learning tasks [8, 9], and do not consider how to fusion the consistency and complementarity characteristics, simultaneously; (2) bases on non-negative matrix factorization (NMF),

I. V. Tetko et al. (Eds.): ICANN 2019, LNCS 11727, pp. 152–165, 2019.
https://doi.org/10.1007/978-3-030-30487-4_13

which is a linear latent factor model, and couldn't find the multi-level abstraction representation of hierarchical non-linear features.

On the one hand, although only consistency or complementarity of multi-view data can be utilized to improve the performance of learning tasks [9–12], both complementarity and consistency of multiple views are meaningful, and the neglect of each aspect will result in the loss of valuable information. In addition, several algorithms also have been proposed to take into account consistency and complementarity at the same time, such as [13, 14], they find latent representations composed of common latent factors shared by multiple views and the specific latent factor of each view. However, they also have a common constraint that the optimization algorithm requires to feed all data in one time, which limits the ability of this algorithm when dealing with large scale data.

On the other hand, most existing multi-view learning algorithms are based on NMF [9, 14, 15], which is an effective latent factor learning method and the nonnegative constraint leads to the parts-based representation of objects [16]. However, the representation learned by NMF also has some inherent weaknesses, such as: (1) numbers of learned subspace dimension are arbitrarily presented, and has less to do with real underlying properties of dataset; (2) it only learn a linear map relationships, thus can't reflect the non-linear relationship in the dataset. this linear assumption is apparently too harsh to be verified, the ground-truth low dimensional structure is very likely to be non-linear.

Motivated by the aforementioned discussion, our objective in this paper is propose a network, which can utilize both consistency and complementarity information of multi-view data to improve the performance of learning tasks, finds out the non-linear mapping relationship and capture real underlying properties of dataset.

Capsule net is a new network proposed by [17], it performs better than the state-of-the-art methods for digit recognition on MNIST dataset by the dynamic routing mechanism between capsules. A capsule represents a set of properties for a particular entity, and routing mechanism aims to implicitly learn global coherence by enforcing part-whole relationships to be learned. For the good performance of capsule net achieved in digit recognition on MNIST dataset, capsule layers show the strong ability of integrating common and special information among feature maps produced by multi-convolution layer.

Therefore, we develop a nonlinear supervised multi-view deep learning algorithm, termed multi-view capsule network (MVCapsNet), which jointly learning the consistency and complementarity information for multi-view data, and finds out the non-linear relationship and real underlying properties of dataset. In detail, multiple views' encoders consider the consistency properties of dataset, the linear mapping in routing process considers the complementarity properties. First, we use encoders to nonlinearly extract feature vectors from multi-view data, and vertically stack feature vectors to combine them into a feature matrix for PrimaryCaps layer, which makes sure each input of primary capsule contains consistency information from different views. Second, we explore the specific features by dynamic routing strategies between PrimaryCaps layer and TargetCaps layer. Finally, experimental results on eight real-world data sets verify the effectiveness of our proposed method.

In addition, there are two different points between MVCapsNet and Capsule Net. First, MVCapsNet use encoders to extract feature vectors from multi-view data, and vertically stack feature vectors to product a feature matrix, while Capsule Net uses convolutional layers to extract feature maps, and product a feature matrix through reshaping all feature maps. Second, considering that reconstructing multi-view data is not necessary in our research, we discard the reconstruction loss in Capsule Net, and just preserve margin loss.

To our best knowledge, this work represents the first attempt to extend capsule net to multi-view learning scenarios. As a result, our contributions we summarize are shown as follows:

(1) different from concatenation, MVCapsNet vertically stack feature vectors extracted by encoders to product a feature matrix, which capture the non-linear relationship and real underlying properties in multi-view dataset;
(2) MVCapsNet is a supervised multi-view deep learning algorithm utilizing both consistency and complementarity of multiple views by capsule layers and dynamic routing mechanism, where multiple views' encoders consider the consistency, and the linear mapping of routing process considers the complementarity;
(3) the mini-batch method can be used to train the model parameters of MVCapsNet, thus unlike traditional multi-view learning methods that based on matrix factorization, MVCapsNet can be applied to large scale data sets;
(4) MVCapsNet avoids the slowly training process because that the number of views is always limited in a small range, and comparing with traditional Capsule Net, the number of parameters in routing process decreased from 10^6 to 10^4.
(5) we also build other baselines deep networks to further analyze MVCapsNet's performance, which explore complementary by mean-pooling, max-pooling and weighted summation. Experimental results show that MVCapsNet outperforms the baselines and factorization base methods, finally achieves better accuracy on all datasets, particularly, comparing with the second best algorithm, the accuracy of our approach is increased by 14.5% on Washington dataset.

2 Capsule Net

Capsule net is a new network framework proposed by [17], and it performs better than the state-of-the-art methods for digit recognition on MNIST dataset. Different from other network, capsule net mainly makes up of capsule layers, and each capsule layer can be divided into many small groups of neurons, called 'capsules' whose activity vector represents the instantiation parameters of a specific type of entity such as an object or an part of object. Besides, capsule net has routing mechanism between two adjacent capsule layers, and routing mechanism is a coupling coefficients updating algorithm, which enables capsule net to select the salient features to improve predictive accuracy.

The capsule net in Fig. 1 consists of three layers, Conv1, PrimaryCaps, and DigitCaps. Conv1 has 256 9×9 convolution kernels with a stride of 1 and ReLU activation, and outputs 256 feature maps that are then used as inputs to the PrimaryCaps. PrimaryCaps is a convolutional capsule layer with 32 channels of convolutional 8D capsules, which means that each primary capsule contains 8 convolutional units with 9×9 convolution kernels and a stride of 2. DigitCaps has one 16D capsule per digit class and each of these capsules receives input from all the capsules in the PrimaryCaps layer, and the length of each capsule represents the probability that the digit class represented by the capsule is present in the current input image. And note that capsule net has routing process between PrimaryCaps and DigitCaps [17].

Routing mechanism is a coupling coefficients updating algorithm. It manages to make capsules in DigitCaps layer to subsume capsules in the PrimaryCaps layer in terms of the entity they identify, and further enables capsule net to make correct predictions. In addition, routing mechanism will be introduced in detail in next section.

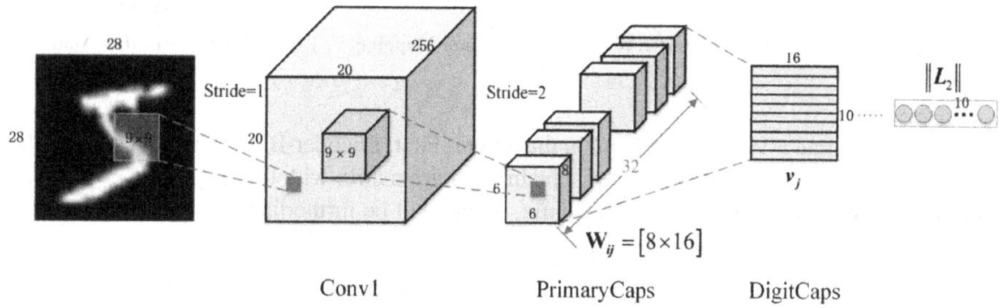

Fig. 1. A sample capsule net [17]

3 Framework

3.1 Notations

In this paper, bold uppercase characters are used to denote matrices, bold lowercase characters are used to denote vectors, and other characters which are not bold are used to denote scalars. Supposed that $\{\boldsymbol{X}^v \in \mathbb{R}^{M^v \times N}, \mathbf{y} \in \mathbb{R}^N\}$ is the sample of view v, where $v = 1, \cdots, V$, and V is the number of views. Among of them, $\boldsymbol{X}^v \in \mathbb{R}^{M^v \times N}$ is view v's input sample, $\mathbf{y} \in \mathbb{R}^N$ is labels, where M^v is the feature dimension of view v, and N is the sample capacity. more specifically, we have V views of raw data, and each view can be expressed as $(\boldsymbol{X}^v, \boldsymbol{y})$, where $\boldsymbol{X}^v = [\boldsymbol{x}_1^v, \cdots, \boldsymbol{x}_N^v]$, $\boldsymbol{x}_1^v \in \mathbb{R}^{M^v}$, $\boldsymbol{y} = [y_1, \cdots, y_N]$.

3.2 MVCapsNet Architecture

In this section, we describe the framework of our proposed MVCapsNet. As shown in Fig. 2, the architecture of MVCapsNet is made up of Encoder-Block, PrimaryCaps, and TargetCaps. What's more, we have some additional operations like linear mapping and routing processes between PrimaryCapsules and TargetCaps. And the detailed training processes are shown in Fig. 2 which can be divided into four stages: A, B, C, and D.

Stage A: As shown in Fig. 2, Encoder-Block is composed with a group of encoders, and we construct V same encoders to extract each view's feature in this stage. And the initial model parameters of each encoder are initialized by the encoder of some

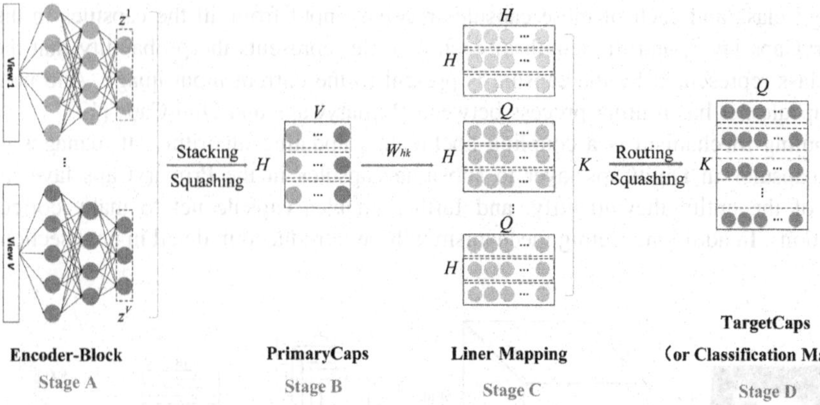

Fig. 2. We illustrate a V-views problem in this figure. First, Encoder-Block parallel connects the output of each encoder in Encoder-Block, obtain a feature matrix with the shape of $H \times V$. Then PrimaryCaps outputs a squashed feature matrix, which will be furtherlinear mapped, routed, and squashed. Finally, TargetCaps outputs a $K \times Q$ classification matrix.

corresponding auto-encoder, which will be explained more detailed in Sect. 4. From these encoders, V hidden features $\left(z^v \in \mathbb{R}^{H \times 1}, v = 1, \cdots, V\right)$ can be obtained and they will be combined into a feature matrix:

$$\boldsymbol{Z} = \left[z^1, \cdots, z^V\right], z^v \in \mathbb{R}^{H \times 1}, \tag{1}$$

where H is the number of dimension of hidden feature vector z^v. Simultaneously, we define each row vector of $\boldsymbol{Z}$ as $\boldsymbol{r}^h \in \mathbb{R}^{1 \times V}$, $h = 1, \cdots, H$, and rename $\boldsymbol{Z}$ as

$$\boldsymbol{R} = \left[\boldsymbol{r}^1; \cdots; \boldsymbol{r}^H\right], \boldsymbol{r}^h \in \mathbb{R}^{1 \times V}, \tag{2}$$

where actually $\boldsymbol{Z}$ equals to $\boldsymbol{R}$, and we use this definition just for convenience of subsequent discussion.

Stage B: The input of this stage is $\boldsymbol{R}$, and we use a non-linear squashing function to transform $\boldsymbol{r}^h$ into a primary capsule, which can be formulated as follows:

$$\boldsymbol{u}^h = \frac{\|\boldsymbol{r}^h\|}{1 + \|\boldsymbol{r}^h\|^2} \frac{\boldsymbol{r}^h}{\|\boldsymbol{r}^h\|}, h = 1, \ldots, H. \tag{3}$$

Obviously, PrimaryCaps has H primary capsule and each of them is a V-dimensional vector as shown in Fig. 2, and we define the set of primary capsule as:

$$\boldsymbol{U} = \left[\boldsymbol{u}^1; \cdots; \boldsymbol{u}^H\right], \boldsymbol{u}^h \in \mathbb{R}^{1 \times V}. \tag{4}$$

Stage C: We use a weight matrix $\boldsymbol{W}_{hk} \in \mathbb{R}^{V \times Q}$ to project each V-dimensional capsule $\mathbf{u}^h$ into Q-dimensional vector called prediction vector $\widehat{\boldsymbol{u}}^{k|h}$, which can be formulated as follows:

$$\widehat{\boldsymbol{u}}^{k|h} = \boldsymbol{u}^h \boldsymbol{W}_{hk} + \boldsymbol{b}_{hk}, \widehat{\boldsymbol{u}}^{k|h} \in \mathbb{R}^{1 \times Q}, \tag{5}$$

where $k = 1, \ldots, K$ represents the k-th classes of the data set. And this stage output a tensor called prediction tensor $\hat{U}$, which consists of prediction vector $\hat{\boldsymbol{u}}^{k|h}$:

$$\widehat{\boldsymbol{U}} = \begin{bmatrix} \widehat{\boldsymbol{u}}^{1|1} & \ldots & \widehat{\boldsymbol{u}}^{1|H} \\ \vdots & \ddots & \vdots \\ \widehat{\boldsymbol{u}}^{K|1} & \ldots & \widehat{\boldsymbol{u}}^{K|H} \end{bmatrix}. \tag{6}$$

Stage D: We first introduce the dynamic routing mechanism between PrimaryCapsules and TargetCaps.

Dynamic routing mechanism is a coupling coefficients updating algorithm. The input of dynamic routing mechanism consists of two parameters: prediction tensor $\widehat{\boldsymbol{U}}$ and iterations number r. And the output of dynamic routing mechanism is coupling coefficients and a matrix weighted by coupling coefficients. For convenience of discussion, in dynamic routing mechanism, we define the output $\boldsymbol{S} = [\boldsymbol{s}^1; \cdots; \boldsymbol{s}^K]$ as follows:

$$\boldsymbol{S} = \begin{bmatrix} \boldsymbol{s}^1 \\ \vdots \\ \boldsymbol{s}^K \end{bmatrix} = \begin{bmatrix} c_{11}\widehat{\boldsymbol{u}}^{1|1} + c_{21}\widehat{\boldsymbol{u}}^{1|2} + \cdots + c_{H1}\widehat{\boldsymbol{u}}^{1|H} \\ \vdots \\ c_{1K}\widehat{\boldsymbol{u}}^{K|1} + c_{2K}\widehat{\boldsymbol{u}}^{K|2} + \cdots + c_{HK}\widehat{\boldsymbol{u}}^{K|H} \end{bmatrix}, \tag{7}$$

where $\boldsymbol{s}^k = \sum_h c_{hk} \hat{\boldsymbol{u}}^{k|h}$ is a weighted sum over all prediction vector $\hat{\boldsymbol{u}}^{k|h}$, and c_{hk} are coupling coefficient that are updated by the iterative dynamic routing process. And for the updating rule of c_{hk}, we define a intermediate vector $\boldsymbol{v}^k$ corresponding to the k-th capsule in TargetCaps in iterative dynamic routing process, it comes from $\boldsymbol{s}^k$ by using a non-linear squashing function

$$\boldsymbol{v}^k = \frac{\left\|\boldsymbol{s}^k\right\|^2}{1 + \left\|\boldsymbol{s}^k\right\|^2} \frac{\boldsymbol{s}^k}{\left\|\boldsymbol{s}^k\right\|}. \tag{8}$$

Based on these definitions above, we further describe the updating process of c_{hk}. The c_{hk} update process is a procedure that iteratively applies the softmax function to log prior probabilities b_{hk}. All b_{hk} are initially set to 0, and then updated based on an agreement computation $\widehat{\boldsymbol{u}}^{kh} \boldsymbol{v}^{k^T}$. The c_{hk} updating process can be formulated as follows:

$$c_{hk} = \frac{\exp(b_{hk})}{\sum_l \exp(b_{hl})}, b_{hk} \leftarrow b_{hk} + \hat{\boldsymbol{u}}^{k|h} \boldsymbol{v}^{k^T}, \tag{9}$$

where the softmax function ensures that $\sum_k c_{hk} = 1$. What's more, the iterative process of the coupling coefficients is listed in Algorithm 1.

In this stage, we set the prediction tensor $\widehat{U}$ obtained by stage C, and iteration r as the input of routing mechanism. Through the dynamic routing mechanism, we also get a matrix $\boldsymbol{S}$ weighted by coupling coefficients, which is further squashed into TargetCaps, and it can be formulated as follows:

$$q^k = \frac{\|s^k\|^2}{1+\|s^k\|^2}\frac{s^k}{\|s^k\|}. \tag{10}$$

Algorithm 1. Routing mechanism

Routing Procedure $\left(\hat{u}^{k|h}, r\right)$ where r is the number of iterations:

for all capsule h in PrimaryCaps and capsule k in TargetCaps:
  $b_{hk} \leftarrow 0$
 for $1,\cdots,r\text{-}1$ iterations **do:**
  for all capsule h in PrimaryCaps:
   $c_{hk} = \frac{\exp(b_{hk})}{\sum_l \exp(b_{hl})}$
  for all capsule k in TargetCaps:
   $s^k = \sum_h c_{hk}\hat{u}^{k|h}$
  for all capsule k in TargetCaps:
   $v^k = \frac{\|s^k\|^2}{1+\|s^k\|^2}\frac{s^k}{\|s^k\|}$
  for all capsule h in PrimaryCaps and capsule k in TargetCaps:
   $b_{hk} \leftarrow b_{hk} + \hat{u}^{k|h} v^{k^T}$
 while r iteration **do:**
  for all capsule h in PrimaryCaps:
   $c_{hk} = \frac{\exp(b_{hk})}{\sum_l \exp(b_{hl})}$
  for all capsule k in TargetCaps:
   $s^k = \sum_h c_{hk}\hat{u}^{k|h}$
 return s^k

According to these four stages we discussed above, we get a classification matrix $Q = \left[q^1;\cdots;q^k\right], k = 1,\cdots,K$, and can further determine the label of instances by comparing the length of row vector.

3.3 Objective Function

We utilize the length of the output vector of a capsule in TargetCaps to represent the probability that the prediction label represented by this capsule is equal to target label of current input $\boldsymbol{X}_i$. And we would like that the k-th capsule's output $\boldsymbol{q}^k$ is the longest vector if the target label of $\boldsymbol{X}_i$ is equal to the prediction label represented by k-th capsule.

To allow for multi-classification, we use a separate margin loss L_k for each capsule in TargetCaps:

$$L_k = T_k \max(0, m^+ - \|\boldsymbol{q}_k\|)^2 + \lambda(1 - T_k)\max(0, \|\boldsymbol{q}_k\| - m^-)^2, \tag{11}$$

where $T_k = 1$ if the target label of $\boldsymbol{X}_i$ is represented by the k-th capsule, and $m^+ = 0.9$, $m^- = 0.1$, and $\lambda = 0.5$. The total loss is simply the sum of the loss of all capsules in TargetCaps:

$$L = \sum_{k=1}^{K} L_K. \tag{12}$$

4 Experiment

In this section, we experimentally evaluate MVCapsNet in classification task on eight real world multi-view data sets, and analyze the convergence of our proposed algorithm.

4.1 Datasets

In this paper, we use eight real-world multi-view data sets to verify the performance of MVCapsNet, including Leaves, Reuters, YaleFace, BBC, Cornell, Texas, Washington, and Wisconsin datasets. And Cornell, Texas, Washington, and Wisconsin dataset are four subset of data sets selected from WebKB data sets. The properties of data sets are summarized in Table 1.

4.2 Configuration and Tricks

In Encoder-Block, structures of all encoders are the same, each encoder has one input layer and three hidden layers l_1, l_2, *and* l_3, and the activation function of all hidden layers is ReLU. Furthermore, as the number of layers of encoder deepens, the number of nodes n_l in each hidden layer is decreasing. In order to make sure that each encoder output contains all the information of the v-th view input $\boldsymbol{x}_i^v$ of $\boldsymbol{X}_i$, n_{l3}, the number of nodes in hidden layers l_3, is selected within the range of $\left[\frac{M^{\max}}{8}, \frac{2M^{\max}}{8}\right]$, where $M^{\max} = \max(M^1, \cdots, M^V)$ is the maximum number of features of all views, and n_{l1}, *and* n_{l2} are selected within ranges of $\left[\frac{2M^{\max}}{4}, M^{\max}\right]$, $\left[\frac{M^{\max}}{4}, \frac{3M^{\max}}{4}\right]$, where $n_{l1} > n_{l2}$. In TargetCaps, the dimensional of capsule is selected from set $\{2V, 3V\}$. And the mini-batch size are $4, 8, 16, 32, 64, 128$, and epoch times is within the range of $[5, 400]$. The gradient descent algorithm we used was Adam, and the learning ratio is set within the range of $\left[10^{-5}, 10^{0}\right]$. The hyperparameter on each data sets are summarized in Table 2.

Table 1. Characteristics of the datasets

Data set	Characteristics			
	The numbers of instances	V	K	The numbers of dimension
Leaves	96	3	6	64 for all
Reuters	1200	5	6	2000 for all
YaleFace	256	2	8	2016 for all
BBC	685	4	5	4659/4633/4665/4684
Cornell	195	2	5	1703/585
Texas	187	2	5	1703/561
Washington	230	2	5	1703/690
Wisconsin	265	2	8	1703/795

Table 2. Hyperparameters on each data sets

Data sets	The numbers of neuron in encoder layers			The numbers of dimension in target capsule	The size of mini-batch
	l_1	l_2	l_3		
Leaves	64	32	16	6	4
Reuters	2048	1024	512	10	32
YaleFace	1024	512	512	2	16
BBC	1024	512	512	4	16
Cornell	1024	512	128	4	6
Texas	1024	512	128	4	6
Washington	1024	512	128	4	6
Wisconsin	1024	512	128	4	16

To boost classification result, the initialization of MVCapsNet's weights is important, since bad initialization can lead to the problem of exploding and vanishing gradients. In Encoder-Block, we begin with pre-trained V auto-encoders, which own the same structure and train by minimizing the reconstruction error of each view, and each encoder in auto-encoders is configured as the same as each encoder in Encoder-Block. Then we use the pre-trained parameters of auto-encoders to initialize the corresponding encoder's weight vectors of Encoder-Block. For auto-encoders, Xavier is used as the weight initialization method [18], the optimizer algorithm we used is Adam, and the learning ratio is set to 0.001. In linear mapping, we initialize weight matrix $\boldsymbol{W}_{hk}$ and bias matrix $\boldsymbol{b}_{hk}$ separately with Xavier.

To avoid over fitting, Encoder-Block was regularized by dropout regularization for all fully-connected layer in training process, and dropout ration was set to 0.5.

4.3 Comparison Algorithms

We evaluate the MVCapsNet performance in classification tasks by comparing it with several baseline multi-view learning algorithms, including GMVNMF [19], multiNMF [16], MVCC [20], DICS [13]. For fair comparison, we choose the parameters of all algorithms within the range that author suggested, and select the number of latent factors k within the range of [5:5:20] for all NMF-based algorithms. And for classification, we first obtain latent representations from all comparison algorithms, then we selected KNN($k = 1$) for classifier.

GMVNMF is an NMF-based algorithm by merging local geometrical structure information of each view in a multi-view feature extraction framework. The extracted feature considered the inner-view relatedness between data, and is further used to produce clustering results. We select parameters λ_f, μ to 0.01, and 10 as author suggested, respectively.

MultiNMF is an NMF-based multi-view clustering algorithm, which can get compatible clustering results across multiple views. We select the values of regularization parameter λ are 10^{-3}, 10^{-2}, 10^{-1}, 10^{0}.

MVCC is a novel multi-view clustering method based on concept factorization with local manifold regularization, which drives a common consensus representation for multiple views. We set parameter α to 100, and both select the values of parameters β and γ are 50, 100, 200, 500, 1000.

DICS is an NMF-based multi-view learning algorithm, by exploring the discriminative and non-discriminative information existing in common and view-specific parts among different views via joint non-negative matrix factorization, and produce discriminative and non-discriminative feature from all subspaces. What's more, discriminative and non-discriminative features are further used to produce classification results. We select parameters α and β within a small range of $[0, 1]$, and set parameter γ to 1.

Due to no publicly available multi-view algorithm based on deep neural network, we generate three baseline models based on deep neural network. These baseline models are exploratory models to validate properties of the dynamic routing in MVCapsNet, they separately use max pooling, mean pooling, and weighted summation to fusion all multiple views representations produced by Encoder-Block, and then input the fusion representation to fully connected layer to make prediction. For fair comparison, we use the same settings for baseline models as what we did in MVCapsNet.

4.4 Result

All datasets divided into training, verification and testing data in a ratio of 0.6:0.2:0.2. For MVCapsNet and all comparison algorithms, we first run each model on each dataset to select hyperparameters that has the best accuracy and generalization performance. Due to randomness, we run all algorithms 10 times on each dataset and report the mean values and standard deviations of accuracy.

All the classification results of eight multi-view datasets are summarized in Table 3, and the best result on each dataset is highlighted in boldface. As we can see, the proposed MVCapsNet achieves better accuracy on all datasets, and it is worth mentioning that, the accuracy that outperforms the second best algorithm is increase by

14.5% on Washington dataset. The promising result may reason from five aspects: (1) compared to factorization based models, Encoder-Block extracts features in a way of effectively fetching consistent information and grasping the underlying common properties of multi-view datasets; (2) compared to deep learning based models, linear mapping and routing mechanism between PrimaryCapsules and TargetCaps are effective in extracting complementary information for multiple views; (3) the pre-trained processes on auto-encoders obtain good initialization weights for Encoder-Block that avoids the instability of gradient descent in back propagation over deep nets and accelerates the convergence speed; (4) non-linear squashing function maps the input of PrimaryCapsules into a better distribution, the length of each vector keep in the range of $[0, 1]$; (5) using dropout technique in the Encoder-Block increases the generalization ability of the MVCapsNet.

Table 3. Accuracy of different methods

Method	ACC (%)							
	Leaves	Reuters	YaleFace	BBC	Cornell	Texas	Washington	Wisconsin
GNMF	95.0 ± 0	40.8 ± 1.2	50.0 ± 2.5	38.0 ± 1.5	41.0 ± 1.8	57.9 ± 1.8	69.6 ± 2.2	52.8 ± 1.4
MultiNMF	95.0 ± 0	52.7 ± 0.2	64.2 ± 4.2	73.1 ± 0.2	49.7 ± 7.7	68.7 ± 3.4	59.3 ± 2.6	50.3 ± 3.5
MVCC	100 ± 0	54.4 ± 1.9	33.3 ± 6.9	95.8 ± 2.6	60.8 ± 5.0	64.7 ± 5.5	62.8 ± 3.8	64.3 ± 2.7
DICS	97.9 ± 2.5	70.3 ± 4.0	89.1 ± 3.2	90.2 ± 2.4	72.8 ± 6.1	81.6 ± 4.0	77.4 ± 6.0	85.1 ± 4.5
Max-Pooling	100 ± 0	90.0 ± 4.6	71.2 ± 3.4	80.5 ± 7.6	71.3 ± 8.7	74.7 ± 5.2	67.5 ± 8.2	86.2 ± 7.7
Mean-Pooling	100 ± 0	90.6 ± 5.3	71.2 ± 4.3	83.3 ± 6.7	70.9 ± 5.5	76.6 ± 4.0	70.0 ± 4.9	84.8 ± 5.2
Weighted Sum	100 ± 0	92.9 ± 4.8	72.8 ± 4.7	87.2 ± 4.5	72.5 ± 13	76.3 ± 4.9	66.9 ± 7.8	86.3 ± 4.3
MVCapsNet	**100 ± 0**	**76.8 ± 3.2**	**95.8 ± 2.3**	**96.2 ± 1.9**	**76.3 ± 3.2**	**84.0 ± 5.9**	**91.9 ± 7.4**	**87.4 ± 3.8**

4.5 Convergence Analysis of Training Process

In order to empirically investigate the convergence property of MVCapsNet, we plot the iterative curves of objective function and the corresponding classification accuracy on three typical data sets in Fig. 3. From Fig. 3, we can observe that: (1) the objective function values drop sharply and meanwhile the classification accuracies increase rapidly within the previous rounds of iterative process, and then the objective function and the accuracy curves begin to decrease/grow mildly, finally converge to a value or fluctuate around a constant; (2) with respect to convergence speed, the objective function values of MVCapsNet converge in the least iterations, in contrast, max-pooling corresponds to the most iterations, because max-pooling operation is lossy compression process and the backpropagation process doesn't make full use of information from multiple views data; (3) in respect of convergence result, all objective functions always finally fluctuate around a constant, what's more, compared to baseline models, we can find that the classification accuracy curves of MVCapsNet often fluctuate within a narrow range. In conclusion, compared to baseline models, MVCapsNet get a better performance on the iterative curves of objective function and the corresponding classification accuracy.

In addition, we can observe that the value of objective function of MVCapsNet decrease as the numbers of epochs increasing, and finally converges to 0 in BBC and

Texas. It means if the label of input is k, the output vector of the k-th capsule in TargetCaps is the most length vector with length greater than 0.9, and the length of the output vectors of other capsules less than 0.1, which can be formulated as:

$$\|\boldsymbol{q}_i\| > m^+, i = k$$
$$\text{and } \|\boldsymbol{q}_i\| < m^-, i = 1, \cdots, k-1, k+1, \cdots, V$$

Thus, with the epoch increases, MVCapsNet can achieve 100% accuracy on some batch of train dataset, which also reflects the strong fitting ability of the neural network, and we used early stopping to avoid over fitting.

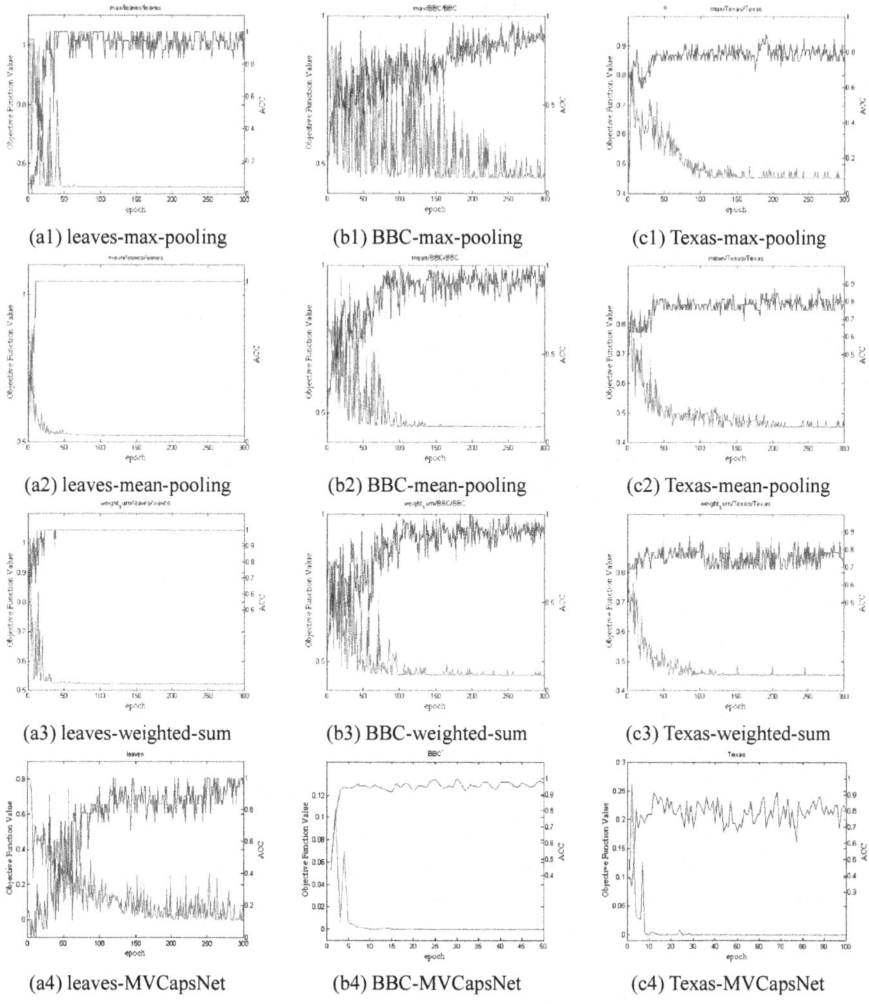

Fig. 3. The convergence property of MVCapsNet and deep learning based models on three datasets

5 Conclusion and Future Work

In this paper, we propose a novel multi-view network, called MVCapsNet. The proposed MVCapsNet aims to utilize both consistency and complementarity to select the salient feature over multi-view for constructing classifiers, and avoids large scale parameters. In detail, we use Encoder-Block to extracts feature vectors for each view, linear mapping and routing mechanism to jointly explore consistent and complementary information of multi-view data, and non-linear squashing function to normalize capsules in each layer. The experimental results on eight real-world data sets have demonstrated the effectiveness of our proposed algorithm.

For future studies, we plan to investigate the possibility of incorporating meta-learning [21] to give better hyperparameters than the human-defined hyperparameters used in this work. Instead of designing routing mechanism according to pre-setting routing strategies, we are also interested in learning to learn not just the learner initialization, but also the learner routing mechanism.

References

1. Blum, A., Mitchell, T.: Combining labeled and unlabeled data with co-training. In: COLT, pp. 92–100. ACM, New York (1998). https://doi.org/10.1145/279943.279962
2. Cai, D., He, X., Han, J., Huang, T.S.: Graph regularized nonnegative matrix factorization for data representation. TPAMI **33**(8), 1548–1560 (2011). https://doi.org/10.1109/TPAMI.2010.231
3. Shao, J., et al.: Common and distinct changes of default mode and salience network in schizophrenia and major depression. Brain Imaging Behav. **12**(6), 1708–1719 (2018). https://doi.org/10.1007/s11682-018-9838-8
4. Sun, S.: A survey of multi-view machine learning. Neural Comput. Appl. **23**(7–8), 2031–2038 (2013). https://doi.org/10.1007/s00521-013-1362-6
5. Li, Y., Yang, M., Zhang, Z.: A Survey of Multi-View Representation Learning. arXiv preprint arXiv:1610.01206 (2016). https://doi.org/10.1109/tkde.2018.2872063
6. Xu, C., Tao, D., Xu, C.: A survey on multi-view learning. arXiv preprint arXiv:1304.5634 (2013). https://doi.org/10.1145/3065386
7. Chao, G., Sun, S., Bi, J.: A Survey on Multi-View Clustering. arXiv preprint arXiv:1712.06246 (2017)
8. Chaudhuri, K., Kakade, S.M., Livescu, K.: Multi-view clustering via canonical correlation analysis. In: ICML, pp. 129–136. ACM, New York (2009). https://doi.org/10.1145/1553374.1553391
9. Kursun, O., Alpaydin, E.: Canonical correlation analysis for multiview semisupervised feature extraction. In: Rutkowski, L., Scherer, R., Tadeusiewicz, R., Zadeh, L.A., Zurada, J.M. (eds.) ICAISC 2010. LNCS (LNAI), vol. 6113, pp. 430–436. Springer, Heidelberg (2010). https://doi.org/10.1007/978-3-642-13208-7_54
10. Sharma, A., Kumar, A., Daume, H., Jacobs, D.W.: Generalized multi-view analysis: a discriminative latent space. In: CVPR, pp. 2160–2167. IEEE, Piscataway (2012). https://doi.org/10.1145/3065386
11. Nie, F., Li, J., Li, X.: Parameter-free auto-weighted multiple graph learning: a framework for multiview clustering and semi-supervised classification. In: IJCAI, pp. 1881–1887. AAAI, Menlo Park (2016)

12. Liu, J., Jiang, Y., Li, Z.: Partially shared latent factor learning with multiview data. IEEE Trans. Neural Networks Learn. Syst. **29**(8), 1233–1246 (2015). https://doi.org/10.1109/TNNLS.2014.2335234
13. Zhang, Z., Qin, Z., Li, P., Yang, Q., Shao, J.: Multi-view discriminative learning via joint non-negative matrix factorization. In: Pei, J., Manolopoulos, Y., Sadiq, S., Li, J. (eds.) DASFAA 2018. LNCS, vol. 10828, pp. 542–557. Springer, Cham (2018). https://doi.org/10.1007/978-3-319-91458-9_33
14. Singh, A.P., Gordon, G.J.: Relational learning via collective matrix factorization. In: KDD, pp. 650–658. ACM, New York (2008). https://doi.org/10.1145/1401890.1401969
15. Gao, J., Han, J., Liu, J., Wang, C.: Multi-view clustering via joint nonnegative matrix factorization. In: SDM, pp. 252–260. SIAM, Philadelphia (2013). https://doi.org/10.1137/1.9781611972832.28
16. Lee, D.D., Seung, H.S.: Learning the parts of objects by nonnegative matrix factorization. Nature **401**, 788–791 (1999). https://doi.org/10.1038/44565
17. Sabour, S., Frosst, N., Hinton, G.E.: Dynamic Routing Between Capsules. In: NIPS, pp. 3859–3869. Curran Associates, New York (2017). https://doi.org/10.1167/8.7.34
18. Glorot, X., Bengio, Y.: Understanding the difficulty of training deep feedforward neural networks. In: AISTATS, pp. 249–256. MIT, Cambridge (2010). 10.1.1.207.2059
19. Wang, Z., Kong, X., Fu, H.: Feature extraction via multi-view non-negative matrix factorization with local graph regularization. In: ICIP, pp. 3500–3504. IEEE, Piscataway (2015). https://doi.org/10.1109/icip.2015.7351455
20. Wang, H., Yang, Y., Li, T.: Multi-view clustering via concept factorization with local manifold regularization. In: ICDM, pp. 1245–1250. IEEE, Piscataway (2016). https://doi.org/10.1109/icdm.2016.0167
21. Finn, C., Abbeel, P., Levine, S.: Model-agnostic meta-learning for fast adaptation of deep networks. In: ICML, pp. 1126–1135. MIT, Cambridge (2017)

Advanced Capsule Networks via Context Awareness

Huu Phong Nguyen(✉) and Bernardete Ribeiro

CISUC, Department of Informatics Engineering, University of Coimbra, Coimbra, Portugal
{phong,bribeiro}@dei.uc.pt

Abstract. Capsule Networks (CN) offer new architectures for Deep Learning (DL) community. Though its effectiveness has been demonstrated in MNIST and smallNORB datasets, the networks still face challenges in other datasets for images with distinct contexts. In this research, we improve the design of CN (Vector version) namely we expand more Pooling layers to filter image backgrounds and increase Reconstruction layers to make better image restoration. Additionally, we perform experiments to compare accuracy and speed of CN versus DL models. In DL models, we utilize Inception V3 and DenseNet V201 for powerful computers besides NASNet, MobileNet V1 and MobileNet V2 for small and embedded devices. We evaluate our models on a fingerspelling alphabet dataset from American Sign Language (ASL). The results show that CNs perform comparably to DL models while dramatically reducing training time. We also make a demonstration and give a link for the purpose of illustration.

Keywords: Capsule Networks · Deep Learning · Transfer Learning · Demonstration

1 Introduction

Capsule Networks arrive in the field of Deep Learning at the time when many issues are considered solved e.g. in image and object recognition, very deep networks with hundreds of layers are able to outperform human. One reason behind the success of DL is the Max Pooling (MP) layer which not only reduces dimension of images but also selects most critical pixels for routing from one layer to another. Though MP works very well, Hinton argues that MP causes loss of useful information. As a consequence, this layer is replaced with a routing algorithm and a new architecture namely Capsule Networks is designed [11]. The CNs can also be referred as Vector CNs since the approach is based on agreements between vectors. The design achieved 0.25% test error on MNIST dataset in comparison with the state of the art using DropConnect 0.39% without data augmentation [16]. The other CN applying Expectation Maximization (Matrix CN) reduces the best error rate by 45% on SmallNORB dataset [5]. However, the networks still face challenges on other datasets e.g. Cifar-10, SVHN and ImageNet.

I. V. Tetko et al. (Eds.): ICANN 2019, LNCS 11727, pp. 166–177, 2019.
https://doi.org/10.1007/978-3-030-30487-4_14

In this research, we choose to build our CNs based on the Vector CN architecture since there are few implementations in literature for Matrix CNs and our preliminary results show that the latter takes longer convergence time in the ASL alphabet dataset.

For DL architecture, we choose several prestige Transfer Learning (TL) models including Inception V3 [15], DenseNet V201 [7], NASNet [17], MobileNet V1 [6] and MobileNet V2 [12] to generate feature maps and compare these models to explore which model is the best in our setting. As TL is a very fast growing field, the models are trained on a wide variety of platforms such as Tensorflow, Caffe, Torch and Theano. In addition, just a year ago, Keras which was one of the biggest independent platforms had been integrated into Tensorflow. As Keras includes pre-trained models for most of leading TLs, we prefer to use this platform to set a unified environment for comparison of all TL models. We also classify models in two groups one that is mainly used for demanding computers (Inception V3, DenseNet V201) and the other for smaller devices (NASNet, MobileNet V1 and V2) since mobiles have become a crucial tool in our daily life.

We perform experiments on static signs of ASL dataset. In ASL, there are two distinct signs namely dynamic signs and static signs. Our aim is to build an action recognition framework to recognize signs in continuous frames (e.g. transcription generators for ASL songs or conversations). In this work, we focus on ASL alphabet signs. For this problem, models are usually based on Convolution Networks [1,2], other Machine Learning techniques like Multilayer Random Forest [9] or Transfer Learning models such as GoogLeNet and AlexNet [3,8].

The rest of this article is structured as follows. We highlight our main contributions in Sect. 2. Next, we describe an ASL dataset for this research in Sect. 3.1. Then we discuss about Vector CNs and TL models' architectures in Sect. 3.2 and Sect. 3.3, accordingly. Experiments and respective results are analyzed and discussed in Sect. 4. We conclude this work in Sect. 5.

2 Contribution

In our research, we improve the design of the Vector Capsule Networks and perform empirical comparisons versus Deep Learning models on accuracy and speed using an ASL fingerspelling alphabet.

First, we propose to modify the Vector CN's architecture to find the most efficient designs. Namely, we extended Convolution layers to better filter input images and varied Fully Connected layers in the Reconstruction to leverage image restoration.

Second, we explore distinct Transfer Learning models for demanding devices (Inception V3 and DenseNet V201) and small devices (NasNet and MobileNets) when integrated with Multilayer Perceptron and Long Short Term Memory. We use the former setting as a baseline to compare with the latter.

Third, Vector CNs are analyzed against DL models. We find out that CNs perform comparatively on both accuracy and speed. In addition, CNs have an advantage as pre-training is not required. Capsules can be trained within an hour compare to days or more for pre-trained TL models.

Finally, we make a demonstration to compare CNs and DLs on videos for teaching ASL alphabets. The results are very promising as our models can recognize almost of all signs without previously seen.

3 Recognition Models

In this section, we first discuss about an ASL dataset that will be used in our experiments. Then we deal with architectures of Vector CNs and DL models.

3.1 ASL Dataset

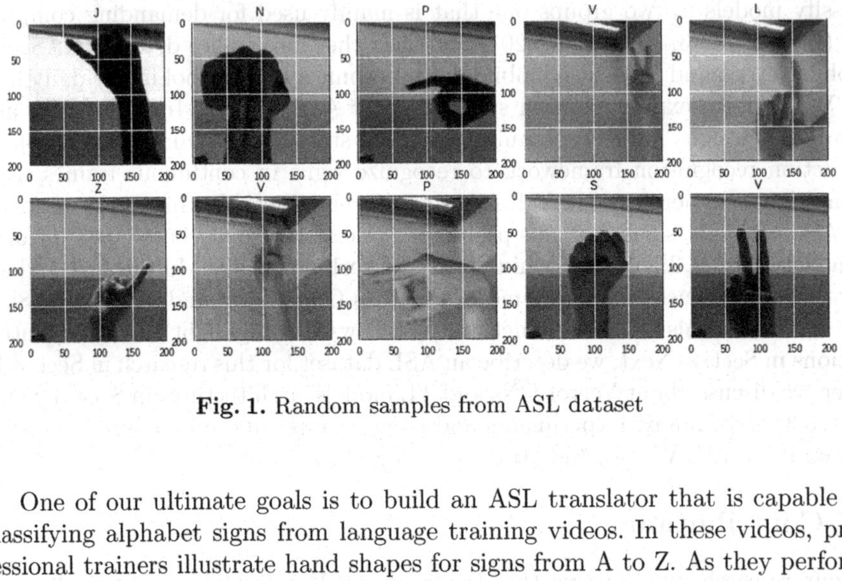

Fig. 1. Random samples from ASL dataset

One of our ultimate goals is to build an ASL translator that is capable of classifying alphabet signs from language training videos. In these videos, professional trainers illustrate hand shapes for signs from A to Z. As they perform demonstrations, the hand is moving around the screen from left to right, up to down and vice versa. To train our models, we search for a dataset that captures similar movements with a large sample size. We expect that each sign should have thousands of instances since a standard MNIST has 60000 samples for 10 classes. With these constraints and since ASL datasets are relatively fewer than for English alphabet, we found only one dataset from Kaggle website[1] that meets our requirements. This set of data includes all 26 signs including dynamic signs “J” and “Z” with 3 additional signs. Each sign includes 3000 samples (200×200 pixels), totally 87000 for all signs. In these images, hands are placed in distinct positions on the screen, distance and lightning are varied.

Figure 1 shows 10 random samples from the dataset. We notice that signs “N” and “P” have different shapes compared to the target video. In stead of replacing them, these signs are retained for the reason mentioned above.

[1] https://www.kaggle.com/grassknoted/asl-alphabet.

The data are selected randomly and split into training and testing sets with the ratio of 70/30. In addition, the value range is re-scaled from $[0, 255]$ to $[0, 1]$. For data augmentation, the rotation, shear, width shift and height shift are set in the ranges of 20, 0.2, 0.2 and 0.2 respectively. Moreover, images' brightness and contrast are spanned using random uniform within distances of 0.6 and 1.5.

3.2 Capsule Networks

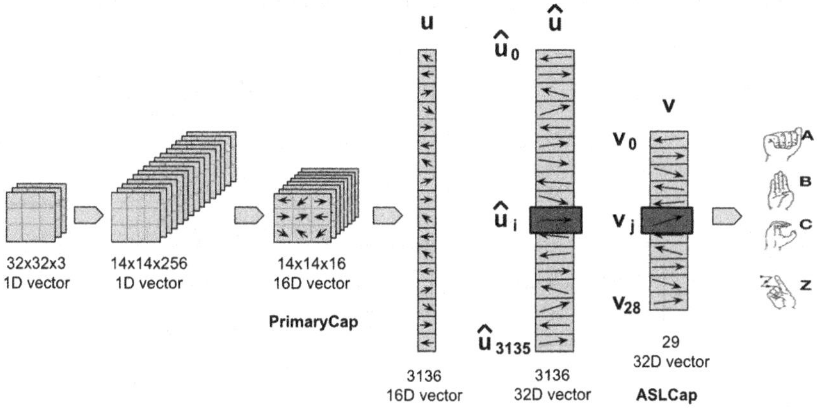

Fig. 2. Vector capsule networks architecture for ASL

Hinton describes a Capsule Networks as a group of neurons that represent distinct properties of the same entity. In Vector CN, a capsule in one layer sends its activity to the capsule in above layer and the method checks which one agrees the most. The essential structure of Capsule Networks is shown in the Fig. 2.

The initial step of Vector CNs is similar to Convolutional Neural Networks where input images are filtered to detect features such as edge and curve. Then, in PrimaryCaps, the generated features are grouped to create multi-dimension vectors. Illustrated in the Figure, 256 feature maps of size 14×14 are transformed into 16 capsules each contains 14×14 vectors of 16 dimensions. Routing from this layer to the ASL Capsule (ASLCap) layer is computed as follows.

$$v_j = \frac{||s_j||^2}{1 + ||s_j||^2} \frac{s_j}{||s_j||}, s_j = \sum_i c_{ij} \hat{u}_{j|i} \tag{1}$$

$$c_{ij} = \frac{exp(b_{ij})}{\sum_k exp(b_{ik})}, \hat{u}_{j|i} = W_{ij} u_i \tag{2}$$

$$b_{ij} \leftarrow b_{ij} + \hat{u}_{j|i} v_j \tag{3}$$

where v_j represents the vector output of capsule j in ASLCap and s_j is its total input produced by a weighted sum of all predictions from layer below. Next, the signal is passed through a squash non-linearity so that the value is in the range of $[0, 1]$. The length of this vector suggests the probability an entity (represented by the capsule) being detected. For example, if the vector v_j is set to represent the sign "L" then the length of this vector indicates if the sign is actually presented. The output of vector u_i is transformed to the vector $\hat{u}_{j|i}$ by multiplying with a weight matrix W_{ij}. The routing coefficient b_{ij} will be increased or decreased based on whether the output v_j has a similar direction with its prediction $\hat{u}_{j|i}$.

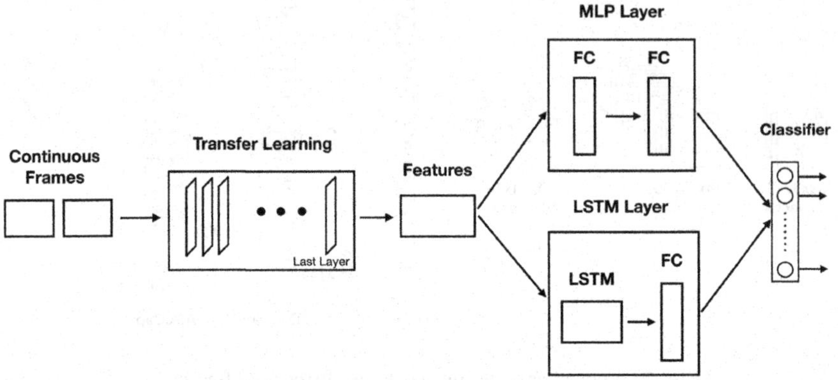

Fig. 3. Transfer learning architecture for ASL

3.3 Deep Learning Models

This section deals with the integration of Transfer Learning models in Deep Learning architecture for ASL recognition to classify alphabet signs in continuous frames. Convolution Neural Networks (ConvNets) were introduced 20 years ago with the notable architecture from LeNet [10]. Throughout the time, ConvNets tended to go deeper e.g. VGG (19 layers). With recent advances in computer hardware, very deep architectures such as Highway Networks [13] and Residual Networks [4] have exceeded 100 layers. Training these models can take days or even months; this gives rise to TL where models are pre-trained on a dataset and re-used on others. In Computer Vision, earlier convolution layers are considered to behave similarly to edge and curve filters. Thus, these frozen weights can be used on our ASL dataset. A modification in the last layer is necessary as the number of signs is 29 compared to 1000 categories in ImageNet.

In our research, we include Inception V3, DenseNet V201, NASNet, MobileNet V1 and MobileNet V2 models in DL Architectures. Inception V1 (or often called GoogLeNet to honor LeCun's Networks) was a winner for image classification challenge in ILSVRC 2014 (ImageNet Large Scale Visual Recognition Competition) and achieved top-5 error of 6.67% [14]. The results for Inception V3 [15] and DenseNet V201 [7] were 5.6% and 6.34%/5.54% (on single-crop/10-crop) respectively.

NASNet was recently introduced and obtained state-of-the-art results on several datasets including Cifar-10, ImageNet and COCO [17]. NASNet comes with two versions one for computers (NASNetLarge) and the other for small devices (NASNetMobile). Since the computation for NASNetLarge takes twice the required time for the slowest models DenseNet V201, we select only NASNet-Mobile in our experiments. Despite of being made for small devices, the model accomplishes 8.4% top-5 error on ImageNet. Additionally, we choose MobileNets [6,12] for comparisons within mobile platform.

As shown in Fig. 3, ASL's signs are illustrated in a video and extracted as a sequence of frames (Please see our demonstration for more information). At the runtime, an active model with trained weights is loaded. Based on each Transfer Learning model, the extracted features have length variations i.e. 2048, 1920, 1056, 1024 and 1280 for Inception V3, DenseNet V201, NASNetMobile, MobileNet V1 and V2.

After this step, the flow goes through either MLP Layer or LSTM Layers. The former comprises two Fully Connected Neural Networks (FC) whereas the latter contains one Long Short Term Memory (LSTM) and one FC. The LSTM has 2048 units with history's lookback of one for classifying one frame per time. Besides, all FCs are composed by 512 neurons. We use MLP in our DL models as a baseline for comparison with Vector CNs. This is also interesting to see performance of DL built on other techniques like LSTM.

4 Experiments and Results

In this section, we first discuss the performances of Vector CNs and DL models on variations of input image size and number of samples. Later, we take two models in DL and compare with two models in Capsule.

4.1 Experiment 1: Effective of Dataset Size and Image Size on Capsule Accuracy

To perform this experiment, we scale the Input images to 64×64, 32×32 and 16×16 pixels and use datasets of $\frac{1}{16}$, $\frac{1}{8}$, $\frac{1}{4}$, $\frac{1}{2}$, and a full size. We vary the size of the dataset so that we can observe the effects when the number of samples is small. We exclude dataset of $\frac{1}{32}$ since this yields fewer than 100 samples per class which may not be enough for recognition. The dataset is split into train and test with the ratio of 70/30. We also use two FCs for Reconstruction, one FC has a half of Input image size and the other has an equal size e.g. when the Input image is 64×64, the two FCs have sizes of 1024 (32×32) and 4096 (64×64), accordingly.

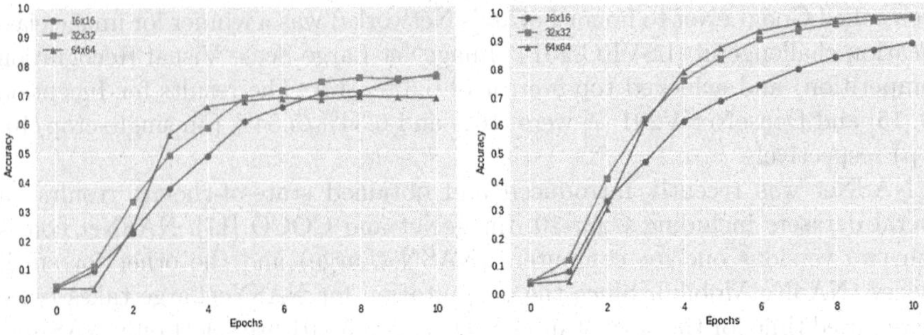

(a) $\frac{1}{16}$ Dataset (b) All Dataset

Fig. 4. Comparisons of capsule networks on image sizes

Figure 4a shows a result of this experiment using $\frac{1}{16}$ dataset. We notice that the accuracy for 64×64 resolution images are lower than for 32×32 and 16×16. This contradicts our expectation since with a larger resolution, the image is clearer and should be recognized better. From Fig. 4b, we see a different approach where 64×64 resolution images perform better than the others. We exclude results for remaining sets to save space.

In summary, these experiments show that a larger image's resolution does not always yield a better accuracy because a small number of samples may affect this performance. With a larger dataset, a higher resolution generally results in a better accuracy. In addition, we can observe that both 64×64 and 32×32 image resolutions achieve an accuracy of approximately 0.99 after 10 epochs using full dataset.

4.2 Experiment 2: Comparisons of Deep Learning Models

In this experiment, we use the same variations of dataset size as in Vector CN models and compare all DL models on MLP and LSTM. Figure 5a shows accuracy of all models with MLP and results from a typical ConvNet using full dataset. We can observe that, despite of being simple, the accuracy approaches 100% on training set. However, this yields only near 60% on test.

Much to our surprise, two versions of MobileNets both outperform Inception V3 and DenseNet 201. This maybe caused by the efficiency of Deepwise Separable Convolution layers. It also can be seen that DenseNet V201 performs better than Inception V3. Perhaps, the model's blocks in which one layer is connected to all other layers helps to reserve more important information. Additionally, a similar trend can be seen using $\frac{1}{16}$ dataset with accuracy be offset approximately 10%–20%. Moreover, we can observe analogous results using LSTM in Fig. 6. Overall, DL models classified with LSTM show faster convergences.

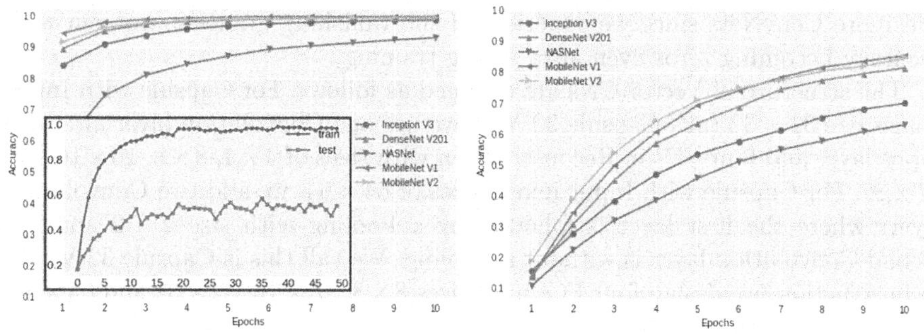

(a) All Dataset

(b) $\frac{1}{16}$ Dataset

Fig. 5. Comparisons of Deep Learning Models on MLP. The Figure on the left hand side also includes a result of training and testing on a typical ConvNet (two Convolution layers each with 32 filters, one FC of 128 neurons, Adam optimizer and 50 epochs)

4.3 Experiment 3: Comparisons of Vector Capsule Networks and Deep Learning Models on Speed

In this experiment, we perform speed tests of Vector CNs and DL models on running times for Feature Extraction and Prediction. Regarding the first metric, all models are executed on GPUs of Tesla K80 and P100. Capsules are excluded since extraction of features is not essential.

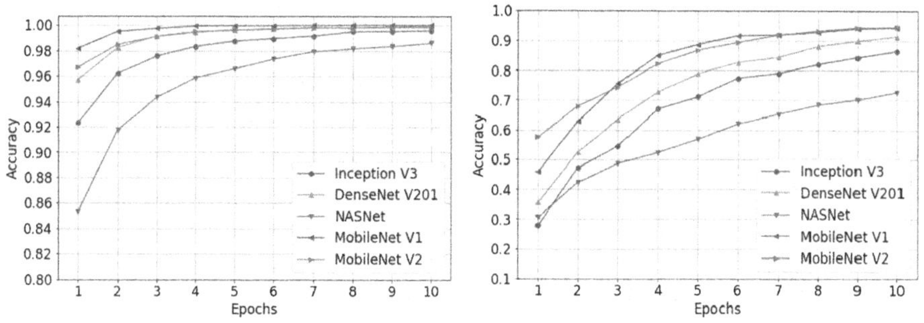

(a) All Dataset

(b) 1/16 Dataset

Fig. 6. Comparisons of deep learning models on LSTM

We observed that with only one ConvNet, the model performed very well on images 64×64 but poorly on the target video. This maybe caused by the model learns very well on the training data but distinct backgrounds between the two hamper its performance. For this reason, we add one more Convolution layer without Pooling after Input image to filter better the backgrounds. We did not add more ConvNets since we experienced the vanishing gradient problem with accuracy becoming zeros even after a long training.

The structure of Vector CNs are changed as follows. For Capsule with Input image size 32 × 32 (aka Capsule 32 V1), we use one Convolution layer after the Input layer and four FCs in Reconstruction with sizes of 4 × 4, 8 × 8, 16 × 16 and 32 × 32. For Capsule with Input image sizes of 64 × 64, we add two Convolution layers where the first layer is followed by a Pooling with size 2 × 2 and the second Convolution layer is without a Pooling. We call this is Capsule 32 V2. In reconstruction, we design four FCs with sizes 8 × 8, 16 × 16, 32 × 32 and 64 × 64.

Table 1. Comparisons of vector CNs and DL models on speed

	Models	Metrics		
		Feature extraction (Tesla K80)	Feature extraction (Tesla P100)	Prediction (CPU 2.7 GHz)
Time (s)	Inception V3	3453	1910	0.248
	DenseNet V201	6250	3199	-
	NASNet	3018	2592	-
	MobileNet V1	870	507	0.070
	MobileNet V2	1175	758	-
	Capsule 32 V1	-	-	0.069
	Capsule 32 V2	-	-	0.086

It can be gleaned from Table 1 that MobileNet V1 runs faster than any other models on both GPUs whereas DenseNet V201 is the slowest. This clearly shows the advantage of Depthwise Separable Convolution in reducing computation. As we expected, all models for mobiles perform faster than models for computers with an exception that NASNet is slower than Inception V3 on Tesla P100.

On prediction speed comparison, we pickup two models from DL. We select MobileNet V1 because of its best accuracy and fastest speed. Besides, Inception V3 is chosen instead of DenseNet V201 based on a faster speed. We perform this experiment on a computer with 4-CPUs of 2.7 GHz. It is unexpected that Capsule 32 V1 is only slightly faster than MobileNet V1 since the model has only 2 CN layers (and 3 ConvNets) compared to 28 ConvNets of its counterpart. It is also noticed that Capsule V2 runs three times faster than Inception 32 V3 but quite slower than MobileNet V1.

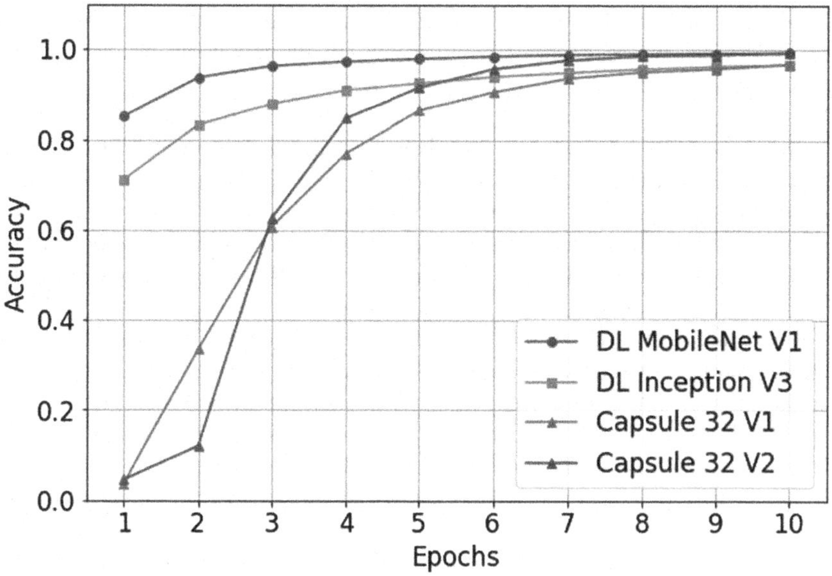

Fig. 7. Capsule networks vs deep learning models on accuracy

4.4 Experiment 4: Comparison of Vector Capsule Networks and Deep Learning Models on Accuracy

This experiment is designed to compare accuracy of Capsules and Deep Learning architectures. We select MobileNet V1, Inception V3, Capsule 32 V1 and Capsule 32 V2 as discussed in the previous section.

As we can see from Fig. 7, MobileNet V1 and Inception V3 perform better than Capsules in first few epochs. However, as number of epochs increases, Capsule 32 V1 achieves a similar accuracy of Inception V3 and Capsule 32 V2 approaches the accuracy of MobileNet V1.

5 Conclusions

In this research, we propose to improve the design of Vector CN by extending ConvNet layers after Input image and vary the number of FCs in Reconstruction to accomplish better accuracy. Having a larger image size is critical in our approach since certain signs are similar. A small change in the position of fingers can yield distinct signs. In addition, variation of background contexts may hamper Capsules' performance. Using our approach we attain the goals as follows. First, our results show that Capsule 32 V2 performs comparatively to DL MobileNet V1 on accuracy and Capsule 32 V1 runs a slightly faster than its counterpart. Second, Vector CNs are greater than DL models in the sense that the latter requires pre-trained weights which can take days or even months for training whereas the former can be trained on-the-fly within an hour. Third, as a result of our exploration, we found that MobileNet V1 even though was mainly built for small devices but is superior to all other DL models both on accuracy and speed in this dataset.

Furthermore, we made a demonstration to illustrate our approach where we compare Vector CN V1 with DL MobileNet V1 in an ASL video. The recorded file can be accessed via the link[2]. Although, Vector CN can recognize most of all signs (excluding signs that we mentioned earlier), the model is more sensitive to changes than the DL model. This suggests pooling in the DL may better than just rescaling as in the Vector CN. In addition, the DL performs better although the accuracy (when testing on the ASL dataset) is similar to that of Vector CN. This can indicate that the DL model is more generative. For this reason, additional samples are needed to improve the overall performance.

Although we demonstrate this approach in the context of ASL alphabet signs, the approach has broader applications to any video recognition tasks where each individual frame's information are crucial.

In the future, we plan to redesign CNs' structure to perform on larger images. We also plan to build Vector CNs and DL MobileNet V1 on mobile devices as the accuracy and speed allow these networks to run in realtime.

Acknowledgements. The reviewers are gratefully acknowledged for their insightful comments. We also thank CISUC - Center of Informatics and Systems of the University of Coimbra for financial support.

References

1. Ameen, S., Vadera, S.: A convolutional neural network to classify American sign language fingerspelling from depth and colour images. Expert Syst. **34**(3), e12197 (2017). https://doi.org/10.1111/exsy.12197
2. Bheda, V., Radpour, D.: Using deep convolutional networks for gesture recognition in American sign language. arXiv preprint arXiv:1710.06836 (2017)
3. Garcia, B., Viesca, S.A.: Real-time American sign language recognition with convolutional neural networks. Convolutional Neural Networks Vis. Recogn. (2016)
4. He, K., Zhang, X., Ren, S., Sun, J.: Deep residual learning for image recognition. In: Proceedings of the IEEE Conference on Computer Vision and Pattern Recognition, pp. 770–778 (2016). https://doi.org/10.1109/CVPR.2016.90
5. Hinton, G.E., Sabour, S., Frosst, N.: Matrix capsules with em routing. In: 6th International Conference on Learning Representations, ICLR (2018)
6. Howard, A.G., et al.: Mobilenets: efficient convolutional neural networks for mobile vision applications. arXiv preprint arXiv:1704.04861 (2017)
7. Huang, G., Liu, Z., Van Der Maaten, L., Weinberger, K.Q.: Densely connected convolutional networks. In: Proceedings of the IEEE Conference on Computer Vision and Pattern Recognition, pp. 4700–4708 (2017). https://doi.org/10.1109/CVPR.2017.243
8. Kang, B., Tripathi, S., Nguyen, T.Q.: Real-time sign language fingerspelling recognition using convolutional neural networks from depth map. In: 2015 3rd IAPR Asian Conference on Pattern Recognition (ACPR), pp. 136–140. IEEE (2015). https://doi.org/10.1109/ACPR.2015.7486481

[2] http://bit.ly/2O4sJSU.

9. Kuznetsova, A., Leal-Taixé, L., Rosenhahn, B.: Real-time sign language recognition using a consumer depth camera. In: Proceedings of the IEEE International Conference on Computer Vision Workshops, pp. 83–90 (2013). https://doi.org/10.1109/ICCVW.2013.18
10. LeCun, Y., Bottou, L., Bengio, Y., Haffner, P., et al.: Gradient-based learning applied to document recognition. Proc. IEEE **86**(11), 2278–2324 (1998). https://doi.org/10.1109/5.726791
11. Sabour, S., Frosst, N., Hinton, G.E.: Dynamic routing between capsules. In: Advances in Neural Information Processing Systems, pp. 3856–3866 (2017)
12. Sandler, M., Howard, A., Zhu, M., Zhmoginov, A., Chen, L.C.: Mobilenetv 2: inverted residuals and linear bottlenecks. In: Proceedings of the IEEE Conference on Computer Vision and Pattern Recognition, pp. 4510–4520 (2018). https://doi.org/10.1109/CVPR.2018.00474
13. Srivastava, R.K., Greff, K., Schmidhuber, J.: Training very deep networks. In: Advances in Neural Information Processing Systems, pp. 2377–2385 (2015)
14. Szegedy, C., et al.: Going deeper with convolutions. In: Proceedings of the IEEE Conference on Computer Vision and Pattern Recognition, pp. 1–9 (2015). https://doi.org/10.1109/CVPR.2015.7298594
15. Szegedy, C., Vanhoucke, V., Ioffe, S., Shlens, J., Wojna, Z.: Rethinking the inception architecture for computer vision. In: Proceedings of the IEEE Conference on Computer Vision and Pattern Recognition, pp. 2818–2826 (2016). https://doi.org/10.1109/CVPR.2016.308
16. Wan, L., Zeiler, M., Zhang, S., Le Cun, Y., Fergus, R.: Regularization of neural networks using dropconnect. In: International Conference on Machine Learning, pp. 1058–1066 (2013)
17. Zoph, B., Vasudevan, V., Shlens, J., Le, Q.V.: Learning transferable architectures for scalable image recognition. In: Proceedings of the IEEE Conference on Computer Vision and Pattern Recognition, pp. 8697–8710 (2018). https://doi.org/10.1109/CVPR.2018.00907

DDRM-CapsNet: Capsule Network Based on Deep Dynamic Routing Mechanism for Complex Data

Jian-wei Liu[1(✉)], Feng Gao[1], Run-kun Lu[1], Yuan-feng Lian[2], Dian-zhong Wang[3], Xiong-lin Luo[1], and Chu-ran Wang[4]

[1] Department of Automation, China University of Petroleum, Beijing Campus (CUP), Beijing, China
{liujw,luoxl}@cup.edu.cn, 814956359@qq.com, 983194327@qq.com

[2] Department of Computer, China University of Petroleum, Beijing Campus (CUP), Beijing, China
lianyuanfeng@cup.edu.cn

[3] Beijing Institute of Space Mechanics and Electricity, Beijing, China
wangdz_bisme@spacechina.com

[4] Academy for Advanced Interdisciplinary Studies, Peking University, Beijing, China
churanwang@pku.edu.cn

Abstract. The Recently proposed CapsNet has attracted the attention of many researchers. It is a potential alternative to convolutional neural networks (CNNs) and achieves significant increase in performance on some simple datasets like MNIST. However, CapsNet gets a poor performance on more complex datasets like CIFAR-10. To address this problem, we focus on the improvement of the original CapsNet from both the network structure and the dynamic routing mechanism. A new CapsNet architecture aiming at complex data called Capsule Network based on Deep Dynamic Routing Mechanism (DDRM-CapsNet) is proposed. For the purpose of extracting better features, we increase the number of convolutional layers before capsule layer in the encoder. We also improve the dynamic routing mechanism in the original CapsNet by expanding it into two stages and increasing the dimensionality of the final output vector. To verify the efficacy of our proposed network on complex data, we conduct experiments with a single model without using any ensembled methods and data augmentation techniques on five real-world complex datasets. The experimental results demonstrate that our proposed method achieves better accuracy results than the baseline and can still improve the reconstruction performance on the premise of using the same decoder structure as the original CapsNet.

Keywords: CapsNet · CNN · Complex data · DDRM-CapsNet

I. V. Tetko et al. (Eds.): ICANN 2019, LNCS 11727, pp. 178–189, 2019.
https://doi.org/10.1007/978-3-030-30487-4_15

1 Introduction

In recent years, convolutional neural networks (CNNs) have shown remarkable results for a wide range of tasks in computer vision such as image classification [1, 2]. Their popularity and effectiveness profit from their powerful ability for detecting distinct features in the receptive field and underlying information implied in the data. However, CNNs also have a few drawbacks and limitations. One is that some spatial information (such as location, pose and orientation) is lost from one layer to another due to max and average pooling. Thus, CNNs do not consider the relative spatial relationships between features while making predictions, e.g. for some person, if we exchange his nose with the mouth on his face, CNNs will still classify this instance as a person because of the appearance of some certain key features. Another major drawback is that CNNs lack the properties of rotation invariance. They seem to easily change their prediction wrongly when the object is rotated.

To overcome aforementioned drawbacks and limitations, Sabour et al. [3] introduced capsule network (CapsNet) as a powerful alternative to CNNs. In CapsNet, the network output exists as vectors instead of scalars as in CNNs, whose length represents the probability of the entity's existence and orientation represents properties of the entity. CapsNet also replaces the max-pooling operation with the concept of dynamic routing mechanism, which only extracts the most active features. CapsNet achieved state-of-the-art performance on MNIST digit classification and performs better than CNNs on highly overlapping digits. CapsNet is considered as a revolution of theory of neural networks and a new direction in the field of deep learning.

The baseline CapsNet architecture is built specifically for MNIST whose image dimensionality is relatively low and image size is not large. In contrast, CapsNet achieved poor results on some more complex datasets not like MNIST. Sabour et al. [3] tested the CapsNet model on CIFAR-10 and achieved 10.6% error with the ensemble of 7 models. This classification result is about what standard CNNs achieved when they were first applied to CIFAR-10 [4]. Using the single CapsNet model same as [3], Xi et al. [5] reached 68.93% validation accuracy over 50 epochs on CIFAR-10. By making a modification based on the original CapsNet which adds an additional convolutional layer before the capsule layer, their best result reaches 71.50% with the ensemble of 4 models. All previous research results verify that if adopting no ensembling methods, the single baseline model achieves poor performance, but it is not worth using ensembling for the sake of better accuracy results because of higher computation complexity. In addition, Mukhometzianov et al. [6] achieved only 18% test accuracy on CIFAR-100 with a single CapsNet model after 18 h of training which is an obvious unsatisfactory result.

Based on the facts above, we analyze and summarize two leading reasons resulting in the performance difference of CapsNet between MNIST and other complex datasets as follows:

(1) Only one convolutional layer before the capsule layer is not enough. In consideration of the complexity of some datasets whose image dimensionality is high or image size is large, the existing number of convolutional layers for CapsNet is not enough. In order to extract more salient features and abstract information, increasing the number of convolutional layers is imperative.

(2) The dimensionality of activity vector is not high enough. The dimensionality size of the activity vector corresponding to each capsule in DigitCaps layer determines the richness of the expression of the features in the image. Therefore, for complex datasets with higher dimensionality, larger size and more categories, the output vector of the original CapsNet is not enough. Allowing the network to output higher-dimensionality activity vector can better represent more complex features.

Based on our above analysis, this paper focuses on the improvement of the original CapsNet from both the network structure and the dynamic routing mechanism. We propose a new architecture for CapsNet which better adapts to more complex datasets than MNIST, termed as Capsule Network based on Deep Dynamic Routing Mechanism (DDRM-CapsNet). Firstly, similar to many CNNs for the task of image classification [7, 8], we add more depth in CapsNet by adding three standard convolutional layers to satisfy the demand of better representing and disentangling complex features in complex image data for higher dimensionality and larger size. Secondly, we improve the dynamic routing mechanism in the original CapsNet and set its output vector as 24*D*. The new mechanism is named Deep Dynamic Routing Mechanism (DDRM) and it is divided into two stages, in which the iterative process of routing protocol in the original CapsNet is adopted.

In conclusion, our contributions are summarized as follows:

(1) We propose a new network architecture called DDRM-CapsNet for complex data, which modifies both the network structure and the dynamic routing mechanism.
(2) No pooling layers are used in our architecture. The encoder only contains four convolutional layers (three standard convolutional layers and one PrimaryCaps layer) and two DigitCaps layers and the decoder adopts the original CapsNet structure which contains three fully connected layers.
(3) We test a single model on all five real-world complex datasets without using any ensembling methods and data augmentation techniques. The experimental results demonstrate that DDRM-CapsNet has a better performance than the previous CapsNet. Especially, DDRM-CapsNet achieves 77.50% and 29.93% test accuracy respectively on CIFAR-10 and CIFAR-100, an obvious promotion of over 11% and 8% respectively compared to the previous CapsNet.
(4) Not only contributing to the improvement of accuracy, our proposed DDRM can also improve the reconstruction performance based on the comparison with the reconstruction of the original CapsNet.

The rest of paper is organized as follows. We start by describing the overall network architecture of DDRM-CapsNet in Sect. 2. In Sect. 3, we illustrate our experimental results and evaluations against the original CapsNet, and analyze the effectiveness of our method. Finally, we conclude our paper and look forward to the future work in Sect. 4.

2 Architecture

Next, we will describe the network architecture of DDRM-CapsNet and Deep Dynamic Routing Mechanism (DDRM) respectively in detail.

2.1 Network Architecture

Our proposed network contains three standard convolutional layers, one PrimaryCaps layer, two DigitCaps layers (DigitCaps1 and DigitCaps2) and three fully connected layers.

Because of the data complexity we aim at, increasing the number of convolutional layers before PrimaryCaps layer is necessary in order to extract more important features and useful information hidden in the dataset. Three standard convolutional layers have 64, 128 and 256 filters respectively according to the requirement of our task and they are all set to size 5×5 and stride 1 by us.

Following three standard convolutional layers, PrimaryCaps layer is a convolutional capsule layer with some channels of convolutional $8D$ capsules, each of which applies 8 convolutional filters of size 9×9 and stride 2. The number of channels is tuned for different datasets.

The next layers are two consecutive DigitCaps layers: DigitCaps1 and DigitCaps2 and their outputs are one $16D$ and one $24D$ capsule respectively for every class. Each of capsules in DigitCaps1 and DigitCaps2 receive input from the PrimaryCaps and DigitCaps1 respectively. DDRM occurs not only between the low-layer capsules in PrimaryCaps and high-layer capsules in DigitCaps1 but also between the ones in DigitCaps1 and DigitCaps2.

Finally, adopting the same way as the original CapsNet, we use an additional reconstruction loss as a regularization method to encourage the capsules in two DigitCaps layers to encode as much information from the input image as possible. During training processes, we mask out all $24D$ vectors of K classes but the one of the correct digit capsule and thus these vectors are flattened into one $K \times 24D$ vector (K is the number of classification class for different datasets, e.g. K is 10 for CIFAR-10 dataset). Then the output from the DigitCaps2 layer is fed to a decoder comprised of three fully connected layers and is converted into a reconstructed image at last. We adopt margin loss for classification and squared error for reconstruction same as [3].

2.2 DDRM

As we know, the length of the activity vector of each capsule in DigitCaps layer indicates existence probability of each class and its direction indicates various properties of each class. Thus, the activity vector of capsules makes the expression of a particular feature richer.

In order to satisfy the demand of better representing complex features in complex image data for higher dimensionality, larger size and more categories, a higher-dimensionality output vector is necessary. Thus, we propose a new mechanism called DDRM based on the original dynamic routing whose output vector is $24D$. DDRM is divided into two stages and routing-by-agreement is used both in these two stages.

Take CIFAR-10 dataset as an example, our proposed network architecture is shown in Fig. 1. The network contains three standard convolutional layers (Conv1, Conv2, Conv3), one PrimaryCaps layer, two DigitCaps layers (DigitCaps1 and DigitCaps2) and three fully connected layers. The input of the whole network is an image from CIFAR-10 dataset whose shape is 32 × 32 × 3. Thus, the input image turns into 256 channels of size 20 × 20 through three standard convolutional layers which have 64, 128 and 256 filters respectively. PrimaryCaps layer outputs 32 channels of convolutional 8*D* capsules into DDRM. Through Stage1, the output of DigitCaps1 is one 16*D* capsule for 10 classes and the final output of DigitCaps2 is one 24*D* vector for 10 classes. During training, we mask out all the 24*D* capsules but the one of the true label and thus the ten 24*D* capsules are flattened into one 240*D* vector. The 240*D* vector is finally converted by three fully connected layers into a 32 × 32 × 3 reconstructed image.

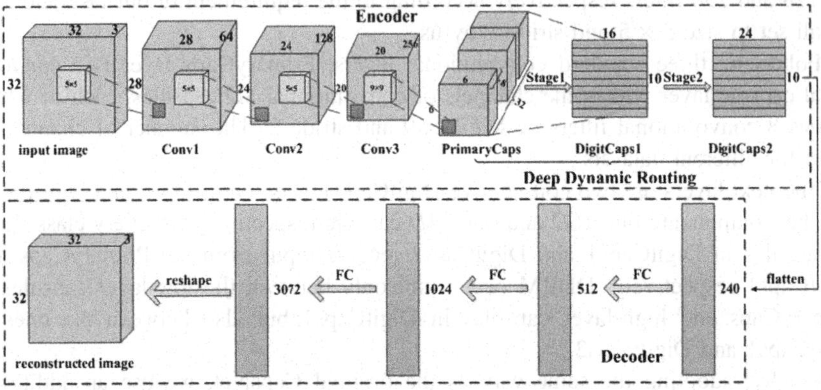

Fig. 1. Network architecture.

3 Experiment

3.1 Datasets and Preprocessing

In this section, we will provide details on the experimental preparation and the datasets we use.

To explore the performance of our proposed network on complex data, we choose five datasets for image classification in total which are respectively CIFAR-10, CIFAR-100 [9], the Extended Yale Face Database B [10], the Cropped Extended Yale Face Database B [11] and BelgiumTS [12]. The characteristics of five datasets including the number of classes, instances, image channels and image size are summarized in Table 1.

Before the experiment, we apply some preprocessing techniques to five datasets above based on their characteristics and our experimental need. Preprocessing techniques we adopt on each of five datasets are summarized in Table 2.

In addition, for CIFAR-10 and CIFAR-100, we both choose 10000 testing images from the official website as our testing data and divide 50000 training images from the official website into our training and validation data as 9:1. We adopt similar division

Table 1. Characteristics of five datasets.

Dataset	Classes	Instances	Channel number	Size (width × height)
CIFAR-10	10	60000	3	32 × 32
CIFAR-100	100	60000	3	32 × 32
Extended Yale Face Database B	28	16380	1	640 × 480
Cropped Extended Yale Face Database B	38	2470	1	168 × 192
BelgiumTS	62	7095	3	Different sizes

Table 2. Preprocessing techniques on each dataset.

Dataset	Min-Max normalization	Resize (width × height)
CIFAR-10	Applied	Not applied
CIFAR-100	Applied	Not applied
Extended Yale Face Database B	Applied	96 × 96
Cropped Extended Yale Face Database B	Applied	96 × 96
BelgiumTS	Applied	48 × 48

on BelgiumTS. As for other two datasets, Training, validation and testing data are divided from the original data as 70%: 15%: 15%. We will use validation data to select hyperparameters for the models in our experiment which achieve best validation results and train each model with the selected hyperparameters.

3.2 Influences of Dimensionality for Output Vector in DigitCaps2

Since the dimensionality for output vector in the DigitCaps2 layer decide how many attributes describe the existence of a particular class which is crucial for the training process and classification accuracy, we evaluate its influences on five datasets above using our proposed method.

We fix the output of the DigitCaps1 layer as a $16D$ vector and choose the dimensionality for output vector in the DigitCaps2 layer as 24, 32 and 40, denoted respectively as the following: (1) "D = 24". (2) "D = 32". (3) "D = 40". We compare these three models on five datasets above. All the classification results on five datasets are summarized in Table 3 and we choose test accuracy as the comparison metric. In our experimental setting, the number of routing iterations is 3 and the weight of reconstruction loss is 0.0005. In addition, we use early stopping to avoid overfitting.

As we can see from Table 3, the model "D = 24" achieves the best accuracy results (at least equally best) among all three models on all five datasets. And we can see that simply increasing the dimensionality for output vector in the DigitCaps2 layer does not work, that is to say, too high- dimensionality output vector cannot help to promote the accuracy result. Based on the fact above, "D = 24" is the most suitable dimensionality for output vector in the DigitCaps2 layer and we choose to use "D = 24" in our experiments.

Table 3. Comparison of test accuracy results (%).

Dataset	D = 24	D = 32	D = 40
CIFAR-10	**76.61**	75.36	74.63
CIFAR-100	**29.48**	26.49	25.71
Extended Yale Face Database B	**100**	**100**	**100**
Cropped Extended Yale Face Database B	**98.64**	98.10	**98.64**
BelgiumTS	**95.66**	94.98	94.98

3.3 Comparisons with Baseline and Influences of Convolutional Layers and DDRM

We fix "D = 24" and attempt different combination modes of the network architecture to train the model including adding different number of standard convolutional layers before PrimaryCaps layer and use DDRM or not. We compare our proposed method to the baseline CapsNet model [3] on all five datasets. We totally evaluate the performance of five models including the baseline: (1) one standard convolutional layer, one PrimaryCaps layer, one DigitCaps layer and three fully connected layers, denoted as "Baseline". (2) one standard convolutional layer, one PrimaryCaps layer, two DigitCaps layers and three fully connected layers, denoted as "1 conv+2 DC". (3) two standard convolutional layers, one PrimaryCaps layer, two DigitCaps layers and three fully connected layers, denoted as "2 conv+2 DC". (4) three standard convolutional layers, one PrimaryCaps layer, two DigitCaps layers and three fully connected layers, denoted as "3 conv+2 DC". (5) four standard convolutional layers, one PrimaryCaps layer, two DigitCaps layers and three fully connected layers, denoted as "4 conv+2 DC".

All the classification results on five datasets are summarized in Table 4. We choose test accuracy as the comparison metric.

Table 4. Comparison of test accuracy results (%).

Dataset	Baseline	1 conv +2 DC	2 conv +2 DC	3 conv +2 DC	4 conv +2 DC
CIFAR-10	66.31	76.61	75.62	**77.50**	74.56
CIFAR-100	21.54	29.48	27.90	**29.93**	27.57
Extended Yale Face Database B	**100**	**100**	**100**	**100**	**100**
Cropped Extended Yale Face Database B	98.37	**98.64**	**98.64**	**98.64**	**98.64**
BelgiumTS	94.98	95.66	95.06	**95.78**	94.06

As we can see from Table 4, no matter which kind of combination mode, our proposed methods achieve better test accuracy results than the baseline model on all five datasets. Especially on CIFAR-10 and CIFAR-100, the best corresponding results of our methods are 77.50% and 29.93%, raising the test accuracy more than 11% and 8%

respectively compared to the baseline model which is an obvious promotion. In addition, with the classification accuracy (69.34% and 18%) for a single model achieved by Xi et al. [5] and Mukhometzianov et al. [6] respectively on CIFAR-10 and CIFAR-100 as a reference to evaluate our results, our accuracy result still achieves an obvious promotion of more than 8% and 11% respectively. It fully proves the effectiveness of our method on improving accuracy although without any data augmentation or ensembling.

In addition, among all the models, "3 conv+2 DC" achieves the best accuracy results (at least equally best) on all five datasets. Based on the fact above, we can conclude that "3 conv+2 DC" has the best generalization performance and it is the most suitable architecture for our network as shown in Fig. 1. The average and total training time of baseline and "3 conv+2 DC" are summarized respectively in Table 5. As we can see from Table 5, "3 conv+2 DC" cost only a little more training time than the baseline.

Table 5. Average and total training time of baseline and "3 conv+2 DC" (seconds/minutes).

Dataset	Baseline	3 conv+2 DC
CIFAR-10	0.16/47.48	0.17/50.38
CIFAR-100	0.17/49.33	0.18/51.26
Extended Yale Face Database B	0.21/122.62	0.23/138.01
Cropped Extended Yale Face Database B	0.25/22.50	0.26/23.49
BelgiumTS	0.06/12.85	0.09/19.28

From the second, third and fifth column in Table 4, we can prove our assumption that increasing the number of standard convolutional layers and our proposed DDRM can help to improve the classification accuracy for complex datasets, which can be a indirect proof that they can extract more features and make the expression of a particular feature richer respectively.

Despite the fact above, "2 conv+2 DC" and "4 conv+2 DC" both respectively cannot achieve better or even achieve lower accuracy results than "1 conv+2 DC" and "3 conv+2 DC" on all five datasets. Thus, simply increasing the number of standard convolutional layers has its limitations and does not always contribute to promote the accuracy result.

3.4 Convergence

The trend curves of training loss for DDRM-CapsNet and baseline on five datasets are shown in Fig. 2. As we can see, DDRM-CapsNet converges faster obviously as the training step increases than the baseline in CIFAR-10, CIFAR-100 and BelgiumTS. In the Extended Yale Face Database B and the Cropped Extended Yale Face Database B, DDRM-CapsNet and the baseline produce similar trend curve. In addition, FSC-CapsNet converges to an obvious lower value than the baseline in CIFAR-10 and CIFAR-100. However, FSC-CapsNet still produces some oscillations on three datasets consisting of RGB images especially on CIFAR-100. Except CIFAR-100, the training loss of FSC-CapsNet approaches 0 at last on other four datasets. Based on all the facts above, DDRM-CapsNet is a model with better and faster convergence overall than the baseline.

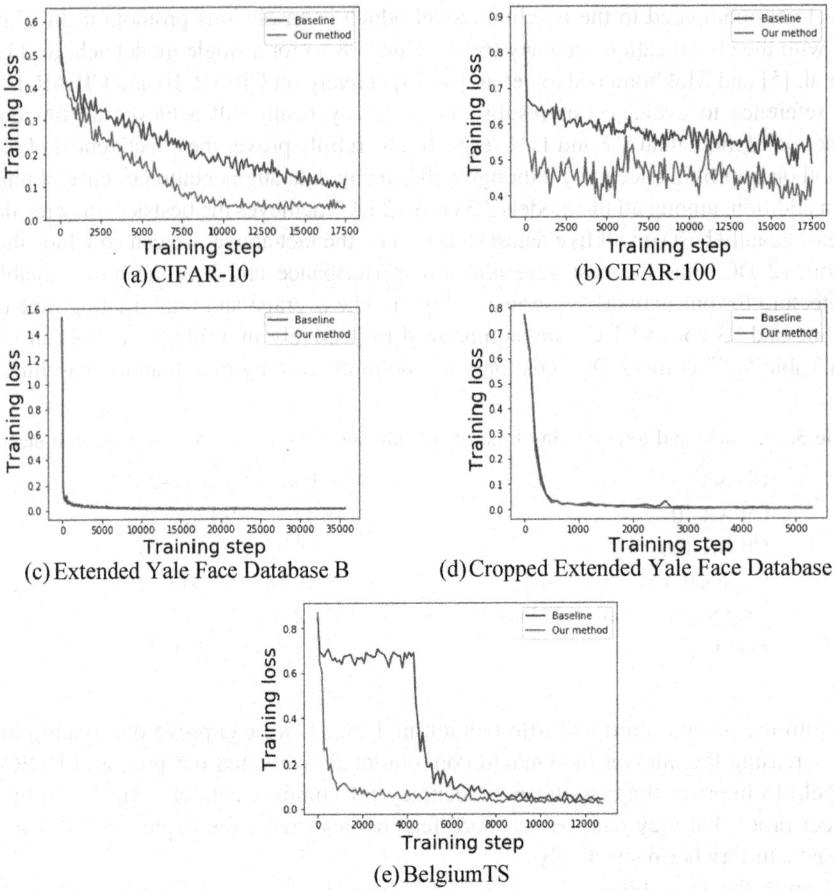

(a) CIFAR-10

(b) CIFAR-100

(c) Extended Yale Face Database B

(d) Cropped Extended Yale Face Database B

(e) BelgiumTS

Fig. 2. Training loss of baseline and our method on five datasets.

3.5 Comparison of Reconstruction Performance

As we can see from Table 4, "1 conv+2 DC" achieves better accuracy results than the baseline model. Their decoder structures are the same which both consist of three fully connected layers and the only difference between them is the encoder part: "1 conv+2 DC" adopts our proposed DDRM which contains two stages and the dynamic routing mechanism of the baseline contains only one stage. Next, we will compare reconstruction performance of them on the Extended Yale Face Database B and CIFAR-10 respectively.

Fifty real images (top half in the figure) from Extended Yale Face Database B and CIFAR-10 and fifty reconstruction images (bottom half in the figure) using trained model of baseline and our method are concatenated shown respectively in Figs. 3 and 5.

For human faces in the Extended Yale Face Database B, although still a little vague, our method reconstructs clearer and more distinct facial features than the baseline, which can prove that our proposed DDRM can not only promote the accuracy

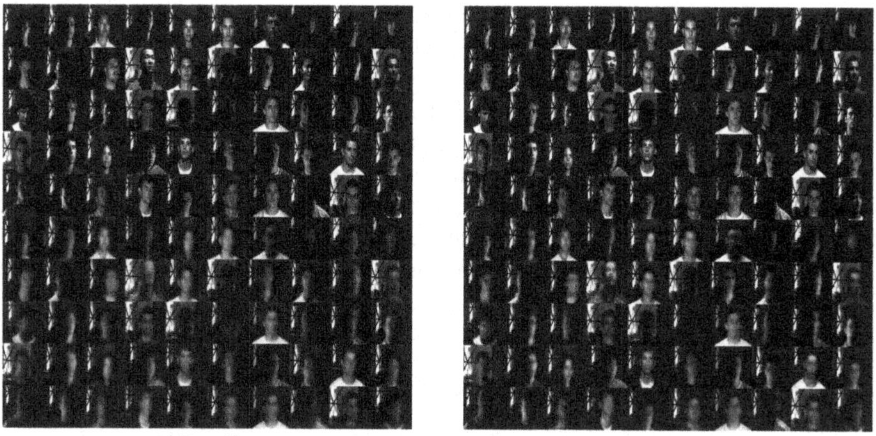

(a) Baseline (b) Our method

Fig. 3. The reconstruction of baseline and our method for Extended Yale Face Database B.

Fig. 4. Comparison of reconstruction performance.

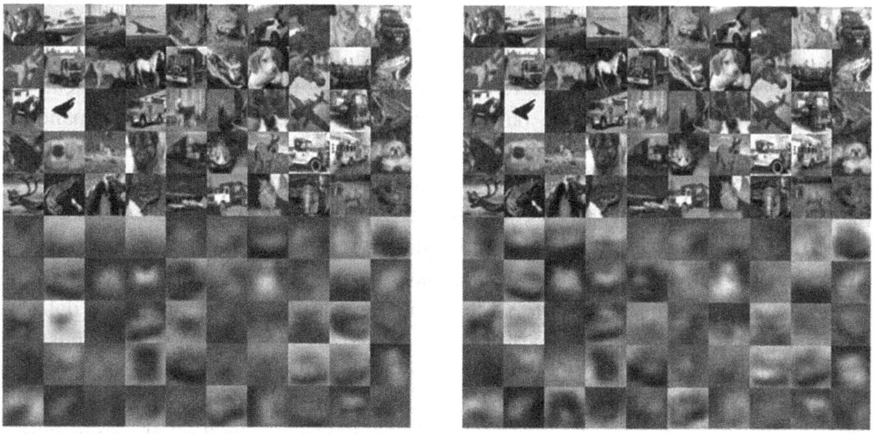

(a) Baseline (b) Our method

Fig. 5. The reconstruction of baseline and our method for CIFAR-10.

result, but also improve the reconstruction performance. We choose eight images under good illumination conditions from Extended Yale Face Database B to explain the reconstruction difference between the baseline and our method. Eight real images (top in the figure) from Extended Yale Face Database B, eight reconstruction images (middle in the figure) using baseline and eight reconstruction images (bottom in the figure) using our method are concatenated shown in Fig. 4. It can be clearly seen that our reconstruction images have clearer organ than the baseline such as eyes and nose. But unfortunately, the reconstruction images using our method on CIFAR-10 are still very vague and lack distinct features, although they have clearer outline than the baseline in most of all fifty pictures.

4 Conclusion and Future Work

In this paper, in order to solve the problem that CapsNet achieves poor results on complex data, we propose a new architecture for CapsNet called DDRM-CapsNet. We modify both the network structure and the dynamic routing mechanism. In detail, we increase the number of convolutional layers before capsule layer in the encoder part to extract better features. We also improve the dynamic routing mechanism based on the original CapsNet, expand the new mechanism into two stages and change its output vector to $24D$. Thus, finally DDRM-CapsNet contains three standard convolutional layers, one PrimaryCaps layer, two DigitCaps layers and three fully connected layers.

We conduct experiments using a single model without any ensembling and data augmentation on five complex datasets. Our experimental results demonstrate the effectiveness of our proposed method compared with the original CapsNet. Our architecture "3 conv+2 DC" achieves the best classification test accuracy among five models including the original CapsNet on all five datasets. Especially on CIFAR-10 and CIFAR-100, the best results of our method are 77.50% and 29.93%, an obvious promotion of more than 11% and 8% respectively compared to the original CapsNet and more than 8% and 11% respectively compared to the single model achieved by Xi et al. [5] and Mukhometzianov et al. [6]. In addition, based on the comparison with the reconstruction of the original CapsNet, we conclude that our proposed DDRM can not only promote the accuracy result, but also improve the reconstruction performance.

Unfortunately, due to limitations of our computational resources and training time, we do not attempt more hyperparameters. Although our proposed method has a significant improvement in accuracy compared to the original CapsNet, it is still difficult to meet CNN's achievements on complex data for image classification. Therefore, we can attempt more hyperparameters such as making more detailed improvements to the network structure in the future. In addition, the reconstruction effect on some datasets such as CIFAR-10 is still unclear and only some outlines can be seen. Thus, the original decoder simply consisting of three fully connected layers is to be modified to a better one to reconstruct input images. At last, the model complexity for CapsNet mainly comes from the dynamic rooting mechanism which costs lots of training time. Thus, in order to achieve better results and explore more possibilities, how to design a more efficient dynamic rooting mechanism is the key, which will become our research emphasis in the future work.

References

1. Krizhevsky, A., Sutskever, I., Hinton, G.E.: Imagenet classification with deep convolutional neural networks. In: Advances in Neural Information Processing Systems, pp. 1097–1105 (2012). https://doi.org/10.1145/3065386
2. Zeiler, Matthew D., Fergus, R.: Visualizing and understanding convolutional networks. In: Fleet, D., Pajdla, T., Schiele, B., Tuytelaars, T. (eds.) ECCV 2014. LNCS, vol. 8689, pp. 818–833. Springer, Cham (2014). https://doi.org/10.1007/978-3-319-10590-1_53
3. Sabour, S., Frosst, N., Hinton, G.E.: Dynamic routing between capsules. In: Advances in Neural Information Processing Systems, pp. 3856–3866 (2017)
4. Zeiler, M.D., Fergus, R.: Stochastic pooling for regularization of deep convolutional neural networks. arXiv preprint arXiv:1301.3557 (2013)
5. Xi, E., Bing, S., Jin, Y.: Capsule network performance on complex data. arXiv preprint arXiv:1712.03480 (2017)
6. Mukhometzianov, R., Carrillo, J.: CapsNet comparative performance evaluation for image classification. arXiv preprint arXiv:1805.11195 (2018)
7. Simonyan, K., Zisserman, A.: Very deep convolutional networks for large-scale image recognition. arXiv preprint arXiv:1409.1556 (2014)
8. Szegedy, C., Liu, W., Jia, Y., et al.: Going deeper with convolutions. In: Proceedings of the IEEE Conference on Computer Vision and Pattern Recognition, pp. 1–9 (2015). https://doi.org/10.1109/cvpr.2015.7298594
9. Krizhevsky, A.: Learning multiple layers of features from tiny images. Technical report, University of Toronto (2009)
10. Georghiades, A.S., Belhumeur, P.N., Kriegman, D.J.: From few to many: illumination cone models for face recognition under variable lighting and pose. IEEE Trans. Pattern Anal. Mach. Intell. **23**(6), 643–660 (2001). https://doi.org/10.1109/34.927464
11. Lee, K.C., Ho, J., Kriegman, D.J.: Acquiring linear subspaces for face recognition under variable lighting. IEEE Trans. Pattern Anal. Mach. Intell. **27**(5), 684–698 (2005). https://doi.org/10.1109/TPAMI.2005.92
12. Timofte, R., Zimmerman, K., Van Gool, L.: Multi-view traffic sign detection, recognition, and 3D localization. Mach. Vis. Appl. **25**(3), 633–647 (2014). https://doi.org/10.1007/s00138-011-0391-3

Embedding Systems

Squeezed Very Deep Convolutional Neural Networks for Text Classification

Andréa B. Duque[(✉)], Luã Lázaro J. Santos, David Macêdo, and Cleber Zanchettin

Centro de Informática - CIn, Universidade Federal de Pernambuco, Recife, Brazil
{abd,lljs,dlm,cz}@cin.ufpe.br

Abstract. Embedding artificial intelligence on constrained platforms has become a trend since the growth of embedded systems and mobile devices, experimented in recent years. Although constrained platforms do not have enough processing capabilities to train a sophisticated deep learning model, like convolutional neural networks (CNN), they are already capable of performing inference locally by using a previously trained embedded model. This approach enables numerous advantages such as privacy, response latency, and no real time network dependence. Still, the use of a local CNN model on constrained platforms is restricted by its storage size. Most of the research in CNNs has focused on increasing network depth to improve accuracy. In the text classification area, deep models were proposed with excellent performance but relying on large architectures with thousands of parameters, and consequently, high storage size. We propose to modify the structure of the Very Deep Convolutional Neural Networks (VDCNN) model to reduce its storage size while keeping the model performance. In this paper, we evaluate the impact of Temporal Depthwise Separable Convolutions and Global Average Pooling in the network parameters, storage size, dedicated hardware dependence, and accuracy. The proposed squeezed model (SVDCNN) is between 10x and 20x smaller than the original version, depending on the network depth, maintaining a maximum disk size of 6MB. Regarding accuracy, the network experiences a loss between 0.4% and 1.3% in the accuracy performance while obtains lower latency over non-dedicated hardware and higher inference time ratio compared to the baseline model.

Keywords: Convolutional Neural Networks · Text classification · Embedded platform · Constrained models

1 Introduction

The general trend in deep learning approaches has been developing models with increasing layers. Deeper neural networks have achieved high-quality results in different tasks, such as image classification, detection, and segmentation.

A. B. Duque and L. L. J. Santos—Equally contributed.

I. V. Tetko et al. (Eds.): ICANN 2019, LNCS 11727, pp. 193–207, 2019.
https://doi.org/10.1007/978-3-030-30487-4_16

Deep models can also learn hierarchical feature representations from images [21]. In the Natural Language Processing (NLP) field, the belief that compositional models can also be used to text-related tasks is more recent.

The increasing availability of text data motivates the research for models able to improve accuracy in different language tasks. Following the image classification Convolutional Neural Network (CNN) tendency, the research in text classification has placed effort into developing deeper networks. The first CNN based approach for text was a shallow network with one layer [10]. Following this work, deeper architectures were proposed [2,22]. Conneau et al. [2] was the first to propose Very Deep Convolutional Neural Networks (VDCNN) applied to text classification. According to the authors, VDCNN accuracy increases with depth. Currently, the approach with 29 layers is the state-of-the-art accuracy of CNNs for text classification [2].

However, regardless of making networks deeper to improve accuracy, little effort has been made to fit text classification models in constrained platforms, like embedded systems and mobile devices. Although constrained platforms do not have enough processing capabilities to train a sophisticated deep learning model, they are capable of processing predictions locally. In this approach, the model is trained on a proper environment for deep learning tasks, and then the trained model is transferred to the target constrained platform so that it performs the inference step.

Still, the model storage size is a limiting factor for constrained platforms [3,5,7]. Concerning embedded systems, FPGAs are a clear example: they usually offer less than 10 MB of on-chip memory and no off-chip memory or storage. Regarding mobile devices, the model size impacts directly on the final application size. Regarding mobile devices, there is a constant effort for developing mobile applications with a smaller size on both entry-level and cutting-edge devices. Concerning entry-level devices, there are operational systems (OS) with several restrictions for maximum application size. For example, on Android GO OS, applications should be less than 40 MB on device, while games should be less than 65 MB on device.

The application size also impacts on the amount of mobile data that the user needs to download and update the application. Therefore, even on cutting-edge smartphones, which count with high internal memory capacity, high storage size applications are undesirable. Additionally, there are numerous benefits of embedding smaller local models as (1) no real-time network dependence, the user can use the application even with no internet connection; (2) lower latency speed, since the inference is performed locally (not on a server), it can be faster and more reliable by avoiding network requests; (3) scalability, no need to worry about scaling or distributed computing, once the processing is performed by each user device; (4) privacy, no personal data needs to leave the device since all processing is performed locally.

The research in deep learning for text classification has been focused on presenting different architectures to obtain state-of-the-art accuracy. To the best of our knowledge, efforts were not made in reviewing text classification models regarding efficiency metrics such as storage size. Despite, several relevant real-world applications depend on text classification tasks such as sentiment analysis, recommendation, and opinion mining. The appeal for these applications combined with the boost in mobile devices usage motivates the need for research in restrained text classification models. In contrast to advances in the text classification field, constrained models have been already proposed to perform image classification [5,7] and it has been demonstrated that size and speed are constraints to an efficient mobile and embedded deployment of deep models [5].

In this paper, we investigate modifications on the network proposed by Conneau et al. [2] intending to reduce its number of parameters and storage size with minimal performance degradation. To achieve these improvements, we used Temporal Depthwise Separable Convolution and Global Average Pooling. Additionally, we also examine the dedicated hardware dependence of the proposed model. Therefore, our main contribution is to propose the Squeezed Very Deep Convolutional Neural Networks (SVDCNN), a very deep text classification model which requires significantly fewer parameters compared to the state-of-the-art CNNs. Furthermore, the reduction of parameters provided by the SVDCNN enables its local usage in constrained platforms, such as embedded systems and mobile devices.

Section 2 provides an overview of deep learning models for text classification. Section 3 presents the VDCNN model. Section 4 explains the proposed model SVDCNN and the subsequent impact in the total number of parameters of the network. Section 5 details the experiments. Section 6 analyses the results and lastly, Sect. 7, presents conclusions and direction for future works.

2 Related Work

Several deep learning architectures were proposed for text and document classification achieving state-of-the-art results in accuracy. Convolutional neural networks (CNNs) and recurrent neural network (RNNs) are two mainstream architectures for such tasks, which have entirely different behaviors.

CNNs are able to learn local response from data and to extract features in a parallel way. CNNs were initially designed for Computer Vision to consider feature extraction and classification as one task [13]. Although CNNs are very successful in image classification tasks, its use in text classification is relatively new and has some peculiarities. Contrasting with the traditional image bi-dimensional representation, texts are one-dimensionally represented. Due to this property, used convolutions are temporal convolutions. Furthermore, it is necessary to generate a numerical representation from the text to training the network. This representation, namely embeddings, is usually obtained through the application of a lookup table, generated from a given dictionary [2].

An early approach for text classification tasks consisted of a shallow neural network working on the word level and using only one convolutional layer [10]. The author reported results in smaller datasets. Later, Zhang et al. [22] proposed the first CNN approach to a character level (Char-CNN), which allowed them to train up to 6 convolutional layers, followed by three fully connected classification layers. Char-CNN uses convolutional kernels of size 3 and 7, as well as simple max-pooling layers.

Conneau et al. (2016) proposed the Very Deep CNN (VDCNN) [2] also on a character level, presenting improvements compared to Char-CNN. Conneau et al. (2016) have shown that text classification accuracy increases when the proposed model becomes deeper. VDCNN uses only small kernel convolutions and pooling operations. The proposed architecture relies on the VGG and ResNet philosophy [4,17]: The number of feature maps and the temporal resolution is modeled so their product is constant. This approach makes it easier to control the memory footprint of the network. Both Zhang and Conneau et al. CNNs utilized standard convolutional blocks and fully connected layers to combine convolution information [2,22]. This architecture increases the number of parameters and storage size of the models. However, size and speed was not the focus of those works.

The idea of developing smaller and more efficient CNNs without losing representative accuracy is a less explored research direction in NLP, but it has already been a trend for computer vision applications [5,7,15]. Most approaches consist of compressing pre-trained networks or training small networks [5]. A recent tendency in image deep models is replacing standard convolutional blocks with Depthwise Separable Convolutions (DSCs). The purpose is to reduce the number of parameters and consequently the model size. DSCs were initially introduced in [16] and since then, they have been successfully applied to image classification, and [1,5,15] machine translation [9] to reduce the computation in convolutional blocks. Another approach is the use of a Global Average Pooling (GAP) layer at the output of the network to replace fully connected layers. This approach has become a standard architectural decision for newer CNNs [4,6].

In contrast to the CNN models, in the RNN models, tokens are usually processed sequentially, considering the text direction to capture these relations. The most common approach for RNN is the Long Short-Term Memory (LSTM model) [18,19]. LSTM is a type of RNN that preserves long term dependency more effectively in comparison to the basic RNN. Attempts to combine both architectures CNNs and RNNs were also proposed such as C-LSTM [23] and RCNN [11]. More recently, the model Transformer based on attention mechanism proposes to compute representations and to dispense the need for convolutions or aligned RNNs [20].

3 VDCNN Model for Text Classification

The VDCNN is a modular architecture for text classification tasks developed to offer different depth levels (9, 17, 29, and 49). Figure 1 presents the architecture for depth 9. The network begins with a lookup table, which generates the embeddings for the input text and stores them in a 2D tensor of size (f_0, s). The number of input characters (s) is fixed to 1,024 while the embedding dimension (f_0) is 16. The embedding dimension can be seen as the number of RGB channels of an image.

The next layer (3, Temp Convolution, 64) applies 64 temporal convolutions of kernel size 3, so the output tensor has size $64 * s$. Its primary function is to fit the lookup table output with the modular network segment input composed by convolutional blocks. Each aforenamed block is a sequence of two temporal convolutional layers, each one accompanied by a temporal batch normalization layer [8] and a ReLU activation. Besides, the different network depths are obtained varying the number of convolutional blocks. As a convention, the depth of a network is given as its total number of convolutions. For instance, the architecture of depth 17 has two convolutional blocks of each level of feature maps, which results in 4 convolutional layers for each level (see Table 1).

Table 1. Number of convolutional layers for each different VDCNN depth architecture

Depth	9	17	29	49
Convolutional block 512	2	4	4	6
Convolutional block 256	2	4	4	10
Convolutional block 128	2	4	10	16
Convolutional block 64	2	4	10	16
First convolutional layer	1	1	1	1

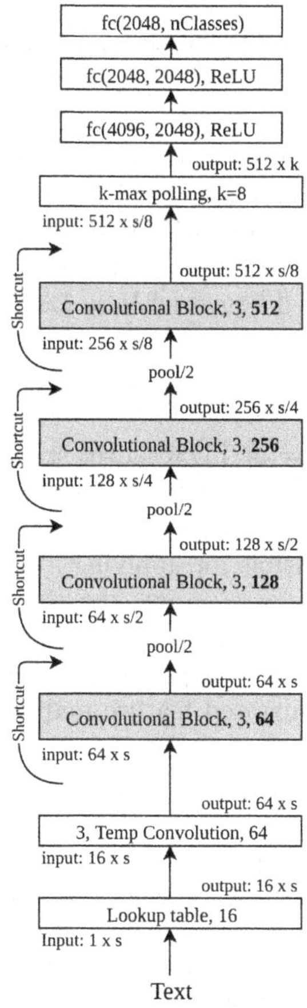

Fig. 1. Depth 9 VDCNN architecture

Considering the first convolutional layer of the network, we obtain the depth $2 * (2 + 2 + 2 + 2) + 1 = 17$. Table 1 summarizes the different depth architectures provided by VDCNN model. The following rule is employed to minimize the network's memory footprint: Before each convolutional block doubling the number of feature maps, a pooling layer halves the temporal dimension. This strategy is inspired by the VGG and ResNets philosophy and results in three levels of feature maps: 128, 256 and 512 (see Fig. 1). Additionally, the VDCNN network also contains shortcut connections [4] for each convolutional blocks implemented through the usage of 1×1 convolutions.

Lastly, for the classification task, the k most valuable features ($k = 8$) are extracted using k-max pooling, generating a one-dimensional vector which supplies three fully connected layers with ReLU hidden units and softmax outputs. The number of hidden units is 2,048, and they do not use dropout but rather batch normalization after convolutional layers perform the network regularization.

4 SVDCNN Model for Text Classification

The primary objective is reducing the number of parameters so the resulting network has a significative lower storage size. We first propose to modify the convolutional blocks of VDCNN model by the use of Temporal Depthwise Separable Convolutions (TDSCs). Next, we apply a Global Average Pooling (GAP) and reduce the number of fully connected layers. The resulting proposed architecture is called Squeezed Very Deep Convolutional Neural Networks (SVDCNN).

4.1 Temporal Depthwise Separable Convolutions (TDSCs)

The use of TDSCs over standard convolutions allowed to reduce the number of parameters without relevant accuracy loss [5]. TDSCs work decompounding the standard convolution into two parts: Depthwise and Pointwise. The first one is responsible for applying a convolutional filter to each channel of the input. For an image as input, the channels are the RGB components, whereas in a text input the dimensions of the embedding are used for representation. The result is one feature map by channel for both cases above. The second convolution unifies the generated feature maps successively applying 1×1 convolutions to achieve the target amount of feature maps.

TDSCs are DSCs which work with one-dimensional convolutions. Although DSCs hold verified results in image classification networks, the use of its temporal version for text related tasks is less explored. Figure 2a presents the architecture of a standard temporal convolution while Fig. 2b presents the TDSC.

For a more formal definition, let P_{tsc} be the number of parameters of a temporal standard convolution, where In and Out are the numbers of Input and Output channels respectively, and D_k is the kernel size:

$$P_{tsc} = In * Out * D_k \tag{1}$$

Alternatively, a TDSC achieves fewer parameters (P_{tdsc}):

$$P_{tdsc} = In * Dk + In * Out \tag{2}$$

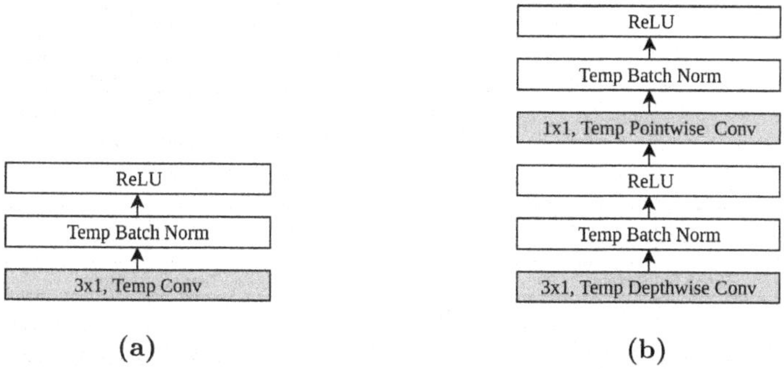

Fig. 2. (a) Temporal Standard Convolution; (b) Temporal Depthwise Separable Convolution.

In the VDCNN model, one convolutional block is composed of two temporal standard convolutional layers. The first one doubles the number of feature maps while the second keeps the same value received as input. Besides, each convolutional layer is followed by a Batch Normalization and ReLU layers. In our model, we proposed changing the temporal standard convolutions by TDSCs.

Figure 3 presents the standard convolutional block on the left and the proposed convolutional block using TDSC on the right. The pattern used in the figure for the convolutional layers is the following: "Kernel Size, Conv type, Output Feature Maps"; as a brief example consider "3×1, Temporal Conv, 256", which means a Temporal Convolution with kernel size 3 and 256 feature maps as output. From Eq. 1, we have the number of parameters of the original convolutional block ($P_{convblock}$) as follows:

$$P_{convblock} = In * Out * 3 + Out * Out * 3 \tag{3}$$

Moreover, from Eq. 2, the number of parameters of the proposed convolutional block ($P_{convblock-tdsc}$) that uses TDSC being:

$$P_{convblock-tdsc} = In * 3 + In * Out + Out * 3 + Out * Out \tag{4}$$

For illustration, following the same characteristics of Fig. 3, consider that the number of input channels In is equal to 128 and the number of output channels Out is equal to 256. Our proposed approach accumulates a total of 99,456 parameters. In contrast, there are 294,912 parameters in the original convolutional block. The use of TDSC yields a reduction of 66.28% in the network size.

Lastly, since each standard temporal convolution turns into two (Depthwise and Pointwise), the number of convolutions per convolutional block has doubled. Nevertheless, these two convolutions work as one because it is not possible to use them separately keeping the same propose. In this way, we count them as one layer in the network depth. This decision holds the provided depth architectures the same as the VDCNN model summarized in Table 1, contributing to a proper comparison between the models.

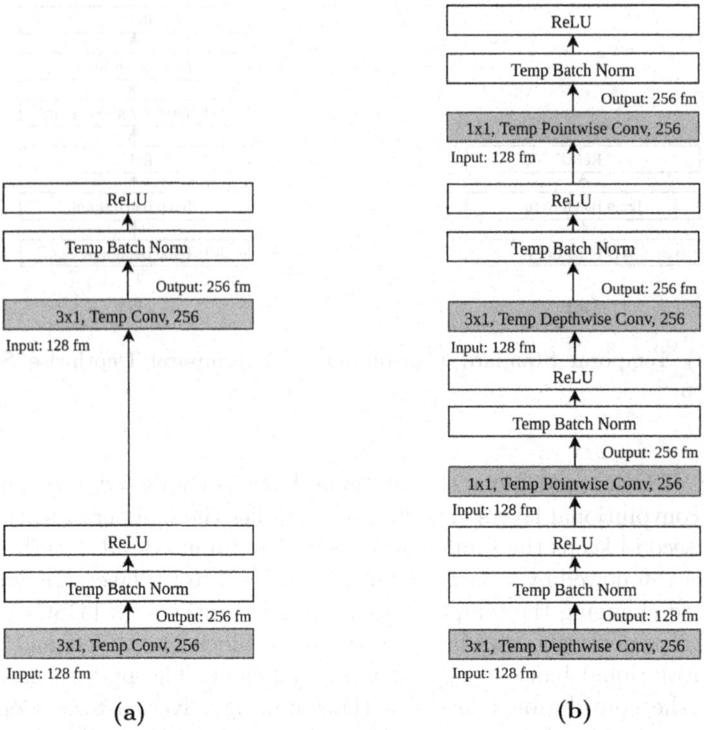

Fig. 3. (a) Standard convolutional block of the VDCNN; (b) Modified convolutional block of the SVDCNN.

4.2 Global Average Pooling (GAP)

The VDCNN model uses a k-max pooling layer ($k = 8$) followed by three fully connected (FC) layers to perform the classification task (Fig. 4a). Although this approach is the traditional architecture choice for text classification CNNs, it introduces a significant number of parameters in the network. A more recent architecture tendency relies on the reduction of fully connected layers. Kaiming et al. used, in ResNet [4], a global average pooling layer followed by one FC layer, while Hoa et al., in DenseNet [12], opted by substitute the FC layers by an average polling layer.

The resulting number of the FC layers parameters (P_{fc}) on the baseline model is presented below, for a problem with four target classes:

$$\begin{aligned} P_{fc} &= 512 * k * 2,048 + 2,048 * 2,048 + 2,048 * 4 \\ P_{fc} &= 12,591,104 \end{aligned} \tag{5}$$

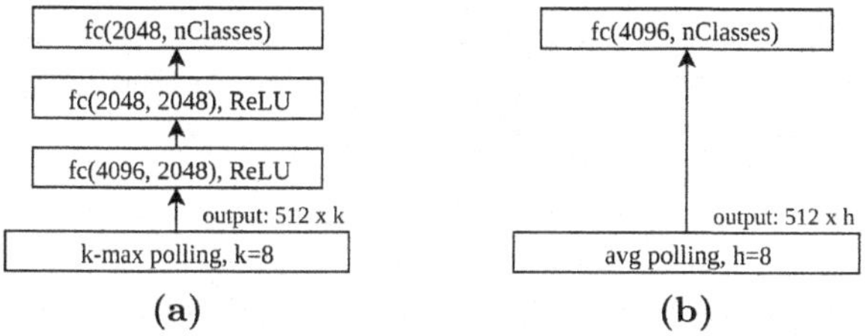

Fig. 4. (a) VDCNN classification layers; (b) SVDCNN classification layers.

Following ResNet philosophy, we directly aggregate the output of the last convolutional block with a Global Average Pooling followed by one fully connected layer with softmax. The option of using a global average pooling layer over fully connected layers contributes substantially to the parameters reduction without significantly degrade of the network accuracy [14].

The number of resulting feature maps given by the average pooling layer was the same as the original k-max pooling layer ($k = h = 8$). Figure 4b presents this proposed modification. The number of parameters using a GAP layer followed by one FC layer (P_{gap}) is calculated as follows:

$$\begin{aligned} P_{gap} &= 4,096 * 4 \\ P_{gap} &= 16,384 \end{aligned} \tag{6}$$

Our proposed approach accumulates a total of 16,384 parameters. In contrast, there are 12,591,104 parameters in the original classification method. This architecture yields a reduction of 99.86%.

5 Experiments

The experiment goal is to investigate the impact of modifying the convolutional block of VDCNN to TDSCs and using GAP with one fully connected layer over the original approach with three fully connected layers. We investigate if the techniques proposed optimize CNNs for text classification concerning constrained platforms, and without degrading accuracy. Therefore, we compare our model with state-of-the-art CNNs. We evaluate Char-CNN, VDCNN, and SVDCNN according to the number of parameters, storage size, inference time, and accuracy. The source code of the proposed model is available in the GitHub repository SVDCNN[1]

The original VDCNN paper reported the number of parameters of the convolutional layers, in which we reproduce in this article. For SVDCNN and Char-CNN, we calculated the abovementioned number of parameters from the network architecture implemented in PyTorch. As for the FC layer's parameters, the number is obtained as the summation of the product of the input and output size of each FC layer for each CNN.

[1] Link: https://github.com/lazarotm/SVDCNN

Considering the network parameters P and assuming that one float number on Cuda environment takes 4 bytes, we can calculate the network storage in megabytes, for all the models, as follows:

$$S = P * 4 \div 1{,}024^2 \tag{7}$$

Regarding the inference time, its average and standard deviation were calculated as the time to predict one instance of the AG's News dataset throughout 1,000 repetitions.

The SVDCNN experimental settings are similar to the original VDCNN paper, using the same dictionary and the same embedding size of 16 [2]. The training is also performed with SGD, utilizing size batch of 64, with a maximum of 100 epochs. We use an initial learning rate of 0.01, a momentum of 0.9, and a weight decay of 0.001. All the experiments were performed on an NVIDIA GTX 1060 GPU + Intel Core i7 4770 s CPU.

Table 2. Datasets used in experiments

Dataset	#Train	#Test	#Classes	Classification task
AG's news	120k	7.6k	4	News categorization
Yelp polarity	560k	38k	2	Sentiment analysis
Yelp full	650k	50k	5	Sentiment analysis

The model's performance is evaluated on three large-scale public datasets also used by Zhang et al. [22] in the introduction of Char-CNN and VDCNN models. Table 2 presents the details of the utilized datasets: AG's News, Yelp Polarity, and Yelp Full.

6 Results

Table 3 presents the number of parameters, storage size, and accuracy for the SVDCNN, VDCNN, and Char-CNN in all datasets. The use of TDSCs promoted a significant reduction in convolutional parameters compared to VDCNN. For the most in-depth network evaluated, which contains 29 convolutional layers (depth 29), the number of parameters of these convolutional layers had a reduction of 66.08%, from 4.6 to 1.56 million parameters. This quantity is slightly larger than the one obtained from the Char-CNN, 1.40 million parameters, but this network has only six convolutional layers (depth 6).

The network size reduction obtained by the use of GAP with only one FC layer is even more representative since both compared models use three FC layers for their classification tasks. Considering a dataset with four target classes, and comparing SVDCNN with VDCNN, the number of parameters of the FC layers has passed from 12.59 to 0.02 million parameters, representing a reduction of

99.84%. Following with the same comparison, but to Char-CNN, the proposed model is 99.82% smaller, 0.02 against 11.36 million of FC parameters.

The reduction of the total parameters impacts directly on the network storage size. While our most in-depth model (29) has only 6MB, VDCNN with the same depth uses 64.16 MB of storage. Likewise, Char-CNN (which has depth 6) occupies 43.25 MB. This reduction is a very significant result for constrained platforms such as embedded systems and mobile devices. For example, FPGAs often have less than 10 MB of on-chip memory and no off-chip memory or storage [5]. Concerting to mobile devices, the usage of a reduced local model offers numerous benefits, such as no real-time network dependence, lower latency speed, increase scalability, privacy, and data saving.

Regarding accuracy results, usually, a model with such parameters reduction should present some loss of accuracy in comparison to the original model. Nevertheless, the difference in accuracy between VDCNN and SVDCNN models varies between 0.4% and 1.3%, which is pretty modest considering the parameters and storage size reduction aforementioned. In Table 3, it is possible to see the accuracy results obtained by the compared models. Another two fundamental results obtained are (a) The base property of VDCNN model is preserved on its squeezed model: the performance still increasing up with the depth and (b) The performance evaluated for the most extensive dataset, i.e., Yelp Review (63.20%), still overcomes the accuracy of the Char-CNN model (62.05%).

Table 3. Number of parameters, storage and accuracy results. For Parameters and Storage, best results in bold by depth. For accuracy, best global results in bold.

	SVDCNN			VDCNN			Char-CNN
	9	17	29	9	17	29	6
Parameters							
#Conv Params [M]	**0.71**	**1.43**	**1.56**	2.20	4.40	4.60	1.37
#FC Params [M]	**0.02**	**0.02**	**0.02**	12.59	12.59	12.59	11.34
#Total Params [M]	**0.73**	**1.45**	**1.58**	14.79	16.99	17.19	12.71
Storage							
Storage Size [MB]	**2.80**	**5.52**	**6.03**	54.75	62.74	64.16	43.25
Accuracy							
Ag News	90.13	90.43	90.55	90.83	91.12	91.27	**92.36**
Yelp Polarity	94.99	95.04	95.26	95.12	95.50	**95.72**	95.64
Yelp Full	61.97	63.00	63.20	63.27	63.93	**64.26**	62.05

Deep learning processing architectures have the property of offering high parallelization power. Therefore, it is expected a fewer inference time while performing predictions on dedicated deep learning hardware in comparison to non-dedicated one. Nevertheless, this is not the only aspect that determines the inference time of a model.

The parallelization potential of a model can vary according to its architecture. As we have more parameters per layers, more parallelizable a model tends to be, while the increase of the depth gets the opposite result. Another natural comprehension fact is that if a model has few parameters, there exists less content to be processed, and then we have a faster inference time. Concerning constrained platforms, like embedded systems and mobile devices, the presence of dedicated deep learning hardware such as a GPU is not entirely feasible. This kind of hardware usually requires more energy and dissipates more heat, two undesirable features for such constrained platforms.

A metric that can be deduced from the inference time is the inference time ratio. This metric is the quotient between CPU and GPU inference times, and it is a general indicator of how independent of dedicated hardware is the inference time performance of a model. The range of values obtained by this metric varies between 0 and 1. The closer to 1, the smaller is the difference of the inference time due to the use of dedicated hardware—the closer to 0 the opposite effect. Consequently, the closer to 1 the inference time ratio of a model, more it tends to be useful for constrained platforms.

Table 4. Time results for AG's News dataset. For GPU, CPU, and Ratio, best results by depth denoted in bold.

	Inference Time		
	GPU	CPU	Ratio
SVDCNN			
9	5.73 ms ± 0.37	**16.83 ms ± 0.82**	**0.34**
17	10.18 ms ± 0.41	**30.65 ms ± 1.71**	**0.33**
29	15.80 ms ± 0.54	48.72 ms ± 2.87	**0.32**
VDCNN			
9	**4.65 ms ± 0.35**	21.06 ms ± 0.62	0.22
17	**7.81 ms ± 0.31**	31.50 ms ± 1.42	0.25
29	**11.27 ms ± 0.43**	**44.30 ms ± 2.94**	0.25
Char-CNN			
6	11.35 ms ± 0.61	216.71 ms ± 4.89	0.05

Concerning to SVDCNN model, each convolutional layer of the convolutional blocks was substituted by two convolutions as shown Fig. 3. As explained in Sect. 4.1, we decided to count the two convolutions as only one layer in the network depth calculus. Nevertheless, compared to the baseline model, the number of convolutions per convolutional block has essentially doubled, for the same depth configuration. Due to this particularity, the SVDCNN tends to show higher inference times compared to the base model on high parallelizable platforms, like GPUs. On the other hand, due to the notable parameter reduction, SVDCNN is expected to obtain better results than the baseline model over constrained platforms, which deal with memory and processing constraints.

The inference times obtained for the three compared models and their respective ratios are available in Table 4. When performing predictions over GPU, the proposed model presented results with a small performance loss compared to the inference time of the baseline. As aforementioned, this result happens due to the architectural change proposed, where two convolutions substituted each convolutional layer of the convolutional blocks. In the other hand, the SVDCNN model presented two desirable properties for constrained systems deployment. First, the SVDCNN obtained lower inference times than VDCNN model when executing on non-dedicated hardware (CPU). Applying the Wilcoxon Paired test, the SVDCNN results for depth 9 and 17 were significantly lower in comparison with the baseline model, with a confidence level of 95%. For depth 9, it was obtained 16.83 ms against 21.06 ms and for depth 17, 30.65 ms against 31.50 ms of the baseline model. Second, the inference time ratio was higher in all depth levels compared, 0.33 against 0.24 on average. It indicates that the SVDCNN model is more undependable of dedicated hardware then the baseline model. Looking to Char-CNN, this model got notably inferior results compared to the proposed method, with 216.71 ms of CPU inference time and Ratio of 0.05.

7 Conclusion

In this paper, we presented the Squeezed Very Deep Convolutional Neural Network (SVDCNN) for text classification model, a squeezed version of the VDCNN model. The primary goal of our work was the reduction of parameters compared to state of the art CNN's for text classification. This reduction made the VDCNN model more feasible of being deployed on constrained platforms, while presenting minimal accuracy loss compared to the baseline model. To achieve this goal, we analyzed the impact of including Temporal Depthwise Separable Convolutions, a Global Average Pooling layer and reduce the number of Fully Connected layers on VDCNN model.

The proposed model reduces about 92.45% the number of parameters and storage size. The size of VDCNN model varies between 54.75 e 64.16 MB while the size of SVDCNN model varies only between 2.80 and 6.03MB. Concerning to accuracy performance, the network experiences an acceptable loss, between 0.4% and 1.3%.

Secondary goals of this work covered the analysis of inference time and deep learning dedicated hardware dependence. Although the difference in inference times obtained by the baseline and the proposed model is small, the difference is still statistically significant. Compared to VDCNN model, SVDCNN model presents lower inference time over CPU processing for depth 9 and 17, while offers a higher inference time ratio, 0.33 against 0.24 on average. Therefore the proposed model is less dependent on dedicated deep learning hardware, which is often a desirable behavior for constrained platforms.

As mentioned before, smaller CNN models enable its deployment on constrained platforms, such as embedded systems and mobile device. FPGAs, for example, usually offer less than 10 MB of on-chip memory and no off-chip memory or storage [5]. Concerning mobile devices, the usage of a reduced local model offers numerous benefits, such as no real-time network dependence, lower latency speed, increase scalability, privacy, and data saving. In the image classification field, several shrunk CNN models were proposed [5,7,15]. However, to the best of our knowledge, works on this direction for the text classification field are still scarce, despite the several critical real-world applications which depend on text classification tasks such as sentiment analysis, recommendation, and opinion mining.

Our work opens several new research directions. We intend to analyze and reduce other network architectures for text classification besides CNNs. We also plan to evaluate other techniques able to reduce storage size, such as model compression [3]. Moreover, the SVDCNN model accuracy over even more massive datasets can be evaluated as well as the efficiency of its depth 49 configuration.

Acknowledgment. We would like to thank CNPq and FACEPE (Brazilian research agencies) for the financial support.

References

1. Chollet, F.: Xception: deep learning with depthwise separable convolutions. In: IEEE Conference on Computer Vision and Pattern Recognition (CVPR), pp. 1251–1258 (2017). https://doi.org/10.1109/cvpr.2017.195
2. Conneau, A., Schwenk, H., Barrault, L., Lecun, Y.: Very deep convolutional networks for text classification. In: Proceedings of the 15th Conference of the European Chapter of the Association for Computational Linguistics: Volume 1, Long Papers. Association for Computational Linguistics (2017). https://doi.org/10.18653/v1/e17-1104
3. Gong, Y., Liu, L., Yang, M., Bourdev, L.: Compressing deep convolutional networks using vector quantization. arXiv preprint arXiv:1412.6115 (2014)
4. He, K., Zhang, X., Ren, S., Sun, J.: Deep residual learning for image recognition. In: 2016 IEEE Conference on Computer Vision and Pattern Recognition (CVPR), pp. 770–778, June 2016. https://doi.org/10.1109/cvpr.2016.90
5. Howard, A.G., et al.: Mobilenets: efficient convolutional neural networks for mobile vision applications. arXiv preprint arXiv:1704.04861 (2017)
6. Huang, G., Liu, Z., van der Maaten, L., Weinberger, K.Q.: Densely connected convolutional networks. In: 2017 IEEE Conference on Computer Vision and Pattern Recognition (CVPR). IEEE, July 2017. https://doi.org/10.1109/cvpr.2017.243
7. Iandola, F.N., Han, S., Moskewicz, M.W., Ashraf, K., Dally, W.J., Keutzer, K.: Squeezenet: alexnet-level accuracy with 50x fewer parameters and <0.5 mb model size. arXiv preprint arXiv:1602.07360 (2016)
8. Ioffe, S., Szegedy, C.: Batch normalization: accelerating deep network training by reducing internal covariate shift. arXiv preprint arXiv:1502.03167 (2015)
9. Kaiser, L., Gomez, A.N., Chollet, F.: Depthwise separable convolutions for neural machine translation. arXiv preprint arXiv:1706.03059 (2017)
10. Kim, Y.: Convolutional neural networks for sentence classification. arXiv preprint arXiv:1408.5882 (2014)

11. Lai, S., Xu, L., Liu, K., Zhao, J.: Recurrent convolutional neural networks for text classification. In: Twenty-Ninth AAAI Conference on Artificial Intelligence (2015)
12. Le, H.T., Cerisara, C., Denis, A.: Do convolutional networks need to be deep for text classification? In: The Workshops of the Thirty-Second AAAI Conference on Artificial Intelligence (2017)
13. Lecun, Y., Bottou, L., Bengio, Y., Haffner, P.: Gradient-based learning applied to document recognition. Proc. IEEE **86**(11), 2278–2324 (1998). https://doi.org/10.1109/5.726791
14. Lin, M., Chen, Q., Yan, S.: Network in network. arXiv preprint arXiv:1312.4400 (2013)
15. Santos, A.G., de Souza, C.O., Zanchettin, C., Macedo, D., Oliveira, A.L.I., Ludermir, T.: Reducing SqueezeNet storage size with depthwise separable convolutions. In: 2018 International Joint Conference on Neural Networks (IJCNN). IEEE, July 2018. https://doi.org/10.1109/ijcnn.2018.8489442
16. Sifre, L., Mallat, S.: Rigid-motion scattering for image classification. Ph.D. thesis, Citeseer (2014)
17. Simonyan, K., Zisserman, A.: Very deep convolutional networks for large-scale image recognition. arXiv preprint arXiv:1409.1556 (2014)
18. Sundermeyer, M., Ney, H., Schluter, R.: From feedforward to recurrent LSTM neural networks for language modeling. IEEE/ACM Trans. Audio Speech Lang. Process. **23**(3), 517–529 (2015). https://doi.org/10.1109/taslp.2015.2400218
19. Tai, K.S., Socher, R., Manning, C.D.: Improved semantic representations from tree-structured long short-term memory networks. In: Proceedings of the 53rd Annual Meeting of the Association for Computational Linguistics and the 7th International Joint Conference on Natural Language Processing (Volume 1: Long Papers). Association for Computational Linguistics (2015). https://doi.org/10.3115/v1/p15-1150
20. Vaswani, A., et al.: Attention is all you need. In: Advances in Neural Information Processing Systems, pp. 5998–6008 (2017)
21. Zeiler, M.D., Fergus, R.: Visualizing and understanding convolutional networks. In: Fleet, D., Pajdla, T., Schiele, B., Tuytelaars, T. (eds.) ECCV 2014. LNCS, vol. 8689, pp. 818–833. Springer, Cham (2014). https://doi.org/10.1007/978-3-319-10590-1_53
22. Zhang, X., Zhao, J., LeCun, Y.: Character-level convolutional networks for text classification. In: Advances in Neural Information Processing Systems, pp. 649–657 (2015)
23. Zhou, C., Sun, C., Liu, Z., Lau, F.: A C-LSTM neural network for text classification. arXiv preprint arXiv:1511.08630 (2015)

NeuroPower: Designing Energy Efficient Convolutional Neural Network Architecture for Embedded Systems

Mohammad Loni[1(✉)], Ali Zoljodi[2], Sima Sinaei[1], Masoud Daneshtalab[1], and Mikael Sjödin[1]

[1] School of Innovation, Design and Engineering, Mälardalen University, Västerås, Sweden
{mohammad.loni,sima.sinaei,masoud.daneshtalab,mikael.sjodin}@mdh.se
[2] Shiraz University of Technology, Shiraz, Iran
ali.zoljodi@sutech.ac.ir

Abstract. Convolutional Neural Networks (CNNs) suffer from energy-hungry implementation due to their computation and memory intensive processing patterns. This problem is even more significant by the proliferation of CNNs on embedded platforms. To overcome this problem, we offer NeuroPower as an automatic framework that designs a highly optimized and energy efficient set of CNN architectures for embedded systems. NeuroPower explores and prunes the design space to find improved set of neural architectures. Toward this aim, a multi-objective optimization strategy is integrated to solve Neural Architecture Search (NAS) problem by near-optimal tuning network hyperparameters. The main objectives of the optimization algorithm are network accuracy and number of parameters in the network. The evaluation results show the effectiveness of NeuroPower on energy consumption, compacting rate and inference time compared to other cutting-edge approaches. In comparison with the best results on CIFAR-10/CIFAR-100 datasets, a generated network by NeuroPower presents up to 2.1x/1.56x compression rate, 1.59x/3.46x speedup and 1.52x/1.82x power saving while loses 2.4%/−0.6% accuracy, respectively.

Keywords: Convolutional Neural Networks (CNNs) · Neural Architecture Search (NAS) · Embedded systems · Multi-objective optimization

1 Introduction

CNNs have penetrated in a wide spectrum of platforms from workstations to embedded devices due to influential learning capabilities. However, modern CNN architectures are becoming more complex to provide superior accuracy leading to remarkable energy consumption. Dealing with huge computing throughput demand of upcoming complex learning models will be more critical where

I. V. Tetko et al. (Eds.): ICANN 2019, LNCS 11727, pp. 208–222, 2019.
https://doi.org/10.1007/978-3-030-30487-4_17

the failure of traditional energy and performance scaling paradigm in affording of modern applications requirements leads computing landscape towards inefficiency [4]. Approximate computing is one possible propitious alternative to cope with these challenges by amortizing output's quality of imprecision-tolerant applications such as objects recognition, image processing, and data analytics. Generally, three different approximation based strategies are proposed to diminish CNN computational complexity and/or improve energy saving: ① pruning network weights and quantization [7,15], ② employing customized hardware accelerators [27], and ③ optimizing network architecture at design-time since the performance (energy consumption and inference time) and output quality of CNNs are immensely affected by network architecture [17–19].

To benefit from these approaches, we propose NeuroPower, a CNN acceleration framework aiming to automatically explore the design space in order to design an energy efficient CNN architecture. NeuroPower solves the NAS problem and explore the design space considering better accuracy level and less network architectural complexity as the optimization objectives. Previous NAS solutions mainly focus on improving the network accuracy, while NeuroPower considers network architectural complexity, represented by the number of parameters in the network, as the second optimization objective since there is a strong correlation between energy consumption and network architectural complexity (see Sect. 3.1). For this, NeuroPower is equipped with a neuro-evolutionary Multi-Objective Optimization (MO^2) mechanism which produces a set of Pareto-optimal curves wherein each point on the curve is a vector with elements of the CNN hyperparameters. NeuroPower adaptively selects a suitable CNN architecture regarding power budget limitations and/or response-time of embedded hardware platform. Network pruning is a popular solution for diminishing the amount of network computation. In addition to design space exploration, NeuroPower can apply a network pruning method on a dense architecture to achieve further level of network optimization. In order to guarantee designing a lightweight architecture and to boost the optimization process, the design space has been trimmed by taking inspirations from DenseNet architecture [12].

Figure 1a illustrates an overview of the proposed NeuroPower framework. The MO^2 starts exploring design space after setting predefined learning and optimization parameters. Displayed NeuroPower controller in Fig. 1a verifies the optimization termination condition by getting energy consumption and/or inference time of candidates. The optimization procedure will be continue until satisfying user criteria or the maximum number of iterations is reached. To verify the impact of NeuroPower on energy consumption and inference time, three COTS embedded platforms are utilized including a many-core NVIDIA Quadro K5100M GPU, a multi-core high-performance Intel Core processor i7-4940MX, and an ARM Cortex-A15. ARM architecture is one of the immensely popular embedded processors due to low power consumption, and providing reasonable performance. However, ARM is not suitable to process computational intensive CNN models. On the other hand, GPUs are popular performance-centric accelerators for machine learning applications refereed as another possibility to

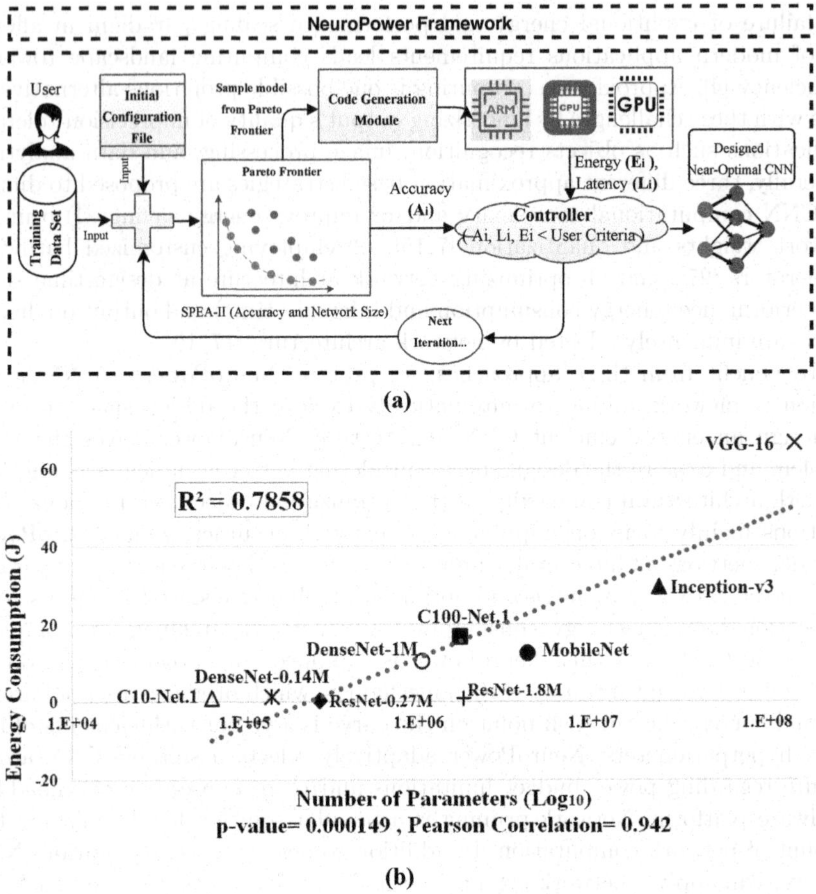

Fig. 1. (a) The overview of NeuroPower framework, (b) Energy consumption vs. # of network parameters.

deal with reducing efficiency trend in the multi-core era. Although GPUs offer a higher level of programmability and memory bandwidth, they suffer from huge power consumption [27]. To tackle these challenges, our proposed framework demonstrates considerable performance gain over GPU, high-performance Intel CPU, and embedded ARM processor. In a nutshell, our main contributions in NeuroPower are:

- Presenting a meta-heuristic MO^2 method to explore energy aware CNN architectures. NeuroPower generates a set of network architectures optimized for a wide range of architectural complexities fitting different hardware resource budgets.
- Proposing novel activation functions which significantly increase the network accuracy.

- Developing a cutting-edge network pruning method on the neural network architecture to obtain less complex network with acceptable accuracy.

The remainder of this paper is organized as follows: Sect. 2 reviews related work in this scope. Section 3 gives background on CNN and the MO^2 algorithm. Details of the proposed framework are presented in Sect. 4 which consist of two solutions for network optimization: Design Space Exploration and Design Space Pruning. The experimental results are presented in Sect. 5, after which Sect. 6 concludes the paper.

2 Related Work

In the field of neural network design space exploration, different automated NAS approaches have been proposed including Bayesian optimization, Reinforcement Learning (RL), and neuro-evolutionary methods. Bayesian-based methods suffer from immense computational cost, suitable only for search models with a fixed-length space, and focuses on low-dimensional continuous problems [3,17]. RL-based NAS methods provides high-quality results for image classification applications compared to the best hand-crafted CNN accuracy results [2,28,29,32]. Despite their success, these models are mainly slow and require considerable computational resources in both exploration and training steps [2]. The most of the neuro-evolutionary methods leverage evolutionary algorithms for optimizing the neural architecture by evolving a population of improved candidates [17–19,21,24]. There has been proposed other multi-objective neuro-evolutionary frameworks [17–19] considering the number of network parameters as the second optimization objective. NeuroPower is more efficient compare to [17,18] in terms of both compression rate and exploration time. Plus, NeuroPower can generate more compact architectures compared to [19], while takes roughly equal exploration time.

Moreover, as mentioned in previous section, the proposed framework has the ability of design space pruning to obtain less complex network with acceptable accuracy. In the field of neural network design space pruning also several methods have been presented. In [15] a method is proposed that prune CNN filters in two levels. It first clusters network filters by enforcing the K-means algorithm, then retain the filter which is the closest to the cluster center and pruning some of the others randomly. In [23] a data-free approach is proposed to carry out CNN model compression. They managed to avoid employing any training data by minimizing the expected squared difference of logits. In [7] a pruning approach by applying L1/L2-norm regularizations is introduced to remove the small weights. Although the performance is inspiring, the pruning would result in unstructured patterns in weights connectivity. Research in [16] tries to select the best filters for pruning, for example, uses absolute weight summation to evaluate the impact of a filter. In this method very low differences in weights are affected too much, thus, the work presented in [10] introduced Average Percentage of Zeros to assess the importance of each filter. This work needs lots of extra calculations and the compression ratio is not satisfying.

3 Background

3.1 An Overview of CNNs

A typical CNN is composed of multiple layers running in sequence, where input data is fed to the first layer and output is a series of feature extraction kernels applied on the input image. Convolution, normalization, pooling, and activation layers are responsible for feature extraction, while fully-connected layers are in charge of classification. VGG-16 [22] is a well-known CNN containing 13 and 3 convolutional and fully-connected layers respectively. Computational analysis of VGG-16 demonstrates that convolutional layers are extremely computation intensive containing 99.3% of the total computation while fully-connected layers are memory-intensive which utilize more than 80% of data movements [17]. Thereby, for optimizing architectural complexity of a CNN, convolutional parameters including *the number of convolutional layers, the sizes of each layer, activation function, convolutional filter size*, and *learning rate* should be considered as the network's optimization hyperparameters.

Table 1. The CNN hyperparameters used as exploring neural design space parameters.

Parameter	Value
Activation Function	Relu, Elu, Sigmoid,
(Left, Right) [20]	Tanh, Swish, Selu, Linear
# Condense Layer	1, 2, 3, 4
# Feature Extraction Layer (FEL)	16, 28, 40, 52
Kernel Size	3×3, 5×5
Optimizer [6]	Adam, SGD, Adagrad, Adamax, Nadam

Table 1 lists considered hyperparameters and their corresponding values where the value range of each parameter has been limited to prune the design space, moreover, huge hyperparameter values does not always provide highly accurate networks [3]. Based on practical evaluations, these selected hyperparameters strongly influence accuracy and inference time [17,18]. In addition, we realized a strong relationship between energy consumption/inference time and the number of parameters of a CNN. Figure 1b illustrates the relationship between energy consumption per each forward query and the number of parameters executed on an NVIDIA Quadro K5100M GPU. The results are plotted in the logarithmic scale to improve visual comprehension. These results imply that the number of parameters in a network is a strong proxy for network architectural complexity [17,19,26]. While the main focus of this paper is on diminishing CNN power consumption, the experimental results indicate that NeuroPower efficiently decreases inference time (see Sect. 5).

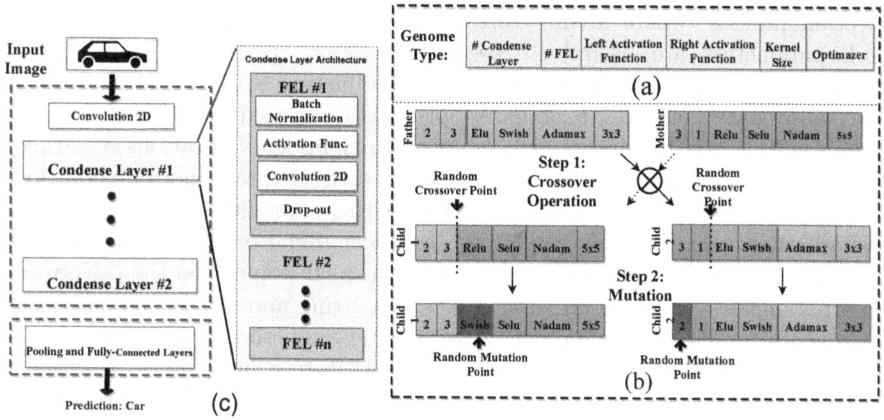

Fig. 2. (a) A genome type representing NAS hyperparameters. (b) Crossover & forced mutation operators between two genomes for SPEA-II optimization algorithm. (c) Inspired template architecture of a generated network.

3.2 Strength Pareto Evolutionary Algorithm-II (SPEA-II)

To make the best balance between the network accuracy and architectural complexity, an optimization approach is needed. Computability is highly challenging especially in complex problems since there is no guarantee that NP-hard complex problems such as NAS problem can be solved in a satisfactory manner in a limited time. To improve solving such problems several techniques have been proposed. Among them, Evolutionary Computing (EC) methods are more prominent [17,21,24]. EC comprises a set of optimization algorithms mimicking the survival of the nature fittest principle, as some characteristics of this process can be utilized in optimization problems. Strength Pareto Evolutionary Algorithm-II (SPEA-II) [31] is a powerful meta-heuristic EC solving MO^2 problems. In this work, accuracy and the number parameters are considered as the optimization objectives. SPEA-II provides slightly superior optimization mechanism compared to NSGA-II [17,30] by obtaining more diverse solutions in the architectural design space of CNNs. Algorithm 1 represents the pseudo-code of NeuroPower framework integrating SPEA-II as the optimization engine. SPEA-II is explained as following steps: ***Step 0:*** Creating an initial population U_0 with size N, and Y_0 as a null population. To generate the initial random population, network hyperparameters are represented as a string of genomes using direct encoding shown as genome type in Fig. 2a. ***Step 1:*** Calculating the fitness values of individuals in the U_0 and Y_0. The fitness function is described in (1) as follows;

$$Score = \frac{Net\_Acc}{\#Net\_Params} \tag{1}$$

where *Net_Acc* is network accuracy and *#Net_Params* is the number of network parameters. The *Score* factor is SPEA-II fitness function for selection process, where architectures with higher accuracy and smaller network parameters are desirable. ***Step 2:*** $Y_{t+1} = \{x_i \mid x_i \in \{Y_t \cup U_t\}$ *AND* x_i *is a nondominant individual*$\}$, and adjusting Y_{t+1} size to N. ***Step 3:*** The NeuroPower controller terminates optimization procedure if one of the individuals in Y_{t+1} satisfies user criteria or maximum number of iterations is reached. otherwise, the procedure progresses as long as satisfying termination condition. ***Step 4:*** Put individuals from Y_{t+1} into the mating pool with substituted binary championship rule. ***Step 5:*** Applying *Crossover* and *ForcedMutation* operators on the mating pool individuals to create the next population U_{t+1}. Network hyperparameters are represented as a genomes string and the recombination of these genes occurs with one-point crossover and one-point mutation operators shown in Fig. 2. We defined the new *ForcedMutation* operator to change at least one hyperparameter node in genome type while guarantee the probability of evaluating equal architectures being zero. *ForcedMutation* operator improves the exploration capability due to pushing the SPEA-II to find new candidates.

Algorithm 1. Pseudo Code of NeuroPower's Design Space Exploration

```
Input: N: Archive Size, G: Max. Number of Iterations, H: Hyperparameters List,
       Eng_user, Acc_user : User Criteria
Output: A Non-Dominated Set of Optimal Architectures on Pareto Frontier
Function Optimization_Engine(N, G, H):
    Step 0: U_0= Random_Population (N, H); Y_0= Empty_Population;
    t = 0; //Iteration Number
    while True do
        Step 1: Fitness_Values_Calculation (U_t, Y_t, N);
        Step 2: Y_{t+1}=Environmental_Selection (U_t, Y_0, N);
        Step 3: if (∃i ∈ Y_{t+1} | E_i, I_i, A_i ¬satisfies Eng_user, Acc_user) then
            BreakWhileLoop; // Terminate NeuroPower
        Step 4: P_t=Mating_Selection (Y_{t+1});
        Step 5: U_{t+1}=Crossover&Forced_Mutation (P_t);
        t = t + 1;
    return Y_{t+1};
```

4 NeuroPower: The Proposed Framework

4.1 Design Space Exploration (DSE) Algorithm

The NeuroPower framework consists of a controller, optimization engine and code generation module (Fig. 1a). Predefined parameters of NeuroPower are specified in the configuration file including optimization and network training parameters such as number of epochs, learning rate, and valid range of network hyperparameters. After providing the input dataset and initiating the configuration file by user, the engine function will start to explore the design space of CNN architectures. At the end of each iteration, the energy consumption and inference time of each individual on Pareto curve will be measured by passing the network configuration to code generation module to generate specific run-time execution code for each platform. The code generation module uses Tensorflow library [1] to automatically generate kernel code for NVIDIA GPUs. Then, the controller checks whether the designed architecture satisfies user criteria or not. In the case of non-satisfaction, the optimization module will be called again to find the next iteration of the optimized solutions (Algorithm 1). SPEA-II explores the design space over a template architecture inspired from DenseNet for decreasing the probability of generating giant architectures. **Template Architecture:** The template consists of multiple Condense Layers where each Condense Layer contains back-to-back Feature Extraction Layers (FELs) [17]. FEL includes *Batch Normalization, Activation Function, 2D Convolution, Drop-out*, respectively. Obviously, for classification max-pooling and fully-connected layers are integrated as the last layers with softmax activation function. To share maximum learned knowledge between layers, all the layers are connected in a feed-forward manner to each other such that each layer receives the additional feature map information from the whole former layers in the Condense Layer and using concatenation layer to merging shared data.

4.2 Design Space Pruning Algorithm

In general, neural network pruning techniques try to reduce the storage and computation required by neural networks without considerable affecting on the network accuracy by learning the influential weights. To take advantages of network pruning on the designed architectures by NeuroPower, we proposed a pruning method which basically uses the idea presented in [15]. This technique tries to select and remove redundant filters which affected zero or very low in the network results by utilizing K-means++ algorithm for selecting appropriate filters for pruning. The proposed pruning algorithm works as follows: First, it employs the K-means++ algorithm to enforce the filters to enter specific clusters. Second, it will retain the filter which is the closest to the cluster center and prune the others in every cluster. Then the pruned model will be fine-tuned to recover accuracy.

5 Experimental Results

In this section the experimental results of design space exploration and design space pruning of the proposed framework are presented respectively. NeuroPower framework has been evaluated using well-known datasets and compare with cutting-edge architectures. The experiments have been performed on the following data sets: MNIST [14], CIFAR-10 [13] and CIFAR-100 [13].

5.1 Training Datasets

MNIST [14]***:*** This is a dataset of black and white images for handwritten digit recognition containing 60,000 training and 10,000 testing images. Each image is a 28×28 pixels with ten labeled output as 0 to 9 numbers. ***CIFAR-10*** [13]***:*** This is a complex colorful dataset of natural images, each with 32 × 32 pixels which is mainly used for object recognition. This benchmark contains ten labeled output classes containing 50000 and 1000 images for training and testing, respectively. ***CIFAR-100*** [13]***:*** CIFAR-100 is similar to CIFAR-10, but with 100 classes while each class has 500 instead of 5,000 as in CIFAR10 making the classification more challenging.

5.2 Design Space Exploration Results

The design space roughly consists of 8000 different design points. The average training time is one hour for each design point by employing NVIDIA GTX 1080ti. Thus, leveraging exhaustive search is not reasonable since exploration takes 8000 GPU-hours, while NeuroPower required 360 GPU-hours for generating the experimental results demonstrating 22x reduction in exploration time. NeuroPower trains each network during exploration step using only 16 epochs since approximately 90% of the maximum achievable accuracy is obtained after 16 epochs [17]. The full training step will be applied to only the best selected architecture with 250 epochs. The NeuroPower's configuration file was set with the following parameters: batch size = 128, maximum number of iterations = 8, and random initial population = 45.

Table 2 presents network designing strategy, error rate, number of parameters and network compression rate of solutions generated by NeuroPower compared to the other cutting-edge approaches. For MNIST dataset, M_Net_1 generated by Neuropower is 2x more compressed (with 0.3% accuracy loss) in comparison

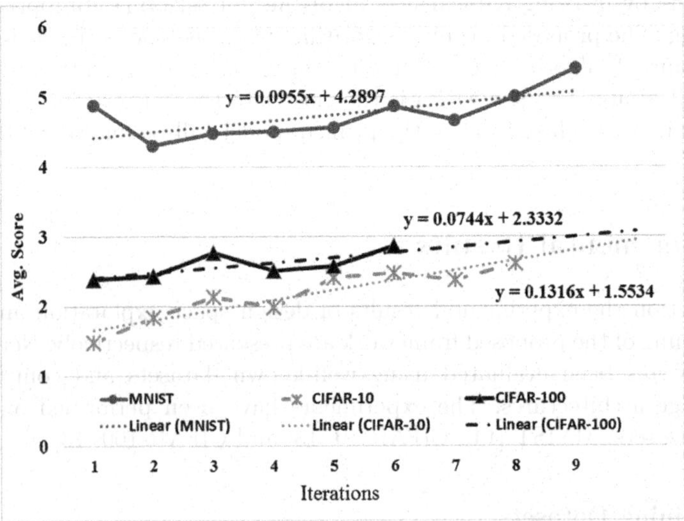

Fig. 3. Score convergence for MNIST, CIFAR-10 and IFAR-100 datasets. The linear equations demonstrate the overall improvement of the *Score* fitness function over proceeding iterations.

with a highly optimized network ADONN-Arch.3 [17]. C10_Net.1, C10_Net.2, and C10_Net.3 are different nodes of Pareto frontier selected from seventh iteration for CIFAR-10 dataset. C10_Net.1 is the most dense architecture provides up to 47.7x compression rate with 13% accuracy loss compared to a cutting-edge squeezed network, named CondenseNet^{Light} [11]. C10-Net.3 provides the best accuracy for CIFAR-10 dataset which is 3.1x compressed with loosing only 3% accuracy. The compression rate of C100-Net.1 and C100-Net.2 architectures for CIFAR-100 dataset is not significant compare to the other solutions, but NeuroPower still provides more accurate networks. In nutshell, NeuroPower strikes better balance between network accuracy and network size compare to RL and EC strategies and hand-crafted designs.

Table 2. Error rate and Compression rate for different datasets.

Dataset	Approach	Solutions	#Params ($\times 10^6$)	Error Rate (%)	Compression Rate*‡
MNIST	Hand-Crafted	Wan et al. [25]	–	0.21	–
	RL	MetaQNN [2]	5.59	0.35	0.023x
	MO^2-EC	* ADONN-Arch.3 [17]	0.13	0.41	–
	MO^2-EC	**Our M_Net_1**	**0.065**	**0.71**	**2x**
CIFAR-10	Hand-Crafted	* CondenseNet^{Light} [11]	3.1	3.46	–
	Hand-Crafted	SimpleNet [8]	5.48	4.68	0.53x
	Hand-Crafted	DenseNet (k = 12)-40 [12]	1.0	7.0	3.1x
	Hand-Crafted	ResNet-20 [9]	0.27	8.75	11.48x
	Hand-Crafted	ResNet-110 [9]	1.7	6.43	1.82x
	Hand-Crafted	Gastaldi et al. [5]	26.4	2.86	0.117x
	RL	Block-QNN-22L [29]	39.8	3.54	0.078x
	RL	MetaQNN [2]	6.92	11.18	0.45x
	RL	NAS-v1/v3 [32]	4.2/37.4	5.50/3.65	0.7x/0.083x
	RL	Block-QNN-S [29]	6.1	4.38	0.5x
	EC	Real et al. [21]	5.4	5.4	0.57x
	MO^2-EC	NSGA-Net [19]	3.3	3.85	0.94x
	MO^2-EC	ADONN-Arch.3 [17]	0.14	14.1	22.14x
	MO^2-EC	Loni et al. [18]	0.56	13.8	5.5x
	MO^2-EC	**Our C10-Net.1**	**0.065**	**16.49**	**47.7x**
	MO^2-EC	**Our C10-Net.2**	**0.21**	**11.05**	**14.7x**
	MO^2-EC	**Our C10-Net.3**	**1.0**	**6.81**	**3.1x**
CIFAR-100	RL	MetaQNN [2]	11.18	27.14	0.28x
	RL	Block-QNN-S [29]	6.1	20.65	0.5x
	Hand-Crafted	* CondenseNet^{Light} [11]	3.1	17.55	–
	Hand-Crafted	DenseNet (k = 12)-40 [12]	1.0	27.55	3.1x
	Hand-Crafted	DenseNet (k = 12)-100 [12]	7.0	23.79	0.44x
	Hand-Crafted	SimpleNet [8]	5.48	26.58	0.53x
	MO^2-EC	NSGA-Net [19]	3.3	20.74	0.94x
	MO^2-EC	**Our C100-Net.1**	**1.1**	**26.63**	**2.82x**
	MO^2-EC	**Our C100-Net.2**	**1.89**	**24.87**	**1.64x**

* The baseline for comparing the compressing rate.

‡ The values more than 1.0 indicate improvement. Best results are in **bold**.

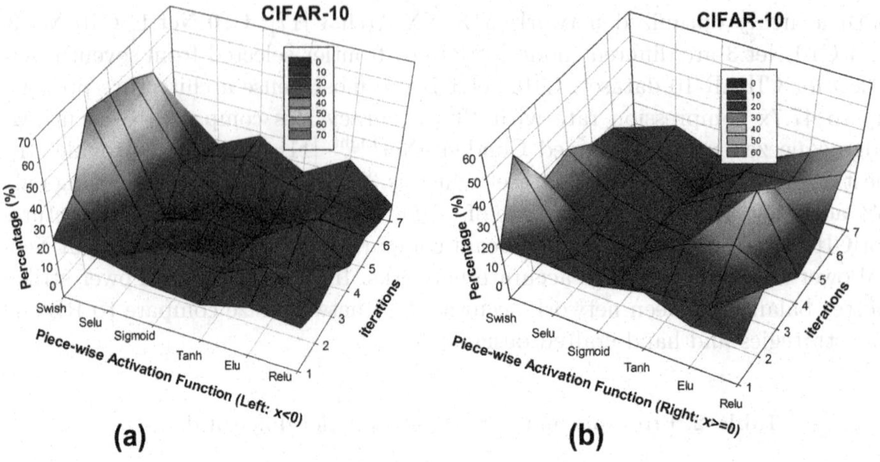

Fig. 4. The percentage of participation of (a) Left activation functions and (b) Right activation functions in the population for the CIFAR-10 dataset.

Figure 3 illustrates the continuous proceeding improvement of the results and demonstrates that the convergency diagram guaranteeing the score/fitness function is approaching toward near-optimal points for the considered datasets. Figure 4 illustrates the tuning of piece-wise activation functions toward designing more accurate architectures for CIFAR-10 dataset. Obviously, Swish is the dominant activation function for the input data greater than zero (right activation function) in initial iterations, however, Relu was replaced after fifth iteration meaning that NeuroPower finds Relu a superior option. However, Swish strongly overcomes other activations functions for the input data less than zero (left activation function) for all iterations.

Table 3 presents the hardware implementation results for MNIST, CIFAR-10 and CIFAR-100 datasets. For each dataset, the architecture with highest *Network-Information-Density* (NID) is employed as the baseline of the comparisons. NID (accuracy per parameters) is a yield factor highlighting that the capacity of an architecture to utilize better its parametric space [26]. In order to measure energy consumption of the tested platforms, we used the NVIDIA Management Library (NVML), Intel Running Average Power Limit (RAPL) and kill-a-watt P4400 device to obtain the average power of GPU, Intel CPU and ARM during benchmark execution. In this paper, the kernel time is used for reporting run-time results, however, the overhead of communication time should be considered for embedded implementations, especially for mainly latency-oriented. Therefore, To demonstrate the positive impact of squeezing network architecture on GPU Device-to-Host (D2H) and Host-to-Device (H2D) data communications, the achieved data communication speedup after leveraging NeuroPower is reported in Table 3.

We can conclude: ① the networks with more NID provide higher energy efficiency. ② For CIFAR-10 and CIFAR-100 our architectures did not obtain maximum achievable energy efficiency, compare to the ResNet architecture. However, if we take the total execution time (kernel + communication) into account, we can achieve higher speedup. In Addition, the obtained energy efficiency results of our designed architectures are showing remarkable improvement on the ARM and CPU platforms. ③ Compacting an architecture potentially diminish the overhead of communication time (D2H/H2D) since less number of data packets need to be copied via PCI-Express Bus. We obtain 1.7x and 1.9x speedup on average for D2H and H2D data communications, respectively.

Table 3. Implementation results for different platforms

Platform			GPU			Intel ® CPU		ARM processor	
Dataset	Network	NID ($\times 10^6$)	Energy efficiency	Speedup (Kernel)	Speedup: D2H/H2D (Comm.)	Energy efficiency	Speedup (Inference Time)	Energy Efficiency	Speedup (Inference Time)
MNIST	* ADONN-Arch.3 [17]	7.06	–	–	–	–	–	–	–
	M_Net_1	**15.25**	**1.55x**	**1.49x**	**1.59x/2.95x**	**1.49x**	**1.51x**	**1.56x**	**1.38x**
CIFAR-10	ResNet-20 [9]	3.37	4.2x	4.25x	0.62x/0.79x	0.75x	0.81x	1.05x	0.87x
	ResNet-110 [9]	0.55	1.53x	1.64x	0.108x/0.15x	0.093x	0.95x	0.16x	0.87x
	DenseNet (k = 12)-100	0.135	0.25x	0.027x	0.05x/0.073x	0.099x	0.112x	0.07x	0.115x
	* ADONN-Arch.3 [17]	6.13	–	–	–	–	–	–	–
	C10_Net_1	**13**	1.54x	1.51x	**1.61x/1.57x**	**1.5x**	**1.59x**	**1.52x**	**1.32x**
	C10_Net_3	0.93	0.14x	0.154x	0.25x/0.313x	0.3x	0.372x	0.3x	0.37x
CIFAR-100	* ResNet-110 [9]	0.43	–	–	–	–	–	–	–
	DenseNet (k = 12)-100	0.109	0.017x	0.016x	0.44x/0.46x	0.92x	1.03x	0.34x	0.74x
	C100-Net.1	**0.66**	0.11x	0.1x	**2.28x/2x**	**3.2x**	**3.46x**	**1.89x**	**2.38x**
	C100-Net.2	**0.4**	0.06x	0.06x	**1.45x/1.39x**	**2.45x**	**2.53x**	**1.35x**	**1.83x**

* The baseline for comparing the energy efficiency of different architectures. The values more than 1.0 indicate improvement. Best results are in **bold**.

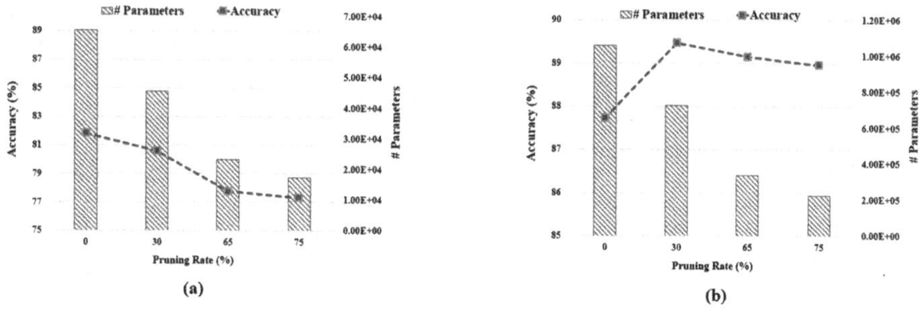

Fig. 5. The impact of the network pruning on the accuracy level of (a) C10-Net.1 and (b) C10-Net.3.

5.3 Pruning Results

The pruning method has been evaluated on two different architectures designed for CIFAR-10 dataset including C10-Net.1 and C10-Net.3. The first architecture is a compressed architecture with 0.065 million parameters, while the second one is a larger architecture with 1 million parameters. First, these two architectures are trained separately with 200 epochs and the accuracy rates are obtained 81.79% for C10-Net.1 and 87.72% for C10-Net.3. Then, the filter pruning technique is used by assuming 'cluster factor = 0.9' and 'number of fine tune epochs = 5' and 'pruning iteration = 10' as the constant configuration and 'maximum pruning percent' is equal to 30, 65, 75 as the threshold on weight pruning for both studied architectures. Figure 5 illustrates the impact of the network pruning on the accuracy level. The number of networks parameters decreases with increasing the pruning rate and the NID of pruned architectures increases with increasing 'maximum pruning percent'. Obviously, the impact of pruning on the accuracy rate of larger architecture, C10-Net.3, is much better than the other one. However, the denser architecture still provides 3.1x higher NID level compared to the pruned architecture of the large network with 75% pruning rate.

6 Conclusion

In this paper, we proposed the NeuroPower framework which automatically generates a highly-optimized CNN for commercial embedded devices. In the presented framework, two algorithms are proposed for design space exploration and design space pruning. NeuroPower alleviates the huge computational cost of CNNs by squeezing the network architecture while delivers acceptable accuracy level. In order to achieve an energy efficient network, a novel fitness function is used to consider energy consumption during exploration procedure. Experimental results show that, in comparison with the best results on CIFAR-10/CIFAR-100 datasets, NeuroPower presents up to 1.59x/3.46x speedup and 1.52x/1.82x power saving while loses 2.4%/-0.6% accuracy, respectively.

Acknowledgment. This Paper is supported by KKS within DeepMaker and DPAC projects.

References

1. Abadi, M., et al.: Tensorflow: a system for large-scale machine learning. In: 12th USENIX Symposium on Operating Systems Design and Implementation (OSDI 2016), pp. 265–283 (2016)
2. Baker, B., Gupta, O., Naik, N., Raskar, R.: Designing neural network architectures using reinforcement learning. arXiv preprint arXiv:1611.02167 (2016)
3. Elsken, T., Metzen, J.H., Hutter, F.: Neural architecture search: a survey. arXiv preprint arXiv:1808.05377 (2018)
4. Esmaeilzadeh, H., Blem, E., Amant, R.S., Sankaralingam, K., Burger, D.: Power-challenges may end the multicore era. Commun. ACM **56**, 93–102 (2013). https://doi.org/10.1145/2408776.2408797. http://dl.acm.org/citation.cfm?doid=2408776.2408797
5. Gastaldi, X.: Shake-shake regularization. arXiv preprint arXiv:1705.07485 (2017)
6. Goodfellow, I., Bengio, Y., Courville, A.: Deep Learning. MIT Press (2016)

7. Han, S., Pool, J., Tran, J., Dally, W.: Learning both weights and connections for efficient neural network. In: Advances in Neural Information Processing Systems, pp. 1135–1143 (2015)
8. Hasanpour, S.H., Rouhani, M., Fayyaz, M., Sabokrou, M.: Lets keep it simple, using simple architectures to outperform deeper and more complex architectures. arXiv preprint arXiv:1608.06037 (2016)
9. He, K., Zhang, X., Ren, S., Sun, J.: Deep residual learning for image recognition. In: Proceedings of the IEEE Conference on Computer Vision and Pattern Recognition, pp. 770–778 (2016)
10. Hu, H., Peng, R., Tai, Y.W., Tang, C.K.: Network trimming: a data-driven neuron pruning approach towards efficient deep architectures. arXiv preprint arXiv:1607.03250 (2016)
11. Huang, G., Liu, S., Van der Maaten, L., Weinberger, K.Q.: Condensenet: an efficient densenet using learned group convolutions. In: Proceedings of the IEEE Conference on Computer Vision and Pattern Recognition, pp. 2752–2761 (2018)
12. Huang, G., Liu, Z., Van Der Maaten, L., Weinberger, K.Q.: Densely connected convolutional networks. In: Proceedings - 30th IEEE Conference on Computer Vision and Pattern Recognition, CVPR 2017 (2017). https://doi.org/10.1109/CVPR.2017.243
13. Krizhevsky, A., Nair, V., Hinton, G.: Cifar-10 and cifar-100 datasets **6** (2009). https://www.cs.toronto.edu/kriz/cifar.html
14. LeCun, Y., Bottou, L., Bengio, Y., Haffner, P., et al.: Gradient-based learning applied to document recognition. Proc. IEEE **86**(11), 2278–2324 (1998)
15. Li, H., Kadav, A., Durdanovic, I., Samet, H., Graf, H.P.: Pruning filters for efficient convnets. arXiv preprint arXiv:1608.08710 (2016)
16. Li, L., Xu, Y., Zhu, J.: Filter level pruning based on similar feature extraction for convolutional neural networks. IEICE Trans. Inf. Syst. **101**(4), 1203–1206 (2018)
17. Loni, M., Daneshtalab, M., Sjodin, M.: ADONN: Adaptive design of optimized deep neural networks for embedded systems. In: Proceedings - 21st Euromicro Conference on Digital System Design, DSD 2018 (2018). https://doi.org/10.1109/DSD.2018.00074
18. Loni, M., Majd, A., Loni, A., Daneshtalab, M., Sjodin, M., Troubitsyna, E.: Designing compact convolutional neural network for embedded stereo vision systems. In: Proceedings - 2018 IEEE 12th International Symposium on Embedded Multicore/Many-Core Systems-on-Chip, MCSoC 2018 (2018). https://doi.org/10.1109/MCSoC2018.2018.00049
19. Lu, Z., et al.: Nsga-net: a multi-objective genetic algorithm for neural architecture search. arXiv preprint arXiv:1810.03522 (2018)
20. Ramachandran, P., Zoph, B., Le, Q.V.: Searching for activation functions. arXiv preprint arXiv:1710.05941 (2017)
21. Real, E., et al.: Large-scale evolution of image classifiers. In: Proceedings of the 34th International Conference on Machine Learning, vol. 70, pp. 2902–2911. JMLR.org (2017)
22. Simonyan, K., Zisserman, A.: Very deep convolutional networks for large-scale image recognition. arXiv preprint arXiv:1409.1556 (2014)
23. Srinivas, S., Babu, R.V.: Data-free parameter pruning for deep neural networks. arXiv preprint arXiv:1507.06149 (2015)
24. Suganuma, M., Shirakawa, S., Nagao, T.: A genetic programming approach to designing convolutional neural network architectures. In: Proceedings of the Genetic and Evolutionary Computation Conference, pp. 497–504. ACM (2017)

25. Wan, L., Zeiler, M., Zhang, S., Le Cun, Y., Fergus, R.: Regularization of neural networks using dropconnect. In: International Conference on Machine Learning, pp. 1058–1066 (2013)
26. Wong, A.: Netscore: towards universal metrics for large-scale performance analysis of deep neural networks for practical usage. arXiv preprint arXiv:1806.05512 (2018)
27. Yazdanbakhsh, A., Park, J., Sharma, H., Lotfi-Kamran, P., Esmaeilzadeh, H.: Neural acceleration for GPU throughput processors (2016). https://doi.org/10.1145/2830772.2830810
28. Zhong, Z., Yan, J., Liu, C.L.: Practical network blocks design with q-learning. arXiv preprint arXiv:1708.05552 **1**(2), 5 (2017)
29. Zhong, Z., Yan, J., Wu, W., Shao, J., Liu, C.L.: Practical block-wise neural network architecture generation. In: Proceedings of the IEEE Conference on Computer Vision and Pattern Recognition, pp. 2423–2432 (2018)
30. Zitzler, E., Deb, K., Thiele, L.: Comparison of multiobjective evolutionary algorithms: empirical results. Evol. Comput. **8**(2), 173–195 (2000)
31. Zitzler, E., Laumanns, M., Thiele, L.: Spea2: Improving the strength paretoevolutionary algorithm. TIK-report **103** (2001)
32. Zoph, B., Le, Q.V.: Neural architecture search with reinforcement learning. arXiv preprint arXiv:1611.01578 (2016)

Swap Kernel Regression

Masaharu Yamamoto and Koichiro Yamauchi(✉)

Chubu University, Matsumoto-cho, Kasugai, Aichi 1200, Japan
tp18014-8600@sti.chubu.ac.jp, k_yamauchi@isc.chubu.ac.jp
http://www.sakura.cs.chubu.ac.jp/

Abstract. Recent developments in the field of artificial intelligence have increased the demand for high performance computation devices. An edge device is highly restricted not only in terms of its computational power but also memory capacity. This study proposes a method that enables both inference and learning on an edge device. The proposed method involves a kernel machine that works in restricted environments by collaborating with its secondary storage system. The kernel parameters, which are not essential for calculating the output values for the upcoming inputs, are stored in the secondary storage to make space in the main memory. The essential kernel parameters stored in the secondary storage are loaded into the main memory when required. With the use of this strategy, the system can realize the recognition/regression tasks without reducing its generalization capability.

Keywords: Swap kernel regression · Regression · Kernel machine · Softmax function · General regression neural network · Secondary storage

1 Introduction

Recently, the computational power of embedded systems has been increasing, which has enabled the execution of heavy computations. However, the computational capability of these systems is still much less when compared to that of enterprise servers. Therefore, almost every artificial intelligence application needs to outsource its heavy computation need to a cloud server. This implies that such edge devices need to be connected to the Internet.

However, using internet communications is usually hesitated due to several reasons. Firstly, Internet communications possess the risk of lack of security. To ensure a safe connection, the system will have to encrypt all streaming data, such as Secure Shell tunneling https://www.openssh.com/. However, to realize such functionality, the computational power for the communication operations will need to include some overhead for the encryption function, to reduce the throughput.

A part of this research was supported by the Chubu University Grant A.

I. V. Tetko et al. (Eds.): ICANN 2019, LNCS 11727, pp. 223–238, 2019.
https://doi.org/10.1007/978-3-030-30487-4_18

This study proposes a new kernel machine that works on a stand-alone system in cooperation with its secondary storage. The proposed method is a variation of the general regression neural networks, whose outputs are calculated as the softmax of the Gaussian kernels. In this method, the kernel parameters that are not needed to calculate the output values for the current inputs are stored in the secondary storage. On the other hand, the essential kernels that are stored in the secondary storage are loaded into the main memory. With the use of this strategy, the system can realize the recognition/regression tasks without reducing its generalization capability. Note that even if the kernels, whose center position is far from current input, are absense, the general regression neural network can calculate appropriate output values because its property is similar to nearest neighbor method.

This remainder of this paper is organized as follows: Sect. 2 denotes the related works, Sect. 3 explains the proposed method, Sect. 4 discusses a suitable distribution for effective inference of this system. Section 5 shows some experimental results and Sect. 6 conclude this paper.

2 Related Works

Memory network (Weston et al. (2015)) is a similar model to our model. Because the memory network is also the neural network cooperation with memory like our proposed model. The network uses the memory as the working memory, where the information is stored temporarily. The proposed method works with the secondary storage system, but it basically stores all information that cannot be stored in the main memory.

Our proposed method manages the swap operation for the kernels. This operation is also similar to the page replacement algorithm (Lee et al. (2001)) proposed for a virtual memory. In this existing system, the target page has to be determined beforehand. However, in our proposed method, the target page cannot be determined expressively, because the kernel parameters stored in the secondary memory cannot be used for the calculation before being loading into the main memory. Therefore, the proposed system will have to determine the essential kernel parameters to be loaded into the main memory before estimating the availability of the kernel.

Another study proposed that a part of the kernel perceptron learns instances for a certain fixed number of kernels (Kivinen et al. (2004); Dekel et al. (2008); Orabona et al. (2008); He and Wu (2012); Yamauchi (2013)). The generalization capabilities of the kernel perceptrons with a fixed number of kernels are restricted because their ability for the learning is also restricted by the fixed number of kernels. On the other hand, our proposed method does not have any such limitation.

3 Swap Kernel Regression

3.1 Outline of the System

This study proposes a virtual kernel machine called 'Swap Kernel Regression.' The proposed method enables the embedded systems to execute a large scaled kernel machine, which is larger than the capacity of the embedded system. To this end, the swap kernel regression collaborates with the secondary storage device and forms a virtual machine learning system (see Fig. 1). Its specifications are:

- It should support one-shot learning to be able to perform easy learning.
- It can be executed with a small computational power.

The swap kernel regression follows the incremental machine learning methodology wherein it records a new instance by allocating a new kernel. If the number of kernels reach the upper bound, it moves a part of the kernel to the secondary storage space to make free space in the main memory. Normally, the learning machine output cannot be calculated correctly if a part of kernels are not active. To overcome this problem, its output is determined as the softmax function of the outputs from the kernels, which is similar to the method of the general regression neural networks. This implies that the property of the swap kernel regression is similar to that of k-nearest neighbors. By using this form, the network output is less affected by the absence of a part of the kernels, whose centroids are far from the current input.

Algorithm 1. Swap kernel regression

Require: new input $\boldsymbol{x}_t$, corresponding label y_t,
current time t,
Cluster kernel set C_{t-1}, Active cluster kernel set C^A,
Numerator functionf^C_{t-1}, denominator function g^C_{t-1},
Support set in the main storage S^1_{t-1},
Support set in the secondary storage S^2_{t-1},
Cumulative error err^{cum}_{t-1}.
$[y, C^A] = CalculateOutput(\boldsymbol{x}_t, t, C_{t-1}, S^1_{t-1}, S^2_{t-1})$ (see Algorithm 2) ▷ y:output
$err = (y_t - y)^2$ ▷ err: residual error
$err^{cum}_t = err^{cum}_{t-1} + err$
$[f^C_t, g^C_t, C_t, S^1_t, S^2_t] = Learning(\boldsymbol{x}_t, y_t, B, C_{t-1}, S^1_{t-1}, S^2_{t-1}, f^C_{t-1}, g^C_{t-1})$ (see Algorithm 3.)
return $[f^C_t, g^C_t, C_t, C^A, S^1_t, S^2_t, err^{cum}_t]$

Note that the calculation of a large scaled network in embedded systems is not impossible if we use the virtual memory system of existing operating systems. To realize an effective calculation, the existing virtual memory systems are not appropriate. The reason being that the related kernels in the secondary memory need to be determined before calculating their kernel outputs. The existing virtual memory system does not care about this fact. So, in the worst case scenario, the system has to repeat several swapping steps to calculate the outputs for each input.

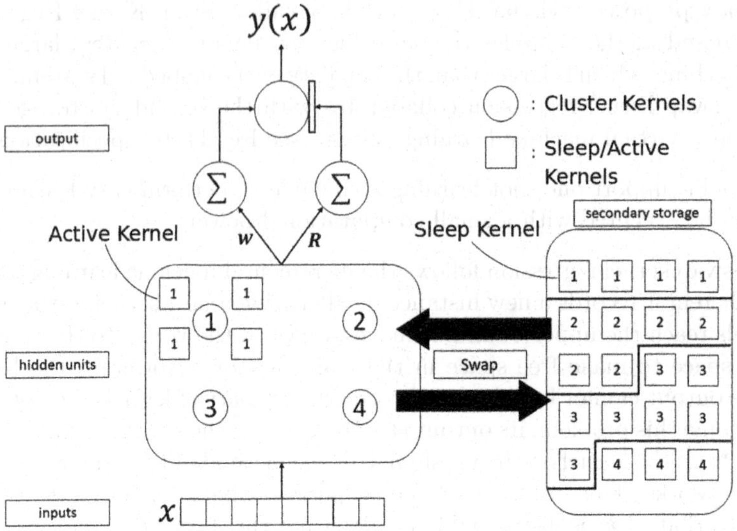

Fig. 1. Structure of swap kernel regression

The swap kernel regression consists of three kinds of units: Cluster, Sleep and Active units. The cluster units are for indexing the sleep units. The sleep units are the kernels stored in the secondary storage. If the sleep units are loaded into the main storage, they are active units. An active unit property is similar to one of the cluster kernels. If the active unit's center position is the closest to one of the cluster unit, the active unit take the ID number of the closest cluster unit. When the active unit is stored in the secondary storage, it becomes to the sleep unit that has the same ID number. The swap-kernel regression method loads the sleep units having the same ID number as that of the maximum activated cluster kernels. The pseudo algorithm is shown in Algorithm 1. This paper explains the swap kernel regression as a single-valued function approximator at first. However, it can be extended to a multivalued function approximator easily.

The experiment section shows an example of the response of the swap-kernel regression method with 10 output values. The extended one was applied for a handwritten digit recognition task (MNIST dataset).

3.2 Learning Algorithm for Cluster-Kernels

Swap kernel regression consists of a limited general regression neural network (LGRNN), which is a kernel machine with fixed number of kernels. The LGRNN has been proposed as the learning method for a small microcomputer (Yamauchi

(2014)). The LGRNN used in this paper is a modification of the existing one to support the swapping kernels.

Before explaining the details of the swap-kernel regression method, let us describe the original LGRNN structure. LGRNN is a variation of the general regression neural network. The general regression neural network (GRNN) output is computed as the softmax function of all the kernel outputs (1). Therefore, if the i-th kernels yields the maximum output value, GRNN output is almost the same as W_i/R_i (the initial value of R_i is 1). It is well known that the GRNN is robust to the noisy inputs. Its output is also less affected by the absence kernels. LGRNN achieves one-shot learning with a fixed number of kernels.

$$y(\boldsymbol{x}) = \frac{\sum_{i \in S^1_{t-1}} W_i K(\boldsymbol{x}_i, \boldsymbol{x})}{\sum_{j \in S^1_{t-1}} R_j K(\boldsymbol{x}_j, \boldsymbol{x})}, \tag{1}$$

where the kernel is a Gaussian kernel function and

$$K(\boldsymbol{x}_i, \boldsymbol{x}) \equiv \exp(-\|\boldsymbol{x} - \boldsymbol{x}_i\|^2/(\sigma^2)) \tag{2}$$

As the Gaussian kernel can be a reproduction kernel, it can also be rewritten as the dot product of two vectors on a Hilbert space: $\langle K(\boldsymbol{x}, \cdot), K(\boldsymbol{x}_i, \cdot)\rangle = \exp(-\|\boldsymbol{x} - \boldsymbol{x}_i\|^2/(\sigma^2))$. By using the dot product form, the learning algorithm can be written using simple algebraic equations.

(1) can be rewritten using the following algebraic equation.

$$y(\boldsymbol{x}) = \frac{\langle (f^c_{t-1} + f^A_{t-1}), K(\boldsymbol{x}, \cdot)\rangle}{\langle (g^c_{t-1} + g^A_{t-1}), K(\boldsymbol{x}, \cdot)\rangle}, \tag{3}$$

Algorithm 2. CalculateOutput

Require: new input $\boldsymbol{x}_t$, current time t, Cluster kernel set C, Support set in the main storage S^1 ($|S^1| \leq B^1$), Support set in the secondary storage S^2.
  $\alpha = 0$, $\beta = 0$
  $i^C_{i*} = \arg\min_{j \in C} \|\boldsymbol{x}_t - \boldsymbol{x}_j\|^2$
  $C^A = C^A \cup i^C_{i*}$
  for all $j^* \in S^2$ where $I^C_{j*} = i^C_{i*}$ and $t^R_{j*} < t$ **do**
    if $|S^1| = B^1$ **then**
      $[\alpha, \beta, C^A, S^1, S^2] = MoveUselessUnits(\boldsymbol{x}_t, \alpha, \beta, C^A, t, S_1, S_2)$; (see Algorithm 6)
    end if
    $S^2 = S^2 \setminus \{j^*\}$
    $S^1 = S^1 \cup \{j^*\}$
  end for
  for $i \in S^1$ **do**
    $\alpha = \alpha + W_i k(\boldsymbol{x}_t, \boldsymbol{x}_i)$; ▷ numerator of (3)
    $\beta = \beta + R_i k(\boldsymbol{x}_t, \boldsymbol{x}_i)$; ▷ denominator of (3)
  end for
  return $[\alpha/\beta, C^A, S^1, S^2]$

---

where $f^C_{t-1} \equiv \sum_{i\in C^1_{t-1}} W_i K(\boldsymbol{x}_i,\cdot)$, $g^C_{t-1} \equiv \sum_{i\in C^1_{t-1}} R_i K(\boldsymbol{x}_i,\cdot)$ denote the vectors for cluster kernels and $f^A_{t-1} \equiv \sum_{i\in S^1_{t-1}\setminus C^1_{t-1}} W_i K(\boldsymbol{x}_i,\cdot)$, $g^A_{t-1} \equiv \sum_{i\in S^1_{t-1}\setminus C^1_{t-1}} R_i K(\boldsymbol{x}_i,\cdot)$ denote the vector for active kernels. $K(\boldsymbol{x}_i,\cdot)$ denotes the vector on Hilbert space, whose number of dimensions is equal to infinity.

The cluster kernels are generated by the LGRNN learning algorithm. As LGRNN kernel centers are distributed sparsely during the learning, the kernel centers are suitable to be used for clustering other kernel centers.

The active kernels sometimes move into the secondary storage, thereby making the essential sleep kernels in the secondary storage to be loaded as the active kernels. Now, let us denote S^1_t and S^2_t as the kernel set in the main memory and the secondary storage after the t-th observation of instance, respectively. The active kernel set is represented by $S^1_t \setminus C_t$, where C_t denotes the set of cluster kernels. The active kernels are also calculated together with the cluster kernels in (3).

In the initial state, $C_0 = \emptyset$. If $(\boldsymbol{x}_t, y_t)$ is a new sample and $|C_{t-1}| < B$, LGRNN allocates a new kernel whose centroid is $\boldsymbol{x}_t$, as shown in the below equations:

$$f^C_t = f^C_{t-1} + y_t K(\boldsymbol{x}_t,\cdot),\quad g^C_t = g^C_{t-1} + K(\boldsymbol{x}_t,\cdot),\quad C_t = C_{t-1}\cup\{t\} \tag{4}$$

Here, B denotes the maximum number of the cluster kernels. However, if $|C_{t-1}| \geq B^C$, the LGRNN cannot allocate new kernel anymore. In such cases, the LGRNN chooses one of the following two learning options: Replacement or Ignore[1].

In the replacement option, the LGRNN replaces the most redundant kernel with a new kernel, whose centroid and weight are $\boldsymbol{x}_t$ and y_t, respectively. On the other hand, in the ignore option, the LGRNN does nothing with the new input.

The most redundant kernel is detected by calculating the approximate linear dependence (ALD). Therefore, if $K(\boldsymbol{u}_i,\cdot)$ is represented by a linear combination of the other kernels: $K(\boldsymbol{u}_j,\cdot)(j \neq i)$, $K(\boldsymbol{u}_i,\cdot)$ is redundant for calculating the LGRNN outputs. More concretely, the LGRNN chooses the kernel whose δ_i is defined in (5) and is the smallest.

$$\delta_i = \min_{a_{ij}} \left\| K(\boldsymbol{u}_i,\cdot) - \sum_{j\neq i} a_{ij} K(\boldsymbol{u}_j,\cdot) \right\|^2, \tag{5}$$

where δ_i and a_i are derivated by the following equation.

$$a_i = K^{-1}k(\boldsymbol{u}_i), \delta_i = \{1 - k^T(\boldsymbol{u}_i)a_i\}, \tag{6}$$

where the matrix K is $[K]_{ij} = K(\boldsymbol{u}_i, \boldsymbol{u}_j)$,

[1] The original LGRNN algorithm has four learning options (Yamauchi (2014)). One of them being the projection operation. However this operation is not useful for the swap kernel regression. Hence, here we only use the replacement and ignore options.

$k(\boldsymbol{x}) = [K(\boldsymbol{u}_1, \boldsymbol{x}), \cdots, K(\boldsymbol{u}_{i-1}, \boldsymbol{x}), K(\boldsymbol{u}_{i+1}, \boldsymbol{x}), \cdots]^T$. The LGRNN chooses the i-th kernel, where $i = argmin_j\{\delta_j\}$ and tries to replace the i-th kernel with a new kernel.

To choose the best learning option from the two, the LGRNN calculates and compares two evaluation functions. These evaluation functions represent losses due to execution of the two learning options. The evaluation function for the replacement option $e_{replace}$ denotes the loss due to the pruning of the most redundant kernel. The output value, which the pruned kernel records, becomes the loss of this learning option. Therefore,

$$e_{replace} \equiv R_{i^*} \left(\frac{W_{i^*}}{R_{i^*}} - \frac{W_{N(\boldsymbol{x}_{i^*})}}{R_{N(\boldsymbol{x}_{i^*})}} \right)^2, \tag{7}$$

where $N(\boldsymbol{x}_{i^*})$ denotes the closest kernel to the i^*-th kernel : $N(\boldsymbol{x}_{i^*}) \equiv \arg\min_{j \in C_t} \|\boldsymbol{x}_{i^*} - \boldsymbol{x}_j\|^2$. Note that R_{i^*} denotes the value, that is proportional to the number of sample that are closest to the i^*-th kernel. This means that (7) is proportional to the probability of having maximum output value of the i^*-th kernel times the error due to the pruning of the i^*-th kernel.

Algorithm 3. Learning

Require: New sample (x_t, y_t), Maximum number of hidden unit kernels:B, set of cluster kernel:C_{t-1}, support set on the main memory:S^1_{t-1}, support set on the secondary storage: S^2_{t-1}, numerator function vector f^C_{t-1}, denominator function vector g^C_{t-1}.

if $|C_{t-1}| < B^C$ **then**
  $f^C_t = f^C_{t-1} + y_t K(\boldsymbol{x}_t, \cdot)$,
  $g^C_t = g^C_{t-1} + K(\boldsymbol{x}_t, \cdot)$,
  $C_t = C_{t-1} \cup \{t\}$
else
  Find the target kernel $i^* = \arg\min_j \delta_j$ where δ_j is defined by (5)
  Calculate $e_{replace}$ and e_{ignore} by (7) and (8).
  if $e_{replace} < e_{ignore}$ **then** ▷ Replacement
    $C_{t-1} = C_{t-1} \setminus \{i^*\}$ ▷ Remove the i^*-th kernel
    $f^C_t = f^C_{t-1-i^*} + y_t K(\boldsymbol{x}_t, \cdot)$, $g^C_t = g^C_{t-1-i^*} + K(\boldsymbol{x}_t, \cdot)$, ▷ Add the new kernel
    $N(\boldsymbol{x}_{i^*}) \equiv \arg\min_{j \in C_{t-1}} \|\boldsymbol{x}_j - \boldsymbol{x}_{i^*}\|^2$
    $R_{N(\boldsymbol{x}_{i^*})} = R_{N(\boldsymbol{x}_{i^*})} + R_{i^*}$.
    $C_t = C_{t-1} \cup \{t\}$
    $[S^1_t, S^2_t] = Store(i^*, C_t, S^1_t, S^2_t)$ (see Algorithm 4)
    $[C_t, S^1_t, S^2_t] = reindex(C_t, S^1_t, S^2_t)$ (see Algorithm 5)
  else ▷ Ignore
    $f^C_t = f^C_{t-1}$, $g^C_t = g^C_{t-1}$, $C_t = C_{t-1}$
    $I^C_t = N(\boldsymbol{x}_t)$.
    $[S^1_t, S^2_t] = Store(t, C_t, S^1_t, S^2_t)$ (see Algorithm 4)
  end if
  return $[f^C_t, g^C_t, C_t, S^1_t, S^2_t]$
end if

On the other hand, the evaluation function for the ignore option denotes the loss due to the LGRNN not learning the new sample. Therefore, let us denote e_{ignore} as the loss, then

$$e_{ignore} \equiv I_w(y_t - y_{t-1}(x_t))^2, \tag{8}$$

where I_w denotes the importance weight for the new input. In this experiment, we set $I_w = 1$.

These two evaluation functions $e_{replace}$ and e_{ignore} are calculated for every input sample. If $e_{replace} \geq e_{ignore}$, the LGRNN executes the replacement option, otherwise the LGRNN chooses the ignore option. In the case of the replacement option,

$$f_t^C = f_{t-1-i^*}^C + y_t K(\boldsymbol{x}_t, \cdot), \quad g_t^C = g_{t-1-i^*}^C + K(\boldsymbol{x}_t, \cdot), \tag{9}$$

where i^* denotes the most redundant kernel index and $f_{t-1-i^*}^C$ is the function that excludes the i^*-th kernel from f_{t-1}^C. At the same time, $R_{N(\boldsymbol{x}_{i^*})}$ is updated to refrect the number of samples distributed around the kernel. Therefore,

$$R_{N(\boldsymbol{x}_{i^*})} = R_{N(\boldsymbol{x}_{i^*})} + R_{i^*} \tag{10}$$

The detailed algorithm is shown in Algorithm 3.

3.3 Data Structure for the Secondary Storage

A part of the kernels is saved into the secondary storage. The data structure of the secondary storage is formed such that it can store the required information for each kernel. Each kernel needs the data listed in Table 1 for this simulation described under the experiment section, SQLite https://www.sqlite.org/index.html.

Table 1. Items required in the database table in the secondary storage (i-th kernel)

No.	Notation	Contents
1	Index	Unique row index
2	I_i^C	Cluster index for this kernel
3	$\boldsymbol{x}_i$	The centroid vector of the i-th kernel
4	w_i/R_i	The extension parameter of the i-th kernel
5	t_i^R	Stored time into the 2nd storage

4 Instance Distribution for Effective Inference

The computational complexity of the swap-kernel-regression method is highly dependent on the distribution of inputs. The swap kernel regression has the two modes: the inference and the learning modes. Both the modes sometimes need kernel swapping. In this section, let us consider the distribution of instances for effective inference. During the inference mode, the swap kernel regression method only calculates the output value. Therefore, if the instances are generated from slowly changing situations, there is a high possibility that they will activate the specified cluster kernel for a while. Also, there is a high possibility that the swap-process will not occur during the continuing current status[2].

In such cases, the computational complexity does not include the cost for the swapping kernels and hence the swap-kernel-regression's inference process can be done with a small computational complexity.

One such environment is modeled as follows. Let us assume that the inputs $\boldsymbol{x}_t$ are generated depending on the status $S(t)$:

$$\boldsymbol{x}_t \sim p(\boldsymbol{x}|S(t)), \quad S(t) \sim p(S|S(t-1)). \tag{11}$$

In many cases, the state changes are based on physical state changes. Therefore, $S(t)$ is similar to the previous $S(t-1)$. This means that the generated input vector $\boldsymbol{x}_t$ is also similar to $\boldsymbol{x}_{t-1}$. Hence, there is a high possibility that the swap-process does not occur if a large state change does not occurred.

Note that the computational cost for the swap kernel regression is affected by the memory capacity and the size of cluster kernels. Therefore, if the number of kernels of the same cluster ID is larger than $|S^1|$, the swapping of kernels will be repeated even if there is no state changes. The capacity for active kernels is $|S^1| - |C|$, where C denotes the cluster kernel set. The average number of active kernels for each cluster is around N/C. Therefore, if the number of active kernel is less than $|S^1| - |C|$, the frequency of swap operation is reduced. The condition is

$$\frac{N}{|C|} \leq |S^1| - |C| \tag{12}$$

Therefore, we obtain following condition for $|C|$.

$$|C| \leq \frac{1}{2}|S^1| + \sqrt{\frac{1}{4}|S^1|^2 - N} \tag{13}$$

Unfortunately, N is unknown in advance. Hence, we need to determine C according to the predicted number of learning samples.

Moreover, σ used in Eq. (2) is also should be determined properly to get highest generalization capability. One way to determine σ is a cross validation like algorithm using existing kernel centers (Yamauchi (2014)). In this study, we set σ value by hand according to preliminary test.

[2] Even under such situations, if the related instance distribution area is wide enough, then the number of kernels of the same cluster is larger than $|S_t^1|$, hence the swap occurs repeatedly (see Algorithm 2).

Algorithm 4. Store

Require: Target kernel index i, Active cluster index C_A, Support set in the main storage S_t^1 Support set in the secondary storage S_t^2
if $|S_t^1| < B^1$ **then**
  $S_t^1 = S_t^1 \cup \{i\}$
else
  for all kernels $j \in S_t^1$ where $I_j^C \notin C_A$. **do**
    $S_t^1 = S_t^1 \setminus \{j\}$
    $S_t^2 = S_t^2 \cup \{j\}$
  end for
  $S_t^1 = S_t^1 \cup \{i\}$
end if
return S_t^1, S_t^2

Algorithm 5. Reindex kernels

Require: Current time t,
 Target kernel index i,
 Corresponding kernel centroid $\boldsymbol{x}_i$,
 Support set in the main storage S_t^1,
 Support set in the secondary storage S_t^2
 Cluster Kernels C_t, Active Cluster Kernels C^A
do
  for all $j \in S_t^1 \setminus C_t$ **do**
    $I_j^C = N(\boldsymbol{x}_j)$ ▷ Reset cluster index.
    $t_j^R = t$ ▷ Set the swap out time.
  end for
  $S_t^2 = S_t^2 \cup \{S_t^1 \setminus C_t\}$ ▷ Move all kernels to the secondary storage except for the cluster kernels.
  $S_t^1 = C_t$
  for all $j \in S_t^2$ where $t_j^R < t$ **do**
    if $|S_t^1| < B^1$ **then**
      $S_t^2 = S_t^2 \setminus \{j\}$
      $S_t^1 = S_t^1 \cup \{j\}$
    else
      break;
    end if
  end for
while $\{S_t^1 \setminus C_t\} \neq \phi$

5 Experiments

5.1 Regression Tasks

At first, we test the swap-kernel-regression method by using the benchmark test dataset recorded in the UCI machine learning repository https://archive.ics.uci.edu/ml/index.php. The datasets for regression used are hearta1, housing, servo, Concrete (See Table 2). Each instance is presented to the swap-kernel-regression one by one. The instances in each dataset are clustered by using an expectation-maximization (EM) algorithm. They are ordered by the clustering result to make the data approximately represent a slowly changing state. The swap-kernel-regression performance is evaluated by using the cumulative error err_t^{cum} calculated in Algorithm 1 and the execution time for the learning of each dataset. The cumulative error err_t^{cum} is the accumulated error before the learning of the current instance was acquired.

Table 2. Dataset used

Dataset	Size of input dimension	Size of output dimension	Dataset size
Concrete	7	1	1030
Servo	12	1	167
Housing	13	1	501
Heartal	35	1	460

The learning for each dataset was repeated for 50 times by changing the order of the instances. An average reading of the cumulative errors for 50 trials is obtained. We also compared the cumulative error with that of the original LGRNN proposed in (Yamauchi (2014)), where the number of kernels is the same as $|S^1|$. The number of cluster kernels is 6, $\sigma = 1$ and $|S^1| \leq 30$. The secondary storage was formed by SQLite.

Figures 2 and 3 show the average cumulative errors of the swap kernel regression and the original LGRNN.

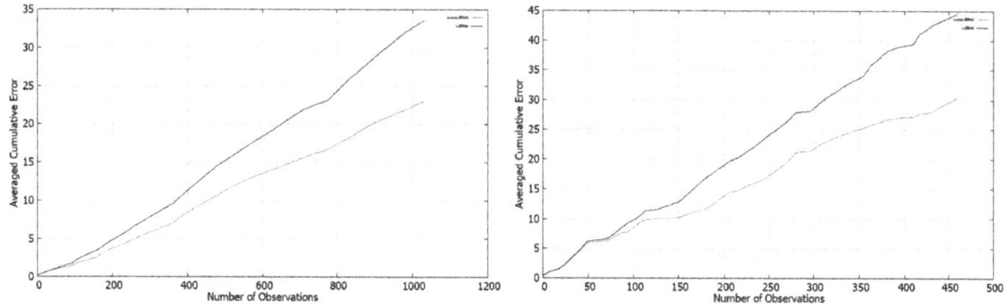

Fig. 2. Average cumulative errors of concrete (left) and heartal (right) datasets: Swap kernel regression (Red) vs original LGRNN (Black) (Color figure online)

From these results, we can see that there is less difference between the swap kernel regression and the original LGRNN, but the cumulative errors of the swap kernel regression are less than those of the original LGRNN in the other datasets.

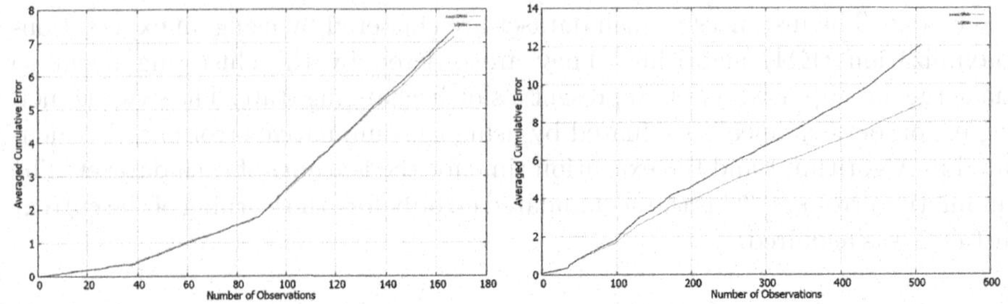

Fig. 3. Average cumulative errors of servo (left) and housing (right) datasets: Swap kernel regression (Red) vs original LGRNN (Black) (Color figure online)

These results suggest that the original LGRNN performance is usually restricted by the limited number of kernels but that of the swap kernel regression is not affected by the number of bounded kernels. The execution times of the swap kernel regression are, however, much longer than those of the original LGRNN. This is because the speed of file operation is much slower than that of memory operation.

We also try to use a solid-state storage memory as the secondary storage. We replace the hard disk with an array on the main memory to approximate the solid-state storage memory. Note that, in this case, the swap kernel regression does not access the files. Hence, we can expect that the speed of the swap kernel regression is increased. Table 3 shows the results for this. We can see from the table that the execution time is faster than the original LGRNN. This is because the swap kernel regression only needs to manage the learning of a small number of cluster kernels. Although the learning algorithm is similar to that of the original LGRNN, the number of the cluster kernels is less than the original one. Therefore, the computational complexity of its learning is smaller than that of the original LGRNN.

Table 3. Comparison of execution time

Dataset	LGRNN [s]	Swap kernel regression (normal secondary storage) [s]	Swap kernel regression (solid-state secondary storage) [s]
Concrete	413.9	4897.6	19.8
Servo	59.7	742.0	2.9
Housing	203.6	2344.4	8.5
Heartal	206.6	2460.6	9.0

5.2 Clustering Task

We have also applied the swap kernel regression to the MNIST dataset http://yann.lecun.com/exdb/mnist/. The MNIST database is a large hand-written digit dataset, which records 60000 image data with corresponding labels. Each data is a 28×28 gray level image data. Such hand written character include deformation in its shape. To ensure the accurate recognition dispute for such deformations, each image data is converted into a feature vector by using the VGG16 model (Simonyan and Zisserman (2015)) (see Fig. 4). We have used the default VGG16 with predetermined parameters.

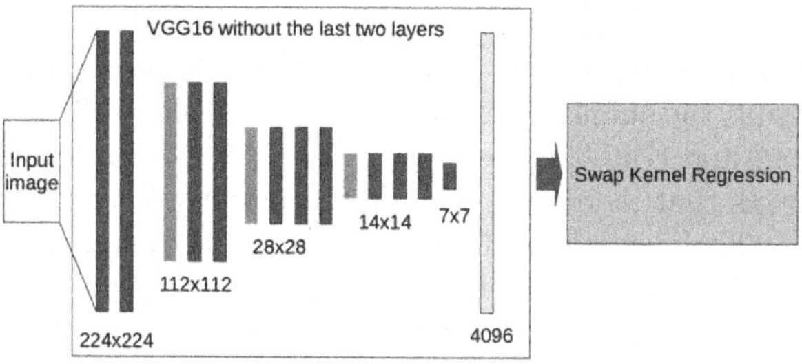

Fig. 4. Swap kernel regression with VGG16: Orange-colored and yellow-colored layers are the max-pooling and full connection layers, respectively. (Color figure online)

Therefore, the images of the MNIST are converted into JPEG images and re-scaled to $224 \times 224 \times 3$[3] as the input for the VGG16 model. We choose the 4096 dimensional vector attained from the first full connection layer.

The label for each data is set as a 10-dimensional vector $\boldsymbol{y}$, whose $(k-1)$-th element represents the k-th class. e.g. If the image is '2', $y^{(1)} = 1$ and $y^{(k)} = 0$, where $k \neq 1$.

In this case, the output size of the swap kernel regression method has to be 10 to realize the clustering of the 10 digit number. Therefore, the equations for the swap kernel regression should also be modified for the 10 output classes. Fortunately, this modification is very easy. We just increase the value of output size. For example, Eq. (3) is extended to

$$y^{(k)}(\boldsymbol{x}) = \frac{\langle (f_{t-1}^{c(k)} + f_{t-1}^{A(k)}), K(\boldsymbol{x}, \cdot) \rangle}{\langle (g_{t-1}^{c} + g_{t-1}^{A}), K(\boldsymbol{x}, \cdot) \rangle}, \tag{14}$$

where k denotes the suffix that is representing the k-th output related parameter. Note that the number of function vectors $f_{t-1}^{c(k)}$ and $f_{t-1}^{A(k)}$ for $k = 1, 2, \cdots, 10$ should also be required. For example, the function vector $f_{t-1}^{c(k)}$ represents the

[3] Although the VGG16 model supports the processing of real color images, we still provide the re-scaled gray-level images as the input.

k-th output related function: $f_{t-1}^{C(K)} \equiv \sum_{i \in C_{t-1}^1} W_i^{(k)} K(\boldsymbol{x}_i, \cdot)$. Therefore, each kernel is connected to $W_i^{(k)}$ for $k = 1, 2, \cdots, 10$.

We also chose 10000 images from the 60000 images present in the MNIST dataset. About 1000 images for each digit character is chosen. We stimulated these 10000 images one by one to the swap kernel regression. The cumulative mistakes are examined using the one-pass learning of them.

σ used in Eq. (2) was set as $\sigma^2 = 1000$, the total number of the kernels was $|S_1| = 30$, the number of cluster kernels was $|C| = 10$.

The clustering result from the swap kernel regression is determined by $C = \arg\max_k y^{(k)}[\boldsymbol{x}]$. Figure 5 shows the cumulative mistakes versus number of observations[4]. We can see that the cumulative number of mistakes was increased gradually. Figure 6 shows an magnified figure of a part of the Figure 5.

We investigated the cumulative number of mistakes at 5000 and 10000 observations. As a result, the cumulative number of mistakes at 5000 and 10000 observations were 892.0 and 1746.0, respectively. Therefore, 1746 is less than two times of 892. This means that increasing ratio of the number of mistakes are reduced during the last 5000 observations. This property was the same as an another test condition: $|S_1| = 30$ and $|C| = 6$. In the latter case, the cumulative number of mistakes at 5000 and 10000 observations were 944 and 1838, respectively. Note that 1838 is less than the two times of 944. We predict that the increase ratio in the cumulative number of mistakes will reduced if the total number of instances becomes large.

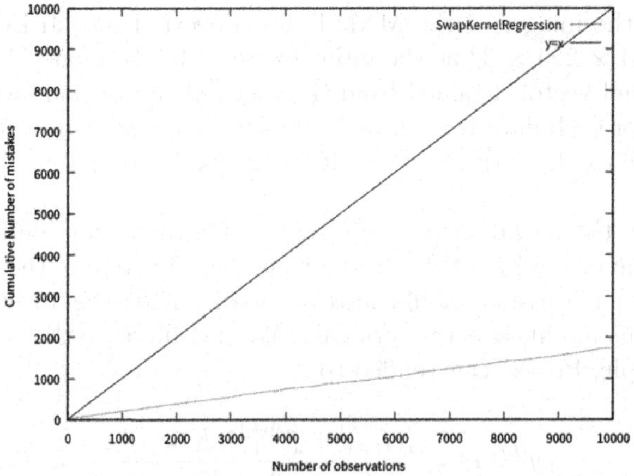

Fig. 5. Cumulative number of mistakes versus number of observations. The line $y = x$ is also plotted for comparison.

[4] Note that each new instance was tested its recognition result before the incremental learning of it, and the swap-kerne-regression learned it incrementally. So, if the swap kernel regression fails to recognize a new instance, the cumulative number of mistakes is incremented.

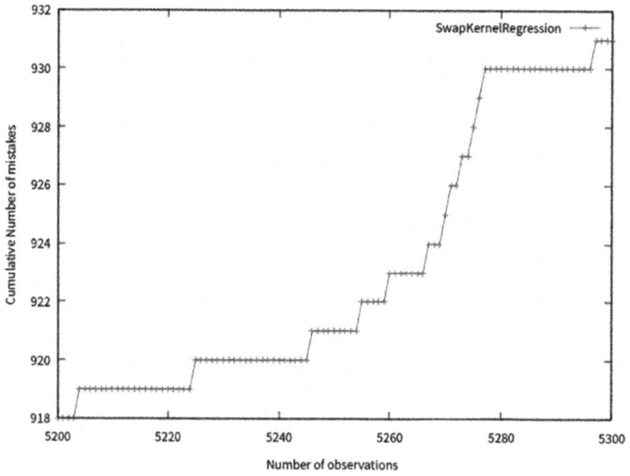

Fig. 6. Magnified figure of Fig. 5 at 5200–5300 observations.

Algorithm 6. MoveUselessUnits

Require: new input $\boldsymbol{x}_t$, numerator α, denominator β, C^A, current time t, Support set in the main storage S^1, Support set in the secondary storage S^2

$r = \arg\max_{j \in C^A} \|\boldsymbol{x}_t - \boldsymbol{x}_j\|^2$ ▷ r:Find the Most far kernel index.

for all i where $I_i^C = r$ **do**

  $\alpha = \alpha + W_i k(\boldsymbol{x}_t, \boldsymbol{x}_i)$

  $\beta = \beta + R_i k(\boldsymbol{x}_t, \boldsymbol{x}_i)$

  $t_i^R = t$

  $S^2 = S^2 \cup \{i\}$ ▷ Swap out

  $S^1 = S^1 \setminus \{i\}$

end for

if $N_r \subseteq S^2$ **then** ▷ N_r : Set of kernels, which are related to the r-th cluster kernel.

  $C^A = C^A \setminus \{r\}$

end if

return $[\alpha, \beta, C^A, S^1, S^2]$

---

6 Conclusion and Discussion

This paper presents the swap-kernel regression method that repeats the incremental learning of new instances within a limited capacity of storage space. To make this possible, the swap-kernel regression method swaps essential and unnecessary kernels for a while. The unnecessary kernels are tentatively stored to the secondary storage. Therefore, if there is no restriction on the capacity of the secondary storage, the swap kernel regression method will not have any limitation in the number of kernels.

In our proposed method, the clustering kernels play a very significant part to enable the swap activity. The cluster ID for each kernel determines the sleep kernels that need to be uploaded from the secondary storage. To realize this, the proposed method consists of cluster kernels and the other kernels. The cluster kernel is used for clustering the other kernels.

The simulation results suggests that the generalization capability is superior to LGRNN. This is because the number of kernels of the swap kernel regression is not bounded to the main memory capacity. Moreover, there are cases wherein the computational complexity of the swap kernel regression is less than the original LGRNN, when the secondary storage consists of a solid-state memory.

Although the swap kernel regression architecture is similar to those of k-nearest neighbors, its generalization capability can be improved by collaborating with an existing DCNN, such as the VGG16 model. The experiments for the one shot learning of the hand-written digit numbers in the MNIST suggested that it can be used for the largescale realworld recognition tasks as well.

Note that if the instance distribution is unbalanced, there is a possibility of reduced frequency of the swap operation. However, so far, the exists for inference only. During the learning, the swap operation is frequently occurred. To reduce the swap operation during the learning, we will need to improve our algorithm.

References

Dekel, O., Shalev-Shwartz, S., Singer, Y.: The forgetron: a kernel-based perceptron on a budget. SIAM J. Comput. (SICOMP) **37**(5), 1342–1372 (2008). https://doi.org/10.1137/060666998

He, W., Wu, S.: A kernel-based perceptron with dynamic memory. Neural Networks **25**, 105–113 (2012). https://doi.org/10.1016/j.neunet.2011.07.008

Kivinen, J., Smola, A.J., Williamson, R.C.: Online learning with kernels. IEEE Trans. Signal Process. **52**(8), 2165–2176 (2004). https://doi.org/10.1109/TSP.2004.830991

Lee, D., et al.: LRFU: a spectrum of policies that subsumes the least recently used and least frequently used policies. IEEE Trans. Comput. **50**(12), 1352–1361 (2001). https://doi.org/10.1109/TC.2001.970573

Orabona, F., Keshet, J., Caputo, B.: The projectron: a bounded kernel-based perceptron. In: ICML 2008, pp. 720–727 (2008)

Simonyan, K., Zisserman, A.: Very deep convolutional networks for large-scale image recognition. In: International Conference on Learning Representations ICLR 2015 (2015), arXiv:1409.1556v6

Weston, J., Chopra, S., Bordes, A.: Memory networks. In: ICLR 2015 (2015)

Yamauchi, K.: An importance weighted projection method for incremental learning under unstationary environments. In: IJCNN2013: The International Joint Conference on Neural Networks 2013, pp. 1–9. The Institute of Electrical and Electronics Engineers, Inc., New York (2013). https://doi.org/10.1109/IJCNN.2013.6706779

Yamauchi, K.: Incremental learning on a budget and its application to quick maximum power point tracking of photovoltaic systems. J. Adv. Comput. Intell. Intell. Inf. **18**(4), 682–696 (2014). https://doi.org/10.20965/jaciii.2014.p0682

Explainable Methods

Model-Agnostic Explanations for Decisions Using Minimal Patterns

Kohei Asano[1(✉)], Jinhee Chun[1], Atsushi Koike[2(✉)], and Takeshi Tokuyama[3]

[1] Graduate School of Information Sciences, Tohoku University, Sendai, Japan
{asano,jinhee}@dais.is.tohoku.ac.jp

[2] National Institute of Technology, Ichinoseki College, Ichinoseki, Japan
koike@ichinoseki.ac.jp

[3] Department of Informatics, Kwansei Gakuin University, Mita, Japan
tokuyama@kwansei.ac.jp

Abstract. Recently, numerous high-performance machine learning models have been proposed. Unfortunately, such models often produce black-box decisions derived using opaque reasons and logic. Therefore, it is important to develop a tool that automatically gives the reasons underlying the black-box model's decision. Ideally, the tool should be model-agnostic: applicable to any machine-learning model without knowing model details. A well-known previous work, LIME, is based on the linear decision. Although LIME provides important features for the decision, the result is still difficult to understand for users because the result might not contain the features required for the decision. We propose a novel model-agnostic explanation method named MP-LIME. The explanation consists of feature sets, each of which can reconstruct the decision correctly. Thereby, users can easily understand each feature set. By comparing our method to LIME, we demonstrate that our method often improves precision drastically. We also provide practical examples in which our method provides reasons for the decisions.

Keywords: Explanation · Interpretability · Machine learning

1 Introduction

Machine learning models, which achieve high accuracy, are applicable to widely various tasks. Nevertheless, such high-performance models are complex and mostly behave as a black-box. This fact engenders a critical *interpretability* issue because these models' decisions are difficult for users to understand. Interpretability is necessary especially when machine learning models are applied to sensitive tasks that entail important responsibilities such as medical diagnosis [5] and education [10].

Nowadays, many studies of interpretability have been reported in the relevant literature [7]. Among the approaches are methods that use another explanatory model that interprets a black-box model. Such methods are preferably model-agnostic: applicable to any machine learning model without knowing the model

I. V. Tetko et al. (Eds.): ICANN 2019, LNCS 11727, pp. 241–252, 2019.
https://doi.org/10.1007/978-3-030-30487-4_19

details. Local interpretable model-agnostic explanation (LIME) is a well-known model-agnostic explanation method proposed by Ribeiro et al. [12]. LIME is applicable to various models for image and sentiment prediction [12]. As an explanatory model that describes the local behavior of a black-box model, LIME uses a linear model. Because the explanatory model is easily interpreted, users can understand the reasons for its decision.

Although LIME is a successful framework, several issues require further improvement. First, although LIME can exploit important features for the decision, the explanation often includes redundant features that do not affect the decision. Consequently, LIME tends to give a low-precision explanation. Second, the LIME explanation is sometimes difficult for users to understand because users cannot always derive the correct decision solely from the presented features. These issues arise because users cannot know the combinations of features that actually contribute to the decision using LIME.

To resolve these issues, we propose a novel explanation method: Minimal Pattern LIME (MP-LIME). The MP-LIME explanation consists of important feature sets we call *minimal patterns*. Users can readily derive the decision only using those minimal patterns because a minimal pattern has neither excess nor deficiency features to make the decision. Because of the property of minimal patterns, the MP-LIME explanation shows higher precision than LIME. Moreover, it is easy for users to understand. Our contributions are the following.

1. We formulate a new explanatory model using feature patterns and propose an effective algorithm to construct the explanatory model (Sect. 4).
2. We show experimentally that our algorithm can build an explanatory model faster and that it has higher precision than the previous LIME (Sect. 5).
3. We demonstrate the application of our method to two tasks: image classification and income prediction using black-box models (Sect. 5).

2 Related Work

One approach to enhancing interpretability is building globally interpretable and highly accurate machine learning models such as those of minimal predictive patterns [2], rule lists [17], and rule sets [11]. Users can clearly comprehend model behavior and explanations of any decision. Because these models become simple to interpret, they present difficulty when performing highly accurate analyses of problems with a complex input domain. Lakkaraju et al. demonstrated that disjoint rule sets provide high interpretability to users through user study [11]. Batal and Hauskrect achieved high accuracy with informative features, so-called minimal predictive patterns, found through frequent pattern mining methodology [2].

As a method to explain any machine learning model, Ribeiro et al. proposed the locally interpretable model-agnostic explanations (LIME) framework [12]. It uses an explanatory model to exhibit the behavior of black-box models to users. In fact, it locally approximates a black-box model using a sparse linear model. Then users can understand the model behavior using weights of the explanatory model. Ribeiro et al. also proposed another local model-agnostic explanation system [13] that uses a rule model as an explanatory model.

Another approach is called model enumeration. Some previous works are a linear model [9], a decision tree [14], and a rule model [8]. Users can select the best model that matches users' prior knowledge by presenting several good models that are semi-optimal solutions.

3 Previous Approach

We introduce the LIME framework [12]. Consider interpreting the decision of an instance $x \in \mathcal{X}$ we obtained from an arbitrary model $f \colon \mathcal{X} \to \mathcal{Y}$. Here, x is the explained instance; $\mathcal{X}$ is the domain of f. Also, $\mathcal{Y}$ is the output space. In the case of binary classification, $\mathcal{Y}$ is simply $\{-1, 1\}$, if we interpret the output as probabilities, then $\mathcal{Y}$ is expected to be $[0, 1]$. The goal of the LIME framework is to identify *interpretable features* that contribute to $f(x)$. In the following, we refer to the class of x with regard to the model f as the *target class* of x.

3.1 Interpretable Representation

Explaining through the original domain $\mathcal{X}$ using any both white-box model [16,17] and an explanatory model [1] does not always engender interpretable models. If the original instance exists in a high-dimensional feature input space and if these features all mutually interact for decisions, then users are unlikely to understand the explanation itself. Consequently, in LIME framework, the original instance $x \in \mathcal{X}$ is converted into a d-dimensional binary vector $\mathbf{x} \in \{0, 1\}^d$ as an interpretable representation. Because of this interpretable representation, it is possible to indicate the existence or absence of a feature. For example, in image classification tasks, the original domain is represented by a 3-channel matrix (third-order tensor). One way to convert x to an interpretable representation is to divide the image into several regions (e.g. superpixels [3]). A missing region corresponds to a 0-element. It is represented as a black area. It is noteworthy that the transformation between an instance in the original domain and an interpretable represented instance must be defined uniquely by users. By converting instances to the interpretable representation and by identifying interpretable features, LIME accommodates a model-agnostic explanation.

3.2 Formulation of LIME Framework

We define a model $g \in \mathcal{G}$ as an *explanatory model*, which describes the local behavior of a given model f, where $\mathcal{G}$ is a family of interpretable models such as linear models or decision trees. Users understand a given decision of $f(x)$ using a specific g. Thereby, we require g to be interpretable while enhancing local fidelity with regard to the original model f in the neighborhood of the input point x. For example, a dense weight vector, such as a few zero elements, might engender better approximation than a sparse weight vector when using a linear model as the explanatory model. However, an explanation with a dense weight vector might be only slightly interpretable because it provides many features to users. Consequently, an explanatory model must not be too complex for interpretability.

The LIME framework is formulated as a tradeoff between local fidelity and interpretability. Letting $\mathcal{L}(f, g, \pi)$ be a local-aware loss between f and g in the locality defined by similarity kernel $\pi\colon \mathcal{X} \times \mathcal{X} \to \mathbb{R}$, then the value $\pi(x, x')$ measures the locality between x and $x' \in \mathcal{X}$. If x' is similar to x in their original domain, then the value of $\pi(x, x')$ becomes larger. Because the explanatory model should be interpretable, a penalty function $\Omega(g)$ is introduced to control the model complexity. Because we must minimize $\mathcal{L}(f, g, \pi)$ and $\Omega(g)$, we are looking for optimization of their relative tradeoff. Consequently, the LIME framework is formulated as

$$\underset{g \in \mathcal{G}}{\operatorname{argmin}} \quad \mathcal{L}(f, g, \pi) + \Omega(g). \tag{1}$$

3.3 Explanations Using a Linear Model

Ribeiro et al. proposed a linear model as an explanatory model [12]. We designate this formulation as Linear-LIME. It obtains $g(\mathbf{x}) = \mathbf{w}^\top \mathbf{x}$, which is formulated as $g\colon \{0, 1\}^d \to \mathbb{R}$ by regressing f with a generated training dataset.

The algorithm generates N neighbor samples denoted by $\mathbf{x}_k$, $k = 1, \ldots, N$. Each sample is generated by setting its components randomly to zero. These samples are used as a training instance of g. Then, sampled vectors $\mathbf{x}_k$ are recovered to instance of original domain $x_k \in \mathcal{X}$, which we call sample instances. Sample instances are input to model f to measure the behavior of f at x_k. Each $f(x_k)$ is used as a label. Thereby, in Linear-LIME, the output space is necessary to satisfy $\mathcal{Y} \subseteq \mathbb{R}$. To construct explanatory model g, training dataset $S = \{(\mathbf{x}_k, \pi(x, x_k), f(x_k)) : k = 1, \ldots, N\}$ is used. When constructing S, we must call model f to get a label. Consequently, it has $\mathcal{O}(N\tau)$ time complexity, where we regard the time complexity of a decision with f as a constant τ because it depends only on the original domain $\mathcal{X}$.

Linear-LIME uses the weighted square loss in Eq. (2) as the local-aware loss. The complexity in Eq. (3) is represented as a condition that constrains the number of nonzero elements of the weight vector $\mathbf{w}$ to be at most $K \in \mathbb{N}$:

$$\underset{g \in \mathcal{G}}{\operatorname{argmin}} \quad \sum_{k=1}^{N} \pi(x, x_k)(f(x_k) - g(\mathbf{x}_k))^2, \tag{2}$$

$$\text{subject to} \quad \|\mathbf{w}\|_0 \leq K, \tag{3}$$

where $\|\mathbf{w}\|_0$ represents the number of nonzero elements of the vector $\mathbf{w}$.

Because the above formulation is computationally difficult to handle, a relaxation method should be considered. In the relaxation, the constraint (3) is replaced with a penalty function $\Omega(g)$ that tends to become large if the constraint is violated. The penalty function is added to the objective function.

This formulation fits the general LIME framework (1). The similarity kernel is formulated as $\pi(x, x_k) = \exp(-D(x, x_k)/\sigma^2)$ with width σ. D is an appropriate distance function (e.g. cosine or L_2 distance). It applies LARS path algorithm [6] to solve Eqs. (2) and (3). Therefore, it has $\mathcal{O}(N\tau + d^3 + d^2N)$ time complexity in addition to the construction time of a training dataset S.

As for the weight vector $\mathbf{w}$, higher weighted features are more important. The weight sign indicates whether the feature promotes or suppresses the decision. Consequently, users can know which features are important. However, it remains unclear which feature patterns are important. Even if the individual weight is small in terms of features, a combination of them might be important. Moreover, no guarantee exists about the explanation of Linear-LIME. If the instance that consists of all positive weighted features are input to model f, then the instance might not be classified as a target class. Furthermore, to give a faithful explanation, we must set an appropriate width of similarity kernel σ. It is impossible to evaluate σ, in which case model f is completely a black box.

4 Proposed Approach

We propose an explanatory model that specifically examines feature combinations and an algorithm that constructs the explanatory model effectively. Because our formulation is based on the LIME framework, it is also a model-agnostic explanation. The proposed explanatory model is defined as a family of important patterns, which we call *minimal patterns*. Therefore, we refer to our formulation as Minimal Patterns LIME (MP-LIME). We present an intuitive illustration of the differences between previous LIME and MP-LIME in Fig. 1.

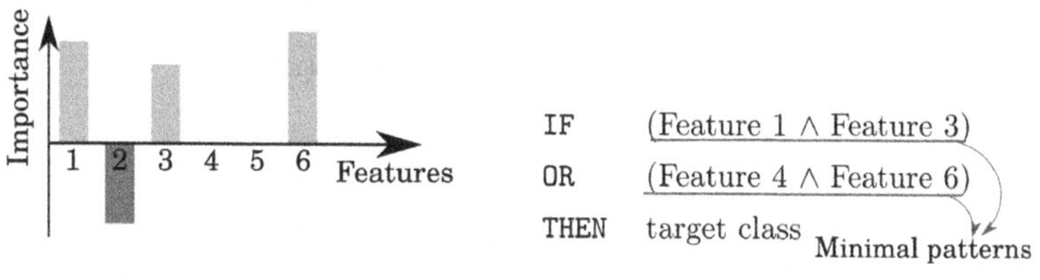

(a) Linear-LIME (b) MP-LIME

Fig. 1. Example of explanations with six interpretable features. (a) Each weight of the interpretable feature represents individual feature importance ($K = 4$). (b) The explanatory model consists of multiple minimal patterns from which the target class is inferred. It behaves as a rule set model using minimal patterns.

4.1 Explanations Using Minimal Patterns

Consider the interpretable representation as a set of features $[d] = \{1, \ldots, d\}$. A subset of nonzero features of $\mathbf{x}$ is regarded as a feature pattern $e \in 2^{[d]}$. A sample instance corresponding to e is denoted by x_e. We use a comparison operator to represent whether x_e is classified to the target class. For this study, c is set as a function that returns a class of x from $f(x)$. It satisfies $f(x_e) \sim f(x) \Leftrightarrow c(f(x_e)) = c(f(x))$ by definition. Because users can decide the class of x using a value of $f(x)$, this representation can be applied to any output space.

First, Definition 1 characterizes minimal patterns.

Definition 1. *A minimal pattern* $e_{\min}$ *satisfies the following.*

$$f(x_{e_{\min}}) \sim f(x), \tag{4}$$

$$\forall i \in e_{\min},\ f(x_{e_{\min} \setminus \{i\}}) \nsim f(x). \tag{5}$$

According to Definition 1, minimal pattern $e_{\min}$ has no extra features to be classified to the target class. We formulate the proposed explanatory model g as a set of rules based on a *minimal patterns family* denoted as $\mathcal{E}_{\min}$. Consequently, it is formulated as $g : 2^{[d]} \to \{0, 1\}$, where 1-output means the target class. Given $\mathcal{E}_{\min}$, $g(e)$ returns 1 if there exists $e_{\min} \subseteq e$ such that $e_{\min} \in \mathcal{E}_{\min}$, and otherwise 0. Users interpret important feature patterns using $\mathcal{E}_{\min}$, such as the weight vector $\mathbf{w}$ in Linear-LIME. The formulation using the rule set eases the interpretation for users compared to other rule models, as stated by Lakkaraju et al. in [11]. Hara [8,9] and Ruggier [14] show that enumerating multiple minimal patterns gives users a complementary perspective compared to the rule model that has a single rule [13]. Let us formulate the desirable properties of $\mathcal{E}_{\min}$. Because every element $e \in \mathcal{E}_{\min}$ must be a minimal pattern, it is clear that instances x_e satisfy $f(x_e) \sim f(x)$ from Eq. (4). However, enumerating all minimal patterns might not improve interpretability because users cannot understand so many patterns. In addition, if we apply Definition 1 to all patterns, then model f is called $\mathcal{O}(2^d)$ times at a worst case. Therefore, we introduce a parameter L to bound the cardinality of $\mathcal{E}_{\min}$ to $|\mathcal{E}_{\min}| \leq L$. MP-LIME is formulated as

$$\operatorname*{argmin}_{g \in \mathcal{G}} \quad \sum_{e \in 2^{[d]}} |\mathbb{1}_{[f(x_e) \sim f(x)]} - g(e)|, \tag{6}$$

$$\text{subject to} \quad e \text{ is a minimal pattern for all } e \in \mathcal{E}_{\min}, \tag{7}$$

$$|\mathcal{E}_{\min}| \leq L. \tag{8}$$

In the expressions presented above, $\mathbb{1}_{[f(x_e) \sim f(x)]}$ returns 1 if it satisfies $f(x_e) \sim f(x)$, and otherwise 0. This formulation fits the general LIME framework shown in Eq. (1) because the constraints (7) and (8) replace the penalty function $\Omega(g)$, which tends to become large if the constraints are violated. To minimize Eq. (6), one must build a model g that classifies all the patterns perfectly. We do not explain the usage of the similarity kernel π yet. However, the local fidelity of the explanation and related concepts are introduced in Sect. 4.2. If Eq. (6) becomes small, then the cardinality of $\mathcal{E}_{\min}$ might be large and $\mathcal{E}_{\min}$ includes many redundant rules. Then Eq. (7) makes all patterns in $\mathcal{E}_{\min}$ minimal patterns. Also, Eq. (8) constrains the cardinality of $\mathcal{E}_{\min}$ to satisfy $|\mathcal{E}_{\min}| \leq L$.

4.2 Construction Algorithm

We propose a search algorithm to construct the minimal pattern family $\mathcal{E}_{\min}$, which is intended to minimize Eq. (6) under constraints (7) and (8). In the proposed algorithm, model f is called $\mathcal{O}(Ld^2)$ in total.

The strategy of the proposed algorithm is similar to hill climbing search: it regards the state as a pattern e. We define an evaluation value of a state e that is computed based on $f(x_e)$ and which takes larger value if $f(x_e)$ indicates the target class strongly (i.e. the probability of the target class is high). We assume the existence of $x_\varnothing$ recovered from the empty set $\varnothing$ and assume that $f(x_\varnothing)$ is not classified as any class: $f(x_\varnothing) \not\sim f(x)$. This assumption is a natural claim because $x_\varnothing$ corresponds to the empty set $\varnothing$ and should therefore have no information. Consequently, the search space is defined as $2^{[d]} \setminus \varnothing$. First the algorithm sets $\mathcal{E}_{\min}$ to the empty set and the pattern corresponding to the explained instance x, i.e., $e = \{\text{indices of nonzero elements of } \mathbf{x}\}$ as the initial state. It evaluates the neighbor patterns: $\{e \setminus \{i\} : i \in e\}$. Next, the pattern that has the highest evaluation value is set to the next state. If no neighbor pattern is classified to the target class, then the current pattern is a minimal pattern. It is appended to $\mathcal{E}_{\min}$. Such a process is repeated until the state reaches a minimal pattern. During the search, the patterns that satisfy Eq. (4) can be a minimal pattern. Therefore, we store these patterns in $\mathcal{E}_{\text{cand}}$ as candidate patterns. After finding a minimal pattern, we must set a new pattern as the next state. However, not all patterns in $\mathcal{E}_{\text{cand}}$ can be a minimal pattern. Therefore, if a pattern e and minimal patterns $e_{\min} \in \mathcal{E}_{\min}$ satisfy the condition

$$e_{\min} \subseteq e, \tag{9}$$

then e cannot be a minimal pattern. For that reason, we remove these patterns from $\mathcal{E}_{\text{cand}}$. The algorithm sets pattern e, which has the highest evaluation score in the candidate set $\mathcal{E}_{\text{cand}}$, and searches for a minimal pattern again. Additionally, we consider the following condition to constraint $\mathcal{E}_{\min}$ to a disjoint pattern set because a disjoint set eases interpretation [11]:

$$e_{\min} \cap e \neq \varnothing. \tag{10}$$

When satisfying $|\mathcal{E}_{\min}| = L$ or $\mathcal{E}_{\text{cand}} = \varnothing$, the algorithm is terminated and returns the minimal pattern family $\mathcal{E}_{\min}$. In the evaluation state e, the model f is called at most $|e| - 1$ times. Consequently, it has $\mathcal{O}(d^2\tau)$ per minimal pattern. Furthermore, because we do not assume anything about f, it still takes $\mathcal{O}(d^2\tau)$ to search for a minimal pattern after the second. Consequently, it takes $\mathcal{O}(Ld^2\tau)$ in total. Finally, we summarize the proposed algorithm as Algorithm 1.

5 Experiments

We next evaluate our explanation method. We present two experiments: quantitative evaluation of faithfulness of explanations (Sect. 5.1) and demonstration of examples of explanations (Sect. 5.2).

Algorithm 1. Construction algorithm for minimal pattern family

Require: Classifier f, Explained instance x, $\mathbf{x}$, Maximum cardinality L
Ensure: Minimal pattern family $\mathcal{E}_{\min}$

$\mathcal{E}_{\min} \leftarrow \varnothing$, $e \leftarrow$ {indices of nonzero elements of $\mathbf{x}$}, $\mathcal{E}_{\text{cand}} \leftarrow \{e\}$
while $(|\mathcal{E}_{\min}| < L) \wedge (\mathcal{E}_{\text{cand}} \neq \varnothing)$ **do**
  if e is a minimal pattern **then** ▷ check conditions (4) and (5) of Definition 1
    $\mathcal{E}_{\min} \leftarrow \mathcal{E}_{\min} \cup \{e\}$ ▷ check the constraint condition (10) optionally
    $\mathcal{E}_{\text{cand}} \leftarrow \mathcal{E}_{\text{cand}} \setminus \{e : e \text{ satisfies (9)}\}$
    $e \leftarrow e$ that has the highest evaluation value in $\mathcal{E}_{\text{cand}}$
  else
    for all e_n: neighbor patterns of e **do**
      if $f(x_{e_n}) \sim f(x)$ **then**
        $\mathcal{E}_{\text{cand}} \leftarrow \mathcal{E}_{\text{cand}} \cup \{e_n\}$
      end if
    end for
    $e \leftarrow$ the neighbor pattern that has the highest evaluation value
  end if
end while

5.1 Evaluation of Reliability

We measure the reliability of the explanatory model by predicting features that white-box models actually used for making the decision. We used two sentiment analysis datasets [4] that consist of 2000 reviews of the productions for *books* and *DVDs*, where the task is to classify a review as positive or negative. We split each dataset into 1600 training instances and 400 test instances. As white-box models, we trained logistic regression (LR) and decision tree (DT) using word-one-hot embedding features. In this experiment, the original domain is equal to the interpretable domain. We set the Linear-LIME parameters as $N = 10000$, $\sigma = 25$ in which the width σ is used in the experiment by Ribeiro[1]. Regarding the parameters of MP-LIME, we set the maximum cardinality as $L = 3$. Both LR and DT are binary classifiers. Thereby we set the relation in Definition 1 as $f(x_e) \sim f(x) \Leftrightarrow f(x_e) = f(x)$. Let F_{true} be a set of true features and F_{pred} be a feature set that is predicted by the explanatory models. F_{true} is observable because LR and DT are interpretable models. F_{true} for LT comprises positively weighted features. Similarly, F_{true} for DT comprises features on the used path for the decision. The faithfulness is measured using the measures: recall $(|F_{\text{true}} \cap F_{\text{pred}}|/|F_{\text{true}}|)$ and precision $(|F_{\text{true}} \cap F_{\text{pred}}|/|F_{\text{pred}}|)$.

Recall, precision, and time expended to get an explanation are shown in Table 1. The row name of Table 1, Linear, MP, MP-dis. mean output of Linear-LIME, MP-LIME with the condition (9) and MP-LIME with the condition (9), (10). Both MP-LIME show a higher recall than Linear-LIME except recall when using DT. The predicted features F_{pred} from MP-LIME consist of the union of minimal patterns. The minimal pattern derives the original decision without extra features. Therefore, for all settings, MP-LIME shows higher precision

[1] https://github.com/marcotcr/lime-experiments.

than Linear-LIME. Lower precision means that irrelevant features exist in the predicted features. Consequently, explanations of MP-LIME are more reliable because the features predicted by MP-LIME are actually used for the decision. Furthermore, MP-LIME constructs explanatory models faster than Linear-LIME does.

Table 1. Comparison of Linear-LIME and our method with the recall, precision, and construction time for the book and DVD dataset

		Recall			Precision			Time [s]		
		Linear	MP	MP-dis.	Linear	MP	MP-dis.	Linear	MP	MP-dis.
Book	LR	0.712	0.945	0.945	0.155	1.0	1.0	20.97	11.53	11.78
	DT	0.922	0.870	0.869	0.115	0.751	0.750	19.03	3.88	3.87
DVD	LR	0.779	0.896	0.896	0.212	1.0	1.0	20.17	8.71	8.62
	DT	0.924	0.880	0.878	0.109	0.709	0.715	18.26	2.44	2.38

5.2 Examples of Explanations

Image Classification Using a Deep Neural Network. When explaining image classification using Linear and MP-LIME, they highlight important regions of the target class, where an image is divided by a superpixel algorithm. Linear-LIME presents superpixels that have positive weight. MP-LIME presents minimal patterns. We classify the image shown in Fig. 2a with Google's pre-trained inception-v3 [15][2]. It is classified as goose with $p = 0.968$. The original image is divided into 40 superpixels with the SEEDS algorithm [3]. The mask of superpixels is also shown with the red line in Fig. 2a. The explanation using Linear-LIME, which is positively weighted superpixels for goose, is shown in Fig. 2b. As parameters of Linear-LIME, we set $N = 10000, \sigma = \sqrt{40}$, and L_2 distance for distance function D of the similarity kernel. We show the explanation using MP-LIME in Fig. 2c. The obtained minimal pattern family consists of two minimal patterns that are colored with the red and blue mask. We regarded the target class of x classified to goose with $p > 0.2$.

Next we discuss the classifications when explanations (Fig. 2b, c) are re-input to the model. Figure 2b is classified as a paper towel with $p = 0.218$. The score of goose is under 0.004, meaning that if users input the interpretable features that have positive weight to the model, users cannot always get the target class. Consequently, users cannot know the reasons for the decision with the explanation of Linear-LIME. The minimal patterns, the red region, and the blue one in Fig. 2c, are classified respectively as goose with $p = 0.397$ and $p = 0.558$ by virtue of the guarantee that each minimal pattern is classified as the target class. In cases with multiple feature patterns (e.g. two geese are in Fig. 2a) contribute to the target class, MP-LIME can detect these patterns.

[2] https://github.com/tensorflow/models/.

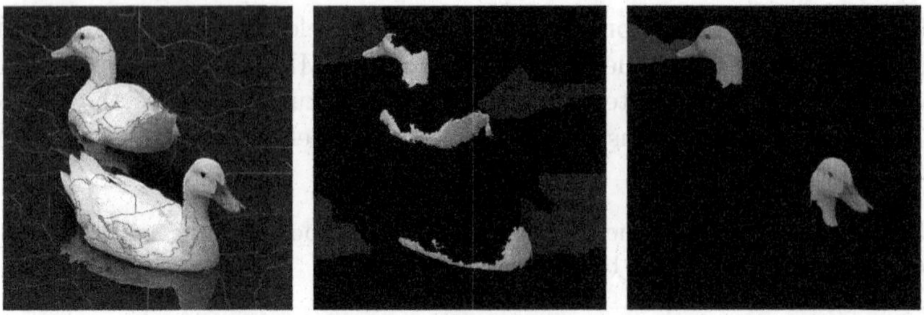

(a) (b) (c)

Fig. 2. Explanation of the image. (a) The mask (red line) is shown with regions by superpixels. The image without a mask is classified as a goose. (b) Important superpixels are explained by Linear-LIME. (c) MP-LIME's explanation. Minimal patterns are colored with red (lower right) and blue (upper left). (Color figure online)

Income Prediction Using Black-Box Models. We applied MP-LIME to income prediction using an adult dataset[3]. The task of the adult dataset is to classify annual income into two classes: >$50K and less than or equal to $50K. The attributes consist of 12 features: 4 numerical features and 8 categorical features. We built a three-layer perceptron as the black-box model. One test instance in the >$50K class is shown in Table 2. The model can predict it correctly.

We show the explanations of MP-LIME in Fig. 3. We divided numerical features into some intervals as an interpretable representation. The characteristics of the instance are that the person has high capital gains, a good job, and a spouse. Intuitively, they seem to imply high income. Because both explanations in Fig. 3 capture these characteristics (e.g. the rules include 0 < `capital gain`), we can understand that it is not an unnatural judgment. The disjoint minimal feature set is shorter than other one in the cardinality of minimal pattern family (Fig. 3b). Although a longer explanation might be redundant, it can present a more detailed description (Fig. 3a).

Table 2. Explained instance

`age`	`capital gain`	`capital loss`	`hours per week`
42	5179	0	50
`workclass`	`education`	`marital status`	`occupation`
Self-emp-inc	HS-grad	Married-civ-spouse	Exec-managerial
`relationship`	`race`	`sex`	`native country`
Husband	White	Male	U.S

[3] https://archive.ics.uci.edu/ml/datasets/adult.

(a)

IF $(0 <$ **capital gain**$)$
OR $($**age** $=$ 40s
$\wedge$ **hours per week** $\in (40, 60]$
$\wedge$ **workclass** $=$ Self-emp-inc
$\wedge$ **maritul status** $=$ Married-civ-spouse
$\wedge$ **occupation** $=$ Exec-managerial
$\wedge$ **native country** $=$ U.S$)$
OR $($**age** $=$ 40s
$\wedge$ **hours per week** $\in (40, 60]$
$\wedge$ **workclass** $=$ Self-emp-inc
$\wedge$ **maritul status** $=$ Married-civ-spouse
$\wedge$ **occupation** $=$ Exec-managerial
$\wedge$ **race** $=$ White$)$
THEN **class** $=$ >$50K

(a)

(b)

IF $(0 <$ **capital gain**$)$
OR $($**age** $=$ 40s
$\wedge$ **hours per week** $\in (40, 60]$
$\wedge$ **workclass** $=$ Self-emp-inc
$\wedge$ **maritul status**$=$Married-civ-spouse
$\wedge$ **occupation** $=$ Exec-managerial
$\wedge$ **native country** $=$ U.S.$)$
THEN **class** $=$ >$50K

(b)

Fig. 3. MP-LIME's explanatory models that fit an instance in the >$50K class shown in Table 2: (a) and (b) respectively present explanations under the constraint conditions (9) and (9), (10). Because of the constraint condition (10), each rule of (b) is disjoint.

6 Conclusion and Future Work

We proposed MP-LIME: a novel model-agnostic explanation for decisions using a minimal pattern family. We defined the minimal pattern family and the explanatory model using them and proposed an algorithm that constructs an explanatory model effectively. In the experiment with a sentiment analysis dataset, our method showed higher precision than that of the previous LIME, with reduced time for the construction of an explanatory model. Some examples suggest that if an explained instance has multiple feature patterns that contribute to a decision, our method can detect these patterns.

Although we only evaluated our method with simulation, using human experiments to measure interpretability is an important task. Our method can only explain individual decisions, not models. It remains an explanation of a black-box model using our formulation.

Acknowledgments. I would like to thank Quentin Labernia Louis Marie and Nguyen Van Quang for their comments on the manuscript. This work was partially supported by JSPS Kakenhi 15H02665 and 17K00002.

References

1. Baehrens, D., Schroeter, T., Harmeling, S., Kawanabe, M., Hansen, K., Müller, K.R.: How to explain individual classification decisions. J. Mach. Learn. Res. **11**, 1803–1831 (2010). http://dl.acm.org/citation.cfm?id=1756006.1859912
2. Batal, I., Hauskrecht, M.: Constructing classification features using minimal predictive patterns. In: Proceedings of the 19th ACM International Conference on Information and Knowledge Management, pp. 869–878. ACM (2010)

3. Van den Bergh, M., Boix, X., Roig, G., Van Gool, L.: Seeds: Superpixels extracted via energy-driven sampling. Int. J. Comput. Vision **111**(3), 298–314 (2015)
4. Blitzer, J., Dredze, M., Pereira, F.: Biographies, bollywood, boom-boxes and blenders: domain adaptation for sentiment classification. In: Proceedings of the 45th Annual Meeting of the Association of Computational Linguistics, pp. 440–447 (2007)
5. Caruana, R., Lou, Y., Gehrke, J., Koch, P., Sturm, M., Elhadad, N.: Intelligible models for healthcare: Predicting pneumonia risk and hospital 30-day readmission. In: Proceedings of the 21th ACM SIGKDD International Conference on Knowledge Discovery and Data Mining, pp. 1721–1730. ACM (2015)
6. Efron, B., Hastie, T., Johnstone, I., Tibshirani, R., et al.: Least angle regression. Ann. Stat. **32**(2), 407–499 (2004)
7. Guidotti, R., et al.: A survey of methods for explaining black box models. ACM Comput. Surv. (CSUR) **51**(5), 93 (2018)
8. Hara, S., Ishihata, M.: Approximate and exact enumeration of rule models. In: AAAI (2018)
9. Hara, S., Maehara, T.: Enumerate lasso solutions for feature selection. In: AAAI, pp. 1985–1991 (2017)
10. Lakkaraju, H., et al.: A machine learning framework to identify students at risk of adverse academic outcomes. In: Proceedings of the 21st ACM SIGKDD International Conference on Knowledge Discovery and Data Mining, pp. 1909–1918. ACM (2015)
11. Lakkaraju, H., Bach, S.H., Leskovec, J.: Interpretable decision sets: a joint framework for description and prediction. In: Proceedings of the 22nd ACM SIGKDD International Conference on Knowledge Discovery and Data Mining, pp. 1675–1684. ACM (2016)
12. Ribeiro, M.T., Singh, S., Guestrin, C.: Why should i trust you? explaining the predictions of any classifier. In: Proceedings of the 22nd ACM SIGKDD International Conference on Knowledge Discovery and Data Mining, pp. 1135–1144. ACM (2016)
13. Ribeiro, M.T., Singh, S., Guestrin, C.: Anchors: high-precision model-agnostic explanations. In: AAAI Conference on Artificial Intelligence (2018)
14. Ruggieri, S.: Enumerating distinct decision trees. In: International Conference on Machine Learning, pp. 2960–2968 (2017)
15. Szegedy, C., Vanhoucke, V., Ioffe, S., Shlens, J., Wojna, Z.: Rethinking the inception architecture for computer vision. In: Proceedings of the IEEE Conference on Computer Vision and Pattern Recognition, pp. 2818–2826 (2016)
16. Tibshirani, R.: Regression shrinkage and selection via the lasso. J. Roy. Stat. Soc. Ser. B (Methodological) **58**, 267–288 (1996)
17. Wang, F., Rudin, C.: Falling rule lists. In: Artificial Intelligence and Statistics, pp. 1013–1022 (2015)

NARPCA: Neural Accumulate-Retract PCA for Low-Latency High-Throughput Processing on Datastreams

Cristian Axenie(✉), Radu Tudoran, Stefano Bortoli, Mohamad Al Hajj Hassan, and Goetz Brasche

Huawei German Research Center, Riesstrasse 25, 80992 Munich, Germany
{cristian.axenie,radu.tudoran,stefano.bortoli, mohamad.alhajjhassan,goetz.brasche}@huawei.com

Abstract. The increasingly interconnected and instrumented world, provides a deluge of data generated by multiple sensors in the form of continuous streams. Efficient stream processing needs control over the number of useful variables. This is because maintaining data structure in reduced sub-spaces, given that data is generated at high frequencies and is typically follows non-stationary distributions, brings new challenges for dimensionality reduction algorithms. In this work we introduce NARPCA, a neural network streaming PCA algorithm capable to explain the variance-covariance structure of a set of variables in a stream through linear combinations. The essentially neural-based algorithm is leveraged by a novel incremental computation method and system operating on data streams and capable of achieving low-latency and high-throughput when learning from data streams, while maintaining resource usage guarantees. We evaluate NARPCA in real-world data experiments and demonstrate low-latency (millisecond level) and high-throughput (thousands events/second) for simultaneous eigenvalues and eigenvectors estimation in a multi-class classification task.

Keywords: Distributed stream processing · PCA · Neural networks

1 Introduction

In many cases, data representations are redundant and the variables are correlated, which means that eventually only a small sub-space of the original representation space is populated by the sample and by the underlying process [24]. Due to considerable practical relevance, there is renewed interest in Principal Component Analysis (PCA), [2,8,34]. PCA is good for maintaining data structure in reduced subspaces in an unsupervised way. It is also useful in updating the decision boundaries and adding discriminately informative features with newly added samples and then updating the feature vectors by incremental eigenvector updates [17,19].

I. V. Tetko et al. (Eds.): ICANN 2019, LNCS 11727, pp. 253–266, 2019.
https://doi.org/10.1007/978-3-030-30487-4_20

The core computational element of PCA is performing a (partial) singular value decomposition, and much work over the last half century has focused on efficient algorithms [11]. The recent focus on understanding streaming high-dimensional data, where the dimensionality of the data can potentially scale together with the number of available sample points, has led to an exploration of the complexity of covariance estimation underlying PCA [4,7,12,16]. Such algorithms have provable complexity guarantees but either store all samples (i.e. for looping through samples) or explicitly maintain the covariance matrix. In high-dimensional applications, where data points are high resolution images, video or bank transactions data, storing all data is prohibitive. Different from previous approaches, our work doesn't only tackle memory constraints, but brings the focus on three critical quantities: latency, throughput and judicious resource allocation.

In the streaming setting, many approaches for incremental or online PCA have been developed, some focusing on replacing the inefficient steps (i.e. high latency of low-rank modifications of the singular value decomposition [18], others on conditioning in householder transformation for QR decomposition etc.) or memory- and computation-efficient operations [5,6,10].

Despite the multitude of successful dedicated algorithms [14,33,35], there is no algorithm that provably recovers the principal components in the same noise and complexity regime as the batch PCA algorithm does and maintains a provably light memory/storage footprint. Moreover, none considers also low-latency and high-throughput at processing streaming data. This work utilizes a new paradigm for stream processing and learning [3] and proposes NARPCA for efficient computation (i.e. incremental learning in neurons) with low-latency and high-throughput (i.e. through orchestration of the stream data flow) while maintaining judicious memory/storage usage.

2 Formalizing the Problem

While much work has focused on memory-constrained PCA, [28,29], there is little work that provides complexity guarantees competitive with batch algorithms, [18], and, to our knowledge, no work on low-latency, high-throughput in large-scale streaming machine learning applications with programmatic resource allocation. In its basic formulation, PCA computes the eigenvectors and eigenvalues of the sample covariance matrix, using a numerical method such as the QR method [24]. This approach requires that all the training data are available before the principal components can be estimated. An incremental method, on the other side, is required to compute the principal components for observations arriving sequentially, where the principal components estimates are updated by each arriving observation [25]. In order to formalize the problem, consider a stream of n-dimensional data vectors $x(t)$. The problem of extracting incrementally the principal components assumes reducing the number of linear combinations of inputs by discarding low variances and only keeping the combinations with large variance: $w_1^T x, w_2^T x, w_3^T x, ..., w_p^T x, p \leq n$ which maximize the expectation

$$E\{(w_i^T x)^2\}_{i=1:p} \tag{1}$$

under the constraints

$$w_i^T w_j = \delta_{ij}, j < i, \tag{2}$$

where δ_{ij} is the Kronecker product. The solution for the vectors $w_1, w_2, w_3, ..., w_p$ are the p dominant eigenvectors of the data covariance matrix calculated incrementally,

$$C = E\{xx^T\}. \tag{3}$$

These are p orthogonal unit vectors $z_1, z_2, z_3, ..., z_p$ given by

$$Cz_i = \lambda_i z_i \tag{4}$$

where $\lambda_1, \lambda_2, \lambda_3, ..., \lambda_p$ are the largest p eigenvalues of C in descending order $\lambda_1 > \lambda_2 > \lambda_3 > ... > \lambda_p$. The first principal component is $c_1^T x$ whereas the minor components are linear combinations $c_n^T x, c_{n-1}^T x$ where c_n is the eigenvector corresponding to the smallest eigenvalue. In a structured form, the basic formulation, PCA follows the following steps:

Data: Stream of n-dimensional data vectors $x(t)$
Result: Eigen features w_p and λ_p
Compute the mean feature vector $\mu = \frac{1}{n}\sum_k^n x_k(t)$;
Compute the covariance matrix $C = E\{x - \mu\}\{x - \mu\}^T$;
Compute eigenvalues λ_i and eigenvectors z_i of C;
while *Estimate high-value eigenvectors* **do**
    Sort eigenvalues λ_i in decreasing order;
    Choose a threshold θ ;
    Choose the first p dominant λ_i to satisfy $(\sum_i^p \lambda_i)(\sum_i^n \lambda_i)^{-1} \geq \theta$;
    Select eigenvectors w_p corresponding to λ_p;
end
Extract principal components from x, $P = V^T x$ where V is the matrix of principal components

For large problems this routine is not computationally efficient and various numerical methods have been used to improve it, using QR decomposition [26] or the Householder reflections [13] replacing Gram-Schmidt, known to lead to cancellation that causes inaccuracy of the computation and a non-orthogonal matrix. In our work we analysed the inefficient operations which impede PCA to achieve the three critical quantities: latency, throughput and memory/storage, when operating on streams. We identified three aspects in the existing approaches which impact a streaming PCA formulation:

- the continuous calculation of the mean μ and other descriptive statistics (i.e. covariance) on the datastream;
- sorting the dominant eigenvalues in the rank update of the QR decomposition and the ordering of lower/upper triangular sub-matrices;
- the complexity of computations performed at each training step.

Stream processing applications distinguish themselves from the traditional store-and-process data analysis through four features: continuous data sources, continuous and long-running analysis, time-to-respond performance requirements, and failure tolerance requirements [1,9]. These characteristics together with the identified bottlenecks will constitute design objectives for our approach that leverage the advantages of PCA for low-latency, high-throughput, resource-efficient stream processing, as shown in the next sections.

3 Materials and Methods

This section covers the design, implementation details, and the motivation to tackle the inherent problems in traditional PCA impeding it to achieve low-latency, high-throughput and fixed memory/storage. Our motivation for this work stems from the need to guarantee performance and efficiency. Dissecting the theory of PCA we found those bottlenecks that kept PCA away from streaming applications.

Employing a novel method and system for online machine learning [3], capable of incrementally computing machine learning models on data streams, we successfully instantiated PCA keeping performance indices (i.e. latency, throughput) and bounded memory allocation in intensive real-world scenarios. The underlying computational mechanism in our approach is the accumulate-retract framework. Such a framework allows for dual model updates as soon as new data comes into the system and leaves the system as the stream progresses. The accumulate-retract framework allows for incremental calculation of the statistical quantities used in the streaming PCA. For example, the average calculation in the eigenvalue update in incremental form can be visualized in Fig. 1.

Such incremental computation tackles successfully the first bottleneck, namely the incremental calculation of the mean μ and other descriptive statistics on the datastream.

The second problem that the accumulate-retract framework solves, is sorting the dominant eigenvalues in the rank update of the QR decomposition. For this, let's assume we need to sort the current list of dominant eigenvalues, as shown in Fig. 2. In this case the caches are used to store contents (i.e. buckets) on updates depending on counts (i.e. histogram). Updates are done in buckets, which contain sorted eigenvalues. Each time new eigenvalues are computed sorting is triggered. In this instantiation the retraction cache stores the last calculated eigenvalues (in time) in each bucket, whereas when the accumulation cache moves according to the sliding convention, new buckets are brought and the entire structure is sorted. Moreover, in this instantiation, the buckets stored on disk or 3rd party storage devices contain data organized based on value/indexes. The last eigenvalue (time-wise) in each bucket has a reference in the retraction cache.

In order to comply with the low-latency, high-throughput requirements of stream processing, our approach uses a single layer neural network, which employs only local, simple operations. There are many models for learning PCA in neurons [22], from stochastic approximation models (i.e. Hebbian and Oja's

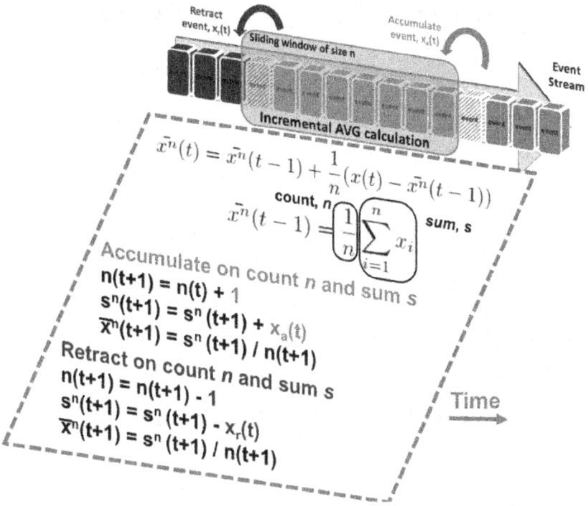

Fig. 1. NARPCA incremental average update using accumulate-retract.

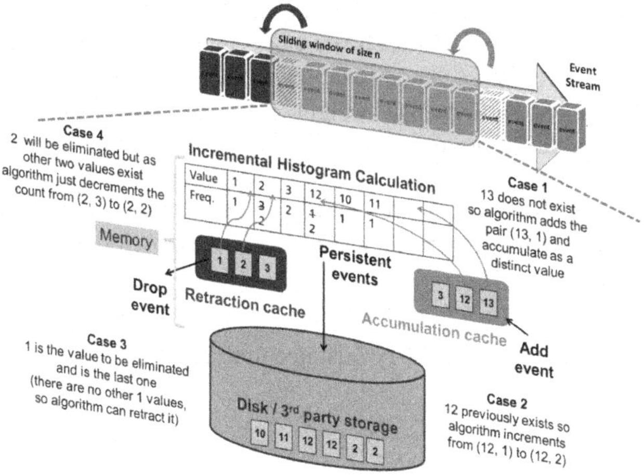

Fig. 2. NARPCA eigenvalues sorting on streams: histogram update.

Learning Rules [20]), to subspace learning [21], nonlinear PCA networks [15] up to denoising autoencoders [27]. NARPCA, Fig. 3, is a single layer neural network based on the Stochastic Gradient Ascent [21]. We chose this model because it efficiently provides a description of the covariance matrix, which is typically too expensive to be estimated online [30]. NARPCA learning rule is given by

$$\Delta w_j(t-1) = \gamma(t) y_j(t)(x(t) - y_j(t) w_j(t-1) - 2\sum_{i<j} y_i(t) w_i(t-1)) \quad (5)$$

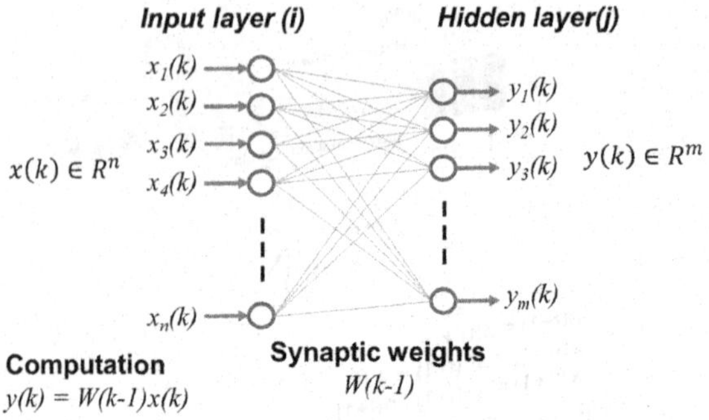

Fig. 3. Neural PCA network.

where $\gamma(t)$ is the learning rate. This learning rule is purely local in the sense that the change in each individual weight only depends on factors that would be locally available at that neuron's position. This rule behaves better for extracting the dominant eigenvectors than other methods [23]. The weight update takes advantage of the accumulate-retract framework, incrementally incorporating new knowledge while decreasing the impact that old data has upon the update, as show in Figure 4. The synaptic weight w_j converge to the eigenvectors c_i as NARPCA finds the unique set of weights which is both optimal and gives uncorrelated outputs. In order to leverage low-latency high-throughput processing on the evolving datastream, we derive the closed form incremental learning rule in the accumulate-retract framework. As shown previously, the eigenvectors $z_1, z_2, z_3, ..., z_p$ are given by

$$Cz_i = \lambda_i z_i, \tag{6}$$

where λ_i are the eigenvalues of the covariance matrix, $C[c_{jk}]$. We can then rewrite C as

$$c_{jk} = \frac{1}{n-1}\sum_{i=1}^{n}(z_{ij} - \bar{z}_j)(z_{ik} - \bar{z}_k) \tag{7}$$

where

$$\bar{z} = \frac{1}{n}\sum_{i=1}^{n} z_i \tag{8}$$

is the incremental average. Hence, we can rewrite the covariance matrix C as

$$C = \frac{1}{n-1}\sum_{i=1}^{n}(z_i - \bar{z})(z_i - \bar{z})^T, \tag{9}$$

which is, in fact, the autocorrelation. The problem is that these measures are not robust statistics and hence not resistant to outliers. We replace z with its estimate at time t $z(t)$ so that $v = \lambda z$ estimate at time t is

$$v(t) = \frac{1}{n}\sum_{i=1}^{n} x(t)x^T(t)z(t). \tag{10}$$

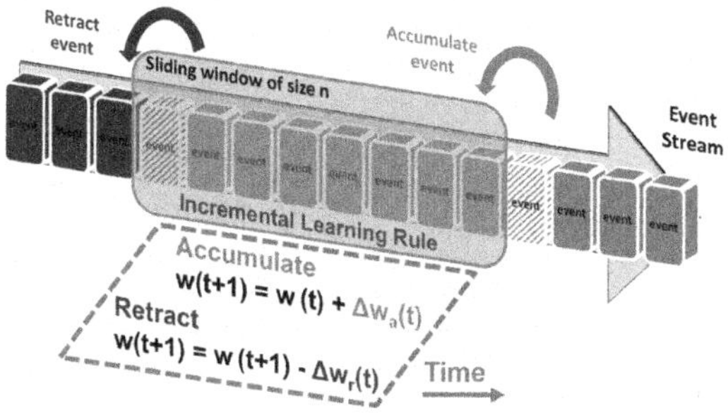

Fig. 4. NARPCA weight update in the accumulate-retract framework.

We can now calculate the eigenvalues and eigenvectors given v as we know that $\lambda = \|v\|$. If we consider

$$z = \frac{v}{\|v\|} \tag{11}$$

we can rewrite

$$v(t) = \frac{1}{n}\sum_{i=1}^{n} x(t)x^T(t)\frac{v(t-1)}{\|v(t-1)\|}. \tag{12}$$

Such computation steps provide a closed form implementation of learning rule in the accumulate-retract framework [3].

NARPCA converges from an initially random set of synaptic weights to the eigenvectors of the input autocorrelation in the eigenvalues order. The optimal weights are found by minimizing the linear reconstruction error $E\{(x-\hat{x})^2\}$ when the rows of W span the first p eigenvectors of C and the Linear Least Squares (LLS) estimate of x given y is

$$\hat{x} = CW^T(WCW^T)^{-1}y. \tag{13}$$

If the rows of W are the first eigenvectors then $WW^T = I$ and $C = W^T\Lambda W$ where Λ is the diagonal matrix of C in descending order. Then, $y = Wx$ is the Karhunen-Loève Transformation (KLT). In the LLS optimization routine, if we have an unknown function f the best estimator of y is

$$\min_f \sum_{i=1}^{n}(y_i - f(x_i))^2. \tag{14}$$

Moreover, if f is linear in x and $y = ax + b$ then the best estimator is the search for the best a, b that minimize

$$\min_f \sum_{i=1}^{n}(y_i - ax_i - b)^2. \tag{15}$$

In the accumulate-retract framework such a problem is incrementally solved as the datastream progresses, using simple updates shown in Fig. 5 Given that covariance can be incrementally calculated as

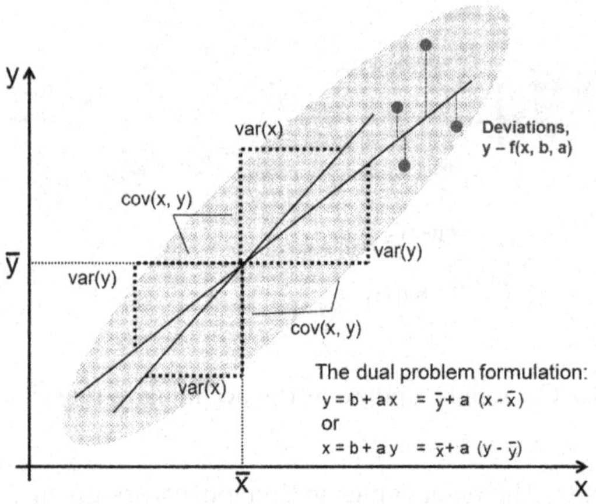

Fig. 5. NARPCA optimization using LLS in accumulate-retract framework.

$$cov_{xy}(t) = \frac{n-2}{n-1} cov_{xy}(t-1) + \frac{1}{n}(x^n(t) - \bar{x}^{n-1}(t))(y^n(t) - \bar{y}^{n-1}(t)), \quad (16)$$

the problem in closed form assumes calculating incrementally a and b as

$$a(t) = \frac{cov_{xy}(t)}{m_2(t)}, b(t) = \bar{y}(t) - a\bar{x}(t) \quad (17)$$

where $m_2(t)$ is the 2nd statistical moment in incremental Yet, up to now we made the assumption that only y values contain errors while x are known accurately. This is not true in practical applications, thus we are seeking the values of a and b that minimize

$$\min_{a,b} \sum_{i=1} \frac{(y_i - ax_i - b)^2}{1 + a^2}, \quad (18)$$

which amounts for the Total Least Squares (TLS). It has been shown that the TLS problem can be solved by performing a Minor Component Analysis (MCA) [32], thus finding the linear combinations (or directions) which contain the minimum variance. Clearly, every eigenvector is a solution of the minimization of TLS error. In the following section we instantiate NARPCA within the accumulate-retract framework for a multi-class classification problem. NARPCA, due to its incremental nature, preserves the discriminant information within the data and can provide classification boundaries [31].

4 Experiments and Discussion

This section introduces the results and the analysis for the instantiation of our framework using Apache Flink [9]. Flink is an open source system for parallel scalable processing on real-time streaming data. At its core, Flink builds on an optimized distributed dataflow runtime that supports our accumulate-retract framework, crucial in obtaining low-latency high-throughput online machine learning. The experimental setup for our tests used 4 machines, each with 24 CPU cores and 196 GB RAM, and Flink for cluster management. During the experiments we consider a fixed sliding window, but the cache-disk orchestration mechanism can support also adaptive windowing. At the same time the caches (i.e. in RAM) mechanism allows to maintain new and old data in order to allow the retraction of individual stream events when sliding. This allows our system to learn from continuous data in a single pass. We used a real-world stream with online bank transactions and queried the eigenvalues and eigenvectors. The data is available online from the PKDD'99 Discovery Challenge - Guide to the Financial Data Set. The dataset and has 10 input features (i.e. transaction id, account id, transaction amount, balance after transaction, transaction bank partner, transaction account partner, transaction type, transaction operation, transaction symbol, transaction date) describing various aspects of the executed transaction. The datastream contained 2M incoming events at 40 kHz. Moreover the datastream had the property that the eigenvalues of the input X are close to the class labels (i.e. $1, 2, ..., d$) and the corresponding eigenvectors are close to the canonical basis of R^d, where d is the number of principal components to extract and the class number for the multiclass classification task (i.e. types of valid and fraud transactions - in our scenario 10 classes). To give the user a sample of the possible output, some sample class labels were, "high-risk fraud", "recurrent fraud", "low-risk valid", "recurrent valid".

In order to evaluate our NARPCA, we implemented an efficient QR-based PCA of [26] using Householder transformation and ran it in the accumulate-retract framework on the same experimental system. Important to note that NARPCA does not need to compute the correlation matrix in advance, since the eigenvectors are derived directly from the data. This is an important feature of NARPCA, particularly if the number of inputs is large. Using the accumulate-retract framework, both algorithms kept the scale of observations and computed the mean of observations incrementally. The scope of our analysis is to emphasize that using simple incremental operations in a single layer neural network and exploiting an efficient data orchestration can leverage low-latency high-throughput streaming PCA with fixed/programmable resource allocation. Such a platform allows NARPCA to learn from datastreams in a single pass. In order to emphasize the advantages the accumulate-retract framework, we now analyse large-scale experiments to extract the eigenfeatures for the multi-class fraud detection scenario (i.e. 2M events streamed at 40 kHz).

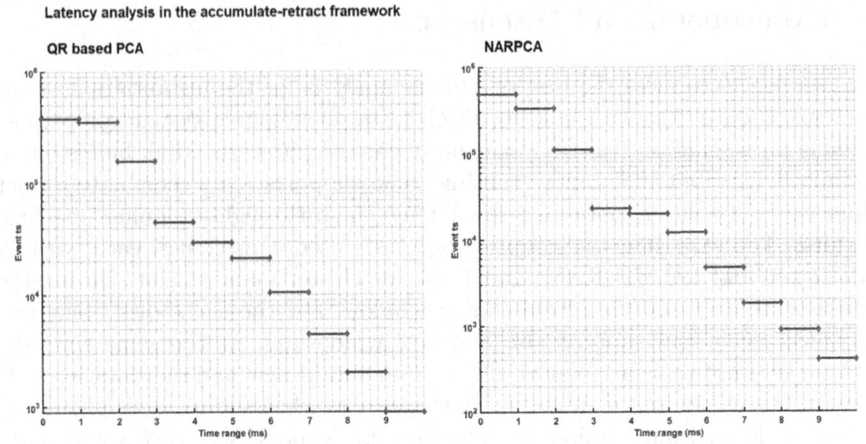

Fig. 6. Comparative analysis of latency in the accumulate-retract framework.

To offer an understanding of the actual estimation performance of the system the next table (Table 1) shows the eigenvalues of the input and how close they are to the class labels (i.e. 1, 2, ..., d=10) and the corresponding eigenvectors variance with respect to the canonical basis of R^d). In terms of latency one can observe that NARPCA outperforms the QR-based PCA, with a substantial distribution of events processed at 1 ms and just a limited number of events processed at over 8 ms, as shown in Fig. 6. This is supported by the gain of 8k events throughput, as shown in Fig. 7. This is also visible in the core distribution of throughput ranges peaking at around 40k events/s. Pushing real-world performance constraints, the accumulate-retract framework instance of NARPCA stands out as a good candidate for low-latency high-throughput systems for dimensionality reduction, in critical applications such as fraud detection. This work is a new instantiation of the accumulate-retract framework [3], promoting a generic streaming machine learning platform with demonstrated potential in real-world applications. The core STARLORD codebase and benchmarking is available at[1] (Table 1).

[1] https://github.com/omlstreaming/icmla2018.

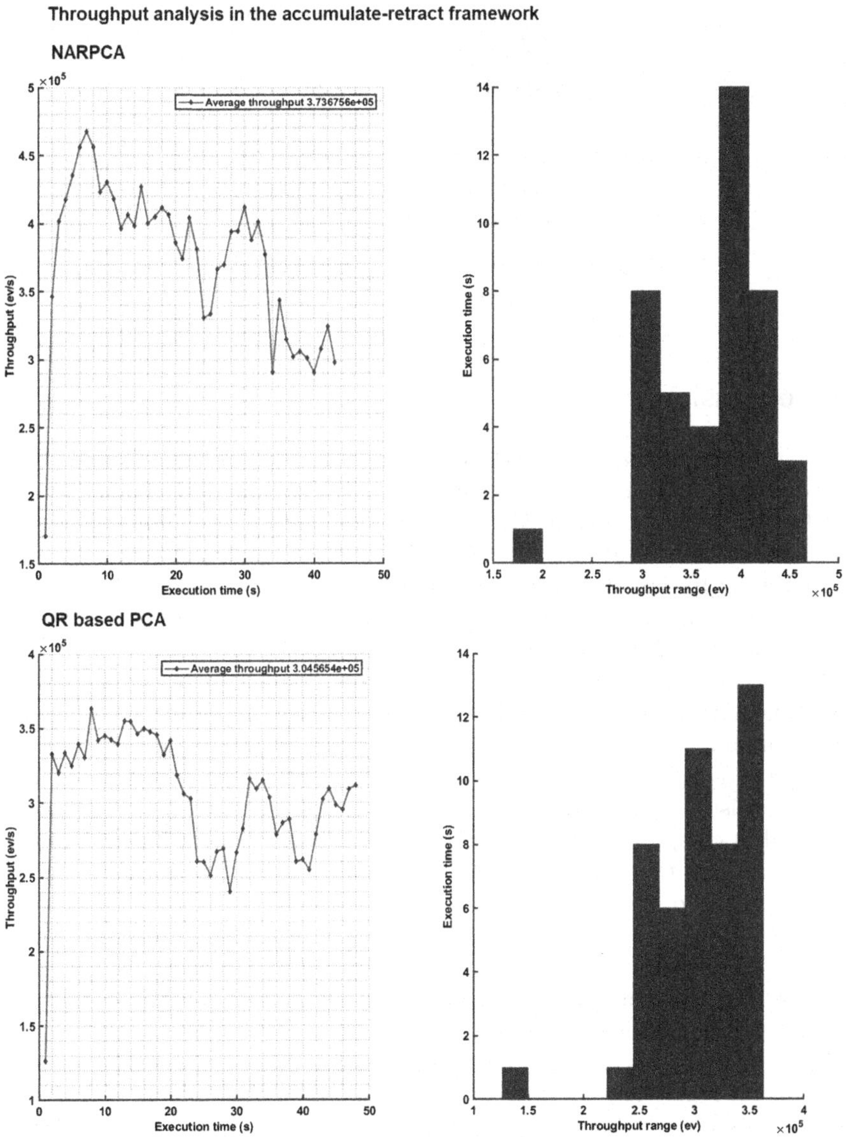

Fig. 7. Comparative analysis of throughput in the accumulate-retract framework.

Table 1. Eigenvalues and Eigenvectors estimates analysis

Eigenvalue	Eigenvalue estimate	Eigenvector variance
1	0.994071965	0.033719458
2	1.99658601	0.023661145
3	3.00600192	0.013884741
4	4.00420688	0.025106736
5	5.04173253	0.022354039
6	5.95475267	0.007637369
7	6.88985141	0.011129644
8	7.87972194	0.015864081
9	8.90795326	0.007244545
10	10.0642228	0.014663302

5 Conclusion

Tackling the theoretical bottlenecks in the traditional PCA algorithm and focusing on three critical quantities, namely latency, throughput and memory/storage, NARPCA supports the renewed interest and performance improvements in streaming machine learning. Traditional statistical packages require to have available prior to the calculation, a batch of examples from the distribution being investigated. While it is possible to run multiple flavours of PCA models with the accumulate-retract framework, neural approaches are capable of performing PCA in real- time, as our experiments show. The adaptive and incremental methodology used in neural approaches is particularly important if storage constraints are important, addressing one of the three critical quantities mentioned before. Strictly speaking, PCA is only defined for stationary distributions. However, in realistic situations, as streaming data, it is often the case that we are interested in compressing data from distributions which are a function of time; in this situation, the NARPCA is a good solution in that it tracks the moving statistics of the distribution and provides as close to batch PCA. Following a distribution's statistics, NARPCA is an example of trade-off between tracking capability and accuracy of convergence. Finally, NARPCA keeps memory usage fixed (i.e. only relevant "hot" data) and disk usage flexible (i.e. processed "cold" data) as the amount of events in the data stream increases. Such a system offers flexibility, allowing for arbitrary combinations of multiple functions (i.e. average, least squares regression, sorting) to be calculated on the stream, with no time and resource penalty, by exploiting the underlying hardware, data processing and data management for true low-latency, high-throughput stream processing.

References

1. Albert, B., Ricard Gavaldà, G.H., Pfahringer, B.: Machine learning for data streams with practical examples. In: MOA. MIT Press (2018)

2. Arora, R., Cotter, A., Livescu, K., Srebro, N.: Stochastic optimization for PCA and PLS. In: 2012 50th Annual Allerton Conference on Communication, Control, and Computing (Allerton), pp. 861–868. IEEE (2012)
3. Axenie, C., Tudoran, R., Bortoli, S., Hassan, M.A.H., Foroni, D., Brasche, G.: STARLORD: sliding window temporal accumulate-retract learning for online reasoning on datastreams. In: 17th IEEE International Conference on Machine Learning and Applications, ICMLA 2018, Orlando, FL, USA, 17–20 December 2018, pp. 1115–1122 (2018)
4. Baker, C.G., Gallivan, K.A., Van Dooren, P.: Low-rank incremental methods for computing dominant singular subspaces. Linear Algebra Appl. **436**(8), 2866–2888 (2012)
5. Balsubramani, A., Dasgupta, S., Freund, Y.: The fast convergence of incremental PCA. In: Advances in Neural Information Processing Systems, pp. 3174–3182 (2013)
6. Boutsidis, C., Garber, D., Karnin, Z., Liberty, E.: Online principal components analysis. In: Proceedings of the Twenty-Sixth Annual ACM-SIAM Symposium on Discrete Algorithms, pp. 887–901 (2015)
7. Brand, M.: Incremental singular value decomposition of uncertain data with missing values. In: Heyden, A., Sparr, G., Nielsen, M., Johansen, P. (eds.) ECCV 2002. LNCS, vol. 2350, pp. 707–720. Springer, Heidelberg (2002). https://doi.org/10.1007/3-540-47969-4_47
8. Bubeck, S., Cesa-Bianchi, N., et al.: Regret analysis of stochastic and nonstochastic multi-armed bandit problems. Found. Trends® in Mach. Learn. **5**(1), 1–122 (2012)
9. Carbone, P., Katsifodimos, A., Ewen, S., Markl, V., Haridi, S., Tzoumas, K.: Apache flink^{TM}: Stream and batch processing in a single engine. IEEE Data Eng. Bull. **38**, 28–38 (2015). https://flink.apache.org/introduction.html
10. Chin, T.J., Suter, D.: Incremental kernel principal component analysis. IEEE Trans. Image Process. **16**(6), 1662–1674 (2007)
11. Golub, G.H., Van Loan, C.F.: Matrix Computations, 3rd edn. Johns Hopkins University Press, Baltimore, MD, USA (1996)
12. Hallgren, F., Northrop, P.: Incremental kernel PCA and the nyström method. arXiv preprint arXiv:1802.00043 (2018)
13. Householder, A.S.: Unitary triangularization of a nonsymmetric matrix. J. ACM **5**(4), 339–342 (1958). https://doi.org/10.1145/320941.320947
14. Jain, P., Jin, C., Kakade, S.M., Netrapalli, P., Sidford, A.: Streaming PCA: matching matrix Bernstein and near-optimal finite sample guarantees for Oja's algorithm. In: Conference on Learning Theory, pp. 1147–1164 (2016)
15. Kramer, M.A.: Nonlinear principal component analysis using autoassociative neural networks. AIChE J. **37**(2), 233–243 (1991)
16. Li, Y.: On incremental and robust subspace learning. Pattern Recogn. **37**(7), 1509–1518 (2004)
17. Lois, B., Vaswani, N.: A correctness result for online robust PCA. In: 2015 IEEE International Conference on Acoustics, Speech and Signal Processing (ICASSP), pp. 3791–3795. IEEE (2015)
18. Mitliagkas, I., Caramanis, C., Jain, P.: Memory limited, streaming PCA. In: Proceedings of the 26th International Conference on Neural Information Processing Systems, NIPS 2013, vol. 2, pp. 2886–2894. Curran Associates Inc., USA (2013)
19. Nadler, B.: Finite sample approximation results for principal component analysis: a matrix perturbation approach. Ann. Statist. **36**(6), 2791–2817 (2008)
20. Oja, E.: Simplified neuron model as a principal component analyzer. J. Math. Biol. **15**(3), 267–273 (1982)

21. Oja, E.: Principal components, minor components, and linear neural networks. Neural Netw. **5**(6), 927–935 (1992)
22. Qiu, J., Wang, H., Lu, J., Zhang, B., Du, K.L.: Neural network implementations for PCA and its extensions. In: 2012 ISRN Artificial Intelligence (2012)
23. Sanger, T.D.: Optimal unsupervised learning in a single-layer linear feedforward neural network. Neural Netw. **2**(6), 459–473 (1989). http://www.sciencedirect.com/science/article/pii/0893608089900440
24. Sarveniazi, A.: An actual survey of dimensionality reduction. Am. J. Comput. Matt. **4**(4), 55–72 (2014)
25. Shamir, O.: Convergence of stochastic gradient descent for PCA. In: International Conference on Machine Learning, pp. 257–265 (2016)
26. Sharma, A., Paliwal, K.K., Imoto, S., Miyano, S.: Principal component analysis using GR decomposition. Int. J. Mach. Learn. Cybern. **4**(6), 679–683 (2013). https://doi.org/10.1007/s13042-012-0131-7
27. Valpola, H.: From neural pca to deep unsupervised learning. In: Advances in Independent Component Analysis and Learning Machines, pp. 143–171. Elsevier (2015)
28. Vershynin, R.: How close is the sample covariance matrix to the actual covariance matrix? J. Theor. Probab. **25**(3), 655–686 (2012)
29. Warmuth, M.K., Kuzmin, D.: Randomized PCA algorithms with regret bounds that are logarithmic in the dimension. In: Advances in Neural Information Processing Systems, pp. 1481–1488 (2007)
30. Weng, J., Zhang, Y., Hwang, W.S.: Candid covariance-free incremental principal component analysis. IEEE Trans. Pattern Anal. Mach. Intell. **25**(8), 1034–1040 (2003)
31. Woo, S., Lee, C.: Incremental feature extraction based on decision boundaries. Pattern Recogn. **77**, 65–74 (2018). http://www.sciencedirect.com/science/article/pii/S003132031730496X
32. Xu, L., Oja, E., Suen, C.Y.: Modified hebbian learning for curve and surface fitting. Neural Netw. **5**(3), 441–457 (1992)
33. Yin, Y., Xu, D., Wang, X., Bai, M.: Online state-based structured SVM combined with incremental PCA for robust visual tracking. IEEE Trans. Cybern. **45**(9), 1988–2000 (2015)
34. Zhan, J., Lois, B., Guo, H., Vaswani, N.: Online (and offline) robust PCA: novel algorithms and performance guarantees. In: Artificial intelligence and statistics, pp. 1488–1496 (2016)
35. Zhao, F., Rekik, I., Lee, S.w., Liu, J., Zhang, J., Shen, D.: Two-phase incremental kernel pca for learning massive or online datasets. Complexity **2019** (2019)

An Evaluation of Various Regression Models for the Prediction of Two-Terminal Network Reliability

Sabina-Adriana Floria[1], Florin Leon[1(✉)], Petru Caşcaval[1], and Doina Logofătu[2]

[1] Department of Computer Science and Engineering, "Gheorghe Asachi" Technical University of Iaşi, Iaşi, Romania
{sabina.floria, florin.leon, cascaval}@tuiasi.ro
[2] Faculty of Computer Science and Engineering, Frankfurt University of Applied Science, Frankfurt, Germany
logofatu@fb2.fra-uas.de

Abstract. Analyzing network data is presently a big challenge for applied machine learning. Many model architectures have been proposed to study or extract information from network data for specific applications. In this paper, we compare the performance of autoencoders, convolutional neural networks and extreme gradient boosting decision trees with different configurations for the task of approximating two-terminal network reliability. The ground truth is generated using an analytical method. Various synthetic datasets containing networks with different configurations are used. The obtained results help us to identify the dataset factors which affect the prediction performance of these models.

Keywords: Two-terminal reliability · Deep learning · Autoencoders · Convolutional Neural Networks · Extreme gradient boosting

1 Introduction

Estimating network reliability is an increasingly important problem, since many types of networks such as IP/optical, transportation, electrical power etc. have requirements regarding high availability rates nowadays. An abstract model for network reliability considers that the nodes and edges have certain probabilities to operate correctly, and their failures are independent events.

Several measures of reliability have been proposed. One of the most common is the so-called *two-terminal reliability*, where one computes the probability that there is at least one path between any two specified nodes that operates successfully, i.e. that a signal can be transmitted from a source to a destination. The exact evaluation of two-terminal network reliability is an NP-hard problem. Therefore, approximate methods are needed in case of large networks.

There is currently a great interest in the analysis of network data in applied machine learning [1–5]. This is a challenging task because it is not easy to find relational patterns when the dataset contains networks with different sizes or topologies.

I. V. Tetko et al. (Eds.): ICANN 2019, LNCS 11727, pp. 267–280, 2019.
https://doi.org/10.1007/978-3-030-30487-4_21

In this work we address the two-terminal reliability estimation as a regression task directly from the adjacency matrix of the underlying graph and the probabilities of nodes and edges. We compare different architectures of several deep learning methods and discuss their performance on several datasets, which contain randomly generated networks. We evaluate the performance of the machine learning techniques and configurations under various circumstances such as: fixed network structure, variable network structure, different topology. The exact reliability values used for training and testing are computed with a deterministic method [6] based on New Multiple Variables Inversion (NMVI) [7].

The rest of the paper is organized as follows. In Sect. 2, we present some related work in this area, Sect. 3 contains a description of our proposed models, the obtained results are discussed in Sect. 4 and finally the conclusions and some ideas for future work are presented in Sect. 5.

2 Related Work

Deep learning is extensively used in real-world applications related to social networks, image classification, facial recognition, health industry, automotive, etc. The data collected from some of these problems can be structured as a graph, and the classification task is difficult.

The actual classification task on graphs varies from one application to another. For example, in [8] a semi-supervised method for classification in network data is presented. Instead of classifying a provided graph, the proposed problem is to classify the nodes within a given graph. The method is able to classify well even if the number of provided labeled instances is small, while the rest of the instances are unlabeled. The idea behind is to get each known class and perform random walks in which the selection of the next visiting node is influenced by the similarity to the current class. After all classes have been iterated, each unlabeled node is classified as the class that most visited the node. The classification performance significantly outperforms other semi-supervised methods and it is competitive with some fully supervised methods.

Another example of network data classification could be the molecular interactions between proteins. In [9] a method that allows the functional clustering of proteins is proposed. The relations between proteins are first described using a graph structure, where the edges represent the functional distances between proteins. Finally, a classification tree is used to obtain the classes.

A mathematical method of classification and regression of graphs, gBoost is presented in [10]. This method consists of two main components: the machine learning part that solves the mathematical program and graph mining that finds optimal patterns. The purpose of using these two components is to progressively collect patterns of graphs in an optimal way and forming a prediction rule. The experimental results on several benchmark data sets show that gBoost is competitive with other state-of-the-art methods.

Paper [11] analyzes the marketing brand awareness of various cellular providers and smartphone products using multiple regression. The network properties, such as density, modularity, clustering coefficient, etc., are used in the model to obtain the coefficient of multiple regression function of brand awareness. Networks are formed by the users of each brand, and conversational data sets are accessed from Twitter. Based on the experiments, a seemingly counterintuitive result is found, i.e. a network has a smaller performance in the spread of information as brand awareness increases.

A graph neural network (GNN) architecture for classifying events on a three-dimensional graph structure is described in [12]. The work is based on a real-world use case in which an ensemble of optical sensors is placed in deep ice in order to detect specific physical events of subatomic particles. The physical geometrical position of sensors can be viewed as a tensor representation and the main signal of interest provided by them is a real number, which reflects the measured energy. The detection of specific events produced by the subatomic particles is difficult to classify because noise is also present. The modeling of this experiment relies on graph structures in which the nodes are represented by the optical sensors and the connections are the distances between the sensors, where this distance is based on their real spatial location. The first major issue is that an event does not produce the activation of all sensors, so there can be many moments of time in which the graph contains inactive nodes, i.e. data is sparse. When these inactive nodes are not taken into account, the occurrence of events provides different graphs, which challenges most classification models. The authors use 3D Convolutional Neural Networks (CNN) and GNN to compare their classification accuracy. GNN have good performance even if the graphs in the input data set have a variable structure. The adjacency matrices of the graphs are provided as the input to the convolution layer sequence, followed by a pooling layer. The final classification is made by applying logistic regression to the output of the pooling layer. The classification results on the test data show that the performance of GNNs is significantly better than that of CNNs.

A novel graph classification method, Substructure Assembling Network (SAN), which is similar to recurrent neural networks, is presented in [13]. The basic idea is to extract small, simple substructures from the original graph within the first Substructure Assembling Unit (SAU) layer; more complex substructures will be obtained when using more SAU layers. These layers are similar to filters and they are progressively applied to each node for edge selection, based on probabilistic decisions. These layers are then followed by a pooling layer to aggregate the obtained substructures into fixed-length vector representation and then a final classical multilayer neural network is used for classification. Beside the fact that this approach can be applied on complex graph structures, it also allows the use of arbitrary size graphs in the data set. The classification performance is compared to several state-of-the-art methods and SAN is found to be competitive or to even outperform others on this specific task of graph classification.

In [14] the Deep Graph Convolutional Neural Network (DCGNN) is presented, which contains two main functions: to extract substructure features and to sort the nodes. The former is achieved by using a proposed form of graph convolution layers, where the node features are aggregated in order to obtain the local substructure information. The latter is a novel SortPooling layer, where nodes are sorted based on their structural roles within the graph. The output of SortPooling can be fed to a classical deep learning structure composed of 1-D convolutional neural network followed by fully connected layers. This deep learning structure is able to learn well the sorted representations, thus the overall model is able to classify well graph structures. Experimental results prove that DGCNN is highly competitive with other state-of-the-art graph classifiers.

A general approach for graph information processing is the use of graph kernels [15], which allow the computation of the similarity between graphs and can thus be used by kernel-based methods such as support vector machines. A recent survey of this type of methods is [16].

Another recent technique is the use of graph embeddings [17, 18], which using the same idea of word embeddings [19, 20], represent the transformation of graphs to a vector or a set of vectors.

Compared to these methods, in our case, the main difference is that we have a regression problem, unlike the classification problems addressed in most of the cited works. Unlike the approaches that use some method of processing the graph information, we directly use the corresponding adjacency matrix and the features of nodes and edges.

3 Model Description

In order to determine the two-terminal network reliability expression, we use an analytical method [6] that is based on the minimal path set between two specified nodes, i.e. source and destination. A minimal path is a communication link between the source and destination nodes, without passing through the same node more than once. The set of minimal paths represents all possible communication links. Based on these minimal paths, the analytical method is used to determine disjoint products. This method is based on complemented variables in order to satisfy the condition that the terms obtained are mutually exclusive. Finally, the reliability expression is computed by summing these disjoint products.

To approximate the two-terminal network reliability, we use three main models: *Autoencoders* (AE) [21, 22], *Convolutional Neural Networks* (CNN) [23, 24] and *eXtreme Gradient Boosting* (XGBoost) [25]. For these models we propose various architectures and compare their performance on generated synthetic datasets. For each architecture, we try different parameter values and we show the configurations that yield the best results. The provided input data for each particular model is a graph structure described by an adjacency matrix, followed by node probabilities. The edge probabilities are included in the adjacency matrix on their specific locations correlated with the node connections. An example of a three-node network and its corresponding adjacency matrix is illustrated in Fig. 1.

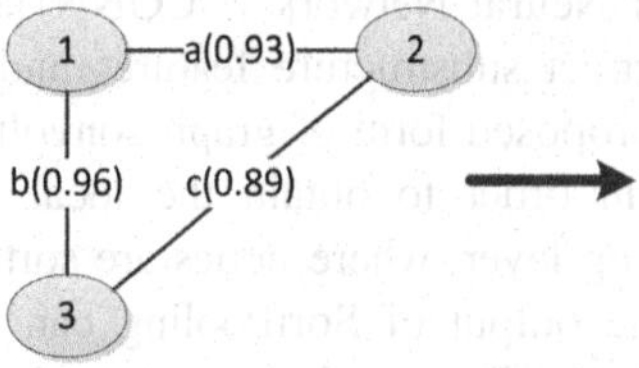

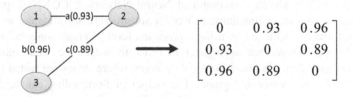

$$\begin{bmatrix} 0 & 0.93 & 0.96 \\ 0.93 & 0 & 0.89 \\ 0.96 & 0.89 & 0 \end{bmatrix}$$

Fig. 1. Example of a network and its corresponding adjacency matrix

3.1 Autoencoders

The AE is a type of artificial neural network with the main purpose of encoding the provided input data and extracting meaningful features from it, followed by a decoding of this latent representation. The structure of an AE consists of: an input layer, one or more hidden layers and an output layer which reconstructs the input data as closely as possible.

The training phase of an AE usually requires a large number of instances in the training dataset. In our case, the input data contains network topology information, both node and edge probabilities and finally, the two-terminal network reliability.

We evaluate two different AE architectures. The first one is denoted as AE_1 and has the following structure: an input layer which represents the actual input data of size 110, followed by two hidden layers of 60 and 40 neurons, respectively. This first half of AE is the encoding part, while the other half, i.e. decoding, contains the mirrored layers of the encoding: a hidden layer of 60 neurons and the output layer of 110 neurons, which provides the reconstructed data. In the rest of the paper we will write the structure of an AE in a more readable way using the layers and their number of neurons. Therefore, this AE has the following structure: 110–60–40–60–110. After the training phase, only its encoding part is used and connected to an output layer containing a layer with a single neuron: 110–60–40–1. Then, a fine tuning phase is applied for this new structure, and this time the neural network provides a single output, i.e. the two-terminal network reliability.

The second architecture, AE_2 has the following structure: 110–200–100–200–110. As in the previous case, the encoding part is connected to a single output neuron, after the AE training is done: 110–200–100–1. At this point, only the last layer of the new structure is trained, followed by a final training of the entire neural network. In this architecture we have a three-phase training, unlike the AE_1 architecture where we have only two training phases.

The structural difference between these architectures is that AE_1 is undercomplete, with the aim to gradually compress the input. AE_2 is overcomplete, in order to project the input in a higher-dimensional space to make the representation easier to process afterwards. Regularization is used to prevent it from directly copying the input.

3.2 Convolutional Neural Networks

CNNs have been originally used for image recognition and classification by hierarchically identifying specific image features, but they are also used to process other types of data, e.g. audio or active power signals. A CNN is comprised of multiple layers such as: convolution, non-linear, pooling and fully connected layers. The network output may be a class or a probability distribution of classes, that best describes the input data. The first layer of a CNN is always a convolution layer, in which various filters are applied in order to extract specific characteristics of the input data. The convolution layer size is strongly influenced by the filter size and is smaller than the original size of the input data. These filters actually contain weights that are used to represent certain features. CNN learns the values of these weights in the training process. A large number of such filters results in a larger number of extracted features from the original input data. Generally, the filter size is chosen to be smaller than the input data size. In order to apply these filters, they are slid repeatedly over the input data, until all the portions of the data are covered. The convolution procedure is characterized by the fact that these filters are used to compute the element wise multiplication between two arrays: a filter and an input region. In our case, we provide the input data as a one-dimensional array. After these filters are applied, smaller one-dimensional arrays are obtained that highlight specific features, depending on the filter used. These obtained arrays are called feature maps and they can be provided as inputs for further convolution layers. By choosing a large number of convolution layers, one can extract higher level features from the original input data. The output of a convolution layer is often passed through an activation function, often the Rectified Linear Unit (ReLU), to ensure the non-linear behavior of the network. Pooling layers are usually employed between the convolution layers, with the purpose of reducing the feature map dimensionality, while the most prominent information is maintained. The pooling layer role is to divide the input into non-overlapping regions and to apply some simple processing in each region, e.g. maximum, average or sum. In case of max pooling, the largest element from each region is fed to the output to create a new feature map of reduced size. Instead, we could also take the average or sum of all elements in each region. Pooling operation is applied to each feature map and this helps to gradually reduce the spatial size of the input representation. The last layer of a CNN is a classic fully connected layer, where each neuron from the previous layer is connected to each neuron in the next layer. This is actually a multilayer perceptron (MLP), which takes as input the obtained feature maps, and outputs a classification for the original input data.

An additional technique that can be used is dropout, which may reduce overfitting. As the name suggests, certain neurons are randomly chosen to be inhibited, i.e. these neurons are not active for some periods in the training phase. So, the training phase is applied on multiple architectures of the neural network with different combinations of neurons.

Table 1. Detailed configuration of layers for CNN_1 through CNN_6

Layers	Parameters	CNN_1	CNN_2	CNN_3	CNN_4	CNN_5	CNN_6
Conv	No. filters	15	15	32	32	32	32
	Kernel size	7	7	5	5	10	10
	Activation	Sigmoid	ReLU	Sigmoid	ReLU	ReLU	ReLU
Pooling	Pool size = 2	Average	Average	Average	Average	Average	Average
Dropout		–	–	–	–	–	Yes
Conv	No. filters	–	–	64	64	64	64
	Kernel size	–	–	5	5	10	10
	Activation	–	–	Sigmoid	ReLU	ReLU	ReLU
Pooling	Pool size = 2	–	–	Average	Average	Average	Average
Dropout		–	–	–	–	Yes	Yes
Dense	Activation	Sigmoid	ReLU	Sigmoid	ReLU	ReLU	ReLU
Dropout		–	–	–	–	Yes	Yes

We use various configurations of CNNs, as shown in Tables 1 and 2. While there are general recommendations for tasks involving image processing, the process of choosing the best combination of CNN parameters remains mainly empirical and problem-dependent. For our problem, we choose different configurations in increasing order of complexity. As shown by the results, there is no unique configuration that gives the best results for all network datasets.

Table 2. Detailed configuration of layers for CNN_7 through CNN_9

Layers	Parameters	CNN_7	CNN_8	CNN_9
Conv	No. filters	15	15	15
	Kernel size	7	7	7
	Activation	Sigmoid	ReLU	Leaky ReLU
Pooling	Pool size = 2	Maximum	Maximum	Maximum
Dense	Activation	Sigmoid	ReLU	Leaky ReLU

3.3 Extreme Gradient Boosting

The last model we use is XGBoost, which is based on gradient boosting decision trees, with various changes and optimizations in order to improve prediction and computing time. When a single decision tree is used, this is prone to overfitting. However, the use of multiple decision trees together in an ensemble can lead to much better results. An example of an ensemble technique is boosting, in which new models are successively added in order to reduce the errors of the previously used models. This is an iterative method that progressively builds new decision trees taking into account the errors made by the tree from the previous iteration. By combining the results of all the decision trees in the ensemble, better results are obtained. This method is called boosting decision trees. Gradient boosting is an extension of boosting, which uses gradient descent in order to optimize a differentiable loss function. The main advantage of XGBoost, in terms of prediction performance, is the use of a regularization term beside the loss function, whose purpose is to provide a measure of the model complexity. If the model is too complex, then it is likely to encounter overfitting issues. Thus, the regularization term can be used as a constraint in order to reduce the model complexity. XGBoost also contains a sparsity aware algorithm for an efficient processing of datasets with missing values or with lots of zero values. These scenarios are often present in datasets, especially when providing adjacency matrices or one-hot encodings. The sparsity aware algorithm detects the patterns of these missing values such that only the relevant features are processed. The use of this algorithm significantly improves the computing time of the overall model. Another advantage of XGBoost is scalability; it can be used as a multi-core or distributed application, and this is especially valuable when very large datasets are analyzed.

We use XGBoost on the regression task with a maximum tree depth of 10. The number of boosted trees for datasets with 10000 instances is set to 150 and 200 for datasets with 20000 instances. These are the only configurations we use in our results, as the other ones proved to be not so good for our task. Our trials show that the number of boosted trees has the largest impact on algorithm performance.

4 Case Studies

4.1 Dataset Generation

In our experiments, we use different model configurations as well as various datasets to see the impact factors which lead to a better learning for each model. In Table 3, we present the chosen datasets that contain 10000 and 20000 networks, respectively, and their chosen topologies.

By fixed connectivity of a dataset we mean that we initially generate a random network and its structure remains constant over the whole dataset, while only the node and edge probabilities are randomly generated between instances. A variable connectivity means that we vary the network structure when generating new instances in a dataset, but keeping the network topology type.

We choose two types of network topologies: random and scale free. When we generate a network with random topology, we choose each node to randomly create connections to the other existing nodes in the network. In the case of scale free topology, we are progressively creating the network by adding one node at a time. Each new node connects to another existing node in the network following a power law distribution, i.e. the new node has a higher chance of connecting to a node with a higher degree: $P(k) \propto k^{-\gamma}$, $2<\gamma<3$, where $P(k)$ is the connection probability to a desired node i and is directly proportional to the degree k (of node i) to the power of γ.

In all datasets, the probabilities of nodes and edges are randomly generated from a uniform distribution in the range [0.9, 1).

In order to compare the results of the different models, cross-validation with 10 folds is employed, i.e. in one fold, 90% of the networks are used for training, while the remaining 10% are used for testing.

Table 3. Description of datasets and their notation

Dataset notation	No. networks	Topology type	Connectivity
D_1	10000	Random	Fixed
D_2	10000	Random	Variable
D_3	20000	Random	Variable
D_4	10000	Scale free	Variable
D_5	20000	Scale free	Variable

4.2 Experimental Results

According to our experiments, the biggest impact factors in learning are the network topology and the number of epochs. Starting from the D_1 dataset (with random topology type, fixed connectivity and random probabilities on both edges and nodes), we can see that the chosen models have a good generalization in terms of reliability estimation. Subsequently, when choosing D_2 and D_3 datasets (with variable connectivity and random topology type), the chosen models do not have good generalization capability because of the increased problem complexity. Similar instances in the dataset, with the same network configuration, may be interpreted as distinct instances because of the fact that the model does not recognize the concept of node ordering. However, in case of D_4 and D_5 datasets, with scale free topology with variable connectivity, we obtain better generalization in comparison to the random topology because the network connectivity to D_4 and D_5 is weaker due to the power law distribution degree of nodes. Thus, the models can learn more efficiently due to a smaller number of features. In the case of random topology type, the models cannot extract dominant network characteristics because they have higher variations in the number of connections between the nodes.

In the following, we first compare the performance of the model with different configurations, and then we make an overall performance comparison by choosing only those configurations with the best results. For each model, we note the correlation coefficient for the training data as r_{train} and for the testing data as r_{test}. This correlation is a similarity measure between the desired and the predicted outputs of the models and it can help one to evaluate the regression performance of each model. When the correlation coefficient tends to 1, the predicted output of a particular model tends to be very close to the desired one. Otherwise, we say that the model will have a weaker prediction performance as the correlation value decreases. In the following results, the chosen models are illustrated on the X axis, while r_{train} and r_{test} are both illustrated on the Y axis with two different colors, according to the legend of figures. We also choose the lower boundary of the Y axis to be higher and closer to the performance of the weakest model in order to observe more easily the performance differences between the studied cases. The configurations used are suggestively labeled with the name of the used method appended with a digit that reflects the configuration number, e.g. CNN_3 represents the third proposed configuration from the convolutional neural networks. Also, for each configuration, we show in Table 4 the optimal number of epochs at which the highest value of r_{test} is obtained and this reflects the maximum learning potential of the model.

For the D_1 dataset, we can see in Fig. 2 that the r_{test} value is close to r_{train}, except for the case of the XGBoost model, whose performance tends to be similar for all datasets, i.e. it learns well on the training dataset, but its regression capability is weaker on the testing set. The approximate mean correlation for D_1 testing dataset is 0.96, which is actually a good performance.

Regarding the AE models, the optimal number of epochs for AE_1 architecture is 2000, while AE_1 architecture required 20000 epochs for the main training phase and 1000 epochs for fine-tuning. In case of CNNs, the CNN_1 model requires the highest number of epochs: 3000. These optimal numbers of epochs are chosen at the point where r_{test} has the highest value, while other neighborhood values for the number of epochs lead to a lower r_{test}. Thus, we get the highest possible value of r_{test} and ignore those cases where certain number of epochs leads to overfitting. D_1 is the only dataset that contains networks with fixed connectivity and we have not used a larger dataset with this type of networks because the performance of models is already good enough.

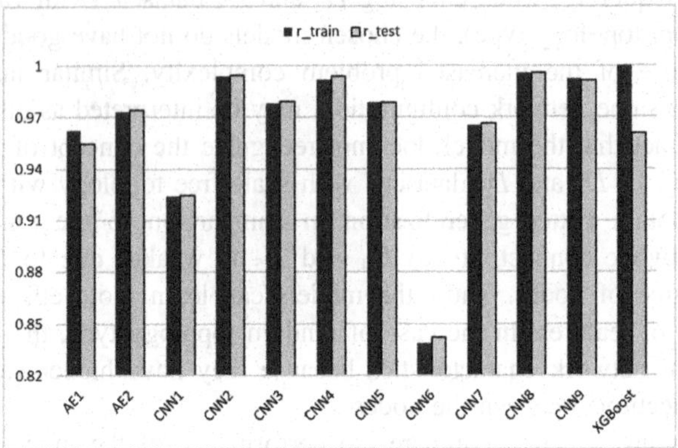

Fig. 2. Prediction performance obtained for dataset D_1

Table 4. Optimal number of epochs for each dataset

Model	Dataset				
	D_1	D_2	D_3	D_4	D_5
AE_1	2000	9000	10000	10000	3000
AE_2 Main phase	20000	10000	10000	10000	10000
AE_2 Fine tuning	1000	100	100	100	100
CNN_1	3000	5000	5000	2000	3000
CNN_2	1000	2000	2000	1000	1000
CNN_3	2000	2000	2000	1000	1000
CNN_4	1000	1000	1000	3000	4000
CNN_5	1000	1000	2000	1000	1000
CNN_6	2000	5000	5000	3000	1000
CNN_7	2000	2000	2000	2000	2000
CNN_8	2000	1000	1000	2000	2000

In case of the D_2 dataset, we can see in Fig. 3a that the obtained performance is lower compared with D_1 (Fig. 2). The AE_1 model has the worst performance and it requires 9000 epochs (Table 4), while AE_2 performs better with only 10000–100 epochs, compared to D_1. The best results are highlighted by XGBoost and CNN models with an approximate r_{test} mean value of 0.75. Using a higher number of instances in the dataset (i.e. D_3 with 20000 networks), the overall performance of models is not significantly improved (Fig. 3). Only a few models have a higher increase in the r_{test} value such as: AE_1, AE_2 and CNN_4. In Table 4, we can see that the optimal number of epochs for the D_2 and D_3 datasets is the same.

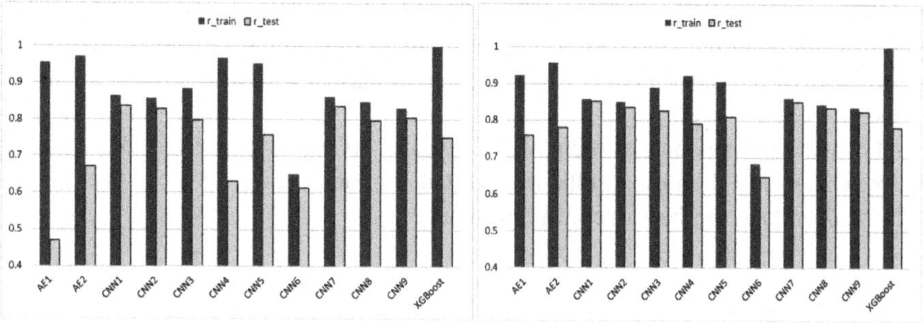

a) b)

Fig. 3. Prediction performance obtained for dataset: (a) D_2; (b) D_3

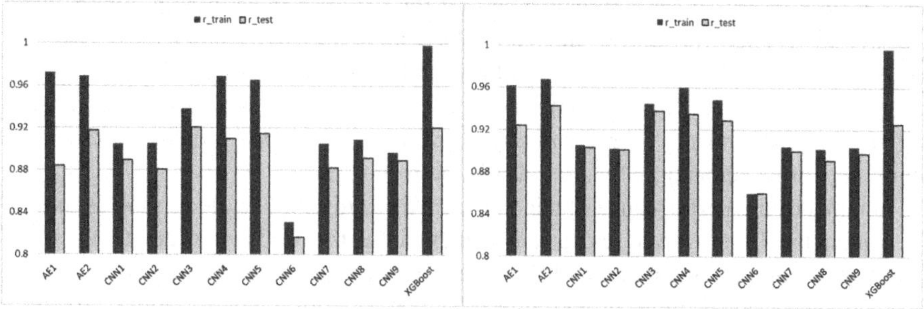

a) b)

Fig. 4. Prediction performance obtained for dataset: (a) D_4; (b) D_5

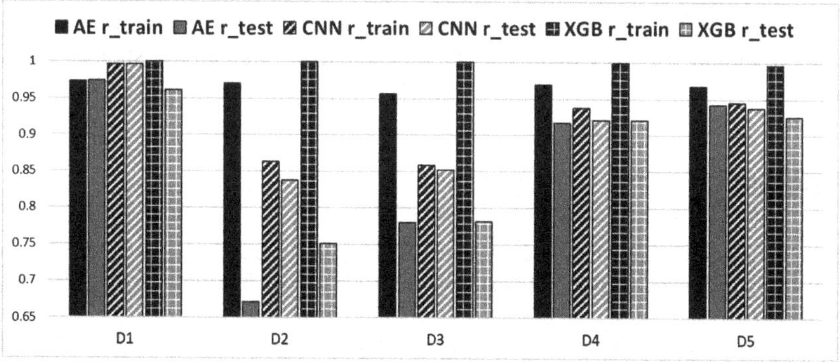

Fig. 5. Overall prediction performance obtained on each dataset

In case of the D_4 and D_5 datasets, the approximate mean r_{test} value is 0.9 (Fig. 4), and we see that AE_1 and AE_2 models have a significant performance increase compared to the D_2 and D_3 datasets. Also, we see that AE_2 is the best model when dataset D_5 is used. These observations show that the AE_1 and AE_2 models are capable of generalizing well on large datasets with a reduced number of features. However, the overall performance of the other models is good, even if datasets with more complex features are used.

The final comparison between AE, CNN and XGBoost models is illustrated in Fig. 5, where only the best results are selected for each dataset. We can see that the CNN models have the best overall performance.

5 Conclusions

Several ideas can be identified from the experimental study. First, the network topology is the main cause of difficulty for learning a good model. If the topology is fixed and only the node and edge probabilities differ, the learning process is much more successful. Conversely, in order to have good results with variable topology, much larger datasets are needed. Secondly, the networks with scale free topology are easier to handle than networks with random topology. This is an important result especially for the study of social networks or other networks which exhibit the scale free property, e.g. software dependency graphs, interbank payment networks, protein-protein interaction networks, semantic networks, airline networks, etc.

In terms of the performance obtained by the three machine learning models used in our study, the best overall results are achieved by the CNN configurations, while XGBoost is competitive in some of the cases. AEs are generally weak predictors even on small datasets. This gives us an intuition that, at least for the two-terminal reliability problem, there is a certain redundancy in the graph structure and certain implicit local relations between adjacent nodes that can be successfully exploited by the CNNs.

A future direction of investigation is the use of graph kernels and graph embeddings instead of the adjacency matrix to evaluate the two-terminal network reliability. Another direction is to analyze the possibility of the predictors to be applied on datasets with a dynamic network size in terms of number of nodes. The accuracy of the predictors should be assessed and their capability limitations should also be determined.

References

1. Sen, P., Namata, G., Bilgic, M., Getoor, L., Galligher, B., Eliassi-Rad, T.: Collective classification in network data. AI Mag. **29**(3), 93–106 (2008). https://doi.org/10.1609/aimag.v29i3.2157
2. Macskassy, S.A., Provost, F.: A brief survey of machine learning methods for classification in networked data and an application to suspicion scoring. In: Airoldi, E., Blei, D.M., Fienberg, S.E., Goldenberg, A., Xing, E.P., Zheng, A.X. (eds.) ICML 2006. LNCS, vol. 4503, pp. 172–175. Springer, Heidelberg (2007). https://doi.org/10.1007/978-3-540-73133-7_13
3. Latouche, P., Rossi, F.: Graphs in machine learning: an introduction. In: 23-th European Symposium on Artificial Neural Networks, Computational Intelligence and Machine Learning (ESANN), Bruges, Belgium, pp. 207–218 (2015). hal-01166849

4. Canning, J.P., et al.: Network classification and categorization (2017). arXiv:1709.04481
5. Hamilton, W.L., Ying, R., Leskovec, J.: Representation learning on graphs: methods and applications. IEEE Data Eng. Bull. **40**(3), 52–74 (2017). arXiv:1709.05584
6. Caşcaval, P., Floria, S.A.: Two approximate approaches for reliability evaluation in large networks. Comparative study. In: 22nd International Conference on System Theory, Control and Computing (ICSTCC), Sinaia, Romania, pp. 541–546. IEEE (2018). https://doi.org/10.1109/icstcc.2018.8540730
7. Caşcaval, P., Floria, S.A.: SDP algorithm for network reliability evaluation. In: 2017 IEEE International Conference on INnovations in Intelligent SysTems and Applications (INISTA), Gdynia, Poland, pp. 119–125. IEEE (2017). https://doi.org/10.1109/inista.2017.8001143
8. Lin, F., Cohen, W.W.: Semi-supervised classification of network data using very few labels. In: 2010 International Conference on Advances in Social Networks Analysis and Mining, Odense, Denmark, pp. 192–199. IEEE (2010). https://doi.org/10.1109/asonam.2010.19
9. Brun, C., Chevenet, F., Martin, D., Wojcik, J., Guénoche, A., Jacq, B.: Functional classification of proteins for the prediction of cellular function from a protein-protein interaction network. Genome Biol. **5**(1), R6 (2003). https://doi.org/10.1186/gb-2003-5-1-r6
10. Saigo, H., Nowozin, S., Kadowaki, T., Kudo, T., Tsuda, K.: gBoost: a mathematical programming approach to graph classification and regression. Mach. Learn. **75**(1), 69–89 (2009). https://doi.org/10.1007/s10994-008-5089-z
11. Peranginangin, Y., Alamsyah, A.: Multiple regression to analyse social graph of brand awareness. Telkomnika **15**(1), 336–340 (2017). https://doi.org/10.12928/telkomnika.v15i1.3460
12. Choma, N., et al.: Graph neural networks for icecube signal classification. In: 17th IEEE International Conference on Machine Learning and Applications (ICMLA), Orlando, FL, pp. 386–391. IEEE (2018). https://doi.org/10.1109/icmla.2018.00064
13. Zhao, X., Zong, B., Guan, Z., Zhang, K., Zhao, W.: Substructure assembling network for graph classification. In: Thirty-Second AAAI Conference on Artificial Intelligence (2018). http://www.cs.ucsb.edu/~bzong/doc/aaai18-san-zong.pdf
14. Zhang, M., Cui, Z., Neumann, M., Chen, Y.: An end-to-end deep learning architecture for graph classification. In: AAAI Conference on Artificial Intelligence, pp. 4438–4445 (2018). https://www.cse.wustl.edu/~muhan/papers/AAAI_2018_DGCNN.pdf
15. Vishwanathan, S.V.N., Schraudolph, N.N., Kondor, R., Borgwardt, K.M.: Graph kernels. J. Mach. Learn. Res. **11**, 1201–1242 (2010). http://www.jmlr.org/papers/volume11/vishwanathan10a/vishwanathan10a.pdf
16. Ghosh, S., Das, N., Gonçalves, T., Quaresma, P., Kundu, M.: The journey of graph kernels through two decades. Comput. Sci. Rev. **27**, 88–111 (2018). https://doi.org/10.1016/j.cosrev.2017.11.002
17. Narayanan, A., Chandramohan, M., Venkatesan, R., Chen, L., Liu, Y., Jaiswal, S.: graph2vec: learning distributed representations of graphs (2017). arXiv:1707.05005
18. Goyal, P., Ferrara, E.: Graph embedding techniques, applications, and performance: a survey. Knowl.-Based Syst. **151**, 78–94 (2018). https://doi.org/10.1016/j.knosys.2018.03.022
19. Mikolov, T., Sutskever, I., Chen, K., Corrado, G., Dean, J.: Distributed representations of words and phrases and their compositionality. In: 26th International Conference on Neural Information Processing Systems, NIPS, Lake Tahoe, pp. 3111–3119 (2013). arXiv:1310.4546
20. Pennington, J., Socher, R., Manning, C.D.: GloVe: global vectors for word representation. In: Conference on Empirical Methods in Natural Language Processing (EMNLP), Doha, Qatar, pp. 1532–1543. Association for Computational Linguistics (2014). https://doi.org/10.3115/v1/d14-1162

21. Rumelhart, D.E., Hinton, G.E., Williams, R.J.: Learning internal representations by error propagation. Parallel Distrib. Process. **1**, 318–362 (1986)
22. Schwenk, H., Milgram, M.: Transformation invariant auto association with application to handwritten character recognition. In: Tesauro, G., Touretzky, D.S., Leen, T.K. (eds.) 7th International Conference on Neural Information Processing Systems (NIPS 1994), pp. 991–998. MIT Press, Cambridge, MA, USA (1994)
23. LeCun, Y., Bottou, L., Bengio, Y., Haffner, P.: Gradient-based learning applied to document recognition. Proc. IEEE **86**(11), 2278–2324 (1998). https://doi.org/10.1109/5.726791
24. LeCun, Y., Haffner, P., Bottou, L., Bengio, Y.: Object recognition with gradient-based learning. Shape, Contour and Grouping in Computer Vision. LNCS, vol. 1681, pp. 319–345. Springer, Heidelberg (1999). https://doi.org/10.1007/3-540-46805-6_19
25. Chen, T., Guestrin, C.: XGBoost: a scalable tree boosting system. In: KDD 2016 Proceedings of the 22nd ACM SIGKDD International Conference on Knowledge Discovery and Data Mining, San Francisco, California, pp. 785–794. ACM (2016). https://doi.org/10.1145/2939672.2939785

Capsule Generative Models

Yifeng Li[1](✉) and Xiaodan Zhu[2]

[1] Digital Technologies Research Centre, National Research Council Canada, Ottawa, ON K1A 0R6, Canada
yifeng.li@nrc-cnrc.gc.ca

[2] Department of Electrical and Computer Engineering, Queen's University, Kingston, ON K7L 3N6, Canada
xiaodan.zhu@queensu.ca

Abstract. Neuroscience studies inspire that structures are needed in the hidden space of deep learning models. In this paper, we propose a capsule restricted Boltzmann machine and a capsule Helmholtz machine by replacing individual hidden variables with encapsulated groups of hidden variables. Our preliminary experiments show that capsule activities in both models can be dynamically determined in context, and these activity spectra exhibit between-class patterns and within-class variations. Our models offer a novel approach to visualizing and understanding the hidden states.

Keywords: Capsule · Restricted Boltzmann machine · Helmholtz machine · Deep generative model

1 Introduction

The development of deep neural networks, based on distributed representations [10], has achieved large successes in a wide range of fields such as computer vision [14,15], speech recognition [8], and natural language processing (e.g., language models [1]), among many others. The limitation on supporting the manipulation of complex semantics and relations [5,7], however, triggers the exploration for revised distributed representations and alternative models. Recently, the concept of *deterministic* capsule networks [12,20] has been proposed to address the limitations of typical *discriminative* models, i.e., convolutional neural networks. In this paper, we further introduce and adapt the concept of capsules to *generative* models. Generative models have evolved from restricted Boltzmann machine (RBM) based models, such as Helmholtz machines (HMs) [4] and deep belief nets [11], to variational auto-encoders (VAEs) [13] and generative adversarial networks (GANs) [6] with prosperity in image and video generation.

In this paper, we propose a capsule RBM model that has *stochastic* capsules in its hidden layer, and a capsule HM where a capsule's status depends on active capsules above it. We also contribute a new wake-sleep algorithm for estimating the model parameters in capsule HM. The paper is organized as follows. We shall first present these models and their learning algorithms, and then show promising benefits of using capsules in deep generative models (DGMs). The paper is finally concluded with improvements and observations made with the proposed models.

I. V. Tetko et al. (Eds.): ICANN 2019, LNCS 11727, pp. 281–295, 2019.
https://doi.org/10.1007/978-3-030-30487-4_22

2 Method

2.1 Capsule RBM

Based on theories of exponential family RBMs (exp-RBMs) [16,17,23] and discriminative capsule nets [12,20], we propose capsule RBM (cap-RBM) replacing hidden variables with stochastic capsules. We use $\boldsymbol{x}$ to represent the visible vector. The k-th capsule in the hidden layer includes $\boldsymbol{h}_k$ which hosts multiple hidden random variables following any distribution from the exponential family, and z_k a binary random variable indicating whether this capsule is active. An example of such network is displayed in Fig. 1a.

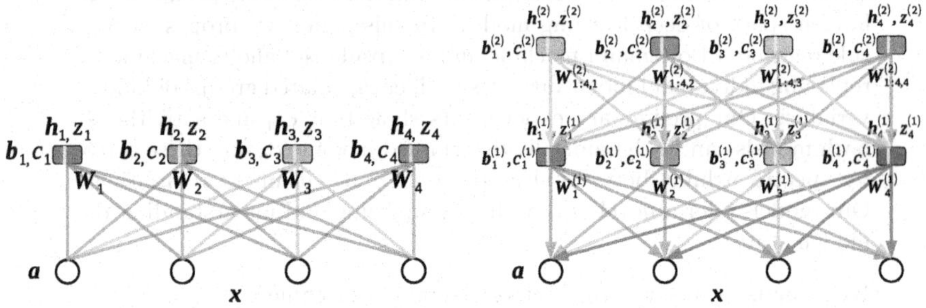

(a) Capsule RBM. (b) Capsule HM.

Fig. 1. Examples of capsule RBM and capsule HM. The meanings of the variables and parameters in capsule RBM are explained as follows. $\boldsymbol{a}$: bias parameters on the visible units. $\boldsymbol{b}_k$: bias parameters on $\boldsymbol{h}_k$. c_k: bias parameter on z_k. $\boldsymbol{W}_k$: interaction matrix between the k-th capsule ($\boldsymbol{h}_k$ and z_k) and $\boldsymbol{x}$. $\boldsymbol{\Omega}$: interaction matrix between $\boldsymbol{x}$ and $\boldsymbol{z}$. Similar meanings apply to capsule HM.

Model Definition. We assume visible vector $\boldsymbol{x}$ has M units, the hidden layer has K capsules (each contains J random variables and one switch variable). For simplicity, we write $\boldsymbol{h} = \{\boldsymbol{h}_1, \cdots, \boldsymbol{h}_K\}$. Following the steps in defining exp-RBMs, first of all, the base distributions of capsule RBM are defined in natural form as

$$\begin{cases} p(\boldsymbol{x}) = \prod_{m=1}^{M} \exp\left(\boldsymbol{a}_m^{\mathrm{T}} \boldsymbol{s}_m + \log f(x_m) - A(\boldsymbol{a}_m)\right) & (1) \\ p(\boldsymbol{h}) = \prod_{k=1}^{K} \prod_{j=1}^{J} \exp\left(\boldsymbol{b}_{k,j}^{\mathrm{T}} \boldsymbol{t}_{k,j} + \log g(h_{k,j}) - B(\boldsymbol{b}_{k,j})\right) & (2) \\ p(\boldsymbol{z}) = \prod_{k=1}^{K} \exp\left(c_k z_k - C(z_k)\right), & (3) \end{cases}$$

where $p(\boldsymbol{x})$ and $p(\boldsymbol{h})$ are from the exponential class, and $p(\boldsymbol{z})$ is Bernoulli distributed. $\boldsymbol{a}_m = [a_m^{(1)}, \cdots, a_m^{(R)}]^{\mathrm{T}}$ and $\boldsymbol{b}_{k,j} = [b_{k,j}^{(1)}, \cdots, b_{k,j}^{(U)}]^{\mathrm{T}}$ are respectively the natural parameters of x_m and $h_{k,j}$, $\boldsymbol{s}_m$ and $\boldsymbol{t}_{k,j}$ are respectively their sufficient statistics, $A(\boldsymbol{a}_m)$ and $B(\boldsymbol{b}_{k,j})$ are corresponding log-partition functions, and $f(x_m)$ and $g(h_{k,j})$ are base measures. For example, if $x_m \sim \mathcal{N}(\mu, \lambda^{-1})$, then $\boldsymbol{a}_m = [a_m^{(1)}, a_m^{(2)}]^{\mathrm{T}} = [\mu\lambda, -\frac{\lambda}{2}]^{\mathrm{T}}$, $\boldsymbol{s}_m = [x, x^2]^{\mathrm{T}}$, $A(\boldsymbol{a}_m) = \frac{1}{2}\log\frac{\pi}{-a_m^{(2)}} - \frac{a_m^{(1)}}{4a_m^{(2)}}$, and $f(x_m) = 1$. If $h_{k,j} \sim \mathcal{BE}(p)$, i.e. Bernoulli, $b_{k,j} = \log\frac{p}{1-p}$, $t_{k,j} = x$, $B(b_{k,j}) = \log\big(1 + \exp(b_{k,j})\big)$, and $g(h_{k,j}) = 1$. Similar notations apply to $p(\boldsymbol{z})$. See [17] for a list of exponential family distributions formulated in natural parameters.

Second, the joint distribution has a similar form as in regular RBM: $p(\boldsymbol{x}, \boldsymbol{h}, \boldsymbol{z}) = \frac{1}{Z}\exp\big(-E(\boldsymbol{x}, \boldsymbol{h}, \boldsymbol{z})\big)$, where Z is the partition function, and the energy function $E(\boldsymbol{x}, \boldsymbol{h}, \boldsymbol{z})$ is defined as

$$\begin{aligned} E(\boldsymbol{x}, \boldsymbol{h}, \boldsymbol{z}) = &-\sum_{m=1}^{M}\big(\boldsymbol{a}_m^{\mathrm{T}}\boldsymbol{s}_m + \log f(x_m)\big) - \sum_{k=1}^{K}\sum_{j=1}^{J}\big(\boldsymbol{b}_{k,j}^{\mathrm{T}}\boldsymbol{t}_{k,j} + \log g(h_{k,j})\big) - \boldsymbol{c}^{\mathrm{T}}\boldsymbol{z} \\ &-\sum_{k=1}^{K} z_k(\boldsymbol{x}^{\mathrm{T}}\boldsymbol{W}_k\boldsymbol{h}_k) - \boldsymbol{x}^{\mathrm{T}}\boldsymbol{\Omega}\boldsymbol{z}, \end{aligned} \tag{4}$$

where the first three terms are bias terms and the last two terms define the interaction between observations and capsules.

Third, we can obtain the conditionals in decomposable forms as given by

$$p(\boldsymbol{x}|\boldsymbol{h}, \boldsymbol{z}) = \prod_{m=1}^{M} p\big(x_m|\eta(\hat{\boldsymbol{a}}_m)\big), \tag{5}$$

$$p(\boldsymbol{h}|\boldsymbol{x}, \boldsymbol{z}) = \prod_{k=1}^{K}\prod_{j=1}^{J} p\big(h_{k,j}|\eta(\hat{\boldsymbol{b}}_{k,j})\big), \tag{6}$$

$$p(\boldsymbol{z}|\boldsymbol{x}, \boldsymbol{h}) = \prod_{k=1}^{K} \mathcal{BE}\big(z_k|\eta(\hat{c}_k)\big), \tag{7}$$

where function $\eta(\cdot)$ maps the natural posterior parameters to the standard forms, and the posterior natural parameters are computed as

$$\hat{a}_m^{(r)} = a_m^{(r)} + \delta(r=1)\Big(\sum_{k=1}^{K} z_k(\boldsymbol{W}_k)_{m,:}\boldsymbol{h}_k + \boldsymbol{\Omega}_{m,:}\boldsymbol{z}\Big), \tag{8}$$

$$\hat{b}_{k,j}^{(u)} = b_{k,j}^{(u)} + \delta(u=1)\Big(z_k(\boldsymbol{W}_k^{\mathrm{T}})_{j,:}\boldsymbol{x}\Big), \tag{9}$$

$$\hat{c}_k = c_k + \boldsymbol{x}^{\mathrm{T}}\boldsymbol{W}_k\boldsymbol{h}_k + (\boldsymbol{\Omega}^{\mathrm{T}})_{k.:}\boldsymbol{x}, \tag{10}$$

where, $r \in \{1, \cdots, R\}$, $u \in \{1, \cdots, U\}$, without loss of generality we assume the first statistics for x_m and $h_{k,j}$ are respectively x_m and $h_{k,j}$, $(\boldsymbol{W}_k)_{m,:}$ means the

m-th row of matrix $\boldsymbol{W}_k$, and $\delta(\cdot)$ is a Kronecker delta function. Transformation tables for exponential family distributions between natural and standard forms can be found in [17].

Variable z_k determines whether the k-th capsule can interact with the visible variables; that is, only when $z_k = 1$, the k-th capsule has an impact on $\boldsymbol{x}$. Thus, the model dynamically decides on which capsules are active depending on the context. The conditional distribution of $\boldsymbol{x}$ is determined by its interactions with the active capsules and the switch variable. The conditional distribution of $\boldsymbol{h}_k$ depends on its interaction with $\boldsymbol{x}$. In turn, the value of the switch variable $\boldsymbol{z}$ depends on all the other variables. Specifically, this model has the following metrics: (1) An observation $\boldsymbol{x}$ will only activate a subset of capsules, some of which can be ubiquitous while some may be specific. (2) This leads to a block-wise structured representation of an observation in the hidden space. (3) Through examining the activity of dozens of capsules, indicated by $\boldsymbol{z}$, it offers a better interpretation compared to disentangling the meaning of hundreds or thousands of individual hidden variables in other generative models.

Model Learning. The model parameters are denoted by $\boldsymbol{\theta} = \{\boldsymbol{a}, \boldsymbol{b}, \boldsymbol{c}, \boldsymbol{W}, \boldsymbol{\Omega}\}$, where we simply write $\boldsymbol{b} = \{\boldsymbol{b}_1, \cdots, \boldsymbol{b}_K\}$ and $\boldsymbol{W} = \{\boldsymbol{W}_1, \cdots, \boldsymbol{W}_K\}$. Similar to exp-RBM, the gradients w.r.t. these parameters can be computed in the form:

$$\Delta_{\theta} = \frac{1}{N}\sum_{n=1}^{N}\Big(\mathrm{E}_{p(\boldsymbol{h},\boldsymbol{z}|\boldsymbol{x}_n)}\big[\frac{\partial E(\boldsymbol{x}_n,\boldsymbol{h},\boldsymbol{z})}{\partial \boldsymbol{\theta}}\big] - \mathrm{E}_{p(\boldsymbol{x},\boldsymbol{h},\boldsymbol{z})}\big[\frac{\partial E(\boldsymbol{x},\boldsymbol{h},\boldsymbol{z})}{\partial \boldsymbol{\theta}}\big]\Big). \tag{11}$$

Derivatives of the energy function w.r.t. these parameters are computed as below:

$$\frac{\partial E(\boldsymbol{x},\boldsymbol{h},\boldsymbol{z})}{\partial a_m^{(r)}} = -s_m^{(r)}, \qquad \frac{\partial E(\boldsymbol{x},\boldsymbol{h},\boldsymbol{z})}{\partial b_{k,j}^{(u)}} = -t_{k,j}^{(u)}, \quad \frac{\partial E(\boldsymbol{x},\boldsymbol{h},\boldsymbol{z})}{\partial \boldsymbol{c}} = -\boldsymbol{z},$$
$$\frac{\partial E(\boldsymbol{x},\boldsymbol{h},\boldsymbol{z})}{\partial \boldsymbol{W}_k} = -z_k\boldsymbol{x}\boldsymbol{h}_k^{\mathrm{T}}, \qquad \frac{\partial E(\boldsymbol{x},\boldsymbol{h},\boldsymbol{z})}{\partial \boldsymbol{\Omega}} = -\boldsymbol{x}\boldsymbol{z}^{\mathrm{T}}. \tag{12}$$

In Eq. 11, the first part is a data-dependent term that can be estimated by mean-field variational approximation using the conditional distributions over $\boldsymbol{h}$ and $\boldsymbol{z}$ while fixing $\boldsymbol{x}_n$. The second part is a data-independent term requiring Monte Carlo approximation where sampling can be performed by Gibbs sampling using the conditional distributions of $\boldsymbol{x}$, $\boldsymbol{h}$, and $\boldsymbol{z}$, alternatingly.

2.2 Capsule HM

Based on the concept of undirected capsule RBM, there exist multiple ways to construct a directed DGM. In this paper, we investigate the most basic idea that the distribution of capsule in layer l depends on its interactions with all active capsules in layer $l+1$. We name this DGM as capsule Helmholtz machine (capsule HM or cap-HM). An example of capsule HM with two hidden capsule layers is illustrated in Fig. 1b. Other sophisticated forms of capsule DGMs are further discussed at the end of this paper.

Model Definition. For a capsule HM with L hidden layers, the joint distribution of visible variables and hidden variables can be decomposed as follows:

$$p(\boldsymbol{x}, \boldsymbol{h}, \boldsymbol{z}) = p(\boldsymbol{x}|\boldsymbol{h}^{(1)}, \boldsymbol{z}^{(1)})\Big(\prod_{l=1}^{L-1} p(\boldsymbol{h}^{(l)}, \boldsymbol{z}^{(l)}|\boldsymbol{h}^{(l+1)}, \boldsymbol{z}^{(l+1)})\Big)p(\boldsymbol{h}^{(L)}, \boldsymbol{z}^{(L)}), \quad (13)$$

where, at the left-hand side, we let $\boldsymbol{h} = \{\boldsymbol{h}^{(1)}, \cdots, \boldsymbol{h}^{(L)}\}$, $\boldsymbol{z} = \{\boldsymbol{z}^{(1)}, \cdots, \boldsymbol{z}^{(L)}\}$ for narrative convenience. The pair $\boldsymbol{h}^{(l)}$ and $\boldsymbol{z}^{(l)}$ host all capsules in layer l, where the k-th capsule can be written as $C_k^{(l)} = \{\boldsymbol{h}_k^{(l)}, z_k^{(l)}\}$. There are three components at the right-hand side of Eq. 13. They are respectively discussed below.

First, the conditional distribution of visible variable is similar to that in capsule RBM:

$$p(\boldsymbol{x}|\boldsymbol{h}^{(1)}, \boldsymbol{z}^{(1)}) = \prod_{m=1}^{M} p(x_m|\eta(\hat{\boldsymbol{a}}_m)), \quad (14)$$

where $\hat{\boldsymbol{a}}^{(r)} = \boldsymbol{a}^{(r)} + \delta(r=1)\big(\sum_{k_1=1}^{K_1} z_{k_1}^{(1)} \boldsymbol{W}_{k_1}^{(1)} \boldsymbol{h}_{k_1}^{(1)} + \boldsymbol{\Omega z}\big)$.

Second, different from the traditional Helmholtz machine and directed DGMs, capsule HM is a mixture of directed and undirected components. The interaction of capsules in two adjacent layers are directed, but the conditional distribution of capsules within an intermediate layer is in fact an undirected sub-model which is defined using a special energy function, as formulated below:

$$p(\boldsymbol{h}^{(l)}, \boldsymbol{z}^{(l)}|\boldsymbol{h}^{(l+1)}, \boldsymbol{z}^{(l+1)}) = \frac{1}{Z_l} \exp\big(-E(\boldsymbol{h}^{(l)}, \boldsymbol{z}^{(l)}|\boldsymbol{h}^{(l+1)}, \boldsymbol{z}^{(l+1)})\big), \quad (15)$$

where the energy is computed as

$$E(\boldsymbol{h}^{(l)}, \boldsymbol{z}^{(l)}|\boldsymbol{h}^{(l+1)}, \boldsymbol{z}^{(l+1)}) = -\sum_{k_l=1}^{K_l} \Big(\sum_{u=1}^{U} \boldsymbol{b}_{k_l}^{(l,u)\mathrm{T}} \boldsymbol{t}_{k_l}^{(l,u)} + \sum_{j=1}^{J} \log g(h_{k_l,j}^{(l)})\Big) - \boldsymbol{c}^{(l)\mathrm{T}} \boldsymbol{z}^{(l)}$$
$$- \sum_{k_l=1}^{K_l} \sum_{k_{l+1}=1}^{K_{l+1}} z_{k_l}^{(l)} z_{k_{l+1}}^{(l+1)} \boldsymbol{h}_{k_l}^{(l)\mathrm{T}} \boldsymbol{W}_{k_l,k_{l+1}}^{(l+1)} \boldsymbol{h}_{l+1}^{(l+1)} - \boldsymbol{z}^{(l)\mathrm{T}} \boldsymbol{\Omega}^{(l+1)} \boldsymbol{z}^{(l+1)}, \quad (16)$$

where $\{\boldsymbol{b}_{k_l}^{(l,u)}, \boldsymbol{c}^{(l)}, \boldsymbol{W}_{k_l,k_{l+1}}^{(l+1)}, \boldsymbol{\Omega}^{(l+1)}\}$ are the parameters in this sub-model, K_l is the number of capsules in layer l, and U is the number of sufficient statistics. In virtue of the exponential family formulation, we can obtain the conditional distributions of individual variables in Eq. 15 for approximation and sampling:

$$p(\boldsymbol{h}^{(l)}|\boldsymbol{z}^{(l)}, \boldsymbol{h}^{(l+1)}, \boldsymbol{z}^{(l+1)}) = \sum_{k_l=1}^{K_l} \sum_{j=1}^{J} p(h_{k_l,j}^{(l)}|\eta(\hat{\boldsymbol{b}}_{k_l,j}^{(l)})), \quad (17)$$

$$p(\boldsymbol{z}^{(l)}|\boldsymbol{h}^{(l)}, \boldsymbol{h}^{(l+1)}, \boldsymbol{z}^{(l+1)}) = \sum_{k_l=1}^{K_l} \mathcal{BE}\big(z_{k_l}|\eta(\hat{c}_{k_l})\big), \quad (18)$$

where J is the number of random variables within a capsule, $\mathcal{BE}(\cdot)$ is Bernoulli probability function, and the posterior natural parameters are computed as

$$\hat{\boldsymbol{b}}_{k_l}^{(u)} = \boldsymbol{b}_{k_l}^{(u)} + \delta(u=1)\Big(\sum_{k_{l+1}=1}^{K_{l+1}} z_{k_l}^{(l)} z_{k_{l+1}}^{(l+1)} \boldsymbol{W}_{k_l,k_{l+1}}^{(l+1)} \boldsymbol{h}_{l+1}^{(l+1)}\Big), \tag{19}$$

$$\hat{c}_{k_l}^{(l)} = c_{k_l}^{(l)} + \sum_{k_{l+1}=1}^{K_{l+1}} z_{k_{l+1}}^{(l+1)} \boldsymbol{h}_{k_l}^{(l)\mathrm{T}} \boldsymbol{W}_{k_l,k_{l+1}}^{(l+1)} \boldsymbol{h}_{k_{l+1}}^{(l+1)} + \boldsymbol{\Omega}_{k,:}^{(l+1)} \boldsymbol{z}^{(l+1)}. \tag{20}$$

From Eq. 19, we can see that the k_{l+1}-th capsule at layer $l+1$ (denoted by $C_{k_{l+1}}^{(l+1)}$) influences the k_l-th capsule at layer l (denoted by $C_{k_l}^{(l)}$), only when both capsules are active. Equation 20 implies that only active capsules at the upper layer can potentially activate capsule $C_{k_l}^{(l)}$.

Finally, the distribution of the top layer can be assumed to be completely factorizable, as formulated below:

$$\begin{aligned} p\big(\boldsymbol{h}^{(L)}, \boldsymbol{z}^{(L)}\big) &= p\big(\boldsymbol{h}^{(L)}\big) p\big(\boldsymbol{h}^{(Z)}\big) \\ &= \sum_{k_L=1}^{K_L} \sum_{j=1}^{J} p\big(h_{k_L,j}^{(L)} | \eta(\boldsymbol{b}_{k_L,j}^{(L)})\big) \sum_{k_L=1}^{K_L} p\big(z_{k_L} | \eta(c_{k_L}^{(L)})\big). \end{aligned} \tag{21}$$

Using sophisticated structure on the top layer is possible, like the case of DBN where RBM is topped on HM. We will pursue this direction in future development.

Given a sample to this capsule HM, a subset of capsules at each layer could be activated. This dynamic context-dependent pattern reflected by $\boldsymbol{z}$ thus offers a novel way to visualize and interpret the hidden representations in DGM. We will prove this concept in the experimental section.

Model Learning. In the same spirit of HM, a corresponding recognition component is introduced to capsule HM to approximate inference $p_{\theta}(\boldsymbol{h}, \boldsymbol{z}|\boldsymbol{x})$ using $q_{\phi}(\boldsymbol{h}, \boldsymbol{z}|\boldsymbol{x})$. The model thus has generative parameters $\boldsymbol{\theta} = \{\boldsymbol{a}^{(r)}, \boldsymbol{b}_{k_l}^{(l,u)}, \boldsymbol{c}^{(l)}, \boldsymbol{W}_{k_{l-1},k_l}^{(l)}, \boldsymbol{\Omega}^{(l)}\}$ and recognition parameters $\boldsymbol{\phi} = \{\boldsymbol{b}_{k_l}^{(R,l,u)}, \boldsymbol{c}^{(R,l)}, \boldsymbol{W}_{k_{l-1},k_l}^{(R,l)}, \boldsymbol{\Omega}^{(R,l)}\}$. We propose a wake-sleep algorithm which is different from HM's wake-sleep algorithm in two aspects: (1) $q(\boldsymbol{h}, \boldsymbol{z}|\boldsymbol{x})$ in wake phase and $p(\boldsymbol{h}^{(l-1)}, \boldsymbol{z}^{(l-1)}|\boldsymbol{h}^{(l)}, \boldsymbol{z}^{(l)})$ in sleep phase are respectively mean-field variational approximations, because each intermediate layer is an energy-based model (note that $p(\boldsymbol{x}|\boldsymbol{h}^{(1)}, \boldsymbol{z}^{(1)})$ does not use variational approximation, but an exponential family distribution); (2) we applied a k-step (persistent) contrastive divergence sampling method [22] (we used $k=1$ in our experiments), such that the states of the top layer $\{\boldsymbol{h}^{(L)}, \boldsymbol{z}^{(L)}\}$ obtained from the wake phase are recycled as the start of the sleep phase. This also implies that Gibbs sampling can be used when generating samples through alternating wake-sleep phases after model learning. Prior work on Helmholtz machine [16] and variational autoencoder [25] has already shown that ancestral sampling often generates unsensible samples. The generative parameters are estimated by maximizing the evidence lower bound (ELBO) which is defined as

$$J(\boldsymbol{\theta}, \boldsymbol{\phi}) = \mathrm{E}_{q_\phi(\boldsymbol{h},\boldsymbol{z}|\boldsymbol{x})}\big[p_{\boldsymbol{\theta}}(\boldsymbol{x}, \boldsymbol{h}, \boldsymbol{z})\big] + H\big(q_\phi(\boldsymbol{h}, \boldsymbol{z}|\boldsymbol{x})\big), \tag{22}$$

where $H(\cdot)$ is the entropy of a distribution. Thus, the gradient w.r.t. the generative parameters can be generally written as

$$\Delta_\theta = \frac{\partial J(\boldsymbol{x})}{\partial \boldsymbol{\theta}} = \mathrm{E}_{q(\boldsymbol{h},\boldsymbol{z}|\boldsymbol{x})}\Big[\frac{\partial \log p(\boldsymbol{x}, \boldsymbol{h}, \boldsymbol{z})}{\partial \boldsymbol{\theta}}\Big]. \tag{23}$$

Since the model is described in the language of exponential family, we can make use of an important property of exponential family distribution (first-order derive of log-partition function w.r.t. natural parameter is the expectation of sufficient statistics) to obtain gradients of the interaction matrices from the first hidden layer to visible layer:

$$\begin{aligned}\frac{\partial \log p(\boldsymbol{x}, \boldsymbol{h}, \boldsymbol{z})}{\partial \boldsymbol{W}_{k_1}^{(1)}} &= \frac{\partial \log p(\boldsymbol{x}|\boldsymbol{h}^{(1)}, \boldsymbol{z}^{(1)})}{\partial \hat{\boldsymbol{a}}^{(1)}} \frac{\partial \hat{\boldsymbol{a}}^{(1)}}{\partial \boldsymbol{W}_{k_1}^{(1)}} \\ &= \Big(\frac{\partial \hat{\boldsymbol{a}}^{(1)\mathrm{T}}\boldsymbol{x}}{\partial \hat{\boldsymbol{a}}^{(1)}} - \frac{\partial A(\hat{\boldsymbol{a}}^{(1)})}{\partial \hat{\boldsymbol{a}}^{(1)}}\Big)\frac{\partial \hat{\boldsymbol{a}}^{(1)}}{\partial \boldsymbol{W}_{k_1}^{(1)}} = (\boldsymbol{x} - \langle \boldsymbol{x} \rangle)(z_{k_1}\boldsymbol{h}_{k_1}^{(1)})^{\mathrm{T}},\end{aligned} \tag{24}$$

where $\langle \boldsymbol{x} \rangle$ denotes expectation under the generative distribution.

It is apparently challenging to compute gradients of the parameters in the intermediate hidden layers ($1 < l < L$). Considering that the corresponding conditionals are undirected energy-based sub-models, we can apply the findings in general Boltzmann machines to derive the gradients:

$$\begin{aligned}\frac{\partial \log p(\boldsymbol{x}, \boldsymbol{h}, \boldsymbol{z})}{\partial \boldsymbol{W}_{k_l,k_{l+1}}^{(l+1)}} &= \frac{\partial \log p(\boldsymbol{h}^{(l)}, \boldsymbol{z}^{(l)}|\boldsymbol{h}^{(l+1)}, \boldsymbol{z}^{(l+1)})}{\partial \boldsymbol{W}_{k_l,k_{l+1}}^{(l+1)}} \\ &= \frac{\partial E(\boldsymbol{h}^{(l)}, \boldsymbol{z}^{(l)})}{\partial \boldsymbol{W}_{k_l,k_{l+1}}^{(l+1)}} - \mathrm{E}_{p(\boldsymbol{h}^{(l)},\boldsymbol{z}^{(l)}|\boldsymbol{h}^{(l+1)},\boldsymbol{z}^{(l+1)})}\Big[\frac{\partial E(\boldsymbol{h}^{(l)}, \boldsymbol{z}^{(l)})}{\partial \boldsymbol{W}_{k_l,k_{l+1}}^{(l+1)}}\Big] \\ &= (z_{k_l}\boldsymbol{h}_{k_l}^{(l)})(z_{k_{l+1}}\boldsymbol{h}_{k_{l+1}}^{(l+1)})^{\mathrm{T}} - \langle (z_{k_l}\boldsymbol{h}_{k_l}^{(l)})(z_{k_{l+1}}\boldsymbol{h}_{k_{l+1}}^{(l+1)})^{\mathrm{T}} \rangle \\ &= \big(z_{k_l}\boldsymbol{h}_{k_l}^{(l)} - \langle z_{k_l}\boldsymbol{h}_{k_l}^{(l)} \rangle\big)(z_{k_{l+1}}\boldsymbol{h}_{k_{l+1}}^{(l+1)})^{\mathrm{T}},\end{aligned} \tag{25}$$

which surprisingly has the same form as in Eq. 24. The gradients of the recognition parameters can be derived in the same way. Thus, we omit them.

3 Experiments

3.1 Capsule RBM

MNIST Data. We here investigate the performance of capsule RBM on the MNIST data (http://yann.lecun.com/exdb/mnist, see Fig. 2a for some examples from the data). We let both base distributions of $\boldsymbol{x}$ and $\boldsymbol{h}_k$ be Bernoulli, and set $K = 40$, $J = 16$, the initial learning rate to be 0.02 (gradually decreased), batch size 100, and the number of epochs 20. We tracked the reconstruction error

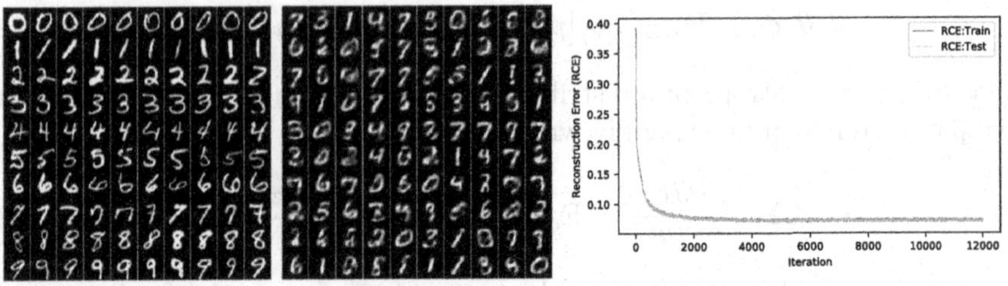

(a) Actual. (b) Generated. (c) Reconstruction errors.

Fig. 2. (a): Actual MNIST images. (b): Generated MNIST images by capsule RBM. (c): Reconstruction errors of training and testing MNIST images during learning capsule RBM.

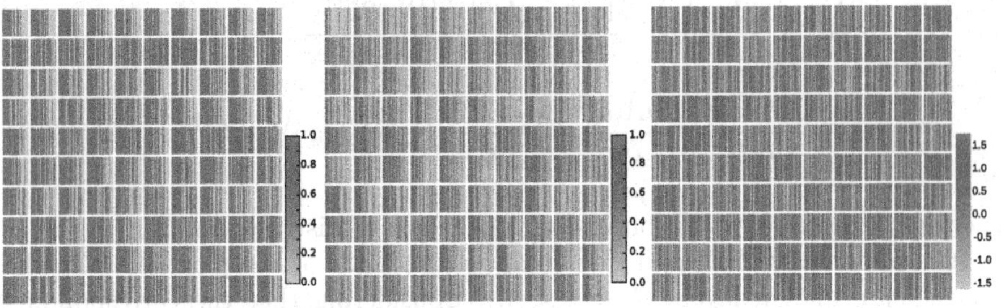

(a) Capsule RBM. (b) RBM. (c) VAE.

Fig. 3. Comparison of hidden representations of MNIST images from Fig. 2a. (a): Capsule activities in capsule RBM. (b): Hidden states in a Bernoulli-Bernoulli RBM without capsules. (c): Hidden states inferred by encoder in VAE.

of training and test samples, which reduced quickly along learning (see Fig. 2c). Figure 2b shows 100 images generated by Gibbs sampling with the learned model.

We obtained the capsule activities (values of $\boldsymbol{z}$) of the actual images as in Fig. 2a using mean-field approximation, and displayed them as spectra in Fig. 3a. Interestingly, class-wise patterns (e.g. patterns in classes 0 and 1) and within-class variations can be observed from the spectra. Furthermore, digits sharing similar parts tend to have partially similar patterns (e.g. digits "1", "4", "7", and "9" all have vertical strokes). By contrast, if a Bernoulli-Bernoulli RBM (without capsules) with 640 hidden variables was used, its hidden states couldn't very clearly exhibit such patterns to the interpretable level (see Fig. 3b). We also learned a VAE with two convolutional layers in its encoder, 40 Gaussian latent variables, and two convolutional layer in its decoder. We then obtained the values of latent variables using the encoder fed by the images from Fig. 2a, and display them in Fig. 3c. The VAE latent space does not show any consistent patterns.

To investigate what information the k-th capsule can represent, we obtained the values of this capsule's projective field by sampling $\boldsymbol{x}$ using Markov chain over $p(\boldsymbol{x}, \boldsymbol{h}|\boldsymbol{z}_k)$ where $\boldsymbol{z}_k$ is a one-hot vector of length K with the k-th element being one. Using this method, we visualize all capsules' projective fields in Fig. 4a, and find that these projective fields do show some distinct signatures. Furthermore, for an actual input image, we can infer the values of each capsule and then plot the reconstructed image and the projective fields of active capsules (see Fig. 4b and c for example). From such plots, we can easily see what kind of capsules are shared among classes or unique to a specific class.

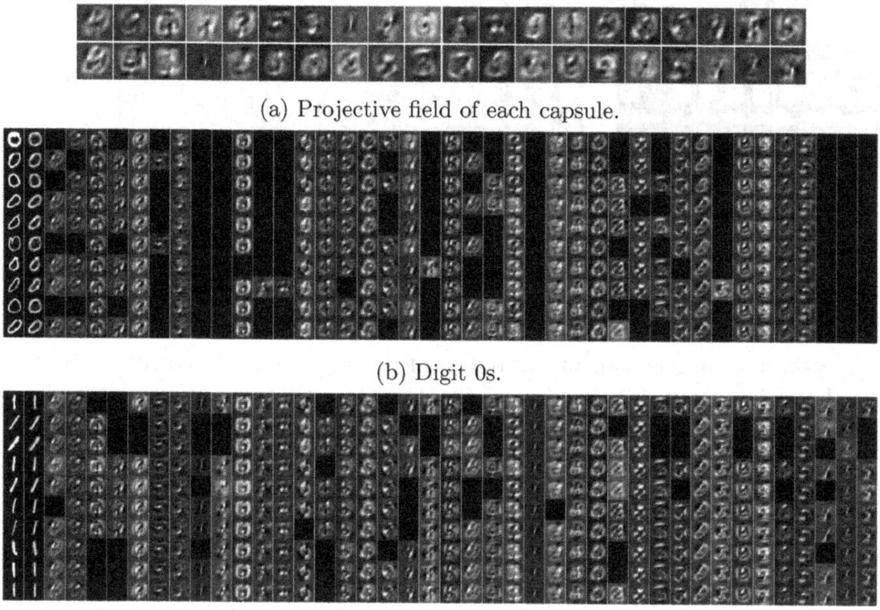

(a) Projective field of each capsule.

(b) Digit 0s.

(c) Digit 1s.

Fig. 4. Visualizing the projective field of each capsule on MNIST data. (a): Visualization of each capsule's projective field. (b): Digit 0s approximated by a linear combination of a subset of capsules' projective fields. (c): Digit 1s approximated by a linear combination of a subset of capsules' projective fields. In (b) and (c), the first columns are actual images; the second columns are corresponding reconstructed images; the rest columns are corresponding to projective fields of individual capsules.

Fashion-MNIST Data. We also explored capsule RBM on the Fashion-MNIST data [24] (see Fig. 5a for some test images). We let both base distributions of $\boldsymbol{x}$ and $\boldsymbol{h}_k$ be Gaussian, and set $K = 20$, $J = 16$, and the initial learning rate to be 0.005. Figure 5b gives some images generated from the capsule RBM model after training. In contrast, Fig. 5c shows some images generated from a Gaussian-Gaussian RBM (without capsules) with 320 hidden units. We can see that this RBM suffers from severe problem of overlapping objects when generating new samples using Gibbs sampling, while our capsule RBM does not suffer from such symptom. We also tried smaller numbers of hidden variables in the Gaussian-Gaussian RBM, but this problem did not disappear. (Interestingly, an RBM, whose hidden states are instead discrete, usually does not have such issue.)

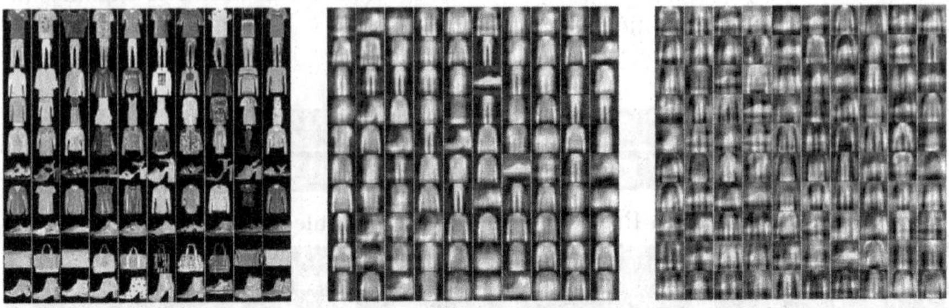

(a) Actual images. (b) Generated by cap-RBM. (c) Generated by RBM.

Fig. 5. Performance of capsule RBM on Fashion-MNIST.

Fig. 6a displays the capsule activities of our capsule RBM corresponding to actual test images in Fig. 5a. Again, the capsule activity spectra exhibit class-specific patterns (e.g. T-shirt/top (row 1) versus Trouser (row 2)). Close classes tend to share similar spectral patterns (e.g. Sandal (row 6) and Sneaker (row 8)). Furthermore, within each class, variations can be observed among capsule activity spectra of samples. When we ran the Gaussian-Gaussian RBM without capsules, the hidden representations in continuous values corresponding to images from Fig. 5a are totally not visually interpretable as shown in Fig. 6c. We trained a VAE with two convolutional layers and 20 latent variables, and find that its latent space corresponding to the same set of actual images does not exhibit consistent patterns. As in the experiments on MNIST data, we also draw the individual capsules' projective fields in Fig. 7 from which we straightforwardly observe shared and specific patterns.

3.2 Capsule HM

We experimented with a two-hidden-layer capsule HM with 40 capsules per layer on the MNIST data. Similarly we also investigated a two-hidden-layer capsule HM with 20 capsules per layer on the Fashion-MNIST data. The distributions, capsule size, and other hyperparameter settings are the same as in the capsule RBMs for the MNIST and Fashion-MNIST data, respectively. Layer-wise pre-training using capsule RBM is essential before running our wake-sleep fine-tuning algorithm. In each iteration of the wake-sleep algorithm, 20 steps are allowed for mean-filed approximation of capsule values. Figure 8 displays the learning curves (quantified by reconstruction errors) during fine-tuning. The pretraining at each layer converges quickly. Importantly, the fine-tuning algorithm is then able to gradually converge further without sign of overfitting.

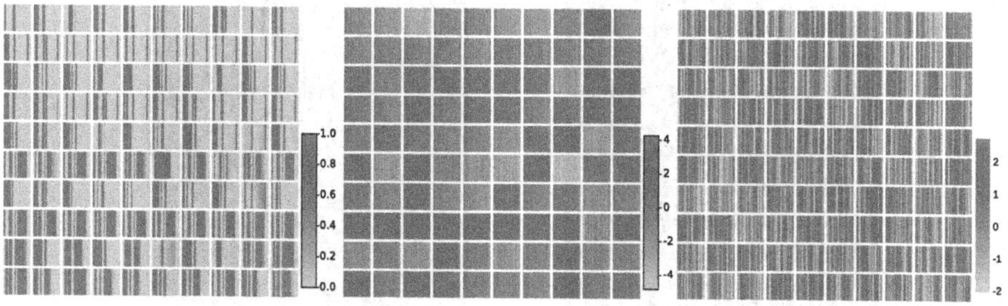

(a) Capsule RBM. (b) Gaussian RBM. (c) VAE.

Fig. 6. Comparison of hidden representations of Fashion-MNIST images from Fig. 5a. (a): Capsule activities in capsule RBM. (b): Hidden states in a Gaussian-Gaussian RBM without capsules. (c): Hidden states inferred by encoder in VAE.

(a) Projective field of each capsule.

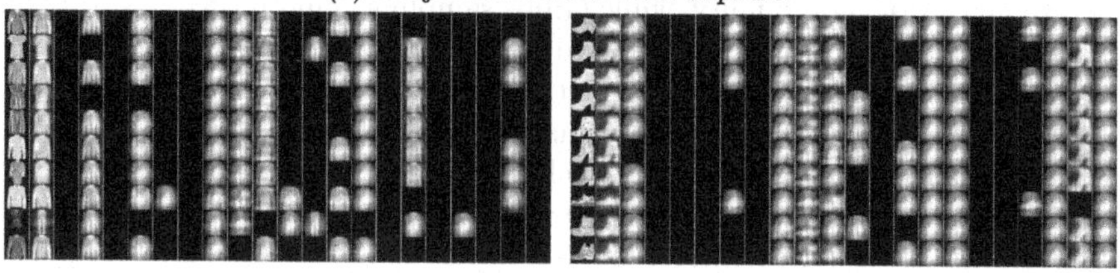

(b) Shirts. (c) Ankle boots.

Fig. 7. Visualizing the projective field of each capsule on Fashion-MNIST data. (a): Visualization of each capsule's projective field. b: Shirts approximated by a linear combination of a subset of capsules' projective fields. c: Ankle boots approximated by a linear combination of a subset of capsules' projective fields. In (b) and (c), the first columns are actual images; the second columns are corresponding reconstructed images; the rest columns are corresponding to projective fields of individual capsules.

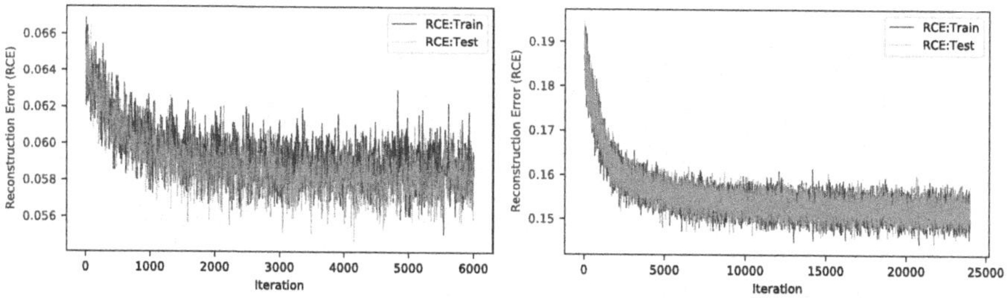

(a) Fine-tuning on MNIST. (b) Fine-tuning on Fashion-MNIST.

Fig. 8. Reconstruction errors in learning processes of capsule HM on MNIST and Fashion-MNIST data.

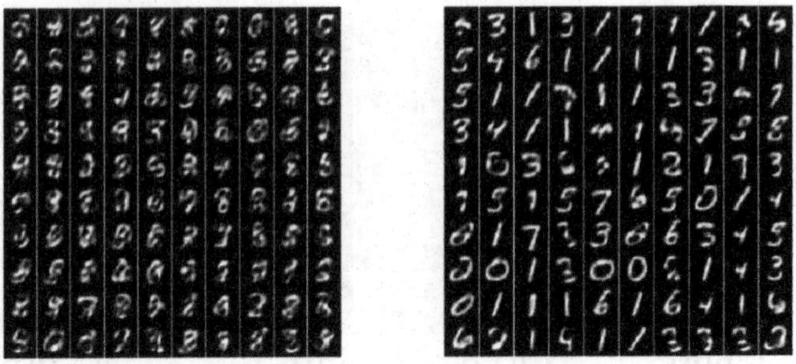

(a) Ancestral sampling. (b) Gibbs sampling.

Fig. 9. Generated images by capsule HM on MNIST.

After the models were trained, we compared two sampling methods, including ancestral sampling using only the sleep phase and Gibbs sampling through long wake-sleep loops. From Fig. 9a and b, we can see that ancestral sampling did not generate images of good quality, while Gibbs sampling could return much better images. This observation is consistent with research on VAE [25].

Figure 10a visualizes the capsule activity spectra inferred using the wake-phase of our algorithm on real MNIST images from Fig. 2a. The two-layer spectra exhibit class-specific patterns and intra-class differences. Interestingly, "1" is the simplest digit, but can activate most capsules at the first layer and least capsules at the second layer. Furthermore, similar classes (such as "7" and "9") could exhibit similar spectra. These observations corroborate that the expressions of capsules are indeed context-dependent. We also investigated capsule activities on the Fashion-MNIST data. Similar results were observed (see Fig. 10b).

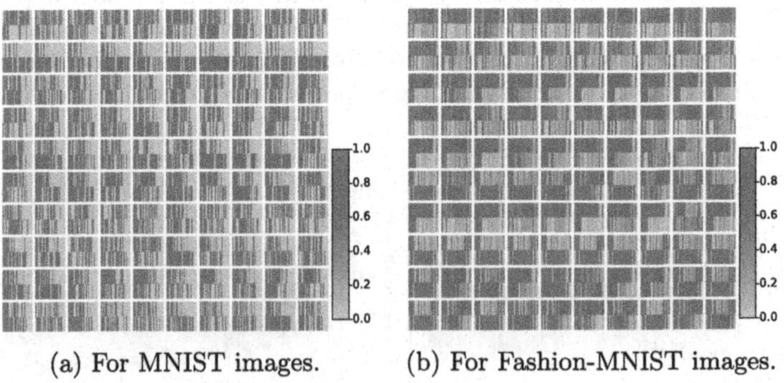

(a) For MNIST images. (b) For Fashion-MNIST images.

Fig. 10. Capsule activities in capsule HM for MNIST images in Fig. 2a and Fashion-MNIST images in Fig. 5a. Each cell in each panel has two rows corresponding to capsule spectra in the 1st (bottom) and 2nd (up) hidden layers.

4 Conclusions and Discussion

This study explored the use of stochastic capsules in shallow and deep generative models. We designed capsule RBMs and capsule HMs by replacing individual hidden units with stochastic capsules and devised new learning algorithms for them. Our empirical results showed that the models are capable of dynamically activating capsules depending on context, and the activity of capsules offers a new way to interpret representations of observations in the hidden space. Furthermore, we find that Gibbs sampling in capsule RBMs and capsule HMs is able to generate samples of good quality. The source code of our implementation is available at https://github.com/yifeng-li/cdgm.

Our current capsule RBM model is accidentally similar to spike-and-slab RBM (ssRBM) [3] which can be viewed as a special case of ours, while the motivations are quite different. The design of ssRBM is motivated by the deficiency of Gaussian-Bernoulli RBM, while our development of capsule RBM is inspired by deterministic capsule nets. In our current design, a collection of active capsules at layer $l+1$ could interact with a capsule at layer l. It would be interesting to enforce a tree structure in the top-down activation path. It can be realized by assigning an activation vector to each capsule at layer l to indicate which capsules at layer $l+1$ could activate the current capsule. This vector should follow multinoulli or multinomial distribution, so that similar capsules at layer l could dynamically form clusters for parent capsules at layer $l+1$. This models transformation in DGMs, in contrast to deterministic capsules introduced in [12,20]. The benefit of such a modification is beyond interpretation of the hidden representations in a dynamic hierarchical activation tree, because more importantly it also offers to generate better samples due to the modelling of transformation.

Our ideas will be tested on more complex data. Sophisticated design of the input layer may be necessary for spatially or temporally correlated data. In the case of large images, stochastic convolution and deconvolution components shall be used as in transforming auto-encoder [9]. We devised a tied wake-sleep algorithm to learn the model parameters in capsule HM, and obtained promising results. It is possible to develop better learning algorithms for capsule DGMs in inspiration of recent ideas for DGMs, such as weighted wake-sleep algorithm [2], neural variational inference and learning algorithm [18], and variational autoencoder based algorithms [13,19]. Reconstruction error was used in this paper to monitor the learning progress. The variational lower bound of likelihood can be computed using Eq. 22 for comparing various capsule DGMs. However, it may be time-consuming because the log-partition function of the joint distribution of each intermediate layer needs to be estimated by using annealed importance sampling methods for exponential family undirected models [17,21].

Acknowledgement. This project was supported by the NRC New Beginnings Ideation Fund. The authors would like to thank the anonymous reviewers for valuable comments.

References

1. Bengio, Y., Ducharme, R., Vincent, P., Jauvin, C.: A neural probabilistic language model. J. Mach. Learn. Res. **2**, 1137–1155 (2003)
2. Bornschein, J., Bengio, Y.: Reweighted wake-sleep. In: International Conference on Learning Representations (2015)
3. Courville, A., Bergstra, J., Bengio, Y.: A spike and slab restricted Boltzmann machine. In: International Conference on Artificial Intelligence and Statistics, pp. 233–241 (2011)
4. Dayan, P., Hinton, G., Neal, R., Zemel, R.: The Helmholtz machine. Neural Comput. **7**, 1022–1037 (1995). https://doi.org/10.1162/neco.1995.7.5.889
5. Fodor, J., Pylyshyn, Z.: Connectionism and cognitive architecture: a critical analysis. Cognition **28**(1–2), 3–71 (1988). https://doi.org/10.1016/0010-0277(88)90031-5
6. Goodfellow, I., et al.: Generative adversarial nets. In: Advances in Neural Information Processing Systems, pp. 2672–2680 (2014)
7. Hinton, G.: Aetherial symbols. In: AAAI Spring Symposium on Knowledge Representation and Reasoning: Integrating Symbolic and Neural Approaches (2015)
8. Hinton, G., et al.: Deep neural networks for acoustic modeling in speech recognition: the shared views of four research groups. IEEE Signal Process. Mag. **29**(6), 82–97 (2012). https://doi.org/10.1109/MSP.2012.2205597
9. Hinton, G., Krizhevsky, A., Wang, S.: Transforming auto-encoder. In: International Conference on Artificial Neural Networks, pp. 44–51 (2011). https://doi.org/10.1007/978-3-642-21735-7_6
10. Hinton, G., McClelland, J., Rumelhart, D.: Distributed representations. In: Rumelhart, D., McClelland, J. (eds.) Parallel Distributed Processing: Explorations in the Microstructure of Cognition, pp. 77–109. MIT Press, Cambridge (1986)
11. Hinton, G., Osindero, S., Teh, Y.: A fast learning algorithm for deep belief nets. Neural Comput. **18**, 1527–1554 (2006). https://doi.org/10.1162/neco.2006.18.7.1527
12. Hinton, G., Sabour, S., Frosst, N.: Matrix capsules with EM routing. In: International Conference on Learning Representations (2018)
13. Kingma, D., Welling, M.: Auto-encoding variational Bayes. In: International Conference on Learning Representations (2014)
14. Krizhevsky, A., Sutskever, I., Hinton, G.E.: ImageNet classification with deep convolutional neural networks. In: Advances in Neural Information Processing Systems, pp. 1097–1105 (2012)
15. LeCun, Y., et al.: Backpropagation applied to handwritten zip code recognition. Neural Comput. **1**(4), 541–551 (1989). https://doi.org/10.1162/neco.1989.1.4.541
16. Li, Y., Zhu, X.: Exploring Helmholtz machine and deep belief net in the exponential family perspective. In: ICML 2018 Workshop on Theoretical Foundations and Applications of Deep Generative Models (2018)
17. Li, Y., Zhu, X.: Exponential family restricted Boltzmann machines and annealed importance sampling. In: International Joint Conference on Neural Networks, pp. 39–48 (2018). https://doi.org/10.1109/IJCNN.2018.8489413
18. Mnih, A., Gregor, K.: Neural variational inference and learning in belief networks. In: International Conference on Machine Learning, pp. II-1791–II-1799 (2014)
19. Rezende, D.J., Mohamed, S., Wierstra, D.: Stochastic backpropagation and approximate inference in deep generative models. In: International Conference on Machine Learning, pp. II-1278–II-1286 (2014)

20. Sabour, S., Frosst, N., Hinton, G.: Dynamic routing between capsules. In: Neural Information Processing Systems, pp. 3856–3866 (2017)
21. Salakhutdinov, R.: Learning and evaluating Boltzmann machines. Department of Computer Science, University of Toronto, Toronto, Canada, Technical report (2008)
22. Tieleman, T.: Training restricted Boltzmann machines using approximations to the likelihood gradient. In: International Conference on Machine Learning, pp. 1064–1071 (2008). https://doi.org/10.1145/1390156.1390290
23. Welling, M., Rosen-Zvi, M., Hinton, G.: Exponential family harmoniums with an application to information retrieval. In: Advances in Neural Information Processing Systems, pp. 1481–1488 (2005)
24. Xiao, H., Rasul, K., Vollgraf, R.: Fashion-MNIST: a novel image dataset for benchmarking machine learning algorithms. ArXiv p. arXiv:1708.07747v2 (2017)
25. Zhao, S., Song, J., Ermon, S.: Towards a deeper understanding of variational autoencoding models. arXiv p. arXiv:1702.08658 (2017)

Evaluating CNNs on the Gestalt Principle of Closure

Gregor Ehrensperger(✉), Sebastian Stabinger, and Antonio Rodríguez Sánchez

University of Innsbruck, Technikerstraße 21a, 6020 Innsbruck, Austria
gregor.ehrensperger@gmx.com, sebastian@stabinger.name
antonio.rodriguez-sanchez@uibk.ac.at
https://iis.uibk.ac.at/

Abstract. Deep convolutional neural networks (CNNs) are widely known for their outstanding performance in classification and regression tasks over high-dimensional data. This made them a popular and powerful tool for a large variety of applications in industry and academia. Recent publications show that seemingly easy classification tasks (for humans) can be very challenging for state of the art CNNs. An attempt to describe how humans perceive visual elements is given by the Gestalt principles. In this paper we evaluate `AlexNet` and `GoogLeNet` regarding their performance on classifying the correctness of the well known Kanizsa triangles and triangles where sections of the edges were removed. Both types heavily rely on the Gestalt principle of closure. Therefore we created various datasets containing valid as well as invalid variants of the described triangles. Our findings suggest that perceiving objects by utilizing the principle of closure is very challenging for the applied network architectures but they appear to adapt to the effect of closure.

Keywords: Convolutional neural network · CNN · Gestalt principles · Principle of closure

1 Introduction and Related Work

Convolutional neural networks have gained enormous interest in industry and research over the past years because they provide outstanding performance in many visual classification tasks. The basic architecture of a CNN was first introduced by LeCun et al. [3] in 1989. Almost a decade later LeCun et al. [4] created `LeNet-5` which was able to classify handwritten digits with an accuracy exceeding 99% on the MNIST dataset. In 2012 Krizhevsky et al. [2] managed to train a deep CNN – later known as `AlexNet` – to classify 1.2 million images into 1000 different classes with an impressive top-5 test error rate of 15%. In 2014 Szegedy et al. [7] introduced the famous `Inception` architectures which are also known as `GoogLeNet` in hommage to `LeNet`. In this paper we experiment with `AlexNet` and `GoogLeNet`[1].

[1] In our case: `Inception v3`.

I. V. Tetko et al. (Eds.): ICANN 2019, LNCS 11727, pp. 296–301, 2019.
https://doi.org/10.1007/978-3-030-30487-4_23

Gestalt psychology explains different perceptual phenomena. In 1923 Wertheimer [8] described a set of rules which are essential for our perception of objects, the so-called *Gestalt principles.* One of these principles is given by the *principle of closure*, which states that humans tend to fill visual gaps to perceive objects as being whole, even when fragments are missing. Another principle is given by the *principle of similarity* which states that shapes that are similar to each other tend to be perceived as a unit. Stabinger et al. [5] could show that neither `LeNet` nor `GoogLeNet` are capable of comparing shapes. Further experiments were performed in the context of the *principle of symmetry*, where Stabinger et al. [6] found variations of a dataset which seem to be at the border of what CNNs can do. Kim et al. [1] just recently adapted tools which are used in psychology to study human brains to analyse the neural responses within CNNs to see whether they utilize the *principle of closure.* They showed that under certain circumstances neural networks do respond to closure effects. In this paper we also experiment with the *principle of closure* by evaluating the ability of the given CNNs to decide whether an image contains a valid or an invalid Kanizsa triangle. Our goal is to gain more insight from a practical point of view into how challenging it is for a CNN to exploit the closure effect and how well it performs.

2 Evaluating CNNs on Datasets Utilizing the Principle of Closure

We decided to use Kanizsa triangles for our datasets since they are commonly used to describe the law of closure. For our tests we generated various datasets with 50.000 images each[2]. One half of each dataset shows valid Kanizsa triangles, the other half invalid variants of the Kanizsa triangle. We created the following scenarios (see Fig. 1).

1. **OFFS**: Translate one of the vertices by a random offset[3].
2. **ANGLE**: Change the opening angle within one vertex.
3. **ROT**: Rotation of one to three vertices by a random angle.
4. **COMB**: Each invalid Kanizsa triangle contains exactly one of the errors out of the set {**ROT**, **ANGLE**, **OFFS**} (picked uniformly random).

We created the datasets with the following parameters and conditions:

- The radii of the circles were chosen by picking a value from 16 to 35 px uniformly random for each image.
- Each angle of the triangle has to be larger than 25° to prevent degenerated triangles.
- Each vertex has to be fully visible (no cut off at the image border).
- The invalid triangles within the **OFFS** dataset were created by translating one of the vertices by 28 to 56 px. It is ensured that no vertices are overlapping or moving outside the visible image region after applying the translation.

[2] 30.000 training, 10.000 validation and 10.000 test images; dimension: 256 × 256 px.

[3] To maximize the visual error, the offset is applied in the direction of the connecting line of the other two vertices.

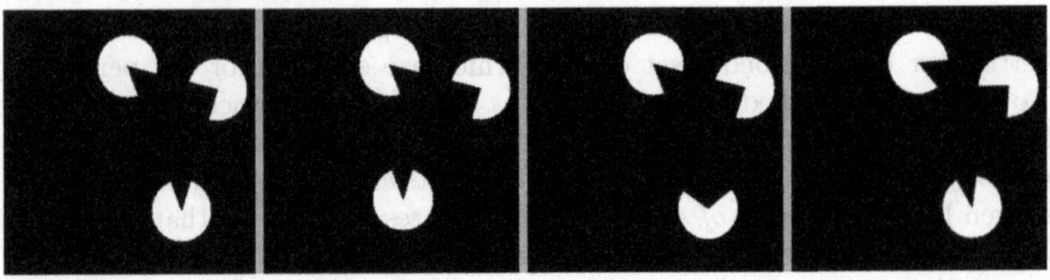

Fig. 1. Illustration of the different datasets. From left to right: Kanizsa triangle without error, **OFFS**, **ANGLE**, **ROT**.

- The invalid triangles within the **ANGLE** dataset were created by opening the angle of one corner by 25 to 35° (picked uniformly random).
- The invalid triangles within the **ROT** dataset were created by rotating one or more of the vertices by 8 to 20° (picked uniformly random).

2.1 Evaluating the CNNs

It took `AlexNet` 140 and `GoogLeNet` 99 epochs[4] to correctly classify 95% of the validation set of **COMB**, which suggests that this problem is rather challenging for the investigated CNN architectures. As a reference we used a subset[5] of the MNIST dataset to train `AlexNet` and `GoogLeNet`. It took `AlexNet` only one epoch and `GoogLeNet` twelve epochs to achieve a test error rate of less than 5%. Please note that one needs to distinguish between ten different classes in the MNIST dataset, while the datasets in this paper only consist of two classes.

To gain more insight, we split the problem into its components and look at the number of epochs the CNNs need to accomplish an accuracy of at least 95% on the validation set[6]:

1. **OFFS**: `AlexNet` 27 epochs, `GoogLeNet` 188 epochs.
2. **ANGLE**: `AlexNet` 12 epochs, `GoogLeNet` 6 epochs.
3. **ROT**: `AlexNet` 6 epochs, `GoogLeNet` 5 epochs.[7]

We observe that `GoogLeNet` needs many epochs to reach sufficient accuracy on **OFFS**, and `AlexNet` requires significantly more epochs to learn to classify **OFFS** than to correctly classify **ANGLE** and **ROT**. Furthermore, we want to

[4] All CNNs were trained using NVIDIA DIGITS https://developer.nvidia.com/digits with the Torch backend and def. settings: fixed learning rate = 0.01, solver = SGD.

[5] While the original MNIST dataset contains 60.000 training images and 10.000 validation images, we moved 10.000 training images to a test image set, and deleted 20.000 of the training images while not changing the distribution of the images among the classes. We did this to be comparable with our own datasets.

[6] Trained multiple times; lowest results are displayed.

[7] In further experiments we also worked with a set where only one of the three vertices was rotated. `AlexNet` needed at least 109 epochs to be able to classify 95% correctly, while `GoogLeNet` needed 6 epochs.

point out that `AlexNet` needed many trials before being able to find a satisfying classifier on the problems involving angles, while `GoogLeNet` needed many trials on the **OFFS** dataset.

3 Interpretation and Further Results

Although the problems seem to be very similar at first glance, **ANGLE** and **ROT** are locally solvable. Basically it suffices to detect the opening angle and its orientation for each vertex. Then, without considering the position of the vertices, comparing these features leads to the classification result. For **OFFS** the CNN needs to use higher-level features since it is not able to decide locally anymore. To make this more evident, if we consider the classification matrices in Table 1, we observe that:

Table 1. Summary of test error rates on the Kanizsa triangle datasets (in %). We trained the CNNs until they converged and evaluated the test sets with a model where the losses on the train and validation set became more stable. The number of epochs that were required to reach this state are indicated in the second column.

	# epochs	tested on / trained on	COMB	OFFS	ANGLE	ROT
AlexNet	142	**COMB**	3.5	11.7	0.7	0
AlexNet	80	**OFFS**	6.2	0.7	6.4	10.1
AlexNet	20	**ANGLE**	15.7	48.8	1.2	4.8
AlexNet	8	**ROT**	15.3	50	4.3	0.3
GoogLeNet	129	**COMB**	0.3	0.8	0	0
GoogLeNet	204	**OFFS**	6.3	0.7	1.4	14.5
GoogLeNet	8	**ANGLE**	14	50	0	0
GoogLeNet	6	**ROT**	13.7	50	1	0.1

1. CNNs trained on **ANGLE** are also able to classify **ROT** and vice versa, but they are not able to classify **OFFS** above chance.
2. CNNs trained on **OFFS** are able to classify **ANGLE**, as well as **ROT** above chance although they did not encounter any of these problems before.

To further analyse this behaviour with another stimulus class, we created datasets with triangles where we removed some sections of the edges. We therefore used the same parameters as described in Sect. 2. The lengths of the visible parts of the edges were chosen by picking a value from 16 to 3 px (uniformly random) for each image. We again created the scenarios **COMB**$^+$, **OFFS**$^+$, **ANGLE**$^+$ and **ROT**$^+$ as illustrated in Fig. 2.

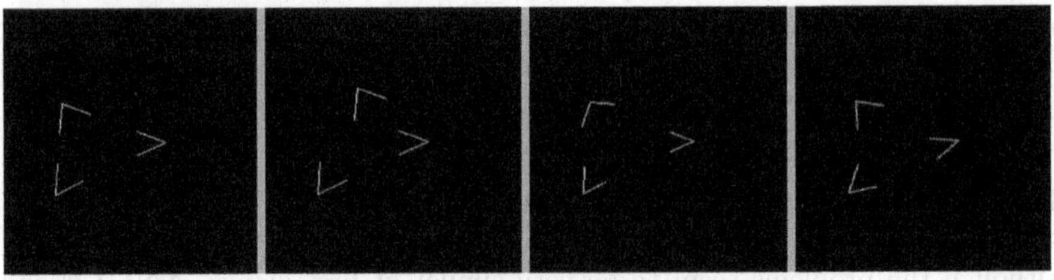

Fig. 2. Illustration of the different incomplete triangle datasets. From left to right: Incomplete triangle without error, **OFFS**$^{+}$, **ANGLE**$^{+}$, **ROT**$^{+}$.

The classification matrices in Table 2 show that CNNs trained on **OFFS**$^{+}$ are able to classify **ANGLE**$^{+}$, as well as **ROT**$^{+}$ significantly above chance. But we also observe that CNNs trained on **ANGLE**$^{+}$ are hardly able to generalize the results to also classify **ROT**$^{+}$ correctly and vice versa. Furthermore `AlexNet` trained on **ANGLE**$^{+}$ also managed to classify some examples of **OFFS**$^{+}$ dataset correctly.

Table 2. Summary of test error rates on the incomplete triangle datasets (in %).

	# epochs	trained on \ tested on	COMB^{+}	OFFS^{+}	ANGLE^{+}	ROT^{+}
`AlexNet`	42	**COMB**$^{+}$	0.9	2	0.8	0.5
`AlexNet`	39	**OFFS**$^{+}$	14.8	1	15.3	13.2
`AlexNet`	25	**ANGLE**$^{+}$	28.9	43.6	2.2	47.9
`AlexNet`	25	**ROT**$^{+}$	32.2	50	50	0.1
`GoogLeNet`	42	**COMB**$^{+}$	0.8	2.3	0.4	0.3
`GoogLeNet`	175	**OFFS**$^{+}$	11.9	0.3	21.5	10
`GoogLeNet`	37	**ANGLE**$^{+}$	26.9	50.1	0.6	37.4
`GoogLeNet`	12	**ROT**$^{+}$	32.2	50	50	0

4 Conclusion

Our findings suggest that in order to discriminate classes in which the positions of the objects matter, the CNNs need to detect higher-level features and generalize. Apparently, CNNs trained on such a problem set also have significantly lower test error rates on previously unseen perturbations of the data, which suggests that – in our case – they are exploiting the principle of closure. Our experiments show that training on these features is quite challenging, needing significantly more epochs than training on the MNIST dataset. We believe that further analysis of the performance of CNNs in the context of the Gestalt principles is a promising area for future research to gain a better understanding of the differences and similarities between human and artificial neural network perception.

Acknowledgment. We want to thank the anonymous reviewers for their constructive suggestions and helpful comments.

References

1. Kim, B., Reif, E., Wattenberg, M., Bengio, S.: Do neural networks show gestalt phenomena? An exploration of the law of closure. arXiv preprint (2019)
2. Krizhevsky, A., Sutskever, I., Hinton, G.E.: Imagenet classification with deep convolutional neural networks. In: Advances in Neural Information Processing Systems (2012)
3. LeCun, Y., et al.: Backpropagation applied to handwritten zip code recognition. Neural Comput. **1**(4), 541–551 (1989). https://doi.org/10.1162/neco.1989.1.4.541
4. LeCun, Y., Bottou, L., Bengio, Y., Haffner, P.: Gradient-based learning applied to document recognition. Proc. IEEE **86**(11), 2278–2324 (1998). https://doi.org/10.1109/5.726791
5. Stabinger, S., Rodríguez-Sánchez, A., Piater, J.: 25 years of CNNs: can we compare to human abstraction capabilities? In: Villa, A.E.P., Masulli, P., Pons Rivero, A.J. (eds.) ICANN 2016. LNCS, vol. 9887, pp. 380–387. Springer, Cham (2016). https://doi.org/10.1007/978-3-319-44781-0_45
6. Stabinger, S., Rodríguez-Sánchez, A.: Evaluation of deep learning on an abstract image classification dataset. In: Proceedings of the IEEE International Conference on Computer Vision, pp. 2767–2772 (2017). https://doi.org/10.1109/iccvw.2017.325
7. Szegedy, C., et al.: Going deeper with convolutions. In: Proceedings of the IEEE Conference on Computer Vision and Pattern Recognition, pp. 1–9 (2015). https://doi.org/10.1109/cvpr.2015.7298594
8. Wertheimer, M.: Laws of organization in perceptual forms. In: A Source Book of Gestalt Psychology, pp. 71–88, London (1938). https://doi.org/10.1037/11496-005

Recovering Localized Adversarial Attacks

Jan Philip Göpfert[1(✉)], Heiko Wersing[2], and Barbara Hammer[1]

[1] Bielefeld University, Research Institute for Cognition and Robotics,
Universitätsstraße 25, 33615 Bielefeld, Germany
jgoepfert@techfak.de
[2] Honda Research Institute Europe GmbH,
Carl-Legien-Straße 30, 63065 Offenbach, Germany

Abstract. Deep convolutional neural networks have achieved great successes over recent years, particularly in the domain of computer vision. They are fast, convenient, and – thanks to mature frameworks – relatively easy to implement and deploy. However, their reasoning is hidden inside a black box, in spite of a number of proposed approaches that try to provide human-understandable explanations for the predictions of neural networks. It is still a matter of debate which of these explainers are best suited for which situations, and how to quantitatively evaluate and compare them [1]. In this contribution, we focus on the capabilities of explainers for convolutional deep neural networks in an extreme situation: a setting in which humans and networks fundamentally disagree. Deep neural networks are susceptible to adversarial attacks that deliberately modify input samples to mislead a neural network's classification, without affecting how a human observer interprets the input. Our goal with this contribution is to evaluate explainers by investigating whether they can identify adversarially attacked regions of an image. In particular, we quantitatively and qualitatively investigate the capability of three popular explainers of classifications – classic salience, guided backpropagation, and LIME – with respect to their ability to identify regions of attack as the explanatory regions for the (incorrect) prediction in representative examples from image classification. We find that LIME outperforms the other explainers.

1 Introduction

In recent years, deep learning has led to astonishing achievements in several domains, including gaming, machine translation, speech processing, and computer vision [2]. The deep neural networks involved act mostly as black boxes, and as a result they are often met with a certain wariness, especially in safety-critical environments, matters where fairness is important, or when rigorous explanations of a decision are legally required. A number of approaches have been proposed which aim to explain the decisions of neural networks to human

This work was supported by Honda Research Institute Europe GmbH, Offenbach am Main, Germany.

I. V. Tetko et al. (Eds.): ICANN 2019, LNCS 11727, pp. 302–311, 2019.
https://doi.org/10.1007/978-3-030-30487-4_24

users. They include methods that determine particularly relevant input regions for a certain decision, methods that locally approximate complex decisions via human-understandable sparse surrogates, classifier visualization techniques, or more general methods that supplement automated decisions by a notion of their domain of expertise, and explicit reject options whenever their validity is questionable [3–6].

Explainers need to address two contradictory goals: they need to preserve the explained (highly nonlinear) model's behavior as much as possible, but simplify it such that it becomes accessible to humans in the form of an explanation. In practice, it is unclear in how far established explainers master this compromise. One problem is that, given an input and a prediction, it is not necessarily clear what *a correct explanation* for the prediction should look like, because the ground truth of which features truly influence the network's prediction is unknown. It might be tempting to judge explanatory methods on whether they succeed in identifying features that a human observer thinks *should* be relevant to the classification, but the existence of adversarial examples shows that the reasoning of humans and neural networks can differ dramatically. In this contribution, we exploit the existence of adversarial examples, using localized adversarial attacks to construct pairs of inputs and predictions together with ground-truth information about which image pixels determine the prediction of the network.

Adversarial attacks are an unsolved challenge for deep neural networks – and more generally for black-box approaches that aim to classify high-dimensional data as is present in computer vision. These attacks result in adversarial examples, which are deliberately generated to fool a classifier. Depending on the specifics of the attack, it may or may not be recognizable by humans, with noticeable artifacts being produced in some cases [7]. In any case, a proper adversarial attack modifies a given input in such a way that the attacked neural network estimates a different (wrong) label, while a human user would assign the same label to the modified input as to the original input.

In this contribution, we use adversarial examples as an extreme setting in which we can investigate the capabilities of explainers with regards to what makes an input adversarial. In other words, we want to understand how adversarial attacks affect explanations of predictions of deep neural networks and make use of them to produce ground-truth explanations, which allows a quantitative evaluation of explainers. For this we explain adversarial attacks in Sect. 2. Then, we take a look at three popular explainers for neural networks in Sect. 3, namely:

- *classic salience* [8] maps, which are based on gradients propagated through a neural network
- *guided backpropagation* [9], which also takes into account the representations that are implicitly learned by neural networks, and
- *LIME* [4], which locally approximates the usually highly nonlinear neural network by a sparse, linear, human-understandable surrogate model.

In Sect. 4, we define the setting and evaluate the behavior of these methods within the field of computer vision: we quantitatively evaluate in how far methods that explain the decision of deep neural networks can locate where an adversarial attack has modified an image. We finish with a conclusion in Sect. 5.

(a) (b) (c)

Fig. 1. An adversarial attack: The original image (a) is classified *flower*. After a localized adversarial attack is performed the resulting adversarial example (b) is classified *wolf spider*. The difference (c) between the two images is seemingly random noise. It is confined to one of the blossoms in the image.

2 Adversarial Attacks

Given a classifier f, a sample x and a label $y = f(x)$ that f assigns to x, the goal of an adversarial attack is to modify x just enough such that f assigns a different label z to the modified sample x', where $z \neq y$ can be *any* other label (in which case the attack is called *untargeted*) or a *specific* label (in which case the attack is called *targeted*). In the simplest setting, f is known to the attacker in its entirety. Black-box attacks, on the other hand, attack deep networks without requiring access to f itself. Instead, they use a surrogate that is inferred from a representative training set. In this work we assume that f is available. Commonly, an untargeted attack on a sample x is formalized as the optimization problem

$$\min \|x' - x\| \quad \text{such that} \quad f(x') \neq f(x), x' \in C(x), \tag{1}$$

where C denotes additional constraints on the adversarial example x', such as box constraints or sparsity. Early approaches aim for an optimization of this problem by standard solvers such as LBFGS, while more recent approaches vary the objective and optimization strategies; software suites available include *foolbox* [10] and *cleverhans* [11].

For our evaluation, we need to efficiently perform targeted adversarial attacks constrained to varying regions within a number of different input images. This process yields adversarial examples together with ground truth as to which region in an example is responsible for its (mis-)classification. We use a targeted, iterative variant of the *Fast Gradient Sign Method* (FGSM) [12], the *Basic Iterative Method* (BIM) [13]. BIM, just as FGSM, relies on the fact that adversarial attacks can be observed also for linear mappings in high dimensional input spaces. Based on this rationale, attacks move an input x along a linear approximation of the objective $J(x, y)$ of the network, adding the change $\epsilon \cdot \text{sign}[\nabla_x J(x, y)]$.

Localized Attacks

We want to investigate whether an explanation can identify the attack as the reason for the prediction of the neural network. For this purpose, we use a modified version of BIM, a localized attack [7], for which a quantitative evaluation of the question, whether an explainer identified the right region, is straightforward: we implement an additional constraint $C(x)$ by allowing x' to deviate from the original input image x only in a specified region of x. This enables us to evaluate the explanation of the resulting adversarial example by measuring the overlap of the pixels (i. e. features) that constitute the explanation with those within the attack region.

3 Explaining Predictions

There exist different methods to explain predictions as produced by black-box mechanisms such as deep networks. Explanations can be either local for the decision $f(x)$ for input x, or they can be global for the function f. They typically focus on either features or prototypes as the basic "language" to explain the model. Here, we are interested in explaining adversarial examples generated by changing a limited number of features. Hence, we focus on local explanations of $f(x)$ where x is an adversarial example, and use for methods that provide a set of features which best explain this decision. Our quantitative evaluation of the results relies on the overlap of features which we changed during generation of an adversarial example x, and the set of features that are used to explain the decision $f(x)$. We compare three different local explanation strategies with respect to their ability in identifying the features where attacks have taken place.

Classic Salience. Salience maps were proposed e. g. by Selvaraju et al. [8] as a visual feedback about the most relevant regions of an image for a specific classification. Essentially, an input feature x_i is highlighted according to its relevance for the classification as given by the gradient $\partial J(x, y)/\partial x_i$.

Guided Backpropagation. One of the reasons for the success of deep convolutional networks is attributed to their ability to learn higher level feature representations of the object as represented within the activation of the hidden layers [14]. A plain gradient as used for salience maps does not focus on these features because it propagates back both positive and negative contributions of the gradients. Guided backpropagation [9] circumvents this problem by truncating negative gradients during backpropagation.

LIME. Ribeiro et al. [4] proposed *Local Interpretable Model-agnostic Explanations* (LIME) as an agnostic method that does not use the specific form of the classifying function f that it explains. It tries to approximate the function f locally around x by an interpretable surrogate in the form of a sparse model in features $\tilde{x}_i$ derived from x. For this purpose, examples are generated around x by jittering, and labeled according to f. The resulting training set is used to infer a sparse, explainable, linear model, which describes f locally around x. For image classification, the basic features $\tilde{x}_i$ are typically superpixels, which are obtained from a perceptual grouping of the image pixels.

4 Experimental Evaluation

We evaluate the information which is provided by these explanations about adversarial attacks for the popular deep neural network *Inception v3* [15] as provided by pytorch's torchvision package. We are interested in two research questions:

R1 Is it possible to uncover substantial information about the location of adversarial attacks in an image by means of explainers?
R2 If the answer is yes, are there substantial differences with regards to the effectiveness of different explanation strategies as introduced above?

Generating Adversarial Examples. To guarantee that our test images were not part of the attacked network's training set, we use crops of 112 images that we took ourselves. For each attack, we set the constraint $C(x)$ such that only a relatively small region within the input image is modified. We obtain those regions by automatic segmentation using the graph-based algorithm proposed by [16] – during this process, semantics are not explicitly taken into account, and regions are instead constructed based on color statistics. When a region contains exactly one object, the attack can resemble the replacement of said object – to illustrate this, we manually segment a small number of input images, e. g. the one seen in Fig. 1. Out of every original input image we generate up to 10 adversarial examples via BIM restricted to the 10 largest regions (Fig. 2). The same target label *wolf spider* is used for every attack. If an attack is not successful or ceases to progress after a certain number of iterations, we discard the attempt. In total, we produce 608 adversarial examples. With this setup we can guarantee that there exist different regions of the same image, which are attacked and should be uncovered, i.e. finding the location of an attack is a non-trivial task, which is not already determined by the image itself.

Evaluation of Explanations. We explain each adversarial example using Classic Salience, Guided Backpropagation, and LIME. LIME segments the adversarial example into disjoint superpixels and ranks those by their influence on the prediction. We look at the 20 most influential superpixels $S_1, \ldots, S_{20}$ and see how well the partial union $\bigcup_{i=1}^{n} S_i$ for $n = 1, \ldots, 20$ recovers the constraint region C.

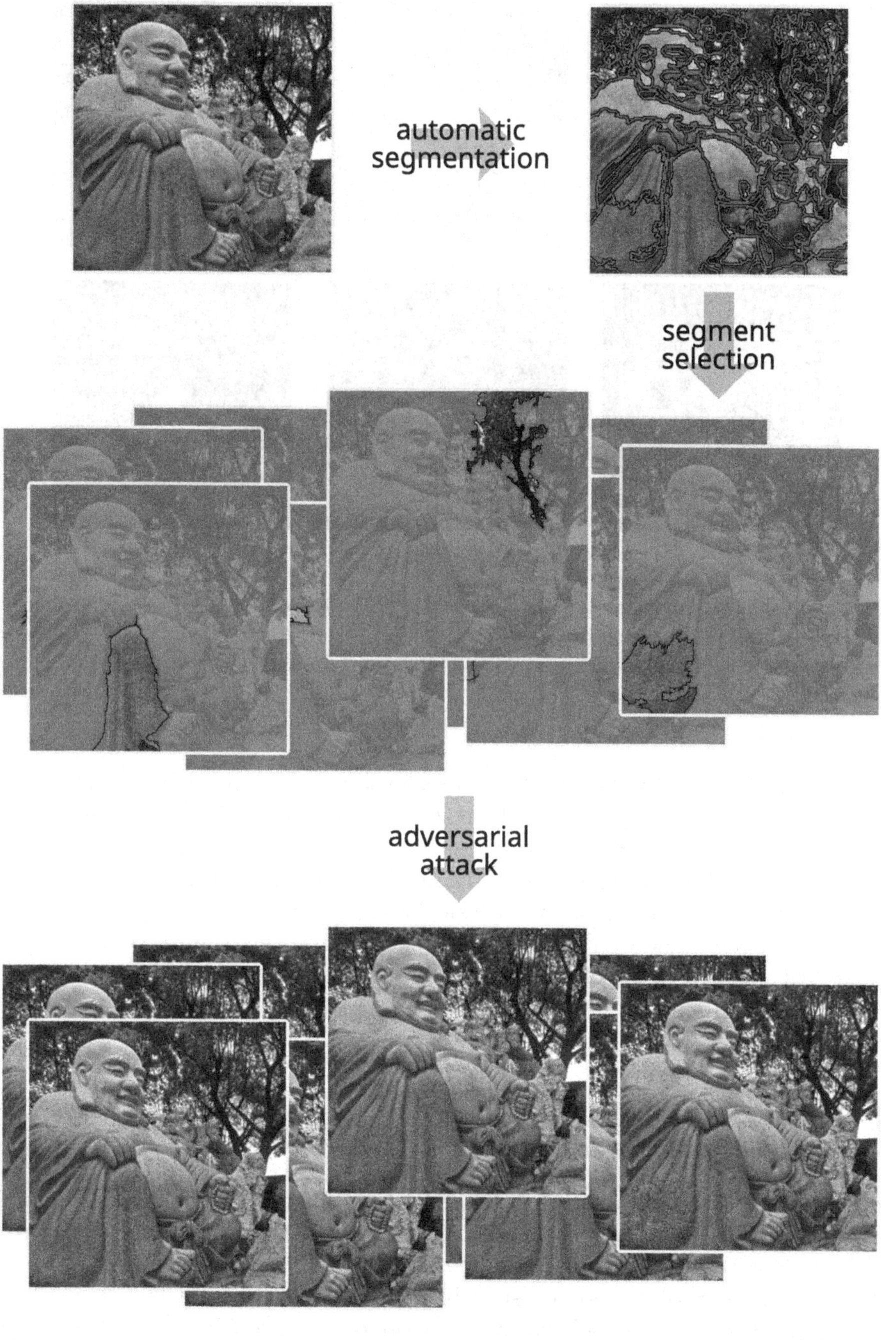

Fig. 2. Overview of our process of generating multiple adversarial examples via localized adversarial attacks from a single input image. First, the image is automatically segmented. Then, the largest segments are chosen and individually used to constrain an adversarial attack.

Fig. 3. Partial explanations for the adversarial example from Fig. 1 for classic salience (d), guided backpropagation (e), and LIME (f). (c) is the ground truth. White indicates pixels relevant for the classification. All explanations contain the same number of white pixels.

For Classic Salience and Guided Backpropagation we sort the pixels in the adversarial example by the ℓ_1 norm of the respective gradients, i. e. by their influence on the prediction. In order to compare the results to those produced by LIME, we look at the $|\bigcup_{i=1}^{n} S_i|$ pixels with the highest influence (Fig. 3). In total, we compare 12 160 explanations for each of the three explainers.

To determine how well such a set of pixels P recovers the region C we calculate the Jaccard Index of the two sets

$$J(P, C) = \frac{P \cap C}{P \cup C} \tag{2}$$

and a likeness

$$H(P, C) = 1 - \frac{\text{Ham}(P, C)}{N} \tag{3}$$

which we base on the Hamming distance between P and C interpreted as binary masks over the entire image with N pixels in total. Both values are between zero and one, with one indicating a perfect match.

LIME distinguishes between superpixels that strongly contribute towards a certain prediction and those that strongly oppose it. We only take into account the former, and in order to interpret the salience maps accordingly, we discard negative gradients in the input layer before we calculate the gradients' magnitudes.

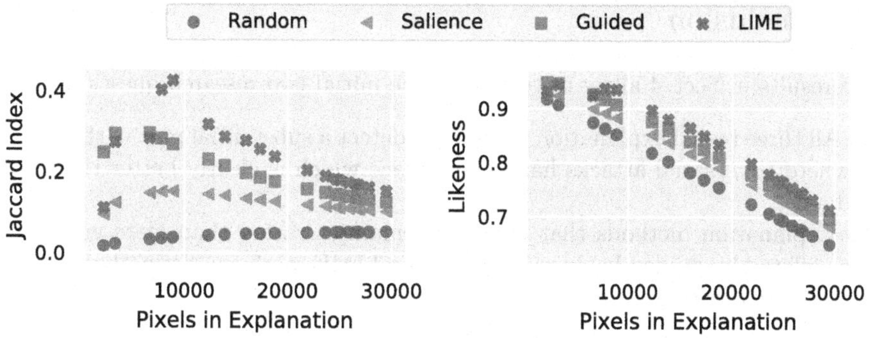

Fig. 4. Jaccard index and Hamming-based likeness for different explanation sizes for the adversarial example from Fig. 1.

Results. When we compare the explanations provided by LIME with the ground truth, if for a certain $n \in \{1, \ldots, 20\}$ the partial union $\bigcup_{i=1}^{n} S_i$ contains all ground-truth pixels, larger unions can only perform worse. We see this in Fig. 4, where the best Jaccard index is reached early for a relatively small number of pixels in the explanation. Classic salience and guided backpropagation behave comparably. To demonstrate that the obtained values are indeed meaningful, we include a random baseline – selecting pixels at random yields a very low Jaccard index.

Note that the default segmentation algorithm inside LIME differs from the one we use to automatically determine regions we attack. Hence, it is almost impossible for LIME to achieve perfect scores.

To compare all three explainers with regards to the entire 608 adversarial examples, we rank them according to the Jaccard index and Hamming index for each example from 1 (best) to 3 (worst). The mean ranks are listed in Table 1. LIME outperforms the other two methods, even though those are based on gradients, just as the adversarial attacks.

All explainers include pixels outside the ground-truth region in their explanations. This is especially noticable for LIME, where entire contiguous segments are selected. This is to be expected, because the neural network's prediction is reached considering the entire input image. Our attacks only change the prediction from one label to a different one. Pixels outside the attacked region can still contribute to both.

Table 1. Mean ranks for all three explainers over all 12 160 explanations with respect to the Jaccard index and the Hamming-based likeness. 1.0 is best, 3.0 is worst.

Explainer	Mean rank	
	Jaccard	Hamming
Classic salience	2.58	2.59
Guided backprop	2.06	2.03
LIME	1.36	1.38

5 Conclusion

The results in Sect. 4 allow us to answer the initial two research questions:

R1 All three tested explanation techniques detect a substantial part of the region where adversarial attacks have taken place which is clearly better than random.

R2 Explanation methods that focus on semantics rather than mere gradients, as offered by guided backpropagation and LIME, perform distinctly better in the tested settings.

The latter finding is particularly interesting in the sense that saliency is essentially based on the same information, which also guides adversarial attacks, namely gradient information. Still, LIME or truncated gradient, both relying on simplifying assumptions, result in a better recovering of the regions where attacks have taken place.

We have investigated the behavior of explanatory methods for deep learning when confronted with adversarial examples. We found that semantics-based approaches in particular are able to identify a substantial part of regions in which an attack has taken place, for a representative set of samples.

In general, we desire a better understanding of adversarial attacks, robustness against them, the certainty of predictions and their explanations, and of how deep convolutional neural networks divide the input space into class regions. With this work, we contribute but a small step towards a more comprehensive grasp of these interlinked concepts. Understanding how labels relate to each other might allow us to construct ground truth with a clearer distinction between strongly and weakly relevant pixels, so that pixels outside attacked regions do not contribute to the prediction as much. Unfortunately, current state-of-the-art classifiers ignore semantic similarities between classes.

Our findings support the idea that it is possible to recover regions that are – by design – the cause for incorrect (adversarial) classifications. In subsequent work we will investigate whether our findings generalize to alternative classification methods and whether explanations of adversarial examples display systematic differences when compared to explanations of proper (correctly classifiable) samples. Furthermore, we will produce an extension towards an interactive scenario in which a human user is aided in understanding principles and pitfalls of automated classification.

References

1. Mohseni, S., Zarei, N., Ragan, E.D.: A survey of evaluation methods and measures for interpretable machine learning (2018). arXiv:1811.11839
2. Schmidhuber, J.: Deep learning in neural networks: an overview. Neural Netw. **61**, 85–117 (2015)
3. Fischer, L., Hammer, B., Wersing, H.: Optimal local rejection for classifiers. Neurocomputing **214**, 445–457 (2016)

4. Ribeiro, M.T., Singh, S., Guestrin, C.: "Why should I trust you?": explaining the predictions of any classifier. In: Proceedings of the 22nd ACM SIGKDD International Conference on Knowledge Discovery and Data Mining (2016). arXiv:1602.04938
5. Samek, W., Wiegand, T., Müller, K.-R.: Explainable artificial intelligence: understanding, visualizing and interpreting deep learning models (2017). arXiv:1708.08296
6. Schulz, A., Gisbrecht, A., Hammer, B.: Using discriminative dimensionality reduction to visualize classifiers. Neural Process. Lett. **42**, 27–54 (2014)
7. Göpfert, J.P., Wersing, H., Hammer, B.: Adversarial attacks hidden in plain sight (2019). arXiv:1902.09286
8. Selvaraju, R.R., Cogswell, M., Das, A., Vedantam, R., Parikh, D., Batra, D.: Grad-CAM: visual explanations from deep networks via gradient-based localization. In: IEEE International Conference on Computer Vision (ICCV), pp. 618–626 (2017)
9. Springenberg, J.T., Dosovitskiy, A., Brox, T., Riedmiller, M.A.: Striving for simplicity: the all convolutional net (2014). arXiv:1412.6806
10. Rauber, J., Brendel, W., Bethge, M.: Foolbox: a python toolbox to benchmark the robustness of machine learning models (2017). arXiv:1707.04131
11. Papernot, N., et al.: Technical report on the CleverHans v2.1.0 Adversarial Examples Library (2016). arXiv:1610.00768
12. Goodfellow, I.J., Shlens, J., Szegedy, C.: Explaining and harnessing adversarial examples (2014). arXiv:1412.6572
13. Kurakin, A., Goodfellow, I.J., Bengio, S.: Adversarial machine learning at scale (2016). arXiv:1611.01236
14. Bengio, Y., Courville, A.C., Vincent, P.: Representation learning: a review and new perspectives. IEEE Trans. Pattern Anal. Mach. Intell. **35**, 1798–1828 (2013)
15. Szegedy, C., Vanhoucke, V., Ioffe, S., Shlens, J., Wojna, Z.: Rethinking the inception architecture for computer vision. In: IEEE Conference on Computer Vision and Pattern Recognition (CVPR), pp. 2818–2826 (2016)
16. Felzenszwalb, P.F., Huttenlocher, D.P.: Efficient graph-based image segmentation. Int. J. Comput. Vis. **59**, 167–181 (2004)

On the Interpretation of Recurrent Neural Networks as Finite State Machines

Christian Oliva(✉) and Luis F. Lago-Fernández

Escuela Politécnica Superior, Universidad Autónoma de Madrid, 28049 Madrid, Spain
christian.oliva@estudiante.uam.es, luis.lago@uam.es

Abstract. The behavior of simple recurrent neural networks trained on regular languages is analyzed in terms of accuracy and interpretability. We use controlled amounts of noise and L1 regularization to obtain stable and accurate responses that are at the same time highly interpretable, and introduce a *shocking* mechanism that reactivates silent neurons when learning stops due to an excessive regularization. Proper parameter tuning allows the networks to develop a strong generalization capacity, and at the same time provides solutions that may be interpreted as finite automata. Experiments carried out with different regular languages show that, in all cases, the trained networks display activation patterns that automatically cluster into a set of discrete states without any need to explicitly perform quantization. Analysis of the transitions between states in response to the input symbols reveals that the networks are in fact implementing a finite state machine that in all cases matches the regular expressions used to generate the training data.

1 Introduction

Recurrent Neural Networks (RNNs) [1,2] have been successfully applied in many domains where it is necessary to model temporal sequences, including in particular the recognition of formal languages [3–7]. Many authors have studied the relationship between this kind of networks and finite state machines, and different methods to extract a finite automaton from a RNN trained on a formal language have been proposed [8–10]. These methods are able to extract an interpretable model associated to a RNN. The performance of the extracted model is comparable to that of the underlying network, and it usually improves its generalization capability [11].

In a previous work [12] we showed that RNNs trained on simple regular languages under proper levels of noise and L1 regularization are able to provide accurate models that are at the same time highly interpretable. The noise accounts for good generalization while the regularization contributes interpretability. The final networks exhibit activity patterns that resemble the discrete states in a deterministic finite automaton (DFA). In this article we extend this work in two different ways. First, we apply the same kind of networks to a more extensive set of languages, the well known *Tomita Grammars* [13], which are a common benchmark in the field. Second, we introduce a new mechanism

I. V. Tetko et al. (Eds.): ICANN 2019, LNCS 11727, pp. 312–323, 2019.
https://doi.org/10.1007/978-3-030-30487-4_25

to avoid over-regularization in the networks. Whenever the learning stops for a sufficiently high number of training epochs, probably due to a high proportion of regularized neurons, the network is awakened by introducing a random signal or *shock* which reactivates the weights. Our results show that this kind of network training applies well to the new set of languages, with the shocking mechanism avoiding the networks getting stuck and making them learn more easily.

We analyze the trained networks using the color activation plots introduced in [14] and making 2-dimensional projections of the networks' activity using the Isomap transformation [15]. We observe that the neurons that survive the regularization process respond to meaningful input patterns, and that their activity tends to form well defined clusters that resemble states in a DFA. Extraction of the transition rules between clusters leads in all the studied cases to deterministic automata that are equivalent to the languages used to train the networks.

The article is organized as follows. In Sect. 2 we introduce the RNN's architecture used in all our experiments. In Sect. 3 we describe the data and the experiments carried out. In Sect. 4 we present and analyze our results. Finally, in Sect. 5 we present the conclusions and discuss future lines of research.

2 Recurrent Neural Network

In all our experiments we use a modified Elman RNN architecture [1] with one single hidden layer, given by the following equations [12]:

$$h_t = tanh(W_{xh}x_t + (W_{hh} + X_\nu)h_{t-1} + b_h) \tag{1}$$

$$y_t = \sigma(W_{hy}h_t + b_y) \tag{2}$$

where x_t, h_t and y_t represent the activation vectors for the input, hidden and output layers, respectively, at time t; W_{xh}, W_{hh} and W_{hy} represent the weight matrices; and b_h and b_y are the bias vectors for each layer. The *tanh* and *sigmoid* functions are used as activations for the hidden and the output layers, respectively. X_ν is a random diagonal matrix whose elements are normally distributed with 0 mean and ν standard deviation. It introduces noise into the recurrent connection. This noise term is multiplied by h_{t-1} in order to ensure that it only affects the active neurons and does not counterbalance the regularization [12].

We train the network to minimize a cross-entropy loss with L1 regularization:

$$L = -\sum_{t=1}^{n}[\hat{y}_t \log(y_t) + (1-\hat{y}_t)\log(1-y_t)] + \gamma(||W_{xh}||_1 + ||W_{hh}||_1 + ||W_{hy}||_1) \tag{3}$$

where $\hat{y}_t$ is the expected output, γ is the regularization parameter and the expression $||\cdot||_1$ denotes the L1 matrix norm. The parameter n is the number of steps in the unrolled version of the network (25 in all our experiments). The size of the input layer depends on the number of input symbols (3 for all the addressed problems), and we consider one single output unit whose interpretation is to accept ($y = 1$) or reject ($y = 0$) a given input string. The number of units in the hidden layer is varied in our experiments in the range $[2, 20]$.

We have observed that regularizing the network sometimes tends to produce too many silent neurons, which makes learning more difficult. In order to avoid this problem, we introduce a form of weight noise [16] that consists of a random reactivation of the network weights whenever the network gets stuck for a sufficient number of training epochs. This random *shock* affects all the network's weights according to the following expression:

$$W = W + X_\zeta \tag{4}$$

where W is any of the weight matrices in Eqs. 1 and 2, and X_ζ is a random matrix whose elements are normally distributed with 0 mean and ζ standard deviation. We will refer to ζ as the *shock parameter*. A shock is applied to the network whenever the training loss has not decreased during the last C training iterations[1].

3 Experiments

In this section we describe the data and the experiments carried out to analyze the network's interpretability in terms of the noise level, the regularization parameter and the shock parameter. For each experimental condition we train 20 networks starting from random weight initialization. In all our experiments the network is initially trained for 50 epochs (100000 iterations), but training may reach a maximum of 150 epochs depending on the number of shocks applied to the network. The cost function is minimized using a standard gradient descent algorithm with a learning rate of 0.01. All the results reported in Sect. 4 are averages over the 20 executions for a given set of parameters.

3.1 Data

We consider seven regular languages on the alphabet of symbols $\{a, b\}$, known as *Tomita Grammars* [13], which have been extensively used in previous studies [11]. Table 1 provides a list of all the Tomita grammars, including the language descriptions and the corresponding regular expressions. For each of the Tomita grammars, we generate problem data as follows. First, a random sequence containing the symbols a, b and \$ is obtained. This sequence represents a set of input strings separated by the \$ symbol. Then, the regular expressions in Table 1 are used to determine whether each partial substring starting at the last \$ belongs or not to the corresponding Tomita language, and the output data is generated as a 1 (accept) or a 0 (reject) respectively. Figure 1 shows the expected output for each of the Tomita grammars for an example input sequence. Acceptance is shown in yellow, rejection is shown in white.

[1] In all the experiments carried out we set $C = 5000$. Whenever the network's weights are shocked the number of training epochs is increased in order to give more time for the training to converge.

Table 1. Description of the 7 Tomita grammars and their corresponding regular expressions.

Name	Regular language	Regular expression
*Tomita*1	Strings with only *a*'s	a^*
*Tomita*2	Strings with only sequences of *ab*'s	$(ab)^*$
*Tomita*3	Strings with no odd number of consecutive *b*'s after an odd number of consecutive *a*'s	$b^*[aa(aa)^*b^* + a(aa)^*bb(bb)^*]^*(a+\lambda)$
*Tomita*4	Strings with fewer than 3 consecutive *b*'s	$(a + ba + bba)^*(bb + b + \lambda)$
*Tomita*5	Strings with even length with an even number of *a*'s	$[aa + bb + (ab + ba)(aa + bb)^*(ab + ba)]^*$
*Tomita*6	Strings where the difference between the number of *a*'s and *b*'s is a multiple of 3	$[ba + (a + bb)(ab)^*(b + aa)]^*$
*Tomita*7	$b^*a^*b^*a^*$	$b^*a^*b^*a^*$

Fig. 1. Expected output (acceptance/rejection) for a set of input strings and all the Tomita grammars. Acceptance is shown in yellow, while rejection is shown in white. The $ symbol represents the end of a string. (Color figure online)

We have generated 5 different datasets to be used in our experiments (see summary in Table 2). The *train* dataset contains 50000 symbols, with equal probabilities for symbols *a* and *b*, and a probability of appearance for the $ symbol of 0.1. The *big* dataset is generated under the same conditions, but it contains 100000 symbols. The *long* dataset contains 20000 characters, but much longer strings. It has been generated by reducing the $ probability to 0.01. Finally, the *all as* (*all bs*) dataset contains 15000 characters and strings composed mainly of *a*'s (*b*'s). All the networks are trained using the *train* dataset, while the remaining datasets are used for validation.

Table 2. Description of the datasets used to train and validate the neural networks. The table shows, for each dataset, the number of input characters, the probability of each input symbol (a, b, \$), and the average, minimum and maximum string lengths.

Data	# chars	a prob.	b prob.	\$ prob.	avg len	min len	max len
train	50000	0.45	0.45	0.1	8.9	0	95
big	100000	0.45	0.45	0.1	9.0	0	81
long	20000	0.495	0.495	0.01	88.3	0	477
all as	15000	0.98	0.01	0.01	113.5	0	566
all bs	15000	0.01	0.98	0.01	95.8	0	475

4 Results and Analysis

In this section we show our results in terms of accuracy and interpretability. The accuracy is evaluated on the validation datasets described in Table 2. The interpretability is analyzed in two ways: (i) by drawing color activation plots of the hidden units in response to an input sequence (Sect. 4.2), and (ii) by plotting the 2-dimensional Isomap projection of the hidden layer activation space in response to accepted input strings (Sect. 4.3).

4.1 Accuracy and Generalization

Following the approach in [12], we first consider the effect of noise and L1 regularization on the network's response. We use the parameter values $\nu = 0.6$ and $\gamma = 10^{-4}$, which were shown to provide a good balance between interpretability and generalization on simpler problems. On further experiments we analyze the effect of network shocks. Table 3 shows the results for networks with 20 hidden neurons trained on each Tomita problem. All the values are averages over 20 different executions. The top 3 subtables correspond to experimental conditions without noise or regularization ($\nu = 0$ and $\gamma = 0$, labeled *Initial*), only noise ($\nu = 0.6$ and $\gamma = 0$, labeled *Noise*) and both noise and regularization ($\nu = 0.6$ and $\gamma = 10^{-4}$, labeled *NoiReg*).

We can observe that the initial configuration provides very good results for all grammars except *Tomita3* and *Tomita7*, with some generalization problems also for *Tomita5* when long strings containing only the b symbol are used. The effect of noise seems to partially mitigate these problems, but it deteriorates the results for *Tomita6*. Finally, the inclusion of regularization, in spite of producing more interpretable networks (results not shown) tends to reduce the accuracy of *Tomita5*, *Tomita6* and *Tomita7*. In these cases it seems that the regularization mechanism is forcing too many neurons to be silent, with the subsequent decrease in accuracy.

In order to avoid this problem, the shocking mechanism allows the network to reactivate the regularized neurons when it is not able to learn during a certain

Table 3. Average accuracy and standard deviation over 20 executions for each *Tomita* problem, under different noise, regularization and shocking conditions. Initial: $\nu = 0$, $\gamma = 0$, $\zeta = 0$. Noise: $\nu = 0.6$, $\gamma = 0$, $\zeta = 0$. NoiReg: $\nu = 0.6$, $\gamma = 10^{-4}$, $\zeta = 0$. Final: $\nu = 0.6$, $\gamma = 10^{-4}$, $\zeta = 0.5$. The number of hidden neurons is 20 in all cases.

Initial	*Tom.1*	*Tom.2*	*Tom.3*	*Tom.4*	*Tom.5*	*Tom.6*	*Tom.7*
train	100.0	100.0	100.0	100.0	100.0	100.0	100.0
big	100.0	100.0	100.0	100.0	100.0	100.0	100.0
long	100.0	100.0	99.98 ± 0.07	100.0	100.0	100.0	99.99 ± 0.02
all as	100.0	100.0	97.03 ± 6.13	100.0	100.0	100.0	92.94 ± 9.8
all bs	100.0	100.0	97.66 ± 5.01	100.0	99.86 ± 0.88	100.0	96.37 ± 6.97
Noise	*Tom.1*	*Tom.2*	*Tom.3*	*Tom.4*	*Tom.5*	*Tom.6*	*Tom.7*
train	100.0	100.0	100.0	100.0	100.0	98.86 ± 2.38	100.0
big	100.0	100.0	100.0	100.0	100.0	98.89 ± 2.34	100.0
long	100.0	100.0	100.0	100.0	100.0	94.52 ± 9.99	100.0
all as	100.0	100.0	100.0	100.0	100.0	99.83 ± 0.74	99.83 ± 0.74
all bs	100.0	100.0	100.0	100.0	100.0	98.18 ± 5.35	100.0
NoiReg	*Tom.1*	*Tom.2*	*Tom.3*	*Tom.4*	*Tom.5*	*Tom.6*	*Tom.7*
train	100.0	100.0	100.0	100.0	78.47 ± 0.0	72.27 ± 0.0	100.0
big	100.0	100.0	100.0	100.0	78.61 ± 0.0	72.02 ± 0.0	100.0
long	100.0	100.0	100.0	100.0	75.26 ± 0.0	67.24 ± 0.0	100.0
all as	100.0	100.0	100.0	100.0	83.65 ± 0.0	66.32 ± 0.0	99.95 ± 0.24
all bs	100.0	100.0	100.0	100.0	81.37 ± 2.77	69.23 ± 2.79	98.26 ± 5.31
Final	*Tom.1*	*Tom.2*	*Tom.3*	*Tom.4*	*Tom.5*	*Tom.6*	*Tom.7*
train	100.0	100.0	100.0	100.0	100.0	100.0	100.0
big	100.0	100.0	100.0	100.0	100.0	100.0	100.0
long	100.0	100.0	100.0	100.0	100.0	100.0	100.0
all as	100.0	100.0	100.0	100.0	100.0	100.0	100.0
all bs	100.0	100.0	100.0	100.0	100.0	100.0	100.0

number of epochs. As an example, we plot in Fig. 2 the average accuracy versus the number of hidden neurons for networks trained on the *Tomita5* problem, both without (left) and with (right) shocks ($\zeta = 0$ and $\zeta = 0.5$, respectively[2]). The noise parameter and the L1 regularization parameter are, as before, $\nu = 0.6$ and $\gamma = 10^{-4}$. Note that when the network is not shocked the learning stops and the accuracy reaches a maximum of about 80% regardless of the number of hidden neurons. However when shocks are introduced the network is able to reach 100% accuracy when the number of hidden neurons is high enough. The same behavior is also observed for the *Tomita6* problem (not shown). The last rows in Table 3 (labeled *Final*) show the results for all the Tomita problems with this final configuration ($\nu = 0.6$, $\gamma = 10^{-4}$, $\zeta = 0.5$), which allows the networks

[2] We have performed experiments with different values of the shocking parameter ζ, and found that any value in the range $[0.5, 1.2]$ provides similar results.

reach a 100% accuracy for all the problems and validation sets. Additionally, we show in next section that the final networks are highly interpretable, with the individual neurons responding to meaningful input patterns.

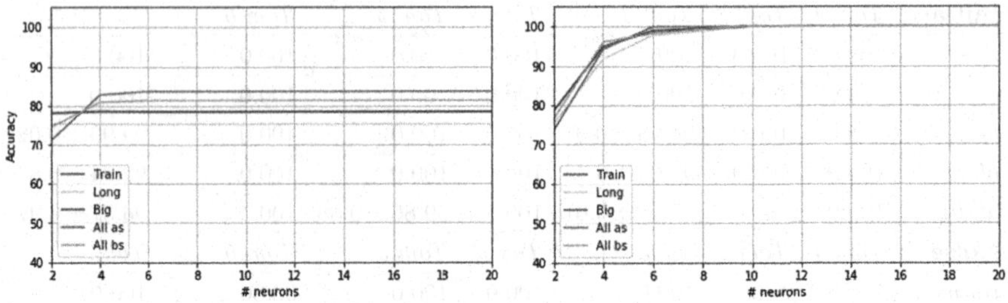

Fig. 2. Average accuracy versus number of hidden neurons for the *Tomita5* problem. Left: shock parameter $\zeta = 0$. Right: shock parameter $\zeta = 0.5$. The noise parameter is $\nu = 0.6$ and the regularization parameter is $\gamma = 10^{-4}$ in both cases.

4.2 Interpretation of Individual Neurons

To analyze the interpretability of the networks we draw color activation plots for the hidden units when a specific input sequence is introduced. Figure 3 shows an example for a network with 20 hidden neurons trained on the *Tomita3* problem, using the final configuration. The first row represents the input sequence, with the color indicating the expected output (yellow = accept, white = reject). The next 4 rows show the response of the 4 hidden neurons that survive the regularization process. The remaining neurons do never become active and they are not included in the plot. The color code is as follows: red means a high positive activation, cyan means a high negative activation.

There are two main conclusions to be extracted from this plot. First, the network is only using 4 of the hidden neurons, while the remaining ones are silent due to the regularization. Second, the active neurons operate in a binary mode, outputting either a +1 (red) or a −1 (cyan). The individual neurons' responses may be interpreted as follows. The first neuron ($N2$) is responding with a positive activation to all odd a's after any sequence of b's. The second one ($N4$) is responding with a positive activation to all even b's after an odd a, and also to all the rejected strings after an odd b. Finally, the logical OR of the activation of the last two neurons ($N5$ and $N6$) corresponds to the expected output. With this interpretation we can easily understand how the network is solving the *Tomita3* problem, with the first two neurons doing auxiliary computations and the last two neurons coding the solution. Similar results have been obtained for the rest of problems, but due to space constraints they are not included here[3].

[3] The results for the complete set of Tomita grammars, including the activation color plots, the Isomap projections of the hidden layer activation space and the extracted automata (see Sect. 4.3) can be publicly accessed at our GitHub repo: https://github.com/slyder095/coliva_llago_icann2019.

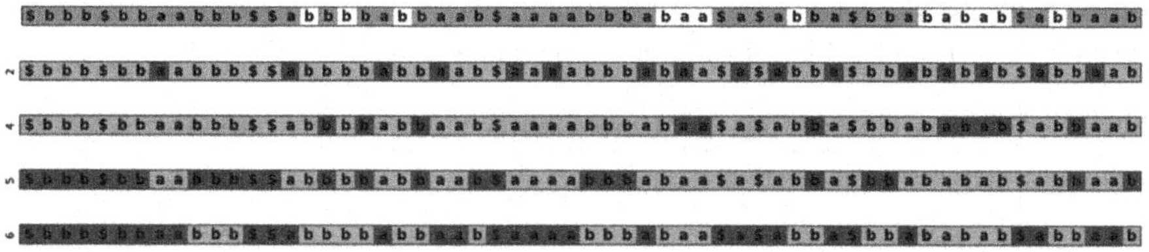

Fig. 3. Color activation plot for a network with 20 hidden neurons trained on the *Tomita3* problem with $\nu = 0.6$, $\gamma = 10^{-4}$ and $\zeta = 0.5$. The first row shows the expected output (yellow means acceptance, white means rejection). The next rows show the hidden neurons' activity (red is positive, cyan is negative). Only the 4 hidden neurons that get activated are shown. (Color figure online)

4.3 Hidden State Analysis and DFA Extraction

In this section we use a 2-dimensional Isomap projection to analyze the activation space in the hidden layer. We have observed that, using the final configuration in Sect. 4.1 ($\nu = 0.6$, $\gamma = 10^{-4}$, $\zeta = 0.5$), the RNN's internal state space becomes discrete, with the network's activity automatically clustered into a finite number of states. Figure 4 shows an example for the *Tomita3* problem, where the network's activation forms 6 clusters. Only input strings that belong to the *Tomita3* language have been used to build this plot. The clusters in cyan represent acceptance states, while the cluster in blue is a rejection one.

The transition rules can be obtained by analyzing the jumps between clusters in response to each input symbol. They are shown in Table 4. Each row in the table represents the transitions departing from a given cluster, which is surrounded by a shaded box in all the figures in that row, and whose name is specified in the first column. Each column from the second to the fourth

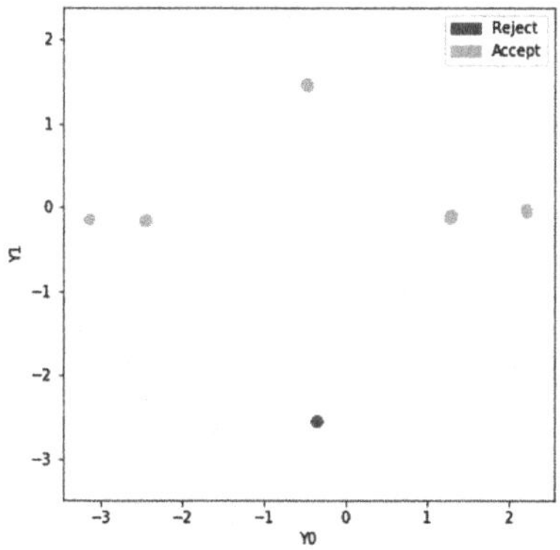

Fig. 4. The 2-dimensional Isomap projection of the activation space of a network trained on the *Tomita3* problem. Acceptance clusters are plotted in cyan, rejection clusters are plotted in blue. This Isomap projection corresponds to the color plot shown in Fig. 3. (Color figure online)

Table 4. Transition rules extracted from the Isomap projection in Fig. 4. The initial clusters are surrounded by a shaded box. The final clusters are shown in red.

Name	Transitions with *a*	Transitions with *b*	Transitions with $
A	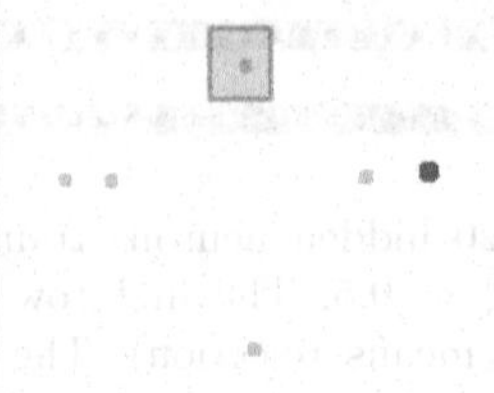	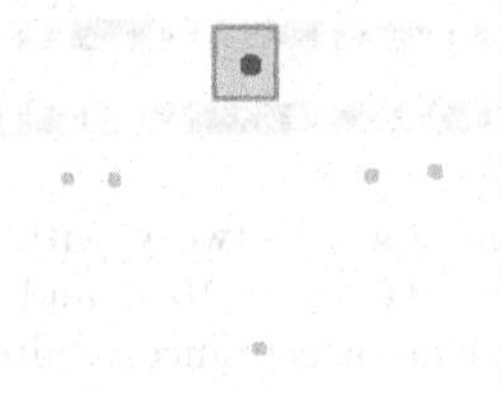	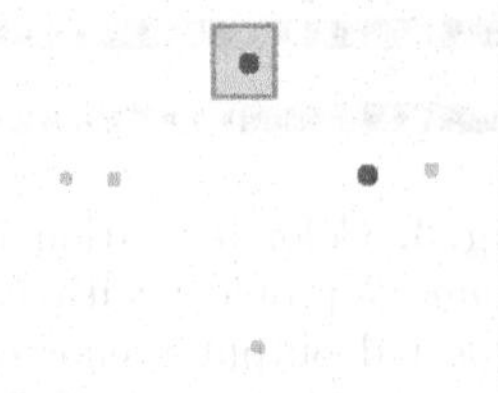
B	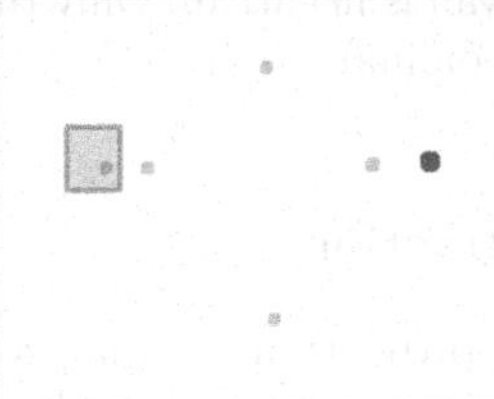		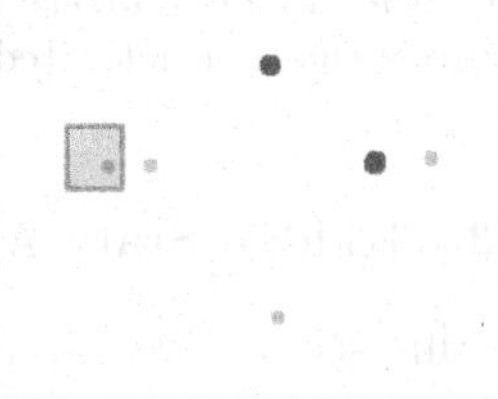
C		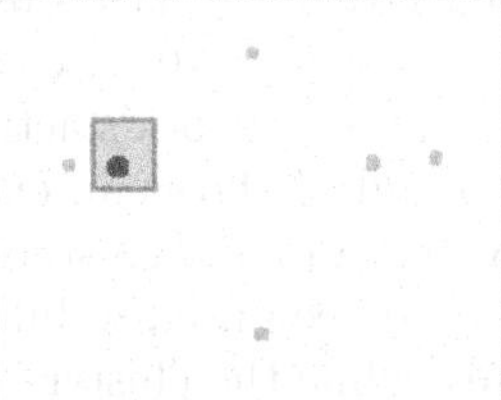	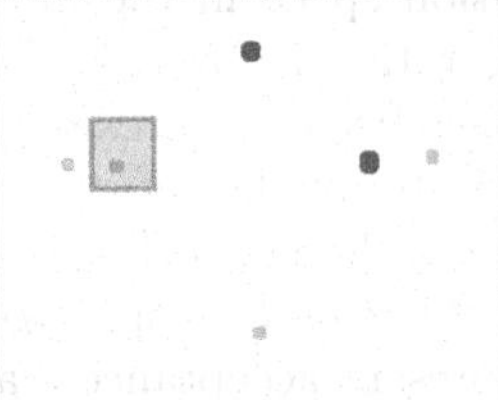
D	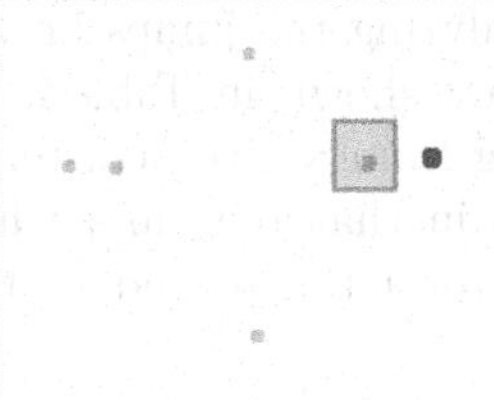	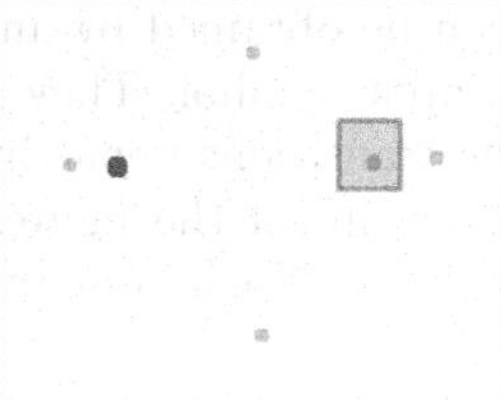	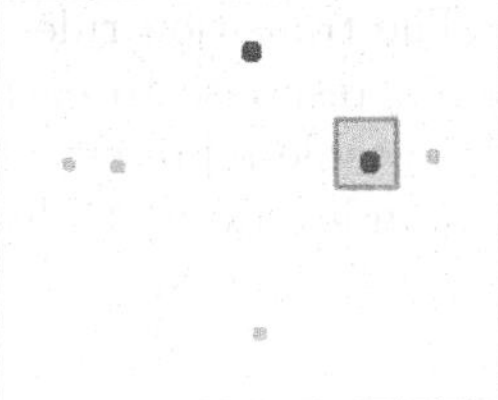
E	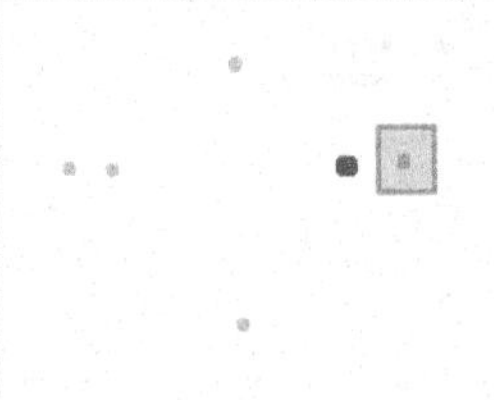	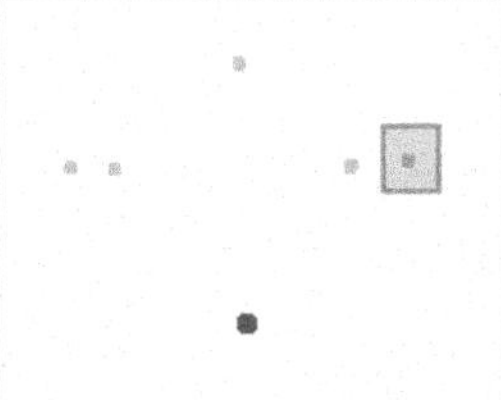	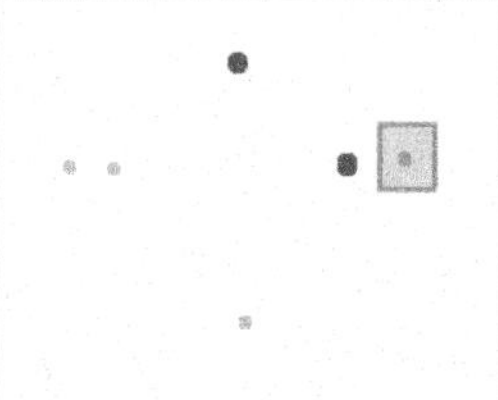
F	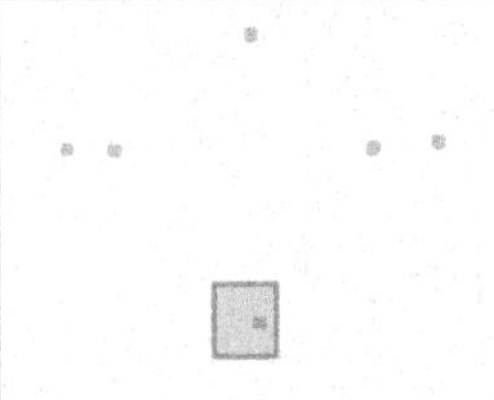		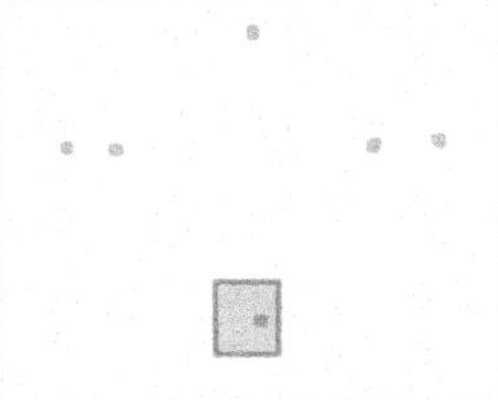

represents the transitions with a given input symbol (a, b or \$), with the destination cluster shown in red. For example, the first row shows that, starting from cluster A, the network moves to cluster E with the symbol a, remains in cluster A with the symbol b, and moves to clusters A and D with the symbol \$. The transition matrix that follows from these plots is shown in Table 5. Note that after a \$ symbol the network always moves to either cluster A or cluster D in an apparently non-deterministic way. These two clusters may be thought of as input states in an automaton associated to the network. From these states, the network initiates a series of deterministic jumps in response to the input symbols a and b. Transitions from cluster F with the symbols a and \$ lead to a *sink* rejection state which does not appear in Tables 4 and 5 because the Isomap projection was obtained using accepted strings only.

The fact that the initial move is non-deterministic does not seem relevant, since the two states A and D are equivalent (they behave exactly in the same way with the same input symbols). It could be explained by noting that the \$ symbol must reset the network to its initial conditions regardless of its past history. So the existence of two equivalent initial states may help the network deal with all the different possibilities. Nevertheless, as shown in Fig. 5 (left), the extracted automaton is correct and recognizes the language generated by the *Tomita*3 grammar. Minimization of this automaton leads to the more compact representation of Fig. 5 (right), which is the minimum DFA for the *Tomita*3 grammar. Similar results are obtained for the rest of problems, but they have been omitted due to space limits. In all the cases we were able to extract finite automata from the trained networks that are equivalent to the corresponding Tomita grammars. All the results can be accessed at our GitHub repo (see footnote in Sect. 4.2).

Table 5. Transition table extracted from the transitions shown in Table 4 for the *Tomita3* problem.

Symbol	State A	State B	State C	State D	State E	State F
a	E	E	E	E	D	–
b	A	F	C	C	F	B
\$	A,D	A,D	A,D	A,D	A,D	–

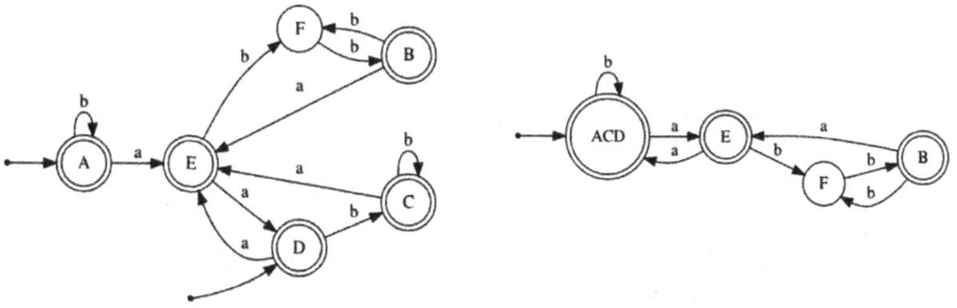

Fig. 5. Left: Finite automaton extracted from the transitions in Table 5 for a network trained on the *Tomita3* grammar. Right: Minimum DFA equivalent to the automaton in the left side. It is also the minimum DFA that recognizes the *Tomita3* grammar.

5 Conclusions and Future Work

In this article we have studied the behavior of RNNs when trained to recognize the Tomita grammars. We tested the networks under different levels of noise and L1 regularization, introducing a *shock* mechanism that reactivates the weights when learning stops due to over-regularization. The networks' responses were analyzed in terms of accuracy and interpretability. Our results show that, using proper values for the noise, regularization and shocking parameters, the trained networks are in general more interpretable and obtain higher accuracy on validation sets. In these conditions, the network's hidden units seem to respond to specific and meaningful input patterns. Additionally, we observe that the RNN's internal activation space becomes automatically clustered into a set of discrete states without the need of explicitly quantizing the network's activity. This set of states, and the corresponding transitions amongst them, can be interpreted as a DFA. In all our tests the extracted DFA match accurately the language associated to the Tomita grammar used to train the network.

It is worth noting that we do not try to explicitly quantize the activation space in order to extract the automata. Most previous works on this field rely on an external quantization to obtain similar results [9], or force the network to form clusters by introducing more or less artificial tricks, such as using non-differentiable activation functions [3], modifying the architecture in order to include a clustering layer [17] or constraining the weight space [18]. We show in this work that it is possible to obtain the same behavior by simply tuning standard parameters such as the noise or regularization levels.

In spite of these promising results, some aspects of the present study still require further analysis. One such aspect is the observation of non-deterministic jumps in response to the $ symbol. Other possible extensions include the analysis of more complex problems, such as non-regular languages or textual information such as programming code or written texts. We also consider the use of different network architectures, such as LSTMs or GRUs.

Acknowledgments. This work has been partially funded by grant S2017/BMD-3688 from Comunidad de Madrid and by Spanish project MINECO/FEDER TIN2017-84452-R (http://www.mineco.gob.es/).

References

1. Elman, J.L.: Finding structure in time. Cogn. Sci. **14**(2), 179–211 (1990)
2. Hochreiter, S., Schmidhuber, J.: Long short-term memory. Neural Comput. **9**(8), 1735–1780 (1997)
3. Zeng, Z., Goodman, R.M., Smyth, P.: Learning finite state machines with self-clustering recurrent networks. Neural Comput. **5**(6), 976–990 (1993)
4. Omlin, C.W., Giles, C.L.: Extraction of rules from discrete-time recurrent neural networks. Neural Netw. **9**(1), 41–52 (1996)
5. Casey, M.: The dynamics of discrete-time computation, with application to recurrent neural networks and finite state machine extraction. Neural Comput. **8**(6), 1135–1178 (1996)

6. Cohen, M., Caciularu, A., Rejwan, I., Berant, J.: Inducing regular grammars using recurrent neural networks. CoRR, abs/1710.10453 (2017)
7. Gers, F.A., Schmidhuber, E.: LSTM recurrent networks learn simple context-free and context-sensitive languages. Trans. Neural Netw. **12**(6), 1333–1340 (2001)
8. Giles, C.L., Miller, C.B., Chen, D., Sun, G., Chen, H., Lee, Y.: Extracting and learning an unknown grammar with recurrent neural networks. In: Advances in Neural Information Processing Systems 4, [NIPS Conference, Denver, Colorado, USA, 2–5 December 1991], pp. 317–324 (1991)
9. Jacobsson, H.: Rule extraction from recurrent neural networks: a taxonomy and review. Neural Comput. **17**(6), 1223–1263 (2005)
10. Weiss, G., Goldberg, Y., Yahav, E.: Extracting automata from recurrent neural networks using queries and counterexamples. CoRR, abs/1711.09576 (2017)
11. Wang, Q., Zhang, K., Ororbia II, A.G., Xing, X., Liu, X., Giles, C.L.: An empirical evaluation of rule extraction from recurrent neural networks. Neural Comput. **30**(9), 2568–2591 (2018)
12. Oliva, C., Lago-Fernández, L.F.: Interpretability of recurrent neural networks trained on regular languages. In: Rojas, I., Joya, G., Catala, A. (eds.) IWANN 2019. LNCS, vol. 11507, pp. 14–25. Springer, Cham (2019). https://doi.org/10.1007/978-3-030-20518-8_2
13. Tomita, M.: Dynamic construction of finite automata from examples using hill-climbing. In: Proceedings of the Fourth Annual Conference of the Cognitive Science Society, Ann Arbor, Michigan, pp. 105–108 (1982)
14. Karpathy, A., Johnson, J., Fei-Fei, L.: Visualizing and understanding recurrent networks. CoRR, abs/1506.02078 (2015)
15. Tenenbaum, J.B., de Silva, V., Langford, J.C.: A global geometric framework for nonlinear dimensionality reduction. Science **290**(5500), 2319 (2000)
16. Adilova, L., Paul, N., Schlicht, P.: Introducing noise in decentralized training of neural networks. CoRR, abs/1809.10678 (2018)
17. Das, S., Mozer, M.: Dynamic on-line clustering and state extraction: an approach to symbolic learning. Neural Netw. **11**(1), 53–64 (1998)
18. Frasconi, P., Gori, M., Maggini, M., Soda, G.: Representation of finite state automata in recurrent radial basis function networks. Mach. Learn. **23**(1), 5–32 (1996)

From Single Neurons to Networks

Neural Field Model for Measuring and Reproducing Time Intervals

Weronika Wojtak[1,2](✉), Flora Ferreira[1], Estela Bicho[1], and Wolfram Erlhagen[2]

[1] Research Centre Algoritmi, University of Minho, Guimarães, Portugal
{w.wojtak,fjferreira,estela.bicho}@dei.uminho.pt
[2] Research Centre of Mathematics, University of Minho, Guimarães, Portugal
wolfram.erlhagen@math.uminho.pt

Abstract. The continuous real-time motor interaction with our environment requires the capacity to measure and produce time intervals in a highly flexible manner. Recent neurophysiological evidence suggests that the neural computational principles supporting this capacity may be understood from a dynamical systems perspective: Inputs and initial conditions determine how a recurrent neural network evolves from a "resting state" to a state triggering the action. Here we test this hypothesis in a time measurement and time reproduction experiment using a model of a robust neural integrator based on the theoretical framework of dynamic neural fields. During measurement, the temporal accumulation of input leads to the evolution of a self-stabilized bump whose amplitude reflects elapsed time. During production, the stored information is used to reproduce on a trial-by-trial basis the time interval either by adjusting input strength or initial condition of the integrator. We discuss the impact of the results on our goal to endow autonomous robots with a human-like temporal cognition capacity for natural human-robot interactions.

Keywords: Neural field model · Interval timing · Neural integrator

1 Introduction

Our successful interaction with an inherently dynamic environment requires the capacity to perceive elapsed time and to produce highly timed motor responses. Humans and other animals are able to generate time intervals in the range of tens of milliseconds to several seconds in anticipation of sensory events (e.g., a color change of a traffic light) without a clock or any external device [6,11]. Moreover, the temporal control of behavior often shows a striking flexibility [15], allowing the adjustment of movement initiation time based on a single or very few observations of environmental changes (e.g. a prolonged amber phase). How the nervous system manages to flexibly process temporal information in the service of behavioral goals is currently an active research field (for a recent review see [14]). A recent experiment in which monkeys were trained to measure

I. V. Tetko et al. (Eds.): ICANN 2019, LNCS 11727, pp. 327–338, 2019.
https://doi.org/10.1007/978-3-030-30487-4_26

different sample intervals (demarcated by two time markers) and immediately afterward reproduce it by a proactive saccade to a predefined target, reveals new insights into the neural processing mechanisms [8]. The main finding during the production epoch is a monotonic increase of neural population activity to a fixed threshold value associated with saccade onset. Such a ramp-to-threshold dynamics has been described previously in a wide range of brain areas during timing tasks [14]. The interesting novelty of this study is the observation that the population activity at the end of the measuring epoch (ME) predicts on a trial-by-trial basis the buildup rate during the production epoch (PE) and consequently anticipates the time of the upcoming motor response. Longer sample intervals are associated with higher firing rates at the end of ME and shallower buildup rates during PE.

Most computational models of ramping activity explain the accumulation of temporal evidence as a result of a network mechanism in which positive and negative feedback is mediated by recurrent connections between neurons [16,18]. However, well known problems with these integrator models are the requirement to fine tune network connections and the lack of robustness to perturbations [10]. Moreover, changes in the network structure (e.g., through Hebbian synaptic modification) are assumed to tune the slope of ramping activity to a new sample interval [16]. Here we use a novel model of a robust neural integrator [22] based on the theoretical framework of dynamic neural fields [17] to test a dynamical systems view on flexible measurement and reproduction of time intervals [15]. The basic assumption is that temporal flexibility can be readily understood in terms of inputs and initial conditions that control the speed with which the neural population activity in the recurrent network evolves. Our primary goal is not to explain in detail the experimental data in [8], but to investigate in numerical model simulations neuro-inspired processing mechanism that may be used in the future to endow autonomous robots with a sophisticated action timing capacity for more natural human-robot interactions [3,5].

2 Dynamic Neural Field (DNF) Model

DNF models explain the existence of self-sustained neural population activity which is commonly believed to represent a neural substrate for higher cognitive functions necessary to fill the gap between sensation and action. They have been used to model aspects of working memory, decision making, planning or learning [17] and to synthesize these cognitive skills in autonomous robots [4]. In the applications, neural fields are typically spanned over continuous dimensions such as direction, position or color. Following the experimental setup in [8], we assume for the present study that the neurons in the field represent the target of the saccadic eye movement triggered at the end of PE which is identified by movement direction. The presentation of the target input triggers the evolution of a localized activation pattern or bump encoding the specific parameter value. To represent not only the nature of the input but also the accumulation of temporal evidence we have to assume that the recurrent interactions between the neurons in the field are able to stabilize a bump solution with a continuum of amplitudes. To ensure this we employ a novel field model [22] consisting of two coupled field equations of classical Amari type [1]. It governs the temporal evolution of two populations, $u(x,t)$ and $v(x,t)$, where x indicates the field position and t represents time:

$$\frac{\partial u(x,t)}{\partial t} = -u(x,t) + v(x,t) + \int_{\Omega} w(|x-y|) f(u(y,t)-h) \mathrm{d}y + S(x,t) + \epsilon^{1/2} \mathrm{d}W(x,t), \quad (1a)$$

$$\frac{\partial v(x,t)}{\partial t} = -v(x,t) + u(x,t) - \int_{\Omega} w(|x-y|) f(u(y,t)-h) \mathrm{d}y, \quad (1b)$$

where $w(|x-y|)$ denotes the distant-dependent connectivity kernel and $f(u)$ is the firing rate function taken here as a Heaviside step function with threshold h. This ensures that only neurons with suprathreshold activity, $f(x) = 1$ for $x \geq h$, contribute to the recurrent excitatory and inhibitory interactions. The function $S(x,t)$ represents the time varying external input to population u. The additive noise term $\mathrm{d}W(x,t)$ describes the increment of a spatially dependent Wiener process with noise amplitude $\epsilon \ll 1$. It allows us, in principle, to test predictions about the variability of time measurements, an interesting issue that goes beyond the scope of this paper.

The lateral inhibition type connectivity kernel has a "Mexican-hat" shape given by the difference of two Gaussians

$$w(x) = A_{ex} e^{\left(-x^2/2\sigma_{ex}^2\right)} - A_{in} e^{\left(-x^2/2\sigma_{in}^2\right)} - g_{in}, \quad (2)$$

with $A_{ex} > A_{in} > 0$, $\sigma_{in} > \sigma_{ex} > 0$, and a constant inhibition $g_{in} > 0$. The parameter values used throughout this study are $A_{ex} = 3$, $A_{in} = 1.5$, $\sigma_{ex} = 1$, $\sigma_{in} = 3$, $g_{in} = 0.5$.

We apply the same coupling function to the v-field with a negative sign. The shape of the distance-dependent synaptic strengths thus represents an inverted Mexican-hat with inhibition dominating at shorter and excitation at longer distances.

Numerical simulations of the model were done in Julia [2] using a forward Euler method with time step $\Delta_t = 0.001$ and spatial step $\Delta_x = 0.005$, on a finite domain Ω with length $L = 60$. To compute the spatial convolution of w and f we employ a fast Fourier transform (FFT), using Julia's package `FFTW` with functions `fft` and `ifft` to perform the Fourier transform and the inverse Fourier transform, respectively.

3 Simulation Results

In the following numerical examples, we consider a target input given by the Gaussian function

$$S(x) = A_S e^{\left(-(x-x_c)^2/2\sigma_S^2\right)}, \quad (3)$$

centered at position $x_c = 0$, with standard deviation $\sigma_S = 2$. The input strength, A_S, differs for the time interval measurement and the time interval reproduction epochs of the experiment (see below). For simplicity, we assume that the interval to measure is defined by the duration of the external input and not by two additional time markers like in the experiments. We leave the interesting issue of potential differences in subjective time measurements with "filled" intervals as opposed to "unfilled" intervals demarcated by time markers for future studies [21]. The temporal integration process thus starts from a homogeneous activity baseline when at time $t = 0$ the suprathreshold target input is presented. Following [8], we use for the numerical tests time intervals in the range of 500 to 1000 ms.

For the reproduction epoch we distinguish two situations. (1) Like for the measurement epoch, the temporal accumulation process starts from a homogeneous initial condition with the presentation of the target input. The input strength is inversely proportional to the bump amplitude reached during ME. (2) The evolution of the population activity starts without external input from a non-homogeneous initial condition. The pre-activation of neurons representing the target direction is inversely proportional to the bump amplitude reached during ME.

3.1 Measuring Time Intervals

The following simulations illustrate how the neural trajectory in the u-field evolves in response to the localized external input specifying the target direction. Figure 1 depicts three examples of steady state solutions that are the result of the temporal input integration over different time intervals. The shape of the self-stabilized bumps reflects the fact that a longer accumulation time results in a higher bump amplitude. A closer inspection of the duration-height dependency using more time intervals reveals that the relationship is approximately linear (Fig. 2).

3.2 Reproducing Time Intervals - Varying Inputs

For the reproduction epoch we apply the same external input, $S(x,t)$, like for the time interval measurement but chose in accordance with the qualitative experimental findings in [8] the input strength in dependence of the bump amplitude reached in ME. The following relation is used for the model simulations:

$$A_S = \frac{1}{\ln(u_{max})}, \tag{4}$$

where u_{max} is maximum of the steady state solution in the u-field in the preceding measurement epoch. Figure 3 shows the input amplitudes, A_S, for the range of measured intervals. The application of the suprathreshold input triggers in all cases the evolution of a bump solution. Figure 4 compares the evolution of population activity for all tested intervals. As can be clearly seen when comparing the slopes of the curves, input strength controls the time course of the neural trajectories. Since the strength of the input is inversely proportional (on a

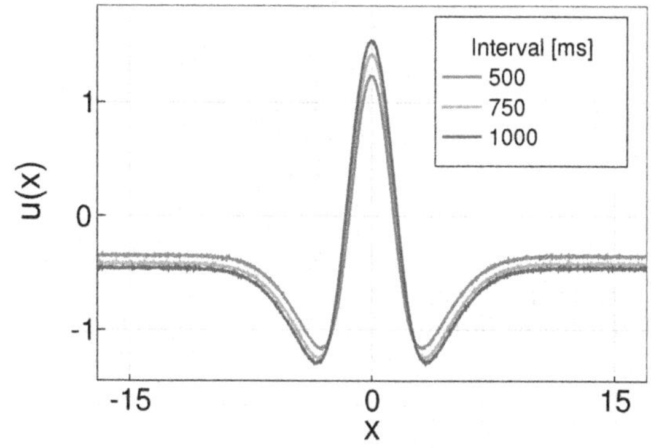

Fig. 1. Example of three steady state solutions of the u-field of (1) resulting from applying three sample intervals of durations $d_{s_j} \in \{500, 750, 1000\}$, respectively. The amplitude of the external input given by (3) is $A_S = 1.75$, the threshold for the Heaviside function $f(u)$ is $h = 0.25$.

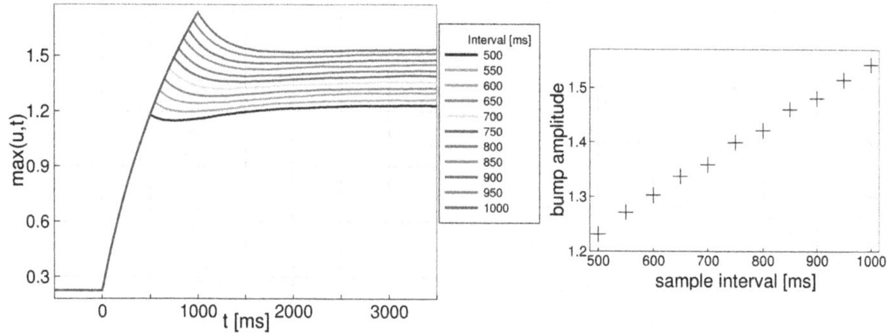

Fig. 2. Left: Time courses of activity in the u-field during the interval measuring epoch. Right: Bump amplitude at the end of the measuring epoch as a function of sample interval length.

logarithmic scale) to interval length, population activity resulting from stronger inputs will reach the fixed read-out threshold, $h_R = 2$, earlier, producing shorter time intervals for movement initiation. Conversely, localized activity integrating weaker inputs reach this threshold later in time, resulting in longer production intervals. After reaching the threshold, h_R, the activity in both fields is reset to the initial resting state. The production interval is measured as the interval between the onset of the input $S(x,t)$ at $t = 0$ and the time when the u-activity reaches the threshold.

Figure 5 compares directly the values of measured and produced intervals. For the tested range, the results reveal a very good match with a slight overestimation of the shortest intervals and a slight underestimation of the longest intervals (see also Table 1).

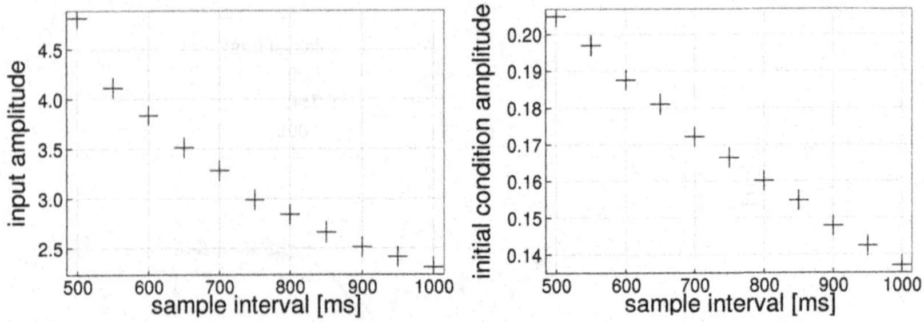

Fig. 3. Left: Strength of the input during the interval production epoch as a function of sample interval length. Right: Strength of the initial condition during the interval production epoch as a function of sample interval length.

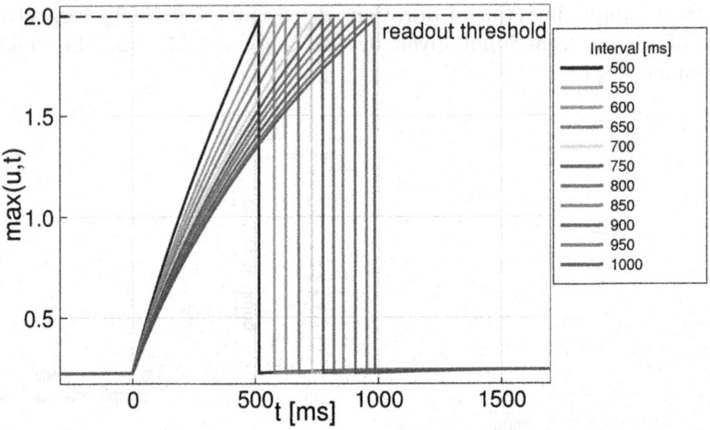

Fig. 4. Time courses of activity in the u-field during the interval production epoch. Threshold reaching time is determined by the input strength.

3.3 Reproducing Time Intervals - Varying Initial Conditions

To test the hypothesis that an adequate choice of initial condition for the population dynamics of the reproduction epoch may be sufficient to account for a flexible reproduction of measured time intervals, we proceed as follows. The numerical simulations do not start from a homogeneous resting state. Instead, the population centered at position x_c representing the planned movement direction appears to be pre-activated at time $t = 0$. The amplitude of the preshape depends on the outcome of the preceding measuring epoch in the following manner:

$$u(x, 0) = \frac{1}{\alpha e^{(u_{max})}} e^{\left(-(x-x_c)^2/8\right)}, \qquad v(x, 0) = K - u(x, 0), \tag{5}$$

where u_{max} is maximum activity of the steady state solution in the u-layer reached during ME, and α is a constant scaling factor for the preshape ampli-

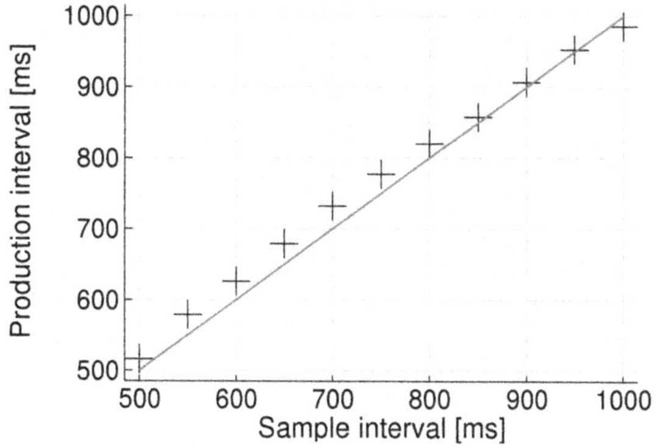

Fig. 5. Production intervals as a function of sample intervals. Goodness of fit $R^2 = 0.99$.

tude which decreases with increasing u_{max}. The role of the constant K can be understood by noting that the subthreshold population dynamics ($f(u) = 0$) has the equilibrium solution $u(x) = v(x)$. By choosing $K > 2h$ one can ensure that the dynamics of the coupled populations will reach the threshold h necessary to drive the evolution of a bump. For the numerical tests we use $K = 0.5$, $h = 0.22$ and $\alpha = 1.25$. The initial condition may be set for instance by a transient input controlling the bell-shaped pre-activation and by a transient "go" signal (e.g., the second flash in the monkey experiment) controlling K and consequently the onset of the temporal evolution at $t = 0$. Figure 6 shows the time course of activity of the u-population for all measured intervals. The initial preshape amplitude predicts motor timing. Stronger preshapes are associated with shorter production intervals. Since no external input is applied, the neural trajectory is identical for all intervals once the threshold for the bump formation is reached. The difference in timing is thus completely explained by the speed with which the subthreshold trajectory reaches threshold, which in turn is determined by the activation gap between $u(x, 0)$ and h. Figure 7 directly compares the measured and produced intervals. The coefficient of determination, $R^2 = 0.95$, indicates that the numerical results fit still quite well the model of a perfect measuring/production match, albeit with larger errors compared to the model with external input (see also Table 1).

Table 1. Values (in milliseconds) of sample and produced intervals.

Sample interval	500	550	600	650	700	750	800	850	900	950	1000
Produced interval (external inputs)	516	579	626	679	732	777	820	858	907	953	986
Produced interval (initial conditions)	518	604	676	741	793	820	862	893	923	950	972

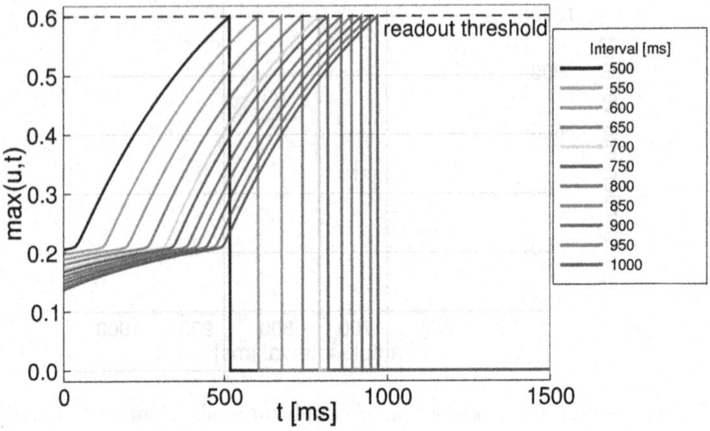

Fig. 6. Time courses of activity in the u-field during the interval production epoch. The instants of reaching the read-out threshold, $h_R = 0.6$, vary systematically in dependence of the initial condition of the field dynamics.

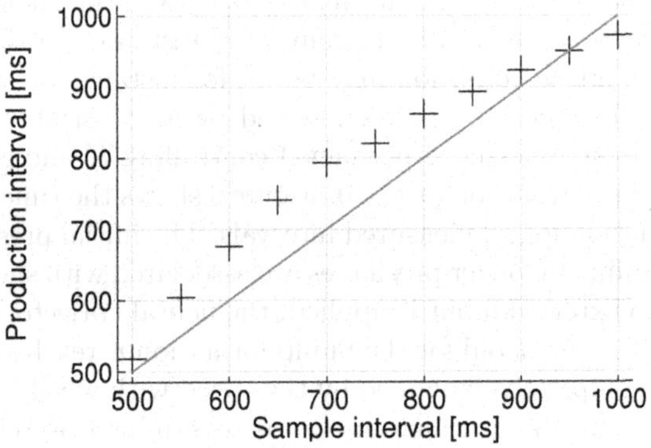

Fig. 7. Production intervals as a function of sample intervals. Goodness of fit $R^2 = 0.95$.

4 Discussion

The results of our simulation study support the notion that neural computational principles of flexible timing may be captured by a dynamical systems perspective. Closely balanced excitation and inhibition in a spatially structured neural network explain the temporal integration and maintenance of external inputs. The information about elapsed time stored in the bump amplitude can be used on a trial-by-trial basis to reproduce the time interval either by adjusting input strength or initial condition of the neural integrator. This affects the speed or the onset of the neural trajectory towards the bump attractor, respectively. The field model shares with other recurrent network models the assumption that the neural mechanisms for timing are closely integrated with the processing of other stimulus attributes like for instance movement direction [12,14].

There are several open issues with the current model implementation. First of all, since the input is continuously integrated, not only its duration but also its strength will influence the bump amplitude and consequently the interval measurement. The "strength normalization" issue can be solved by not integrating the input directly but instead a bump from a connected neural field which is triggered and deleted by transient signals (e.g., input onset and offset). In classical neural field models, the shape of such a memory bump is exclusively determined by the recurrent interactions within the network [1,4]. Moreover, recurrent interactions are known to increase the signal-to-noise ratio, making the integration process more robust compared to the direct integration of a potentially weak and noisy input. Interestingly, the usage of a memory bump in the integration process might also explain the finding that "filled" intervals are typically judged as lasting longer than "unfilled" intervals of the same duration [21]. Since a stationary bump solution of the field equation with a lasting external input has a slightly larger amplitude compared to a bump triggered by a brief, transient input, the temporal integration in the "filled" condition predicts a larger bump amplitude in the measurement field compared to the "unfilled" condition.

A second issue concerns the scaling of intervals to values outside the measured range by instruction or symbolic cues [20]. The effective bump height during reproduction should reflect this additional information. We have recently proposed and tested a simple and effective adaptation rule for the bump height based on the comparison between the produced time course of population activity and the neural trajectory of a reference or synchronization signal indicating the expected timing [23].

Our ultimate application goal for the model is to advance towards a human-like temporal cognition capacity for autonomous robots [13]. We are planning to test the model as part of an existing dynamic field control architecture for natural human-robot cooperation [5]. The continuous real-time synchronization of decision and actions with a human partner requires flexible perception and production of time intervals, fully integrated in other cognitive processes without reference to external computer clocks. A concrete example of human-robot collaboration is an assembly paradigm in which a robot assistant hands over a series of objects to the human worker. Findings in recent experiments directly comparing human-human and human-robot handovers stress the importance of temporal aspects of the robot's actions [7,9]. Being able to adapt to the user by minimizing the human's waiting time is considered crucial for user acceptance and satisfaction. Figure 8 presents a sketch of a possible model implementation in the context of a cooperative object transfer task. The robot has first to measure the duration of individual assembly steps. This could be achieved for instance in a learning by demonstration paradigm in which the robot watches a human teacher executing the assembly work (assuming that all objects are within reach, [19]). Time measurement starts when the robot observes the teacher reaching for a specific object and stops when he/she reaches for the next one. The input to the

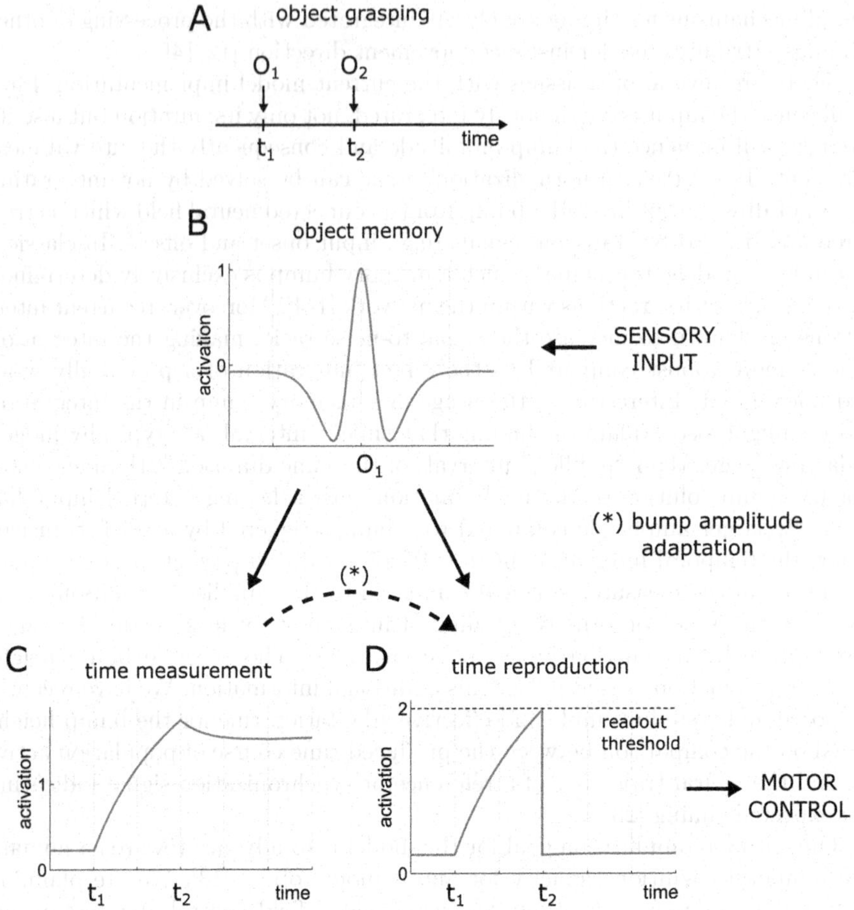

Fig. 8. Object handover task. (A) The robot has to measure the time interval, $[t_1, t_2]$, between two consecutive graspings of object O_1 and object O_2. (B) Visual input from the camera system, characterizing the first object (e.g., object color), drives the evolution of a bump in an object memory field. (C) Time course of the temporal integration of the object memory in the measurement field during the interval $[t_1, t_2]$. (D) The measured duration is recalled in the reproduction field by integrating the memory bump with an amplitude defined by the measurement bump in (C). Reaching the readout threshold is associated with the initiation of the object transfer to the exchange position.

measurement field is thus a self-stabilized bump in a memory field representing the object currently manipulated. During joint task execution, the robot uses the temporal information stored in the bump amplitude to prepare the complementary action of holding out the next object for the user. The temporal integration of the object memory bump with an amplitude given by Eq. 4 causes ramping activity in the time reproduction field. Reaching the pre-defined activation threshold at the end of the interval to be estimated is associated with the initiation of the object transport to the exchange position. Due to motor delays, the object exchange may still not be in perfect synchrony. A perceived temporal mismatch between the expected and the realized event timing (e.g., user picking object from robot hand) can be used to adapt in a single trial the initial resting state in the reproduction field in order to compensate systematic motor delays [23]. We are currently studying how the choice of the time scale of the robust neural integrator ($\tau = 1$ in the present study) affects precision timing for time intervals that are relevant for human-robot interactions.

Acknowledgments. The work received financial support from FCT through the PhD fellowship PD/BD/128183/2016, the project "Neurofield" (POCI-01-0145-FEDER-031393) and the research centre CMAT within the project UID/MAT/00013/2013.

References

1. Amari, S.: Dynamics of pattern formation in lateral-inhibition type neural fields. Biol. Cybern. **27**(2), 77–87 (1977). https://doi.org/10.1007/BF00337259
2. Bezanson, J., Edelman, A., Karpinski, S., Shah, V.B.: Julia: a fresh approach to numerical computing. SIAM Rev. **59**(1), 65–98 (2017). https://doi.org/10.1137/141000671
3. Bicho, E., Louro, L., Erlhagen, W.: Integrating verbal and nonverbal communication in a dynamic neural field architecture for human-robot interaction. Front. Neurorobotics **4**, 5 (2010). https://doi.org/10.3389/fnbot.2010.00005
4. Erlhagen, W., Bicho, E.: The dynamic neural field approach to cognitive robotics. J. Neural Eng. **3**, 36–54 (2006). https://doi.org/10.1088/1741-2560/3/3/R02
5. Erlhagen, W., Bicho, E.: A dynamic neural field approach to natural and efficient human-robot collaboration. In: Coombes, S., beim Graben, P., Potthast, R., Wright, J. (eds.) Neural Fields, pp. 341–365. Springer, Heidelberg (2014). https://doi.org/10.1007/978-3-642-54593-1_13
6. Gallistel, C.R., Gibbon, J.: Time, rate, and conditioning. Psychol. Rev. **107**(2), 289–344 (2000). https://doi.org/10.1037//0033-295X.107.2.289
7. Glasauer, S., Huber, M., Basili, P., Knoll, A., Brandt, T.: Interacting in time and space: investigating human-human and human-robot joint action. In: RO-MAN, 2010 IEEE, pp. 252–257. IEEE (2010). https://doi.org/10.1109/ROMAN.2010.5598638
8. Jazayeri, M., Shadlen, M.N.: A neural mechanism for sensing and reproducing a time interval. Curr. Biol. **25**(20), 2599–2609 (2015). https://doi.org/10.1016/j.cub.2015.08.038
9. Koene, A., et al.: Relative importance of spatial and temporal precision for user satisfaction in human-robot object handover interactions. In: Proceedings of the New Frontiers in Human-Robot Interaction, vol. 14 (2014)
10. Lim, S., Goldman, M.S.: Balanced cortical microcircuitry for maintaining information in working memory. Nat. Neurosci. **16**(9), 1306 (2013). https://doi.org/10.1038/nn.3492
11. Machado, A., Malheiro, M.T., Erlhagen, W.: Learning to time: a perspective. J. Exp. Anal. Behav. **92**(3), 423–458 (2009). https://doi.org/10.1901/jeab.2009.92-423

12. Machens, C.K., Romo, R., Brody, C.D.: Functional, but not anatomical, separation of "what" and "when" in prefrontal cortex. J. Neurosci. **30**(1), 350–360 (2010). https://doi.org/10.1523/JNEUROSCI.3276-09.2010
13. Maniadakis, M., Trahanias, P.: Temporal cognition: a key ingredient of intelligent systems. Front. Neurorobotics **5**, 2 (2011). https://doi.org/10.3389/fnbot.2011.00002
14. Paton, J.J., Buonomano, D.V.: The neural basis of timing: distributed mechanisms for diverse functions. Neuron **98**(4), 687–705 (2018). https://doi.org/10.1016/j.neuron.2018.03.045
15. Remington, E.D., Egger, S.W., Narain, D., Wang, J., Jazayeri, M.: A dynamical systems perspective on flexible motor timing. Trends Cogn. Sci. **22**(10), 938–952 (2018). https://doi.org/10.1016/j.tics.2018.07.010
16. Reutimann, J., Yakovlev, V., Fusi, S., Senn, W.: Climbing neuronal activity as an event-based cortical representation of time. J. Neurosci. **24**(13), 3295–3303 (2004). https://doi.org/10.1523/JNEUROSCI.4098-03.2004
17. Schöner, G., Spencer, J.: Dynamic Thinking: A Primer on Dynamic Field Theory. Oxford University Press, Oxford (2016). https://doi.org/10.1093/acprof:oso/9780199300563.001.0001
18. Simen, P., Balci, F., deSouza, L., Cohen, J.D., Holmes, P.: A model of interval timing by neural integration. J. Neurosci. **31**(25), 9238–9253 (2011). https://doi.org/10.1523/JNEUROSCI.3121-10.2011
19. Sousa, E., Erlhagen, W., Ferreira, F., Bicho, E.: Off-line simulation inspires insight: a neurodynamics approach to efficient robot task learning. Neural Netw. **72**, 123–139 (2015). https://doi.org/10.1016/j.neunet.2015.09.002
20. Wang, J., Narain, D., Hosseini, E.A., Jazayeri, M.: Flexible timing by temporal scaling of cortical responses. Nat. Neurosci. **21**(1), 102 (2018). https://doi.org/10.1038/s41593-017-0028-6
21. Wearden, J.H., Norton, R., Martin, S., Montford-Bebb, O.: Internal clock processes and the filled-duration illusion. J. Exp. Psychol. Hum. Percept. Perform. **33**(3), 716 (2007). https://doi.org/10.1037/0096-1523.33.3.716
22. Wojtak, W., Coombes, S., Bicho, E., Erlhagen, W.: Combining spatial and parametric working memory in a dynamic neural field model. In: Villa, A.E.P., Masulli, P., Pons Rivero, A.J. (eds.) ICANN 2016. LNCS, vol. 9886, pp. 411–418. Springer, Cham (2016). https://doi.org/10.1007/978-3-319-44778-0_48
23. Wojtak, W., Ferreira, F., Erlhagen, W., Bicho, E.: Learning joint representations for order and timing of perceptual-motor sequences: a dynamic neural field approach. In: 2015 International Joint Conference on Neural Networks (IJCNN), pp. 3082–3088. IEEE (2015). https://doi.org/10.1109/IJCNN.2015.7280717

Widely Linear Complex-Valued Autoencoder: Dealing with Noncircularity in Generative-Discriminative Models

Zeyang Yu(✉), Shengxi Li, and Danilo Mandic

Department of Electrical and Electronic Engineering, Imperial College London, London, UK
{z.yu17,shengxi.li17,d.mandic}@imperial.ac.uk

Abstract. We propose a new structure for the complex-valued autoencoder by introducing additional degrees of freedom into its design through a widely linear (WL) transform. The corresponding widely linear backpropagation algorithm is also developed using the $\mathbb{CR}$ calculus, to unify the gradient calculation of the cost function and the underlying WL model. More specifically, all the existing complex-valued autoencoders employ the strictly linear transform, which is optimal only when the complex-valued outputs of each network layer are independent of the conjugate of the inputs. In addition, the widely linear model which underpins our work allows us to consider all the second-order statistics of inputs. This provides more freedom in the design and enhanced optimization opportunities, as compared to the state-of-the-art. Furthermore, we show that the most widely adopted cost function, i.e., the mean squared error, is not best suited for the complex domain, as it is a real quantity with a single degree of freedom, while both the phase and the amplitude information need to be optimized. To resolve this issue, we design a new cost function, which is capable of controlling the balance between the phase and the amplitude contribution to the solution. The experimental results verify the superior performance of the proposed autoencoder together with the new cost function, especially for the imaging scenarios where the phase preserves extensive information on edges and shapes.

Keywords: Complex-valued neural networks · Widely linear backpropagation · Spectrum reconstruction

1 Introduction

With the significant improvement of computational power and the exponential growth of data, deep learning has become the most rapidly growing area in the field of artificial intelligence. Numerous techniques have been proposed in this area, which enable a deep neural network model to even surpass human-level performance. Driven by these outstanding opportunities, extensive research has been conducted on the use of deep learning for image and voice recognition.

I. V. Tetko et al. (Eds.): ICANN 2019, LNCS 11727, pp. 339–350, 2019.
https://doi.org/10.1007/978-3-030-30487-4_27

An autoencoder is an unsupervised deep learning structure, proposed by Hinton *et al.* [7,8,18]. It automatically learns to compress the original high-dimensional data and extract meaningful features, which can then be used as an input for other models. Essentially, the autoencoder is a neural network which can be divided into two parts - an encoder and a decoder. The encoder maps the original data into a low-dimensional representation, whilst the decoder learns to reconstruct the original data from this low-dimensional representation. This is one of the most widely applied deep learning algorithms for dimensionality reduction and feature extraction.

Recently, complex-valued neural networks have received increasing attention due to their potential for easier optimization, faster learning and robustness, compared to real-valued ones [1,9,19]. Applications include radar image processing, antenna design, and forecasting in smart grid, to mention but a few [10]. In this context, Arjovsky *et al.* [2] showed that using a complex representation in recurrent neural networks can increase the representation capacity. Călin-Adrian Popa [16] verified that the complex-valued convolutional neural network (CVCNN) outperforms the real-valued one, with the biggest improvement in performance for the bigger kernel sizes. In terms of autoencoders, Hata *et al.* [6] illustrated that a complex-valued autoencoder can extract better features than the real-valued one. However, all the existing complex-valued neural networks are designed using the strictly linear transform, which assumes the complex outputs of each layer are independent of the conjugate parts of the inputs. This assumption limits the structure of the covariance matrix of the output of the complex linear transform, restricts the number of degrees of freedom, and thus may possibly lead to sub-optimum or unstable optimization process.

In this paper, we propose a new structure for the complex-valued autoencoder, referred to as the widely linear complex-valued autoencoder (WLCAE). The proposed autoencoder makes use of the widely linear transform [13] for the linear part of the autoencoder, which provides more degrees of freedom in the analysis and enhanced performance. To optimize the parameters in such autoencoder, we derive the corresponding widely linear backpropagation algorithm using the $\mathbb{CR}$ calculus [11,13]. In order to further improve the performance of the proposed autoencoder in the complex domain, instead of the standard mean squared error, a phase-magnitude cost function is also proposed to improve the performance of the complex-valued autoencoder.

2 Preliminaries

2.1 Widely Linear Transform

In a real-valued autoencoder, the linear transform of a single layer is defined as $\mathbf{z} = \mathbf{W}\mathbf{a}$ where $\mathbf{a}$ is the input to this layer, $\mathbf{W}$ is the transform matrix, and $\mathbf{z}$ is the output of the linear transform. By applying this linear transform, the features from the previous layer are combined according to specific weighting, which to a great extend determines the behavior of the neural network as a whole. However, in the complex domain, it has recently been recognized that there are two types of linear transforms - strictly linear transform and widely linear transform.

In a way similar to the real-valued transform, with complex-valued $\mathbf{z}, \mathbf{W}$ and $\mathbf{a}$, the strictly linear transform in the complex domain is defined as

$$\mathbf{z} = \mathbf{W}\mathbf{a} \tag{1}$$

The so called "augmented representation" of the strictly linear transform then clearly shows the lack of its degrees of freedom, as two of the block diagonal matrices below are zero, that is

$$\underline{\mathbf{z}} = \begin{bmatrix} \mathbf{z} \\ \mathbf{z}^* \end{bmatrix} = \begin{bmatrix} \mathbf{W}, \mathbf{0} \\ \mathbf{0}, \mathbf{W}^* \end{bmatrix} \begin{bmatrix} \mathbf{a} \\ \mathbf{a}^* \end{bmatrix} \tag{2}$$

The widely linear transform in complex domain is defined as

$$\mathbf{z} = \mathbf{W}_1\mathbf{a} + \mathbf{W}_2\mathbf{a}^* \tag{3}$$

and its augmented representation is given by

$$\underline{\mathbf{z}} = \begin{bmatrix} \mathbf{z} \\ \mathbf{z}^* \end{bmatrix} = \begin{bmatrix} \mathbf{W}_1, \mathbf{W}_2 \\ \mathbf{W}_2^*, \mathbf{W}_1^* \end{bmatrix} \begin{bmatrix} \mathbf{a} \\ \mathbf{a}^* \end{bmatrix} = \underline{\mathbf{W}\mathbf{a}} \tag{4}$$

Compared to the strictly linear transform in (2), one additional transfer matrix is added to merge the information from the conjugate of the input.

Complex-valued $\mathbf{z}$ and $\mathbf{a}$ can also be represented via the following form

$$\begin{aligned} \mathbf{z} &= \mathbf{m} + j\mathbf{n} \\ \mathbf{a} &= \mathbf{u} + j\mathbf{v} \end{aligned} \tag{5}$$

where $\mathbf{m}$ and $\mathbf{u}$ are the real parts, $\mathbf{n}$ and $\mathbf{v}$ are the imaginary parts.

Then, the augmented representation of both of these two complex linear transforms is equivalent to the following real linear transform

$$\begin{bmatrix} \mathbf{m} \\ \mathbf{n} \end{bmatrix} = \begin{bmatrix} \mathbf{M}_{11}, \mathbf{M}_{12} \\ \mathbf{M}_{21}, \mathbf{M}_{22} \end{bmatrix} \begin{bmatrix} \mathbf{u} \\ \mathbf{v} \end{bmatrix} \tag{6}$$

where

$$\begin{aligned} \mathbf{W}_1 &= \frac{1}{2}[\mathbf{M}_{11} + \mathbf{M}_{22} + j(\mathbf{M}_{21} - \mathbf{M}_{12})] \\ \mathbf{W}_2 &= \frac{1}{2}[\mathbf{M}_{11} - \mathbf{M}_{22} + j(\mathbf{M}_{21} + \mathbf{M}_{12})] \end{aligned} \tag{7}$$

By inspecting (2) and (7), the strictly linear transform assumes $\mathbf{M}_{11} = \mathbf{M}_{22}$ and $\mathbf{M}_{21} = \mathbf{M}_{12} = \mathbf{0}$, which imposes a very stringent constraint during the optimization process [14]. On the other hand, the widely linear transform exhibits sufficient degrees of freedom to capture the full available second-order information, the so called augmented complex statistics.

2.2 Generalized Derivatives in the Complex Domain

Consider a complex-valued function $f(z) = u(x, y) + jv(x, y)$ where $z = x + jy$. This function is differentiable at z if it simultaneously satisfies the Cauchy-Riemann Equations [17]

$$\begin{aligned} \frac{\partial u(x,y)}{\partial x} &= \frac{\partial v(x,y)}{\partial y} \\ \frac{\partial v(x,y)}{\partial x} &= -\frac{\partial u(x,y)}{\partial y} \end{aligned} \tag{8}$$

However, these conditions are too stringent for general optimization in autoencoders. In particular, it is obvious that any function that depends on both z and z^* does not satisfy the Cauchy-Riemann conditions, which means that it is not differentiable in the standard complex way. Unfortunately, the most widely applied cost function, the mean squared error, belongs to this type: it is a real function of complex variables which is defined via the multiplication between the residual and its conjugate. To address this issue, the $\mathbb{CR}$ calculus was proposed to calculate the gradient.

Specifically, $\mathbb{CR}$ calculus assumes that z and z^* are mutually independent. Therefore, we need to calculate two gradients termed the $\mathbb{R}$-derivative and the $\mathbb{R}^*$-derivative [13]. The $\mathbb{R}$-derivative is calculated by

$$\frac{\partial f}{\partial z}_{|z^*=const} = \frac{1}{2}\left(\frac{\partial f}{\partial x} - j\frac{\partial f}{\partial y}\right) \tag{9}$$

while the $\mathbb{R}^*$-derivative has the form

$$\frac{\partial f}{\partial z^*}_{|z=const} = \frac{1}{2}\left(\frac{\partial f}{\partial x} + j\frac{\partial f}{\partial y}\right) \tag{10}$$

Correspondingly, the chain rule is derived as

$$\frac{\partial f(g(z))}{\partial z} = \frac{\partial f}{\partial g}\frac{\partial g}{\partial z} + \frac{\partial f}{\partial g^*}\frac{\partial g^*}{\partial z} \tag{11}$$

3 Proposed Widely Linear Complex-Valued Autoencoder

The widely linear complex-valued autoencoder is an extension of the traditional complex-valued autoencoder which accounts for second-order data noncircularity (improperness). The structure of one single layer of the proposed widely linear network is shown in Fig. 1. The widely linear complex-valued autoencoder includes two main building blocks: the widely linear transform component and an enhanced cost function which separates phase and amplitude for spectrum reconstruction. We first present the structure of the widely linear complex-valued autoencoder in Sect. 3.1, then we show in Sect. 3.2 that the phase is not well balanced when using the mean squared error cost function, which may lead to sub-optimality of complex-valued autoencoders when using the mean squared error as the cost. To this end, we derive the novel phase-amplitude cost function on the basis of the popular mean squared error cost function in Sect. 3.2 to further improve the performance of the proposed autoencoder.

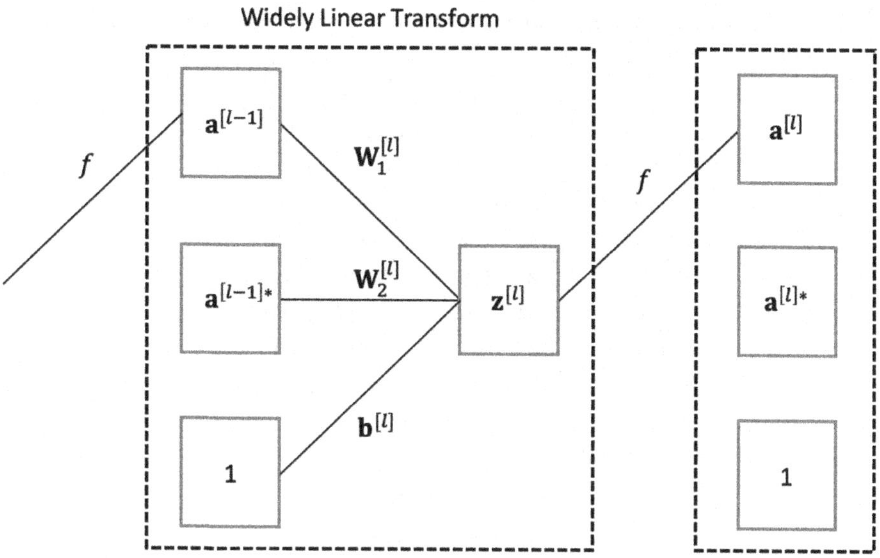

Fig. 1. The structure of a single layer of the proposed widely linear complex-valued autoencoder.

3.1 Widely Linear Complex-Valued Autoencoder

Since the strictly linear transform limits the structure of the covariance matrix of the merged features, we propose to introduce a widely linear transform component into the complex-valued autoencoder. Let $\mathbf{a}^{[0]}$ be the input vector, $\mathbf{a}^{[l]}$ the output of the activation function, $\mathbf{z}^{[l]}$ the result for the widely linear transform, $\mathbf{W}_1^{[l]}, \mathbf{W}_2^{[l]}$ the complex-valued weight matrices, and $\mathbf{b}^{[l]}$ the bias vector. Moreover, $l \in [1, 2, \ldots, L]$ designates the index of each layer. The output vector of the activation function is then calculated as

$$\begin{aligned}\mathbf{z}^{[l]} &= \mathbf{W}_1^{[l]}\mathbf{a}^{[l-1]} + \mathbf{W}_2^{[l]}\mathbf{a}^{[l-1]*} + \mathbf{b}^{[l]} \\ \mathbf{a}^{[l]} &= f(\mathbf{z}^{[l]})\end{aligned} \tag{12}$$

where $f(\cdot)$ is the activation function. The mean squared error cost function for one sample is given by

$$J = \frac{1}{N}(\mathbf{a}^{[L]} - \mathbf{x})^H(\mathbf{a}^{[L]} - \mathbf{x}) \tag{13}$$

where N is the dimension of $\mathbf{a}^{[L]}$.

Then, the widely linear backpropagation algorithm can be derived using the $\mathbb{CR}$ calculus as follows

$$\begin{aligned}\frac{\partial J}{\partial \mathbf{z}^{[l]}} &= \frac{\partial J}{\partial \mathbf{a}^{[l]}}\frac{\partial \mathbf{a}^{[l]}}{\partial \mathbf{z}^{[l]}} + \frac{\partial J}{\partial \mathbf{a}^{[l]*}}\left[\frac{\partial \mathbf{a}^{[l]}}{\partial \mathbf{z}^{[l]*}}\right]^* \\ \frac{\partial J}{\partial \mathbf{z}^{[l]*}} &= \frac{\partial J}{\partial \mathbf{a}^{[l]}}\frac{\partial \mathbf{a}^{[l]}}{\partial \mathbf{z}^{[l]*}} + \frac{\partial J}{\partial \mathbf{a}^{[l]*}}\left[\frac{\partial \mathbf{a}^{[l]}}{\partial \mathbf{z}^{[l]}}\right]^* \\ \frac{\partial J}{\partial \mathbf{a}^{[l-1]}} &= \frac{\partial J}{\partial \mathbf{z}^{[l]}}\frac{\partial \mathbf{z}^{[l]}}{\partial \mathbf{a}^{[l-1]}} + \frac{\partial J}{\partial \mathbf{z}^{[l]*}}\left[\frac{\partial \mathbf{z}^{[l]}}{\partial \mathbf{a}^{[l-1]*}}\right]^* \\ \frac{\partial J}{\partial \mathbf{a}^{[l-1]*}} &= \frac{\partial J}{\partial \mathbf{z}^{[l]}}\frac{\partial \mathbf{z}^{[l]}}{\partial \mathbf{a}^{[l-1]*}} + \frac{\partial J}{\partial \mathbf{z}^{[l]*}}\left[\frac{\partial \mathbf{z}^{[l]}}{\partial \mathbf{a}^{[l-1]}}\right]^*\end{aligned} \tag{14}$$

When the activation function satisfies the Cauchy-Riemann equations, then $\frac{\partial \mathbf{a}^{[l]}}{\partial \mathbf{z}^{[l]*}} = \mathbf{0}$. In this case, the first two equations of the widely linear backpropagation can be simplified as follows

$$\begin{aligned}\frac{\partial J}{\partial \mathbf{z}^{[l]}} &= \frac{\partial J}{\partial \mathbf{a}^{[l]}}\frac{\partial \mathbf{a}^{[l]}}{\partial \mathbf{z}^{[l]}} \\ \frac{\partial J}{\partial \mathbf{z}^{[l]*}} &= \frac{\partial J}{\partial \mathbf{a}^{[l]*}}\left[\frac{\partial \mathbf{a}^{[l]}}{\partial \mathbf{z}^{[l]}}\right]^*\end{aligned} \tag{15}$$

It should be pointed out that the main decent direction of the cost function in the complex domain is in the direction of the conjugate gradient [3]. Since the conjugate gradients of the parameters with respect to $\mathbf{z}^{[l]}$ all vanish, the gradient of the cost function with respect to the weight matrices and the bias vector can be expressed as

$$\begin{aligned}\nabla_{\mathbf{W}_1^{[l]}} J &= \frac{\partial J}{\partial \mathbf{z}^{[l]*}}\left[\frac{\partial \mathbf{z}^{[l]}}{\partial \mathbf{W}_1^{[l]}}\right]^* \\ \nabla_{\mathbf{W}_2^{[l]}} J &= \frac{\partial J}{\partial \mathbf{z}^{[l]*}}\left[\frac{\partial \mathbf{z}^{[l]}}{\partial \mathbf{W}_2^{[l]}}\right]^* \\ \nabla_{\mathbf{b}^{[l]}} J &= \frac{\partial J}{\partial \mathbf{z}^{[l]*}}\left[\frac{\partial \mathbf{z}^{[l]}}{\partial \mathbf{b}^{[l]}}\right]^*\end{aligned} \tag{16}$$

3.2 Importance of Phase Information

The complex number consists of the phase and the amplitude parts, where the phase of the frequency spectrum has been proven to play a more important role than the magnitude. Indeed, Oppenheim and Lim [15] verified that the information encoded in the magnitude of an image can be approximately recovered by the information encoded in its phase. For illustration, consider the surrogate images in Fig. 2 with I_1 and I_2 denoting the two original images in the top panel of Fig. 2. The 2D Fourier transform is first applied to these two images and their phase parts are swapped, which results in the new images at the bottom of Fig. 2, that is

$$\begin{aligned}\hat{I}_1 &= \mathscr{F}^{-1}(|\mathscr{F}(I_1)|e^{j\angle \mathscr{F}(I_2)}) \\ \hat{I}_2 &= \mathscr{F}^{-1}(|\mathscr{F}(I_2)|e^{j\angle \mathscr{F}(I_1)})\end{aligned} \tag{17}$$

Fig. 2. Effects of phase on images. (a) and (b): original images I_1 and I_2; (c) and (d): images $\hat{I}_1$ and $\hat{I}_2$ generated by swapping the phase spectra and keeping the original magnitude spectra.

The example in Fig. 2 makes it obvious that the phase preserves the information of edges and shapes while the amplitude preserves the information about pixel intensity. Inspired by this idea, we propose a new cost function for the complex-valued autoencoder in order to make it possible to balance the cost between amplitude and phase.

Mean squared error is one of the most widely used cost functions for the complex-valued autoencoder. However, this cost function suffers from the lack of ability to measure the difference in the frequency domain. As mentioned above, the importance of different frequency components in an image should not be treated on equal terms. In order to further enhance the performance of spectrum reconstruction, we propose to normalize the cost at each neuron by the amplitude of the corresponding input component, which from the above discussion is physically meaningful. To prevent the gradient from exploding, a lower bound, β, is added to the normalization factor, to yield a normalized cost for a single neuron in the form

$$J_i = \frac{(a_i^{[L]} - x_i)(a_i^{[L]} - x_i)^*}{\max(x_i x_i^*, \beta)} \tag{18}$$

where all the variables correspond to the neuron with index i.

Since the information contained in the phase is comparably important, we propose to separate the cost function into two costs - one of the amplitude and the other one of the phase. A similar practice has already yielded advantages in linear adaptive filtering [4]. Let $x = A_x e^{j\theta_x}$ and $y = A_y e^{j\theta_y}$ be the values of two corresponding input and output neurons, where A is the amplitude and θ is the phase. We start from the mean squared error of this pair of neurons which can be factorized as

$$\begin{aligned} J &= (y - x)(y - x)^* \\ &= (A_y e^{j\theta_y} - A_x e^{j\theta_x})(A_y e^{j\theta_y} - A_x e^{j\theta_x})^* \\ &= (A_y - A_x)^2 + A_y A_x \big(2 - 2\cos(\theta_y - \theta_x)\big) \end{aligned} \tag{19}$$

The first term above is the cost of the amplitude, and the second term is the cost of the phase weighted by the amplitude of the input and output components. Then, we can adjust the weight of the second term to control the importance of phase during the reconstruction of the frequency spectrum.

By combining the idea of normalizing the cost of reconstruction by amplitude and manipulating the cost of phase, we develop a new cost function which is specific for frequency spectrum reconstruction and has the form

$$J = \frac{(\sqrt{yy^*} - \sqrt{xx^*})^2 + \alpha(2\sqrt{yy^* xx^*} - xy^* - x^* y)}{\max(xx^*, \beta)} \tag{20}$$

4 Experiments

The performances of a strictly linear and the proposed widely linear complex-valued autoencoder were evaluated on the benchmark MNIST database [12]. For simplicity, both these types of autoencoder were implemented with only one hidden layer, and the performance was measured by peak signal-to-noise ratio (PSNR) of the reconstructed images.

4.1 Experimental Setup

For the training data, we randomly selected 250 samples for each digital number, and then normalized the pixel values between 0 and 1. The complex image data can be generated in two ways. The first way is to combine adjacent pixels into

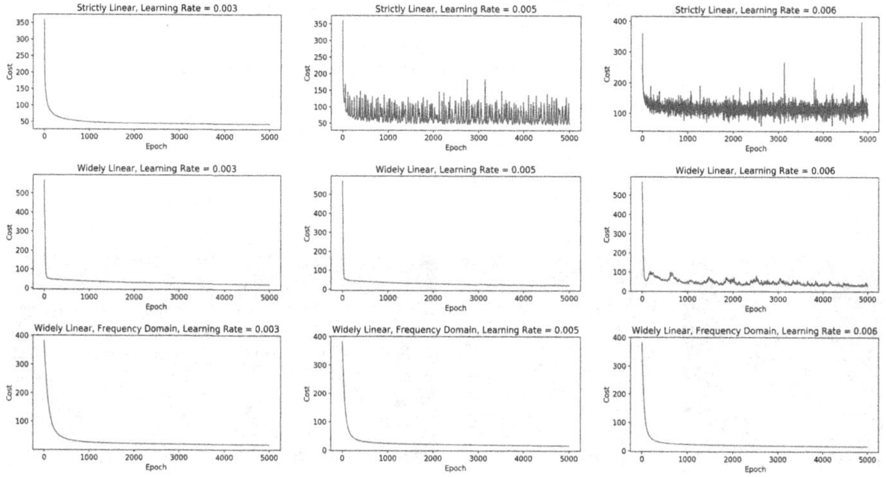

Fig. 3. Training performance of the proposed widely linear autoencoder vs the standard one. Top: Strictly linear autoencoder, combining adjacent pixels into one complex number. Middle: Widely linear autoencoder, combining adjacent pixels into one complex number. Bottom: Widely linear autoencoder, Fourier transform. Learning rate from left to right: 0.003, 0.005 and 0.006.

one complex number, the most widely used way to generate complex data. The second way is to apply the 2D Fourier transform and discard the conjugate symmetric part of the data. The frequency spectrum was reconstructed via the output of the autoencoders and an inverse Fourier transform was applied to obtain the original image.

In our experiments, the strictly linear autoencoder had 196 hidden units while the widely linear autoencoder had 98 hidden units. As a result, both of these two autoencoders had the same number of parameters. For the activation function, we used the inverse tangent function $f(\cdot) = arctan(\cdot)$. For the initialization, we used Xavier initialization [5] for both the real and imaginary parts, with the same random seed.

To train the autoencoder, three cost functions were used - mean squared error, mean squared error normalized by amplitude shown in Eq. (18), and the phase-amplitude cost function shown in Eq. (20). Each autoencoder was trained over 5000 epochs. For simplicity, the lower bound of normalization β was set to 0.1.

4.2 Experimental Result

Figure 3 shows the training process of each types of autoencoders with different learning rates. Observe that under the same type of the input, the proposed widely linear autoencoder was more stable than the strictly linear autoencoder. In addition, the use of the Fourier transform to generate complex data was able to stabilize the auto-encoder for large learning rates, which allows the acceleration of the training process.

Table 1. PSNR values with different cost functions

Input data	Cost function	PSNR (dB)
Complex pixels	MSE	15.68
DFT	MSE	16.20
DFT	Normalized MSE	18.47

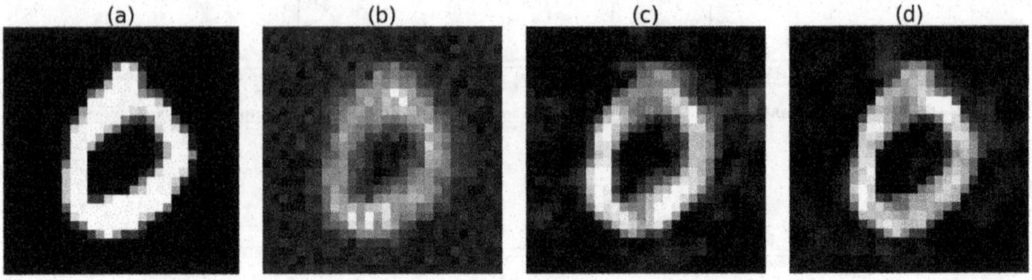

Fig. 4. Examples of the reconstructed images. (a): Original image. (b): Combining adjacent pixels into one complex number as the input, mean squared error as the cost function. (c): Frequency spectrum as the input, mean squared error as the cost function. (d): Frequency spectrum as the input, mean squared error normalized by amplitude as the cost function.

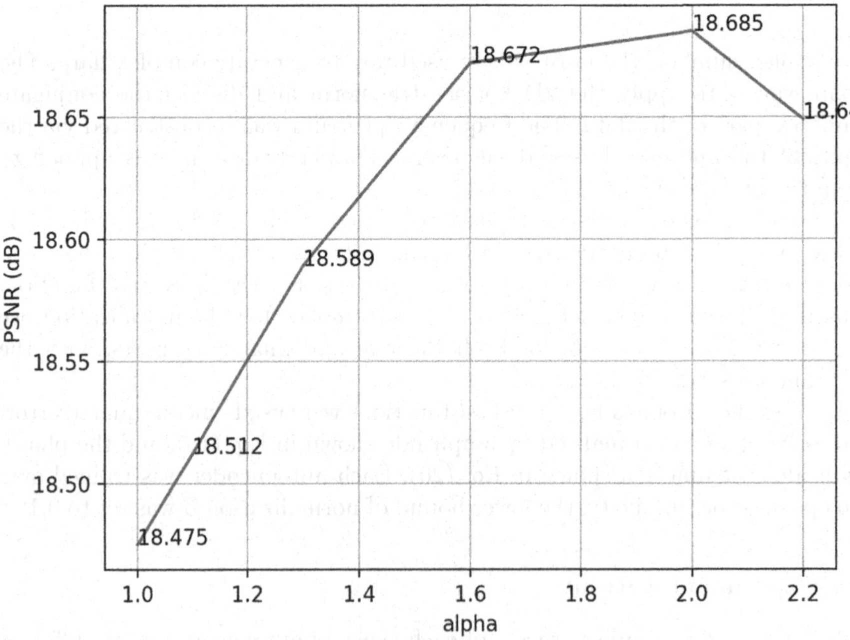

Fig. 5. The effect of phase weighting, α, on reconstruction.

Table 1 shows the effect on the PSNR of normalizing frequency components by their magnitude. We can see from the table that the PSNR was significantly reduced by using the normalized cost function. After applying the Fourier transform to the input data, the original data was transferred to an orthogonal representation, which is much easier to learn. However, the magnitude of different frequency components are no longer of the same scale. Normalizing the reconstruction error in the frequency domain with the magnitude was thus capable of significantly improving the performance of reconstruction of the original images. Figure 4 shows the examples of the reconstructed images of these three algorithms.

Figure 5 shows the advantageous effects of tuning separately the phase term in the cost function on PSNR. By increasing the weight parameter, α, the performance was further improved.

5 Conclusions

We have proposed the widely linear complex-valued autoencoder to enhance the degrees of freedom in the design, and have introduced the phase-amplitude cost function, to math the requirements of spectrum reconstruction. Since the strictly linear transform in the complex domain cannot capture the whole second-order statistics as it uses only the covariance matrix, such optimization process is significantly unstable. By using the widely linear transform in the complex-valued autoencoder or deep neural network, we have shown that the stability can be significantly improved through the underlying augmented complex statistics. In addition, when applying the Fourier transform to the input data and training the autoencoder with the proposed phase-amplitude cost function, the reconstruction error has been shown to be significantly reduced.

References

1. Aizenberg, I.: Complex-Valued Neural Networks with Multi-valued Neurons, vol. 353. Springer, Heidelberg (2011). https://doi.org/10.1007/978-3-642-20353-4
2. Arjovsky, M., Shah, A., Bengio, Y.: Unitary evolution recurrent neural networks. In: International Conference on Machine Learning, pp. 1120–1128 (2016)
3. Brandwood, D.H.: A complex gradient operator and its application in adaptive array theory. In: IEE Proceedings H-Microwaves, Optics and Antennas, vol. 130, pp. 11–16. IET (1983)
4. Douglas, S.C., Mandic, D.P.: The least-mean-magnitude-phase algorithm with applications to communications systems. In: 2011 IEEE International Conference on Acoustics, Speech and Signal Processing (ICASSP), pp. 4152–4155. IEEE (2011)
5. Glorot, X., Bengio, Y.: Understanding the difficulty of training deep feedforward neural networks. In: Proceedings of the thirteenth international conference on artificial intelligence and statistics, pp. 249–256 (2010)
6. Hata, R., Murase, K.: Multi-valued autoencoders for multi-valued neural networks. In: 2016 International Joint Conference on Neural Networks (IJCNN), pp. 4412–4417. IEEE (2016)

7. Hinton, G.E., Osindero, S., Teh, Y.W.: A fast learning algorithm for deep belief nets. Neural Comput. **18**(7), 1527–1554 (2006)
8. Hinton, G.E., Salakhutdinov, R.R.: Reducing the dimensionality of data with neural networks. Science **313**(5786), 504–507 (2006)
9. Hirose, A.: Complex-Valued Neural Networks, vol. 400. Springer, Heidelberg (2012). https://doi.org/10.1007/978-3-642-27632-3
10. Hirose, A.: Complex-Valued Neural Networks: Advances and Applications, vol. 18. Wiley, Hoboken (2013)
11. Kreutz-Delgado, K.: The complex gradient operator and the CR-calculus. arXiv preprint arXiv:0906.4835 (2009)
12. LeCun, Y., Bottou, L., Bengio, Y., Haffner, P.: Gradient-based learning applied to document recognition. Proc. IEEE **86**(11), 2278–2324 (1998)
13. Mandic, D.P., Goh, V.S.L.: Complex Valued Nonlinear Adaptive Filters: Noncircularity, Widely Linear and Neural Models, vol. 59. Wiley, Hoboken (2009)
14. Mandic, D.P., Still, S., Douglas, S.C.: Duality between widely linear and dual channel adaptive filtering. In: 2009 IEEE International Conference on Acoustics, Speech and Signal Processing, pp. 1729–1732. IEEE (2009)
15. Oppenheim, A.V., Lim, J.S.: The importance of phase in signals. Proc. IEEE **69**(5), 529–541 (1981)
16. Popa, C.: Complex-valued convolutional neural networks for real-valued image classification. In: 2017 International Joint Conference on Neural Networks (IJCNN), pp. 816–822. IEEE (2017)
17. Riemann, B.: Grundlagen für eine allgemeine Theorie der Functionen einer veränderlichen complexen Grösse. Ph.D. thesis, EA Huth (1851)
18. Rumelhart, D.E., Hinton, G.E., Williams, R.J.: Learning internal representations by error propagation. California Univ San Diego La Jolla Inst for Cognitive Science, Technical report (1985)
19. Trabelsi, C., et al.: Deep complex networks. arXiv preprint arXiv:1705.09792 (2017)

NatCSNN: A Convolutional Spiking Neural Network for Recognition of Objects Extracted from Natural Images

Pedro Machado(✉), Georgina Cosma, and T. Martin McGinnity

Computational Neurosciences and Cognitive Robotics Group,
School of Science and Technology, Nottingham Trent University, Nottingham, UK
{pedro.baptistamachado,georgina.cosma,martin.mcginnity}@ntu.ac.uk

Abstract. Biological image processing is performed by complex neural networks composed of thousands of neurons interconnected via thousands of synapses, some of which are excitatory and others inhibitory. Spiking neural models are distinguished from classical neurons by being biological plausible and exhibiting the same dynamics as those observed in biological neurons. This paper proposes a Natural Convolutional Neural Network (NatCSNN) which is a 3-layer bio-inspired Convolutional Spiking Neural Network (CSNN), for classifying objects extracted from natural images. A two-stage training algorithm is proposed using unsupervised Spike Timing Dependent Plasticity (STDP) learning (phase 1) and ReSuMe supervised learning (phase 2). The NatCSNN was trained and tested on the CIFAR-10 dataset and achieved an average testing accuracy of 84.7% which is an improvement over the 2-layer neural networks previously applied to this dataset.

Keywords: SNN · CSNN · Bio-inspired neural networks · Object classification · Unsupervised learning · Supervised learning · ReSuMe · STDP

1 Introduction

The mammalian visual cortex is responsible for performing advanced, complex and low-power (about 20 watts [13]) image processing. Neuromorhpic architectures (neuro-biological architectures that can run bio-inspired models of neural systems) have evolved as a consequence of the rapid miniaturisation of electronic components, lithography manufacturing process and the developments of cognitive applications [1]. In particular, Spiking Neural Networks (SNN), which are characterised by displaying similar spike-timing encoding and plasticity as real neurons [5], offer a sophisticated low-power and high performance computational processing paradigm. However, the use of SNN for classification of natural images with a high accuracy remains a complex task on typical machine/deep learning benchmarks such as CIFAR-10 [8].

I. V. Tetko et al. (Eds.): ICANN 2019, LNCS 11727, pp. 351–362, 2019.
https://doi.org/10.1007/978-3-030-30487-4_28

This paper proposes NatCSNN, a bio-inspired Convolutional Spiking Neural Network for natural image object classification. The proposed architecture, includes a two phase training approach where: in phase 1, unsupervised Spike Timing Dependent Plasticity (STDP) learning is used for training the middle layers; and in phase 2, the ReSuMe supervised learning algorithm is used to train the Layer 3 neurons. A systematic method for searching for the initial synaptic weights is also proposed.

The paper is structured as follows: the literature review is discussed in Sect. 2, the NatCSNN architecture is discussed in Sect. 3, the experimental training of the NatCSNN is discussed in Sect. 4, the results are shown in Sect. 5 and a discussion and future work are provided in Sect. 6.

2 Literature Review

The majority of previous works have focused on conventional CSNN and the MNIST dataset. Wang *et al.* [20], proposed a similarity search method using a forward SNN with successively connected encoding. The authors claim an accuracy of 100%, 100% and 92% for noise levels of 5%, 20% and 40% respectively when tested on the MNIST dataset [11]. The authors proposed a new method for training multi-layer spiking convolution neural networks (CSNN) incorporating supervised and unsupervised learning. The training process includes two components for unsupervised feature extraction and supervised classification using adapted versions of the Spike-Timing Dependent Plasticity (STDP). Tavanaei *et al.* [19] claim that their proposed CSNN achieved an accuracy of 98.60% on the MNIST dataset [11]. Kheradpisheh *et al.* [6], designed an STDP-based spiking deep CSNN composed of one Difference of Gaussians (DoG) layer (temporal encoding) three convolutional layers and three pooling layers, using unsupervised STDP learning. The paper proposes an eight layer architecture SNN and claim an accuracy of 98.4% when tested in the MNIST dataset. Kulkarni *et al.* [10], proposed a three layer architecture trained with a supervised learning approach using the spike triggered Normalised Approximate Descendent algorithm with an accuracy of 98.17% on the MNIST dataset. In [12], a deep spiking CSNN (SpiCNN) composed of a hierarchy of stacked convolution layers, a spatial-pooling layer and a fully-connected layer is proposed. The SpiCNN was trained using unsupervised STDP with an accuracy of 91.1% on the MNIST dataset.

Relevant literature on CSNNs [6,10,12,19,20] for image processing have in common: (i) multiple-layer CSNNs, (ii) use of the Leaky-integrate-and-fire (LIF) neuron model, (iii) use of unsupervised/supervised STDP (or an STDP adaptation) for training and (iv) all of the relevant work was tested on the MNIST hand-written black-and-white dataset.

The MNIST dataset is one of the commonly used benchmark datasets, composed only of simple black-and-white images (containing hand-written numbers from 0 to 9). In contrast, the CIFAR-10 [8] dataset is composed of 50,000 coloured natural images with natural backgrounds and thus represents a significantly more challenging test for image processing algorithms.

More recent works, Sengupta *et al.* [16] and Hu *et al.* [4] have proposed hybrid architectures by combining classical deep learning architectures with spiking neural networks. Sengupta *et al.* [16] proposed an ANN to SNN conversion technique that is claimed to outperform state-of-the-art techniques, reporting an 12.54% error on the CIFAR-10 dataset when combined with Residual network architectures. Hu *et al.* [4], proposed a shortcut normalisation mechanism to convert continued-valued activation's to match firing rates in SNN; Their proposed architecture receives the continued-valued activation's from a Residual Network and converts them into spiking rates which are fed into a spiking residual network architecture. Their experiments achieved an accuracy of 92.85% when tested on the CIFAR-10 dataset. Despite the accuracy obtained on the CIFAR-10 using these hybrid architectures, the proposed architectures are all composed of several layers and none of the architectures uses biological spiking neuron parameters, reducing therefore the bio-plausibility of the proposed architectures.

Other work published on the CIFAR-10 has utilised classical deep neural networks. Krizhevsky *et. al.* [9] describe how to train a two-layer convolutional Deep Belief Network (DBN) on the CIFAR-10 and obtained 78.90% accuracy using a 2 layer architecture similar to the NatCSNN proposed in this paper. In [18], a 32-layer network, designated as highway networks inspired in Long Short-Term Memory (LSTM), is proposed and the authors reported an accuracy of 92.40% on the CIFAR-10 dataset. Springenberg *et al.* [17], proposed a 10-layer Network, designated as All-CNN, with an accuracy of 92.40% without data augmentation on the CIFAR-10 dataset.

The NatCSNN proposed in this paper is a compact, low-layer count (3) bio-inspired architecture, target at processing natural images where the network must perform the task of extracting features from CIFAR-10. It is implemented as a multi-hierarchical SNN composed of three SNN layers connected via excitatory and inhibitory synapses and trained using unsupervised STDP learning (layers 1 and 2) and supervised learning using ReSuMe (details are presented in Sect. 3). This paper also proposes a systematic method to search for the initial synaptic weights and a 2-phase training approach, using a mixture of unsupervised and supervised learning. NatCSNN was compared to two adaptations of the architecture proposed in [8].

3 NatCSNN Architecture

3.1 Spiking Neuron Model

The neuron model used in this work is based on the Leaky-Integrate-and-Fire (LIF) neuron model was selected because it is considered to be one of the simplest spiking neuron models describing the biological neuronal cells dynamics [3]. More complex models with higher computational requirements are available (*e.g.* Izhikevich [5]) but demand higher computational requirements. The LIF dynamics can be represented as a RC (Resistance, Capacitance) electronic circuit as depicted in picture Fig. 1.

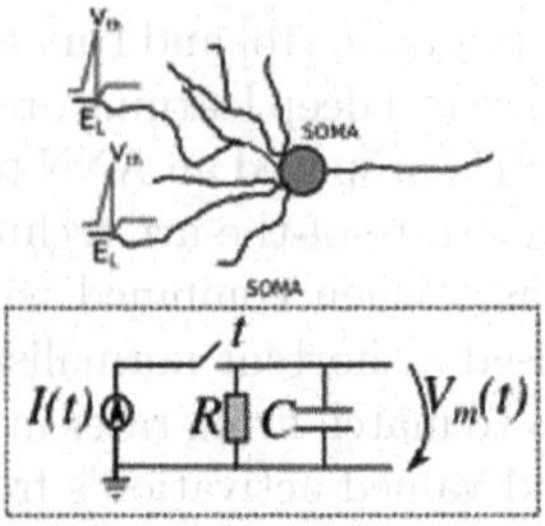

Fig. 1. Equivalent electronic circuit of the leaky-integrate-and-fire neuron model. Let a current $I(t)$ charge the RC circuit. Spikes are generated when the voltage $V_m(t)$ at the terminals of the capacitance is greater or equal to the threshold V_{th} making $V_m(t)$ dropping to E_L (reset voltage) during a t_{ref} (refractory period).

The LIF neuron model is governed by the Eq. 1.

$$\tau_m \frac{\delta V_m}{\delta t} = -V_m + RI(t) \tag{1}$$

where $\tau_m = RC$ is the time constant, R the membrane resistance, C the membrane capacitance, $V_m(t)$ the membrane voltage and $I(t)$ is the current at time t. When $V_m(t)$ reaches the V_{th} (threshold voltage), the membrane voltage is set to the reset membrane potential ($V_m(t) = E_L$).

Equation 1 can be improved using the multi-timescale adaptive threshold predictor and non-resetting leaky integrator (MAT) as described in [7]. MAT provides an adaptive threshold and prevents the neuron from over-spiking when exposed to high continuous currents. The adaptive threshold is described by Eqs. 2 and 3 and taken from the implemented version of the MAT in the NEST framework [14].

$$V_{th}(t) = \sum_k H(t - t_k) + E_L \tag{2}$$

where

$$[h]H(t) = \sum_{j=1}^{L} w_j^{(-t\tau_{mj})} \tag{3}$$

where V_{th}(t) is the threshold voltage in time t, t_k is the kth spike time, L is the number of threshold time constants, τ_{mj} ($j = 1, ..., L$) are the jth time constants, w_j ($j = 1, ..., L$) are the weights of the jth time constants, and E_L is the reset membrane potential value [7].

The MAT model, implemented in NEST[1], was used in our work as the neuron model for providing the desired adaptive threshold dynamics.

[1] Retrieved from https://nest-simulator.readthedocs.io/en/latest/models/neurons/integrate_and_fire/iaf_psc_alpha.html?highlight=iaf_psc_alpha, last accessed on the 26/03/2019.

3.2 Layers and Synaptic Connectivity

The input layer receives an image of n rows × m columns (n and m ∈ $\mathbb{Z}$); Layer 1 performs the encoding of the pixel intensity values to spike events, Layer 2a extracts features, Layer 2b provides lateral inhibition, Layer 3 classifies the object type. The proposed architecture is shown in Fig. 2.

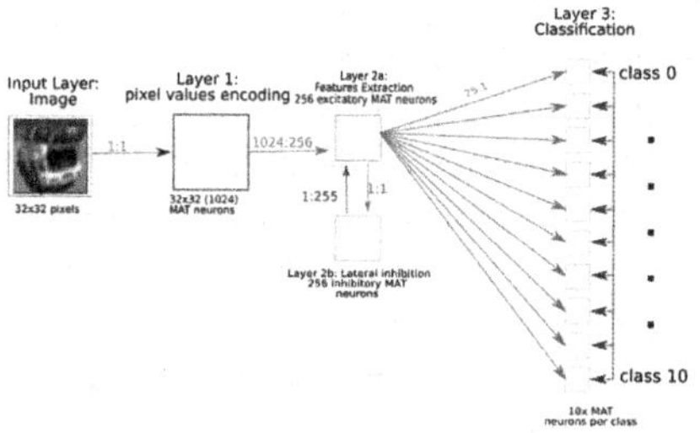

Fig. 2. NatCSNN with (i) n × m (n and m ∈ $\mathbb{Z}$) (image input followed by the three processing layers. Layer 1: Encoding of pixel intensity values to spike events, Layer 2a: features extraction, Layer 2b: lateral inhibition and Layer 3: classification layer.

Input Images to the NatCSNN

Each image is converted into grayscale, normalised (pixel intensity values in the range of 0.0 up to 1.0) and its pixel intensity value converted into spike train events. The image pixel intensity values are feed to the Layer 1 neurons using a one-to-one (1:1) connectivity. Each pixel intensity value is converted into a current given by Eq. 4

$$[h]I(i,j) = p(i,j).I_K \tag{4}$$

where I(i,j) is the current for a the neuron in row i and column j, p(i,j) is the pixel intensity value in row i and column j and I_K is a current constant for producing the desirable spike rate.

Layer 1: Pixel Intensity Values Encoding. Each neuron, in Layer 1, receives a current proportional to a pixel intensity value given by Eq. 4. The frequency of spikes is linearly proportional to the pixel intensity value and therefore a neuron will spike up to 10 times during a simulation time step if the pixel intensity value is near the maximum (1.0) or none if near the minimum value (0.0). The neurons in Layer 1 connect to the neurons in Layer 2a (features extraction group) via all-to-all connections.

STDP synapses are used during phase 1 training to adjust the weights of the connections between the pre-neurons (Layer 1) to the post-neurons (Layer 2a). The weights change based on the STDP parameters (detailed in Sect. 4) and trained on the training dataset of 50,000 images during 5 epochs (runs).

Layer 2: Feature Extraction. Layer 2 is composed of 2 groups of neurons, one called the features extraction group and the other the lateral inhibition group. Layer 2a and Layer 2b have the same number of neurons, which is 25% of the Layer 1 neurons. Each neuron in the feature extraction group receives input from all Layer 1 neurons. Each neuron in the feature extraction group presents its output to a single neuron of the lateral inhibition group via one excitatory synapse and receives incoming spike events from all the other neurons in the lateral inhibition group.

STDP synapses are used during phase 1 of training to connect the Layer 2a neurons (features extraction group) to the Layer 2b neurons (lateral inhibition group) and vice-versa. The number of neurons in both Layer 2a and 2b is the same. The weights of Layer 2a and 2b neuron's synapses change accordingly to the STDP parameters (detailed in Sect. 4) when trained on the training dataset of 50,000 images during 5 epochs. The number of epochs was experimentally obtained and 5 epochs was the value that produced better results. Values above 5 epochs made the synaptic weights to saturate in the maximum weights allowed for each synapse and values below 5 epochs produced lower accuracy.

Layer 3: Classification. Layer 3 is composed of 10 groups (one group per class) of 10 LIF neurons. Each neuron of the Layer 2a feature extraction group is connected to all the Layer 3 neurons. The 10 LIF neurons per class are used to improve the classification accuracy by increasing the resolution.

Layer 3 neurons are only trained in phase 2 training after training the Layer 2 neurons (phase 1 training) during the initial 5 epochs. During phase 2 training, the synapses of the Layer 2 neurons are converted into static synapses with fixed weights where the final Phase 1 trained weights are used. During phase 2, the neurons of the feature extraction group are connected using STDP synapses and their weights are trained on the training dataset during 5 further epochs. As before, the 5 epochs were selected experimentally.

ReSuMe [15], a supervised learning algorithm, was used for training the response of the Layer 3 neurons. In ReSuMe, teacher signals are used for producing the desired spike pattern in response to a stimulus [15]. Figure 3 shows the teacher signal (desired spike pattern) n_{teach} being presented to a neuron n_{post} for delivering a spike pattern by adjusting the synaptic weight w between the pre-neuron n_{pre} and the post-neuron n_{post}. The learning occurs with modification of the weights.

The ReSuMe [15] equations are as follows:

$$[h]W_{ex}(s_{ex}) = \begin{cases} A_{ex}e^{\left(\frac{-s_{ex}}{\tau_{ex}}\right)}, & \text{if } s_{ex} > 0, \\ 0, & \text{if } s_{ex} \le 0, \end{cases} \tag{5}$$

$$W_{ih}(s_{ih}) = \begin{cases} A_{ih}e^{\left(\frac{-s_{ih}}{\tau_{ih}}\right)}, & \text{if } s_{ih} > 0, \\ 0, & \text{if } s_{ih} \le 0, \end{cases} \tag{6}$$

where A_{ex}, A_{ih}, τ_{ex} and τ_{ih} are constants. A_{ex} and A_{ih} are positive in excitatory synapses and negative in inhibitory synapses. In both cases τ_{ex} and τ_{ih} are positive time constants [15].

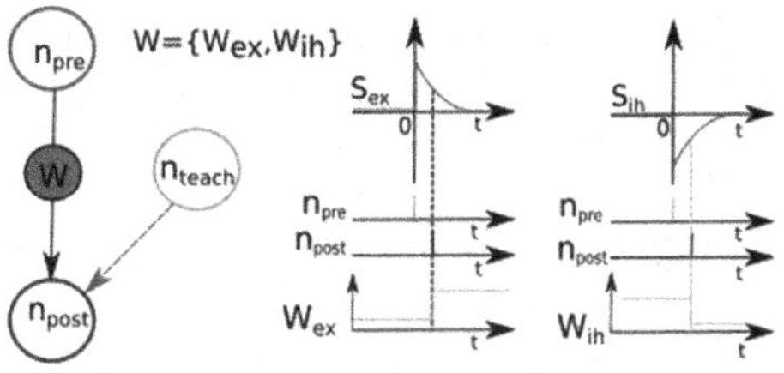

Fig. 3. ReSuMe learning: (A) Remote supervision. (B) Learning windows [15].

4 Training the NatCSNN

This section specifies the methodology that was followed for training the NatC-SNN network and evaluating its performance on the CIFAR-10 dataset [8]. The simulation was performed using the NEST (NEural Simulator Tool) version 2.16.0 [14].

4.1 Building the NatCSNN

The simulation setup included the following steps:

Step 1 - Load dataset to memory: The dataset is loaded to memory and the images converted to grey-scale. The conversion of the images into grey-scale reduces substantially (a third) the required number of neurons and synapses. Grey-scale images were used for reducing the number of spiking neurons and its synapses.

Step 2 - Convert pixel intensity values to currents: Pixel intensity values have to be multiplied by a current constant I_k to get a spike pattern proportional to the pixel intensity value and the spikes are regularly spaced during the period of 100 ms (simulation time-step). I_k was modelled so that a given neuron spikes up to 10 times over a period of 100 ms.

Step 3 - Create the network: The NatCSNN architecture is created as follows: Layer 1: 1024 neurons (32 rows $\times$ 32 columns), Layer 2: 512 neurons ($1024 \div 4 \times 2$ groups), Layer 3: 100 neurons (10 classes $\times$ 10 neurons).

Step 4 - Create synaptic connectivity using: L1 to L2 are connected via all-to-all connectivity, L2a (features extraction group) to L2b (lateral inhibition group) via one-to-one connectivity, L2b to L2a via one-to-(n-1) (all the neurons with exception of the neuron that is connected to the neuron in L2a) and L2a to L3 via all-to-all connectivity.

Step 5 - Connect the L2a to L3 neurons: The L2 neurons are connected to the L3 neurons via all-to-all connections. Each L3 neuron of each class receives connection of one 10% of the L2a neurons). Overall, the 10 neurons per classifier receives outputs of the L2b neurons. Each L3 neurons of a given class connect to all the other L3 neurons classes via inhibitory synapses.

Step 6 - Set the simulation parameters: The simulation is configured with a time step of $t = 100$ ms and the neurons with the parameters are as follows: initial $V_m = -70.0$ mV, $E_L = -70.0$ mV, $C_m = 100.0$ pF, $\tau_m = 5.0$ ms, $\tau_{syn_{ex}} = 1.0$ mV, $\tau_{syn_{in}} = 3.0$ ms, $t_{ref} = 2.0$ ms, $t_{spike} = -1.0$ ms, $\tau_1 = 10.0$ ms, $\tau_2 = 20.0$ ms, $\alpha_1 = 37.0$ mV, $\alpha_2 = 2.0$ mV, $\omega = -51.0$ mV, $V_{th} = -51.0$ mV and $V_{reset} = -70.0$ mV.

Training phase 1: During phase 1 training the synapses of L1 to L2a, L2a to L2b and L2b to L2a are trained using unsupervised STDP with the parameters listed in Table 1. The STDP parameterisation was selected from the parameters suggested by Gerstner *et al.* [3] that have been observed in the Visual Cortex and Hippocampal.

The 50,000 training images of the training batch were presented, one-by-one, for a period of 100 ms (one simulation timestep) to the network in 5 epochs and during the phase 1 of training the weights were adjusted accordingly to the STDP rules. The weights were stored, into files, every 500 simulation time steps (or 50000 ms of simulation).

Training phase 2: The synapses of L1 to L2a, L2a to L2b and L2b to L2a are converted to static synapses using the weights trained in phase 1. The excitatory and inhibitory synapses are of STDP type. During Phase 2 training, the weights of the neurons in Layer 3 STDP synapses are trained using the ReSuMe algorithm and parameters were set as listed in Table 1.

Table 1. Unsupervised STDP and ReSuMe parameters

Parameter	Description	Unsupervised STDP	ReSuMe
W_{ex}	Initial excitatory weight excitatory synapse	Random $(600.0 \pm 10\%)^a$ Random $(490.84 \pm 10\%)^b$	241.
W_{ih}	Initial inhibitory weight inhibitory synapse	Random $(-100.0 \pm 10\%)$	−120.
τ_{ex}	Time constant of short pre-synaptic trace	10. ms	10.0 ms
A^+_{ex}	Weight of pair potentiation rule of the excitatory synapse	0.001	0.001
A^-_{ex}	Weight of pair depression rule of the excitatory synapse	0.0005	0.0
A^+_{ih}	Weight of pair potentiation rule of the inhibitory synapse	0.001	0.001
A^-_{ih}	Weight of pair depression rule of the inhibitory synapse	0.0005	0.0
$Wmax_{ex}$	Maximum allowed weight of the excitatory synapse	1200.	1200.
$Wmax_{ih}$	Maximum allowed weight of the inhibitory synapse	−1200.	1200.

[a] L1 to L2a neurons
[b] from L2a to L2b neurons

Ten extra neurons (one per class) are used to provide the teaching signals to the classifier neurons as specified using the ReSuMe algorithm. Each teaching neuron will only spike when a picture being exposed to the neurons in Layer 1 belongs to that class. The 50,000 training images of the training batch were presented to the network during 5 epochs and during that period the weights were adjusted accordingly to the STDP rules and to the teaching signals applied by the teaching neurons to the Layer 3 classifier neurons.

Testing mode: All the STDP synapses were replaced by static synapses using the weights trained in phases 1 and 2.

5 Results

The NatCSNN was trained using the 50,000 testing images in two phases, phase 1, training of the Layer 2 neurons synapses, using unsupervised STDP learning for 5 epochs and phase 2, training of the excitatory and inhibitory synapses of the layer 3 neurons, using supervised learning using ReSuMe for 5 epochs.

The remaining 10,000 CIFAR-10 images were reserved for testing. One of the most challenging tasks in spiking neural network simulations is the definition of the starting weights for the network. In this case we have used the Monte Carlo algorithm to select the initial weight values for the STDP synapses between the L2a features extraction group and the L3 neurons. The initial values of the L2a to L3 synapses is crucial because the selection of a low or high value will impact on the overall accuracy. The initial value was selected using the Monte Carlo algorithm. The accuracy of the NatCSNN was improved by using 100 neurons (10 per classifier) and using the connectivity shown in Table 2. The average value of the obtained accuracy using the 10 neurons per classifier (100 neurons) was 84.70% with a standard deviation of 1.579%.

All neurons' action potentials were reset before exposing the next image to the NatCSNN. Forcing the neurons to start with the reset voltage is necessary to prevent receipt of an inhibitory stimulus (*i.e.* neurons from Layer 2a and Layer 3), which would cause a drop in membrane action potential to a very low value preventing neurons from spiking when exposed to the excitatory stimulus. The neuron parameters are the same for all the neurons. The initial minimum weight of the STDP excitatory synapses was selected experimentally. Neurons with all-to-all connectivity receive spike contributions from many neurons and therefore the initial weight must below the current required to make the neuron spike (see Table 1) and below the maximum value (1200.0 μA, see Table 1) that makes neurons spike constantly.

Table 2 compares the performance of NatCSNN with other relevant approaches. The works in [2,17] and [9] have tested their methods on the colour images while the NatCSNN was tested on grey-scale images. To enable a grey-scale comparison, we have re-implemented CDBN [9] o utilise grey-scale images and applied it to the CIFAR-10 dataset, because it has the same number of layers as NatCSNN, resulting in two variants (a) CDBN-ANN 1 with two convolutional layers followed by a dense layer with 10 neurons and CDBN-ANN 2 with three

Table 2. Classification accuracy of the NatCSNN compared with other classical CNNs tested on the CIFAR-10 dataset

Architecture	CIFAR-10 accuracy [%]	Number of layers	Images type
All-CNN [17]	92.75	10	Colour
Highway network [2]	92.40	32	Colour
CDBN [9]	78.90	3	Colour
NatCSNN (grey)	**84.70**	**3**	**Grey**
CDBN-ANN 1 (grey)	80.54	3	Grey
CDBN-ANN 2 (grey)	82.4	4	Grey

Table 3. Classification accuracy of the NatCSNN using 10 neurons per classifier

Class	NatCSNN [%]	CDBN-ANN 1 [%]	CDBN-ANN 2 [%]
Airplane	84.005	83	84
Automobile	87.021	92	91
Bird	86.119	75	74
Cat	85.3	67	66
Deer	83.436	78	81
Dog	83.421	74	78
Frog	86.732	73	81
Horse	82.502	88	88
Ship	83.35	88	88
Truck	85.115	87	89

convolutional layers followed by a dense layer of 10 neurons. Both CDBN-ANN 1 and CDBN-ANN 2 receive grey images. For a fair comparison the CDBN was tuned to achieve its highest accuracy. Both the CDBN-ANN 1 and CDBN-ANN2 implementations were trained with 100 epochs. Table 2 shows that the networks with better accuracy are the ones with more layers and that the NatCSNN has a better accuracy when compared with the colour CDBN [9], the CDBN-ANN 1 (re-implemented by the authors) and the CDBN-ANN 2 (re-implemented by the authors). It can be seen that the number of layers and the conversion of colour to grey-scale images negatively affects the classification accuracy. Therefore, it will be possible to improve the accuracy of the NatCSNN by adding more layers, although this would increase the complexity of training with the increase of neuron and its synaptic connectivity. We also note that Table 3 illustrates a more uniform level of accuracy of NatCSNN across classes, as compared to CDBN.

6 Discussion and Future Work

This paper proposes, NatCSNN, a bio-inspired convolutional spiking neural networks trained and tested on the CIFAR-10 dataset. The CIFAR-10 dataset was selected because the authors aim to use the target architecture in robotics applications and processing live images captured by RGB cameras. The proposed architecture incorporates 2 types of learning, namely, *phase 1:* unsupervised STDP learning for training the synaptic connections between the L1 and L2a, L2a and L2b, and L2b and L2a; Inhibitory synapses are used to connect the neurons from L2b to L2a for providing lateral inhibition and *phase 2:* ReSuMe is used for training the synaptic connections between the L2a and L3, and intra L3 neurons connectivity. LIF neurons with adaptive threshold were used to inhibit neurons from spiking with very high spike rates when exposed to very high currents. The CIFAR-10 pixel intensity values were normalised and the current constant I_k was tuned for producing a spike rate proportional to the pixel intensity value. Also, the Monte Carlo algorithm was used for selecting the initial STDP weights for synapses connecting L2a and L3 neurons. Static synapses were used during the testing phase and the trained weights loaded into those synapses. Only the spike rate was used to select the correct class using the winner-takes-all. The NatCSNN was trained on the 50,000 training batch and tested on the 10,000 testing batch of the CIFAR-10 dataset. The NEST-simulator was used to implement the NatCSNN because, it is currently being used by the Neurorobotics platform for emulating bio-inspired neural networks. The main contributions of this paper are (a) a 3-layer bio-inspired convolutional neural network architecture designed to process natural images with no pre-processing required that exhibits a better accuracy than 3-layer classical CNN or ANN. (b)the use of combination of unsupervised learning for training the middle layers, (c)incorporation of lateral inhibition for reducing the background interference and (d) a flexible architecture that enables the possibility of processing live captured images (during test mode). Future work, includes expanding the current work to live-captured images and process such images on-the-fly. A more detailed analysis of the pre-trained weights and a pruning approach for synapses/neurons that have no influence over the simulation (weights not trained during the training phases) will be conducted. The adaptation of the NatCSNN to work with coloured images may include the use of hybrid approaches where the convolution layers could be replaced by efficient computer vision and deep learning approaches. Further testing under different test conditions (*e.g.* different light conditions, different image size, more objects per scene, etc.) will also be conducted. Finally we intend to apply the NatCSNN in both robotic simulation (*i.e.* Gazebo) and in real robotic applications.

References

1. Chen, Y., et al.: Neuromorphic computing's yesterday, today, and tomorrow - an evolutional view. Integration **61**, 49–61 (2018). https://doi.org/10.1016/j.vlsi.2017.11.001

2. Coates, A., et al.: Text detection and character recognition in scene images with unsupervised feature learning. In: 2011 International Conference on Document Analysis and Recognition, pp. 440–445. IEEE, September 2011. https://doi.org/10.1109/ICDAR.2011.95
3. Gerstner, W., Kistler, W.M., Naud, R., Paninski, L.: Neuronal Dynamics: From Single Neurons to Networks and Models of Cognition. Cambridge University Press, New York (2014)
4. Hu, Y., Tang, H., Wang, Y., Pan, G.: Spiking deep residual network (2018)
5. Izhikevich, E.: Which model to use for cortical spiking neurons? IEEE Trans. Neural Netw. **15**(5), 1063–1070 (2004)
6. Kheradpisheh, S.R., Ganjtabesh, M., Thorpe, S.J., Masquelier, T.: STDP-based spiking deep convolutional neural networks for object recognition. Neural Netw. **99**, 56–67 (2018). https://doi.org/10.1016/j.neunet.2017.12.005
7. Kobayashi, R., Tsubo, Y., Shinomoto, S.: Made-to-order spiking neuron model equipped with a multi-timescale adaptive threshold. Front. Comput. Neurosci. **3**, 9 (2009). https://doi.org/10.3389/neuro.10.009.2009
8. Krizhevsky, A.: Learning multiple layers of features from tiny images. Technical report (2009)
9. Krizhevsky, A.: Convolutional deep belief networks on CIFAR-10 (2010)
10. Kulkarni, S.R., Rajendran, B.: Spiking neural networks for handwritten digit recognition-Supervised learning and network optimization. Neural Netw. **103**, 118–127 (2018). https://doi.org/10.1016/j.neunet.2018.03.019
11. LeCun, Y., Cortes, C.: MNIST handwritten digit database (2010)
12. Lee, C., Srinivasan, G., Panda, P., Roy, K.: Deep spiking convolutional neural network trained with unsupervised spike timing dependent plasticity. IEEE Trans. Cogn. Dev. Syst. **8920**(c), 1 (2018)
13. Ling, J.: Power of a Human Brain - The Physics Factbook (2001)
14. Linssen, C., Peyser, A., et al.: Nest 2.16.0 (neural simulation tool). Zenodo **2**(4), 1430 (2018). https://doi.org/10.4249/scholarpedia.1430
15. Ponulak, F., Kasiński, A.: Supervised learning in spiking neural networks with ReSuMe: sequence learning, classification, and spike shifting. Neural Comput. **22**(2), 467–510 (2010). pMID: 19842989
16. Sengupta, A., Ye, Y., Wang, R., Liu, C., Roy, K.: Going deeper in spiking neural networks: VGG and residual architectures. Front. Neurosci. **13**, 1–10 (2018)
17. Springenberg, J.T., Dosovitskiy, A., Brox, T., Riedmiller, M.: Striving for simplicity: the all convolutional net, pp. 1–14 (2014)
18. Srivastava, R.K., Greff, K., Schmidhuber, J.: Training very deep networks, pp. 1–9, July 2015. https://doi.org/10.1109/CVPR.2016.90
19. Tavanaei, A., Kirby, Z., Maida, A.S.: Training spiking convnets by STDP and gradient descent. In: 2018 International Joint Conference on Neural Networks (IJCNN), pp. 1–8. IEEE, July 2018. https://doi.org/10.1109/IJCNN.2018.8489104
20. Wang, Z., Ma, Y., Dong, Z., Zheng, N., Ren, P.: Spiking locality-sensitive hash: spiking computation with phase encoding method. In: 2018 International Joint Conference on Neural Networks (IJCNN), pp. 1–7. IEEE, July 2018

Deep Semantic Asymmetric Hashing

Mian Zhang, Cheng Cheng, and Xianzhong Long(✉)

School of Computer Science and Technology, School of Software,
Nanjing University of Posts and Telecommunications, Nanjing 210023, China
{b16090832,1217043024,lxz}@njupt.edu.cn

Abstract. Deep hashing, which combines binary codes learning and convolutional neural network, has achieved promising performance for highly efficient image retrieval. Asymmetric deep hashing methods, which treat query points and database points in an asymmetric way perform better than symmetric deep hashing methods on retrieval tasks in both time complexity and accuracy. However, most existing asymmetric deep hashing methods do not sufficiently discover semantic correlation from label information, which results in reducing the discrimination of learned binary codes. In this paper, we propose a novel Deep Semantic Asymmetric Hashing (DSAH) approach, which exploits semantic correlation between query points and their labels in a common semantic space to form more discriminative and similarity-preserving binary codes. Experiments show that DSAH outperforms current state-of-the-art non-deep hash methods and deep hashing methods, especially asymmetric deep hashing methods.

Keywords: Deep hashing · Semantic learning · Image retrieval

1 Introduction

With rapid growth of multimedia data on web, retrieving the relevant multimedia content from massive database has been an urgent need. To enable accurate retrieval under efficient computation, approximate nearest neighbors (ANN) search has attracted increasing attention, which transform high-dimensional media data into compact binary codes and generates similar binary codes for similar data items. By using binary hash codes to represent the original data, the storage cost can be dramatically reduced. Furthermore, we can achieve a constant or sub-linear time complexity for search by using hash codes to construct an index. Hence, hashing has become more and more popular for ANN search in large scale datasets.

Based on whether supervised information is used or not, hashing methods can be further categorized into supervised and unsupervised methods. Unsupervised methods use unlabeled data to learn a set of hash functions. Typical learning criteria include reconstruction error minimization [4] and graph learning [17]. Compared to the unsupervised methods, supervised hashing methods explores supervised information such as the similarity relationship between database points,

I. V. Tetko et al. (Eds.): ICANN 2019, LNCS 11727, pp. 363–374, 2019.
https://doi.org/10.1007/978-3-030-30487-4_29

to learn compact hash codes. Supervised Hashing with Kernels (KSH) [12] and Supervised Discrete Hashing (SDH) [16] build discrete binary codes by minimizing the Hamming distances across similar pairs and maximizing the Hamming distances across dissimilar pairs. Minimal Loss Hashing (MLH) [13] and Hamming Distance Metric Learning [14] learn hash codes by minimizing the triplet loss functions based on similarity of database points. However, the quality of hash codes generated is highly dependent on the way feature selection is done, and these methods use hand-crafted features for representation. The need to perform manual feature selection has been a big limitation to the success of these methods.

With the fast development of Convolutional Neural Network (CNN), which can learn the rich mid-level image representation, several CNN-based hashing methods have been proposed. Deep supervised hashing (DNNH) [8] is the first end-to-end framework which can perform simultaneous feature learning and hash code learning for applications with pairwise labels. Deep Pairwise Supervised Hashing (DPSH) [15] and Deep Supervised Hashing (DSH) [11] follows similar framework as DNNH, thus yielding similar retrieval performance. HashNet [1] use continuation method to attack the ill-posed gradient problem in optimizing deep networks with non-smooth binary activations and yield better performance than DPSH and DSH.

Up to now, Most existing deep hashing methods are symmetric. These methods try to learn one deep hash function for both query points and database points. On the contrary, Deep asymmetric pairwise hashing (DAPH) [15] and Asymmetric Deep Supervised Hashing (ADSH) [5] treat the query points and database points in an asymmetric way, which learn a deep hash function only for query points, while the binary hash codes for database points are directly learned. Asymmetric deep hashing methods perform better than most symmetric deep hashing methods in both time complexity and retrieval accuracy.

However, most existing asymmetric deep hashing methods do not sufficiently discover semantic correlation from label information. For multi-label datasets such as MS-COCO and NUS-WIDE, a sample is annotated with multiple labels, existing asymmetric deep hashing methods only use similarity relationship between query points and database points constructed from label annotations. Given any pair of samples, existing asymmetric deep hashing methods regard them as similar pair if two samples share at least one label. Therefore, multiple labels in current asymmetric deep hashing methods are oversimplified to single-label case, which removes many useful semantic information and can not maintain the original similarity relationship of sample pairs. As a result, the learned binary codes are less discriminative. Therefore, we should exploit more semantic information from labels to indicate the accurate similarity relationship between samples and produce more discriminative binary codes.

In this paper, we propose a novel deep supervised hashing method, Deep Semantic Asymmetric Hashing (DSAH) for large-scale nearest neighbor search. The main contributions of DSAH are summarized as follows:

1. A novel architecture for hashing, consisting of a label auto-encoder (LAE) and an image network (ImgNet). The LAE encodes labels into semantic codes in semantic space, and then decodes them to reconstruct the labels. The ImgNet tries to learn a function from query points to discriminative binary codes.
2. Several novel constrains to guarantee robust binary codes for retrieval tasks.
3. An novel efficient training strategy to alternatively optimize the parameters of LAE and ImgNet while learning the binary codes of database points directly.

Experiments demonstrate that DSAH can generate high-quality hash codes and yield state-of-the-art image retrieval performance on three benchmark datasets, CIFAR-10, MS-COCO and NUS-WIDE.

2 Deep Semantic Asymmetric Hashing

2.1 Task Definition

In image similarity retrieval, we are given n query points $Q = \{q_i\}_{i=1}^n$, m database points $X = \{x_i\}_{i=1}^m$, label annotations of query points $Z = \{z_i\}_{i=1}^n$ and label annotations of database points $Y = \{y_i\}_{i=1}^m$. $z_i = [z_{i1}, \cdots, z_{ic}]^T (i = 1, \cdots, n)$ and $y_i = [y_{i1}, \cdots, y_{ic}]^T (i = 1, \cdots, m)$, where c represents the number of classes. If point q_i (x_i) belongs to class $j = 1, \cdots, c$, $z_{ij}(y_{ij}) = 1$ otherwise, $z_{ij}(y_{ij}) = 0$. Using label information, we can easily obtain pairwise similarity labels $S \in \{0, 1\}^{n \times m}$ between points, where $s_{ij} = 1$ if q_i and x_j are similar or $s_{ij} = 0$ if q_i and x_j are dissimilar.

The goal of deep hashing is to learn similarity-preserving binary hash codes for both query points and database points. We use $U \in \{-1, 1\}^{n \times r}$ to denote the learned binary codes for query points and $B \in \{-1, 1\}^{m \times r}$ to denote the learned binary codes for database points, where r is the length of binary codes.

2.2 Architecture of DSAH

As it is showed in Fig. 1, the architecture of the proposed method consists two parts, a label auto-encoder (LAE) and an image network (ImgNet), along which a common semantic space is constructed. LAE is an end-to-end fully connected deep neural network which takes label codes of query points Z as inputs and outputs reconstructed label codes $\hat{Z}^a$. ImgNet is also an end-to-end neural network which takes query points Q as inputs and outputs constructed label codes $\hat{Z}^p$. We use $H^a = \{h_i^a\}_{i=1}^n$, $H^p = \{h_i^p\}_{i=1}^n$ to denote the outputs of LAE and ImgNet at semantic layer (semantic codes), which are in blue. We use $L = \{l_i\}_{i=1}^n$ to denote the outputs of ImgNet at hash layer, which are in green. The binary codes of query points $U = sign(L)$. Please note that all the label codes are in orange.

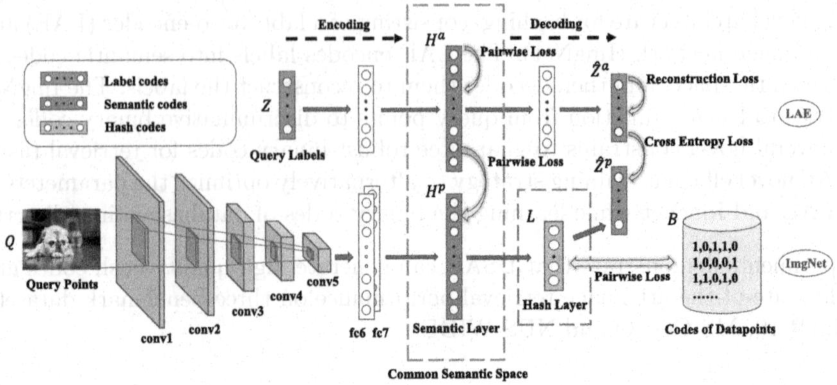

Fig. 1. The Architecture of DSAH

2.3 Feature Learning

For image feature learning, We adopt CNN-F model [2] to extract image features. The CNN-F model contains 5 convolutional layers and 3 fully-connected layers. In DSAH, we use the first seven layers for feature learning. Other CNN architectures can also be used to for feature learning, but it is not the focus of this paper. The detailed configuration of the feature learning part of DASH is shown in Table 1. In Table 1, "filter" specifies the number of convolution filters and their receptive field size, denoted as "num × size × size"; "stride" indicates the convolution stride which is the interval at which to apply the filters to the input;"pad" indicates the number of pixels to add to each side of the input; "LRN" indicates whether Local Response Normalization (LRN) [7] is applied; "pool" indicates the down sampling factor. "4096" in the fully-connected layer indicates the dimensionality of the output. The activation function for all layers is the REctification Linear Unit (RELU) [7].

Table 1. Configuration of the feature learning part of DSAH.

Layer	Configuration
conv1	filter 64 × 11 × 11, stride 4 × 4, pad 0, LRN, pool 2 × 2
conv2	filter 256 × 5 × 5, stride 1 × 1, pad 2, LRN, pool 2 × 2
conv3	filter 256 × 3 × 3, stride 1 × 1, pad 1
conv4	filter 256 × 3 × 3, stride 1 × 1, pad 1
conv5	filter 256 × 3 × 3, stride 1 × 1, pad 1, pool 2 × 2
fc6	4096
fc7	4096

2.4 Loss Functions of LAE

To exploit abundant semantic information from label information. We train LAE at semantic level using both original label codes Z and pairwise labels $S \in \{-1, 1\}^{n \times n}$ of query points.

By feeding LAE with Z, we can get the semantic codes of query points H^a at the semantic layer. Then the likelihood of the pairwise labels between query points $S \in \{0, 1\}^{n \times n}$ can be defined as follows:

$$p(s_{ij}|H^a) = \begin{cases} \sigma(\Omega_{ij}), & \text{if } s_{ij} = 1 \\ 1 - \sigma(\Omega_{ij}) & \text{if } s_{ij} = 0 \end{cases} \tag{1}$$

where $\Omega_{ij} = (h_i^a)^T h_j^a$, and $\sigma(\Omega)_{ij} = \frac{1}{1+e^{-\Omega_{ij}}}$ is the sigmoid function. We can find out that the larger inner product $(h_i^a)^T h_j^a$ is, the greater the similarity of them is, which is reflected by larger $p(1|h_i^a, h_j^a)$. Also, the smaller the inner product $(h_i^a)^T h_j^a$ is, the lesser the similarity of them is, which is reflected by larger $p(0|h_i^a, h_j^a)$.

By taking the negative log-likelihood of the pairwise labels S, we get the following optimization problem:

$$\begin{aligned} \min_{\Theta^a} J_1^a &= -log\, p(S|H^a) = -\sum_{s_{ij} \in S} log\, p(s_{ij}|H^a) \\ &= -\sum_{s_{ij} \in S} (s_{ij}(h_i^a)^T h_j^a - log(1 + e^{(h_i^a)^T h_j^a})) \end{aligned} \tag{2}$$

By minimize J_1^a, the semantic codes can well preserve the original similarity relationship. And we take Mean Square Error (MSE) to guarantee that LAE can well reconstruct the original label codes $Z = \{z_i\}_{i=1}^n$:

$$\min_{\Theta^a} J_2^a = \left\| \hat{Z}^a - Z \right\|_2^2 \tag{3}$$

where $\hat{Z}^a = \{\hat{z}_i^a\}_{i=1}^n$ are the reconstructed label codes and Θ^a are the parameters of LAE. The overall loss function for LAE can be derived as follows:

$$\min_{\Theta^a} J^a = J_1^a + \alpha J_2^a \tag{4}$$

where α is the hyper-parameter which determines the relative significance of J_1^a and J_2^a.

2.5 Loss Functions of ImgNet

The goal of ImgNet is to learn binary codes which can preserve the similarity between query points and database points, it is natural to minimize the L_2

loss between the supervised information S and inner product of query-database binary code pairs [12], which can be formulated as follows:

$$\min_{\Theta^p, B} J_1^p = \sum_{i=1}^{m}\sum_{j=1}^{n}(b_i^T u_j - r s_{ij})^2 \quad s.t.\ B \in \{-1,1\}^{m\times r} \tag{5}$$

where Θ^p are the parameters of ImgNet. Please note that, we will use $s_{ij} = -1$ to denote the dissimilar pairs when training ImgNet for the convenience of learning binary codes of database points. For binary codes of query points $\{u_i\}_{i=1}^n \in U$ are not continuous, we cannot use gradient back-propagation (BP) algorithm to update Θ^p. It is natural to use $tanh(L)$ to approximate U, where $L = \{l_i\}_{i=1}^n$ are the outputs at hash layer. Then, J_1^p can be rewritten as follows:

$$\min_{\Theta^p, B} J_1^p = \sum_{i=1}^{m}\sum_{j=1}^{n}(b_i^T tanh(l_j) - r s_{ij})^2 \quad s.t.\ B \in \{-1,1\}^{m\times r} \tag{6}$$

Because binary codes of query points U are obtained by $sign(L)$, we modify J_1^p as follows to control the quantization error of the binarizition operation:

$$\min_{\Theta^p, B} J_1^p = \sum_{i=1}^{m}\sum_{j=1}^{n}(b_i^T tanh(l_j) - r s_{ij})^2 + \beta(b_i - tanh(l_j))^2 \quad s.t.\ B \in \{-1,1\}^{m\times r} \tag{7}$$

where β is a hyper-parameter.

As we introduced above, most asymmetric deep hashing methods do not sufficiently discover semantic correlation from label information. To conquer this, we combine LAE and some proper constrains between LAE and ImgNet to guide the training process of ImgNet to learn more discriminative binary codes at semantic level.

In the common semantic space, the query points and their labels should share the same codes, namely, for query points $\{q_i\}_{i=1}^n$, the outputs of LAE and ImgNet at semantic layer, $\{h_i^a\}_{i=1}^n$ and $\{h_j^p\}_{j=1}^n$, should share same representation if $s_{ij} = 1$, and different if $s_{ij} = -1$. To achieve this goal, we design a loss function which share the similar form as (6) and can be written as follows:

$$\min_{\Theta^p} J_2^p = \sum_{i=1}^{n}\sum_{j=1}^{n}((h_i^a)^T h_j^p - r s_{ij})^2 \tag{8}$$

Further more, for high dicriminative binary hash codes can not only perform well in retrieval tasks but also in classification tasks [16], which means the better reconstructed label codes we can get from binary codes, the more discriminative binary codes the ImgNet can learn. Therefore, We use the reconstructed label codes from LAE to guide the learning of binary codes by reducing the following cross-entropy loss:

$$\min_{\Theta^p} J_3^p = \sum_{i=1}^{n}\sum_{j=1}^{r} \hat{z}_{ij}^a log \frac{1}{\hat{z}_{ij}^p} \tag{9}$$

where $\{\hat{z}^a\}_{i=1}^n$ are the reconstructed label codes from LAE and $\{\hat{z}^p\}_{i=1}^n$ are the reconstructed label codes from ImgNet. The second subscript j refer to the specific class annotation indexed by j of the label codes.

Finally, the overall loss function for ImgNet can be written as follows:

$$\min_{\Theta^p, B} J^p = J_1^p + \gamma J_2^p + \eta J_3^p \tag{10}$$

where γ, η are hyper-parameters to balance three function terms.

2.6 Learning Algorithm

We design an alternating optimization algorithm to learn the parameters of LAE (Θ^a), parameters of ImgNet (Θ^p) and binary hash codes of database points B. Please note that, in most real applications, we are given both query points and database points. Here we randomly sample database points to construct query points at every iteration.

Learning B with Θ^a, Θ^p Fixed. When Θ^a and Θ^p are fixed, we use the same optimization strategy as ADSH [5] to update the binary codes of database points, which can be formulated as follows:

$$B_{*k} = -sign(2\hat{B}_k \hat{U}_k^T U_{*k} - 2rS^T U - 2\beta\bar{U}) \tag{11}$$

where B_{*k} denote the kth column of B and $\hat{B}_k$ denote the matrix of B excluding colunm k. U_{*k} denote the kth column of U and $\hat{U}_k$ denote the matrix of U excluding colunm k. And $\bar{U} = \{\bar{u}\}_{j=1}^n$ where $\bar{u}_j = \bar{u}_j$ if database point x_j is sampled as query point in current iteration, otherwise, $\bar{u}_j = 0$. S is the similarity matrix.

Learning Θ^a, Θ^p with B Fixed. When B is fixed, we use back-propagation (BP) algorithm to update Θ^a and Θ^p, which is widely used in existing deep learning methods. The pseudocode of the whole algorithm can be find in Algorithm 1.

3 Experiments

3.1 Datasets

We conduct extensive experiments to evaluate DSAH with several state-of-the-art hashing methods on three benchmark datasets, CIFAR-10 [6], MS-COCO [10] and NUSWIDE [3].

Algorithm 1. The Learning Algorithm for DSAH

Data: $X = \{x_i\}_{i=1}^m$: m database points.
$Y = \{y_i\}_{i=1}^m$: label codes of database points.
$S \in \{-1, 1\}^{m \times m}$: Supervised similarity matrix.
Result: Parameters for LAE and ImgNet: Θ^a, Θ^p
B: Binary codes for database points.
Initialization : Θ^a, Θ^p, B
Binary code length r
Mini-batch size w
Iteration number t_l, t_s
Hyper-parameter α, β, γ, η
Learning rate for LAE and ImgNet μ^a, μ^p

```
while LAE is not convergence do
    Randomly sample w database points to construct a mini-batch.
    Calculate J^a
    Update Θ^a by BP algorithm:
    Θ^a ← Θ^a − μ^a · ∇_{Θ^a} (1/w)(J^a)
end
for t_1 = 1 → t_l do
    Random sample database points to construct query points.
    for t_2 = 1 → t_s do
        for k = 1 → n/w do
            Randomly sample w query points to construct a mini-batch.
            Calculate J^a, J^p
            Update Θ^a by BP algorithm:
            Θ^a ← Θ^a − μ^a · ∇_{Θ^a} (1/w)(J^a)
            Update Θ^a by BP algorithm:
            Θ^p ← Θ^p − μ^p · ∇_{Θ^p} (1/w)(J^p)
        end
        for i = 1 → r do
            Update B_{*i} according to (11)
        end
    end
end
```

CIFAR-10 is a single-label dataset with 60,000 tiny images. These images are manually labeled into 10 classes, which are airplane, automobile, bird, cat, deer, dog, frog, horse, ship, and truck. The size of each image is 32×32 pixels.

NUS-WIDE contains nearly 270,000 images,each image is associated with one or multiple labels from 81 semantic concepts. We use the 21 most frequent concepts are used, where each concept has as least 5,000 images, resulting in a total of 166,047 images.

MS-COCO is a dataset for image recognition, segmentation and captioning. The current release contains 82,783 training images and 40,504 validation images, where each image is labeled by some of the 80 semantic concepts. For training images, we discard the images which have no category information.

Following standard evaluation protocol as previous work [1,8], the similarity information for hash function learning and for ground-truth evaluation is constructed from image labels: if two images share at least one label, they are regarded as a similar pair, otherwise they are a dissimilar pair.

3.2 Setting

For LAE and ImgNet share the common semantic space, we set their semantic layer are both 1024-dimensional. The structure configuration are as follows:

LAE ($c \rightarrow 512 \rightarrow 1024 \rightarrow 512 \rightarrow c$)

ImgNet ($Q \rightarrow CNN \rightarrow 4096 \rightarrow 4096 \rightarrow 1024 \rightarrow r \rightarrow c$)

For parameters Θ^a and Θ^p, we initialize layers copied from the CNN-F model from pre-trained model on ImageNet. For hyper-parameters, we use cross-validation strategy on all datasets to search the optimal values and the best values for α, β, γ, η are 1, 100, 0.5, 0.1. Because LAE are pre-trained and most layers of the ImgNet are trained from scratch, we set the learning rate of ImgNet ten times that of LAE. The learning rate of LAE ranges from 10^{-5} to 10^{-1} and the learning rate of ImgNet ranges from 10^{-6} to 10^{-2}. Finally, the batch size of LAE and ImgNet are set to 64.

3.3 Baselines

We compare the retrieval performance of DSAH with eight state-of-the-art hashing methods, including traditional hashing methods KSH [12], SDH [16], ITQ [4], FastH [9] and deep hashing methods DNNH [8], HashNet [1], ADSH [5], DAPH [15], among which ADSH and DAPH are asymmetric deep hashing methods. We evaluate the proposed DSAH by Mean Average Precision (MAP), Top-5K precision and correlation between bits of binary codes.The MAP results are calculated based on the Top-5K returned samples.

3.4 Results and Discussions

The results of MAP and Top-5K precision are shown in Table 2 and Fig. 2.

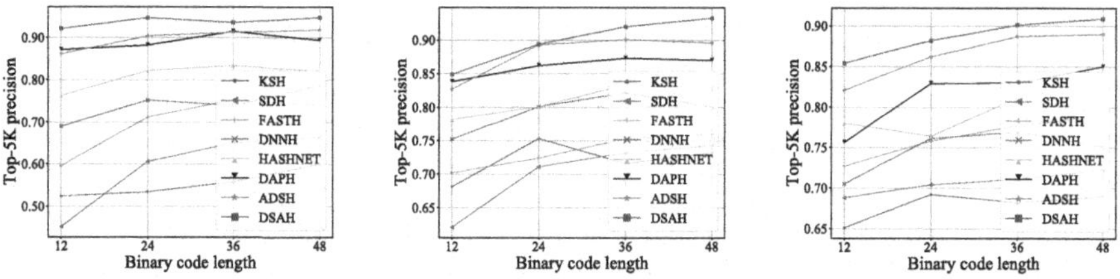

(a) CIFAR-10 (b) MS-COCO (a) NUS-WIDE

Fig. 2. Top-5K precision on three datasets.

Table 2. MAP on three datasets. The best results for MAP are shown in bold.

Method	CIFAR-10				MS-COCO				NUS-WIDE			
	12 bits	24 bits	36 bits	48 bits	12 bits	24 bits	36 bits	48 bits	12 bits	24 bits	36 bits	48 bits
KSH	0.524	0.534	0.558	0.601	0.681	0.753	0.716	0.732	0.651	0.692	0.682	0.690
SDH	0.461	0.606	0.650	0.664	0.621	0.711	0.732	0.743	0.688	0.704	0.711	0.723
ITQ	0.354	0.371	0.414	0.423	0.483	0.492	0.499	0.511	0.572	0.579	0.588	0.591
FATH	0.596	0.712	0.753	0.741	0.702	0.724	0.753	0.760	0.727	0.758	0.777	0.789
DNNH	0.690	0.752	0.740	0.788	0.752	0.801	0.822	0.801	0.705	0.761	0.769	0.751
HashNet	0.763	0.822	0.834	0.821	0.782	0.801	0.837	0.830	0.780	0.764	0.812	0.830
DAPH	0.871	0.887	0.915	0.894	0.788	0.802	0.811	0.820	0.726	0.778	0.791	0.822
ADSH	0.890	0.924	0.932	0.934	0.834	0.858	0.863	0.864	0.836	0.876	0.897	0.903
DSAH	**0.911**	**0.930**	**0.943**	**0.948**	**0.847**	**0.870**	**0.879**	**0.885**	**0.849**	**0.889**	**0.901**	**0.909**

As it is illustrated in Table 2 and Fig. 2, more frequently the deep hash methods outperform the traditional non-deep hash methods for the advantages of deep neural networks and end-to-end training framework. The asymmetric deep hashing methods outperform the symmetric deep hashing methods for the reason that the asymmetric deep hashing methods only take query points for training and learn the binary codes of database points directly. And the proposed method, DSAH, which also treat query points and database points in the asymmetric way, outperform all the non-deep hashing methods and deep hashing methods, especially, the asymmetric deep hashing methods because DSAH sufficiently exploit the semantic correlation between query points and their labels.

From Fig. 2, we can find that for most existing deep hashing methods, they perform well when binary code length is short and their performance get promoted when increasing the binary code length from 12 bits to 36 bits. But when binary code length increase to 48 bits, their performance advance little, some of which even fail down. This phenomenon violates the intuition that longer hash codes can encode more information such that the intrinsical similarity structure can be better preserved. In contrast, the performance of the proposed method, DSAH, keep rising significantly when increasing binary code length, even to 48 bits. We will experimentally prove that with semantic correlation from labels exploited sufficiently, the proposed method can significantly reduce correlation between binary code bits such that longer binary hash codes can encoded more information, leading to better performance on retrieval accuracy. We use mean Absolute Correlation as metric to reflect the correlation between binary code bits at a specific binary code length, which can be formulated as follows:

$$mAC = \frac{2\sum_{i=1}^{r}\sum_{j>i}|C_{ij}|}{r(r-1)} \tag{12}$$

where C is the correlation matrix (absolute value) of binary code bits, C_{ij} is the correlation coefficient between binary code bit i and j and r is the binary code length. We report the mAC and correlation matrix of binary codes learned by DNNH, DAPH, and our method DSAH at 32 bits (first row) and 48 bits (second row) in Fig. 3.

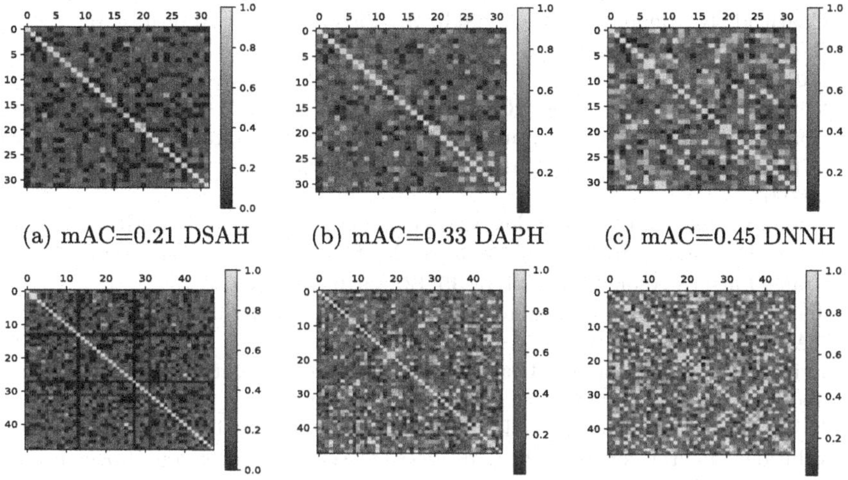

(a) mAC=0.21 DSAH (b) mAC=0.33 DAPH (c) mAC=0.45 DNNH

(d) mAC=0.19 DSAH (e) mAC=0.40 DAPH (f) mAC=0.51 DNNH

Fig. 3. Correlation matrix and mAC values at 32 Bits and 48 Bits.

The results show that at long binary code length, the proposed method, DSAH, can significantly reduce the correlation between binary code bits, experimentally proving that with semantic correlation from labels sufficiently exploited, the correlation between binary code bits can be significantly reduced, which indicates that our proposed method can be applied when sometimes we need longer binary codes in order to improve the retrieval accuracy if larger memory or faster computing device are available.

4 Conclusion

In this paper, we proposed a novel deep hashing method, DSAH, for image retrieval, which can sufficiently exploit label information to help promoting semantic correlation between labels and database points. Experiments show that DSAH can achieve state-of-the-art performance on three real datasets and DSAH can be applied to retrieval tasks which needs long binary codes to encode more information for high retrieval accuracy.

Acknowledgment. This work is supported in part by the Innovation and Entrepreneurship Training Program for College Students of NJUPT (Grant No.XZD2018082), the Postdoctoral Research Plan of Jiangsu Province (Grant No. 1501054B), the Postdoctoral Science Foundation of China (Grant No. 2016M591840).

References

1. Cao, Z., Long, M., Wang, J., Yu, P.S.: Hashnet: deep learning to hash by continuation. In: Proceedings of the IEEE International Conference on Computer Vision, pp. 5608–5617 (2017)

2. Chatfield, K., Simonyan, K., Vedaldi, A., Zisserman, A.: Return of the devil in the details: delving deep into convolutional nets. arXiv preprint arXiv:1405.3531 (2014)
3. Chua, T.S., Tang, J., Hong, R., Li, H., Luo, Z., Zheng, Y.: NUS-WIDE: a real-world web image database from national university of Singapore. In: Proceedings of the ACM International Conference on Image and Video Retrieval, p. 48. ACM (2009)
4. Gong, Y., Lazebnik, S., Gordo, A., Perronnin, F.: Iterative quantization: a procrustean approach to learning binary codes for large-scale image retrieval. IEEE Trans. Pattern Anal. Mach. Intell. **35**(12), 2916–2929 (2013)
5. Jiang, Q.Y., Li, W.J.: Asymmetric deep supervised hashing. In: Thirty-Second AAAI Conference on Artificial Intelligence (2018)
6. Krizhevsky, A., Hinton, G.: Learning multiple layers of features from tiny images. Tech. rep. Citeseer (2009)
7. Krizhevsky, A., Sutskever, I., Hinton, G.E.: Imagenet classification with deep convolutional neural networks. In: Advances in Neural Information Processing Systems, pp. 1097–1105 (2012)
8. Lai, H., Pan, Y., Liu, Y., Yan, S.: Simultaneous feature learning and hash coding with deep neural networks. In: Proceedings of the IEEE Conference on Computer Vision and Pattern Recognition, pp. 3270–3278 (2015)
9. Lin, G., Shen, C., Shi, Q., Van den Hengel, A., Suter, D.: Fast supervised hashing with decision trees for high-dimensional data. In: Proceedings of the IEEE Conference on Computer Vision and Pattern Recognition, pp. 1963–1970 (2014)
10. Lin, T.-Y., et al.: Microsoft COCO: common objects in context. In: Fleet, D., Pajdla, T., Schiele, B., Tuytelaars, T. (eds.) ECCV 2014. LNCS, vol. 8693, pp. 740–755. Springer, Cham (2014). https://doi.org/10.1007/978-3-319-10602-1_48
11. Liu, H., Wang, R., Shan, S., Chen, X.: Deep supervised hashing for fast image retrieval. In: Proceedings of the IEEE Conference on Computer Vision and Pattern Recognition, pp. 2064–2072 (2016)
12. Liu, W., Wang, J., Ji, R., Jiang, Y.G., Chang, S.F.: Supervised hashing with kernels. In: 2012 IEEE Conference on Computer Vision and Pattern Recognition, pp. 2074–2081. IEEE (2012)
13. Norouzi, M., Blei, D.M.: Minimal loss hashing for compact binary codes. In: Proceedings of the 28th International Conference on Machine Learning (ICML-11), pp. 353–360. Citeseer (2011)
14. Norouzi, M., Fleet, D.J., Salakhutdinov, R.R.: Hamming distance metric learning. In: Advances in Neural Information Processing Systems, pp. 1061–1069 (2012)
15. Shen, F., Gao, X., Liu, L., Yang, Y., Shen, H.T.: Deep asymmetric pairwise hashing. In: Proceedings of the 25th ACM International Conference on Multimedia, pp. 1522–1530. ACM (2017)
16. Shen, F., Shen, C., Liu, W., Tao Shen, H.: Supervised discrete hashing. In: Proceedings of the IEEE Conference on Computer Vision and Pattern Recognition, pp. 37–45 (2015)
17. Weiss, Y., Torralba, A., Fergus, R.: Spectral hashing. In: Advances in Neural Information Processing Systems, pp. 1753–1760 (2009)

A Neural Network for Semi-supervised Learning on Manifolds

Alexander Genkin[1(✉)], Anirvan M. Sengupta[2,3], and Dmitri Chklovskii[1,2]

[1] Neuroscience Institute, NYU Langone Medical Center, 435 E 30th St, New York, NY 10016, USA
alexander.genkin@nyumc.org

[2] Flatiron Institute, Simons Foundation, 162 5th Ave, New York, NY 10010, USA
dchklovskii@flatironinstitute.org

[3] Department of Physics and Astronomy, Rutgers University, 136 Frelinghuysen Rd, Piscataway, NJ 08854, USA
anirvans@physics.rutgers.edu

Abstract. Semi-supervised learning algorithms typically construct a weighted graph of data points to represent a manifold. However, an explicit graph representation is problematic for neural networks operating in the online setting. Here, we propose a feed-forward neural network capable of semi-supervised learning on manifolds without using an explicit graph representation. Our algorithm uses channels that represent localities on the manifold such that correlations between channels represent manifold structure. The proposed neural network has two layers. The first layer learns to build a representation of low-dimensional manifolds in the input data as proposed recently in [8]. The second learns to classify data using both occasional supervision and similarity of the manifold representation of the data. The channel carrying label information for the second layer is assumed to be "silent" most of the time. Learning in both layers is Hebbian, making our network design biologically plausible. We experimentally demonstrate the effect of semi-supervised learning on non-trivial manifolds.

Keywords: Semi-supervised learning · Online learning · Manifold learning

1 Introduction

When labeled data are scarce or expensive to obtain, we often resort to semi-supervised learning which exploits the abundance of unlabeled data. For data concentrating on a lower dimensional manifold, it is often reasonable to assume smoothness, i.e., that data points adjacent on the manifold are likely to have similar values of the target variable (the label). Then, learning the manifold structure from both labeled and unlabeled data can assist in label prediction. [1–3,11].

I. V. Tetko et al. (Eds.): ICANN 2019, LNCS 11727, pp. 375–386, 2019.
https://doi.org/10.1007/978-3-030-30487-4_30

In machine learning, an online method updates the model incrementally as it receives training data in a sequential manner. This approach is to be contrasted with offline machine learning, which generates the best model by learning on the entire training data set at once. Online learning is used either because it is computationally infeasible to train over the entire dataset, or it is used where the algorithm has to dynamically adapt to new patterns in the data, e.g. when the data itself is generated in real time. The last situation is particularly relevant in the context of neuronal networks.

Our brains likely rely on online semi-supervised learning to generate behavior. As our sensory organs stream data about the world they are analyzed in real time to produce behaviorally relevant output. While most of the sensory data lack labels, some supervision is available from other sources such as inter-personal communication.

To represent a data manifold, semi-supervised learning algorithms typically construct an adjacency graph whose vertices are labeled and unlabeled data points and edge weights represent their adjacency on the manifold. However, such representation is impractical in the online setting where the data are streamed sequentially and the labels are predicted on the fly. Furthermore, the online setting does not have the memory capacity to store the past data.

Thus, there is a need for online semi-supervised algorithms both for modeling neural computation and solving general machine learning tasks. Whereas existing online algorithms [4] can rely on a sparse representation, they still require memory quadratic in the dimensionality of data. In addition, these algorithms rely on the availability of an adjacency measure between new and stored data points.

In this paper, we propose a biologically plausible neural network for online semi-supervised learning (Fig. 1, left). By avoiding explicit representation of the adjacency graph our network can process unlimited-size datasets in online setting. Moreover, as required by biology, the network relies only on local learning rules meaning that synaptic weight update depends on the activity of only the two neurons this synapse connects.

The network has two layers. The first layer learns the manifold structure of the data by representing each datum as a sparse vector whose components represent overlapping localities on the manifold. The manifold structure is captured by the correlations between the components carried by corresponding channels. Because most existing algorithms for sparse representations, such as [10], do not have natural neural implementations we base our work on the recently developed manifold tiling algorithm [8]. Inspiration for such design comes from biological neural networks such as place cells in the rodent hippocampus.

The second layer learns a classifier using both occasional supervision and the similarity of the manifold representation of the data provided by the first layer. In our neural network, the supervision signal is not fed back from downstream layers of the network like in perceptron or back-propagation networks, but comes along and synchronously with the data from the previous layer. To make it semi- (rather than fully) supervised, the label signal is assumed to be "silent" most of the time. The output attempts to predict the correct label when that signal is not available, otherwise it just reproduces the label.

We derive both the activity dynamics and the learning rules in each layer from the principle of similarity preservation [6] which was previously used in the unsupervised setting. Starting with a similarity preserving objective function allows us to analyze the output of the algorithm and obtain biologically plausible local learning rules.

We demonstrate experimentally the effectiveness of this semi-supervised network compared to fully supervised online learning. Moreover, we observe that online semi-supervised learning may be competitive with offline methods, especially on smaller samples. This is an important advantage allowing our network to adapt quickly when the manifold shape or the labels are changing with time.

2 Review of the Manifold-Tiling Network Derived from Non-negative Similarity Matching

To introduce our notation, let the input to the network be a set of vectors, $\mathbf{x}_t \in R^n, t = 1, \ldots, T$, coming from n channels at time t. In response, the manifold learning network layer outputs an activity vector, $\mathbf{h}_t \in R^m, t = 1, \ldots, T$, m being the number of output channels, or hidden units in our two-layer network, Fig. 1, left.

Manifold-tiling networks have been derived [8] from similarity-preserving objectives [5] with a non-negativity constraint. Similarity preservation postulates that similar input pairs, $\mathbf{x}_t$ and $\mathbf{x}_{t'}$, evoke similar output pairs, $\mathbf{h}_t$ and $\mathbf{h}_{t'}$. Similarity of a pair of vectors can be quantified by their scalar product. Nonlinear manifolds can be learned by constraining the sign of the output and introducing a similarity threshold α. [8] propose an optimization problem:

$$\min_{\substack{\mathbf{H} \geq 0 \\ \text{diag}\mathbf{H}^\top \mathbf{H} \leq \mathbf{I}}} -\text{Tr}((\mathbf{X}^\top \mathbf{X} - \alpha \mathbf{E})\mathbf{H}^\top \mathbf{H}) \tag{1}$$

$$= \min_{\mathbf{h}_t \geq 0,\ \|\mathbf{h}_t\|_2^2 \leq 1} -\sum_{t,t'} (\mathbf{x}_t^\top \mathbf{x}_{t'} - \alpha)\mathbf{h}_t^\top \mathbf{h}_{t'}.$$

Here matrix notation was introduced: $\mathbf{X} \equiv [\mathbf{x}_1, \ldots, \mathbf{x}_T] \in R^{n \times T}$ and $\mathbf{H} \equiv [\mathbf{h}_1, \ldots, \mathbf{h}_T] \in R^{m \times T}$, and $\mathbf{E}$ is a matrix of all ones.

Intuitively, (1) attempts to preserve similarity for similar pairs of input samples but orthogonalizes the outputs corresponding to dissimilar input pairs. Indeed, if the input similarity of a pair of samples t, t' is above a specified threshold, $\mathbf{x}_t^\top \mathbf{x}_{t'} > \alpha$, then the output vectors $\mathbf{h}_t$ and $\mathbf{h}_{t'}$ would prefer to have $\mathbf{h}_t^\top \mathbf{h}_{t'} \approx \mathbf{x}_t^\top \mathbf{x}_{t'} - \alpha$, i.e., they would be similar. If, however, $\mathbf{x}_t^\top \mathbf{x}_{t'} < \alpha$, then they would tend to be orthogonal, $\mathbf{h}_t^\top \mathbf{h}_{t'} = 0$, since the lowest value of $\mathbf{h}_t^\top \mathbf{h}_{t'}$ for $\mathbf{h}_t, \mathbf{h}_{t'} \geq 0$ is zero. As $\mathbf{h}_t$ and $\mathbf{h}_{t'}$ are nonnegative, to achieve orthogonality, the output activity patterns for dissimilar patterns would have non-overlapping sets of active output channels. In the context of manifold representation, (1) strives to preserve in the $\mathbf{h}$-representation the local geometry of the input data cloud

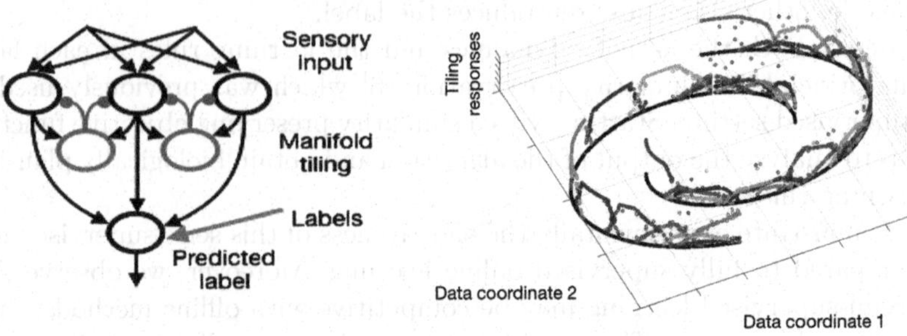

Fig. 1. *Left:* Two-layer network for semi-supervised learning. The first layer learns manifolds (the upper layer with interneurons in red), the second layer is one neuron that learns a classifier in the semi-supervised manner. The output of the network predicts the label value when the labels channel is silent, otherwise it reproduces the label. *Right:* Receptive fields of manifold tiling. Data are 2000 points sampled from two arcs in 2D (black dots); in the third dimension we show responses of individual channels to the corresponding data points, each channel is assigned a color (Color figure online).

in $\mathbf{x}$-space and let the global geometry emerge out of the nonlinear optimization process.

Figure 1 illustrates manifold tiling on a two spiral arcs in two dimensions, showing the receptive fields of output channels in the third dimension. Receptive fields tile the arcs with overlaps, but there is no overlap between separate arcs.

To derive a neural network that optimizes (1), we express the norm constraint in the Lagrangian form:

$$\min_{\forall t:\,\mathbf{h}_t\geq 0}\ \max_{\forall t:\,\mathbf{u}_t\geq 0}\ -\frac{1}{T}\sum_{t,t'}(\mathbf{x}_t^\top\mathbf{x}_{t'}-\alpha)\mathbf{h}_t^\top\mathbf{h}_{t'} \\ +\sum_t \mathbf{u}_t^\top\mathbf{u}_t(1-\mathbf{h}_t^\top\mathbf{h}_t). \tag{2}$$

Here, unconventionally, the non-negative Lagrange multipliers that impose the inequality constraints are factorized into inner products of two non-negative vectors ($\mathbf{u}_t^\top\mathbf{u}_t$). In the second step, we introduce auxiliary variables, $\mathbf{W}, \mathbf{b}, \mathbf{V}_t$ [7]:

$$\min_{\forall t:\,\mathbf{h}_t\geq 0}\ \max_{\forall t:\,\mathbf{u}_t\geq 0}\ \min_{\mathbf{W}}\max_{\mathbf{b}}\ \min_{\forall t:\,\mathbf{V}_t\geq 0}\ T\,\mathrm{Tr}(\mathbf{W}^\top\mathbf{W})-T\|\mathbf{b}\|_2^2+ \\ +\sum_t\Big(-2\mathbf{x}_t\mathbf{W}^\top\mathbf{h}_t+2\sqrt{\alpha}\mathbf{h}_t^\top\mathbf{b}+\|\mathbf{u}_t\|_2^2-2\mathbf{u}_t\mathbf{V}_t\mathbf{h}_t+\mathrm{Tr}(\mathbf{V}_t^\top\mathbf{V}_t)\Big) \tag{3}$$

The equivalence of (3) to (2) can be seen by performing the $\mathbf{W}, \mathbf{b}$, and $\mathbf{V}_t$ optimizations explicitly and plugging back in the optimal values. Equation (3) suggests a two-step online algorithm (see [8] for full derivation). For each input $\mathbf{x}_t$, in the first step, one solves for $\mathbf{h}_t$, $\mathbf{u}_t$ and $\mathbf{V}_t$, by projected gradient descent-ascent-descent,

$$\begin{bmatrix} \mathbf{h}_t \\ \mathbf{u}_t \\ \mathbf{V}_t \end{bmatrix} \longleftarrow \begin{bmatrix} \mathbf{h}_t + \gamma_h \left(\mathbf{W}\mathbf{x}_t - \mathbf{V}_t^\top \mathbf{u}_t - \sqrt{\alpha}\mathbf{b}\right) \\ \mathbf{u}_t + \gamma_u \left(-\mathbf{u}_t + \mathbf{V}_t \mathbf{h}_t\right) \\ \mathbf{V}_t + \gamma_V \left(\mathbf{u}_t \mathbf{h}_t^\top - \mathbf{V}_t\right) \end{bmatrix}_+, \tag{4}$$

where $\gamma_{h,u,V}$ are step sizes. This iteration can be interpreted as the dynamics of a biologically plausible neural circuit (Fig. 1, right, the upper layer), where components of $\mathbf{h}_t$ are activities of excitatory neurons, $\mathbf{b}$ is a bias term, components of $\mathbf{u}_t$ are activities of inhibitory neurons (shown in red), and $\mathbf{W}$ is the feedforward connectivity matrix. $\mathbf{V}_t$ is the synaptic weight matrix from excitatory to inhibitory neurons, which undergoes a fast time-scale anti-Hebbian plasticity, which in computer simulation means repeated updates within one t step. In the second step, $\mathbf{W}$ and $\mathbf{b}$ are updated by gradient descent-ascent:

$$\mathbf{W} \leftarrow \mathbf{W} + \eta \left(\mathbf{h}_t \mathbf{x}_t^\top - \mathbf{W}\right), \qquad \mathbf{b} \leftarrow \mathbf{b} + \eta \left(\sqrt{\alpha}\mathbf{h}_t - \mathbf{b}\right),$$

where $\mathbf{W}$ is going through a slow time-scale Hebbian plasticity and $\mathbf{b}$ through homeostatic plasticity. The parameter η is a learning rate.

3 A Neural Network for Semi-supervised Learning

In this section, we propose a neural network architecture for semi-supervised learning. In our approach, contrary to the widely accepted schemes, the label signal is not fed back from downstream layers of the network but comes along and synchronously with the rest of the data. To make it semi- (rather than fully) supervised, the signal is assumed to be "silent" most of the time.

Consider a classification problem with the input stream of data, $\{\mathbf{h}_1, \ldots, \mathbf{h}_t, \ldots\}$, where $\mathbf{h}_t \in R^m$, and the corresponding class labels $\{\tilde{z}_1, \ldots, \tilde{z}_t, \ldots\}$, where in a binary case $\tilde{z}_t \in \{-1, +1\}$. The labels are occasionally signalled by a channel carrying values $z_t = \theta_t \tilde{z}_t$, where $\theta_t \in \{0, 1\}$ either masks or reveals the true label. The data from the previous layer and the label channel are combined in the semi-supervised learning neuron, Fig. 1, right, bottom layer.

Consider a time period of $1, \ldots, T$, where the inputs are organized into a matrix $\mathbf{H} = [\mathbf{h}_1, \ldots, \mathbf{h}_T]$ and a vector of (partly hidden) labels $\mathbf{z}^\top = (z_1, \ldots, z_T)$. The output $\mathbf{y}^\top = (y_1, \ldots, y_T)$ needs to reproduce the label signal, so we employ a quadratic loss function $\|\mathbf{y} - \mathbf{z}\|^2$. We express the assumption of smoothness of predicted label $\mathbf{y}$ on the manifold using the similarity alignment [7] between the input and output Gramians: $\mathrm{Tr}(\mathbf{H}^\top \mathbf{H} \mathbf{y} \mathbf{y}^\top)$. Also, as the label only takes values 1 and -1, we restrict the output to stay within those limits. This gives rise to the following optimization problem:

$$\begin{aligned} &\min_{\mathbf{y}} \|\mathbf{y} - \mathbf{z}\|^2 - \frac{\mu}{T} \mathrm{Tr}(\mathbf{H}^\top \mathbf{H} \mathbf{y} \mathbf{y}^\top), \\ &\text{s.t.} \quad -1 \le y_t \le 1, \;\; t = 1, \ldots, T, \end{aligned} \tag{5}$$

where we also introduced a regularization coefficient μ controlling the relative importance of the two parts of the objective function.

To derive an online algorithm, following [7], we introduce an auxiliary variable $\mathbf{w}$ and expand in time:

$$\min_{\mathbf{y}} \min_{\mathbf{w}} \frac{1}{T} \sum_t \left[\frac{1}{2}(y_t - z_t)^2 - \mu y_t \mathbf{w}^\top \mathbf{h}_t \right] + \frac{\mu}{2} \mathbf{w}^\top \mathbf{w} \tag{6}$$

$$\text{s.t.} \quad -1 \le y_t \le 1, \;\; t = 1 \dots T.$$

Optimizing over $\mathbf{w}$, we obtain: $\mathbf{w} = \frac{1}{T} \sum_t y_t \mathbf{h}_t$, which makes it clear the new formulation is equivalent to Eq. (5). The advantage of this formulation is that it suggests a two-step online algorithm. For each input $\mathbf{h}_t$, on the first step, one solves for the instantaneous output y_t under fixed $\mathbf{w}$:

$$y_t = \max(-1, \min(1, \mu \mathbf{w}_t^\top \mathbf{h}_t + z_t)) \tag{7}$$

On the second step, $\mathbf{w}$ is updated as:

$$\mathbf{w} \leftarrow \frac{t}{t+1} \mathbf{w} + \frac{1}{t+1} y_t \mathbf{h}_t \tag{8}$$

This also maps well onto a biologically plausible neural network where components of $\mathbf{w}$ are interpreted as synapse weights, updated by local Hebbian rule. We assume that the synapse weight of the z channel is not changing, thus differentiating it from the other input channels. We set this weight to be equal to 1 without loss of generality. The algorithm is initialized with $\mathbf{w} = 0$, assuming no prior information.

An alternative objective function can be obtained by expressing the loss as $-\mathbf{y}^\top \mathbf{z}$ and adding an entropy-like regularizer treating $(y_t + 1)/2$ as a probability estimate for $\tilde{z}_t = 1$:

$$\begin{aligned} \min_{\mathbf{y}} & - \mathbf{y}^\top \mathbf{z} - \frac{\mu}{2T} \mathrm{Tr}(\mathbf{H}^\top \mathbf{H} \mathbf{y} \mathbf{y}^\top) \\ & - \sum_t \left[\frac{1 + y_t}{2} \log(\frac{1 + y_t}{2}) + \frac{1 - y_t}{2} \log(\frac{1 - y_t}{2}) \right] \end{aligned} \tag{9}$$

The solution of this optimization problem is the familiar sigmoidal neuron rule:

$$y_t = \tanh\left(\mu \mathbf{w}_t^\top \mathbf{h}_t + z_t\right)) \tag{10}$$

with the same update for $\mathbf{w}$ as in Eq. (8). The behavior of both algorithms is almost indistinguishable, so we only report the results from Eq. (7).

4 Numerical Experiments

We apply our algorithm to the synthetic dataset designed as “two moons”: two classes are sets of points in 2D, each concentrated around a spiral arc, Fig. 2, top. Such a synthetic dataset is widely used as a test for semi-supervised learning algorithms (see, e.g., [2,4]). Note that the classes are not linearly separable, and can be separated only when their manifold structure is discovered. Upon discovering the manifold structure, intuitively, the data can be classified using only one labeled example for each class, see red asterisks in Fig. 2, top.

Our network solves this highly non-linear classification problem. The first layer learns units that tile each "moon" with overlaps while no unit is shared between the two moons. The second layer propagates labeling information along links formed by correlations in the tile responses. We generated data points randomly and uniformly, only placing two labeled points early in the data stream. We used tiling layer with 40 neurons and semi-supervised neuron with $\mu = 1000$. The Fig. 2, bottom row, illustrates the working of the semi-supervised neuron. As seen on Fig. 2, bottom left, the output is zero until labeled points arrive. Then there is a transition period, during which the label signals propagate along correlated tiles. Finally, the responses stabilize to correct values: 1 for green, -1 for blue. Figure 2, bottom right, illustrates propagation of the labeling information. Initially, all weights are zero. When a labeled point arrives, weights corresponding to the tiles overlapping this point increase in absolute value. That signal gradually propagates until all synapses corresponding to "green moon" get positive weights and, all "blue" ones - negative weights.

Next, we apply our network to a larger dataset, a 3D Chessboard on a Swiss roll, Fig. 3, left. All the data live on a 2D Swiss roll manifold and the two classes are defined by the squares of the chessboards. We consider chessboards with varying square sizes with the most fine-grained chessboard being most difficult for classification. Whereas linear classifiers per se can not solve this problem, after learning the manifold classification is linear.

We compare our semi-supervised algorithm with an online fully supervised classifier – logistic regression. Both algorithms get the same input stream of 2000 data points, of which 50, 100, or 200 randomly selected are labeled and the rest are unlabeled. The input for both classification algorithms is the output of tiling with 200 neurons. Parameters μ for our neuron and learning rate for logistic regression are selected for best results of each algorithm. All runs repeated 10 times to obtain error bars.

Both algorithms classify each input using their current weights. However, the fully supervised algorithm cannot update its weights when an unlabeled example arrives, unlike the semi-supervised algorithm. Indeed, experiments show that the semi-supervised neural network performs better than the supervised classifier (Fig. 3, center), demonstrating its ability to take advantage of unlabeled data.

Next, we compare our online algorithm with an offline semi-supervised learning algorithm. For the latter, we use a state of the art linear SVM with Laplacian penalty following [2], but with a twist [1]: for the linear case we assume smoothness of weights rather than labels. This means that components of the separating vector $\mathbf{w}$ should have similar values when corresponding tiling components have highly overlapping receptive fields. The degree of overlap between receptive fields can be measured by dot products between tiling components, and can be calculated on both labeled and unlabeled data. Then the Gramian $S = \frac{1}{T}\mathbf{H}\mathbf{H}^\top$

[1] In a separate experiment we made sure this twist only improves the results.

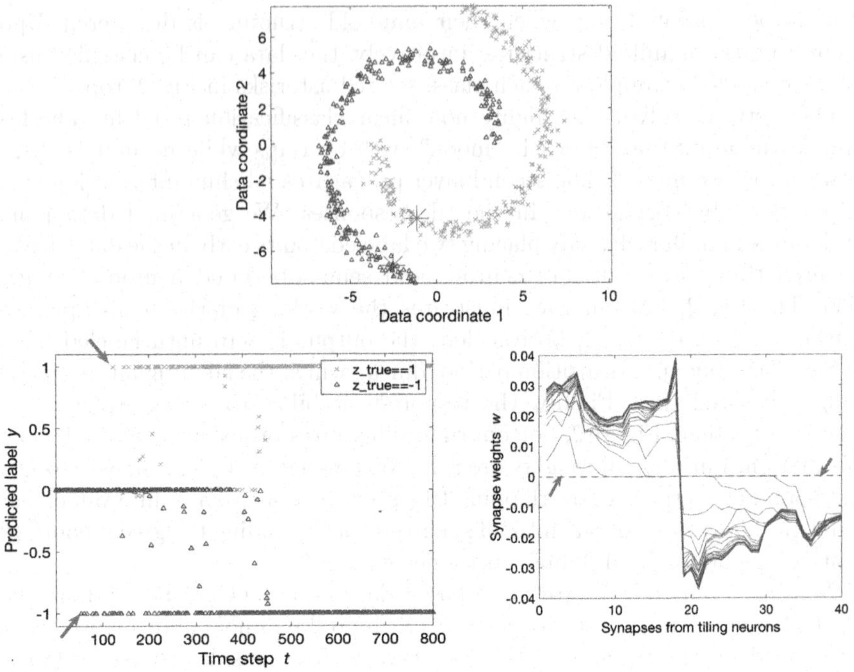

Fig. 2. Semi-supervised learning on the "two moons" dataset with two labeled points. *Top:* "Two moons" in 2D, classes - green crosses and blue triangles; red asterisks indicate two labeled points. *Bottom left:* Label predicted by the semi-supervised neuron (y_t values) in time, green crosses and blue triangles as the true class of the input. Labeled points indicated by arrows. *Bottom right:* Propagation of labels is shown by the weights of the tiles in time. Tiles are ordered along the x axis according to their locations on the "moons": "crosses" on the left and "triangles" - on the right. Lines show temporal dynamics of the weights, and only every 100th time point is shown. Arrows indicate tiles where labeled points fall.

can be thought of as the adjacency matrix of a graph where vertices are tiling components. The graph will be fairly sparse due to the nature of tiling. The graph Laplacian penalty is then:

$$\sum_{i,j}(w_i - w_j)^2 S_{i,j} = 2\mathbf{w}^\top L\mathbf{w}, \quad \text{where } L = \text{diag}(S\mathbf{1}) - S, \tag{11}$$

and the objective function of linear SVM with Laplacian penalty takes the form:

$$\min_{\mathbf{w},b} \sum_t [1 - z_t(\mathbf{w}^\top \mathbf{h}_t + b)]_+ + \lambda\|\mathbf{w}\|^2 + \mu\mathbf{w}^\top L\mathbf{w} \tag{12}$$

where the index t runs through the labeled samples only, with $z_t \in \{-1, 1\}$ being labels.

In this experiment, the online algorithm is fed a data stream with 0.05% of samples randomly labeled. Then at every 500th step the classification rule

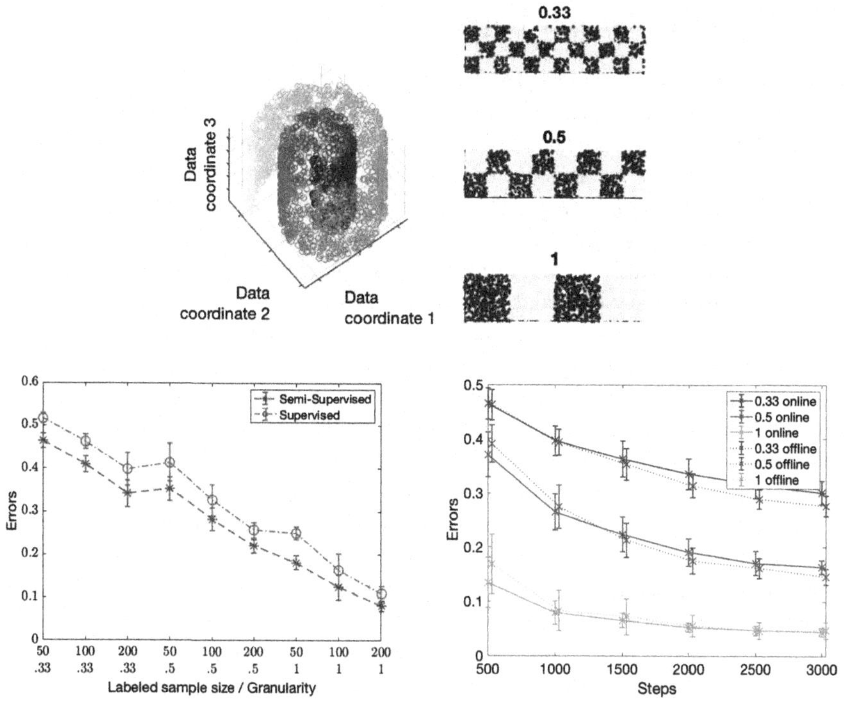

Fig. 3. *Left:* 3D Swiss roll manifold and three binary classification problems on the unrolled manifold. Granularity of the chessboard decreases from top to bottom. *Center:* Semi- vs. fully supervised: comparison of our semi-supervised algorithm with a fully supervised algorithm in the online setting. *Right:* Online vs. offline: comparison of our online semi-supervised learning algorithm with the offline semi-supervised algorithm (see text) for different granularity levels of the chessboard.

obtained up to this point is applied to a separate test set of 2000 samples. At the same step, the SVM with Laplacian regularization, Eq. (12), is trained on all data seen online so far and tested against the same test set. As before, the input for both algorithms is the output of tiling with 200 neurons. Parameters μ for our neuron and learning rate for logistic regression are selected for best results of each algorithm. All runs repeated 10 times to obtain error bars.

Offline algorithm has an advantage of considering all data samples before taking decision on labeling, while online algorithm has to assign a label estimate to each data sample as it appears. Results on Fig. 3, right, show, however, that with enough smoothness (i.e., coarser granularity in the "Chessboard" example), the online algorithm perform closely to the offline one. Moreover, online algorithm can perform better than the offline one while the number of presented data points is small (e.g., less than approximately 1200 with granularity 0.5). But small sample sizes is exactly the situation where semi-supervised learning is supposed to be helpful. The ability of the online algorithm to adapt quickly is also important when there is a drift in the manifold shape or the labels.

5 Relation to Graph Laplacian

Existing algorithms for semi-supervised learning on manifolds typically utilize the graph Laplacian for smoothness regularization [2,3,11], see the last term in Eq. (12). This follows from the analysis of [9], which showed that graph Laplacian regularization results in classifier corresponding to normalized graph cut, which helps avoid heavily imbalanced classes. In contrast, our smoothness term, last term, in Eq. (6), lacks diagonal normalization of Laplacian. When optimized exactly, it should lead to the minimum cut of the graph, which is prone to generate classes of very different size [9]. Consider a simple example of a square, where two labeled points for two classes are close to diagonally opposite corners. Laplacian regularization would cut the square in half approximately along the other diagonal, Fig. 4, left, while the minimum graph cut would lead to highly asymmetric solution: one predicted label concentrates closely around one of the labeled points, all the rest occupied by the other label.

However in our experiments we very rarely observe this trend towards asymmetrical solutions. To develop an intuition for why this happens, consider a period in the learning process during which labels channel is silent ($z_t = 0$), and y_t is not reaching the limits yet. This is the decisive period, where the label information propagates between the synapse weights, see Fig. 2, bottom left. Then (7) becomes simply $y_t = \mu \mathbf{w}_t^\top \mathbf{h}_t$. Assume the input points arrive i.i.d., then so are $\mathbf{h}_t$ vectors. Then substituting expression for y_t into (8) we can write an expectation for one component of $\mathbf{w}$:

$$\mathrm{E}(\Delta w_i) = \eta\Big(\sum_j \mu\,\mathrm{E}(h_i h_j) w_j - w_i\Big) = \eta\Big(\mu \sum_j s_{i,j} w_j - w_i\Big), \tag{13}$$

where we defined $s_{i,j} \equiv \mathrm{E}(h_i h_j)$, and $\eta = 1/(t+1)$. Now $(s_{i,j})$ can be seen as the adjacency matrix of a weighted graph, where vertices are tiling channels, in a manner analogous to the matrix $(S_{i,j})$, appearing in Eq. (11) in the previous section. The term $\mu \sum_j s_{i,j} w_j$, appearing in the right hand side of Eq. (13), has the effect of "smoothing" out $\mathbf{w}$ in over the tiling channels, in a manner analogous to the effect of the Laplacian penalty presented in (12). Essentially, the Laplacian penalty causes the components of $\mathbf{w}$ diffuse over the graph [11]. So, in expectation, the evolution of $\mathbf{w}$ in our algorithm would share some features with the gradient descent of $\mathbf{w}$ to optimize the expression in (12). "Smoothness" of the resulting $\mathbf{w}$ over channels translate to smoothness of prediction over input space, thereby reducing the likelihood of extremely imbalanced solutions.

We illustrate this with a simulation experiment on the square in Fig. 4. Ideally, there should be equal number of predicted labels for both classes. We, therefore, measure the imbalance, by looking at fraction associated with the majority class among predictions. This measure of imbalance ranges from 0.5 to 1.0. For each run, we generate 2000 unlabeled sample points uniformly on the square, plus 2 labeled points near the corners. These data were fed to our network with 50 tiling channels and $\mu = 10$ in (6). For comparison, the output of tiling layer is also used as input to linear classifier with Laplacian regularization. The histogram of results, after 100 such runs, is presented in Fig. 4, right.

While indeed the results for our network fluctuate more, compared to those of the Laplacian regularization approach, the extreme imbalances are rare in both approaches.

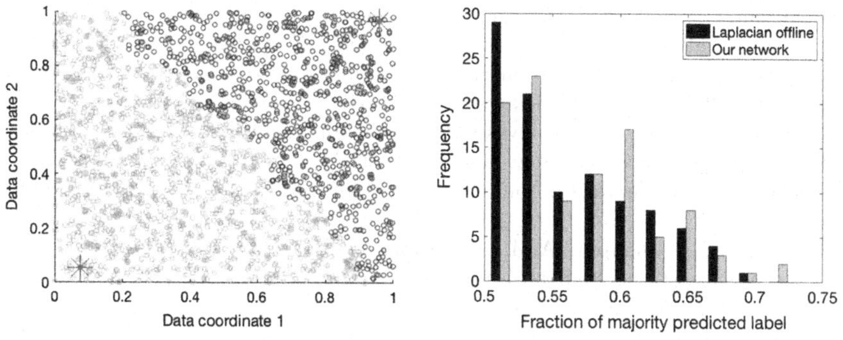

Fig. 4. *Left:* Linear classification with Laplacian regularization, points colored by predicted label; labeled points are red arrows. *Right:* The histogram of 100 repetitions of simulation of our measure of imbalance, namely, the fraction of the majority predicted label for Laplacian solution offline and for our network. Note that the frequencies fall off in both methods as the fraction moves up from 0.5.

6 Conclusion

We presented a neural network that learns low-dimensional manifolds in the data stream, then learns a classifier in a semi-supervised setting, where only small part of inputs are labeled. The network operates in an online fashion, producing an output immediately after seeing every input. Weights are updated by a biologically plausible local Hebbian-type rule. We demonstrated the effectiveness of the network in simulations, comparing it with fully supervised online algorithm and with a semi-supervised offline algorithm.

Acknowledgements. The authors are grateful to Victor Minden and Mariano Tepper for their insightful comments. We thank Johannes Friedrich, Tiberiu Tesileanu and Charles Windolf for helpful discussions.

References

1. Ando, R.K., Zhang, T.: Learning on graph with laplacian regularization. In: Advances in Neural Information Processing Systems, pp. 25–32 (2007). https://doi.org/10.7551/mitpress/7503.003.0009
2. Belkin, M., Niyogi, P., Sindhwani, V.: Manifold regularization: a geometric framework for learning from labeled and unlabeled examples. J. Mach. Learn. Res. **7**, 2399–2434 (2006)
3. Bengio, Y., Delalleau, O., Le Roux, N.: Label propagation and quadratic criterion. In: Semi-Supervised Learning. MIT Press (2006). https://doi.org/10.7551/mitpress/9780262033589.001.0001

4. Goldberg, A.B., Li, M., Zhu, X.: Online manifold regularization: a new learning setting and empirical study. In: Daelemans, W., Goethals, B., Morik, K. (eds.) ECML PKDD 2008. LNCS (LNAI), vol. 5211, pp. 393–407. Springer, Heidelberg (2008). https://doi.org/10.1007/978-3-540-87479-9_44
5. Pehlevan, C., Chklovskii, D.: A normative theory of adaptive dimensionality reduction in neural networks. In: Cortes, C., Lawrence, N.D., Lee, D.D., Sugiyama, M., Garnett, R. (eds.) Advances in Neural Information Processing Systems, vol. 28, pp. 2269–2277. Curran Associates, Inc. (2015)
6. Pehlevan, C., Hu, T., Chklovskii, D.: A hebbian/anti-hebbian neural network for linear subspace learning: a derivation from multidimensional scaling of streaming data. Neural Comput. **27**, 1461–1495 (2015). https://doi.org/10.1162/neco_a_00745
7. Pehlevan, C., Sengupta, A.M., Chklovskii, D.B.: Why do similarity matching objectives lead to hebbian/anti-hebbian networks? Neural Comput. **30**(1), 84–124 (2018). https://doi.org/10.1162/neco_a_01018
8. Sengupta, A., Pehlevan, C., Tepper, M., Genkin, A., Chklovskii, D.: Manifold-tiling localized receptive fields are optimal in similarity-preserving neural networks. In: Bengio, S., Wallach, H., Larochelle, H., Grauman, K., Cesa-Bianchi, N., Garnett, R. (eds.) Advances in Neural Information Processing Systems, vol. 31, pp. 7080–7090. Curran Associates, Inc. (2018)
9. Shi, J., Malik, J.: Normalized cuts and image segmentation. IEEE Trans. Pattern Anal. Mach. Intell. **22**(8) (2000). https://doi.org/10.1109/cvpr.1997.609407
10. Yu, K., Zhang, T., Gong, Y.: Nonlinear learning using local coordinate coding. In: Advances in Neural Information Processing Systems, pp. 2223–2231 (2009)
11. Zhu, X., Ghahramani, Z., Lafferty, J.D.: Semi-supervised learning using Gaussian fields and harmonic functions. In: Proceedings of the 20th International Conference on Machine Learning (ICML-03), pp. 912–919 (2003)

Neural Network Theory

Counting with Analog Neurons

Jiří Šíma(✉)

Institute of Computer Science, Czech Academy of Sciences,
P. O. Box 5, 18207 Prague 8, Czech Republic
sima@cs.cas.cz

Abstract. We refine the analysis of binary-state neural networks with α extra analog neurons (αANNs). For rational weights, it has been known that online 1ANNs accept context-sensitive languages including examples of non-context-free languages, while offline 3ANNs are Turing complete. We now prove that the deterministic (context-free) language containing the words of n zeros followed by n ones, cannot be recognized offline by any 1ANN with real weights. Hence, the offline 1ANNs are not Turing complete. On the other hand, we show that any deterministic language can be accepted by a 2ANN with rational weights. Thus, two extra analog units can count to any number which is not the case of one analog neuron.

Keywords: Neural computing · Analog state · Deterministic pushdown automaton · Deterministic context-free language · Chomsky hierarchy

1 Introduction

The computational power of (recurrent) neural networks with the saturated-linear activation function[1] depends on the descriptive complexity of their weight parameters [10,18]. Neural nets with *integer* weights, corresponding to binary-state networks, coincide with finite automata [1,3,4,7,14,20]. *Rational* weights make the analog-state networks computationally equivalent to Turing machines [4,12], and thus (by a real-time simulation [12]) polynomial-time computations of such networks are characterized by the fundamental complexity class P. Moreover, neural nets with arbitrary *real* weights can even derive "super-Turing" computational capabilities [10]. In particular, their polynomial-time computations correspond to the nonuniform complexity class P/poly while any input/output mapping (including undecidable problems) can be computed within exponential time [11]. In addition, a proper hierarchy of nonuniform complexity classes between P and P/poly has been established for polynomial-time computations of neural nets with increasing Kolmogorov complexity of real weights [2].

[1] Some of the results are valid for more general classes of activation functions [6,13,21] including the logistic function [5].

Research was done with institutional support RVO: 67985807 and partially supported by the grant of the Czech Science Foundation No. 19-05704S.

I. V. Tetko et al. (Eds.): ICANN 2019, LNCS 11727, pp. 389–400, 2019.
https://doi.org/10.1007/978-3-030-30487-4_31

As can be seen, our understanding of the computational power of recursive (Turing complete) neural networks is satisfactorily fine-grained when changing from rational to arbitrary real weights. In contrast, there is still a gap between integer and rational weights which results in a jump from regular to recursively enumerable languages in the Chomsky hierarchy. In the effort of refining the analysis of subrecursive neural nets we have introduced a model of binary-state networks extended with α extra analog-state neurons (αANNs) [15], as already *three* additional analog units allow for Turing universality [16]. Although this model of αANNs has been inspired by theoretical issues, neural networks with different types of units/layers are widely used in practical applications, e.g. in deep learning [9], and they thus require a detailed mathematical analysis.

In our previous work, we have characterized syntactically the class of languages accepted online by the 1ANNs with one extra analog neuron [17] in terms of so-called cut languages [19]. The *online* (real-time) input/output protocol means that a (potentially infinite) input word $\mathbf{x}$ is sequentially read symbol after symbol, each being processed with a *constant-time overhead*, while a neural network simultaneously signals via its output neuron whether the prefix of $\mathbf{x}$ that has been read so far, belongs to the respective language [3,20]. By using the underlying syntactic characterization we have shown that the languages recognized online by the 1ANNs with rational weights are context-sensitive, and we have presented explicit examples of such languages that are not context-free. Furthermore, we have formulated a sufficient condition when a 1ANN accepts only a regular language in terms of quasi-periodicity of its real weight parameters. For example, 1ANNs with weights from the smallest field extension $\mathbb{Q}(\beta)$ over rational numbers including a Pisot number $\beta = 1/w$ where w is the self-loop weight of the analog unit, have only a power of finite automata. These results [17] refine the classification of subrecursive neural networks with the weights between integer and rational weights, within the Chomsky hierarchy.

In addition, we have shown [16] that any language accepted by a Turing machine in time $T(n)$ can be accepted offline by a binary-state neural network with *three* extra analog units (3ANNs) having rational weights in time $O(T(n))$. The *offline* input/output protocol assumes that an input word $\mathbf{x}$ is read by a neural network either sequentially, each symbol on request with no time bounds for its processing (possibly with the recognition of each input prefix), or $\mathbf{x}$ is already encoded in a real initial state of the analog neuron. The neural network then carries out its computation until it possibly halts and decides whether $\mathbf{x}$ belongs to the underlying language, which is indicated by its output neurons [12]. Thus, for rational weights, the languages accepted online by 1ANNs or offline by 3ANNs are context-sensitive or recursively enumerable, respectively.

In this paper, we further refine the analysis of αANNs by showing that the deterministic (context-free) language $L = \{0^n1^n \mid n \geq 1\}$, containing the words of n zeros followed by n ones, cannot be recognized even offline by any 1ANN with one extra analog neuron having arbitrary real weights. Hence, the offline 1ANNs are not Turing complete. The proof is based on an asymptotic analysis of computations by 1ANNs whose dynamics is quite restricted for recalling a stored number. It follows that 1ANNs cannot count to an arbitrarily large number, although we know 1ANNs with rational weights accept some context-sensitive cut languages that are not context-free [17].

On the other hand, we prove that the deterministic languages (including L) which are accepted by the deterministic pushdown automata (DPDA) can be recognized by 2ANNs with *two* extra analog neurons and rational weights. This means that two extra analog units can count to any number which is not the case of one analog neuron. The proof exploits the classical technique of implementing the stack of a DPDA by analog units, including the encoding of stack contents based on a Cantor-like set [12]. The synchronization of a fully parallel computation by 2ANNs is implemented by alternating the storage of stack contents between two analog neurons so that the first neuron realizes the `top` and `push` operations while the second one carries out the `pop` operation.

The paper is organized as follows. In Sect. 2, we introduce a formal model of binary-state neural networks αANNs with α extra analog units. Section 3 shows an example of a deterministic language that cannot be recognized by any 1ANN with real weights, while Sect. 4 presents a simulation of any DPDA by a 2ANN with rational weights. We present some open problems in Sect. 5.

2 Neural Networks with a Few Extra Analog Units

For a small integer constant $\alpha \geq 0$ (e.g. $\alpha \leq 3$), we specify a computational model of a *binary-state neural network αANN with α extra analog units*, $\mathcal{N}$, which will be used as a formal language acceptor. The network $\mathcal{N}$ consists of $s \geq \alpha$ *units (neurons)*, indexed as $V = \{1, \ldots, s\}$. The units in $\mathcal{N}$ are assumed to be binary-state (shortly *binary*) neurons (i.e. *perceptrons, threshold gates)* except for the first α neurons $1, \ldots, \alpha \in V$ which are *analog* units. The neurons are connected into a directed graph representing an *architecture* of $\mathcal{N}$, in which each edge $(i, j) \in V^2$ leading from unit i to j is labeled with a real *weight* $w(i, j) = w_{ji} \in \mathbb{R}$. The absence of a connection within the architecture corresponds to a zero weight between the respective neurons, and vice versa.

The *computational dynamics* of $\mathcal{N}$ determines for each unit $j \in V$ its *state (output)* $y_j^{(t)}$ at discrete time instants $t = 0, 1, 2, \ldots$. The outputs $y_1^{(t)}, \ldots, y_\alpha^{(t)}$ from analog units $1, \ldots, \alpha \in V$ are real numbers from the unit interval $\mathbb{I} = [0, 1]$, whereas the states $y_j^{(t)}$ of the remaining $s - \alpha$ neurons $j \in V' = V \setminus \{1, \ldots, \alpha\}$ are binary values from $\{0, 1\}$. This establishes the *network state* $\mathbf{y}^{(t)} = \left(y_1^{(t)}, \ldots, y_\alpha^{(t)}, y_{\alpha+1}^{(t)}, \ldots, y_s^{(t)}\right) \in \mathbb{I}^\alpha \times \{0, 1\}^{s-\alpha}$ at each discrete time instant $t \geq 0$. For notational simplicity, we assume a synchronous fully parallel mode without loss of efficiency [8]. At the beginning of a computation, the neural network $\mathcal{N}$ is placed in an *initial state* $\mathbf{y}^{(0)} \in \{0, 1\}^s$. At discrete time instant $t \geq 0$, an *excitation* of any neuron $j \in V$ is defined as $\xi_j^{(t)} = \sum_{i=0}^{s} w_{ji} y_i^{(t)}$, including a real *bias* value $w_{j0} \in \mathbb{R}$ which can be viewed as the weight $w(0, j)$ from a formal constant unit input $y_0^{(t)} \equiv 1$ for every $t \geq 0$ (i.e. $0 \in V'$). At the next instant $t+1$, all the neurons $j \in V$ compute their new outputs $y_j^{(t+1)}$ in parallel by applying an *activation function* $\sigma_j : \mathbb{R} \longrightarrow \mathbb{I}$ to $\xi_j^{(t)}$, that is, $y_j^{(t+1)} = \sigma_j\left(\xi_j^{(t)}\right)$ for $j \in V$. The analog units $j \in \{1, \ldots, \alpha\}$ employ the *saturated-linear* function $\sigma_j(\xi) = \sigma(\xi)$ where $\sigma(\xi) = \xi$ for $0 \le \xi \le 1$, while $\sigma(\xi) = 1$ for $\xi > 1$, and $\sigma(\xi) = 0$ for $\xi < 0$. For neurons $j \in V'$ with binary states $y_j \in \{0, 1\}$, the *Heaviside* activation function $\sigma_j(\xi) = H(\xi)$ is used where $H(\xi) = 1$ for $\xi \ge 0$ and $H(\xi) = 0$ for $\xi < 0$. This determines the new network state $\mathbf{y}^{(t+1)} \in \mathbb{I}^\alpha \times \{0, 1\}^{s-\alpha}$ at time $t+1$.

The computational power of neural networks has been studied analogously to the traditional models of computations so that the networks are exploited as acceptors of formal languages $L \subseteq \Sigma^*$ [18]. For simplicity, we assume the binary alphabet $\Sigma = \{0, 1\}$ and for a finite αANN $\mathcal{N}$, we use the following offline input/output protocol employing its special neurons nxt, inp, out $\in V'$. An input word (string) $\mathbf{x} = x_1 \ldots x_n \in \{0, 1\}^n$ of arbitrary length $n \ge 0$, is sequentially presented to $\mathcal{N}$, bit after bit, via the so-called *input neuron* inp $\in V'$, at the time instants $0 < \tau_1 < \tau_2 < \cdots < \tau_n$ when queried by $\mathcal{N}$. Thus, once the prefix $x_1, \ldots, x_{k-1}$ of $\mathbf{x}$ for $1 \le k \le n$, has been read, the next input bit $x_k \in \{0, 1\}$ is presented to $\mathcal{N}$ one computational step after $\mathcal{N}$ activates the neuron nxt $\in V'$, that is, $y_{\mathrm{inp}}^{(t)} = x_k$ and $y_{\mathrm{nxt}}^{(t-1)} = 1$ if $t = \tau_k$, and $y_{\mathrm{inp}}^{(t)} = y_{\mathrm{nxt}}^{(t-1)} = 0$, otherwise, for $k = 1, \ldots, n$. At the same time, $\mathcal{N}$ carries its computation deciding about each prefix of the input word $\mathbf{x}$ whether it belongs to L, which is indicated by the output neuron out $\in V'$ when the neuron nxt is active, i.e. $y_{\mathrm{out}}^{(\tau_{k+1}-1)} = 1$ if $x_1 \ldots x_k \in L$, and $y_{\mathrm{out}}^{(\tau_{k+1}-1)} = 0$ if $x_1 \ldots x_k \notin L$, where $\tau_{n+1} > \tau_n$ is the time instant when the input word $\mathbf{x}$ is decided. We say that a language $L \subseteq \{0, 1\}^*$ is *accepted (recognized)* by αANN $\mathcal{N}$, which is denoted by $L = \mathcal{L}(\mathcal{N})$, if for any input word $\mathbf{x} \in \{0, 1\}^*$, $\mathbf{x} \in L$ iff $\mathcal{N}$ halts and accepts $\mathbf{x}$.

3 One Analog Neuron Cannot Count

In this section, we prove that the deterministic language L, containing the words of n zeros followed by n ones, which imitates counting, cannot be accepted by any 1ANN $\mathcal{N}$ with one extra analog unit. The main idea of the proof is based on the fact that $\mathcal{N}$ must keep the count of the initial segment of zeros in an input word because this must later be compared to the number of subsequent ones in order to decide whether the input is accepted. However, this count is unbounded while $\mathcal{N}$ has only finitely many possible binary states. Thus, this number can just be stored by using a real state of the analog neuron. On the contrary, suppose $L = \mathcal{L}(\mathcal{N})$ is accepted by $\mathcal{N}$. By presenting a series of zeros as an input to $\mathcal{N}$, we obtain an infinite bounded sequence of real analog-state values which has a monotone convergent subsequence according to the Bolzano-Weierstrass theorem. This subsequence is further pruned so that it remains infinite while the following condition is satisfied. Starting with any analog value from this pruned convergent subsequence, the binary states enter the same cycle in a while after a subsequent series of ones is presented to $\mathcal{N}$, which induces a periodic behavior in the limit. This periodicity provides only a finite number of thresholds for separating an infinite number of analog values from each other, which represent the counts of zeros. This means that $\mathcal{N}$ would accept two input words composed of different number of zeros followed by the same number of ones, which is a contradiction. The technical details are presented in the following proof sketch.

Theorem 1. *The deterministic context-free language* $L = \{0^n1^n \mid n \geq 1\}$ *cannot be recognized by a neural network 1ANN with one extra analog unit having real weights.*

Proof. (Sketch.) On the contrary, assume that $\mathcal{N}$ is a neural network 1ANN with one extra analog unit such that $L = \mathcal{L}(\mathcal{N})$. Let $y_j^{(t)}(\mathbf{x})$ and $\xi_j^{(t)}(\mathbf{x})$ be the state and the excitation of neuron $j \in V$ at time instant $t \geq 0$, respectively, when an input word $\mathbf{x} \in \{0,1\}^n$ of length n is presented to $\mathcal{N}$, which satisfies $t < \tau_{n+1}$ by the input protocol (formally, we also allow infinite input strings $\mathbf{x} \in \{0,1\}^\omega$). Denote by $\mathbf{y}^{(t)}(\mathbf{x}) = \left(y_1^{(t)}(\mathbf{x}), \ldots, y_s^{(t)}(\mathbf{x})\right) \in \mathbb{I} \times \{0,1\}^{s-1}$ and $\tilde{\mathbf{y}}^{(t)}(\mathbf{x}) = \left(y_2^{(t)}(\mathbf{x}), \ldots, y_s^{(t)}(\mathbf{x})\right) \in \{0,1\}^{s-1}$ the corresponding network state, respectively, restricted to binary neurons. For the infinite input string 0^ω, there exists $t_0 \geq 0$ such that the state of analog unit meets $y_1^{(t_0)}(0^\omega) \in \{0,1\}$ (we know $y_1^{(0)}(0^\omega) \in \{0,1\}$ by definition) and $0 < y_1^{(t)}(0^\omega) < 1$ for every $t > t_0$, since otherwise there would be infinitely many time instants t with the same network state $\mathbf{y}^{(t)}(0^\omega)$ due to $\{0,1\}^s$ is finite, which provides $n_1 < n_2$ such that $\mathcal{N}$ would accept incorrectly the input word $0^{n_2}1^{n_1} \notin L$. For the same reason, the self-loop weight meets $w_{11} \neq 0$ since for $w_{11} = 0$, the analog unit could produce only a finite number of output values $y_1^{(t)} \in \left\{\sum_{i \in V'} w_{1i} y_i \,\middle|\, (y_2, \ldots, y_s) \in \{0,1\}^{s-1}\right\}$ for $t > t_0$. Define the *base* $\beta = 1/w_{11}$ and the set of *digits*, $A = \left\{\beta \sum_{i \in V'} w_{1i} y_i \,\middle|\, (y_2, \ldots, y_s) \in \{0,1\}^{s-1}\right\} \cup \{0, \beta\}$. We introduce an infinite sequence of digits, $a_1 a_2 a_3 \ldots \in A^\omega$ as $a_1 = \beta y_1^{(t_0)}(0^\omega) \in \{0, \beta\} \subseteq A$ and $a_k = \beta \sum_{i \in V'} w_{1i} y_i^{(t_0+k-2)}(0^\omega) \in A$ for $k \geq 2$. For every $t \geq t_0$, we have $y_1^{(t+1)}(0^\omega) = \sum_{i=0}^{s} w_{1i} y_i^{(t)}(0^\omega) = \beta^{-1}\left(a_{t-t_0+2} + y_1^{(t)}(0^\omega)\right)$, which implies $y_1^{(t)}(0^\omega) = \sum_{k=1}^{t-t_0+1} a_{t-t_0-k+2}\, \beta^{-k}$. It follows that $|\beta| > 1$ because $0 < y_1^{(t)}(0^\omega) < 1$ for every $t > t_0$.

Consider an infinite sequence of time instants $0 < t_1 < t_2 < t_3 < \cdots$ such that for each n, $t_n = \tau_{n+1} - 1$ is the last time instant before the next $(n+1)$th bit is presented to $\mathcal{N}$ after the input 0^n has been read, that is, $y_{\text{nxt}}^{(t_n)}(0^n) = 1$. Since the infinite sequence of real numbers $y_1^{(t_n)}(0^n) \in \mathbb{I}$ for $n \geq 1$, is bounded, there exists its monotone convergent subsequence $y_1^{(t_{n_p})}(0^{n_p}) \in (0,1)$ for $p \geq 1$, where $t_{n_1} > t_0$, $n_1 < n_2 < n_3 < \cdots$, and $c_0 = \lim_{p \to \infty} y_1^{(t_{n_p})}(0^{n_p})$, according to Bolzano-Weierstrass theorem. We assume that this subsequence is nondecreasing, that is, $y_1^{(t_{n_p})}(0^{n_p}) \leq y_1^{(t_{n_{p+1}})}(0^{n_{p+1}})$ for every $p \geq 1$, while the argument for a nonincreasing subsequence is analogous. In the following considerations, we will repeatedly remove some elements from the sequence (n_p) given by Bolzano-Weierstrass theorem, so that infinitely many elements remain, which satisfy additional conditions. For simplicity, we will keep the original notation (n_p) for these pruned sequences without loss of generality.

There are only finitely many possible states of binary neurons taken from $\{0,1\}^{s-1}$, and hence, there exists $\tilde{\mathbf{u}} \in \{0,1\}^{s-1}$ which occurs infinitely many times in the corresponding subsequence $\tilde{\mathbf{y}}^{(t_{n_p})}(0^{n_p})$ for $p \geq 1$. By skipping the remaining elements, we can assume without loss of generality that $\tilde{\mathbf{y}}^{(t_{n_p})}(0^{n_p}) = \tilde{\mathbf{u}}$ for every $p \geq 1$. It follows that the subsequence $y_1^{(t_{n_p})}(0^{n_p})$ for $p \geq 1$, is increasing since for $y_1^{(t_{n_p})}(0^{n_p}) = y_1^{(t_{n_{p+1}})}(0^{n_{p+1}})$, we have $\mathbf{y}^{(t_{n_p})}(0^{n_p}) = \mathbf{y}^{(t_{n_p})}(0^{n_{p+1}})$, and hence, the input $0^{n_{p+1}}1^{n_p} \notin L$ would be incorrectly accepted by $\mathcal{N}$.

We will inductively construct an increasing infinite sequence (m_p) of natural numbers $m_p \geq 0$ such that for each $p \geq 1$ and for every $q > p$,

$$\tilde{\mathbf{y}}^{(t_{n_p}+k)}(0^{n_p}1^{n_p}) = \tilde{\mathbf{y}}^{(t_{n_q}+k)}(0^{n_q}1^{n_p}) \quad \text{for every } k = 0, \ldots, m_p \tag{1}$$

$$\tilde{\mathbf{y}}^{(t_{n_p}+m_p+1)}(0^{n_p}1^{n_p}) \neq \tilde{\mathbf{y}}^{(t_{n_q}+m_p+1)}(0^{n_q}1^{n_p}), \tag{2}$$

while pruning the corresponding sequence (n_p) so that the number of elements in (n_p) remains infinite. Observe that by definition, $m_p \leq m_{p+1}$, and condition (1) holds at least for $k = 0$, whereas condition (2) is met before the next input bit is presented to $\mathcal{N}$ after the input $0^{n_p}1^{n_p} \in L$ has been read, due to $0^{n_q}1^{n_p} \notin L$ for $q > p$. Suppose $m_1 < m_2 < \cdots < m_{p-1}$ have been constructed, satisfying (1) and (2). For the next index $p \geq 1$, let $\tilde{m}_p \geq 0$ be the maximal natural number that meets (1) with m_p replaced by $\tilde{m}_p$, which means $\tilde{m}_p \geq m_{p-1}$. On the contrary assume that $\tilde{m}_p = m_{p-1}$. There exists $\tilde{\mathbf{u}}' \in \{0,1\}^{s-1}$ such that the set $Q = \left\{q \geq p \,\middle|\, \tilde{\mathbf{y}}^{(t_{n_q}+\tilde{m}_p+1)}(0^{n_q}1^{n_p}) = \tilde{\mathbf{u}}'\right\}$ is infinite since there are only 2^{s-1} possible states of binary neurons. We omit all the elements n_q in (n_p) such that $p \leq q \notin Q$, while the pruned sequence (n_p), including the indices from infinite Q, remains infinite, and $p = \min Q$ is the new succeeding index in the pruned (n_p). In addition, the new maximal value of $\tilde{m}_p$ satisfying (1) for this index p, increases by at least 1, and hence, we have $\tilde{m}_p > m_{p-1}$. Moreover, we can assume without loss of generality that there are infinitely many indices q that meet (2) with m_p replaced by $\tilde{m}_p$, since otherwise we could skip them in (n_p), while increasing $\tilde{m}_p$. Thus, the constructed sequence $m_1, \ldots, m_{p-1}$ is extended with $m_p = \tilde{m}_p > m_{p-1}$ and the sequence (n_p) is further pruned by removing those indices $q > p$ for which (2) is not satisfied. This completes the inductive construction which ensures the sequence (m_p) which corresponds to (n_p) and satisfies (1) and (2), is increasing, and hence unbounded. Hereafter, we assume there are infinitely many even numbers in (m_p) while the proof for the opposite case when there are infinitely many odd numbers in (m_p), is analogous. Thus, by pruning the sequence (n_p) we can assume without loss of generality that m_p is even for every $p \geq 1$.

In addition, for each $p \geq 1$, define m'_p to be the maximum number such that $0 \leq m'_p \leq m_p$ and $0 \leq \xi_1^{(t_{n_p}+k)}(0^{n_p}1^{n_p}) \leq 1$ for every $k = 0, \ldots, m'_p$, which holds at least for $k = 0$ because $\xi_1^{(t_{n_p})}(0^{n_p}1^{n_p}) = y_1^{(t_{n_p}+1)}(0^{n_{p+1}}) \in (0,1)$. We introduce $b_k = \beta \sum_{i \in V'} w_{1i} y_i^{(t_{n_p}+k-1)}(0^{n_p}1^{n_p}) \in A$ for $k = 1, \ldots, m_p + 1$, which is a consistent definition for every $p \geq 1$, due to (1). We have $y_1^{(t_{n_p}+k)}(0^{n_p}1^{n_p}) =$

$\sum_{i=0}^{s} w_{1i} y_i^{(t_{n_p}+k-1)}(0^{n_p}1^{n_p}) = \beta^{-1}\left(b_k + y_1^{(t_{n_p}+k-1)}(0^{n_p}1^{n_p})\right)$ for $1 \leq k \leq m'_p+1$. Hence, $\xi_1^{(t)}(0^{n_p}1^{n_p}) = \beta^{-(t-t_{n_p}+1)} y_1^{(t_{n_p})}(0^{n_p}) + \sum_{k=1}^{t-t_{n_p}+1} b_{t-t_{n_p}-k+2}\,\beta^{-k}$ for each $p \geq 1$ and $t_{n_p} \leq t \leq t_{n_p} + \min(m'_p+1, m_p)$. One can prove that $m'_p = m_p$ for every $p \geq 1$.

Since the sequence $y_1^{(t_{n_p})}(0^{n_p})$ is increasing, we have for every $p \geq 1$,

$$
\begin{aligned}
y_1^{(t_{n_p}+m_p)}(0^{n_p}1^{n_p}) &= \beta^{-m_p}\, y_1^{(t_{n_p})}(0^{n_p}) + \sum_{k=1}^{m_p} b_{m_p-k+1}\,\beta^{-k} \\
< \ \beta^{-m_p}\, y_1^{(t_{n_{p+1}})}(0^{n_{p+1}}) &+ \sum_{k=1}^{m_p} b_{m_p-k+1}\,\beta^{-k} = y_1^{(t_{n_{p+1}}+m_p)}(0^{n_{p+1}}1^{n_p}) \qquad (3)
\end{aligned}
$$

due to $y_1^{(t_{n_p}+m_p)}(0^{n_p}1^{n_p}) = \xi_1^{(t_{n_p}+m_p-1)}(0^{n_p}1^{n_p})$ and m_p is even. There exists $\tilde{\mathbf{v}} \in \{0,1\}^{s-1}$ such that $\tilde{\mathbf{y}}^{(t_{n_p}+m_p)}(0^{n_p}1^{n_p}) = \tilde{\mathbf{v}}$ for infinitely many $p \geq 1$, since there are only 2^{s-1} states of binary neurons, and by pruning the sequence (n_p), we can assume without loss of generality that $\tilde{\mathbf{y}}^{(t_{n_p}+m_p)}(0^{n_p}1^{n_p}) = \tilde{\mathbf{v}}$ for every $p \geq 1$. Similarly, assume there exists a binary neuron $j_0 \in \{2,\ldots,s\}$ such that $y_{j_0}^{(t_{n_p}+m_p+1)}(0^{n_p}1^{n_p}) \neq y_{j_0}^{(t_{n_{p+1}}+m_p+1)}(0^{n_{p+1}}1^{n_p})$ for every $p \geq 1$, according to (2), since there are only $s-1$ binary neurons. It follows that $w_{j_0,1} \neq 0$ because $\tilde{\mathbf{y}}^{(t_{n_p}+m_p)}\ (0^{n_p}1^{n_p}) = \tilde{\mathbf{y}}^{(t_{n_{p+1}}+m_p)}(0^{n_{p+1}}1^{n_p})$ by (1), and we define $c = -\frac{1}{w_{j_0,1}} \sum_{i \in V'} w_{j_0,i}\, y_i^{(t_{n_p}+m_p)}(0^{n_p}1^{n_p})$, which is a consistent definition due to $\tilde{\mathbf{y}}^{(t_{n_p}+m_p)}(0^{n_p}1^{n_p}) = \tilde{\mathbf{v}}$ for every $p \geq 1$. Assume $w_{j_0,1} > 0$, while the argument for $w_{j_0,1} < 0$ is analogous. We have $y_{j_0}^{(t_{n_p}+m_p+1)}(0^{n_p}1^{n_p}) = 1$ iff $\xi_{j_0}^{(t_{n_p}+m_p)}(0^{n_p}1^{n_p}) \geq 0$ iff $y_1^{(t_{n_p}+m_p)}(0^{n_p}1^{n_p}) \geq c$, and similarly, $y_{j_0}^{(t_{n_{p+1}}+m_p+1)}(0^{n_{p+1}}1^{n_p}) = 1$ iff $y_1^{(t_{n_{p+1}}+m_p)}(0^{n_{p+1}}1^{n_p}) \geq c$, which implies

$$
y_1^{(t_{n_p}+m_p)}(0^{n_p}1^{n_p}) < c \leq y_1^{(t_{n_{p+1}}+m_p)}(0^{n_{p+1}}1^{n_p}) \qquad (4)
$$

by (3). We obtain $y_1^{(t_{n_p})}(0^{n_p}) < \beta^{m_p}\left(c - \sum_{k=1}^{m_p} b_{m_p-k+1}\,\beta^{-k}\right) \leq y_1^{(t_{n_{p+1}})}(0^{n_{p+1}})$ for every $p \geq 1$, which implies $\lim_{p\to\infty} \sum_{k=1}^{m_p} b_{m_p-k+1}\,\beta^{-k} = c$.

For $p \geq 1$, $c_p = \lim_{q\to\infty} y_1^{(t_{n_q}+m_p)}(0^{n_q}1^{m_p}) = \beta^{-m_p} c_0 + \sum_{k=1}^{m_p} b_{m_p-k+1}\beta^{-k}$ according to (3), which implies $\lim_{p\to\infty} c_p = c$. We introduce the intervals, $I_{p,r} = \left[\beta^{-r}c + \sum_{k=1}^{r} b_{m_p+r-k+1}\beta^{-k}\,,\ \beta^{-r}c_p + \sum_{k=1}^{r} b_{m_p+r-k+1}\beta^{-k}\right)$ for every $p \geq 1$ and $r = 0,\ldots,\ell_p - 1$, where $\ell_p = m_{p+1} - m_p$ is even. Note that for notational simplicity, we assume $\beta > 1$ while for $\beta < -1$ when the interval lower and upper bounds are swapped for odd r, the argument is similar. It follows from (4) that $y_1^{(t_{n_q}+m_p+r)}(0^{n_q}1^{m_p}) \in I_{p,r}$ for every $q > p$. For all sufficiently large $p \geq p_0$, we will prove by induction on $r = 0,\ldots,\ell_p - 1$ that $I_{p+1,r} \subset I_{p,r}$ and

$$
\tilde{\mathbf{y}}^{(t_{n_{p+1}}+m_p+r)}(0^{n_{p+1}}1^{n_{p+1}}) = \tilde{\mathbf{y}}^{(t_{n_{p+2}}+m_{p+1}+r)}(0^{n_{p+2}}1^{n_{p+2}})\,. \qquad (5)
$$

For the base case $r = 0$, the length of $I_{p,0} = [c, c_p)$ is β^{ℓ_p} times greater than that of the interval $I_{p+1} = \left[\beta^{-\ell_p}c + \sum_{k=1}^{\ell_p} b_{m_{p+1}-k+1}\beta^{-k}\,,\ c_{p+1}\right)$ because $c_{p+1} =$

$\beta^{-\ell_p} c_p + \sum_{k=1}^{\ell_p} b_{m_{p+1}-k+1}\beta^{-k}$. According to (4), $\beta^{-\ell_p} c + \sum_{k=1}^{\ell_p} b_{m_{p+1}-k+1}\beta^{-k} \leq \beta^{-\ell_p} y_1^{(t_{n_{p+1}}+m_p)}(0^{n_{p+1}}1^{n_p}) + \sum_{k=1}^{\ell_p} b_{m_{p+1}-k+1}\beta^{-k} = y_1^{(t_{n_{p+1}}+m_{p+1})}(0^{n_{p+1}}1^{n_{p+1}}) < c$, which means $I_{p+1,0} = [c, c_{p+1}) \subset I_{p+1}$. Hence, $c_{p+1} < c_p$ and $I_{p+1,0} \subset I_{p,0}$. In addition, $\tilde{\mathbf{y}}^{(t_{n_{p+1}}+m_p)}(0^{n_{p+1}}1^{n_{p+1}}) = \tilde{\mathbf{y}}^{(t_{n_{p+2}}+m_{p+1})}(0^{n_{p+2}}1^{n_{p+2}}) = \tilde{\mathbf{v}}$ by (1).

For the induction step, assume $I_{p+1,k} \subset I_{p,k}$ and $\tilde{\mathbf{y}}^{(t_{n_{p+1}}+m_p+k)}(0^{n_{p+1}}1^{n_{p+1}}) = \tilde{\mathbf{y}}^{(t_{n_{p+2}}+m_{p+1}+k)}(0^{n_{p+2}}1^{n_{p+2}})$ for $k = 0, \ldots, r-1$. By definition of b_k, we know $b_{m_p+k} = b_{m_{p+1}+k}$ for $k = 1, \ldots, r$. Hence, the intervals $I_{p,r}$ and $I_{p+1,r}$ have the same lower bound by definition, which ensures $I_{p+1,r} \subset I_{p,r}$ due to their upper bounds satisfy $c_{p+1} < c_p$. On the contrary assume $\tilde{\mathbf{y}}^{(t_{n_{p+1}}+m_p+r)}(0^{n_{p+1}}1^{n_{p+1}}) \neq \tilde{\mathbf{y}}^{(t_{n_{p+2}}+m_{p+1}+r)}(0^{n_{p+2}}1^{n_{p+2}})$, which means there is $j_1 \in \{2, \ldots, s\}$ such that $y_{j_1}^{(t_{n_{p+1}}+m_p+r)}(0^{n_{p+1}}1^{n_{p+1}}) \neq y_{j_1}^{(t_{n_{p+2}}+m_{p+1}+r)}(0^{n_{p+2}}1^{n_{p+2}})$. It follows that $w_{j_1,1} \neq 0$ because $\tilde{\mathbf{y}}^{(t_{n_{p+1}}+m_p+r-1)}(0^{n_{p+1}}1^{n_{p+1}}) = \tilde{\mathbf{y}}^{(t_{n_{p+2}}+m_{p+1}+r-1)}(0^{n_{p+2}}1^{n_{p+2}})$. We define $c' = -\frac{1}{w_{j_1,1}} \sum_{i \in V'} w_{j_1,i}\, y_i^{(t_{n_{p+1}}+m_p+r-1)}(0^{n_{p+1}}1^{n_{p+1}})$. For example, consider the case when $w_{j_1,1} > 0$ and $y_{j_1}^{(t_{n_{p+1}}+m_p+r)}(0^{n_{p+1}}1^{n_{p+1}}) = 1$, while the argument for the remaining cases is similar. By the analogy to c, we have $y_1^{(t_{n_{p+2}}+m_{p+1}+r-1)}(0^{n_{p+2}}1^{n_{p+2}}) < c' \leq y_1^{(t_{n_{p+1}}+m_p+r-1)}(0^{n_{p+1}}1^{n_{p+1}})$. If $c' \in I_{p+1,r-1} \subset I_{p,r-1}$, then $y_1^{(t_{n_q}+m_{p+1}+r-1)}(0^{n_q}1^{n_{p+2}}) \geq c'$ for sufficiently large $q > p+2$, which implies $y_{j_1}^{(t_{n_{p+2}}+m_{p+1}+r)}(0^{n_{p+2}}1^{n_{p+2}}) \neq y_{j_1}^{(t_{n_q}+m_{p+1}+r)}(0^{n_q}1^{n_{p+2}})$, contradicting (1). If $c' \notin I_{p+1,r-1}$, then $c' \notin I_{q,r-1} \subseteq I_{p+1,r-1}$ for every $q > p$, which gives $y_{j_1}^{(t_{n_{q+1}}+m_q+r)}(0^{n_{q+1}}1^{n_{q+1}}) = y_{j_1}^{(t_{n_{q+2}}+m_{q+1}+r)}(0^{n_{q+2}}1^{n_{q+2}})$ for every $q > p$. Thus, for all sufficiently large $p \geq p_0$, we have $\tilde{\mathbf{y}}^{(t_{n_{p+1}}+m_p+r)}(0^{n_{p+1}}1^{n_{p+1}}) = \tilde{\mathbf{y}}^{(t_{n_{p+2}}+m_{p+1}+r)}(0^{n_{p+2}}1^{n_{p+2}})$ since there are only 2^{s-1} possible values of c', which completes the induction step.

We conclude that for all sufficiently large $p \geq p_0$, $b'_r = b_{m_p+r} = b_{m_{p+1}+r}$ for $r = 1, \ldots, \ell_p = \ell$, according to (5), which implies $c = B\sum_{q=1}^{\infty} \beta^{-\ell(q-1)} = \frac{B}{1-\beta^{-\ell}}$ where $B = \sum_{r=1}^{\ell} b'_{\ell-r+1}\beta^{-r}$. Hence, one can show that the expression $\beta^{m_p}\left(c - \sum_{k=1}^{m_p} b_{m_p-k+1}\,\beta^{-k}\right) = \beta^{m_{p_0}}\left(c - \sum_{k=1}^{m_{p_0}} b_{m_{p_0}-k+1}\beta^{-k}\right) = C$ is constant for every $p \geq p_0$. Thus, $y_1^{(t_{n_p})}(0^{n_p}) < C \leq y_1^{(t_{n_{p+1}})}(0^{n_{p+1}})$ for every $p \geq p_0$, which is a contradiction. This completes the proof of the theorem. □

4 Two Analog Neurons Accept Deterministic Languages

In this section, we show that a deterministic pushdown automaton can be simulated by a 2ANN with two extra analog unit.

Theorem 2. *For any deterministic context-free language $L \subseteq \{0,1\}^*$, there is a neural network 2ANN with two extra analog units having rational weights, $\mathcal{N}$, which accepts $L = \mathcal{L}(\mathcal{N})$.*

Proof. Let $L = \mathcal{L}(\mathcal{M})$ be accepted by a DPDA $\mathcal{M} = (Q, \Sigma, \Gamma, q_0, Z_0, F, \delta)$ where $Q \neq \emptyset$ is a finite set of states, Σ and Γ are finite sets of input and stack symbols, respectively, which are assumed for simplicity to be the binary alphabet $\Sigma = \Gamma = \{0, 1\}$. In addition, $q_0 \in Q$ is the start state, $Z_0 \in \Gamma$ is the starting stack symbol, and $F \subseteq Q$ is the set of accepting states. Moreover, $\delta : (Q \times (\Sigma \cup \{\varepsilon\}) \times \Gamma) \longrightarrow \mathcal{P}(Q \times \Gamma^*)$ is a transition function that given a current state $q \in Q$ of $\mathcal{M}$, a next symbol $x \in \Sigma \cup \{\varepsilon\}$ of an input word which is read from left to right (including the empty string ε, which means no symbol is read), and a symbol $Z \in \Gamma$ on the top of the stack, produces either the empty set $\delta(q, x, Z) = \emptyset$ (i.e. $\mathcal{M}$ halts), or a one-element set $\delta(q, x, Z) = \{(q', \gamma)\}$ with a new state $q' \in Q$ and a string $\gamma \in \Gamma^*$ that replaces Z on the top of the stack where the first symbol of γ becomes the top element. In order to ensure that $\mathcal{M}$ is truly deterministic, it is assumed that for any $q \in Q$, $Z \in \Gamma$, if $\delta(q, \varepsilon, Z) \neq \emptyset$, then $\delta(q, x, Z) = \emptyset$ for every $x \in \Sigma$. An input word $\mathbf{x} \in \Sigma^*$ is accepted by $\mathcal{M}$ if there is a (unique) sequence of transitions of $\mathcal{M}$ defined by δ, from the start state q_0 with the starting symbol Z_0 on the stack, which, while reading $\mathbf{x}$, terminates in an accepting state $q_f \in F$. We assume without loss of generality that if $\delta(q, x, Z) = \{(q', \gamma)\}$, then the length $|\gamma|$ of string γ is at most 2, whereas $\gamma = Z'Z$ for some $Z' \in \Gamma$, if $|\gamma| = 2$.

We will construct a neural network 2ANN with two extra analog units, $\mathcal{N}$, which accepts the same language $L = \mathcal{L}(\mathcal{N}) = \mathcal{L}(\mathcal{M})$ by simulating the deterministic pushdown automaton $\mathcal{M}$. The stack of $\mathcal{M}$ is realized by the two analog neurons $1, 2 \in V$ of $\mathcal{N}$, where the first unit implements the `top` and `push` operations while the `pop` operation is performed by the second analog neuron. The current contents of the stack, $Z_1 \dots Z_p \in \Gamma^p$ are encoded by the state of an analog neuron,

$$y_k^{\mathrm{cur}} = \sum_{i=1}^{p} \frac{2Z_i + 1}{4^i} \in \mathbb{I} \qquad \text{for } k \in \{1, 2\}\,, \tag{6}$$

using a Cantor-like set which allows an efficient neural implementation of the stack operations [12], producing the new state of analog neurons:

$$\mathtt{top} = H(2y_1 - 1) \tag{7}$$

$$\mathtt{push}(Z): \quad y_1^{\mathrm{new}} = \sigma\left(\frac{1}{4} y_1^{\mathrm{cur}} + \frac{1}{2} Z + \frac{1}{4}\right) \tag{8}$$

$$\mathtt{pop}: \quad y_2^{\mathrm{new}} = \sigma(4y_2^{\mathrm{cur}} - 2\mathtt{top} - 1)\,. \tag{9}$$

The finite control of $\mathcal{M}$ which is defined by the transition function δ, is implemented by binary neurons. We will describe its functionality while the omitted technical details are ensured using known techniques of implementing finite automata by neural networks with only integer weights [1,3,4,7,14,20]. At the beginning of the simulation of $\mathcal{M}$ by $\mathcal{N}$, the stack is initialized by the starting stack symbol Z_0. This is implemented by a special binary neuron init $\in V'$ which is only initially active, that is, $y_{\mathrm{init}}^{(t)} = 1$ iff $t = 0$. Thus, init is connected to the first analog neuron $1 \in V$ via the weight $w(\mathrm{init}, 1) = (2Z_0 + 1)/4$, which encodes the stack contents Z_0 by analog state $y_1^{(1)} = (2Z_0 + 1)/4$, according to (6). Then, each transition of $\mathcal{M}$ is realized by one so-called *macrostep* $\tau \geq 1$ which is composed of 12 computational steps of $\mathcal{N}$, starting at the discrete time instant

Table 1. The macrostep of 2ANN $\mathcal{N}$ simulating one transition of DPDA $\mathcal{M}$ (including the pop and push operations)

t	$y_1^{(t)}$	$y_2^{(t)}$	$y_{\mathrm{ctrl}}^{(t)}$	$y_{z_0}^{(t)}$	$y_{z_1}^{(t)}$	$y_{z'_0}^{(t)}$	$y_{z'_1}^{(t)}$	$y_{\mathrm{top}}^{(t)}$	$y_{\mathrm{nxt}}^{(t)}$	$y_{\mathrm{out}}^{(t)}$	$y_{inp}^{(t)}$
0	z	0	1	0	0	0	0		0	0	0
1	0	z	0	0	0	0	0	Z	0	0	0
2	z	0	1	0	0	0	0		0	0	0
3	0	z	0	0	0	0	0		1	$q \in F$	0
4	z	0	1	0	0	0	0		0	0	x
5	0	z	0	0	0	0	0		0	0	0
6	z	0	1	0	0	0	0		0	0	0
7	0	z	1	0	0	0	0		0	0	0
8	0	$2z$	1	$Z = 0$	$Z = 1$	0	0		0	0	0
9	0	$z' = 4z - 2Z - 1$	0	0	0	0	0		0	0	0
10	z'	0	0	0	0	0	0		0	0	0
11	$\frac{z'}{2}$	0	0	0	0	$Z' = 0$	$Z' = 1$		0	0	0
$12 \equiv 0$	$z'' = \frac{z'}{4} + \frac{Z'}{2} + \frac{1}{4}$	0	1	0	0	0	0		0	0	0

$t = 12(\tau - 1) + 2$ (including the first two steps $t = 0, 1$ for the stack initialization). Hereafter, the computational time $t = 0, 1, 2, \ldots, 12$ of $\mathcal{N}$ is for simplicity related to the macrostep. The state evolution of selected neurons during the macrostep is presented in Table 1.

At the beginning of the macrostep when $t = 0$, the state of the first analog neuron $1 \in V$ encodes the current contents of the stack, that is, $y_1^{(0)} = z \in \mathbb{I}$ by (6). The storage of the stack contents alternates between the two analog neurons which are connected by the weights $w(1, 2) = w(2, 1) = 1$. These unit weights copy the state from the first analog neuron to the second one and back, under the control of binary neuron ctrl $\in V'$. During the macrostep, the output of ctrl produces a sequence of binary states given by the regular expression $1(01)^3(110 + 010)(001 + 101)$ starting with $y_{\mathrm{ctrl}}^{(0)} = 1$, where the strings 110 and 001 deviating from the regular signal $(01)^*$ correspond to the pop and push operations, respectively, if they occur as described below. For this purpose, the weights $w(\mathrm{ctrl}, 1) = -W$, $w(\mathrm{ctrl}, 2) = W$, and $w(0, 2) = -W$ are introduced, where $W > 0$ is a sufficiently large positive parameter excluding the influence from other neurons. It follows that $z = y_1^{(0)} = y_2^{(1)} = y_1^{(2)} = y_2^{(3)} = y_1^{(4)} = \cdots$ and $0 = y_2^{(0)} = y_1^{(1)} = y_2^{(2)} = y_1^{(3)} = y_2^{(4)} = \cdots$, as shown in Table 1.

At time instant $t = 1$ of the macrostep, the binary neuron top $\in V'$ reads the top element $Z \in \Gamma$ from the stack, that is, $y_{\mathrm{top}}^{(1)} = Z \in \{0, 1\}$, which is implemented by the weight $w(1, \mathrm{top}) = 2$ and the bias $w(0, \mathrm{top}) = -1$, according to (7). If $\delta(q, x, Z) \neq \emptyset$ for some $x \in \Sigma$, where $q \in Q$ is a current state of $\mathcal{M}$ encoded by binary neurons of $\mathcal{N}$, which is tested at time instant $t = 2$, then $y_{\mathrm{nxt}}^{(3)} = 1$, $y_{\mathrm{out}}^{(3)} = 1$ iff $q \in F$ is a final state, and $y_{\mathrm{inp}}^{(4)} = x \in \{0, 1\}$ is the next input symbol, by the input/output protocol. Anyway, the next two steps $t = 5, 6$ of the macrostep are exploited for evaluating the transition function $\delta(q, x, Z)$ where $x = \varepsilon$ is the empty word if $\delta(q, \varepsilon, Z) \neq \emptyset$. If $\delta(q, x, Z) = \emptyset$, then the simulation by $\mathcal{N}$ terminates since the computation of $\mathcal{M}$ halts.

Thus, assume $\delta(q,x,Z) = \{(q',\gamma)\}$ where $q' \in Q$ is the new state of $\mathcal{M}$, which substitutes the old one encoded by binary neurons of $\mathcal{N}$, and $\gamma \in \Gamma^*$ should replace the top symbol on the stack. If $|\gamma| \leq 1$, then the top symbol Z is popped from the stack during time instant $t = 7, 8, 9$ of the macrostep. At time instant $t = 7$, the current contents of the stack are stored by the second analog neuron as $y_2^{(7)} = z$. The pop operation is implemented by the weights $w(2,2) = 2$, $w(z_0, 2) = -1$, and $w(z_1, 2) = -3$ from the binary neurons $z_0, z_1 \in V'$ whose outputs are activated at time instant $t = 8$ of the macrostep so that $y_{z_b}^{(8)} = 1$ iff $Z = b \in \{0,1\}$. Moreover, we know $y_{\text{ctrl}}^{(7)} = y_{\text{ctrl}}^{(8)} = 1$ and $y_{\text{ctrl}}^{(9)} = 0$ when the pop operation applies (otherwise, $y_{\text{ctrl}}^{(7)} = 0$). Hence, $y_2^{(8)} = 2z$ by $w(2,2) = 2$, and $y_2^{(9)} = 4z - 2\texttt{top} - 1 = z' \in \mathbb{I}$ due to $w(z_0, 2) = -1$ and $w(z_1, 2) = -3$, which pops the top symbol $Z = \texttt{top}$ from the stack according to (9).

If $|\gamma| \geq 1$, then either $\gamma = Z'$ or $\gamma = Z'Z$, where $Z' \in \Gamma$ is the new top symbol which is pushed to the stack during time instant $t = 10, 11, 12$ of the macrostep. At time instant $t = 10$, the current contents of the stack are stored by the first analog neuron as $y_1^{(10)} = z'$. The push(Z') operation is implemented by the weights $w(1,1) = \frac{1}{2}$, $w(z_0', 1) = \frac{1}{4}$, and $w(z_1', 1) = \frac{3}{4}$ from the binary neurons $z_0', z_1' \in V'$ whose outputs are activated at time instant $t = 11$ of the macrostep so that $y_{z_b'}^{(11)} = 1$ iff $Z' = b \in \{0,1\}$. Moreover, we know $y_{\text{ctrl}}^{(10)} = y_{\text{ctrl}}^{(11)} = 0$ and $y_{\text{ctrl}}^{(12)} = 1$ when the push operation applies (otherwise, $y_{\text{ctrl}}^{(10)} = 1$). Hence, $y_1^{(11)} = \frac{z'}{2}$ by $w(1,1) = \frac{1}{2}$, and $y_2^{(12)} = \frac{z'}{4} + \frac{Z'}{2} + \frac{1}{4} = z'' \in \mathbb{I}$ due to $w(z_0', 1) = \frac{1}{4}$ and $w(z_1', 1) = \frac{3}{4}$, which pushes the symbol Z' to the stack according to (8). At time instant $t = 12$, the macrostep of $\mathcal{N}$ simulating one transition of $\mathcal{M}$ using rational weights is finished while the new contents z'' of the stack are stored by the first analog neuron as required for the next macrostep. This completes the simulation and the proof of the theorem. □

5 Conclusion

In this paper, we have refined the analysis of the computational power of binary-state neural networks αANNs extended with α analog-state neurons. We have proven that the deterministic (context-free) language $L = \{0^n1^n \mid n \geq 1\}$ which imitates counting to any number n, cannot be recognized offline by any 1ANN with real weights. It is an open question whether a 1ANN can recognize any non-regular context-free language and whether there is a non-context-sensitive language that can be accepted offline by a 1ANN. In addition, we have shown that any deterministic language can be accepted by a 2ANN with rational weights. It is an open problem whether two extra rational-weight analog units suffice for simulating any Turing machine. Another challenge for further research is to prove a proper "natural" hierarchy of neural networks between integer and rational weights similarly as it is known between rational and real weights [2] and possibly, map it to known hierarchies of regular/context-free languages. This problem is related to a more general issue of finding suitable complexity measures of subrecursive neural networks establishing the complexity hierarchies, which could be employed in practical neurocomputing, e.g. the precision of weight parameters, energy complexity [14], temporal coding etc.

References

1. Alon, N., Dewdney, A.K., Ott, T.J.: Efficient simulation of finite automata by neural nets. J. ACM **38**(2), 495–514 (1991)
2. Balcázar, J.L., Gavaldà, R., Siegelmann, H.T.: Computational power of neural networks: A characterization in terms of Kolmogorov complexity. IEEE Trans. Inf. Theory **43**(4), 1175–1183 (1997)
3. Horne, B.G., Hush, D.R.: Bounds on the complexity of recurrent neural network implementations of finite state machines. Neural Netw. **9**(2), 243–252 (1996)
4. Indyk, P.: Optimal simulation of automata by neural nets. In: Mayr, E.W., Puech, C. (eds.) STACS 1995. LNCS, vol. 900, pp. 337–348. Springer, Heidelberg (1995). https://doi.org/10.1007/3-540-59042-0_85
5. Kilian, J., Siegelmann, H.T.: The dynamic universality of sigmoidal neural networks. Inf. Comput. **128**(1), 48–56 (1996)
6. Koiran, P.: A family of universal recurrent networks. Theoret. Comput. Sci. **168**(2), 473–480 (1996)
7. Minsky, M.: Computations: Finite and Infinite Machines. Prentice-Hall, Englewood Cliffs (1967)
8. Orponen, P.: Computing with truly asynchronous threshold logic networks. Theoret. Comput. Sci. **174**(1–2), 123–136 (1997)
9. Schmidhuber, J.: Deep learning in neural networks: An overview. Neural Netw. **61**, 85–117 (2015)
10. Siegelmann, H.T.: Neural Networks and Analog Computation: Beyond the Turing Limit. Birkhäuser, Boston (1999)
11. Siegelmann, H.T., Sontag, E.D.: Analog computation via neural networks. Theoret. Comput. Sci. **131**(2), 331–360 (1994)
12. Siegelmann, H.T., Sontag, E.D.: On the computational power of neural nets. J. Comput. Syst. Sci. **50**(1), 132–150 (1995)
13. Šíma, J.: Analog stable simulation of discrete neural networks. Neural Netw. World **7**(6), 679–686 (1997)
14. Šíma, J.: Energy complexity of recurrent neural networks. Neural Comput. **26**(5), 953–973 (2014)
15. Šíma, J.: The power of extra analog neuron. In: Dediu, A.-H., Lozano, M., Martín-Vide, C. (eds.) TPNC 2014. LNCS, vol. 8890, pp. 243–254. Springer, Cham (2014). https://doi.org/10.1007/978-3-319-13749-0_21
16. Šíma, J.: Three analog neurons are turing universal. In: Fagan, D., Martín-Vide, C., O'Neill, M., Vega-Rodríguez, M.A. (eds.) TPNC 2018. LNCS, vol. 11324, pp. 460–472. Springer, Cham (2018). https://doi.org/10.1007/978-3-030-04070-3_36
17. Šíma, J.: Subrecursive neural networks. Neural Netw. **116**, 208–223 (2019)
18. Šíma, J., Orponen, P.: General-purpose computation with neural networks: A survey of complexity theoretic results. Neural Comput. **15**(12), 2727–2778 (2003)
19. Šíma, J., Savický, P.: Quasi-periodic β-expansions and cut languages. Theoret. Comput. Sci. **720**, 1–23 (2018)
20. Šíma, J., Wiedermann, J.: Theory of neuromata. J. ACM **45**(1), 155–178 (1998)
21. Šorel, M., Šíma, J.: Robust RBF finite automata. Neurocomputing **62**, 93–110 (2004)

On the Bounds of Function Approximations

Adrian de Wynter(✉)

Amazon Alexa, 300 Pine St., Seattle, Washington 98101, USA
dwynter@amazon.com

Abstract. Within machine learning, the subfield of Neural Architecture Search (NAS) has recently garnered research attention due to its ability to improve upon human-designed models. However, the computational requirements for finding an exact solution to this problem are often intractable, and the design of the search space still requires manual intervention. In this paper we attempt to establish a formalized framework from which we can better understand the computational bounds of NAS in relation to its search space. For this, we first reformulate the function approximation problem in terms of sequences of functions, and we call it the Function Approximation (FA) problem; then we show that it is computationally infeasible to devise a procedure that solves FA for all functions to zero error, regardless of the search space. We show also that such error will be minimal if a specific class of functions is present in the search space. Subsequently, we show that machine learning as a mathematical problem is a solution strategy for FA, albeit not an effective one, and further describe a stronger version of this approach: the Approximate Architectural Search Problem (a-ASP), which is the mathematical equivalent of NAS. We leverage the framework from this paper and results from the literature to describe the conditions under which a-ASP can potentially solve FA as well as an exhaustive search, but in polynomial time.

Keywords: Neural networks · Learning theory · Neural Architecture Search

1 Introduction

The typical machine learning task can be abstracted out as the problem of finding the set of parameters of a computable function, such that it approximates an underlying probability distribution to seen and unseen examples [19]. Said function is often hand-designed, and the subject of the great majority of current machine learning research. It is well-established that the choice of function heavily influences its approximation capability [5,55,59], and considerable work has gone into automating the process of finding such function for a given task

I. V. Tetko et al. (Eds.): ICANN 2019, LNCS 11727, pp. 401–417, 2019.
https://doi.org/10.1007/978-3-030-30487-4_32

[9,10,18]. In the context of neural networks, this task is known as Neural Architecture Search (NAS), and it involves searching for the best performing combination of neural network components and parameters from a set, also known as the *search space.* Although promising, little work has been done on the analysis of its viability with respect to its computation-theoretical bounds [14]. Since NAS strategies tend to be expensive in terms of their hardware requirements [23,40], research emphasis has been placed on optimizing search algorithms, [14,32], even though the search space is still manually designed [14,26,27,60]. Without a better understanding of the mathematical confines governing NAS, it is unlikely that these strategies will efficiently solve new problems, or present reliably high performance, thus leading to complex systems that still rely on manually engineering architectures and search spaces.

Theoretically, learning has been formulated as a function approximation problem where the approximation is done through the optimization of the parameters of a given function [12,19,37,38,52]; and with strong results in the area of neural networks in particular [12,16,21,42]. On the other hand, NAS is often regarded as a search problem with an optimality criterion [10,14,40,50,59], within a given search space. The choice of such search space is critical, yet strongly heuristic [14]. Since we aim to obtain a better insight on how the process of finding an optimal architecture can be improved with relation to the search space, we hypothesize that NAS can be enunciated as a function approximation problem. The key observation that motivates our work is that all computable functions can be expressed in terms of combinations of members of certain sets, better known as models of computation. Examples of this are the μ-recursive functions, Turing Machines, and, of relevance to this paper, a particular set of neural network architectures [31].

Thus, in this study we reformulate the function approximation problem as the task of, for a given search space, finding the procedure that outputs the computable sequence of functions, along with their parameters, that best approximates any given input function. We refer to this reformulation as the Function Approximation (FA) problem, and regard it as a very general computational problem; akin to building a fully automated machine learning pipeline where the user provides a series of tasks, and the algorithm returns trained models for each input.[1] This approach yields promising results in terms of the conditions under which the FA problem has optimal solutions, and about the ability of both machine learning and NAS to solve the FA problem.

1.1 Technical Contributions

The main contribution of this paper is a reformulation of the function approximation problem in terms of sequences of functions, and a framework within the context of the theory of computation to analyze it. Said framework is quite flexible, as it does not rely on a particular model of computation and can be applied

[1] Throughout this paper, the problem of data selection is not considered, and is simply assumed to be an input to our solution strategies.

to any Turing-equivalent model. We leverage its results, along with well-known results of computer science, to prove that it is not possible to devise a procedure that approximates all functions everywhere to zero error. However, we also show that, if the smallest class of functions along with the operators for the chosen model of computation are present in the search space, it is possible to attain an error that is globally minimal.

Additionally, we tie said framework to the field of machine learning, and analyze in a formal manner three solution strategies for FA: the Machine Learning (ML) problem, the Architecture Search problem (ASP), and the less-strict version of ASP, the Approximate Architecture Search problem (a-ASP). We analyze the feasibility of all three approaches in terms of the bounds described for FA, and their ability to solve it. In particular, we demonstrate that ML is an ineffective solution strategy for FA, and point out that ASP is the best approach in terms of generalizability, although it is intractable in terms of time complexity. Finally, by relating the results from this paper, along with the existing work in the literature, we describe the conditions under which a-ASP is able to solve the FA problem as well as ASP.

1.2 Outline

We begin by reviewing the existing literature in Sect. 2. In Sect. 3 we introduce FA, and analyze the general properties of this problem in terms of its search space. Then, in Sect. 4 we relate the framework to machine learning as a mathematical problem, and show that it is a weak solution strategy for FA, before defining a stronger approach (ASP) and its computationally tractable version (a-ASP). We conclude in Sect. 5 with a discussion of our work.

2 Related Work

The problem of approximating functions and its relation to neural networks can be found formulated explicitly in [38], and it is also mentioned often when defining machine learning as a task, for example in [2,4,5,19,52]. However, it is defined as a parameter optimization problem for a predetermined function. This perspective is also covered in our paper, yet it is much closer to the ML approach than to FA. For FA, as defined in this paper, it is central to find the sequence of functions which minimizes the approximation error.

Neural networks as function approximators are well understood, and there is a trove of literature available on the subject. An inexhaustive list of examples are the studies found in [12,16,21,22,25,35,36,38,42,44,50]. It is important to point out that the objective of this paper is not to prove that neural networks are function approximators, but rather to provide a theoretical framework from which to understand NAS in the contexts of machine learning, and computation in general. However, neural networks were shown to be Turing-equivalent in [31,45,46], and thus they are extremely relevant this study.

NAS as a metaheuristic is also well-explored in the literature, and its application to deep learning has been booming lately thanks to the widespread availability of powerful computers, and interest in end-to-end machine learning pipelines. There is, however, a long standing body of research on this area, and the list of works presented here is by no means complete. Some papers that deal with NAS in an applied fashion are the works found in [1,9,10,29,43,48,49,51], while explorations in a formal fashion of NAS and metaheuristics in general can also be found in [3,10,44,58,59]. There is also interest on the problem of creating an end-to-end machine learning pipeline, also known as AutoML. Some examples are studies such as the ones in [15,20,23,57]. The FA problem is similar to AutoML, but it does not include the data preprocessing step commonly associated with such systems. Additionally, the formal analysis of NAS tends to be as a search, rather than a function approximation, problem.

The complexity theory of learning and neural networks has been explored as well. The reader is referred to the recent survey from [33], and [2,7,13,17,53]. Leveraging the group-like structure of models of computation is done in [39], and the Blum Axioms [6] are a well-known framework for the theory of computation in a model-agnostic setting. It was also shown in [8] that, under certain conditions, it is possible to compose some learning algorithms to obtain more complex procedures. Bounds in terms of the generalization error was proven for convolutional neural networks in [28]. None of the papers mentioned, however, apply directly to FA and NAS in a setting agnostic to models of computation, and the key insights of our work, drawn from the analysis of FA and its solution strategies, are, to the best of our knowledge, not covered in the literature. Finally, the Probably Approximately Correct (PAC) learning framework [52] is a powerful theory for the study of learning problems. It is a slightly different problem than FA, as the former has the search space abstracted out, while the latter concerns itself with finding a sequence that minimizes the error, by searching through combinations of explicitly defined members of the search space.

3 A Formulation of the Function Approximation Problem

In this section we define the FA problem as a mathematical task whose goal is–informally–to find a sequence of functions whose behavior is closest to an input function. We then perform a short analysis of the computational bounds of FA, and show that it is computationally infeasible to design a solution strategy that approximates all functions everywhere to zero error.

3.1 Preliminaries on Notation

Let **R** be the set of all total computable functions. Across this paper we will refer to the finite set of *elementary functions* $\mathcal{E} = \{\psi^1, ..., \psi^m\}$ as the smallest class of functions, along with their operators, of some Turing-equivalent model of computation.

Let $S = \{\phi_j : dom(\phi_j) \to img(\phi_j)\}_{j \in J}$ be a set of functions defined over some sets $dom(\phi_j), img(\phi_j)$, such that S is indexed by a set J, and that $S \subset \mathbf{R}$. Also let $f(x) = (\phi_{i_1}, \phi_{i_2}, ..., \phi_{i_k})(x)$ be a sequence of elements of S applied successively and such that $i_1, ..., i_k \in I$ for some $I \subset J$. We will utilize the abbreviated notation $f = (\phi_i)_{i=1}^k$ to denote such a sequence; and we will use $\mathcal{S}^{\star,n} = \{(\phi_i)_{i=1}^k | \ \phi_i \in S, k \leq n\}$ to describe the set of all n-or-less long possible sequences of functions drawn from said S, such that $f \in \mathcal{S}^{\star,n} \Leftrightarrow f \in \mathbf{R}$.

For consistency purposes, throughout this paper we will be using Zermelo-Fraenkel with the Axiom of Choice (ZFC) set theory. Finally, for simplicity of our analysis we will only consider continuous, real-valued functions, and beginning in Sect. 3.3, only computable functions.

3.2 The FA Problem

Prior to formally defining the FA problem, we must be able to quantify the behavioral similarity of two functions. This is done through the *approximation error* of a function:

Definition 1 (The approximation error). *Let f and g be two functions. Given a nonempty subset $\sigma \subset dom(g)$, the* approximation error *of a function f to a function g is a procedure which outputs 0 if f is equal to g with respect to some metric $d : \mathbb{R} \times \mathbb{R} \to \mathbb{R}_{\geq 0}$ across all of σ, and a positive number otherwise:*

$$\varepsilon_\sigma(f, g) = \frac{1}{|\sigma|} \sum_{x \in \sigma} d(f(x), g(x)) \tag{1}$$

where we assume that, for the case where $x \notin dom(f)$, $d(f(x), g(x)) = g(x)$.

Definition 2 (The FA Problem). *For any input function $\mathcal{F}$, given a function set (the* search space*) $\mathcal{S}$, an integer $n \in \mathbb{N}_{>0}$, and nonempty sets $\sigma \subset dom(\mathcal{F})$, find the sequence of functions $f = (\phi_i)_{i=1}^k$, $\phi_i \in \mathcal{S}$, $k \leq n$, such that $\varepsilon_\sigma(f, \mathcal{F})$ is minimal among all members of $\mathcal{S}^{\star,n}$ and σ.*

The FA problem, as stated in Definition 2, makes no assumptions regarding the characterization of the search space, and follows closely the definition in terms of optimization of parameters from [37,38]. However, it makes a point on the fact that the approximation of a function should be given by a sequence of functions.

If the input function were to be continuous and multivariate, we know from [24,34] that there exists at least one exact (i.e., zero approximation error) representation in terms of a sequence of single-variable, continuous functions. If such single-variable, continuous functions were to be present in $\mathcal{S}$, one would expect that the FA problem could solved to zero error for all continuous multivariate inputs, by simply comparing and returning the right representation.[2] However, it is infeasible to devise a generalized algorithmic procedure that outputs such representation:

[2] With the possible exception of the results from [54].

Theorem 1. *There is no computable procedure for FA that approximates all continuous, real-valued functions to zero error, across their entire domain.*

Proof. Solution strategies for FA are parametrized by the sequence length n, the subset of the domain σ, and the search space $\mathcal{S}$.

Assume $\mathcal{S}$ is infinite. The input function $\mathcal{F}$ may be either computable or uncomputable. If the input $\mathcal{F}$ is uncomputable, by definition it can only be estimated to within its computable range, and hence its approximation error is nonzero. If $\mathcal{F}$ is a computable function, we have guaranteed the existence of at least one function within $\mathcal{S}^{\star,n}$ which has zero approximation error: $\mathcal{F}$ itself. Nonetheless, determining the existence of such a function is an undecidable problem. To show this, it suffices to note that it reduces to the problem of determining the equivalence of two halting Turing Machines by asking whether they accept the same language, which is undecidable.

When n or σ are infinite, there is no guarantee that a procedure solving FA will terminate for all inputs.

When n, σ, or $\mathcal{S}$ are finite, there will always be functions outside of the scope of the procedure that can only be approximated to a nonzero error.

Therefore, there cannot be a procedure for FA that approximates all functions, let alone all computable functions, to zero error for their entire domain. □

It is a well-known result of computer science that neural networks [12,16,19, 21,22], and PAC learning algorithms [52], are able to approximate a large class of functions to an arbitrary, non-zero error. However, Theorem 1 does not make any assumptions regarding the model of computation used, and thus it works as more generalized statement of these results.

For the rest of this paper we will limit ourselves to the case where n, σ, and $\mathcal{S}$ are finite, and the elements of $\mathcal{S}$ are computable functions.

3.3 A Brief Analysis of the Search Space

It has been shown that the solutions to FA can only be found in terms of finite sequences built from a finite search space, whose error with respect to the input function is nonzero. It is worth analyzing under which conditions these sequences will present the smallest possible error.

For this, we note that any solution strategy for FA will have to first construct at least one sequence $f \in \mathcal{S}^{\star,n}$, and then compute its error against the input function $\mathcal{F}$. It could be argued that this "bottom-up" approach is not the most efficient, and one could attempt to "factor" a function in a given model of computation that has explicit reduction formulas, such as the Lambda calculus. This, unfortunately, is not possible, as the problem of determining the reduction of a function in terms of its elementary functions is well-known to be undecidable [11]. However, the idea of "factoring" a function can still be leveraged to show that, if the set of elementary functions $\mathcal{E}$ is present in the search space $\mathcal{S}$, any sufficiently clever procedure will be able to get the smallest possible theoretical error for $\mathcal{S}$, for any given input function $\mathcal{F}$:

Theorem 2. *Let $\mathcal{S}$ be a search space such that it contains the set of elementary functions, $\mathcal{E} \subset \mathcal{S}$. Then, for any input function $\mathcal{F}$, there exists at least one sequence $f_o \in \mathcal{S}^{\star,n}$ with the smallest approximation error among all possible computable functions of sequence length up to and including n.*

Proof. By definition, $\mathcal{E}$ can generate all possible computable functions. If $\mathcal{E} \not\subset \mathcal{S}$, then $|\mathcal{S}^{\star,n}| < |\mathcal{E}^{\star,n}|$, and so there exist input functions whose sequence with the smallest approximation error, f_o, is not contained in $\mathcal{S}^{\star,n}$. □

In practice, constructing a space that contains $\mathcal{E}$, and subsequently performing a search over it, can become a time consuming task given that the number of possible members of $\mathcal{S}^{\star,n}$ grows exponentially with n. On the other hand, constructing a more "efficient" space that already contains the best possible sequence requires prior knowledge of the structure of a function relating $\mathcal{S}$ to $\mathcal{F}$–the problem that we are trying to solve in the first place. That being said, Theorem 2 implies that there must be a way to quantify the ability of a search space to generalize to any given function, without the need of explicitly including $\mathcal{E}$. To achieve this, we first look at the ability of every sequence to approximate a function, by defining the *information capacity* of a sequence:

Definition 3 (The Information Capacity). *Let $f = (\phi_i)_{i=1}^n$ be a finite sequence, where every ϕ_i has associated a finite set of possible parameters π_i, and a restriction set ρ_i in its domain: $\phi_i\colon dom(\phi_i) \times \pi_i \rightarrow img(\phi_i) \setminus \rho_i$, so that the next element in the sequence is a function ϕ_{i+1} with $dom(\phi_{i+1}) = img(\phi_i) \setminus \rho_i$.*

Then the information capacity *of a sequence f is given by the Cartesian product of the domain, parameters, and range of each ϕ_i:*

$$C(f) = dom(\phi_1) \times \Big(\prod_{i=1}^{n-1} \pi_i \times (img(\phi_i) \setminus \rho_i) \Big) \times \pi_n \times img(\phi_n) \tag{2}$$

Note that the information capacity of a function is quite similar to its graph, but it makes an explicit relationship with its parameters. Specifically, in the case where $\pi_i \subset \Pi$ for every π_i in some f, $C(f) = dom(\phi_1) \times \Pi \times img(\phi_n)$.

At a first glance, Definition 3 could be seen as a variant of the VC dimension [7,53], since both quantities attempt to measure the ability of a given function to generalize. However, the latter is designed to work on a fixed function, and our focus is on the problem of building such a function. A more in-depth discussion of this distinction, along with its application to the framework from this paper, is given in Sect. 4.1, and in Appendix B.

A search space is comprised of one or more functions, and algorithmically we are more interested about the quantifiable ability of the search space to approximate any input function. Therefore, we define the *information potential* of a search space as follows:

Definition 4 (The Information Potential). *The* information potential of a *search space $\mathcal{S}$, is given by all the possible values its members can take for a given sequence length n:*

$$U(\mathcal{S}, n) = \bigcup_{f \in \mathcal{S}^{\star,n}} C(f) \tag{3}$$

The definition of the information potential allows us to make the important distinction between comparing two search spaces S_1, S_2 containing the same function f, but defined over different parameters $\pi_1, \pi_2 \subset \Pi$; and comparing S_1 and S_2 with another space, S_3, containing a different function g: the information potentials will be equivalent on the first case, $U(S_1, n) = U(S_2, n)$, but not on the second: $U(S_3, n) \neq U(S_1, n)$.

For a given space $\mathcal{S}$, as the sequence length n grows to infinity, and if the search space includes the set of elementary functions, $\mathcal{E} \subset \mathcal{S}$, its information potential encompasses all computable functions:

$$\lim_{n \to \infty} U(\mathcal{S}, n) = \mathbf{R} \tag{4}$$

In other words, the information potential of such $\mathcal{S}$ approaches the information capacity of a universal approximator, which depending on the model of computation chosen, might be a universal Turing machine, or the universal function from [41], to name a few.

In the next section, we leverage the results shown so far to evaluate three different procedures to solve FA, and show that there exists a best possible solution strategy.

4 The FA Problem in the Context of Machine Learning

In this section we relate the results from analyzing FA to the field of machine learning. First, we show that the machine learning task can be seen as a solution strategy for FA. We then introduce the Architecture Search Problem (ASP) as a theoretical procedure, and note that it is the best possible solution strategy for FA. Finally, we note that ASP is unviable in an applied setting, and define a more relaxed version of this approach: the Approximate Architecture Search Problem (a-ASP), which is the analogous of the NAS task commonly seen in the literature.

4.1 Machine Learning as a Solver for FA

The Machine Learning (ML) problem, informally, is the task of approximating an input function $\mathcal{F}$ through repeated sampling and the parameter search of a predetermined function. This definition is a simplified, abstracted out version of the typical machine learning task. It is, however, not new, and a brief search in the literature [4,5,19,37] can attest to the existence of several equivalent formulations. We reproduce it here for notational purposes, and constrain it to computable functions:

Definition 5 (The ML Problem). *For an unknown, continuous function $\mathcal{F}$ defined over some domain $dom(\mathcal{F})$, given finite subsets $\sigma \subset dom(\mathcal{F})$, a function f with parameters from some finite set Π, and a function $m\colon \mathbb{R} \times \mathbb{R} \to \mathbb{R}_{\geq 0}$, find a $\pi_o \in \Pi$ such that $m(f(x, \pi_o), \mathcal{F}(x))$ is minimal for all $x \in \sigma$.*

As defined in Definition 2, any procedure solving FA is required to return the sequence that best approximates any given function. In the ML problem, however, such sequence f is already given to us. Even so, we can still reformulate ML as a solution strategy for FA. For this, let the search space be a singleton of the form $\mathcal{S}_{ML} = \{f\}$; set m to be the metric function d in the approximation error; and leave σ as it is. We then carry out a "search" over this space by simply picking f, and then optimizing the parameters of f with respect to the approximation error $\varepsilon_\sigma(f, \mathcal{F})$. We then return the function along with the parameters π_o that minimize the error.

Given that the search is performed over a single element of the search space, this is not an effective procedure in terms of generalizability. To see this, note that the procedure acts as intended, and "finds" the function that minimizes the approximation error $\varepsilon_\sigma(f, \mathcal{F})$ between f and any other $\mathcal{F}$ in the search space $\mathcal{S}_{ML}$. However, being able to approximate an input function $\mathcal{F}$ in a single-element search space tells us nothing about the ability of ML to approximate other input functions, or even whether such $f \in \mathcal{S}_{ML}$ is the best function approximation for $\mathcal{F}$ in the first place. In fact, we know by Theorem 2 that for a given sequence length n, for every $\mathcal{F}$ there exists an optimal sequence f_o in $\mathcal{E}^{\star,n}$, which is may not be present in $\mathcal{S}_{ML}$.

Since we are constrained to a singleton search space, one could be tempted to build a search space with one single function that maximizes the information potential, such as the one as described in Eq. 4, say, by choosing f to be a universal Turing Machine. There is one problem with this approach: this would mean that we need to take in as an input the encoding of the input function $\mathcal{F}$, along with the subset of the domain σ. If we were able to take the encoding of $\mathcal{F}$ as part of the input, we would already know the function and this would not be a function approximation problem in the first place. Additionally, we would only be able to evaluate the set of computable functions which take in as an argument their own encoding, as it, by definition, needs to be present in σ.

In terms of the framework from this paper we can see that, no matter how we optimize the parameters of f to fit new input functions, the information potential $U(\mathcal{S}_{ML}, n)$ remains unchanged, and the error will remain bounded. This leads us to conclude that measuring a function's ability to learn through its number of parameters [19,47,53] is a good approach for a fixed f and single input $\mathcal{F}$, but incomplete in terms of describing its ability to generalize to other problems. This is of critical importance, because, in an applied setting, even though nobody would attempt to use the same architecture for all possible learning problems, the choice of f remains a crucial, and mostly heuristic, step in the machine learning pipeline.

The statements regarding the information potential of the search space are in accordance with the results in [55], where it was shown that–in the terminology of this paper–two predetermined sequences f and f', when averaging their approximation error across all possible input functions, will have equivalent performance. We have seen that ML is unable to generalize well to any other possible input function, and is unable to determine whether the given sequence f is the best for the given input. This leads us to conclude that, although ML is a computationally tractable solution strategy for FA, it is a weak approach in terms of generalizability.

4.2 The Architecture Search Problem (ASP)

We have shown that ML is a solution strategy for FA, although the nature of its search space makes it ineffective in a generalized setting. It is only natural to assume that a stronger formulation of a procedure to solve FA would involve a more complex search space.

Similar to Definition 5, we are given the task of approximating an unknown function $\mathcal{F}$ through repeated sampling. Unlike ML, however, we are now able to select the sequence of functions (i.e., architecture) that best fits a given input function $\mathcal{F}$:

Definition 6 (The Architecture Search Problem (ASP)). *For an unknown, continuous function $\mathcal{F}$ defined over some domain $dom(\mathcal{F})$, given a finite subset $\sigma \subset dom(\mathcal{F})$, a sequence length n, a search space $\mathcal{S}_{ASP}$, and a function $m\colon \mathbb{R} \times \mathbb{R} \to \mathbb{R}_{\geq 0}$, find the sequence $f = (\phi_i)_{i=1}^{k}$, $\phi_i \in \mathcal{S}_{ASP}$, $k \leq n$ such that $m(f(x), \mathcal{F}(x))$ is minimal for all $x \in \sigma$, and all $f \in \mathcal{S}_{ASP}^{\star,n}$.*

Note that we have left the parameter optimization problem implicit in this formulation, since, as pointed out in Sect. 4.1, a single-function search space f would be ineffective for dealing with multiple input functions $\mathcal{F}$, no matter how well the optimizer performed for a given subset of these inputs.

At a first glance, ASP looks similar to the PAC learning framework [52]. However, FA is the task about finding the right sequence of computable functions for all possible functions, while PAC is a generalized, tractable formulation of learning problems, with the search space abstracted out. A more precise analysis of the relationship between FA and PAC is described in Appendix A.

As a solution strategy for FA, ASP is also subject to the results from section Sect. 3. The key difference between ML and ASP is that ASP has access to a richer search space, which allows it to have a better approximation capability. In particular, ASP could be seen as a generalized version of the former, since for any n-sized sequence present in $\mathcal{S}_{ML}$, one could construct a space with bigger information potential in ASP, but with the same constrains in sequence length. For example, we could use $\mathcal{E}$ as our search space, choose a sequence length n, and so $U(\mathcal{S}_{ML}, n) \subset U(\mathcal{E}, n)$.

Since ASP has no explicit constraints on time and space, this procedure is essentially performing an exhaustive search. Theorem 2 implies that, for fixed n and any input $\mathcal{F}$, ASP will always return the best possible sequence within that space, as long as the search space contains the set of elementary functions, $\mathcal{E} \subset \mathcal{S}$.

On the other hand, it is a cornerstone of the theory and practice of machine learning that learning algorithms must be tractable–that is, they must run in polynomial time. Given that the search space for ASP grows exponentially with the sequence length, this approach is an interesting theoretical tool, but not very practical. We will still use ASP as a performance target for the evaluation of more applicable procedures. However, it is desirable to formulate a solution strategy for FA that can be used in an applied setting, but can also be analyzed within the framework of this paper.

To achieve this, first we note that any other solution strategy for FA which terminates in polynomial time will have to be able to avoid verifying every possible function in the search space. In other words, such procedure would require a function that is able to choose a nonempty subset of the search space. We denote such function as $\mathcal{B}$, such that for a search space $\mathcal{S}$, $\mathcal{B}(\mathcal{S}) \subset \mathcal{S}^{\star,n}$. We can now define the Approximate Architecture Search Problem (a-ASP) as the formulation of NAS in terms of the FA framework:

Definition 7 (The Approximate ASP (a-ASP)). *If $\mathcal{F}$ is an unknown, continuous function defined over some domain dom($\mathcal{F}$), given a finite subset $\sigma \subset dom(\mathcal{F})$, a sequence length n, a search space $\mathcal{S}_{ASP}$, a function $m\colon \mathbb{R}\times\mathbb{R} \to \mathbb{R}_{\geq 0}$, and a set builder function $\mathcal{B}(\mathcal{S}_{ASP}) \subset \mathcal{S}^{\star,n}_{ASP}$, find the sequence $f = (\phi_i)_{i=1}^{k}$, $\phi_i \in \mathcal{B}(\mathcal{S}_{ASP})$, $k \leq n$ such that $m(f(x), \mathcal{F}(x))$ is minimal for all $x \in \sigma$ and $f \in \mathcal{B}(\mathcal{S}_{ASP})$.*

Just as the previous two procedures we defined, a-ASP is also a solution strategy for FA. The only difference between Definitions 6 and 7 is the inclusion of the set builder function to traverse the space in a more efficient manner. Due to the inclusion of this function, however, a-ASP is weaker than ASP, since it is not guaranteed to find the functions f_o that globally minimizes $\varepsilon_\sigma(f_o, \mathcal{F})$, for all given $\mathcal{F}$. Additionally, the fact that this function must be included into the parameters for a-ASP implies that such procedure requires some design choices. Given that everything else in the definition of a-ASP is equivalent to ASP, it can be stated that the set builder function is the only deciding factor when attempting to match the performance of ASP with a-ASP.

It has been shown [56] that certain set builder functions perform better than others in a generalized setting. This can be also seen from the perspective of the FA framework, where we have available at our disposal the sequences that make up a given function. In particular, if $\mathcal{S} = \{\phi_1, ..., \phi_m\}$ is a search space, and $\mathcal{B}$ is a function that selects elements from $\mathcal{S}^{\star,n}$, a-ASP not only has access to the performance of all the k sequences chosen so far, $\{\varepsilon_\sigma(f_i, F), f_i \in \mathcal{B}(\mathcal{S}^{\star,n})\}_{i\in\{1,...,k\}}$, but also the encoding (the configurations from [56]) of their composition. This means that, given enough samples, when testing against a subset of the input, $\sigma' \subset \sigma$, such an algorithm would be able to learn the expected output $\phi(s)$ of the functions $\phi \in \mathcal{S}$, and their behavior if included in the current sequence $f_{k+1} = (f_k, \phi)(s)$, for $s \in \sigma'$. Including such information in a set builder function could allow the procedure to make better decisions at every step, and this approach has been used in applied settings with success [26,30].

It can be seen that these design choices are not necessarily problem-dependent, and, from the results of Theorem 2, they can be done in a theoretically motivated manner. Specifically, we note that the information potential of the search space remains unchanged between a-ASP and ASP, and so, by including $\mathcal{E}$, a-ASP could have the ability to perform as well as ASP.

5 Conclusion

The FA problem is a reformulation of the problem of approximating any given function, but with finding a sequence of functions as a central aspect of the task. In this paper, we analyzed its properties in terms of the search space, and its applications to machine learning and NAS. In particular, we showed that it is impossible to write a procedure that solves FA for any given function and domain with zero error, but described the conditions under which such error can be minimal. We leveraged the results from this paper to analyze three solution strategies for FA: ML, ASP, and a-ASP. Specifically, we showed that ML is a weak solution strategy for FA, as it is unable to generalize or determine whether the sequence used is the best fit for the input function. We also pointed out that ASP, although the best possible algorithm to solve for FA, is intractable in an applied setting.

We finished by formulating a solution strategy that merged the best of both ML and ASP, a-ASP, and pointed out, through existing work in the literature, complemented with the results from this framework, that it has the ability to solve FA as well as ASP in terms of approximation error.

One area that was not discussed in this paper was whether it would be possible to select *a priori* a good subset σ of the input function's domain. This problem is important since a good representative of the input will greatly influence a procedure's capability to solve FA. This is tied to the data selection process, and it was not dealt with on this paper. Further research on this topic is likely to bear great influence on machine learning as a whole.

Acknowledgments. The author is grateful to the anonymous reviewers for their helpful feedback on this paper, and also thanks Y. Goren, Q. Wang, N. Strom, C. Bejjani, Y. Xu, and B. d'Iverno for their comments and suggestions on the early stages of this project.

Appendices

A PAC Is a Solver for FA

PAC learning, as defined by Valiant [52], is a slightly different problem than FA, as it concerns itself with whether a *concept class* C can be described with high probability with a member of a *hypothesis class* H. It also establishes bounds in terms of the amount of samples from members $c \in C$ that are needed to learn C. On the other hand, FA and its solution strategies concern themselves with finding a solution that minimizes the error, by searching through sequences of explicitly defined members drawn from a search space.

Regardless of these differences, PAC learning as a procedure can still be formulated as a solution strategy for FA. To do this, let H be our search space. Then note that the PAC error function $e_{pac}(h, c) = Pr_{x \sim \mathcal{P}}[h(x) \neq c(x)]$, $c \in C$, $h \in H$, is equivalent to computing $\varepsilon_\sigma(h, c)$ for some subset $\sigma \subset dom(c)$, and choosing the frequentist difference between the images of the functions as the metric d. Our objective would be to return the $h \in H$ that minimizes the approximation error for a given subset $\sigma \subset C$. Note that we do not search through the expanded search space $H^{\star,n}$.

Finding the right distribution for a specific class may be NP-hard [7], and so e_{pac} requires us to make certain assumptions about the distribution of the input values. Additionally, any optimizer for PAC is required to run in polynomial time. Due to all of this, PAC is a weaker approach to solve FA when compared to ASP, but stronger than ML since this solution strategy is fixed to the design of the search space, and not to the choice of function. Nonetheless, it must be stressed that the bounds and paradigms provided by PAC and FA are not mutually exclusive, either: the most prominent example being that PAC learning provides conditions under which the choice subset σ is optimal.

With the polynomial constraint for PAC learning lifted, and letting the sample and search space sizes grow infinitely, PAC is effectively equivalent to ASP. However, that defies the purpose of the PAC framework, as its success relies on being a tractable learning theory.

B The VC Dimension and the Information Potential

There is a natural correspondence between the VC dimension [7,53] of a hypothesis space, and the information capacity of a sequence.

To see this, note that the VC dimension is usually defined in terms of the set of concepts (i.e., the input function $\mathcal{F}$) that can be shattered by a predetermined function f with $img(f) = \{0, 1\}$. It is frequently used to quantify the ability of a procedure to learn the input function $\mathcal{F}$.

In the FA framework we are more interested in whether the search space–also a set–of a given solution strategy is able to generalize well to multiple, unseen input functions. Therefore, for fixed $\mathcal{F}$ and f, the VC dimension and its variants provide a powerful insight on the ability of an algorithm to learn. When f is not fixed, it is still possible to utilize this quantity to measure the capacity of a search space $\mathcal{S}$, by simply taking the union of all possible $f \in \mathcal{S}^{\star,n}$ for a given n. However, when the the input functions are not fixed either, we are unable to use the definition of VC dimension in this context, as the set of input concepts is unknown to us. We thus need a more flexible way to model generalizability, and that is where we leverage the information potential $U(\mathcal{S}, n)$ of a search space.

References

1. Angeline, P.J., Saunders, G.M., Pollack, J.B.: An evolutionary algorithm that constructs recurrent neural networks. Trans. Neur. Netw. **5**(1), 54–65 (1994). https://doi.org/10.1109/72.265960
2. Bartlett, P., Ben-David, S.: Hardness results for neural network approximation problems. In: Fischer, P., Simon, H.U. (eds.) EuroCOLT 1999. LNCS (LNAI), vol. 1572, pp. 50–62. Springer, Heidelberg (1999). https://doi.org/10.1007/3-540-49097-3_5
3. Baxter, J.: A model of inductive bias learning. J. Artifi. Intell. Res. **12**, 149–198 (2000). https://doi.org/10.1613/jair.731
4. Ben-David, S., Hrubes, P., Moran, S., Shpilka, A., Yehudayoff, A.: A learning problem that is independent of the set theory ZFC axioms. CoRR abs/1711.05195 (2017). http://arxiv.org/abs/1711.05195
5. Bengio, Y.: Learning deep architectures for AI. Found. Trends Mach. Learn. **2**(1), 1–127 (2009). https://doi.org/10.1561/2200000006
6. Blum, M.: A machine-independent theory of the complexity of recursive functions. J. ACM **14**(2), 322–336 (1967). https://doi.org/10.1145/321386.321395
7. Blumer, A., Ehrenfeucht, A., Haussler, D., Warmuth, M.K.: Learnability and the vapnik-chervonenkis dimension. J. Assoc. Comput. Mach. **36**, 929–965 (1989). https://doi.org/10.1145/76359.76371
8. Bshouty, N.H.: A new composition theorem for learning algorithms. In: Proceedings of the Thirtieth Annual ACM Symposium on Theory of Computing, STOC 1998, pp. 583–589. ACM, New York (1998). https://doi.org/10.1145/258533.258614
9. Carpenter, G.A., Grossberg, S.: A massively parallel architecture for a self-organizing neural pattern recognition machine. Comput. Vis. Graph. Image Process. **37**, 54–115 (1987). https://doi.org/10.1016/S0734-189X(87)80014-2
10. Carvalho, A.R., Ramos, F.M., Chaves, A.A.: Metaheuristics for the feedforward artificial neural network (ANN) architecture optimization problem. Neural Comput. Appl. (2010). https://doi.org/10.1007/s00521-010-0504-3
11. Church, A.: An unsolvable problem of elementary number theory. Am. J. Math. **58**, 345–363 (1936)
12. Cybenko, G.: Approximation by superpositions of a sigmoidal function. Math. Control Signals Systems **2**, 303–314 (1989). https://doi.org/10.1007/BF02551274
13. Cybenko, G.: Complexity theory of neural networks and classification problems. In: Almeida, L.B., Wellekens, C.J. (eds.) EURASIP 1990. LNCS, vol. 412, pp. 26–44. Springer, Heidelberg (1990). https://doi.org/10.1007/3-540-52255-7_25
14. Elsken, T., Metzen, J.H., Hutter, F.: Neural architecture search: a survey (2019). https://doi.org/10.1007/978-3-030-05318-5_3
15. Feurer, M., Klein, A., Eggensperger, K., Springenberg, J., Blum, M., Hutter, F.: Efficient and robust automated machine learning. In: Cortes, C., Lawrence, N.D., Lee, D.D., Sugiyama, M., Garnett, R. (eds.) Advances in Neural Information Processing Systems, vol. 28, pp. 2962–2970. Curran Associates, Inc. (2015)
16. Funahashi, K.: On the approximate realization of continuous mappings by neural networks. Neural Netw. **2**, 183–192 (1989). https://doi.org/10.1016/0893-6080(89)90003-8
17. Girosi, F., Jones, M., Poggio, T.: Regularization theory and neural networks architectures. Neural Comput. **7**, 219–269 (1995). https://doi.org/10.1162/neco.1995.7.2.219

18. Golovin, D., Solnik, B., Moitra, S., Kochanski, G., Karro, J., Sculley, D.: Google vizier: a service for black-box optimization (2017). https://doi.org/10.1145/3097983.3098043
19. Goodfellow, I., Bengio, Y., Courville, A.: Deep Learning. MIT Press, Cambridge (2016). http://www.deeplearningbook.org
20. He, Y., Lin, J., Liu, Z., Wang, H., Li, L.J., Han, S.: AMC: autoML for model compression and acceleration on mobile devices. In: Proceedings of the European Conference on Computer Vision (ECCV), pp. 784–800 (2018)
21. Hornik, K.: Approximation capabilities of multilayer feedforward networks. Neural Netw. **4**, 251–257 (1991). https://doi.org/10.1016/0893-6080(91)90009-T
22. Hornik, K., Stinchcombe, M., White, H.: Multilayer feedforward networks are universal approximators. Neural Netw. **2**, 359–366 (1989). https://doi.org/10.1016/0893-6080(89)90020-8
23. Jin, H., Song, Q., Hu, X.: Auto-keras: Efficient neural architecture search with network morphism (2018)
24. Kolmogorov, A.N.: On the representation of continuous functions of several variables by superposition of continuous function of one variable and addition. Dokl. Akad. Nauk SSSR **114**, 953–956 (1957)
25. Leshno, M., Lin, V.Y., Pinkus, A., Shocken, S.: Multilayer feedforward networks with a nonpolynomial activation function can approximate any function. Neural Netw. **6**, 861–867 (1993). https://doi.org/10.1016/S0893-6080(05)80131-5
26. Liu, H., Simonyan, K., Yang, Y.: Hierarchical representations for efficient architecture search. In: International Conference on Learning Representations (2018)
27. Liu, H., Simonyan, K., Yang, Y.: DARTS: differentiable architecture search. In: International Conference on Learning Representations (2019)
28. Long, P.M., Sedghi, H.: Size-free generalization bounds for convolutional neural networks. CoRR abs/1905.12600 (2019). https://arxiv.org/pdf/1905.12600v1.pdf
29. Luo, R., Tian, F., Qin, T., Liu, T.Y.: Neural architecture optimization. In: NeurIPS (2018)
30. Miller, G.F., Todd, P.M., Hegde, S.U.: Designing neural networks using genetic algorithms. In: Proceedings 3rd International Conference Genetic Algorithms and Their Applications, pp. 379–384 (1989)
31. Neto, J.P., Siegelmann, H.T., Costa, J.F., Araujo, C.P.S.: Turing universality of neural nets (revisited). In: Pichler, F., Moreno-Díaz, R. (eds.) EUROCAST 1997. LNCS, vol. 1333, pp. 361–366. Springer, Heidelberg (1997). https://doi.org/10.1007/BFb0025058
32. Ojha, V.K., Abraham, A., Snášel, V.: Metaheuristic design of feedforward neural networks: a review of two decades of research. Eng. Appl. Artif. Intell. **60**(C), 97–116 (2017). https://doi.org/10.1016/j.engappai.2017.01.013
33. Orponen, P.: Computational complexity of neural networks: a survey. Nordic J. Comput. **1**(1), 94–110 (1994)
34. Ostrand, P.A.: Dimension of metric spaces and hilbert's problem 13. Bull. Am. Math. Soc. **71**, 619–622 (1965). https://doi.org/10.1090/S0002-9904-1965-11363-5
35. Park, J., Sandberg, I.W.: Universal approximation using radial-basis-function networks. Neural Comput. **3**, 246–257 (1991). https://doi.org/10.1162/neco.1991.3.2.246
36. Pham, H., Guan, M., Zoph, B., Le, Q., Dean, J.: Efficient neural architecture search via parameters sharing. In: Dy, J., Krause, A. (eds.) Proceedings of the 35th International Conference on Machine Learning. Proceedings of Machine Learning Research, 10–15 July 2018, vol. 80, pp. 4095–4104. PMLR (2018)

37. Poggio, T., Girosi, F.: A theory of networks for approximation and learning. A.I. Memo No. 1140 (1989)
38. Poggio, T., Girosi, F.: Networks for approximation and learning. Proc. IEEE **78**(9), 1481–1497 (1990). https://doi.org/10.1109/5.58326
39. Rabin, M.O.: Computable algebra, general theory and theory of computable fields. Trans. Amer. Math. Soc. **95**, 341–360 (1960). https://doi.org/10.1090/S0002-9947-1960-0113807-4
40. Real, E., et al.: Large-scale evolution of image classifiers. In: Proceedings of the 34th International Conference on Machine Learning (2017)
41. Rogers Jr., H.: The Theory of Recursive Functions and Effective Computability. MIT Press, Cambridge (1987)
42. Schäfer, A.M., Zimmermann, H.G.: Recurrent neural networks are universal approximators. In: Kollias, S.D., Stafylopatis, A., Duch, W., Oja, E. (eds.) ICANN 2006. LNCS, vol. 4131, pp. 632–640. Springer, Heidelberg (2006). https://doi.org/10.1007/11840817_66
43. Schaffer, J.D., Caruana, R.A., Eshelman, L.J.: Using genetic search to exploit the emergent behavior of neural networks. Physics D **42**, 244–248 (1990). https://doi.org/10.1016/0167-2789(90)90078-4
44. Siegel, J.W., Xu, J.: On the approximation properties of neural networks. arXiv e-prints arXiv:1904.02311 (2019)
45. Siegelmann, H.T., Sontag, E.D.: Turing computability with neural nets. Appl. Math. Lett. **4**, 77–80 (1991). https://doi.org/10.1016/0893-9659(91)90080-F
46. Siegelmann, H.T., Sontag, E.D.: On the computational power of neural nets. J. Comput. Syst. Sci. **50**, 132–150 (1995). https://doi.org/10.1006/jcss.1995.1013
47. Sontag, E.D.: VC dimension of neural networks. Neural Netw. Mach. Learn. **168**, 69–95 (1998)
48. Stanley, K.O., Clune, J., Lehman, J., Miikkulainen, R.: Designing neural networks through evolutionary algorithms. Nat. Mach. Intell. **1**, 24–35 (2019)
49. Stanley, K.O., Miikkulainen, R.: Evolving neural networks through augmenting topologies. Evol. Comput. **10**(2), 99–127 (2002). https://doi.org/10.1162/106365602320169811
50. Sun, Y., Yen, G.G., Yi, Z.: Evolving unsupervised deep neural networks for learning meaningful representations. IEEE Trans. Evol. Comput. **23**, 89–103 (2019). https://doi.org/10.1109/TEVC.2018.2808689
51. Tenorio, M.F., Lee, W.T.: Self organizing neural networks for the identification problem. In: Touretzky, D.S. (ed.) Advances in Neural Information Processing Systems 1, pp. 57–64. Morgan-Kaufmann, San Mateo (1989)
52. Valiant, L.G.: A theory of the learnable. Commun. ACM **27**, 1134–1142 (1984). https://doi.org/10.1145/1968.1972
53. Vapnik, V.N., Chervonenkis, A.Y.: On the uniform convergence of relative frequencies of events to their probabilities. In: Vovk, V., Papadopoulos, H., Gammerman, A. (eds.) Measures of Complexity, pp. 11–30. Springer, Cham (2015). https://doi.org/10.1007/978-3-319-21852-6_3
54. Vitushkin, A.: Some properties of linear superpositions of smooth functions. Dokl. Akad. Nauk SSSR **156**, 1258–1261 (1964)
55. Wolpert, D.H., Macready, W.G.: No free lunch theorems for optimization. IEEE Trans. Evol. Comput. **1**(1), 67–87 (1997). https://doi.org/10.1109/4235.585893
56. Wolpert, D.H., Macready, W.G.: Coevolutionary free lunches. IEEE Trans. Evol. Comput. **9**, 721–735 (2005). https://doi.org/10.1109/TEVC.2005.856205

57. Wong, C., Houlsby, N., Lu, Y., Gesmundo, A.: Transfer learning with neural autoML. In: Proceedings of the 32nd International Conference on Neural Information Processing Systems, NIPS 2018, pp. 8366–8375 (2018)
58. Yang, X.S.: Metaheuristic optimization: algorithm analysis and open problems. In: Proceedings of the 10th International Symposium on Experimental Algorithms, vol. 6630, pp. 21–32 (2011). https://doi.org/10.1007/978-3-642-20662-7_2
59. Yao, X.: Evolving artificial neural networks. Proc. IEEE **87**(9), 1423–1447 (1999). https://doi.org/10.1109/5.784219
60. Zoph, B., Le, Q.V.: Neural architecture search with reinforcement learning. CoRR abs/1611.01578 (2016)

Probabilistic Bounds for Approximation by Neural Networks

Věra Kůrková(✉)

Institute of Computer Science of the Czech Academy of Sciences,
Pod Vodárenskou věží 2, 18207 Prague, Czech Republic
vera@cs.cas.cz

Abstract. A probabilistic model describing relevance of tasks to be computed by a class of feedforward networks is studied. Bounds on correlations of network input-output functions with almost all randomly-chosen functions are derived. Impact of sizes of function domains on correlations are analyzed from the point of view of the concentration of measure phenomenon. It is shown that on large domains, errors of approximation of randomly chosen functions by fixed input-output functions are almost deterministic.

Keywords: Approximation of random functions · Feedforward networks · Dictionaries of computational units · High-dimensional geometry · Concentration of measure · Azuma-Hoeffding inequalities

1 Introduction

Feedforward networks compute parameterized families of input-output functions. In practical applications, function domains are finite, although typically quite large. They can be formed by pixels of pictures, discretized cubes, or scattered vectors of data. It has long been known that under a mild condition on dictionary of computational units, feedforward networks have the *universal representation property*, i.e., they can *exactly* compute any real-valued function on a finite domain [1]. In particular, shallow networks with one hidden layer of computational units of many common types satisfy this condition (see, e.g., [2] and the references therein). However, the arguments proving this property assume that the number of network units is potentially as large as the size of the domain. For large domains, such networks might be too large for efficient implementations.

Obviously, representations of not all functions on a given domain require networks with the large numbers of units needed for universality-type results. These results include worst cases, but for various classes of functions much smaller numbers of network units or parameters are sufficient. Moreover by a proper choice of computational units or a network architecture, these numbers can be considerably reduced (in some cases even from exponential to linear). For example, a

I. V. Tetko et al. (Eds.): ICANN 2019, LNCS 11727, pp. 418–428, 2019.
https://doi.org/10.1007/978-3-030-30487-4_33

one-hidden-layer network with Gaussian support vectors requires for a classification of vectors of the d-dimensional Boolean cube $\{0,1\}^d$ according to the parity at least 2^{d-1} units [3]. On the other hand, it is easy to verify that a shallow network with signum perceptrons can accomplish this task using only d units. Using Hadamard matrices and pseudo-noise sequences, we constructed classes of functions whose computation can be accomplished by two-hidden-layer signum perceptron network with numbers of units depending on the input dimension only linearly, while computation by one-hidden-layer perceptron networks needs numbers of units growing with the dimension exponentially [4,5].

Thus to identify and explain efficient network designs, it is desirable to obtain some theoretical understanding to suitability of types of network architectures and units for approximation of various classes of classification and regression tasks. Even on sets of moderate sizes, there is an enormous number of binary classification tasks. Comparison with the estimated number 10^{80} of atoms in the Universe (see, e.g., [6]) shows how enormous is the number $2^{267} > 10^{80}$ of all binary classifiers on a domain of size 267. The number of highly uncorrelated regression tasks grows exponentially with the size m of the domain. While there are only m exactly orthogonal unit vectors in m-dimensional space, the number of ε-orthogonal vectors (which have inner products at most ε) grows with m exponentially. A lower bound $e^{\frac{m\varepsilon^2}{2}}$ on this number, called quasiorthogonal dimension $\dim_\varepsilon m$, was proven in [7]. The linear space of real-valued functions on a domain of size m is isomorphic to the m-dimensional Euclidean space $\mathbb{R}^m$ and so there is an exponentially growing number of highly uncorrelated functions on the domain.

In practical applications, most functions from the large sets of all classification or regression functions on a given domain are not likely to model any task of interest. Thus relevance of most functions for a choice of a class of networks suitable for an efficient computation of tasks from a given application area is very low or negligible. In [8] we introduced a probabilistic approach modeling a prior knowledge that a binary classification is likely to occur in a given application. Using the Chernogff-Hoeffding Bound on sums of independent random variables, we derived lower bounds on approximate measures of network sparsity holding for almost all functions randomly chosen according to product probabilities.

In this paper, we extend investigation of probabilistic models of relevance of functions for a given application domain also to regression tasks. We analyze effects of increasing sizes of function domains on probabilities of correlations of randomly chosen functions with input-output functions of a feedforward network. Geometry of high-dimensional spaces implies concentration of values of sufficiently smooth functions of many variables close to their mean values or medians. This property of high-dimensional spheres is called the concentration of measure phenomenon. Similar property was also discovered in probability theory, where it has been studied in terms of bounds on large deviations of sums of random variables by Hoeffding [9], Chernoff [10], and Azuma [11]. It implies that randomized techniques work almost deterministically [12]. We employ the Lévy Lemma for regression tasks selected randomly from uniform distributions and the Azuma-Hoeffding Inequality for tasks selected from product probability distributions. We show that correlations of randomly chosen functions with a fixed input-output function are sharply concentrated around their mean value. Thus on large domains, errors in approximation of randomly chosen functions by feedforward networks behave almost deterministically. Suitability of a given class of networks for a regression task described by the probability distribution depends on the largest mean value of the inner products of randomly chosen functions with an input-output function from the class.

The paper is organized as follows. In Sect. 2, we introduce notations and basic concepts on feedforward networks and approximation. In Sect. 3, the probabilistic model of relevance of regression tasks is introduced and effects of increasing sizes of function domains are studied for regression tasks selected uniformly. In Sect. 4, the case of non uniform distributions is studied. Section 5 is a brief discussion.

2 Approximation of Functions by Feedforward Networks

In practical applications, domains $X \subset \mathbb{R}^d$ are finite, but their sizes $\operatorname{card} X = m$ and/or input dimensions d can be large. We denote by

$$\mathcal{F}(X) := \{f \mid f : X \to \mathbb{R}\}$$

the *set of all real-valued functions on* X, by

$$\mathcal{B}(X) := \{f \mid f : X \to \{-1, 1\}\}$$

its subset formed by the *all functions on* X *with values in* $\{-1, 1\}$, and

$$C_1(X) = \{f \in \mathcal{F}(F) \mid (\forall i = 1, \dots, m)\, f(x_i) \in [0, 1]\}.$$

For a linear ordering $\{x_1, \dots, x_m\}$ of elements of X, we define an isomorphism $\iota : \mathcal{F}(X) \to \mathbb{R}^m$ as $\iota(f) := (f(x_1), \dots, f(x_m))$ and thus we identify $\mathcal{F}(X)$ with the finite dimensional Euclidean space $\mathbb{R}^m$. On $\mathcal{F}(X)$, we denote the induced inner product by

$$\langle f, g \rangle := \sum_{u \in X} f(u)g(u)$$

and the Euclidean norm $\|f\|_2 := \sqrt{\langle f, f \rangle}$. By

$$S_1(X) = \{f \in \mathcal{F}(X) \mid \|f\|_2 = 1\}$$

we denote the unit sphere in $\mathcal{F}(X)$, which is an isomorphic image of the sphere S^{m-1} in $\mathbb{R}^m$.

We investigate approximation of real and binary-valued functions on X by *feedforward networks with single linear outputs.* Such networks compute input-output functions from the set

$$\operatorname{span} G := \left\{ \sum_{i=1}^{n} w_i g_i \,\middle|\, w_i \in \mathbb{R},\ g_i \in G,\ n \in \mathbb{N} \right\}, \tag{1}$$

where G, called a *dictionary*, is a parameterized family of functions. In *shallow (one-hidden-layer) networks*, G is formed by functions computable by a given type of computational units, whereas in *deep networks* with several hidden layers, it is formed by combinations and compositions of functions representing units from lower layers. By

$$\operatorname{span}_n G := \left\{ \sum_{i=1}^{n} w_i g_i \,\middle|\, w_i \in \mathbb{R},\ g_i \in G \right\}$$

we denote the set of functions computable by networks with at most n units in the last hidden layer.

In the analysis of approximation capabilities of neural networks computing function from sets of the form (1), it has to be taken into account that the approximation error $\|f - \operatorname{span}_n G\|$ in any norm $\|.\|$ can be made arbitrarily large by multiplying f by a scalar. Indeed, for every $c > 0$,

$$\|cf - \operatorname{span}_n G\| = c\|f - \operatorname{span}_n G\|\,. \tag{2}$$

Further,

$$\|f - \operatorname{span}_n G\| = \|f - \operatorname{span}_n \xi G\|, \tag{3}$$

where $\xi : G \to \mathbb{R}_+$ is any mapping and $\xi G = \{\xi(g)g \mid g \in G\}$.

The equality (2) shows that approximation errors by networks with linear output have to be considered in sets of normalized functions or in sets of functions of a given fixed norm and (3) shows that approximation errors are invariant under multiplication of elements of a dictionary by scalars.

Euclidean distance between functions of the same norm depends on their *correlation* defined as the inner product $\langle f^o, g^o \rangle$, where $f^o = \frac{f}{\|f\|}$. It can be studied in terms of the *angular pseudometrics* ρ on $S_1(X)$ defined as

$$\rho(f,g) = \arccos |\langle f, g \rangle|.$$

Note that ρ is not a metrics, it is merely a pseudometrics, because the distance between f and $-f$ is zero. The more correlated normalized functions are, the better they can approximate each other in l_2-norm as

$$\|f^o - g^o\|_2 = 2\sin(\alpha/2) \quad \text{where} \quad \alpha = \arccos |\langle f^o, g^o \rangle|.$$

3 Probability of Relevance of Computational Tasks

A prior knowledge about relevance of computational tasks for a given application area can be modeled by a probability measure. For the classification task we assume that there is a discrete probability measure Pr on the set $\mathcal{B}(X)$, while for regression task we assume that there is a probability measure Pr on the sigma algebra of subsets of $S_1(X)$ or $C_1(X)$ which are isometric images of Lebesgue measures on corresponding subsets of $\mathbb{R}^m$. A binary or real-valued function f on $X = \{x_1, \ldots, x_m\}$ can be represented as a vector $(f(x_1), \ldots, f(x_m)) \in \mathbb{R}^m$. So a randomly chosen function f can be expressed by m random variables

$$Y_1 := f(x_1), \ldots, Y_m := f(x_m).$$

Without any prior knowledge on the type of tasks to be performed by a neural network, we have to assume that the probability measure is uniform. When the size $\operatorname{card} X = m$ of the domain X is large, then $S_1(X)$ is isometric to the high-dimensional sphere S^{m-1}. The geometry of high-dimensional spaces has many counter-intuitive properties. In particular, most of the area of a high-dimensional sphere is concentrated around the equator. Let

$$C(g, \varepsilon) := \{f \in S^{m-1} \mid \langle f, g \rangle \geq \varepsilon\}$$

denote the *"polar cap"* centered at a fixed vector g containing all vectors within a fixed angular distance $\alpha = \arccos \varepsilon$ (see Fig. 1). Integration in spherical polar coordinates gives the following upper bound on the normalized surface area λ^o of the polar cap $C(g, \varepsilon)$.

$$\lambda^o(C(g, \varepsilon)) \leq e^{-\frac{m\varepsilon^2}{2}} \tag{4}$$

(see, e.g., [13]).

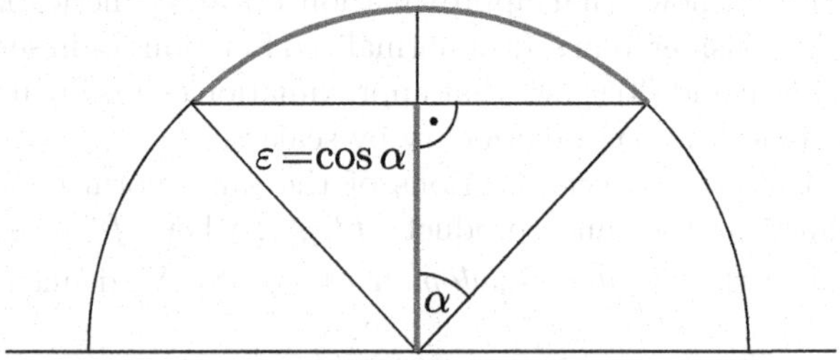

Fig. 1. Polar cap

So for a fixed ε, the fraction of the surface of a high-dimensional sphere occupied by a polar cap $C(g, \varepsilon)$ decreases exponentially fast to zero with increasing dimension m.

A generalization of the upper bound (4) obtained by replacing the inner product $\langle ., g \rangle$ with any 1-Lipschitz function (satisfying for all $x, y \in S^{m-1}$, $|h(x) - h(y)| \leq |x - y|$)) is the essence of the Lèvy Lemma [14] on concentration of values of Lipschitz functions on high-dimensional spheres. By $\operatorname{med}(h)$ is denoted the *median* of h, i.e., $\Pr[u \in S^{m-1} \mid h(u) < \operatorname{med}(h)] = 1/2$ and $\Pr[u \in S^{m-1} \mid h(u) > \operatorname{med}(h)] = 1/2$.

Theorem 1 (Lévy Lemma). *Let m be a positive integer,* Pr *be a uniform probability measure (normalized surface measure) on S^{m-1}, and $h : S^{m-1} \to \mathbb{R}$ be 1-Lipschitz. Then for every $\varepsilon \in [0,1]$*

$$\Pr[u \in S^{m-1} \mid |h(u) - \mathrm{med}(h)| > \varepsilon] \leq 2e^{-\frac{m\varepsilon^2}{2}}.$$

The Lévy Lemma states that almost all values of a Lipschitz function on a high-dimensional sphere are close to the median of the function. This property of high-dimensional spheres is called the *concentration of measure phenomenon.*

It follows from the Cauchy-Schwartz Inequality that on $S_1(X)$ the inner product with a fixed function g is 1-Lipschitz. By symmetry, both its median and expectation are equal to zero. Thus we get the following corollary.

Theorem 2. *Let* Pr *be the uniform probability measure on $S_1(X)$ and $g \in S_1(X)$. Then for every $\varepsilon \in [0,1]$*

$$\Pr[f \in S_1(X) \mid |\langle f, g\rangle| > \varepsilon] \leq 2e^{\frac{-m\varepsilon^2}{2}}.$$

Theorem 2 shows that for any fixed normalized function g on a large domain X, almost all uniformly randomly chosen functions in $S_1(X)$ are highly uncorrelated with g (Fig. 2).

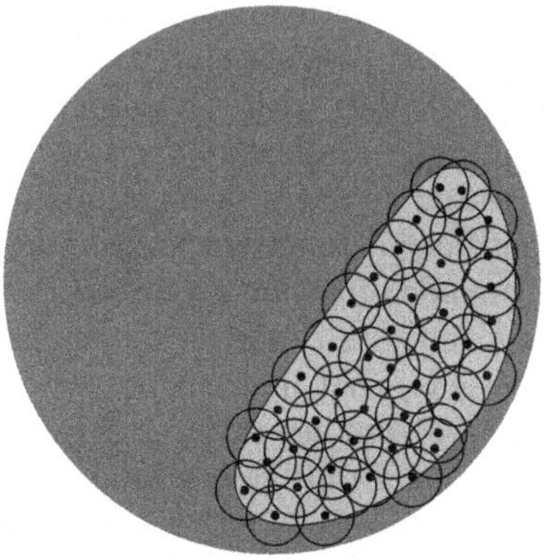

Fig. 2. Covering of a subset of a sphere

If we have no prior knowledge about the type of tasks to be performed, we have to search for a class of networks capable to compute with a desirable accuracy any uniformly randomly chosen function in $S_1(X)$. By Theorem 2, in this case a class of networks has to have a very large capacity to contain input-output functions which are close within an angular distance to any uniformly randomly chosen function in $S_1(X)$. Capacity of networks can be described in terms of covering numbers of sets of their input-output functions.

For a subset F of a metric space $\mathcal{X}$ and $\varepsilon > 0$, an *ε-net in F* is a set $\{f_1, \dots, f_n\}$, such that the family of the closed balls $B_\varepsilon(f_i)$ of radii ε centered at f_i covers F. The *ε-covering number* denoted $\mathcal{N}_\varepsilon(F)$ of a subset F of a metric space $\mathcal{S}$ is the cardinality of a minimal ε-net in F, i.e.,

$$\mathcal{N}_\varepsilon(F) = \min\{n \in \mathbb{N}_+ \mid F \subseteq \bigcup_{i=1}^{n} B_\varepsilon(f_i),\ (\forall i = 1, \dots, n)(f_i \in F)\}.$$

When the set over which the minimum is taken is empty, then $\mathcal{N}_\varepsilon(F) = +\infty$. Note that any compact set has finite covering numbers. Thus any closed subset of $S_1(X)$ has finite covering numbers.

The following corollary of Theorem 2 estimates the probability that a uniformly randomly chosen function is nearly orthogonal to all elements of a dictionary.

Corollary 1. *Let d be a positive integer, $X \subset \mathbb{R}^d$ with* $\operatorname{card} X = m$, Pr *be a uniform probability measure on $S_1(X)$, $\varepsilon > 0$, and $F \subset S_1(X)$ has finite covering numbers in the angular pseudometrics ρ on $S_1(X)$. Then*

$$\Pr[f \in S_1(X) \mid (\forall g \in F)\,(\rho(f,g) \geq 2 \arccos \varepsilon)] \geq 1 - 2\mathcal{N}_{\arccos \varepsilon}(F)\, e^{-\frac{m\varepsilon^2}{2}}.$$

Corollary 1 shows that if we do not have any prior knowledge about a type of task, we have to estimate approximation capabilities of a class of networks from its covering numbers. Because the sizes of polar caps on high-dimensional spheres are small (decrease exponentially fast with m), to contain input-output functions approximating well all uniformly randomly functions in $S_1(X)$, a class of networks must have large covering numbers (growing exponentially with m). Note that for finite sets of input-output functions (having finite sets of parameters), all covering numbers are bounded from above by sizes of such sets. However, for some values of ε, covering numbers can even be smaller. This can happen for highly coherent sets in the sense that many pairs of input-output functions are close to each other. Corollary 1 implies that for networks with sets of parameters growing with sizes of domains only polynomially, most functions are nearly orthogonal to all input-output functions and thus cannot be well approximated by such networks.

Covering numbers of sets of the form $\operatorname{span}_n G$ depend on n. In [15] we derived upper bounds on the sizes of sets of binary-valued functions computable by perceptron networks in dependence on n. Various estimates of covering numbers in l_2-norm are known. For example, any subset F of the set of functions on a finite domain X with range $\{0, 1\}$ which has a finite VC-dimension has power-type covering numbers in l_2 [16].

4 Tasks Modeled by Non Uniform Probability Distributions

In the previous section, we showed that without a prior knowledge of a type of tasks, satisfactory performance can only be guaranteed when networks with large numbers of parameters are available. However in real applications, often probabilities modeling relevance of functions are far from being uniform. Typically, they are non zero only on relatively small subsets of $S_1(X)$. Some insights into cases where tasks are selected from non uniform distributions can be obtained using some concentration results, which were discovered in probability theory. There, they have been studied in terms of bounds on large deviations of sums of random variables by Hoeffding [9] and Chernoff [10]. Some extensions holding not merely for sums but also for functions of several random variables, which satisfy certain smoothness conditions, follow from bounds proven by Azuma [11]. Most of these results assume that the random variables $Y_1, \ldots, Y_m$ are independent.

Here, we apply the *method of bounded differences.* A function Φ of m real variables satisfies the *Bounded Difference Condition (BDC) with parameters* $c_i, i = 1, \ldots, m$, if for every $i = 1 \ldots, m$, and random variables $Y = (Y_1, \ldots, Y_m)$ and $\bar{Y} = (\bar{Y}_1, \ldots, \bar{Y}_m)$, which differ only in the i-th coordinate,

$$\left|\Phi(Y) - \Phi(\bar{Y})\right| \leq c_i.$$

The next theorem from [12, p.70] states that most values of a function of many random variables satisfying the BDC are concentarted around its mean value.

Theorem 3. *If Φ satisfies the BDC condition with parameters $c_i, i = 1, \ldots, m$, $c := \sum_{i=1}^m c_i^2$, and random variables Y_i are independent, then*

$$\Pr\left(|\Phi - E(\Phi)| > t\right) \leq e^{-2t^2/c}.$$

Applying this theorem to inner products of a fixed function h with functions randomly chosen according to a product probability Pr on $C_1(X)$, we obtain the following probabilistic estimate.

Theorem 4. *Let $X = \{x_1, \ldots, x_m\} \subset \mathbb{R}^d$ and $h \in S_1(X)$. Then the inner product of h with f randomly chosen from $C_1(X)$ according to a product probability* Pr *satisfies for every $\lambda > 0$*

$$\Pr\Big(\Big|\Big\langle \frac{f}{\sqrt{m}}, h\Big\rangle - \frac{E(\langle ., h\rangle)}{\sqrt{m}}\Big| > \lambda\Big) \leq e^{-\frac{m\lambda^2}{2}}.$$

Proof. Let Φ_h be a function of m random variables defined as $\Phi_h(Y_1, \ldots, Y_m) = \sum_{i=1}^m h(x_i)Y_i$. Let $Y_1 = f(x_1), \ldots, Y_m = f(x_m)$ be random variables induced by a function $f \in C_1(X)$ selected according to the probability Pr. For all $i = 1, \ldots, m$, values of $Y_i = f(x_i)$ are in the interval $[-1, 1]$ and so Φ_h satisfies the bounded difference condition with parameters $2h(x_i)$. As $\|h\|_2 = 1$, we have $\sum_{i=1}^m (2h(x_i))^2 = 4\sum_{i=1}^m h(x_i)^2 = 4$. Pr is a product probability and thus the random variables $Y_i = f(x_i)$ are independent. Setting $t = \sqrt{m}\lambda$ we obtain by Theorem 3

$$\Pr[|\langle f, h\rangle - E(\langle ., h\rangle)| > \sqrt{m}\lambda] \leq e^{-\frac{m\lambda^2}{2}}$$

and the statement follows. □

We apply Theorem 4 to investigation of approximation by sets of the form $\mathrm{span}_n\, G$. If $h \in \mathrm{span}_n\, G$, then also $\frac{h}{\sqrt{m}} \in \mathrm{span}_n\, G$. As $\langle \frac{f}{\sqrt{m}}, h\rangle = \langle f, \frac{h}{\sqrt{m}}\rangle$, large inner product between a randomly selected f with $\frac{h}{\sqrt{m}}$ implies that f can be well approximated by $\mathrm{span}_n G$.

In contrast to the case of uniform probability when all mean values are equal to zero, in the case of non uniform probability, the mean values of inner products with some input-output functions computable by a class of networks might be non zero, even might be quite large. Theorem 4 shows that in such cases, the class of networks can approximate well most functions randomly chosen according to the probability. Inner products of most randomly chosen functions with an input-output function with large mean value are sharply concentrated around this mean value. For large function domains, approximation of randomly chosen functions is almost deterministic.

5 Discussion

To get some insight how neural networks can efficiently approximate functions from sets containing exponentially growing numbers of uncorrelated functions, we investigated a probabilistic model of relevance of regression tasks for a given application area. We proved that performance of a given class of networks on a randomized set of functions on large domains is almost deterministic in the sense that either a given class of networks can approximate well almost all randomly selected functions according to a given probability or none of them, unless its sets of input-output functions have exponentially growing covering numbers. The dual problem of investigation of approximation of fixed functions with randomly selected input-output functions according to probability distributions on sets of network parameters are subject of our future research. Almost deterministic behavior of correlations of functions with large numbers of parameters might provide some insight into performance of randomized learning algorithms.

We assumed that the probability distribution is a product of independent probabilities. In machine learning, typically the data are assumed to be independent and identically distributed (i.i.d.) [17,18]. Under this assumption, stochastic separation theorems for classification were derived in [19,20]. However, independence of random variables is a strong assumption. The hypothesis that a probability distribution can be expressed as a product probability is called the "naive Bayes assumption" [21]. However in some practical applications, probabilities describing a prior knowledge do not satisfy the independence assumption. Suitability of some tools based on theory of martingales for investigation of such cases are subject of our future work.

Acknowledgments. V. K. was partially supported by the Czech Grant Foundation grant GA19-05704S and the institutional support of the Institute of Computer Science RVO 67985807.

References

1. Ito, Y.: Finite mapping by neural networks and truth functions. Math. Sci. **17**, 69–77 (1992)
2. Pinkus, A.: Approximation theory of the MLP model in neural networks. Acta Numer. **8**, 143–195 (1999). https://doi.org/10.1017/S0962492900002919
3. Bengio, Y., Delalleau, O., Roux, N.L.: The curse of highly variable functions for local kernel machines. In: Advances in Neural Information Processing Systems, vol. 18, pp. 107–114. MIT Press (2006)
4. Kůrková, V.: Constructive lower bounds on model complexity of shallow perceptron networks. Neural Comput. Appl. **29**, 305– 315 (2018). https://doi.org/10.1007/s00521-017-2965-0
5. Kůrková, V.: Limitations of shallow networks representing finite mappings. Neural Comput. Appl. (2018). https://doi.org/10.1007/s00521-018-3680-1
6. Lin, H., Tegmark, M., Rolnick, D.: Why does deep and cheap learning work so well? J. Stat. Phys. **168**, 1223–1247 (2017). https://doi.org/10.1007/s10955-017-1836-5
7. Kainen, P.C., Kůrková, V.: Quasiorthogonal dimension of Euclidean spaces. Appl. Math. Lett. **6**, 7–10 (1993). https://doi.org/10.1016/0893-9659(93)90023-G
8. Kůrková, V., Sanguineti, M.: Classification by sparse neural networks. IEEE Trans. Neural Netw. Learn. Syst. (2019). https://doi.org/10.1109/TNNLS.2018.2888517
9. Hoeffding, W.: Probability inequalities for sums of bounded random variables. J. Am. Stat. Assoc. **58**, 13–30 (1963). https://doi.org/10.1080/01621459.1963.10500830
10. Chernoff, H.: A measure of asymptotic efficiency for tests of a hypothesis based on the sum of observations. Ann. Math. Stat. **23**, 493–507 (1952). https://doi.org/10.1214/aoms/1177729330
11. Azuma, K.: Weighted sums of certain dependent random variables. Tohoku Math. J. **19**, 357–367 (1967). https://doi.org/10.2748/tmj/1178243286
12. Dubhashi, D., Panconesi, A.: Concentration of Measure for the Analysis of Randomized Algorithms. Cambridge University Press, Cambridge (2009). https://doi.org/10.1017/CBO9780511581274
13. Ball, K.: An elementary introduction to modern convex geometry. In: Levy, S. (ed.) Flavors of Geometry, pp. 1–58. Cambridge University Press, Cambridge (1997)
14. Matoušek, J.: Lectures on Discrete Geometry. Springer, New York (2002). https://doi.org/10.1007/978-1-4613-0039-7
15. Kůrková, V., Sanguineti, M.: Probabilistic lower bounds for approximation by shallow perceptron networks. Neural Netw. **91**, 34–41 (2017). https://doi.org/10.1016/j.neunet.2017.04.003
16. Haussler, D.: Sphere packing numbers for subsets of the Boolean n-cube with bounded Vapnik-Chervonenkis dimension. J. Comb. Theory A **69**(2), 217–232 (1995). https://doi.org/10.1016/0097-3165(95)90052-7
17. Cucker, F., Smale, S.: On the mathematical foundations of learning. Bull. Am. Math. Soc. **39**, 1–49 (2002). https://doi.org/10.1090/S0273-0979-01-00923-5
18. Vapnik, V.: The Nature of Statistical Learning Theory. Springer, New York (1997). https://doi.org/10.1007/978-1-4757-3264-1

19. Gorban, A., Tyukin, I.: Stochastic separation theorems. Neural Netw. **94**, 255–259 (2017). https://doi.org/10.1016/j.neunet.2017.07.014
20. Gorban, A.N., Golubkov, A., Grechuk, B., Mirkes, E.M., Tyukin, I.Y.: Correction of AI systems by linear discriminants: probabilistic foundations. Inf. Sci. **466**, 303–322 (2018). https://doi.org/10.1016/j.ins.2018.07.040
21. Rennie, J., Shih, L., Teevan, J., Karger, D.: Tackling the poor assumptions of naive Bayes classifiers. In: Proceedings of 20th International Conference on Machine Learning (ICML 2003), pp. 616–623 (2003)

New Architectures

Tree Memory Networks for Sequence Processing

Frederik Diehl[1(✉)] and Alois Knoll[2]

[1] fortiss GmbH, Munich, Germany
diehl@fortiss.org
[2] Chair for Robotics and Embedded Systems,
Technische Universität München, Munich, Germany

Abstract. Long-term dependencies are difficult to learn using Recurrent Neural Networks due to the vanishing and exploding gradient problems, since their hidden transform operation is applied linearly in sequence length. We introduce a new layer type (the Tree Memory Unit), whose weight application scales logarithmically in the sequence length. We evaluate this on two pathologically hard memory benchmarks and two datasets. On those three tasks which require long-term dependencies, it strongly outperforms Long Short-Term Memory baselines. However, it does show weaker performance on sequences with few long-term dependencies. We believe that our approach can lead to more efficient sequence learning if used on sequences with long-term dependencies.

1 Introduction

Deep Recurrent Neural Networks (RNNs) have shown great success in various applications such as speech recognition, translation, or reinforcement learning. However, they still suffer from difficulties in learning long-term dependencies, mostly due to the vanishing or exploding gradient problem [11] which means the gradient norm scales linearly with the sequence length. Similarly, Convolutional Neural Network (CNN)-based architectures achieve good results on real-world sequence problems [22] but have a sharply delimited horizon.

Inspired by Pollack [19], we argue that processing a sequence using a tree structure of merging steps allows us to greatly lessen the issue of vanishing gradients, since merging scales logarithmically with sequence length. However, in our experiments Recursive Neural Networks (RvNNs) were unable to solve some very simple tasks like outputting the currently seen symbol of a sequence.

Therefore, we propose a new layer type: The Tree Memory Unit (TMU), which aims to combine the advantages of both RNNs and RvNNs. Our model consists of an ordered list of binary tree state representations. Our architecture ensures that:

(a) contrary to RNNs, which scale with $O(t)$, the number of gradient applications for t timesteps scales with $O(\log t)$.

I. V. Tetko et al. (Eds.): ICANN 2019, LNCS 11727, pp. 431–443, 2019.
https://doi.org/10.1007/978-3-030-30487-4_34

(b) the number of gradient applications is at most equal to the number of gradient applications in an RNN.
(c) contrary to RvNNs, the computation structure is similar for every timestep.

We empirically evaluate several choices for the TMU layer architecture and compare it with RNN architectures on a number of different problems.

2 Related Work

The history of RNNs has been shaped by the exploding and vanishing gradient issues [3,11], both of which can cause learning to misbehave either through learning instability or lack of a gradient for early elements of the sequence. While gradient clipping [18] is effective at alleviating exploding gradients, vanishing gradients have been the focus of much research, whether through new memory units, attention mechanisms, or by engineering properties of the transition functions.

One of the first proposed solutions were Long Short-Term Memory (LSTM) units [11]. Since their inception, multiple variations like Gated Recurrent Units (GRUs) [5] have been proposed (for a comprehensive overview see Greff et al. [10]). All of them share the design paradigm of a core state whose updating is dependent on gating functions.

Orthogonal to this redesign, attention mechanisms have been proposed [2]. These alleviate the vanishing gradient since the attention centre can be moved without incurring additional gradient applications. Relatedly, external memory can be introduced in sequence processing [9], and similarly avoids gradient decreases over longer times.

RvNNs [19] have seen their main application in natural language processing, for example by Socher et al. [20]. They process sequences in a tree structure, which should cause gradient applications to scale only logarithmically in the sequence length. Specialized variants of these RvNN have been used in natural language processing [4] with convincing results, and have been combined with LSTMs for application on parse trees [21].

While RvNNs have not found much use outside of natural language processing, dilated convolutions [23] and especially WaveNet's dilated causal convolutions [22] can be seen as an explicit height-limited tree structure without weight sharing.

3 Tree Memory Unit

TMU layers are based on three ideas: (i) Hidden states in a recurrent model can be merged by an operation in vector space, (ii) older states probably contain information that is less relevant to the present, and (iii) well-chosen rules allow us to restrict merge operations to at most $O(\log n)$ per timestep.

3.1 Base TMU Model

TMUs are a neural network layer. Like simple recurrent or LSTM layers, they combine an in-layer memory with transformations which take new inputs and old states to produce a new state and new output. However, a TMU state is not a single vector but a list of vectors in the shared memory space $\mathbb{R}^n$.

We define three transformations operating on the memory space:

$$e: \mathbb{R}^i \rightarrow \mathbb{R}^n, \quad m: \mathbb{R}^{2*n} \rightarrow \mathbb{R}^n, \quad s: \mathbb{R}^{2*n} \rightarrow \mathbb{R}^n.$$

The embedding transformation e embeds an input sample from the input space $\mathbb{R}^i$ into hidden space. Both the merging transformation m and the summary transformation s take two states to create a new state. Throughout this work, we represent these transformations as neural networks, parameterized by θ_e, θ_m, and θ_s. Usually, these are single-layer fully-connected networks using the ReLU activation function. The whole model is then parameterized by $\theta = (\theta_e, \theta_m, \theta_c)$.

Internally, each TMU contains an ordered list of state cells. Each of these cells is either empty or contains one state. This is shown in Fig. 1a. By using the merging transformation recursively, we combine several states, each of which represents several timesteps from the original sequence.

We restrict each internal cell to only contain states with a certain horizon (number of timesteps it represents). Specifically, each pair of internal state cell contains states of exactly 2^i steps, where i is the zero-indexed pair index. As an example, the first state cell pair in Fig. 1a contains two states with a one-step horizon, and the second and third pair contain one state each with a horizon of two and four steps respectively.

New states are inserted into the front pair of the memory list. If a pair is not completely filled, the new state will be inserted in the first cell, displacing the old state to the second cell. If the pair is already filled, the old states will be merged using the merging transformation m—producing a state of double the horizon of the old ones—and the procedure continues recursively in the next pair. This is shown in Fig. 1b. At the end of the list, a new pair is created and the last state inserted.

A TMU's memory size is unbounded. However, because memory is organized as a balanced binary tree, memory size only grows logarithmically in the number of timesteps.

To generate the output for a timestep, the summary transformation is applied recursively to all states, starting with the oldest. This ensures that more recent timesteps have fewer transformations applied to them.

Since the actual structure of a TMU layer does not depend on the input and is instead fixed for the number of timesteps, we can unroll a TMU layer into a fixed computation graph. Figure 2 depicts such a computation graph. Each perfect binary tree is visible by following the merging representations (black arrows). This also shows the efficiency we can achieve through this procedure: Every merge and summary operation on the same level can be batched and executed in parallel.

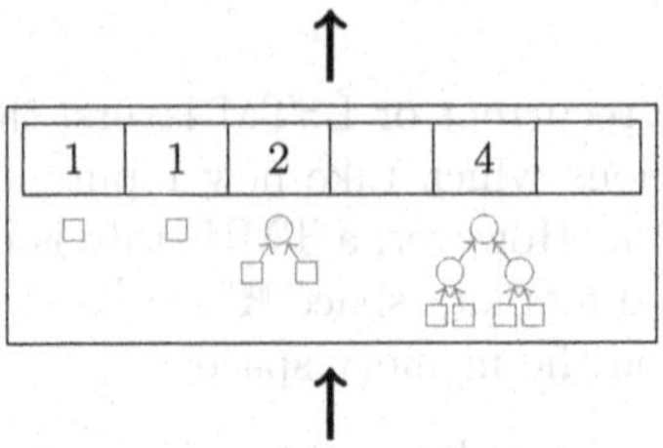

(a) Internal memory of a TMU layer. Each pair of state cells (rectangles) contains one or two states with a certain horizon. The represented tree for each state (gray) is shown with merging as circles and the encoded inputs as rectangles.

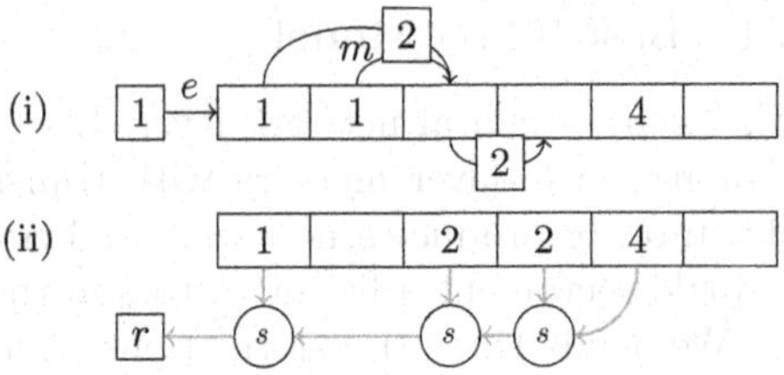

(b) Insertion procedure. (i) *Merging Phase*: A new state of horizon 1 is inserted. Since the first pair is full, its states are merged. The new state (with horizon 2) is inserted into the next pair. (ii) *Summary Phase*: After inserting the new state, iterative summarizing produces the new output r.

Fig. 1. Internals of a TMU.

3.2 Number of Gradient Applications

The application of the hidden-to-hidden transformation in RNNs (both simple and more advanced architecture like LSTMs) scales linearly in the sequence length t. This can easily result in a vanishing or exploding gradient.

In contrast, the underlying memory structure of a TMU layer is a balanced binary tree. Since transformations follow the leaf-root path (see Fig. 2), they scale only logarithmically with the sequence length. It is therefore much more robust to both vanishing and exploding gradients.

More specifically, the maximum number of transformations is applied to the chronologically first sequence element. In the computation graph, this first sequence element is part of the largest perfect binary tree, whose size scales with $O(\log t)$. Therefore, both merging and summary transformations are also applied $O(\log t)$ times. The total number of transformations therefore scales with $O(\log t)$.

3.3 Architecture Variations

In this section, we report a number of different architecture choices we evaluated. These include the influence of increasing depth, several strategies to decrease the number of parameters, and a restricted memory size.

Increasing Depth: Deep Neural Networks (DNNs), both CNNs and RNNs, greatly benefit from using more layers. We evaluate increasing depth both by stacking more TMU layers sequentially and by using deeper networks for the embedding, merging, and summary transformations.

Reducing Parameters: Another approach is to reduce the number of parameters per state complexity. To achieve this, we can combine the merging and

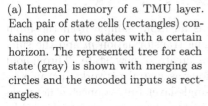

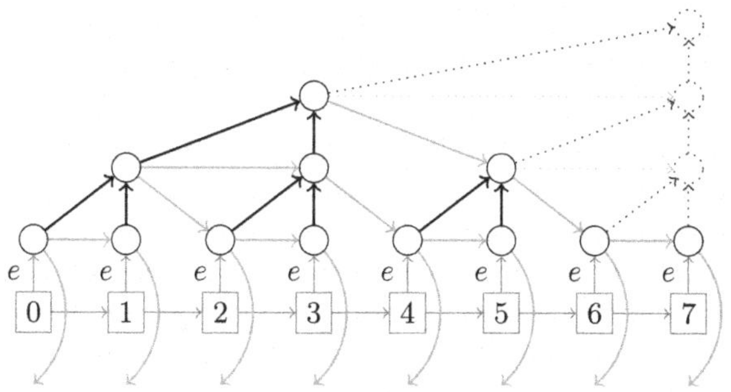

Fig. 2. Unrolled computation graph of a TMU layer on a sequence of length 8. Each sequence element (gray rectangle) is first encoded using the encoding transformation e. Afterwards, the nodes are merged consecutively in an upwards pass (black arrows). In the downward pass, we then successively summarize two nodes (represented by blue arrows) and finally produce the sequence output. Each arrow type represents applying the same transformation. As an example, timestep 0 has two merge and three summary operations applied to produce the output at timestep 7. Dotted operations are unnecessary, but have been drawn to show future growth. (Color figure online)

the summary transformations, since their input and output space is identical. We have also experimented with treating each memory dimension as separate (i.e. diagonal matrices for merging and summary transforms). However, this performed significantly worse than any alternative. We therefore did not pursue this further.

Limited Memory: The base model assumes an unbounded and resizable memory. A limited-memory variant of the TMU can be implemented by restricting the number of states stored in the memory. For this, we change the procedure for introducing new states: We keep an overflow state and whenever a merge occurs which would break the memory limit, we instead merge it with the overflow state. While this breaks the property of similarly-growing memory horizons, it allows us to add an effectively unlimited number of states during inference without increasing memory size or forgetting previous states.

4 Experiments

We evaluate the TMU on a total of four different task: An adaption of the adding task [11], the copy task [1], the pixel-wise permutated MNIST task [16], and the Wikipedia character prediction task.

4.1 Evaluation Procedure

As a baseline, we use both a simple RNN and LSTM network with the same hyperparameters as the TMUBase model. Using the same number of parameters as the TMU models, they have 200 and 100 units respectively. To ensure a fair comparison between our results, we conduct each training three times, using the random seeds 0, 1, and 2 to avoid seed-hacking. Where we mention or plot confidence bounds, these are 95% bounds.

Except for the architecture evaluation described in Sect. 4.4, we did not vary the architecture of the TMU network. Neither did we conduct extensive hyper-parameter optimization. Instead, we reused the LSTM's hyperparameter choices as given by Arjovsky et al. [1] and did not change them for TMUs. This indicates that TMUs should be fairly tolerant of hyperparameter choice. We used the Adam optimizer [14] with default parameters and trained with a batchsize of 64 and clip gradients at a magnitude of 5.

We implemented our experiments using Tensorflow. We use the Singularity containerizer [15] to enable reproducible experiments.

4.2 Synthetic Datasets

On both the adding and the copy task, we generate training (100k samples, from which we draw 5k and 10k respectively for each epoch), validation (5k), and test sets (5k).

Adding Task. The adding task provides a sequence of t pairs of numbers. The first number is sampled uniformly at random between $[0, 1)$. The second is 0 everywhere except for two timesteps, one in each half of the sequence. The goal is to output the sum of the two random numbers indicated by the two set indices.[1] A memoryless evaluation will achieve a mean squared error of 0.167.

Copy Task. The copy task, introduced by Arjovsky et al. [1], provides a sequence of length $T+20$ of one-hot encoded symbols from an alphabet of 10 (8 characters, 1 delimiter, and the 0 symbol). The first ten elements of the sequence are chosen at random from the eight characters. The remainder is set to 0 except for one set to the delimiter symbol, ten symbols before the end. The goal is to produce the 0 symbol until reading the delimiter and then copying the first ten symbols of the input. The categorical cross-entropy of the memoryless strategy, outputting 0 until reading the delimiter and then drawing the last ten characters at random, is $\frac{10 \log 8}{T+20}$.

Permutated MNIST. The MNIST dataset [17] has long served as a simple baseline for computer vision tasks. The Sequential MNIST task [16] converts this dataset into a simple sequence problem. Like a scanning beam sweeping the MNIST image line by line and pixel by pixel, it produces a sequence of dimensionality 1. Each entry contains the value of the corresponding pixel.

The Permutated MNIST task is a variation of the Sequential MNIST task. Here, a random (but fixed) permutation of pixel order is applied to every sample. This removes much of the local structure, meaning that a classifier has to be able to reason over longer distances.

[1] We note that this setup, which has become a standard for RNN evaluation, differs from the original implementation by Schmidhuber [11].

4.3 Wikipedia Dataset

The *enwik8* dataset, used in the so-called Hutter challenge [12], contains the first 10^8 bytes of the English version of Wikipedia from 2006-03-03. This includes text, markup, and links. Following Graves [8], we treat each byte as a separate character for a total of 205 distinct characters. We use the first 90 M characters as training data, and evenly split the remainder between validation and test set.

We evaluate the model using the *bits-per-character* metric

$$\sum_{t=0}^{T} - \log_2 p(x_t | x_{0:t-1}, \theta),$$

where T is the number of characters in the sequence, x_t is the tth character, and $p(x_t|x_{0:t-1}, \theta)$ is the model output conditioned on the previous characters. This is equivalent to the categorical cross-entropy scaled by $1/\log_e 2$.

We use a significantly bigger model for this dataset. Following the model setup from Chung et al. [6], we use a three-layer LSTM with a memory complexity of 191 as a baseline. We train two TMU models, both also with 1.4 M parameters. One uses a single layer with memory complexity 545, the other three layers, each with a memory complexity of 300. We also test the three-layer network with dropout with a rate of 0.2. Contrary to Chung et al. [6], we train the models on sequence lengths of 500, and reset the initial state every 100 sequences. To allow us to evenly divide the data into batches, we also reduce the batch size to 50.

4.4 Architecture Evaluation

We evaluate different choices of our architecture (see Sect. 3.3) on the permutated MNIST dataset. All of our models have approximately 41k parameters (see also Table 1 for a comparison).

For our base model, which is the model as described in Sect. 3.1, this is a memory complexity of 100. We use a singlefully-connected layer with the Rectified Linear Units (ReLUs) non-linearity for the transformations, and a fully-connected layer as output. We call this model **TMUBase**.

To evaluate the performance of increasing depth in the models, we introduce two variations. The first network, called **TMUStack**, uses three stacked TMU layers, each with a memory complexity of 54. **TMUTransform** increases the depth of the transformations, each of which is replaced by three fully-connected layers with the same dimensionality.

We also measure the effect of reducing parameters by using the same parameters for merging and summary transformations (**TMUTied**). Lastly, we also evaluate the effect of limited memory.

Table 1. Memory dimensionality and number of trainable parameters by architecture permutation. Layers is the number of full TMU layers. Int. Layers is the number of internal layers per TMU. Weights specifies whether the two transformation functions have separate parameters.

Model	Parameters	Complexity	Layers	Int. Layers	Weights
TMUBase	41 410	100	1	1	Separate
TMUStack	41 914	54	3	1	Separate
TMUTransform	41 914	54	1	3	Separate
TMUTied	41 030	140	1	1	Tied

5 Results

We report our results in three sections: We first optimize the TMU model's architecture, then apply it to three synthetic benchmarks. Afterwards, we report the results on a language-modelling dataset. We also introduce a significantly smaller model (**TMUSmall**), with only about 8.5k parameters.

5.1 Architecture Evaluation

The performance of the four different architectures from Sect. 4.4 are depicted in Fig. 3a. We see that deeper transformation networks (TMUTransform) are more difficult to optimize and leads to a worse result. Similarly, at least for this problem, stacking multiple TMU layers (TMUStack) is not worth the loss in memory complexity. Neither is parameter-sharing (TMUTied). Accordingly, we use TMUBase for subsequent experiments.

Figure 3b shows the effect of limiting the TMU's memory. As can be seen, a higher memory generally results in a better performance. However, even with a memory limit of 4, the TMU network outperforms a comparable LSTM network.

5.2 Synthetic Tasks

We report the result of a comparison of the TMU with the baseline models on the three synthetic tasks. On all three, the TMU models strongly outperform the recurrent baselines.

Adding Task. As Fig. 4a shows, both TMU models are able to solve every adding task within the provided 50 epochs. Note especially that learning appears to scale roughly logarithmically with the sequence length, supporting our assumption on the gradient scaling. uRNNs [1] need 5x as many samples for smaller $t = 200$ and fail to solve the $t = 750$ adding task.

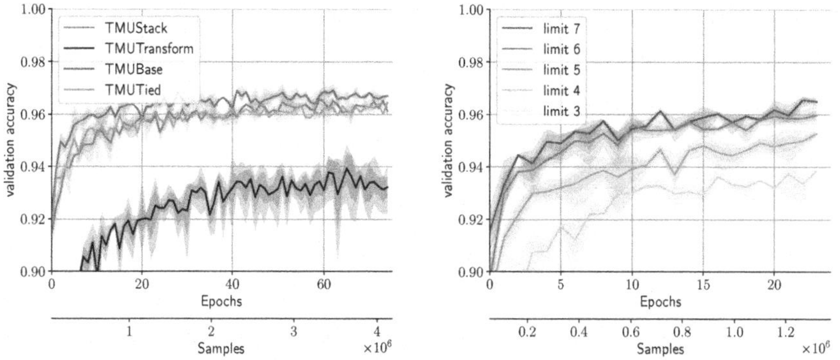

(a) Validation accuracy using different architectures. Note that most architectures perform similar, except for more complicated transforms.

(b) Validation accuracy for different memory limits. Note that smaller memory limits performed much worse, and have therefore not been plotted.

Fig. 3. Validation accuracy on the pMNIST task for different architecture choices.

Copy Task. Both TMUBase and TMUSmall are able to solve the copy task for sequence lengths of 100 and 200. However, they fail to solve the task for a length of 1000. Despite this, they still consistently outperform the LSTM and RNN models, which fail to solve the task for any length. The bad performance of LSTMs is perhaps surprising, but consistent with literature [1]. Jing et al. [13] show a comparison between three different implementations of unitary RNNs which do solve the $t = 1000$ copy task.

Permutated MNIST. Figure 5 compares the performance of a TMU model with both an Simple RNN (sRNN) and an LSTM model. As can be seen, the TMU model both converges significantly faster and to a better value. In fact, they achieve a higher performance than both of the baseline models' final result after just one epoch. This result is also close to TMUBase's performance on the sequential MNIST task (98.2% vs 96.2%). This further confirms our assumption of resilience against long-term dependencies. To our knowledge, TMUBase achieves a new state-of-the-art performance on the permutated MNIST task, performing better than the batch-normalized LSTM model from Cooijmans et al. [7].

5.3 Language Modelling

We report our results and the original baseline from Chung et al. [6] in Table 3 and Fig. 6. Here, stacking multiple TMU results in better performance compared to single-layer TMUs. We can also see the faster convergence of the TMU models. However, the LSTM model still achieves slightly greater final accuracy.

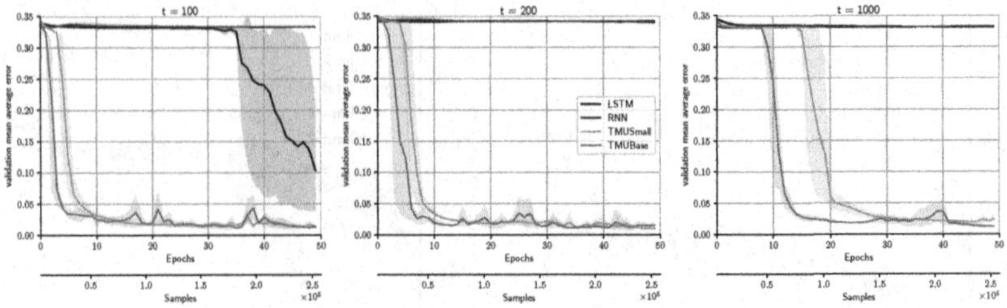

(a) Performance on the adding task.

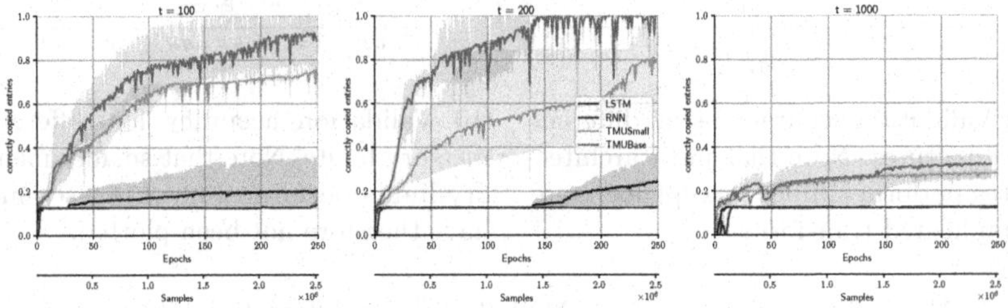

(b) Performance on the copy task.

Fig. 4. Performance comparison on the memory tasks. Each shows three different sequence lengths of 100, 200, and 500.

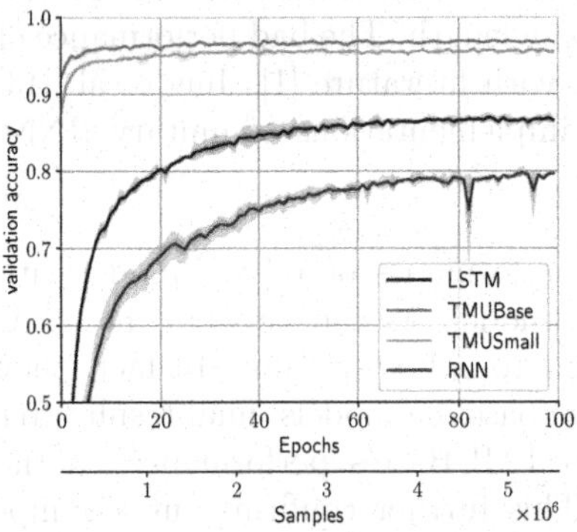

Fig. 5. Performance comparison of TMU with two RNN models on pMNIST task.

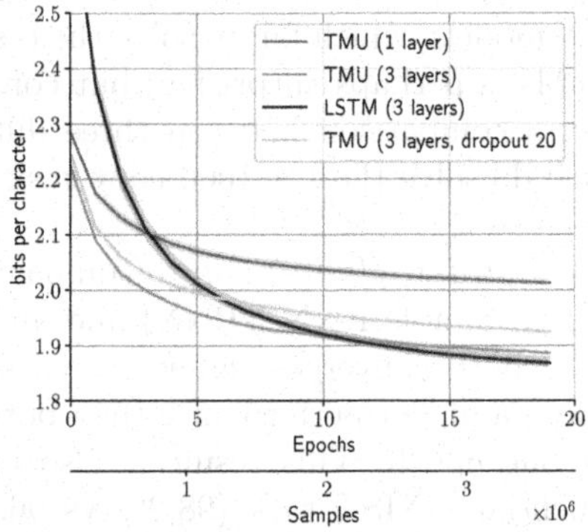

Fig. 6. Validation bits-per-character for three different models on the enwik8 dataset.

Interestingly, the LSTM model performs worse on the training set, which suggests that regularization should make the TMU model perform better. However, our experiments with dropout apparently over-regularized, resulting in worse performance.

Table 2. Accuracy on the pMNIST task. (*) Results are from Arjovsky et al. [1], Jing et al. [13], and Cooijmans et al. [7] respectively.

Model	Parameters	Test Acc
RNN	42.4k	0.798 ± 0.005
LSTM	42.1k	0.866 ± 0.004
URNN*	~9k	0.914
EURNN*	13.3k	0.937
BN-LSTM*	42.1k	0.954
TMUBase	41.4k	0.962 ± 0.003
TMUSmall	8.7k	0.953 ± 0.003

Table 3. Performance of different models on the *enwik8* dataset. (*) Result is from Chung et al. [6].

Model	Val BPC
LSTM* (3 layers)	1.868
LSTM (3 layers)	1.868 ± 0.012
TMU (1 layer)	2.003 ± 0.004
TMU (3 layers)	1.884 ± 0.003
TMU (3 layers, dropout)	1.915 ± 0.005

We also note that we saw significant speed differences between TMU and LSTM models. Particularly, we saw a less-than-linear speed increase in sequence length for the TMU, which happens due to intelligent batching of matrix multiplications and mostly independent computations per timestep.

We also conducted several experiments using TMUs with translations, but were unable to achieve satisfactory results. We believe this is due to a lack of long-term dependencies.

6 Conclusion

We proposed a novel layer type for neural network sequence processing which, by storing several states, allows gradients to scale logarithmically in the sequence length. We validated this on a total of two pathologically hard benchmark datasets and two real-world datasets.

On all but one task, our model strongly outperformed comparable LSTM models. On the last task, it performed comparably, if slightly worse. However, we were unable to achieve satisfactory results on a translation task.

We believe the Tree Memory Unit to provide an excellent tool to tackle sequence processing with long-term dependencies. At the same time, many of the approaches previously applied to RNNs can potentially also be applied to our approach, and we believe their application will further improve the results of TMUs. Especially the question of regularization remains open.

The TMU, as a drop-in layer, should be able to replace any type of RNN layer in already-developed neural networks. Based on our experiments, TMU-based models are a viable alternative to LSTM models on sequences with long-term dependencies.

References

1. Arjovsky, M., Shah, A., Bengio, Y.: Unitary evolution recurrent neural networks. In: Proceedings of the 33rd International Conference on Machine Learning, vol. 48, pp. 1120–1128 (2016). http://arxiv.org/abs/1511.06464
2. Bahdanau, D., Cho, K., Bengio, Y.: Neural Machine Translation by Jointly Learning to Align and Translate. arXiv preprint arXiv:1409.0473 (2014). https://doi.org/10.1146/annurev.neuro.26.041002.131047. ISSN 0147–006X
3. Bengio, Y., Simard, P., Frasconi, P.: Learning Long-Term Dependencies with Gradient Descent is Difficult (1994). ISSN 19410093
4. Bowman, S.R., Gauthier, J., Rastogi, A., Gupta, R., Manning, C.D., Potts, C.: A Fast Unified Model for Parsing and Sentence Understanding. arXiv preprint arXiv:1603.06021 (2016). https://doi.org/10.18653/v1/P16-1139
5. Cho, K., et al.: Learning phrase representations using RNN encoder-decoder for statistical machine translation. In: Proceedings of the 2014 Conference on Empirical Methods in Natural Language Processing, pp. 1724–1734 (2014). https://doi.org/10.3115/v1/D14-1179, http://arxiv.org/abs/1406.1078. ISBN 9781937284961
6. Chung, J., Gulcehre, C., Cho, K., Bengio, Y.: Gated feedback recurrent neural networks. In: International Conference on Machine Learning, pp. 2067–2075 (2015). https://doi.org/10.1145/2661829.2661935, http://arxiv.org/abs/1502.02367. ISBN 9781634393973
7. Cooijmans, T., Ballas, N., Laurent, C., Gülçehre, Ç., Courville, A.: Recurrent Batch Normalization. arXiv preprint arXiv:1603.09025 (2016). https://doi.org/10.1227/01.NEU.0000210260.55124.A4. ISSN 16113349
8. Graves, A.: Generating Sequences with Recurrent Neural Networks. arXiv preprint arXiv:1308.0850, August 2013. https://doi.org/10.1145/2661829.2661935. ISSN 18792782
9. Graves, A., Wayne, G., Danihelka, I.: Neural Turing Machines. arXiv preprint arXiv:1410.5401 (2014). https://doi.org/10.3389/neuro.12.006.2007. ISSN 2041–1723
10. Greff, K., Srivastava, R.K., Koutnik, J., Steunebrink, B.R., Schmidhuber, J.: LSTM: a search space odyssey. IEEE Trans. Neural Netw. Learn. Syst. (2016). https://doi.org/10.1109/TNNLS.2016.2582924. ISSN 21622388
11. Hochreiter, S., Schmidhuber, J.: Long short-term memory. Neural Comput. **9**(8), 1735–1780 (1997). https://doi.org/10.1162/neco.1997.9.8.1735, http://www7.informatik.tu-muenchen.de/~hochreit%5Cnwww.idsia.ch/~juergen. ISSN 0899–7667
12. Hutter, M.: The human knowledge compression contest, p. 6 (2012). http://prize.hutter1.net
13. Jing, L., et al.: Tunable Efficient Unitary Neural Networks (EUNN) and their application to RNNs. arXiv preprint arXiv:1612.05231 (2016). ISSN 1938–7228
14. Kingma, D., Ba, J.: Adam: A method for stochastic optimization. arXiv preprint arXiv:1412.6980 (2014)
15. Kurtzer, G.M., Sochat, V., Bauer, M.W.: Singularity: Scientific containers for mobility of compute. PLoS ONE **12**(5), e0177459 (2017)
16. Le, Q.V., Jaitly, N., Hinton, G.E.: A Simple Way to Initialize Recurrent Networks of Rectified Linear Units. arXiv preprint arXiv:1504.00941 (2015). https://doi.org/10.1109/72.279181. ISSN 1045–9227
17. LeCun, Y., Bottou, L., Bengio, Y., Haffner, P.: Gradient-based learning applied to document recognition. Proc. IEEE **86**(11), 2278–2324 (1998). https://doi.org/10.1109/5.726791. ISSN 00189219

18. Pascanu, R., Mikolov, T., Bengio, Y.: On the difficulty of training recurrent neural networks. In: International Conference on Machine Learning, pp. 1310–1318 (2013). https://doi.org/10.1109/72.279181, http://arxiv.org/abs/1211.5063. ISBN 08997667 (ISSN)
19. Pollack, J.B.: Recursive distributed representations. Artif. Intell. **46**(1), 77–105 (1990). https://doi.org/10.1016/0004-3702(90)90005-K. ISSN 00043702
20. Socher, R., Perelygin, A., Wu, J.: Recursive deep models for semantic compositionality over a sentiment treebank. In: Proceedings of the 2013 Conference on Empirical Methods in Natural Language Processing, pp. 1631–1642 (2013). https://doi.org/10.1371/journal.pone.0073791, http://nlp.stanford.edu/~socherr/EMNLP2013_RNTN.pdf%5Cnwww.aclweb.org/anthology/D13-1170%5Cnaclweb.org/supplementals/D/D13/D13-1170.Attachment.pdf%5Cnoldsite.aclweb.org/anthology-new/D/D13/D13-1170.pdf. ISBN 9781937284978
21. Tai, K.S., Socher, R., Manning, C.D.: Improved Semantic Representations From Tree-Structured Long Short-Term Memory Networks. arXiv preprint arXiv:1503.00075 (2015). https://doi.org/10.1515/popets-2015-0023. ISSN 9781941643723
22. van den Oord, A., et al.: WaveNet: A Generative Model for Raw Audio. arXiv preprint arXiv:1609.03499 (2016). https://doi.org/10.1109/ICASSP.2009.4960364. ISSN 0899–7667
23. Yu, F., Koltun, V.: Multi-Scale Context Aggregation by Dilated Convolutions. arXiv preprint arXiv:1511.07122 (2015). https://doi.org/10.16373/j.cnki.ahr.150049. ISSN 00237205

On Deep Set Learning and the Choice of Aggregations

Maximilian Soelch(✉), Adnan Akhundov, Patrick van der Smagt, and Justin Bayer

argmax.ai, Volkswagen Group Machine Learning Research Lab, Munich, Germany
m.soelch@argmax.ai

Abstract. Recently, it has been shown that many functions on sets can be represented by sum decompositions. These decompositons easily lend themselves to neural approximations, extending the applicability of neural nets to set-valued inputs—Deep Set learning. This work investigates a core component of Deep Set architecture: aggregation functions. We suggest and examine alternatives to commonly used aggregation functions, including learnable recurrent aggregation functions. Empirically, we show that the Deep Set networks are highly sensitive to the choice of aggregation functions: beyond improved performance, we find that learnable aggregations lower hyper-parameter sensitivity and generalize better to out-of-distribution input size.

Keywords: Set functions · Deep learning · Representation learning

1 Introduction

Machine learning algorithms make implicit assumptions on the data set encoding. For instance, feed-forward neural networks assume that data is encoded in a unique vector representation, e. g. by one-hot encoding categorical variables. Yet, many interesting learning tasks revolve around data sets consisting of sets: depth vision with 3D point clouds, probability distributions represented by finite samples, or operations on unstructured sets of tags [16,21,26].

Naively, a population[1] is embedded by ordering and concatenating particle vectors into a matrix. While standard neural networks can learn to *imitate* order-invariant behavior, e.g. by random input permutation at each gradient step, such architectures are no true set functions. Further, they cannot easily handle varying population sizes. This motivated research into order-invariant neural architectures [4,6,20,24]. From this, the Deep Set framework emerged, proving that many interesting invariant functions allow for a sum decomposition [18,25, 29]. It allows for straightforward application of neural networks that are order-invariant by design, and can handle varying population sizes.

[1] Disambiguating terms like *set* and *sample*, we discuss *data sets* of *populations* of *particles*.

I. V. Tetko et al. (Eds.): ICANN 2019, LNCS 11727, pp. 444–457, 2019.
https://doi.org/10.1007/978-3-030-30487-4_35

In this work, we study aggregations—the component of a Deep Set architecture that induces order invariance by mapping a variable-sized population to a fixed-sized description. After discussing desirable properties and extending the theory around aggregation functions, we suggest multiple alternatives, including learnable recurrent aggregation functions. Studying them in several experimental settings, we find that the choice of aggregation impacts not only the performance, but also hyper-parameter sensitivity and robustness to varying population sizes. In the light of these findings, we argue for new evaluation techniques for neural set functions.

2 Order-Invariant Deep Architectures

We discuss populations $\mathcal{X}$ of particles $\mathbf{x}$ from a particle space $\mathscr{X} \subset \mathbb{R}^d$, i. e. $\mathbf{x} \in \mathcal{X}$ and $\mathcal{X} \subset \mathscr{X} \subset \mathbb{R}^d$. We are further interested in representations $\mathbf{X} \in \mathbb{R}^{p \times d}, p = |\mathcal{X}|$, achieved by concatenating the particles of $\mathcal{X}$. A permutation of the particle axis with a permutation π is denoted by $\mathbf{X}_\pi$, i. e. $\mathbf{X} \neq \mathbf{X}_\pi$ but $\mathbf{X} \equiv \mathcal{X} \equiv \mathbf{X}_\pi$. Data sets $\mathcal{D}$ consist of finite populations $\mathcal{X}_i$ of potentially varying size.

2.1 Invariance, Equivariance, and Decomposition of Invariant Functions

We study invariant functions according to

Definition 1 (Invariance). *A function f on the power set $\mathcal{P}(\mathscr{X})$ is* order-invariant *if for any permutation π and input $\{\mathbf{x}_1, \ldots, \mathbf{x}_N\} \in \mathcal{P}(\mathscr{X})$*

$$f\left(\{\mathbf{x}_1, \ldots, \mathbf{x}_N\}\right) = f\left(\{\mathbf{x}_{\pi(1)}, \ldots, \mathbf{x}_{\pi(N)}\}\right).$$

If it is clear from the context, we will call such functions *invariant*. When the input is embedded as a matrix, Definition 1 can be formulated as $f(\mathbf{X}) = f(\mathbf{X}_\pi)$. A related, important notion is that of *equivariant* functions:

Definition 2 (Equivariance). *A function f is* equivariant *if input permutation results in equivalent output permutation, i. e. for any $\mathbf{X}$ and $\mathbf{X}_\pi$*

$$f(\mathbf{X}_\pi) = (f(\mathbf{X}))_\pi.$$

In [29], a defining structural property of order-invariant functions was proven:

Theorem 1 (Deep Sets, [29]). *A function f on populations $\mathcal{X}$ from* countable *particle space $\mathscr{X}$ is invariant if and only if there exists a decomposition,*

$$f(\mathcal{X}) = \rho \sum_{\mathbf{x} \in \mathcal{X}} \phi(\mathbf{x}),$$

with appropriate functions ϕ and ρ.

We call such functions *sum-decomposable*; this follows [25], where severe pathologies for *uncountable* input spaces are pointed out:

1. There exist invariant functions that have no sum decomposition.
2. There exist sum decompositions that are everywhere-discontinuous.
3. Even relevant functions such as $\max(\mathcal{X})$ cannot be *continuously* decomposed when the image space of the embedding ϕ is smaller than the population size $|\mathcal{X}|$.

As a consequence they refine Theorem 1 to

Theorem 2 (Uncountable Particle Spaces, [25]). *A* continuous *function f on* finite *populations $\mathcal{X}$, $|\mathcal{X}| \leq p$, is invariant if and only if it is sum-decomposable via $\mathbb{R}^p$.*

That is, for arbitrary f, the image space of ϕ has to have at least dimension p, which is both necessary and sufficient. More restrictive in scope than Theorem 1, it is more applicable in practice where most function approximators—neural networks, Gaussian processes—are continuous.

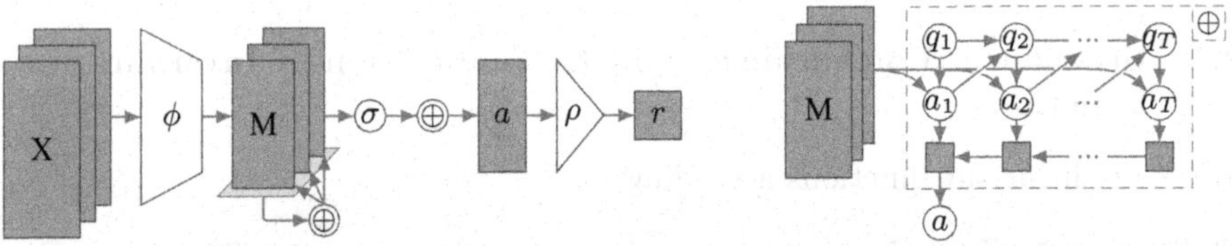

(a) Deep Set Framework. (b) Recurrent Aggregation.

Fig. 1. *Left*: Deep Set architecture, Eqs. (2) to (5), with a single equivariant layer, Eq. (1). Aggregation functions are depicted by $\oplus$. *Right*: Recurrent aggregation function, Eqs. (11) to (15). Queries to memory are produced in a forward pass, responses aggregated in a backward pass.

2.2 Deep Sets

A generic invariant neural architecture emerges from Theorems 1 and 2 by using neural networks for ρ and ϕ, respectively. In practice, to allow for higher-level particle interaction during the embedding ϕ, *equivariant* neural layers are introduced [29],

$$\text{equivariant}(\mathbf{X}) = \sigma\left(\mathbf{X} - \mathbf{1}\alpha(\mathbf{X})\right), \tag{1}$$

where $\sigma(\cdot)$ denotes a per-particle feed-forward layer, and $\alpha(\cdot)$ denotes an aggregation. Aggregations—our object of study—induce invariance by mapping a population to a fixed-size description, typically e. g. sum, mean, or max. The full architecture is

$$\mathbf{m}_i = \mathrm{embed}(\mathbf{x}_i) \tag{2}$$

$$\mathbf{C} = \mathrm{combine}(\mathbf{M}) \qquad (\mathbf{M} = [\mathbf{m}_i^\top]) \tag{3}$$

$$\mathbf{a} = \mathrm{aggregate}(\mathbf{C}) \tag{4}$$

$$\mathbf{r} = \mathrm{process}(\mathbf{a}), \tag{5}$$

with ϕ implemented by a per-particle embedding followed by an equivariant combination function consisting of equivariant layers. Summation is replaced by a generic aggregation operation. In [18,29], the max operation is suggested as an alternative summation. Lastly, ρ can be implemented by arbitrary functions, since the aggregation in Eq. (4) is already invariant. This framework is depicted in Fig. 1a.

2.3 Order Matters

Recurrent neural networks can handle set-valued input by feeding one particle at a time. However, it has been shown that the result is sensitive to order, and an invariant *read-process-write* architecture has been suggested as a remedy [24]:

$$\mathbf{q}_t = \mathrm{LSTM}(\mathbf{q}_{t-1}, \mathbf{a}_{t-1}) \tag{6}$$

$$\hat{w}_{i,t} = \mathrm{attention}(\mathbf{m}_i, \mathbf{q}_t) \qquad (=\mathbf{m}_i^\top \mathbf{q}_t) \tag{7}$$

$$\mathbf{w}_t = \mathrm{softmax}(\hat{\mathbf{w}}_t) \tag{8}$$

$$\mathbf{a}_t = \sum w_{i,t}\mathbf{m}_i \tag{9}$$

$$\mathbf{a} = \mathbf{a}_T \tag{10}$$

An embedded memory is queried The invariant result $\mathbf{a}_t$ is iteratively used to refine subsequent queries with an LSTM [8]. It is not obvious how to cast the recurrent structure into the setting of Eqs. (2) to (5) and Theorems 1 and 2. To the best of our knowledge, this model has only been discussed in its sequence-to-sequence context. We will revisit and refine this architecture in Sect. 3.3.

2.4 Further Related Work

Several papers introduce and discuss a Deep Set framework for dealing with set-valued inputs [18,29]. A driving force behind research into order-invariant neural networks are point clouds [17–19], where such architectures are used to perform classification and semantic segmentation of objects and scenes represented as point clouds in $\mathbb{R}^3$. It is further shown that a max decomposition allows for arbitrarily close approximation [18].

Generative models of sets have been investigated: in an extension of variational auto-encoders [11,22], the inference of latent population statistics resembles a Deep Sets architecture [4]. Generative models of point clouds are proposed by [1] and [28].

Permutation-invariant neural networks have been used for predicting dynamics of interacting objects [6]. The authors propose to embed the individual object positions in pairs using a feed-forward neural network. Similar pairwise approaches have been investigated by [2,3], and applied to relational reasoning in [23].

Weighted averages based on attention have been proposed and applied to multi-instance learning [10]. Several works have focused on higher-order particle interaction, suggesting computationally efficient approximations of Janossy pooling [15], or propose set attention blocks as an alternative to equivariant layers [14].

3 The Choice of Aggregation

The invariance of the Deep Set architecture emerges from invariance of the *aggregation function*— Eq. (4). Theorem 1 theoretically justifies summing the embeddings $\phi(\mathbf{x}_i)$. In practice, mean or max-pooling operations are used. Equally simple and invariant, they are numerically favorable for varying population sizes, controlling input magnitude to downstream layers. This section discusses alternatives and their properties.

3.1 Alterantive Aggregations

We start by justifying alternative choices with an extension of Theorems 1 and 2:

Corollary 1 (Sum Isomorphism). *Theorems 1 and 2 can be extended to aggregations of the form* $\alpha_g = g \circ \sum \circ g^{-1}$*, i. e. summations in an isomorphic space.*

Proof. From $\rho \circ \sum \circ \phi = (\rho \circ g^{-1}) \circ g \circ \sum \circ g^{-1} \circ (g \circ \phi)$, sum decompositions can be constructed from α_g-decompositions and vice versa.

This class includes, e. g., mean (with $g((x_1, \dots, x_{n+1})) = (x_1, \dots, x_n)/x_{n+1}$ and $g^{-1}(\mathbf{x}) = (\mathbf{x}^\top, 1)^\top$) and logsumexp (LΣE) (with $g = \ln$). In that light, there is an interesting case to be made for LΣE: depending on the input magnitudes, LΣE can behave akin to max (cf. Figs. 2a to c) or like a linear function akin to summation (cf. Figs. 2d to f). Operating in log space, LΣE further exhibits *diminishing returns*: N identical scalar particles x_i yield $\mathrm{L\Sigma E}(\{x_i\}) = \ln(N) + x_1$. The larger N, the smaller the output change from additional particles. Beyond making LΣE a numerically useful aggregation, diminishing returns are a desirable property from a statistical perspective, where we would like to have asymptotically consistent results.

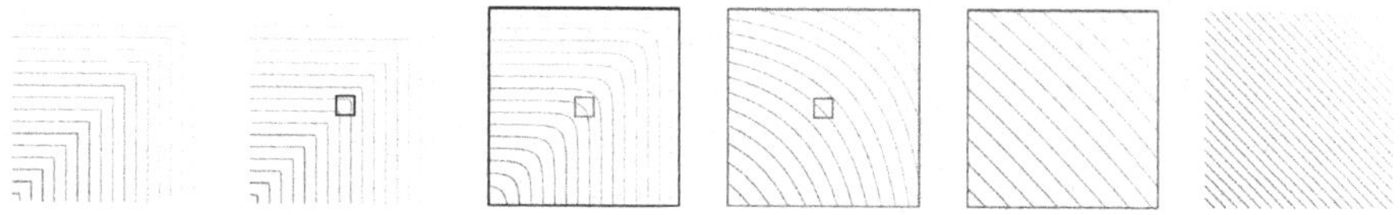

(a) max on $[-10, 10]^2$ (b) LΣE on $[-100, 100]^2$ (c) LΣE on $[-10, 10]^2$ (d) LΣE on $[-1, 1]^2$ (e) LΣE on $[-.1, .1]^2$ (f) sum on $[-10, 10]^2$

Fig. 2. Contour plots for max (left), sum (right), and logsumexp (LΣE) on two inputs. For large ranges, LΣE acts like max, shifting towards sum with decreasing input range. Matching square boxes indicate zoom between plots. Plots (a), (c), and (f) on range $[-10, 10]^2$ share contour levels.

Divide and Conquer. Commutative and associative binary operations like addition and multiplication yield invariant aggregations. Widening this perspective, we see that divide-and-conquer style operations yield invariant aggregations: order invariance is equivalent to conquering being invariant to division. Examples beyond the previously mentioned operations are logical operators such as any or all, but also sorting (generalizing max and min, and any percentile, e. g. median). While impractical for typical first-order optimization, we note that aggregations can be of very sophisticated nature.

3.2 Learnable Aggregation Functions

In [29], cf. Eqs. (2) to (5), the aggregation is the only non-learnable component. We will now investigate ways to render the aggregations learnable. In Sect. 2.3, we have seen that due to the structure of Theorem 1, recurrent architectures as suggested by [24] had been overlooked as it is not straightforward to cast them into the Deep Sets framework. Inspired by the read-process-write architecture, we suggest *recurrent aggregations*:

Definition 3 (Recurrent and Query Aggregation). *A* recurrent aggregation *is a function* $f(\mathcal{X}) = \mathbf{a}$ *that can be written recursively as:*

$$\mathbf{q}_t = \text{query}(\mathbf{q}_{t-1}, \mathbf{a}_{t-1}) \tag{11}$$

$$\hat{w}_{i,t} = \text{attention}(\mathbf{m}_i, \mathbf{q}_t) \tag{12}$$

$$\mathbf{w}_t = \text{normalize}(\hat{\mathbf{w}}_t) \tag{13}$$

$$\mathbf{a}_t = \text{reduce}\left(\{w_{i,t}\mathbf{m}_i\}\right) \tag{14}$$

$$\mathbf{a} = g\left(\mathbf{a}_{1:T}\right), \tag{15}$$

where $\mathbf{m}_i = \phi(\mathbf{x}_i)$ *is an embedding of the input population* $\{\mathbf{x}_i\}$ *and* $\mathbf{q}_1$ *is a constant. We further call the special case* $T = 1$ *(i. e. a single query* $\mathbf{q} \equiv \mathbf{q}_1$*) a* query aggregation.

As long as reduce is invariant and normalize is equivariant, recurrent and query aggregations are invariant. This architectural block is depicted in Fig. 1b.

Building upon Eqs. (6) to (10), recurrent aggregations introduce two modifications: firstly, we replace a weighted sum by a general weighted aggregation—giving us a rich combinatorial toolbox on the basis of simple invariant functions such as those mentioned in Sect. 3.1. Secondly, we add post-processing of the step-wise results $\mathbf{a}_{1:T}$. In practice, we use another recurrent network layer that processes $\mathbf{a}_{1:T}$ in reversed order. Without this modification, later queries tend to be more important, as their result is not as easily forgotten by the forward recurrence. The backward processing reverses this effect, so that the first queries tend to be more important, and the overall architecture is more robust to common fallacies of recurrent architectures, in particular unstable gradients.

Observing Eq. (14), we note that our learnable aggregation functions wrap around the previously discussed simpler non-learnable aggregations. A major benefit is that the inputs are weighted—sum becomes weighted average, for instance. This also allows the model to effectively exploit non-linearities as discussed with LΣE (cf. Fig. 2).

3.3 A Note on Universal Approximation

The key promise of *universal* approximation is that a family of approximators (e. g. neural nets, or neural sum decompositions) is dense within a wider family of interesting functions [7,9,12]. The universality granted by Theorems 1 and 2, through constructive proofs, hinges on sum aggregation. Corollary 1 grants flexibility, but does not apply to arbitrary aggregations, like max or the suggested learnable aggregations. (Note that max allows for arbitrary approximation [18].) It remains open to what extent the sum can be replaced. As such, the suggested architectures might not grant universal approximators. As we will see in Sect. 4, however, they provide useful inductive biases in practical settings, much like feed-forward neural nets are usually replaced with architectures targeted towards the task. It is worth noting that the embedding dimension constraint of Theorem 2 is rarely met, trading theoretical guarantees for test-time performance.

4 Experiments

We consider three simple aggregations: mean (or weighted sum), max, and LΣE. These are used in equivariant layers and final aggregations, and may be be wrapped into a recurrent aggregation. This combinatorially large space of configurations is tested in four experiments described in the following sections.

4.1 Mininmal Enclosing Circle

In this supervised experiment, we are trying to predict the minimal enclosing circle of a population of size 20 from a Gaussian mixture model (GMM). A sample population with target circle is depicted in Fig. 3. The sample mean does not approximate the center of the minimal enclosing circle well, and the correct solution is defined by at least three particles. The models are trained by

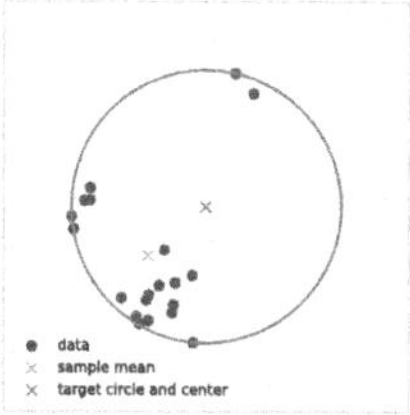

Fig. 3. Minimal enclosing example population

Table 1. Minimal enclosing circle results.

Recurrent equiv./aggr.	Best MSE	Radius MSE	Center MSE	Median best MSE
✗ / ✗	0.71	0.06	0.66	1.57
✗ / ✓	1.02	0.14	0.88	1.30
✓ / ✗	0.54	0.08	0.47	0.87
✓ / ✓	0.42	0.09	0.33	0.58

minimizing the mean squared error (MSE) towards the center and radius of the true circle (computable in linear time [27]).

Results are given in Table 1. Each row shows the best result out of 180 runs (20 runs for each of the 9 combinations of aggregations). We can see that both recurrent equivariant layers and recurrent aggregations improve the performance, with equivariant layers granting the larger performance boost. The challenge lies mostly in a better approximation of the center.

The top row indicates that an entirely non-recurrent model performs better than its counterpart with recurrent aggregation (second row). To test for a performance outlier, we compute a bootstrap estimate of the expected peak performance when only performing 20 experiments: we subsample all available experiments (with replacement) into several sets of 20 experiments, recording the best performance in each batch. The last column in Table 1 reports the median of these best batch performances. The result shows increased robustness to hyper-parameters, despite having more hyper-parameters.

4.2 GMM Mixture Weights

In this experiment, our goal is to estimate the mixture weights of a Gaussian mixture model directly from particles. The GMM populations of size 100 in our data set are sampled as follows: each mixture consists of two components; the mixture weights are sampled from [.05, .95]; the means span a diameter of the unit circle, their position is drawn uniformly at random; component variances are a fixed to the same diagonal value such that the clusters are not linearly separable. An example population is shown in Fig. 4a. The model outputs concentrations a and b of a Beta distribution. We train to maximize the log-likelihood of the smaller ground truth weight under this Beta distribution. At training time, for every gradient step the batch population size N is chosen randomly, with $(N = n) \propto n$. In Fig. 4a, we show how an estimator based on the learned model behaves with growing population size.

We were again interested in the robustness of the models. We compare to expectation maximization (EM)—the classic estimation technique for mixture weights—as a baseline by gathering 100 estimates each from EM and the model for each population size by subsampling (with replacement) the original population. Then we compare the likelihood of the true weight under a kernel density

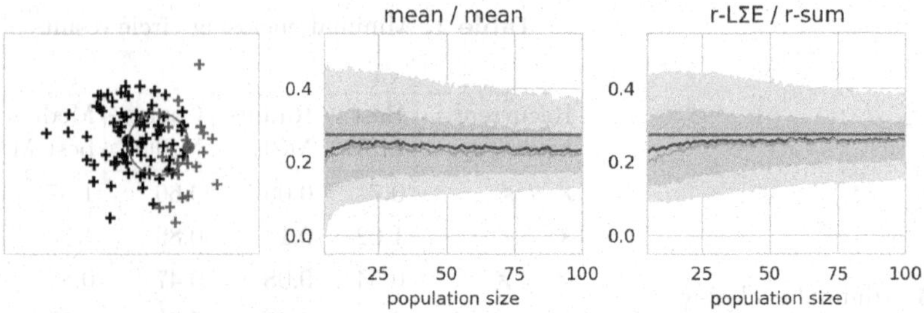

(a) *Left*: Example population. *Middle and Right*: Estimator development for increasing populations size for a non-learnable and a learnable model, with 50% and 90% empirical confidence intervals.

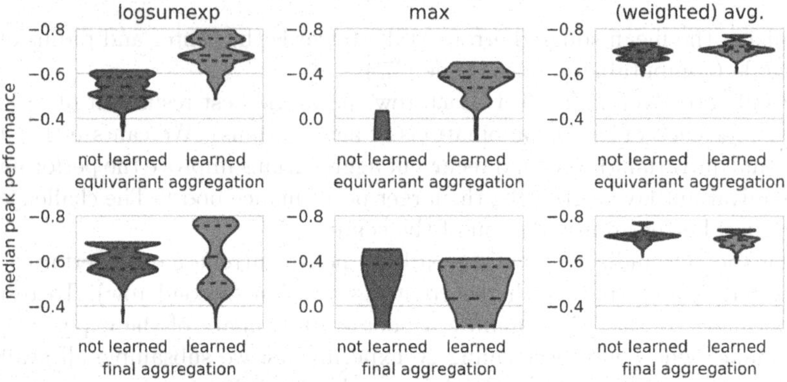

(b) Robustness analysis. Metric is the score ratio of the true mixture weight under a neural model compared to expectation maximization (negative sign indicates EM is outperformed; the more negative, the better). Each violin shows the peak performance distribution for batches of 5 experiments. Top row: equivariant layer aggregations. Bottom row: final aggregations.

Fig. 4. Results for the Gaussian mixture model mixture weights experiment.

estimate (KDE) of these estimates. The final metric is the log ratio of the scores under the two KDEs. Then, as in the previous section, we compute the peak performance for batches of 5 experiments in order to see which configurations of models consistently perform well.

The results of this analysis are shown in Fig. 4b. The top row indicates that learnable equivariant layers lead to a significant performance boost across all reduction operations. Note that the y-axis is in log scale, indicating *multiples* of improvements over the EM baseline. We note that LΣE benefits most drastically from learnable inputs. Notably, the middle column, which depicts max-type aggregations, indicates that this type of aggregation significantly falls behind the alternatives. Notice that we had to scale the y-axes to even show the violins, and that a significant amount of *peak* performances perform *worse* than EM (indicated by sign flip of the metric).

4.3 Point Clouds

The previous experiment extensively tested the effect of aggregations in controlled scenarios. To test the effect of aggregations on a more realistic data set, we tackle classification of point clouds derived from the ModelNet40 benchmark data set [30]. The data set consists of CAD models describing the surfaces of objects from 40 classes. We sample point cloud populations uniformly from the surface. The training is performed on 1000 particles. For this experiment, we fixed all hyper-parameters—including optimizer parameters and learning rate schedules—as described in [29], and only exchanged the aggregation functions in the equivariant layers and the final aggregation.

Table 2. Test set accuracy on ModelNet40 classification.

$\vert\mathcal{X}\vert$	Equivariant layer type & aggregation type									
	max max	max r-LΣE	max r-sum	max q-max	max q-sum	r-sum r-sum	max r-max	r-max r-max	r-LΣE r-LΣE	q-sum q-sum
1000	87.3	85.8	85.7	83.8	83.5	82.0	81.7	81.2	78.0	77.5
100	66.5	75.3	73.0	69.5	68.4	71.9	45.3	22.0	64.0	60.3
50	47.0	62.8	58.4	52.4	51.3	61.0	35.5	14.6	51.9	46.8

The results for the 10 best configurations are summarized in Table 2. The original model (max/max column) performs best in the training scenario ($|\mathcal{X}| = 1000$, first row)—as expected on hyper-parameters that were optimized for the model. Otherwise, learnable final aggregations outperform all non-learnable aggregations. We further observe that max-type aggregations in equivariant layers seem crucial for good final performance. This contrasts the findings from Sect. 4.2. We believe this to be a result of either (i) the hyper-parameters being optimized for max-type equivariant layers, or (ii) the classification task (as opposed to a regression task), favoring max-normalized embeddings that amplify discriminative features.

The second and third row highlight an insufficiently investigated problem with invariant neural architectures: the top-performing model overfits to the training population size. Despite sharing all hyper-parameters except the aggregations, the test scenarios with fewer particles show that learnable aggregation functions generalize favorably. Compare the first two columns: both drops for the original model are comparable to the total drop for the learnable model.

4.4 Spatial Attention

In the previous experiments, we investigated models trained in isolation on supervised tasks. Here, we will test the performance as a building block of a larger model, trained end-to-end and unsupervised. The data consists of canvases containing multiple MNIST digits, cf. Fig. 5a. In [5], an unsupervised algorithm

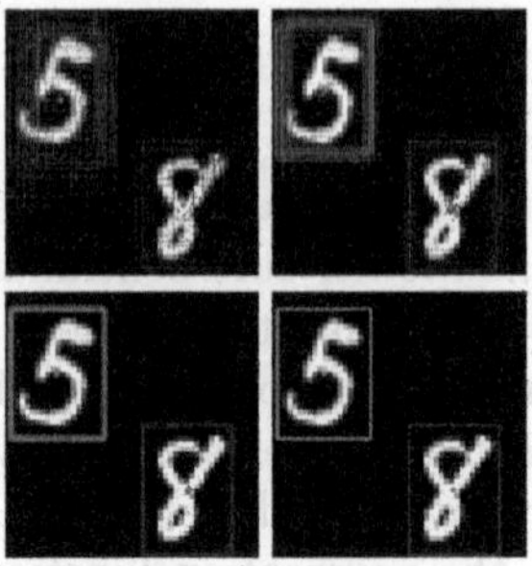

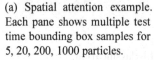

(a) Spatial attention example. Each pane shows multiple test time bounding box samples for 5, 20, 200, 1000 particles.

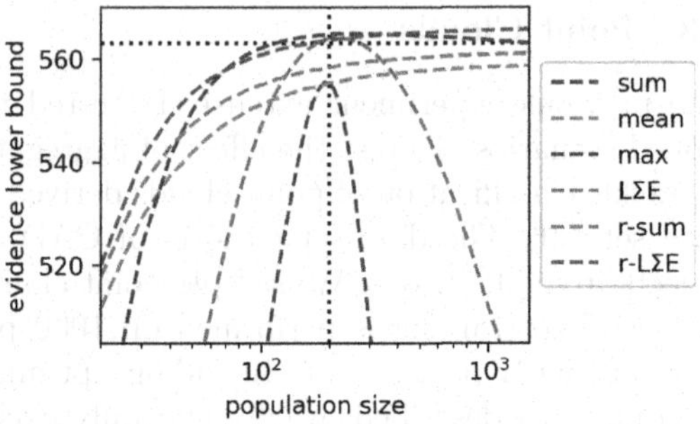

(b) Test-time evidence lower bound values against various population sizes. Dashed vertical line: training population size. Dashed horizontal line: best baseline model.

Fig. 5. Results of the spatial attention experiment.

for scene understanding of such canvases was introduced. We plug an invariant model as the localization module, which repeatedly attends to the input image, at each step returning the bounding box of an object. To turn a canvas into a population, we interpret the gray-scale image as a two-dimensional density and create populations by sampling 200 particles proportional to the pixel intensities. Remarkably, the set-based approach requires an order of magnitude fewer weights, and consequently has a significantly lower memory footprint compared to the original model, which repeatedly processes the entire image.

The task is challenging in several ways: the loss is a lower bound to the likelihood of the input canvas, devoid of localization information. The intended localization behavior needs to emerge from interaction with downstream components of the overall model. As with enclosing circles, the bounding box center is correlated with the sample mean of isolated particles from one digit. However, depending on the digit, this can be inaccurate.

As Fig. 5b indicates, the order-invariant architecture on 200 particles (as in training, vertical line) can serve as a drop-in replacement, performing on a par or slightly improved compared to the original model baseline, indicated by the vertical line. This is remarkable, with the original model being notoriously hard to train [13].

We investigate the performance of the model when the population size varies. We observe that the effect on performance varies with different aggregation functions. Learnable aggregation functions exhibit strictly monotonic performance improvements. This is reflected by tightening bounding boxes for increasing population sizes, Fig. 5a. Similar behavior cannot be found reliably for non-learnable aggregations. Note that we can trade off performance and inference speed *at test time* by varying the population size.

Lastly, we note that in both this and the point cloud experiment, Sect. 4.3, learnable LΣE-aggregations performed well. We attribute this to the properties of diminishing returns and sum-max-interpolation amplified by weighted inputs, cf. Sect. 4.

5 Discussion and Conclusion

We investigated aggregation functions for order-invariant neural architectures. We discussed alternatives to previously used aggregations. Introducing recurrent aggregations, we showed that each component of the Deep Set framework can be learnable. Establishing the notion of sum isomorphism, we created ground for future aggregation models.

Our empirical studies showed that aggregation functions are indeed an orthogonal research axis within the Deep Set framework worth studying. The right choice of aggregation function may depend on the type of task (e. g. regression vs. classification). It affects not only training performance, but also model sensitivity to hyper-parameters and test time performance on out-of-distribution population sizes. We showed that the learnable aggregation functions introduced in this work are more robust in their performance and more consistent in their estimates with growing population sizes. Lastly, we showed how to exploit these features in larger architectures by using neural set architectures as drop-in replacements. In the light of our experimental results, we strongly encourage emphasizing desirable properties of invariant functions, and in particular actively challenge models in non-training scenarios in future research.

References

1. Achlioptas, P., Diamanti, O., Mitliagkas, I., Guibas, L.: Learning Representations and Generative Models for 3D Point Clouds, February 2018. https://openreview.net/forum?id=BJInEZsTb
2. Chang, M.B., Ullman, T., Torralba, A., Tenenbaum, J.B.: A Compositional Object-Based Approach to Learning Physical Dynamics. arXiv:1612.00341 [cs], December 2016
3. Chen, X., Cheng, X., Mallat, S.: Unsupervised deep haar scattering on graphs. In: Ghahramani, Z., Welling, M., Cortes, C., Lawrence, N.D., Weinberger, K.Q. (eds.) Advances in Neural Information Processing Systems, vol. 27, pp. 1709–1717. Curran Associates, Inc. (2014). http://papers.nips.cc/paper/5545-unsupervised-deep-haar-scattering-on-graphs.pdf
4. Edwards, H., Storkey, A.: Towards a Neural Statistician. arXiv:1606.02185 [cs, stat], June 2016
5. Eslami, S.M.A., et al.: Attend, infer, repeat: fast scene understanding with generative models. In: Proceedings of the 30th International Conference on Neural Information Processing Systems NIPS 2016, pp. 3233–3241. Curran Associates Inc., USA (2016). http://dl.acm.org/citation.cfm?id=3157382.3157459
6. Guttenberg, N., Virgo, N., Witkowski, O., Aoki, H., Kanai, R.: Permutation-equivariant neural networks applied to dynamics prediction. arXiv:1612.04530 [cs, stat], December 2016
7. Hecht-Nielsen, R.: Theory of the backpropagation neural network. In: International Joint Conference on Neural Networks, vol. 1, pp. 593–605. IEEE, Washington (1989). https://doi.org/10.1109/IJCNN.1989.118638, http://ieeexplore.ieee.org/document/118638/

8. Hochreiter, S., Schmidhuber, J.: Long short-term memory. Neural Comput. **9**(8), 1735–1780 (1997).https://doi.org/10.1162/neco.1997.9.8.1735,https://www.mitpressjournals.org/doi/10.1162/neco.1997.9.8.1735
9. Hornik, K., Stinchcombe, M., White, H.: Multilayer feedforward networks are universal approximators. Neural Netw. **2**(5), 359–366 (1989). https://doi.org/10.1016/0893-6080(89)90020-8, http://www.sciencedirect.com/science/article/pii/0893608089900208
10. Ilse, M., Tomczak, J.M., Welling, M.: Attention-based Deep Multiple Instance Learning, February 2018. https://arxiv.org/abs/1802.04712
11. Kingma, D.P., Welling, M.: Auto-Encoding Variational Bayes. arXiv:1312.6114 [cs, stat], December 2013
12. Kolmogorov, A.N.: On the representation of continuous functions of many variables by superposition of continuous functions of one variable and addition. Doklady Akademii Nauk SSSR **114**, 953–956 (1957). https://zbmath.org/?q=an%3A0090.27103, mSC2010: 26B40 = Representation and superposition of functions of several real variables
13. Kosiorek, A., Kim, H., Teh, Y.W., Posner, I.: Sequential attend, infer, repeat: generative modelling of moving objects. In: Bengio, S., Wallach, H., Larochelle, H., Grauman, K., Cesa-Bianchi, N., Garnett, R. (eds.) Advances in Neural Information Processing Systems, vol. 31, pp. 8606–8616. Curran Associates, Inc. (2018). http://papers.nips.cc/paper/8079-sequential-attend-infer-repeat-generative-modelling-of-moving-objects.pdf
14. Lee, J., Lee, Y., Kim, J., Kosiorek, A.R., Choi, S., Teh, Y.W.: Set Transformer, October 2018. https://arxiv.org/abs/1810.00825
15. Murphy, R.L., Srinivasan, B., Rao, V., Ribeiro, B.: Janossy Pooling: Learning Deep Permutation-Invariant Functions for Variable-Size Inputs. arXiv:1811.01900 [cs, stat], November 2018
16. Poczos, B., Singh, A., Rinaldo, A., Wasserman, L.: Distribution-free distribution regression. In: Artificial Intelligence and Statistics, pp. 507–515, April 2013. http://proceedings.mlr.press/v31/poczos13a.html
17. Qi, C.R., Liu, W., Wu, C., Su, H., Guibas, L.J.: Frustum PointNets for 3D Object Detection from RGB-D Data. arXiv:1711.08488 [cs], November 2017
18. Qi, C.R., Su, H., Kaichun, M., Guibas, L.J.: PointNet: deep learning on point sets for 3D classification and segmentation. In: 2017 IEEE Conference on Computer Vision and Pattern Recognition (CVPR), pp. 77–85, July 2017. https://doi.org/10.1109/CVPR.2017.16
19. Qi, C.R., Yi, L., Su, H., Guibas, L.J.: PointNet++: deep hierarchical feature learning on point sets in a metric space. In: Guyon, I. et al. (eds.) Advances in Neural Information Processing Systems, vol. 30, pp. 5099–5108. Curran Associates, Inc. (2017). http://papers.nips.cc/paper/7095-pointnet-deep-hierarchical-feature-learning-on-point-sets-in-a-metric-space.pdf
20. Ravanbakhsh, S., Schneider, J., Poczos, B.: Deep Learning with Sets and Point Clouds. arXiv:1611.04500 [cs, stat], November 2016
21. Reed, S., Akata, Z., Yan, X., Logeswaran, L., Schiele, B., Lee, H.: Generative adversarial text to image synthesis. In: International Conference on Machine Learning, pp. 1060–1069, June 2016. http://proceedings.mlr.press/v48/reed16.html
22. Rezende, D.J., Mohamed, S., Wierstra, D.: Stochastic Backpropagation and Approximate Inference in Deep Generative Models, January 2014. https://arxiv.org/abs/1401.4082
23. Santoro, A., et al.: A simple neural network module for relational reasoning. arXiv:1706.01427 [cs], June 2017

24. Vinyals, O., Bengio, S., Kudlur, M.: Order Matters: Sequence to sequence for sets. arXiv:1511.06391 [cs, stat], November 2015
25. Wagstaff, E., Fuchs, F.B., Engelcke, M., Posner, I., Osborne, M.: On the Limitations of Representing Functions on Sets. arXiv:1901.09006 [cs, stat], January 2019
26. Wang, Y., Sun, Y., Liu, Z., Sarma, S.E., Bronstein, M.M., Solomon, J.M.: Dynamic Graph CNN for Learning on Point Clouds. arXiv:1801.07829 [cs], January 2018
27. Welzl, E.: Smallest enclosing disks (balls and ellipsoids). In: Maurer, H. (ed.) New Results and New Trends in Computer Science. LNCS, vol. 555, pp. 359–370. Springer, Heidelberg (1991). https://doi.org/10.1007/BFb0038202
28. Yi, L., Zhao, W., Wang, H., Sung, M., Guibas, L.: GSPN: Generative Shape Proposal Network for 3D Instance Segmentation in Point Cloud. arXiv:1812.03320 [cs], December 2018
29. Zaheer, M., Kottur, S., Ravanbakhsh, S., Poczos, B., Salakhutdinov, R.R., Smola, A.J.: Deep sets. In: Guyon, I., et al. (eds.) Advances in Neural Information Processing Systems, vol. 30, pp. 3391–3401. Curran Associates, Inc. (2017). http://papers.nips.cc/paper/6931-deep-sets.pdf
30. Wu, Z., et al.: 3D ShapeNets: a deep representation for volumetric shapes. In: 2015 IEEE Conference on Computer Vision and Pattern Recognition (CVPR), pp. 1912–1920. IEEE, Boston, June 2015. https://doi.org/10.1109/CVPR.2015.7298801, http://ieeexplore.ieee.org/document/7298801/

Hilbert Vector Convolutional Neural Network: 2D Neural Network on 1D Data

Nasrulloh R. B. S. Loka(✉), Muthusubash Kavitha, and Takio Kurita

Hiroshima University, Higashi-Hiroshima, Japan
satrialoka@gmail.com, {kavitha,tkurita}@hiroshima-u.ac.jp

Abstract. Two-Dimensional Neural Network (2D CNN) has become an alternative method for one-dimensional data classification. Previous studies are focused either only on sequence or vector data. In this paper, we proposed a new 2D CNN classification method that suitable for both, sequence and vector data. The Hilbert space-filling curve was used as a 1D to 2D transfer function in the proposed method. It is used for two reasons: (i) to preserve the spatial locality of 1D data and (ii) to reduce the distance of far-flung data elements. Furthermore, a 1D convolution layer was added in the first stage of our proposed method. It can capture the correlation information of neighboring elements, which is effective for sequence data classification. Consequently, the trainable property of 1D convolutions is very helpful in extracting relevant information for vector data classification. Finally, the performance of the proposed Hilbert Vector Convolutional Neural Network (HVCNN) was compared with two 2D CNN based methods and two non-CNN based methods. Experimental results showed that the proposed HVCNN method delivers better numerical accuracy and generalization property than the other competitive methods. We also did weight distribution analysis to support this claim.

Keywords: Deep learning · Convolutional neural network · Learning representation

1 Introduction

Recently, convolutional neural network (CNN) [8] shows a subtle impact on the two dimensional (2D) data classification task. Convolution layer inside the CNN become an essential module in modern deep learning architectures, and used in a broad range of applications such as large scale image recognition [7,15], object detection [12] , image segmentation [13], etc. Despite CNN popularity on 2D data classification, several study propose to use 2D CNN on one-dimensional (1D) data, e.g., sequence-to-sequence prediction [1], 1D feature based medical image recognition [5], and 1D DNA sequence classification [17].

Yin et al. [17] compare different space filling-curve algorithms as a 1D to 2D transfer function on data pre-processing stage for DNA classification using

I. V. Tetko et al. (Eds.): ICANN 2019, LNCS 11727, pp. 458–470, 2019.
https://doi.org/10.1007/978-3-030-30487-4_36

2D CNN. Later, they claimed that the Hilbert space-filling curve produced the best performance for such tasks, and propose the Hilbert space-filling curve CNN (HCNN) for DNA classification. The Hilbert space-filling curve has been widely applied in data compression, data indexing, and image representation in geographic information system. The key advantage of using Hilbert space-filling curve as a 1D to 2D transfer function is the preservation of locality property from the original 1D data. Moreover, it reduces the distance between far-flung data elements. Therefore, HCNN performs well for sequence data classification.

Kavitha et al. [5] propose a vector based convolutional neural network (V-CNN) in which a vector to a matrix transformation is added as pre-processing layer of the 2D CNN. The transformation is realized by using a fully connected layer and the weights of the transformation are trained to minimize the loss function. The effectiveness of the V-CNN is shown by applying to automatic recognition of colonies of induced pluripotent stem (iPS) cells. The main difference between V-CNN and HCNN is the learning possibility of the 1D to 2D transformation stage. In the HCNN, the 1D to 2D transformation is fixed in pre-processing stage, whereas in the V-CNN, 1D to 2D transformation is trainable. Thus, V-CNN is suitable for vector data.

It is known that the correlations between the values of the local sub-sequences in the sequence data are usually high. Whereas, the correlation of far away data points is comparatively low. The implementation of 1D convolution is effective in extracting important correlation in local sub-sequences within the data. Keeping that in mind, this study proposed to apply 1D convolution before the Hilbert space-filing curve transformation, which is suitable for sequence data classification. The 1D convolution weights are trainable for minimizing the loss value of the target task. The trainable property will also benefit for vector data for extracting useful information for classification, which is similar to the function of fully connected layer in V-CNN.

The effectiveness of the proposed approach is evaluated and compared in terms of classification accuracy and the sparseness of the weights over conventional HCNN and V-CNN. Using the weights of the 1D convolution, the HVCNN can efficiently extract the most relevant information of the local neighboring points in the sequence data. Furthermore, it helps to minimize the number of trainable parameters compared to V-CNN and thus maximize the generalization ability of HVCNN. Additionally, the performance of the HVCNN model in classifying both sequence data and vector data is compared with two non-CNN based classification methods using Support Vector Machine (SVM) [3] and Long Short Term Memory (LSTM) methods [4]. The result showed that HVCNN give competitive performance even with minimal 2D CNN settings.

2 Related Work

In this section we review two previous classification methods based on 2D CNN 1D vector data and sequence data using 2D CNN.

2.1 V-CNN

The vector-based convolutional neural network (V-CNN) is proposed by Kavitha et al. [5] for automatic recognition of the colonies status of the induced pluripotent stem cell images. The morphological and textural feature vectors of cell colonies are classified by transforming it into 2D data space and feed it into 2D CNN. The 1D vector data to the 2D data space transformation is done using fully connected trainable vector-to-matrix pre-processing layer. The pre-processing layer added additional capacity to the network to classify the vector data though there were no relationships between the neighboring data elements. Moreover, the study claims that the V-CNN produced better performance compared to the SVM for classification. The merit of the trainable pre-processing layer of the V-CNN is adopted in our proposed model.

2.2 HCNN

The Hilbert space-filling curve CNN (HCNN) is developed for DNA classification by Yin et al. [17]. They use the Hilbert space-filling curve for mapping 1D into 2D data in data pre-processing stage. It preserves the distance between the data points which are close to each other and reduce the distance between those which are far away from each other. Furthermore, Yin et al. shows that the Hilbert space-filling curve is superior than the other space-filling curve methods for 1D to 2D data transformation in CNN based classification method. Therefore, we adopted the Hilbert space-filling curve method as a transformation layer in our proposed network to improve the performance of the 2D CNN on 1D data classification.

3 Method

This section explains the proposed HVCNN method and its various components.

Fig. 1. Hilbert space filling curve of order 1, 2, 3 and 4.

3.1 Hilbert Space Filling Curve

Hilbert space-filling curve is proven to produce best performance in preserving the locality information of 1D data to 2D data space transformation [10]. The pseudo code of Hilbert space-filling curve is presented in algorithm 1 and 2.

Algorithm 1 takes 1D data index d and 2D side length n (we can also consider n as the order of the curve) as its input. The outputs are corresponding two-dimensional coordinates x and y. Algorithm 2 flip and rotate the coordinate system appropriately to create a connection between every sub region in the 2D space which is obtained from Hilbert space-filling curve. The size of the 2D space produced by Hilbert space-filling curve is a square of $2^n \times 2^n$. For example, Hilbert curve with order of 1, 2, 3 and 4 is illustrated in Fig. 1.

Algorithm 1: Hilbert Space-filling curve

```
Input: n, d
Output: x,y
s=1, t=d, x=y=0;
while s less than n do
    rx = 1 ∧ t/2 ;
    ry = 1 ∧ t^rx ;
    x,y = rot(s,x,y,rx,ry);
    x = x+(s*rx);
    y = y+(s*ry);
    t = t/4;
    s = s*2;
return x,y
```

Algorithm 2: rot function for rotating and flipping x and y coordinates

```
Input: s,x,y,rx,ry
Output: x,y
if ry = 0 then
    if ry = 1 then
        x = n-1-x ;
        y = n-1-y ;
        return y,x
    return x,y
```

In the proposed network, Hilbert space-filling curve is placed after the first layer of 1D convolution that preserves the spatial correlations between the outputs of 1D convolution in 2D convolution stage. Additionally, its capability to reduce the distance of far-flung data elements, helps the proposed network can effectively learn the distant points correlations [17].

3.2 2D CNN

CNN architecture consists of three-layer components: convolution, rectifier linear unit (ReLu), and pooling. The convolutional weights are shared to reduce the number of trainable weights. Hence, it can detect similar patterns on different locations on a 2D data. The convolution layer use a kernel function which is defined as:

$$h_{i,j} = \sum_{k=1}^{m}\sum_{l=1}^{m} w_{k,l}x_{i+k-1,j+l-1} + w_0 \tag{1}$$

where $h_{i,j}$ is convolution output at position i and j, m is kernel width and height, x indicates its input, w is the weight of the kernel and w_0 is bias.

The second layer is ReLU, which is inspired from a biological cortical neuron [11]. The advantage of using ReLU as an activation function is its ability to introduce sparsity for the network. It also introduces non-linearity to the output of the previous layer. It returns 0 if input $x < 0$. ReLu function is defined as:

$$ReLu(x) = max(0, x) \tag{2}$$

Lastly, Max pooling layer is used for reducing the resolution of the feature maps. As a result, the feature maps becomes spatially invariant [14]. Max pooling layer takes the maximum value of elements in $n \times n$ window for the output. All these layers makes the 2D CNN effectively classifying 2D data, for example image classification [7]. Therefore, we use 2D CNN at our proposed model after transforming the 1D data to 2D data using Hilbert space-filling curve.

3.3 1D Convolutions

One-dimensional convolution layer has the same mechanism as the 2D convolution layer, except it operates on 1D data. For example, let us consider the data x convolved using a filter with length n and trainable weight w and the output can be computed using:

$$h_i = \sum_{k=1}^{n} w_k x_{i+k-1} + w_0 \tag{3}$$

1D convolution is used in our proposed method, because of its capability in extracting neighboring points correlations in the sequence data [6].

3.4 Proposed 2D CNN Architectures for 1D Data

Our proposed architecture consists of one 1D convolution layer, a 1D to 2D transfer function by Hilbert space-filling curve, and one 2D CNN block. The 2D CNN block consists of 2D convolution layer, ReLU, max pooling, full connection layer and final softmax layer to calculate the probabilities of data being a certain class. The overview of our proposed method is illustrated in Fig. 2. The 2D CNN

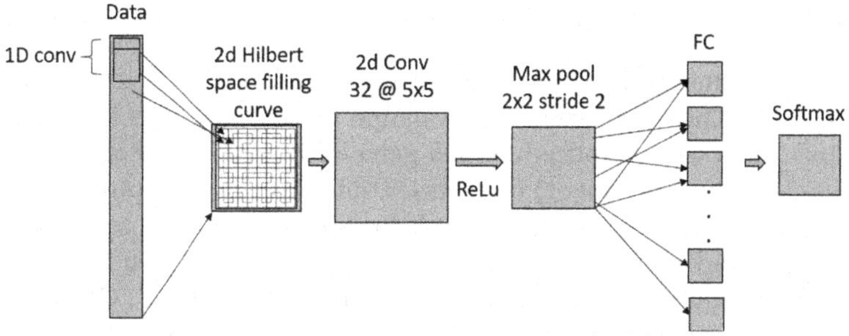

Fig. 2. Proposed HVCNN architecture

block was set to minimal setting to observe the effectiveness of our HVCNN method over the HCNN and V-CNN.

The intuition behind adding a 1D convolution layer in our proposed network is to introduce trainable parameters in the transformation process. This trainable parameters aggregates neighboring elements, hence it makes the local subsequence correlation more important for the learning process. In addition, by transforming 1D convolution output into the 2D space using the Hilbert space-filling curve, our model can able to learn the correlations between the local subsequences data elements that are far from each other.

3.5 Optimization Method and Loss Function

In this study we use mini-batch Stochastic Gradient Descent (SGD) as an optimization method to update the model parameters, which is defined as:

$$\theta = \theta - \alpha.\nabla L(\theta; \mathbf{x}^{(i)}; \mathbf{y}^{(i)}) \tag{4}$$

where θ is model weights, L indicate the loss function, and α is learning rate. The parameters $\mathbf{x}^{(i)}$ and $\mathbf{y}^{(i)}$ represents input and target class on batch i, respectively. Loss function used in this study is softmax cross entropy with weight decay loss to avoid overfitting. The total loss is defined as:

$$L(\theta; \mathbf{x}^{(i)}; \mathbf{y}^{(i)}) = CE(\theta; \mathbf{x}^{(i)}; \mathbf{y}^{(i)}) + \lambda.WD(\theta) \tag{5}$$

where CE indicates cross entropy loss, λ is weight decay term, and WD represents weight decay loss.

4 Experiments

In this section we discuss about the data sets, data representation, experimental settings and weight analysis. In the last part of this section, the results of our study will be discussed.

4.1 Data Sets and Experimental Setup

In this study, sequence (i.e splice-junction gene) and vector (i.e spam base) data sets were used. These data sets are available in UCI machine learning repository [9,16]. The task for splice-junction gene data set is to recognize the given sequence is exon/intron (donor) boundaries, intron/exon (acceptors) boundaries or neither. On the other hand, the task for spam base data set is to classify between spam and non-spam email. In the splice-junction gene data, the features are DNA sequence, a combination of nucleobase {A, G, T, C}, while in the vector data the features are frequency of specific words, special characters, and uninterrupted capital letters. Detailed information of the data sets is presented in Table 1.

Table 1. Data specification

Data set	Splice junction	Spam base
Data characteristic	Sequence	Vector
Number of instances	3190	4601
Number of attributes	61	57
Number of classes	3	2

K-Mers one-hot encoding representation is used for splice junction DNA data set. It represent the sequence combinations of DNA data. In this study 1-Mers one-hot encoding is used to encode one character of DNA sequence to 4-bit representation. Hence the embedded data size becomes $n \times 4^k$, where n is the length of the sequence, and k is the mers length.

In our experiment train and test set ratio are set to 9:1. The proposed model is implemented using tensorflow 1.7 [2] on 4 GB Geforce GTX 980 GPU, the computer specification is 8GB RAM, Intel® Core^{TM} i7-3960X CPU @3.30 GHz × 12.

4.2 Weight Analysis

The weights distributions in 2D convolution and full connection layer were analyzed after training the model. In sequence data set classification, weight distribution of HVCNN layer was less sparse compared with V-CNN. Contrarily, it is more sparse compared to HCNN as shown in Fig. 3(a) and (b). It is because in V-CNN, the number of trainable weights are higher than the HVCNN. Therefore, the degree of freedom in V-CNN method are higher than the other two methods. On the other hand, the degree of freedom in HCNN is limited, because its 1D to 2D transformation are handcrafted in data pre-processing stage. Hence, there was no trainable parameters on its transformation process. However, the handcrafted transformation process in HCNN has a locality preservation properties.

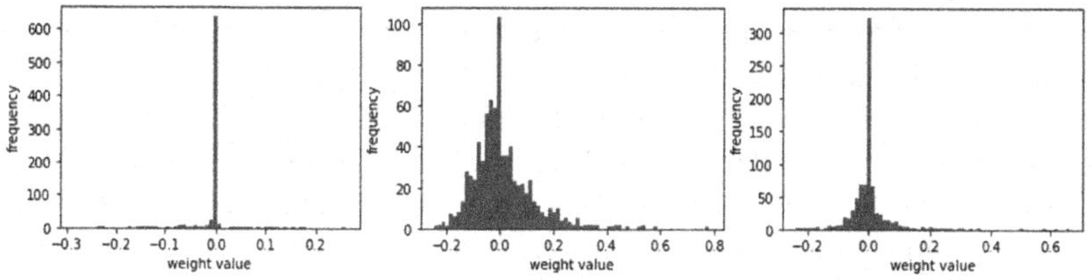

(a)

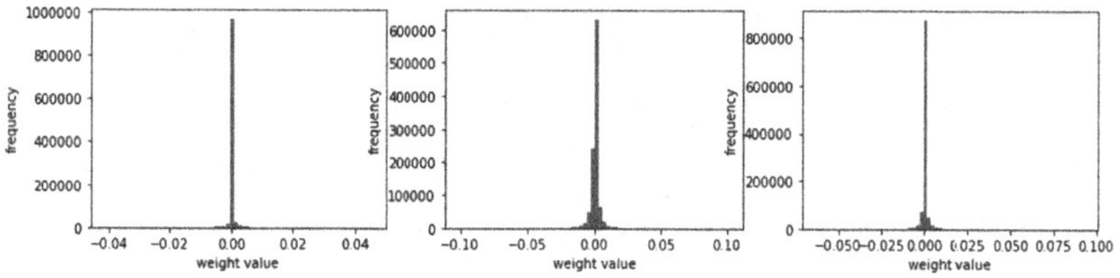

(b)

Fig. 3. Distributions of weight histograms for sequence data set. From left to right: V-CNN, HCNN, Proposed HVCNN. (a) 2D convolution layer, (b) full connected layer.

In this sense, our proposed HVCNN combines the flexibility of trainable weights as well as the locality preservation property by Hilbert space-filling curve. Additionally, our proposed HVCNN method consists of lower number of trainable weights than V-CNN by using 1D convolution layer. It makes our HVCNN sparsity level is in between the V-CNN and HCNN method. For vector data set. The proposed HVCNN method produce less sparse weights in 2D convolution layer than the other two methods. It is because there were no correlations between the neighboring data points. Hence the 1D convolution layer does not introduce more sparsity for the following layers.

The weight sparsity of the proposed method on sequence data shows that it generalize better than V-CNN and HCNN. The high sparse weights in V-CNN may introduce underfitting to the model, while less sparse wight in HCNN can introduce overfitting to the model. Therefore, the proposed HVCNN method is more suitable to sequence data classification. However, it also has competitive results on vector data, as shown in the later section.

4.3 Experimental Results

The performance of our HVCNN method was analyzed in terms of the best kernel size and compared it with V-CNN and HCNN classification methods on sequence and vector data. We also compared the proposed method to two non-CNN classification methods, namely SVM and LSTM.

HVCNN Performance Analysis with Different Kernel Size on Sequence Data. In 1D convolution layer we used four different kernel size to check the best kernel size based on accuracy and loss, using sequence data. In this experiment we set the learning rate to 0.02, weight decay term to 0.1 and the number of epoch used is 2500. The four 1D kernel size used are 1, 3, 6, and 12. The accuracy and loss values of four different 1D convolution kernel size is shown in Fig. 4(a) and (b), respectively. HVCNN with filter size of 3 generates higher accuracy and lower loss values compared to the other filter sizes. The average accuracy and loss values calculated for the last 100 epoch is presented in Table 2.

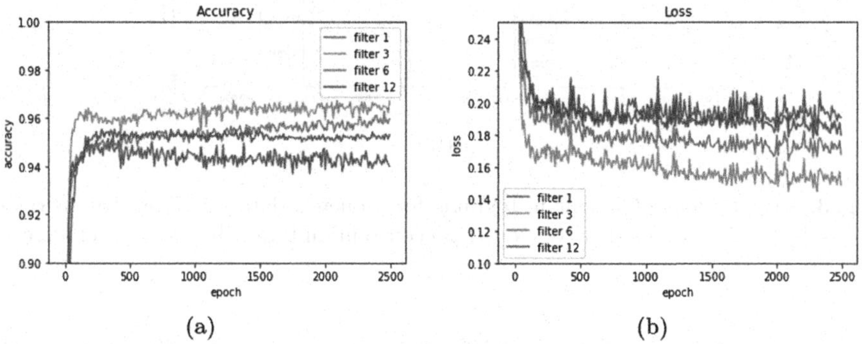

Fig. 4. Performance comparisons of the proposed HVCNN using different size 1D convolution filter for sequence data set (a) accuracy, and (b) loss.

Performance Comparisons of Different Methods on Sequence Data. In this experiment we set the learning rate to 0.02 with 2500 epoch. For HVCNN we used 1D kernel size of 3. Tuning the regularizer to avoid overfitting we got regularizer term 0.01, 0.1, and 0.3 respectively for HCNN, HVCNN and VCNN. The comparisons of accuracy of proposed method with other two methods using sequence data classification is shown in Fig. 5(a). The proposed HVCNN method shows higher accuracy and lower loss values compared to HCNN and V-CNN methods. Comparisons of loss values of HVCNN with HCNN and V-CNN using sequence data classification is shown in Fig. 5(b).

Average accuracy and loss values for the final 100 epoch is shown in Table 3. It is observed that the proposed HVCNN shows best performance with 0.965 accuracy and 0.152 loss values.

Performance Comparisons of Different Methods on Vector Data. The vector data set is normalized before training. For training, we use learning rate of 0.02, and epoch of 2500 in all the three methods. From the tuning results, we set the regularizer term to 0.01. The proposed HVCNN for vector data set classification based on four different 1D convolution kernel size filter was evaluated. It was found that the kernel size 3 yielded better performance than other kernel sizes as similar

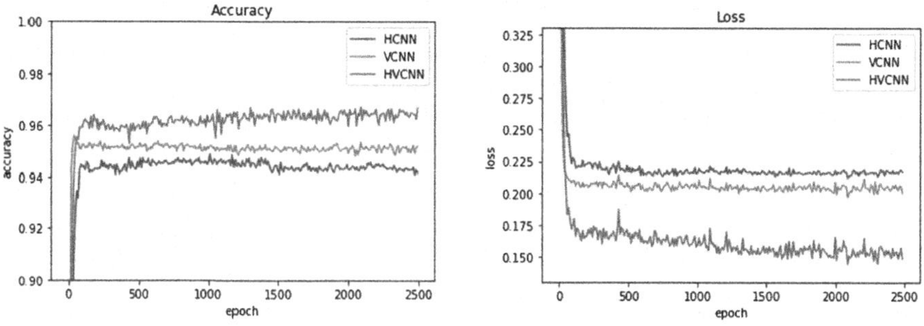

(a) (b)

Fig. 5. Performance comparisons of the proposed HVCNN with HCNN and VCNN for sequence data set, (a) accuracy, and (b) loss.

Table 2. Performance of HVCNN using different size 1D convolution filter based on sequence data

Kernel size	1	3	6	12
Accuracy	0.942	**0.965**	0.960	0.952
Loss	0.192	**0.152**	0.172	0.184

with the sequence data evaluation. The proposed HVCNN perform better than the other two CNN-based methods used in this study. The average accuracy and loss values for the last 100 epoch is described in Table 3. HVCNN yields best performance compared to other two methods with accuracy of 0.930 and loss of 0.205. Comparisons of accuracy and loss values of HVCNN with HCNN and V-CNN for vector data classification is shown in Fig. 6(a) and (b).

We also compared our proposed method over two non-CNN based approach, specifically SVM and LSTM. We use SVM with radial basis function kernel and LSTM with 128 cell number. Our proposed method showed better performance than the non-CNN based models on sequential data. HVCNN produced competitive results on vector data, it is because vector data does not have high correlations between neighboring data points.

Table 3. Performance of different methods on both data

Measurements	V-CNN		HCNN		HVCNN		SVM		LSTM	
	Seq	Vec	Seq	Vec	Seq	Vec	Seq	Vec	Seq	Vec
Accuracy	0.943	0.925	0.951	0.924	**0.965**	**0.930**	0.956	**0.937**	0.943	0.922
Loss	0.217	**0.196**	0.204	0.243	**0.152**	0.205	-	-	0.345	0.445

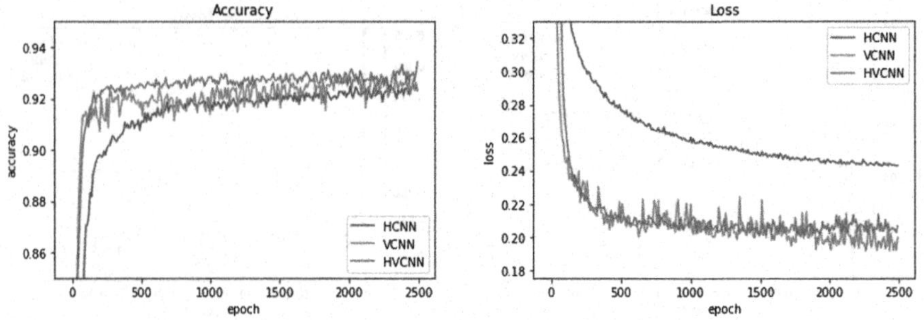

(a) (b)

Fig. 6. Performance comparisons of the proposed HVCNN using different size 1D convolution filter for vector data set (a) accuracy, and (b) loss.

5 Conclusions

We have shown in our experimental results that our proposed method gain better performance in both vector and sequence dataset compared to the two other conventional 2D CNN based methods. Our proposed method work best on sequence data because of its 1D convolution which capture the correlation between neighboring points and also the Hilbert space-filling curve ability to preserve the spatial locality information of the data. On the other hand, HVCNN performs slightly better than V-CNN on vector data. It is because of the nature of vector data in which every neighboring value is less related to each other. Nevertheless, the trainability property 1D convolution can be a good use to vector data classification. Additionally we compare our method to non-CNN approach method, namely SVM and LSTM. The experimental result suggest that our method are better in sequence data, and still got competitive results on vector data, even though we only use minimal 2D CNN setting.

Using minimal 2D CNN architecture settings, the combination of 1D convolution and Hilbert space-filling curve helps the 2D convolution layer to generalize better. In sequence data, our proposed method gains 0.965 accuracy and 0.152 loss, which is higher than the other CNN based and non-CNN based methods. In the future, we plan to scale up our study on various data sets and more complex 2D CNN architecture settings, to test the robustness of our proposed HVCNN network model on different cases.

Acknowledgment. This work was partly supported by JSPS KAKENHI Grant Number 16K00239. The authors also thank the Institute of Education Fund Management (LPDP) of the Ministry of Finance of Indonesia, which has provided scholarship support for the first author to undertake the master program.

References

1. Elbayad, M., Besacier, L., Verbeek, J.: Pervasive attention: 2D convolutional neural networks for sequence-to-sequence prediction. In: Conference on Computational Natural Language Learning (2018). https://arxiv.org/abs/1808.03867
2. GoogleResearch: TensorFlow: a system for large-scale machine learning. GoogleResearch (2015). http://dl.acm.org/citation.cfm?id=3026877.3026899
3. Hearst, M.A., Dumais, S.T., Osuna, E., Platt, J., Scholkopf, B.: Support vector machines. IEEE Intell. Syst. Appl. **13**(4), 18–28 (1998). https://doi.org/10.1109/5254.708428
4. Hochreiter, S., Schmidhuber, J.: Long short-term memory. Neural Comput. **9**(8), 1735–1780 (1997). https://doi.org/10.1162/neco.1997.9.8.1735
5. Kavitha, M., Kurita, T., Park, S.Y., Chien, S.I., Bae, J.S., Ahn, B.C.: Deep vector-based convolutional neural network approach for automatic recognition of colonies of induced pluripotent stem cells. PLoS ONE **12**(12), 1–18 (2017). https://doi.org/10.1371/journal.pone.0189974
6. Kiranyaz, S., Ince, T., Gabbouj, M.: Real-time patient-specific ECG classification by 1-D convolutional neural networks. IEEE Trans. Biomed. Eng. **63**(3), 664–675 (2016). https://doi.org/10.1109/TBME.2015.2468589
7. Krizhevsky, A., Sutskever, I., Hinton, G.E.: ImageNet classification with deep convolutional neural networks. In: Advances in Neural Information Processing Systems, pp. 1–9 (2012). https://doi.org/10.1016/j.protcy.2014.09.007
8. LeCun, Y.: Generalization and network design strategies (1989). http://yann.lecun.com/exdb/publis/pdf/lecun-89.pdf
9. Mark, H., Erik, R., George, F., Jaap, S.: UCI Machine Learning Repository (1999). https://archive.ics.uci.edu/ml/datasets/spambase
10. Moon, B., Jagadish, H.V., Faloutsos, C., Saltz, J.H.: Analysis of the clustering properties of the Hilbert space-filling curve. IEEE Trans. Knowl. Data Eng. **13**(1), 124–141 (2001). https://doi.org/10.1109/69.908985
11. Nair, V., Hinton, G.E.: Rectified linear units improve restricted boltzmann machines. In: Proceedings of the 27th International Conference on Machine Learning (ICML) (2010). https://doi.org/10.1.1.165.6419
12. Redmon, J., Divvala, S., Girshick, R., Farhadi, A.: You only look once: unified, real-time object detection. In: 2016 IEEE Conference on Computer Vision and Pattern Recognition (CVPR) (2015). https://doi.org/10.1109/CVPR.2016.91
13. Ronneberger, O., Fischer, P., Brox, T.: U-Net: convolutional networks for biomedical image segmentation. In: Navab, N., Hornegger, J., Wells, W.M., Frangi, A.F. (eds.) MICCAI 2015. LNCS, vol. 9351, pp. 234–241. Springer, Cham (2015). https://doi.org/10.1007/978-3-319-24574-4_28
14. Scherer, D., Müller, A., Behnke, S.: Evaluation of pooling operations in convolutional architectures for object recognition. In: Diamantaras, K., Duch, W., Iliadis, L.S. (eds.) ICANN 2010. LNCS, vol. 6354, pp. 92–101. Springer, Heidelberg (2010). https://doi.org/10.1007/978-3-642-15825-4_10
15. Simonyan, K., Zisserman, A.: Very deep convolutional networks for large-scale image recognition. In: ICLR, pp. 1–14 (2014). https://doi.org/10.1016/j.infsof.2008.09.005

16. Towell, G., Noordewier, M., Shavlik, J.: UCI Machine Learning Repository (1992). https://archive.ics.uci.edu/ml/datasets/Molecular+Biology+(Splice-junction+Gene+Sequences)
17. Yin, B., Balvert, M., Zambrano, D., Schönhuth, A., Bohte, S.M.: An Image Representation based Convolutional Network for DNA Classification. CoRR abs/1806.04931 (2018). http://arxiv.org/abs/1806.04931

The Same Size Dilated Attention Network for Keypoint Detection

Yuan Chang[1(✉)], Zixuan Huang[1(✉)], and Qiwei Shen[1,2]

[1] State Key Laboratory of Networking and Switching Technology, Beijing University of Posts and Telecommunications, Beijing 100876, China
{changyuan,huangzixuan0508,shenqw}@bupt.edu.cn
[2] EBUPT Information Technology Company, Ltd., Beijing 100191, China

Abstract. In recent years, convolution neural networks have significant progress on keypoint detection. However, lots of approaches require multiple upsampling of small featuremaps to produce the final output. The huge information loss in the upsampling process is the key to restrict the accuracy. This work presents a new network architecture, which is designed to solve the problem of information loss in the process of upsampling and feature fusion compared with the previous approaches. We replace the normal convolution in the backbone network by using dilated convolution with stride of one to keep featuremaps' size consistent, which avoids the multi-times upsampling during prediction. We also explore the feature fusion methods and propose a feature fusion block (AFB), which improves the accuracy and accelerates the convergence of model with the help of multi-scale resampling and attention mechanism. Excellent results are achieved on MsCOCO 2017 dataset and Ali apparel keypoints dataset. The code will be released for further research.

Keywords: Keypoint detection · Pose estimation · Dilated convolution · Attention · Feature fusion

1 Introduction

Keypoint detection is a fundamental task of computer vision. It is mostly applied to pose estimation and face alignment. After predicting the keypoints of human body, human posture can be easily estimated. Recently, due to the rapid development of deep learning, convolutional neural network has greatly improved the accuracy of the keypoints detection. CPN [6] and Hourglass [20], for example, have shown remarkable results. However, the size of featuremaps will gradually decrease with the expanding receptive field because of maxpooling and convolution stride. Since the keypoints location belong to the precise classification at the pixel level, when small featuremaps are finally reverted to a larger size heatmap outputs through upsampling, the lost information cannot be completely restored. These losses can be ignore in target detection, but they are fatal for delicate tasks such as keypoint detection.

I. V. Tetko et al. (Eds.): ICANN 2019, LNCS 11727, pp. 471–483, 2019.
https://doi.org/10.1007/978-3-030-30487-4_37

In order to solve this problem, we propose a new network architecture, which uses dilated convolution [37] instead of normal convolution in backbone. Due to the characteristics of dilated convolution, the receptive field can expand exponentially. Therefore, even if the stride is one, it can also guarantee that the top layer has a large receptive field. And the advantage of stride one is that featuremap does not shrink during delivery. The stack of dilated convolution with the same expansion rate will make sampling too sparse to capture the information which is known as gridding issue [28]. For keypoint task, it is possible to miss a point. Accordingly, we assign different expansion rates to the dilated convolution at the same stage, and explore the different combinations of expansion rates.

We also resample the output of backbone at multiple scales, which can effectively enhance its expression ability. At present, feature fusion methods are mostly adopted channel concatenate or element-wise add, but directly add or reducing the number of channels by 1×1 convolution may lead to the loss of useful information. We introduce attention mechanism to enable network to autonomously learn the weights of each fusion component instead of simple average contribution, which effectively improves the performance of feature fusion.

At present, keypoint detection approaches mostly predict heatmaps which are finally converted to coordinates. The output size of heatmaps are generally one quarter of the input image size. We keep this regular setting. In the backbone network, when the featuremaps are reduced to 1/4 of the original input, we use dilated convolution whose stride is one to keep the size of featuremap unchanged in the subsequent stage, which avoid the upsampling operation during generating the final prediction.

The main contributions of this work are twofold.

We design a new network which is different from the traditional encoder-decoder architecture as shown in Fig. 1. It eliminates the upsampling operation of the network and avoids the information loss caused by bilinear interpolation.

We propose a new feature fusion block named AFB which first resamples the input at multiple scales and then uses the attention mechanism to allow network to learn the weights of the components to be fused.

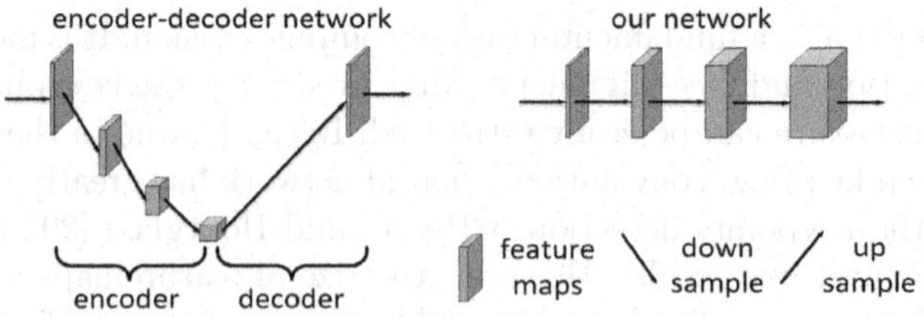

Fig. 1. The architectures of encoder-decoder network and ours.

2 Related Work

With the increase of demand, human keypoint detection have been a popular field in computer vision. Before the development of deep learning, keypoints detection tasks are transformed into a tree-structured or graphical model in the traditional way [2,7,9,14,22–24,36]. With the development of deep learning, convolutional neural networks have gradually gained a dominant position in such tasks [3,6,8,10,12,19–21,29,32,33,35]. At present, the use of CNN for human keypoint detection mainly adopts the top-down pipeline. This pipeline [6,20,33] uses the target detection algorithm to cut out the human region in the picture, and then detects the keypoints.

2.1 Keypoint Detection

Toshev et al. [26] first use CNN to solve the problem of human keypoint detection. Tompson et al. [25] introduce heatmaps of keypoints as prediction in this field. Wei et al. [29] use a deep neural network and propose to generate rough results first, and continuously improve the prediction in the follow-up network phase. Newell et al. [20] propose a u-shaped network to generate accurate predictions by stacking several hourglass modules. Chen et al. [6] utilize the idea of intermediate supervision and multi-scale pyramid cascade, which reach the state-of-the-art at that time. Xiao et al. [33] fuse the results of bilinear interpolation and deconvolution, reducing the information loss in upsampling.

2.2 Dilated Convolution

Yu et al. [37] first put forward the concept of dilated convolution, sampling every few units to improve the receptive field. Wang et al. [28] point out that there is a gridding issue in the dilated convolution with the same expansion rate. If the dilated convolution is too sparse, the distance between two adjacent sampling of top convolution will be greater than the length of the target. The dilated convolution with unequal expansion rate is proposed to homogenize sampling. Li et al. [15] analyze that the effect of multi-column network is not significant, and then propose a deeper network. In this network, VGG16 is used to extract features and dilated convolution is used to understand highly congested scenes. They also explore the difference between upsampling and dilated convolution in their study. Wei et al. [30] integrate various dilated convolution of different rate by using classification activation maps to generate corresponding localization maps. This network is used to deal with the semantic segmentation of weak supervision and semi-supervision.

2.3 Attention

Attention mechanism originally came about in natural language processing and then migrated to computer vision [18,34]. Jie et al. [13] enhance the model expressiveness by weighting channels. Wang et al. [27] assign weights to each pixel of the featuremap by adding branches, which form an attention mechanism of spatial dimension. Woo et al. [31], based on SENet, retains the attention of channel dimension and adds attention of lightweight spatial dimension to improve model accuracy.

3 Our Approach

Before introducing our network, let us take a look at the two outstanding methods of human keypoint detection: Cascaded Pyramid Network (CPN) [6] and Simplebaseline [33].

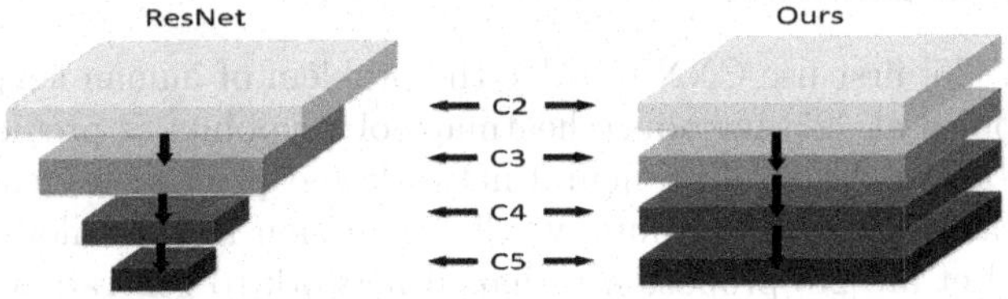

Fig. 2. ResNet and our backbone.

The backbone of Simplebaseline and CPN mostly use the ResNet [11] series, we name ResNet different stages C2-C5 in the Fig. 2, the output size of C2 is a quarter of original picture and the output of C5 is only 1/8 of C2. In order to predict heatmap, the final result needs to be upsampled eight times. Bilinear interpolation for upsampling uses four surrounding pixel values for estimation, which inevitably leads to errors in the process of multiple upsampling. When the distance between two keypoints is less than eight pixels, information cannot be restored by bilinear interpolation. In CPN, in order to compensate for this, the cascade mode is adopted to upsample through step by step fusion. As for the Simplebaseline, they improve the performance by merging the results of bilinear interpolation and deconvolution.

From this perspective, we adopt the dilated convolution with stride one to maintain the consistent size of C2-C5 outputs and eliminate upsampling operation in the network.

3.1 Network Architecture

Our network architecture is shown in Fig. 3. In order to avoid the gridding issue mentioned above, we use dilated convolutions of unequal expansion rates in the same stage in the backbone.

According to [6] and our experiments, intermediate supervision can improve the accuracy and accelerate network convergence. We follow this idea, adding intermediate supervision after the merging block.

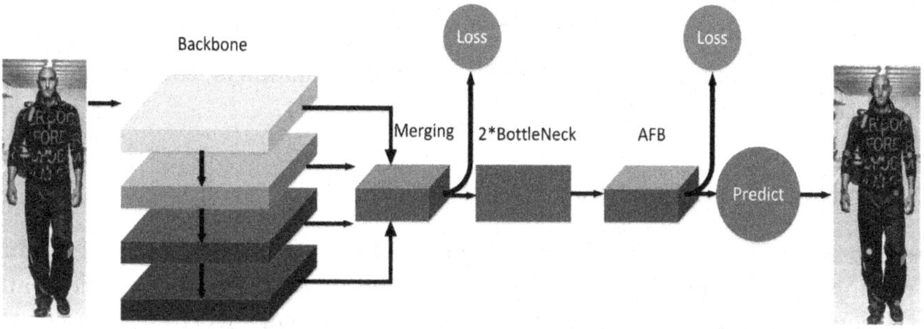

Fig. 3. Our network architecture for keypoint detection.

In Merging block, we use extra dilated convolutions for the outputs of C2-C5 to extract features respectively in a more refined way. Subsequently, the above four featuremaps are merged to make the output feature have low-level semantic information according to the Feature Pyramid Networks [16]. Finally, the featuremaps go through two bottleneck blocks and an attention fusion block (AFB) to predict the result.

3.2 Merging Block

This block merges the featuremaps of four stages in backbone and transmit fusion result to the next block.

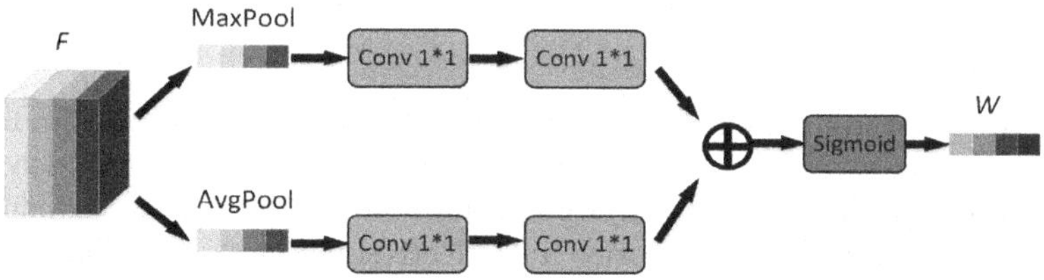

Fig. 4. Channel attention module.

Before merging, we perform different dilated convolution on the outputs of C2-C5 stages according to the receptive fields at different stages. We concatenate featuremaps and get F. In order to minimize the information loss during compressing the channels, we use the channel dimension attention (Fig. 4). We aggregate the spatial information by using max-pooling and average-pooling operations. The channel attention W is computed blow, and σ denotes sigmoid function, $\mathcal{G}$ denotes convolution functions:

$$W = \sigma\left(\mathcal{G}_1\left(MaxPool\left(F\right)\right) + \mathcal{G}_2\left(AvgPool\left(F\right)\right)\right) \tag{1}$$

$$Outputs = F + W \cdot F \tag{2}$$

Finally, we compress the number of output channels to 256 with 1*1 convolution.

3.3 Attention Fusion Block (AFB)

Deeplab series [4,5] propose the atrous spatial pyramid pooling (ASPP) module to resample featuremap by using dilated convolution of different expansion rates in the semantic segmentation. Multi-scale resampling can effectively enhance the expression ability of featuremap. In our study, ASPP module is used for reference and modified to apply to the keypoint detection task. We propose the AFB as shown in Fig. 5, we make the following two improvements:

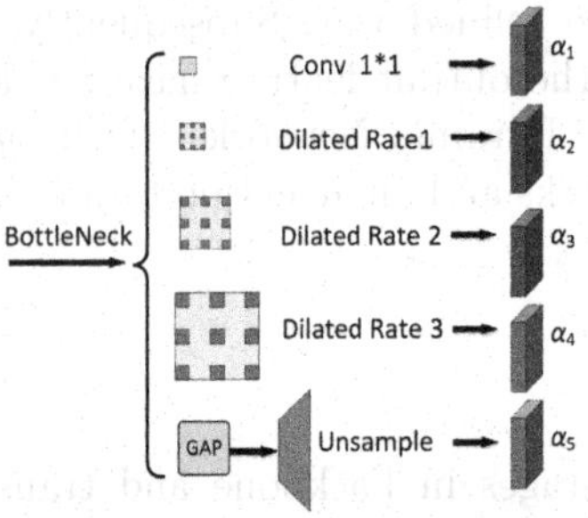

Fig. 5. Multi-scale resampling.

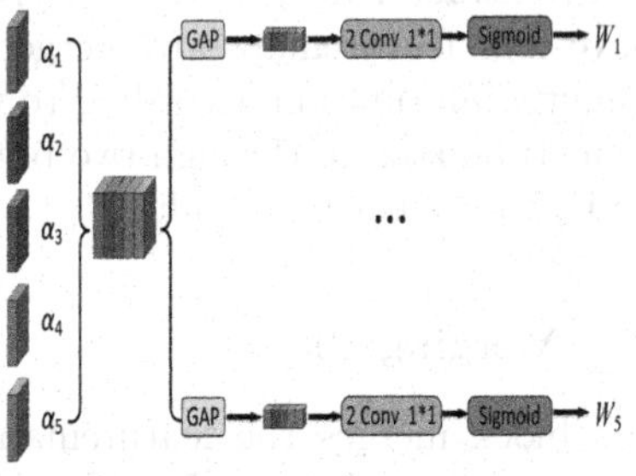

Fig. 6. Computing different fusion components' weights with attention.

Firstly, we study the expansion rates of ASPP and find that the traditional large expansion rates such as 12, 18 are not effective in keypoint detection, because the expansion rate is too large to skip some groundtruth. Reducing the expansion rate of dilated convolution will effectively improve its performance in the model which using heatmap with a Gaussian kernel of 7.

Secondly, we explore the method of feature fusion. At present, there are two direct feature fusion methods: element-wise add or channel concatenate. Experiments show when the features to be fused are similar, the element-wise add method is better than concatenate. However, in the remaining scenes where the features are not similar, the concatenate may be better than the element-wise add. For example, when fusing different stages' outputs of ResNet [11], concatenate is better than the element-wise add. As shown in the Fig. 5, AFB needs to fuse five components. Because the features of each component to be merged are similar, we adopt the method of element-wise add. Direct addition operation means that the weights of the fusion components are the same as the below Eq. 3, but some components are more suitable for the groundtruth, and other components only play a supporting role. Differentiating the fusion components' weights can speed up network convergence and play a positive role in the result.

$$\beta = \alpha_1 + \alpha_2 + \alpha_3 + \alpha_4 + \alpha_5 \tag{3}$$

As shown in Fig. 6, we use the attention mechanism to enable the network to automatically learn the proportion of each fusion component in the final output. The Attention module connects $\alpha_1 - \alpha_5$ to be fused in the channel dimension, and performs global average pooling (GAP) to obtain the result with global features. Then the results is compressed by 1×1 convolutions and activated by sigmoid respectively as the weight of each fusion component in Eq. 4. So this allows the network to learn the trade-offs in the fusion process, and the output is shown in Eq. 5, where α_i represents the components to be fused, W_i represents the weight of each component, and β represents the output.

$$W_i = \sigma\left(\mathcal{G}_i\left(GAP\left(Concat\left(\alpha_{1\ldots5}\right)\right)\right)\right) \tag{4}$$

$$\beta = \sum_{i=1}^{5} W_i \cdot \alpha_i \tag{5}$$

4 Experiment

4.1 Dataset and Experimental Setup

Coco2017. The MsCOCO dataset [17] is the most authoritative dataset in the keypoint detection field. Almost all 2D keypoint detection algorithms will be evaluated using COCO. The latest dataset is COCO2017. The COCO train, validation, and test sets contain more than 200k images and 250k person instances labeled with keypoint. 150k instances of them are publicly available for training and validation. Our models are only trained on COCO train2017 dataset (includes 57K images and 150K person instances), no extra data involved.

The COCO evaluation uses the mean average precision (AP) over 10 OKS thresholds as main competition metric. The OKS is defined as:

$$\text{OKS} = \frac{\sum_i \exp\left(-d_i^2/2s^2k_i^2\right)\delta\left(v_i > 0\right)}{\sum_i \delta\left(v_i > 0\right)}$$

Ali Apparel Keypoints Dataset. We use the Ali apparel keypoints dataset [1] as an aid to verify that our keypoint detection algorithm is robust in other scenarios. In this dataset, a set of clothing keypoints is defined on the basis of fashion design. The set is further refined into six subsets, including 41 sub-categories and 24 kinds of keypoints in total. There are altogether 100,000 annotated images in this dataset.

Normalized Error (NE) is used for evaluating the results. NE is the average normalized distance between predicted keypoint position and annotation position.

Training. Our backbone network is initialized by ResNet pre-training on ImageNet. We train our all models using adam algorithm with an initial learning rate of 5e-4 while batchsize is 36. The default resolution of ground truth in COCO is 384×288, and 512×512 in Ali dataset. Data augmentation includes rotation (± 45 degrees) and random flip. It is the same as the state-of-the-art method [6,33] for a fair comparison. Due to the consistent size of the featuremap and attention mechanism, our network has a faster convergence speed and shorter training cycle to achieve good results.

Testing. We directly evaluate the prediction of the model without TTA and model stacking. The heatmap size is a quarter of input size.

4.2 Comparison with Other State-of-the-Art Methods

We compare our results with a 8-stage Hourglass, CPN and Simplebaseline on COCO val2017 and Ali apparel keypoints dataset respectively without any extra data. All the methods use a similar top-down paradigm. For reference, the person detection AP of Hourglass and CPN is 55.3, which is comparable to Simplebaseline's and ours 56.4.

Table 1. Comparisons of different methods on COCO2017 val dataset. - indicates only use dilated convolution at stage C4,C5 so the featuremap size of each stage are (96, 72), (48, 36), (48, 36), (48, 36). * means using the human groundtruth bbox of COCO instead of detector. Note that the results of CPN and Simplebaseline are cited from [33] and not implemented by us.

Models	Backbone	Inputsize	AP
8-stage Hourglass	–	256×256	67.1
CPN	ResNet50	384×288	71.6
Simplebaseline	ResNet50	384×288	72.2
Ours	ResNet50	384×288	**73.4**
Our*	ResNet50	384×288	75.3
Our-	ResNet50	384×288	73.1

Compared with CPN as shown in Table 1, our network has an improvement of 1.8 in AP, and compared with Simplebaseline, we has an improvement of 1.2 in AP. If do not use detector but directly use the character bbox groundtruth, our model will achieve 75.3 in AP. When we only use dilated convolution at stage C4,C5, AP will slightly decrease from 73.4 to 73.1.

From the Table 2, we have achieved an excellent result in the Ali dataset. Our algorithm still gets good results in other keypoint detection scenarios, and also performs well on face keypoint detection task.

Table 2. Comparisons of different methods on Ali apparel dataset.

Models	Backbone	Inputsize	Error Rate
CPN	ResNet50	512 × 512	0.045
Simplebaseline	ResNet50	512 × 512	0.042
Ours	ResNet50	512 × 512	**0.038**
Our-	ResNet50	512 × 512	0.039

4.3 Ablation Study

The Effect of Dilated Convolution. In this section, we explore the advantages of dilated convolution. In the case where the number of convolution layers is same, the theoretical receptive field of dilated convolution is much larger than the normal convolution. Therefore, the stacking of normal convolutional layers will make the top layer of network unable to perceive global information. To prove this view, we replace the dilated convolution in our network with normal convolution whose stride is one.

Table 3. Different backbone on COCO2017 val dataset.

Models	Inputsize	AP
Normal convolution with stride one	388 × 288	63.1
Dilated convolution with stride one	384 × 288	**73.4**

As shown in Table 3, dilated convolution can expand the receptive field without depending on the stride. Both large receptive field and reducing information loss are the key to solve this task.

Attention Fusion Block. We have designed three schemes for comparative tests of AFB on COCO val2017. (1) Remove AFB for direct prediction. (2) Replace the AFB with ASPP. (3) Our original network architecture.

Table 4. Comparisons of different blocks on COCO2017 val dataset.

Models	Inputsize	AP
Network without AFB	384 × 288	72.8
Network with ASPP	384 × 288	72.9
Network with AFB	384 × 288	**73.4**

It can be seen from Table 4 that in the absence of AFB, the network can reach 72.8 AP only by backbone. Adding ASPP module will improve 0.1 AP, while adding AFB will improve the AP from 72.8 to 73.4.

Feature Fusion Method. We also explore the feature fusion method on COCO val2017, which is divided into two parts.

First we compare the results of element-wise add and concatenate in the Merging block as shown in the Table 5.

Then we explore the difference between element-wise add and concatenate in AFB shown in the Table 6.

For reference, the final featuremaps size is unified to 96 × 72 (W × H).

Table 5. Different fuse methods in Merging block on COCO2017 val dataset.

Models	Inputsize	AP (avg)
Merge with element-wise add	384 × 288	73.1
Merge with concatenate	384 × 288	**73.4**

Table 6. Different fuse methods in AFB on COCO2017 val dataset.

Models	Inputsize	AP (avg)
AFB with element-wise add	384 × 288	**73.4**
AFB with concatenate	384 × 288	73.2

We repeat several tests to ensure the accuracy of the results and record the mean of results in the table. It can be concluded from Tables 5 and 6 when the features to be merged are similar, e.g. for multi-scale resampling, the element-wise add method is better than concatenate. However, in the remaining scenes where the features are not similar, the concatenate may be better than the element-wise add. This conclusion is obtained under our model and requires more experiments to ensure its universality.

5 Conclusion

This research proposes a new keypoint detection network which inspires new ideas for the field. We use dilated convolution to overcome the disadvantage of upsampling. Multi-scale resampling and attention mechanism are introduced to improve network's performance. Our algorithm has reached perfect result on COCO2017 dataset and Ali apparel dataset. Finally, we will continue to explore the optimization of our method to achieve higher precision in keypoint detection.

Acknowledgements. This work was supported in part by the National Natural Science Foundation of China under Grant 61771068 and Grant 61671079, in part by the Beijing Municipal Natural Science Foundation under Grant 4182041, in part by the Fundamental Research Funds for the Central Universities under Grant 2018RC20.

References

1. Ali apparel keypoints dataset. https://tianchi.aliyun.com/competition/entrance/231670/information/
2. Andriluka, M., Roth, S., Schiele, B.: Pictorial structures revisited: people detection and articulated pose estimation. In: 2009 IEEE Conference on Computer Vision and Pattern Recognition, pp. 1014–1021. IEEE (2009). https://doi.org/10.1109/cvprw.2009.5206754
3. Bulat, A., Tzimiropoulos, G.: Human pose estimation via convolutional part heatmap regression. In: Leibe, B., Matas, J., Sebe, N., Welling, M. (eds.) ECCV 2016. LNCS, vol. 9911, pp. 717–732. Springer, Cham (2016). https://doi.org/10.1007/978-3-319-46478-7_44
4. Chen, L.C., Papandreou, G., Kokkinos, I., Murphy, K., Yuille, A.L.: Deeplab: semantic image segmentation with deep convolutional nets, atrous convolution, and fully connected crfs. IEEE Trans. Pattern Anal. Mach. Intell. **40**(4), 834–848 (2018). https://doi.org/10.1109/tpami.2017.2699184
5. Chen, L.C., Papandreou, G., Schroff, F., Adam, H.: Rethinking atrous convolution for semantic image segmentation. arXiv preprint arXiv:1706.05587 (2017). https://doi.org/10.4271/2018-01-1635
6. Chen, Y., Wang, Z., Peng, Y., Zhang, Z., Yu, G., Sun, J.: Cascaded pyramid network for multi-person pose estimation. In: Proceedings of the IEEE Conference on Computer Vision and Pattern Recognition, pp. 7103–7112 (2018). https://doi.org/10.1109/cvpr.2018.00742
7. Dantone, M., Gall, J., Leistner, C., Van Gool, L.: Human pose estimation using body parts dependent joint regressors. In: Proceedings of the IEEE Conference on Computer Vision and Pattern Recognition, pp. 3041–3048 (2013). https://doi.org/10.1109/cvpr.2013.391
8. Dong, X., Yan, Y., Ouyang, W., Yang, Y.: Style aggregated network for facial landmark detection. In: Proceedings of the IEEE Conference on Computer Vision and Pattern Recognition, pp. 379–388 (2018). https://doi.org/10.1109/cvpr.2018.00047
9. Gkioxari, G., Arbelaez, P., Bourdev, L., Malik, J.: Articulated pose estimation using discriminative armlet classifiers. In: Proceedings of the IEEE Conference on Computer Vision and Pattern Recognition, pp. 3342–3349 (2013). https://doi.org/10.1109/cvpr.2013.429
10. Gkioxari, G., Toshev, A., Jaitly, N.: Chained predictions using convolutional neural networks. In: Leibe, B., Matas, J., Sebe, N., Welling, M. (eds.) ECCV 2016. LNCS, vol. 9908, pp. 728–743. Springer, Cham (2016). https://doi.org/10.1007/978-3-319-46493-0_44
11. He, K., Zhang, X., Ren, S., Sun, J.: Deep residual learning for image recognition. In: Proceedings of the IEEE Conference on Computer Vision and Pattern Recognition, pp. 770–778 (2016). https://doi.org/10.1109/cvpr.2016.90
12. Insafutdinov, E., Pishchulin, L., Andres, B., Andriluka, M., Schiele, B.: DeeperCut: a deeper, stronger, and faster multi-person pose estimation model. In: Leibe, B., Matas, J., Sebe, N., Welling, M. (eds.) ECCV 2016. LNCS, vol. 9910, pp. 34–50. Springer, Cham (2016). https://doi.org/10.1007/978-3-319-46466-4_3
13. Jie, H., Li, S., Gang, S., Jie, H., Li, S., Gang, S.: Squeeze-and-excitation networks (2017). https://doi.org/10.1109/cvpr.2018.00745
14. Johnson, S., Everingham, M.: Learning effective human pose estimation from inaccurate annotation. In: CVPR 2011, pp. 1465–1472. IEEE (2011). https://doi.org/10.1109/cvpr.2011.5995318

15. Li, Y., Zhang, X., Chen, D.: Csrnet: Dilated convolutional neural networks for understanding the highly congested scenes (2018). https://doi.org/10.1109/cvpr.2018.00120
16. Lin, T.Y., Dollár, P., Girshick, R., He, K., Hariharan, B., Belongie, S.: Feature pyramid networks for object detection. In: Proceedings of the IEEE Conference on Computer Vision and Pattern Recognition, pp. 2117–2125 (2017). https://doi.org/10.1109/cvpr.2017.106
17. Lin, T.-Y., et al.: Microsoft COCO: common objects in context. In: Fleet, D., Pajdla, T., Schiele, B., Tuytelaars, T. (eds.) ECCV 2014. LNCS, vol. 8693, pp. 740–755. Springer, Cham (2014). https://doi.org/10.1007/978-3-319-10602-1_48
18. Liu, N., Han, J., Yang, M.H.: Picanet: learning pixel-wise contextual attention for saliency detection. In: Proceedings of the IEEE Conference on Computer Vision and Pattern Recognition, pp. 3089–3098 (2018). https://doi.org/10.1109/cvpr.2018.00326
19. Merget, D., Rock, M., Rigoll, G.: Robust facial landmark detection via a fully-convolutional local-global context network. In: Proceedings of the IEEE Conference on Computer Vision and Pattern Recognition, pp. 781–790 (2018). https://doi.org/10.1109/cvpr.2018.00088
20. Newell, A., Yang, K., Deng, J.: Stacked hourglass networks for human pose estimation. In: Leibe, B., Matas, J., Sebe, N., Welling, M. (eds.) ECCV 2016. LNCS, vol. 9912, pp. 483–499. Springer, Cham (2016). https://doi.org/10.1007/978-3-319-46484-8_29
21. Papandreou, G., et al.: Towards accurate multi-person pose estimation in the wild. In: Proceedings of the IEEE Conference on Computer Vision and Pattern Recognition, pp. 4903–4911 (2017). https://doi.org/10.1109/cvpr.2017.395
22. Pishchulin, L., Andriluka, M., Gehler, P., Schiele, B.: Poselet conditioned pictorial structures. In: Proceedings of the IEEE Conference on Computer Vision and Pattern Recognition, pp. 588–595 (2013). https://doi.org/10.1109/cvpr.2013.82
23. Sapp, B., Taskar, B.: Modec: multimodal decomposable models for human pose estimation. In: Proceedings of the IEEE Conference on Computer Vision and Pattern Recognition, pp. 3674–3681 (2013). https://doi.org/10.1109/cvpr.2013.471
24. Sapp, B., Jordan, C., Taskar, B.: Adaptive pose priors for pictorial structures. In: 2010 IEEE Computer Society Conference on Computer Vision and Pattern Recognition, pp. 422–429. IEEE (2010). https://doi.org/10.1109/cvpr.2010.5540182
25. Tompson, J.J., Jain, A., LeCun, Y., Bregler, C.: Joint training of a convolutional network and a graphical model for human pose estimation. In: Advances in Neural Information Processing Systems, pp. 1799–1807 (2014). https://doi.org/10.1063/1.5024463
26. Toshev, A., Szegedy, C.: Deeppose: human pose estimation via deep neural networks. In: Proceedings of the IEEE Conference on Computer Vision and Pattern Recognition, pp. 1653–1660 (2014). https://doi.org/10.1109/cvpr.2014.214
27. Wang, F., et al.: Residual attention network for image classification. In: Proceedings of the IEEE Conference on Computer Vision and Pattern Recognition, pp. 3156–3164 (2017). https://doi.org/10.1109/cvpr.2017.683
28. Wang, P., et al.: Understanding convolution for semantic segmentation (2017). https://doi.org/10.4271/2018-01-1635
29. Wei, S.E., Ramakrishna, V., Kanade, T., Sheikh, Y.: Convolutional pose machines. In: Proceedings of the IEEE Conference on Computer Vision and Pattern Recognition, pp. 4724–4732 (2016). https://doi.org/10.1109/cvpr.2016.511

30. Wei, Y., Xiao, H., Shi, H., Jie, Z., Feng, J., Huang, T.S.: Revisiting dilated convolution: A simple approach for weakly- and semi- supervised semantic segmentation (2018). https://doi.org/10.1109/cvpr.2018.00759
31. Woo, S., Park, J., Lee, J.-Y., Kweon, I.S.: CBAM: convolutional block attention module. In: Ferrari, V., Hebert, M., Sminchisescu, C., Weiss, Y. (eds.) ECCV 2018. LNCS, vol. 11211, pp. 3–19. Springer, Cham (2018). https://doi.org/10.1007/978-3-030-01234-2_1
32. Wu, W., Qian, C., Yang, S., Wang, Q., Cai, Y., Zhou, Q.: Look at boundary: a boundary-aware face alignment algorithm. In: Proceedings of the IEEE Conference on Computer Vision and Pattern Recognition, pp. 2129–2138 (2018). https://doi.org/10.1109/cvpr.2018.00227
33. Xiao, B., Wu, H., Wei, Y.: Simple baselines for human pose estimation and tracking. In: Ferrari, V., Hebert, M., Sminchisescu, C., Weiss, Y. (eds.) ECCV 2018. LNCS, vol. 11210, pp. 472–487. Springer, Cham (2018). https://doi.org/10.1007/978-3-030-01231-1_29
34. Xu, J., Zhao, R., Zhu, F., Wang, H., Ouyang, W.: Attention-aware compositional network for person re-identification. In: Proceedings of the IEEE Conference on Computer Vision and Pattern Recognition, pp. 2119–2128 (2018). https://doi.org/10.1109/cvpr.2018.00226
35. Yang, W., Li, S., Ouyang, W., Li, H., Wang, X.: Learning feature pyramids for human pose estimation. In: Proceedings of the IEEE International Conference on Computer Vision, pp. 1281–1290 (2017). https://doi.org/10.1109/iccv.2017.144
36. Yang, Y., Ramanan, D.: Articulated pose estimation with flexible mixtures-of-parts. In: CVPR 2011, pp. 1385–1392. IEEE (2011). https://doi.org/10.1109/cvpr.2011.5995741
37. Yu, F., Koltun, V.: Multi-scale context aggregation by dilated convolutions. arXiv preprint arXiv:1511.07122 (2015). https://doi.org/10.1007/s11042-018-5653-x

Gradient-Based Learning of Compositional Dynamics with Modular RNNs

Sebastian Otte[1(✉)], Patricia Rubisch[2], and Martin V. Butz[1]

[1] Cognitive Modeling Group, University of Tübingen, Sand 14, 72076 Tübingen, Germany
sebastian.otte@uni-tuebingen.de

[2] Institute for Adaptive and Neural Computation, University of Edinburgh, 10 Crichton Street, Edinburgh EH8 9AB, Scotland

Abstract. Learning compositional dynamics with *recurrent neural networks* (RNNs) trained with *back-propagation through time* (BPTT) is usually a difficult task. Typically RNNs learn the consecutive shape along target sequences from time step to time step, focusing on local temporal correlations. When the challenge is to identify and model independent, unknown data subcomponents, that is, data generating causes on-the-fly during training, however, this local temporal shape-oriented inductive learning bias is obstructive. We propose a modular, compositional RNN architecture and derive simple procedures to automatically infer the source subdynamics that generate the data. We show that the involved error signal separation can be used for both teacher forcing and model-distinct target signal provision in the compositional RNN architecture. As a result, the entire network is able to learn compositional dynamics, developing emergent, flexibly adaptable signal decompositions within the distributed modules. We demonstrate that in this way simple RNNs trained with BPTT can learn sequences that could so far only be solved effectively with reservoir computing approaches. Moreover we show that these RNNs are much more robust against signal noise when compared to traditional BPTT or reservoir computing approaches.

Keywords: Signal decomposition · Recurrent neural networks · Teacher forcing · Back-propagation through time

1 Introduction

Over the recent years *recurrent neural networks* (RNNs) have become quite popular for their powerful sequence learning abilities. There are essentially two major paradigms for training RNNs. On the one hand, there is gradient-based learning, which is usually based on *back-propagation through time* (BPTT) [14] in combination with an appropriate gradient descent optimization technique, such as Adam [7]. On the other hand, there is reservoir computing—the most

I. V. Tetko et al. (Eds.): ICANN 2019, LNCS 11727, pp. 484–496, 2019.
https://doi.org/10.1007/978-3-030-30487-4_38

prominent representative of which are *echo state networks* (ESNs) [5], which provide a reservoir of recurrent dynamics, which are tuned by optimizing a linear output mapping.

Recent research focus lies on the former paradigm—not least due to the groundbreaking success of *long short-term memory* (LSTM) RNNs [4] and similar architectures. But even though LSTMs perform better than ESN-like approaches in various problem scenarios—particularly on sequence labeling tasks—there are drawbacks. Among other things, it appeared to be difficult to learn compositional or chaotic dynamics via BPTT—a task that is solved rather well by ESNs [10,11]. Nonetheless, there is so far no real explanation why this is case.

One aspect that could at least partially explain the superiority over BPTT when facing compositional or chaotic dynamics is that the attractor space of neural reservoirs is naturally shaped by random (or globally tuned) connectivity patterns a priori in a data-uncorrelated manner. In contrast, the inherent inductive learning biases in gradient-based RNNs cause them to focus on local temporal correlations within the data, focusing on learning the consecutive local shape along the sequence. When looking at compositional dynamics, however, this is particularly detrimental as it obstructs the identification and respective neural reflection of potentially independent subdynamics during training. As a result, when learning compositional problems via BPTT, the results are often mediocre and, on top of that, the decomposition of the target signal into dynamic subcomponents remains elusive. Nonetheless, the automatic decomposition into (partially) independent subdynamics is an important requisite towards the development of more generalized and better interpretable neural representations.

This paper addresses these challenges (i) by using a pre-structured RNN architecture, namely, a basin of RNN modules, which contribute compositionally to a common output, (ii) by deriving a novel scheme that infers individual subdynamics on-the-fly during training, individualizing teacher forcing and gradient signals. As a result, we demonstrate that it becomes possible to effectively learn compositional dynamics with BPTT. Moreover, the proposed system is able to decompose superimposed dynamics automatically and also appears to be significantly more robust to noise than, for instance, ESNs.

This paper is organized as follows. In Sect. 2.1 the modular RNN architecture is motivated and the procedure for inferring the subdynamics is derived. Section 3 demonstrates the capabilities of our system in the context of a representative signal decomposition problem and also provide further analyses of the system's behavior. Finally, in Sect. 4 recapitulates the proposed method and the achieved results and points out most relevant future objectives.

2 Learning Compositional Dynamics

Prestructuring neural networks is an important requisite for the success of their application. An obvious motivation comes from the human brain's modularity. Signal sources are separated and processed in highly modularized interactive manners, shaped by evolutionary-tuned developmental predispositions. As a consequence, specialized pathways can be identified, for example, deep sensory processing (e.g. dorsal/ventral visual processing), local sensory and motor processing in body-respective topologies (as illustrated by the sensory and motor homunculi), local forward model processing in the cerebellum, distinct hippocampal structures, or complementary activation patterns in nuclei that are involved in volitional movement [1,2,6,13].

For RNNs it has been shown that controlled connectivity can facilitate the learning capabilities tremendously, as well known from very deep ANN structures [3] as well as the superior performance of LSTMs over standard RNNs [4,15]. Even though unnecessary connections can in principle be deactivated by tuning down the respective weights, in practice the neural crosstalk can effectively hinder reaching and maintaining certain levels of performance quality and stability. Moreover, statistical correlations that are useful for generating particular input output mappings may be disruptive when mapping other inputs to similar outputs. This effect is clearly visible in the evaluation of fully-connected RNN variants Sect. 3—they entirely fail to learn the given compositional dynamics.

2.1 Modularized RNN

In this paper we propose a loosely prestructured network, namely, a modularized RNN, which matches the nature of compositional dynamics structurally. The base architecture is shown in Fig. 1. In accordance with the considered problem we assume a target signal that is composed of a certain number n of (independent) superimposed subdynamics, each much simpler than the overall signal. This is reflected by $m \geq n$ submodules within the RNN architecture. Each submodule, in the following indexed by i, can be considered as an RNN for itself with rather limited complexity.

In this paper we focus on oscillator networks: they do not have an explicit, separate input, but they feed their own output back into the network. Oscillator RNNs are typically initialized by *teacher forcing*, which means that the output is overwritten with the desired output signal. As a result, the hidden state of the network evolves as if the network would have created the desired output, tuning the network into the target dynamics.

Each module i has H hidden units (here non-linear, fully-connected) and K output neurons (here linear and fully-connected from as well as back into the hidden layer). x_{ik}^t refers to the k-th output of the i-th module at time step t. The final output layer, which has also K linear outputs, just sums element-wise over the respective outputs of all modules (without weighting):

$$y_k^t = \sum_i x_{ik}^t \tag{1}$$

Note that K also represents the dimensionality of the considered target signal (which is 1 within the experiments in Sect. 3).

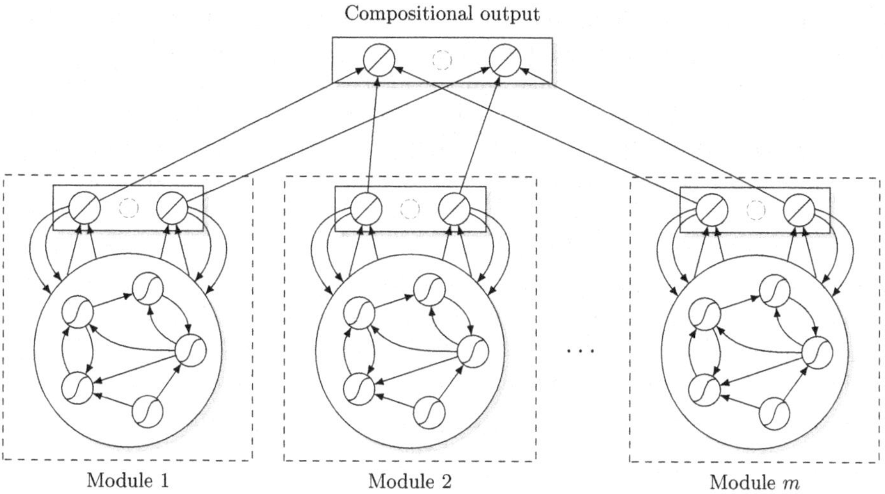

Fig. 1. Modular RNN architecture consisting of m separate oscillator RNN modules, indexed i, which contribute to a common output composition with K output neurons, indexed k. Each module is driven by its own output feedback and its recurrent hidden dynamics.

2.2 Adaptive Subdynamics Inference

We focus our task space on predicting the progression of a sequence. Specifically, several time steps of a time series are presented to the RNN sequentially via teacher forcing (tuning phase). Afterwards, the network continues the time series without further input, one and even multiple time steps ahead. In case of a regular monolithic RNN architecture its output during the tuning phase is just overwritten with the desired output $\mathbf{z}^t$. In our case, we want to achieve that the submodules reflect single subdynamics of the compositional signal. Consequently, it would be necessary to tune the modules with respective subtarget signals separately. These are, however, unknown as we only see the composed overall target signal. Hence, it is therefore necessary to simultaneously deduce the dynamic subcomponents and train the respective modules accordingly.

Let us consider one particular module i. Assuming that at the current time step all other modules generate correct outputs and all modules contribute additively to the common output, we can deduce the desired target signal $\tilde{\mathbf{z}}_i^t$ for module i by

$$\tilde{z}_{ik}^t = z_{ik}^t - \left[\left(\sum_{i'=1}^{m} x_{i'k}^t \right) - x_{ik}^t \right] \tag{2}$$

This is basically the compositional target minus the summed output of all submodules other than i. Note, however, that within an untrained RNN the particular outputs x_{ik}^t may be imprecise or even wrong. Recapitulate that, on the one hand, our goal is to synchronize the modules with the target signal.

On the other hand, we want to achieve an increasingly progressive separation of the subdynamics within the different modules. This requires a balance between the maintenance of local stability and the focus on the common, compositional output. For this reason we propose to perform the subtarget inference adaptively and gradually based on the current individual module dynamics. This can be accomplished by simply calculating adapted outputs x_{ik}^t at each time step with

$$\tilde{x}_{ik}^t = x_{ik}^t + \gamma^t \left(\tilde{z}_{ik}^t - x_{ik}^t\right) \tag{3}$$

where $0 < \gamma^t \leq 1$ is a time-varying step width. The essential aspect is now that we use the adapted outputs $\tilde{x}_{ik}^t$ for both (i) as teacher forcing signals for the respective modules (overwriting all x_{ik}^t) and (ii) as a desired output for individual sublosses, e.g, the squared error

$$\mathcal{L}_i^t = \frac{1}{2} \sum_k \left(\tilde{x}_{ik}^t - x_{ik}^t\right)^2 \tag{4}$$

Training the weights $w_{jj'}$ of the RNN via BPTT depends on the gradient

$$\frac{\partial \sum_t \sum_i \mathcal{L}_i^t}{\partial w_{jj'}} \tag{5}$$

The intuition of the outlined procedure is as follows: the modules are trained to generate outputs matching the current conception of their own contribution to compositional wholes. The smaller γ^t, the more the modules are driven by their own prediction of the particular subdynamics and the less they are influenced by each other as well as by the discrepancy between the overall compositional output and the target signal. On the other hand, a large γ^t leads to a strong pull towards approaching a common consensus and the target signal. It is due to this contrastive process that subdynamics can progressively emerge within separate modules, which is demonstrated in the next section.

3 Experiments

The experimental part of this paper (the presented results were obtained using the JANNLab framework [9]) addresses the *multiple superimposed oscillator* (MSO) benchmark. The MSO dynamics are generated using the equation

$$\text{MSO}_n(t) = \sum_{i=1}^{n} a_i \sin(f_i t + \varphi_i) \tag{6}$$

where n gives the number of superimposed waves, f_i the frequency, a_i the amplitude, and φ_i the phase-shift of each particular wave. Usually waves with the following frequencies are considered [8,10]:

$$\begin{array}{llll} f_1 = 0.2, & f_2 = 0.311 & f_3 = 0.42 & f_4 = 0.51 \\ f_5 = 0.63 & f_6 = 0.74 & f_7 = 0.85 & f_8 = 0.97 \\ f_9 = 1.08 & f_{10} = 1.19 & f_{11} = 1.27 & f_{12} = 1.32 \end{array}$$

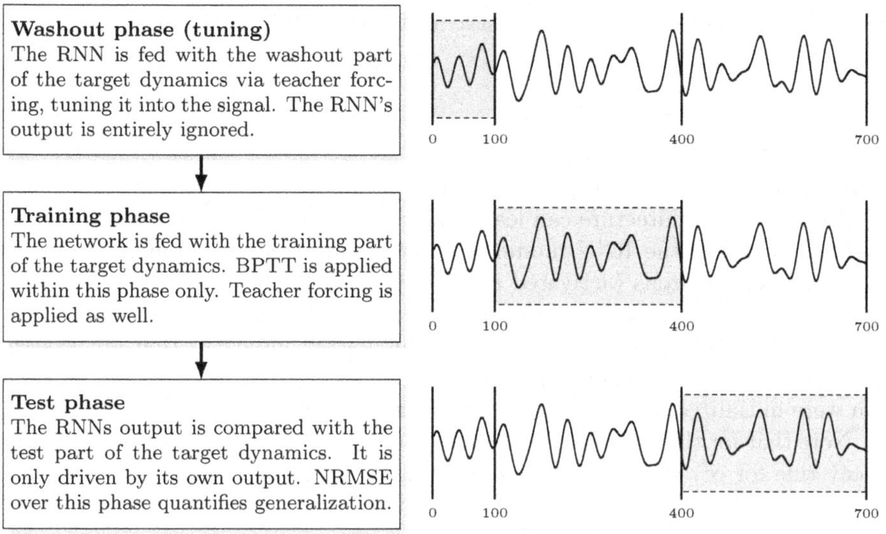
Washout phase (tuning)
The RNN is fed with the washout part of the target dynamics via teacher forcing, tuning it into the signal. The RNN's output is entirely ignored.
0 100 400 700
Training phase
The network is fed with the training part of the target dynamics. BPTT is applied within this phase only. Teacher forcing is applied as well.
0 100 400 700
Test phase
The RNNs output is compared with the test part of the target dynamics. It is only driven by its own output. NRMSE over this phase quantifies generalization.
0 100 400 700

Fig. 2. Overview over the three phases of the MSO benchmark.

For instance, MSO_5 contains the frequencies from f_1 to f_5, MSO_6 contains the frequencies from f_1 to f_6 and so on.

The usual MSO benchmark consists of the first 700 time steps of one particular time series (see Fig. 2). The first 100 time steps are used as a *washout phase*. Here, the target signal of the previous time step is injected back into the network via teacher forcing, while the original network output is completely ignored. The next 300 time steps are the *training phase*, in which the computed neural activations are used to accomplish the respective weight modification. We back-propagate the occurred error over this time window. Moreover, we continue to apply teacher forcing with the target signal. The last 300 time steps are used as the *test phase*, where the network is exclusively driven by its own output from the previous time step and its internal hidden dynamics.

To measure the test phase performance we compute the *normalized root mean square error* (NRMSE). Given a K-dimensional target sequence $\mathbf{z}$ with variance σ_z^2 an the generated output sequence $\mathbf{y}$ it is calculated by

$$\text{NRMSE}(\mathbf{y}, \mathbf{z}) = \sqrt{\frac{1}{KT\sigma_z^2}\left[\sum_{t=1}^{T}\sum_{k=1}^{K}(z_k^t - y_k^t)^2\right]} \tag{7}$$

For our purposes the MSO benchmark is ideally suited. Even though its formulation is relatively simple, it is surprisingly hard to be learned with RNNs, particularly when trained via BPTT. As stated more than ten years ago, this problem requires the development of individual, independent oscillators [12]. As an alternative, ESNs can be tued such that the development of linear attractors is fostered [10]. For incremental gradient-based learning, however, this problem remains challenging and thus can serve as a very useful, representative example for compositional dynamics.

3.1 Results

The first series of experiments is intended to provide a quantitative evaluation of how well our architecture can learn different MSO instances. In order to keep the complexity of the RNN modules as low as possible, we fixed their size to five non-linear neurons (activated by the hyperbolic tangent function). At first we used $m = n$ (number of modules is equal to the number of subdynamics). Additional experiments (not included in this paper) indicated that our system learns even with more modules than subsignals ($m > n$). The weights in each run were initialized normally distributed with a standard deviation of 0.1.

Note that for the experiments in this paper, we consistently used the following decay rule for γ^t, which turned out to work well during preliminary investigations. In the first time step of each sequential cycle (begin of washout) we set $\gamma^1 = 1$. After that γ^t is decayed using

$$\gamma^t = \alpha\gamma^{t-1} + (1 - \alpha)\gamma_{lo} \tag{8}$$

with $0 < \alpha < 1$ (potentially closely below 1). Thus, γ^t (slowly) converges towards the final step width γ_{lo}, which should be chosen significantly smaller than 1.

The training set consisted of only one single example of the respective MSO instance with no phase shifts ($\phi_i = 0$). This makes the benchmark particularly difficult as it requires the RNN to generalize from very little data. In contrast, the test set contained 100 MSO sequences with random phase shifts in order to probe the generalization abilities of the network. We used the Adam optimizer [7] for weight tuning, more or less with the default parameters (first and second moment smoothing factors $\beta_1 = 0.9$ and $\beta_2 = 0.999$). The learning rate η varied for the different problems as detailed below.

Table 1. Achieved error rates of our system for various MSO instances in comparison with regular RNNs/LSTMs (with direct teacher forcing).

MSO_n	Modular RNN				RNN (TF)	LSTM (TF)
	γ_{lo}	η	Success rate	NRMSE	NRMSE	NRMSE
1	0.9	10^{-3}	100 %	$7.09 \cdot 10^{-4}$	$6.25 \cdot 10^{-4}$	$1.47 \cdot 10^{-3}$
2	0.4	10^{-3}	100 %	$9.46 \cdot 10^{-4}$	0.921	0.980
3	0.2	$5 \cdot 10^{-4}$	76.92 %	$7.23 \cdot 10^{-3}$	0.995	0.988
4	0.1	$5 \cdot 10^{-4}$	71.43 %	$9.60 \cdot 10^{-3}$	–	–
5	0.1	$5 \cdot 10^{-4}$	47.62 %	$1.13 \cdot 10^{-2}$	–	–
6	0.1	10^{-4}	40.00 %	$2.06 \cdot 10^{-2}$	–	–
7	0.1	10^{-4}	34.48 %	$3.26 \cdot 10^{-2}$	–	–

Table 1 reports the achieved error rates (average over ten runs) and well-suited configuration parameters for MSO instances after 50.000 training iterations. Note that below an NRMSE of 0.1 it becomes difficult to visually see the difference between the output and the target signal, which we can therefore consider as a threshold indicating a precise prediction (see Fig. 3 for reference: an error of ≈ 0.1 corresponds to deviation of between the time steps 50–75, after time step 100 the error is on average at a level of 0.01).

Also, it is important to mention that the success of a training run strongly depends on the weight initialization—the learning process is obviously very sensitive to the starting conditions. These cases, in which the training error does not improve have been left out for computing the average error and are reported in the table as *success rate* separately. As it is trivial to learn a single wave, the first row in Table 1 can be seen as a minimal achievable error baseline for gradient-based training. Note, for comparison, that linear ESNs can model these dynamics much more precisely (with error rates around 10^{-8} for seven waves).

Nevertheless, it can be seen that the system is able to learn MSO instances precisely up to seven superimposed waves (it was to us so far not possible to sufficiently reproducibly learn eight or more waves). This is still—to the best of our knowledge—the first time that such error rates have been reported for this benchmark with that many waves for simple RNNs purely trained via BPTT. In contrast, monolithic oscillator RNNs (including LSTMs) with fully connected output feedback could not even learn an MSO_2 (for reference: an NRMSE between the respective MSO signal and a zero signal is ≈ 1).

More importantly, a closer inspection of the modules' activities reveals the real advantage of our system. Figure 3 shows the compositional output of a modular RNN trained on MSO_5 while the corresponding subdynamics are tuned into a presented target signal. It appears that (here in less than 25 time steps) the tuning scheme stabilizes the neural activities so that the RNN is synchronized with the compositional target signal, whereas each submodule clearly generates a distinct wave with a specific frequency—the original dynamic subcomponents. This is really remarkable, because the network did never received this information during training—the decomposition emerged spontaneously due to the adapted error-processing mechanism.

3.2 Emerging Decomposition

In the following we attempt to shed further light on how and when this signal decomposition actually starts to emerge. For this purpose we investigated a representative training process of the modular architecture learning MSO_5 more closely. Specifically, after each training iteration, we performed 100 time steps of signal tuning and, afterwards, recorded the compositional output as well as the submodule outputs of the next 1024 time steps during which self-driven signal prediction is performed. From these output trains we computed the respective frequency spectra using *fast Fourier transform* (FFT). Looking at the spectral representation provides information about the frequencies, which are generated within the RNN at a certain stage of training.

Figure 4 presents the outcome of this investigation. It shows the development of frequency spectra (six lower segments) paired with the respective test loss (most top segment) over the first 800 training iterations.

There are several interesting aspects to discover. First, it appears that after a short initialization period in which neither the modules nor the entire RNN produce any distinct spectral pattern, the final frequencies suddenly emerge surprisingly early during training (already after the first 200 iterations). This is significantly before the loss starts to drop. The latter only happens after the frequencies do not noticeably change any more. Note that at this time, there is still an overall error of ≈ 1, which is visually far away from a correct output. Second, frequencies can change: the output of the second module changes its main frequency significantly during training over iteration 100 until approx. 200 (it kind of swaps the frequency with the fourth module), while most others modules more or less remain at their initial frequency. Third, harmonics: the first

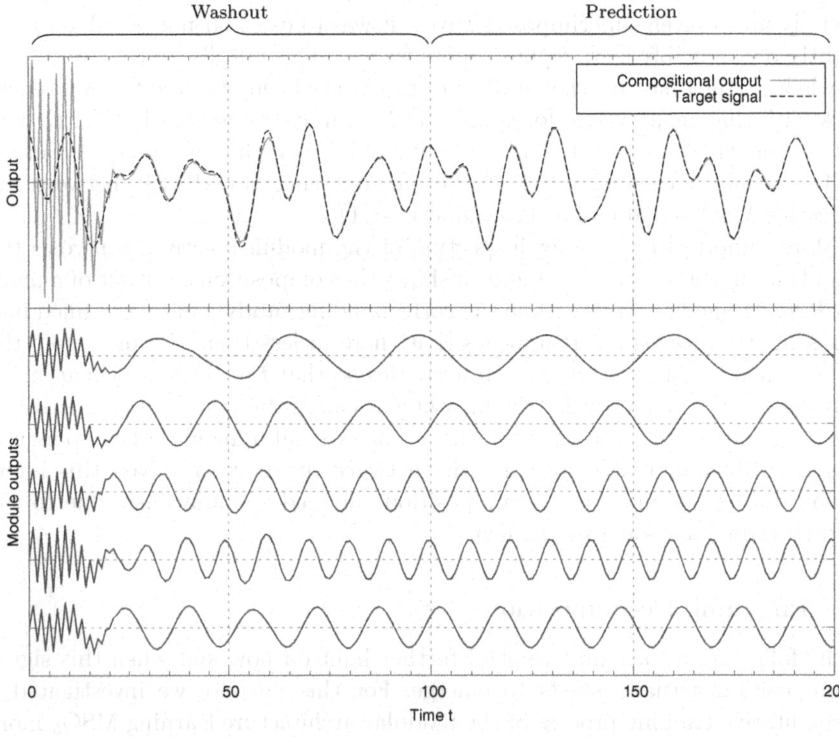

Fig. 3. Exemplary visualization of the tuning behavior within the modular RNN trained on MSO_5. Over the first 100 time steps washout (tuning) is performed. Over the subsequent 100 time steps the RNN predicts the sequence progression only driven by its own output. To upper part shows the compositional output plotted against the target sequence. To lower part shows the output development of the individual modules, achieving the signal decomposition into single waves.

module resonates also with the third harmonic, and, less visibly, even with the fourth harmonic, of its base frequency (0.2). Fourth, it seems that the medium frequencies (modules one and three particularly) were learned in tendency earlier than the higher or lower frequencies (modules 2, 5).

3.3 On the Robustness to Noise

It has been reported in [10] that ESNs, which learned MSO instances, are extremely sensitive to any sort of minimal noise. This is because they learn to approximate linear attractors in which all components are finely adjusted to each other. Consequently, the networks are not able to compensate any numerical deviation that is not specifically part of this linear dynamic process.

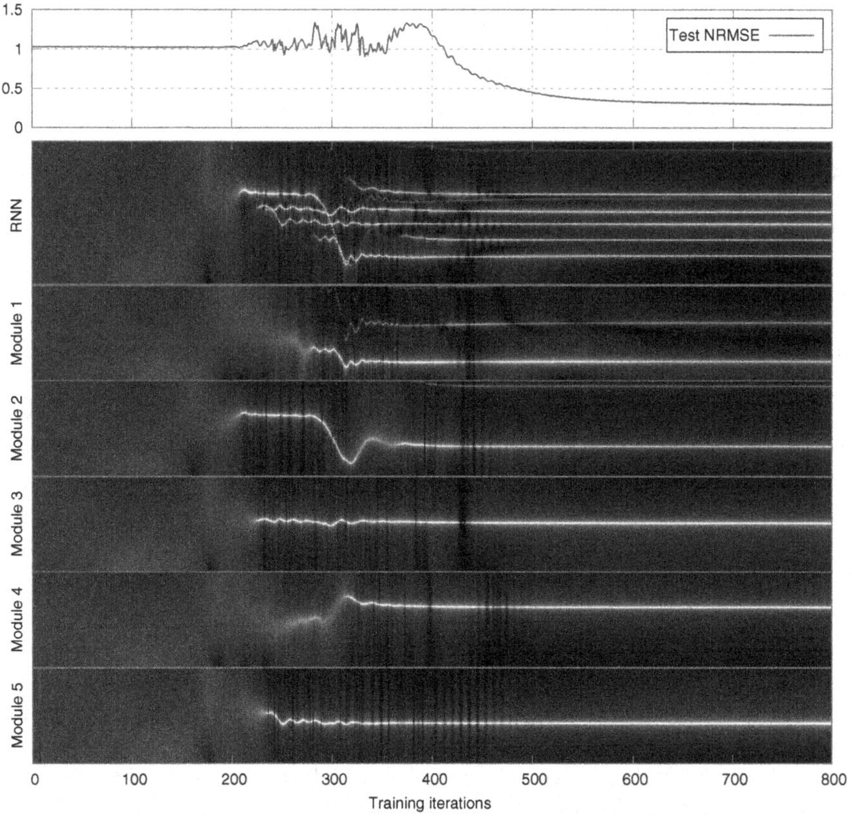

Fig. 4. Frequency development during the first 800 training iterations for MSO_5. The frequency range (y-axis) per row is $[0, 1]$. A high intensity close to the top border within a row indicates a high frequency. After each iteration the output spectrum of the overall RNN as well as of all five submodules is generated from 1024 times steps after tuning. The top row shows the corresponding error rate.

However, noise robustness is usually of crucial interest in practice. Therefore, we give a brief outlook on the robustness of our system to noise.

It turned out that once the RNN is trained, its modularized structure in combination with the adaptive tuning scheme exhibits an impressive noise robustness, as exemplarily shown in Fig. 5. Obviously, the network can easily tune its neural activities into the target dynamics, which requires not only activating the respective frequency components, but also an individual phase synchronization. Note that the network did not experience any noise during training.

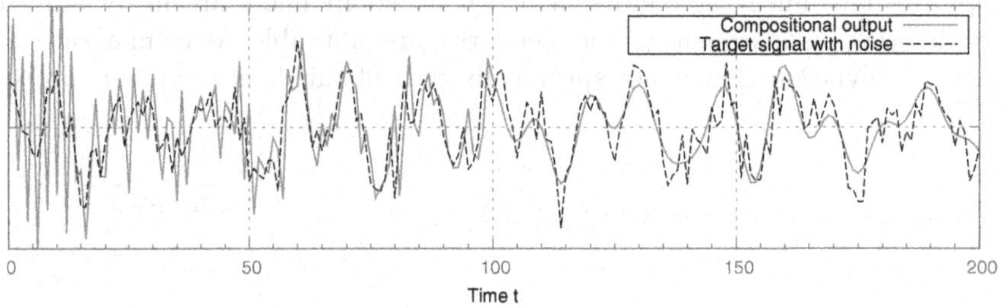

Fig. 5. A trained modular RNN tuning into a noisy MSO_5 (noise level $\sigma = 1$, standard deviation of ground truth is 1.58). Over the first 100 time steps the RNN is tuned with decreasing γ^t. The second 100 time steps are self-driven.

This robustness could be explained by the fact that a single module provides only a small capacity and cannot be influenced by other modules directly. Hence, it is not so prone to interferences as, in contrast, a more complex, monolithic network, and it thus falls into its learned attractor dynamics more easily. Additionally, the modules are not fully driven by teacher forcing but also (depending on γ^t) by their own prediction. This blend leads to the development of compositional outputs while pursuing global plausibility.

4 Conclusion

In this study we demonstrated that it is possible to effectively learn compositional dynamics with an RNN, while simultaneously identifying independent unknown data subcomponents on-the-fly during training. Our solution involves a modular compositional RNN architecture and a novel simple procedure to automatically infer the source subdynamics, which can be used for both teacher forcing and target signal provision for respective neural modules. In this way, simple RNNs trained with BPTT can learn problems that could so far only be solved effectively with reservoir computing approaches. We showed that the trained network performs a perfect separation of superimposed subdynamics and that it is able to quickly synchronize the individual modules accordingly. Moreover, our RNN model provides a remarkable robustness to noise, even though it was never opposed to noise during training.

In our upcoming research investigations we will focus on questions like, how the tuning rate γ^t can be adapted optimally based on the current statistics of the internal dynamics and the error signal, or how the sensitivity to starting conditions can be reduced. Of particular interest will also be to discover whether it is possible to let the modularization emerge within the process as well. This would certainly be useful in the context of compositional dynamics in which the subcomponents are partially correlated.

With the presented approach it was possible to overcome a specific drawback of gradient-based RNNs in a restricted problem scenario. Nonetheless, we think that the subtarget emergence in combination with a certain degree of modularization could be of general interest for RNN learning. Specifically, in the near future, we intend to investigate whether the procedure could be a generally beneficial supplement for teacher forcing based learning.

Acknowledgments. The authors would like to thank Sander Bothé, CWI Amsterdam, for helpful comments and suggestions regarding this work.

References

1. Butz, M.V., Kutter, E.F.: How the Mind Comes Into Being: Introducing Cognitive Science from a Functional and Computational Perspective. Oxford University Press, Oxford (2017)
2. Gao, Z., et al.: A cortico-cerebellar loop for motor planning. Nature **563**(7729), 113 (2018)
3. He, K., Zhang, X., Ren, S., Sun, J.: Deep residual learning for image recognition. In: The IEEE Conference on Computer Vision and Pattern Recognition (CVPR), June 2016
4. Hochreiter, S., Schmidhuber, J.: Long short-term memory. Neural Comput. **9**(8), 1735–1780 (1997). https://doi.org/10.1162/neco.1997.9.8.1735
5. Jaeger, H.: The "echo state" approach to analysing and training recurrent neural networks. Technical report, GMD Report, 148, Fraunhofer Institute for Analysis and Information Systems AIS, Sankt Augustin, Germany (2001)
6. Kandel, E.R., Schwartz, J.H., Jessell, T.M., Jessell, M.B.T., Siegelbaum, S., Hudspeth, A.: Principles of Neural Science. McGraw-hill, New York (2000)
7. Kingma, D.P., Ba, J.L.: Adam: a method for stochastic optimization. 3rd International Conference for Learning Representations abs/1412.6980 (2015)
8. Koryakin, D., Lohmann, J., Butz, M.V.: Balanced echo state networks. Neural Netw. **36**, 35–45 (2012)
9. Otte, S., Krechel, D., Liwicki, M.: JANNLab neural network framework for Java. In: Poster Proceedings of MLDM 2013, pp. 39–46. ibai-publishing, New York (2013)
10. Otte, S., Butz, M.V., Koryakin, D., Becker, F., Liwicki, M., Zell, A.: Optimizing recurrent reservoirs with neuro-evolution. Neurocomputing **192**, 128–138 (2016)
11. Pathak, J., Hunt, B., Girvan, M., Lu, Z., Ott, E.: Model-free prediction of large spatiotemporally chaotic systems from data: a reservoir computing approach. Phys. Rev. Lett. **120**, 024102 (2018)
12. Schmidhuber, J., Wierstra, D., Gagliolo, M., Gomez, F.: Training recurrent neural networks by evolino. Neural Comput. **19**, 757–779 (2007)

13. Svoboda, K., Li, N.: Neural mechanisms of movement planning: motor cortex and beyond. Curr. Opin. Neurobiol. **49**, 33–41 (2018)
14. Werbos, P.: Backpropagation through time: what it does and how to do it. Proc. IEEE **78**(10), 1550–1560 (1990). https://doi.org/10.1109/5.58337
15. Wu, Y., et al.: Google's Neural Machine Translation System: Bridging the Gap between Human and Machine Translation. ArXiv e-prints 1609.08144 (2016)

Transfer Learning with Sparse Associative Memories

Quentin Jodelet[1,2(✉)], Vincent Gripon[1], and Masafumi Hagiwara[2]

[1] IMT Atlantique, Technopole Brest Iroise, 29238 Brest, France
quentin.jodelet@imt-atlantique.net
[2] Keio University, Yagami Campus, Yokohama 223-8522, Japan

Abstract. In this paper, we introduce a novel layer designed to be used as the output of pre-trained neural networks in the context of classification. Based on Associative Memories, this layer can help design deep neural networks which support incremental learning and that can be (partially) trained in real time on embedded devices. Experiments on the ImageNet dataset and other different domain specific datasets show that it is possible to design more flexible and faster-to-train Neural Networks at the cost of a slight decrease in accuracy.

Keywords: Neural Networks · Associative Memories · Self-organizing Maps · Deep learning · Transfer learning · Incremental learning · Computer vision

1 Introduction

During the past decade, deep neural networks, and more specifically Deep Convolutional Neural Networks have been established as the state-of-the-art solution for various problems of Computer Vision such as image classification [13,19,31,33], image segmentation [3,12,22] and object tracking [2,34].

A standard Deep Neural Network relies on millions of trained parameters and thus requires millions of floating point operations in order to compute the output corresponding to a given input. Consequently, the use of deep neural networks for inference in real time tasks requires massive computing power and large amounts of memory. However embedded devices have important limitations in terms of computing power, memory and battery usage, so that deep neural networks are difficult to implement. Many research works have been carried out in order to produce faster deep neural networks architectures at run-time; new specific architectures have been developed specifically for real-time execution [28] and embedded systems [14,30]. Quantization [10,11,36,39], and more generally binarization [4,26,40], of deep neural networks is the preferred solution for running inference on embedded devices. It permits, at the cost of a little decrease of the accuracy, to replace the computationally intensive floating-point operations by low-bit operations which can be more efficiently implemented, especially on FPGA.

I. V. Tetko et al. (Eds.): ICANN 2019, LNCS 11727, pp. 497–512, 2019.
https://doi.org/10.1007/978-3-030-30487-4_39

Nevertheless, those research are mostly focused on the efficient execution of the inference on the embedded device and not on the even more complex training procedure which requires going through a large dataset multiple time. As of today, this procedure is generally performed offline using specific hardware such as GPUs or TPUs. Moreover, neural networks trained sequentially using backpropagation algorithm have a high propensity to steeply forget previous tasks when learning new ones regardless of whether they are used for reinforcement learning or supervised learning. This situation, referred to as catastrophic forgetting [7,8], happens because the weights of the network previously optimized for the first tasks are overwritten in order to correctly achieve the new task. Thus, adding new elements to the dataset (or new classes) can be handled only by restarting the training from scratch.

In order to benefit from the accuracy of deep neural networks without having to train them, a common solution is to rely on transfer learning [24]. In the context of computer vision, transfer learning consists in using deep neural networks pre-trained on a large dataset such as ImageNet [5], Microsoft COCO [21] or Google OpenImages [20], in order to obtain a generic image representation for other tasks. It is then possible to address new classification tasks on a different dataset by using pre-trained models as feature extractors, which may then be fine-tuned and combined with a simple, sometimes incremental, classifier [1,6,27,38].

In this paper, by using Self-Organizing Maps and Sparse Associative Memories, we propose a new Neural Network model meant to be used for classification tasks using transfer learning with pre-trained deep neural networks. The method we introduce comes with the following interests:

- It is able to incrementally learn new classes, while achieving competing accuracy with off-the-shelf non-incremental transfer methods
- It performs learning with a very limited complexity compared to existing counterparts, making it a competitive solution for embedded devices
- It builds on top of well-known models of Associative Memories and Self-Organizing Maps, each with its own set of hyperparameters that can be advantageously tuned in order to adapt to the ad-hoc constraints of a given problem

We experimentally prove these points in Sect. 4 by performing experiments using competitive vision transfer benchmarks.

2 Self-organizing Maps and Sparse Associative Memories

2.1 Self-organizing Maps

Presentation. A Self-Organizing Map (SOM) [18] is a fully connected layer of N neurons that associates a d-dimensional input vector $\mathbf{x}$ with an N-dimensional output vector $\mathbf{q}(\mathbf{x})$. These neurons are organized on a 2D-grid of q by r units in a way that each neuron but those on the edges has 4 direct neighbors.

All these neurons are entirely connected with the d neurons of the previous layer. The weights corresponding to a given neuron i are denoted $\mathbf{w}_i$. Figure 1 depicts an example of such an input layer and a map layer.

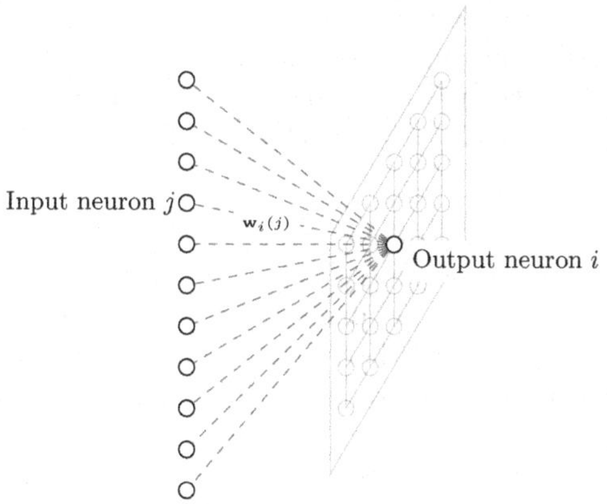

Fig. 1. Depiction of a self-organizing map layer.

Inference. When an input vector $\mathbf{x}$ is presented to the map layer, the corresponding output is computed as a vector $q(x) \in \{0,1\}^N$ containing a single 1. The coordinate i^* which value is 1 is defined as $i^* = \arg\min_{i=1}^{N} dist(\mathbf{w}_i, x)$. This i^*-th neuron is referred to as the Best-Matching Unit (BMU). Note that when the vector x and the vectors $\mathbf{w}_i$ all have a unit norm, the dynamics of self-organizing maps is equivalent to:

$$\mathbf{q}(\mathbf{x}) = h(W \cdot \mathbf{x}) , \tag{1}$$

where h is a Winner-Takes-All (WTA) operator (all values are put to 0 except for the maximal one, which is put to 1) and W is the matrix which lines are the vectors $\mathbf{w}_i$.

Training. In contrast with classic fully-connected layers used in deep neural networks, SOMs are built so that neighbor units contain strong inner dependencies, as explained below. The learning algorithm is performed for a specific number of epoch E and a specific batch size. The parameters $\mathbf{w}_i$ are first initialized at randoms. The learning procedure is then performed by iterating the following operations for t from 0 to E:

1. The training set $\mathcal{X}$ is randomly shuffled.
2. For each input vector $\mathbf{x}$ in $\mathcal{X}$, the corresponding output vector $\mathbf{y}$ is computed. Denoting i^* as the neuron where $\mathbf{y}(i^*) = 1$, we perform the following update of all weights:

$$\forall i, \mathbf{w}_i \leftarrow \mathbf{w}_i + (\mathbf{x} - \mathbf{w}_i)A(t)\Theta(t, i^*, i) . \tag{2}$$

where A is the learning decay function expressed as $A(t) = \alpha T(t)$ with α is the learning rate and T is a function which decreases with t that can be expressed as $T(t) = 1 - \frac{t}{E}$ or $T(t) = e^{-\frac{t}{E}}$; Θ the neighborhood function which decreases with t and the distance in the grid between neurons i and i' defined as $\Theta(t, i, i') = e^{-\frac{d_{i,i'}^2}{2(\theta T(t))^2}}$ where T is the decreasing function defined above and $d_{i,i'}$ is the distance between the i-th and the i'-th neurons in the grid independently of their associated vectors $\mathbf{w}_i$ and $\mathbf{w}_j$. Note that the latter depends only on the topology of the chosen self-organizing map.

Quantizing with Multiple SOMs. A popular way to quantize a vector is to use Product Quantization [15] (PQ). PQ consists in the following: (a) splitting the input vectors into k distinct subparts and (b) quantizing each part individually and independently from the others. The term "product" comes from the fact that the initial space is divided into a Cartesian product of lower dimensional subspaces.

In this section we propose to use multiple SOMs in order to perform PQ, using one for each subspace. The study is restricted to the case where vectors in each subspace all have the same dimension and where each SOM contains the same number N of neurons, such that the number of anchor vectors in the product (initial) space is N^k.

Concretely, let us consider dk-dimensional input vectors. Our methodology is summarized as follows:

- Training:
  1. Initialize k SOMs with input dimension d (indexed from 1 to k). They each contain N neurons,
  2. Split training vectors regularly into k d-dimensional subvectors each. The first subvector of each train vector is used to train the first SOM, the second subvector of each train vector to train the second SOM, etc.
- Quantizing:
  1. Split the input vector x into the k corresponding subvectors,
  2. For each subvector, obtain the corresponding output subvector using the associated SOM,
  3. Concatenate the output subvectors to obtain a kN-dimensional binary vector containing exactly k 1s, denoted $Q(x)$.

2.2 Sparse Associative Memories

Sparse Associative Memories [9] (SAMs) are neural networks able to store and retrieve sparse patterns from incomplete inputs. They consist of a neural network made of p distinct groups composed of variable numbers of units bound by binary connections. SAMs are able to store patterns which have exactly one active neuron in each group. Although not optimized for this problem, SAMs are also able to retrieve "close" patterns, meaning that some initially active neurons are changed during the retrieving procedure to find a stored pattern.

The learning procedure is as follows: The connections between the neurons are initialized empty; then for each pattern to store, the corresponding connections are added to the network. Since connections are binary (they either exist or not), they are not reinforced if shared by more than a single pattern.

The retrieving procedure starts from a partial pattern, meaning that some of its active neurons are initially not activated. Then, an iterative procedure is started. This procedure consists in finding in each group of neurons, the neuron (or the neurons) that has the maximum number of connections with the active neurons. Hopefully, after a few iterations, the network stabilizes to the stored pattern.

3 Proposed Model: Combining SOMs and SAMs

3.1 Presentation

We propose a new model by combining SAMs with multiple SOMs. The proposed model is a sparse associative memory composed of $p = k+1$ groups, where the k first groups correspond to k self-organizing maps composed of N neurons each, and the last group is the output layer containing M neurons. Since we are only interested in finding the active neuron in the last group, connections between the first k groups are ignored and the retrieving procedure is not iterated.

The proposed model has two hyper-parameters: k the number of SOMs and N the number of neurons on each SOM (as stated before, we assume that each SOM has the same number of neurons).

3.2 Training

The proposed model is expressed as k weight matrices Ws corresponding to each SOM and one sparse matrix Ω representing the connections between the k SOMs and the output layer. We denote $\mathcal{X}$ the training set containing pairs ($\mathbf{x}$, $\mathbf{y}$), where $\mathbf{x}$ is a dk-dimensional vector and $\mathbf{y}$ is an integer value between 1 and M corresponding to the label. The learning procedure consists in two distinct steps:

1. Training the multiple SOMs as described in the Sect. 2.1 on the training dataset $\mathcal{X}$ in order to compute the weight matrix W associated with each SOM.
2. The sparse matrix Ω is made of M lines and kN columns, initially containing only 0s. Two methods are proposed in order to train Ω:
   - **Binary method:** the sparse matrix Ω is a binary matrix containing only 1s and 0s. Then for each couple ($\mathbf{x}$, $\mathbf{y}$) in the training set $\mathcal{X}$, the following equation is obtained:

$$\Omega = \max_{(x,y)\in\mathcal{X}} \mathbf{e}_y \cdot Q(\mathbf{x})^\top \tag{3}$$

     where $^\top$ is the transpose operator, the max is applied componentwise, $\mathbf{e}_\ell$ is the vector of size M containing only 0s except for one 1 at the ℓ-th coordinate and Q is the quantization function which uses the k SOMs of the model as defined in the Sect. 2.1.

- **Integer method:** the sparse matrix Ω is an integer matrix containing only positive integer values. Then for each couple $(\mathbf{x}, \mathbf{y})$ in the training set $\mathcal{X}$, the following equation is obtained:

$$\Omega = \sum_{(x,y)\in\mathcal{X}} \mathbf{e}_y \cdot Q(\mathbf{x})^\top \tag{4}$$

where $^\top$ is the transpose operator, $\mathbf{e}_\ell$ is the vector of size M containing only 0s except for one 1 at the ℓ-th coordinate and Q is the quantization function which uses the k SOMs of the model as defined in the Sect. 2.1.

For reasons of clarity, we denote kxN-AL the proposed model composed of k SOMs with N neurons on each SOM if it was trained using the binary method and kxN-IAL if it was trained using the integer method.

The binary method is the faster one because it takes advantage of the fact that both Ω and $Q(x)$ are binary variables, implying that the computation of the product of both can be highly optimized during implementation. However, it is important to notice that a lot of information is lost due the binary representation of elements inside the matrix Ω and the integer method has been designed to mitigate this loss. Although it is no longer possible to take advantage of binary operations to optimize the implementation, integer operations remain faster than floating-point operations.

3.3 Inference

The retrieving procedure is also twofold and does not depend on the method used for the training. By considering an input vector $\mathbf{x}'$, the following prediction can be obtained by:

$$h\left(\Omega \cdot Q(\mathbf{x}')\right) \tag{5}$$

where h is an activation function, the Winner-Takes-All (WTA) function is the most commonly used and Q is the quantization function which uses the k SOMs of the model as defined in the Sect. 2.1.

When used this way, the sparse associative memory basically emulates a majority vote among the multiple self-organizing maps.

3.4 Proposed Model Used as Classifier

Presentation. The model composed of multiple self-organizing maps and one sparse associative memory proposed in the previous section has been designed to be used as a new neural network classifying layer for a conventional Deep Neural Network. The proposed model is a neural network classifier that relies on Transfer Learning and it has to be combined with a feature extractor. In general, the feature extractor is a Convolutional Neural Network pre-trained on a universal dataset, such as ImageNet for image classification, which classification layer has been removed.

Training. We denote $\mathcal{U}$ the universal training dataset used to train the feature extractor. $\mathcal{U}$ contains pairs ($\mathbf{x}$, $\mathbf{y}$), where $\mathbf{x}$ is a training vector and $\mathbf{y}$ is the corresponding label, and $\mathcal{U}'$ the dataset containing pairs ($\mathbf{x}'$, $\mathbf{y}$) where $\mathbf{x}'$ is a k-dimensional vector obtained as the output when $\mathbf{x}$ is passed as the input to the feature extractor. Similarly, we denote $\mathcal{T}$ the domain specific training set and $\mathcal{T}'$.

As described in Sect. 3.2, the first step is to train the SOMs of the proposed model on the universal dataset $\mathcal{U}'$. The second step consists in training from scratch the matrix Ω using the domain specific training set $\mathcal{T}'$. The first step, training the SOMs, is the most computationally expensive task and has to be done ahead; while the second step, the training on the domain specific dataset, takes fully advantage of the fast incremental learning algorithm described above and has been designed to be done in real-time on the edge.

Application. The strengths of this learning procedure is that it is simple and fast: once the feature extractor and the self-organizing maps have been trained on the universal dataset, each training element of the specific dataset has to be processed only one time in order to be learned and the procedure is limited to two sparse matrix products and non-linear functions if the input of the model is a unit vector. Moreover, the learning of each element is independent, and thus it is possible to learn new elements in parallel and incrementally. This means that contrary to deep neural networks which rely on the gradient decent algorithm, it is not required to restart the training from scratch in order to learn new classes or new elements for a previously learned class. Therefore in the situation where the proposed model has already been trained on several classes and has to learn a new one, it is just required to process the elements of the new class. While for a standard deep neural network trained using gradient decent algorithm, in order to avoid catastrophic forgetting it is required to restart the learning from scratch and to process again the elements of the previously learned classes in addition to the elements of the new class.

4 Experiments

4.1 Protocol

In the following subsections, the impact of the different hyper-parameters of the proposed model is evaluated and the proposed model is compared with other methods on several small domain-specific datasets.

In order to be able to express the complete layer as matrix products, inputs of the proposed model are normed: this does not significantly impact the accuracy of the model in this case.

Because the accuracy and the time required for the training may slightly vary, every experiment has been done thirty times. The mean and the standard deviation are reported for each measure. Measures of the training time only consider the time required to train the classifiers and do not take the time required to extract the features into account.

Competing Methods. In order to evaluate our method, the proposed model is compared with different classifiers: a brute-force K-Nearest Neighbor classifier, a Support Vector Machine and a simple deep neural network classifier (denoted DNN classifier). The C-SVM with a Gaussian kernel has been used and it has been trained using a One-vs-Rest policy. The deep neural network is composed of three densely connected layers and it has been trained using three different optimizers: stochastic gradient descent, stochastic gradient descent combined with Cyclical Learning rates [32] and Adam [17]. All classifiers, just like the proposed model, are trained using transfer learning with the same feature extractor. The feature extractor used in all the experiments below is a VGG-16 model trained on ILSVRC dataset [29] whose dense classification layer has been removed, thus the feature vector is a 4096-dimensional floating point vector. In order to compare the four solutions, it has been decided to not use augmentation on training data or fine-tuning of previous layers of the pre-trained VGG-16 model: the use of these techniques will improve the performance of every method.

Datasets. The proposed model has been compared with the other classifiers on several domain specific dataset: 102 Category Flower Dataset [23] (denoted by Flower102), the Indoor Scene Recognition Dataset [25] (denoted by Indoor67), the Caltech-UCSD Birds 200 dataset [35] (denoted by CUB200), the Stanford Dogs Dataset [16] (denoted by Dog120) and the Stanford 40 Actions Dataset [37] (denoted by Stanford40). These datasets contain highly similar images divided into a lot of classes containing only few images each:

- Flower102 dataset contains images of 102 different flower species: the training set is composed of 2040 images and the test set is composed of 6149 images.
- Indoor67 dataset contains images of 67 different indoor places: the training set is composed of 5360 images and the test set is composed of 1340 images.
- CUB200 dataset contains images of 200 different bird species: the training set is composed of 3000 elements and the test set is composed of 3033 elements.
- Dog120 dataset contains images of 120 different dog species: the training set is composed of 12000 elements and the test set is composed of 8580 elements.
- Stanford40 dataset contains images of 40 distinct type of actions performed by humans: the training set is composed of 4000 elements and the test set is composed of 5532 elements.

4.2 Impact of Hyper-parameters

The first series of experiments consist in comparing the accuracy of the proposed model on the classification of the Stanford Dogs Dataset depending on the two hyper-parameters of the proposed model: k the number of self-organizing maps and N the number of neuron in each self-organizing map.

Figures 2 and 3 compare the Top-5 accuracy of different versions of the proposed model on the classification of Dog120. Figure 2 compares versions of the proposed model which each has a different number of SOMs and Fig. 3 compares versions of the proposed model which each has a different number of neurons

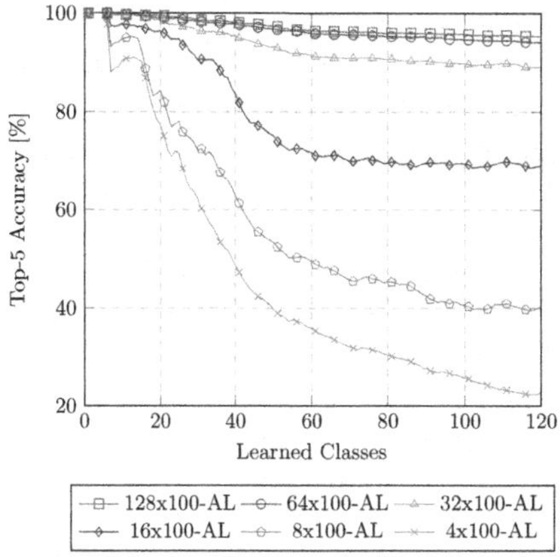

Fig. 2. Comparison of the Top-5 accuracy of the proposed model on classification task on Dog120 depending on the number of self-organizing maps composing the model.

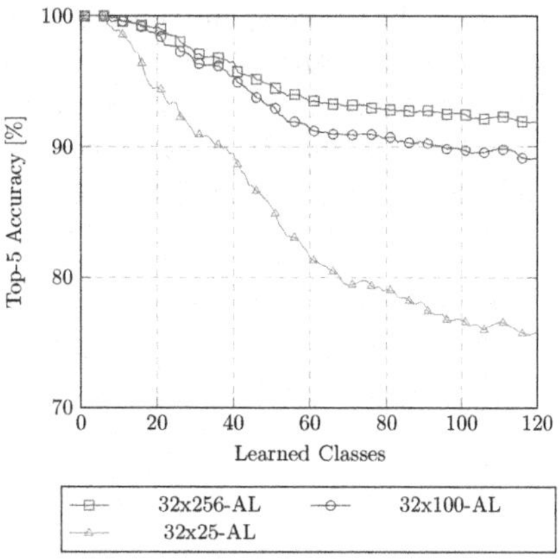

Fig. 3. Comparison of the Top-5 accuracy of the proposed model on classification task on Dog120 depending on the number of neurons on each self-organizing map composing the model.

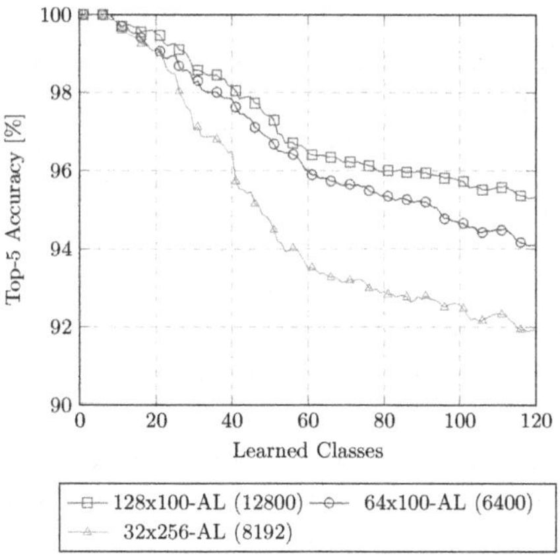

Fig. 4. Comparison of the Top-5 accuracy of the proposed model on classification task on Dog120 depending on the total number of neurons.

in each SOM. It appears that, both the increase of the number of SOMs composing the model and the increase of the number of neurons in each SOM will increase the accuracy of the model. This is tied to the fact that they will reduce the loss of information induced by the quantization. However, the computational cost of both the training procedure and the inference procedure of the proposed model is directly correlated to the total number of neurons in the model: the sum of the number of neurons in each SOM. Thus, increasing the number of SOMs or the number of neurons per SOM will also increase the cost. It should be noted that increasing the number of neurons is not necessarily synonymous with increasing the accuracy of the model. As shown in Fig. 4, the 32×256-AL is outperformed by the 64×100-AL even though the latter has 28% less neurons than the first one. In general, for a fixed number of neurons, the model using the largest number of SOMs should be preferred.

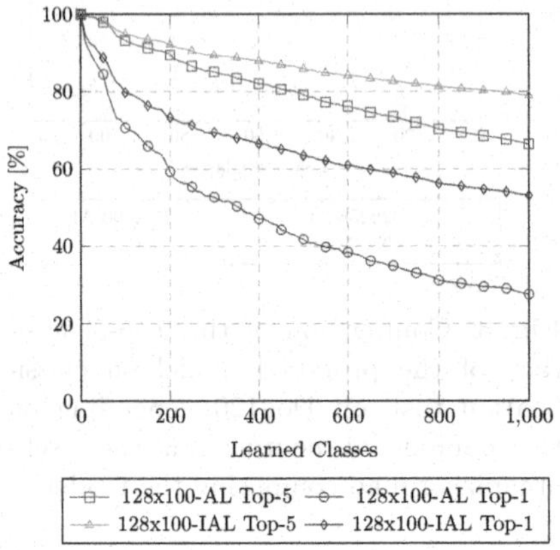

Fig. 5. Comparison of the binary (128×100-AL) and integer (128×100-IAL) version of proposed model on classification task on ILSVRC 2012 dataset.

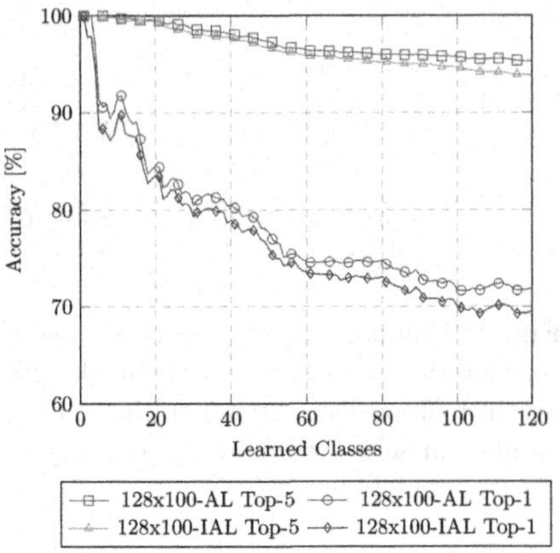

Fig. 6. Comparison of the binary (128×100-AL) and integer (128×100-IAL) version of proposed model on classification task on Dog120.

Figures 5 and 6 compare the original proposed model with the improved version which uses integer values instead of binary values on two different classification tasks. The binary model is more accurate than the integer one on the Dog120 dataset while the integer model is more accurate on the ILSVRC dataset. In fact the binary model is more efficient for datasets containing few images per classes whereas the integer model is more efficient on larger datasets containing more images per classes.

4.3 Comparison with Other Methods

Figure 7 compares the accuracy of the proposed model with the accuracy of the deep neural network classifier trained on the Dog120 dataset using stochastic gradient descent depending on the number of learned classes. Both classifier have been trained on all the considered classes at once: this means that each time a new class is added to the training set, the learning procedure is restarted from scratch and the classifier has to learn again the previously learned classes in addition to the new class. It appears that both models have nearly the same accuracy: they have the same Top-5 accuracy and the Top-1 accuracy of proposed model is slightly inferior to the one of the deep neural network classifier. In the

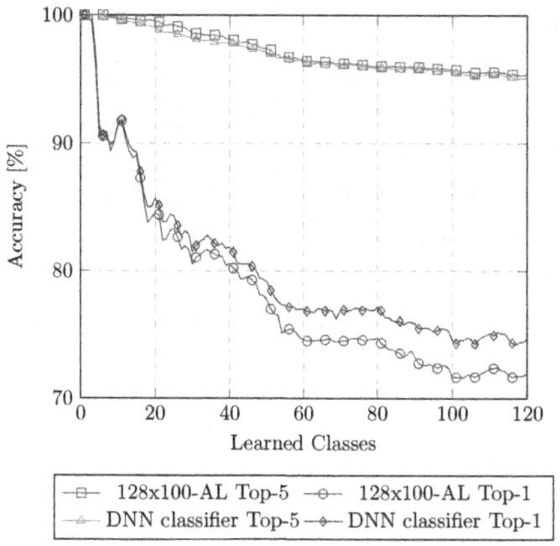

Fig. 7. Comparison of 128×100-AL with the DNN classifier trained using SGD on classification task on the Dog120 dataset depending on the number of classes learned. Both classifiers have been trained on all the considered classes at once.

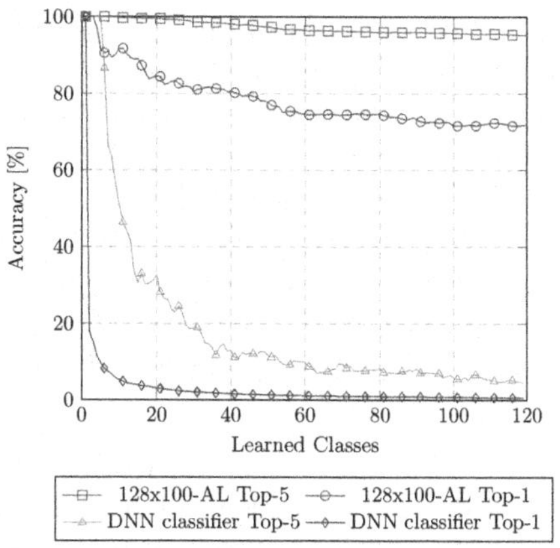

Fig. 8. Comparison of 128×100-AL with the DNN classifier trained using SGD on classification task on the Dog120 dataset depending on the number of classes learned. Both classifiers have been trained sequentially.

case where the number of learned classes equals 120, the loss in accuracy is about 2.7%: the Top-1 accuracy of the proposed model is 71.9% and the Top-1 accuracy of the deep neural network classifier is 74.6%.

However, as explained in the Sect. 3.4, contrary to the deep neural network classifier, the proposed model supports incremental learning. Figure 8 compares the accuracy of the proposed model with the accuracy of the deep neural network classifier trained on the Dog120 dataset using stochastic gradient descent depending on the number of learned classes. Nevertheless, in this case both classifiers have been trained sequentially: this means that each time a new class is added to the training set, the classifier is only trained on the new elements. As expected, the accuracy of the proposed model is exactly the same because of the learning algorithm used: it does not change if the proposed model is trained on all the dataset at once or sequentially. However, the accuracy of the deep neural network classifier crashed and dropped to 0.66% for Top-1 accuracy and 4.55% for Top-5 accuracy in the case where the number of learned classes equals 120. This is due to catastrophic forgetting: since the deep neural network classifier was trained sequentially, each time it learns a new class it also inevitably forgets all the previously learned classes. Therefore, the deep neural network classifier always predicts the last learned class independently of the input image.

As a result, the proposed model is more flexible than the deep neural network classifier because it supports incremental learning at the cost of the slight decrease of accuracy. The proposed model can be more easily retrained and adapted to a new situation compared to the deep neural network classifier. For example, if the proposed model has already been trained on the first 119 classes of the Dog120 dataset and has to learn the last one, it is just required to process the elements of the new class, while for the deep neural network classifier, it is required to restart the learning from scratch and to process the elements of all the 120 classes of the dataset in order to avoid catastrophic forgetting. In this case, it will be up to approximately 2600 times faster for the proposed model to learn the new class compared to the deep neural network classifier, as shown in Table 3.

The proposed model has also been compared with the other classifiers on several additional domain specific dataset:

Table 1. Comparison of the accuracy of 128 × 100-AL with different transfer learning methods on classification task on different domain specific datasets when learning the complete dataset at once. Values are averaged over 30 runs.

		Non incremental methods				Incremental methods	
		DNN classifier (SGD)	DNN classifier (SGD + CycleLR)	DNN classifier (Adam)	SVM	K-NN	Proposed model 128 × 100-AL
Flower102	Top-1	**75.71% (±0.97)**	70.52% (±2.08)	72.12% (±0.96)	73.80% (±0.0)	57.13% (±0.0)	66.92% (±0.0)
	Top-5	**91.89% (±0.56)**	89.07% (±1.25)	90.17% (±0.69)	90.94% (±0.0)	80.34% (±0.0)	87.48% (±0.0)
Indoor67	Top-1	65.43% (±0.83)	64.05% (±0.93)	61.86% (±1.48)	**67.24% (±0.0)**	52.76% (±0.0)	56.49% (±0.0)
	Top-5	90.21% (±0.50)	89.57% (±0.56)	87.86% (±0.52)	**90.90% (±0.0)**	78.36% (±0.0)	87.31% (±0.0)
CUB200	Top-1	37.31% (±0.97)	32.69% (±1.21)	31.97% (±1.20)	38.02% (±0.0)	24.70% (±0.0)	**41.51% (±0.0)**
	Top-5	66.74% (±1.05)	61.83% (±1.46)	61.61% (±1.50)	66.74% (±0.0)	50.31% (±0.0)	**76.18% (±0.0)**
Dog120	Top-1	74.56% (±0.34)	73.81% (±0.29)	70.80% (±0.65)	**76.35% (±0.0)**	68.83% (±0.0)	71.91% (±0.0)
	Top-5	95.06% (±0.14)	94.63% (±0.15)	93.37% (±0.30)	**95.90% (±0.0)**	87.74% (±0.0)	95.34% (±0.0)
Stanford40	Top-1	68.05% (±0.54)	67.81% (±0.42)	66.21% (±0.70)	**69.54% (±0.0)**	57.36% (±0.0)	59.06% (±0.0)
	Top-5	90.67% (±0.34)	90.61% (±0.28)	89.46% (±0.39)	**91.68% (±0.0)**	79.10% (±0.0)	87.02% (±0.0)

Table 1 shows that the proposed model is slightly inferior to the others methods in terms of performance on the tested datasets except for the CUB200 dataset. However, due to the learning algorithm used, it is considerably faster to train as shown in Table 2. In order to moderate these results, it may be possible to decrease a bit the training time of the other models by using a more aggressive early stop function and different hyper-parameters but the order of magnitude will remain similar: generally the proposed model is 10 times faster to train than

Table 2. Comparison of the training time of 128×100-AL with different classifiers on different domain specific datasets when learning the complete dataset at once. Training time duration is expressed relatively to the one of the proposed model: the lower is the value, the better it is. Values are averaged over 30 runs.

	DNN classifier (SGD)	DNN classifier (SGD + CycleLR)	DNN classifier (Adam)	SVM	Proposed model 128×100-AL
Flower102	45 (±8.5)	18 (±3.8)	32 (±5.9)	87 (±5.3)	**1**
Indoor67	20 (±3.1)	9 (±1.6)	18 (±3.2)	127 (±8.2)	**1**
CUB200	24 (±3.6)	9 (±1.15)	16 (±2.2)	87 (±3.1)	**1**
Dog120	18 (±4.1)	9 (±0.5)	15 (±2.2)	214 (±12.4)	**1**
Stanford40	12 (±2.2)	8 (±0.63)	14 (±2.4)	79 (±5.4)	**1**

Table 3. Comparison of the training time of 128×100-AL with different classifiers on different domain specific datasets when learning the last class of the dataset after having learned the previous classes. Training time duration is expressed relatively to the one of the proposed model: the lower is the value, the better it is. Values are averaged over 30 runs.

	DNN classifier (SGD)	DNN classifier (SGD + CycleLR)	DNN classifier (Adam)	SVM	Proposed model 128×100-AL
Flower102	5410 (±977)	2222 (±428)	3867 (±655)	10460 (±247)	**1**
Indoor67	1602 (±248)	762 (±120)	1474 (±238)	10207 (±101)	**1**
CUB200	4632 (±836)	1836 (±271)	3197 (±411)	17111 (±1028)	**1**
Dog120	2703 (±582)	1333 (±22)	2222 (±337)	31239 (±376)	**1**
Stanford40	667 (±111)	409 (±16)	737 (±126)	4220 (±44)	**1**

the others when trained on the whole dataset at once. However, as explained above, if it is required to only learn a new class, both the deep neural network classifier and the SVM have to be retrained from scratch and thus, the proposed model is exceptionally faster to train, as shown in Table 3.

5 Conclusion

We introduced a new classifier model primarily composed of Self-Organizing Maps and Sparse Associative Memories. By combining the proposed layer with a pre-trained Deep Neural Network, it is possible to design flexible deep neural networks with a considerably faster learning algorithm as well as the support of incremental learning at the cost of a slight decrease of the accuracy. Using the proposed model can help the development and the deployment of new intelligent embedded devices which can learn new elements in real time and adapt themselves to their environment without the help of an external agent responsible for the execution of the training algorithm.

References

1. Azizpour, H., Razavian, A.S., Sullivan, J., Maki, A., Carlsson, S.: Factors of transferability for a generic ConvNet representation. IEEE Trans. Pattern Anal. Mach. Intell. **38**(9), 1790–1802 (2016). https://doi.org/10.1109/tpami.2015.2500224
2. Bertinetto, L., Valmadre, J., Henriques, J.F., Vedaldi, A., Torr, P.H.S.: Fully-convolutional siamese networks for object tracking. In: Hua, G., Jégou, H. (eds.) ECCV 2016. LNCS, vol. 9914, pp. 850–865. Springer, Cham (2016). https://doi.org/10.1007/978-3-319-48881-3_56
3. Chen, L.C., Papandreou, G., Schroff, F., Adam, H.: Rethinking atrous convolution for semantic image segmentation. arXiv preprint arXiv:1706.05587 (2017)
4. Courbariaux, M., Hubara, I., Soudry, D., El-Yaniv, R., Bengio, Y.: Binarized neural networks: Training deep neural networks with weights and activations constrained to+ 1 or −1. arXiv preprint arXiv:1602.02830 (2016)
5. Deng, J., Dong, W., Socher, R., Li, L.J., Li, K., Fei-Fei, L.: ImageNet: a large-scale hierarchical image database. In: 2009 IEEE Conference on Computer Vision and Pattern Recognition. IEEE, June 2009. https://doi.org/10.1109/cvprw.2009.5206848
6. Donahue, J., et al.: DeCAF: a deep convolutional activation feature for generic visual recognition. In: International Conference on Machine Learning, pp. 647–655 (2014)
7. French, R.: Catastrophic forgetting in connectionist networks. Trends Cogn. Sci. **3**(4), 128–135 (1999). https://doi.org/10.1016/s1364-6613(99)01294-2
8. Goodfellow, I.J., Mirza, M., Xiao, D., Courville, A., Bengio, Y.: An empirical investigation of catastrophic forgetting in gradient-based neural networks. arXiv preprint arXiv:1312.6211 (2013)
9. Gripon, V., Berrou, C.: Sparse neural networks with large learning diversity. IEEE Trans. Neural Netw. **22**(7), 1087–1096 (2011). https://doi.org/10.1109/tnn.2011.2146789
10. Han, S., Mao, H., Dally, W.J.: Deep compression: Compressing deep neural networks with pruning, trained quantization and huffman coding. arXiv preprint arXiv:1510.00149 (2015)
11. Han, S., Pool, J., Tran, J., Dally, W.: Learning both weights and connections for efficient neural network. In: Advances in Neural Information Processing Systems, pp. 1135–1143 (2015)
12. He, K., Gkioxari, G., Dollar, P., Girshick, R.: Mask r-CNN. In: 2017 IEEE International Conference on Computer Vision (ICCV). IEEE, October 2017. https://doi.org/10.1109/iccv.2017.322
13. He, K., Zhang, X., Ren, S., Sun, J.: Deep residual learning for image recognition. In: 2016 IEEE Conference on Computer Vision and Pattern Recognition (CVPR). IEEE, June 2016. https://doi.org/10.1109/cvpr.2016.90
14. Howard, A.G., et al.: Efficient convolutional neural networks for mobile vision applications. arXiv preprint arXiv:1704.04861 (2017)
15. Jégou, H., Douze, M., Schmid, C.: Product quantization for nearest neighbor search. IEEE Trans. Pattern Anal. Mach. Intell. **33**(1), 117–128 (2011). https://doi.org/10.1109/TPAMI.2010.57
16. Khosla, A., Jayadevaprakash, N., Yao, B., Fei-Fei, L.: Novel dataset for fine-grained image categorization. In: First Workshop on Fine-Grained Visual Categorization, IEEE Conference on Computer Vision and Pattern Recognition. Colorado Springs, CO, June 2011

17. Kingma, D.P., Ba, J.: Adam: A method for stochastic optimization. arXiv preprint arXiv:1412.6980 (2014)
18. Kohonen, T.: The self-organizing map. Proc. IEEE **78**(9), 1464–1480 (1990). https://doi.org/10.1109/5.58325
19. Krizhevsky, A., Sutskever, I., Hinton, G.E.: Imagenet classification with deep convolutional neural networks. In: Advances in Neural Information Processing Systems 25, pp. 1097–1105. Curran Associates, Inc. (2012)
20. Kuznetsova, A., et al.: The open images dataset v4: Unified image classification, object detection, and visual relationship detection at scale. arXiv:1811.00982 (2018)
21. Lin, T.-Y., et al.: Microsoft COCO: common objects in context. In: Fleet, D., Pajdla, T., Schiele, B., Tuytelaars, T. (eds.) ECCV 2014. LNCS, vol. 8693, pp. 740–755. Springer, Cham (2014). https://doi.org/10.1007/978-3-319-10602-1_48
22. Long, J., Shelhamer, E., Darrell, T.: Fully convolutional networks for semantic segmentation. In: Proceedings of the IEEE Conference on Computer Vision and Pattern Recognition, pp. 3431–3440 (2015). https://doi.org/10.1109/CVPR.2015.7298965
23. Nilsback, M.E., Zisserman, A.: Automated flower classification over a large number of classes. In: 2008 Sixth Indian Conference on Computer Vision, Graphics & Image Processing. IEEE, December 2008. https://doi.org/10.1109/icvgip.2008.47
24. Pan, S.J., Yang, Q.: A survey on transfer learning. IEEE Trans. Knowl. Data Eng. **22**(10), 1345–1359 (2010). https://doi.org/10.1109/TKDE.2009.191
25. Quattoni, A., Torralba, A.: Recognizing indoor scenes. In: 2009 IEEE Conference on Computer Vision and Pattern Recognition. IEEE, June 2009. https://doi.org/10.1109/cvprw.2009.5206537
26. Rastegari, M., Ordonez, V., Redmon, J., Farhadi, A.: XNOR-net: ImageNet classification using binary convolutional neural networks. In: Leibe, B., Matas, J., Sebe, N., Welling, M. (eds.) ECCV 2016. LNCS, vol. 9908, pp. 525–542. Springer, Cham (2016). https://doi.org/10.1007/978-3-319-46493-0_32
27. Razavian, A.S., Azizpour, H., Sullivan, J., Carlsson, S.: CNN features off-the-shelf: an astounding baseline for recognition. In: 2014 IEEE Conference on Computer Vision and Pattern Recognition Workshops. IEEE, June 2014. https://doi.org/10.1109/cvprw.2014.131
28. Redmon, J., Divvala, S., Girshick, R., Farhadi, A.: You only look once: unified, real-time object detection. In: 2016 IEEE Conference on Computer Vision and Pattern Recognition (CVPR). IEEE, June 2016. https://doi.org/10.1109/cvpr.2016.91
29. Russakovsky, O., et al.: ImageNet large scale visual recognition challenge. Int. J. Comput. Vis. (IJCV) **115**(3), 211–252 (2015). https://doi.org/10.1007/s11263-015-0816-y
30. Sandler, M., Howard, A., Zhu, M., Zhmoginov, A., Chen, L.C.: MobileNetV2: inverted residuals and linear bottlenecks. In: 2018 IEEE/CVF Conference on Computer Vision and Pattern Recognition. IEEE, June 2018. https://doi.org/10.1109/cvpr.2018.00474
31. Simonyan, K., Zisserman, A.: Very deep convolutional networks for large-scale image recognition. arXiv preprint arXiv:1409.1556 (2014)
32. Smith, L.N.: Cyclical learning rates for training neural networks. In: 2017 IEEE Winter Conference on Applications of Computer Vision (WACV). IEEE, March 2017. https://doi.org/10.1109/wacv.2017.58

33. Szegedy, C., Vanhoucke, V., Ioffe, S., Shlens, J., Wojna, Z.: Rethinking the inception architecture for computer vision. In: 2016 IEEE Conference on Computer Vision and Pattern Recognition (CVPR). IEEE, June 2016. https://doi.org/10.1109/cvpr.2016.308
34. Wang, L., Ouyang, W., Wang, X., Lu, H.: Visual tracking with fully convolutional networks. In: 2015 IEEE International Conference on Computer Vision (ICCV), pp. 3119–3127, December 2015. https://doi.org/10.1109/ICCV.2015.357
35. Welinder, P., et al.: Caltech-UCSD Birds 200. Technical report, CNS-TR-2010-001, California Institute of Technology (2010)
36. Wu, J., Leng, C., Wang, Y., Hu, Q., Cheng, J.: Quantized convolutional neural networks for mobile devices. In: 2016 IEEE Conference on Computer Vision and Pattern Recognition (CVPR), pp. 4820–4828, June 2016. https://doi.org/10.1109/CVPR.2016.521
37. Yao, B., Jiang, X., Khosla, A., Lin, A.L., Guibas, L., Fei-Fei, L.: Human action recognition by learning bases of action attributes and parts. In: 2011 International Conference on Computer Vision. IEEE, November 2011. https://doi.org/10.1109/iccv.2011.6126386
38. Yosinski, J., Clune, J., Bengio, Y., Lipson, H.: How transferable are features in deep neural networks? In: Advances in Neural Information Processing Systems, pp. 3320–3328 (2014)
39. Zhou, A., Yao, A., Guo, Y., Xu, L., Chen, Y.: Incremental network quantization: towards lossless CNNS with low-precision weights. arXiv preprint arXiv:1702.03044 (2017)
40. Zhou, S., Wu, Y., Ni, Z., Zhou, X., Wen, H., Zou, Y.: Dorefa-net: training low bitwidth convolutional neural networks with low bitwidth gradients. arXiv preprint arXiv:1606.06160 (2016)

Linear Memory Networks

Davide Bacciu[1], Antonio Carta[1(✉)], and Alessandro Sperduti[2]

[1] Università di Pisa, Pisa, Italy
{bacciu,antonio.carta}@di.unipi.it
[2] Università di Padova, Padua, Italy
sperduti@math.unipd.it

Abstract. Recurrent neural networks can learn complex transduction problems that require maintaining and actively exploiting a memory of their inputs. Such models traditionally consider memory and input-output functionalities indissolubly entangled. We introduce a novel recurrent architecture based on the conceptual separation between the functional input-output transformation and the memory mechanism, showing how they can be implemented through different neural components. By building on such conceptualization, we introduce the Linear Memory Network, a recurrent model comprising a feedforward neural network, realizing the non-linear functional transformation, and a linear autoencoder for sequences, implementing the memory component. The resulting architecture can be efficiently trained by building on closed-form solutions to linear optimization problems. Further, by exploiting equivalence results between feedforward and recurrent neural networks we devise a pretraining schema for the proposed architecture. Experiments on polyphonic music datasets show that the pretraining schema consistently improves the performance of the LMN and outperforms LSTM architectures by up to 3.7 frame-level accuracy percentage points despite using about one fifth of the number of parameters of an equivalent LSTM.

Keywords: Recurrent neural networks · Learning algorithms · Autoencoders · Memory

1 Introduction

Recurrent Neural Networks (RNNs) are one of the pillars of the deep learning revolution, thanks to their statefulness which allows to learn complex computational tasks requiring the ability to memorize and "reason over" past inputs activations, such as with sequential data processing.

The diffusion of RNN architectures has initially been restrained by the well known difficulties in learning long-term sequential dependencies due to gradient vanishing and explosion issues [4]. Nonetheless, in the recent past, these issues have been addressed by a number of solutions exploiting gating units to control access and update of the state component, such as in the seminal LSTM model [10] and the follow-up GRU networks [7]. A different line of research has tried tackling

I. V. Tetko et al. (Eds.): ICANN 2019, LNCS 11727, pp. 513–525, 2019.
https://doi.org/10.1007/978-3-030-30487-4_40

with the problem by resorting to articulated modular architectures, reducing the distance between long-term dependencies and introducing explicit multiscale time dynamics, such as in Clockwork RNN [13] and Hierarchical multiscale RNNs [6]. Alternatively, RNN have been augmented with attention mechanisms [2] in the attempt of optimizing the state encoding by allowing to focus only on past memories at certain timesteps that are deemed relevant for the task. Attention mechanisms typically come at the cost of an increased computational effort, motivating recent attempts to improve it through hierarchical approaches [1].

The common thread running through the solutions proposed so far is that of resorting to complex architectures, either at the level of the memory cell, such as with the gating units in LSTM, or at the network level, such as with multi-scale RNN and attention-based models. This results in models that, even if end-to-end differentiable, are often difficult to train, in practice.

We introduce a novel RNN paradigm, dubbed Linear Memory Networks (LMN), which aims at simplifying the design and training of RNNs while retaining the ability to learn long-term dependencies. The model is based on the intuition that, in order to efficiently solve a sequence processing problem, recurrent models need to solve two associated tasks: a functional task, which concerns mapping the input sequence into a sequence of outputs, and a memory task, exploiting a memorization mechanism to remember past states that can serve for the functional task [18]. Recurrent models typically solve these two tasks together, by learning the mapping from inputs to outputs and the memorization mechanism at the same time. The LMN puts forward a novel approach based on the explicit separation between the functional and memory components of a recurrent model. The key intuition is that by explicitly separating the two tasks it is possible to simplify both the architecture and the learning algorithms used to train these models, while acquiring a deeper understanding of the inner workings, for example exploiting explicit memorization.

The literature reports several attempts to introduce a separate memory for recurrent architectures, such as in Memory Networks [19] and in Neural Turing Machines [8]. Differentiable Neural Computers [9]. However, the memory mechanism in these models is used to augment architectures that are already recurrent, rather than to simplify them, and it typically involves non-trivial addressing and memory access schemes. The end result is that these architectures become easily quite complex and difficult to train.

The LMN, on the other hand, proposes a simple architecture comprising a non-linear feedforward network to model the functional component of the RNN, while the memory component is realized by means of a linear autoencoder for sequences. The choice of these components allows us to exploit closed-form solutions for linear autoencoder training by [17] and the equivalence results between certain classes of RNN and their unrolled feedforward version [18] to efficiently train the linear memory to reconstruct the hidden states computed by the nonlinear feedforward part. We will show how this allows to define a simple multi-stage learning scheme, comprising an effective pretraining phase that cannot be realized in gated architectures, such as LSTM. Through an experimental analysis on complex sequence processing tasks, we show how the simple LMN architecture is capable of obtaining competitive results with respect to complex recurrent models, including gated RNN.

2 Linear Autoencoder for Sequences

We begin by summarizing the linear autoencoder for sequences [17], that is the building block for realizing the LMN memory component. A linear autoencoder for sequences is a recurrent linear model designed to encode an input sequence into an hidden state, computed using a linear transformation. Given a set of n sequences, where each sequence s^q in the set is composed of l^q vectors $x_1^q...x_l^q$, $x_i^q \in \mathbb{R}^a$, where q is the index of the sequence and a the dimension of the vectors. A linear autoencoder computes the state vector $y_t \in \mathbb{R}^p$, i.e. the encoding of the input sequence up to time t, using the following equations:

$$y_t = Ax_t + By_{t-1} \tag{1}$$

$$\begin{bmatrix} x_t \\ y_{t-1} \end{bmatrix} = Cy_t, \tag{2}$$

where p is the hidden state size, $A \in \mathbb{R}^{p\times a}$, $B \in \mathbb{R}^{p\times p}$ and $C \in \mathbb{R}^{(a+p)\times p}$ are the model parameters, which can be trained by exploiting a decomposition of the output data matrix Y. Let us assume that the training set consists of a single sequence $\{x_1, \ldots, x_l\}$ and define $Y \in \mathbb{R}^{l\times p}$ as the matrix containing the state vectors at each timestep. From Eqs. (1) and (2) it follows that:

$$\underbrace{\begin{bmatrix} y_1^T \\ y_2^T \\ y_3^T \\ \vdots \\ y_l^T \end{bmatrix}}_{Y} = \underbrace{\begin{bmatrix} x_1^T & 0 & \ldots & 0 \\ x_2^T & x_1^T & \ldots & 0 \\ \vdots & \vdots & \ddots & \vdots \\ x_l^T & x_{l-1}^T & \ldots & x_1^T \end{bmatrix}}_{\Xi} \underbrace{\begin{bmatrix} A^T \\ A^T B^T \\ \vdots \\ A^T B^{l-1^T} \end{bmatrix}}_{\Omega}. \tag{3}$$

The matrix Ξ contains the reversed subsequences of x and Y contains the state vectors at each timestep. The encoding matrices A and B can be identified by exploiting the truncated SVD decomposition $\Xi = V\Sigma U^T$, where imposing $U^T\Omega = I$ yields $\Omega = U$. We can then exploit the structure of Ξ to obtain A, B, and the associated matrix $C = \begin{bmatrix} A^T \\ B^T \end{bmatrix}$, as shown in [17]. Specifically, $\Omega = U$ is satisfied by using matrices

$$P \equiv \begin{bmatrix} I_a \\ 0_{a(l-1)\times a} \end{bmatrix}, \text{ and } R \equiv \begin{bmatrix} 0_{a\times a(l-1)} & 0_{a\times a} \\ I_{a(l-1)} & 0_{a(l-1)\times a} \end{bmatrix},$$

to define $A \equiv U^T P$ and $B \equiv U^T RU$, where I_u is the identity matrix of size u, and $0_{u\times v}$ is the zero matrix of size $u \times v$.

The algorithm can be easily generalized to multiple sequences by stacking the data matrix Ξ_q for each sequence s^q and padding with zeros to match sequences length.

The sequence autoencoding scheme in Eqs. (1) and (2) can be used to reconstruct the input sample and the past state given the current state vector. It should be clear how the iterative application of this process allows to reconstruct (an approximation of) the past input sequence. In particular, the training algorithm guarantees an optimal encoding when $p = rank(\Xi)$. The computational cost of the algorithm is dominated by the SVD decomposition computed on the matrix Ξ. In the following sections, we show how such properties can be used to efficiently memorize and gather access to the history of the hidden states in a recurrent network.

3 Linear Memory Networks

The Linear Memory Network (LMN) is a recurrent architecture where the memory and the functional components are explicitly separated: a sketch of the LMN structure is depicted in Fig. 1a. The network combines a non-linear feedforward model (Functional box in Fig. 1a) with a separate memory component implemented through a linear sequential autoencoder (Memory box in Fig. 1a). Therefore, the memory is entirely linear while the feedforward component allows to model nonlinear dependencies between the input vectors. Note that the functional component comprises a number of feedforward neurons which is, in general, different from the number of recurrent linear units in the memory component. The relationships between the functional activation $h_t \in \mathbb{R}^p$ and the memory state $h_t^m \in \mathbb{R}^m$ are regulated by the following equations:

$$h_t = \sigma(W^{xh} x_t + W^{mh} h_{t-1}^m) \tag{4}$$

$$h_t^m = W^{hm} h_t + W^{mm} h_{t-1}^m \tag{5}$$

where a, p, m are respectively the input size, hidden size and memory size, while $W^{xh} \in \mathbb{R}^{p \times a}$, $W^{mh} \in \mathbb{R}^{p \times m}$, $W^{hm} \in \mathbb{R}^{m \times p}$, $W^{mm} \in \mathbb{R}^{m \times m}$ are the model parameters matrices, and σ is a non-linear activation function (tanh for the purpose of this paper). The catch of the LMN architecture is using the linear autoencoder to linearly encode the history of the nonlinear functional activation h_t, i.e. the input to the autoencoder, in the state h_t^m. The architecture is based on the equivalence results described in the previous section. The separation of the memory component allows to train the network to explicitly store the past activations of the functional component by training the corresponding linear autoencoder. A possible instantiation of this approach will be given in the next section, where we describe a pretraining scheme that exploits the properties of the network.

The network output (or a successive layer in a deeply layered architecture) can be wired to the LMN recurrent layer in two different ways, denoted as LMN-A and LMN-B in Fig. 1a. The first approach, exploits the activation of the functional component h_t, while the second has direct access to the memory h_t^m, resulting in the following (alternative) output activations

$$y_t^m = \sigma(W^{mo} h_t^m) \tag{6}$$
$$y_t^h = \sigma(W^{ho} h_t), \tag{7}$$

where σ is the activation function (sigmoid in this paper), o the output size, $W^{mo} \in \mathbb{R}^{o \times m}$ and $W^{ho} \in \mathbb{R}^{o \times h}$ are the functional-to-output and memory-to-output parameter matrices, respectively.

We provide experimental results for both variants of the model. The definition given here and the experimental results cover only the case where the functional component is made of a single layer, but the approach can be easily extended to deep networks by adding layers to the feedforward component and connecting them with the memory.

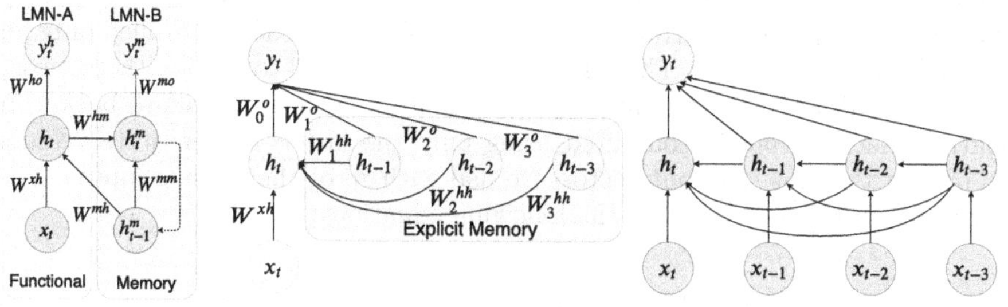

(a) (b) (c)

Fig. 1. Schematic representation of the memory layouts in the different network architectures. Figure 1a shows the architecture of the LMN, highlighting the separation between the functional and memory components and showing how the memory component is efficiently encoded using a linear autoencoder. Figure 1b shows the corresponding network with a (highly parameterized) explicit memory. Since the previous hidden states are explicitly memorized the architecture is feedforward and no gradients can flow through the previous hidden states. Figure 1c shows the unfolded network for $k = 3$ timesteps, where there is no explicit memory and, instead, we have explicit connections between hidden states.

3.1 Training and Pretraining Algorithm

The LMN is differentiable end-to-end and it can be trained with standard backpropagation. If the memory component is trained using backpropagation there are no theoretical guarantees on its memorization properties. Therefore we are interested in alternative algorithms to train separately the memory of the network. Since the memory component is equivalent to a linear autoencoder, it can be trained separately, through an ad-hoc algorithm, to reconstruct the hidden representation of the functional component at previous time steps. By building on the explicit solution for linear autoencoders given in [17] and presented in Sect. 2, it is possible to construct an optimal encoding of the hidden states sequences with the minimal number of memory units. In this section, we propose a pretraining algorithm that can be used to initialize the model parameters based on the considerations above.

The pretraining algorithm works in three steps. First, we construct through unfolding an equivalent network to generate an approximation of the functional component activations. Second, we use these activations as inputs to the linear autoencoder. Finally, we initialize the LMN by transferring to the LMN the output weights from the unfolded network, and the encoding weights from the linear autoencoder.

More in detail, the first step of the pretraining algorithm constructs an unfolded version of the LMN, shown in Fig. 1c, where the memory is substituted by an explicit representation of the previous hidden states and their relationship with the current state is explicitly represented by a parameterized transformation. To allow an efficient training of the network, the model is unrolled only for a fixed number of steps k. The unfolded model is trained to predict the network output y_t and its parameters are adjusted accordingly, using standard backpropagation. Each output is computed using only the last k hidden state vectors. To predict the first k output vectors we pad with zeros the missing inputs. The unrolled network is defined by the following equations:

$$h_t = \sigma(W^{xh} x_t + \sum_{i=1}^{k} W_i^{hh} h_{t-i}), \quad t = 1, \dots, k \tag{8}$$

$$y_t = \sigma(\sum_{i=0}^{k} W_i^{o} h_{t-i}), \tag{9}$$

where $W_i^{hh} \in \mathbb{R}^{h \times h}$ explicitly represents the relationship between the current hidden state and the hidden state at time $t-i$, while $W_i^o \in \mathbb{R}^{o \times h}$ represents the relationship between the current output y_t and the hidden state at time $t-i$.

The second step of the pretraining algorithm is based on previous equivalence results between recurrent and feedforward networks in [18]. While their results are focused on RNN, they can be easily adapted to the LMN architecture. Given a trained unfolded network as defined in Eqs. (8) and (9), we want to create a new neural network with an explicit memory. Figure 1b shows a feedforward neural network, equivalent to the unfolded one in Fig. 1c, where previous hidden states are explicitly stored in a separate memory and used to compute the new hidden state. Previous hidden states are considered constants during the backpropagation.

The explicit memory representation in Fig. 1b is inefficient because the computational cost and the number of parameters scale linearly with the memory size, which is explicitly bound by the finite length k. Instead, by using the compressed representation of the linear autoencoder in the LMN (see Fig. 1a) we obtain a more efficient memory, since the hidden states are stored and compressed using a basis of principal components, as discussed in [17]. Note how the compressed representation does not depend on the original unfolding length k, whereas it allows to adaptively accommodate longer term dependencies up to the limits of memory capacity.

In essence, the second step of the pretraining algorithm amounts to training a linear autoencoder to reconstruct the hidden states h_i (obtained from step one) for each sequence in the training set, by constructing the matrix H of hidden state subsequences and using the linear autoencoder training algorithm. As a result, we obtain the matrices A and B, corresponding to the parameters of the trained linear autoencoder.

In the third step, we use the parameter matrices obtained in the previous two steps to initialize an LMN. The parameters of the autoencoder A and B can be used to update the LMN memory state h^t, while the connecting between the hidden states and the connections into the output can be represented by decoding the sequence $h^t, \dots, h^{t-k}$ using the matrix $U = [A^T, A^T B^T, \dots, A^T B^{k-1}]$ using the relationship $Uh_t^m = \left[h_t^\top, \dots, h_{t-k}^\top\right]^\top$. The LMN W^{xh} matrix is initialized using the corresponding matrix W^{xh} of the unfolded network. The remainder of the LMN matrices is initialized as

$$
\begin{aligned}
W^{hm} &= A, \\
W^{mm} &= B, \\
W^{mh} &= \left[W_1^{hh} \dots W_k^{hh}\right] U, \\
W^{mo} &= \left[W_1^{o} \dots W_k^{o}\right] U.
\end{aligned}
$$

Using the pretraining procedure the memory is initialized to reconstruct the entire sequence of hidden states computed by the unrolled network. While the unrolled network requires a number of parameters that scales linearly with the unrolling length k, the LMN is more efficient and can use the linear autoencoder to reduce the number of parameters without reducing the memory length. The choice of k is a tradeoff between the ability to explicitly represent hidden-to-hidden connections at increasing delays and the computational resources needed to train the unrolled model. Notice that even for a small k the memory h_t^m still encodes the entire sequence. However, in this setting the memory-to-hidden connection $(W^m h)$ will need to decode only the last timestep. In the following experiments we fix $k = 10$ to provide a good tradeoff between the computational cost and the ability to explicitly represent connections between delayed hidden states.

3.2 A Comparison with Gated Recurrent Architectures

The main difference between the LMN model and other recurrent architectures in the literature is the conceptual separation between the memory and the functional component. The state dynamics is captured by the linear memory component without the need for multiplicative gates like in LSTM and GRU units, leading to a simple, easily trainable architecture, without unwanted exponential decay effects due to the presence of gates. The number of model parameters, having fixed the number of neurons, is also smaller in LMN: LSTM requires $4(x+h)h$ parameters, GRU requires $3(x+h)h$ parameters, and LMN requires $(x+m)f+(f+m)m$ parameters, where x is the input size, h the number of hidden units, f and m the number of functional and memory units (only for LMN). If we set $h = m + f$, we obtain that the number of parameters for the LMN architecture is maximized when $m = f = h/2$. The total number of parameters for the LMN architecture in this case becomes $\frac{1}{2}((x+\frac{h}{2})h+h^2)$, less than LSTM and GRU architectures with the same number of hidden units. In order to give a more intuitive understanding of the relationship, Fig. 2 shows the ratio between the number of parameters of an LSTM and those of an LMN against the ratio between the input and the hidden size, for the special case where $m = f = h/2$. We notice that when $x = h$ the LSTM use 6.4 parameters more than an equivalent LMN.

Furthermore, the linear dynamics of the memory allows the design of ad-hoc, optimized training algorithms. As an example of this possibility, this paper presents a pretraining algorithm. Another interesting possibility is the development of second order optimization methods [14] which exploit the linearity of the memory to yield an efficient closed form solution.

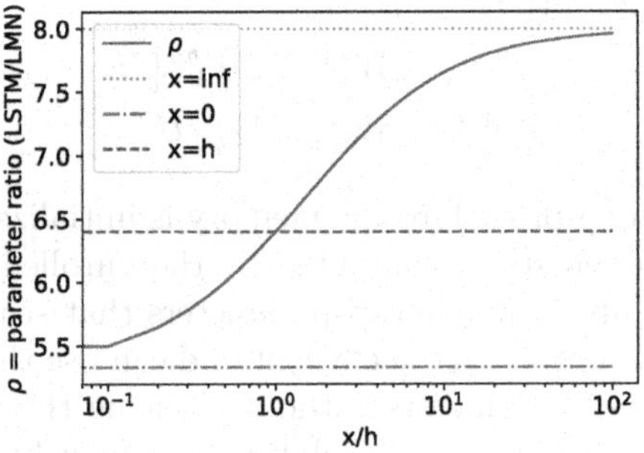

Fig. 2. Ratio between the number of parameters of the LSTM and LMN (ρ) against the ratio between the hidden size and the input size. The dotted lines indicate points of interest along the curve.

4 Experimental Results

We evaluated LMN on sequence prediction tasks using four different datasets of polyphonic music representing piano roll versions of songs in different styles and with different degrees of polyphony [5]. Each sequence is sampled at equal timesteps to obtain a feature vector composed of 88 binary values representing the piano notes from A0 to C8. Each note is set to 1 if it is currently being played or 0 if it is not. The task is to predict the notes played at the next timestep given the sequence of previous notes. The performance of each model is evaluated using frame-level accuracy as defined in [3]. We used the same train-validation-test split as in [5]. Even if all datasets contain music represented in piano roll style, they are different from each other, ranging from classical music to folk music, composed for piano, orchestra or chorales. This generates widely different performance results depending on the dataset.

We compare the output configurations of the LMN architecture in Fig. 1a using a random initialization of the model parameters (LMN-A and LMN-B, in the following). In addition, we have tested the LMN-B output configuration with parameters initialized using the pretraining scheme (pretraining results are shown only for the LMN-B configuration as including those of pre-trained LMN-A would not add much to the analysis). The LMN results are compared versus a number of reference models from literature. Specifically, we consider an RNN with random initialization or using the pretraining scheme described in [15], an LSTM network, and the RNN-RBM model (for which we report the original results from [5]). Note that the Nottingham dataset has been expanded since the publication of [5] and therefore the results are not fully comparable. All the networks have been optimized using Adam [11]

Table 1. Frame-level accuracy computed on the test set for each model. RNN-RBM results are taken from [5]

	JSB Chorales	MuseData	Nottingham	Piano MIDI
RNN	31.00	35.02	72.29	26.52
pret-RNN	30.55	35.47	71.70	27.31
LSTM	32.64	34.40	72.45	25.08
RNN-RBM*	33.12	34.02	**75.40**	**28.92**
LMN-A	30.61	33.15	71.16	26.69
LMN-B	33.98	35.56	72.71	28.00
pret-LMN-B	**34.49**	**35.66**	**74.16**	28.79

with a fixed learning rate of 0.001 using early stopping on the validation set to limit the number of epochs. Except for the RNN-RBM, all the architectures have a single layer. For the RNN and LSTM models, we have selected the number of hidden recurrent neurons/cells with a grid search over the range $\{50,\ 100,\ 250,\ 500,\ 750\}$. For the LMN architecture, we have searched the number of nonlinear functional units and of the linear memory units over the range $\{(50,50),\ (50,100),\ (100,100),\ (100,250),\ (250,250),\ (250,500)\}$, where the first number refers to functional units and the second to the memory units. All models have been regularized using L2 weight decay, selecting the regularization hyperparameter by grid search over the range $\{10^{-4},\ 10^{-5},\ 10^{-6},\ 10^{-7},\ 0\}$.

The unrolled network used in pretraining is trained with an unfolding length set to $k = 10$, with hidden sizes equal to the corresponding LMN. We found useful to use the SeLU activation function, as defined in [12], to improve the convergence of the training procedure for the unfolded model only. Other models, including the final LMN, use a tanh activation function for the hidden units and a sigmoid activation for the outputs. During preliminary experiments we did not find any significant performance improvement when training LMN using different activation functions.

All models are implemented using Pytorch[1] [16]. The test performances for the best configuration of each model (selected on validation) are reported in Table 1.

Looking at the results, we notice that the LMN-B model is competitive when confronted with other recurrent architectures with gating units, even without pretraining. The pretrained model outperforms the LSTM on all the 4 datasets by up to 3.7 frame-level accuracy percentage points despite using about one fifth of the parameters of a corresponding LSTM. The LMN architecture obtains also better results in two different datasets when compared to the RNN-RBM, a more complex architecture which comprises multiple layers. On the Piano MIDI the difference in performance with respect to RNN-RBM is relatively small, while the Nottingham dataset is tested using the updated version, and therefore the results are not exactly comparable. The RNN and LMN performance has also been tested when using a pretraining scheme (note that RNN-RBM uses pretraining as well [5]). For the LMN architecture, we notice a more consistent improvement induced by the pretraining algorithm than for the RNN architecture. This is not surprising since the LMN pretraining scheme follows naturally from the equivalence results in [18]. LSTM models are not pretrained, and the same pretraining scheme used for RNN and LMN cannot be easily adapted to gating units. We argue that this is an example where it can be clearly appreciated the advantage of dealing with an architecture of lesser complexity which, despite its apparent simplicity, leads to excellent performance results.

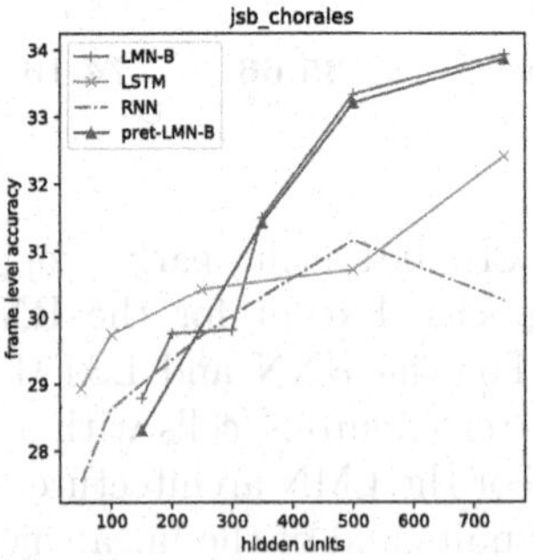

Fig. 3. Frame level accuracy on the validation set against the number of hidden units for different models trained on the JSB Chorales dataset. For the LMN variants the number of hidden units corresponds to the sum of functional and memory units.

[1] https://gitlab.itc.unipi.it/AntonioCarta/icann19.

To assess the behavior of the LMN architecture as a function of the parameter space size, Fig. 3 shows the performance of different models on the validation set for the JSB Chorales. Each curve represents the performance of a model for a given number of hidden units. Again, we focus on the LMN-B architecture both in its basic and pretrained version. For the LMN, we consider the number of hidden units to be the sum of functional and memory units in the configuration under test. We notice a consistent improvement of the LMN models with respect to both LSTM and RNN, starting from 350 hidden units. Please, notice that, as pointed out in Sect. 3.2, with the same number of hidden units LMN-B has significantly less free parameters than the other architectures under comparison.

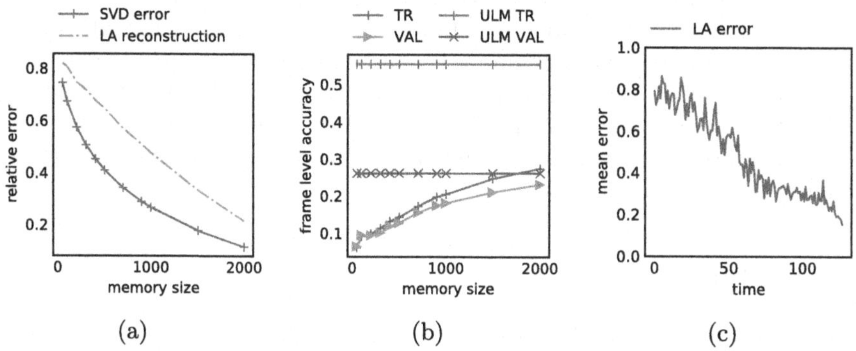

Fig. 4. Performance of the pretrained network computed for the JSB Chorales dataset at different stages of the pretraining procedure. Figure 4a shows the SVD reconstruction error and the linear autoencoder (LA) reconstruction error for the training set hidden state sequences. Figure 4b shows the pretrained LMN error after the initialization, compared against the unfolded network (ULM) on the train (TR) and validation (VAL) sets. Figure 4c shows the linear autoencoder reconstruction error for a single hidden state sequence corresponding to the first sample of the training set.

5 Pretraining Analysis

In previous sections, we have discussed how, by training a linear autoencoder on the hidden sequences generated by the unfolded network, we can obtain the optimal reconstruction of the hidden states while keeping the minimal amount of hidden units.

To gain a better understanding of the effect of the pretraining procedure, in the following, we study the performance of the model after each step of the algorithm. Figure 4a shows the average reconstruction error related to the SVD factorization of H, i.e. the matrix containing the hidden states subsequences used to train the corresponding linear autoencoder, for the training set sequences of the JSB Chorales. On the same plot, we overlay the reconstruction error of the corresponding trained linear autoencoder (LA). As expected, the reconstructions error steadily decreases for both models as the number of memory units h_t^m grows.

The parameter matrices of the linear autoencoder are then used to initialize the LMN. Figure 4b shows the performance obtained by the original unfolded network (ULM) and the corresponding pretrained LMN on the training and validation sets of JSB Chorales. The performance is computed after initialization by pretraining and before the fine-tuning phase. It can be seen how the pretrained-LMN performance on the validation set is close to that obtained by the unfolded network, while LMN greatly reduces the number of parameters used with respect to the ULM configuration. It must also be noted that the performance of the unfolded network is lower than that of a randomly initialized and then trained LMN model: this highlights the need of a fine tuning phase after the pretraining initialization.

Finally, Fig. 4c shows the autoencoder reconstruction error for the first training sequence of the JSB Chorales obtained by a pretrained LMN with hidden state size 50 and 1000 memory units. It can be noticed that most of the errors are concentrated on the first steps of the sequence, while the second part of the input has a much lower error. This shows that the linear autoencoder needs a burn-in period to recover from the state initialization and after such period becomes fairly accurate.

6 Conclusion

We have introduced a novel recurrent architecture, the Linear Memory Network (LMN), designed on a conceptual separation of the memory-related functionalities from the non-linear functional transformations. We build our model on sound theoretical results concerning the equivalence of certain classes of RNN architectures and their unfolded feedforward counterpart. We exploit the same intuition to suggest an effective pretraining scheme to initialize both LMN components in an efficient way. Experimental results show that the model is competitive on difficult tasks against various recurrent architectures and the associated analysis provides insights into the dynamics and properties of the memory component. We think that the LMN model has the potential of fostering renewed interest in the study of novel, simplified architectures for recurrent neural networks. The availability of a fully linear recurrent dynamics opens up interesting research lines in the direction of efficient training algorithms exploiting closed-form solutions of linear optimization problems. Further, the LMN model can be used as a building block to construct deep or modular architectures or as a replacement of vanilla and gated recurrent units in existing models. Finally, the concept of a recurrent linear memory for sequences can be easily generalized to a recursive autoencoder, allowing to extend the LMN model to the treatment of tree-structured data.

Acknowledgments. This work has been partially supported by the University of Padova, Department of Mathematics, DEEPer project and by the Italian Ministry of Education, University, and Research (MIUR) under project SIR 2014 LIST-IT (grant n. RBSI14STDE).

References

1. Andrychowicz, M., Kurach, K.: Learning efficient algorithms with hierarchical attentive memory. CoRR abs/1602.03218 (2016)
2. Bahdanau, D., Cho, K., Bengio, Y.: Neural machine translation by jointly learning to align and translate. In: ICLR (2015)
3. Bay, M., Ehmann, A.F., Downie, J.S.: Evaluation of multiple-F0 estimation and tracking systems. In: ISMIR (2009)
4. Bengio, Y., Simard, P.Y., Frasconi, P.: Learning long-term dependencies with gradient descent is difficult. IEEE Trans. Neural Networks **5**(2), 157–166 (1994). https://doi.org/10.1109/72.279181
5. Boulanger-Lewandowski, N., Bengio, Y., Vincent, P.: Modeling temporal dependencies in high-dimensional sequences: Application to polyphonic music generation and transcription. In: ICML (2012)
6. Chung, J., Ahn, S., Bengio, Y.: Hierarchical multiscale recurrent neural networks. In: ICLR (2017)
7. Chung, J., Gulcehre, C., Cho, K., Bengio, Y.: Empirical evaluation of gated recurrent neural networks on sequence modeling. In: NIPS 2014 Workshop on Deep Learning, December 2014
8. Graves, A., Wayne, G., Danihelka, I.: Neural turing machines. arXiv preprint arXiv:1410.5401 (2014)
9. Graves, A., et al.: Hybrid computing using a neural network with dynamic external memory. Nature **538**(7626), 471 (2016). https://doi.org/10.1038/nature20101
10. Hochreiter, S., Schmidhuber, J.: Long short-term memory. Neural Comput. **9**(8), 1735–1780 (1997). https://doi.org/10.1162/neco.1997.9.8.1735
11. Kingma, D.P., Ba, J.: Adam: a method for stochastic optimization. CoRR abs/1412.6980 (2014)
12. Klambauer, G., Unterthiner, T., Mayr, A., Hochreiter, S.: Self-normalizing neural networks. In: NIPS (2017)
13. Koutník, J., Greff, K., Gomez, F.J., Schmidhuber, J.: A clockwork RNN. In: ICML (2014). http://proceedings.mlr.press/v32/koutnik14.html
14. Martens, J.: Deep learning via hessian-free optimization. In: ICML (2010)
15. Pasa, L., Sperduti, A.: Pre-training of recurrent neural networks via linear autoencoders. In: NIPS (2014)
16. Paszke, A., et al.: Automatic differentiation in PyTorch (2017)
17. Sperduti, A.: Linear autoencoder networks for structured data. In: International Workshop on Neural-Symbolic Learning and Reasoning (2013)
18. Sperduti, A.: Equivalence results between feedforward and recurrent neural networks for sequences. In: IJCAI (2015). http://dl.acm.org/citation.cfm?id=2832747.2832783
19. Sukhbaatar, S., Weston, J., Fergus, R., et al.: End-to-end memory networks. In: Advances in Neural Information Processing Systems, pp. 2440–2448 (2015)

Reinforcement Learning

A Multi-armed Bandit Algorithm Available in Stationary or Non-stationary Environments Using Self-organizing Maps

Nobuhito Manome[1,2(✉)], Shuji Shinohara[2], Kouta Suzuki[1,2], Kosuke Tomonaga[1,2], and Shunji Mitsuyoshi[2]

[1] SoftBank Robotics Group Corp., Tokyo, Japan
manome@bioeng.t.u-tokyo.ac.jp
[2] The University of Tokyo, Tokyo, Japan

Abstract. Due to the multitude of potential courses of action, communication robots designed to satisfy the users facing them must take appropriate action more rapidly. In practice however, user requests often change while these robots are determining the most appropriate actions for these users. Therefore, it is difficult for robots to derive an appropriate course of action. This issue has been formalized as the "multi-armed bandit (MAB) problem." The MAB problem points to an environment featuring multiple levers (arms) where pulling an arm has a certain probability of yielding a reward; the issue is to determine how to select the levers to pull to maximize the rewards gained. To solve this problem, we considered a new MAB problem algorithm using self-organizing maps that is adaptable to stationary and non-stationary environments. For this paper, numerous experiments were conducted considering a stochastic MAB problem in both stationary and non-stationary environments. As a result, we determined that the proposed algorithm demonstrated equivalent or improved capability in stationary environments with numerous arms and consistently strong effectiveness in a non-stationary environment compared to the existing UCB1, UCB1-Tuned, and Thompson Sampling algorithms.

Keywords: Multi-armed bandit problem · Self-organizing maps · Sequential decision making

1 Introduction

The "multi-armed bandit (MAB) problem" points to an environment with numerous levers (arms), where each arm has a certain probability of yielding a reward when pulled. The problem, assuming that a succession of arms is pulled, is to select which arms to pull to maximize rewards gained [1]. This problem points to a model featuring an intrinsic trade-off between searching for arms with a high probability of reward and using previous knowledge to pull arms that have been confirmed to have a high reward probability [2]. MAB problems, where rewards yielded by each arm are determined by a set probability distribution for each arm, are termed "stochastic MAB problems."

Applications of the MAB framework include online advertisements [3–6], recommendation systems [7–10], and robots [11, 12]. In particular, with communication

I. V. Tetko et al. (Eds.): ICANN 2019, LNCS 11727, pp. 529–540, 2019.
https://doi.org/10.1007/978-3-030-30487-4_41

robots designed to satisfy the users facing them, robot's possible courses of action are considered to rest in their arms, and user's satisfaction is considered the reward; they should choose an arm with a high reward probability more rapidly when there are more arms in the environment. Moreover, in practice, users can end up making changes even as robots are considering what action would be most appropriate; despite this, robots are expected to continue their search for an arm with a high reward probability even in this dynamic environment. Problems in which the arms' individual reward probability changes during the problem are called "non-stationary MAB problems."

Representative algorithms for dealing with the MAB problem include the ε-greedy algorithm [2], the softmax algorithm [2], upper-confidence bound (UCB) policies [13], and the Thompson Sampling algorithm [14]. These algorithms show satisfactory capability in stationary environments; however, as they prove to be unsatisfactory in non-stationary environments, algorithms tailored to dynamic environments such as sliding window UCB [15] and Bayesian Adaptive Greedy (BAG1) [16] have been proposed. It is clear that the development of algorithms that demonstrate superior functionality in both stationary and non-stationary environments is not a straightforward task.

One online learning method is the self-organizing map (SOM) [17]. The SOM is one of the artificial neural networks developed by Kohonen; it is frequently used in data mining [18–20].

We considered a new (SOM-based) algorithm to solve MAB problems; it is capable of adapting to both stationary and non-stationary environments using Kohonen's most basic SOM. Furthermore, to evaluate the algorithm's capability, we conducted numerical experiments in both stationary and non-stationary environments using a stochastic MAB framework. In this paper, we shall compare the capability of the proposed algorithm with that of the UCB1 [13], UCB1-Tuned [13], and Thompson Sampling algorithms, which effectiveness is known to be superior to the ε-greedy and softmax algorithms in stationary environments.

This research has two purposes: to propose a new approach to solving MAB problems using SOMs, and to propose an effective multi-armed bandit algorithm that is useful in both stationary and non-stationary environments.

2 Multi-armed Bandit Algorithms

2.1 UCB1

In MAB problems, to maximize reward, it is important to strike a balance between searching for arms with high reward probability and applying previous knowledge by pulling arms for which the high reward probability has been confirmed. UCB1 demonstrates a superior balance between search and knowledge application. It is also an algorithm with a guaranteed upper limit on expected loss; it is therefore the standard algorithm used for stochastic MAB problems.

With this algorithm, initially, each arm is pulled once; subsequently, the algorithm opts to pull the arm j with the highest value according to the formula in (1).

$$j = \text{argmax}_i\left(\bar{X}_i + \sqrt{\frac{2\log n}{T_i(n)}}\right) \tag{1}$$

where $\bar{X}_i$ is the expected value of arm i; n is the number of times all arms have been selected; and $T_i(n)$ is the number of times arm i has been selected.

2.2 UCB1-Tuned

UCB1-Tuned is an updated UCB1 model.

In this algorithm, as with UCB1, each arm is initially pulled once; subsequently, the algorithm opts to pull arm j with the highest value as defined in (2):

$$j = \text{argmax}_i\left(\bar{X}_i + \sqrt{\frac{\log n}{T_i(n)}\min\left\{\frac{1}{4}, V_i(T_i(n))\right\}}\right) \tag{2}$$

where $\bar{X}_i$ is the expected value of arm i; n is the number of times all arms have been selected; $T_i(n)$ is the number of times arm i has been selected; and V_i is defined as per (3):

$$V_i(s) = \left(\frac{1}{s}\sum\nolimits_{\gamma=1}^{s} X_{i,\gamma}^2\right) - \bar{X}_{i,s}^2 + \sqrt{\frac{2\log n}{s}} \tag{3}$$

where $X_{i,\gamma}$ is the reward for pulling arm i at point γ.

2.3 Thompson Sampling

Thompson Sampling is a method that hypothesizes that the arm reward parameter μ_i is generated in accordance with a certain probability distribution. Thompson Sampling is a probability-matching method where the arm to pull is determined stochastically based on each arm's hypothesized parameters. In addition, in most cases, it is known to be capable of a favorable impact within a finite number of trials as opposed to UCB policies [21].

This algorithm samples a random number $\tilde{\mu}_i$ generated according to a given probability distribution for each arm, then selects the arm with the highest value. In this paper, the reward parameter μ_i for each arm is implemented according to a beta distribution.

2.4 Proposed Algorithm

This section will begin by explaining Kohonen's most basic SOM. Next, we will discuss the algorithm designed to solve MAB problems using SOMs.

Self-organizing Map

A SOM is an artificial neural network developed by Kohonen aimed at unsupervised learning. Outlines of the SOM architecture and the algorithm are shown in Fig. 1.

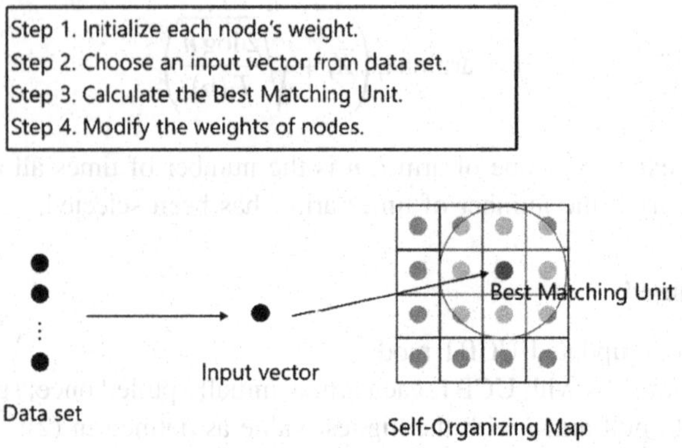

Fig. 1. Overview of the self-organizing map architecture and algorithm

A SOM consists of two layers: an input layer and a competitive layer. The purpose of a SOM is to map a high-dimensional observed data set onto the low-level space of the competitive layer. The competitive layer of the SOM is divided into a square grid, with a node attributed to each cell. In addition, each node contains a vector that has the same size as the number of dimensions in the corresponding observed data, labelled as "weight."

The SOM algorithm is presented below.

Step 1. The weight of each node is given an initial value of $\mathbf{y}_k(0)$. Also, the learning frequency is set at $t = 1$.

Step 2. A data value $\mathbf{x}$ is selected from the observed data set as an input vector.

Step 3. A best matching unit c with the weight closest to the input vector $\mathbf{x}$ is set as per (4):

$$c = \mathrm{argmin}_k \|\mathbf{x} - \mathbf{y}_k(t-1)\|^2 \tag{4}$$

Step 4. The weight of each node is updated as per (5):

$$\mathbf{y}_k(t) = \mathbf{y}_k(t-1) + \alpha(t)h_{ck}(t)\{\mathbf{x} - \mathbf{y}_k(t-1)\} \tag{5}$$

where α is the learning rate; h_{ck} is the neighborhood function. Each is defined in (6)–(8).

$$\alpha(t) = \alpha_0\left(1 - \frac{t}{T}\right) \tag{6}$$

$$h_{ck}(t) = \exp\left(-\frac{d_{ck}^2}{2\sigma(t)^2}\right) \tag{7}$$

$$\sigma(t) = \max\left\{\sigma_0 \exp\left(-\frac{t}{\tau}\right), \sigma_{\min}\right\} \tag{8}$$

where α_0 is the initial value of the learning rate; T is the time constant that sets the minimum speed for the learning rate; and d_{ck} is the Euclidean distance between the best matching unit c and the neighborhood node k. Additionally, σ is the neighborhood radius; σ_0 is the initial value for the neighborhood radius; $\sigma_{\min}$ is the minimum value for the neighborhood radius; and τ is the time constant that sets the minimum speed for the neighborhood radius. Furthermore, as the algorithm returns to Step 2 with learning frequency $t = t + 1$, the processing is repeated.

SOM-Based Algorithm

The proposed algorithm estimates the reward probability by factoring in the reward gained when arm i is selected as the SOM^i input value for arm i, then sequentially determining the arm to select. The algorithm works as follows:

Step 1. A SOM^i for arm i is prepared for each arm. Here, the initial value of $\mathbf{y}_k^i(0)$ for the weight of each node in the SOM^i shall be a one-dimensional vector, $\mathbf{y}_k^i(0) = (1)$. Also, the time step shall be $t = 1$.

Step 2. The arm j with the highest valuation as determined by (9) is selected.

$$j = \mathrm{argmax}_i \frac{1}{N^i} \sum\nolimits_{k=1}^{N^i} \left\| \mathbf{y}_k^i(t-1) \right\| \tag{9}$$

where N^i is the number of SOM^i nodes. Furthermore, if multiple arms reach the maximum valuation, the arm will be selected based on which arm has the lowest arm number i.

Step 3. The reward gained when arm j is selected is confirmed. If the reward is 1, then $\mathbf{x} = (1)$; if the reward is 0, then $\mathbf{x} = (0)$.

Step 4. For the SOM^j for the selected arm j, the best matching unit c for $\mathbf{x}$ is determined as per (10).

$$c = \mathrm{argmin}_k \left\| \mathbf{x} - \mathbf{y}_k^j(t-1) \right\|^2 \tag{10}$$

Here, if there are multiple candidates as the best matching unit, then the candidate with the lowest node number k will be selected.

Step 5. For SOM^j, the node weight is revised as per (11):

$$\mathbf{y}_k^j(t) = \mathbf{y}_k^j(t-1) + \alpha\left(t^j\right) h_{ck}\left(t^j\right) \left\{ \mathbf{x} - \mathbf{y}_k^j(t-1) \right\} \tag{11}$$

where t^j represents the number of times arm j has been selected; α and h_{ck} are calculated as per (6)–(8). For the non-selected arm $i (i \neq j)$, $\mathbf{y}_k^i(t) = \mathbf{y}_k^i(t-1)$. Furthermore, as the algorithm returns to Step 2 with time step $t = t + 1$, the processing is repeated.

In accordance with the flow in this algorithm, each arm is estimated to have a high valuation at the start; the valuation is then adjusted based on the results of the arm selection.

Moreover, in this algorithm, the weight of each individual SOM node corresponds to the valuation for the arm. An overview of the way weights of SOM nodes are updated is shown in Fig. 2. As shown in item 2 in (11), the greater the difference between the node's value and the actual reward gained, the more drastic the update on the weight of the node. Therefore, even if the reward ratio for an arm suddenly changes, the environmental change is automatically detected, and adaptations can occur.

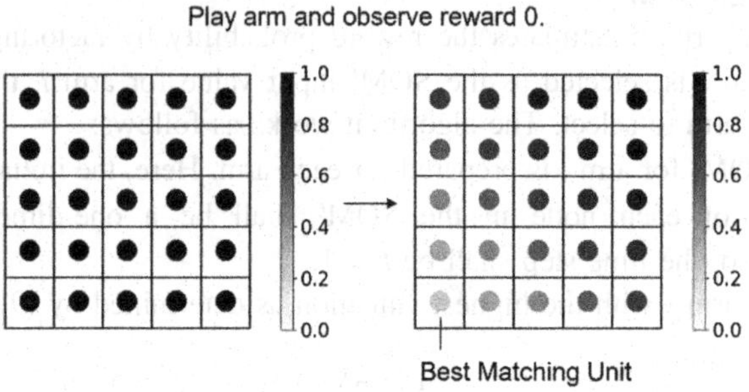

Fig. 2. An overview of the way the weight of the SOM nodes is updated in the proposed algorithm. The figure shows the weight of nodes being updated in a SOM corresponding to a given arm in a case where the reward gained from the arm is 0.0. Each circle in the grid represents a node; the node color corresponds to the weight.

If continual adaptation to environmental change is a primary objective, then the learning rate and neighborhood radius in (5) should be constants. In (9), the valuation for each arm is set to the average of the weight of all nodes; in practice, however, the weight of one node can also be used as the valuation for an arm. Therefore, this algorithm can be described as a simple model for a single node. However, in this paper, given the objectives for this research, we implement Kohonen's most basic, unaltered, SOM.

3 Experimental Setup

This section describes the numerical experiment conducted for this paper. The numerical experiment was conducted in both a stationary and a non-stationary environment using a stochastic MAB framework.

The reward attributed to an arm is determined based on a reward ratio P_i set for each arm i. When a player selects an arm i, it is possible to gain a reward of 1.0 at a probability of P_i and a reward of 0.0 at a probability of $1 - P_i$. Here, the number of times an arm is selected is called a "step"; a player can only select one arm per step. In a stationary environment, the reward ratio P_i for each arm is determined using a uniform random number from the interval $[0, 1]$ for each trial run. In a non-stationary environment, not only is the reward ratio P_i for each arm determined using a random number from the interval $[0, 1]$ for each trial run, but the reward ratio for each arm is also reshuffled at each step using a uniform random number from the interval $[0, 1]$.

The evaluation of the effectiveness of the algorithm involves a representative metric of "regret" in the MAB problem. "Regret" represents the disparity between the rewards that would have been gained if the arm with the maximum probability of reward had been selected at every step and the expected value of the reward gained by the arms that were actually selected. The smaller the value of regret, the better the algorithm is considered to be.

In this experiment, to evaluate the performance of the algorithm, cases were presented where the number of arms was set at 2, 10, 100, and 200; a 10,000-step simulation was performed 10,000 times for each, and an average value for regret was calculated. The average value for regret is summed at each step for each trial; the total is then divided by 10,000, the total number of trials. In addition, in a non-stationary environment, the reward ratios for all arms were reshuffled in all trials every 1,000 steps.

4 Results

In cases where the number of arms was set to 2, 10, 100, and 200, the results for regret in a stationary environment are shown in Fig. 3; the results for regret in a non-stationary environment are shown in Fig. 4. Here, the competitive layer in the proposed algorithm's SOM has an overall size of 10 × 10 in the shape of a non-torus square grid, with $\alpha_0 = 0.1, \mathrm{T} = 10,000, \sigma_0 = 10, \sigma_{\min} = 5,$ and $\tau = 50$.

In Fig. 3, in a stationary environment, in a case with 2 arms, the UCB1-Tuned and Thompson Sampling algorithms both yielded the minimal value for regret. In a case with 10 arms, Thompson Sampling yielded the minimal value for regret. In cases with 100 or 200 arms, Thompson Sampling and the proposed algorithm both equally yielded the lowest value for regret. However, in cases with 100 or 200 arms, in the earliest steps (from step 0 to step 1,000), the proposed algorithm yielded the lowest value for regret.

In Fig. 4, in a non-stationary environment, in all cases, with 2, 10, 100, or 200 arms, the proposed algorithm yielded the lowest value for regret in a dynamic environment after the first 1,000 steps.

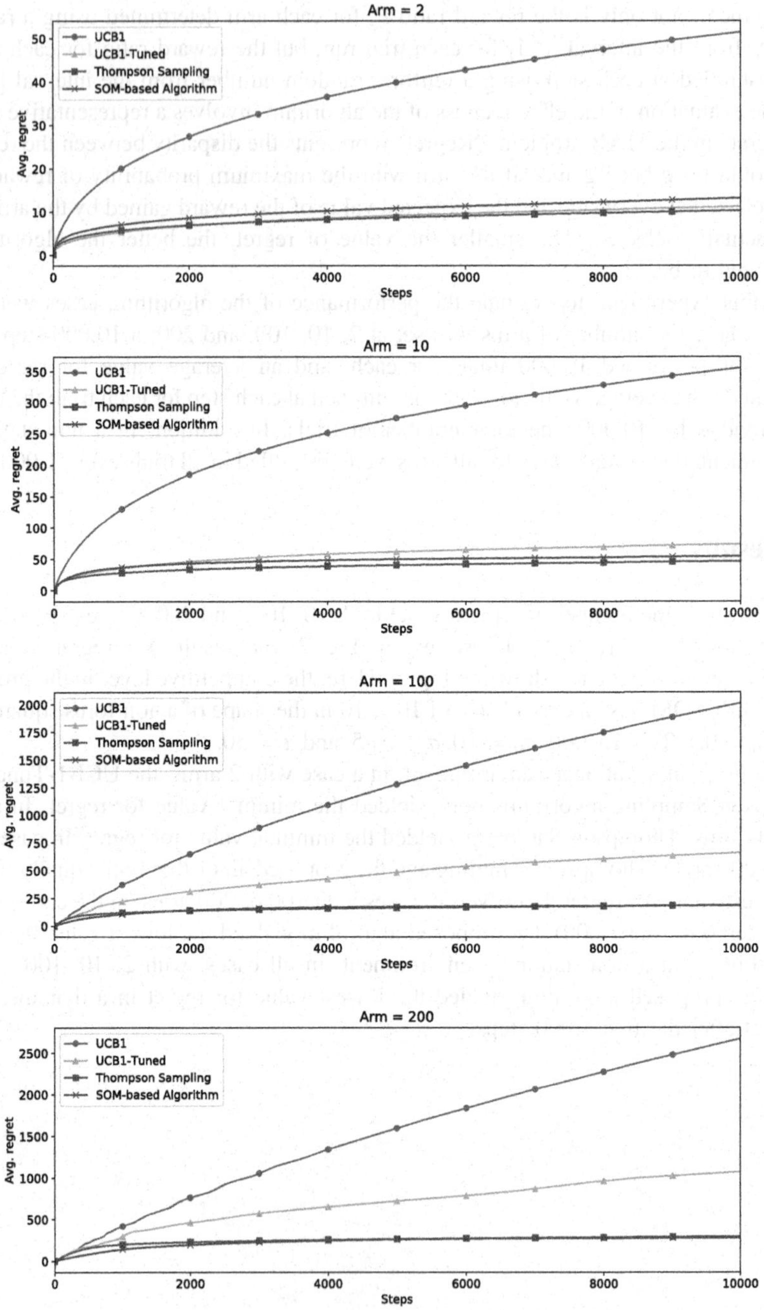

Fig. 3. A comparison of results for regret from UCB1, UCB1-Tuned, Thompson Sampling, and SOM-based algorithms in a stationary environment. Charts display the average value of regret over 10,000 trials with, from top to bottom, 2, 10, 100, and 200 arms.

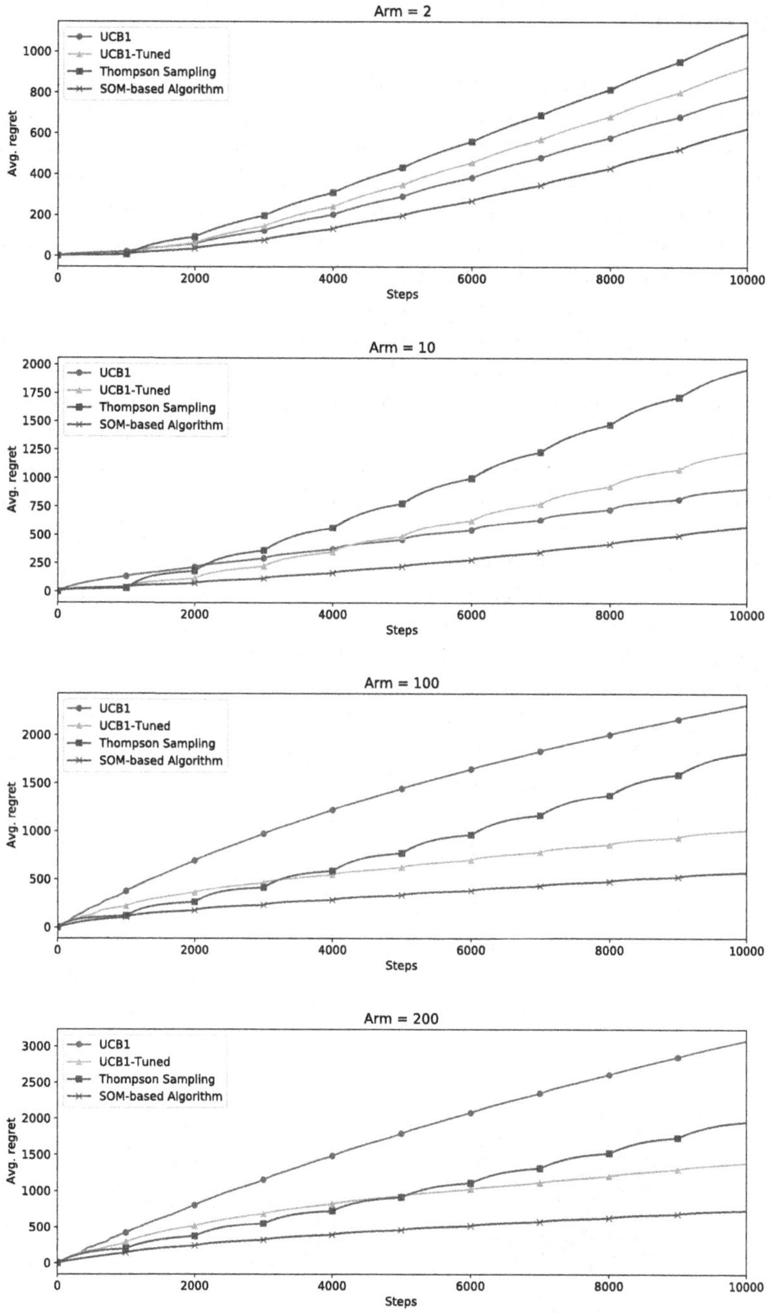

Fig. 4. A comparison of results for regret from UCB1, UCB1-Tuned, Thompson Sampling, and SOM-based algorithms in a non-stationary environment. Charts display the average value of regret over 10,000 trials with, from top to bottom, 2, 10, 100, and 200 arms.

5 Discussion

Based on these results, in a stationary environment, one can conclude that the proposed algorithm demonstrates equivalent or superior effectiveness compared with UCB1, UCB1-Tuned, and Thompson Sampling algorithms in cases with numerous arms. In particular, the proposed algorithm confirmed it was capable of selecting arms with high reward ratios at earlier stages in cases with numerous arms. Furthermore, in a non-stationary environment, the proposed algorithm has shown to be capable of selecting arms with high reward ratios consistently, regardless of the number of arms, in contrast with UCB1, UCB1-Tuned, and Thompson Sampling algorithms.

The proposed algorithm featured in this paper used Kohonen's unaltered SOM. We will discuss its benefits and limitations below.

Some of the advantages the algorithm has lie in the way it can efficiently estimate an arm's reward probability within a finite time by reducing the neighborhood radius. By nature, in using a SOM, one presumes that the data from the observation target will not change. Therefore, if the observation target does change from time to time, the learning rate and neighborhood radius should not be reduced. On the other hand, as stated above, the greater the difference between the valuation at the current point in time and the actual reward gained, the more drastic the revision in valuation; therefore, the proposed algorithm demonstrates strong capability in both a stationary environment and a non-stationary environment. Moreover, the algorithm is different from sliding window UCB and BAG1 for the reason that it does not need to set a time window.

The approach also yields benefits from a data mining perspective. SOMs excel at visualizing data characteristics. Therefore, through visualization of the SOM, the approach helps better understand information concerning the arm: the rewards that it yields, and the frequency with which those rewards can be expected to appear. Examples of the results of visualization for the SOM are shown in Figs. 5 and 6. Figure 5 shows the visualization of a SOM after an arm with two reward value outputs, 0.0 and 1.0, is pulled 1,000 times. Figure 6 shows the visualization of a SOM after an arm with three reward value outputs, 0.0, 0.5, and 1.0, is pulled 1,000 times. In both Figs. 5 and 6, the SOM provides an intuitive visual display of the rewards that appear and the frequency with which those rewards can be expected to appear.

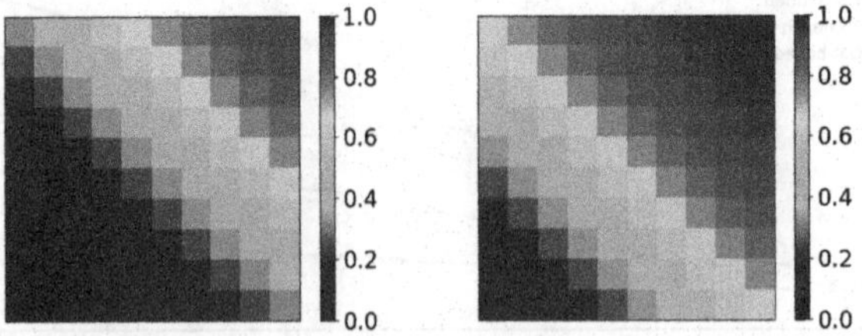

Fig. 5. Results visualization for a SOM for the proposed algorithm where arm rewards have two possible values. The graphic on the left shows SOM results visualization after an arm, for which the probability of gaining a reward of 0.0 or 1.0 is 0.7 or 0.3 respectively, has been pulled 1,000 times. The graphic on the right shows SOM results visualization after an arm, for which the probability of gaining a reward of 0.0 or 1.0 is 0.3 or 0.7 respectively, has been pulled 1,000 times. The color of a grid cell represents the weight of the corresponding node.

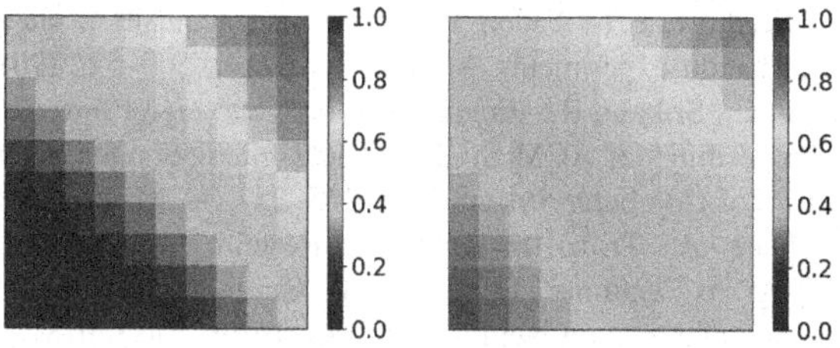

Fig. 6. Results visualization for a SOM for the proposed algorithm where arm rewards have three possible values. The graphic on the left shows SOM results visualization after an arm, for which the probability of gaining a reward of either 0.0, 0.5, or 1.0 is 0.5, 0.2, or 0.3 respectively, has been pulled 1,000 times. The graphic on the right shows SOM results visualization after an arm, for which the probability of gaining a reward of 0.0, 0.5, or 1.0 is 0.2, 0.6, or 0.2 respectively, has been pulled 1,000 times. The color of a grid cell represents the weight of the corresponding node.

One of the algorithm's limitations is that it requires as many SOMs to be prepared as there are arms. Therefore, if the problem features 200 arms, then 200 SOMs must be prepared, consuming a large amount of memory. However, with regard to the calculation speed, as calculations for each step only involve the weight of a single SOM, no significant delay is created. Moreover, since this algorithm changes the performance greatly due to the way we set SOM parameters, there is undeniable necessity that these parameters need further research.

6 Conclusions

This paper proposed a MAB algorithm using Kohonen's most basic SOM capable of adaptation to stationary and non-stationary environments. It also conducted a numerical experiment using a stochastic MAB framework in both a stationary and non-stationary environment. As a result, the proposed algorithm demonstrated equivalent or improved effectiveness in stationary environments with numerous arms and consistently strong capability in non-stationary environments regardless of the number of arms in contrast with existing UCB1, UCB1-Tuned, and Thompson Sampling algorithms.

In the future, we will look to conduct further analysis on situations where SOM parameters change, and develop a refined algorithm based on SOM formulas.

References

1. Robbins, H.: Some aspects of the sequential design of experiments. Bull. Am. Math. Soc. **58**(5), 527–535 (1952)
2. Sutton, R.S., Barto, A.G.: Introduction to Reinforcement Learning. MIT Press, Cambridge (1998)
3. Xu, M., Qin, T., Liu, T.Y.: Estimation bias in multi-armed bandit algorithms for search advertising. Adv. Neural Inf. Process. Syst. **26** (2013)

4. Schwartz, E.M., Bradlow, E.T., Fader, P.S.: Customer acquisition via display advertising using multi-armed bandit experiments. Market. Sci. **36**(4), 500–522 (2017)
5. Combes, R., Jiang, C., Srikant, R.: Bandits with budgets: regret lower bounds and optimal algorithms. In: Proceedings of ACM SIGMETRICS International Conference on Measurement and Modeling of Computer Systems, pp. 245–257. ACM, Portland (2015)
6. Gasparini, M., Nuara, A., Trovò, F., Gatti, N., Restelli, M.: Targeting optimization for internet advertising by learning from logged bandit feedback. In: Proceedings of International Joint Conference on Neural Networks. IEEE, Rio (2018)
7. Li, L., Chu, W., Langford, J., Schapire, R.E.: A contextual-bandit approach to personalized news article recommendation. In: Proceedings of the 19th International Conference on World Wide Web, Raleigh, North Carolina, pp. 661–670, (2010)
8. Meshram, R., Gopalan, A., Manjunath, D.: Optimal recommendation to users that react: online learning for a class of POMDPs. In: Proceedings of 55th Conference on Decision and Control, pp. 7210–7215. IEEE, Las Vegas (2016)
9. Balakrishnan, A., Bouneffouf, D., Mattei, N., Rossi, F.: Using contextual bandits with behavioral constraints for constrained online movie recommendation. In: Proceedings of the Twenty-Seventh International Joint Conference on Artificial Intelligence, Stockholm, Sweden, pp. 5802–5804 (2018)
10. Wang, Q., Li, T., Iyengar, S.S., Shwartz, L., Grabarnik, G.Y.: Online IT Ticket automation recommendation using hierarchical multi-armed bandit algorithms. In: Proceedings of the 2018 SIAM International Conference on Data Mining, San Diego, CA, USA, pp. 657–665 (2018)
11. Korein, M., Veloso, M.: Multi-armed bandit algorithms for spare time planning of a mobile service robot. In: Proceedings of the 17th International Conference on Autonomous Agents and Multi Agent Systems, Stockholm, Sweden, pp. 2195–2197 (2018)
12. Eppner, C., Brock, O.: Visual detection of opportunities to exploit contact in grasping using contextual multi-armed bandits. In: Proceedings of the IEEE/RSJ International Conference on Intelligent Robots and Systems, Vancouver, Canada, pp. 273–278 (2017)
13. Auer, P., Cesa-Bianchi, N., Fischer, P.: Finite-time analysis of the multiarmed bandit problem. Mach. Learn. **47**(2–3), 235–256 (2002)
14. Thompson, W.R.: On the likelihood that one unknown probability exceeds another in view of the evidence of two samples. Biometrika **25**, 285–294 (1933)
15. Garivier, A., Moulines, E.: On upperconfidence bound policies for non-stationary bandit problems. Algorithmic Learn. Theor., 174–188 (2011)
16. Larkin, L., Richard, D., Joshua, R.: Multi-armed bandit strategies for non-stationary reward distributions and delayed feedback processes. arXiv preprint arXiv:1902.08593 (2019)
17. Kohonen, T.: Self-organizing Maps. Springer, Heidelberg (1995). https://doi.org/10.1007/978-3-642-56927-2
18. Li, T., Sun, G., Yang, C., Liang, K., Ma, S., Huang, L.: Using self-organizing map for coastal water quality classification: towards a better understanding of patterns and processes. Sci. Total Environ. **628–629**(1), 1446–1459 (2018)
19. Belkhiri, L., Mouni, L., Tiri, A., Narany, T.S., Nouibet, R.: Spatial analysis of groundwater quality using self-organizing maps. Groundwater Sustain. Dev. **7**, 121–132 (2018)
20. Camara-Turull, X., Fernández-Izquierdo, M.Á., Sorrosal-Forradellas, M.T.: Analysing capital structure of spanish chemical companies using self-organizing maps. Kybernetes **46**(6), 947–965 (2017)
21. Kaufmann, E., Korda, N., Munos, R.: Thompson sampling: an asymptotically optimal finite-time analysis. Algorithmic Learn. Theor., 199–213 (2012)

Cooperation and Coordination Regimes by Deep Q-Learning in Multi-agent Task Executions

Yuki Miyashita[1,2](✉) and Toshiharu Sugawara[1](✉)

[1] Computer Science and Engineering, Waseda University, Tokyo 1698555, Japan
{y.miyashita,sugawara}@isl.cs.waseda.ac.jp
[2] Shimizu Corporation, Tokyo 1040031, Japan

Abstract. We investigate the coordination structures generated by deep Q-network (DQN) with various types of input by using a distributed task execution game. Although cooperation and coordination are mandatory for efficiency in multi-agent systems (MAS), they require sophisticated structures or regimes for effective behaviors. Recently, deep Q-learning has been applied to multi-agent systems to facilitate their coordinated behavior. However, the characteristics of the learned results have not yet been fully clarified. We investigate how information input to DQNs affect the resultant coordination and cooperation structures. We examine the inputs generated from local observations with and without the estimated location in the environment. Experimental results show that they form two types of coordination structures—the division of labor and the targeting of near tasks while avoiding conflicts—and that the latter is more efficient in our game. We clarify the mechanism behind and the characteristics of the generated coordination behaviors.

Keywords: Multi-agent deep reinforcement learning · Coordination · Cooperation · Divisional cooperation

1 Introduction

Cooperation and coordination for improving overall efficiency in multi-agent systems is an important issue. However, their appropriate strategic regime for cooperation is influenced by a variety of factors such as task structures, frequency of task occurrence, and environmental characteristics, which makes it a challenging issue. Even in a simple case, it is wasteful for multiple agents to target a certain task that just one agent would be able to handle, but it is not easy to decide which agent among a group should do it. Because appropriate coordinated behaviors that consider such complicated factors cannot be defined in the design phases of the systems, it is desirable for the agents themselves to identify the cooperative actions appropriately and form a regime for cooperation according to the many environmental factors.

I. V. Tetko et al. (Eds.): ICANN 2019, LNCS 11727, pp. 541–554, 2019.
https://doi.org/10.1007/978-3-030-30487-4_42

Deep reinforcement learning (DRL) has produced many successful results in fields such as robotics [1,3] and games [4,6,7]. However, it needs a very large number of positive and negative training data, which requires a very long learning/training time. It is also affected by the quality of input data; e.g., noisy or partially missing training data severely degrade the learning results. In particular, when we apply DRL to multi-agent systems, we always need to consider the fact that the appropriate behaviors in cooperation/coordination are highly dependent on the behaviors of the other agents, and thus, the current positive training data may become negative or noisy data next time. Such instability of data characteristics affects the convergence and correctness of the learning results. Although the issues facing coordination and cooperation have been extensively studied in multi-agent system contexts, despite this difficulty, few studies addressed those issues using the DRL technique [2,5,8]. For example, Leibo *et al.* [5] analyzed the relationship between learned (un)competitive policies and resource scarcity in multi-agent DRL (MA-DRL), i.e., agents have their own *deep Q-network* (DQN). Palmer *et al.* [8] proposed an extension of MA-DRL called *lenient learning* in which agents possess the temperature value of each state-action pair and decay the value when the pair is applied in order to avoid the use of outdated pairs. However, it is still not clear how the observations of agents and data input to the DQN affects the generated coordination structures in MA-DRL.

Our contribution is to examine what kinds of strategic cooperative behaviors emerge in multiple agents by changing the observable view of each agent as the inputs to the DQNs. We use the *distributed task execution game*. Although simple, this game is appropriate to understand the characteristics of emerging coordination regimes. In our model, agents have their own DQNs. To examine how various state information to DQNs affect the results of coordination, we compare the locally observable environmental data with and without the agent's location in the environment. Note that even if we limit the observational area, the number of states for learning become huge, and thus learning results hardly converge in the case of naive reinforcement learning.

Our experimental results show that if agents could add the absolute locations, they were able to establish division of labor in a bottom-up manner, in the sense that they determined individual areas that each agent would be responsible for. However, in unbusy environments, they could not generate such divisional cooperation and the entire performance stayed low. Moreover, when they did not include the locational information, they did not induce the division and allocation of responsible areas, but the entire performance finally outperformed the cases when agents did include the locations because they were able to tactfully avoid conflicts and wasteful behaviors. We discuss why the regime with division of labor could not deliver a better performance. We also show that agents in the generated regime executed tasks very efficiently by comparing it with the performance induced by a naive and intuitive allocation algorithm in unbusy environments.

2 Problem Formulation

We consider a multi-agent problem called the *distributed task execution game* in which tasks continuously appear somewhere in an environment at a certain rate and multiple agents move around to select and execute the tasks concurrently. An example of our problem environment is shown in Fig. 1(a). The environment is a lattice consisting of $N \times N$ cells where black squares are agents and red circles are tasks they have to execute. The possible actions are one of $A = \{up, right, down, left\}$. If one of the agents moves onto a cell containing a task, it can execute the task and receives a positive reward, r. Then, the task disappears and a new task is placed on another cell. If more than two agents attempt to move onto the same cell, one of them can successfully move and the other remains in the original position.

This problem is specified as a tuple $\langle I, m, N, E, \{S_i\}, \{A_i\}\rangle$, where $I = \{1, \ldots, n\}$ is the set of n agents, m is the number of tasks deployed in the environment, N is the lattice size of the environment, and $E(\ni e)$ is the set of all possible environmental states including all agents working there. We assume that agent $\forall i \in I$ can observe the limited local area whose center is i itself; the state of this local area at time t is denoted by $s_{i,t}$, which is the subset of the entire state e_t $(s_{i,t} \subset e_t)$ and whose center is i itself. Let S_i be the set of all local states of i. We assume that agents are *perfect* observers, i.e., agent i can correctly identify the local state, $s_{i,t}$. Finally, we define $\mathcal{A} = A_1 \times \cdots \times A_n \ni a_t = (a_{1,t}, \ldots, a_{n,t})$ as a product of actions, where A_i is the set of all possible actions in i. In our problem, $A_i = A$, so all agents have the same possible actions.

Every time agents take joint actions a_t in e_t they may receive a *reward* $r_i(e_t, a_t)$, and then, the environmental state transits to e_{t+1}. The value of the reward they receive only depends on the current state $e_t \in E$ and joint action $a_t \in \mathcal{A}$. Then, because i is the autonomous learner, it has to select and take the action only on the basis of observed local state at t. Because we consider MA-DRL, the agents individually learn the Q-values (or their policies) in order to improve the entire performance, i.e., agents autonomously identify appropriate coordinated/cooperative behaviors to obtain more rewards using their own DQNs. The policy π_i of i is usually expressed as the function whose domain is the set of the local state S_i.

We introduce discrete time $t \geq 0$, and the distributed task execution game proceeds as follows. Initially $(t = 0)$, n agents $I = \{1, \ldots, n\}$ and m tasks $\Psi = \{\psi_1, \cdots, \psi_m\}$ are scattered in the environment. Let e_t be the entire state of the environment at t. All agents take the following steps simultaneously.

(1) At time t, agent $\forall i \in I$ decides action $a_{i,t}$ in e_t on the basis of its own *policy*, so $a_{i,t} = \pi_i(s_{i,t}) \in A$.
(2) When i moves to a cell where task ψ_u exists, i executes ψ_u and ψ_u is deleted. Then i receives reward $r_{i,t} = r$.
(3) After all agents move at t, if the number of tasks in environment e_t is less than m, new tasks are generated and placed on the empty cells selected randomly in the lattice, until the number of tasks is equal to m. The resulting environment is e_{t+1}.

(4) If $t \geq H$, an epoch of the game ends; otherwise, $t = t + 1$ and go back to Step (1), where H is a positive integer.
(5) After one epoch has ended, the environment is initialized and another epoch will start from Step (1).

We iterate this game for F epochs, where F is also a positive integer. The objective of the agents is to maximize the number of rewards they receive, so they learn which action will result in higher rewards by using a certain learning technique.

3 Learning Methods

3.1 Deep Q-Network with Local Belief

DQN is the reinforcement learning method in which a Q-function or policy is learned using a deep neural network. We take the concurrent learning approach, meaning that individual agents have their own network for learning.

In conventional reinforcement learning, an agent learns the action-value function (i.e., Q-function) and the associated policy π to maximize the sum of the cumulative expected rewards. When we denote the discounted future reward at t step as $R_t = \sum_{t'=t}^{T} \gamma^{t'-t} r_{t'}$, where T is the horizon step and $\gamma \in [0, 1)$ is the discount factor, the action-value function Q for policy π is defined as

$$Q^{\pi}(s, a) = \mathbb{E}[R_t | s = s_t, a = \pi(s_t) = a_t].$$

Furthermore, the optimal action value $Q^*(s, a)$ is defined as

$$Q^*(s, a) = \max_{\pi} \mathbb{E}[R_t | s = s_t, a = \pi(s_t) = a_t].$$

Q-learning [11] is a sample-based approximation method to estimate optional Q-value $Q^*(s, a)$, where

$$Q^*(s, a) = \mathbb{E}[r + \gamma \max_{a'} Q^*(s', a') | s, a],$$

and $Q^*(s', a')$ is the estimated optimal Q-value for the next state s'. However, Q-learning is often slow when the problem space is large.

In DQN, the Q-function (or the associated policy π) is estimated by a set of neural network parameters θ whose values are updated by using agent experience. At time t, to obtain the optimal Q-value approximation from the network, parameters $\theta_{i,t}$ in the network of agent i are updated to minimize the mean squared loss function $L_{i,t}(\theta_{i,t})$, which is defined as

$$L_{i,t}(\theta_{i,t}) = \mathbb{E}_{(s_i, a_i, r_i, s'_i)}[(r_i + \gamma \max_{a'_i} Q_i(s'_i, a'_i; \theta^-_{i,t}) - Q_i(s_i, a_i; \theta_{i,t}))^2],$$

Note that we use the fixed target Q-network, i.e., target network parameters $\theta^-_{i,t}$ are periodically copied from the main Q-network parameters θ to stabilize learning for the DQN; this is particularly important when learning the coordinated behavior of multiple agents should avoid confusion due to outdated and noisy training data. In our problem, $\theta_{i,*}$ is copied to $\theta^-_{i,*}$ every H time steps (i.e., 1 epoch).

Then, we propose a policy based on the combination of observations and additional information to examine various inputs to DQNs. Because we apply MA-DRL to this game, each agent decides its next action by using the policy associated with the learned Q-values from its own DQN. Usually, the policy should be decided on the basis of the observation $s_{i,t}$. By defining the *view* of i at time t, $v_{i,t}$, as the aggregation of the observed state $s_{i,t}$ and the locational information, which is the part of the local belief, we want to extend the domain of Q_i and π_i by

$$Q_i : \mathcal{V}_i \times A_i \longrightarrow \mathbb{R}, \text{ and } \pi_i : \mathcal{V}_i \longrightarrow A_i,$$

where $\mathcal{V}$ is the set of observed state with the local belief in i. Examples of these views are described in Sect. 3.3.

3.2 Experience Replay

We apply experience replay in DQN learning in order to avoid overfitting. Agent i stores the experienced data $c_{i,t} = (s_{i,t}, a_{i,t}, r_{i,t}, s_{i,t+1})$ into its own memory $D_{i,t-1} = \{c_{i,t-d}, \cdots, c_{i,t-1}\}$, where $d > 0$ is memory capacity, at t steps. Then, i updates parameters $\theta_{i,t}$ at every step to minimize loss $L_{i,t}(\theta_{i,t})$, which is denoted by

$$L_{i,t}(\theta_{i,t}) = \mathbb{E}_{(s_i,a_i,r_i,s'_i)\sim U(D_{i,t})}[(r_i + \gamma_q \max_{a'_i} Q_i(s'_i, a'_i; \theta^-_{i,t}) \\ -Q_i(s_i, a_i; \theta_{i,t}))^2],$$

where $U(D_{i,t})$ indicates the minibatch, i.e., the random sampling from experience memory $D_{i,t}$.

To reduce the value of loss function $L_{i,t}(\theta_{i,t})$, we calculate the gradient of loss function $\nabla L_{i,t}(\theta_{i,t})$. We adopted RMSprop [10] here because its learning rate for parameter updates does not change; this might be useful because independent multi-agent learning is likely to be unsteady.

3.3 View Representation

Agent i has a limited range of observation that is specified by the *observable range size* V_i, where V_i is a non-negative integer. Agents can or cannot locate tasks and other agents correctly within this range depending on their abilities. This means that individual agents assume that the observed data $s_{i,t}$ within V_i is their own current state. Figure 1(a) shows an example of i's observable range, which is sized $V_i = V$. The green square is the observable range in the environment, and its center is itself. In this example, the range covers the outside of the environment whose size is $(2V + 1) \times V'$, and of course, i cannot obtain any information on this part.

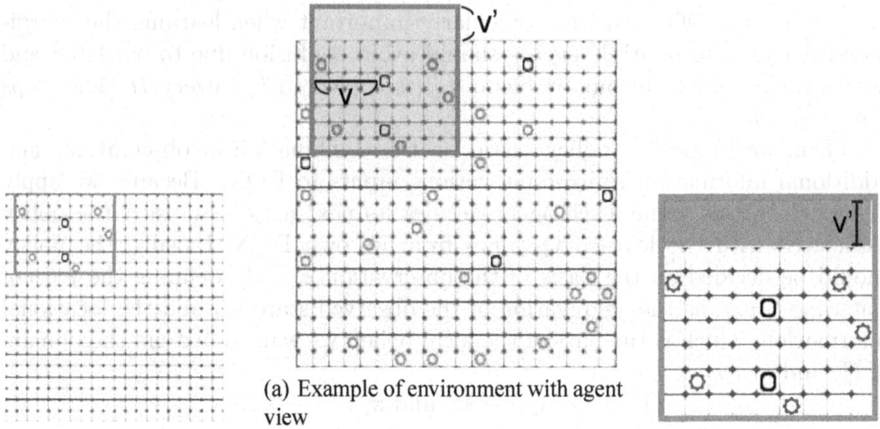

(b) Relative view

(a) Example of environment with agent view

(c) Local view

Fig. 1. Environmental state and relative/local views.

Table 1. Network architecture.

Layer	Input	Filter size	Stride	Activation	Output
Convolutional		2×2	1		$20 \times 20 \times 8$
Max pooling	$20 \times 20 \times 8$	2×2	2		$10 \times 10 \times 8$
Convolutional	$10 \times 10 \times 8$	2×2	1		$10 \times 10 \times 16$
Max pooling	$10 \times 10 \times 16$	2×2	2		$5 \times 5 \times 16$
FCN	$5 \times 5 \times 16$			ReLu	100
FCN	100			Liner	4

We consider two types of inputs to the DQNs, *relative views* and *local views*, based on the observable ranges.

Relative Views. Agent i with the relative view generates its view $v_{i,t}$ for input to the local DQN by composing its observed state $s_{i,t}$ and the entire map, as shown in Fig. 1(b). Since i cannot observe outside of its range, the unobservable regions are assumes to be blank (filled up by 0). However, we assume that this relative view includes the abstract map of the environment and that i's current location is a part of its belief $b_{i,t}$. The actual input to the local DQN consists of three $N \times N$ lattices, with the first lattice containing only the location of itself, the second one containing only other agents in the observable range, and the third one including only tasks in the observable range.

Local Views. Agent i with the local view just inputs the observed state (so $v_i = s_i$) to the DQN, as shown in Fig. 1(c). We assume that i can see the wall of the environment and that the cells outside of this wall are filled with -1.

Since i is located at the center of the observation, the input to the DQN consists of two $(2V_i + 1)^2$ sublattices: one including only other agents in the observable range and the other including only tasks in the observable range.

3.4 Architecture of Neural Network

In MA-DRL, each agent uses its own policy derived by the DQN to decide its action independently. The architecture of the deep neural network is, as specified in Table 1, composed of convolutional network layers, max pooling layers, and fully connected network (FCN) layers. The convolutional network can enhance an agent's visual recognition, as reported in many papers on image recognition. The shape of the first input layer of the network depends on the size and the shape of agent's views, so its value is not shown in Table 1. The output data from the DQN are the collections of action-value pairs, and agents select the actions whose values are highest.

As the learning strategy, we use the ε-greedy strategy with decay to choose actions on the basis of the learning results so far with probability $1 - \varepsilon_{i,t}$ or randomly with probability $\varepsilon_{i,t}$. In our learning method, we assume that agent i decays its own $\varepsilon_{i,t}$ gradually by $\varepsilon_{i,t} = \varepsilon_{i,t-1} * \gamma_\varepsilon$, where γ_ε is the decay rate. By starting with a large value of ε, the ε-greedy strategy with decay enables agents to take various actions in the initial stages of learning.

Table 2. Learning parameters.

Parameter	Value
Discount factor γ_q	0.99
Initial value $\varepsilon_i = \varepsilon_{i,0}$	0.9999
Decay rate γ_ε	0.9999995
Learning rate for RMSprop l_r	0.0001
Momentum for RMSprop α	0.90
ε for RMSprop ε_{rms}	1e-07

Table 3. Experimental parameters.

Parameter	Value
Size of environment N	20
No. of agents n	6
Reward r	1
Memory capacity d	2000
Mini batch size $\|U(D_{i,t})\|$	32
Epoch length H	200
Sum of epochs F	60,000

4 Experiments and Discussion

4.1 Experimental Setting

We experimentally compare the performances (i.e., the total rewards earned by all agents) and analyze the coordination behavior when the DQNs have various types of inputs. We conduct three experiments. In the first experimental scenario (Exp. 1), we examine the performances of agents with the relative views by changing their observable range size V in a busy environment where the number of tasks is 25 ($m = 25$). Note that when m is larger, agents have more chances to execute tasks and thereby get more rewards. This also means that they have more chances to learn.

In the second experiment (Exp. 2), we investigate the performance of agents with local views and discuss the differences in performance and the coordination structure of agents with the relative views. Finally, in the third experiment (Exp. 3), we conduct the same experiments in Exps. 1 and 2 in the unbusy environments specified by $m = 1, 2$, and 4. In this case, agents with local or relative views have fewer chances to learn and more difficulty in finding tasks. We also compare the performances of our methods with that of a naive task allocation method that calculates all combinations of shortest paths to reach all tasks; this naive method may not be optimal, but it delivers considerably good performance. The parameters for these experiments are listed in Tables 2 and 3. The number of agents n is six in all experiments. Note that because we change the observable range size V and the number of tasks m in these experiments, they are not listed.

4.2 Experiment 1: Relative View Input

We first examine whether six agents ($n = 6$) with relative views improve their performance over time and how the observable range size V affects the performance when the number of tasks in the environment is large ($m = 25$). The results of the earned rewards per epoch from 1 to 60,000 epochs (12,000,000 time steps) are plotted in Fig. 2, where each plot is the average value of the earned rewards every 100 epochs when $V = 4, 8, 15$, and 19. Note that agents with $V = 19$ can observe the entire environment correctly. These results clearly indicate that the total earned rewards increased along with epochs in all cases, but their performances were almost identical regardless of the observable range sizes (agents with $V = 8$ exhibited the best performance).

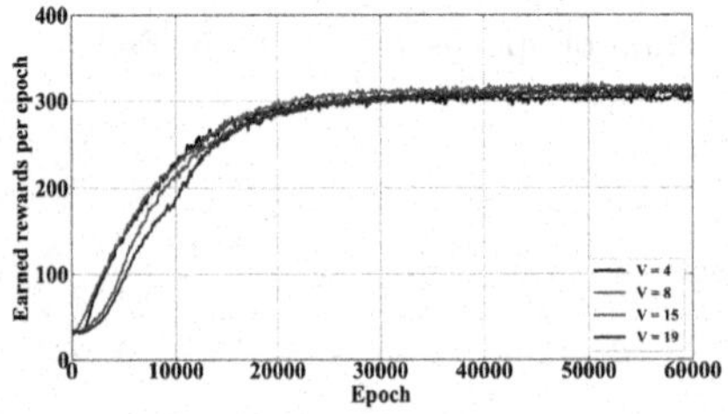

Fig. 2. Earned rewards per epoch (relative views, $m = 25$).

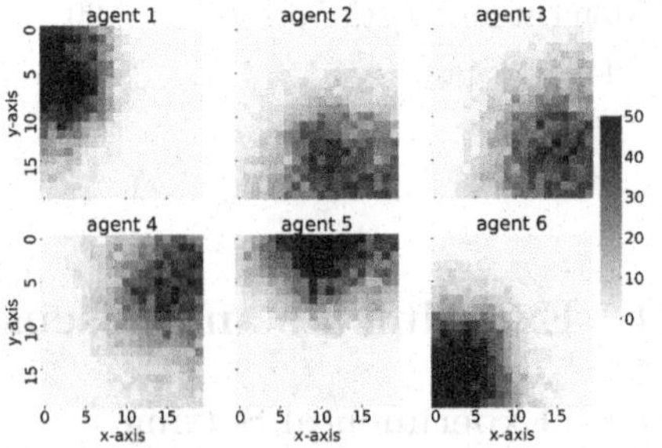

Fig. 3. Locations of executed tasks (relative views). (Color figure online)

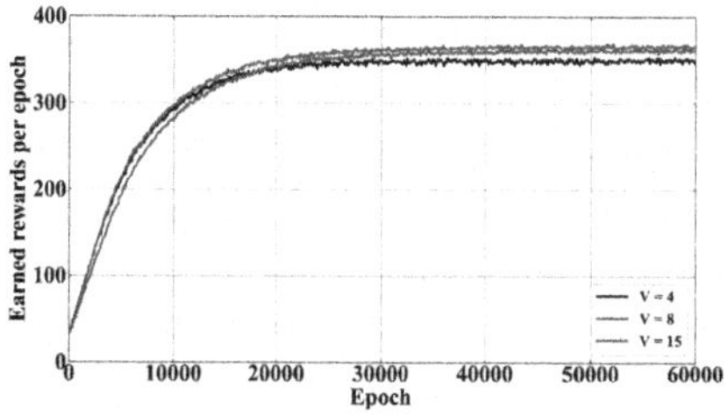

Fig. 4. Earned rewards per epoch (local views, $m = 25$).

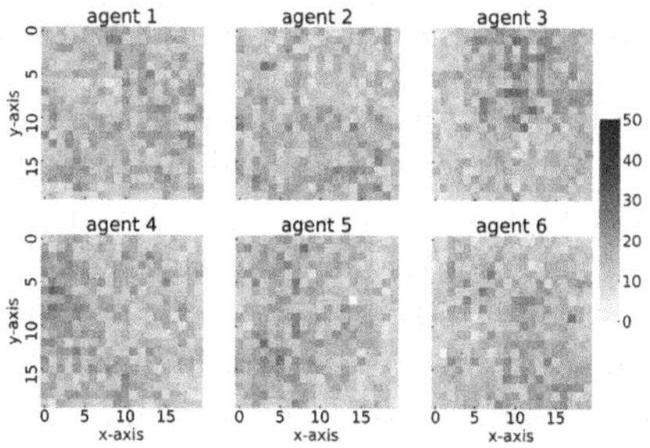

Fig. 5. Locations of executed tasks (local views).

To analyze the structure of coordinated behavior, we investigate where each agent was working in the environment. We counted the number of tasks that each agent executed in individual cells between 55,000 and 60,000 epochs when $V = 8$ and visualized these data using heat maps. This is shown in Fig. 3, where the darker blue cells indicate that the corresponding agent executed more tasks, and white and faint blue cells indicate that it seldom or never executed tasks, respectively. We can see that the movements of all agents were localized, and the agents tended to execute tasks in specific regions; it seems that they form a division of labor by segmentation in a bottom-up manner. We call these segmented regions, where mainly just one agent is moving around, the *responsible regions*. When multiple agents try to do the same task, only one agent can earn the reward and the attempt of the other agents go to waste. Therefore, they generate their working regions to avoid such conflicts. In the earlier epochs (around 10,000 epochs), agents already started to execute only in specific regions, but the regions are unclear and indistinct. Then, they gradually formed shapes and the locations became stable. Note that we also confirmed that when $V = 4$, 15, and 19, similar divisional cooperation appeared.

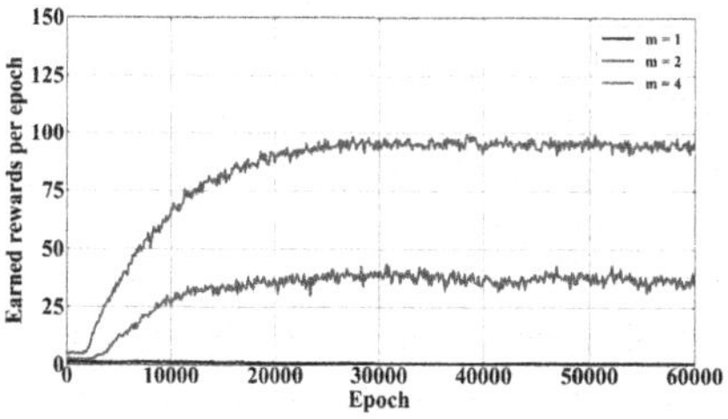

Fig. 6. Earned rewards per epoch (relative views).

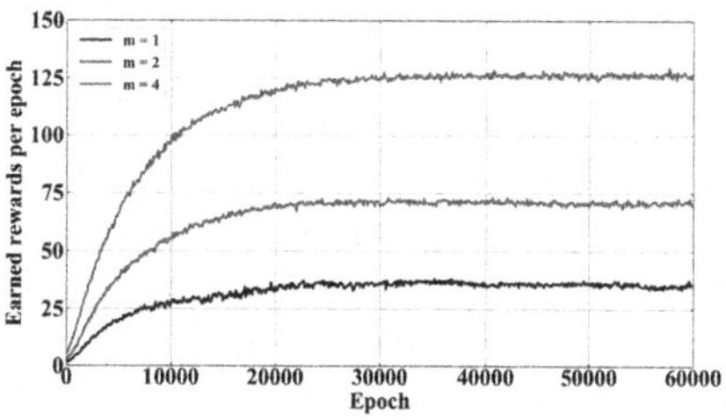

Fig. 7. Earned rewards per epoch (local views).

4.3 Experiment 2: Local View Input

In Exp. 2, the experimental setting is identical to that of Exp. 1 except that the agents input the local views to their DQNs. Figure 4 plots the total rewards earned at every epoch from $t = 1$ to 60,000 when $V = 4, 8$, and 15. As shown, the agents with the local views could also improve performance and earned game rewards mostly did not depend on the observable range sizes (the performance when $V = 8$ was slightly higher). In addition, if we compare these results with those in Fig. 2, the earned total rewards in Exp. 2 were approximately 20% higher than those in Exp. 1.

We also counted where each agent executed the tasks to see what kind of coordination structure emerged. The results are shown as the heatmaps in Fig. 5. Unlike the case of relative view (Fig. 3), agents did not form responsible regions. The divisional cooperation in terms of segmentation improved to a certain level of performance, but in this particular problem, flexible coordination without segmentation achieved better performance (discussed in more detail in Sect. 4.5).

4.4 Experiment 3: Unbusy Environment

Because there are so many tasks in a busy environment, agents could pursue and execute tasks in a distributed and independent way. However, if the number of tasks are limited, e.g., less than the number of agents, it is probable that agents will target the same task to earn more rewards, and thus they may not be able to learn coordinated activities. To see what happens in such an environment, we conducted the distributed task execution game in an environment where m is 1 to 4. The observable range size of all agents is fixed to 8 ($V = 8$). The performance results are plotted in Fig. 6 (relative views) and Fig. 7 (local views).

As shown in Fig. 6, agents with relative views could not learn appropriate behavior when $m = 1$ (the total rewards remained almost zero). However, when $m = 2$ and 4, they could execute tasks to some degree. In contrast, we can see that agents with local views could work quite well even when m was very small, as shown in Fig. 7. Their final performances were much better than those of agents with relative views (approximately 25% higher when $m = 4$ and almost double when $m = 2$).

It is not shown here, but agents with relative views could generate divisional cooperation by partitioning and allocating the responsible regions to each agent (although their boundaries were not so clear), but when $m = 1$, they could not form divisional cooperation and agents could seldom earn rewards. Agents with local views did not generate divisional cooperation like in the busy environment; specifically, when V was large ($V = 15$ in our experiments), we observed the divided areas, but divided areas were gradually blurry with progression of agent's learning and finally disappeared.

To check whether the resulting coordinated behaviors exhibited a reasonable performance, we compare the earned rewards with those earned using a naive centralized method when $m = 1, 2$, and 4. This method calculates the shortest time steps in all combinatorial cases when these tasks are allocated to agents.

Table 4. Comparison of earned rewards per epoch.

Number of tasks	Naive	Local view	Relative view
$m = 1$	38.7	35.3	0.4
$m = 2$	73.6	70.7	36.7
$m = 4$	129.3	126.4	94.5

For example, when $m = 2$ and $n = 6$, the number of possible assignments is 6^2. We calculate the required time to execute all tasks for all possible assignments, i.e., the shortest time steps to reach the locations of tasks. Then, agents select the best one whose required time is the smallest (randomly selected in breaking tie) and move according to the selected assignment; other agents stay in their current positions. When one of the tasks disappeared and another task was added, we repeat the same calculation mentioned above, and (re)allocate tasks to appropriate agents. This assignment may not be optimal but is reasonable in a dynamically changing environment. We list the results of the earned rewards per epoch in Table 4, where the naive centralized method is labeled as "naive." The data in this table are the average of the earned rewards of 100 epochs for the naive method and the averages during 55,000 to 60,000 epochs for the agents with relative and local views.

As indicated in Table 4, the performance of agents with local view was almost identical to that using the centralized method, and the coordinated behaviors generated by the DQN with local views performed quite well even in unbusy environments. However, the performance of agents with the relative views was much lower than the others.

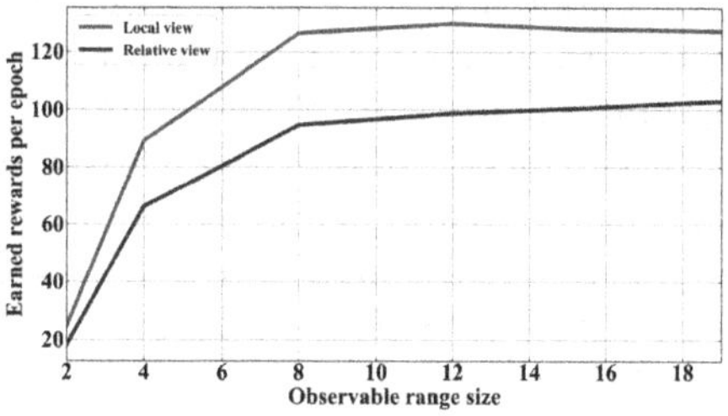

Fig. 8. Correlation between performance and observable range size when $m = 4$.

Finally, we investigate the relationship between the observable range size and the resulting average performance during 55,000 to 60,000 epochs. This result is plotted in Fig. 8. As shown, if the observable range size V was larger, the performances increased. In particular, when $V = 2$, the performance was quite low, probably because it took more time to find tasks. Note that when $V = 2$, agents with the relative views could not form divisional cooperation. However, when $V \geq 8$, their performances were not much different. Tasks were inside the observable range of at least one of the agents. However, they had a peak value ($V = 12$ when agents used the local view and $V = 15$ when agents used the relative view). Agents with a large observable range size would find the same tasks and move to one of them; this resulted in redundant movements.

4.5 Discussion

We gleaned a number of interesting insights from our experiments. First, agents were able to learn different coordination strategies. In our game, redundant or useless actions are caused by conflicts, meaning that multiple agents target the same tasks, so agents attempted to identify strategies to reduce such conflicts. Therefore, agents that had the absolute location in the entire environment established divisional cooperation on the basis of locational segmentation, and agents with local view learned how to target nearby tasks by paying attention to the locations of other agents. In addition, we can see from the results of Exp. 3 that, to establish divisional cooperation, having a sufficient number of tasks to identify the segmentation of work areas resulted in better performance. In the environment where only a small number of tasks was generated, it was difficult for agents to form divisional cooperation and the performance suffered as a result.

Second, we analyzed the difference in performance between relative views and local views, which was the reason why divisional cooperation in this game had a lower performance. In this particular game, it seems that the strategy based on divisional cooperation was not bad but not excellent. For example, suppose that agent i is responsible for area R_i and is located near the fringe of R_i. When a task appears on the opposite side of R_i, the agent will take some time to detect and move toward the task. Even when another agent finds this task, the agent may not approach it because it is outside of the responsible area. However, since agents with local view do not form responsible areas, the agent near the task can approach and execute it if no other agents exist nearby.

We conducted another experiment in which information on other agents' locations were removed from the inputs, although the details of the results were omitted. Its results indicated that locational information on other agents was essential to generate the coordination strategy that targets nearby tasks by paying attention to the others' locations (local views), but that information was not so important to establish divisional cooperation (relative views). In the latter case, two agents might closely exist, but they would execute fewer tasks, and they were likely to move away, like a repulsive force. So, agents could indirectly know the existence of other agents. This phenomenon is quite similar to the divisional cooperation by normal reinforcement learning reported by Sugiyama *et al.* [9], where although the agent in their paper did not care about the locations of other agents, it could identify a certain area as not so important because other agents were moving around and executing tasks in that area.

5 Conclusion

We discussed which strategic coordination/cooperation structures emerge in a distributed task execution game with MA-DRL in accordance with input to the DQNs. In MA-DRL, agents have their own DQNs to learn action-value pairs, and we examined a number of inputs based on the observable views with the local beliefs. Our experimental results indicated that inputs with absolute locations in the environment could form a divisional cooperation structure by segmentation. At the same time, inputs that contained only the local view could not generate divisional cooperation but instead formed flexible coordination in which agents near tasks targeted these tasks by paying attention to the locations of other agents in their view to avoid conflicts. These results also demonstrate that flexible coordination by avoiding conflicts outperformed coordination by divisional cooperation in our game.

We would like to extend our environments, agents, network structures, and games for our future work. For example, we will explore situations where the environment has an obstacle, task generation is biased in a certain area, tasks have structures that should be done cooperatively with a number of different agents, and agents have their specialties.

Acknowledgements. This work was partly supported by JSPS KAKENHI Grant Number 17KT0044.

References

1. Amarjyoti, S.: Deep reinforcement learning for robotic manipulation - the state of the art. CoRR abs/1701.08878 (2017). https://doi.org/10.1109/ICRA.2017.7989385, http://arxiv.org/abs/1701.08878
2. Gupta, J.K., Egorov, M., Kochenderfer, M.: Cooperative multi-agent control using deep reinforcement learning. In: Sukthankar, G., Rodriguez-Aguilar, J.A. (eds.) AAMAS 2017. LNCS (LNAI), vol. 10642, pp. 66–83. Springer, Cham (2017). https://doi.org/10.1007/978-3-319-71682-4_5
3. Hüttenrauch, M., Sosic, A., Neumann, G.: Guided deep reinforcement learning for swarm systems. CoRR abs/1709.06011 (2017). http://arxiv.org/abs/1709.06011
4. Lample, G., Chaplot, D.S.: Playing FPS games with deep reinforcement learning. In: Proceedings of the Thirty-First AAAI Conference on Artificial Intelligence, 4–9 February 2017, San Francisco, California, USA, pp. 2140–2146 (2017). http://aaai.org/ocs/index.php/AAAI/AAAI17/paper/view/14456
5. Leibo, J.Z., Zambaldi, V., Lanctot, M., Marecki, J., Graepel, T.: Multi-agent reinforcement learning in sequential social dilemmas. In: Proceedings of the 16th Conference on Autonomous Agents and MultiAgent Systems, pp. 464–473. IFAAMAS, Richland (2017). http://dl.acm.org/citation.cfm?id=3091125.3091194
6. Mnih, V., et al.: Playing Atari with deep reinforcement learning. CoRR abs/1312.5602 (2013). http://arxiv.org/abs/1312.5602
7. Mnih, V., et al.: Human-level control through deep reinforcement learning. Nature **518**(7540), 529 (2015). https://doi.org/10.1038/nature14236
8. Palmer, G., Tuyls, K., Bloembergen, D., Savani, R.: Lenient multi-agent deep reinforcement learning. In: Proceedings of the 17th International Conference on Autonomous Agents and MultiAgent Systems, AAMAS 2018, IFAAMAS, Richland, SC, pp. 443–451 (2018). http://dl.acm.org/citation.cfm?id=3237383.3237451
9. Sugiyama, A., Sugawara, T.: Improvement of robustness to environmental changes by autonomous divisional cooperation in multi-agent cooperative patrol problem. In: Advances in Practical Applications of Cyber-Physical Multi-Agent Systems: The PAAMS Collection - 15th International Conference, PAAMS 2017, Porto, Portugal, 21–23 June 2017, Proceedings, pp. 259–271 (2017). https://doi.org/10.1007/978-3-319-59930-4_21

10. Tieleman, T., Hinton, G.: Lecture 6.5-RMSProp: divide the gradient by a running average of its recent magnitude. COURSERA Neural Netw. Mach. Learn. **4**(2), 26–31 (2012). https://doi.org/10.1007/BF00992698
11. Watkins, C.J., Dayan, P.: Q-Learning. Mach. Learn. **8**(3–4), 279–292 (1992). https://doi.org/10.1007/BF00992698

Boosting Reinforcement Learning with Unsupervised Feature Extraction

Simon Hakenes(✉) and Tobias Glasmachers

Institute for Neural Computation, Ruhr University Bochum, Bochum, Germany
{simon.hakenes,tobias.glasmachers}@ini.rub.de

Abstract. Learning to process visual input for Deep Reinforcement Learning is challenging and training a neural network with nothing else but a sparse and delayed reward signal seems rather inappropriate. In this work, Deep Q-Networks are leveraged by several unsupervised machine learning methods that provide additional information for the training of the feature extraction stage to find a well suited representation of the input data. The influence of convolutional filters that were pretrained on a supervised classification task, a Convolutional Autoencoder and Slow Feature Analysis are investigated in an end-to-end architecture. Experiments are performed on five ViZDoom environments. We found that the unsupervised methods boost Deep Q-Networks significantly depending on the underlying task the agent has to fulfill. While pretrained filters improve object detection tasks, we find that Convolutional Autoencoders leverage navigation and orientation tasks. Combining these two approaches leads to an agent that performs well on all tested environments.

Keywords: Deep Reinforcement Learning · Unsupervised learning

1 Introduction

When thinking about an autonomous agent acting in the real world, deep Reinforcement Learning (RL) algorithms, that are able to efficiently process visual input, are of central importance. In order to learn an intelligent behaviour, high level information about the environment has to be extracted from the input data. Learning both, feature extraction and policy, from nothing else than a scalar, sparse and delayed reward signal seems to be inefficient. Especially in three dimensional environments with an agent that is able to move around, the state space is huge and impossible to discover completely. Similar to humans and animals, which learn mostly unsupervised [11], combining unsupervised machine learning methods with reinforcement learning algorithms into an end-to-end solution is promising in terms of accelerated training while keeping the training procedure simple.

We therefore apply several unsupervised machine learning techniques with the goal to learn meaningful visual filters quickly, so that reinforcement learning can focus on learning a policy expressed by the higher (dense) layers of

I. V. Tetko et al. (Eds.): ICANN 2019, LNCS 11727, pp. 555–566, 2019.
https://doi.org/10.1007/978-3-030-30487-4_43

the network. We compare several unsupervised machine learning techniques in combination with reinforcement learning in an end-to-end framework for their suitability towards this goal. As a baseline, a Deep Q-Network (DQN) is trained from scratch, i.e., with randomly initialized weights and without any auxiliary method, as in the work of Mnih et al. [19]. As a first step, the opportunities of transfer learning are explored by pretraining the convolutional layers of the DQN with real world images in a supervised classification task. Furthermore, we add two different unsupervised auxiliary objective functions to the DQN: a Convolutional Autoencoder (CAE) [18] and a gradient-based variant of Slow Feature Analysis (SFA) [24]. CAEs operate on single images and ignore the rich temporal structure of visual input. SFA is based on the idea that the most informative signals are slowly changing over time compared to the raw sensor signals, and hence takes the temporal structure into account. All three methods affect only the convolution filters. After initial experimentation, the pretrained filters and the CAE were found to be most promising, however, for different tasks. Hence, we also explored the combination of both with a joint feature set.

For reproducibility, the code is publicly available at https://github.com/shakenes/unsupervised-drl.

The remainder of this work is organized as follows. After discussing related work we introduce the background and the environments in Sects. 3 and 4. We describe our experiments, present and discuss the results in Sects. 5, 6, and 7, and finally draw conclusions.

2 Related Work

The combination of unsupervised learning with reinforcement learning was explored by several authors.

Unsupervised auxiliary tasks for RL that each yield a reward by themselves are proposed in [12,21]. However, the visual input is only exploited indirectly with an additional reward function, in contrast to using established unsupervised learning algorithms.

The authors of [3] decoupled feature extraction from policy learning. They proposed two new methods based on vector quantization and sparse coding to learn the features separately but simultaneously to the policy. Some interesting results on Atari games were shown as a neural network consisting of only 6–18 neurons was necessary to learn the policy. One may conclude that the actual RL part is nearly trivial when fed with high level and low dimensional features. However, the vector quantization methods are unsuitable for quickly changing scenes of 3D environments like ViZDoom.

In [1,16] an autoencoder is used for dimensionality reduction of visual input data and learning a policy based on the encoded data. However, the study aimed for a bottleneck as small as possible, while we only aim for efficient training of the convolutional layers. Similarly, in [15] the CAE features are used to predict the immediate rewards and to compute the Successor Representation for each possible action.

3 Theoretical Background

3.1 Reinforcement Learning

Many sequential decision making processes can be formulated as a Markov Decision Process (MDP) defined by the state space $\mathcal{S}$, the set of possible actions $\mathcal{A}$, the state transition probability $\mathcal{P}(s_{t+1}|s_t, a_t)$, the reward function $\mathcal{R}(s, a)$ and the discount factor $\gamma \in (0, 1]$, which represents the preference of immediate rewards over future rewards. An agent receiving ego-perspective visual input in a three dimensional environment can only observe the state partially. The future discounted reward at time t is $R_t = \sum_{t'=t}^{T} \gamma^{t'-t} r_t$, where T is the time step at which the MDP terminates and r_t is the reward received in time step t.

The most prominent class of deep RL algorithms are temporal difference methods, in particular Q-Learning [25]. Key to Q-Learning is approximating the optimal action-value function, that returns the expected R_t after seeing some state s, taking an action a and following a policy π thereafter:

$$Q^*(s, a) = \max_{\pi} \mathbb{E}\left[R_t | s_t = s, a_t = a, \pi\right] \tag{1}$$

For high-dimensional visual inputs, this function can be approximated with a CNN, which makes it dependent on the network weights θ [19]: $Q^*(s, a; \theta)$. The Q-Learning loss is then:

$$L_i(\theta_i) = \mathbb{E}\left[(y_i - Q(s, a; \theta_i))^2\right] \tag{2}$$

with the target

$$y_i = \mathbb{E}\left[r + \gamma \max_{a'} Q(s', a'; \theta_{i-1} | s, a)\right] \tag{3}$$

In this work, double Q-Learning [9] is applied to avoid overestimation of the Q-values.

3.2 Transfer Learning

The general idea of transfer learning is to gain knowledge about one task and exploit it in a different but related task. In the case of a CNN, instead of training it from scratch with randomly initialized weights, it can be pretrained on an arbitrary visual task. The weights, especially the last layers, are then fine-tuned with respect to the new task. This is more data efficient and often leads to better performance and faster convergence than training from scratch [8,20,28,29]. This fact suggests that the features extracted by a CNN are generic and not specific for any task.

3.3 Convolutional Autoencoders

An autoencoder is a neural network with a small central layer, which is used to learn a low-dimensional representation of high-dimensional input data.

To achieve this, the autoencoder is trained to approximate the identity function in a least squares sense. It can hence be thought of as a non-linear extension of principal component analysis for dimensionality reduction. Since the central layer is smaller than the input and output layers, it acts as an information bottleneck, which forces the encoder to transform the input into a low dimensional representation. The decoder needs to back-transform the data such that the output data is as similar as possible to the input data [10]. For visual data, it makes sense to exploit the local correlation between the pixels by using (stacked) convolutional layers [18].

3.4 Slow Feature Analysis

Slow Feature Analysis follows the intuition that the most informative features are slowly changing over time compared to raw input/sensor signals [26,27]. It was shown that SFA is able to encode and disentangle object identity, rotation and position in visual tasks [5], as well as position and orientation from visual first person recordings [6].

SFA can be formally described as a sequence of optimization problems. Considering a time series $\{x_t\} \in \mathbb{R}^d$ with $t = 0, \ldots, \tau$, SFA aims at finding input-output functions $g_i : \mathbb{R}^d \to \mathbb{R}$ that minimize $\left\langle (g_i(x_{t+1}) - g_i(x_t))^2 \right\rangle_t$ where $\langle \cdot \rangle_t$ being the average over time. To avoid the trivial constant solution, to ensure normalization and to avoid redundant features, zero mean $\langle g_i(x_t) \rangle_t = 0$, unit variance $\langle g_i(x_t)^2 \rangle_t = 1$ and decorrelation, $\langle g_i(x_t) g_j(x_t) \rangle_t = 0$ are enforced.

Schüler et al. [24] proposed a method for gradient-based end-to-end training of SFA. In order to do that, a differentiable loss as well as a differentiable whitening procedure enforcing the constraints (zero mean, unit variance and decorrelation) are designed.

4 Environments

Our experiments were carried out on five ViZDoom [13] environments which are described in this section. Screenshots are given in Fig. 1. The simplest environment is *Basic* where the agent is supposed to hit an immobile enemy with a gun while moving only left and right. If hit, the episode terminates and a reward is given. Missing the enemy, timeout and time passing are punished. To solve the task, the agent only needs to detect the target object's location on a static background, which is quite easy.

In *Defend the Center*, the agent is spawned in the center of a circular room together with several enemies. The agent cannot move around, but only turn left and right. The goal is to kill the monsters before they reach the agent. Each kill is rewarded while dying is punished. Here, the agent has to detect the locations of multiple objects at once on a static background. Additionally, since enemies might be behind the agent, it has to keep track of its complete surrounding area.

Health Gathering consists of a rectangular room with an acid floor that damages the agent over time. To survive, the agent has to gather health packs that are randomly distributed on the floor. Increasing the health by collecting such a health pack is rewarded. In contrast to the preceding environments, the agent has three degrees of freedom instead of one. Therefore, the agent needs to actually navigate in the room and detect objects on a dynamically changing background.

Health Gathering Supreme is similar to *Health Gathering* except for maze-like walls in the room. That means, simple (input ignoring) policies like running in a circle become useless. Additionally, there are poisonous potions that lower the agent's health when collected. This constellation makes navigation much more challenging and demands the ability to distinguish between different kinds of objects.

The environment *My Way Home* places the agent in a maze with several connected rooms. A green vest is placed as a target in one of the rooms. The agent is spawned in a random room facing in a random direction. When the agent finds the vest, it gets a reward. Navigation and orientation by recognizing the rooms are the key challenges in this environment.

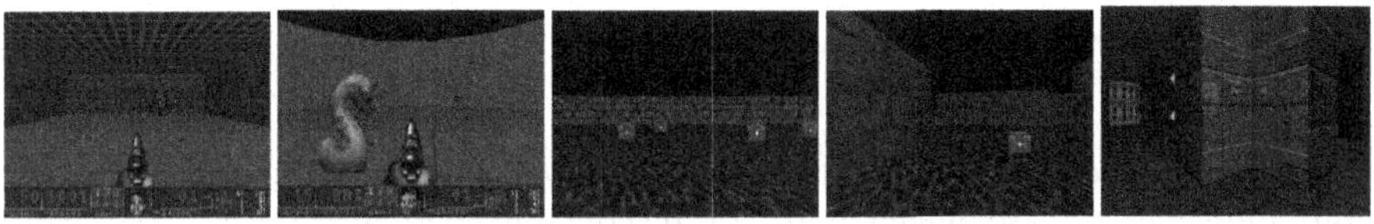

(a) (b) (c) (d) (e)

Fig. 1. Screenshots of the environments: (a) Basic, (b) Defend the Center, (c) Health Gathering, (d) Health Gathering Supreme, (e) My Way Home. (Color figure online)

5 Experiments

We carried out experiments aiming to answer the following research question: can unsupervised methods exploit the rich visual data to quickly evolve useful visual filters and speed up reinforcement learning? And if so, which method works best?

To this end, five experiments were carried out in each environment. As a baseline, the DQN was trained from scratch, i.e. with randomly initialized weights without any auxiliary method. The feed-forward CNN contains two convolutional layers with 32 7×7 filters and 4×4 strides in the first, and 32 5×5 filters with 2×2 strides in the second layer. They are followed by a dense layer with 1024 units. Each layer has a ReLU activation, $f(x) = \max(0, x)$. The last layer is dense (fully connected) with as many units as there are possible actions in the environment with linear activations representing the Q-values. The DQN is fed with 128×128 px grayscale images.

In order to exploit the capabilities of transfer learning, the convolutional layers of the DQN are pretrained on a subset of the ImageNet data set [22] in a supervised classification task. The data set contains real world images of animals and objects. The evolved convolutional filters form the initialization of the DQN. The fully connected layers are initialized at random.

To combine a CAE with the DQN, the decoder branch is placed on top of the last convolutional layer (Fig. 2a). Two dense layers with 1024 and 128^2 units, respectively, reconstruct the input image and propagate their gradients into the encoding convolutional layers. The DQN branch stays unaltered. Both branches are trained alternately. The training of the CAE is stopped after some time to prevent overfitting.

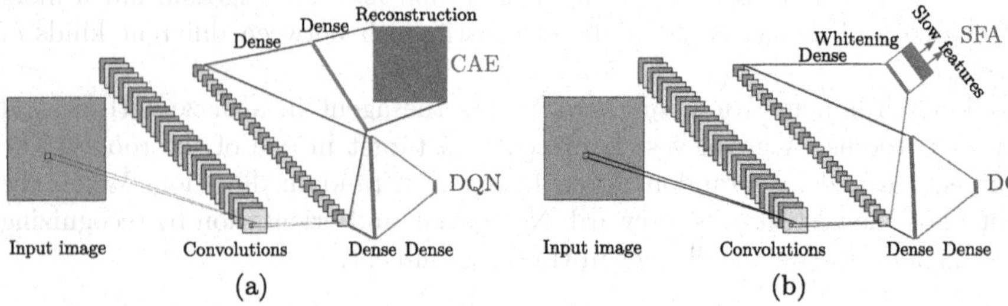

Fig. 2. Visualization of the CAE (a) and SFA (b) architecture.

Similar to the CAE architecture, a dense layer with 16 units and the power whitening layer [24] are placed on top of the convolutional layers (Fig. 2b). In contrast to previous work [17] the slow features are not fed into the value function. Their slowness just serves as an objective function for training more powerful filters. Note that the batches for DQN and SFA differ, because the SFA needs data from consecutive time steps.

Initial experiments showed that the pretrained filters and the CAE show the most promising results, however, on different environments. Therefore, we implemented a combination of both methods. Our architecture contains two parallel filter banks, one with pretrained filters and one trained by the CAE (which does not impact the pretrained filters). The dense layers connect to both filter banks, allowing the DQN to decide which set of features to use for which task – or to use both simultaneously. This architecture is referred to as the *Combination* in the following.

6 Results

6.1 Reward

All proposed methods improve the performance of the agent in terms of reward in the *Basic* environment as shown in Fig. 3a. They all manage to learn a sensible behaviour after less episodes than the baseline method which stagnates in the beginning. This scenario is mostly an object detection task as the agent can only move left and right and needs to align its gun with the still standing enemy to shoot it.

In *Defend the Center*, the Combination and the pretrained filters alone improve the performance greatly (Fig. 3b). The CAE and the SFA are not able to bring any benefit. Here, the agent solves an object detection task with multiple enemies that need to be shot in order to survive. However, the agent stands in a circular room and can only turn itself left and right, so there is no navigation involved.

In contrast to *Basic* and *Defend the Center*, the agent faces the challenges of an ego perspective 3D environment in *Health Gathering*, where it can move freely through the room. Here, training from scratch, the CAE, and the Combination work well. Surprisingly, SFA and the pretrained filters harm the performance significantly. The DQN apparently learns to choose the features from the CAE branch to determine the policy, as the pretrained filters have a far worse performance (Fig. 3c).

In *Health Gathering Supreme* the same task has to be solved in a maze like environment. The agent also has to distinguish between health kits and poisonous potions. The CAE improves the agent's performance, while the Combination shows the same performance as the baseline. Again, the pretrained filters and the SFA lead to a worse result (Fig. 3d).

In *My Way Home*, the agent needs to navigate through a labyrinth. The Combination of CAE and pretrained filters is the only method that really improves the agent's performance compared to the baseline (Fig. 3e).

6.2 Convolutional Filters

Since our central aim was to evolve filters quickly so a policy can be learned on top, we investigate the filters of the convolution layers in more details. Big differences between methods and environments can be observed. When trained from scratch without any auxiliary method, the DQN did not evolve a meaningful structure in the convolutional layers, see Fig. 4a. A more detailed investigation showed that they only changed negligibly compared to their initialization.

The pretrained filters behave similarly. Although minor changes are visible, their overall structure remains the same during the training procedure (Fig. 4b).

In the challenging environments *Health Gathering* and *Health Gathering Supreme*, the CAE encodes the features using well structured filters (Fig. 4c). One can observe edge detectors, centre-surround filters and cross-shaped structures, suitable for the detection of health packs. In contrast, the filters after training on *Basic* and *Defend the Center* are quite unstructured. The second convolutional layer still lacks meaningful structures.

As the only method, the SFA develops filters in both convolutional layers (Fig. 4d). However, their functional "meaning" is not obvious from visual inspection. The slowness loss drops significantly throughout the training, showing that the CNN successfully evolves slow features.

As expected, the combination of pretrained filters and CAE develop similar filters compared to the individual approaches, because they cannot interfere with each other.

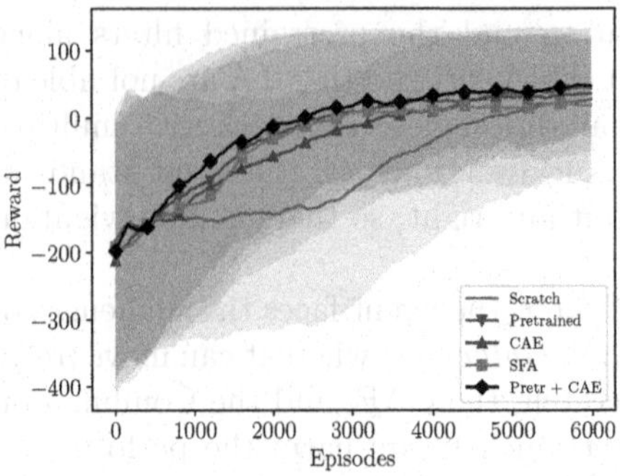

(a) *Basic*

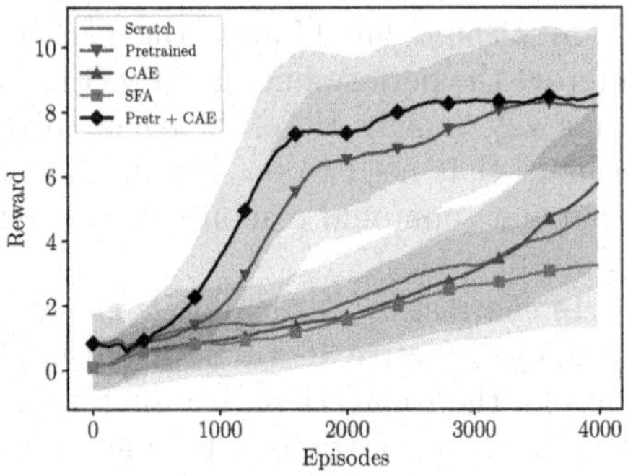

(b) *Defend the Center*

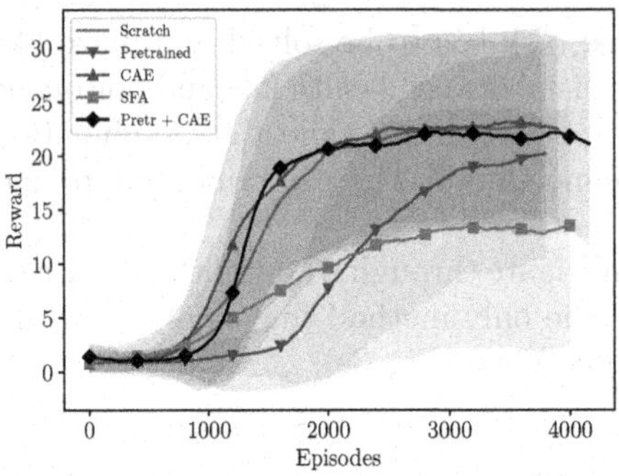

(c) *Health Gathering*

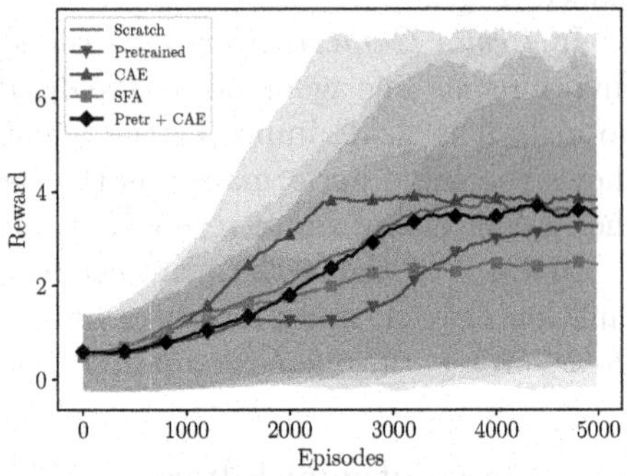

(d) *Health Gathering Supreme*

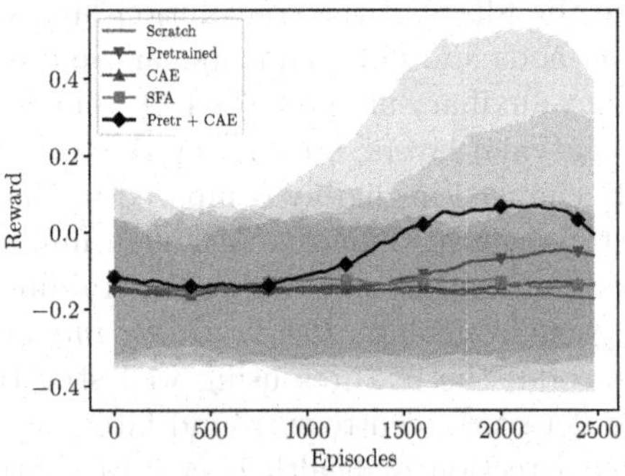

(e) *My Way Home*

Fig. 3. The mean reward per episode with standard deviation over 15 runs.

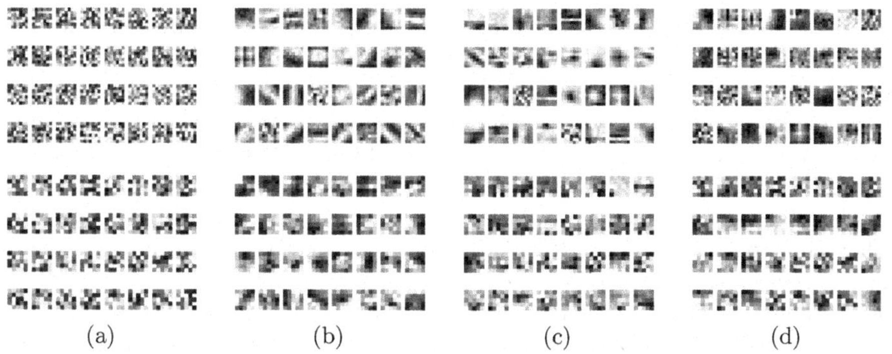

Fig. 4. Examples of evolved filters after training. The upper mosaics show the filters of the first convolutional layer while the lower mosaics belong to the second layer.

7 Discussion

The results show that unsupervised auxiliary methods can accelerate the training of a DQN significantly. The impact highly depends on the method and the environment. None of the methods works well in isolation across all environments. However, the proposed Combination of pretrained convolutional filters and a CAE seems to be a good and universally applicable choice. This can be explained by the joint set of features that specialize in different tasks: the pretrained filters perform better in object detection tasks, which is unsurprising because that is the task they were initially trained on, while the CAE focuses on global properties of the scene, which helps the agent to navigate in three dimensional environments.

The fact that the filters did not change during training and stayed as initialized implies that the DQN on its own is not able to generate useful gradients to develop actually meaningful filters. This suggests that it is important to somehow solve the problem of feature extraction when attacking complex reinforcement learning tasks. This is underlined by the findings of [3]. Their work implies that the reinforcement learning part itself is rather easy when there is a well suited representation of the input data.

The SFA shows disappointing results. Although it seems beneficial to exploit the temporal characteristics of the input signals, the used method was not able to develop a well suited representation for reinforcement learning. It is worth noting that the authors of [24] use far deeper architectures than we did.

Taking a closer look at the evolved filter kernels in the convolutional layers, one can conclude that unsupervised methods do help to develop more powerful filters, with the CAE showing the most impressive results. At this point two questions have to be answered: First, how is the quality of a filter kernel determined? And second, how should one interpret the still random looking filters in the second layer, and in the first layer when training from scratch? To answer the first question, filters from the literature are investigated [14,30]. Well evolved filters in CNNs often show some kind of structure with the weights being locally correlated. They usually can easily be distinguished from the randomly initialized ones. Similar to filters used in computer vision, it is often possible to assign functions like edge detection or templates to good filters. However, the results of this work show that even random looking filters can lead to a good performance in visual RL. As [23] stated, CNNs can perform surprisingly well with random filters, nevertheless outperformed by a pretrained and fine-tuned one. They showed that random filters are frequency selective, which might already be a decent enough feature in our case. Another explanation can be the findings of [2]. They investigated Random Projections of high dimensional data onto a lower-dimensional subspace using a random matrix. This does usually not distort the data in a significant way. Possibly, the filters stayed random looking due to a too high number of parameters of the model, which would suggest to lower the number of hidden units in the network, for example by decreasing the number of filters in the second layer. A short, qualitative study on this hypothesis shows that scaling the number of filters in the second convolutional layer in our DQN down by a factor of two leads to results comparable to the full network. Training time and maximum performance only suffer slightly, but the method based on SFA becomes quite unstable. However, it is worth mentioning here that [19] used even three convolutional layers with 32, 64 and 64 filters in their DQN, while testing their algorithm on Atari 2600 games, which are less challenging in terms of exploiting visual input than the ones explored in this work. We therefore hypothesize that their results could possibly also be achieved with a DQN with fewer parameters.

8 Conclusion

Returning to our initial question, it is now possible to state that unsupervised auxiliary methods can actually improve deep RL from visual input. While pretrained convolutional filters accelerate the training in environments that mostly require object detection and localization, CAEs greatly improve the performance in three dimensional worlds where it is crucial for the agent to fulfill navigation tasks. The Combination of both shows good results on all tested environments. Although these methods are completely unsupervised and can therefore not know which features are useful for the task, they still help developing meaningful filters to extract features that are well suited to learn sensible behavior.

An explanation for the poor performance of the DQN is given by pointing out that it was not able to develop meaningful filters on its own. Therefore, the importance of a powerful feature extraction stage for RL on complex problems is emphasized.

In future work we will develop our approach further by considering additional feature sets that are generated by objective functions aiming for monocular depth or optical flow estimation, since these take the spatial properties of the three dimensional environments into account [4, 7].

References

1. Alvernaz, S., Togelius, J.: Autoencoder-augmented neuroevolution for visual Doom playing. CoRR abs/1707.03902 (2017). http://arxiv.org/abs/1707.03902
2. Bingham, E., Mannila, H.: Random projection in dimensionality reduction: applications to image and text data. In: ACM SIGKDD International Conference on Knowledge Discovery and Data Mining, pp. 245–250. ACM, New York (2001). https://doi.org/10.1145/502512.502546
3. Cuccu, G., Togelius, J., Cudré-Mauroux, P.: Playing atari with six neurons. In: International Conference on Autonomous Agents and MultiAgent Systems, pp. 998–1006. International Foundation for Autonomous Agents and Multiagent Systems, Richland, SC (2019)
4. Dosovitskiy, A., et al.: FlowNet: learning optical flow with convolutional networks. In: IEEE International Conference on Computer Vision (ICCV), pp. 2758–2766, December 2015. https://doi.org/10.1109/ICCV.2015.316
5. Franzius, M., Sprekeler, H., Wiskott, L.: Slowness and sparseness lead to place, head-direction, and spatial-view cells. PLoS Comput. Biol. **3**(8), 1–18 (2007)
6. Franzius, M., Wilbert, N., Wiskott, L.: Invariant object recognition and pose estimation with slow feature analysis. Neural Comput. **23**, 2289–2323 (2011)
7. Godard, C., Aodha, O.M., Brostow, G.J.: Unsupervised monocular depth estimation with left-right consistency. In: IEEE Conference on Computer Vision and Pattern Recognition (CVPR), pp. 6602–6611, July 2017. https://doi.org/10.1109/CVPR.2017.699
8. Goodfellow, I., Bengio, Y., Courville, A.: Deep Learning. MIT Press, Cambridge (2016)
9. Hasselt, H.V., Guez, A., Silver, D.: Deep reinforcement learning with double Q-learning. In: AAAI Conference on Artificial Intelligence, pp. 2094–2100. AAAI Press (2016)
10. Hinton, G.E., Salakhutdinov, R.R.: Reducing the dimensionality of data with neural networks. Science **313**(5786), 504–507 (2006). https://doi.org/10.1126/science.1127647
11. Hinton, G., Sejnowski, T., Poggio, T.: Unsupervised Learning: Foundations of Neural Computation. A Bradford Book. MCGRAW HILL BOOK Company (1999)
12. Jaderberg, M., et al.: Reinforcement learning with unsupervised auxiliary tasks. CoRR abs/1611.05397 (2016)
13. Kempka, M., Wydmuch, M., Runc, G., Toczek, J., Jaśkowski, W.: ViZDoom: a doom-based AI research platform for visual reinforcement learning. In: IEEE Conference on Computational Intelligence and Games, pp. 341–348. IEEE, Santorini, September 2016
14. Krizhevsky, A., Sutskever, I., Hinton, G.E.: Imagenet classification with deep convolutional neural networks. In: Pereira, F., Burges, C.J.C., Bottou, L., Weinberger, K.Q. (eds.) Advances in Neural Information Processing Systems 25, pp. 1097–1105. Curran Associates, Inc. (2012)
15. Kulkarni, T.D., Saeedi, A., Gautam, S., Gershman, S.J.: Deep successor reinforcement learning. CoRR abs/1606.02396 (2016). http://arxiv.org/abs/1606.02396
16. Lange, S., Riedmiller, M.: Deep auto-encoder neural networks in reinforcement learning. In: International Joint Conference on Neural Networks (IJCNN), pp. 1–8, July 2010. https://doi.org/10.1109/IJCNN.2010.5596468
17. Legenstein, R., Wilbert, N., Wiskott, L.: Reinforcement learning on slow features of high-dimensional input streams. PLoS Comput. Biol. **6**(8), e1000894 (2010)

18. Masci, J., Meier, U., Cireşan, D., Schmidhuber, J.: Stacked convolutional auto-encoders for hierarchical feature extraction. In: Honkela, T., Duch, W., Girolami, M., Kaski, S. (eds.) ICANN 2011. LNCS, vol. 6791, pp. 52–59. Springer, Heidelberg (2011). https://doi.org/10.1007/978-3-642-21735-7_7
19. Mnih, V., et al.: Human-level control through deep reinforcement learning. Nature **518**(7540), 529–533 (2015)
20. Oquab, M., Bottou, L., Laptev, I., Sivic, J.: Learning and transferring mid-level image representations using convolutional neural networks. In: 2014 IEEE Conference on Computer Vision and Pattern Recognition, pp. 1717–1724, June 2014
21. Papoudakis, G., Chatzidimitriou, K.C., Mitkas, P.A.: Deep reinforcement learning for Doom using unsupervised auxiliary tasks. CoRR abs/1807.01960 (2018). http://arxiv.org/abs/1807.01960
22. Russakovsky, O., et al.: ImageNet large scale visual recognition challenge. Int. J. Comput. Vis. (IJCV) **115**(3), 211–252 (2015)
23. Saxe, A.M., Koh, P.W., Chen, Z., Bhand, M., Suresh, B., Ng, A.Y.: On random weights and unsupervised feature learning. In: International Conference on Machine Learning, pp. 1089–1096. Omnipress (2011)
24. Schüler, M., Hlynsson, H.D., Wiskott, L.: Gradient-based training of slow feature analysis by differentiable approximate whitening. CoRR abs/1808.08833 (2018). http://arxiv.org/abs/1808.08833
25. Watkins, C.J.C.H.: Learning from delayed rewards. Ph.D. thesis, King's College, Cambridge (1989)
26. Wiskott, L.: Learning invariance manifolds. In: Niklasson, L., Bodén, M., Ziemke, T. (eds.) ICANN 1998. PNC, pp. 555–560. Springer, London (1998). https://doi.org/10.1007/978-1-4471-1599-1_83
27. Wiskott, L., Sejnowski, T.: Slow feature analysis: unsupervised learning of invariances. Neural Comput. **14**(4), 715–770 (2002)
28. Wohlfarth, K., et al.: Dense cloud classification on multispectralsatellite imagery. In: IAPR Workshop on Pattern Recognition in Remote Sensing (PRRS), August 2018. https://doi.org/10.1109/PRRS.2018.8486379
29. Yosinski, J., Clune, J., Bengio, Y., Lipson, H.: How transferable are features in deep neural networks? In: Ghahramani, Z., Welling, M., Cortes, C., Lawrence, N.D., Weinberger, K.Q. (eds.) Advances in Neural Information Processing Systems, pp. 3320–3328. Curran Associates, Inc. (2014)
30. Zeiler, M.D., Fergus, R.: Visualizing and understanding convolutional networks. In: Fleet, D., Pajdla, T., Schiele, B., Tuytelaars, T. (eds.) ECCV 2014. LNCS, vol. 8689, pp. 818–833. Springer, Cham (2014). https://doi.org/10.1007/978-3-319-10590-1_53

A Multi-objective Reinforcement Learning Algorithm for JSSP

Beatriz M. Méndez-Hernández[1(✉)], Erick D. Rodríguez-Bazan[2], Yailen Martinez-Jimenez[1], Pieter Libin[3], and Ann Nowé[3]

[1] Universidad Central "Marta Abreu" de Las Villas, Santa Clara, Cuba
beatrizm87@gmail.com, yailenm@uclv.edu.cu
[2] Inria Méditerranée Valbonne, Valbonne, France
erick-david.rodriguez-bazan@inria.fr
[3] Vrije Universiteit Brussel, Brussels, Belgium
{pieter.libin,ann.nowe}@vub.ac.be

Abstract. Scheduling is a decision making process that takes care of the allocation of resources to tasks over time. The Job Shop scheduling problem is one of the most complex scheduling scenarios and is commonly encountered in manufacturing industries. Most of the existing studies are based on optimizing one objective, but in real-world problems, multiple criteria often need to be optimized at once. We propose a Multi-Objective Multi-Agent Reinforcement Learning Algorithm that aims to obtain the non-dominated solutions set for Job Shop scheduling problems. The proposed algorithm is used to solve a set of benchmark problems optimizing makespan and tardiness. The performance of our algorithm is evaluated and compared to other algorithms from the literature using two measures for evaluating the Pareto front. We show that our algorithm is able to find a set of diverse and high quality non-dominated solutions, that significantly and consistently improves upon the results obtained by other state-of-the-art algorithms.

Keywords: Job Shop Scheduling Problems · Multi-objective · Multi-agent · Reinforcement Learning · Pareto front

1 Introduction

The Job Shop Scheduling Problem (JSSP) refers to the problem of allocating a number of jobs to machines such that one or more criteria are optimized. The jobs are conformed by different tasks which have an order that must be respected (i.e., precedence constraints). Such problems can be identified in a variety of real-world environments, mainly in the manufacturing industry. For instance, a printing company has different work centers and there are jobs that must be processed

P. Libin and A. Nowé—Contributed equally.

I. V. Tetko et al. (Eds.): ICANN 2019, LNCS 11727, pp. 567–584, 2019.
https://doi.org/10.1007/978-3-030-30487-4_44

by the work centers in a specific order. Jobs have a promised delivery date (i.e., a due date) assigned. In this example settings, both the completion time and the tardiness need to be optimized in order to satisfy the user's preferences [1].

As the JSSP is an NP-Hard problem [2], exact optimization techniques are computationally intractable and for larger instances, the use of meta-heuristics is required.

Most of the research on scheduling focuses on minimizing the makespan (i.e., completion time of all the jobs) [3,4] and therefore approaches the JSSP as a single-objective problem. However, these studies do not take into account the real world constraints which renders them less suitable for applications [5]. For that reason, more recently the interest in addressing several objectives at once (i.e., solving Multi-objective JSSP) has increased. The proposed solutions to solve Multi-objective JSSP (MOJSSP) can be classified into two distinct approaches: an approach that uses an multi-objective aggregation function (i.e., scalarization) and a Pareto-based approach.

In this work, we use Reinforcement Learning (RL) to solve the JSSP. RL is a technique that learns to solve a problem by trial-and-error [6]. The principles of the algorithms are simple and the algorithms can be applied to multi-batch dynamic scheduling with unpredictable entry time [7]. In [8], a new algorithm is developed to solve the single JSSP using Multi-Agent Reinforcement Learning (MARL), and this new algorithm optimized the makespan and obtained excellent experimental results. Furthermore, in [9], the authors proposed an algorithm to solve a logistic manufacturing problem with distributed resources using Multi-Agent Systems (MAS). Inspired by these successes, this paper presents a new Multi-Objective Multi-Agent Reinforcement Learning Approach (MOMARLA) to solve the JSSP. Each agent represents a specific objective to optimize and we use two action selection strategies to find a diverse and accurate Pareto front.

Our new method solves the JSSP as a multi-objective problem, which is essential to address real world problems. Furthermore, our method returns the Pareto front, and thus provides flexibility with respect to the preference of utility of a particular setting. Finally, our method significantly outperforms the state-of-the-art algorithms, and has the potential to improve how the JSSP is solved, in a variety of industrial settings.

The remainder of this paper is organized as follows: Sect. 2 presents background knowledge about the JSSP and Multi-objective optimization. Section 3 gives a literature review about techniques and algorithms used to solve MOJSSP. Section 4 introduces Reinforcement Learning from a Multi-Agent point of view and in Sect. 5 we propose our new method. In Sect. 6, the experiments and the results obtained are analyzed, and finally, conclusions are formulated in Sect. 7.

2 Background

2.1 Formal Description of the JSSP

A JSSP considers a set of n jobs $\mathcal{J} = \{J_j\}_{1 \leq j \leq n}$ which must be processed on a set of m machines $\mathcal{M} = \{M_i\}_{1 \leq i \leq m}$. Each job needs to be processed by all the machines in a given order ($k = 1, \ldots, m$). We refer to the processing of job J_j on machine M_i as the operation o_{kij}. Operation o_{kij} is the $k-th$ operation of job J_j which requires the exclusive use of M_i, for an uninterrupted duration p_{kij} (i.e., the processing time). A schedule allocates operations to machines at certain times, which is typically expressed by specifying the starting time ($t_{kij} \geq 0$) for each operation on a machine M_i.

The goal is to find the optimal schedule, i.e., the schedule of the ordered operations and the starting times on each machine such that one or more criteria are optimized. For a MOJSSP, a set of objectives should be considered simultaneously. However, some of the considered objectives may be conflicting, that is, an improvement in one objective may worsen another. In this paper we take into account two objectives:

- Makespan, the total time required to complete all jobs: $C^*_{\max} = max_{1\leq j \leq |\mathcal{J}|} C_j$, where $C_j = \max_{1\leq i \leq |\mathcal{M}|} c_{kij}$ and c_{kij} is the end time of the operation o_{kij}.
- Tardiness, the sum of all differences between the completion time of a job and its due date: $T = \sum_{j=1}^{|\mathcal{J}|} \max(0, C_j - d_j)$, where d_j is the due date of the job J_j.

2.2 Multi-objective Optimization

Solving a multi-objective optimization problem implies finding a vector of decision variables which satisfies constraints, and optimizes a vector-valued function whose elements represent the objective functions. A multi-objective problem can be defined as:

$$\begin{aligned} \min F(x) = \ & [f_1(x), f_2(x), \ldots, f_q(x)] \\ \text{subject to} \ \ & x \in S \end{aligned} \tag{1}$$

where $x = (x_1, x_2, \ldots, x_h)^T$ is the vector of the h decision variables, q is the number of objectives and S is the feasible region (i.e., the region defined by the constraints).

A solution a is said to dominate another solution b ($a \preceq b$) if the following conditions are true: (i) the solution a is no worse than the solution b in all objectives, and (ii) the solution a is strictly better than solution b in at least one objective.

When relative preferences are known in advance, an intuitive approach is to combine multiple criteria into a linear aggregation (i.e., scalarization). In this case, the problem to solve is: $\min F(x) = \sum_{i=1}^{q} w_i \cdot f_i(x)$. However, in order to provide a suitable scalarization function, the preferences of the user (i.e., the weights in the linear combination) need to be known [10]. Another approach is to obtain the Pareto front (Λ), which consists of finding the compromise (i.e., trade-off) solutions based on the Pareto optimality concept [11]. This set consists of the non-dominated solutions.

3 Related Work

As said in the introduction, most of the research approaches the JSSP as a single-objective problem. These approaches include different meta-heuristics as well as hybrid methods. Some of these approaches include genetic algorithms [12,13], tabu search [14], neural networks [15], Ant Colony Optimization [16,17], Bee Colony Optimization [18] and Particle Swarm optimization (PSO) [3,19,20].

In [21], the authors present a hybrid PSO and Tabu Search algorithm for JSSP. They use an improved PSO, that performs more exploration at the beginning and more exploitation at the end, to provide diverse solutions for the Tabu Search algorithm. In [4], the authors use an enhanced harmony search which combines the differential-based enhance mechanism and the variable neighborhood search based on the blocks on the critical path. In [22], the author proposes an agent-based local search genetic algorithm for solving JSSP. A MAS containing various agents each with special behaviors is developed to implement the genetic local search algorithm. However, more recently, we see an increase in research that focuses on the JSSP as a multi-objective problem. Studies on how to solve MOJSSP can be divided into the two approaches: scalarization and Pareto-based.

3.1 Scalarization Approach

In [23], the authors propose a two-stage genetic algorithm, which uses a scalarization function to optimize: makespan, total weighted tardiness and earliness. Also, in [24], a new objective function is proposed which contains the sum of the maximum earliness and tardiness criteria. The authors develop a new approximate optimization approach which is based on the imperialist competitive algorithm hybridized with an efficient neighborhood search. An effective hybrid dual PSO algorithm including leading-population and searching-population with a greedy strategy is proposed in [25]. The authors use simulated annealing to avoid falling into local optima. Also, in [26] a Multi-Objective PSO algorithm (MOPSO) is proposed, in which they modify the representation of the particles and optimize the makespan, the idle time and the tardiness. This approach improves the results obtained by the Multi-Objective Genetic Algorithm (MOGA) [27], which uses a genetic algorithm to derive optimal machine-wise priority dispatching rules and minimizes the makespan, the tardiness and the idle time using a weighted sum function. In [28], the author proposes an improved memetic algorithm with a new naturally inspired cooperation phase. This algorithm optimizes the makespan, total weighted tardiness, and total weighted earliness using the weighting approach.

3.2 Pareto-Based Approach

The evolutionary algorithms have also been applied to multi-objective JSSP using a Pareto-based approach. An example is NSGA-II, a non-dominated sorting-based multi-objective evolutionary algorithm which improves the computational complexity of the evolutionary algorithms and the need to specify a sharing parameter [29]. Also, there exists an extension of NSGA-II algorithm [30] which incorporates a genetic algorithm with local SA operators to solve the proposed bi-criteria problem. The genetic operators adopt the binary tournament selection, the multi-point crossover and the inverse mutation to generate offspring individuals. The designed local simulated annealing operators are performed for each generation individuals to improve offspring population significantly.

To solve MOJSSPs, in [31], the authors presented an algorithm, Pareto Archived Simulated Annealing (PASA), which aims to minimize the makespan and the flow time. Besides, in [32], the authors constructed an algorithm to optimize makespan, flow time and tardiness. In [33], the authors propose an application of the MOPSO algorithm which uses the behavior of a swarm as a set of non-dominated solutions. The objectives used are makespan and tardiness. A strength Pareto evolutionary algorithm (SPEA) emphasizing the importance of elitism (i.e., to reserve a place to the best individuals in the next generation) is proposed by [34]. In [35], the authors use a measure to describe the relative position among different individuals, to adjust the external population and assign different fitness values to individuals. The Pareto Archive Particle Swarm Optimization (PAPSO) converting the JSSP into a continuous problem is presented in [36]. In their work, the objectives to optimize are makespan and total tardiness. Also in [37], the authors propose an effective multi-objective algorithm for solving the bi-criteria job shop scheduling problem with the uncertainty of processing time. In that case, the objectives used are expected makespan and tardiness.

4 Multi-agent Reinforcement Learning

Reinforcement Learning is a machine learning technique that allows agents to learn how to behave optimally in a determinate environment. At each time step, the agent is located in a particular state of the environment (i.e., $s \in S$, S represents the set of states) and needs to choose an action (i.e., $a \in A$, A represents the set of actions). The agent's actions determine its immediate reward, and the next state. The objective of the agent is to optimize the accumulation of reward that it receives over time. Therefore, the agent should not only take into account the immediate reward but also the delayed reward.

Q-Learning is an important RL algorithm that was proposed in [38]. Its main idea is to learn, through an action-value update rule, how good an action is in a given state. Each state-action pair has a Q-value associated ($Q : S \text{ x } A \rightarrow \mathbb{R}$). At each step t, an action a is selected according to a policy. The function $Q(s, a)$ is the estimated utility function, telling us how good an action is in a given state. More formally, the Q-values update rule is:

$$Q(s,a) \leftarrow Q(s,a) + \alpha[r + \gamma max_{a'} Q(s',a') - Q(s,a)], \tag{2}$$

where α $(0 \leq \alpha \leq 1)$ is the learning rate, which determines to what extent the newly acquired information will update the Q-value, r is the immediate reward received after taking action a from state s. The discount factor $(0 \leq \gamma \leq 1)$ represents the importance of future rewards. The state s' is the state in which we end up after executing action a. The action a' is the best according to the current Q-values in the next state s'.

One of the challenges that arises in RL is the trade-off between exploration and exploitation. To obtain a high reward, a RL agent must prefer actions that it has tried in the past and found to be effective in producing reward. But to discover such actions, it has to try actions that it has not selected before. The agent has to exploit what it already knows in order to obtain better rewards, but it also has to explore in order to make better action selection decisions in the future. The dilemma is that neither exploration nor exploitation can be pursued exclusively [39].

MARL involves multiple agents learning in the same environment. Learning in a multi-agent setting is more complex when the actions of one agent might influence the rewards and transitions experienced by the other agents. Multiple agents are interacting with the environment, where the next state is given by the result of the combination of the action taken by all the agents. The interaction among the agents is also necessary to obtain global good results because the agent only has a local view of the environment.

5 MOMARLA Applied to JSSP

In this section we introduce our multi-objective algorithm which is inspired by the single objective RL algorithm introduced in [8].

This proposal uses the Q-Learning algorithm to solve JSSPs. The agents are associated with the resources (i.e., there exists an agent for each resource) and take decisions about the future actions (i.e., which is the next operation to process by the corresponding resource). An agent only has information about its associated resource (i.e., a local view).

Based on these concepts we introduce MOMARLA, whose general idea is to have an agent for each objective. A state is represented by a pair, $s = (\Omega_i, M_i)$, where the first element is the set of available operations (i.e., the operations that are waiting to be processed by the machine M_i) and the second element is the machine M_i. An agent's action is to select the next operation that has to be processed. In each iteration, the agents build a schedule (i.e., a set of operations which have associated start times t_i) according to their objective and a selection strategy. The method involves two phases which differ in the way to select the next operation to process $(\pi(M_i, e))$. In the first phase, the agents act as independent units, each optimizing their respective objective. In the second phase, the agents collaborate to find the best solution for all the objectives combined. For each of the phases, we run the algorithm for which we show the pseudocode in Algorithm 1. The method is parameterized by the JSSP properties, the Q-learning parameters, the objectives and the selecting strategy e. Algorithm 1 is run twice to obtain the Pareto front.

For the first phase, ϵ-greedy is used as the action selection strategy, which instructs the agent to choose the best action according to its own objective most of the time. With probability ϵ it chooses a uniformly random action.

Algorithm 1. MOMARLA

Input: number of machines (m), number of jobs (n), JSSP instance, Q-Learning parameters (α), objectives (q), action selection strategy (e), action policy ($\pi()$)
Output: ordered Pareto front (Λ)
repeat
  for $l = 1$ to q **do**
    $X \leftarrow$ empty solution
    Insert o_{1ij} of each J_j in Ω_i
    while $\bigcup_{i=1}^{m} \Omega_i \neq \emptyset$ **do**
      Select M_i randomly such that $\Omega_i \neq \emptyset$
      Select the next operation o_{kij} using $\pi(M_i, e)$
      $t_i \leftarrow \max(t_i, c_{(k-1)ij})$
      $X \leftarrow X \bigcup (o_{kij}, t_i)$
      Update the time of M_i, $t_i \leftarrow t_i + p_{kij}$
      Update the final time of the operation selected $c_{kij} \leftarrow t_i$
      if $agent_l =$ "$Makespan$" **then**
        $r_l \leftarrow \frac{1}{c_{ij}}$
      else
        $r_l \leftarrow \frac{1}{d_{kij}}$
      for $s = (\Omega_i, M_i)$ **do**
        $Q(s,a) \leftarrow Q(s,a) + \alpha[r_l - Q(s,a)]$
      Update the machines' queues
        Remove o_{kij} from the machine queue
        Find the next machine M_{i^*} to process the J_j
        Add $o_{(k+1)i^*j}$ to the queue of the machine M_{i^*}
    for each (s,a) visited **do**
      Update the reward (r_l)
      $r_l \leftarrow \dfrac{1}{f_l(X)}$
      Take into account future actions and states
      $Q'(s',a') \leftarrow max_{a'} Q(s',a')$
      Update the Q-values
      $Q(s,a) \leftarrow Q(s,a) + \alpha[r_l + Q'(s',a') - Q(s,a)]$
    if X is non dominated **then**
      $\Lambda \leftarrow X$
until Λ does not change for 1000 iterations **return** Λ

We use a dynamic value for ϵ, which is calculated using the Value-Difference Based Exploration method proposed by [40]. The general idea is to consider the temporal-difference errors observed from the value function as a measure of the agent's uncertainty about the environment, which directly affects the exploration probability. The desired behavior is to render the agent more explorative in situations where the knowledge about the environment is uncertain (i.e., at the beginning of the learning process) which is recognized as large changes in the value function. On the other hand, the exploration rate should be reduced as the agent's knowledge about the environment becomes less uncertain, which can be recognized as the value function not changing significantly anymore [40]. This phase will generate schedules that are constructed focusing on only one of the objectives.

In the second phase, as we want to diversify the Pareto front by finding compromise solutions between the objectives, it is necessary for the different agents to interact. During this interaction, when an agent chooses the next action a, it takes into account how good the action is for the other agents. To find the compromise solutions, the selection strategy is the Borda-rule [41]. This rule allows to combine preferences of various agents focusing on different objectives. Assume that there are t voters, r candidates and a fixed list of r integers $s_1 \geq \ldots \geq s_r$. Each voter i ranks the first candidate with a score s_1, the second one with a score s_2 and so on, where $s_i = r - i + 1$. The total score of a candidate is the sum of all the scores received. The candidate with the highest sum is the winner. Each agent is a voter, the candidates are the available operations in a state and the agent ranks an operation according to its Q-value. Then, the operation with the highest sum of scores is the operation selected to be processed. If there exists more than one action with the same score, one of them will be selected uniformly random.

The stop condition is the same for the end of both the first and second phase. This condition is determined by the Pareto front convergence, when the Pareto front does not change anymore during 1000 iterations.

The agent selects the action with highest sum of scores and receives a reward from the environment according to its preferences. Each time the agent selects an action the machine time is updated (steps 12–13), which guaranties to have only one operation executing in the machine at the same time. The job's operations are managed according to the order that have into the job, an operation will only be processed if the previous operation in the job was selected by an agent (steps 20–23).

Our algorithm uses two update schemes: local and global. In RL, the extent to which rewards observed earlier are valued compared to rewards that are observed later, is modulated by the discount factor γ, that takes a value in [0,1]. For the local update (step 19), our aim is to maximize the agent's immediate reward, this can be obtained by choosing $\gamma = 0$ [8]. This update is done when the agent selects an action. The global update is used after a schedule has been built. For this global view (step 30), we need to equally value the future and current actions, which can be obtained by choosing $\gamma = 1$ [8].

For the local update, we propose a cost function (i.e., feedback signal) for each agent according to its objective. When an agent selects an action, a reward is assigned based on the quality of the solution it is able to obtain. We use the following reward functions:

- ***Makespan:*** $r = 1/c_{ij}$ [8].
- ***Tardiness:*** $r = 1/d_{kij}$, where d_{kij} is the due date of operation o_{kij} which is calculated as $d_j - (m - k + p_{kij}) + p_{mwj}$, where d_j is the due date of J_j, p_{mwj} is the processing time of the last operation of J_j which must be processed by the machine M_w and $m - k$ is the distance between the operation k and the operation m (i.e., last operation) [42].

Once an iteration finishes (i.e., a complete schedule is obtained) the Q-values of the state-action pairs that have been visited are updated. This global update allows us to know how good the schedule is, and its reward associated in this case is $1/f_l(X)$ [8], where X is the current schedule and f_l is the objective function associated to the $agent_l$. It is possible to see that according to this formula, if the objective function value increases, the reward decreases. As the goal is to maximize the reward and both objectives have to be minimized, with this formula we guarantee a higher reward for small values of the objective function.

The algorithm records a Q-tuple with the values for each objective of the constructed schedule. The schedule will be included in the Pareto front if its values compose a non-dominated solution [11]. The size of the Q-tuple will be the number of objectives that the user aims to optimize. If the new solution obtained is dominated, it will not dominate any other existing solutions [11]. If the current solution dominates any solution on the front, those solutions will be removed. Finally, if the new solution is non-dominated it will be added to the Pareto front.

The Pareto front is ordered (ascending order) according to the distance between the solution and the ideal solution [43]. An ideal solution represents the utopian solution that minimizes all the objectives at once.

The algorithm stops when the Pareto front converges, i.e., Λ has not changed for 1000 iterations. This number was selected because we tested the changes into the Pareto front using different values and this was the most suitable value for all instances tested.

An important aspect to solve the JSSP problem is that scheduling constraints need to be honored. Therefore, we will explicitly list the constraints and show how these are dealt with in our algorithm. Firstly, no task for a job can be started until the previous task for that job is completed. Secondly, a machine can only work on one task at a time. Thirdly, a task, once started, must run to completion. The first constraint is dealt with in two locations of the algorithm, i.e., steps 12–13 and steps 20–23. In steps 12–13, after selecting an operation the global time is updated. In steps 20–23, the operation is removed from the queue of the machine and the next operation of this job is sent to the machine that must process it. For the second constraint, we solve the problem updating the global time of the system each time an operation is selected, so it is impossible to send two operations to the same machine at the same time (step 12 in the algorithm). For the third constraint, we do a global modification of the time, such that pre-emption is not allowed (steps 12–13 in the algorithm).

6 Experimental Results

The algorithm was implemented in Java and its performance was evaluated using 15 benchmarks instances obtained from the OR Library [44]. This library contains the instances most commonly used by the JSSP research community. The instances belong to four classes of standard JSSP benchmark problems: (i) ft06 [45] (6 jobs and 6 machines); (ii) ft10 [45], abz5-abz6 [46] and orb01-orb05 [47] (10 jobs and 10 machines); (iii) ft20 [45] (20 jobs and 5 machines); abz7-abz8 [46] (20 jobs and 15 machines) and (iv) la26-la28 [48] (20 jobs and 10 machines).

These instances were selected as they exhibit the highest complexity throughout the OR library, according to the metrics proposed by [49,50]. We present details on these complexities in Appendix A. Appendix B contains the results obtained for other instances. As these instances were designed to minimize only the makespan, it is necessary to add a due date for each job to include the tardiness objective as well. The due date for the instance ft06 is set according to [27]. For the remaining problems, the due dates are set according to [35].

In this experiment, we compare MOMARLA to three other algorithms from the literature: SPEA [34], CMEA [35] and MOPSO [33]. The parameter settings are the ones used in the original papers. We use two metrics to evaluate the quality of the non-dominated solutions: Hypervolume [51] and Two Set Coverage (C-metric) [52].

The Hypervolume metric is the most popular metric in the Multi-Objective optimization literature [51]. Hypervolume is the only indicator of scalar performance that is compatible with the Pareto dominance and the maximization of this metric achieves the convergence to the optimal Pareto front. In this paper, the objectives are normalized into $[0, 1]$, to remove the effect of scale difference.

According to the literature, the best values for α parameter are 0.1 and 0.2, which ensure that the agents do not fall into local optima [53]. We ran the instances using the different α values and we show in Fig. 1a the mean of the Hypervolume metric for the different values of this parameter. In accordance with the recommendations in literature [53], we found that the best value for α is 0.2.

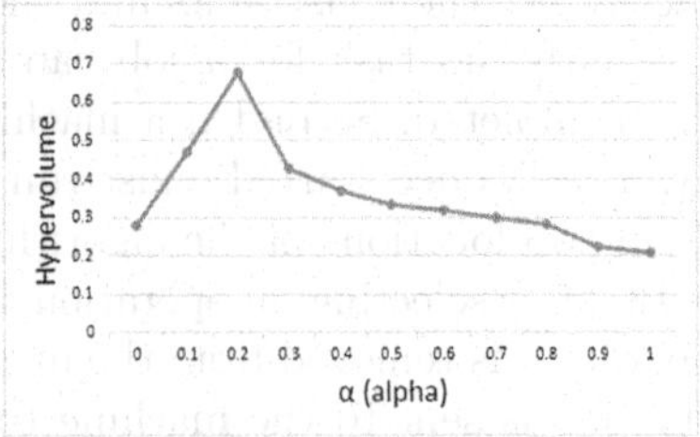

(a) The Hypervolume behavior according to different values of the learning rate parameter (α).

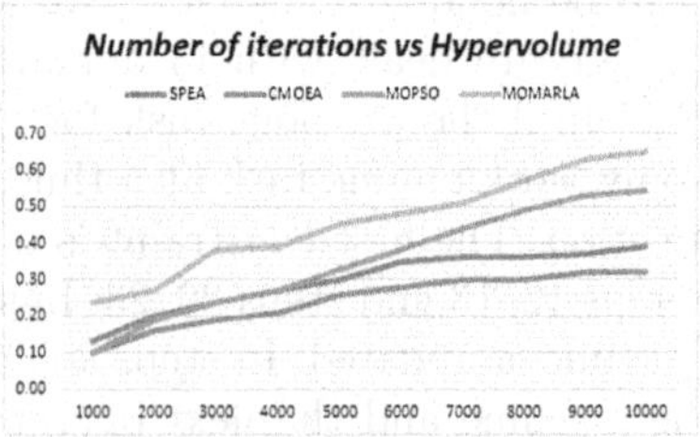

(b) Ranking of each agent to the operations according its Q-value.

Fig. 1. The behavior of the algorithms overtime.

Figure 1b shows our algorithm has a better behavior than the three other algorithms for the same number of iterations. We include this graphic because the stop conditions are not the same ones for all algorithms and the graphic allows us to understand the algorithms' anytime behavior.

Table 1 shows the results achieved when we calculate the Hypervolume to the Pareto fronts obtained. Our algorithm is equally good or better than the other evaluated algorithms for all of the analyzed instances. The best results are shown in bold (no significant differences). The last row shows the mean for this metric by each algorithm, where MOMARLA got the higher mean. The variance values are low and very similar for the four algorithms, as is shown in Appendix C.

Table 1. Comparison among SPEA, CMEA, MOPSO and MOMARLA according to Hypevolume.

Inst	Algo			
	SPEA	CMEA	MOPSO	MOMARLA
ft06	0.07	0.07	0.50	**0.65**
ft10	0.17	0.26	0.87	**0.96**
ft20	**0.20**	**0.20**	**0.21**	**0.25**
abz5	0.34	0.33	**0.36**	**0.4**
abz6	0.22	0.36	0.31	**0.42**
abz7	0.51	0.45	**1**	**1**
abz8	0.88	0.36	**0.99**	**0.99**
la26	0.33	**0.39**	**0.47**	**0.47**
la27	**0.58**	**0.56**	0.41	**0.6**
la28	**0.48**	0.42	**0.48**	**0.54**
orb01	0.62	**0.74**	0.59	**0.80**
orb02	0.20	0.04	0.30	**0.53**
orb03	0.69	0.31	**0.85**	**0.86**
orb04	**0.63**	0.28	0.52	**0.79**
orb05	0.00	0.023	0.22	**0.90**
Mean	*0.39*	*0.32*	*0.54*	***0.68***

We also use a Wilcoxon test to find significant differences among the results (see Table 2). According to this test, we can demonstrate whether our approach has significant differences with the other state-of-the-art algorithms. The comparison shows that there exist significant differences (ρ-value < 0.05) and the bigger value of R^- rang means that our approach obtains better results than the other algorithms, i.e., obtains a bigger Hypervolume value.

Table 2. Comparison among SPEA, CMEA, MOPSO and MOMARLA according to the Wilcoxon test.

Algorithms	R+	R−	ρ-value
SPEA-CMEA	64	27	0.2079
SPEA-MOPSO	30.5	74.5	0.177
SPEA-MOMARLA	15	105	0.008362
CMEA-MOPSO	16	104	0.01025
CMEA-MOMARLA	0	120	0.0007247
MOPSO-MOMARLA	0	78	0.002526

The C-metric [52] is a binary indicator that can be described as follows: let A and B be two approximation sets. $C(A, B)$ gives the fraction of solutions in B that are dominated by at least one solution in A. Hence, $C(A, B) = 1$ means that all solutions in B are dominated by at least one solution in A while $C(A, B) = 0$ implies that no solution in B is dominated by a solution in A.

Table 3. Comparison between SPEA, CMEA, MOPSO and MOMARLA according to C-metric.

Inst	Met					
	C(S,M)	C(M,S)	C(C,M)	C(M,C)	C(P,M)	C(M,P)
ft06	0.208	0.549	0.291	0.397	0.394	0.532
ft10	0.157	0.548	0.267	0.271	0.382	0.559
ft20	0.165	0.602	0.26	0.352	0.435	0.388
abz5	0.124	0.563	0.391	0.346	0.335	0.347
abz6	0.201	0.481	0.409	0.266	0.367	0.452
abz7	0.211	0.368	0.322	0.335	0.324	0.432
abz8	0.208	0.529	0.305	0.399	0.364	0.441
la26	0.199	0.509	0.333	0.34	0.417	0.574
la27	0.154	0.576	0.338	0.352	0.409	0.492
la28	0.162	0.536	0.282	0.373	0.313	0.516
orb01	0.269	0.448	0.222	0.352	0.462	0.466
orb02	0.167	0.505	0.322	0.404	0.377	0.409
orb03	0.184	0.463	0.275	0.355	0.411	0.422
orb04	0.134	0.451	0.275	0.265	0.396	0.533
orb05	0.182	0.504	0.33	0.396	0.418	0.494
Mean	*0.19*	*0.50*	*0.31*	*0.35*	*0.40*	*0.45*
Sum of dominated fraction	*2.725*	*7.632*	*4.597*	*5.203*	*5.804*	*7.057*

S:SPEA, C:CMEA, P:MOPSO, M:MOMARLA

Table 3 shows the values obtained when we apply the metric on the Pareto fronts that were returned by the different algorithms. By analyzing these values, it is possible to conclude that our algorithm only obtains lower values than the other algorithms for four out of fifteen instances. However, it is worth noting that the mean of the dominated fraction of the solution obtained by SPEA, CMEA and MOPSO is higher than MOMARLA. This indicates that the solutions obtained by the other three algorithms are mostly dominated by the solutions of our algorithm.

Our experimental results demonstrate that our algorithm outperforms the state-of-the-art. The major reason for our superior performance can be explained by the fact that we model the problem as a multi-agent system. In the first phase, each agent optimizes the objective for which it is responsible, which allows it to find the extreme solutions of the Pareto front. In the second phase, the agents interact, which allows our algorithm to find the compromise solutions of the Pareto front, which eventually converges to a diverse and wide Pareto front.

7 Conclusions

In this paper, we propose a Multi-Objective Multi-Agent Reinforcement Learning algorithm to obtain the Pareto front to solve MOJSSPs. The algorithm is divided in two phases. In the first phase, the agents work as independent units seeking to optimize the objectives they are responsible for. In the second phase, the agents work together to find compromise solutions. The algorithm uses two updates, i.e., a local and a global scheme. The local scheme gives rewards according to how good an action is for a given state. The global scheme evaluates how good a schedule is and for this scheme the reward is based on the complete schedule. Also, the Pareto front is ordered using the distance between the solution found and the ideal solution. The algorithm has been tested on 15 benchmark problems taking into account two objectives: makespan and tardiness. The results obtained were compared to three other algorithms from the literature using two metrics to measure Pareto-based algorithms. For both metrics, our algorithm improves the results of the state-of-the-art consistently and significantly, as demonstrated in our experiments.

Acknowledgment. This work was supported by the Vlaamse InterUniversitaire Raad, Flemish InterUniversity Council, Belgium (VLIR) under the UIC program VLIR-UCLV. Pieter Libin was supported by a PhD grant of the FWO (Fonds Wetenschappelijk Onderzoek - Vlaanderen). Erick D. Rodríguez-Bazan was supported by a PhD grant of INRIA. We thank the four anonymous reviewers for their suggestions, that allowed us to improve the manuscript.

Appendices

A Instance complexity

The instances used were selected according to the complexities proposed by [49,50], as we show in Table 4.

Table 4. Complexity of the instances used.

Instances	Complexity 1 [50]	Complexity 2 [49]
ft06	36	1.64
ft10	100	16.67
ft20	100	23.31
abz5	100	23.77
abz6	100	18.89
abz7	300	21.87
abz8	300	22.77
la26	200	20.32
la27	200	21.51
la28	200	18.45
orb01	100	17.22
orb02	100	16.43
orb03	100	17.04
orb04	100	19.07
orb05	100	16.71

B Supplementary Instances

We tested the algorithms for other instances but with less complexity. Tables 5 and 6 show the results obtained according to Hypervolume and C-metric respectively. For these instances, our algorithm also shows a better performance.

Table 5. Comparison among SPEA, CMEA, MOPSO and MOMARLA according to Hypevolume for supplementary instances.

Inst	Algo			
	SPEA	CMEA	MOPSO	MOMARLA
la01	0.17	0.28	0.88	0.97
la02	0.05	0.06	0.59	0.85
la03	0.19	0.19	0.23	0.38
la04	0.27	0.29	0.41	0.45
la05	0.31	0.33	0.37	0.5
la06	0.46	0.51	0.88	0.9
la07	0.74	0.87	1	1
la08	0.28	0.3	0.45	0.59
la09	0.12	0.22	0.25	0.41
la10	0.14	0.14	0.3	0.52

Table 6. Comparison between SPEA, CMEA, MOPSO and MOMARLA according to C-metric for supplementary instances.

Inst	Met					
	C(S,M)	C(M,S)	C(C,M)	C(M,C)	C(P,M)	C(M,P)
la01	0.125	0.625	0.235	0.425	0.421	0.555
la02	0.204	0.714	0.241	0.341	0.336	0.428
la03	0.136	0.586	0.293	0.326	0.397	0.51
la04	0.154	0.576	0.271	0.471	0.453	0.523
la05	0.203	0.625	0.245	0.501	0.434	0.51
la06	0.175	0.511	0.305	0.52	0.426	0.455
la07	0.21	0.621	0.288	0.531	0.391	0.465
la08	0.184	0.574	0.273	0.476	0.485	0.51
la09	0.105	0.641	0.291	0.399	0.38	0.611
la10	0.127	0.632	0.21	0.426	0.425	0.527
Mean	*0.17*	*0.61*	*0.27*	*0.44*	*0.41*	*0.51*
Sum of dominated fraction	*1.659*	*6.105*	*2.652*	*4.416*	*4.148*	*5.094*

S:SPEA, C:CMEA, P:MOPSO, M:MOMARLA

C Hypervolume variance

Figure 2 shows the Hypervolume and the variance of the algorithms for the different instances.

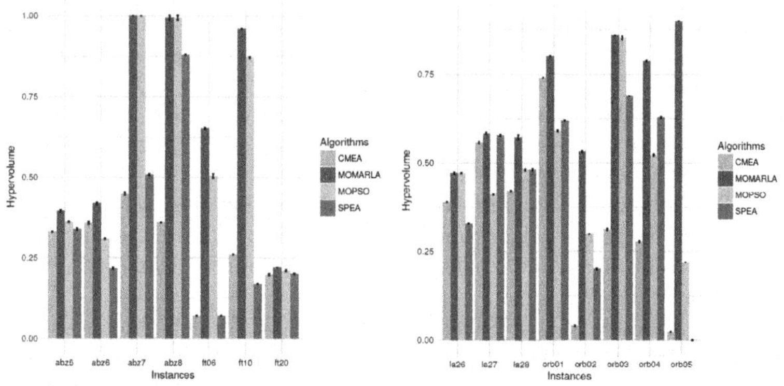

Fig. 2. Hypervolume and variance of the algorithms.

References

1. Fayad, C., Petrovic, S.: A fuzzy genetic algorithm for real-world job shop scheduling. In: Ali, M., Esposito, F. (eds.) IEA/AIE 2005. LNCS (LNAI), vol. 3533, pp. 524–533. Springer, Heidelberg (2005). https://doi.org/10.1007/11504894_71
2. Garey, M.-R., Johnson, D.-S., Sethi, R.: The complexity of flowshop and jobshop scheduling. Math. Oper. Res. **1**(2), 117–129 (1976)
3. Rameshkumar, K., Rajendran, C.: A novel discrete PSO algorithm for solving job shop scheduling problem to minimize makespan. In: IOP Conference Series: Materials Science and Engineering, vol. 310, no. 1, p. 012143. IOP Publishing, February 2018
4. Zhao, F., Qin, S., Yang, G., Ma, W., Zhang, C., Song, H.: A differential-based harmony search algorithm with variable neighborhood search for job shop scheduling problem and its runtime analysis. IEEE Access (2018)
5. Urlings, T.: Heuristics and Metaheuristics for heavily constrained hybrid Flowshop problems. Ph.D. Universitat Politcnica de Valncia (2010)
6. Gabel, T., Riedmiller, M.: Adaptive reactive job-shop scheduling with reinforcement learning agents. Int. J. Inf. Technol. Intell. Comput. **24**(4) (2008)
7. Cao, Y., Yang, Y., Wang, H., Yang, L.: Intelligent job shop scheduling based on MAS and integrated routing wasp algorithm and scheduling wasp algorithm. JSW **5**(4), 487–494 (2009)
8. Martinez Jimenez, Y.: A generic multi-agent reinforcement learning approach for scheduling problems. Ph.D., Vrije Universiteit Brussel, p. 128 (2012)
9. Li, K., Zhou, T., Liu, B.-H., Li, H.: A multi-agent system for sharing distributed manufacturing resources. Expert Syst. Appl. **99**, 32–43 (2018)
10. Roijers, D., Vamplew, P., Whiteson, S., Dazeley, R.: A survey of multi-objective sequential decision-making. J. Artif. Intell. Res. **48**, 67–113 (2013)
11. Rey Horn, J., Nafpliotis, N., Goldberg, D.-E.: A niched Pareto genetic algorithm for multiobjective optimization. In: Proceedings of the First IEEE Conference on Evolutionary Computation, IEEE World Congress on Computational Intelligence, vol. 1, pp. 82–87. IEEE, June 1994
12. Watanabe, M., Ida, K., Gen, M.: A genetic algorithm with modified crossover operator and search area adaptation for the job-shop scheduling problem. Comput. Ind. Eng. **48**(4), 743–752 (2005)
13. Zhang, R., Chiong, R.: Solving the energy-efficient job shop scheduling problem: a multi-objective genetic algorithm with enhanced local search for minimizing the total weighted tardiness and total energy consumption. J. Clean. Prod. **112**, 3361–3375 (2016)
14. Nowicki, E., Smutnicki, C.: Some new ideas in TS for job shop scheduling. In: Sharda, R., Voß, S., Rego, C., Alidaee, B. (eds.) Metaheuristic Optimization via Memory and Evolution. Operations Research/Computer Science Interfaces Series, vol. 30, pp. 165–190. Springer, Boston (2005)
15. Weckman, G.-R., Ganduri, C.-V., Koonce, D.-A.: A neural network job-shop scheduler. J. Intell. Manuf. **19**(2), 191–201 (2008)
16. Udomsakdigool, A., Kachitvichyanukul, V.: Two-way scheduling approach in ant algorithm for solving job shop problems. Int. J. Ind. Eng. Manag. Syst. **5**(2), 68–75 (2006)
17. Udomsakdigool, A., Kachitvichyanukul, V.: Multiple colony ant algorithm for job-shop scheduling problem. Int. J. Prod. Res. **46**(15), 4155–4175 (2008)

18. Wong, L.-P., Puan, C.-Y., Low, M.-Y.-H., Chong, C.-S.: Bee colony optimization algorithm with big valley landscape exploitation for job shop scheduling problems. In: 40th Conference on Winter Simulation on Proceedings, pp. 2050–2058. Winter Simulation Conference (2008)
19. Surekha, P., Sumathi, S.: Solving fuzzy based job shop scheduling problems using GA and ACO. J. Emerg. Trends Comput. Inf. Sci. (2010)
20. Pratchayaborirak, T., Kachitvichyanukul, V.: A two-stage PSO algorithm for job shop scheduling problem. Int. J. Manag. Sci. Eng. Manag. **6**(2), 83–92 (2011)
21. Gao, H., Kwong, S., Fan, B., Wang, R.: A hybrid particle-swarm tabu search algorithm for solving job shop scheduling problems. IEEE Trans. Industr. Inf. **10**(4), 2044–2054 (2014)
22. Asadzadeh, L.: A local search genetic algorithm for the job shop scheduling problem with intelligent agents. Comput. Ind. Eng. **85**, 376–383 (2015)
23. Kachitvichyanukul, V., Sitthitham, S.: A two-stage genetic algorithm for multi-objective job shop scheduling problems. J. Intell. Manuf. **22**(3), 355–365 (2011)
24. Yazdani, M., Aleti, A., Khalili, S.-M., Jolai, F.: Optimizing the sum of maximum earliness and tardiness of the job shop scheduling problem. Comput. Ind. Eng. **107**, 12–24 (2017)
25. Meng, Q., Zhang, L., Fan, Y.: Research on multi-objective job shop scheduling with dual particle swarm algorithm based on greedy strategy. Wireless Pers. Commun. **103**(1), 255–274 (2018)
26. Sha, D.-Y., Lin, H.-H.: A multi-objective PSO for job-shop scheduling problems. Expert Syst. Appl. **37**(2), 1065–1070 (2010)
27. Ponnambalam, S.G., Ramkumar, V., Jawahar, N.: A multiobjective genetic algorithm for job shop scheduling. Prod. Planning Control **12**(8), 764–774 (2001)
28. Kurdi, M.: An improved island model memetic algorithm with a new cooperation phase for multi-objective job shop scheduling problem. Comput. Ind. Eng. **111**, 183–201 (2017)
29. Deb, K., Pratap, A., Agarwal, S., Meyarivan, T.-A.-M.-T.: A fast and elitist multi-objective genetic algorithm: NSGA-II. IEEE Trans. Evol. Comput. **6**(2), 182–197 (2002)
30. Wang, B., Xie, H., Xia, X., Zhang, X.-X.: A NSGA-II algorithm hybridizing local simulated-annealing operators for a bicriteria robust job-shop scheduling problem under scenarios. IEEE Trans. Fuzzy Syst. (2018)
31. Suresh, R.K., Mohanasundaram, K.M.: Pareto archived simulated annealing for job shop scheduling with multiple objectives. The Int. J. Adv. Manuf. Technol. **29**(1–2), 184–196 (2006)
32. Niu, S.-H., Ong, S.-K., Nee, A.-Y.: An improved intelligent water drops algorithm for solving multi-objective job shop scheduling. Eng. Appl. Artif. Intell. **26**(10), 2431–2442 (2013)
33. Wisittipanich, W., Kachitvichyanukul, V.: An efficient PSO algorithm for finding Pareto-frontier in multi-objective job shop scheduling problems. Ind. Eng. Manag. Syst. **12**(2), 151–160 (2013)
34. Zitzler, E., Thiele, L.: Multiobjective evolutionary algorithms: a comparative case study and the strength Pareto approach. IEEE Trans. Evol. Comput. **3**(4), 257–271 (1999)
35. Lei, D., Wu, Z.: Crowding-measure-based multiobjective evolutionary algorithm for job shop scheduling. Int. J. Adv. Manuf. Technol. **30**(1–2), 112–117 (2006)
36. Lei, D.: A Pareto archive particle swarm optimization for multi-objective job shop scheduling. Comput. Ind. Eng. **54**(4), 960–971 (2008)

37. Hao, X., Gen, M., Lin, L., Suer, G.-A.: Effective multiobjective EDA for bi-criteria stochastic job-shop scheduling problem. J. Intell. Manuf. **28**(3), 833–845 (2017)
38. Watkins, C.-J., Dayan, P.: Q-learning. Mach. Learn. **8**(3–4), 279–292 (1992)
39. Sutton, R.S., Barto, A.G.: Introduction to Reinforcement Learning, vol. 135. MIT Press, Cambridge (1998)
40. Tokic, M.: Adaptive ϵ-Greedy exploration in reinforcement learning based on value differences. In: Dillmann, R., Beyerer, J., Hanebeck, U.D., Schultz, T. (eds.) KI 2010. LNCS (LNAI), vol. 6359, pp. 203–210. Springer, Heidelberg (2010). https://doi.org/10.1007/978-3-642-16111-7_23
41. Young, P.: Optimal voting rules. J. Econ. Perspect. **9**(1), 52–64 (1995)
42. Cheng, H.C., Chiang, T.C., Fu, L.C.: Multiobjective job shop scheduling using memetic algorithm and shifting bottleneck procedure. In: Computational Intelligence in Scheduling, CI-Sched 2009, pp. 15–21. IEEE, April 2009
43. Opricovic, S., Tzeng, G.-H.: Compromise solution by MCDM methods: a comparative analysis of VIKOR and TOPSIS. Eur. J. Oper. Res. **156**(2), 445–455 (2004)
44. Beasley, J.-E.: OR-Library (2014). http://people.brunel.ac.uk/mastjjb/jeb/info.html
45. Fisher, H.: Probabilistic learning combinations of local job shop scheduling rules. Ind. Sched., 225–251 (1963)
46. Adams, J., Balas, E., Zawack, D.: The shifting bottleneck procedure for job shop scheduling. Manage. Sci. **34**(3), 391–401 (1988)
47. Applegate, D., Cook, W.: A computational study of the job-shop scheduling problem. ORSA J. Comput. **3**(2), 149–156 (1991)
48. Lawrence, S.: Resource constrained project scheduling: an experimental investigation of heuristic scheduling techniques (Supplement). Graduate School of Industrial Administration, Carnegie-Mellon University (1984)
49. Ruiz-Vanoye, J.A., Diaz-Parra, O., Perez-Ortega, J., Salgado, G.R., Gonzalez-Barbosa, J.J.: Complexity of instances for combinatorial optimization problems. In Computational Intelligence and Modern Heuristics, IntechOpen (2010)
50. Yamada, T., Nakano, R.: Genetic algorithms for job-shop scheduling problems. In: Proceedings of Modern Heuristic for Decision Support, pp. 67–81 (1997)
51. Riquelme, N., Von Lücken, C., Baran, B.: Performance metrics in multi-objective optimization. In: Computing Conference (CLEI), Latin American, pp. 1–11. IEEE (2015)
52. Zitzler, E.: Evolutionary Algorithms for Multiobjective Optimization: Methods and Applications, vol. 63. Shaker, Ithaca (1999)
53. Tsitsiklis, J.-N.: Asynchronous stochastic approximation and Q-learning. Mach. Learn. **16**(3), 185–202 (1994)

A Reinforcement Learning Approach for Sequential Spatial Transformer Networks

Fatemeh Azimi[1,2(✉)], Federico Raue[1], Jörn Hees[1], and Andreas Dengel[1,2]

[1] TU Kaiserslautern, Kaiserslautern, Germany
{fatemeh.azimi,federico.raue,joern.hees,andreas.dengel}@dfki.de
[2] Smart Data and Knowledge Services, German Research Center for Artificial Intelligence (DFKI), Kaiserslautern, Germany

Abstract. Spatial Transformer Networks (STN) can generate geometric transformations which modify input images to improve classifier's performance. In this work, we combine the idea of STN with Reinforcement Learning (RL). To this end, we break the affine transformation down into a sequence of simple and discrete transformations. We formulate the task as a Markovian Decision Process (MDP) and use RL to solve this sequential decision making problem. STN architectures learn the transformation parameters by minimizing the classification error and backpropagating the gradients through a sub-differentiable sampling module. In our method, we are not bound to differentiability of the sampling modules. Moreover, we have freedom in designing the objective rather than only minimizing the error; e.g., we can directly set the target as maximizing the accuracy. We design multiple experiments to verify the effectiveness of our method using cluttered MNIST and Fashion-MNIST datasets and show that our method outperforms STN with proper definition of MDP components.

Keywords: Reinforcement Learning · Policy Gradient · Spatial Transformer Networks

1 Introduction

Invariance against different transformations is crucial in many tasks such as image classification and object detection. Previous works have addressed this challenge, from early work on feature descriptors [1] to modeling geometric transformations [2]. It is also very beneficial if the network can detect the important content in the image and distinguish it from the rest [3]. To this end, there are different approaches such as searching through region proposals in object detection [4,5], and using various attention mechanisms for both classification and detection tasks [6–9].

With recent advance in deep learning, there has been a breakthrough in various areas of Computer Vision mainly caused by the advances in Convolution Networks [10,11]. Introducing deeper and more complex classification network

I. V. Tetko et al. (Eds.): ICANN 2019, LNCS 11727, pp. 585–597, 2019.
https://doi.org/10.1007/978-3-030-30487-4_45

architectures [12–14] has led to achieving high accuracy in challenging datasets such as ImageNet [15]. However, another approach for improving the performance is to simplify the classification by transforming the input image [16]. Hence, an important question to ask is *"what are the suitable transformations?"*.

In [16], the authors introduced the STN method for improving the classification accuracy. In STN, a network is trained to generate parameters of an affine transformation which is applied to the input image. They showed that this modification simplified the task and improved the performance. In their work, affine parameters were searched locally by differentiating the classification loss and backpropagating the gradients through a sub-differentiable sampling module.

Similar to STN, we address improving the classifier accuracy by applying an affine transformation to the input. Different from their approach, we model the task as a Markovian Decision Process. We break the affine transformation to a sequence of discrete and simple transformations and use RL to search for a combination of transformations which minimizes the classification error. This way, the task is simplified to a search problem in discrete search space. Using RL, we are not dependent on differentiability of different sampling modules and not limited to minimizing the classification loss as the optimization objective.

Since the breakthrough in RL [17], many works have successfully utilized it for solving different vision problems [18–21]. Combining RL methodology with deep learning as well as significant improvement in RL algorithms [22,23] has made it a powerful search method for different applications [18,24]. Moreover, RL can serve as a learning method which is not dependent on differentiability of the utilized modules [6]. For example, [25] adapted an RL solution for Image Restoration (IR), in which the goal is maximizing the Peak Signal to Noise Ratio (PSNR). For this task, they provide a set of IR tools and use RL to search for the optimal combination of applying these tools, aiming to maximize PSNR. In another application, Bahdanau et al. adapted RL for language sequence prediction [26]. In RL framework, one can design a reward for different objectives; they used this characteristic to directly search for a sequence which maximizes the test time metrics such as BLEU score.

To sum up, we formulate the transformation task as a sequential decision-making problem, in which instead of finding a one-step transformation, the model searches for a combination of discrete transformations to improve the performance. We use RL for solving the search problem and apply both Policy Gradient and Actor-Critic algorithms [27,28]. We experiment with different reward designs including maximizing classification accuracy and minimizing the classification loss.

In the following, we provide related work and the required background for our approach. Afterwards, we explain our method followed by experiments and an ablation study.

2 Related Work

Our work is mainly related to STN model and the RL algorithms that we utilize for solving the sequential transformation task. In this part, we focus on explaining the main ideas of STN paper as well as the required background about RL algorithms.

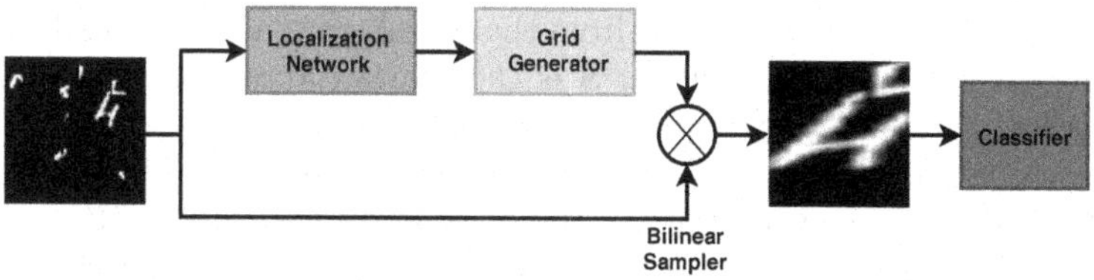

Fig. 1. An overview of the components in STN architecture. The localization network generates the parameters of an affine transformation. The grid generator together with the sampler module generates the transformed image.

2.1 Spatial Transformer Network (STN)

In STN architecture [16], the model learns a geometric transformation and modifies the input image to minimize the classification error. Although it is possible to use different transformations, here we focus only on affine transformation. The main components of an STN are the *localization network*, the *grid generator* and the *sampler module*. Figure 1 shows an overall view of STN architecture. The *localization network* takes the input image and generates the affine transformation parameters. The *grid generator* computes the location of each output pixel in the input image. To warp the input image based on the estimated transformation, each pixel in the output should be computed using a sampling kernel applied to the input image. The *sampler* uses the grid generator output and the bilinear sampling kernel to generate output pixels from the input image:

$$V_{ij} = \sum_{n}^{H} \sum_{m}^{W} U_{nm} max(0, 1 - |x_i - m|) max(0, 1 - |y_j - n|) \; \forall i, j \in [1 \dots H], [1 \dots W], \tag{1}$$

where H and W are the height and width of the image respectively, and V and U are the corresponding pixel values in the output and input image. The coordinate (x_i, y_i) is the location in the input where the sampling kernel is applied. The sampling module is differentiable within the local neighborhood, as can be seen in Eq. 2.

$$\frac{\delta V_{ij}}{\delta x_i} = U_{nm} max(0, 1 - |y_j - n|) \begin{cases} 0 & \text{if } |m - x_i| \geq 1 \\ 1 & \text{if } m \geq x_i \\ -1 & \text{if } m \leq x_i \end{cases} \tag{2}$$

and similarly for $\frac{\delta V_{ij}}{\delta y_j}$. Therefore, the parameters of the localization network are gradually updated using backpropagation through the classification loss within a local window. For more information, please refer to the original paper [16].

2.2 Reinforcement Learning (RL)

The main components in an RL framework are the State Space (**S**), the Action Space (**A**), and the Reward Signal (**R**) [29]. Additionally, an *episode* refers to a sequence of state-action transitions from the initial state until the final state. An important consideration in defining **S** is the Markovian assumption; it implies that selecting an action only requires information from the current state. Having this framework, a network (or an agent) is trained to learn picking the right action (or a policy) at every state in the episode. In training an RL agent, the objective is maximizing the expected total reward at the end of each episode:

$$J(\theta) = E_{\tau \sim \pi_\theta}[r(\tau)], \tag{3}$$

where $r = \sum_{t=0}^{t=T} R_t$, T is the episode length, and τ is an episode sampled from policy π_θ.

RL provides two main training algorithms: Policy Gradient (PG) and Q-learning. Additionally, there are Actor-Critic (AC) algorithms, which combine PG and Q-learning to merge the advantages of both algorithms. In PG algorithms, the policy is often approximated using a neural network which is trained by maximizing the objective in Eq. 3, using gradient ascent. Using backpropagation for maximizing this objective leads to the update rule below, with α as the learning rate.

$$\theta_{new} = \theta_{old} + \alpha \nabla_\theta J(\theta) \tag{4}$$

$$\nabla_\theta J(\theta) = E_{\tau \sim \pi_\theta}[\nabla_\theta (\log \pi_\theta(\tau)) r(\tau)] \tag{5}$$

In Q-learning the optimal policy is found by estimating the Q function. The Q function approximates the expected total reward from the current state for each possible action:

$$Q^\pi(s_t, a_t) = E_{\pi_\theta}\left[\sum_{t'=t}^{T} r(s_{t'}, a_{t'} | s_t, a_t)\right] \tag{6}$$

Therefore, one can find the optimal policy by always selecting the action leading to higher Q value.

PG methods are simple and effective, but they suffer from high variance. In AC, this issue is addressed by subtracting a baseline from $r(\tau)$ in Eq. 5, and shifting it around the zero mean. More precisely, the baseline in AC is the expected value of the Q function as

$$V^\pi(s_t) = E_{a_t \sim \pi_\theta}[Q^\pi(s_t, a_t)] \tag{7}$$

This value is also approximated using another neural network. The value network is supposed to estimate the total reward from time-step t onward. Therefore, the sum of rewards from t to the end of the episode ($\sum_{t=t'}^{T} r(t)$) can serve as the ground-truth for training the value network using a proper loss function. More details can be found in [29]. In this paper, we experiment with both PG and AC algorithms.

3 Sequential Spatial Transformer Network (SSTN)

Our goal is to learn a sequence of image transformations $T = T_n \cdot T_{n-1} \cdot ... \cdot T_0$, which is applied to the input image and helps the classifier achieve a better performance. There are different image adjustments including geometric transformations and filtering methods. In this paper, we only consider affine transformations.

In this paper, we decompose the affine transformation into a sequence of specific and discrete transformations instead of applying it in one step as in [16]. We formulate the problem of finding the affine parameters as an MDP and aim to learn picking the right transformation at every time-step of the sequence. The policy network is trained together with the classifier on the cluttered data, and the sequence of transformations is learned only by maximizing the reward signal. Figure 2 shows our proposed architecture.

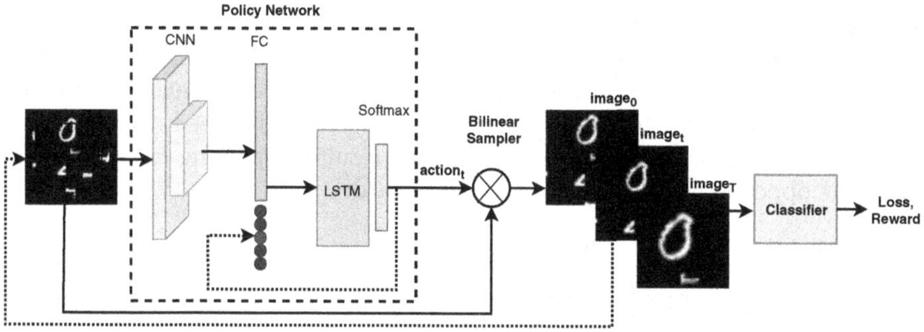

Fig. 2. SSTN architecture for finding the sequential affine transformation $T = T_n \cdot T_{n-1} \cdot ... \cdot T_0$. We compare the performance of different policy architectures with and without using LSTM. The last layer of the policy network is a softmax which outputs the probability distribution of the actions. When using LSTM, the one-hot encoded action from the previous time-step is merged into the feature map of $image_t$. At each time-step an action corresponding to transformation T_i is sampled from the policy and applied to the image.

3.1 MDP Framework for SSTN

As mentioned in Sect. 2.2, the main parts in an RL framework are **S**, **A**, and **R**. In this section, we elaborate on these elements in formulating our task.

State Space: We consider two state space definitions and experiment with both of them. First, we define a state as the transformed image at step t ($image_t$ in Fig. 2). Second, we define the state as a combination of the current transformed image ($image_t$) and the previous action (a_{t-1}). We merge the one-hot encoded action from the last time-step into the state as: $s_t = (image_t, action_{t-1})$. To keep track of the order of sampled actions in different time-steps, the model utilizes an LSTM module [30], which is a recurrent neural network with gate functions to avoid vanishing gradient problem. This formulation is closer to the Markovian assumption as the information from the past actions helps the network to learn the proper order of applying the transformations.

Action Space: Every action $action_t$ is a specific transformation sampled from the policy which is applied at time-step t and slightly transforms the image and the state. In order to construct an affine transformation, we define the action space as $A = \{Translation, Rotation, Scale, Identity\}$. The episode length is fixed to T for all images, and having the *Identity* transformation allows for stopping the process for individual images before reaching T. Having a fixed episode length allows us to train our model in mini-batches.

Reward: The agent learns the task while maximizing the reward; therefore, the reward definition has to enfold the objective of the task. An intuitive reward definition would be based on classification accuracy, since the goal is achieving higher accuracy. Accordingly, we give a discrete reward of **+1** when a label prediction changes from false to correct as the result of applying an action, and **-1** for the opposite case; other cases get **0** reward:

$$r_1 = \begin{cases} \mathbf{1} & \text{if } (pred_{t-1} \neq label \wedge pred_t = label) \\ \mathbf{-1} & \text{if } (pred_{t-1} = label \wedge pred_t \neq label) \\ \mathbf{0} & \text{otherwise} \end{cases} \tag{8}$$

Here $pred_{t-1}$ and $pred_t$ are predicted labels before and after applying the action at time-step t a_t.

Moreover, we can address maximizing the accuracy by minimizing the classification loss similar to [16]. This way the reward design is simply the negated loss:

$$r_2 = -loss \tag{9}$$

In this case, the reward is always negative as loss is a positive value; therefore, the maximum expected reward would be zero. It means that the model tries to learn a policy which pushes the classification loss toward zero.

Additionally, we can consider the reward as the loss difference between consecutive time-steps:

$$r_3 = loss_{t-1} - loss_t, \tag{10}$$

where t is the time-step. With this reward definition, the model tries to maximize the difference in loss values between every two following steps, toward a positive reward. In other words, the model tries to pick an action which results in a smaller loss value compared to the previous time-step.

3.2 Training

Having **S**, **A**, and **R** defined, we use the algorithms introduced in Sect. 2.2 to learn combining a set of discrete transformations for improving the classifier performance. First, we use PG algorithm mainly due to its effectiveness and simplicity. Then we extend our implementation to AC algorithm. More details about AC training algorithm for one epoch is presented in Algorithm 1. PG algorithm is similar, but it does not include the critic network and baseline reduction.

Algorithm 1: Actor-Critic Training Algorithm for SSTN

Input : Images and classification labels
Output: Classifier and sequential spatial transformer policy

Initialize classifier (ψ), *actor* (θ), *and critic* (ϕ) *networks*
for *Image = 1 : N* **do**
  initialize state $\boldsymbol{s}$, $t = 0$, $RewardValueList = [empty]$
  while $t <$ *episode-length* **do**
    $\pi(a_t|s_t) = actor(s_t)$
    sample the action : $a_t \sim \pi(a_t|s_t)$
    $image_{t+1} = \boldsymbol{apply\_ction}(image_t, a_t)$
    $s_{t+1} = (image_{t+1}, \boldsymbol{one\_hot}(a_t))$
    $predictions_t, loss_t = \boldsymbol{classify}(image_t, labels)$
    $reward_t = \boldsymbol{compute\_reward}^a$
    $value_t = critic(s_t)$
    append $(reward_t, value_t)$ *to* $RewardValueList$
    $t += 1$
  end
  Update parameters:
  $\Delta\phi = \frac{d}{d\phi} MSE\_loss(v_t, \sum_{t=t'}^{t=T} \gamma^{T-t} r_t)^b$
  $\Delta\theta = \frac{d}{d\theta} E[log\pi_\theta(\sum_{t=t'}^{t=T} \gamma^{T-t} r_t - v_t)]$
  $\Delta\psi = \frac{d}{d\psi} CrossEntropy\_loss(predicted\_labels, labels)$
  $\boldsymbol{Empty}(RewardValueList)$
end

[a] Depending on the used reward definition (Equations 8 to 10)
[b] γ is a discount factor, here set to 0.98

4 Experiments

In this section, we present the experimental setup for testing the performance of our method in improving the classification accuracy by applying a sequence of discrete transformations to the input image. We proceed with a discussion on results and an ablation study on the impact of reward design and episode length.

Dataset: We evaluate our method using cluttered MNIST [6] and cluttered Fashion-MNIST datasets. cluttered MNIST has been used by several works to demonstrate visual attention [6,31]. We followed the same procedure for generating cluttered Fashion-MNIST which includes ten clothing categories. We generate 80×80 grayscale images using the publicly available code[1]. The generated images are covered by clutter and the main content is located at a random location within the image boundaries. Both datasets include 500K training and 100K test images.

4.1 Network Architecture and Experiment Description

Our action space includes 10 transformations, including ± 4 *pixels* translation in x and y direction, scaling of 0.8 in x, y, and xy direction (since transformation is applied in backward mapping manner, $scale < 1$ has zoom-in effect), rotation of ± 10 degrees and *Identity* transformation. In Sect. 4.2, we show a comparison of the classification accuracies using different reward definitions. Here we present results using reward definition in Eq. 10.

We evaluate our model in the following settings. First, we take a 2-layer fully connected network as the classifier (referred as MLP in the following). The reason for choosing this simple classifier is to examine the improvement in classification accuracy based on only image transformations. Keeping the classifier architecture unchanged, we experiment with different policy architectures including LeNet and LeNet combined with LSTM. We also experiment with both PG and AC training algorithms.

For comparison, we implement our own version of the STN model and train it on our dataset (the size of cluttered MNIST images is 60×60 in STN paper). For the localization network in Fig. 1, we use the same LeNet architecture as in policy network. In STN paper [16], they used SGD as optimizer; however, we reached better results using Adam optimizer and we report the best observed performance.

Table 1. Experiments with MLP classifier and STN as the baseline, followed by the SSTN approach results. For all the experiments the classifier architecture is the same. The episode length for SSTN is set to 40. Our experiments cover PG algorithm with different architectures as well as applying AC algorithm on the best architecture. CMNIST and CFMNIST columns are the classification accuracies (%) for cluttered MNIST and Fashion-MNIST datasets, respectively. We observe that with proper definition of the state space, our approach outperforms the STN method.

Method	CMNIST	CFMNIST
MLP classifier	54.01	30.74
MLP classifier with STN	94.49	62.54
MLP classifier with LeNet policy (PG)	91.04	58.70
MLP classifier with LeNet+LSTM policy (PG)	95.88	70.27
MLP classifier with LeNet+LSTM policy (AC)	**96.83**	**71.61**

The utilized LeNet architecture consists of two convolution layers with 32 and 64 kernels, followed by max pooling and two fully-connected layers with ReLU

[1] https://github.com/deepmind/mnist-cluttered.

non-linearity. In policy network, the last layer is a softmax which generates the action probabilities. The actions are sampled from a *Categorical* distribution fitted to the softmax output. For all experiments we use Adam optimizer with learning rate of $10e-4$ and the episode length is 40. In the next experiment setup, we change the classifier to LeNet and repeat similar experiments.

Table 2. Experiment results when using LeNet for the classifier network and the episode length of 40. CMNIST and CFMNIST columns are the classification accuracies (%) for cluttered MNIST and Fashion-MNIST datasets, respectively.

Method	CMNIST	CFMNIST
LeNet classifier	95.94	72.40
LeNet classifier with STN	97.72	77.38
LeNet classifier with LeNet policy (PG)	95.82	74.59
LeNet classifier with LeNet+LSTM policy (PG)	98.23	83.16
LeNet classifier with LeNet+LSTM policy (AC)	**98.29**	**83.27**

Tables 1 and 2 show the results of our experiments using MLP and LeNet classifiers. We note that the impact of both policy network in SSTN and localization network in STN is only to transform the image before feeding it to the classifier and not to increase the power of the classifier.

For the policy network, first we use a LeNet architecture and then combine it with LSTM. We aim to investigate if considering the state as the current single image satisfies the Markovian assumption. Based on the experiments with LSTM module, we observe that this is an essential element and the single image does not include all the required information. The reason is that the RL agent is supposed to learn the sequence of actions constructing the optimal affine transformation; therefore, it needs the tool for remembering the order of applying actions. The input to LSTM is the extracted feature map from the current transformed image, concatenated with one-hot encoded previous action. Finally, we take the best architecture from these experiments and train it with AC algorithm. In AC algorithm, we use the same network as policy for the critic. Although it is possible to share weights between the actor and the critic, it is more stable if separate networks are used [26]. As expected, applying AC training algorithm leads to further improvement; since it addresses some of the shortcomings in PG as mentioned in Sect. 2.2. As results in Table 2 show, the LeNet classifier serves as a strong baseline and achieves high accuracy, especially in cluttered MNIST dataset. However, we still can get an improvement by modifying the input image before classifying.

4.2 Ablation Study

In this section, we present an ablation study on the impact of the reward design and episode length on the performance.

Reward: Figure 3 shows the epoch-accuracy curve for different reward definitions. Although the performance is close, r_3 outperforms the others.

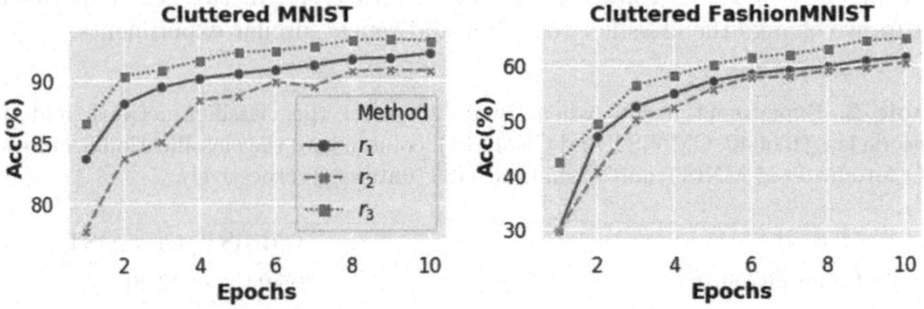

Fig. 3. Comparison between three different reward definitions using MLP classifier and LeNet+LSTM policy network using PG algorithm and episode length of 20.

We believe this behavior is because r_3 provides more concise information about the taken action compared to the discrete reward in Eq. 8. We observe that the performance using r_2 is worse than the others. We argue that in reward r_1 and r_3, we consider the change caused by taking the action between every two time-steps; while, in r_2 we only consider the loss value at current time-step and not the change. The results indicate that this formulation incorporates less information compared to the other two.

Episode Length: Another important hyper-parameter is the number of time-steps per episode. Figure 4 shows the performance of AC and PG algorithms for different time-steps. As the results illustrate, the accuracy is better for more extended episodes. However, this can be seen as a trade-off between speed and accuracy. Another observation is that when using LeNet as classifier, the performance of PG and AC algorithms are very similar. This indicates that using a stronger classifier decreases the variance in reward signal.

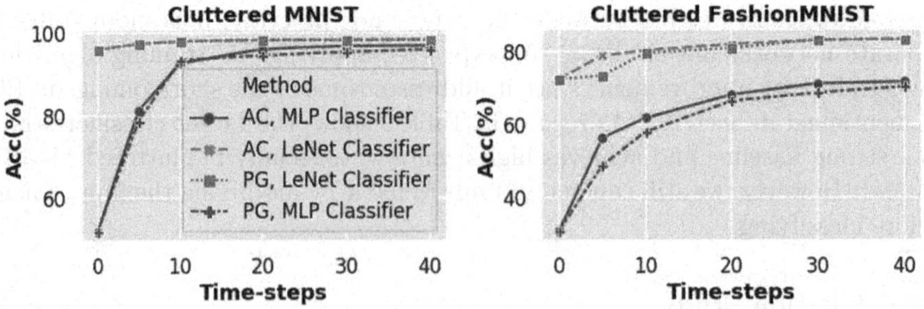

Fig. 4. Results for AC and PG algorithms with MLP and LeNet classifiers using different episode lengths.

5 Conclusion and Future Work

In this work, we present an extension of the STN model, in which we model the problem as a sequence of discrete transformations. We formulate finding the affine transformation as a search problem and aim to learn a combination of discrete transformations which improves the classification accuracy. We use both Policy Gradient and Actor-Critic training algorithms and compare our method with extensive experiments on cluttered MNIST and Fashion-MNIST datasets. For future work, we would like to extend this work to more complex datasets such as SVHN and PASCAL VOC. Moreover, we plan to extend our approach to more general transformations beyond geometric alterations, e.g., morphological operations; this extension can be done by merely extending the action space. Another exciting direction is adapting this method for other relevant tasks such as detection.

Acknowledgement. This work was supported by TU Kaiserslautern CS PhD scholarship program, the BMBF project DeFuseNN (Grant 01IW17002), and the NVIDIA AI Lab (NVAIL) program.

References

1. Lowe, D.G.: Distinctive image features from scale-invariant keypoints. Int. J. Comput. Vision **60**(2), 91–110 (2004). https://doi.org/10.1023/B:VISI.0000029664.99615.94
2. Dai, J., et al.: Deformable convolutional networks. In: Proceedings of the IEEE International Conference on Computer Vision, pp. 764–773 (2017). https://doi.org/10.1109/ICCV.2017.89
3. Redmon, J., Divvala, S., Girshick, R., Farhadi, A.: You only look once: unified, real-time object detection. In: Proceedings of the IEEE Conference on Computer Vision and Pattern Recognition, pp. 779–788 (2016). https://doi.org/10.1109/cvpr.2016.91
4. Girshick, R.: Fast R-CNN. In: Proceedings of the IEEE International Conference on Computer Vision, pp. 1440–1448 (2015). https://doi.org/10.1109/iccv.2015.169
5. Ren, S., He, K., Girshick, R., Sun, J.: Faster R-CNN: towards real-time object detection with region proposal networks. In: Advances in Neural Information Processing Systems, pp. 91–99 (2015). https://doi.org/10.1109/TPAMI.2016.2577031
6. Mnih, V., Heess, N., Graves, A., et al.: Recurrent models of visual attention. In: Advances in Neural Information Processing Systems, pp. 2204–2212 (2014)
7. Ba, J., Mnih, V., Kavukcuoglu, K.: Multiple object recognition with visual attention. arXiv preprint arXiv:1412.7755 (2014)
8. Sermanet, P., Frome, A., Real, E.: Attention for fine-grained categorization. arXiv preprint arXiv:1412.7054 (2014)
9. Bueno, M.B., Giró-i Nieto, X., Marqués, F., Torres, J.: Hierarchical object detection with deep reinforcement learning. Deep Learn. Image Process. Appl. **31**(164), 3 (2017). https://doi.org/10.3233/978-1-61499-822-8-164
10. LeCun, Y., Bottou, L., Bengio, Y., Haffner, P.: Gradient-based learning applied to document recognition. Proc. IEEE **86**(11), 2278–2324 (1998). https://doi.org/10.1109/9780470544976.ch9

11. Krizhevsky, A., Sutskever, I., Hinton, G.E.: ImageNet classification with deep convolutional neural networks. In: Advances in Neural Information Processing Systems, pp. 1097–1105 (2012)
12. He, K., Zhang, X., Ren, S., Sun, J.: Deep residual learning for image recognition. In: Proceedings of the IEEE Conference on Computer Vision and Pattern Recognition, pp. 770–778 (2016). https://doi.org/10.1109/CVPR.2016.90
13. Szegedy, C., et al.: Going deeper with convolutions. In: Proceedings of the IEEE Conference on Computer Vision and Pattern Recognition, pp. 1–9 (2015). https://doi.org/10.1109/cvpr.2015.7298594
14. Huang, G., Liu, Z., Van Der Maaten, L., Weinberger, K.Q.: Densely connected convolutional networks. In: Proceedings of the IEEE Conference on Computer Vision and Pattern Recognition, pp. 4700–4708 (2017). https://doi.org/10.1109/cvpr.2017.243
15. Deng, J., Dong, W., Socher, R., Li, L.-J., Li, K., Fei-Fei, L.: ImageNet: a large-scale hierarchical image database. In: IEEE Conference on Computer Vision and Pattern Recognition, CVPR 2009, pp. 248–255. IEEE (2009). https://doi.org/10.1109/cvprw.2009.5206848
16. Jaderberg, M., Simonyan, K., Zisserman, A., et al.: Spatial transformer networks. In: Advances in Neural Information Processing Systems, pp. 2017–2025 (2015)
17. Mnih, V., et al.: Playing atari with deep reinforcement learning. arXiv preprint arXiv:1312.5602 (2013)
18. Zoph, B., Le, Q.V.: Neural architecture search with reinforcement learning. arXiv preprint arXiv:1611.01578 (2016)
19. Baker, B., Gupta, O., Naik, N., Raskar, R.: Designing neural network architectures using reinforcement learning. arXiv preprint arXiv:1611.02167 (2016)
20. Liang, X., Lee, L., Xing, E.P.: Deep variation-structured reinforcement learning for visual relationship and attribute detection. In: 2017 IEEE Conference on Computer Vision and Pattern Recognition (CVPR), pp. 4408–4417. IEEE (2017). https://doi.org/10.1109/cvpr.2017.469
21. Park, J., Lee, J.-Y., Yoo, D., So Kweon, I.: Distort-and-recover: color enhancement using deep reinforcement learning. In: Proceedings of the IEEE Conference on Computer Vision and Pattern Recognition, pp. 5928–5936 (2018). https://doi.org/10.1109/cvpr.2018.00621
22. Schulman, J., Wolski, F., Dhariwal, P., Radford, A., Klimov, O.: Proximal policy optimization algorithms. arXiv preprint arXiv:1707.06347 (2017)
23. Wu, Y., Mansimov, E., Grosse, R.B., Liao, S., Ba, J.: Scalable trust-region method for deep reinforcement learning using kronecker-factored approximation. In: Advances in Neural Information Processing Systems, pp. 5279–5288 (2017)
24. Cubuk, E.D., Zoph, B., Mane, D., Vasudevan, V., Le, Q.V.: AutoAugment: learning augmentation policies from data. arXiv preprint arXiv:1805.09501 (2018)
25. Yu, K., Dong, C., Lin, L., Change Loy, C.: Crafting a toolchain for image restoration by deep reinforcement learning. In: Proceedings of the IEEE Conference on Computer Vision and Pattern Recognition, pp. 2443–2452 (2018). https://doi.org/10.1109/cvpr.2018.00259
26. Bahdanau, D., e al.: An actor-critic algorithm for sequence prediction. arXiv preprint arXiv:1607.07086 (2016)
27. Sutton, R.S., McAllester, D.A., Singh, S.P., Mansour, Y.: Policy gradient methods for reinforcement learning with function approximation. In: Advances in Neural Information Processing Systems, pp. 1057–1063 (2000)
28. Sutton, R.S.: Temporal credit assignment in reinforcement learning (1984)

29. Sutton, R.S., Barto, A.G.: Reinforcement Learning: An Introduction. MIT Press, Cambridge (2018)
30. Hochreiter, S., Schmidhuber, J.: Long short-term memory. Neural Comput. **9**(8), 1735–1780 (1997)
31. Gregor, K., Danihelka, I., Graves, A., Rezende, D.J., Wierstra, D.: Draw: a recurrent neural network for image generation. arXiv preprint arXiv:1502.04623 (2015)

Deep Recurrent Policy Networks for Planning Under Partial Observability

Zixuan Chen[1(✉)] and Zongzhang Zhang[2]

[1] School of Computer Science and Technology, Soochow University, Suzhou, China
cczxqueen@gmail.com
[2] National Key Laboratory for Novel Software Technology, Nanjing University, Nanjing, China
zhangzongzhang@gmail.com

Abstract. QMDP-net is a recurrent network architecture that combines the features of model-free learning and model-based planning for planning under partial observability. The architecture represents a policy by connecting a partially observable Markov decision process (POMDP) model with the QMDP algorithm that uses value iteration to handle the POMDP model. However, as the value iteration used in QMDP iterates through the entire state space, it may suffer from the "curse of dimensionality". Besides, as the policies based on the QMDP will not take actions to gain information, this may lead to bad policies in domains where information gathering is necessary. To address these two issues, this paper introduces two deep recurrent policy networks, asynchronous QMDP-net and ReplicatedQ-net, based on the plain QMDP-net. The former takes advantage of the idea of asynchronous update into the value iteration process of QMDP to learn a smaller abstract state space representation for planning. The latter partially replaces the QMDP with the replicated Q-learning algorithm to take informative actions. Experimental results demonstrate the proposed networks perform better than the plain QMDP-net on the robotic tasks in simulation.

Keywords: POMDP · QMDP · Value iteration · Replicated Q-learning

1 Introduction

In the field of artificial intelligence, building intelligent agents is one major target [1]. For a given task, an intelligent agent should be able to observe the environment, integrate information to decide what to do and execute the chosen action in the next step [2]. However, in tasks with partially observable environments, the agent is uncertain about the exact consequence of its actions, furthermore, it cannot determine with full certainty the environmental state based on

This work is in part supported by the National Natural Science Foundation of China under Grant Nos. 61876119 and 61502323, and the Natural Science Foundation of Jiangsu under Grant No. BK20181432.

I. V. Tetko et al. (Eds.): ICANN 2019, LNCS 11727, pp. 598–610, 2019.
https://doi.org/10.1007/978-3-030-30487-4_46

the current observation. As a consequence, for intelligent agents, planning optimal actions under uncertainty is a challenging problem as it requires reasoning over all possible futures given the past history of actions and observations [2]. To fulfill the goal of planning under uncertainty, two kinds of approaches, i.e., model-based and model-free approaches, can be applied [3]. In model-based approaches, partially observable Markov decision process (POMDP) provides a mathematical framework for acting optimally in such partially observable environments [4–6]. A variety of approximate POMDP algorithms exist for approximately solving POMDPs [2, 7–10], but because the problem is so computationally challenging, manually constructing POMDP models or learning them from data remains very difficult. In model-free approaches, an optimal policy is directly searched within a policy class, but lots of data and computational cost are required for the searching process [3].

QMDP-net is a fully differentiable neural network architecture for planning under partial observability [3]. It is a recurrent policy network, which simulates the structure of recurrent neural network (RNN) to combine the strengths of model-based planning and model-free learning. QMDP-net represents a policy by connecting a POMDP model with the QMDP algorithm [12] that treats the POMDP as if its state were fully observable after one time step and solves the model using value iteration [13], thus it is embedded with the solution structure of planning and is able to successfully plan in POMDPs. After trained on different parameterized sets of tasks, QMDP-net can generalize to new tasks in these sets and transfer to other similar tasks beyond these sets.

Even though QMDP-net successfully deals with some POMDPs and generates policies with great generalization ability, the QMDP algorithm that used in QMDP-net still exists some inadequacies that can be improved. First, its value iteration process involves the entire state space in each iteration, which means it may get into meaningless sweeping [11] and suffer from the "curse of dimensionality" [3]. Second, QMDP assumes that any state uncertainty will disappear at the next time step, which may cause bad policies in domains where repeated information gathering is necessary [12]. To address the above problems and further improve the recurrent policy network for better planning under uncertainty, based on the plain QMDP-net, we introduce the asynchronous QMDP-net and the ReplicatedQ-net in this paper. The former integrates the idea of asynchronous update [14] into QMDP's value iteration process to learn a smaller abstract state space representation for planning, which significantly alleviates the problem of "curse of dimensionality" and improves the efficiency of each iteration. The latter partially replaces the QMDP with the replicated Q-learning [12], a more complicated approximate POMDP algorithm, to consider current belief when the agent selects actions, making the computed policies take informative action to further improve the planning performance of the network.

2 Background and Related Work

2.1 POMDP Model

A POMDP is formally defined as a tuple $< S, A, T, R, O, \Omega >$, where S is a set of states, A is a set of actions, and O is a set of observations. The transition function, $T(s, a, s') = p(s'|s, a)$, defines the probability of the agent being in state s' after taking action a in state s. The agent's decisions are made based on information from its observations formalized by the observation function $\Omega(s', a, o) = p(o|a, s')$, which defines the probability of receiving observation o in state s' after taking action a. The agent's immediate reward for taking action a in state s is given by $R : S \times A \rightarrow \mathbb{R}$.

A POMDP can be transformed to a belief-state MDP in which the agent gathers all information about its past history using a belief b according to the transition function and the observation function. The belief b is a probability distribution over S, which provides a Markovian signal for the planning task. Each POMDP problem assumes an initial belief b_0, at every time step t the agent takes an action a and observes o, and updates the belief b_t with a Bayesian filter:

$$b_t(s') = \tau(b_{t-1}, a_t, o_t) = \eta\Omega(s', a_t, o_t) \sum\nolimits_{s \in S} T(s, a_t, s')b_{t-1}(s), \quad (1)$$

where η is a normalizing constant. The belief b_t recursively integrates the information of environment in the entire past history $(a_1, o_1, a_2, o_2, \ldots, a_t, o_t)$.

The goal of the agent is to choose actions which can compute an optimal plan, such a plan is called a policy $\pi(b)$ and the policy maps beliefs to actions. A policy π can be characterized by a value function V_π which is defined as the expected total discounted reward $V_\pi(b)$ that the agent can summarize by following π starting from belief b_0:

$$V_\pi(b) = \mathbb{E}\big[\sum\nolimits_{t=0}^{\infty} \gamma^t R(b_t, a_{t+1})|b_0 = b, \pi\big], \quad (2)$$

where $R(b_t, a_{t+1}) = \sum_{s \in S} R(s_t, \pi(b_t))b_t(s)$, s_t is the state at time t, $a_{t+1} = \pi(b_t)$ is the action that policy π chooses at time t, and $\gamma \in (0, 1)$ is a discount rate. The discount rate ensures a finite sum and is usually chosen close to 1.

2.2 QMDP-Net

Figure 1 shows the main modules of QMDP-net. It consists of two modules. The Bayesian filter module encodes the Bayesian filter, which is used to estimate states through integrating information from the past actions and observations of agent into a belief. The QMDP planner module encodes the QMDP algorithm. QMDP makes use of the Q-values of the underlying fully observable MDP, that is, it temporarily ignores the observation model and finds the Q-values for the MDP consisting of the transitions and rewards only, actions are then selected by weighting the Q-value with the belief. In the QMDP planner, by using the Bellman equation, Q-values can be computed iteratively, as bellow:

$$Q_{k+1}(s, a) = R(s, a) + \gamma \sum\nolimits_{s' \in S} T(s, a, s')V_k(s'), \quad (3)$$

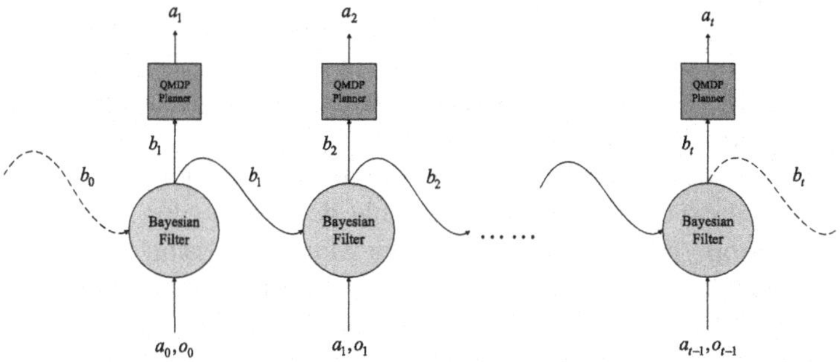

Fig. 1. QMDP-net architecture. A QMDP-net consists of two modules and is an RNN that imposes structure priors for decision making under partial observability.

$$V_k(s) = \max_{a \in A} Q_k(s,a). \tag{4}$$

In the QMDP planner, Eq. 3 is implemented by convolutional layer f_T whose kernel weights encode the transition function T, followed by an addition operation with $R(s,a)$ which is obtained by an f_R mapping. Equation 4 is expressed by a max pooling layer, where $Q_k(s,a)$ is the input and $V_k(s)$ is the output. Equations 3 and 4 jointly simulate the convolutional neural network (CNN) layer. The two equations are implemented K iterations by stacking the convolutional and max pooling layers K times with tied weights. The final approximate Q-value $Q_K(s,a)$ is obtained after K iterations. The estimated Q-value for the current belief state $b_t(s)$ is defined as: $q(a) = \sum_{s \in S} Q_K(s,a) b_t(s)$. Through the mapping of a policy function f_π, the chosen action a_t will be output.

2.3 Related Work

Asynchronous update methods provide reasonable solutions to alleviate the problem of meaningless sweeping. It prioritizes the updates for certain states according to the importance of states, making some important states be updated more frequently. The efficiency of asynchronous update is related to the order of updating, as a consequence, how to define the importance of states becomes very important. The idea of applying asynchronous update to improve the efficiency of algorithm has been gaining a lot of attentions. Prioritized sweeping [15], a typical asynchronous planning algorithm, utilizes the temporal-difference (TD) error as the state importance to prioritize the updates and performs them in the order of priority. In it a priority queue is applied to store the prioritized state-action pairs. Once the top state-action pair in the queue has been updated, the importance of its predecessor states will be updated thereupon. Real-time dynamic programming (RTDP) [16] is a representative example of an asynchronous dynamic programming algorithm. Its update order is determined by the order of states encountered in real or simulated trajectories. Prioritized experience replay [17], a new replay mechanism applied in Deep Q-Networks (DQN), defines the priority of the transition probability by TD error and samples the transitions from the replay memory by their priorities. On many Atari games, DQN with prioritized experience replay can achieve a better performance, outperforming vanilla DQN with uniform experience replay.

We turn to progresses in embedding unique computation structure in a neural network architecture. In fully observable domains, value iteration network (VIN) [18] is proposed to do planning under Markov decision processes (MDPs) where the agent knows its exact state. Based on VIN, asynchronous value iteration network (AVIN) [14] is proposed by adopting the asynchronous update method to achieve a better planning performance under MDPs. Value prediction network (VPN) [19] replaces the value iteration process with the Monte-Carlo tree search to predict the future values on the semi-MDPs, meanwhile eliminates the limitation of the fixed topology of the state space. For the partially observable domains, cognitive mapping and planner (CMP) [20] constructs a belief map for the environment and applies a differentiable hierarchical planner to produce the next action at each time step.

3 Asynchronous QMDP-Net

We propose the asynchronous QMDP-net, a recurrent policy network that applies the idea of asynchronous update into the QMDP planner to improve the plain QMDP-net for planning better under uncertainty. Asynchronous QMDP-net effectively reduces the possibility of meaningless sweeping that happens in the value iteration process of QMDP and alleviates the "curse of dimensionality". Since QMDP makes use of the underlying fully observable MDP to perform the computation of the final Q-values of POMDP, in asynchronous QMDP-net, we choose to use the Bellman error to favour the sampling of certain states in every round of update process so as to learn a much smaller abstract state set for more efficient planning. The Bellman error is the absolute value of the difference between the state value obtained before and after one round of value iteration. The Bellman error for state s in the nth value iteration is defined as:

$$BE_n(s) = |V_{n-1}(s) - \max_{a \in A} Q_n(s, a)| = |V_n^{\text{be}}(s) - V_n^{\text{af}}(s)|,$$

where $V_n^{\text{be}}(s)$ is the state value before the nth value iteration and $V_n^{\text{af}}(s)$ is the state value after the nth value iteration.

The main reason of using the Bellman error to define the importance of states is that between two rounds of value iteration, there are some states whose state values may change significantly, whereas others whose state values may change little, and the predecessor states connected to those that have changed a lot are more likely to also change a lot. According to the definition of the above equation, the greater the change of the state value, the larger the Bellman error, which suggests that for those have relatively large Bellman errors we should give them high priorities in updating their state values.

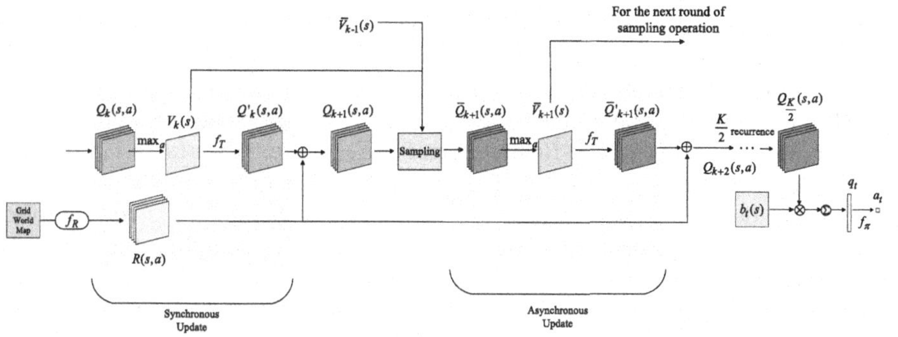

Fig. 2. Asynchronous QMDP planner module in asynchronous QMDP-net. Each update process of this module consists of synchronous update and asynchronous update, where synchronous update is equivalent to the original value iteration process. After $\frac{K}{2}$ recurrence, the module selects an action according to the current belief b_t.

According to the defined state importance, states to be updated in each round of asynchronous update are sampled with a threshold, that is, states whose Bellman errors are greater than the threshold will be sampled, whereas others will not be sampled and their values remain unchanged. The threshold is defined as $\rho = \frac{\sqrt{\mathrm{maxE}^2 + \mathrm{minE}^2}}{N}$, where maxE is the maximum value of state importance for the entire state space, minE is the minimum value of state importance for the entire state space, and N is the total number of states for the entire state space. By considering the maximum importance and the minimum importance, this threshold fully neutralizes the state importance over the entire state space. Based on this threshold, the network can effectively distinguish between the less important states and the more important states and successfully sample states with relatively higher priorities during each iteration, this allows the asynchronous updates to be performed more reasonably.

Asynchronous QMDP-net consists of a Bayesian filter module and an asynchronous QMDP planner module. Figure 2 shows the main innovation part of the asynchronous QMDP-net, namely the asynchronous QMDP planner module. In order to avoid the phenomenon where some really trivial states will never be updated, or the phenomenon where the distribution of update times of certain states is unfair, for the whole iteration process in the asynchronous QMDP-net, we adopt the update mode of "synchronous → asynchronous → ⋯ → synchronous → asynchronous" to average the number of synchronous updates and asynchronous updates, and the total number of iterations is halved to $\frac{K}{2}$. This operation ensures the states with relatively higher priorities can be updated more times, making the planned policies more goal-directed and thus enabling the network has better planning performance. The specific explanation of the update process in Fig. 2 is as follows: During the synchronous update, the value function for each state on the state space is updated with the Bellman equation.

Here, f_T denotes the convolutional layer, whose kernel weights encode the transition function T, f_R maps both the goal and the obstacles of a grid world map to the reward function $R(s,a)$, $Q'_k(s,a) = \gamma \sum_{s' \in S} T(s,a,s')V_k(s')$. After the synchronous update, the states to be updated in the asynchronous update can be sampled according to the Bellman error $BE_k(s)$, i.e. $|\overline{V}_{k-1}(s) - V_k(s)|$, and the current threshold ρ. The function corresponding to the sampling operation in Fig. 2 is defined as $\overline{S} = f_{\text{sp}}(BE_k(s), \rho; S)$, where $\overline{S}$ represents the sampled state set, and S represents the whole state space. After sampling the states to be updated, the asynchronous update can be performed. In Fig. 2, $\overline{Q}_{k+1}(s,a)$ represents the Q-values to be updated asynchronously, where the value functions of those states that are not sampled are "blocked" and keep the original values, while the value functions of those sampled states are updated using the Bellman equation. After $\frac{K}{2}$ rounds of such updates and being weighted by the current belief $b_t(s)$, the final Q-value q_t will be obtained.

4 ReplicatedQ-Net

To enable the policies that the network computes to take informative actions, we propose ReplicatedQ-net. Same as QMDP-net and asynchronous QMDP-net, ReplicatedQ-net is also a recurrent policy network that is obtained by partially replacing the QMDP algorithm used in QMDP-net with the value update rule of replicated Q-learning. It is worth noting that, in order to prevent the algorithmic sophistication from increasing the difficulty of learning, instead of directly using the replicated Q-learning to solve POMDPs, in ReplicatedQ-net, we masterly combine the value update rule used in replicated Q-learning with the value iteration algorithm to achieve better planning performance while reducing the difficulty of learning. Replicated Q-learning is an extension of Q-learning, which is used to learn the approximate Q-values of the learned POMDP model [12]. Replicated Q-learning generalizes Q-learning to apply to vector-valued states and uses a single vector to approximate the POMDP's Q-value for each action a. This feature allows us to successfully apply the algorithm to the calculation process of the plain QMDP-net framework. Specifically, we use the value update rule of replicated Q-learning to compute the final Q-values of the POMDP model at each time step, while the value iteration algorithm that is used to compute the Q-values of the underlying MDP remains unchanged.

A ReplicatedQ-net consists of two modules, a Bayesian filter module and a ReplicatedQ planner module. Figure 3 shows the main innovation part of the ReplicatedQ-net, namely the ReplicatedQ planner module. In it we use the Q-value of the underlying MDP as the single vector value to compute the POMDP model's Q-value, this approximation is simple and can be remarkably effective. The initial single vector value $Q_0(s,a)$ for time step $t = 0$ is directly computed by iteratively applying the value iteration K times. For each time step $t > 0$, as shown in Fig. 3, the component of the value $Q_t(s,a)$ is updated by using the next update rule:

$$\Delta Q(s,a) = \alpha b_{t-1}(s)[R(s,a) + \gamma \max_{a \in A} \hat{q}_t(a) - Q_{t-1}(s,a)], \tag{5}$$

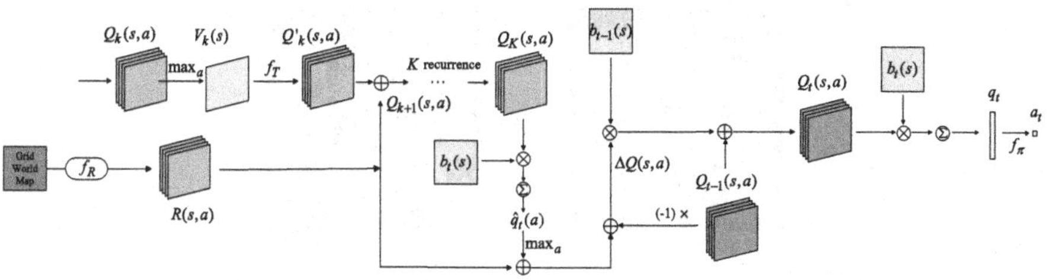

Fig. 3. The ReplicatedQ planner module of ReplicatedQ-net.

where α is a learning rate and $b_{t-1}(s)$ is the belief at time step $t-1$. The update rule is evaluated for every $s \in S$ at each time step after the agent performs K-round value iterations.

Then the vector value is updated by $Q_t(s,a) \leftarrow Q_{t-1}(s,a) + \Delta Q(s,a)$. For current time step t, the final POMDP model's Q-value $q_t(a)$ is computed by weighting the current belief b_t: $q_t(a) = \sum_{s \in S} Q_t(s,a) b_t(s)$. In Eq. 5, we use $\hat{q}_t(a) = \sum_{s \in S} Q_K(s,a) b_t(s)$ to estimate the Q-value for the POMDP model at current time step t after the agent performs K-round value iterations, and this estimated Q-value serves as a medium for computing the vector value $Q_t(s,a)$. This update rule applies the Q-learning update rule to each component of $Q(\cdot, a)$ in proportion to the probability that the agent is currently occupying the state associated with that component. Using this update rule to compute the POMDP model's Q-value of each time step enables the network to generate policies that can take actions to gain information about the past history, such that the network has better planning.

See again Fig. 3, in the ReplicatedQ planner module, before each round of updates begins, the Q-value of underlying MDP, i.e. $Q_K(s,a)$, is iteratively computed by the Bellman equation. After obtaining the Q-value of underlying MDP, the current estimated Q-value of the POMDP model, i.e. $\hat{q}_t(a)$, can also be obtained. According to the update rule shown above, the current vector value $Q_t(s,a)$ will be updated, as a consequence, the final POMDP model's Q-value $q_t(a)$ that integrates the past information will also be updated.

5 Experiments

The specific experimental task models a robot learning to navigate in partially observable grid worlds (see Fig. 4 for examples). The robot possesses a map corresponding to the current grid world environment. For the robot, only the local information around it can be observed. These local observations are ambiguous and insufficient for the robot to determine where it is exactly located.

The main objective of the experiments is to verify the effectiveness of asynchronous QMDP-net and ReplicatedQ-net. We compare the performance of asynchronous QMDP-net and ReplicatedQ-net with QMDP-net and its untied variant, untied QMDP-net, on simulated robot navigation task. Untied QMDP-net is obtained by untying the kernel weights in the convolutional layers that

Fig. 4. Two specific visual grid world maps where a robot is learning to navigate. Red circle indicates the goal and green circles indicate the possible initial states of the robot. The exact initial state is unknown. The robot only has a belief over the initial state. (Color figure online)

implement value iteration in the planner module of QMDP-net. While the robot navigation task is relatively simple compared with the Atari games, it is still very challenging, as dealing with partial observability and distant future rewards requires complex long-term reasoning [3]. Because the exact state of the robot is unknown, a successful policy must be inferred through many steps to gather information and improve state estimation through partial observation.

5.1 Experimental Setup

In our robot navigation example, the map of the environment, the goal, and the belief over the robot's initial state are represented as an $N \times N$ images with three channels. The first channel encodes the obstacles in the environment, the second channel encodes the goal, and the belief over the robot's initial state is encoded by the third channel. During the navigation, the robot has five actions: moving up, moving down, moving left, moving right or staying in place. We consider deterministic and stochastic variants of the domain. The stochastic domain adds uncertainties to robot's actions and observations, i.e., the robot has a possibility of 0.2 to fail to execute the specified move action and stay in place, and the observations are faulty with probability 0.1 independently in each direction [3]. In this work, we only use imitation learning to perform training. We trained the policies with expert trajectories from 10,000 random environments, and 5 trajectories in each environment. Then we tested these trained networks on a separate set of 500 random environments to examine their generalization abilities.

The internal structure and the settings of each network parameter of asynchronous QMDP-net and ReplicatedQ-net are the same as the plain QMDP-net. In particular, f_T is represented by CNN components with 3×3 and 5×5 kernels depending on the task, f_π is a single softmax layer and f_R is the identity function. The amount of planning for each network can be adjusted by the setting of K, and K depends on the problem size, specifically, $K = 3 \times N$. The larger the value of K, the more distant states that information can be propagated to.

5.2 Experimental Results and Analysis

The main results are reported in Fig. 5, Tables 1 and 2. For each domain, we use the training loss that is computed by the spare softmax cross entropy between the predicted value and the expert label to demonstrate the training performance of networks, and use the task's success rate and the average number of time steps for task completion to quantify the testing performance of networks. When the success rates are similar, the completion time can be used to do comparison.

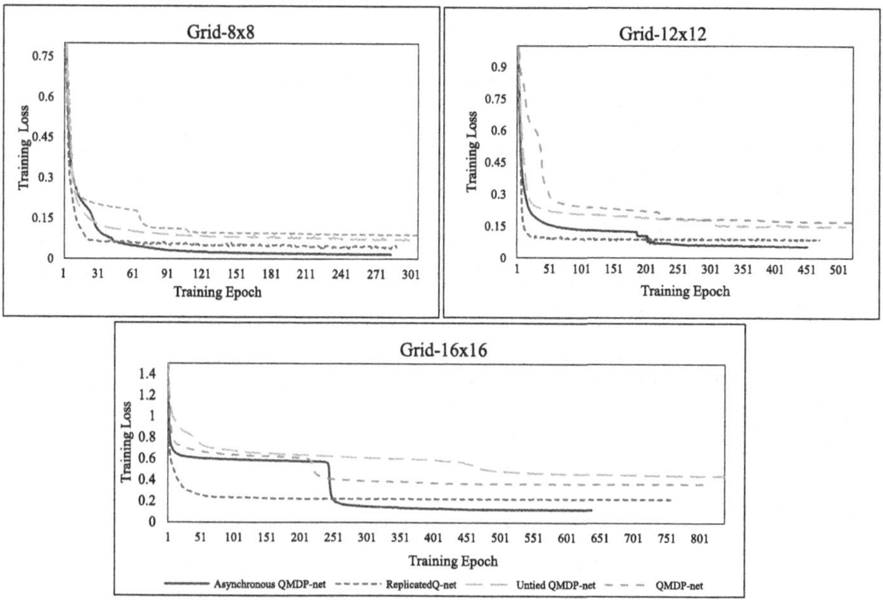

Fig. 5. Comparison of training performance of the recurrent policy networks. Untied QMDP-net relaxes the POMDP structure priors on the network architecture, which may degrade the training performance of network as shown in Grid-16 × 16, but sometimes strong priors may overstrain the network and degrade the training performance as shown in Grid-8 × 8 and Grid-12 × 12.

Figure 5 shows the comparison of training performance among asynchronous QMDP-net, ReplicatedQ-net, QMDP-net and untied QMDP-net in 8×8, 12×12 and 16×16 deterministic navigation tasks. As the training epoches increase, the training losses of networks will decrease and reach convergence after a certain number of epoches. When the convergence is reached, the training losses of asynchronous QMDP-net and ReplicatedQ-net are smaller than the training losses of QMDP-net and untied QMDP-net, indicating that the first two networks can be trained better than the latter two networks. In addition, asynchronous QMDP-net and ReplicatedQ-net require fewer training epoches to reach convergency, and the training epoches which are needed to complete the whole training process for these two networks are also significantly fewer. The above results show

Table 1. Testing performance comparison of recurrent policy networks. The policy networks used for testing are trained under Grid-8 × 8. SR denotes the success rate in percentage. Time denotes the average number of time steps for task completion. Grid-$N \times N$ and Grid-S-$N \times N$, respectively, denote the deterministic and stochastic variants of environment with size $N \times N$.

Grid	Asy. QMDP-net		ReplicatedQ-net		QMDP-net		Untied QMDP-net	
	SR	Time (s)	SR	Time (s)	SR	Time (s)	SR	Time (s)
8 × 8	100.00	5.5	100	5.7	99.0	5.6	100	5.8
16 × 16	96.00	24.3	92.00	24.8	91.00	24.3	91.00	24.1
18 × 18	95.00	32.6	91.00	32.3	88.00	34.1	82.00	38.8
S-18 × 18	94.00	41.2	91.00	42.4	86.00	50.6	81.00	51.9

Table 2. Testing performance comparison of recurrent policy networks. The policy networks used for testing are trained under Grid-16 × 16.

Grid	Asy. QMDP-net		ReplicatedQ-net		QMDP-net		Untied QMDP-net	
	SR	Time (s)	SR	Time (s)	SR	Time (s)	SR	Time (s)
16 × 16	98.00	24.0	97.00	24.1	86.00	33.5	78.00	42
32 × 32	98.00	110.5	95.00	104.4	58.00	253.9	47.00	339.7
S-32 × 32	97.00	117.6	86.00	188.8	59.00	290.8	22.00	377.7
64 × 64	92.00	1029.5	85.00	972.8	15.00	3207.6	–	–

that asynchronous QMDP-net and ReplicatedQ-net have better training performance than QMDP-net and untied QMDP-net.

Tables 1 and 2 show the comparison of testing performance between asynchronous QMDP-net, ReplicatedQ-net, QMDP-net and untied QMDP-net. As we can see from these two tables, when evaluated on new environments, asynchronous QMDP-net and ReplicatedQ-net have higher success rates and faster completion time than QMDP-net and untied QMDP-net. In tasks with relatively small environment sizes, the performance of these four networks is comparable. However, as the environment size increases, the superiorities of asynchronous QMDP-net and ReplicatedQ-net are gradually revealed. For QMDP-net and untied QMDP-net, as the size of the environment increases, the strong structure priors will bring better testing performance to the recurrent policy network. It is worth noting that as the value iteration process used in the ReplicatedQ planner module is still synchronous, it causes a certain negative impact on the training performance and the testing performance of network.

6 Conclusion

In this paper, we proposed two recurrent policy networks, asynchronous QMDP-net and ReplicatedQ-net, based on the plain QMDP-net for planning under partial observability. Asynchronous QMDP-net is obtained by integrating the asynchronous update process into the planner module of the plain QMDP-net. This significantly alleviates the problem of "curse of dimensionality" that value iteration may suffer, making the planning process more efficient and more effective in partially observable tasks. ReplicatedQ-net is obtained by partially replacing the value update rule of the QMDP algorithm used in QMDP-net with replicated Q-learning, which not only enables the network to generate policies that can take informative actions, but also reduces the difficulty of the online learning process. In the experiments, we apply some partially observable robot navigation tasks to demonstrate the effectiveness of the two proposed networks.

As future topics, we would like to explore better ways for sampling the states to be updated in the asynchronous QMDP-net to further improve the network performance. Besides, the proposed recurrent policy networks are still limited in imitation learning, we are trying to extend them to reinforcement learning.

References

1. Russell, S.J., Norvig, P.: Artificial Intelligence - A Modern Approach, 2nd Edn. Prentice Hall (2003). https://doi.org/10.1016/0004-3702(96)00007-0
2. Spaan, M.T.J., Vlassis, N.A.: Perseus: randomized point-based value iteration for POMDPs. J. Artif. Intell. Res. **24**, 195–220 (2005). https://doi.org/10.1613/jair.1659
3. Karkus, P., Hsu, D., Lee, W.S.: QMDP-Net: deep learning for planning under partial observability. In: 30th Advances Neural Information Processing Systems (NIPS), pp. 4697–4707. arXiv preprint arXiv:1703.06692 (2017)
4. Sondik, E.J.: The optimal control of partially observable markov processes over the infinite horizon: discounted costs. Oper. Res. **26**, 282–304 (1978). https://doi.org/10.1287/opre.26.2.282
5. Lovejoy, W.S.: Computationally feasible bounds for partially observed markov decision processes. Oper. Res. **39**, 162–175 (1991). https://doi.org/10.1287/opre.39.1.162
6. Kaelbling, L.P., Littman, M.L., Cassandra, A.R.: Planning and acting in partially observable stochastic domains. Artif. Intell. **101**, 99–134 (1998). https://doi.org/10.1016/S0004-3702(98)00023-X
7. Kurniawati, H., Hsu, D., Lee, W.S.: SARSOP: efficient point-based POMDP planning by approximating optimally reachable belief spaces. In: Robotics: Science and Systems (2008). https://doi.org/10.15607/rss.2008.iv.009
8. Pineau, J., Gordon, G.J., Thrun, S.: Applying metric-trees to belief-point POMDPs. In: 16th Advances Neural Information Processing Systems (NIPS), pp. 759–766 (2003)
9. Silver, D., Veness, J.: Monte-carlo planning in large POMDPs. In: 24th Advances Neural Information Processing Systems (NIPS), pp. 2164–2172 (2010)
10. Ye, N., Somani, A., Hsu, D., Lee, W.S.: DESPOT: online POMDP planning with regularization. J. Artif. Intell. Res. **58**, 231–266 (2017). https://doi.org/10.1613/jair.5328
11. Bertsekas, D.P.: Distributed asynchronous computation of fixed points. Math. Program. **27**, 107–120 (1983). https://doi.org/10.1007/bf02591967

12. Littman, M.L., Cassandra, A.R., Kaelbling, L.P.: Learning policies for partially observable environments: scaling up. In: 12th International Conference on Machine Learning (ICML), pp. 362–370 (1995). https://doi.org/10.1016/b978-1-55860-377-6.50052-9
13. Bellman, R.: Dynamic Programming. Princeton University Press, Princeton (1957)
14. Pan, Z., Zhang, Z., Chen, Z.: Asynchronous value iteration network. In: Cheng, L., Leung, A.C.S., Ozawa, S. (eds.) ICONIP 2018. LNCS, vol. 11302, pp. 169–180. Springer, Cham (2018). https://doi.org/10.1007/978-3-030-04179-3_15
15. Moore, A.W., Atkeson, C.G.: Prioritized sweeping: reinforcement learning with less data and less time. Mach. Learn., 103–130 (1993). https://doi.org/10.1007/bf00993104
16. Barto, A.G., Bradtke, S.J., Singh, S.P.: Learning to act using real-time dynamic programming. Artif. Intell. **72**, 81–138 (1995). https://doi.org/10.1016/0004-3702(94)00011-O
17. Schaul, T., Quan, J., Antonoglou, I., Silver, D.: Prioritized experience replay. In: 4th International Conference on Learning Representations (ICLR). arXiv preprint arXiv:1511.05952 (2016)
18. Aviv, T., Yi, W., Garrett, T., Sergey, L., Pieter, A.: Value iteration networks. In: 29th Advances in Neural Information Processing Systems (NIPS), pp. 2154–2162 (2016)
19. Oh, J., Singh, S., Lee, H.: Value prediction network. In: 30th Advances in Neural Information Processing Systems (NIPS), pp. 6120–6130 (2017)
20. Gupta, S., Davidson, J., Levine, S., Sukthankar, R., Malik, J.: Cognitive mapping and planning for visual navigation. In: 35th Conference on Computer Vision and Pattern Recognition (CVPR), pp. 7272–7281 (2017). https://doi.org/10.1109/cvpr.2017.769

Mixed-Reality Deep Reinforcement Learning for a Reach-to-grasp Task

Hadi Beik Mohammadi(✉), Mohammad Ali Zamani, Matthias Kerzel, and Stefan Wermter

Knowledge Technology, Department of Informatics, University of Hamburg, Hamburg, Germany
{6beik,zamani,kerzel,wermter}@informatik.uni-hamburg.de
http://www.knowledge-technology.info

Abstract. Deep Reinforcement Learning (DRL) has become successful across various robotic applications. However, DRL methods are not sample-efficient and require long learning times. We present an approach for online continuous deep reinforcement learning for a reach-to-grasp task in a mixed-reality environment: A human places targets for the robot in a physical environment; DRL for reaching these targets is carried out in simulation before actual actions are carried out in the physical environment. We extend previous work on a modified Deep Deterministic Policy Gradient (DDPG) algorithm with an architecture for online learning and evaluate different strategies to accelerate learning while ensuring learning stability. Our approach provides a neural inverse kinematics solution that increases over time its performance regarding the execution time while focusing on those areas of the Cartesian space where targets are often placed by the human operator, thus enabling efficient learning. We evaluate reward shaping and augmented targets as strategies for accelerating deep reinforcement learning and analyze the learning stability.

Keywords: Deep reinforcement learning · Visuomotor learning · Neuro-robotic models

1 Introduction

Deep continuous reinforcement learning enables physical robots to acquire visuomotor abilities by interacting with their environment. Following the paradigm of developmental robotics, this would enable the robots to master more and more challenging tasks in complex environments [3]. However, deep reinforcement learning depends on extended periods of trial-and-error learning [10] that expose robots and their environment to physical stress. Virtual environments

The authors gratefully acknowledge partial support from the German Research Foundation DFG under project CML (TRR 169) and the European Union under project SECURE (No 642667).

I. V. Tetko et al. (Eds.): ICANN 2019, LNCS 11727, pp. 611–623, 2019.
https://doi.org/10.1007/978-3-030-30487-4_47

and simulations overcome this challenge by offering fast and safe training, but transferring learned abilities from simulation to the real world can be challenging. Furthermore, neural deep reinforcement learning approaches can struggle with stability [13] and catastrophic forgetting [12], i.e., "unlearning" of acquired skills through new experiences.

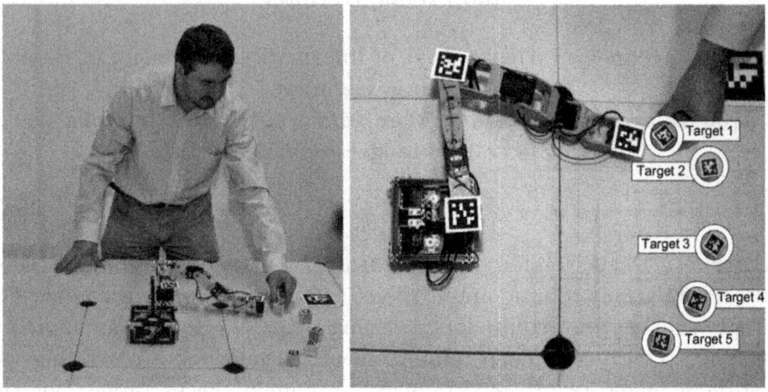

Fig. 1. Learning setup: (left) A robot arm with two degrees of freedom for planar movement uses continuous deep reinforcement learning to reach for objects marked with QR codes. Our architecture extracts the environmental information including the robot's joint length and target position, and learns to solve the specific reach-to-grasp task in its simulator. Once the learner is confident about the solution, it is deployed on the real robot. (right) Experimental setup: The robot repeatedly reaches for the targets T_1 to T_5, always in the same order. We evaluate the learning speed and the stability of different deep reinforcement learning strategies.

To address these issues we propose an architecture for online learning: usually, reach-to-grasp abilities are trained with a large number of random positions. In contrast, our approach focuses on online learning of interactively provided targets, thus avoiding extensive initial training times and attention to unused parts of the workspace. We evaluate different strategies for fast and stable learning based on a modified Deep Deterministic Policy Gradient (DDPG) [11] algorithm. We extend previous work on task simplification in a virtual simulation [9] with an integrated mixed-reality architecture that allows task-specific learning. In our experimental setup, an experimenter provides a visual target to the robot. The geometry of the arm and the target are transferred to a simulation model, where solving the specific task instance is learned. This solution is then executed with the real arm, as depicted in Fig. 1(left). The entire trial-and-error learning phase is carried out in simulation; only the final result is executed on the real robot. One advantage of this approach is that, over time, past experiences enhance the performance of the system leading to faster results as learning is progressing. We present an interactive mixed-reality experimental setup and a modified neural architecture for deep continuous reinforcement learning that takes into account task-focused learning. We evaluate different strategies to accelerate the simulated learning process. Experimental results demonstrate the ability of the approach to produce correct reach-to-grasp solutions and perform stable learning from past experiences over time.

2 Background and Related Work

2.1 Inverse Kinematics

Inverse kinematics is defined as finding a joint configuration $\Theta = \Theta_{i=1,\ldots,n}$ that moves the end effector of a robotic arm into a specified pose, e.g., reaching for a graspable object. Though this problem can be solved analytically for a small number of degrees of freedom (DoFs), it becomes intractable when the complexity of the robotic arm increases. Therefore, state-of-the-art inverse kinematics approaches utilize pseudoinverse Jacobians to minimize the pose error of a current joint configuration. Strategies like random restarts are used to overcome local minima; this is for instance used by the inverse kinematics solver TRAC-IK [2]. In contrast, solvers based on feed-forward neural networks offer constant computation time. However, they require a large amount of training data and can suffer from relatively high pose errors [5,8]. These issues can be addressed with deep reinforcement learning.

2.2 Continuous Deep Reinforcement Learning

Reinforcement learning is based on trial-and-error explorations. In the past, tabular Q-learning [18] approximates the optimal state-action value function for an agent which interacts with its environment. The policy of the agent can converge to an optimal policy which maps the given state s_t to the action a_t for which the expected return is the maximum. Tabular Q-learning was limited to a discrete state and action representation; it had no possibility for generalization over states and actions. Mnih et al. [13] introduced Deep Q-Network learning, which applies function approximation to use high dimensional raw input data, e.g., unprocessed pixel data as the state, thus enabling q-learning in a continuous state space. However, it is still limited to discrete actions.

Finally, the DDPG introduced by Lilicrap et al. [11] is an actor critic RL which uses two separate neural networks to predict the return of an action (critic: $Q(s_t, a_t; \theta^Q)$) and to suggest optimal actions (actor: $\mu(s_t; \theta^\mu)$). Like DQN, the DDPG agent uses a memory replay to record its experience, *state*, *action*, *next state* and *reward* (s_t, a_t, s_{t+1}, r_t). Since, direct using of the actor and critic networks may cause instability in target value, two target networks, actor $Q'(s_t, a_t; \theta^{Q'})$ and critic $\mu'(s_t; \theta^{\mu'})$ were used. The target networks are updated gradually toward the primary actor and critic networks. In each update, a batch of experience is sampled and the target networks are used to calculate the target value

$$y_t = r_t + \gamma Q'(s_{t+1}, \mu'(s_{t+1}; \theta^{\mu\prime}); \theta^{Q\prime}) \tag{1}$$

to train the critic network and its parameters by optimizing the following loss.

$$\min_{\theta^Q} \frac{1}{N} \sum_i (y_t - Q(s_t, a_t; \theta^Q))^2 \tag{2}$$

The actor network parameter is updated using the sampled policy gradient.

$$\nabla_{\theta^\mu} J \approx \frac{1}{N} \sum_i \nabla_a Q(s, a|\theta^Q)|_{s=s_i}^{a=\mu(s_i)} \nabla_{\theta^\mu} \mu(s|\theta^\mu)|_{s_i} \tag{3}$$

After updating both networks, the target network parameters are slowly updated

$$\theta^{Q'} \leftarrow \tau\theta^Q + (1-\tau)\theta^{Q'}, \; and \; \theta^{\mu'} \leftarrow \tau\theta^\mu + (1-\tau)\theta^{\mu'} \tag{4}$$

where $\tau \ll 1$ is the weight to slowly transfer the parameters from trainable models to a target model to gain more stability [11].

Though the proposed mixed-reality architecture can be applied to most variants of (continuous) deep reinforcement learning algorithms like the continuous actor critic learning algorithm (CACLA) [17] and continuous deep q-learning with model-based acceleration [6], we focus on the widely-used and well-established DDPG algorithm [11] and extend the work of Kerzel et al. [9] on a modified DDPG.

2.3 Accelerating Learning and Reward Shaping

One of the major challenges of deep reinforcement learning is the need for extended training periods [10]. Several approaches have been proposed to minimize the learning time: Hafez et al. [7] reward the exploration of novel areas of the state space in a curiosity-driven approach. Schaul et al. [16] implement prioritized memory sweeping [14] to select those samples from the memory that are best suited to drive the learning process.

Reward shaping [15] can guide the learning process by giving small rewards that are, e.g., proportional to the inverse of the distance to a goal. The reward-sparse task of finding a target through random exploration is transformed into the reward-rich task of following the *scent* of the strongest reward, thus accelerating learning. Kerzel et al. [9] suggest a related strategy: instead of creating a reward-rich environment, they augment the virtual size of the target in the simulation according to the difficulty of reaching the target, thus making hard-to-reach targets less difficult to reach. In our experiments, we focus on *reward shaping* and *augmented targets*, as they are representative of learning acceleration strategies that directly simplify the learning task. We evaluate the ability of these strategies especially in the context of task-specific online learning of interactively provided targets.

3 Methodology

Our proposed architecture for online deep reinforcement learning is composed of two major components, as shown in Fig. 2(left). A modified DDPG learner forms the core of the architecture. The DDPG core is connected via the *mixed-reality interface* to a physical robot, a virtual simulator of the physical robot and *visual inspector.* The robot arm and positions of possible targets, which are both marked with QR code tags, are visually analyzed by the *visual inspector.* The geometry and current configuration, as well as the position of targets, are transferred to the simulator which is used for the trial-and-error stage of deep reinforcement learning. Once the algorithm has learned to reach a given target, the commands are carried out on the real robot.

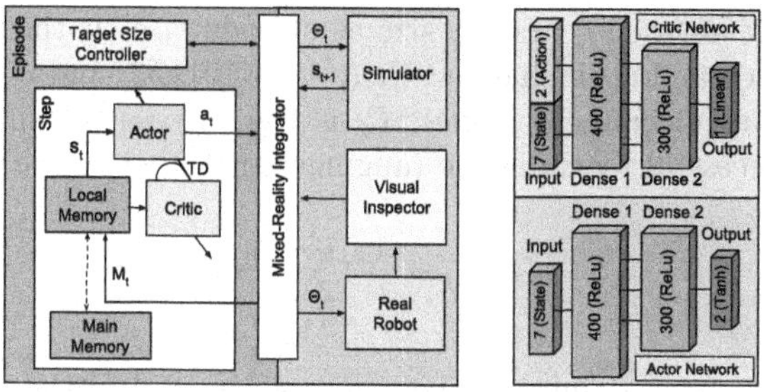

Fig. 2. Left: Architecture for online continuous deep reinforcement learning based on modified DDPG algorithm. Right: Detailed neural architecture of actor and critic.

3.1 Problem Description

Given a target position in 2D, $X^T = [x_1, x_2]$, the joint lengths $L = [l_1, l_2]$ and the initial joint configuration $\Theta_0 = [\theta_0^1, \theta_0^2]$, our goal is to find the final joint configuration $\Theta_t = [\theta_t^1, \theta_t^2]$ where $\|X_{\Theta_t} - X^T\| \leq \rho$ and X_{Θ_t} is the end-effector position corresponding to Θ_t joint configuration at the time step t and ρ is the tolerated error which is the radius of the circle around the object.

3.2 Accelerating Learning with Augmented Targets

One approach to solve this problem (3.1) is to use vanilla DDPG [11]. The agent receives a big reward (here 10) when the end-effector is within the tolerated distance to the target position, and a small reward for every time step (here −0.01).

$$r_t = \begin{cases} 10, & if\ \|X_{\Theta_t} - X^T\| \leq \rho \\ -0.01, & otherwise \end{cases} \tag{5}$$

However, this reward is too sparse to train the agent efficiently. Therefore, we propose an adaptive approach that adjusts the reachability of the target based on the approach by Kerzel et al. [9]. We simplify the task by training a "larger-than-life" target. Keeping the previous reward function, we adjust the augmented target size based on the obtained success during the training. We increase the target size if the agent fails consecutively to reach the target and decrease it when the agent succeeds consecutively to reach the target.

The adaptive target size defined as

$$\tilde{\rho}(e) = \begin{cases} \rho, & if\ e < e_\zeta \\ \tilde{\rho}(e-1) + \delta^+, if & \eta(10,\ e) < P_\zeta,\ \ e \geq e_\zeta,\ \tilde{\rho}(e) < \tilde{\rho}_{max} \\ \tilde{\rho}(e-1) - \delta^-, if & \eta(10,\ e) \geq P_\zeta,\ \ e \geq e_\zeta,\ \tilde{\rho}(e) < \tilde{\rho}_{min} \\ \rho, & if\ \ \eta(10,\ e) = 1,\ \ \ e \geq e_\zeta,\ \tilde{\rho}(e) = \rho \\ \tilde{\rho}(e-1), & otherwise \end{cases} \tag{6}$$

where $\tilde{\rho}(e)$ is the augmented target size at episode e, e_ζ is the episode number which the size remaining unchanged (here it is 10). δ^+ and δ^- are the target size increment and decrement values. P_ζ is the success threshold and $\eta(k,\ e)$ indicates the success in reaching the (augmented) target in the past k episodes

$$\eta(k,\ e) = \frac{1}{k} \sum_{e'=e-k}^{e} S_{e'} \tag{7}$$

where S_e is the success/failure of the agent at the end of the episode e (when the episode terminates $t = Tr$).

$$S_e = \begin{cases} 1, if\ \|X_{\Theta_{t=Tr}} - X^T\| \leq \tilde{\rho}(e) \\ 0, if\ \|X_{\Theta_{t=Tr}} - X^T\| > \tilde{\rho}(e) \end{cases} \tag{8}$$

We chose $\delta^+ > \delta^-$ so that the augmented target size grows fast but shrinks slowly to ensure that the difficulty to reach the target does not increase abruptly.

3.3 Accelerating Learning with Reward Shaping

For comparison, we also evaluated a more direct form of reward shaping by giving small rewards based on the change in the distance between the end-effector and the target according to the following formula:

$$rs_t = \frac{\|X_{\Theta_{t-1}} - X^T\| - \|X_{\Theta_t} - X^T\|}{\|X_{\Theta_{t-1}} - X^T\|} \tag{9}$$

where rs_t is the reward calculated by reward shaping at the time step t; however, rs_t is limited to the interval $[-0.05, 0.05]$ to stabilize the rewards.

3.4 Modified DDPG

The agent's experiences (s_t, a_t, r_t, s_{t+1}) are recorded in a memory. The state (s_t) is composed of

$$\begin{aligned} s_t = [&sin(\theta_t^1),\ cos(\theta_t^1),\ sin(\theta_t^2),\ cos(\theta_t^2), \\ &r_t^{target},\ sin(\theta_t^{target}),\ cos(\theta_t^{target})] \end{aligned} \tag{10}$$

where $(r^{target},\ \theta^{target})$ is the polar coordinate of the target position. If the target is augmented, these experiences are also among the recorded samples. Since these

Algorithm 1 Modified DDPG Algorithm [11]

Initialize critic θ^Q and actor θ^μ networks
Create target networks $\theta^{Q'} \leftarrow \theta^Q$ and $\theta^{\mu'} \leftarrow \theta^\mu$
Initialize main and local replay buffer R_M, R_L
while Agent has NOT learned all *Objects* **do**
  for *object* in *Objects* **do**
    obtain the position of the *object*
    $R_L \leftarrow R_M$
    while Agent has NOT finished the fine tune **do**
      Receive initial observation state s_0
      Define the augmented target size $\tilde{\rho}_e$
      for t = 0, MaxStepNumber **do**
        Perform action $a_t = \mu(s_t; \theta)$
        if $\tilde{\rho}_e > \rho$ **then**
          $R_L \overset{Store}{\leftarrow} (s_t, a_t, r_t, s_{t+1})$
        else
          $R_L, R_M \overset{Store}{\leftarrow} (s_t, a_t, r_t, s_{t+1})$
        end if
        Update the actor and critic network (eq. 1-4)
      end for
    end while
  end for
end while

experiences are only transient goals to help the agent, we clean the main memory from the augmented target experiences after the agent has learned to reach the object. However, the local memory which is initialized by the main memory at the beginning of each task-specific learning cycle records every experience [9]. In other words, the local memory's content is used for learning to reach one specific target. Therefore, a mixture of novel and old experiences enables learning to reach the new target without catastrophic forgetting [12] regarding the already learned targets.

4 Experiments, Results, Discussion

4.1 Robot Platform and Simulator

The robot platform used for our experiments is a 2 DoFs serial manipulator. The joints are rotational servo motors with absolute encoders, and they are specially designed for accurate target angle controlling. The length of each link is adjustable. The setup also provides a ceiling camera to capture top-view images which facilitate the detection process, as depicted in Fig. 1. Each target object is associated with a unique QR code The physical specification of the manipulator like the base coordinate frame and the length of each link is calculated and stored to be transferred to the simulator. The link length is calculated by the distance between the centroids of two consecutive joints and end-effector The simulator is the central executing component for learning. The input of the simulator is a relative angle command, and the output is the position of the end-effector. The control frequency is about one KHz and therefore well suited for the requirements of deep reinforcement learning.

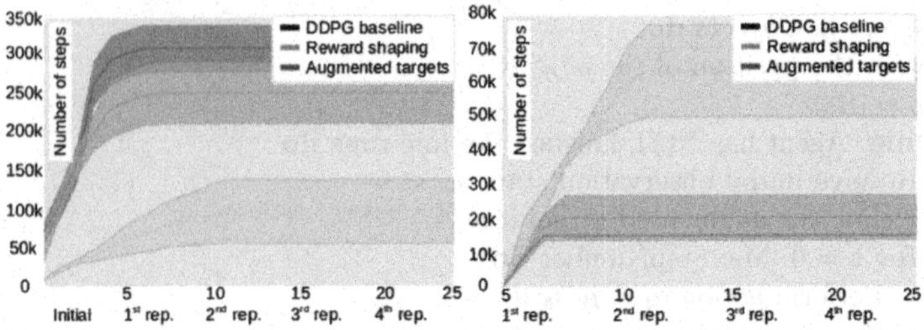

Fig. 3. The accumulated number of training steps to reach the targets T_1 to T_5 five times. Left: The number of all training steps. The X-axis indicates the target number, we train the network to reach each of the five objects repeatedly. The unmodified DDPG baseline requires the most training steps, and the reward shaping condition requires the least. Right: When only accumulating the steps for re-learning already visited targets, the *baseline*, and *augmented targets* condition provide more stable learning.

4.2 Experimental Design

As shown in Fig. 1(right), five targets are placed in the robot's workspace. In our mixed-reality setup, first, the joint lengths and target positions are extracted through the *Vision Inspector* to construct the simulator robot model.

We evaluate the use of three different learning strategies: in the *baseline* condition, we use an unmodified DDPG algorithm, in the *augmented targets* condition, we adapt the target size dynamically according to learning success as described in Sect. 3.2, and in the *reward shaping* condition we give direct rewards for just approaching the target as detailed in Sect. 3.3. Each experimental condition is executed five times to avoid confounding effects or random initialization.

The robot starts with the first target T_1; in simulation, a solution to reach for the target is learned and then executed on the real robot. The architecture then moves on to learn a solution for the second target T_2 and so on until all five targets have been reached. This is the initial phase, in which each target is novel for the agent. We evaluate the number of (simulated) learning steps it takes in each condition to learn to reach all five targets. In the second phase, the targets are re-visited in the same order four times. This way, we evaluate if learning to reach a target accelerates over the lifetime of the DRL agent. We hypothesize that every time the same target is supplied, the agent learns to reach the object faster.

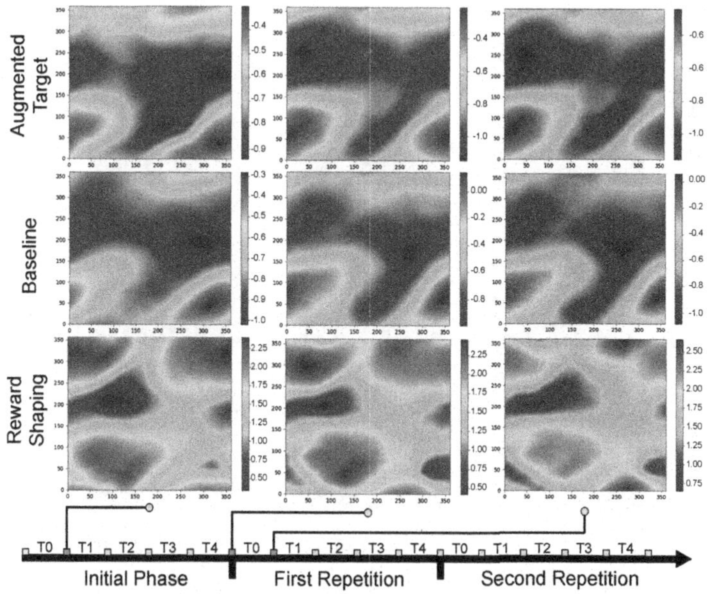

Fig. 4. Visualization of the critic network in joint space. For each experimental condition, the maps show the expected reward for each configuration in the joint space given the target T_1. The rows indicate the training approach and the columns indicate different phases of learning. In each small plot, the X-axis indicates the values of the first joint and the Y-axis indicates the values of the second joint. Regarding the critic value, the *baseline* and *augmented target* approaches are less sensitive compared to *reward shaping* when they are introduced to four new targets.

4.3 Implementation

We implemented our modified DDPG model in Keras [4] with a Tensorflow back end [1]. The hyper-parameters and neural network architecture are adapted from Kerzel et al. [9]. The networks for critic and actor both consist of two dense layers with 400 and 300 units, see Fig. 2(right). We use a low-level input feature vector of the target position in polar space and the current joint configuration in joint space. The outputs are the relative joint values in the range from -1 to 1 from the current value of the motor. For training, we use the Adam optimizer with a learning rate of 10^{-4} for the actor and 2×10^{-4} for the critic. Rectified Linear Unit (ReLU) is used as activation function for all layers except for the last layer of the actor network which produces the joint angles with a hyperbolic tangent function (tanh).

4.4 Results

The results are depicted in Fig. 3(left). As expected, the DDPG *baseline* requires the most training steps to reach all five targets for the first time while the strong

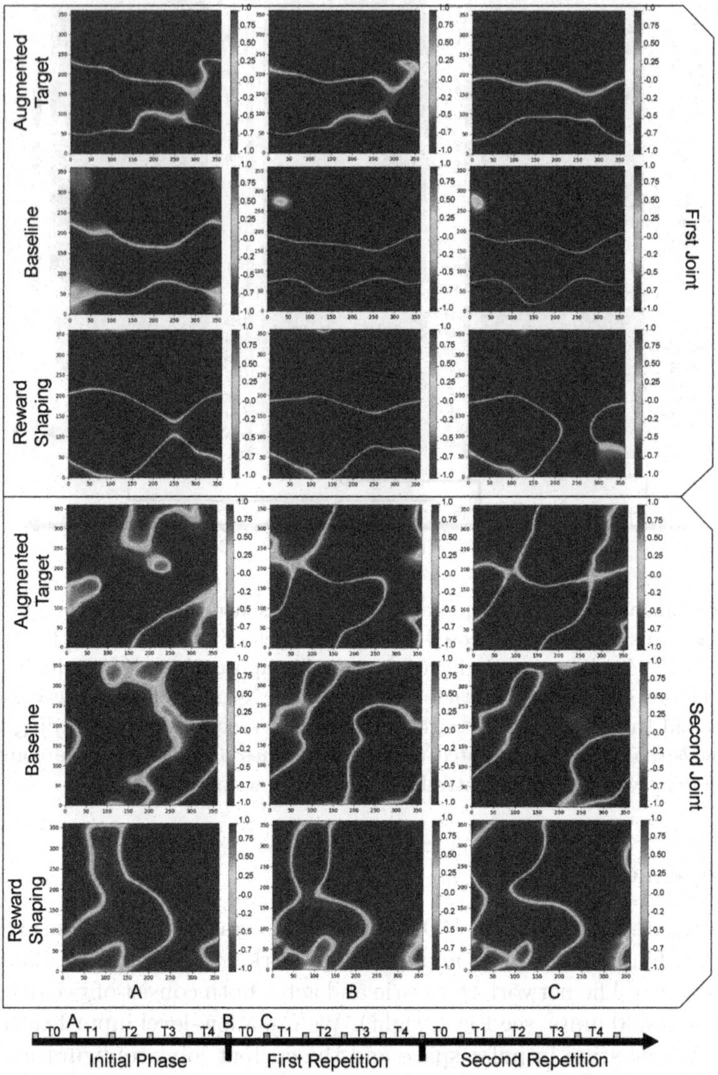

Fig. 5. Visualization of the actor network in joint space. For each experimental condition, the maps show the best action for each state (configuration in the joint space given the targets T_1). The rows indicate the training approach and the columns indicate different phases of learning. In each small plot, the X-axis indicates the values of the first joint and the Y-axis indicates the values of the second joint. The colors in the maps indicate the relative joint values. Similar to critic maps, the actor maps of *baseline* and *augmented target* for the first joint are less sensitive after new targets are introduced. For the second joint, interestingly, learning new targets has improved the action map. This means that despite generating a visually irregular map in the initial phase, the agent has relatively improved the policy. (Color figure online)

reward shaping needs the least number of training steps. The *augmented targets* strategy performs slightly better than the *baseline*. To analyze the stability of the learning, we accumulate the number of training steps it takes to re-learn the targets in the repetitions following the initial learning phase, as shown in Fig. 3(right). The *reward shaping* turns out to be less stable than the other two conditions and needs to relearn targets while the *baseline* and *augmented targets* conditions remain mostly stable. We believe the instability in *reward shaping* is caused by the strong reward signal guiding the agent toward the target and satisfying the learning objective immaturely. For further analysis, we take a closer look at the learning process by visualizing the critic network as expected reward maps, see Fig. 4. Figure 5 shows a visual representation of an actor map (Policy) for every possible given action to reach a specific target (T_1) in workspace. As our experimental setup uses a 2-DoFs robot arm, it is easy to visualize what the critic learned as a planar map. We focus on the critic network as the actor network is indirectly trained by a gradient transfer from the critic network.

For each experimental condition, we depict the *critic map* for the first and second visit to target T_1. Other targets serve as a distractor to perturb the learning. For stable learning, we expect the initial critic map for the repeated visit of T_1 to be mostly identical to the final map from the first visit. This is not the case for the *reward shaping condition* but true for the other two conditions. Meanwhile in actor map *baseline* and *augmented target* for the first joint are less sensitive after new targets are introduced. For the second joint, learning new targets helped the agent to relatively improve the policy. This means that despite generating a visually irregular map in the initial phase, the agent has relatively improved the policy. Our approach faces the same limitations for transferring learned policies from simulation to the real world based on the accuracy of sensors, actuators and the simulation itself. However, by using the simulation only when requested, we focus the learning process more precisely towards the actions requested by the user.

In summary, the results show that our approach enables stable online learning in a reach-to-grasp task. Different strategies to accelerate the learning can be used depending on the task requirements: learning novel targets can be strongly accelerated by *reward shaping* or more stable learning can be achieved with *augmented targets*. Our approach can be generalized to related deep reinforcement tasks, as long as a suitable way of transferring the state of the physical system into a virtual simulation and a strategy to accelerate learning (by reward shaping, augmenting the targets or another method) are available.

5 Conclusion

We present an approach for online continuous deep reinforcement learning in a mixed-reality environment for a reach-to-grasp task. Based on visual markers, the geometry of the robotic arm and target are transferred to an internal simulation. The approach enables an interactive and secure human-robot collaboration.

A non-expert user can operate a physical robot by intuitive instructions via placing a sequence of physical targets. Our modified DDPG algorithm focuses on learning to reach the interactively supplied target; once a solution is found, it is carried out on a real robot.

In contrast to other neural approaches, our online learning approach does not require initial training. Once a target is given, the algorithm focuses on learning to reach it. With each new target, more training samples are generated and used for learning. The approach can use different strategies to speed up the learning process. Depending on priorities, reward shaping can accelerate learning novel targets, or adaptive targets can lead to more stable learning. In future work, we will evaluate dynamic mechanisms to balance strategies for learning acceleration and automated adaptation of hyper-parameters according to the learning progress. Also, the approach will be applied to a more complex robot arm.

References

1. Abadi, M., et al.: TensorFlow: large-scale machine learning on heterogeneous distributed systems. arXiv preprint arXiv:1603.04467 (2016)
2. Beeson, P., Ames, B.: TRAC-IK: an open-source library for improved solving of generic inverse kinematics. In: 2015 IEEE-RAS 15th International Conference on Humanoid Robots (Humanoids), pp. 928–935. IEEE (2015). https://doi.org/10.1109/HUMANOIDS.2015.7363472
3. Cangelosi, A., Schlesinger, M.: Developmental Robotics: From Babies to Robots. MIT Press, Cambridge (2015). https://doi.org/10.7551/mitpress/9320.001.0001
4. Chollet, F., et al.: Keras (2015). https://github.com/keras-team/keras
5. Daya, B., Khawandi, S., Akoum, M.: Applying neural network architecture for inverse kinematics problem in robotics. J. Softw. Eng. Appl. **3**(03), 230 (2010). https://doi.org/10.4236/jsea.2010.33028
6. Gu, S., Lillicrap, T., Sutskever, I., Levine, S.: Continuous deep Q-learning with model-based acceleration. In: International Conference on Machine Learning, pp. 2829–2838 (2016). http://dl.acm.org/citation.cfm?id=3045390.3045688
7. Hafez, B., Weber, C., Wermter, S.: Curiosity-driven exploration enhances motor skills of continuous actor-critic learner. In: Proceedings of the 7th Joint IEEE International Conference on Development and Learning and on Epigenetic Robotics (ICDL-EpiRob), pp. 39–46 (2017). https://doi.org/10.1109/DEVLRN.2017.8329785
8. Jha, P., Biswal, B.: A neural network approach for inverse kinematic of a scara manipulator. IAES Int. J. Rob. Autom. **3**(1), 52 (2014). https://doi.org/10.11591/ijra.v3i1.3201
9. Kerzel, M., Beik-Mohammadi, H., Zamani, M.A., Wermter, S.: Accelerating deep continuous reinforcement learning through task simplification (2018). https://doi.org/10.1109/IJCNN.2018.8489712
10. Levine, S., Pastor, P., Krizhevsky, A., Quillen, D.: Learning hand-eye coordination for robotic grasping with large-scale data collection. In: Kulić, D., Nakamura, Y., Khatib, O., Venture, G. (eds.) ISER 2016. SPAR, vol. 1, pp. 173–184. Springer, Cham (2017). https://doi.org/10.1007/978-3-319-50115-4_16

11. Lillicrap, T.P., et al.: Continuous control with deep reinforcement learning. arXiv preprint arXiv:1509.02971 (2015)
12. McCloskey, M., Cohen, N.J.: Catastrophic interference in connectionist networks: the sequential learning problem. Psychol. Learn. Motiv. **24**, 109–165 (1989). https://doi.org/10.1016/S0079-7421(08)60536-8
13. Mnih, V., et al.: Human-level control through deep reinforcement learning. Nature **518**(7540), 529–533 (2015). https://doi.org/10.1038/nature14236
14. Moore, A.W., Atkeson, C.G.: Prioritized sweeping: reinforcement learning with less data and less time. Mach. Learn. **13**(1), 103–130 (1993). https://doi.org/10.1007/BF00993104
15. Ng, A.Y., Harada, D., Russell, S.J.: Policy invariance under reward transformations: theory and application to reward shaping. In: Proceedings of the Sixteenth International Conference on Machine Learning, pp. 278–287, ICML 1999. Morgan Kaufmann Publishers Inc., San Francisco (1999). http://dl.acm.org/citation.cfm?id=645528.657613
16. Schaul, T., Quan, J., Antonoglou, I., Silver, D.: Prioritized experience replay. arXiv preprint arXiv:1511.05952 (2015)
17. Van Hasselt, H., Wiering, M.A.: Reinforcement learning in continuous action spaces. In: IEEE International Symposium on Approximate Dynamic Programming and Reinforcement Learning, ADPRL 2007, pp. 272–279. IEEE (2007). https://doi.org/10.1109/ADPRL.2007.368199
18. Watkins, C.J., Dayan, P.: Q-learning. Mach. Learn. **8**(3–4), 279–292 (1992). https://doi.org/10.1007/BF00992698

FMNet: Multi-agent Cooperation by Communicating with Featured Message Network

Jiheng Jiang, Shuangjiu Xiao(✉), and Linling Xun

Shanghai Jiao Tong University,
No. 800, Dongchuan Road, Minhang District, Shanghai, China
fidy1995@sjtu.edu.cn, xsjiu99@cs.sjtu.edu.cn,
xl194@163.com

Abstract. Multi-agent systems are taking great part in nowadays industries. Cooperative environments may help agents perform better, but the training process is usually time consuming and costly. Although the training process can be speeded up by communicating with important information (such as observations, action sequence, model data and other potential data) between agents, redundant information is still a disturbance term. In this paper, we present a method, called Featured Message Network, which uses a fixed random network to extract features of information from agents as featured message. By communicating with featured messages, agents can cooperate more efficiently while not suffering from useful information loss or redundant information disturbing. We optimized a traditional Deep Q-learning system with our method. We tested our method on Meeting in a Grid problem and experimental results show that training process becomes faster and more stable with our method.

Keywords: Cooperative multi-agent system · Multi-agent reinforcement learning · Featured message · Deep Q-learning

1 Introduction

Multi-agent systems are having a wide range of uses in nowadays industries, including self-driving automobiles, robot swarms, smart home, etc. Many of the recent researches showed that agents in a cooperative environment may perform better [14, 31, 37]. However, these models usually need long time to train, and always rely on excellent hardware resources.

Agent communication is proved to help agents cooperate better in many environments with different tasks. The communication needs information from the other agent including observations, action sequence, model data, and other potential information. Sukhbaatar et al. sends the information to a mean filter, and then communicate among all agents, to make them aware of joint action [35]. Foerster et al. has introduced a communicate mechanism where every agent send all raw information every frame to other agents, solving a few social dilemmas and riddles efficiently [13].

Although agent communication achieved success, there are still problems that could disrupt the training progress. The most serious problem is that agent information

I. V. Tetko et al. (Eds.): ICANN 2019, LNCS 11727, pp. 624–635, 2019.
https://doi.org/10.1007/978-3-030-30487-4_48

is always redundant, which makes training and communication inefficient. The agent's Q-learning network should not only determine the next action, but also needed to calculate the information from other agents. If agents communicate with not raw information but more concise messages which can still express the situation of agents, the amount of computation could be reduced, and the communication efficiency could be guaranteed. Inspired by this idea, we present a supplement network in a Deep Q-learning system to improve the communication efficiency and the training speed, called Featured Message Network or FMNet, which makes communication messages simple and clear by extracting feature of information from each agent separately.

Our FMNet receives raw information from the agent as its input. Then the input is processed with a fixed random network, which can roughly extract the features of the information and outputs a low-dimensioned featured message. Similar featured messages should be output from FMNet while agents meet similar situations, which indicate experience refining. The faster and more stable the experience formed, the faster and more stable training is guaranteed for effective multi-agent cooperation.

There are several main contributions in this paper. Firstly, we proposed a featured message network used in cooperative multi-agent system to make agents cooperation perform better. Secondly, we present an optimized multi-agent Deep Q-Learning system to achieve agent cooperation in a partial-observable environment. We tested our method by a series of experiments, comparing with other information exchanging methods. The result showed that our method could shorten the training processing and reduce the fail rate in the course of Deep Q-learning multi-agent cooperating.

2 Related Work

2.1 Multi-agent Reinforcement Learning Frameworks

Reinforcement Learning, or RL, is a well-developed category in machine learning. It focus on learning how to react with a certain environment [36]. Multi-agent RL, however, is much more difficult than single agent situations. Bowling and Veloso has pointed out that multi-agent environments are inherently non-stationary, which could cause unstableness in the learning process [6].

The problem still remains when Mnih et al. introduced deep neural networks into Q-learning [27]. They then established the experience replay technique which sample from previous experience to ensure the data is independent, and thus improve the stableness in single agent settings [28]. Foerster et al. has introduced stabilized experience replay in MARL [15]. Yang et al. implements a mean field Q-learning, which approximates agents as a single agent [39].

There are also works based on policy gradient. Benerjee and Peng has extended the WoLF(Win or Learn Fast) [7] with policy gradient, which makes it accurate in more complex games [3]. The deep learning approach occurred when Lillicrap et al. introduced the actor-critic architecture with DQN, named Deep Deterministic Policy Gradient [25]. After that, several algorithms has been proposed, including TRPO [33] and PPO [34]. OpenAI trained their agents with these methods and has beaten amateur human players in Dota2, a five to five competitive game [26]. These methods are straightforward to find the optimal, which need huge amount of calculation resources.

Most of the multi-agent systems in real world is partially observable. Bernstein et al. defined it mathematically as Dec-POMDP, or Decentralized Partially Observable Markov Decision Progress [4]. After that, several standard Dec-POMDP problems are introduced, including Decentralized Tiger [29], Broadcast Channel [16], Meeting in a Grid [1, 2, 5] and other problems. Ishii et al. has developed an approximation method to estimate unobservable states [19]. Omidshafiei et al. has worked on Meeting in a Grid problem with multi-task settings with modified DRQN and achieved success on high dimensions [30]. We tested our method on these problems, but with quite different settings, where communications are not allowed in the original problems.

Google has proposed a toolbox called Tensorforce, which implements DQN and policy gradients with their own training framework Tensorflow [32]. In our experiments, we use this to implement our neural agents.

2.2 Cooperative Multi-agent Systems

Multi-agent system is a system that contains a running environment, objects and agents which are the only ones to act [12]. For years researchers work on the topic of finding out how agents can really cooperate with each other.

One of the most popular topics is to solve the social dilemmas, or general-sum games. De Cote et al. has introduced several modified principles of Q-learning to make the agents more cooperative [10]. Yu et al. claimed unmodified algorithm of reinforcement learning would lead to converge to the Nash equilibrium. They proposed emotional learning to modify the learning behaviors of agents so that they can cooperate [40]. Foerster has noticed the importance of data from other agents, and raised Learning with Opponent-Learning Awareness [14]. Although communication is forbidden in these problems, information of other agents can still help them to cooperate.

Another cooperate method is to train a global value function, where agents are influenced by not only the environment but also a global policy. Before the introduction of neural networks, Kok and Vlassis implemented the traditional Q-learning method. They used a sparse representation of the joint state-action space make the agents learn a global policy [21, 22]. Varshavskaya et al. implemented an agreement algorithm to take the average value of robot parameters as the whole controller, which could be considered as global policy [38]. QMIX which took a central network that combined all the Q-values of agents and outputs a joint action can help agents perform tactics [31].

Neural agents are proved to have the potential to communicate in (natural) language and cooperate. Lazaridou et al. and Havrylov et al. implemented a descriptive problem and make agents guess from the information from others [17, 24]. Cao et al. has implemented the negotiate problem where two agents have to take things from the table and achieve highest points [9]. The two communicate channels, proposal and language can both help agents negotiate and cooperate, but from the test result we know objective information is more stable than language.

3 Method

3.1 Featured Message Network

Information from other agents is helpful, but also could be redundant, which can disturb the Q-network with huge amount of calculation and could cause waste in time. If information could be represented in a concise form and not suffering information loss at the same time, then the training efficiency could be improved.

We also argue that this is more likely to be the way when human communicate to each other in a collaborative task solving situation. Imagine when in a football game, the coach or players want to play a certain tactic, they would not say all the details about the play – players already know how to deal with it, and a whole play needs lots of time to explain. Instead, they could only say a few keywords, or just yell out some specific numbers, then all players should know the meaning. In that case, that short form of the tactic is a featured message sending to all players (Fig. 1).

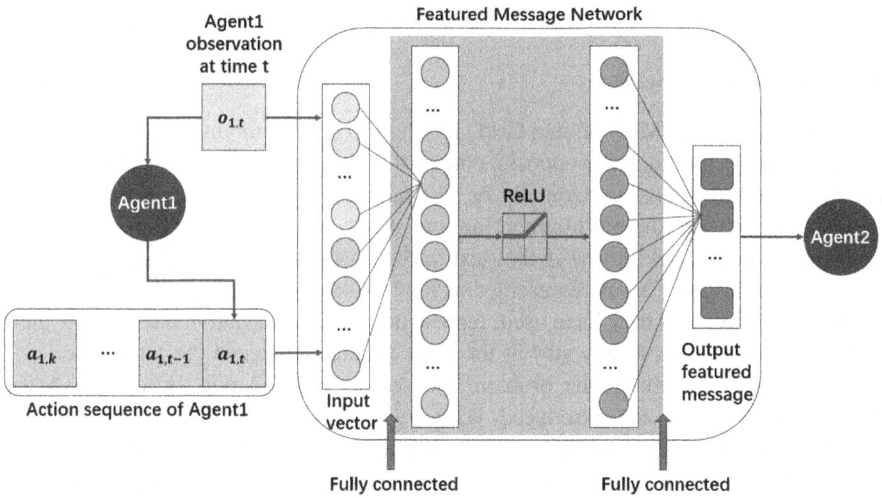

Fig. 1. Workflow with featured message network

Inspired by this idea, we propose a Featured Message Network pre-processing the information before sending to the other agent to reduces the calculation and improve the accuracy. We introduce a fixed function $f(\theta) : \{\mathcal{O}, \mathcal{A}\} \rightarrow \mathbb{R}^k$ before the information is sent. The function takes the observation and action sequence of one agent as input, and outputs a feature vector representing the agent's states. The function could be considered as a black box to the other agent. Agents do not need to be aware of how the information forms. The only thing they should do is to learn the feature by their own observations and rewards, and turn them into convinced experience.

In our practice, we used a fixed random network as the function. This ensures when meeting similar situations, the function generates similar output [8]. The network consist of two fully connected layer, where the parameters $\hat{\theta}$ is chosen randomly according to the normalized Gaussian distribution. There is a ReLU activation function between two layers to avoid negative outputs. Then it goes through another fully connected layer. Finally, we do a floor operation to the output to easier the calculation. We presented the mathematical form of our network as

$$f(x;\theta) = \lfloor F_2(ReLU(F_1(x;\theta_1));\theta_2) \rfloor, \quad (1)$$

where $x = (o_{1,t}, a_{1,k}, \ldots, a_{1,t})$, and $ReLU(z) = \max(0, z)$.

We have noticed that in the traditional classification methods, the classifier is evolving during the training. This is not a suitable case in our method. Firstly, the neural agents will be easier to train when they receive the same observation in the same states. If a different message is given under a similar situation, the network would be unstable. Secondly, we cannot tell the features are correct or not, or there is not a standard for the features. The features are automatically learnt according to the running rewards by the neural network of agents. Adjusting parameters of the function is difficult and unnecessary.

3.2 Environment Setting

We have chosen the "Meeting in a Grid" problem to be our running environment. Two smart agents are placed at the opposite corner of a finite square chess board with length L, where they can move horizontally or vertically one unit at a time. Before moving, they should observe the environment around them. Although agents are invisible to each other, they should know if they can move to the adjacent squares on their up, down, left and right. This is represented as a 4d vector as $v_i \in \{0, 1\}$. They also know about how many turns they have used, represented as a non-negative integer. The game ends when two agents finally stay at the same square, or exceed the turn limit T.

In the very beginning, the problem focused on a 2 * 2 grid. After that, higher dimensioned problems are introduced. We have chosen both 2 * 2 and 3 * 3 grid. The coordinate of the grid starts at (1, 1), which can make the calculation easier.

We have set the turn limit T to restrict the explore space of one complete run. This may cause the network not to converge in a very short period of time, but a proper limit can avoid stochastic policies. The total possible states of the grid can be measured as $S = (L^2)^2$, which equals 81 different states in our experiment. We have chosen $T = L^3$ as the limit.

The agents receive a fixed penalty $-r_p$ every turn unless they meet at the same position. In order to normalize the reward easily, agents will be rewarded $r_m = T \times r_p$ when they succeed in meeting in time. In conclusion, the total reward in one run would be $R = r_m - t \times r_p = (T - t) \times r_p$. The normalization is used for data statistics, in which we divide the reward with the max possible reward. We can clearly see that the value closest to 1 achieves the best policy.

3.3 Agent Architecture

The agents are implemented with an optimized Deep Q-learning architecture. We have implemented our FMNet as a supplement module of the traditional DQN. We only show how agent 1 sends featured message and how agent 2 act with featured message in one turn in Fig. 2, because the workflow of both agents are the same.

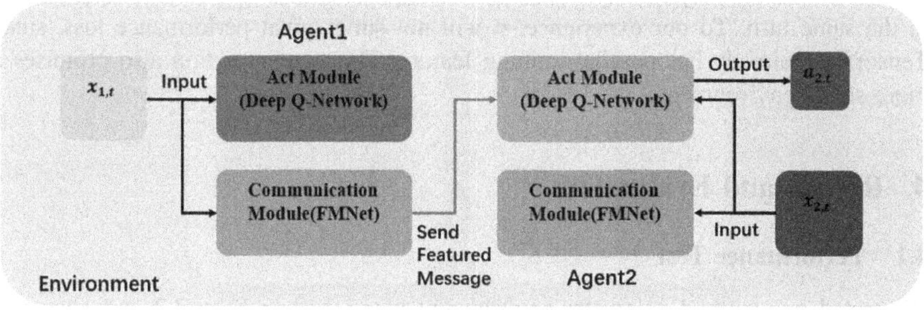

Fig. 2. Agent2 workflow in one turn

Agents are initially placed at the two opposite corners of the grid, with position coordinates $(1, L)$ and $(L, 1)$. For every turn, every agent i receives a vector $o_{i,t} = (\boldsymbol{p}, t)$ as its observation, where 4d vector $\boldsymbol{p}$ represents the adjacent square of the current position of the agent, and non-negative integer t represents turns they have used. Agents are unaware of which position they are currently staying at, but with other information, the position can be easily judged.

After the observation, agents are intended to send a message to the other. The observation $o_{i,t}$ and the action sequence $A_{i,t} = \{a_{i,k}, \ldots, a_{i,t}\}$ is combined and sent to the FMNet as input. The network outputs a vector $\boldsymbol{c}_i$, which stands for the featured message as mentioned in Sect. 3.1. In order to make comparison, we have also tested no information exchange and all raw information exchange. In these cases, $\boldsymbol{c}_i$ is replaced according to communication method, and the length of it may vary.

Then agents are intended to move either up, left, right, down, or stay at where they are. These actions are represented as continuous integers where $a_i \in [0, 4], a_i \in \mathbb{N}$. The movements are chosen by the agent's neural network. The network receives the observation and the featured message from the other agent as input. The network aims at predicting the Q-value as the Bellman equation [11] goes:

$$Q(s_t, a_t) = r_{t+1} + \gamma\, max_a\, Q(s_{t+1}, a) \quad (2)$$

The DQN is combined with an RNN and four dense layers with different activation functions. Firstly, the input vector is sent into the RNN part with two LSTM cells. The RNN outputs a vector as its learnt feature. Then the vector inputs in a network combined with four fully connected layers, two as a group. In each group, the activation function is ReLU and Softmax sequentially. Finally, the network outputs a Q-table, and choose the action with the maximum future Q-value.

Thanks to Google Tensorforce [23], we built the network easily without caring about the implementation of the network and its loss function. The loss function is just as usual [27]:

$$L = \{r_t + \gamma \times max_{a'} Q'\left(s_{t+1}, a'\right) - Q(s_t, a_t)\}^2 \tag{3}$$

We did not have a parallel architecture. The agents choose their actions sequentially in the same turn. To our experience, it will not suffer great performance loss, since Tensorforce already has parallel training feature. The sequent action also promises a more stable environment.

4 Results and Evaluation

4.1 Performance Test

We tested our method using the environment mentioned in Sect. 3.2 and agents in Sect. 3.3. We have set the fixed reward r_p to 1, so that the calculation will be easier. We chose $\gamma = 0.95$ and learning rate 0.001 with Adam optimizer [20]. The agents' neural network is rather small, so the difference will be significant.

Our FMNet is established as Sect. 3.1 described, where we have two fixed dense layers connected by a ReLU activation function. The input of the network is $\boldsymbol{x} = (o_{1,t}, a_{1,k}, \ldots, a_{1,t})$, as we took $k = t - 4$ which makes $\boldsymbol{x}$ a 8d vector. The network outputs a 4d featured message which means we reduced the volume of communication by 50%. The network is initialized with random numbers from normal distribution. Parameters of our FMNet are all fixed since the same observations will always generate the same output, which makes the DQN stable. We also argue that random parameter have little effect to the result. We will prove it with a random parameter influence test in Sect. 4.2.

During our experiment, we observed the output and reward of the network. There are several states of the network: (1) Running. The network is not stable and the policy is still stochastic. (2) Not converging. The network does not converge to a stable state, as the policy does not always lead to finishing the task. (3) Converging. The agents have learnt the policy and finish the task every time with same actions.

Due to the unstableness of the neural networks, we have set the training limit up to 2×10^4 episodes. If the network could not converge in time, this training will be marked as failed to converge. Otherwise, if the network is stable (e.g. continuously outputs same action and gain same reward in 1000 episodes), the episode number and final converging reward would be recorded. In order to get a convinced result, we repeatedly run the game with different initial values of the Q-network of agents. During the training, our FMNet is not re-generated.

We chose three other methods as comparison: no information exchanged, all raw information exchanged, and an agreement method. We run the game 250 times for each method. Table 1 showed the converging episode and reward and fail rate of the three method in 3 * 3 grid running environment.

Table 1. Results in 3 * 3 grid of different communication methods.

Information type	Average converging episode	Average converging reward	Fail to converge in time rate (%)
No information	8019	**0.950**	11
Raw information	7464	**0.949**	11
Agreement/Mean	7253	**0.950**	25
Our method	**6030**	**0.952**	**6**

The result showed that our method can roughly reduce the fail rate by half. Our method also has the lowest average converging episode. Although we have seen a very small fluctuate in the converging reward, we think that is caused by system error, and we can say all methods can achieve the best policy. We also seen the agreement method which use a mean Q-learning framework fails far more than other situations. That is because calculating the joint action directly need much more calculation resources which we did not provide, since the action space increases exponentially. We can conclude from the result that training process is the fastest and the most stable with our method among all the tested methods.

4.2 Optimizing FMNet

Our FMNet reduces the volume of the communication by compressing complex information into a simpler feature vector form. There are two possible factors that could influence the effect of our FMNet. One is the volume of the featured messages; the other is the quality of random number. So we designed a volume of communication test and a random parameter test.

Since our method does not reduce the number of communications, we tested how different volume of messages could affect agents. The volume of output must be smaller than input, otherwise it would be meaningless. We chose three typical volumes: 25%, 50% and 75% of input. That makes the network output a 2d, 4d or 6d feature message. The result of our volume test is shown as follows (Table 2).

Table 2. Results in 3 * 3 grid of different volume of communication.

Output volume (of input)	Average converging episode	Average converging reward	Fail to converge in time rate (%)
25%	6714	**0.949**	9
50%	**6030**	**0.952**	**6**
75%	6585	**0.948**	10
(Raw)	7464	**0.949**	11

This result is in line with our expectations. Longer messages would disturb the DQN with more amount of calculation, while messages that are too compressed would possibly suffer information loss. The 50% of original input has the fastest training speed and lowest fail rate.

Since the method needs a fixed random network, we wonder how random parameters influenced our method. We run the test 3000 times with 100 times as an epoch. Before every epoch began, we re-generate our FMNet parameters. We have extremely lowered the episode limit in order to speed up the test. We calculated how much difference between the minimum, maximum, median and average. The training environment is the 2 * 2 grid, which takes less time.

From the result, we know that all training epochs can reach a good policy, but there exist differences in average episodes among separate experiments. However, the differences were also shown in previous results. That means the parameters has little effect on the method (Table 3).

Table 3. Results of random parameter influence test.

Data	Average converging episode	Normalized episode	Average converging reward	Normalized reward
Average	2995 ± 232	1.000 ± 0.077	0.961 ± 0.022	1.000 ± 0.025
Maximum	3243	1.082	0.998	1.039
Minimum	2460	0.821	0.931	0.969
Median	2992	0.999	0.972	1.011

5 Conclusion

In the paper, we proposed a featured message network used in a cooperative multi-agent system to make agents cooperation perform better. An optimized multi-agent Deep Q-Learning system is brought out to achieve agent cooperation in a partial-observable environment. We tested our method on a traditional "Meeting in a Grid" problem, and the result showed our method can make the network more stable and learn quicker. Our FMNet could be used to many practical scenario in the future such as autonomous driving, competitive video games and industrial automation.

However, to our experience, our method could be improved by a self-augmenting approach by the previous work of our team [18]. Since FMNet of every agent is the same, agents could learn from themselves. This could potentially shorten the learning progress. Other future works including, for example, testing our method with more complex experiment environments. Last but not least, intelligent oriented messaging mechanism should be further studied in practical problems with numerous agents.

References

1. Amato, C., Bernstein, D.S., Zilberstein, S.: Optimal fixed-size controllers for decentralized pomdps. In: Proceedings of the AAMAS Workshop on Multi-Agent Sequential Decision Making in Uncertain Domains (MSDM) (2006)

2. Amato, C., Zilberstein, S.: Achieving goals in decentralized POMDPs. In: Proceedings of The 8th International Conference on Autonomous Agents and Multiagent Systems, International Foundation for Autonomous Agents and Multiagent Systems, vol. 1, pp. 593–600 (2009)
3. Banerjee, B., Peng, J.: Adaptive policy gradient in multiagent learning. In: Proceedings of the Second International Joint Conference on Autonomous Agents and Multiagent Systems, ACM, pp. 686–692 (2003). https://doi.org/10.1145/860575.860686
4. Bernstein, D.S., Givan, R., Immerman, N., Zilberstein, S.: The complexity of decentralized control of markov decision processes. Math. Oper. Res. **27**(4), 819–840 (2002). https://doi.org/10.1287/moor.27.4.819.297
5. Bernstein, D.S., Hansen, E.A., Zilberstein, S.: Bounded policy iteration for decentralized pomdps. In: Proceedings of the Nineteenth International Joint Conference on Artificial Intelligence (IJCAI), pp. 52–57 (2005)
6. Bowling, M., Veloso, M.: An analysis of stochastic game theory for multiagent reinforcement learning. Technical report, Carnegie-Mellon Univ Pittsburgh Pa School of Computer Science (2000)
7. Bowling, M., Veloso, M.: Multiagent learning using a variable learning rate. Artif. Intell. **136**(2), 215–250 (2002). https://doi.org/10.1016/s0004-3702(02)00121-2
8. Burda, Y., Edwards, H., Storkey, A., Klimov, O.: Exploration by random network distillation. arXiv preprint arXiv:1810.12894 (2018)
9. Cao, K., Lazaridou, A., Lanctot, M., Leibo, J.Z., Tuyls, K., Clark, S.: Emergent communication through negotiation. arXiv preprint arXiv:1804.03980 (2018)
10. de Cote, E.M., Lazaric, A., Restelli, M.: Learning to cooperate in multi-agent social dilemmas. In: AAMAS, vol. 6, pp. 783–785 (2006). https://doi.org/10.1145/1160633.1160770
11. Dolcetta, I.C., Ishii, H.: Approximate solutions of the bellman equation of deterministic control theory. Appl. Math. Optim. **11**(1), 161–181 (1984). https://doi.org/10.1007/bf01442176
12. Ferber, J., Weiss, G.: Multi-agent Systems: An Introduction to Distributed Artificial Intelligence, vol. 1, Addison-Wesley Reading (1999)
13. Foerster, J., Assael, I.A., de Freitas, N., Whiteson, S.: Learning to communicate with deep multi-agent reinforcement learning. In: Advances in Neural Information Processing Systems, pp. 2137–2145 (2016)
14. Foerster, J., Chen, R.Y., Al-Shedivat, M., Whiteson, S., Abbeel, P., Mordatch, I.: Learning with opponent-learning awareness. In: Proceedings of the 17th International Conference on Autonomous Agents and MultiAgent Systems, International Foundation for Autonomous Agents and Multiagent Systems, pp. 122–130 (2018)
15. Foerster, J., et al.: Stabilising experience replay for deep multi-agent reinforcement learning. In: Proceedings of the 34th International Conference on Machine Learning, vol. 70. pp. 1146–1155 (2017) JMLR.org
16. Hansen, E.A., Bernstein, D.S., Zilberstein, S.: Dynamic programming for partially observable stochastic games. In: AAAI, vol. 4, pp. 709–715 (2004)
17. Havrylov, S., Titov, I.: Emergence of language with multi-agent games: Learning to communicate with sequences of symbols. In: Advances in Neural Information Processing Systems, pp. 2149–2159 (2017)
18. Huang, X., Xiao, S.: Self-augmenting strategy for reinforcement learning. In: Proceedings of the 2017 International Conference on Computer Science and Artificial Intelligence, ACM, pp. 1–4 (2017). https://doi.org/10.1145/3168390.3168392

19. Ishii, S., Fujita, H., Mitsutake, M., Yamazaki, T., Matsuda, J., Matsuno, Y.: A reinforcement learning scheme for a partially-observable multi-agent game. Mach. Learn. **59**(1–2), 31–54 (2005). https://doi.org/10.1007/s10994-005-0461-8
20. Kingma, D.P., Ba, J.: Adam: a method for stochastic optimization. arXiv preprint arXiv: 1412.6980 (2014)
21. Kok, J. R., Vlassis, N.: Sparse cooperative q-learning. In: Proceedings of the Twenty-First International Conference on Machine Learning, ACM, p. 61 (2004). https://doi.org/10.1145/1015330.1015410
22. Kok, J.R., Vlassis, N.: Collaborative multiagent reinforcement learning by payoff propagation. J. Mach. Learn. Res. **7**, 1789–1828 (2006)
23. Kuhnle, A., Schaarschmidt, M., Fricke, K.: Tensorforce: a tensorflow library for applied reinforcement learning (2017). https://github.com/tensorforce/tensorforce
24. Lazaridou, A., Peysakhovich, A., Baroni, M.: Multi-agent cooperation and the emergence of (natural) language. arXiv preprint arXiv:1612.07182 (2016)
25. Lillicrap, T.P., et al.: Continuous control with deep reinforcement learning. arXiv preprint arXiv:1509.02971 (2015)
26. McCandlish, S., Kaplan, J., Amodei, D., Team, O.: An Empirical Model of Large-Batch Training. arXiv preprint arXiv:1812.06162 (2018)
27. Mnih, V., et al.: Playing atari with deep reinforcement learning. arXiv preprint arXiv:1312.5602 (2013)
28. Mnih, V., et al.: Human-level control through deep reinforcement learning. Nature **518** (7540), 529 (2015)
29. Nair, R., Tambe, M., Yokoo, M., Pynadath, D., Marsella, S.: Taming decentralized POMDPs: Towards efficient policy computation for multiagent settings. In: IJCAI, vol. 3, pp. 705–711 (2003)
30. Omidshafiei, S., Pazis, J., Amato, C., How, J.P., Vian, J.: Deep decentralized multi-task multi-agent reinforcement learning under partial observability. In: Proceedings of the 34th International Conference on Machine Learning, vol. 70, pp. 2681–2690 (2017). JMLR.org
31. Rashid, T., Samvelyan, M., de Witt, C.S., Farquhar, G., Foerster, J., Whiteson, S.: QMIX: monotonic value function factorisation for deep multi-agent reinforcement learning. arXiv preprint arXiv:1803.11485 (2018)
32. Schaarschmidt, M., Kuhnle, A., Ellis, B., Fricke, K., Gessert, F., Yoneki, E.: Lift: reinforcement learning in computer systems by learning from demonstrations. arXiv preprint arXiv:1808.07903 (2018)
33. Schulman, J., Levine, S., Abbeel, P., Jordan, M.I., Moritz, P.: Trust region policy optimization. In: ICML, vol. 37, pp. 1889–1897 (2015)
34. Schulman, J., Wolski, F., Dhariwal, P., Radford, A., Klimov, O.: Proximal policy optimization algorithms. arXiv preprint arXiv:1707.06347 (2017)
35. Sukhbaatar, S., Fergus, R.: Learning multiagent communication with backpropagation. In: Advances in Neural Information Processing Systems, pp. 2244–2252 (2016)
36. Sutton, R.S., Barto, A.G.: Reinforcement learning: an introduction (1998). https://doi.org/10.1109/tnn.1998.712192
37. Tampuu, A., et al.: Multiagent cooperation and competition with deep reinforcement learning. PLoS ONE **12**(4), e0172395 (2017). https://doi.org/10.1371/journal.pone.0172395
38. Varshavskaya, P., Kaelbling, L.P., Rus, D.: Efficient distributed reinforcement learning through agreement. In: Asama, H., Kurokawa, H., Ota, J., Sekiyama, K. (eds.) Distributed Autonomous Robotic Systems, vol. 8, pp. 367–378. Springer, Heidelberg (2009). https://doi.org/10.1007/978-3-642-00644-9_33

39. Yang, Y., Luo, R., Li, M., Zhou, M., Zhang, W., Wang, J.: Mean field multi-agent reinforcement learning. arXiv preprint arXiv:1802.05438 (2018)
40. Yu, C., Zhang, M., Ren, F.: Emotional multiagent reinforcement learning in social dilemmas. In: Boella, G., Elkind, E., Savarimuthu, B.T.R., Dignum, F., Purvis, M.K. (eds.) PRIMA 2013. LNCS (LNAI), vol. 8291, pp. 372–387. Springer, Heidelberg (2013). https://doi.org/10.1007/978-3-642-44927-7_25

Robots

Inferring Event-Predictive Goal-Directed Object Manipulations in REPRISE

Martin V. Butz([✉]), Tobias Menge, Dania Humaidan, and Sebastian Otte

Cognitive Modeling Group, Department of Computer Science and Department of Psychology, Faculty of Science, Tübingen University, Sand 14, 72076 Tübingen, Germany
martin.butz@uni-tuebingen.de
https://cm.inf.uni-tuebingen.de

Abstract. The recently introduced REtrospective and PRospective Inference SchEme (REPRISE) infers contextual event states in the form of neural parametric biases retrospectively in recurrent neural networks (RNNs), distinguishing, for example, different sensorimotor control dynamics. Moreover, it actively infers motor commands prospectively in a goal-directed manner, minimizing anticipated future loss signals—such as the distance to a goal location. REPRISE struggles, however, when multiple, somewhat competing goals are active in parallel—such as when an object is to-be picked up and carried to a goal location. Moreover, unsuitable statistical correlations in the training data can prevent successful goal-directed motor inference, failing to reach particular goal constellations. We scrutinize this challenge and propose that appropriate gradient separation techniques are missing. First, we show that relative encodings and suitable training schedules can alleviate the problem. Most robust behavior, however, is achieved when the RNN architecture is suitably modularized. In the future, emergent RNN modularizations and more direct gradient separation mechanisms need to be developed. Moreover, we expect that REPRISE will shed further light onto the hierarchical neuro-cognitive structure of human thought.

Keywords: Recurrent neural networks · Active inference · Parametric biases · Sensorimotor codes · Event-predictive cognition · Neurocognitive modeling

1 Introduction

Over the last two decades, our mind has been portrayed as a predictive inference system, which plans and controls highly adaptive, goal-directed behavior by anticipating upcoming states and sensations [1,7,9,10,14]. Despite initial promising results with predictively encoded, generative artificial neural networks in computer vision [26], the development of generative recurrent artificial neural

Supported by Humboldt Foundation.

I. V. Tetko et al. (Eds.): ICANN 2019, LNCS 11727, pp. 639–653, 2019.
https://doi.org/10.1007/978-3-030-30487-4_49

networks (RNNS) that are suitably structured for the invocation of dexterous, adaptive goal-directed control remains highly challenging. Recently, a promising retrospective and prospective active inference scheme (REPRISE) has been proposed, which learns sensorimotor forward models and exploits those models for the invocation of goal-directed behavioral control [5,6].

Various strands of research suggest that our brain develops generative models of the encountered sensorimotor streams of information. These models appear to be loosely hierarchically structured, which is the case when moving from primary to deeper visual processing areas [17,26], revealing structures that can be related to Gestalt perceptions [16]. When focusing on generative models that predict information over time, however, evidence has corroborated suggesting that the involved temporally-predictive generative encodings are structured in an event-predictive manner [3,4,15,32]. *Events*, which can be described as predictive neural attractors that encode distinct sensorimotor dynamics, and *event boundaries*, which encode the conditions under which events typically commence, end, or transition into each other, are considered to constitute fundamental units of thought [25,27]. With respect to anticipatory, goal-directed behavior, such event structures offer themselves well for the development of conceptually abstracted, hierarchical structures, that can be suitably exploited for the generation and modeling of human-like model-based planning. Moreover, close relations can be drawn to hierarchical reinforcement learning [2,7,18]. REPRISE develops hidden stable structures, which can be closely related to event encodings, and which may be exploitable for the invocation of conceptual reasoning, planning, and deeper goal-directed behavioral control [5].

It has been shown that sensorimotor temporally predictive models learned by an RNN can be used to compute inverse, goal-directed motor commands by means of active inference [22], approximating model-predictive control [8]. The active inference process uses prospective, back-propagation through time (BPTT) to infer the motor commands believed to be necessary to reach a desired goal-state. This mechanism was not only used to control flying vehicles towards particular locations in space [22], but also to control a many-joint robot arm towards a particular end-point location and orientation, in which case the forward kinematics is predicted [20,23]. The REPRISE adaptation process [5,6] adds retrospective inference, fostering the emergent distinction of several robotic systems during learning, and thus enabling the control of several systems by one RNN architecture without the provision of information about which system is currently being controlled.

The RNN to be analyzed and improved in this paper uses the REPRISE adaptation process to achieve goal directed behavior for different systems. The scenario consists of several flying and gliding vehicles, which can be controlled by means of thrust-like motors. The general scenario was detailed and investigated elsewhere [5,20,23]. In addition, a transportable object is introduced, which can be attached to and thus transported by the controlled vehicle. Figure 1 shows typical scenes in our simulator. A video about the scenario in which REPRISE controls the vehicles can be found online.[1]

Here, we show that the original architecture struggles when multiple, competing objectives are activated. For example, when the goal is to transport an object through space, the architecture fails to reach and hold on to the object. To scrutinize this challenge, we first evaluate performance in the light of different goal objectives. Moreover, we investigate to which extent a velocity encoding of the sensorimotor dynamics—instead of a location-based encoding—can alleviate the problem. Despite some performance improvements, the main challenge remains and appears to be due to competing gradient signals, which lead to the inference of unsuitable motor control commands. We thus introduce a modularized RNN structure, which solves the gradient interference problem, confirming our interference hypothesis. In conclusion, we discuss alternatives to the introduced hard modularization. In particular, we believe that gradient separation techniques need to be developed to enable the concurrent pursuance of multiple objectives, possibly by a technique introduced concurrently at ICANN 2019 [21].

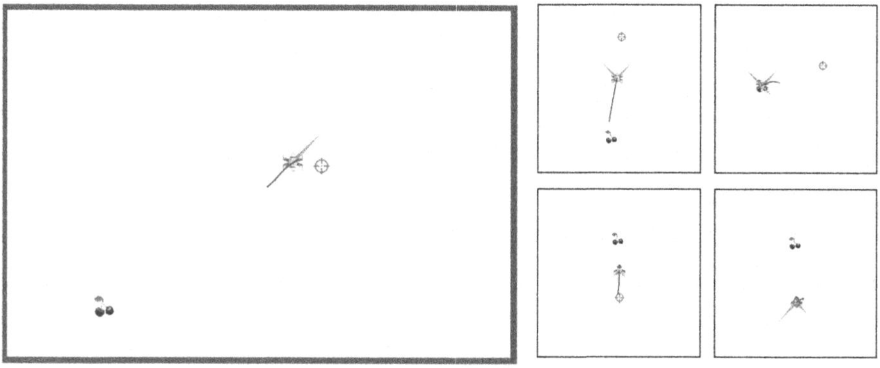

Fig. 1. Exemplar scene with whole training/testing area (an areas of 3 × 2 units, left image) and, furthermore, four zoomed-in exemplar scenes (right) with green circular goal locations and the red cherry target object. The vehicles are controlled by REPRISE. Left: REPRISE currently attempts to reach the cherry object controlling the "glider" vehicle, which undergoes simulated inertia and can be controlled by four thrust-like motors (yellow lines emanating from the vehicle). Right: REPRISE controlling the "glider" picking up and transporting the cherry (top); REPRISE controlling the "rocket"heading towards the goal location (bottom). The rocket undergoes inertia and gravity and can be controlled by two thrust motors pushing the vehicle obliquely upwards. The red line extending from the vehicles depicts the flight trajectory REPRISE currently anticipates (Color figure online).

[1] https://www.youtube.com/watch?v=KDK94qOaaTE.

2 REPRISE Model and Setup

The used RNN model mostly corresponds to the REPRISE architecture introduced elsewhere [5,6]. For simplicity purposes, we first introduce the mechanism that is applied to train the sensorimotor temporal forward models. Afterwards, we detail the mechanisms that unfold while actively inferring vehicle properties retrospectively and goal directed motor control commands prospectively.

2.1 Forward Model Process

The forward model assumes a discrete-time dynamical system, with the states being dependent on the time step t. The model furthermore assumes a *partially observable Markov decision process* (POMDP), such that the states have to be separated into perceivable states $s^t \in \mathbb{R}^n$ and hidden states $\sigma^t \in \mathbb{R}^m$. The system controls are represented by the component $x^t \in \mathbb{R}^k$. The next system state is determined by the previous state and the mapping Φ (1). Throughout this paper, we use an LSTM-like RNN architecture [13] for training the mapping Φ:

$$(s^t, \sigma^t, x^t) \xrightarrow{\Phi} (s^{t+1}, \sigma^{t+1}). \tag{1}$$

Note that in accordance to [6], the hidden state $\sigma^t \in \mathbb{R}^m$ is separated into more stable contextual state estimations $c^t \in \mathbb{R}^u$ and dynamic LSTM hidden cell states $\sigma_c^t \in \mathbb{R}^h$ with $h + u = m$ (we use $h = 16$, $u = 5$ in this work).

2.2 Inference of the Action Sequence

A trained forward model can be used to predict a series of T system-states $\{s^{t+1}, s^{t+2}, ..., s^{t+T}\}$ into the future (1), depending on the sequence of controls $\{x^{t+1}, x^{t+2}, ..., x^{t+T}\}$. Following [22], the inference of the control sequence needed to reach the desired system states $\{g^{t+1}, g^{t+2}, ..., g^{t+T}\}$ is achieved by using *back propagation through time* (BPTT) in combination with sensorimotor anticipations of control-dependent future system states. The control-sequence is thereby updated each time step t with the motor command-respective propagated errors $\frac{\partial \mathcal{L}}{\partial x_i^{t'}}$:

$$\frac{\partial \mathcal{L}}{\partial x_i^{t'}} = \sum_{h=1}^{H} \left[\frac{\partial net_h^{t'}}{\partial x_i^{t'}} \frac{\partial \mathcal{L}}{\partial net_h^{t'}} \right] = \sum_{h=1}^{H} w_{ih} \frac{\partial \mathcal{L}}{\partial net_h^{t'}}, \tag{2}$$

where the loss $\mathcal{L}$ is defined as the squared discrepancy between future desired system states and predicted states $\{s^{t+1}, s^{t+2}, ..., s^{t+T}\}$ (e.g., vehicle and goal locations) under a temporal future horizon T, that is, $\mathcal{L} = \frac{1}{2} \sum_{t'=t+1}^{T} \left(g^{t'} - s^{t'} \right)^2$, $net_h^{t'}$ denotes the value of the weighted summed activity reaching hidden neuron h at time t', and H the number of hidden neurons in the RNN. Each time step t, the process of prediction, inference, and update is iterated a small number of times to achieve a convergence towards the desired states.

2.3 System Architecture and Scenario

The RNN evaluated in this paper is trained to learn a forward mapping for several types of systems $\phi = \{\phi_1, \ldots, \phi_u\}$ (see Table 1). All systems are controlled by five motor commands, that is, $x^t \in \mathbb{R}^5$, which are composed of four thrust-like motor commands [0..1], which are causing forces in four oblique directions, and one signal to attach the target [0..1]. In the case of system ϕ_1, that is, the "rocket", two of the motor commands are ignored, while the other two induce oblique upwards impulses. All systems generate five state information signals, that is, $s^t \in \mathbb{R}^5$, which includes the current $(x, y) \in \Re^2$ position of the system, the current relative distance to an object in the scene $(d_x, d_y) \in \Re^2$, and a binary attachment signal $a \in \{0, 1\}$.

Following [6], REPRISE maintains a neural system context $c^t \in \mathbb{R}^u$ – elsewhere referred to as parametric bias neurons [28,29,31]. Previous work with parametric bias neurons has typically focused on imitation learning and particularly the progressively compact encoding of particular motion sequences, such as approaching an object from a certain direction or grasping an object [24,28,30], or moving the own body along trajectories generated by another robot [19]. In contract, REPRISE infers neural context activities such that the sensorimotor dynamics of the currently active system ϕ_i can be predicted accurately. The system's context c^t is initialized randomly and not preset but updated each time step during the training and inference procedure by using BPTT retrospectively over recent time steps with a retrospective temporal horizon R, similar to the motor control inference (cf. Sect. 2.5) but projecting and accumulating the gradient in the context neurons, enforcing a constant activity over R.

Table 1. Systems used for training and control

System	Type	Gravity	Inertia	Thrusts	Attach	Sensors
ϕ_1	Rocket	Yes	Yes	2	1	5
ϕ_2	Glider	No	Yes	4	1	5
ϕ_3	Stepper	No	No	4	1	5

2.4 Training the Forward Model

With the perceivable state s^t, the context neurons $c^t \in \mathbb{R}^u$, and the motor control commands m^t as input, and the changes in s^t as target output, the architecture is trained sequentially with a learning rate of $1e-3$ and $1e-4$ with 150 blocks each. The blocks are composed of 2.001 time steps, after which the hidden states of the neurons are reset to zero activities. We trained thirty RNNs independently, where we initialized the weight values by means of randomly, normally-distributed values with a standard deviation of 0.1. Training behavior is similar to [5], ensuring that the motor repertoire and motions are explored in a sufficiently distributed manner. Additionally, a heuristic script was implemented to induce goal object reaching trajectories, such that the vehicle moves to the object in a typically suboptimal manner, often circling the object first, but eventually reaching it and thus attaching and transporting the object.

As a result, three training modes are used during a block to change the controls of the vehicle: free flight, seek, and transport. During the *free flight* training mode, the vehicle moves randomly through the environment. It thereby uses either random controls (50%), keeps the last ones (30%), or sets them to zero (20%). During the *seek* training mode, the controls are set to move the vehicle towards a target object. When the object's distance is below a certain threshold, the system attaches the object. During the *transport* training mode, the controls are set randomly in the same way as in the free flight mode while the object is kept attached. The mode switches either when an object is attached/detached, after 50 time steps, or by chance with a probability of 1%.

2.5 Evaluating the Active Control Inference

The trained RNN is evaluated during active, goal-directed inference. Throughout the evaluations, we successively probe the ability to reach a random goal location $(x_g, y_g, a = 0)$, to reach an object location and holding onto the object $(x_o, y_o, a = 1)$, and to transport an object to a goal location, that is, to reach a random goal location with the object being attached $(x_g = x_o, y_g = y_o, a = 1)$, in which case the object needs to be transported to the current goal location. Each goal constellation is activated for 150 time steps. Moreover, vehicles switch during training and goal-directed behavior every 150 time steps. Please note, though, that a robustness for random vehicle switches has been confirmed elsewhere, as long as the switches do not occur overly frequently [5]. After each goal location reaching trial, the goal location is reset to a random position. The performance is determined by calculating the mean and standard deviation over all RNNs and runs for each goal inference-type respectively.

3 Evaluations and System Modifications

With the task and system in hand, we now first evaluate the original system from [5]. We show that it is able to reach not only absolute goal locations as already shown in [5], but also relatively encoded object locations as long as no additional objectives are applied. However, we also show that the system struggles to issue and maintain the attachment command to transport the object and it cannot pursue two somewhat competing goals in parallel. We then evaluate the reason for this failure, exploring the effect of a velocity-based encoding, instead of a location-based one. The corroborated results, which improve but do not come near to optimality, suggests that the active inference mechanism suffers from a *gradient interference problem*, which applies when multiple somewhat disjunctive objectives are being pursued. Thus, we modularize the RNN architecture to prevent the gradient interference and in fact reach near optimal, goal-directed transport behavior.

3.1 Gradient Interference and Simple Alleviations

We first evaluate the REPRISE's active inference performance with the training schedule detailed above. In the first experiment, the standard training schedule and the successive objectives are applied as detailed above. We report results of the consequent goal-directed behavioral control performance.

Figure 2 shows the obtained results. During the goal location approach, a distance of .042 units on average is maintained during the last 50 of the 150 time steps. Thus, the goal is reached and proximity is being maintained rather well. In contrast, the target object is reached with a mean of only 0.535 units during the last 50 time steps while attempting to reach it. As a partial consequence of this failure, also the transport behavior fails. Although the desired behavior and the error signal magnitude is similar for inferring the goal location and the target object location, the results show strongly differing performance values.

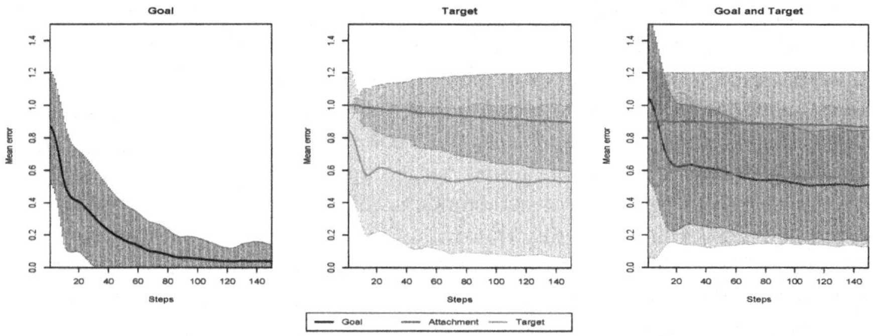

Fig. 2. The black colored graphs depict the Euclidean distance to the goal location, the green ones show the Euclidean distance to the target object, while the red ones report the error in the currently encountered attachment signal. Each of the graphs additionally shows respective standard deviations. (Color figure online)

Thus, the question is where this discrepancy comes from. One addition to the error signal in the object reaching task is that an additional error is induced, which signals that an object should be attached. Might it be due to the error signal from the attachment objective?

We thus re-evaluated the trained networks' active inference abilities without attachment objective during target object reaching trials. Figure 3 shows that the obtained results during target object reaching clearly improve (center figure). The goal location/target object are now reached with an average Euclidean distance of .080/0.145 units during the last 50 of 150 reaching time steps of each respective trial. The only variable in contrast to the default case above is the absence of the back-propagated error signal from the attachment objective (i.e. $a = 1$ versus no loss via a).

The results suggest that the attachment objective-based error signal (during prospective, active inference) might be back-projected onto particular relative

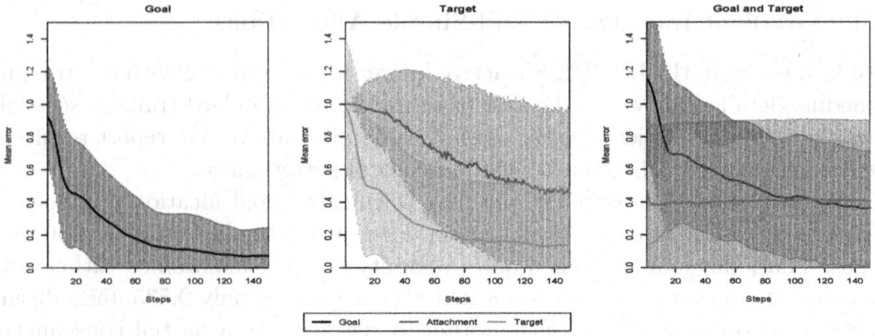

Fig. 3. Default mode without attachment control inference during *target inference*.

target object distances, due to biased statistical correlations encountered during training. In fact, these statistics must be biased simply because an actual attachment can only occur when sufficiently close to the object, because attachments typically occur when flying slowly (due to the seek algorithm implementation), and attachment maintenance implies that the target object stays close to the vehicle. As a result, the skewed statistics between successful target attachments and flying behavior interrupt actual target approaching behavior, preventing actual successful target object attachments. This interpretation is further supported by results when changing the training schedule to *free flight* only: similar performance is reached in the target object reaching trials even when the attachment objective (i.e. $a = 1$) is applied (results not shown). This latter result is most likely the case because there is no statistical bias in the velocity and relative location encodings when correlated with the attachment signal.

However, the solution to the first and second objective should still be improved. Moreover, the third objective, that is, transporting the approached object to the goal location is still far from being solved. In fact, in typical trials when both objectives are set, but the vehicle starts not close enough to the target object, the vehicle usually moves to a point exactly between object and goal locations, indicating the dynamics of two competing gradients. Thus, these results and observations point to a *multiobjective interference problem*, partially combined with the problem of *biased training statistics*. In the next section, we further focus on these issues and consider additional solution options.

3.2 Prediction of Velocities

One statistical bias that must be reflected in the training statistics is the location of the vehicle: besides being often close to the transportable object, also the distribution of absolute locations will be non-uniformly distributed. Apart from the non-appealing option to artificially optimize motor training, we explored the option to encode velocities instead of locations as the sensory information, while still applying the same training schedule. The sensory state $s^t \in \mathbb{R}^5$ is changed from location and relative distance to the target object encodings, to velocity encodings of the vehicle and the target.

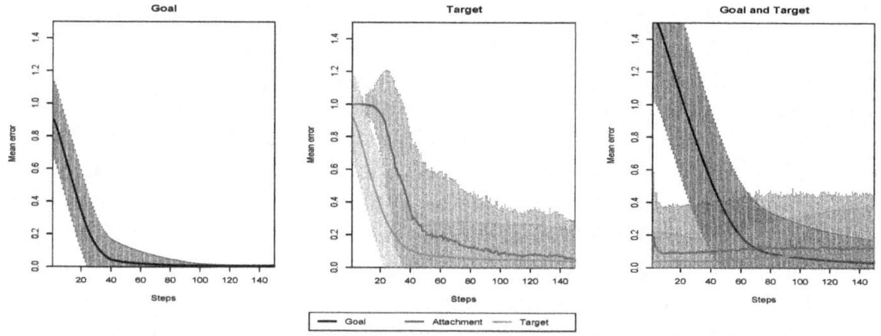

Fig. 4. Performance of a velocity based RNN with a constant velocity error signal towards the goal or target object.

The inference modes for the velocity based RNN are the same as for the location based architecture above. However, there is the additional need to transform the desired goal reaching objectives into a desired velocity objective during active inference. This need can also be viewed as being advantageous, since it offers better control over the converging speed of the system towards the goal and target position. We apply a simple constant target velocity encoding of unit per second pointing towards the target. Please note that the stepper system cannot be used with the velocity based architecture since it has no inertia and therefore no velocity. Thus, the reported results in the velocity encoding below are about glider and rocket only.

The results shown in Fig. 4 imply a huge performance improvement in the goal location and target object reaching trials. Goal locations are now reached with a mean of 0.006 units during the last 50 time steps, while the target objects are reached with a mean of 0.045 units, while the target is attached with a mean of 93% during the last 50 time steps. During the *transport to goal objective*, however, this value decreases to 88%, implying accidental disruptive detachment events. Interestingly, when changing the target velocity from the applied constant to a distance-linear or even -exponential mapping, the object and target location approach performance stays comparable, while the object attachment during transport strongly decreases to values below 20% (not shown).

These results show that with a velocity based forward model, the *goal location* and *target location* reaching objectives are achieved more accurately and reliably when compared to the location-based runs. However, attached targets are still rather frequently lost during the transport trials, that is, the *goal and target* inference trials – particularly when the velocity gradient signal is linearly or exponentially enhanced. This suggests that stronger velocity objectives can negatively affect attachment behavior. Once again, this is likely due to the training statistics, seeing that the linear or exponential error signal focuses backpropagation more strongly on velocity control than the constant setting, such that this error signal affects the attachment motor command inadequately.

3.3 Modularized Network

All results so far have pointed towards interacting, interdependent gradient information, which affects motor inference in unsuitable manners. To avoid the interaction of the object attachment with the object and goal location reaching objectives, we now modularize the RNN architecture. The main difference between the modularized architecture and the one used above is that the position/velocity of the system as well as the distance to the target object are predicted by one of the modularized sub-networks, while the attachment-status is predicted independently by the other modularized sub-network (see Fig. 5). The active inference of the motor control commands is done in these two sub-networks, thereby separating the back-propagated errors of motor thrust commands from the attachment control command. The sub-networks have eight memory cells each, that is, combined the same number of LSTM-cells as the monolithic network. The inferred context, motor controls, and attachment control, and furthermore the whole system state is fed into both sub-networks, in the same way as was done in the default RNN.

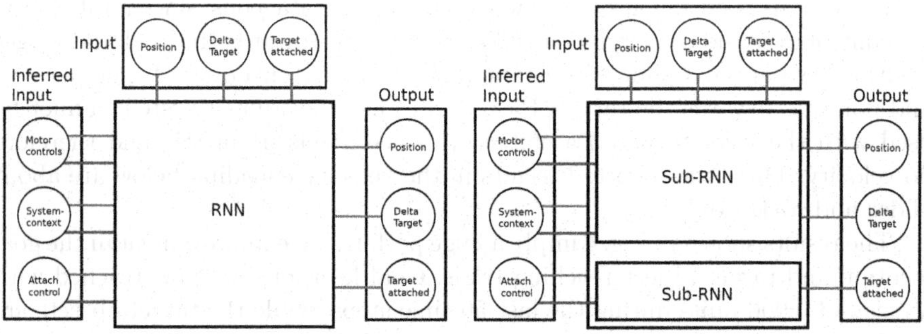

Fig. 5. Model of the default RNN (left) and the modularized RNN (right): Grey connections are used for forward-passes and blue connections for inference. The system-state input is connected to the whole RNN in both cases. For the modularized RNN, the output and the inferred input (motor controls, system state, and attachment control) are connected to either one (but not both) of the two sub-RNNs, effectively modularizing the back-propagated error signals. (Color figure online)

In the first experiment, the modularized architecture is used to infer the goal-directed behavior for velocity based system states using the constant target velocity mapping used above. Figure 6 shows that the goal and target object locations are reached effectively with a mean of 0.018 and 0.028 units during the last 50 trials. Furthermore, the goal location is reached with a mean of 0.036 units during the transport trial with the target still being attached in 98% of the cases. Thus, the gradient interference problem is solved to a large extent.

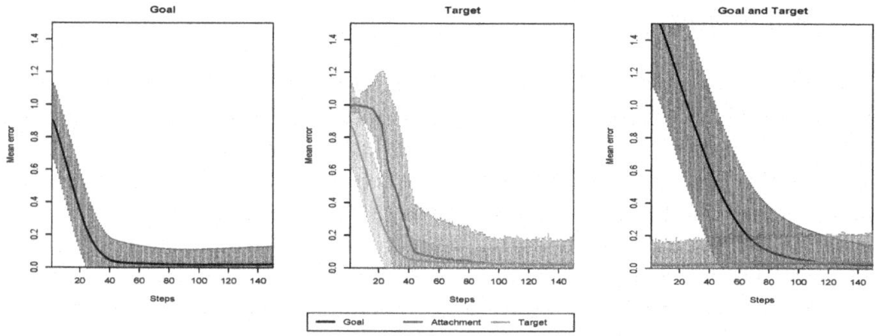

Fig. 6. Performance with velocity state signals in the modularized RNN architecture.

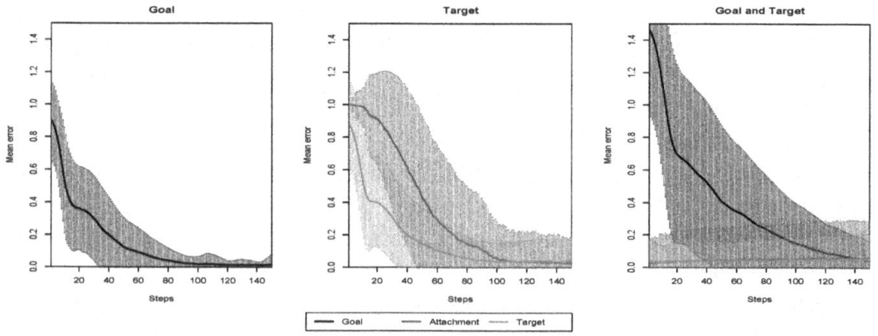

Fig. 7. Performance with location state signals in the modularized RNN architecture.

Besides the velocity-based encoding, we were also interested in the performance gain from the modularization with the spatial encoding used above. The results in Fig. 7 show that an error of 0.014 and 0.037 units is reached during the last 50 steps of each trial while pursuing a goal location and a target object location, respectively. During the transport trials, the goal location is reached with a mean of 0.086 units, the deterioration of which is mostly due to the approx. 6% of trials during which the object is accidentally detached. The performance with the location-based modularization of the RNN model is thus largely comparable to the velocity-based one, albeit more detachments occur. Note that the slower goal and target approach behavior is due to the trials with the stepper.

Overall, the modularized RNN yields improved performance particularly in reaching, attaching, and transporting the target object. Thus, it appears that gradient interference was prevented even more successfully due to the modularized architecture.

4 Conclusion

This paper has evaluated, analyzed, and modified the neuro-cognitive architecture REPRISE [5], focusing on its goal-directed active inference mechanism. Control performance decreases when attempting to pursue competing objectives concurrently. This competition in the back-propagated goal-error-based gradient may be either due to subtle and unexpected biases resulting from the sensorimotor statistics encountered during training or due to inherently competing gradients. The latter is, for example, the case when the objective is to transport the object to the goal, which is only possible once the object is held by the vehicle. When all three objectives, that is, vehicle at goal location, target object close to the vehicle, and target object attached to the vehicle are activated but not satisfied yet, the vehicle typically flies towards a position between goal location and target object location, hovering between the two locations. The observed successful performance in the modularized architecture was only possible because the system's objective was first to move to the target object and then to transport it to the goal location. We thus essentially informed the system about the hierarchical nature of the problem, inducing hierarchical planning somewhat artificially.

These results and interpretations imply two fundamental and critical future work directions, addressing (i) the identified gradient interference problem and (ii) the necessary hierarchical planning mechanism. The gradient interference problem was solved by modularizing the RNN architecture, while the hierarchical planning challenge was solved by inducing successive goals in an appropriate sequence. Both of these solutions essentially induce hand-crafted learning and inference biases. The successful solution confirms that we identified the problem correctly. However, the hand-craftedness is obviously not satisfactory or even applicable in other scenarios and system architectures. Clearly, a suitable network modularization is not always possible and often not known in advance. We believe that the further exploration of emergent modularizations based on predictability signals and the inference of not only temporal but causal correlations between sensory and motor structures will be essential. Moreover, such modularizations may be fostered further by contextual neurons and their selective activation dependent on the goal-respective event context. REPRISE currently only utilizes contextual neurons to modify the active sensorimotor forward model. It may well be the case that enhancements of this approach, with a further focus on respective goals, will enable the necessary modularization. Thereby, surprise signals may need to be processed in a dedicated manner as suggested in [3] and successfully done in more explicit event-predictive architectures in [12] and [11]. Complementary to this, however, also modifications of back-propagation that directly prevent gradient interferences may be possible. A first approach in this direction that separates error gradient-based backpropagation over a modularized RNN architecture was able to extract the individual sine waves from time series data that consists of multiple superimposed sine-waves without informing the system about the number of contained waves [21]. We believe that the suggested modularization mechanisms and gradient separation mechanisms may be well-suited to identify individual events and possible event transitions, while simultaneously forming conceptual, event-specific neural modules.

In [11,12] strict modularizations were learned solving simple object transportation tasks and complex robot behavioral control tasks. Our current goal is to develop such modularizations without clear-cut separations of event- and event-boundary-predictive encodings in suitably structured RNN architectures. Once we have accomplished this, we expect that the system will be able to naturally plan on deeper, conceptual levels, which would enable it to plan and execute sequential object manipulations and to use tools in highly versatile, goal-directed manners. Seeing that our human brain develops conceptual structures from sensorimotor experiences, REPRISE offers one possible neuro-computational model of this learning process, the developing event-predictive structures, and the processing dynamics that unfold within them.

References

1. Bar, M.: Predictions: a universal principle in the operation of the human brain. Philos. Trans. Royal Soc. B Biol. Sci. **364**(1521), 1181–1182 (2009). https://doi.org/10.1098/rstb.2008.0321
2. Botvinick, M., Weinstein, A.: Model-based hierarchical reinforcement learning and human action control. Philos. Trans. Royal Soc. Lond. B Biol. Sci. **369**(1655) (2014). https://doi.org/10.1098/rstb.2013.0480
3. Butz, M.V.: Towards a unified sub-symbolic computational theory of cognition. Front. Psychol. **7**(925) (2016). https://doi.org/10.3389/fpsyg.2016.00925
4. Butz, M.V.: Which structures are out there? Learning predictive compositional concepts based on social sensorimotor explorations. MIND Group, Frankfurt am Main (2017). https://doi.org/10.15502/9783958573093
5. Butz, M.V., Bilkey, D., Humaidan, D., Knott, A., Otte, S.: Learning, planning, and control in a monolithic neural event inference architecture. Neural Networks **117**, 135–144 (2019). https://doi.org/10.1016/j.neunet.2019.05.001
6. Butz, M.V., Bilkey, D., Knott, A., Otte, S.: Reprise: a retrospective and prospective inference scheme. In: Proceedings of the 40th Annual Meeting of the Cognitive Science Society, pp. 1427–1432 (2018)
7. Butz, M.V., Kutter, E.F.: How the Mind Comes Into Being: Introducing Cognitive Science from a Functional and Computational Perspective. Oxford University Press, Oxford (2017)
8. Camacho, E.F., Bordons, C.: Model Predictive Control. Springer, London (1999). https://doi.org/10.1007/978-1-4471-3398-8
9. Clark, A.: Surfing Uncertainty: Prediction, Action and the Embodied Mind. Oxford University Press, Oxford (2016)
10. Friston, K.: The free-energy principle: a rough guide to the brain? Trends Cogn. Sci. **13**(7), 293–301 (2009). https://doi.org/10.1016/j.tics.2009.04.005
11. Gumbsch, C., Butz, M.V., Martius, G.: Autonomous identification and goal-directed invocation of event-predictive behavioral primitives (2019)
12. Gumbsch, C., Otte, S., Butz, M.V.: A computational model for the dynamical learning of event taxonomies. In: Proceedings of the 39th Annual Meeting of the Cognitive Science Society, Cognitive Science Society, pp. 452–457. (2017)

13. Hochreiter, S., Schmidhuber, J.: Long short-term memory. Neural Comput. **9**, 1735–1780 (1997)
14. Hohwy, J.: The Predictive Mind. Oxford University Press, Oxford (2013)
15. Hommel, B., Müsseler, J., Aschersleben, G., Prinz, W.: The theory of event coding (TEC): a framework for perception and action planning. Behav. Brain Sci. **24**, 849–878 (2001)
16. Jäkel, F., Singh, M., Wichmann, F.A., Herzog, M.H.: An overview of quantitative approaches in Gestalt perception. Vis. Res. **126**, 3–8 (2016). https://doi.org/10.1016/j.visres.2016.06.004
17. Khaligh-Razavi, S.M., Kriegeskorte, N.: Deep supervised, but not unsupervised, models may explain IT cortical representation. PLoS Comput. Biol. **10**(11), e1003915 (2014). https://doi.org/10.1371/journal.pcbi.1003915
18. McClelland, J.L., et al.: Letting structure emerge: connectionist and dynamical systems approaches to cognition. Trends Cogn. Sci. **14**(8), 348–356 (2010). https://doi.org/10.1016/j.tics.2010.06.002
19. Murata, S., Yamashita, Y., Arie, H., Ogata, T., Sugano, S., Tani, J.: Learning to perceive the world as probabilistic or deterministic via interaction with others: a neuro-robotics experiment. IEEE Trans. Neural Networks Learn. Syst. **28**(4), 830–848 (2017). https://doi.org/10.1109/TNNLS.2015.2492140
20. Otte, S., Hofmaier, L., Butz, M.V.: Integrative collision avoidance within RNN-driven many-joint robot arms. In: Kůrková, V., Manolopoulos, Y., Hammer, B., Iliadis, L., Maglogiannis, I. (eds.) ICANN 2018. LNCS, vol. 11141, pp. 748–758. Springer, Cham (2018). https://doi.org/10.1007/978-3-030-01424-7_73
21. Otte, S., Rubisch, P., Butz, M.V.: Gradient-based learning of compositional dynamics with modular RNNs. In: Tetko, I.V., et al. (eds.) ICANN 2019, LNCS, vol. 11727, pp. 484–496. Springer, Cham (2019)
22. Otte, S., Schmitt, T., Friston, K., Butz, M.V.: Inferring adaptive goal-directed behavior within recurrent neural networks. In: 26th International Conference on Artificial Neural Networks (ICANN 2017), pp. 227–235 (2017)
23. Otte, S., Zwiener, A., Butz, M.V.: Inherently constraint-aware control of many-joint robot arms with inverse recurrent models. In: 26th International Conference on Artificial Neural Networks (ICANN 2017), pp. 262–270 (2017)
24. Park, J., Kim, D., Nagai, Y.: Learning for goal-directed actions using RNNPB: developmental change of "what to imitate". IEEE Trans. Cognitive Dev. Syst. **10**(3), 545–556 (2018). https://doi.org/10.1109/TCDS.2017.2679765
25. Radvansky, G.A., Zacks, J.M.: Event Cognition. Oxford University Press, Oxford (2014)
26. Rao, R.P., Ballard, D.H.: Predictive coding in the visual cortex: a functional interpretation of some extra-classical receptive-field effects. Nature Neurosci. **2**(1), 79–87 (1999). https://doi.org/10.1038/4580
27. Richmond, L.L., Zacks, J.M.: Constructing experience: event models from perception to action. Trends Cogn. Sci. **21**(12), 962–980 (2017). https://doi.org/10.1016/j.tics.2017.08.005
28. Sugita, Y., Tani, J., Butz, M.V.: Simultaneously emerging braitenberg codes and compositionality. Adapt. Behav. **19**, 295–316 (2011). https://doi.org/10.1177/1059712311416871
29. Tani, J.: Model-based learning for mobile robot navigation from the dynamical systems perspective. IEEE Trans. Syst. Man Cybern. (Part B) **26**(3), 421–436 (1996). Special Issue on Learning Autonomous Systems

30. Tani, J.: Learning to generate articulated behavior through the bottom-up and the top-down interaction processes. Neural Networks **16**(1), 11–23 (2003). https://doi.org/10.1016/S0893-6080(02)00214-9
31. Tani, J.: Exploring Robotic Minds. Oxford University Press, Oxford (2017)
32. Zacks, J.M., Speer, N.K., Swallow, K.M., Braver, T.S., Reynolds, J.R.: Event perception: a mind-brain perspective. Psychol. Bull. **133**(2), 273–293 (2007). https://doi.org/10.1037/0033-2909.133.2.273

On Unsupervised Learning of Traversal Cost and Terrain Types Identification Using Self-organizing Maps

Jan Faigl(✉) and Miloš Prágr

Faculty of Electrical Engineering, Czech Technical University in Prague,
Technicka 2, 166 27 Prague, Czech Republic
{faiglj,pragrmi1}@fel.cvut.cz
https://comrob.fel.cvut.cz

Abstract. This paper reports on the deployment of self-organizing maps in unsupervised learning of the traversal cost for a hexapod walking robot. The problem is motivated by traversability assessment of terrains not yet visited by the robot, but for which shape and appearance features are available. The perception system of the robot is used to extract terrain features that are accompanied by traversal cost characterization captured from the real experience of the robot with the terrain, which is characterized by proprioceptive features. The learned model is employed to predict the traversal cost of new terrains based only on the shape and appearance features. Based on the experimental deployment of the robot in various terrains, a dataset of the traversal cost has been collected that is utilized in the presented evaluation of the traversal cost modeling using self-organizing map approach. In comparison with the Gaussian process, the self-organizing map provides competitive results and the found paths using the predicted traversal costs are close to the optimal path based on reference traversal cost of the particular terrain types. Besides, the self-organizing map can also be utilized for unsupervised identification of the terrain types, and it further supports incremental learning, which is more suitable for practical deployments of the robot in a priory unknown environments where reference traversal costs are not available.

1 Introduction

The work reported in this paper is motivated by a deployment of the multi-legged walking robot (depicted in Fig. 1) in an unknown environment, where the robot is requested to perform data collection missions or long-term environmental monitoring. In the motivational deployment, it is expected the robot continuously operates while it also improves its motion performance by avoiding hard to traverse areas. The robot can perceive its surrounding environment using

This work was supported by the Czech Science Foundation under research project No.18-18858S. The authors acknowledge the support of the OP VVV MEYS funded project CZ.02.1.01/0.0/0.0/16_019/0000765 "Research Center for Informatics".

I. V. Tetko et al. (Eds.): ICANN 2019, LNCS 11727, pp. 654–668, 2019.
https://doi.org/10.1007/978-3-030-30487-4_50

its exteroceptive sensors such as RGB-D camera [18] while the proprioceptive signals (e.g., energy consumed, velocity, attitude stability) can be utilized to model the robot experience with the traversed terrain. A fundamental requirement to improve the robot motion performance is to avoid difficult terrains [2], and therefore, it is desirable to model the robot traversal cost and extrapolate the cost for seen but not yet visited areas to avoid costly terrains [11].

The herein reported empirical evaluation on unsupervised learning of the terrain traversability assessment is a part of our ongoing effort on terrain learning [10,12] for which we aim to develop computationally efficient unsupervised learning system to model and predict the robot traversal cost. Although models based on Gaussian Processes (GPs) [13] can be utilized for the traversal cost learning and prediction, e.g., modeling elevation maps [16], GP-based approach can be considered computationally demanding, and it does not scale with incremental deployment. In this paper, we focus on the evaluation of the Self-Organizing Map (SOM) [8] for unsupervised model learning and prediction of the traversal cost in a priory unknown environments, where the information about the ground truth traversal cost is not available. Based on our recent results on the evaluation of traversal cost learning reported in [4], we identified that combining data from similar terrain types might improve traversal cost estimates based on new exteroceptive measurements. Therefore, we employ SOM in traversal cost prediction, and we further investigate the clustering of the learned SOM [17] to identify prototypes corresponding to the similar terrain types. Moreover, the traversal cost defined as the attitude stability in [4] is extended by two additional cost indicators (the required power and achieved velocity) in the herein reported model learning, which supports the generalizability of the presented approach.

The remainder of the paper is organized as follows. A brief description of the addressed problem and utilized evaluation methodology is presented in the following section. The studied unsupervised terrain types identification is discussed in Sect. 3. The empirical results and description of the found evaluation insights are reported in Sect. 4. Concluding remarks are dedicated to Sect. 5.

2 Problem Specification

The addressed problem of traversal cost modeling follows our previous work reported in [4], and therefore, a brief problem specification is presented here to make the paper self-contained. The terrain characterization from exteroceptive measurements is described by the three shape features [9] and two appearance features of the ab channel means of the Lab color space. The exteroceptive feature descriptor $\boldsymbol{d}_{sa}$ is thus a vector $\boldsymbol{d}_{sa} = (s_1, s_2, s_3, a_1, a_2)$. In the learning phase, the descriptor is further accompanied by three traversal cost estimates c_1, c_2, and c_3, where c_1 is the mean value of the instantaneous power consumption, c_2 is the mean forward velocity, and c_3 characterizes the attitude stability determined as the variance of the robot roll; and all the cost indicators are computed from 10 s long period corresponding to the one motion gait cycle of the multi-legged robot. The full descriptor $\boldsymbol{d}$ is thus eight dimensional vector $\boldsymbol{d} = (s_1, s_2, s_3, a_1, a_2, c_1, c_2, c_3)$.

The learning is performed for a sequence of descriptors called trail $\mathcal{T}$, e.g., $\mathcal{T} = (\boldsymbol{d}(1), \ldots, \boldsymbol{d}(n))$, to learn the traversal cost model $\mathcal{M}(\mathcal{T})$. The model is used to predict the traversal cost using a new exteroceptive feature $\boldsymbol{d}_{sa}$ that can be expressed as

$$(c_1, c_2, c_3) \leftarrow \text{predict}(\mathcal{M}, \boldsymbol{d}_{sa}). \tag{1}$$

For the traversability assessment of a new environment, the features correspond to a grid map of the environment. Hence, we consider the model evaluation for a set of m descriptors characterizing the new terrain $\mathcal{G} = \{\boldsymbol{d}_{sa}(1), \ldots, \boldsymbol{d}_{sa}(m)\}$.

Although a ground truth traversal cost is not available in the motivational deployment in a priory unknown environment, a reference value of the traversal cost can be considered for the evaluation of the selected unsupervised learning approaches. In the case labels of the particular terrain types in the trails used for the learning are available, e.g., provided by a human, the real measured traversal costs can be grouped for individual terrains, and "*ground-truth*" traversal costs can be estimated as the mean values of the traversal costs that can be further accompanied by the standard deviation. Thus, it is assumed the traversal costs are from normal distributions. However, such a reference value cannot be utilized for evaluation of the predicted traversal costs from explicitly unknown terrains, where the trails are not annotated, and thus the explicit terrain type labels are not available. In such a case, we can follow the approach based on the results reported in [4], and we can consider a GP-based model compound from the individual GPs for particular terrain types to model a probability distribution of the traversal costs per particular labeled terrain type. Since an individual GP is learned for each cost indicator and the terrain type trail, such a reference model is compounded from three times more GPs than the number of terrain types considered. Then, the compounded model can be utilized to provide a reference traversal cost for unlabeled data as the predicted traversal cost with the lowest variance of the predicted mean value.

The reference traversal cost model is denoted $\mathcal{M}_{\text{ref}}$ for the case of the mean and standard deviation values computed from the labeled trails, and $\mathcal{M}_{\text{GP}}^{tt}$ for the compounded GP-based model. The reference model $\mathcal{M}_{\text{ref}}$ can be used to estimate the traversal cost of the testing data $\mathcal{G}$, which consists of partially (human) labeled descriptors with the particular terrain types. For the unlabeled descriptors, the traversability cost is provided by the individual GP-based model with the lowest variance of the predicted mean value.

Even though we can utilize the root-mean-square error to evaluate the quality of the prediction, in a practical deployment, the traversal costs and also the exteroceptive descriptors are random variables. Therefore, we measure the performance of the model $\mathcal{M}$ by the ratio $R(\mathcal{M})$ defined as

$$R(\mathcal{M}) = \frac{|\{\boldsymbol{d}_{sa}|\boldsymbol{d}_{sa} \in \mathcal{G} \text{ and } |\text{predict}(\mathcal{M}, \boldsymbol{d}_{sa}) - \mu(\boldsymbol{d}_{sa})| \leq 2\sigma(\boldsymbol{d}_{sa})\}|}{|\mathcal{G}|} \cdot 100\%, \tag{2}$$

where $\mu(\boldsymbol{d}_{sa})$ and $\sigma(\boldsymbol{d}_{sa})$ correspond to the reference "*ground-truth*" if the terrain type for each $\boldsymbol{d}_{sa}$ is known, or they are provided by the compounded GP-based model $\mathcal{M}_{\text{GP}}^{tt}$. The ratio R is motivated to measure "correctness" of the predicted values according to the reference model, where the prediction is considered correct if it fits about 95% values of the reference GP-based model prediction, and thus the ratio (2) is called the *correctness ratio.*

3 Unsupervised Terrain Types Identification

Even though we can imagine explicit terrain labels, e.g., flat ground and grass, the robot does not have such explicit terrain types when it is deployed in an unknown environment where it can only see its surroundings and perceive the terrain by the proprioceptive measurements. Therefore, we can imagine that similar terrain features can belong to the same "terrain type", and thus we can perform unsupervised clustering of the data to identify similarities.

For the SOM, we can consider a visualization of the learned lattices, e.g., using U-matrix [15]. Besides, we can also cluster the learned prototypes according to the smallest cluster separation measure [3] as suggested in [17]. In particular, we consider 2–30 clusters determined in 100 iterations of [7] initialized by [1]. The number of determined clusters can be considered as the number of terrain types in the dataset used for the learning. We propose the following procedure to evaluate the unsupervised identification of the terrain types.

First, we consider the dataset trail $\mathcal{T}$ is annotated by a human operator who provides explicit terrain type labels. The clusters of SOM prototypes are then examined for the terrain labels using the annotated descriptors of the trail $\mathcal{T}$. The learned prototypes do not precisely match the descriptors of $\mathcal{T}$ because of learning error, and therefore, we propose to annotate each prototype according to the label of the closest $d \in \mathcal{T}$. Thus, for each cluster, we compute a histogram of the specific terrain types of the given labels, and the cluster can be labeled according to the terrain type with the largest histogram bin. However, the robot experience with the terrain captured by the descriptors in $\mathcal{T}$ can be different from the human labels, and we can also expect a different number of clusters than the number of labels provided by the human. Therefore, we evaluate the identified terrain types as the percentage ratio of each terrain type label within each particular cluster and the total number of the clustered prototypes.

Let the total number of prototypes be M, the number of clusters be N, and the number of prototypes within the i-th cluster be m_i; then, the percentage ratio $T_{i,l}$ of the terrain type label l in the cluster i is computed as

$$T_{i,l} = \frac{|\{\boldsymbol{w}|\boldsymbol{w} \in \mathcal{N}_i, \text{ such that } label(\text{argmin}_{\boldsymbol{d} \in \mathcal{T}}(\|(\boldsymbol{w}, \boldsymbol{d})\|)) \text{ is } l\}|}{M} \cdot 100\%, \quad (3)$$

where $\mathcal{N}_i$ is the i-th cluster of all prototypes in the SOM lattice $\mathcal{N}$, i.e., $\mathcal{N}_i \subseteq \mathcal{N}$, and $label(\cdot)$ is the label of the corresponding descriptor $\boldsymbol{d}$ of the trail $\mathcal{T}$. Since the sum of all $T_{i,l}$ gives one hundred percentage points, the ratios $T_{i,l}$ describe a distribution of the human labels across the terrain types identified by the unsupervised procedure.

A similar evaluation can be directly performed on the trail descriptors using the same hierarchical clustering as for the SOM prototypes. Notice that the number of prototypes of the learned SOM is considerably smaller than the size of the input dataset, and thus continuous clustering of the trail descriptors can be demanding for a practical deployment with online learning. The evaluation results on the collected dataset with the real hexapod walking robot are reported in the following section.

4 Results

Individual trails for seven particular terrain types have been collected with the real hexapod walking robot. These trails are combinations of flat terrain and wooden blocks that are further covered by artificial turf and black fabric, which change the visual appearance of the terrain and impact the traversal costs, see Fig. 1. In addition, the seventh terrain is a wooden sloped surface with a visual appearance similar to wooden blocks.

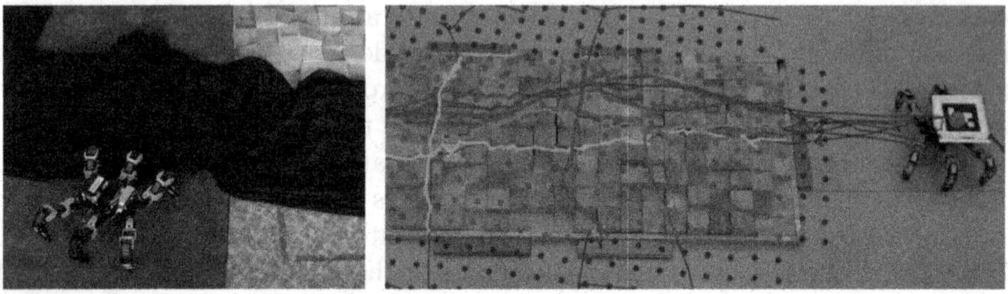

Fig. 1. Utilized hexapod walking robot and terrains types – flat floor and wooden blocks considered uncovered but also covered by artificial turf and black fabric. The terrain types are further accompanied by a single wooden sloped surface (not shown in the photo). The parts of the labeled trail on wooden blocks are visualized as color curves. The unlabeled descriptors are small blue disks. (Color figure online)

Since an explicit human label of the terrain types is available, we can compute the "*ground-truth*" reference traversal costs as mean values accompanied by the standard deviations from all measured traversal costs indicators per individual terrain types. The particular reference costs are depicted in Table 1 where the forward velocity c_2 and attitude stability c_3 costs are multiplied by 100 to scale them to a competitive value to the power cost c_1 because their absolute measured values are relatively small. From the listed values, we can notice that some of the terrains are equal regarding the required energy cost c_1, such as wooden blocks covered by artificial turf and flat floor, which is because of the employed adaptive locomotion control [5], but the stability of the motion (captured by the cost c_2) differs. On the other hand, the most energy demanding terrains are flat floor covered by black fabric, which causes slippage of the foot end-points, and wooden sloped surface. The increased slippage of these terrains corresponds to the relatively small velocity c_2 and high instability of the motion c_3. Regarding the navigation and avoiding difficult terrains, the most distinguishable real measured values are for the energy consumption c_1, which is thus suitable for weighting the traversed distance in the path planning. However, the weights of individual traversal costs can be further tuned according to a particular deployment scenario.

Table 1. Reference traversal costs – average measured traversal cost values

Terrain	$\text{costs}_{average}$			$\text{costs}_{std.dev.}$		
	$\overline{c_1}$	$\overline{c_2}'$	$\overline{c_3}'$	σ_{c_1}	σ'_{c_2}	σ'_{c_3}
Flat floor covered by black fabric	13.2	1.6	2.2	0.75	0.57	0.99
Wooden blocks covered by black fabric	11.0	1.5	2.2	0.68	0.62	0.74
Wooden blocks	11.1	1.7	2.2	0.64	0.68	0.76
Wooden blocks covered by artificial turf	10.7	1.6	1.9	0.54	0.47	0.68
Flat floor	10.6	2.3	0.9	0.85	0.53	0.22
Wooden sloped surface	13.3	1.9	2.4	0.77	0.92	1.12
Flat floor covered by artficial turf	10.6	1.8	1.0	0.37	0.65	0.23

Presented values for c_2 and c_3 are multiplied by 100 because absolute measured values are relatively small.

In addition to the direct computation of the reference model $\mathcal{M}_{\text{ref}}$, the compound GP-based reference model $\mathcal{M}^{tt}_{\text{GP}}$ is learned from the labeled trails, but all these trails are concatenated into a single trail $\mathcal{T}_{all}$ with 2177 feature descriptors for the evaluation of the learned GP and SOM from the unlabeled data. The evaluation is performed for the testing set $\mathcal{G}$ with 4355 descriptors from which only 1153 are labeled by the terrain type. The correctness ratio (2) computed only from the labeled test descriptors is thus denoted $\mathcal{R}$, and the ratio computed from all descriptors is denoted $\mathcal{R}_{all}$.

The standard SOM [8] with the three sizes of the squared lattice (10×10, 20×20, and 30×30) is utilized with the initial learning gain $g_0 = 10$ and the fixed learning rate $\mu = 0.99$. The gain is decreased $g \leftarrow (1 - \alpha)g$ after each learning epoch according to the gain decreasing rate $\alpha = 0.05$. A single learning epoch is considered as the adaptation of SOM to all input terrain descriptors (in random order), and the total number of learning epochs is limited to 300. The descriptors are used as they have been computed from the measured signals without any normalization.

The SOM learning procedure has been implemented in C++ and learning the complete model for $\mathcal{T}_{all}$ takes about 1.1 s, 3.9 s, and 8.6 s depending on the lattice size using the Intel i7-8550U CPU. GP-based learning utilizes GPy [6] and it takes about 113.9 s to learn $\mathcal{T}_{all}$ within the same computational environment. The prediction of the cost for a single feature using SOM is negligible as it takes about 0.5 μs, 2.0 μs, and 4.5 μs depending of the lattice size, while a single cost prediction using GP-based model takes about 8.7 ms.

First, the prediction of the learned SOM has been compared with the GP-based models using the correctness ratio (2) and the reference models $\mathcal{M}_{\text{ref}}$

Table 2. Correctness ratios R for labeled data of $\mathcal{T}_{all}$

Ratio	Cost	Model learned from $\mathcal{T}_{all}$							
		$\mathcal{M}_{\mathrm{GP}}^{tt}$	$\mathcal{M}_{\mathrm{GP}}$	$\mathcal{M}_{\mathrm{SOM}}^{10\times10}$	$\mathcal{M}_{\mathrm{SOM}}^{20\times20}$	$\mathcal{M}_{\mathrm{SOM}}^{30\times20}$	$\mathcal{M}_{\mathrm{SOM}_3}^{10\times10}$	$\mathcal{M}_{\mathrm{SOM}_3}^{20\times20}$	$\mathcal{M}_{\mathrm{SOM}_3}^{30\times30}$
R - $\mathcal{M}_{\mathrm{ref}}$	c_1	80.1	56.3	78.2	75.3	77.3	87.5	83.9	73.4
	c_2	78.6	78.0	89.0	85.0	85.0	85.3	85.9	73.5
	c_3	91.6	89.8	73.0	72.5	72.5	73.4	86.4	73.5
R - $\mathcal{M}_{\mathrm{GP}}^{tt}$	c_1	-	42.6	48.1	45.5	45.8	59.8	61.5	59.7
	c_2	-	69.7	77.3	75.7	74.5	79.2	81.7	80.4
	c_3	-	46.7	61.3	57.6	50.6	69.4	66.1	64.5

and $\mathcal{M}_{\mathrm{GP}}^{tt}$. Two types of prediction using the learned SOM are considered. The prediction using the closest prototype is denoted $\mathcal{M}_{\mathrm{SOM}}$. Besides, we consider prediction using the weighted average from k closest prototypes. Based on the empirical evaluation, we found that the best performance is for computing the average from three closest prototypes, and therefore, we report only results for $k = 3$ that are denoted $\mathcal{M}_{\mathrm{SOM}_3}$. Since SOM is randomized, the correctness ratios are computed from 20 trials, and the average values for the labeled data are reported in Table 2 and for the unlabeled data in Table 3, where the lattice size is encoded in the superscript. The standard deviations are in units of percentage points of the average values, and thus they are omitted for clarity.

Table 3. Correctness ratios R_{all} for unlabeled data using the reference $\mathcal{M}_{\mathrm{GP}}^{tt}$

Ratio	Cost	Model learned from $\mathcal{T}_{all}$						
		$\mathcal{M}_{\mathrm{GP}}$	$\mathcal{M}_{\mathrm{SOM}}^{10\times10}$	$\mathcal{M}_{\mathrm{SOM}}^{20\times20}$	$\mathcal{M}_{\mathrm{SOM}}^{30\times20}$	$\mathcal{M}_{\mathrm{SOM}_3}^{10\times10}$	$\mathcal{M}_{\mathrm{SOM}_3}^{20\times20}$	$\mathcal{M}_{\mathrm{SOM}_3}^{30\times30}$
R_{all}	c_1	46.7	51.5	50.8	51.3	56.0	56.8	56.6
	c_2	76.4	82.3	79.7	78.9	83.1	83.8	83.1
	c_3	55.5	56.4	55.2	49.1	60.7	59.9	58.4

The achieved correctness ratios reported in Tables 2 and 3 indicate that all predictors provide competitive performance. Although a better performance is indicated for the reference "*ground-truth*" model $\mathcal{M}_{\mathrm{ref}}$ than for the compounded GP-based model $\mathcal{M}_{\mathrm{GP}}^{tt}$, explicit terrain types might not be available for deployment scenarios in a priory unknown environments. Therefore the compounded model is suitable for the evaluation of learned models without labeled trails shown in Table 3, because it provides the best performance for the labeled trails, see Table 2. The weighted average from three closest prototypes $\mathcal{M}_{\mathrm{SOM}_3}$ provides noticeably better prediction than $\mathcal{M}_{\mathrm{SOM}}$. On the other hand, increasing the size of the lattice does not improve the prediction correctness, and thus small and less computationally demanding 10×10 large SOM is sufficient.

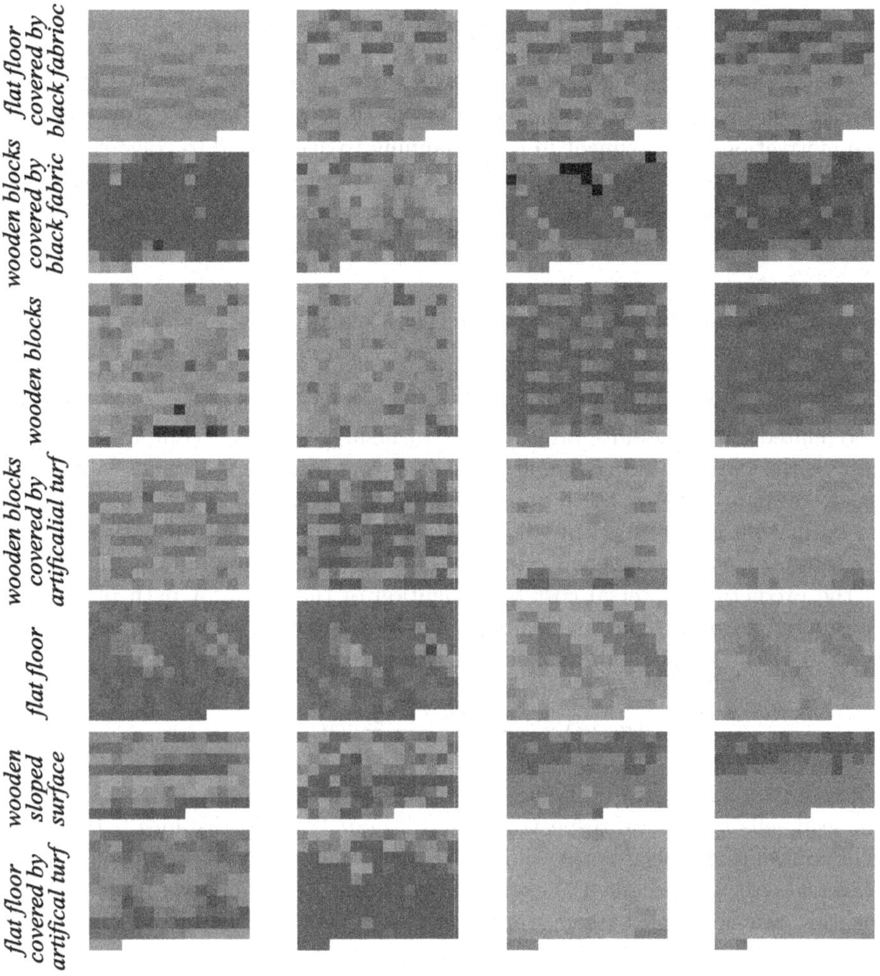

(b) Reference $\mathcal{M}_{\mathrm{GP}}^{tt}$ (c) $\mathcal{M}_{\mathrm{GP}}$ (d) $\mathcal{M}_{\mathrm{SOM}}^{10\times10}$ (e) $\mathcal{M}_{\mathrm{SOM}_3}^{10\times10}$

Fig. 2. Predicted values of the velocity cost c_2 for the labeled part of the testing data $\mathcal{G}$ that are organized into separate (possibly) equally large grids according to the particular terrain types from top to down as *flat floor covered by black fabric*, *wooden blocks covered by black fabric*, *wooden blocks*, *wooden blocks covered by artificial turf*, *flat floor*, *wooden sloped surface*, and *flat floor covered by artificial turf*. The absolute values of the prediction c_2 are colorized using the jet color palette (low values are in the blue and high values are in the red). (Color figure online)

The prediction correctness ratios vary for the individual traversal costs c_1, c_2, and c_3, and there is not a single best performing model among the performed trials of the SOM. Therefore, we select the particular learned model $\mathcal{M}_{\mathrm{SOM}_3}^{10\times10}$ with $R(c_1) = 64.7\%$, $R(c_2) = 79.3\%$, and $R(c_3) = 71.0\%$ for further investigation of the unsupervised terrain types identification using SOM. Similarly, we select $\mathcal{M}_{\text{SOM}}^{10\times10}$ with $R(c_1) = 47.5\%$, $R(c_2) = 75.4\%$, and $R(c_3) = 63.2\%$ that is used for detail examination of the predicted values, which is shown in Fig. 2 for the expected velocity cost c_2 on the testing grid $\mathcal{G}$. Notice, that even though the prediction is not perfect regardless of the GP or SOM method, for the motivational deployment in path planning to avoid hard to traverse regions, the main important property of the traversal cost prediction is distinguishability of the hard to traverse areas, which seems satisfiable for all the predictions and it is further detailed in the following section.

4.1 Predicted Traversal Cost in Path Planning Scenario

The possible impact of the traversal cost prediction to navigation of the robot in the environment is related to the ability to avoid hard to traverse areas, which is also related to the absolute values of the traversal cost and the computed distance cost in the path planning. Regarding the reference costs shown in Table 1, the most distinguishable is the required power cost c_1 and since this paper focuses on evaluation of the SOM in traversal cost learning and not on path planning, we select c_1 as the traversal cost weight to demonstrate the possible impact of the prediction traversal cost to navigation of the robot. A path planning is considered for a grid-like environment, where the motion cost from moving from the cell ν_1 to the neighboring cell ν_1 is computed as

$$c(\nu_1, \nu_2) = \frac{c_1(\nu_1) + c_1(\nu_2)}{2} \cdot \|(\nu_1, \nu_2)\|, \tag{4}$$

where $c_1(\nu_1)$ and $c_1(\nu_2)$ is the predicted (or reference) required power cost c_1 of the grid cells ν_1 and ν_2, respectively, and $\|(\nu_1, \nu_2)\|$ is the distance between the cells considering 8-neighborhood. Having a grid map of the environment with the traversal cost assessment, the optimal path from the initial location to the goal location can be found by any graph search such as A* or Dijkstra's algorithm.

Fig. 3. Testing grid map of the size 380 × 30 cells with two terrain types that are hard to traverse: the flat ground covered by black fabric and wooden sloped surface (shown in the red); that are accompanied by the wooden blocks and wooden blocks covered by the black fabric (shown in the blue) that are all placed on the flat ground (shown in the white here to highlight hard to traverse areas). (Color figure online)

The robot avoids hard to traverse area if the total cost (using (4)) of traversing the more difficult area is higher than the travel cost of avoiding the area. If the hard to traverse area is small, it might be still optimal to traverse it rather than avoid it. Therefore, an artificial scenario with several hard to traverse areas with the dimensions of the 200 × 20 grid cells are placed in an environment

Table 4. Average path costs found using traversal cost prediction of c_1

Prediction model	Path cost			
	$\overline{C}$	σ_C	$\overline{\Delta}$ [%]	σ_Δ [%]
$\mathcal{M}_{\mathrm{GP}}^{tt}$	4318.1	18.2	1.5	0.4
$\mathcal{M}_{\mathrm{GP}}$	4259.2	5.7	0.2	0.1
$\mathcal{M}_{\mathrm{SOM_3}}^{10\times10}$	4281.8	23.9	0.7	0.6
$\mathcal{M}_{\mathrm{clustering}}$ - classification	4325.2	23.2	1.7	0.5
$\mathcal{M}_{\mathrm{SOM}}^{10\times10}$ - classification	4494.7	9.2	5.7	0.2

Δ is the difference of the path cost from the reference path cost.

with a flat ground to form a zig-zag pattern, see Fig. 3. For the map shown in Fig. 3, the optimal path from the grid cell $(0, 10)$ to $(379, 15)$ can be found using the particular traversal cost prediction C_{pred}; however, the final cost path C is determined as the cost over the grid map that is assessed using the reference "*ground-truth*" model $\mathcal{M}_{\mathrm{ref}}$. The assessment for the learned models is performed based on shape and appearance features that are randomly selected from the features of the trails with the corresponding terrain types, and 20 grids with randomly chosen feature descriptors have been created. Thus, the path costs in Table 4 are reported as the average values $\overline{C}$, the standard deviations σ_C, and also as the average percentage difference $\overline{\Delta}$ of the final path cost found using the predicted traversal cost from the cost of the optimal reference path found using the $\mathcal{M}_{\mathrm{ref}}$ traversal cost model with the standard deviation denoted σ_Δ. Selected found path with the corresponding path costs are depicted in Fig. 4.

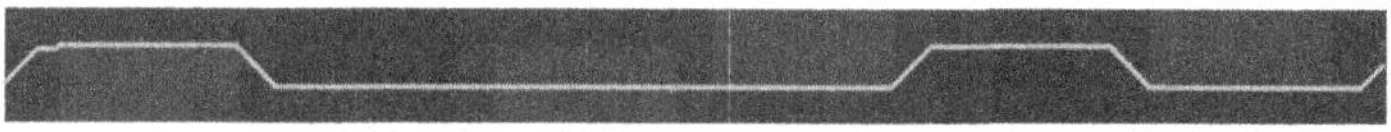

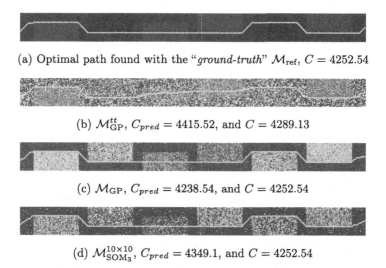

(a) Optimal path found with the "*ground-truth*" $\mathcal{M}_{\mathrm{ref}}$, $C = 4252.54$

(b) $\mathcal{M}_{\mathrm{GP}}^{tt}$, $C_{pred} = 4415.52$, and $C = 4289.13$

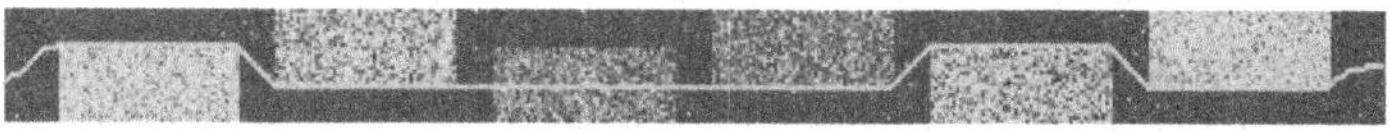

(c) $\mathcal{M}_{\mathrm{GP}}$, $C_{pred} = 4238.54$, and $C = 4252.54$

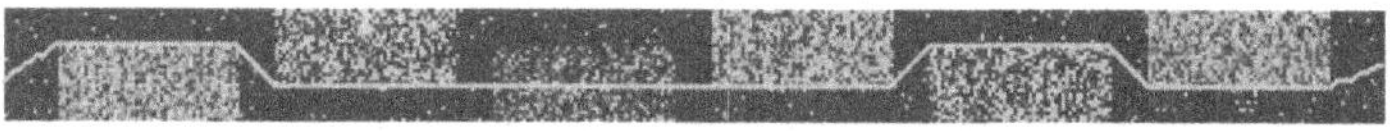

(d) $\mathcal{M}_{\mathrm{SOM_3}}^{10\times10}$, $C_{pred} = 4349.1$, and $C = 4252.54$

Fig. 4. Selected best found optimal paths using different traversal cost model of the cost c_1 (required power) with the predicted cost C_{pred} and the final path cost C computed using the reference traversal costs.

Both $\mathcal{M}_{\text{GP}}$ and SOM-based traversal cost predictions are capable of determining the same solution as the optimal reference path using $\mathcal{M}_{\text{ref}}$ with a lower standard deviation of the GP-based model. The compound $\mathcal{M}_{\text{GP}}^{tt}$ is not able to provide the same solution as the reference model $\mathcal{M}_{\text{ref}}$ in any of the twenty generated grid maps. The maps are randomly created, and also particular features vary in real observations. Therefore, the single reported case does not necessarily mean the compounded model is not a suitable predictor of the traversal costs, especially when the overall difference of the path cost is about 1.5% of the reference optimal path costs for the model $\mathcal{M}_{\text{ref}}$. Notice, the last two rows in Table 4 is for the predictions using classification based on the identified terrains, which is described in the following section.

4.2 Terrain Types Identification

Unsupervised clustering has been firstly performed for the feature descriptors of the trail $\mathcal{T}_{all}$ to compute the terrain type ratio (3) and study differences between the human labeled terrain types and identified types from the data. Even though the trail is composed of seven terrain types, the smallest cluster separation measure [3] is achieved for six clusters. The corresponding distribution of the labeled terrain types among these clusters is depicted in Table 5.

Table 5. Terrain type ratios of the clustered feature descriptors of $\mathcal{T}_{all}$

Cluster	*Flat floor covered by black fabric*	*Wooden blocks covered by black fabric*	*Wooden blocks*	*Wooden blocks covered by artif. turf*	*Flat floor*	*Wooden sloped surface*	*Flat floor covered by artif. turf*
1	1.5	21.5	2.2	0.2	14.0	0.2	0.3
2	0.0	0.0	18.7	0.0	0.0	1.9	0.0
3	0.0	0.0	0.0	6.5	0.0	0.0	12.2
4	16.4	0.0	0.0	0.0	0.0	0.2	0.5
5	0.0	0.0	0.0	0.0	0.0	3.5	0.0
6	0.0	0.0	0.0	0.0	0.0	0.2	0.0

The largest cluster includes almost 40% of the features, and the results indicate that *wooden blocks covered by black fabric* might be considered similar to the *flat floor*, which is not expected behavior. The wooden blocks terrain type is identifiable in the second cluster. The third cluster indicates that probably the appearance features are significant for the artificial turf, which is green. The flat floor covered by the black fabric is dominant in the fourth cluster. Finally, two additional clusters cover the wooden sloped surface. The means of the determined clusters can be utilized for the classification with the prediction of the traversal cost determined as the means of the particular cluster traversal cost. However, regarding the results for such $\mathcal{M}_{\text{clustering}}$ in Table 4, the terrain distinguishability is lower than for the traversal cost regression.

Table 6. Terrain type ratios of the clustered prototypes of the learned $\mathcal{M}_{\text{SOM}}^{10\times10}$

Cluster	*Flat floor covered by black fabric*	*Wooden blocks covered by black fabric*	*Wooden blocks*	*Wooden blocks covered by artif. turf*	*Flat floor*	*Wooden sloped surface*	*Flat floor covered by artif. turf*
1	17	15	2	0	6	0	2
2	0	0	0	6	0	0	12
3	0	0	13	0	0	5	0
4	0	0	0	3	0	0	6
5	0	0	0	0	0	6	0
6	0	0	0	2	0	1	0
7	0	0	0	0	0	2	0
8	0	0	0	0	0	2	0

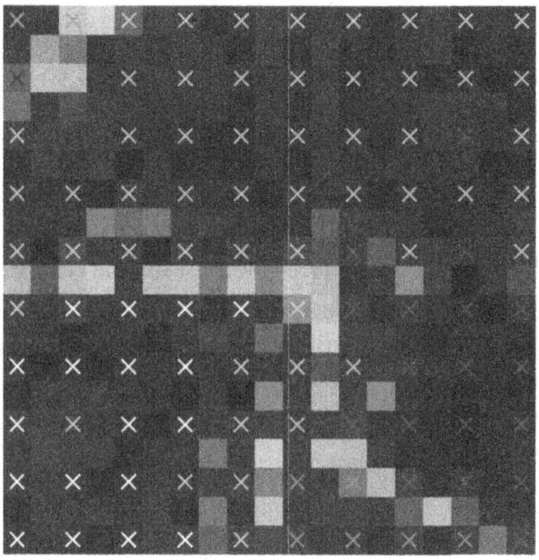

Fig. 5. Visualization of the clustered learned SOM on top of the U-matrix. The individual clusters are shown as small color crosses at the centers of cells corresponding to the prototypes of the SOM lattice.

The terrain type ratios of clustered learned prototypes from the 10×10 large SOM are depicted in Table 6 and corresponding U-matrix is visualized in Fig. 5. In this case, the smallest separation measure is for eight clusters, and we can read from the results that black fabric is dominant for the first cluster while the artificial turf is dominant for the second cluster. The wooden blocks might be considered similar to the wooden sloped surface. Similarly to Table 5, the wooden sloped surface can be found in several clusters.

Having clustered SOM prototypes, individual costs per each cluster can be computed as the average cost value among the cluster, that can be then utilized for traversal cost assessment based on classification of the feature descriptor $\boldsymbol{d}_{sa}$ according to the closest prototype of the learned SOM. Regarding the overview of the path cost in Table 4, such a traversal cost prediction is noticeably worse than the SOM-based regression. However, terrain type identification can be suitable in the scenario where the "*ground-truth*" reference traversal costs are not available because of missing explicit terrain type labels.

4.3 Discussion

The reported results support the feasibility of using SOM for unsupervised learning of the traversal cost model and even relatively small lattice with the size 10×10 provides competitive results to significantly more demanding GP. Moreover, SOM also provides a straightforward prediction of multi-dimensional cost indicators. Although only a relatively simple evaluation of the traversal cost prediction in path planning has been performed, the results support sufficient distinguishability of the hard to traverse areas that can be achieved even for predictors with relatively low correctness ratios. It is especially important in the cases where the reference traversal costs are not explicitly available, e.g., because of a priory unknown environments in robotic exploration missions [12]. SOM-based unsupervised learning can be considered as a suitable technique for traversal cost learning, and we further plan to consider on-line variants of SOM such as [14] to follow the motivational deployments with incremental learning.

Moreover, based on the reported results, we can observe that the robot can perceive the terrain differently than the natural labels derived from the particular terrains the robot traversed. It is also because the proprioceptive sensing can be similar for two terrains that can appear differently, e.g., like wooden blocks and a wooden sloped surface which are different mainly in shape features but look similar in ab channels of the Lab color space. Hence, we can speculate that the human labels for the terrain types might be misleading, albeit they seem to be a natural choice, which is used for learning the reference model $\mathcal{M}_{\text{ref}}$ and also the compounded GP-based model $\mathcal{M}^{tt}_{\text{GP}}$. The most important part of the "*ground-truth*" is the fact that in the motivational deployment of the robot in a priory unknown environment, the explicit labels are not available, and the robot has to rely solely on unsupervised learning, where the most important quality measure is a sufficient distinguishability of the hard to traverse areas regarding the particular cost. The presented results indicate that a combination of several traversal costs is probably necessary, as considering a single cost might now provide sufficient distinguishability. The evaluation of the traversal cost predictors in such setups is considered as a subject of our future work.

5 Conclusion

In this paper, we report on unsupervised learning of robot traversal cost predictors. The results support that SOM can provide competitive predictions to the GP-based model, but it is less computationally demanding. Moreover, the unsupervised terrain types identification provides a different view on the natural human labels of the terrains, and it seems to be suitable to focus on how the terrain types are perceived by the robot rather than human labeling, which is particularly important in the deployments without known terrain types. Besides, the results further support that prediction based on the weighted average from the closest prototypes improves the predicted values concerning the reference model. However, there is still an open question of how the predictors for incremental and unsupervised learning should be evaluated because of the stochastic nature of the cost variables and also the exteroceptive features. Therefore, we plan to investigate the alternative feature descriptors and further ways how to create the reference model in addition to improving the predictors.

References

1. Arthur, D., Vassilvitskii, S.: K-means++: the advantages of careful seeding. In: Eighteenth Annual ACM-SIAM Symposium on Discrete Algorithms (SODA), pp. 1027–1035 (2007)
2. Bartoszyk, S., Kasprzak, P., Belter, D.: Terrain-aware motion planning for a walking robot. In: International Workshop on Robot Motion and Control (RoMoCo), pp. 29–34 (2017). https://doi.org/10.1109/RoMoCo.2017.8003889
3. Davies, D.L., Bouldin, D.W.: A cluster separation measure. IEEE Trans. Pattern Anal. Mach. Intell. PAMI **1**(2), 224–227 (1979). https://doi.org/10.1109/TPAMI.1979.4766909
4. Faigl, J., Prágr, M.: Incremental traversability assessment learning using growing neural gas algorithm. In: Advances in Self-Organizing Maps, Learning Vector Quantization, Clustering and Data Visualization, pp. 166–176 (2020). https://doi.org/10.1007/978-3-030-19642-4_17
5. Faigl, J., Čížek, P.: Adaptive locomotion control of hexapod walking robot for traversing rough terrains with position feedback only. Robot. Auton. Syst. **116**, 136–147 (2019). https://doi.org/10.1016/j.robot.2019.03.008
6. GPy: a Gaussian process framework in python (2012). http://github.com/SheffieldML/GPy. Accessed 28 Mar 2019
7. Hartigan, J.A., Wong, M.A.: A k-means clustering algorithm. JSTOR Appl. Stat. **28**(1), 100–108 (1979). https://doi.org/10.2307/2346830
8. Kohonen, T.: Self-organizing Maps, 3rd edn. Springer, Heidelberg (2001). https://doi.org/10.1007/978-3-642-56927-2
9. Kragh, M., Jørgensen, R.N., Pedersen, H.: Object detection and terrain classification in agricultural fields using 3D lidar data. In: International Conference on Computer Vision Systems (ICVS), vol. 9163, pp. 188–197 (2015). https://doi.org/10.1007/978-3-319-20904-3_18
10. Prágr, M., Čížek, P., Faigl, J.: Cost of transport estimation for legged robot based on terrain features inference from aerial scan. In: IEEE/RSJ International Conference on Intelligent Robots and Systems (IROS), pp. 1745–1750 (2018). https://doi.org/10.1109/IROS.2018.8593374
11. Prágr, M., Čížek, P., Faigl, J.: Incremental learning of traversability cost for aerial reconnaissance support to ground units. In: Modelling and Simulation for Autonomous Systems (MESAS), pp. 412–421 (2019). https://doi.org/10.1007/978-3-030-14984-0_30
12. Prágr, M., Čížek, P., Faigl, J.: Online incremental learning of the terrain traversal cost in autonomous exploration. In: Robotics: Science and Systems (RSS) (2019). https://doi.org/10.15607/RSS.2019.XV.040

13. Rasmussen, C.E., Williams, C.K.I.: Gaussian Processes for Machine Learning. MIT Press, Cambridge (2006)
14. Rougier, N., Boniface, Y.: Dynamic self-organising map. Neurocomputing **74**(11), 1840–1847 (2011). https://doi.org/10.1016/j.neucom.2010.06.034
15. Ultsch, A., Siemon, H.P.: Kohonen's self organizing feature maps for exploratory data analysis. In: International Neural Network Conference (INNC), pp. 305–308 (1990)
16. Vasudevan, S., Ramos, F., Nettleton, E., Durrant-Whyte, H., Blair, A.: Gaussian process modeling of large scale terrain. In: IEEE International Conference on Robotics and Automation (ICRA), pp. 1047–1053 (2009). https://doi.org/10.1002/rob.20309
17. Vesanto, J., Alhoniemi, E.: Clustering of the self-organizing map. IEEE Trans. Neural Networks **11**(3), 586–600 (2000). https://doi.org/10.1109/72.846731
18. Čížek, P., Faigl, J.: On localization and mapping with RGB-D sensor and hexapod walking robot in rough terrains. In: IEEE International Conference on Systems, Man, and Cybernetics (SMC), pp. 2273–2278 (2016). https://doi.org/10.1109/SMC.2016.7844577

Scaffolding Haptic Attention with Controller Gating

Alexandra Moringen, Sascha Fleer[(✉)], and Helge Ritter

Neuroinformatics Group, EXC Cognitive Interaction Technology (CITEC), Bielefeld University, Bielefeld, Germany
{abarch,sfleer,helge}@techfak.uni-bielefeld.de
https://ni.www.techfak.uni-bielefeld.de

Abstract. A powerful concept that emerged within the field of educational psychology is scaffolding. Characterizing favourable expert-learner interaction, it can be defined as a temporal support that provides a novice an adaptable guidance to either learn tasks that would usually be beyond own capabilities or to speed up and refine the learning of manageable problems. In this work we apply the above-mentioned concept to implement a novel multi-strategy haptic exploration controller that is able to perform object identification using a robot.

In our previous work we have proposed a reinforcement learner that acquires haptic exploration capabilities for a goal-directed task by optimizing motor control in a strongly restricted attentional framework, called the *haptic attention model* (HAM). The resulting policy however was not characterized by a smooth energy-efficient exploration suitable for execution on a robot. In this work, we scaffold the designed learning architecture by imposing the so-called *controller gating* that is trained to switch between orientation and position control. Integrated in the same reinforcement learning setting as the HAM, controller gating guides and monitors the data acquisition. Inspired by the human expert scaffolding, it analyzes the HAM internal data representation, modulates the HAM weight update process, and forces data acquisition that achieves efficient and successful completion of the goal. Our computational scaffold adapts to the learner model, while it masters the skill. The evaluation demonstrated that it is more likely for the trained model to change either location or orientation than simultaneously change both, which significantly improves the smoothness and the energy-efficiency of the resulting exploration.

Keywords: Haptic exploration · Reinforcement learning · Scaffolding · Gating · Haptic glances · Exploratory procedures · Robotics

A. Moringen and S. Fleer—Contributed equally to this work.

Electronic supplementary material The online version of this chapter (https://doi.org/10.1007/978-3-030-30487-4_51) contains supplementary material, which is available to authorized users.

I. V. Tetko et al. (Eds.): ICANN 2019, LNCS 11727, pp. 669–684, 2019.
https://doi.org/10.1007/978-3-030-30487-4_51

1 Introduction

Efficient and successful execution of almost any daily task heavily relies on haptic interaction with the environment. Although this capacity is essential to humans, haptic interaction is still a great challenge even for very advanced robotic platforms. Ideally we need a general modeling approach to learn a goal-directed policy based on haptic data, thus enabling a robot to acquire haptic skills without or with little supervision. This process should be performed preferably in simulation that enables to address time and security concerns.

Recent work [10,24] towards implementing contact-rich interaction with the environment proposes methods to learn, to generalize and to make the policy robust. The authors outline multiple encountered difficulties, such as restrictions through sample size, insufficient quality or resolution of the tactile sensors, or the absence of physics models of contact and collisions. Another major challenge is the multimodal integration [19] illustrated on an example of object identification. The learned policies perform a robust peg insertion [10] and rotation of a dice [24]. Work by these authors shows that implementing haptic interaction is still an open question in the case, in which we do not hard code the haptic interaction process, as done in e.g. [3], but learn it. The demonstrated applications, constrained to a small number of shapes, show that there is still a need for an approach to learn haptic interaction with unknown 3D shapes without human guidance or demonstrations. This poses a challenge, due to the fact that common shapes are often represented by a spatially distributed mixture of local geometrical features, such as different types of curvature, vertices, edges, etc. Therefore, an efficient haptic exploration policy should not only control the pose of a given tactile sensor while optimizing the information intake, but also integrate both the temporal, the spatial and the multimodal aspects of the data gained throughout the exploration.

The target of our work is to further foster a generalized approach to learning of haptic interaction for robots employing simulation. In [4] we have proposed a computational approach that addresses the above-mentioned aspects and performs the learning in a physics-driven simulation environment Gazebo. In this work we extend the previous work with two contributions. Firstly, we employ a simulated KUKA robot arm with an attached tactile sensor array Myrmex [20] to perform haptic interaction. To enable a rigorous exploratory behavior, the original HAM model yields a stochastic location policy resulting in a behavior that could be described casually as jumpy. Regulating this stochasticity for more smooth and efficient trajectory in Cartesian space as well as a more focused exploration of the local shape features is the second contribution of this work. Inspired by human behavior[1], we introduce the so-called scaffolded HAM, or *S*-HAM. We demonstrate the success of our approach on gated policy learning to classify four objects.

---

[1] A visualization of a participant performing haptic search [13] includes both jumps and a focused local shape explorations can be found in the supplementary material (`Haptic_Search_MHSB.mp4`).

2 Background and Terminology

To form the theoretical foundation of our approach, we combine three building blocks (described in detail in the following sections):

- primitive haptic actions termed **haptic glances** (HGs) to perform the most elementary haptic interaction,
- **haptic attention model** to execute an optimal sequence of haptic glances,
- **computational scaffolding** to guide the learning and performance of the above model.

Implementation of the above concepts is described in detail in Sects. 3 and 4.

2.1 Haptic Glances and Exploratory Procedures

The first building block of our approach is the concept of haptic glances [9]. Klatzky and Lederman present the original definition of a haptic glance as a brief, spatially constrained contact that involves little or no movement of the fingers. We interpret a haptic glance as an element of a functional basis of haptic interaction, from which *haptic exploratory procedures* (EPs) [8] or other haptic manipulations can be constructed. Inspired by the functionality of the finger, our first implementation of haptic glances for control of the tactile sensor array Myrmex [4] employs the parameter pose as an input. The corresponding pose is then taken up by Myrmex when it establishes contact with the environment (see Fig. 1). In our setup, the objects are designed to have only a one-dimensional curvature feature (see Fig. 2). Therefore, we can employ a one-dimensional translation and orientation to parameterize the target pose without loss of generality. A haptic glance is then characterized by a tuple $(\boldsymbol{p}, x, \varphi)$, where $\boldsymbol{p}$ describes the pressure profile of the sensor after the contact has been established.

2.2 Haptic Attention Model

Building upon the *haptic glances*, HAM performs a goal-directed optimization over a sequence of target poses controlling the tactile sensor. In other words, it generates a robotic exploratory procedure. Although our previously presented model HAM is leading to fruitful results when learning the object identification task, the generated exploratory procedure may be executed more time-efficiently and smoothly. For an execution on a robot, we therefore pursue a behavior that resembles the contour following EP [8] in a small local environment. When describing contour following w.r.t. the translation and orientation, a sliding movement along a flat surface changes the translation but leaves the orientation of the finger roughly unchanged. On the other hand, while we explore a salient edge, the translation of the finger remains unchanged, while the orientation changes. HAM, characterized by a stochastic location policy, is very likely to vary both parameters at the same time. Therefore, firstly, this enables only one type of strategy designed to explore by sampling pose from a Gaussian.

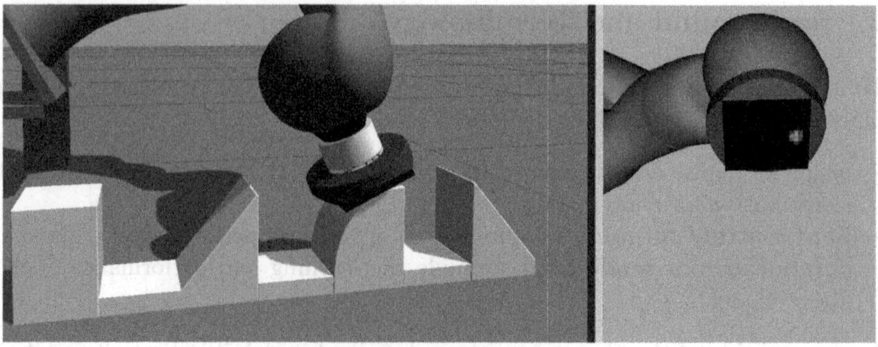

Fig. 1. KUKA arm performing a haptic glance in a Gazebo simulation environment. Left: Myrmex moves down from above until a collision with a simulated object is detected. Right: Corresponding output of the simulated sensor array. The strength of the raw signal determines the color mapping from green to red. (Color figure online)

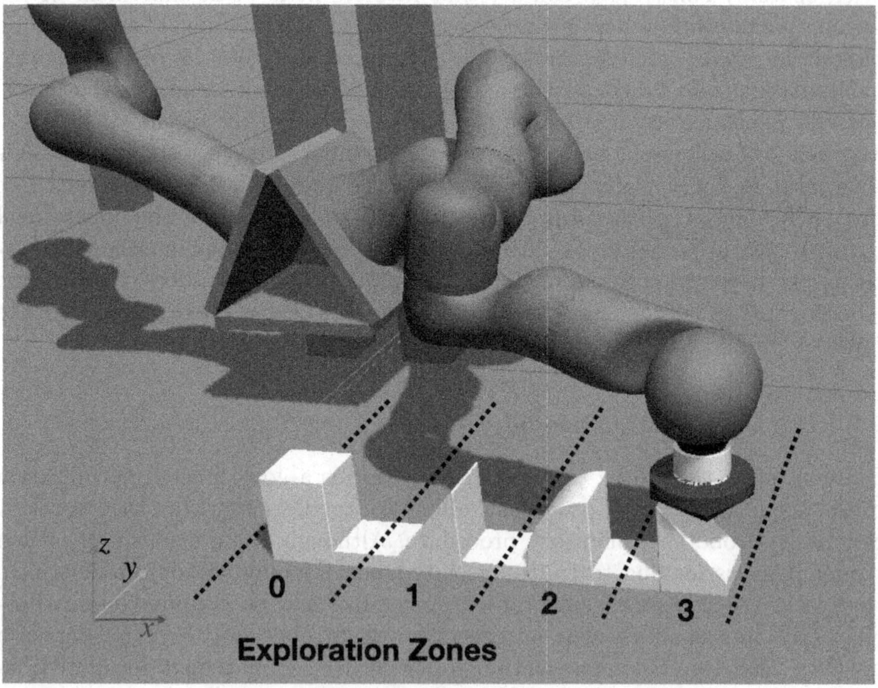

Fig. 2. Simulated environment with four objects 0–3. The simulated Myrmex sensor array is depicted in red. The simulated tactile sensor grid is facing down. The *exploration zone* for each object is visualized by the dotted lines. (Color figure online)

Secondly, there is no mechanism to control the efficiency of policy in terms of energy or smoothness. To address the above issues, we extend HAM with an extra gating network S that at each point in time decides about the type of control strategy to be executed based on representation and success of HAM.

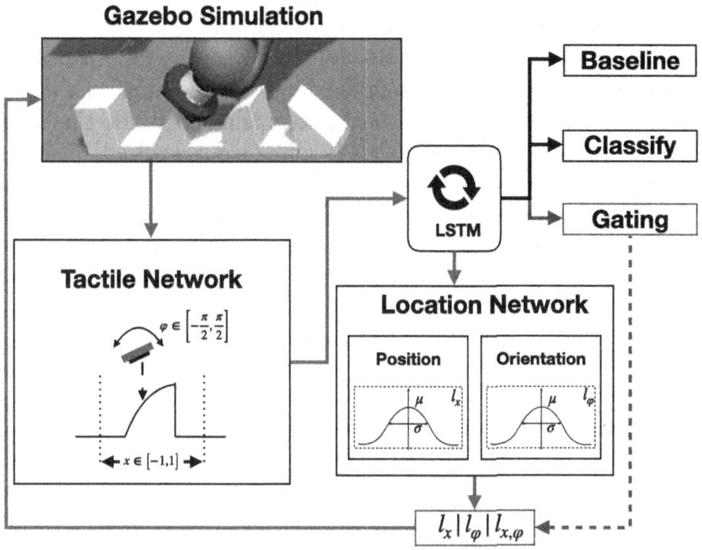

Fig. 3. HAM architecture (red and black). Gating extension S (green). Overall neural network architecture S-HAM performs control of a tactile sensor array Myrmex in a simulation environment Gazebo. The main control loop is depicted with red arrows. The sensor array (in red) is controlled by a KUKA arm. Gazebo outputs the sensor reading together with the corresponding sensor pose for each haptic glance. The tactile network merges the pose and the tactile data to a single representation provided further to the LSTM. The LSTM is responsible for accumulating data over time and is optimized to provide features to the classifier that enable it to perform an optimal classification. The location network closes the loop by generating the next target pose for the sensor in the simulation environment. The gating network implements the scaffolding, and is trained to decide which exploration strategy to employ in the next step based on the training process. (Color figure online)

2.3 Scaffolding

Scaffolding is a term commonly employed to describe a process of guidance performed by the expert to enable the learner to acquire a new skill [5,17,27]. Our implementation presented in this work is strongly aligned with this description. In general, scaffolding employs a range of techniques, such as ongoing diagnosis and assessment, fading out of guidance, and hierarchical increase of the complexity level for the performed tasks. It can be considered central to describe fostering expert-learner interaction. Although there is no existing theoretical framework for scaffolding in machine learning, some concepts are built on similar ideas although the direct link to scaffolding has never been established. One of this approaches is the so-called curriculum learning [2]. It can be described by a gradual increase of the task complexity given to the learning algorithm. It is implemented by e.g. a careful selection of sub-tasks employed in the course of the model training. Our scaffolding implementation with a gating network S guides the learner during the data acquisition and optimization process (see detailed description in the sections below). Importantly, the scaffold S is itself integrated into the same reinforcement learning framework as the learner HAM, and optimizes its output towards reward maximization. While there exists work were the learning process of an artificial intelligence is scaffolded using a human teacher [22,23] or the psychological concept of scaffolding is used in order to design a novel meta-cognitive scaffolding classifier using Fuzzy Neural Networks [18], we propose scaffolding as a continuous self-regulating module that is able to directly interact with the exploration policy of the regular model. It can thus be seen as a continuous self-guiding approach that enables the agent to learn to use abilities that it is usually not capable of.

3 Experimental Setup and Robot Control

The experimental setup consists of two parts: the simulation environment and the haptic control policy. The simulated robotic setup consist of a KUKA LRW4 robot arm. It has 7 degrees of freedom and its end-effector is equipped with the square-shaped tactile sensor array, called Myrmex, mounted on an ATI force-torque sensor (Fig. 2). The simulation environment Gazebo[2] contains both, the simulated robot, as well as the four simulated three-dimensional objects that are placed within individual exploration zones for classification. The interaction between the policy and the simulation environment takes place over the Gazebo-ROS interface. The haptic policy provides a target pose for Myrmex in the exploration zone's local coordinate system, which is then executed by Gazebo (see a detailed description in the section below). After the sensor-object collision is detected, the values of the simulated tactile grid are sent back to the control policy via ROS[3].

Myrmex is a rigid tactile sensor array that exists both in simulation and as real sensor array. It is a 16×16 grid of tactile sensors. The movement of Myrmex in this work is restricted to performing haptic glances[4]. As one can see in the provided video, a haptic glance is performed by moving the sensor down until a collision with the object can be detected. The sensor readings are generated after applying the Myrmex sensor simulation library[5] to the raw collision information

[2] http://gazebosim.org.
[3] https://www.ros.org.
[4] An example of several haptic glances can be found in the supplementary material (`KUKA.mp4`).
[5] `Myrmex-Gazebo` plugin library: https://github.com/ubi-agni/gazebo_tactile_plugins.

generated by Gazebo. Once a collision has been established, the sensor is moved up again. A new target pose is then generated by the network.

Haptic glance is a primitive controller that is parameterized by two inputs, the rotation around y-axis and a translation along the x-axis resulting in a pose vector $\boldsymbol{l} = (\varphi, x)$. Task-oriented meta-control is then performed by the network architecture that executes a closed-loop control, and generates new target poses based on the tactile sensor readings (see section below). In order to learn an exploration policy that is independent of the object's pose within the global coordinate system, we introduce *exploration zones*. Exploration zones are pre-defined regions in front of the robot with their own local coordinate systems, in which the objects are placed for exploration. After specification of the exploration zone, two out of six pose parameters of the tactile sensor can be modified by the HAM: the position $x \in [-1, 1]$ along the x-axis within the coordinate frame of the corresponding exploration zone, and the orientation angle $\varphi \in [-0.3\pi, 0.3\pi]$ around the y-axis.

The new controller gating S selects one of the following options: $\boldsymbol{l}_{\boldsymbol{x}} = (\varphi_{t-1}, x)$, $\boldsymbol{l}_{\varphi} = (\varphi, x_{t-1})$, or $\boldsymbol{l}_{\boldsymbol{x},\varphi} = (\varphi, x)$. Here, the index $t-1$ denotes that the parameter from the previous loop execution $t-1$ is employed (it remains constant), and only the other parameter generated by the network is employed to control the sensor.

3.1 Dataset

Available haptic simulation is still only slightly faster than real-time. It is, however, possible to replace the data acquisition in live simulation by using a dataset pre-recorded with the same simulation. The sensor is interacting within the same regions of the location-orientation space multiple times leading to almost the same pressure readings. To enable an efficient evaluation of the model for a different configurations of hyperparameters, e.g. the number of haptic glances, we tesselate the location-orientation space that can be accessed by the sensor. We then generate a cache of haptic glances that are stored in a dataset for learning and hyperparameter optimization.

The dataset is generated by recording tuples $d_o = (\boldsymbol{p}, x, \varphi)$ of the normalized pressure data $\boldsymbol{p}$, together with the corresponding location x and orientation φ of the sensor. In order to generate data of each object that is independent of its positioning, the location data $x \in [-1, 1]$ is given within the location space of the exploration zone. After reaching the corresponding exploration zone with the robot, the recording of the data points starts at $x = -1$ with the orientation $\varphi = -0.3\pi$. After covering the orientation space by recording φ while incrementing it with a step size of $\Delta_{\varphi} = \pi \cdot 0.05$, the location is incremented by $\Delta_x = 0.05$ and the recording of the orientations starts anew at $\varphi = -0.3\pi$. Leading to 41×41 pre-recordings per object (41 orientation recordings per position), our full dataset has a size of about 6724 data points. During training, the model generates location-orientation pairs (x, φ) for which the corresponding pressure vector $\boldsymbol{p}$ is extracted from the dataset. This is performed by taking the data point d_o that best matches (x, φ), instead of re-measuring the pressure vector in simulation.

4 Methods

Instead of seeing their environment as a whole image, humans are only able to recognize small parts of the scene, while the location of the fixations depends on the current task [6,11]. In machine learning, this human-like way of perception is modeled in approaches like the *recurrent model of visual attention* [1,12]. As "visual perception is a touch-like process" [16], we used the above-mentioned model as an inspiration for a haptic controller that is able to learn efficient haptic exploration. While a detailed description of the learner model can be found in [4] we only give a brief recap of the model structure in this work. Instead, the focus is set on the description of the model extension with scaffolding mechanism, which is implemented by means of a gating network sub-module.

4.1 Network Architecture

Our core network architecture HAM is built out of three sub-modules: The "tactile network", the "location network" and the "classification network". The modules are all connected to a single *Long short-term memory unit* (LSTM) [7] with a hidden state of 256 neurons (see Fig. 3). Additionally, the HAM is integrated in a control loop with Gazebo. Each executed haptic glance, executed within the Gazebo simulation, is represented by the pose and the corresponding pressure vector, $\boldsymbol{l}$ and $\boldsymbol{p}$, resp. This data is processed by the tactile network, which is in charge of merging and representing both data modalities, the pose and the pressure profile, with equally-sized feature vectors. By merging the pose of the sensor and the corresponding sensor reading, the "what" and "where", in one feature vector it performs a **bimodal integration**. The features of the network are then provided to the LSTM module to perform **integration of the input features over time**. This is an important part of the strategy, as it is focused on optimizing the sequential information intake. While the very first glance is always random, the location network then provides the target pose for the next haptic glance. It generates a adaptable stochastic policy, based on a two-dimensional Gaussian with adaptable mean μ and standard deviation σ. After generating a certain number of glances, the classification network uses the accumulated information, stored within the LSTM to perform classification of the current object. As the model is trained using *reinforcement learning* [21], it receives a reward of $r_t = 1$ if the object was correctly classified and $r_t = 0$ otherwise.

Tactile Network. The task of this module is to combine the information about the sensor's pose $\boldsymbol{l}$ with the corresponding pressure data $\boldsymbol{p}$ that were measured during the execution of the haptic glance. Therefore, the pressure data is normalized and then processed through one linear layer of 64 neurons. Likewise, the vector $\boldsymbol{l}$ is altered. The features of both layers are then concatenated and again streamed through two additional layers with 64 neurons and one with 256 in order to get the correct number of features for the LSTM network.

Location Network. This module uses the feature vector that is computed by the LSTM network for generating a new location-orientation pair that is then used for the next haptic glance. Therefore, Gaussian distributions are used for sampling the position x and orientation φ respectively by adapting the mean μ and standard deviation σ. For computing the four necessary variables μ_x, μ_φ, σ_x and σ_φ, the features of the LSTM are propagated through an independent linear layer with 64 neurons for each of them. The means are sampled within the range $\mu \in [-1, 1]$ using the *tanh* as the activation function. For the standard deviations $\sigma \in [0, 1]$ we employ the *sigmoid* function. To ensure that the location and position of the sensor is valid, the sampled values of the Gaussians are restricted to the range $[-1, 1]$. Thus, if the sampled x or φ is sampled outside this range, it is resampled using the same mean and standard deviation.

Gating Network. The extension of the model S-HAM with the gating network performs scaffolding by guiding the controller selection process: orientation change, location change, or both. As the location network generates a stochastic policy in order to facilitate exploration of the object, generation of the exact same x or φ so that $x \approx x_{t-1}$ or $\varphi \approx \varphi_{t-1}$ is unlikely. Consequently, the gating network can be seen as a supportive module that extends the policy and enables to perform three distinct types of shape exploration to suite main types of curvature: locally flat (constant orientation φ), curvy (change of both φ and x) or edgy (constant translation x). Figure 4 visualizes an exemplary data flow within the network. The gating network is built out of a single linear layer with 64 neurons and three output neurons, using the *softmax* function as the activation function. Thus, it generates a probability density $\pi_g(\boldsymbol{h}_S; \theta_g)$, estimating the type of the controller using the feature vector $\boldsymbol{h}_S$ that is generated by the LSTM unit after S consecutive glances. θ_g denotes the weights of the gating network.

4.2 Network Training

One training step is given through the sequence of a pre-defined number of haptic glances, followed by a classification attempt. The classifier and the location network are trained together using an update rule (4) that is derived from a hybrid-loss, while the gating network is trained independently. The update rule (4) is built out of a *cross-entropy* term, penalizing misclassification on the one hand. On the other hand, an additional term is added that rates the stochastic policy that is generated by the location network. This part of the update rule is computed using the *REINFORCE algorithm* [25,26], where the plain update rule is given by

$$\Delta_\theta = \alpha_t (r_t - b_t) \cdot \zeta, \tag{1}$$

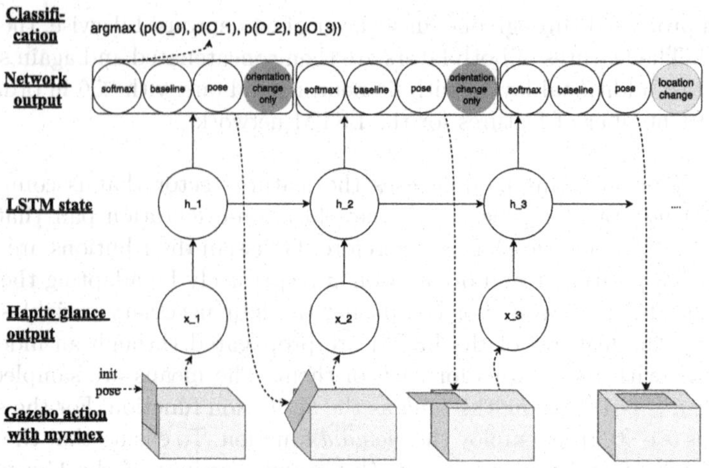

Fig. 4. Unfolded representation of the *S*-HAM network architecture illustrating the data flow. In the bottom row Myrmex is depicted by a red square. The network output presented in the upper row consist of the classifier output (softmax), the baseline, the new target pose (location and orientation) and, finally, the output of the gating network corresponding to the type of the primitive controller. An exemplary output of the gating network is depicted with green and yellow. (Color figure online)

where α_t is the learning rate, and $\zeta = \frac{\partial \log f}{\partial \theta}$ the *characteristic eligibility* of the function f that characterizes the to-be-learned policy. In order to reduce the variance within the loss, the REINFORCE algorithm uses a learned baseline b_t that estimates the performance of the model. The baseline, like the gating network, is optimized independently from the main architecture by minimizing the averaged mean-squared-error with respect to the reward r_t.

Location network uses Gaussians $\mathcal{N}(x; \mu, \sigma)$ with adaptable mean μ and standard deviation σ for generating the stochastic policy that controls the position and orientation of the haptic glances. Therefore, the means (μ_x, μ_φ) and standard deviations $(\sigma_x, \sigma_\varphi)$ of the sampled position and orientation can directly be seen as the adaptable variables of the network instead of the weights θ. The characteristic eligibilities for μ and σ are then given by

$$\zeta_\mu = \frac{\partial \log \mathcal{N}(x; \mu, \sigma)}{\partial \mu} = \frac{x - \mu}{\sigma^2} \tag{2}$$

and

$$\zeta_\sigma = \frac{\partial \log \mathcal{N}(x; \mu, \sigma)}{\partial \sigma} = \frac{(x - \mu)^2 - \sigma^2}{\sigma^3}. \tag{3}$$

The update rule for the classification and location policy can be summarized as:

$$
\begin{aligned}
\Delta_\theta = &-\alpha \cdot \sum_{o=0}^{O} \log(\pi_c(o)) \cdot y_o \\
&-\alpha \cdot \beta \cdot (r_t - b_t) \cdot \begin{cases} \zeta_{\mu_x} + \zeta_{\mu_\varphi} + \zeta_{\sigma_x} + \zeta_{\sigma_\varphi} & \text{if } \boldsymbol{l}_{x,\varphi} \leftarrow \pi_g(\boldsymbol{h}_S) \\ \zeta_{\mu_x} + \zeta_{\sigma_x} & \text{if } \boldsymbol{l}_x \leftarrow \pi_g(\boldsymbol{h}_S) \\ \zeta_{\mu_\varphi} + \zeta_{\sigma_\varphi} & \text{if } \boldsymbol{l}_\varphi \leftarrow \pi_g(\boldsymbol{h}_S) \end{cases}
\end{aligned} \quad (4)
$$

The first part is the supervised cross-entropy misclassification penalty. The function $\pi_c(o)$ gives the computed classification probability that the to-be-classified object is object o, while y_o is 1 if o corresponds to the correct object and 0 otherwise. In the second part, reinforcement learning is used for judging the generated location policy of the haptic glances. ζ_{μ_x} and ζ_{μ_φ} are the characteristic eligibilities, rating the generated means (μ_x, μ_φ), while ζ_{σ_x} and ζ_{σ_φ} are rating the generated standard deviations $(\sigma_x, \sigma_\varphi)$ respectively. The parameter β controls the contribution of the different parts of the update, while the characteristic eligibilities are included in the update based on the decision of the gating network $\pi_g(\boldsymbol{h}_S)$. E.g. $\boldsymbol{l}_x \leftarrow$ is indicating that the gating network has decided to only employ the position control, while the orientation remains constant. Hence, only "active" components of the update rule defined by the selected strategy (4) are employed. In case the orientation change is selected by the gating network, the weight update is performed only for the layers of the location network that are effectively used within the current training step for the orientation generating part (see Fig. 3).

The gating network is also trained using the REINFORCE update rule (1) with the characteristic eligibility

$$\zeta_g = \nabla_{\theta_g} \log \pi_g(\boldsymbol{h}_S; \theta_g). \quad (5)$$

The overall network model is trained using stochastic gradient descent with Nesterov momentum [14,15]. The chosen learning rate of $\alpha_0 = 8 \cdot 10^{-4}$ decays exponentially towards $\alpha_{\min} = 10^{-4}$ every training-step t with a decay factor of $\delta_\alpha = 0.99$ and a step-size of $T = 800$.

5 Experiments and Results

Our experiment is split in two parts. In the first part, we train our model by using the dataset. The results are then taken to analyse the learned policy of the gating network and compare the achieved classification accuracy with our baseline model. In the second part we study the energy consumption of both HAM and S-HAM by exploiting the pre-trained models for evaluating the joint changes during the classification task on the full robot simulation.

5.1 Training on the Dataset

For the experimental evaluation of our approach we train a haptic policy to explore and classify the four above-mentioned objects while relying on the information of 8 consecutive glances. For each training step, a batch size of 64 is used. It is important to notice that the current batch only specifies the to-be-classified objects and their corresponding exploration zones by randomly choosing from the four provided ones. Except for the first random haptic glance, the locations and the corresponding pressure vectors are chosen by the location policy of the network. The next important remark is that the network is processing all to-be-classified objects within the batch sequentially which is a relevant feature for the application on a real/simulated robot. The emerging policy is therefore interco-ordinated for the current object and the generated sequence of haptic glances. At the beginning of the classification process for each object within the batch, the exploration zone of the given object is set as active. The pre-defined number of glances is performed one after another within the interval corresponding to the selected zone. Two adjustable pose parameters of the sensor are generated by the (S)-HAM for each, except the first, glance.

For training, the gradients are computed for every classification attempt within the batch. In the end, the gradients are accumulated and a single update is performed. For evaluating the performance of the designed approach, the learning is stopped after a predefined number of steps. Using the current policy, the model has then to classify 100 batches which are then used to compute the average success rate. The results are then averaged over eleven distinct learning runs while the standard deviation of the mean is used as an error. Thus all runs are executed the same number of training steps that is likely to ensure a good final performance instead of using techniques like "early stopping" to have the same amount of data for all runs.

Figure 5 shows the controllers selected by the gating network averaged over all four objects (see again Fig. 2). After a short learning process, it decides to mainly use the generated location $\boldsymbol{l}_x$ with a probability of about $\approx 45\%$. Generated orientation $\boldsymbol{l}_\varphi$ is used with a probability of about $\approx 25\%$. A new position and orientation $\boldsymbol{l}_{x,\varphi}$ at the same time is only chosen with a probability lower than 20%.

Figure 6 compares the average performance of the regular HAM and the extended architecture. It clearly shows that the initial classification accuracy of both architectures corresponds to random walk. While the original HAM is able to achieve a nearly perfect score of $\approx 100\%$, the HAM using the gating network learns slower and seems to saturate at an accuracy of $\approx 97\%$. This evaluation shows a trade off between a less scattered exploration policy targeting smoothness and execution efficiency on the one side, and classification accuracy. To improve both classification accuracy and smoothness is the focus of our future work.

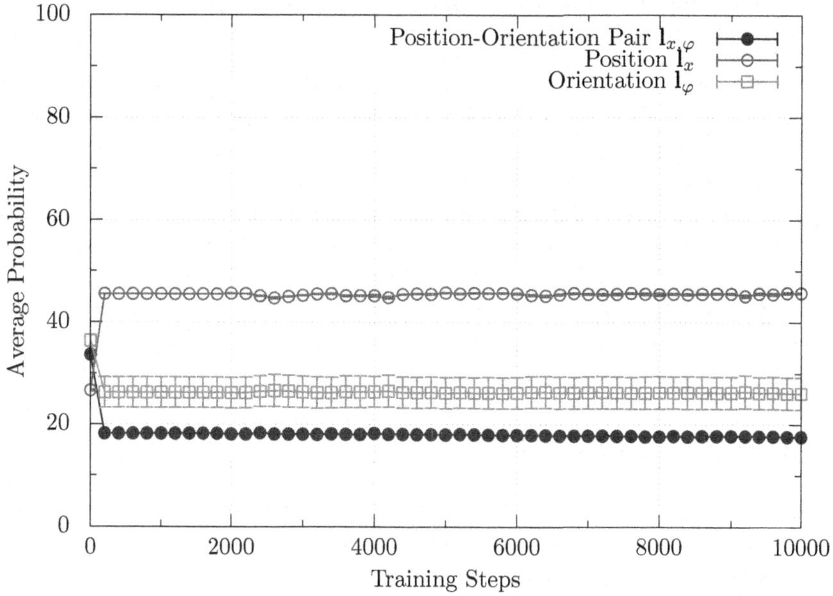

Fig. 5. Average choice of the gating network to either choose only the generated position $\boldsymbol{l}_x$, the orientation $\boldsymbol{l}_\varphi$ or both $\boldsymbol{l}_{x,\varphi}$ for the four classified objects.

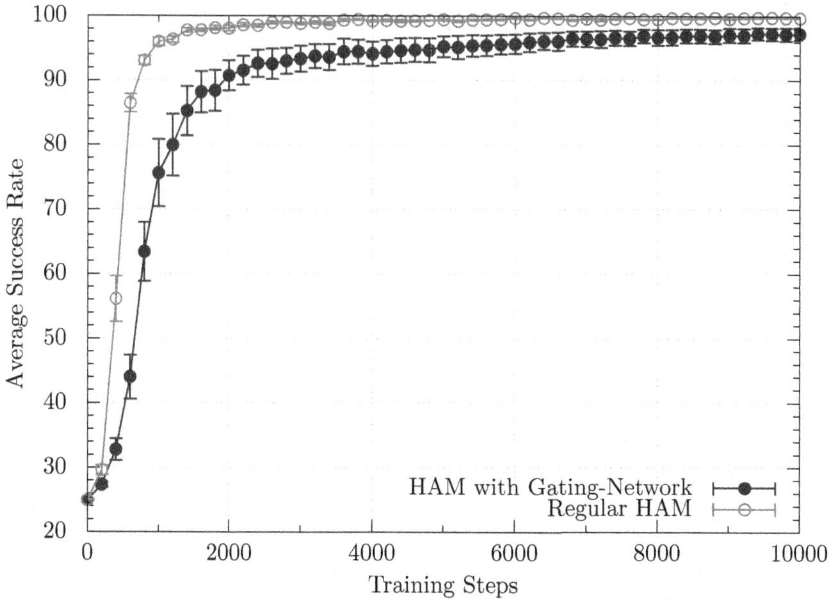

Fig. 6. Comparison of the classification performance for HAM and *S*-HAM that are both trained with 8 haptic glances.

5.2 Measuring the Energy Efficiency of the (S)-HAM on a Simulated KUKA Arm

In this evaluation we employ a pre-trained HAM and a pre-trained S-HAM to compare the resulting control of the robot w.r.t. the rotational change. For the evaluation, all four objects are classified 20 times with 8 glances. Here the absolute change of all seven joints of the arm is read out at every time step. All seven scalars are then added together and again summed up over all time steps. We employ this value denoted by Δ_{joints} as an efficiency indicator of the model. In the above-mentioned trial, the overall rotational change is $\Delta_{\text{joints}} = 1036.93$ for the HAM and $\Delta_{\text{joints}} = 898.53$ for the S-HAM. The resulting measurement for the trained S-HAM is roughly 10% smaller and is thus indicating a better efficiency.

6 Summary and Outlook

The work extended the stochastic control policy of the previously introduced model HAM to perform switching between multiple strategies of shape exploration. Inspired by the psychological research, we showed how to pursue this goal by computationally scaffolding HAM with a gating network. What distinguishes our computational approach from the human expert scaffolding is the fact that the scaffolding network is not a temporal and fading support, but remains with the learner model after the goal-directed optimization process converges.

The proposed multi-module neural network architecture S-HAM consists of the haptic attention learner HAM and its scaffold S. HAM learns to explore three-dimensional objects with a rigid tactile sensor array in a physics-driven simulation environment Gazebo. The environment contains a KUKA robot arm equipped with a simulated tactile sensor array Myrmex. In each loop run, it acquires new data from the environment, integrates it with the previously available representation in the LSTM unit, performs classification and generates a target pose for the next haptic glance. Integrated in the main loop is the scaffold S, a gating network that, based on the internal HAM state, operates on the location network and activates one of the three available primitive types of the haptic glance controller: orientation change, position change, or both. The evaluation showed that for a trained S-HAM less than 20% of the operations corresponded to both location and orientation change. This yielded a more energy-efficient exploration w.r.t. the joint change and is therefore more suitable for an execution on a robot.

The proposed method is likely to enable further optimization of the robot control. An interesting direction of future work is to optimize the execution of movement between two glances, e.g. to perform the movement between two poses generated by the S-HAM without going up and down again. If only an orientation change should be performed, the robot will perform this orientation change "in-place" by pivoting around the contact. This type of optimization yields both new challenges and new benefits. Such re-orientation performed with minimal contact loss may yield new tactile data for every point in time during the execution of rotation. Therefore, an extended modeling approach should accommodate not only for one haptic glance data point, but for all the data that the new control yields during the movement from one pose to the other.

Acknowledgments. This research/work was supported by the Cluster of Excellence Cognitive Interaction Technology 'CITEC' (EXC 277) at Bielefeld University, which is funded by the German Research Foundation (DFG). We would also like to express our great appreciation to Guillaume Walck.

References

1. Ba, J., Mnih, V., Kavukcuoglu, K.: Multiple object recognition with visual attention. CoRR abs/1412.7755 (2014). http://arxiv.org/abs/1412.7755
2. Bengio, Y., Louradour, J., Collobert, R., Weston, J.: Curriculum learning. In: Proceedings of the 26th Annual International Conference on Machine Learning, ACM, pp. 41–48 (2009)
3. Chu, V., et al.: Using robotic exploratory procedures to learn the meaning of haptic adjectives. In: 2013 IEEE International Conference on Robotics and Automation (ICRA), IEEE, pp. 3048–3055 (2013)
4. Fleer, S., Moringen, A., Klatzky, R.L., Ritter, H.J.: Learning efficient haptic shape exploration with a rigid tactile sensor array. CoRR abs/1902.07501 (2019). http://arxiv.org/abs/1902.07501
5. Hammond, J.: Scaffolding: teaching and learning in language and literacy education. ERIC (2001)
6. Hayhoe, M., Ballard, D.: Eye movements in natural behavior. Trends Cogn. Sci. **9**(4), 188–194 (2005)
7. Hochreiter, S., Schmidhuber, J.: Long short-term memory. Neural Comput. **9**(8), 1735–1780 (1997)
8. Klatzky, R.L., Lederman, S.J., Reed, C.L.: There's more to touch than meets the eye: the salience of object attributes for haptics with and without vision. J. Exp. Psychol. **116**, 356 (1987)
9. Klatzky, R.L., Lederman, S.J.: Identifying objects from a haptic glance. Percept. Psychophysics **57**(8), 1111–1123 (1995). https://doi.org/10.3758/BF03208368
10. Lee, M.A., et al.: Making sense of vision and touch: self-supervised learning of multimodal representations for contact-rich tasks. arxiv (2019)
11. Mathe, S., Sminchisescu, C.: Action from still image dataset and inverse optimal control to learn task specific visual scanpaths. In: Advances in Neural Information Processing Systems, pp. 1923–1931 (2013)
12. Mnih, V., Heess, N., Graves, A., Kavukcuoglu, K.: Recurrent models of visual attention. CoRR abs/1406.6247 (2014). http://arxiv.org/abs/1406.6247
13. Moringen, A., Aswolinskij, W., Buescher, G., Walck, G., Haschke, R., Ritter, H.: Modeling target-distractor discrimination for haptic search in a 3D environment. In: BioRob (2018)
14. Nesterov, Y.: A method for solving the convex programming problem with convergence rate $O(1/k^2)$. In: Dokl. Akad. Nauk SSSR, pp. 543–547 (1983)
15. Nesterov, Y.: Introductory Lectures on Convex Optimization: A Basic Course. Applied Optimization. Springer, Boston (2004). https://doi.org/10.1007/978-1-4419-8853-9

16. Noë, A.: Action in Perception. Representation and Mind. MIT Press, Cambridge (2004)
17. van de Pol, J., Volman, M., Beishuizen, J.: Scaffolding in teacher-student interaction: a decade of research. Educ. Psychol. Rev. **22**(3), 271–296 (2010)
18. Pratama, M., Lu, J., Lughofer, E., Zhang, G., Anavatti, S.: Scaffolding type-2 classifier for incremental learning under concept drifts. Neurocomputing **191**, 304–329 (2016). https://doi.org/10.1016/j.neucom.2016.01.049
19. Rouhafzay, G., Cretu, A.: Object recognition from haptic glance at visually salient locations. IEEE Trans. Instrum. Measur. 1–11 (2019). https://doi.org/10.1109/TIM.2019.2905906
20. Schurmann, C., Koiva, R., Haschke, R., Ritter, H.: A modular high-speed tactile sensor for human manipulation research. In: 2011 IEEE World Haptics Conference (WHC 2011), IEEE, pp. 339–344 (2011)
21. Sutton, R.S., Barto, A.G.: Reinforcement Learning: An Introduction, 2nd edn. MIT Press, Cambridge (2018)
22. Thomaz, A.L.: Socially guided machine learning. Ph.D. thesis, Computer Science Department Faculty Publication Series (2006)
23. Thomaz, A.L., Breazeal, C.: Reinforcement learning with human teachers: evidence of feedback and guidance with implications for learning performance. In: Association for the Advancement of Artificial Intelligence - 2006, Boston, MA, pp. 1000–1005 (2006)
24. Tian, S., et al.: Manipulation by feel: touch-based control with deep predictive models. arxiv (2019)
25. Williams, R.J.: Toward a theory of reinforcement-learning connectionist systems. Technical Report NU-CCS-88-3, Northeastern University (1988)
26. Williams, R.J.: Simple statistical gradient-following algorithms for connectionist reinforcement learning. Mach. Learn. **8**(3–4), 229–256 (1992)
27. Zydney, J.M.: Scaffolding. In: Seel, N.M. (ed.) Encyclopedia of the Sciences of Learning, pp. 2913–2916. Springer, Boston (2012). https://doi.org/10.1007/978-1-4419-1428-6

Benchmarking Incremental Regressors in Traversal Cost Assessment

Miloš Prágr(✉) and Jan Faigl

Department of Computer Science, Faculty of Electrical Engineering, Czech Technical University in Prague, Technická 2, 166 27 Prague 6, Czech Republic
{pragrmi1,faiglj}@fel.cvut.cz
https://comrob.fel.cvut.cz/

Abstract. Motivated by the deployment of multi-legged walking robots in traversing various terrain types, we benchmark existing online and unsupervised incremental learning approaches in traversal cost prediction. The traversal cost is defined by the proprioceptive signal of the robot traversal stability that is combined with appearance and geometric properties of the traversed terrains to construct the traversal cost model incrementally. In the motivational deployment, such a model is instantaneously utilized to extrapolate the traversal cost for observed areas that have not yet been visited by the robot to avoid difficult terrains in motion planning. The examined approaches are Incremental Gaussian Mixture Network, Growing Neural Gas, Improved Self-Organizing Incremental Neural Network, Locally Weighted Projection Regression, and Bayesian Committee Machine with Gaussian Process Regressors. The performance is examined using a dataset of the various terrains traversed by a real hexapod walking robot. A part of the presented benchmarking is thus a description of the dataset and also a construction of the reference traversal cost model that is used for comparison of the evaluated regressors. The reference is designed as a compound Gaussian process-based model that is learned separately over the individual terrain types. Based on the evaluation results, the best performance among the examined regressors is provided by Incremental Gaussian Mixture Network, Improved Self-Organizing Incremental Neural Network, and Locally Weighted Projection Regression, while the latter two have the lower computational requirements.

Keywords: Terrain characterization · Multi-legged walking robot · Incremental learning

1 Introduction

The addressed traversal cost assessment is motivated by the deployment of mobile robots in long-term autonomous missions, where robots have to plan their motion in the environment and identify hard to traverse areas [1,2]. Our particular interest in the traversal cost assessment problem stems from the deployment

I. V. Tetko et al. (Eds.): ICANN 2019, LNCS 11727, pp. 685–697, 2019.
https://doi.org/10.1007/978-3-030-30487-4_52

of a hexapod walking robot (see Fig. 1), that can benefit from the ability to plan the motion of each leg [20] and thus traverse rough terrains. More specifically, in this paper, we focus on traversable areas since untraversable terrains such as walls, extreme slopes, or ravines can be easily recognized in a 3D terrain map build as a part of the robot localization [9]. Thus, we investigate approaches to improve the efficiency of the robot motion over traversable areas by learning models for prediction of the traversal cost based on the perceived terrain geometry and appearance features.

In our previous work [13,14], we have deployed the Incremental Gaussian Mixture Network Model (IGMN) [11] to learn the cost of transport [17]. However, the IGMN suffers from the quadratic time complexity regarding the input dimension. On the other hand, the recent deployments of the Gaussian Process (GP) regression in robotic applications such as occupancy mapping [10] can motivate for GP-based traversal cost model, but the deployment of GPs in incremental life-long setups is hampered by their cubic learning time complexity regarding the training set size. Therefore, there is a need for efficient unsupervised incremental learning approaches that would provide competitive results to the IGMN or GP-based models, but would be computationally less demanding.

Our early results on incremental learning are reported in [4], and the herein presented work extends therein proposed evaluation, and we report on benchmarking of five incremental learning approaches for traversal cost prediction using geometry and appearance terrain descriptors. Five competing approaches include the Growing Neural Gas (GNG) [5], Improved Self-Organizing Incremental Neural Network (ISOINN) [15], Locally Weighted Projection Regression (LWPR) [18], IGMN [11], and an incrementally learned product of the GP regressor experts constructed using the Bayesian Committee Machine (BCM-GP) [16] which we have previously deployed in an exploration setup in [12]. All the regressors are evaluated using a real dataset that has been collected by a hexapod walking robot in a testing environment with seven terrain types. The performance of the incremental learners is benchmarked over areas observed but not necessarily traversed by the robot. Therefore, the traversal cost ground truth is not readily available, and the examined approaches are compared with a compound reference GP-based model that is prepared offline from the collected dataset for which an individual model is created for each particular terrain type.

The rest of the paper is organized as follows. Section 2 describes the used dataset of the real terrain traversal cost. The proposed benchmarking methodology for evaluation of the regressors in the addressed problem is presented in Sect. 3. The evaluation results together with the description of the learning approaches and their parametrizations are reported in Sect. 4. Finally, the paper is concluded in Sect. 5.

2 Terrain Traversal Dataset

The dataset for the benchmarking of the terrain traversal cost learning consists of learning data and testing data that both have been collected by the real hexapod walking robot in a laboratory test site. The learning data, which are called trails, are sequences of terrain descriptors accompanied by the proprioceptive measure of the robot traversal cost over the terrains. The testing data are considered as terrain descriptors organized into grids that represent maps of seen environments for which the traversal cost is not available and has to be predicted.

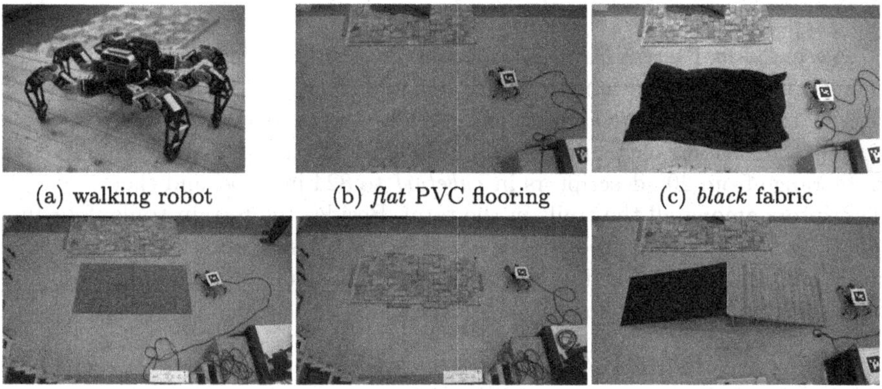

(a) walking robot (b) *flat* PVC flooring (c) *black* fabric

(d) artificial *turf* (e) wooden *cubes* (f) *slope* terrains

Fig. 1. The (a) hexapod walking robot and some of the (b–f) traversed terrains. The *cubeblack* and *cubeturf* terrains are created by covering the (e) wooden cubes with the (c) black fabric and (d) artificial turf, respectively.

The used hexapod walking robot is shown in Fig. 1 together with the seven particular terrains denoted: *flat*, *slope*, *cubes*, *turf*, *black*, *cubeblack*, and *cubeturf*. The terrains have been set with the intention to confuse the learners. For example, using only appearance and geometric features, it is hard to distinguish whether the black fabric and artificial turf cover the cubes (*cubeblack* and *cubeturf*) or similarly the flat ground (*black* and *turf*, respectively). Moreover, the *slope* terrain consists of two distinct sloped areas that are both descended and ascended by the robot, and thus provide different robot experience.

The robot trails are sequences of terrain feature descriptors that are paired with traversal cost measurement. The terrain descriptor $\boldsymbol{d}_t = (s_1, s_2, s_3, a_1, a_2)$ is based on our previous work [13], and it comprises of a three-dimensional shape descriptor [7] and two-dimensional Lab space color descriptor. The features characterize 0.2 m radius around the robot at the particular location for which the traversal cost c is measured as the square root of the robot roll variance for a 10 s period. The traversal cost measurements are computed from inertial measurements sampled with the frequency 400 Hz. Overall, the robot terrain traversal experience is captured by the descriptor $\boldsymbol{d}_e = (s_1, s_2, s_3, a_1, a_2, c)$, where the traversal cost c is experienced over the area characterized by $\boldsymbol{d}_t$. Thus, each terrain descriptor is reported with the cost experienced over the period the robot is present at the described location.

Since some of the benchmarked approaches compute Euclidean distance over the feature space, both $\boldsymbol{d}_t$ and c are normalized to be roughly zero mean and unit variance to assure that each dimension is represented equally. Even though the work is motivated by incremental life-long learning, where the variance of the incoming data is not known a priori, we leverage our expert knowledge of the data which are presumed to be distributed normally with $(\mu_s, \sigma_s) = (0.5, 0.2)$ for the shape features, $(\mu_a, \sigma_a) = (0.0, 10.0)$ for the appearance, and $(\mu_c, \sigma_c) = (0.02, 0.01)$ for the cost.

An individual terrain trail is collected for each particular terrain type, and therefore, the seven terrain trails are denoted $\mathcal{T}_{black}, \ldots, \mathcal{T}_{turf}$. Moreover, each terrain trail $\mathcal{T}_{\mathrm{t}}$ is divided into three equally length parts $\mathcal{T}_{\mathrm{t}} = (\mathcal{T}_{\mathrm{t}}^1, \mathcal{T}_{\mathrm{t}}^2, \mathcal{T}_{\mathrm{t}}^3)$, where t stands for a particular terrain type. The lengths of the individual terrain trails range from 202 descriptors in *cubeturf* to 824 in *slope*, and there are 3522 descriptors among all the trails in the total. Besides the terrain trails, four full-length (with all terrain types) trails are created that simulate the traversal of all the available terrains. The full-length trails are constructed as different orderings of the terrain trails as follows

$$\begin{aligned} \mathcal{T}_1 &= (\mathcal{T}_{black}, \mathcal{T}_{cubeblack}, \mathcal{T}_{cubes}, \mathcal{T}_{cubeturf}, \mathcal{T}_{flat}, \mathcal{T}_{slope}, \mathcal{T}_{turf}), \\ \mathcal{T}_2 &= (\mathcal{T}_{flat}, \mathcal{T}_{black}, \mathcal{T}_{turf}, \mathcal{T}_{cubes}, \mathcal{T}_{cubeblack}, \mathcal{T}_{cubeturf}, \mathcal{T}_{slope}), \\ \mathcal{T}_3 &= (\mathcal{T}_{flat}, \mathcal{T}_{black}, \mathcal{T}_{cubeblack}, \mathcal{T}_{turf}, \mathcal{T}_{cubeturf}, \mathcal{T}_{cubes}, \mathcal{T}_{slope}), \\ \mathcal{T}_4 &= (\mathcal{T}_{black}^1, \mathcal{T}_{cubeblack}^1, \mathcal{T}_{cubes}^1, \mathcal{T}_{cubeturf}^1, \mathcal{T}_{flat}^1, \mathcal{T}_{slope}^1, \mathcal{T}_{turf}^1, \mathcal{T}_{black}^2, \ldots, \mathcal{T}_{turf}^3). \end{aligned} \tag{1}$$

The testing data are terrain descriptors organized into grid maps with the size of the squared cell 0.1 m. The individual grids are denoted $\mathcal{G}_{black}, \ldots, \mathcal{G}_{turf}$. All seven individual terrain grids are merged into a single grid $\mathcal{G}_{merged}$ for evaluation of the regressors on the whole testing dataset.

3 Benchmark Methodology

The addressed problem is to construct the terrain traversal cost model using a set of experience descriptors $\boldsymbol{d}_e$, and instantaneously use the model for predicting the traversal cost c using the terrain descriptor $\boldsymbol{d}_t$ determined from the available model of the environment. In the motivational deployment scenario, the model is constructed incrementally as new data about the terrain traversability are collected during the robot movement over the terrain, and thus the model is sequentially learned from descriptors of the trail $\mathcal{T}$. Thus the model $\mathcal{M}(\mathcal{T}, k)$ at the learning step k incorporates the k-th observation $\boldsymbol{d}_{\mathrm{e}}^k$ from the trail $\mathcal{T}$, i.e., $\boldsymbol{d}_{\mathrm{e}}^k \in \mathcal{T}$, and the learning process can be defined as the iterative update

$$\mathcal{M}(\mathcal{T}, k) \leftarrow update(\mathcal{M}(\mathcal{T}, k-1), \boldsymbol{d}_{\mathrm{e}}^k | \boldsymbol{d}_{\mathrm{e}}^k \in \mathcal{T}), \tag{2}$$

where the initial model $\mathcal{M}(\mathcal{T}, 0)$ carries no information for any trail $\mathcal{T}$.

The prediction of each examined regressor is evaluated over the terrain descriptor grid maps. However, the robot has not traversed all the represented areas, and thus the ground truth traversal cost is not available for the grid maps. Therefore, the quality of the individual models is evaluated using a reference model $\mathcal{M}_{\text{ref}}$, and we follow the evaluation based on the correctness ratio [4]. The cost prediction $pred(\mathcal{M}, \boldsymbol{d}_t)$ of the model $\mathcal{M}$ for the terrain descriptor $\boldsymbol{d}_t$ is considered correct if it corresponds to 95 % confidence interval of the reference model $\mathcal{M}_{\text{ref}}$, and the correctness $correct(\mathcal{M}, \mathcal{M}_{\text{ref}}, \boldsymbol{d}_t)$ is defined as

$$correct(\mathcal{M}, \mathcal{M}_{\text{ref}}, \boldsymbol{d}_t) = \begin{cases} 1 & \text{if} \quad |pred(\mathcal{M}, \boldsymbol{d}_t) - \mu(\mathcal{M}_{\text{ref}}, \boldsymbol{d}_t)| < 2\sigma(\mathcal{M}_{\text{ref}}, \boldsymbol{d}_t) \\ 0 & \text{otherwise} \end{cases}, \tag{3}$$

where $\mu(\mathcal{M}_{\text{ref}}, \boldsymbol{d}_t)$ and $\sigma(\mathcal{M}_{\text{ref}}, \boldsymbol{d}_t)$ are the predictive mean and square root of the predictive variance of the reference $\mathcal{M}_{\text{ref}}$. The predicted cost is assumed to be a random variable that is modeled by the mean and variance, and therefore, the reference model is based on the individual GP for each particular terrain type. A particular reference model for the dataset described in Sect. 2 is thus a compound model of seven GPs.

The prediction of each examined regressor is evaluated over the terrain descriptor grid maps. In particular, each terrain grid map $\mathcal{G}_t$ is associated with the reference GP-based model $\mathcal{M}_{\mathcal{G}_t}$, which is learned using the particular terrain type trail $\mathcal{T}_t$. Although the individual terrain trails are ordered differently in the four full-length trails $\mathcal{T}_1, ..., \mathcal{T}_4$, it does not affect the reference models, because the reference models are not learned incrementally.

The prediction of the model $\mathcal{M}$ over $\mathcal{G}$ is quantified by the correctness ratio $\mathcal{R}$

$$\mathcal{R}(\mathcal{M}, \mathcal{G}) = \frac{\sum_{\boldsymbol{d}_t \in \mathcal{G}} correct(\mathcal{M}, \mathcal{M}_{\mathcal{G}}, \boldsymbol{d}_t)}{|\mathcal{G}|}, \tag{4}$$

where $|\mathcal{G}|$ is the number of descriptors in the grid $\mathcal{G}$.

4 Evaluation Results

Five incremental learning algorithms are benchmarked for the terrain traversal cost modeling with the hexapod walking robot. Namely, we use the Incremental Gaussian Mixture Network Model (IGMN) [11], the Robust Bayesian Committee Machine with Gaussian Process Regressors (BCM-GP) [3], the Growing Neural Gas (GNG) [5], the Improved Self-Organizing Incremental Neural Network (ISOINN) [15], and the Locally Weighted Projection Regression (LWPR) [18]. In the rest of this section, the used parametrizations of the individual models are described, and we report on the performance of the models in terms of their correctness ratios and interpret their traversal cost predictions.

4.1 Parametrization of the Examined Traversal Cost Models

Except for the LWPR, which performs better when tuned manually, the parametrizations of the individual models are selected by maximizing the correctness ratio $R(\mathcal{M}(\mathcal{T}_1), \mathcal{G}_{merged})$ evaluated on the merged grid map $\mathcal{G}_{merged}$ using a grid search. Therefore, the selected parametrizations may not suit the other trails perfectly; however, we consider this transfer of parametrization to be a part of the evaluation of the incremental learners.

The IGMN is an incremental approximation of the EM algorithm which learns a set of Gaussian components. The algorithm is parameterized with the grace period $v_{\min} = 5$, scaling factor $\delta = 0.1$, and is allowed up to 100 components. The minimal accumulated posterior is fixed to $sp_{\min} = 3$ to enforce that any $sp_{\min}$ and $v_{\min}$ combination allows adding new components. The IGMN has been implemented in Python as all the other algorithms.

The framework [19] implemented in Python has been used for the GNG [5] and ISOINN [15] algorithms. The GNG is parameterized with the learning step $\lambda = 10$ and maximal age $a_{\max} = 10$. The framework utilizes Gaussian kernel smoother parameterized with $K = 1000$ smoothing neurons and smooth parameter $smooth = 0$. The ISOINN is parameterized with the learning step $\lambda = 10$ and maximal age $a_{\max} = 1000$, and it also utilizes smoother with $K = 1000$, but with the smooth parameter $smooth = -0.75$. It is worth noting that $a_{\max} = 1000$ effectively inhibits edge deletion given the lengths of the trails.

Python bindings of the LWPR implementation [8] are used to compute the LWPR models. In the best performing parametrization on $R(\mathcal{M}(\mathcal{T}_1), \mathcal{G}_{merged})$, the initial distance metric is set as $\mathbf{D}_{\text{init}} = 0.1\mathbf{I}$, where $\mathbf{I}$ is an identity matrix, and the distance metric learning rate is $\alpha_{\text{init}} = 1000$. However, such parametrization is prone to overfitting when learning on other trails, and exhibits poor performance overall. Therefore, we further report on results for the manually tuned parametrization $\mathbf{D}_{\text{init}} = 10\mathbf{I}$ and $\alpha_{\text{init}} = 10$ that is denoted LWPR$^+$.

The BCM-GP [16] learns Gaussian Process regressor experts, which are combined using the Robust Bayesian committee machine. Experts are constructed incrementally one at a time, and after the expert is constructed, it is not further modified. The BCM-GP is parameterized with the maximal expert size of 25 observations and uses the Matérn $\frac{3}{2}$ kernel. The GPy toolbox [6] is used to learn the individual experts and the BCM-GP is also implemented in Python.

Finally, the reference GP-based models are learned using the GPy toolbox with the RBF kernel.

4.2 Correctness Ratios of the Examined Regressors

The correctness ratios R of the examined regressor on $\mathcal{G}_{merged}$ for four trails $\mathcal{T}_1, \ldots, \mathcal{T}_4$ are depicted in Table 1 and they range between approx. 55 % and 75 %.

Table 1. Correctness ratio R on the *merged* grid $\mathcal{G}_{merged}$ for different trails

Trail	BCM-GP	GNG	IGMN	ISOINN	LWPR	LWPR$^+$
$\mathcal{T}_1$	0.59	0.74	0.70	0.77	0.72	0.68
$\mathcal{T}_2$	0.62	0.57	0.71	0.59	0.48	0.69
$\mathcal{T}_3$	0.57	0.57	0.71	0.64	0.58	0.69
$\mathcal{T}_4$	0.72	0.63	0.67	0.69	0.70	0.66

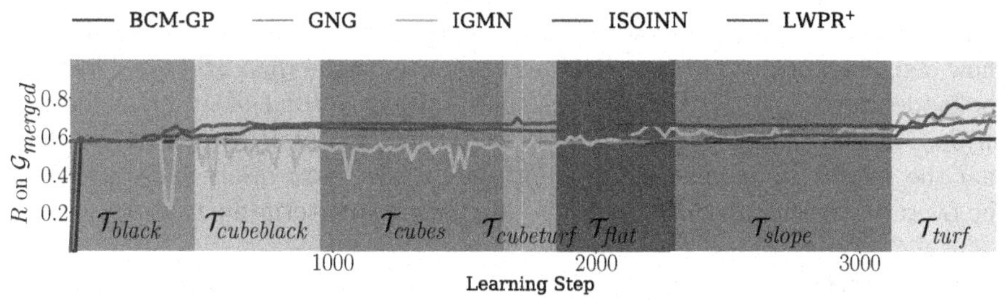

Fig. 2. The evolution of the correctness ratio R computed on $\mathcal{G}_{merged}$ for the incrementally learned traversal cost models on $\mathcal{T}_1$.

The IGMN and hand-tuned LWPR$^+$ appear to be the most stable incremental regressors as their results are similar regardless of the trail ordering used for learning. The GNG and ISOINN appear to be much more affected by the trail ordering and are outperformed by the IGMN for $\mathcal{T}_2$ and $\mathcal{T}_3$. On the other hand, the GNG and ISOINN outperform the IGMN for $\mathcal{T}_1$, and ISOINN also performs slightly better for $\mathcal{T}_4$. The best performance for $\mathcal{T}_4$ is provided by the BCM-GP, but its overall performance is not convincing, especially when compared to the IGMN, ISOINN, and LWPR$^+$.

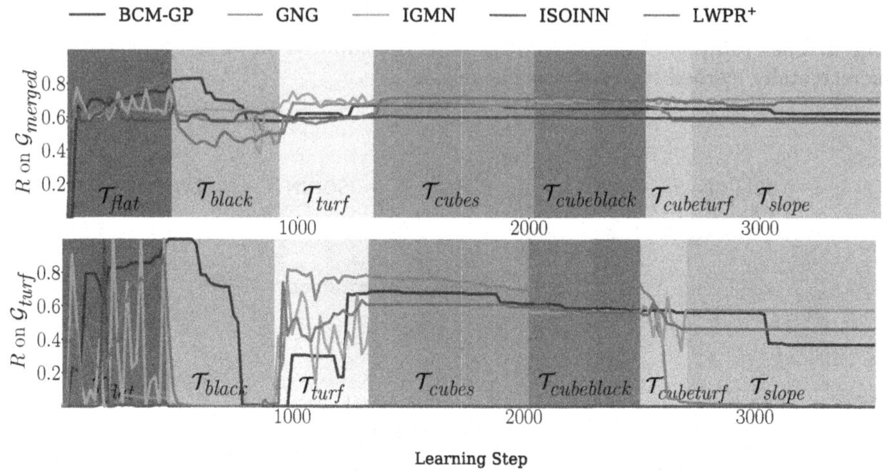

Fig. 3. The evolution of the correctness ratio R computed on $\mathcal{G}_{merged}$ and $\mathcal{G}_{turf}$ for the incrementally learned traversal cost models on $\mathcal{T}_2$.

The incremental nature of the learners can be observed in the evolution of the correctness ratio R presented in Figs. 2, 3, 4 and 5. A drop in the correctness ratio is expected behavior because of new information is incorporated into the models. It is especially prevalent for the performance evaluation on the individual terrain grids, where the GNG notably suffers by the dropout. Figures 3 and 4 show a significant drop in the GNG performance on the $\mathcal{G}_{turf}$ grid after learning the model from $\mathcal{T}_{cubeturf}$. Arguably, the performance of some of the other learners on $\mathcal{G}_{turf}$ is also relatively poor. The showed evolution of R reinforces the claim that the IGMN is the most stable approach, as new data rarely cause a drop in the overall correctness, although there are some short term fluctuations.

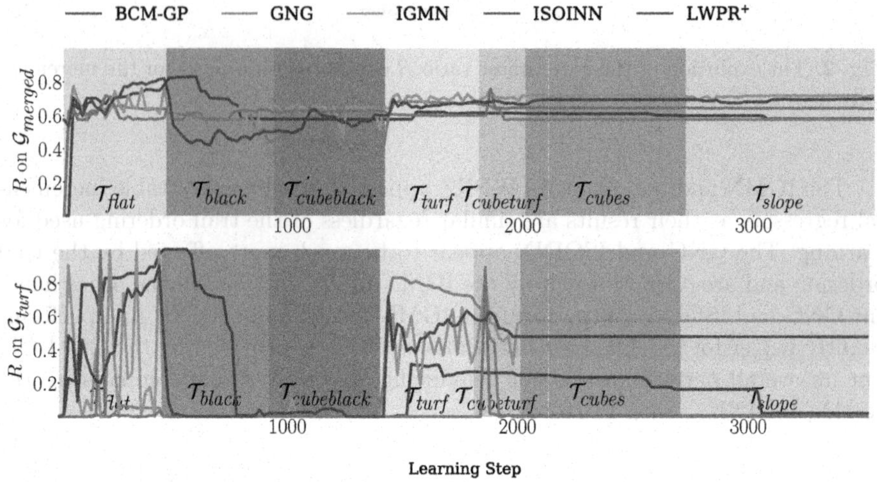

Fig. 4. The evolution of the correctness ratio R computed on $\mathcal{G}_{merged}$ and $\mathcal{G}_{turf}$ for the incrementally learned traversal cost models on $\mathcal{T}_3$.

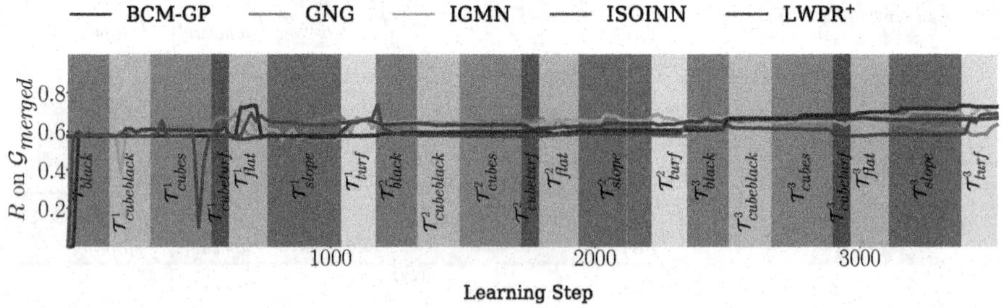

Fig. 5. The evolution of the correctness ratio R computed on $\mathcal{G}_{merged}$ for the incrementally learned traversal cost models on $\mathcal{T}_4$.

4.3 Qualitative Analysis

In our experience, the most significant ability of a traversal cost model is the inference of the traversal cost values that can be used to identify hard to traverse terrains. The adherence to the GP-based reference traversal cost model

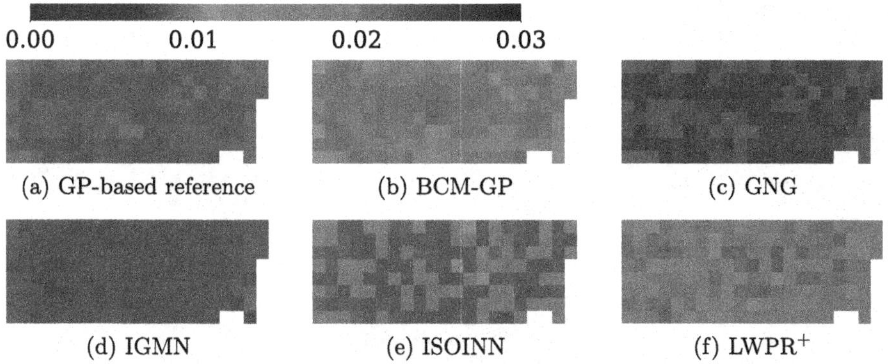

Fig. 6. The (a) mean of the GP reference model, and (b) BCM-GP, (c) GNG, (d) IGMN, (e) ISOINN, (f) LWPR$^+$ predictions over $\mathcal{G}_{flat}$ learned on $\mathcal{T}_1$. Only grid cells corresponding to the spatial allocation of the *flat* terrain are shown.

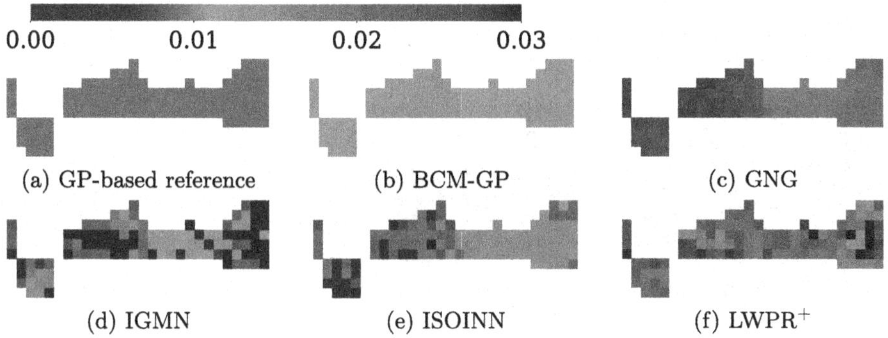

Fig. 7. The (a) mean of the GP reference model, and (b) BCM-GP, (c) GNG, (d) IGMN, (e) ISOINN, (f) LWPR$^+$ predictions over $\mathcal{G}_{slope}$ learned on $\mathcal{T}_1$. Only grid cells corresponding to the spatial allocation of the *slope* terrain are shown.

is not necessary, even though the reference model provides baseline predictions. Therefore, we investigate the predicted values over individual terrains.

The grid maps in Figs. 6 and 8 indicate that the reference, IGMN, ISOINN, and LWPR$^+$ learned on $\mathcal{T}_1$ predict a higher cost on $\mathcal{G}_{cubes}$ than on $\mathcal{G}_{flat}$, and thus they provide desired information for path planning to avoid difficult terrains.

The differences between predictions on $\mathcal{G}_{slope}$ showed in Fig. 7 are not surprising given that the predictive variance of the reference is higher than on other terrains. Notice, the ISOINN and LWPR$^+$ predictions are noisy over all the terrains, but the median values are applicable to path planning. However, several failed predictions on $\mathcal{G}_{flat}$ can be seen in Fig. 9. These are especially prevalent when learning on $\mathcal{T}_2$ and $\mathcal{T}_3$, where $\mathcal{T}_{flat}$ is traversed first. The overall performance of the GNG is considered mediocre, and it fails to predict distinctively low values on $\mathcal{G}_{flat}$ even when learned on $\mathcal{T}_1$. Nevertheless, its predictions on

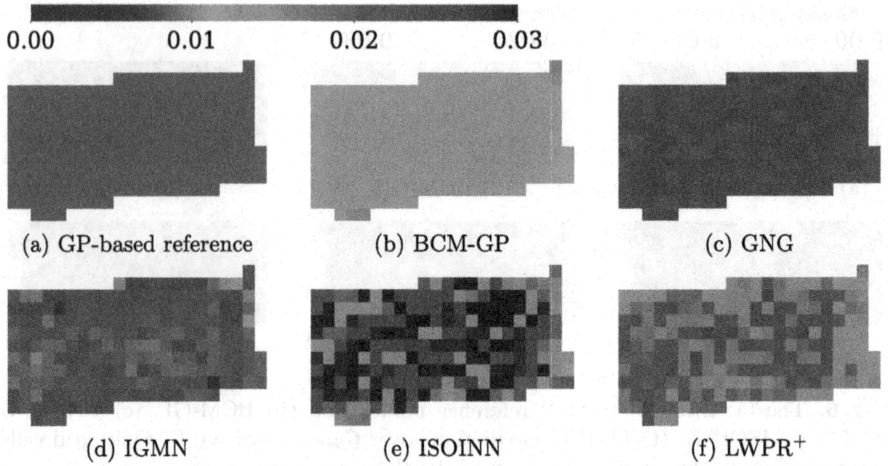

Fig. 8. The (a) mean of the GP reference model, and (b) BCM-GP, (c) GNG, (d) IGMN, (e) ISOINN, (f) LWPR$^+$ predictions over $\mathcal{G}_{cubes}$ learned on $\mathcal{T}_1$. Only grid cells corresponding to the spatial allocation of the *cubes* terrain are shown.

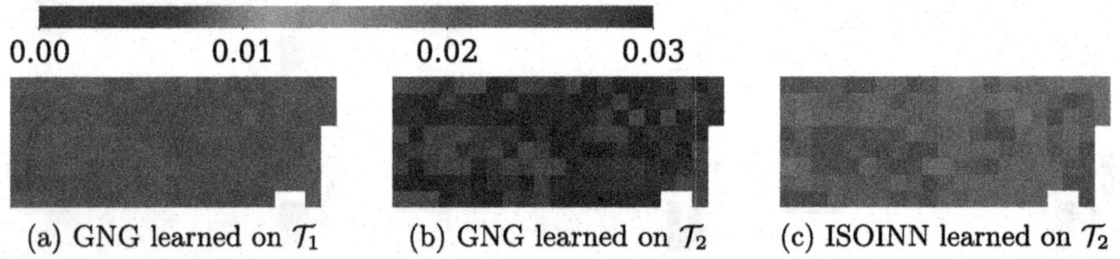

Fig. 9. Examples of high-cost predictions over $\mathcal{G}_{flat}$ which make it hard to discriminate the flat terrain from rough terrains.

$\mathcal{G}_{cubes}$ and $\mathcal{G}_{slope}$ are considered well-suited for path planning. Finally, the BCM-GP fails to provide distinctive costs for most terrains, and therefore, it cannot discriminate the hard to traverse areas.

4.4 Discussion

Based on the reported results, the IGMN, ISOINN, and LWPR$^+$ provide satisfiable performance in traversal cost inference for the considered hexapod walking robot, although ISOINN is more prone to forgetting or concept drift, see Fig. 9. The BCM-GP and GNG provide competitive results in terms of the correctness ratio and outperform the IGMN and LWPR$^+$ on some trails, but they do not provide predictions applicable to path planning. A close inspection indicates that the individual BCM-GP predictions are almost uniform and correspond to the most commonly observed traversal cost, i.e., the cost over the various easy to traverse terrains. Considering the previous deployment of the BCM-GP model in the exploration task in [12], these results are somewhat underwhelming.

However, in the exploration task, the robot actively perceives the environment until all observed terrains are sufficiently known. In our case, the terrains on the test grids may remain unknown to the model. Nevertheless, the inability of the BCM-GP to extrapolate the predictions for such terrains is disappointing.

Table 2. $\mathcal{T}_1$ learning and $\mathcal{G}_{merged}$ prediction wall times T_{wall} [s]. (Intel i5-4460 CPU)

Method/Phase	BCM-GP	GNG	IGMN	ISOINN	LWPR$^+$	Compound GP
Learning	5.27	1.14	3.95	1.26	0.71	8.94
Prediction	22.44	0.62	4.54	0.60	0.59	8.64

The best performing regressors among the examined approaches are considered IGMN, ISOINN, and LWPR$^+$. The final IGMN and LWPR$^+$ predictions are the most stable, exhibiting only a very small difference when learning over permuted trails. The ISOINN outperforms the IGMN in few tested trails in terms of the correctness ratio. Moreover, according to the learning and inference times reported in Table 2, the ISOINN and LWPR$^+$ offer performance speedup over the IGMN in high dimensional learning, as they do not suffer from the quadratic time complexity with regards to the input dimension which hampers the IGMN.

5 Conclusion

In this paper, we present results on benchmarking five incremental learning approaches in traversal cost estimation of the hexapod walking robot. The main motivation of the presented work is to find alternatives to the IGMN algorithm we have used previously. The examined approaches include the Growing Neural Gas, Improved Self-Organizing Incremental Neural Network, Bayesian Committee Machine with Gaussian Process regressors, and Locally Weighted Projection Regression. Based on the presented results, the BCM-GP performs poorly, contradicting our initial intuition. The GNG performance is ambiguous, and it seems the used approach suffers from the concept drift for certain ordering of the learning sequences. The ISOINN and the hand-tuned LWPR$^+$ perform similarly to the IGMN in terms of the prediction correctness ratio, and all the three methods provide distinguishable cost prediction that is applicable in path planning. However, a possible drawback of the LWPR is the necessity of tuning the parameters and the grid search on $\mathcal{G}_{merged}$ provides significantly worse results in the case of $\mathcal{T}_2$ and $\mathcal{T}_3$ trails. Moreover, the ISOINN and LWPR offer better potential in high dimensional feature spaces, where the IGMN suffers from quadratic time complexity. Therefore, we consider the ISOINN and LWPR as the primary traversal cost learners for further deployments.

Acknowledgments. This work was supported by the Czech Science Foundation under research project No. 18-18858S.

References

1. Bartoszyk, S., Kasprzak, P., Belter, D.: Terrain-aware motion planning for a walking robot. In: International Workshop on Robot Motion and Control (RoMoCo), IEEE, pp. 29–34 (2017). https://doi.org/10.1109/RoMoCo.2017.8003889
2. Brunner, M., Brüggemann, B., Schulz, D.: Rough Terrain Motion Planning for Actuated, Tracked Robots. In: International Conference on Agents and Artificial Intelligence (ICAART), pp. 40–61 (2013). https://doi.org/10.1007/978-3-662-44440-5_3
3. Deisenroth, M.P., Ng, J.W.: Distributed Gaussian processes. In: International Conference on International Conference on Machine Learning (ICML), pp. 1481–1490 (2015)
4. Faigl, J., Prágr, M.: Incremental traversability assessment learning using growing neural gas algorithm. In: Advances in Self-Organizing Maps, Learning Vector Quantization, Clustering and Data Visualization, pp. 166–176 (2020). https://doi.org/10.1007/978-3-030-19642-4_17
5. Fritzke, B.: A growing neural gas network learns topologies. In: Neural Information Processing Systems (NIPS), pp. 625–632 (1994)
6. GPy: A Gaussian process framework in Python (2012). http://github.com/SheffieldML/GPy. Accessed 28 Mar 2019
7. Kragh, M., Jørgensen, R.N., Pedersen, H.: Object detection and terrain classification in agricultural fields using 3D lidar data. In: International Conference on Computer Vision Systems (ICVS), vol. 9163, pp. 188–197 (2015). https://doi.org/10.1007/978-3-319-20904-3_18
8. LWPR library (2007). https://github.com/jdlangs/lwpr. Accessed 28 May 2019
9. Nowicki, M.R., Belter, D., Kostusiak, A., Čížek, P., Faigl, J., Skrzypczynski, P.: An experimental study on feature-based SLAM for multi-legged robots with RGB-D sensors. Ind. Robot **44**(4), 428–441 (2017). https://doi.org/10.1108/IR-11-2016-0340
10. O'Callaghan, S., Ramos, F.T., Durrant-Whyte, H.: Contextual occupancy maps using Gaussian processes. In: IEEE International Conference on Robotics and Automation (ICRA), pp. 1054–1060 (2009). https://doi.org/10.1109/ROBOT.2009.5152754
11. Pinto, R., Engel, P., Alegre, P.: A fast incremental Gaussian mixture model. PLoS ONE e0141942 (2015). https://doi.org/10.1371/journal.pone.0139931
12. Prágr, M., Čížek, P., Bayer, J., Faigl, J.: Online incremental learning of the terrain traversal cost in autonomous exploration. In: Robotics: Science and Systems (RSS) (2019). https://doi.org/10.15607/RSS.2019.XV.040
13. Prágr, M., Čížek, P., Faigl, J.: Cost of transport estimation for legged robot based on terrain features inference from aerial scan. In: IEEE/RSJ International Conference on Intelligent Robots and Systems (IROS), pp. 1745–1750 (2018). https://doi.org/10.1109/IROS.2018.8593374
14. Prágr, M., Čížek, P., Faigl, J.: Incremental learning of traversability cost for aerial reconnaissance support to ground units. In: Modelling and Simulation for Autonomous Systems (MESAS), pp. 412–421 (2019). https://doi.org/10.1007/978-3-030-14984-0_30
15. Shen, F., Yu, H., Sakurai, K., Hasegawa, O.: An incremental online semi-supervised active learning algorithm based on self-organizing incremental neural network. Neural Comput. Appl. **20**(7), 1061–1074 (2011). https://doi.org/10.1007/s00521-010-0428-y

16. Tresp, V.: A Bayesian committee machine. Neural Comput. **12**(11), 2719–2741 (2000). https://doi.org/10.1162/089976600300014908
17. Tucker, V.A.: The energetic cost of moving about: walking and running are extremely inefficient forms of locomotion. Much greater efficiency is achieved by birds, fish-and bicyclists. Am. Sci. **63**(4), 413–419 (1975)
18. Vijayakumar, S., Schaal, S.: Locally weighted projection regression: an O(n) algorithm for incremental real time learning in high dimensional space. In: International Conference on International Conference on Machine Learning (ICML), pp. 1079–1086 (2000)
19. Xiang, Z., Xiao, Z., Wang, D., Xiao, J.: Gaussian kernel smooth regression with topology learning neural networks and Python implementation. Neurocomputing **260**, 1–4 (2017). https://doi.org/10.1016/j.neucom.2017.01.051
20. Čížek, P., Masri, D., Faigl, J.: Foothold placement planning with a hexapod crawling robot. In: IEEE/RSJ International Conference on Intelligent Robots and Systems (IROS), pp. 4096–4101 (2017). https://doi.org/10.1109/IROS.2017.8206267

CPG Driven RBF Network Control with Reinforcement Learning for Gait Optimization of a Dung Beetle-Like Robot

Matheshwaran Pitchai[1(✉)], Xiaofeng Xiong[1], Mathias Thor[1], Peter Billeschou[1], Peter Lukas Mailänder[2], Binggwong Leung[3], Tomas Kulvicius[2], and Poramate Manoonpong[1,3(✉)]

[1] Embodied AI and Neurorobotics Lab, Centre for BioRobotics, The Mærsk Mc-Kinney Møller Institute, University of Southern Denmark, Odense M, Denmark
matheshwaranpitchai@gmail.com, {xizi,mathias,pebil,poma}@mmmi.sdu.dk

[2] Department of Computational Neuroscience, University of Goettingen, Goettingen, Germany
tomas.kulvicius@phys.uni-goettingen.de

[3] Bio-inspired Robotics and Neural Engineering Lab, School of Information Science and Technology, Vidyasirimedhi Institute of Science and Technology, Rayong, Thailand
Binggwong.L_s17@vistec.ac.th

Abstract. In this paper, we employ a central pattern generator (CPG) driven radial basis function network (RBFN) based controller to learn optimized locomotion for a complex dung beetle-like robot using reinforcement learning approach called "Policy Improvement with Path Integrals (PI^2)". Our CPG driven RBFN controller is inspired by rhythmic dynamic movement primitives (DMPs). The controller can be also seen as an extension to a traditional CPG controller, which usually controls only the frequency of the motor patterns but not the shape. Our controller uses the CPG to control the frequency while the RBFN takes care of the shape of the motor patterns. In this paper, we only focus on the shape of the motor patterns and optimize those with respect to walking speed and energy efficiency. As a result, the robot can travel faster and consume less power than using only the CPG controller.

Keywords: Brain inspired computing · Reinforcement learning · Artificial neural networks

1 Introduction

Limitations of wheeled robots on unstructured terrains lead to the necessity of legged robots, and the ubiquitous coarse nature of our environment explains the importance of legged robots. When designing a legged robot, nature serves to be the primary influence, inspired by the morphology of various multi-legged

I. V. Tetko et al. (Eds.): ICANN 2019, LNCS 11727, pp. 698–710, 2019.
https://doi.org/10.1007/978-3-030-30487-4_53

creatures [1]. The applications of walking robots are quite diverse like employing them in a search and rescue operation [2], planetary exploration [3]. However, they could be used in even more activities if the robots are versatile enough to adopt them. Rather than mimicking the versatility of the insect, multi-legged robots settle on just locomotion most of the time. In this work, we will use a six-legged dung beetle-like robot, named ALPHA, introducing for the first time, which is inspired by the morphology of a dung beetle. The dung beetle is of particular interest here primarily because of its versatility in mobility and object handling capabilities that it can effectively manipulate objects such as a ball of dung, and roll it using its two hind legs, effortlessly changing from a hexapod gait to a quadruped gait, achieving all this moving backwards [4]. Achieving this level of flexibility in a robot could be of great help, for instance, in a planetary exploration task when the robot has to move a reasonably big object to investigate or to collect samples. When it comes to generating locomotion for legged robots, using central pattern generators (CPG) is one of the preferred methods and it has only been increasing in the recent years [5]. The problem of motor pattern optimization is essentially a problem of finding the optimal foothold transfer trajectory. The CPG controller provides rhythmic patterns as inputs to the motors resulting in a foothold transfer trajectory that are good enough to make the robot walk stably, but might not be an optimal solution. In order to search for optimal motor patterns that result in an optimal foothold transfer trajectory, we would need several arbitrary patterns to try on the robot, which the CPG controller is not capable of. For this purpose, a CPG driven RBFN controller is introduced to generate arbitrary motion patterns for learning optimized locomotion, in terms of velocity and power consumption, using the PI^2 reinforcement learning approach. The main advantage of the PI^2 method is that it is simple to implement and doesn't involve matrix inversions or any other complex mathematical operations, making it less susceptible to numerical instability. Due to its simpler structure, it adapts easily to higher dimensional control policies. Also, the positive results of several other robot learning tasks [6–9] support the use of this method.

1.1 Paper Structure

The following sections will start by introducing the ALPHA robot used in our study, in Sect. 2. Section 3 introduces the proposed CPG driven RBFN controller, which itself is an extended version of the CPG controller so it also covers the CPG controller introduction. All the steps involved in implementing the PI^2 learning to the proposed controller will be explained in Sect. 4. Sections 5 and 6 will go through the procedure carried out to perform the testing and the results obtained from the testing, respectively. The paper concludes with a brief discussion about the obtained results, comparison with a similar method, and future works.

2 Dung Beetle-Like Robot

Figure 1 shows the basic structure of the ALPHA. It is simulated and tested in the V-REP robot simulator from Coppelia Robotics. The robot has six legs with three revolute joints in each, namely TC, CF, and FT joints. Each joint has one degree of freedom, making each leg operate with three degrees of freedom. The robot also has a revolute abdomen joint, which could be helpful in object manipulation tasks. Since the objective here is to make the robot move forward, the abdomen joint is considered to be a fixed joint (set at 20°). To start testing with the robot, a typical walking pose of a real dung beetle is considered for the initial joint positions. Different operating angle ranges for each joint were considered based on the initial joint bias, and the joint range values that would not collide with other legs are chosen and can be found in Table 1.

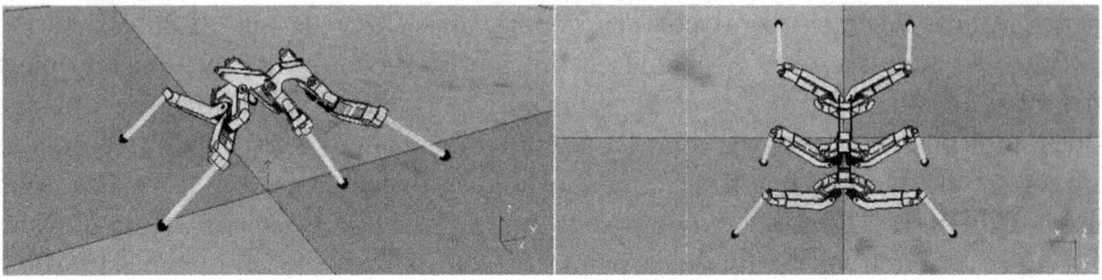

Fig. 1. The ALPHA in a simulation environment with initial joint position

Table 1. Initial joint angles and operating angle range biases

Joint types	Front legs (in deg)		Mid legs (in deg)		Hind legs (in deg)	
	Joint angle	Angle range	Joint angle	Angle range	Joint angle	Angle range
TC joint	0	[−15, 15]	20	[5, 35]	−30	[−30, −15]
CF joint	−75	[−90, −60]	−65	[−80, −50]	−30	[−80, −30]
FT joint	−21	[−36, −6]	30	[15, 45]	−21	[−36, −6]

3 CPG Driven RBFN Controller

The purpose of a CPG driven RBFN controller (Fig. 2) arises from the inability of the CPG controller to generate arbitrary motor patterns. The purpose of arbitrary motor patterns arises from the necessity to learn optimized locomotion for a complex robot, like the ALPHA. With the outputs from the CPG as inputs to an RBFN, any arbitrary pattern could be generated by changing the output weights of the RBFN as shown in Fig. 4. Table 2 describes the notations used in this study. The following sections will explain briefly about the construction of the controller.

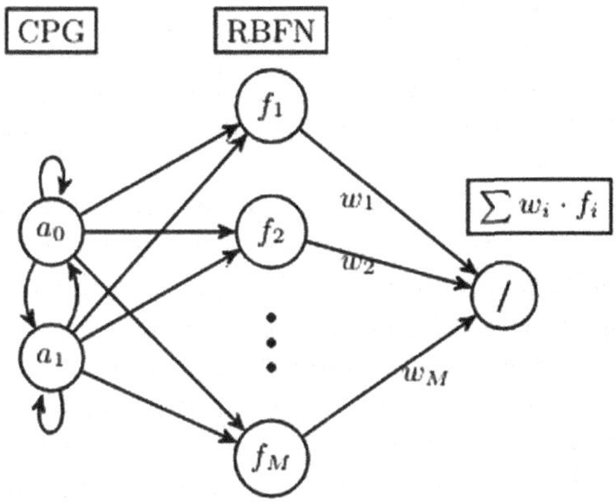

Fig. 2. CPG driven RBFN controller

Table 2. Notations

Notations	Description
U	Parameter vector
U_k	Noisy parameter vector of kth roll-out
δU_k	Set of Gaussian noises added to the parameter vector at k^{th} roll-out
K	Number of roll-outs
I	Number of iterations
T	Phase length of the robot (stance time + swing time)
S	Number of time-steps in one phase length
t	Simulation time of one roll-out
M	Number of Gaussian kernels
W_1	Set of weights representing the motor patterns to the TC joints for 1 T
W_2	Set of weights representing the motor patterns to the CF joints for 1 T
W_3	Set of weights representing the motor patterns to the FT joints for 1 T

3.1 Central Pattern Generator (CPG)

The central pattern generator is a biological neural circuit that produces rhythmic outputs which are responsible for rhythmic motions like breathing and walking. The SO(2) controller [10] is an artificial neural network based central pattern generator with two neurons connected to each other, as shown in Fig. 3(a). The recurrent connections of the SO(2) controller result in a quasi-periodic pattern with frequency control for specific weight parameter configurations. The SO(2) controller will be referred to as a CPG controller hereafter in the paper, to avoid confusion. The activation function of the neurons is as follows,

$$a_i(t) = \sum_{j=0,1} h_{ij} \cdot tanh(a_j(t-1)) + B_i \qquad ; i = 0, 1 \tag{1}$$

With the biases set to $B_0 = B_1 = 0.01$ and by using the following weights,

$$\begin{pmatrix} h_{00} & h_{01} \\ h_{10} & h_{11} \end{pmatrix} = \begin{pmatrix} 1.01 & 0.0314 \\ -0.0314 & 1.01 \end{pmatrix} \tag{2}$$

the resulting neural outputs a_0 and a_1 oscillate in a near sinusoidal shape for every 205 steps with an offset of approximately 50 steps between each other. The results of the same can be found in Fig. 3(b). For a forward motion of the robot using the outputs from the CPG controller, the neural output a_0 is applied to the *TC* joints of the robot and the neural output a_1 to the *CF* joints. The *FT* joints of the robot are fixed initially, as the robot performed poorly when either of the neural outputs applied to the *FT* joints. The motion signals are sent to the joints with an offset to obtain a tripod gait like dung beetle walking. This corresponds to the performance of the robot using the CPG controller and the results of the same in comparison with the CPG driven RBFN controller can be found in the results section. By passing the outputs from the CPG as the inputs to the RBFN, this results in our CPG driven RBFN controller explained in the next section.

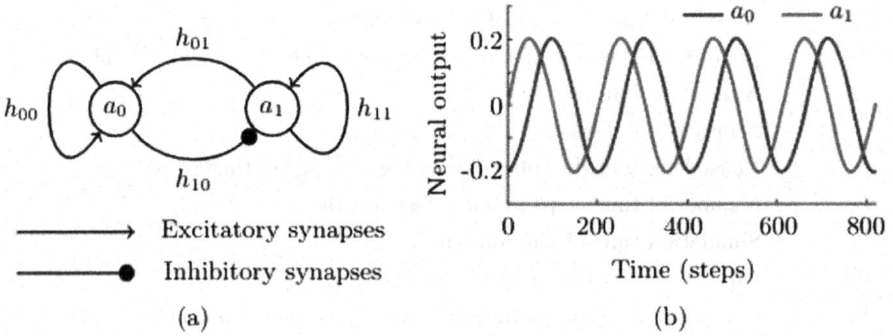

Fig. 3. (a) CPG controller. (b) CPG outputs

3.2 Radial Basis Function Network (RBFN)

The RBFN used in our controller has M Gaussian kernels with each of its means spaced equally but with the same standard deviation σ. The means of the Gaussian kernels are obtained using the phase length T as follows,

$$\mu_i^{a_j} = a_j(T * (i-1)/(M-1)); \qquad \forall i = 1, 2, .., M; \quad \forall j = 0, 1. \tag{3}$$

Using the calculated means and standard deviations, the Gaussian kernels needed for the function is generated using the following Gaussian distribution,

$$f_i((a_0, a_1)|(\mu_i^{a_0}, \mu_i^{a_1}, \sigma_i)) = \frac{1}{\sigma_i\sqrt{2\pi}} e^{-((a_0-\mu_i^{a_0})^2+(a_1-\mu_i^{a_1})^2)/2\sigma_i^2} \quad ; \forall i = 1, 2, .., M \tag{4}$$

The inputs of the RBFN come from the CPG, and the network uses a delta rule to update the weights in every iteration, resulting in a weighted linear combination of the M radial basis functions after N iterations as described in Eq. 5. By adjusting the weights, any arbitrary pattern could be generated as shown in Fig. 4. This resulting network is called as the CPG driven RBFN controller and can be seen in Fig. 2.

$$y(x) = \sum_{i=1}^{M} w_i \cdot f_i \tag{5}$$

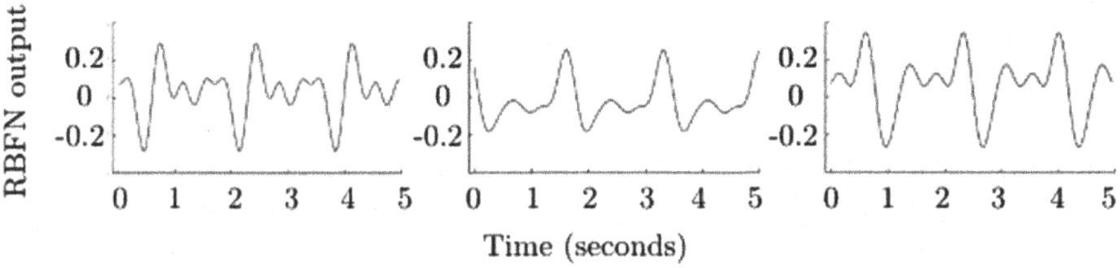

Fig. 4. Examples of arbitrary motor patterns that could be created by using the CPG driven RBFN controller. The weights were set manually to obtain these patterns.

4 Optimization of Motion Patterns Using PI^2

The CPG driven RBFN controller adapts easily to the ALPHA robot, forming three RBFNs for three types of the joints (TC, CF, and FT joints) of the robot but uses the same CPG outputs for all the three networks (Fig. 5). The controller outputs with three sets of weights W_1, W_2, and W_3 representing the motor patterns to the TC, CF, and FT joints, respectively. It is then followed by a PI^2 learning process to learn optimized motor patterns. Now, we apply the PI^2 approach as the learning method to find the motor patterns of the TC, CF, and FT joints that allow the robot to move forward faster and consume less power in comparison with the pure CPG controller. The control policy to be optimized in this learning problem is defined as a set of all motor patterns to the TC, CF, and FT joints needed for one phase length (T) of the robot. We parameterize the control policy by substituting the motor patterns to the TC, CF, and FT joints for the sets of weights (W_1, W_2, and W_3 respectively) used to represent those signals and is defined as the parameter vector U in Eq. 6.

$$U = [W_1, W_2, W_3] \tag{6}$$

where, $\quad W_j = [w_{j1}, w_{j2}, ..., w_{jM}] \qquad \forall j = 1, 2, 3.$

The learning process involves generating arbitrary patterns by adding random noise to the parameter vector U. The random noise is obtained from a Gaussian distribution with a mean of zero and a standard deviation of 0.001.

The process involved is mathematically represented as,

$$\delta w_{jkm} \epsilon \mathcal{N}\ (0{,}0.001) \tag{7}$$
$$\delta W_{jk} = [\delta w_{jk1}\ ,\ \delta w_{jk2}\ , ...,\ \delta w_{jkM}] \tag{8}$$
$$\delta U_k = [\delta W_{1k}, \delta W_{2k}, \delta W_{3k}] \tag{9}$$
$$\forall j = 1,2,3;\ \forall m = 1,2,..,M;\ \forall k = 1,2,..,K$$

The resulting noisy parameter vector U_k is

$$U_k = U + \delta U_k \tag{10}$$

$$U_k = [W_1 + \delta W_{1k}, W_2 + \delta W_{2k}, W_3 + \delta W_{3k}] \tag{11}$$
$$\forall k = 1,2,..,K.$$

The same is done for K number of roll-outs for each iteration. Now, each of the newly generated K sets of patterns is tested on the simulated robot for t seconds, and all the relevant data needed for calculating the fitness of the roll-out is obtained. The fitness of each roll-out is defined in Eq. 15 as a function of the normalized values of both the power consumed by the robot for a displacement of 1 m along the positive y-axis and the displacement of the robot along the positive y-axis, during the roll-out.

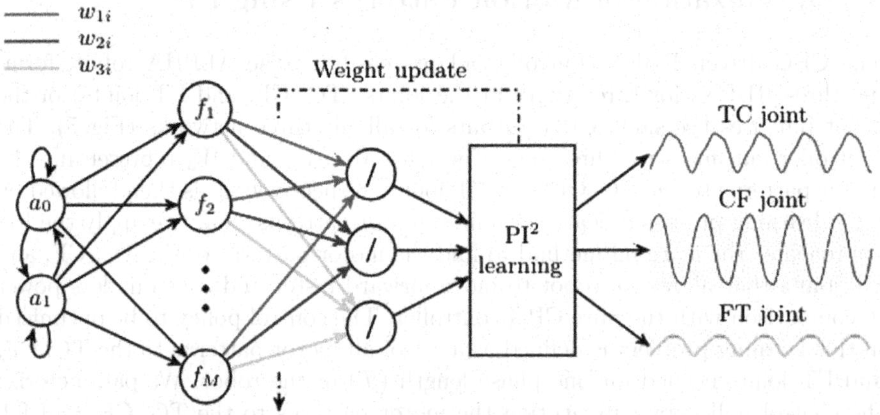

Fig. 5. CPG driven RBFN controller implementation for the ALPHA

$$total\_power_{ik} = \sum_{j=1}^{18} \sum_{s=1}^{tS} \tau_{js} \cdot \omega_{js} \tag{12}$$

$$pow_{ik} = \frac{total\_power_{ik}}{dis_{ik}} \tag{13}$$

$$d_{ik} = \frac{dis_{ik}}{dis_{cpg}}; \qquad p_{ik} = \frac{pow_{cpg}}{pow_{ik}} \tag{14}$$

$$F_{ik} = (1-c) \cdot d_{ik} + c \cdot p_{ik} \tag{15}$$
$$\forall i = 1, 2, .., I; \ \forall k = 1, 2, .., K$$

The constant term c in Eq. 15 is used to specify the percentage of influence of the parameters on the resulting fitness value. The total power consumed by the robot during the roll-out in Eq. 12 is calculated as a sum of power consumed by each of the 18 joints. The power consumed by the motor at each joint is calculated as a sum of the product of torque and angular velocity of the motor obtained at each simulation step. The total power consumed by the robot during the roll-out is then divided by the total displacement along the positive y-axis (in metres) to obtain the power consumed to travel 1 metre, as in Eq. 13.

The objective is to compare and obtain a higher fitness value than the CPG controller. The average displacement along the positive y-axis and the average power consumed to travel one metre by the robot using the CPG controller, averaged over ten roll-outs, are used for the normalization as in Eq. 14.

After K number of roll-outs and calculating the corresponding fitness values, an exponential value is calculated on the fitness value F_{ik} of all the current iteration roll-outs as,

$$E_{ik} = e^{\lambda \frac{F_{ik} - \min_k(F_{ik})}{\max_k(F_{ik}) - \min_k(F_{ik})}}. \tag{16}$$

The constant term λ is set to 10 for all the calculations. Now, the probability weighting P_{ik} is calculated from E_{ik} as follows,

$$P_{ik} = \frac{E_{ik}}{\sum_{k=1}^{K} E_{ik}}. \tag{17}$$

The parameter vector can be updated now using the probability weighting as,

$$U = U + \sum_{k=1}^{K} P_{ik} \cdot \delta U_k. \tag{18}$$

The same continues for I number of iterations and the updated parameter vector at the end of Ith iteration is the output of the PI^2 learning process.

5 Experimental Procedure

The experiment is carried out in the V-REP simulation environment with ROS interface to communicate data and instructions. Each roll-out is simulated for a duration of 5 s with the parameters as specified in Table 3.

At the start of each roll-out, the robot was dropped on the floor at *(x,y) = (0,0)*, facing towards the positive *y-axis*. And at the end of each simulation, the displacement of the robot along the positive *y-axis* and also the power consumed by the robot for travelling that distance were obtained for further processing. The learned parameter vector was obtained at the end of I iterations.

Table 3. Parametric values used in the experiment.

I	100	N	100
K	10	σ	0.1
c	0.5	M	20
t	5 s	T	1 s

6 Results

The progress of mean and standard deviation of fitness, velocity, and power consumption per metre after each weight update, averaged over ten instances of the learning experiment, is shown in Fig. 6(a), (b), and (c) respectively. For comparison, fitness, velocity and power consumption per metre value of the robot performance using the CPG controller is shown as a green line. It shows us that the CPG driven RBFN controller resulted in higher fitness value consuming less power and moving faster than the CPG controller.

The motor patterns that are generated using the CPG controller and the motor patterns generated by the CPG driven RBFN controller after learning are shown in Fig. 7. It is interesting to see that the operational angle range of

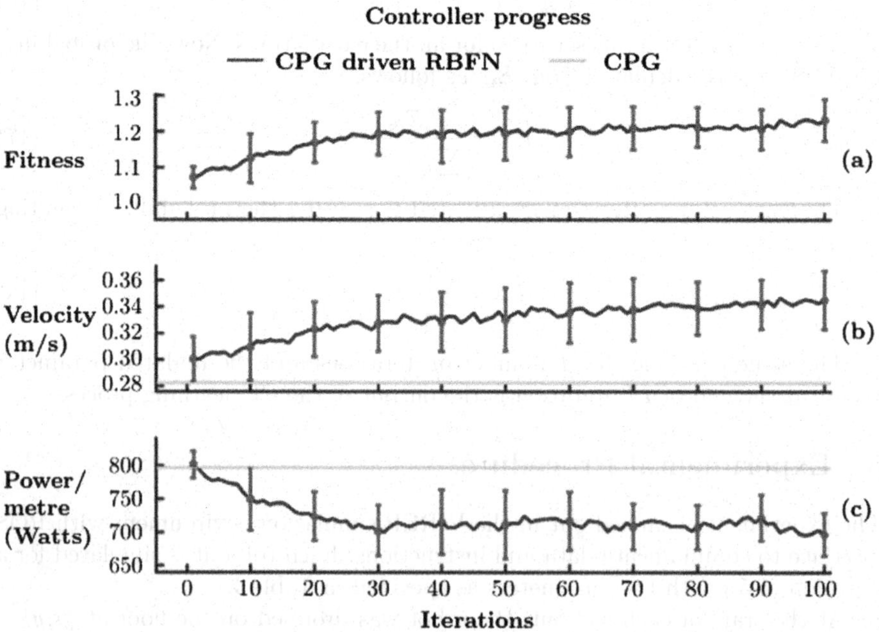

Fig. 6. Progress of mean and standard deviation of (a) fitness, (b) velocity and (c) power consumption/metre, after every update, averaged over 10 PI^2 learnings. The green line indicates the reference values of the CPG controller. (Color figure online)

the TC joints, responsible for forward and backward movement of the leg, has evolved to be shorter than the CPG controller. This might explain the increase in fitness value due to lesser power consumption and the changes in the FT joints pattern, responsible for extension and flexion of the leg, giving the needed extension in co-ordination with the TC joints to travel faster. The CF joints, responsible for upward and downward movement of the leg, remain with the slightest changes.

Similarly, the performance of the robot in simulation using the signals from the CPG controller and the CPG driven RBFN controller are shown in Fig. 8(a) and (b), respectively. It can be seen that the robot with CPG driven RBFN controller has evolved into travelling approximately 0.3 metres more than the robot with CPG controller, in the same time. In addition to the results presented, the videos of the simulated ALPHA locomoting using the CPG controller and the proposed CPG driven RBFN controller for 10 s each, can be found at http://www.manoonpong.com/ICANN2019/.

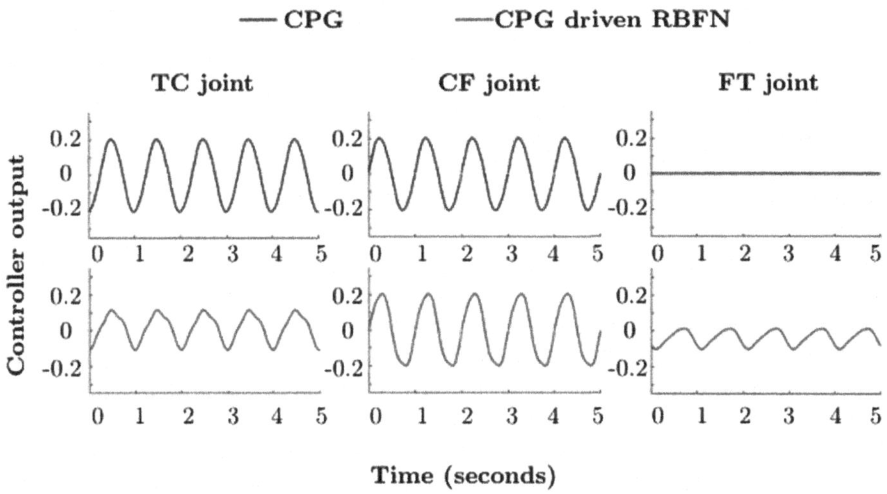

Fig. 7. Motor patterns generated by (a) the CPG controller and (b) the CPG driven RBFN controller. This corresponds to the performance represented in Fig. 8, (a) and (b), respectively.

7 Discussion

In this paper, we introduced the CPG driven RBFN controller inspired by rhythmic DMPs [11,12], which differs mainly as the former is a neural implementation of the latter. The mentioned rhythmic DMPs uses a phase oscillator to provide the phase signal to the fixed basis functions with adjustable weights that result in producing non-linear periodic patterns. However, our controller uses an ANN-based CPG to introduce periodicity and be able to control its frequency [13]

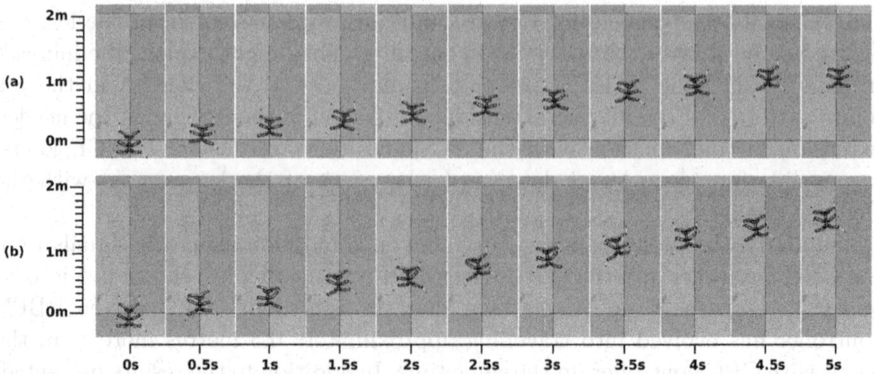

Fig. 8. Aerial snapshots of the simulated robot moving along the positive *y-axis* using (a) the CPG controller and (b) the CPG driven RBFN controller.

while an RBFN takes the CPG outputs as its inputs to produce arbitrary non-linear periodic patterns to learn optimized motor patterns. Another difference is that the phase signal sent to the basis functions in rhythmic DMPs is one dimension whereas, in our controller the CPG sends both the outputs as inputs to the RBFN, making it a two-dimensional phase signal. The advantage of taking a neural approach is that it allows us to apply and test other neural learning mechanisms like neural plasticity [14], which will be investigated in our future work.

Another approach similar to our controller is discussed in [15], in which the periodic patterns are generated as a weighted linear combination of several CPGs with different frequencies. One advantage of using our controller over the other is that the CPG driven RBFN controller is modular with the CPG part controlling the frequency and the RBFN part controlling the shape of the pattern. This modular structure enables using different methods to learn one part or the other independently. Another advantage of using our controller over combining multiple CPGs is that the former uses fewer parameters than the latter.

We have successfully implemented the CPG driven RBFN controller for the ALPHA with the PI^2 method to learn an optimal gait. There is a slight deviation of the robot from the *y-axis* in Fig. 8(b), which might be rectified by continuing the learning above 100 iterations or by introducing a negative reward in the fitness function based on the deviation. However, from Figs. 6 and 8, it shows that the CPG driven RBFN controller results in making the robot travel faster and consume less power than using the CPG controller. The results obtained from the performed experiment also imply that the CPG driven RBFN controller can be used to generate an optimal gait for other complex legged robots.

Acknowledgements. This research was supported partly by the Human Frontier Science Program under Grant agreement no. RGP0002/2017, Startup Grant-IST Flagship research of Vidyasirimedhi Institute of Science & Technology (VISTEC), the European Community H2020 Programme (Future and Emerging Technologies, FET) under grant agreement no. 732266, Plan4Act.

References

1. Tenreiro Machado, J.A., Silva, M.F.: An overview of legged robots. In: International Symposium on Mathematical Methods in Engineering, MME 2006 (2006). https://www.researchgate.net/publication/258972509_An_Overview_of_Legged_Robots
2. Bellicoso, C.D., et al.: Advances in real-world applications for legged robots. J. Field Rob. **35**(8), 1311–1326 (2018). https://doi.org/10.1002/rob.21839
3. Görner, M., Chilian, A., Hirschmüller, H.: Towards an autonomous walking robot for planetary exploration. In: Proceedings of the 10th International Symposium on Artificial Intelligence, Robotics and Automation in Space (i-SAIRAS), September 2010. http://robotics.estec.esa.int/i-SAIRAS/isairas2010/PAPERS/036-2798-p.pdf
4. Ignasov, J., et al.: Bio-inspired design and movement generation of dung beetle-like legs. Artif. Life Rob. (2018). https://doi.org/10.1007/s10015-018-0475-5
5. Ijspeert, A.J.: Central pattern generators for locomotion control in animals and robots: a review. Neural Netw. **21**(4), 642–653 (2008). https://doi.org/10.1016/j.neunet.2008.03.014
6. Theodorou, E., Buchli, J., Schaal, S.: Reinforcement learning of motor skills in high dimensions: a path integral approach. In: Proceedings of the IEEE International Conference on Robotics and Automation (ICRA), pp. 2397–2403 (2010). https://doi.org/10.1109/ROBOT.2010.5509336
7. Stulp, F., Schaal, S.: Hierarchical reinforcement learning with movement primitives. In: 11th IEEE-RAS International Conference on Humanoid Robots, pp. 231–238 (2011). https://doi.org/10.1109/Humanoids.2011.6100841
8. Chatterjee, S., et al.: Reinforcement learning approach to generate goal-directed locomotion of a snake-like robot with screw-drive units. In: 2014 23rd International Conference on Robotics in Alpe-Adria-Danube Region (RAAD) (2014). https://doi.org/10.1109/RAAD.2014.7002234
9. Stulp, F., Sigaud, O.: Robot skill learning: from reinforcement learning to evolution strategies. Paladyn J. Behav. Rob. **4**(1), 49–61 (2013). https://doi.org/10.2478/pjbr-2013-0003
10. Pasemann, F., Hild, M., Zahedi, K.: SO(2)-networks as neural oscillators. In: Mira, J., Álvarez, J.R. (eds.) IWANN 2003. LNCS, vol. 2686, pp. 144–151. Springer, Heidelberg (2003). https://doi.org/10.1007/3-540-44868-3_19
11. Ijspeert, A.J., Nakanishi, J., Hoffmann, H., Pastor, P., Schaal, S.: Dynamical movement primitives: learning attractor models for motor behaviors. Neural Comput. **25**(2), 328–373 (2013). https://doi.org/10.1162/NECO_a_00393
12. Ijspeert, A.J., Nakanishi, J., Schaal, S.: Learning attractor landscapes for learning motor primitives. In: Advances in Neural Information Processing Systems, Vancouver, BC, CA, vol. 15, pp. 1547–1554 (2003). https://papers.nips.cc/paper/2140-learning-attractor-landscapes-for-learning-motor-primitives.pdf

13. Manoonpong, P., Pasemann, F., Woergoetter, F.: Sensor-driven neural control for omnidirectional locomotion and versatile reactive behaviors of walking machines. Rob. Auton. Syst. **56**(3), 265–288 (2008). https://doi.org/10.1016/j.robot.2007.07.004
14. Grinke, E., Tetzlaff, C., Wörgötter, F., Manoonpong, P.: Synaptic plasticity in a recurrent neural network for versatile and adaptive behaviors of a walking robot. Frontiers Neurorobotics **9** (2015). https://doi.org/10.3389/fnbot.2015.00011
15. Righetti, L., Ijspeert, A.J.: Programmable central pattern generators: an application to biped locomotion control. In: Proceedings 2006 IEEE International Conference on Robotics and Automation, ICRA 2006 (2006). https://doi.org/10.1109/ROBOT.2006.1641933

Spiking Networks

Training Delays in Spiking Neural Networks

Laura State[1,2](✉) and Pau Vilimelis Aceituno[2]

[1] University of Tübingen, Tübingen, Germany
[2] Max Planck Institute for Mathematics in the Sciences, Leipzig, Germany
{state,pau.aceituno}@mis.mpg.de

Abstract. Spiking Neural Networks (SNNs) are a promising computational paradigm, both to understand biological information processing and for low-power, embedded chips. Although SNNs are known to encode information in the precise timing of spikes, conventional artificial learning algorithms do not take this into account directly. In this work, we implement the spike timing by training the synaptic delays in a single layer SNN. We use two different approaches: a classical gradient descent and a direct algebraic method that is based on a complex-valued encoding of the spikes. Both algorithms are equally able to correctly solve simple detection tasks. Our work provides new optimization methods for the data analysis of highly time-dependent data and training methods for neuromorphic chips.

1 Introduction

Artificial Neural Networks are state-of-the-art techniques in machine learning tasks. However, they come at the cost of large computational resources, both in terms of training and execution. To overcome this challenge, Spiking Neural Networks (SNNs) have been proposed as an alternative. The low amount of power needed to run SNNs [5] and their similarity to biological nervous systems are promising, but their performance is still below that of their conventional counterparts (see [8] and [2]). Therefore, SNNs remain a second choice for machine learning tasks.

Typical training algorithms for SNNs modify the weights of the connections between the neurons, in line with the classical training in machine learning. However, the output of a SNN depends also crucially on the timing of single spikes. To improve the performance of SNNs, we therefore propose to extend the classical training algorithms and adapt both the time delays and the weights of the connections.

As a proof of concept, we implemented a single-layer perceptron and designed two training algorithms. The first algorithm is based on a complex representation of spikes whereas the second method uses standard gradient descent. Both frameworks are able to efficiently train the latencies and the weights of the SNN for a simple detection task, showing that an additional optimization of the delays is not only beneficial but also surprisingly easy.

I. V. Tetko et al. (Eds.): ICANN 2019, LNCS 11727, pp. 713–717, 2019.
https://doi.org/10.1007/978-3-030-30487-4_54

2 Problem Statement

Spiking neurons are implemented as Leaky Integrate-and-Fire (LIF) neurons [4]. In this model, the state of a neuron is described by its membrane potential $v(t)$, which evolves according to the equation

$$\tau \frac{dv(t)}{dt} = -v(t) + v_{rest} + i(t) \tag{1}$$

where $\tau > 1$ refers to the decay constant, $v_{rest} < 0$ to the resting potential and $i(t)$ to the current input of the neuron. When the membrane potential reaches the threshold $v_{th} > 0$, the neuron emits a spike. After firing, the potential is reset to its resting voltage $v_{rest} < v_{th}$.
The firing of a neuron generates instantaneous pulses of current, which can be described by the dirac function $\delta(t)$. Those pulses are transmitted to other neurons via synapses. The connections are characterized by weights w and delays d which correspond, respectively, to the gain and the latency of a pulse of current going to another neuron. Therefore, the input to a postsynaptic neuron can be described as

$$i(t) = \sum_k w_k \delta(t - t_k + d_k)$$

where w_k is the weight, t_k the time at which the presynaptic spike was generated and d_k the transmission delay (see also Fig. 2A). Thus, training a LIF neuron means to find the parameters of the N synapses that yield an output spike train as close as possible to a desired output.

We simplify the model as follows: first, we assume that the spike trains are sparse, meaning that only a few spikes occur over the whole train. This idea is generally accepted in the neuroscience community and crucial for a possible application on neuromorphic hardware chips. As SNNs consume energy only when there is a spike, they are advantageous only when there are few spikes. Second, we break the time intervals of the spike trains in small intervals of length T, where T is in order of magnitude of the decay constant τ or larger, meaning that the intervals are effectively independent. Combined with the sparsity constraint, we obtain many independent time intervals with at most one spike.

We start by training the single-layer perceptron for a simple detection task, i.e. to detect a specific input pattern within a multitude of possible inputs.

3 Approach and Results

After implementing the single-layer perceptron, we introduce two different ways to train its weights and delays. First, we use a complex representation of the

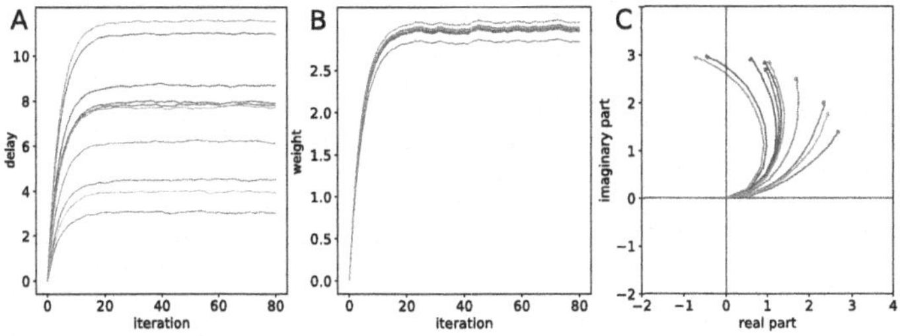

Fig. 1. Panel A and B: Evolution of the delays and real weights during gradient descent. Delays (A) and weights (B) converge to the linear solution of the complex analysis. **Panel C: Evolution of the weights during gradient descent in the complex representation.** Dots indicate convergence points.

pre- and postsynaptic spikes, allowing us to solve for the delays and weights of the synapses directly. A single spike is encoded as

$$w_k e^{j\varphi_k}$$

where $\varphi_k = t_k \pi / 2T$ yields the complex phase for a spike emitted at time t_k and a time interval of T. The parameter w_k refers to the weight of the spike and j to the complex unit. Using this representation, the training algorithm of the LIF neuron reduces to a linear regression problem with the following solution

$$W = X^{+} Y$$

with X referring to the vector of the presynaptic and Y to the vector of the postsynaptic spikes. As we can compute the pseudoinverse X^{+} of X, we can directly calculate W, denoting to the vector of N complex weights. The phases of those weights W_n can be converted to the delays d_n and their modulus to the real weights w_n of the synapses.

Our second training method uses standard gradient descent [1] on the weights and delays, independently for both parameters. The results for $N = 10$ presynaptic neurons are shown in Fig. 1.

We simulated the response of the single-layer perceptron to two different input spike trains, using the weights and delays from the gradient descent approach. Results are displayed in Fig. 2, panel B to D. Using a spike train from the test set, a spike is postsynaptically generated as the membrane potential reaches the threshold. Feeding in a different, randomly generated pattern, the LIF neuron remains silent.

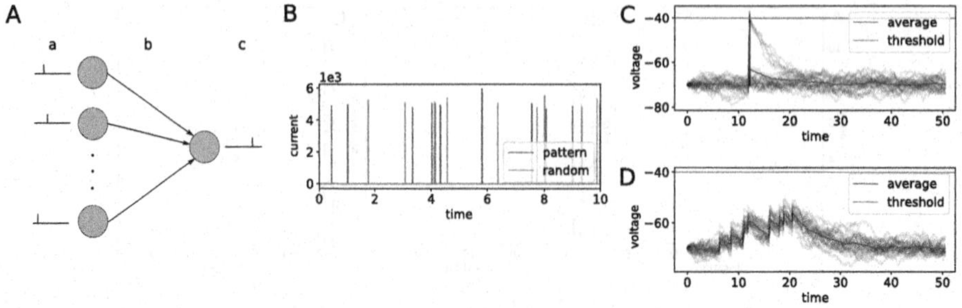

Fig. 2. Panel A: LIF neuron. The input of $N = 10$ presyn. neurons (a) is transmitted via synapses with weights w and delays d (b) to the postsyn. neuron, producing a spike pattern (c). **Panel B: Presyn. spike patterns (input currents).** A spike train from the test set (labelled 'pattern') and an arbitrary, randomly generated spike train (labelled 'random'). Train and test data were generated by adding independent noise on a basic pattern, the basic pattern by randomly drawing one spike time per presyn. neuron from a uniform distribution between zero and $T = 10$. **Panel C and D: Membrane responses.** Spikes arrive at the same time postsynaptically when the test spike train is fed in (panel C), lead to increase in membrane potential over the threshold and the LIF neuron fires. Spikes do not arrive at the same time postsynaptically when a different, arbitrary pattern is fed in (panel D), increase in membrane potential is not sufficiently high to evoke a spike. The membrane potential was calculated multiple times and averaged, each realization thereby following Eq. 1 with additional Gaussian noise.

4 Conclusion

By implementing a single LIF neuron that is trained in the weights and delays of the individual synapses, we could show that the SNN framework can be used to detect input spike patterns. Using a complex representation of the spikes thereby allowed us to derive the solutions directly.

At the moment, we work on applying the newly introduced framework to the classification of the MNIST dataset of handwritten digits [7]. Using a simple, random feature-extracting approach which converts every digit to 180 spike trains, the algorithm already achieves 80% and 66% accuracy for the gradient descent and linear algebra approach respectively.

Another idea is to apply our framework on a triangulation task that determines the origin of ground vibrations. Our approach could also be used to test the hypothesis of latency decrease due to Spike-Timing-Dependent Plasticity, as for example proposed in [6]. Training the framework on experimental data that was recorded over time and both on the pre-and postsynaptic side, the hypothesized latency decrease should be visible in the time evolutions of the trained delays.

We believe that the above-outlined ideas are the first step towards more general methods, including multi-layer networks and accounting for multiple spikes in a spike train. Finally, our framework provides new optimization strategies for neuromorphic computation, specifically for neuromorphic chips that implement adaptable delays such as the Loihi chip that was developed by the Intel Corporation [3].

References

1. Bishop, C.M.: Pattern Recognition and Machine Learing. Springer, New York (2006)
2. Cao, Y., Chen, Y., Khosla, D.: Spiking deep convolutional neural networks for energy-efficient object recognition. Int. J. Comput. Vis. **113**(1), 54–66 (2014). https://doi.org/10.1007/s11263-014-0788-3
3. Davies, M., et al.: Loihi: A neuromorphic manycore processor with on-chip learning. IEEE Micro **38**(1), 82–99 (2018). https://doi.org/10.1109/mm.2018.112130359
4. Dayan, P., Abbott, L.F.: Theoretical Neuroscience: Computational and Mathematical Modeling of Neural Systems. The MIT Press (2001)
5. Diehl, P.U., Zarrella, G., Cassidy, A., Pedroni, B.U., Neftci, E.: Conversion of artificial recurrent neural networks to spiking neural networks for low-power neuromorphic hardware. In: 2016 IEEE International Conference on Rebooting Computing (ICRC), IEEE, October 2016. https://doi.org/10.1109/icrc.2016.7738691
6. Guyonneau, R., VanRullen, R., Thorpe, S.J.: Neurons tune to the earliest spikes through STDP. Neural Comput. **17**(4), 859–879 (2005). https://doi.org/10.1162/0899766053429390
7. Lecun, Y., Bottou, L., Bengio, Y., Haffner, P.: Gradient-based learning applied to document recognition. Proc. IEEE **86**(11), 2278–2324 (1998). https://doi.org/10.1109/5.726791
8. O'Connor, P., Welling, M.: Deep spiking networks. arxiv (2016)

An Izhikevich Model Neuron MOS Circuit for Low Voltage Operation

Yuki Tamura(✉), Satoshi Moriya, Tatsuki Kato, Masao Sakuraba, Yoshihiko Horio, and Shigeo Sato

Research Institute of Electrical Communication, Tohoku University, 2-1-1 Katahira, Aoba-ku, Sendai, Miyagi 980-8577, Japan
yuki-tam@riec.tohoku.ac.jp

Abstract. The Izhikevich neuron model has attracted attention because it can reproduce various neural activities although it is described by simple differential equations and is expected to be applied to engineering. Among a few MOS circuits inspired by the Izhikevich model, the circuit proposed by Wijekoon and Dudek in 2008 exhibits the simplest structure, and it is practical. However, the power supply voltage of the circuit is 3.3 V. To implement such a neuron MOS circuit using state-of-the-art semiconductor manufacturing process, we must redesign the circuit to operate it with a lower supply voltage. Thus, we analyzed their circuit operation by SPICE simulation assuming a 1.0 V supply voltage and found that the bias voltage ranges to generate specific spike activities were limited. In addition, we clarified the discrepancies between the Izhikevich neuron model and the original circuit. In this study, we propose a new Izhikevich model neuron circuit based on these findings and investigate the circuit dynamics by null-cline analysis and SPICE simulation. The dynamics of the proposed MOS circuit are close to those of the Izhikevich model and various spikes are generated. Furthermore, we successfully enlarged the bias voltage range for specific spikes.

Keywords: Izhikevich neuron model · Analog neuron circuit · SPICE simulation · Null-cline analysis

1 Introduction

Information processing of biological brain nervous systems has attracted significant attention for their merits such as high-level information processing and adaptive response to fluctuating environments even with low power consumption. In recent years, LSIs inspired by biological nervous systems such as IBM's TrueNorth and Google's TensorFlow have been developed.

The mechanism of the electrophysiological activity of neurons has been widely studied for many years, and various mathematical models that describe neuron activity have been proposed hitherto. Among the models, the Izhikevich model [1] has attracted attention because it can reproduce various neural activities although it is described by simple differential equations and is expected to be applied to engineering. Among the MOS circuits inspired by the Izhikevich model, the circuit proposed by Wijekoon and

I. V. Tetko et al. (Eds.): ICANN 2019, LNCS 11727, pp. 718–723, 2019.
https://doi.org/10.1007/978-3-030-30487-4_55

Dudek in 2008 [2] exhibits the simplest structure and is practical. Their analog circuit operates with a 3.3 V voltage supply and reproduces various spikes. However, in state-of-the-art LSIs, the power supply voltage decreases. Therefore, we verified the operation of their circuit using SPICE simulation and a power supply voltage of 1.0 V. Subsequently, we found that the range of bias voltage that reproduces specific spike activities is limited and the discrepancies between the Izhikevich model and their circuit. In this study, we propose a new Izhikevich model neuron circuit based on these findings and investigate the circuit dynamics by null-cline analysis and SPICE simulation.

2 Izhikevich Model

The Izhikevich neuron model [1] is described by the following equations:

$$\dot{v} = 0.04v^2 + 5v + 140 - u + I, \tag{1}$$

$$\dot{u} = a(bv - u), \tag{2}$$

$$\text{if } v \geq 30\,\text{mV, then} \begin{cases} v \leftarrow c \\ u \leftarrow u + d \end{cases}. \tag{3}$$

Equation 1 describes the time change of the membrane potential v of a neuron, where u and I are the recovery variable and synapse current, respectively. Equation 2 describes the recovery variable u and Eq. 3 corresponds to the reset operation. This model reproduces the known neural activities of cortical neurons, such as regular spiking (RS), intrinsically bursting (IB), chattering (CH), fast spiking (FS), and low-threshold spiking (LTS) by properly adjusting the four parameters: *a, b, c,* and *d*.

3 Previous Study

In 2008, Wijekoon and Dudek reported an analog circuit [2] operating similar to the Izhikevich model. Because MOS transistors in the circuit operate in the strong inversion region, the circuit is effective for implementing the Izhikevich model described by a quadratic function. They successfully reproduced the RS, FS, IB, CH, and LTS of the Izhikevich model. The circuit comprises three subcircuits. The first subcircuit corresponds to Eq. 1 and generates spikes by rapidly changing the membrane potential V. The second subcircuit corresponds to Eq. 2. This circuit feeds the recovery variable U back to the first subcircuit and adjusts the spike timing depending on U. The third subcircuit is a comparator that generates reset pulses for resetting the membrane potential V and the recovery variable U. Although the circuit is well optimized, some discrepancies exist. The dynamics related to V and the reset operation of U are different from those of the original. For example, an unnecessary U-squared term exists in the right-hand side of Eq. 1.

4 Proposed Circuit

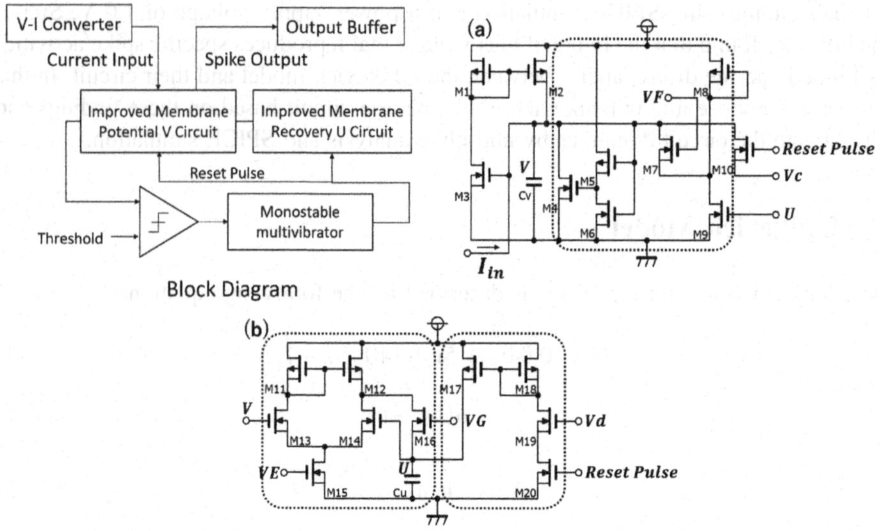

Fig. 1. Block diagram and schematics of the subcircuits. (a) Membrane potential V circuit and (b) Membrane recovery U circuit.

To solve the discrepancies between the original circuit and the Izhikevich model and to enable the circuit to operate with a low voltage supply, we redesigned the subcircuits. The fundamental function of each subcircuit is the same as that of the original circuit. Figure 1 shows the block diagram of our proposed circuit and the subcircuit schematics. We redesigned the three parts surrounded by dotted lines. The mathematical model of the proposed circuit is deduced as follows:

$$C_v * \dot{V} = \alpha(V - V_t)^2 - \beta\left\{(1 - V_t)V - \frac{1}{2}V^2\right\} - \gamma\left[VF - V_t - \frac{n}{2}(V - U + 1)\right](V + U - 1) + I, \quad (4)$$

$$C_u * \dot{U} = \delta\left[VG - V_t - \frac{n}{2}V\right](V - \varepsilon U), \quad (5)$$

where $\alpha, \beta, \gamma, \delta$, and ε depend on the gate width-to-length ratio of the MOSFET, *W/L*; n and I are the slope factor and post-synaptic current, respectively.

In the subcircuit related to V (Fig. 1(a)), the transistor M7 operates in the linear region to remove an unnecessary U-squared term unlike the original circuit. The subcircuit related to U (Fig. 1(b)) comprises a differential pair in the left block and a current mirror circuit in the right block. In the left part, the gate voltage VE of the transistor M15 and the *W/L* ratio of the MOSFETs constituting the differential pair corresponds to *a* and *b* in Eq. 2, respectively. Note that because the parameter *b* is proportional to the *W/L* ratio, it is not possible to reproduce some dynamics of the Izhikevich model that are obtained by setting the parameter *b* negative [3]. In the right part, the current mirror circuit generates *d* in Eq. 3 as desired, while *d* in the original circuit is a function of *U*. In the third subcircuit, which is not shown in Fig. 1, we added a monostable multivibrator for a stable reset operation by converting an unstable pulse generated by a comparator to a firm reset pulse with fixed duration.

5 Experimental Results

5.1 Null-Cline Analysis

We used a mathematical model to investigate the dynamics of the circuit and compared the dynamics of the proposed circuit with those of the Izhikevich model and the original circuit. As shown in Fig. 2, the null-cline of the proposed circuit becomes closer to that of the Izhikevich model. In particular, the shape of the *V* null-cline becomes quadratic.

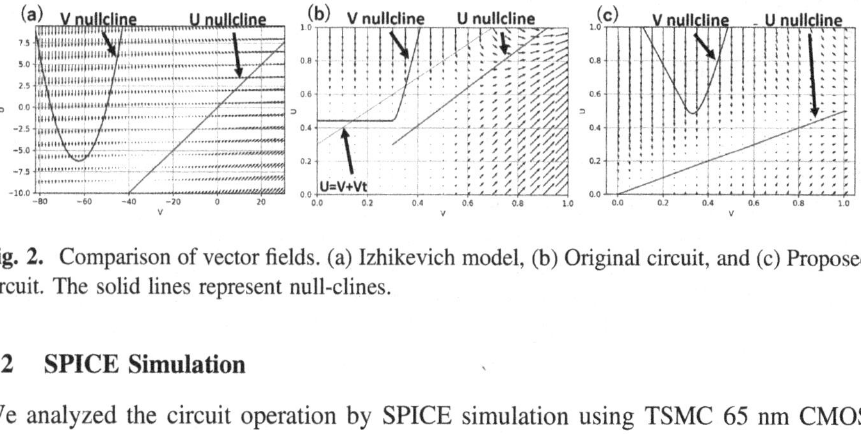

Fig. 2. Comparison of vector fields. (a) Izhikevich model, (b) Original circuit, and (c) Proposed circuit. The solid lines represent null-clines.

5.2 SPICE Simulation

We analyzed the circuit operation by SPICE simulation using TSMC 65 nm CMOS technology. The power supply voltage was set to 1.0 V. The proposed circuit generated various types of spikes similar to those of the Izhikevich model after we adjusted two voltage parameters *Vc* and *Vd*, which are related to the reset operation. Figure 3 shows the relation between spike type and *Vc* and *Vd,* in addition to the values of the other parameters and the shape of each spike. The parameter ranges of the proposed circuit for CH and IB are enlarged and various pulses can be generated even with a low supply voltage. The shape of each spike of the proposed circuit is similar to that of the Izhikevich model.

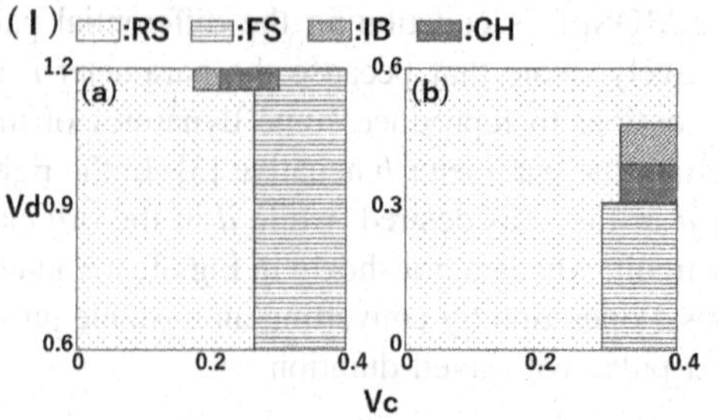

(II)

M1	5/1	M11	2.5/1	Cv	0.1pF
M2	5/1	M12	2.5/1	Cu	1pF
M3	2/1	M13	1/1	VDD	1.0V
M4	0.1/1	M14	1/1	VE	0.4V
M5	3.5/1	M15	0.1/1	VF	1.0V
M6	1/1	M16	0.1/1	VG	1.0V
M7	0.1/2	M17	2.5/1	I	4μA
M8	3.5/1	M18	2.5/1		
M9	1/1	M19	1/1		
M10	4/1	M20	1/1		

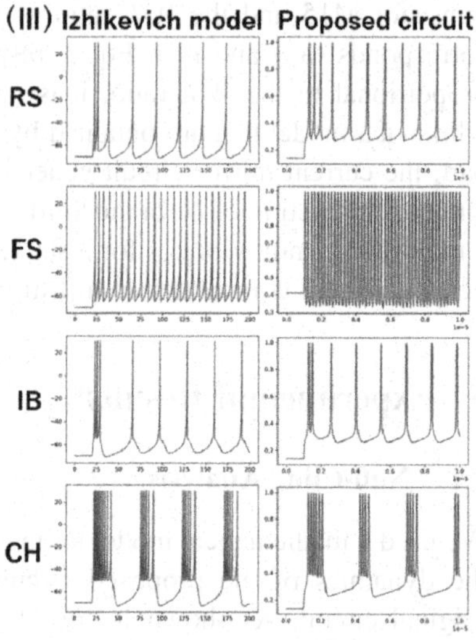

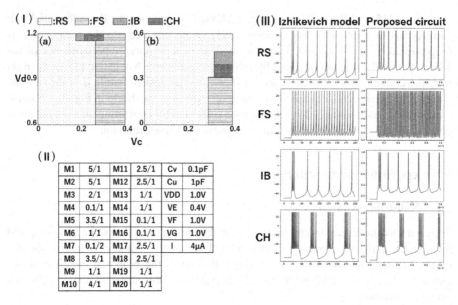

Fig. 3. (I) Relation between spike type and parameters *Vc* and *Vd.* (a) Original circuit, (b) Proposed circuit. (II) Circuit parameters. The size of transistors is expressed in micrometer. (III) Comparison of spike shapes between the Izhikevich model and the proposed circuit.

6 Conclusion

We proposed an improved neuron MOS circuit by solving the discrepancies between the Izhikevich model and the previously studied circuit. The dynamics of the proposed circuit resembled the Izhikevich model and various spikes were generated. However, the power consumption of the proposed circuit was approximately 20 μW that resulted in difficulty in large-scale integration. The consideration of MOS operations in the subthreshold region to reduce power consumption remains as future work. In some cases, it is worth considering an exponential integrate-and-fire neuron (EIaF model [4]) because exponential function is naturally realized in the subthreshold operation.

Acknowledgments. This study was supported by the Cooperative Research Project Program of the Research Institute of Electrical Communication, Tohoku University; the Program on Open Innovation Platform with Enterprises, Research Institute and Academia (OPERA) from Japan Science and Technology Agency (JST); JSPS KAKENHI (Grant Nos, 17K18864 and 18J12197); and JST CREST Grant Number JPMJCR18K4, Japan.

References

1. Izhikevich, E.M.: Simple model of spiking neurons. IEEE Trans. Neural Networks **14**(6), 1569–1572 (2003). https://doi.org/10.1109/TNN.2003.820440

2. Jayawan, H.B. Wijekoon, P.D.: Compact silicon neuron circuit with spiking and bursting behavior. Neural Networks **21**, 524–534 (2008). https://doi.org/10.1016/j.neunet.2007.12.037
3. Izhikevich, E.M.: Which model to use for cortical spiking neurons? IEEE Trans. Neural Networks **15**(5), 1063–1070 (2004). https://doi.org/10.1109/TNN.2004.832719
4. Brette, R., Gerstner, W.: Adaptive exponential Integrate-and-Fire model as an effective description of neuronal activity. J. Neurophysiol. **94**(5), 3637–3642 (2005). https://doi.org/10.1152/jn.00686.2005

UAV Detection: A STDP Trained Deep Convolutional Spiking Neural Network Retina-Neuromorphic Approach

Paul Kirkland[1(✉)], Gaetano Di Caterina[1], John Soraghan[1], Yiannis Andreopoulos[2], and George Matich[3]

[1] The University of Strathclyde, Glasgow, UK
paul.kirkland@strath.ac.uk
[2] University College London, London, UK
[3] Leonardo, London, UK

Abstract. The Dynamic Vision Sensor (DVS) has many attributes, such as sub-millisecond response time along with a good low light dynamic range, that allows it to be well suited to the task for UAV Detection. This paper proposes a system that exploits the features of an event camera solely for UAV detection while combining it with a Spiking Neural Network (SNN) trained using the unsupervised approach of Spike Time-Dependent Plasticity (STDP), to create an asynchronous, low power system with low computational overhead. Utilising the unique features of both the sensor and the network, this result in a system that is robust to a wide variety in lighting conditions, has a high temporal resolution, propagates only the minimal amount of information through the network, while training using the equivalent of 43,000 images. The network returns a 91% detection rate when shown other objects and can detect a UAV with less than 1% of pixels on the sensor being used for processing.

Keywords: CNN · SNN · STDP · UAV

1 Introduction

Consumer UAVs and micro-UAVs are increasingly available at low cost, allowing their use in commercial applications (inspection, filming and deliveries) [14] and social use by the general public to become more frequent [19]. However, as the number of UAVs in circulation increases, so does the concern for misuse and accidents. A prime example in the UK recently was the closure of airports due to UAV flying over this restricted area [1], with near misses recorded in the UK in 2018 as 117, up 10 times from 4 years ago [5]. Nonetheless, a number of other concerns, other than collisions, exist due to the UAVs ability to carry a small

Supported by Leonardo, Data Collection in collaboration with University College London.

I. V. Tetko et al. (Eds.): ICANN 2019, LNCS 11727, pp. 724–736, 2019.
https://doi.org/10.1007/978-3-030-30487-4_56

payload: these could contain potentially harmful chemical or explosives or could be used to smuggle illegal goods [6].

Detection of UAVs is not trivial due to their small form factor, coupled with the expanse of the search space. They also possess a high range of manoeuvrability while being difficult to discriminate against birds at distant ranges. These features make it difficult for typical detection approaches such as visual, infra-red, audio and radar to detect the UAV in a wide range of situations [6].

This paper presents a novel UAV Detection system, utilising the features of both the Dynamic Vision Sensor (DVS) and Spiking Neural Network (SNN). This end-to-end spiking Neuromorphic system possesses the following range of features: asynchronous functionality, low power consumption, low computational throughput, high dynamic range, high temporal resolution and dynamic relationship with scene environment. The results of a pilot study show that this system is ideal for the task of UAV detection, displaying features that are unmatched by any other single sensor systems.

The remainder of the paper is organised as follows. Section 2 provides background on the sensor and the spiking network used and explaining the unsupervised learning mechanism. Section 3 provides details about the experimental set-up, Sect. 4 shows off the results of the system and Sect. 5 has the discussion of these results.

2 Background

Neuromorphic engineering combines research from both the neuroscience and computational neuroscience fields that is exploited within an Engineering aspect. The proposed system makes use of three such Neuromorphic approaches, the event-based camera, spiking neural network and spike time dependent plasticity. The respective sensor, neuron model and learning mechanism combine with a traditional Deep Convolutional Neural Network (DCNN) architecture, to capitalise on the characteristic unique to each.

2.1 Dynamic Vision Sensor - Event Based Camera

The Dynamic Vision Sensor is a biologically-inspired sensor (silicon retina) created to mimic how human eye perceives motion with their retina: as such the sensor asynchronously transmits the logarithmic light intensity difference (events) on a pixel by pixel level. This replaces the fixed frame rate traditional camera images, with a far more compressed and sparse output, resulting in 1 to 3 orders of magnitude increase in output rate (33 ms traditional to 15 μs Event Based) [4]. This allows the sensor to have a much higher temporal resolution (in essence a 66000 frames per second super slow-motion camera for up to 800 pixels, as compared to real world frames per second closer to 1–2,000) but without the caveat of the extra processing required for the pixels that didn't change. Another feature is the DVS's high dynamic range, rated at >120 dB vs the <60 dB of traditional cameras [4,11]. This allows the event based camera to see in a wide variety of lighting conditions, from quickly changing brightness conditions, to low light ones, where traditional cameras would not be able to detect anything. A comparison of images captured from a DSLR and the DVS, showing UAVs flying in a well lit and low light scene, are illustrated in Fig. 1. It can be seen that the DVS camera is able to capture the shape of the UAV in a well lit situation Fig. 1(b) and (c) and is also able to capture the shape in the low light situation when the outline of the UAV is indistinguishable in Fig. 1(e) and (f). The images in Fig. 1(c) and (f) show a typical post processing median filtering of the images to give better sensor noise suppression.

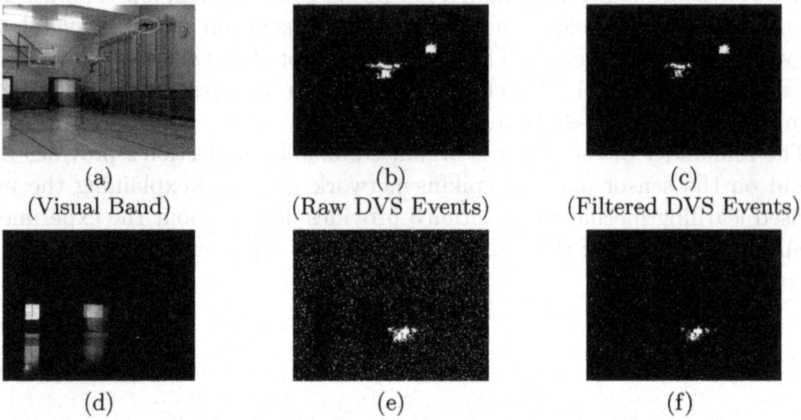

Fig. 1. Use of the high dynamic range within the DVS to capture stark lighting differences. (TOP) indoor well lit scene (BOTTOM) low light scene.

The advantages of the DVS leads to the main attribute exploited within this paper, that relates the dynamic relationship to the visual source. This attribute is how the sensor can deliver a sparse yet detailed account of the scene, minimising computation and power. An example of this is shown in Fig. 2 highlights the ability to change the integration time of the events captured to create a frame (for visual representation and training). The top row shows a slow-moving UAV, where a higher integration time is required to collect enough event to represent the UAV, as not as many changes in light intensity occur. While the bottom row illustrates the removal of motion blur, in a fast-moving UAV collision, by decreasing the integration time. The integration times can also be overlapped allowing a combination of both a longer integration time to capture events and the fine temporal resolution changes in the scene. The main drawback to the current DVS technology is the low spatial resolution. However, active research in this area has shown cameras with a sensor size of 640×480 [16] and 384×320 [9] pixels can be produced while maintaining the useful features.

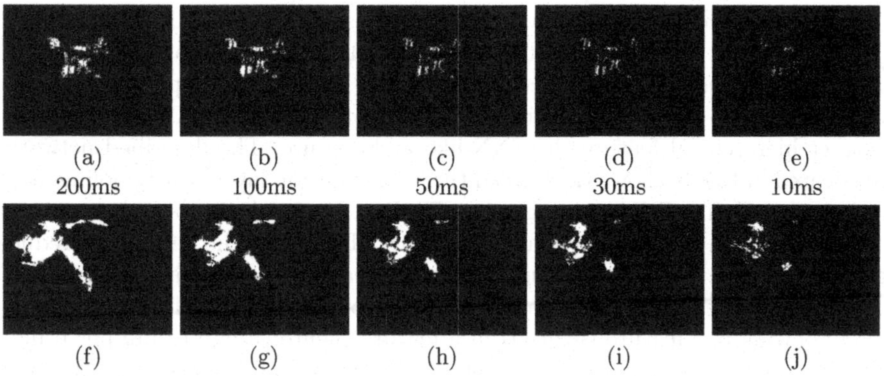

Fig. 2. DVS filtered events captured in a range of time frames for a low speed (TOP) and high speed scene (BOTTOM)

2.2 Spiking Neural Network

The network used within this paper makes use of both the benefits of convolutional and spiking neural networks.

The CNN brings a local spatial coherence and parameter/weight sharing method, that allows an image to be compressed, such that it can be represented by a respectively smaller number of features versus the number of pixel in the image. Combining these features within progressive layers allows further compression to occur. The SNN allows sparsity to occur through changing of the neuron model, and learning mechanism. The new neuron model converts the floating point values travelling through the network with 1 bit binary spikes. These spikes are far more simplistic in nature, with constant amplitude and duration of individual spikes. Their information is characterised entirely by their emission time (when a neuron fired), and frequency of firing (how often a neuron fires). The neurons have a threshold to reach before passing information forward, but further information can be inferred from the timing of frequency of the neuron firing. In other words, only passing a small amount of important information through the network, but in a timely manner. This can be seen as similar to that of the primate visual system, which has been shown to have spike rates on the order of a few hertz [15].

The change in the neuron model leads to a very important paradigm shift in the network: from looking for content, to looking for context. This reiterates the usefulness of the sparse information transfer that can relate importance into it's time dependency. In that, a few import pieces of context can be used to build content, but no amount of content

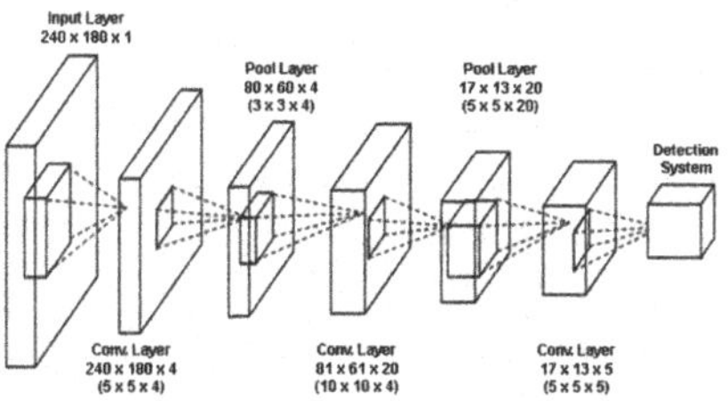

Fig. 3. SNN architecture 3 layer convolution and pooling

can give you context. This type of sparse, spike-time-based deep network [10,12,17] is not as suited for a backpropagation learning mechanism as a CNN. It then makes use of a simplified unsupervised Spike-Time Dependent Plasticity (STDP) rule [2] in combination with a winner-takes-all (WTA) approach, to extract hierarchical features in CNN-like architecture. The described network, illustrated in Fig. 3, shows the typical three convolution layers with pooling layer in-between. Unlike CNN learning, with STDP each convolution layer has an intra and inter lateral inhibition mechanism [10,18]. This helps the network to reduce the information propagated, especially redundant and repeating information, while ensuring that the most salient information is maintained. It operates by only allowing one feature (neuron) in a feature (neuron) map to fire per frame, seen as an intra map competition. This WTA approach then moves onto the inter map inhibition. Only allowing one spike to occur in any given spatial region, typically the size of the convolution kernel, throughout all the maps. When not training the convolution and pooling layers operate in a standard procedure, with the pooling also following the WTA theme with a max pool operation.

3 Methodology

Two different methods of capturing data were used in this work. Actual events captured from a DVS and simulated events generated from data captured from a higher resolution DSLR camera. The following describes the set up for the experimental data collection and simulated sensor data creation along with any specifics pertaining to the network and learning mechanism.

3.1 Dynamic Vision Sensor Data

The data was captured within a small (basketball court sized) gymnasium, as seen in Fig. 4, in order to be able to control the amount of light in a given scene. Two different sized UAVs (DJI Phantom [without propellers - 290 × 290 × 195 mm] and DJI Tello [98 × 92.5 × 41 mm]) were used which allowed a wider range of test scenarios to be replicated. The event data was captured using a DVS240 Neuromorphic Vision Sensor with a spatial resolution of 240 × 180 and asynchronous event output. It was mounted on top of a DSLR Camera, producing a 1920 × 1080 output at 60 Frames per Second (FPS), both pictured in Fig. 4. This was used for ground truth data and use within the simulated data as a means of comparison. The DVS camera is set up to give out a tuple for each spike event, these contain the xy coordinate, the timestamp of when the event occurred, and the polarity of the change in intensity. However, during training and testing of the proposed system the polarity

Fig. 4. Indoor test set up

value was ignored, compressing all the spike information into one channel instead of two. The time-stamp data was embedded into each of the frames used for the dataset, this provides a significant advantage over simulated event data [10] as the earlier events are no longer just the highest contrast, but actually, still represent the spatio-temporal domain they were captured in. To further improve this temporal aspect a range of integration time for the dataset frame collection was used, ranging from 10 ms up to 200 ms with overlaps in the time windows of 10%, 50% and 90%. This wide variety in the frames allows the sensor to capture a diverse range of speed variability within the sensor field of view. This allows the temporal data, usually lost in the snapshot of a frame to be instilled within event capture.

3.2 Simulated Dynamic Vision Sensor Data

There are two sources of UAV footage used for the simulated event data: Video recorded from a DSLR camera as explained in the previous section. The other footage is captured from some outside testing using a DSLR (1920 × 1080 @ 30–60 fps).

An example of the simulated data is provided in Fig. 5, which shows a simulated events frame, along with the pre and post the processing stage when the resolution is down-sampled to 240 × 180.

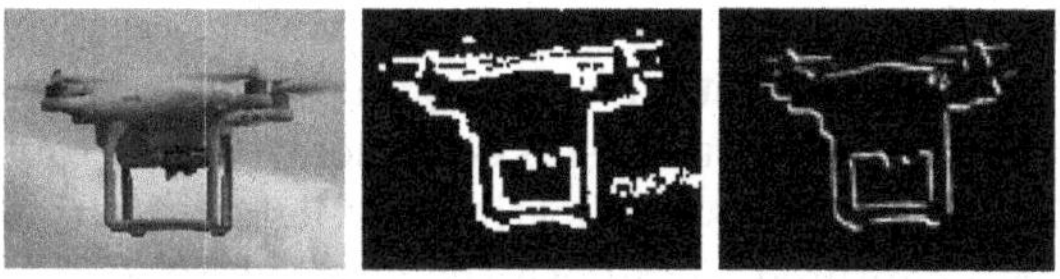

Fig. 5. Simulated UAVs

The outdoor footage provides a wide range of lighting conditions per frame and a number of different background disturbances to cause noise and clutter in the data (clouds and ground objects). The only issue with simulating the event data is the inherent lack of temporal resolution (missing information between each frame that needs to be interpolated). A number of simulators already exist [3,7,13], with PIX2NVS [3] being the event simulator used in this paper. The event sensor simulator takes the frame rate and interpolates the events that would exist between the frames. This is limited to the actual recorded frame rate of the footage, so to further enhance the temporal resolution, some extra post processing is carried out to reduce the number of spikes. Allowing a higher fidelity capture of only the edges of the moving objects.

Table 1. Table of network parameters.

Layer	Conv. 1	Pool 1	Conv. 2	Pool 2	Conv. 3
Filter Size	5	5	10	5	5
Number of Maps	4	4	20	20	10
Stride	1	5	1	5	1
Propagation Threshold	$\propto$ Input Spikes	1	45	1	3
Initial Weights	Mean of 0.8 with STD 0.08				

3.3 Proposed UAV Detection System

As mentioned in Sect. 3.1 the asynchronous data produced by the DVS camera is converted into a frame, embedded with the temporal data (a image where the value of a pixel is the time-stamp of the event occurrence). This frame is then used within a layer-wise learning methodology to extract and build features to allow the network to successfully identify a UAV. A list of the network parameters is shown in Table 1, which also highlights a novel feature of the proposed system, pre-emptive neuron thresholding (PENT). The PENT takes the typically reactive neuron thresholding concept [8], but allows it to work in advance of the spikes reaching a neuron. This concept is to overcome the potential of spikes saturating the first layer of the SNN causing a false detection in the system. A typical reactive system would adapt the neuron thresholds if the saturation continued over time, but with the PENT approach, the system is able to act in a timely manner to prevent such saturation from propagating false features through the network. The detection parameters for finding a UAV are embedded within the network itself. As the network enforces a WTA approach to convolution and pooling, the last convolution layer as seen in Fig. 3, has a highly sparse input and output. This allows it to act as a detection layer. In this situation, it is able to forgo usage of a fully connected layer [18] or support vector machine [10] as classification isn't required. The network's evaluation will be based upon the number of successful detections and its robustness to a range of highly spiking noisy inputs, replicating low light conditions. The proposed system will use data captured from both the actual DVS and the simulated DVS. The aim is to show how a network can be trained to deliver a higher accuracy from extending training data with simulated DVS data. This data would often be easier to obtain or would already exist, highlighting the ease at which a traditional visual detection system could be converted to an event camera and SNN. With this conversion resulting in a notable reduction in computational, processing and power, promoting its use within an environment where resources are limited.

4 Testing Results

This section shows the results of training from three UAV detection networks, using only actual DVS event data, only simulated DVS event data, and our proposed system which utilises both of the previous datasets together. Each of the networks is then tested on a series of actual DVS Event frames, comparing the benefit of additional training data, even if it is simulated data.

DVS Trained Network - During initial testing the network trained on real DVS event data struggled to converge to useful feature within the second layer, due to the sparse feature maps that were learned in the first layer. A set of pre-trained weights representing Gabor features, shown in Fig. 6, indicative

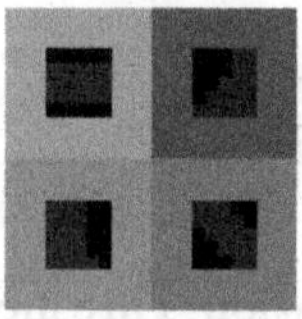

Fig. 6. Synthetic gabor features

of that seen in other first layer SNNs [10,18], allowed all the networks to have better building blocks to create more complex features in the second and third layers. Throughout all of the further testing, this method was used, using the four features presented in Fig. 6 as the first layer of each network. Training the network using the events captured from the DVS results in a low resolution feature combination for the second layer. These feature maps resemble low fidelity UAV shapes as seen in Fig. 7. It also shows the progression of these shapes into the third layer used for detection. This network produced an overall accuracy of 90% when using PENT (50–54% with static thresholding depending on the focus of true or false positives). Results of all 3 networks are located in Table 2, showing results of testing against 1,000 UAV images and 1,000 images of empty or noisy scenes (background clutter or a person in the scene).

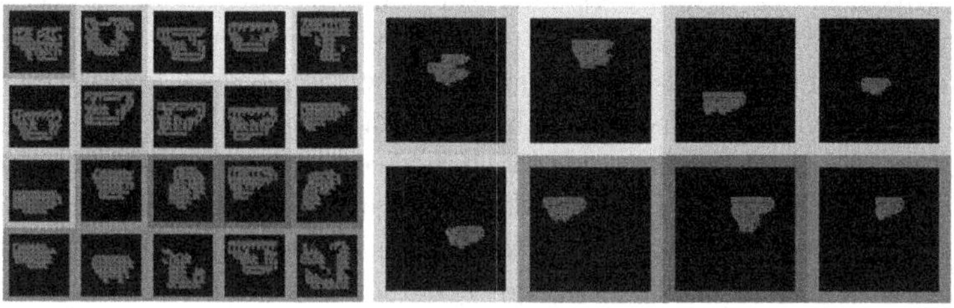

Fig. 7. Second and third layer of the actual DVS event trained network

Table 2. Results data in the confusion matrix for the three trained networks, each being tested with the same 2000 images (1000 with UAV, 1000 without)

N = 2000	UAV Predicted								
		True	False		True	False		True	False
Actual UAV	True	850	150	True	610	490	True	880	120
	False	50	950	False	40	960	False	60	940
Overall Accuracy	Actual DVS = 90%			Simulated DVS = 78%			Proposed System = 91%		

Simulated DVS Trained Network - The network trained using simulated DVS event data was then tested for comparison. These simulated events are originating from a higher resolution image then being scaled to the same resolution as the actual DVS. As the scene is derived from a higher resolution, a higher fidelity feature can occur in the second layer, as seen in Fig. 8. These higher fidelity features combine with the low, to create features more representative of a UAV in the third layer. This seemingly qualitative improvement results in a quantitative drop in overall accuracy down to 78% with full results in Table 2. The drop in accuracy is a result of the features of the network having to fine a fidelity compared to the actual DVS test set. However, this network did return the best false positive results, suggesting these more complex features were better at discriminating objects in the images without UAVs.

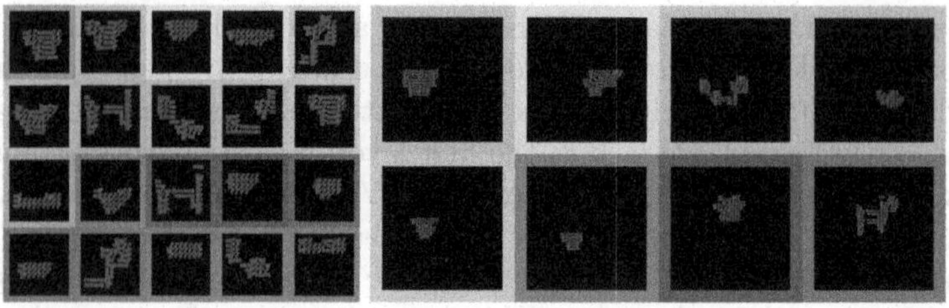

Fig. 8. Second and third layer of the simulated DVS event trained network

Proposed System Trained Network - The proposed detection system is the third network to be trained, utilising both datasets, real and simulated. At first this network exhibits visually very similar features in the second and third layers as seen in Fig. 9(d) and (h) to that of the simulation data network shown in Fig. 8. Figure 9 also demonstrates how the network learns the features seen in these layers, started with the random weight Fig. 9(a) and (e), then refining the important features in UAV shaped component parts seen in Fig. 9(b), (c), (f) and (g). While the proposed system and previous network trained on simulated data appear to have learned the same feature mapping, the accuracy results show otherwise with an overall accuracy of 91% exhibiting the highest number of correct detection, results shown in Table 2. To help visualise how these features help to detect the UAV, an example of an event image from both the actual and simulated DVS data is shown in Fig. 10, indicating where the pooled mapping of the features map onto the UAV. The image also highlights how an improvement in spatial resolution of the sensor could open up the possibilities of UAV classification system rather than just detection systems. By using the higher fidelity features from the extra spatial resolution, it allows a better realisation on the component part of the UAV allowing more distinct feature to exist.

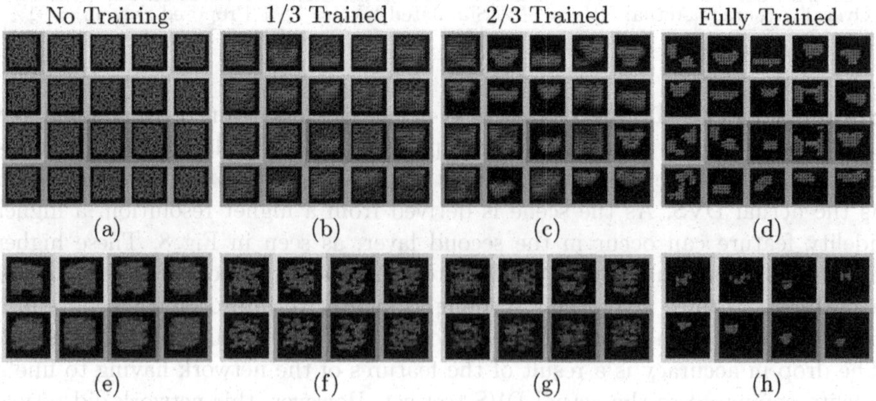

Fig. 9. Illustration of training in the UAV detection network

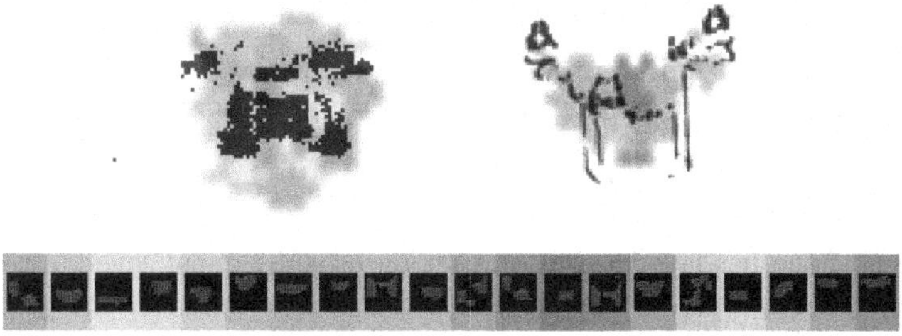

Fig. 10. Feature mapping and their activations on UAV image

This demonstrates the main contribution of this paper that simulated DVS events can be a useful training tool for the desired network, when used in conjunction with actual DVS event data, improving upon the network trained only on DVS events. Since traditional video is more regularly available, this can prove an excellent starting point for new ideas and concepts that might not have DVS event footage. This could be ideal in situations where new data is either difficult to generate or obtain.

The proposed system was also able to show robustness to noise with the second contribution of this paper being the introduction of PENT (Pre-Emptive Neuron Thresholding). A visualisation of how noise is handled by the PENT is shown in Fig. 11, depicting events captured from a low light scene with a UAV flying, similar to that shown in the low light scene Fig. 1(d). Demonstrating how when PENT is active, only the features of the UAV are captured as shown in Fig. 11(b), while when PENT is off, the UAV features are masked by noise seen in Fig. 11(f). The reduced propagation of features through the network due to

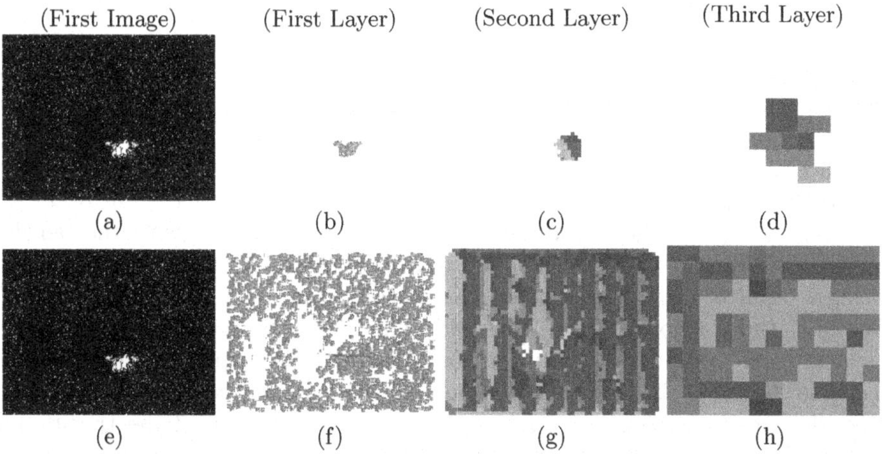

Fig. 11. Active threshold stops the saturation of layer one features propagation through the network causing false detections.

Table 3. Table of accuracy with additive noise.

SNR Level (dB)	23	15	7	0.1	-9	-15
Accuracy (%)	85	83	82	72	62	46

saturation of the fist layer has an impact on all subsequent layers as shown in Fig. 11(c), (d), (g) and (h). Testing this feature over a range of noise levels shows that is can maintain an accuracy over 80% for SNR levels above 1 dB, as seen in Table 3.

The results from the SNN resemble those from a CNN, thanks partially to the convolution and pooling layers. Furthermore, the system is built upon a sparse spiking neuron model which only further sparsifies throughout the network, while in an unsupervised fashion learns distinctive feature to identify a UAV. This sparsity instils the ethos of only transmitting important information, which results in a lower computational throughput, for both runtime and training. On average less than 200 pixels are active per frame that succeeded in detection, a mere 0.5% of the overall sensor size then moves on for processing. This computation reduction then results in a significant reduction within the SNN compared to a CNN counterpart, with over 270,000 calculation needed for the CNN's convolution layers and only 1,300 required for the SNN on average, over 200 times the difference. A similar reduction in calculation is also seen within the pooling layers thus further reducing the amount of computations needing to be done and resulting in a reduction in power used. This reduction in information transfer allows the system to converge to useful feature quickly. This results in using only 20,000 images each to train the second and third layer (3000 required if you want to train layer one), so 40–43,000 in total.

5 Conclusion

Consumer UAVs and micro-UAVs have presented security and defence with a new-age problem. This paper presents a robust detection system for UAVs, that has many of the useful features of other sensors, while fewer of the drawbacks. The overall accuracy of 91%, coupled with an enhanced resilience to noise due to PENT, make the proposed system a feasible alternative for the future. From utilising the sparse nature of the SNN, this accuracy comes with the benefit of also providing a far lower computation load than a traditional CNNs, this being a result of not having to pass information from every neuron in the layer, but only those who pass the threshold. The SNN also pairs nicely with the asynchronous event driven nature of the DVS. With its output also representing a sparse version of the traditional frame based camera. The system to that effect then delivers high accuracy, while being the sparse version of the traditional system. This sparsity can deliver many benefits with reductions in computational processing leading to a reduction in overall size, weight, power and cost, therefore improving overall application system viability.

References

1. BBC News: Gatwick Airport: Drones ground flights - BBC News. https://www.bbc.co.uk/news/uk-england-sussex-46623754
2. Bi, G.Q., Poo, M.M.: Synaptic modifications in cultured hippocampal neurons: dependence on spike timing, synaptic strength, and postsynaptic cell type. J. Neurosci. **18**(24), 10464–10472 (1998). https://doi.org/10.1523/JNEUROSCI.18-24-10464.1998
3. Bi, Y., Andreopoulos, Y.: PIX2NVS: parameterized conversion of pixel-domain video frames to neuromorphic vision streams. In: 2017 IEEE International Conference on Image Processing (ICIP), pp. 1990–1994. IEEE, September 2017. https://doi.org/10.1109/ICIP.2017.8296630
4. Brandli, C., Berner, R., Yang, M., Liu, S.-C., Delbruck, T.: A 240 × 180 130 dB 3 μs latency global shutter spatiotemporal vision sensor. IEEE J. Solid-State Circuits **49**(10), 2333–2341 (2014). https://doi.org/10.1109/JSSC.2014.2342715
5. Civil Aviation Authority: Airprox involving UAS Drones—UK Airprox Board (2019). https://www.airproxboard.org.uk/Reports-and-analysis/Statistics/Airprox-involving-UAS-Drones
6. G4S: drones: threat from above. Technical report (2017). www.g4s.us
7. Garcia, G.P., Camilleri, P., Liu, Q., Furber, S.: pyDVS: an extensible, real-time dynamic vision sensor emulator using off-the-shelf hardware. In: 2016 IEEE Symposium Series on Computational Intelligence (SSCI), pp. 1–7. IEEE, December 2016. https://doi.org/10.1109/SSCI.2016.7850249
8. Huang, C., Resnik, A., Celikel, T., Englitz, B.: Adaptive spike threshold enables robust and temporally precise neuronal encoding. PLoS Comput. Biol. **12**(6), e1004984 (2016). https://doi.org/10.1371/journal.pcbi.1004984. https://dx.plos.org/10.1371/journal.pcbi.1004984
9. Huang, J., Guo, M., Chen, S.: A dynamic vision sensor with direct logarithmic output and full-frame picture-on-demand. In: 2017 IEEE International Symposium on Circuits and Systems (ISCAS), pp. 1–4. IEEE, May 2017. https://doi.org/10.1109/ISCAS.2017.8050546
10. Kheradpisheh, S.R., Ganjtabesh, M., Thorpe, S.J., Masquelier, T.: STDP-based spiking deep convolutional neural networks for object recognition. Neural Netw. **99**, 56–67 (2018). https://doi.org/10.1016/J.NEUNET.2017.12.005. https://www.sciencedirect.com/science/article/pii/S0893608017302903?via%3Dihub
11. Mueggler, E., Rebecq, H., Gallego, G., Delbruck, T., Scaramuzza, D.: The event-camera dataset and simulator: event-based data for pose estimation, visual odometry, and SLAM. Technical report (2016). http://rpg.ifi.uzh.ch/davis_data.html
12. Panda, P., Srinivasan, G., Roy, K.: Convolutional spike timing dependent plasticity based feature learning in spiking neural networks. Technical report (2017). https://arxiv.org/pdf/1703.03854.pdf
13. Rebecq, H., Gehrig, D., Scaramuzza, D.: ESIM: an open event camera simulator. Technical report (2018). https://www.blender.org/
14. Shakhatreh, H., et al.: Unmanned aerial vehicles: a survey on civil applications and key research challenges. IEEE Access **7**, 48572–48634 (2018)
15. Shoham, S., O'Connor, D.H., Segev, R.: How silent is the brain: is there a "dark matter" problem in neuroscience? J. Comp. Physiol. A. **192**(8), 777–784 (2006). https://doi.org/10.1007/s00359-006-0117-6

16. Son, B., et al.: 4.1 A 640 × 480 dynamic vision sensor with a 9 µm pixel and 300Meps address-event representation. In: 2017 IEEE International Solid-State Circuits Conference (ISSCC), pp. 66–67. IEEE, February 2017. https://doi.org/10.1109/ISSCC.2017.7870263
17. Tavanaei, A., Maida, A.S.: Bio-inspired spiking convolutional neural network using layer-wise sparse coding and STDP learning. Technical report (2017). https://arxiv.org/pdf/1611.03000.pdf
18. Thiele, J.C., Bichler, O., Dupret, A.: Event-based, timescale invariant unsupervised online deep learning with STDP. Front. Comput. Neurosci. **12**, 46 (2018). https://doi.org/10.3389/fncom.2018.00046
19. Department for Transport, UK: Taking Flight: The Future of Drones in the UK Government Response (2019). https://assets.publishing.service.gov.uk/government/uploads/future-of-drones-in-uk-consultation-response-web.pdf

Autonomous Learning Paradigm for Spiking Neural Networks

Junxiu Liu[1(✉)], Liam J. McDaid[1], Jim Harkin[1], Shvan Karim[1], Anju P. Johnson[2], David M. Halliday[2], Andy M. Tyrrell[2], Jon Timmis[2], Alan G. Millard[2], and James Hilder[2]

[1] School of Computing, Engineering and Intelligent Systems, Ulster University, Derry BT48 7JL, Northern Ireland, UK
{j.liu1,lj.mcdaid,jg.harkin,haji_karim-s}@ulster.ac.uk

[2] Department of Electronic Engineering, University of York, York YO10 5DD, UK
{anju.johnson,david.halliday,andy.tyrrell,jon.timmis,alan.millard, james.hilder}@york.ac.uk

Abstract. Compared to biological systems, existing learning systems lack the ability to learn autonomously, especially in changing and dynamic environments. This paper addresses the issue of autonomous learning by developing a self-learning spiking neural network (SNN) and demonstrating its autonomous learning capability using a simple robot controller application. Our proposed learning rule exploits an inherit property of the existing Spike-Timing-Dependent Plasticity (STDP) rule in that if the instantaneous presynaptic frequency decreases, then for a conventional Hebbian window the STDP rule potentiates. Conversely if the instantaneous frequency increases the STDP rule depresses: the opposite is true for anti-Hebbian window. This paper will also show that obstacle avoidance is achievable using a conventional Hebbian learning window while object tracking can be learned using an anti-Hebbian learning window. Hence the proposed learning paradigm is novel in that it does not require external supervisions for either these tasks. The proposed learning paradigm also uses a previously explored astrocyte neuron interaction where a periodic Slow Inward Current (SIC) from an astrocyte can potentiate a postsynaptic neuron for a period of time: this time window can be used to strengthen/weaken synaptic pathways. An obstacle avoidance task is used for the performance analysis and results show that the SNN based robot controller has autonomous learning capabilities under the dynamic conditions.

Keywords: SNN · Learning · Plasticity windows · Robots

1 Introduction

Spiking neural networks (SNNs) are a third generation networks which closely resemble their biological counterparts. SNNs comprise of neurons and synapses where the former releases a transient voltage spike when excited. When action

I. V. Tetko et al. (Eds.): ICANN 2019, LNCS 11727, pp. 737–744, 2019.
https://doi.org/10.1007/978-3-030-30487-4_57

potentials arrive at the presynaptic terminal, the membrane potential of the postsynaptic neuron increases under the stimuli and a spike event occurs when the postsynaptic potential exceeds a threshold level. SNNs have good temporal data processing capability and are used in many applications such as the pattern recognition [1], data analytics [2], fault-tolerant computing [3,4] and robotic control [5,6]. Various learning algorithms have been proposed for SNNs and the choice of algorithm is critically dependant of the application domain. Most SNN applications use some form of supervision for the learning phase where the learning data is preselected from a dataset. However, the requirement for a supervised approach constrains the design, development and deployment of the SNN systems, especially for applications operating within a dynamic environment, e.g. robots [7].

The Spike-Timing-Dependent plasticity (STDP) [8] and Bienenstock, Cooper, and Munro (BCM) [9] learning rules are two commonly used learning rules for SNNs. A combined STDP/BCM learning rule, termed BSTDP, has be demonstrated in an SNN-based robotic controller application to implement learning, e.g. in the approach of [7] the spiking astrocyte neural network used BSTDP to implement both learning and self-repair in the robotic applications. However, it required supervisory signals to achieve the correct input/output mapping. In this paper we address the issue of autonomous learning. This paper revisits earlier work and proposes a novel autonomous learning strategy which uses the Hebbian/anti-Hebbian learning approach where the novelty is a decision capability that can potentiate or depress as a function of instantaneous previous synaptic spike frequency. Furthermore, we draw on the concept of an SIC which is a postsynapitc stimulus current released by astrocytes: note that SIC model used in this work is a high level abstraction of the biological SIC function. This approach avoids the complexity involved in modelling many astrocyte processes. This autonomous learning strategy is demonstrated on a simple SNN robotic controller.

The rest of the paper is organized as follows. Section 2 describes the autonomous learning strategy and Sect. 3 presents simulation results which demonstrate the proposed autonomous learning concept for obstacle avoidance. Section 4 concludes the paper.

2 Autonomous Learning Principle

This section presents an SNN that demonstrates a plausible autonomous learning paradigm.

2.1 Autonomous Learning Strategy

We consider as a demonstrator an SNN-based robotic controller deployed in an obstacle avoidance application. In the present case our SNN controller senses one input and learns over time to respond with an appropriate output action to avoid an obstacle. To put this in context we will consider a robot moving in a forward direction with an obstacle placed in its path. We also assume that the sensor input data is mapped to a linear spike train and the actuator output neurons drive the robot in either the forward direction or to motion a left turn (the left turn was chosen arbitrarily). Hence our SNN controller has one presynaptic neuron and two postsynaptic actuator neurons: the proposed autonomous learning algorithm will learn to respond with either a forward or left turn motion. A key signalling pathway is the slow inwards current (SIC) emitted by an excited astrocyte cell [10]. Because astrocyte interacts with many neurons we assume that the SIC continually stimulates both postsynaptic neurons, which propels the robot initially towards the obstacle. When the robot becomes in proximity to the object, the sensor becomes active and the presynaptic neuron fires. However, because of morphology we assume that astrocyte processes are of different lengths with different associated delays and therefore the SIC signal will cause only one of the actuator neurons to become active for a period of time followed by the other: none of the two actuator neurons are active at the same time. In the current case this will cause the two postsynaptic neurons to enter into a "toggling action" where one actuator neuron becomes active for a period of time followed by the other and then this process repeats. Hence each pathway between the presynaptic neuron and the postsynaptic neurons will be periodically strengthened or weakened. If the activity of one of the postsynaptic neuron causes the instantaneous presynaptic firing frequency Δf_{pre} to increase then the synaptic pathway will be depressed: in the present case the SNN based controller is learning an obstacle avoidance task and consequently motion towards an object needs to be avoided. Our simulations will show that a conventional Hebbian learning window in conjunction with STDP will train an SNN to implement obstacle avoidance without the need for a learning signal. Consequently for obstacle avoidance we require that for $\Delta f_{pre} > 0$ the weights associated with active actuator neurons are depressed and potentiated only for $\Delta f_{pre} < 0$. This condition is satisfied by adopting a conventional Hebbian learning window. Conversely the SNN will learn an object tracking task using an anti-Hebbian learning window. In the present case the former is adopted and a Hebbian window is selected.

Figure 1 shows a synaptic connection between the input sensory neuron and output actuator neuron (forward motion). Each time the postsynaptic neuron fires, the robot will move forward decreasing the distance to the obstacle which increases the input sensory neuron spike frequency. Therefore, the inter spike interval (ISI) decreases, as shown in Fig. 1. Spikes at times a, b and c show a steadily reducing ISI where the time period between spike a and b is greater than the time period between spike b and c, $t_1 > t_2$ and $\Delta f_{pre} > 0$. The proposed rule effectively uses the sign of Δf_{pre} to implement either potentiation if Δf_{pre} is negative or depression if Δf_{pre} is positive. Note that in the present case our approach uses all correlations between pre and post firing times that are within the plasticity window except for the presynaptic spike time that causes the postsynaptic response to cross the firing threshold. This spike time when correlated with postsynaptic firing tends to favour weight potentiation strongly

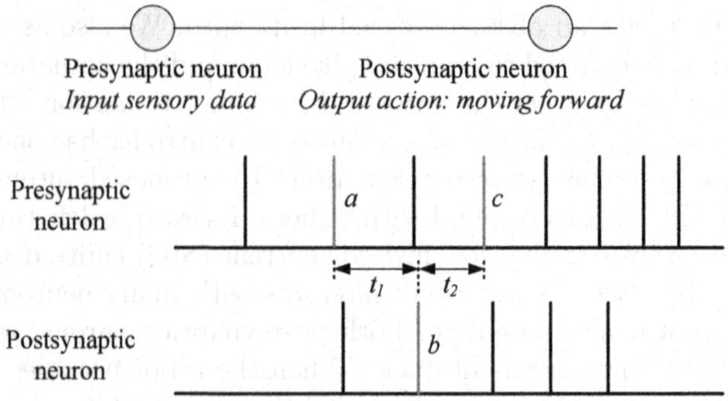

Fig. 1. Temporal changing between the input sensory spikes and output spikes for obstacle avoidance where the output neuron is to move forward.

and swamps out other correlations within the plasticity. Therefore, to avoid this and make learning more sensitive to ISI we only consider before and after spike correlations.

2.2 Models

The STDP learning rule with different kernel structures can be used for synaptic long-term potentiation (LTP) or long-term depression (LTD). Based on the Hebbian STDP learning rule, LTP occurs when the presynaptic neuron fires before the postsynaptic firing, whereas LTD occurs when the temporal firing order is reversed [11]. STDP based learning is described by

$$\delta w^i_{syn}(\Delta t) = \begin{cases} A_0 exp(\frac{\Delta t}{\tau_+}), & \Delta t \leq 0 \\ -A_0 exp(\frac{\Delta t}{\tau_-}), & \Delta t > 0 \end{cases} \tag{1}$$

where $\delta w^i_{syn}(\Delta t)$ is the ith synaptic weight to be updated, Δt is the time difference between post and presynaptic spikes, A_0 is the height of STDP learning window, τ_+ and τ_- are the widths of the plasticity window. In addition, the postsynaptic neuron was modelled using the Leaky Integrate and Fire (LIF) approach, due to its simplistic nature, and this neuron model is expressed as

$$\tau_m \frac{dv}{dt} = -v(t) + R_m \sum_{i=1}^{n} I^i_{syn}(t), \tag{2}$$

where τ_m and v are the time constant and membrane potential respectively, R_m is the membrane resistance, $I^i_{syn}(t)$ is the current injected to the neuron membrane at synapse i, and the firing threshold voltage is 9 mV. The neuron model also includes a refractory period of 2 ms, and the current injected to the neuron from the ith synapse, $I^i_{syn}(t)$, is calculated by

$$I^i_{syn}(t) = r_I * w^i_{syn}(t) + I_s, \tag{3}$$

where r_I is the synaptic current production rate, I_s is the SIC signal from astrocyte, $w^i_{syn}(t)$ is the synaptic weight of the ith synapse, which is modulated by the STDP learning rule, i.e.

$$w^i_{syn}(t) = w^i_{syn}(t-1) + \delta w^i_{syn}. \tag{4}$$

Note that I_s is the SIC signal and because the formulation of a biologically plausible model for this current takes into account many factors, we will assume for simplicity an SIC spike of duration 1 ms. Additionally, since SIC currents correlate with neuron activities, but on a slow time scale, we choose arbitrary an SIC interspike interval of 1/6 of the presynaptic spike frequency.

3 Results

In this section a simple robotic demonstrator is used to showcase the proposed autonomous learning algorithm where the data was collected using the Psi swarm robot developed by the York Robotics Laboratory, University of York, UK [12]. An infrared sensor placed at the front of the robot provided the sensory input data for the SNN-based controller. This data was converted to a linear spike train which modelled the presynaptic neuron: a rate-based encoding scheme is used where the distance between the mobile robot and obstacle (or object), d, is proportional to the reciprocal of input spike train frequency, $1/f_{pre}$. Figure 2 shows the SNN structure for the obstacle avoidance task, where two output neurons are synaptically connected to the input of a sensory neuron. The input neuron senses the output of the front sensor and, in response, the output neurons A and B will, when active, motion the robot to move forward and turn left.

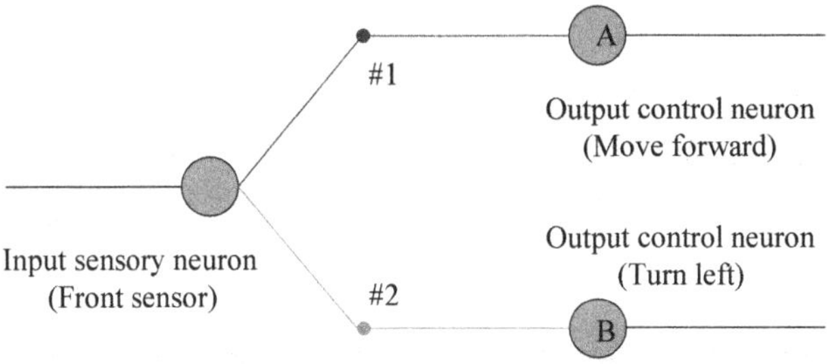

Fig. 2. Synaptic connections between the input and output neurons.

The output actuator neurons are periodically firing due to the astrocyte signal SIC. Also, we initiate the learning process with neuron A (forward motion) becoming active before neuron B, as shown in Fig. 3(c): neuron A is active for 3 s followed by neuron B for a further 3 s and this process continually repeats. In the time period when neuron A is active, the synaptic pathway (#1) is depressed from an initial synaptic weight of 20, see Fig. 3(f). Under the input stimuli, the postsynaptic neuron fires at ~ 0.6 s as shown in Fig. 3(d), then the robot moves forward to the obstacle and Δf_{pre} is positive, see Fig. 3(b). An STDP window with equally balanced LTP and LTD kernel structure is used for the learning. When the output neuron A continues to fire from ~ 0.6 s, the robot continually moves towards the obstacle and the frequency of input sensory spike train increases. This leads to the LTD, as shown by Fig. 3(f). Each time neuron A is stimulated the synaptic pathway #1 is further depressed and eventually pathway (#1) becomes inactive and postsynaptic neuron A ceases to fire (~ 6.5 s in Fig. 3(d)). This we define as autonomous learning as weight depression does not require the external supervision.

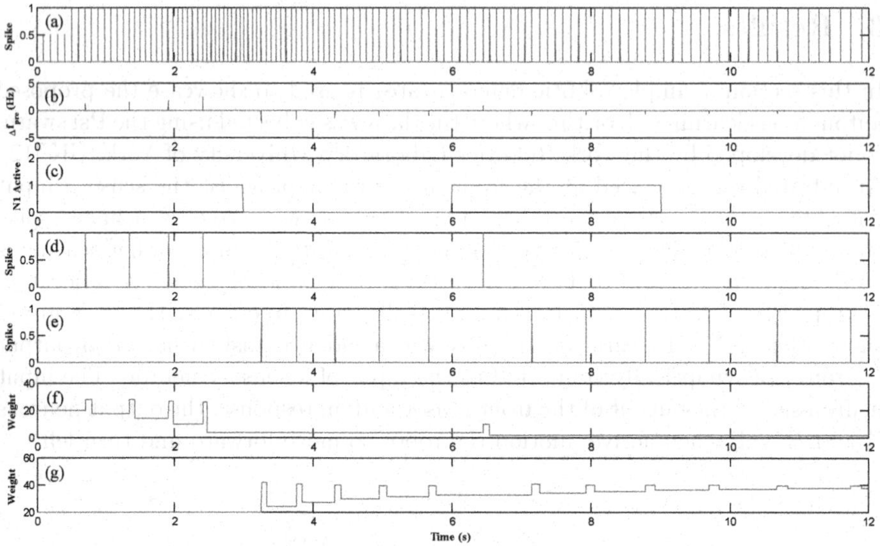

Fig. 3. SNN activities between input sensor neuron and output action neurons. (a). Input spike train. (b). Δf_{pre}. (c). Neuron A active status where 1 represents active and value 0 represents inactive. (d, e). Spikes of output neuron A and B. (f, g). Synapse #1 and #2 weights.

Now consider the connection between input sensor and output neuron B (left turn motion) when synaptic pathway #2 is active due to SIC. The initial weight for the synapse #2 is also set to 20 (see Fig. 3(g)). The synaptic pathway #2 is active between 3 and 6 s. Under the input stimuli, the output neuron B fires at $\sim$3.4 s, i.e. the robot turns slightly to the left and therefore away from the obstacle. Thus, the frequency of input sensory spike train decreases (negative Δf_{pre} in Fig. 3(b)). Note the same plasticity window is used in all pathways. The weight of synapse #2 starts to be potentiated, as shown by Fig. 3(g) and as the synaptic weight increases, the SNN continues to promote a left turning motion, see the output spikes in Fig. 3(e). As the robot turns to the left moving away from the obstacle, Δf_{pre} approaches zero, learning ceases and the synaptic weights stabilize, see Fig. 3(g). Results demonstrate the autonomous learning process favours strengthening the pathway to neuron B, which is a left turning motion, and the weight associated with this pathway is potentiated accordingly. Note that during the initial learning phase, one of the actuator neurons is active for a period of time followed by the other due to the delays in the SIC spikes. However, after a period of learning, only one actuator neuron will be active (left turn motion) due to the potentiated synaptic weight, and the other actuator neuron becomes inactive as the associated synaptic weight is depressed. Compared to other approaches such as [7], the proposed method can learn and adapt to the surrounding environmental conditions based on the STDP kernel structures. Therefore, the proposed learning approach does not require an input to output mapping table and thus points to a possible future direction for SNN metaplasticity.

4 Conclusion

A novel autonomous learning strategy for SNNs has been presented which uses the STDP with kernel structures. It exploits an inherit property of STDP where if $\Delta f_{pre} < 0$, the STDP rule potentiates for conventional Hebbian window. Conversely if the $\Delta f_{pre} > 0$ the STDP rule depresses: the opposite is true for anti-Hebbian window. This novel learning strategy, demonstrated using an obstacle avoidance task, used a conventional Hebbian learning window. However, the SNN could be reconfigured to learn an object tracking task using an anti-Hebbian learning window. Another novel feature of the proposed learning paradigm is an astrocyte associated SIC. The SIC potentiates postsynaptic actuator neurons periodically and in each time window weight potentiation/depression occurs. Results of an SNN under an obstacle avoidance robotic task show that the proposed paradigm is able to learn autonomously within a dynamic environment. The authors recognise that the proposed SNN demonstrator requires much refinement to allow scaling to a useful SNN. Despite this our SNN fragment does demonstrate a new approach to autonomous learning. Furthermore, this approach could be taken further but would require a significant body of research involving experimentalists to determine the time course of SICs and other associated secondary messengers. However, with current data on astrocyte process morphology it may be possible to model delays but this would in itself be a challenge well beyond the scope of this paper. Overcoming this challenge in future work would permit scaling the network to a more useful SNN controller with the capability to continually learn more complex input/output patterns and operate in a real-world environment.

Acknowledgments. This work is part of the EPSRC funded SPANNER project (EP/N007141X/1) (EP/N007050/1).

References

1. Hu, J., Tang, H., Tan, K.C., Li, H., Shi, L.: A spike-timing-based integrated model for pattern recognition. Neural Comput. **25**(2), 450–472 (2013). https://doi.org/10.1162/NECO-a-00395
2. Mashford, B.S., Yepes, A.J., Tang, J., Harrer, S.: Neural-network-based analysis of EEG data using the neuromorphic TrueNorth chip for brain-machine interfaces. IBM J. Res. Dev. **61**(2), 1–6 (2017). https://doi.org/10.1147/JRD.2017.2663978
3. Liu, J., Harkin, J., Maguire, L.P., McDaid, L.J., Wade, J.J.: SPANNER: a self-repairing spiking neural network hardware architecture. IEEE Trans. Neural Netw. Learn. Syst. **29**(4), 1287–1300 (2018). https://doi.org/10.1109/TNNLS.2017.2673021
4. Liu, J., Harkin, J., Maguire, L.P., McDaid, L.J., Wade, J.J., Martin, G.: Scalable Networks-on-Chip interconnected architecture for astrocyte-neuron networks. IEEE Trans. Circuits Syst. I Regul. Pap. **63**(12), 2290–2303 (2016). https://doi.org/10.1109/TCSI.2016.2615051
5. Liu, J., Harkin, J., McElholm, M., McDaid, L., Jimenez-Fernandez, A., Linares-Barranco, A.: Case study: bio-inspired self-adaptive strategy for spike-based PID controller. In: 2015 IEEE International Symposium on Circuits and Systems (ISCAS), pp. 2700–2703. IEEE (2015). https://doi.org/10.1109/ISCAS.2015.7169243
6. Johnson, A.P., et al.: Homeostatic fault tolerance in spiking neural networks: a dynamic hardware perspective. IEEE Trans. Circuits Syst. **65**(2), 687–699 (2018). https://doi.org/10.1109/TCSI.2017.2726763
7. Liu, J., et al.: Exploring self-repair in a coupled spiking astrocyte neural network. IEEE Trans. Neural Netw. Learn. Syst. **30**(3), 865–875 (2019). https://doi.org/10.1109/TNNLS.2018.2854291
8. Feldman, D.E.: The spike-timing dependence of plasticity. Neuron **75**(4), 556–571 (2012). https://doi.org/10.1016/j.neuron.2012.08.001
9. Bienenstock, E.L., Cooper, L.N., Munro, P.W.: Theory for the development of neuron selectivity: orientation specificity and binocular interaction in visual cortex. J. Neurosci. **2**(1), 32–48 (1982). https://doi.org/10.1523/JNEUROSCI.02-01-00032.1982
10. Kovács, A., Pál, B.: Astrocyte-dependent slow inward currents (SICs) participate in neuromodulatory mechanisms in the pedunculopontine nucleus (PPN). Frontiers Cell. Neurosci. **11**, 1–16 (2017). https://doi.org/10.3389/fncel.2017.00016
11. Song, S., Miller, K.D., Abbott, L.F.: Competitive Hebbian learning through spike-timing-dependent synaptic plasticity. Nat. Neurosci. **3**, 919–926 (2000). https://doi.org/10.1038/78829
12. Hilder, J., Horsfield, A., Millard, A.G., Timmis, J.: The Psi Swarm: a low-cost robotics platform and its use in an education setting. In: Alboul, L., Damian, D., Aitken, J.M.M. (eds.) TAROS 2016. LNCS (LNAI), vol. 9716, pp. 158–164. Springer, Cham (2016). https://doi.org/10.1007/978-3-319-40379-3_16

Multi-objective Spiking Neural Network Hardware Mapping Based on Immune Genetic Algorithm

Junxiu Liu[1], Xingyue Huang[1], Yongchuang Huang[1], Yuling Luo[1(✉)], and Su Yang[2]

[1] School of Electronic Engineering, Guangxi Normal University, Guilin, China
yuling0616@mailbox.gxnu.edu.cn
[2] School of Computing, Engineering and Intelligent Systems, Ulster University, Londonderry, UK

Abstract. For the Spiking Neuron Network (SNN) systems, the hardware implementation has unique advantages in terms of performance, energy, and scalability. The Networks-on-Chip (NoC) interconnection strategy has been widely used in hardware SNNs as it provides excellent interconnection mechanism for interneuronal communications. However, the mapping between the SNN models and NoC hardware systems remains a research challenge. In this paper, a multi-objective immune genetic algorithm is proposed for the mapping of SNN hardware system, which is based on the Immune Algorithm (IA) and Genetic Algorithm (GA). It can optimize the SNN hardware systems by reducing the energy consumption and communication delays. In the experiments, the spiking astrocyte neuron network model and the Star-Subnet-Based-3D Mesh (3D-SSBM) NoC hardware system are used for testing. Results demonstrate that the proposed algorithm provides an effective mapping solution for hardware SNNs with low energy consumption and communication delay.

Keywords: Particle swarm algorithm · Genetic Algorithm · Spiking Neural Networks · Networks-on-Chip

1 Introduction

Spiking Neuron Networks (SNNs) are based on the spiking sequence encoding and are close to the biological understanding of nervous system [1,2]. Compared to traditional neural networks, SNNs exhibit stronger bionics properties and computational power [3]. Based on the good biological properties and powerful computational abilities, researchers hope to develop brain-like systems that can mimic the information processing mechanisms of mammalian brain. However, due to the limitations of execution speed and scalabilities of traditional computers [4], the parallel advantages of SNNs cannot be fully exploited if they

I. V. Tetko et al. (Eds.): ICANN 2019, LNCS 11727, pp. 745–757, 2019.
https://doi.org/10.1007/978-3-030-30487-4_58

are implemented by software-based approaches. Additionally, the conventional hardware implementations, such as parallel GPUs, are suffering from the problems of high energy consumption [5]. Therefore, in order to overcome the existing problems of SNNs implementations, it is necessary to explore alternative custom hardware architectures [6–10].

The Networks-on-Chip (NoC) has been widely used for communications inside the chips [11,12], and provides a good solution for large-scale SNN hardware systems [13–15]. The typical NoC architecture consists of a computing and communication sub-system. The former contains many processing elements (PEs), which are responsible for the generalized computing tasks. The latter is constructed by the routers and channels (between the routers). It is responsible for the communication interconnection of the PEs, and can realize the high-speed interaction of the data resources. PEs and routers are connected to each other according to a certain topology [16]. In the process of realizing SNNs, the PEs are adopted to realize the spiking neurons where spiking neurons need to be assigned to the appropriate PEs in NoCs. In this paper, this assignment process is defined as the SNN mapping. The spiking neurons and PEs in the NoC are one-to-one correspondent, which belongs to the typical quadratic assignment problem (QAP) in the NP-hard class [17]. Meanwhile, for the high-performance hardware systems, energy consumption and communication delay affect the performance of the hardware systems. High energy consumption and heat dissipation have brought severe challenges to the system reliabilities [18].

Research shows that intelligent optimization algorithms such as ant colony optimization [19], Genetic Algorithm (GA) [20] and Immune Algorithm (IA) [21] can be used to solve QAPs [17,19–21]. In this paper based on the immune algorithm and genetic algorithm [20,21], a novel multi-objective SNN mapping algorithm is proposed for hardware SNN mapping, with the aim to improve the performance and reliability of hardware SNN systems. Different from the state-of-the-art metaheuristics method such as the approach of [22], in this paper the quadratic assignment problem is optimized by a combination of GA and IA method based on our previous work [23]. Experimental results demonstrate that the proposed multi-objective SNN mapping algorithm can significantly reduce the energy consumption and communication delays of SNN hardware systems. The rest of this paper is organized as follows: Sect. 2 describes the problems and models for the SNN mapping. The multi-objective SNN mapping algorithm is presented in Sect. 3 in detail, and the experimental results are given in Sect. 4 where the mapping algorithm is applied to a 3D-SSBM NoC architecture. The summary of the paper and the future work are provided in Sect. 5.

2 Problems, Models and Objective Function of SNN Mapping

In this section, the multi-objective SNN mapping algorithm, energy/delay models and the objective function are introduced in detail.

2.1 SNN Mapping Problem

SNN mapping assigns neurons in the network to the PEs in the NoC architecture based on the optimization rules. The purpose is to generate the mapping for specific applications and minimize the energy consumption and communication delays between the neurons. In order to clearly describe the mapping problem, it is assumed that neurons and PEs correspond to each other, i.e. the function of each neuron is only performed by one PE. An example is shown in Fig. 1, where the mapping problem of the SNN is abstracted as a mapping problem between the SNN communication graph (SNNCG) and the NoC architecture graph (NoCAG) [24].

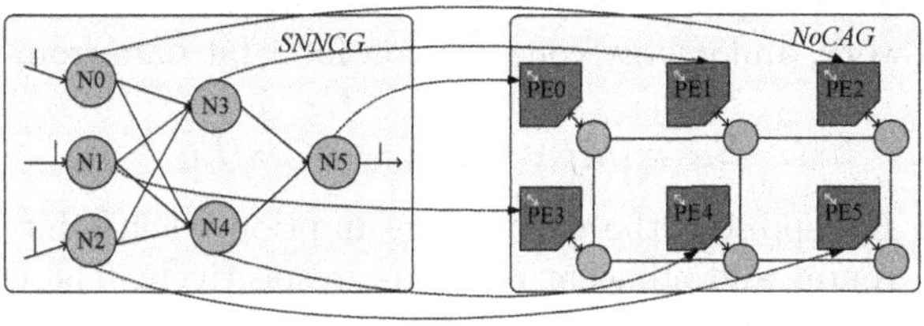

Fig. 1. SNN mapping process.

Definition 1: In the SNNCG (N, E) directed graph, each vertex $N_i \in N$ corresponds to one neuron while each edge $E_{ij} \in E$ corresponds to one communication path between the directly connected N_i and N_j neurons. Particularly, the communication traffic from N_i to N_j is denoted by the value t_{ij} of each edge E_{ij}, where the maximum communication delay between N_i and N_j is denoted by L_{ij}. Moreover, only the direct links between neurons lead to edges in SNNCG.

In this paper, a communication matrix $T = [t_{ij}]$ is used to describe the communication traffic between the directly connected neurons from N_i to N_j. Then an example matrix of T between n neurons $(0 \leq i \leq n-1, 0 \leq j \leq n-1)$ is given by

$$T = \begin{bmatrix} 0 & t_{01} & t_{02} & \cdots t_{0,n-1} \\ t_{10} & 0 & t_{12} & \cdots t_{1,n-1} \\ t_{20} & t_{21} & 0 & \cdots t_{2,n-1} \\ \cdots & \cdots & \cdots & \cdots \quad \cdots \\ t_{n-1,0} & t_{n-1,1} & t_{n-1,2} & \cdots \quad 0 \end{bmatrix}, \tag{1}$$

where if $t_{ij} = 0$, there is no communication occurred between the directly connected N_i and N_j neurons.

Definition 2: Similarly, each vertex $v_i \in V$ in the NoCAG (V, P) directed graph represents a PE in the NoC, where the communication path from v_i to v_j of PE is represented by the edge $p_{ij} \in P$. The communication traffic between the PE

v_i and v_j is denoted by f_{ij} of the edge p_{ij}. B_{ij} denotes the maximum bandwidth provided by the path p_{ij}, where h_{ij} denotes the distance between v_i and v_j, i.e. the number of hops in this approach.

In summary, according to the SNNCG (N, E) and NoCAG (V, P), the problem of SNN mapping ($N \rightarrow V$) is given by $v_j = map(N_j)$, where the neuron N_j is assigned to the processing elements v_j, i.e. N_j is mapped to v_j in the NoC system.

2.2 Objective Function

In this subsection, the energy and delay models for the hardware NoC systems are provided. The energy model of NoC communication in the approach of [25] is used in this work, and energy consumption for 1-bit data from PE v_i to v_j is defined as

$$E_{ij} = (h_{ij} + 1) \times E_s + h_{ij} \times E_l, \tag{2}$$

where E_s and E_l represent the energy consumption when 1-bit data is transmitted by the router and adjacent channels, respectively. The communication energy E of NoC system is given by

$$\begin{aligned} E &= \sum [(h_{ij} + 1) \times E_s + h_{ij} \times E_l] \times t_{ij} \\ &= \sum t_{ij} \times h_{ij} \times (E_s + E_l) + \sum E_s \times t_{ij}. \end{aligned} \tag{3}$$

where $0 \leq i \leq n-1$, $0 \leq j \leq n-1$. Obviously, the parameters in Eq. (3) are constants except $\sum t_{ij} \times h_{ij}$. The aim of optimization in this paper is to find the minimum weighted sum of h_{ij}, i.e. the minimum energy consumption E. The weight t_{ij} represents the communication traffic between PE_i and PE_j where the neurons N_i and N_j are located, respectively. Finally,the objective function can be described as

$$\min\{\sum t_{ij} \times h_{ij}\}, 0 \leq i \leq n-1, 0 \leq j \leq n-1. \tag{4}$$

The delay model in the approach of [26] is used in this work. Assume that in the NoC architecture using mesh topology, the XY routing algorithm and the wormhole switching technology are used. Then the transmission delay is denoted by $T_{i,j}$ when a single data is transmitted from the source node r_i to the target node r_j. $T_{i,j}$ is the time period between sending the packet header from r_i and when the packet tail reaches r_j. The delay model is defined as

$$T_{i,j} = (T_b + T_w) \times h_{i,j} + T_b \times (B - 1), \tag{5}$$

where T_b represents the time that a frame of data passes through a switch and a link when the network is not blocked. T_w is the average time the packet header waits at the switch node when the network is blocked. $h_{i,j}$ denotes the Manhattan distance from the network node r_i to r_j. B is the number of data frames contained in the data packet. T_b and B are constant coefficients.

In Eq. (5), the first term is the total time that the data packet header arrives at the destination network node. The second term is the total time elapsed since the remaining frames arrived at the destination network node which is constant. Therefore, the optimization space for $T_{i,j}$ lies in the first term, depending on the parameters T_w and $h_{i,j}$. However, it is very difficult to accurately model T_w. Therefore, the approach of [26] optimizes T_w by balancing the link load, reducing the transmission delay which results in a less data transmission time.

According to [26], the objective function for energy and delay is given by

$$cost = \lambda \times E(C) + (1 - \lambda) \times VAR(L), \tag{6}$$

where λ is the proportional coefficient, which is used to adjust the proportion between the communication energy consumption and the delay, and its value ranges from 0 to 1. If $\lambda = 0$, only the system delay is optimized, and if λ is set between 0 and 1, the system energy and delay are optimized at the same time. $E(C)$ denotes the energy consumption of the system. Obviously, optimizing $E(C)$ is equivalent to optimizing the total weighted Manhattan distances between network nodes. $VAR(L)$ is the link load variance and it can be calculated by

$$VAR(L) = \sum_{i=1}^{M} [Load(l_i) - Load(L)_{avg}]^2 / M, \tag{7}$$

where l_i is the i_{th} link in the NoC, M is the total number of links, $Load(l_i)$ is the load of link l_i, and $Load(L)_{avg}$ is the average link load. $Load(l_i)$ and $Load(L)_{avg}$ can be calculated by

$$Load(l_k) = \sum_{i=1}^{N}\sum_{j=1}^{N} w_{i,j} \times pass_{i,j}^{k}, \tag{8}$$

$$pass_{i,j}^{k} = \begin{cases} 1, when\ p_{i,j}\ pass\ by\ l_k \\ 0, else \end{cases}, \tag{9}$$

$$Load(l)_{avg} = \sum_{i=1}^{N} Load(l_i)/M, \tag{10}$$

where $p_{i,j}$ represents the path from node i to j in the NoC, $w_{i,j}$ represents the amount of traffic from neuron i to j.

Particularly, the one-to-one mapping requirements of the neuron and PE can be met if the $\forall N_i \in N \Rightarrow map(N_i) \in V$ and $\forall N_i \neq N_j \Rightarrow map(N_i) \neq map(N_j)$ are satisfied, where the requirements of the network size and bandwidth are ensured by size(SNNCG) $\leq$ size(NoCAG) and $\forall t_{ij} \leq B_{ij}$. Reducing energy consumption essentially minimizes the total weighted distance between PEs.

2.3 Multi-objective Optimization Problems

In various engineering practices, it is often necessary to solve multiple goal optimization problems that are composed of various sub-goals. However, these sub-goals are always in conflict with each other. Therefore, for multi-objective optimization, the aim is to solve the conflicting relationship among these sub-goals so that the actual problem can be addressed optimally.

Generally, the multi-objective optimization can be briefly described as: given a set of decision vector $X = (x_1, x_2, \cdots, x_n)$, it satisfies the constraints of

$$g_i(X) \geq 0 \ (i = 1, 2, \cdots, k), \tag{11}$$

and

$$h_i(X) \geq 0 \ (i = 1, 2, \cdots, l). \tag{12}$$

Assuming that there are r optimization goals with conflicting relationships. In this case, the multi-objective optimization problem can be described as

$$f(X) = (f_1(X), f_2(X), \cdots, f_r(X)). \tag{13}$$

If there exists a vector $X^* = (x_1^*, x_2^*, \cdots, x_n^*)$ which can meet the constraints of (11) and (12), the $f(X^*)$ has an optimal solution.

The traditional methods generally include linear weighted sum method, constraint and goal planning methods, etc. In this paper, the two former methods are briefly introduced as follows.

(1). The linear weighted sum method. It combines the objective functions of multiple sub-objectives into a new objective function by adding weight coefficients, which transforms the multiple optimization problems into a single optimization problem. Its corresponding descriptions are given by

$$max \ f(x) \sum_{i=1}^{k} w_i f_i(x), \tag{14}$$

$$s.t.: \ x \in X_f, \tag{15}$$

where X denotes the decision space, weight coefficient w_i denotes the weights, and $w_i \geq 0$ which represents the degree of importance among the various sub-goals. In particular, the coefficients satisfy $\sum_{i=1}^{r} w_i = 1$.

Linear weighted sums are easy to understand and calculate. At the same time, many adjustment methods are proposed for the weight coefficient w_i, such as fixed weight, random weight and adaptive weight methods, etc. The objective function used in this work is based on the linear weighted sum method.

(2). The constraint method. Any $(r-1)$ sub-objects in r sub-objectives of this method are converted into constraints, and the remaining one is treated as the objective function (i.e. the constraint method). This method can be described as

$$max \ f(X) = f_j(x), \tag{16}$$

$$s.t.: e_i(x) = f_i(x) \geq \varepsilon_i, 1 \leq i \leq k, i \neq j, \tag{17}$$

where ε and i can have different values in the optimization process.

3 Multi-objective Mapping Algorithm for SNNs

Based on immune genetic algorithm, a multi-objective SNN mapping algorithm is proposed in this paper. The immune system makes natural organisms be able to withstand the adverse effects of bacteria and viruses on themselves, i.e. immunity. Additionally, *B* and *T* lymphocytes play an important role in the immune system, and the specific antibodies in the immune system are produced by *B* lymphocytes. When the organism is invaded by bacteria, viruses, or antigens, the biological immune system will produce antibodies to destroy the antigen. The immune response mechanism and its many functional features are the important parts of the biological immune system. Particularly, the immune algorithm is inspired by the working process of the biological immune system: the antigen is regarded as a practical engineering problem, while the antibody is regarded as a candidate solution to that problem. Then the fitness is calculated, and the best antibody is retained according to the fitness. The algorithm is continuously iterated until the optimal solution set for this problem is obtained [21,27]. In a short summary, the basic components in the biological immune system are: (a) Antigen. It corresponds to the practical engineering problems, such as numerical functions, constraints, etc.; (b) Antibody. A candidate solution to a practical problem; (c) Fitness. It is used to characterize the performance of antibody, which is represented as the power consumption in this paper; and (d) Vaccine. It refers to a prior knowledge of the evolutionary environment or practical problems and is the best estimate of an individual's genes. For the initial solution generation, if there is already a solution existing in the current memory file, then it will be extracted. Additionally, the initial solution can be randomly optimized if it cannot solve the problem. Otherwise, all of the initial solutions will be randomly generated.

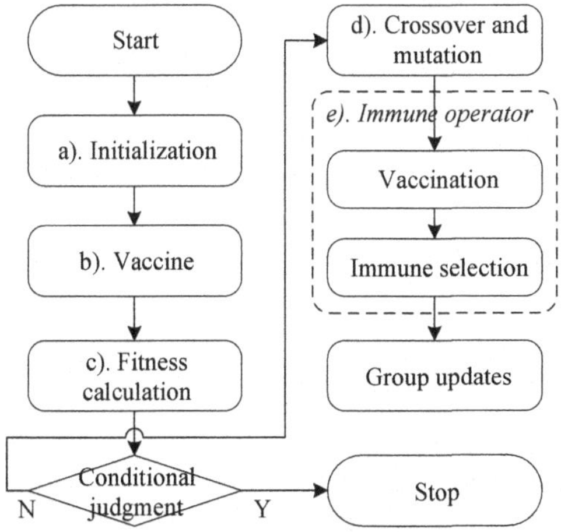

Fig. 2. Basic Immune Genetic algorithm running process.

In this paper, the multi-objective immune genetic algorithm for SNN mapping is proposed. Figure 2 shows the operation process including (a) The immune genetic algorithm is firstly initialized to extract the basic characteristics of the problem to be solved (i.e. the mapping of hardware SNN). (b) The vaccine in the algorithm is the description of the objective function and constraints of the practical problem. Meanwhile, the extraction of such prior knowledge is to take a vaccine. (c) Then the algorithm calculates the fitness. If the termination conditions are satisfied, the algorithm is ceased. (d) Otherwise, it will cross and mutate. (e) The immune operator includes the vaccination and immune selection in the immune genetic algorithm.

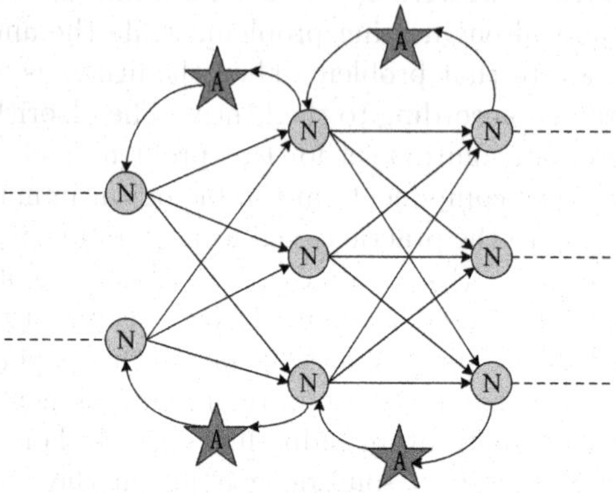

Fig. 3. Spiking astrocyte neural networks.

4 Results

In this section, the experimental process and results are shown in detail, where the spiking astrocyte neural network and 3D-SSBM on-chip network architecture are used as an example application. The multi-objective immune algorithm is implemented by C++ and the Microsoft Visual Studio 2010 is used for all simulations. In order to evaluate the performance of the proposed algorithm, experiments are also carried out by using two benchmarks of random and sequential mappings.

4.1 SNN and 3D-SSBM Structures

The spiking astrocyte neural network structure is shown in Fig. 3, which is based on our previous work of [28]. Unlike feedforward neural networks, each neuron in the spiking astrocyte neural network is associated with an astrocyte. The data can be fed back through the shape of glial cells during delivery. At the same time, the transmission data on each communication path are set to be uniform in this work. Similar to the Star-Subnet-Based-2D Mesh NoC architecture [23], the Star-Subnet-Based-3D Mesh NoC architecture (3D-SSBM) is used in this paper which is shown in Fig. 4. Compared to 2D-SSBM, the 3D-SSBM has more advantages in hardware interconnection. The 3D-SSBM NoC architecture employs the XYZ routing algorithm at the top layer, where the node routing algorithm in the bottom layer (i.e. star subnet) is same as the approach of [23].

As shown in Table 1, the numbers of neurons in the input and hidden layers of the spiking astrocyte neural network are experimentally set to 9 and 10 respectively, where there is only one neuron in the output layer. Specially, the neurons are numbered sequentially from top to bottom in a forward direction from 0. The size of the 3D-SSBM is $3 \times 3 \times 3$, which includes 27 tile routers. Each star subnet can accommodate 5 neurons, i.e. each node router connects 5 PEs.

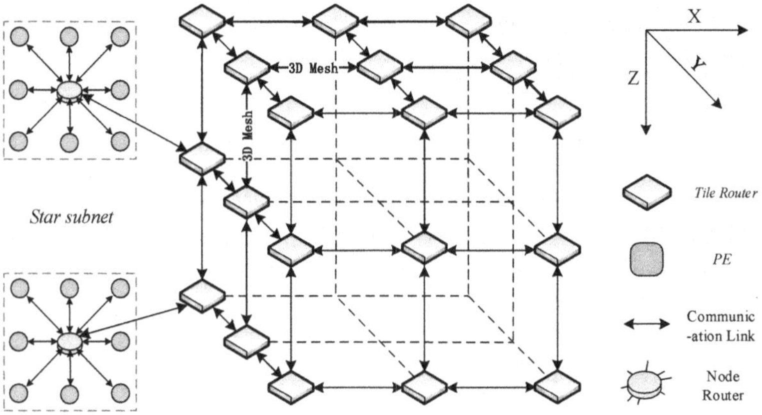

Fig. 4. The 3D-SSBM NoC architecture.

4.2 Analysis of Results

Table 1 shows that the algorithm performs 1000 iterations in the experiment, and the objective function scaling factor λ is set to from 0.1 to 0.9. In order to evaluate the performances on energy and delay, the comparison between the random, sequential and the proposed mapping algorithms is provided in this paper. The random mapping method in the approach of [23] is used in this paper. The sequential mapping assigns the spiking neurons sequentially to the PEs in the same order.

Figure 5(a) shows the fitness variations of different mapping methods with the number of iterations, where the objective function scaling factor is set at $\lambda = 0.5$. It can be seen that the fitness of the random and sequential mapping algorithms are higher than the proposed mapping algorithm, which indicates that the energy consumption and delay are higher. Obviously, with the increasing number of iterations the energy consumption and delay are continuously reduced, i.e. the system performance optimized by the proposed algorithm is much better. The metric of reduction ratio is used in this paper for the performance analysis, which represents the reduction percentage of energy consumption/delay of the proposed algorithm compared to other benchmarks. Figure 5(b) shows the energy/delay ratios under different values of λ, using the benchmarks of random and sequential mapping schemes. It can be seen that as the λ increases, the energy reduction ratios become larger, i.e. the proposed algorithm has a much lower energy consumption compared to random and sequential mapping schemes. However, the delay reduction ratios increases when the λ grows, as expected.

Obviously, the proposed method in this paper has much better performance than the conventional methods. Results show that the proposed algorithm can optimize the energy consumption and communication delays of the SNNs simultaneously, and can also focus on the optimization of the energy consumption or delay of the networks to different degrees by adjusting the coefficient λ of the target function.

Table 1. Experiment parameter setting

	Parameters	Random mapping	Sequential mapping	This work
3D-SSBM NoC	3D mesh NoC scale	$3 \times 3 \times 3$		
	Star subnet size	5		
	Total location	135		
Spiking astrocyte neural networks	Neural network scale	$9 \times 10 \times 1$		
	Total neurons	20		
Algorithm	λ	*N/A*	*N/A*	0.1–0.9
	Number of iterations	1000	1000	1000

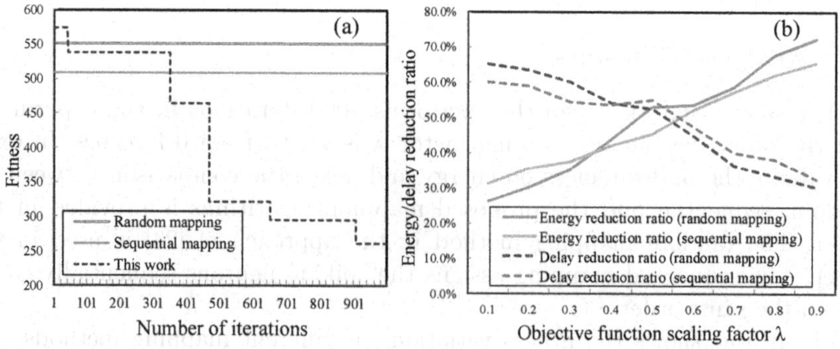

Fig. 5. Experimental results. (a) The change of fitness with different iterations. (b) Energy/delay reduction ratios under different objective function scale factor λ.

5 Conclusions

A multi-objective SNN mapping algorithm is proposed in this paper, which aims to optimize the energy consumption and delays of SNN hardware systems during the mapping processes. The SNN and 3D-SSBM NoC system are used to evaluate the performance of the proposed multi-objective SNN mapping method. Results demonstrated that the proposed SNN mapping algorithm can effectively reduce the energy consumptions and delays of the SNN hardware systems compared to the conventional random and sequential mapping methods. In particular, the energy consumption and delay can be optimized to different degrees by adjusting the scaling factor λ of objective function. Furthermore, more efficient multi-objective metaheuristics will be considered in our future work for further improving the mapping performance.

Acknowledgments. This research was partially supported by the National Natural Science Foundation of China under Grants 61603104 and 61661008, the Guangxi Natural Science Foundation under Grants 2016GXNSFCA380017 and 2017GXNSFAA198180, the funding of Overseas 100 Talents Program of Guangxi Higher Education under Grant F-KA16035, 2018 Guangxi One Thousand Young and Middle-Aged College and University Backbone Teachers Cultivation Program, and the Innovation Project of Guangxi Graduate Education under Grant YCSW2019076.

References

1. Maass, W.: Fast sigmoidal networks via spiking neurons. Neural Comput. **9**(2), 279–304 (1997). https://doi.org/10.1162/neco.1997.9.2.279
2. Liu, J., Huang, Y., Luo, Y., Harkin, J., McDaid, L.: Bio-inspired fault detection circuits based on synapse and spiking neuron models. Neurocomputing **331**, 473–482 (2019). https://doi.org/10.1016/j.neucom.2018.11.078
3. Paugam-Moisy, H., Bohte, S.: Computing with spiking neuron networks. In: Rozenberg, G., Bäack, T., Kok, J.N. (eds.) Handbook of Natural Computing. Springer, Heidelberg (2012). https://doi.org/10.1007/978-3-540-92910-9_10
4. De Garis, H., Shuo, C., Goertzel, B., Ruiting, L.: A world survey of artificial brain projects, part i: large-scale brain simulations. Neurocomputing **74**(1), 3–29 (2010). https://doi.org/10.1016/j.neucom.2010.08.004
5. Moctezuma, J.C., McGeehan, J.P., Nunez-Yanez, J.L.: Biologically compatible neural networks with reconfigurable hardware. Microprocess. Microsyst. **39**(8), 693–703 (2015). https://doi.org/10.1016/j.micpro.2015.09.003
6. Wan, L., Liu, J., Harkin, J., McDaid, L., Luo, Y.: Layered tile architecture for efficient hardware spiking neural networks. Microprocess. Microsyst. **53**, 21–32 (2017). https://doi.org/10.1016/j.micpro.2017.07.005
7. Liu, J., Harkin, J., Li, Y., Maguire, L.: Low cost fault-tolerant routing algorithm for Networks-on-Chip. Microprocess. Microsyst. **39**(6), 358–372 (2015). https://doi.org/10.1016/j.micpro.2015.06.002
8. Liu, J., Harkin, J., Maguire, L.P., McDaid, L.J., Wade, J.J., Martin, G.: Scalable networks-on-chip interconnected architecture for astrocyte-neuron networks. IEEE Trans. Circuits Syst. I Regul. Pap. **63**(12), 2290–2303 (2016). https://doi.org/10.1109/TCSI.2016.2615051

9. Luo, Y., et al.: Low cost interconnected architecture for the hardware spiking neural networks. Front. Neurosci. **12**, 1–14 (2018). https://doi.org/10.3389/fnins.2018.00857
10. Liu, J., Harkin, J., Maguire, L.P., McDaid, L.J., Wade, J.J.: SPANNER: a self-repairing spiking neural network hardware architecture. IEEE Trans. Neural Netw. Learn. Syst. **29**(4), 1287–1300 (2018). https://doi.org/10.1109/TNNLS.2017.2673021
11. Monchiero, M., Palermo, G., Silvano, C., Villa, O.: Exploration of distributed shared memory architectures for NoC-based multiprocessors. J. Syst. Architect. **53**(1), 719–732 (2007). https://doi.org/10.1109/icsamos.2006.300821
12. Liu, J., Harkin, J., Li, Y., Maguire, L.P.: Fault-tolerant networks-on-chip routing with coarse and fine-grained look-ahead. IEEE Trans. Comput. Aided Des. Integr. Circuits Syst. **35**(2), 260–273 (2016). https://doi.org/10.1109/TCAD.2015.2459050
13. Liu, J., Harkin, J., McDaid, L.J., Martin, G.: Hierarchical networks-on-chip interconnect for astrocyte-neuron network hardware. In: International Conference on Artificial Neural Networks (ICANN), pp. 382–390 (2016). https://doi.org/10.1007/978-3-319-44778-0_45
14. Carrillo, S., Harkin, J., McDaid, L.J., Morgan, F., Pande, S., Cawley, S., McGinley, B.: Scalable hierarchical network-on-chip architecture for spiking neural network hardware implementations. IEEE Trans. Parallel Distrib. Syst. **24**(12), 2451–2461 (2013). https://doi.org/10.1109/tpds.2012.289
15. Firuzan, A., Modarressi, M., Daneshtalab, M.: Reconfigurable communication fabric for efficient implementation of neural networks. In: International Symposium on Reconfigurable Communication-centric Systems-on-Chip (ReCoSoC), pp. 1–8 (2015). https://doi.org/10.1109/recosoc.2015.7238097
16. Benini, L., Micheli, G.D.: Networks on chips: a new SoC paradigm. Computer **35**(1), 70–78 (2002). https://doi.org/10.1109/2.976921
17. Lim, W.L., Wibowo, A., Desa, M.I., Haron, H.: A biogeography-based optimization algorithm hybridized with tabu search for the quadratic assignment problem. Comput. Intell. Neurosci. **2016**, 1–12 (2016). https://doi.org/10.1155/2016/5803893
18. Liu, J., Harkin, J., Li, Y., Maguire, L.: Online traffic-aware fault detection for networks-on-chip. J. Parallel Distrib. Comput. **74**(1), 1984–1993 (2014). https://doi.org/10.1016/j.jpdc.2013.09.001
19. Gambardella, L.M., Taillard, É.D., Dorigo, M.: Ant colonies for the quadratic assignment problem. J. Oper. Res. Soc. **50**(2), 167–176 (1999). https://doi.org/10.2307/3010565
20. Misevicius, A.: An improved hybrid genetic algorithm: new results for the quadratic assignment problem. Knowl.-Based Syst. **17**(1), 65–73 (2004). https://doi.org/10.1016/j.knosys.2004.03.001
21. Sepúlveda, J., Gogniat, G., Sepúlveda, D., Pires, R., Chau, W., Strum, M.: 3DMIA : a multi-objective artificial immune algorithm for 3d-mpsoc multi-application 3D-NoC mapping. In: 15th Annual Conference Companion on Genetic and Evolutionary Computation, pp. 167–168 (2013). https://doi.org/10.1145/2464576.2464659
22. Franco-Sepúlveda, G., Del Rio-Cuervo, J.C., Pachón-Hernández, M.A.: State of the art about metaheuristics and artificial neural networks applied to open pit mining. Res. Policy **60**(1), 125–133 (2019). https://doi.org/10.1016/j.resourpol.2018.12.013

23. Liu, J., Huang, X., Luo, Y., Cao, Y.: An energy-aware hybrid particle swarm optimization algorithm for spiking neural network mapping. In: International Conference on Neural Information Processing (ICONIP), pp. 805–815 (2017). https://doi.org/10.1007/978-3-319-70090-8_82
24. Singh, A.K., Srikanthan, T., Kumar, A., Wu, J.: Communication-aware heuristics for run-time task mapping on NoC-based MPSoC platforms. J. Syst. Architect. **56**(7), 242–255 (2010). https://doi.org/10.1016/j.sysarc.2010.04.007
25. Hu, J., Marculescu, R.: Energy-aware mapping for tile-based NoC architectures under performance constraints. In: Proceedings of Asia South Pacific Design Automation Conference, pp. 233–239 (2003). https://doi.org/10.1109/aspdac.2003.1195022
26. Yang, S., Li, L., Gao, M., Zhang, Y.: An energy- and delay-aware mapping method of NoC. Acta Electronica Sinica **36**(5), 937–942 (2008)
27. Sepúlveda, M.J., Chau, W.J., Gogniat, G., Strum, M.: A multi-objective adaptive immune algorithm for multi-application NoC mapping. Analog Integr. Circ. Sig. Process **73**(3), 851–860 (2012). https://doi.org/10.1007/s10470-012-9869-9
28. Liu, J., et al.: Exploring self-repair in a coupled spiking astrocyte neural network. IEEE Trans. Neural Netw. Learn. Syst. **30**(3), 865–875 (2019). https://doi.org/10.1109/tnnls.2018.2854291

The Importance of Self-excitation in Spiking Neural Networks Evolved to Recognize Temporal Patterns

Muhammad Yaqoob[1], Volker Steuber[2], and Borys Wróbel[1(✉)]

[1] Evolving Systems Laboratory, Adam Mickiewicz University in Poznan, Poznan, Poland
{yaqoob,wrobel}@evosys.org
[2] University of Hertfordshire, Hatfield, UK
v.steuber@herts.ac.uk

Abstract. Biological and artificial spiking neural networks process information by changing their states in response to the temporal patterns of input and of the activity of the network itself. Here we analyse very small networks, evolved to recognize three signals in a specific pattern (ABC) in a continuous temporal stream of signals (...CABCACB...). This task can be accomplished by networks with just four neurons (three interneurons and one output). We show that evolving the networks in the presence of noise and variation of the intervals of silence between signals biases the solutions towards networks that can maintain their states (a form of memory), while the majority of networks evolved without variable intervals between signals cannot do so. We demonstrate that in most networks, the evolutionary process leads to the presence of superfluous connections that can be pruned without affecting the ability of the networks to perform the task and, if the unpruned network can maintain memory, so does the pruned network. We then analyse how these small networks can perform their tasks, using a paradigm of finite state transducers. This analysis shows that self-excitatory loops (autapses) in these networks are crucial for both the recognition of the pattern and for memory maintenance.

Keywords: Temporal pattern recognition · Spiking neural networks · Ex-loops · Self-loops · Artificial evolution · Minimal cognition · Complex networks · Genetic algorithm · Finite state transducer

1 Introduction

The current understanding of information processing in biological brains postulates that this processing is accomplished thanks to constant transitions of biological networks from one pattern of spiking activity to another [1,3,5,11,12, 15,23]. Temporal input patterns in all sensory modalities, including smell [25], sight [34], and hearing [14], influence these patterns of activity; and the patterns

I. V. Tetko et al. (Eds.): ICANN 2019, LNCS 11727, pp. 758–771, 2019.
https://doi.org/10.1007/978-3-030-30487-4_59

of neural activity determine the animal behaviour. One of the central problems in neuroscience is how biological neural circuits can accomplish such temporal processing. Answering this question may help in designing bio-inspired artificial cognitive systems. Of special interest is how this processing, which also involves the maintenance of the spiking activity (a form of memory), while depending on the precise timing of spikes, can be accomplished in the presence of noise [8,10]; and indeed may necessitate noise [6,13,29,37].

In this work, we analyse very small spiking neural networks (SNNs) evolved to perform a simple temporal pattern recognition task. We have shown previously that without noise, two interneurons are sufficient for this task, but such networks are fragile to even the slightest variation of the timing of inputs [39]. In contrast, networks with three interneurons can be evolved to recognize patterns consisting of three stimuli in the presence of noise, and they are robust to a change of neuronal parameters or duration of intervals of silence between the stimuli [38,40]. In this work, we use the same model of noise (on the membrane voltage) as previously; while its level is biologically realistic, and so including it adds to the biological plausibility of our model, our primary concern is to aid in the evolution of networks that can maintain their states (a form of memory) even as the intervals between stimuli are hugely increased when testing the evolved network. One of the original contributions of this paper is that evolving the networks both in the presence of noise and the variation of intervals between stimuli biases the networks towards those that can maintain their states.

We observe that a variety of network topologies resulting from an artificial evolutionary process can perform the same computational task [38–40]. This is also the case for biological networks [18,22]. By using artificial evolution, we are able to find the commonalities between the networks that can accomplish simple, but not trivial, computational tasks.

The recognition of temporal pattern requires temporal storage of the stimulus or delays [16,30–33]. Since our networks are very small, delays caused by synaptic delays are minimal. The main contribution of this paper is that the crucial connections that maintain the network state and memory in the presence of variable silent intervals are self-excitatory loops (autapses), which sheds new light on the importance of these connections that are commonly found in biological neural systems [26,36]. Furthermore, persistent spiking activity in response to short sensory input is common in all areas of brain [17] which perhaps is responsible for keeping short-term memory in accumulating tasks [27].

2 Methods

Each network in our model is encoded in a linear genome, and consists of three inputs, three interneurons, and one output neuron [38–40]. Inputs are not allowed to connect to the output neuron directly and only interneurons can have self-loops. A fully connected network with this structure can have up to 21 connections (up to nine connections from inputs to interneurons, six connections between the interneurons, three self-loops, and three connections from the interneurons to the output neuron).

Each input is dedicated to one signal (stimulus type), denoted as A, B and C. The interneurons and output neuron are modelled using Euler integration with 1 ms steps of the differential equations for adaptive exponential integrate and fire neurons [20]; we use the same parameter values as in [38–40]; these values result in tonic spiking in response to constant input current. Since this study focuses on the effect of network connectivity, the neuronal parameters are kept constant (allowing them to evolve would hugely increase the search space of the artificial evolutionary process). To simulate noisy synaptic background at a biologically realistic level [2,7,9,21], we add a random value taken from a normal distribution with standard deviation 2 mV and mean 0 to the membrane potential of each neuron at every 1 ms simulation step. When a neuron receives a spike the excitatory g_E or inhibitory g_I conductance is updated by the connection weight multiplied by the respective conductance gain. The value of the excitatory and inhibitory gain is 7 nS.

The task of the networks is to recognize three signals in a particular order (ABC) in a continuous random sequence (...BCACACC**ABC**ACBAC...), in which all signals appear with equal probability, and thus the correct patterns take up about 10% of time. To generate a variety of solutions, we use a genetic algorithm with a population of 300 individuals, with 100 independent runs for each of the two settings: in the first setting signals are followed by a constant interval of silence (16 ms), in the second setting the intervals vary, with a uniform distribution between 16 and 32 ms (in previous work, [38,40], we used noise on the membrane potential, but did not vary the interval of silences). In both settings the length of a each signal is 6 ms. We use the same genetic operators as in [40]; they can result in changes of weights, deletion and addition of edges (synapses) and the nodes (neurons) in the network (through deletion and duplication, respectively, of consecutive elements in the linear genomes; however, the maximum size of the network was limited as described above).

Each individual in the population in each generation is evaluated on six sequences. Four out of these six sequences are generated randomly with equiprobable occurrence of three signals A, B and C; the remaining two sequences consist of four concatenated patterns in random order: ABC and three patterns that are hard to distinguish from this target (ABA, ABB, and BBC). The fitness function [38,40] rewards networks in which the output neuron spiked (at least once) in the correct intervals, and did not spike in the incorrect intervals: $f_{fitness} = 1 - R + 4P$, where R, reward (P, penalty) is the fraction of correct (incorrect) intervals in which output spiked. P is multiplied by 4 in this formulation because its denominator is much larger than the numerator for the networks that have correct performance or are close to it (when the input sequence is random, 90% of intervals are incorrect). The correct intervals are those that start at the onset of the last signal (C) of the correct pattern (ABC) and end with the end of the silence that follows. Similarly, incorrect intervals start at the onset of each signal that is not C in ABC. Both correct and incorrect intervals last either 22 ms or, in the setting with variable silence intervals, 22–38 ms.

The false discovery rate (FDR) of the network is defined as the number of incorrect intervals in which output spiked divided by the sum of both incorrect and correct intervals in which the output spiked. The true positive rate (TPR) of the network is the same as R. We define a champion in a run as a perfect recognizer if its TPR is above 0.99 and FDR below 0.01 for the settings (constant or variable interval of silence between the signals) under which a champion was evolved.

In order to simplify the network analysis, we use pruning of superfluous edges in the network. Our pruning algorithm removes excessive connections in two steps in a loop: (i) a random connection is removed for testing; (ii) if TPR < 0.95 or FDR > 0.05, the connection is reinstated and labelled as vital; the loop is terminated when all the connections are labelled as vital.

3 Results and Discussion

Out of 100 independent runs in the presence of noise on membrane potential but with constant interval of silence between the signals, 15 ended with champions that were perfect recognizers; when in addition to noise the intervals of silence varied during evolution, the yield was 12%.

Even though our artificial evolutionary process allows for deletion of nodes (neurons) in the network, none of the perfect recognizers had less than three interneurons. In addition, even though pruning can result in a disconnection of a node, no network ended up with less than three interneurons after pruning. Perfect recognizers evolved only with noise had slightly more (19.20 on average; Table 1) edges than the perfect recognizers evolved also with variation of silences (18.83). This difference persisted after pruning (14.26 and 13.08 edges, respectively). None of these differences were statistically significant.

We tested both the evolved and pruned networks on a random sequence with 100,000 signals and 100 ms intervals of silence between signals. Our results (Table 1) show, firstly, that evolving the networks with both noise and variation of silences resulted in more perfect recognizers that can keep memory (11 out of 12) than for evolving only with noise (4 out of 15). Secondly, all these $11 + 4 = 15$ perfect recognizers kept memory also after pruning, demonstrating that the removed connections are unnecessary not only for recognizing the pattern but also for keeping memory.

Interestingly, while the perfect recognizers that kept memory had fewer self-excitatory loops after pruning (all had 2; Table 1) than the champions which did not keep memory (which on average had 2.42), the sum of weights of the self-excitatory loops was significantly higher in recognizers that kept memory (mean sum 14.6 vs. 12.3; $p = 0.002$, one-sided Wilcoxon test). This suggests that the memory is maintained in these networks through self-excitation; we will explore this issue further below by analysing the mechanisms by which some networks keep memory while other fail to do so.

Based on the TPR and FDR with 100 ms intervals of silence (Table 1), we can divide the 27 perfect recognizers into four groups: (i) 15 memory-keepers

Table 1. The number of edges and self-excitatory loops in perfect recognizers evolved with noise and constant (top, 15 champions) or variable (bottom, 12 champions) silences, and their robustness to the increase of silences to 100 ms

Champions evolved in the presence of constant (16 ms) silence intervals

	0	1	2	3	4	5	6	7	8	9	10	11	12	13	14
evolved edges	19	21	20	19	18	19	19	18	21	16	20	20	19	20	19
edges after pruning	10	14	15	13	11	14	16	15	16	16	17	16	15	13	13
self ex-loops	1	3	2	3	2	2	2	2	3	3	3	2	2	2	2
100 ms TPR	0.02	0.98	0.98	0.97	0.96	0.95	0.99	0.55	0.99	0.00	0.00	0.00	0.96	0.99	0.96
100 ms FDR	0.99	0.37	0.01	0.12	0.56	0.01	0.03	0.90	0.20	1.00	1.00	0.99	0.58	0.01	0.56

Champions evolved in the presence of noise and variable (16-32 ms) intervals of silence

	0	1	2	3	4	5	6	7	8	9	10	11
evolved edges	19	21	20	19	20	18	16	20	18	19	18	18
edges after pruning	13	12	14	14	14	13	11	13	15	12	13	13
self ex-loops	2	2	2	2	3	2	2	2	2	2	2	2
100ms TPR	0.99	0.99	0.99	0.98	0.90	0.98	0.99	0.98	0.99	0.97	0.98	0.99
100ms FDR	0.04	0.01	0.01	0.01	0.40	0.04	0.01	0.01	0.04	0.01	0.02	0.01

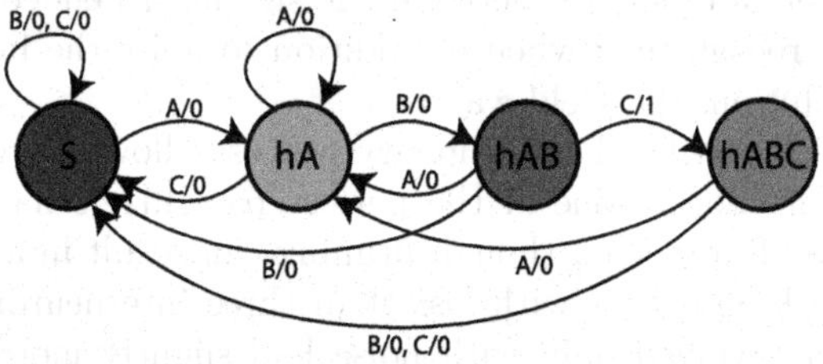

Fig. 1. Finite state transducer for recognizing ABC. The symbols above each arrow correspond to the input (A, B, C) and output (0: no spiking, 1: spiking of the output neuron).

(TPR remains high, and FDR low; evolved only with noise: number 2, 5, 6, 13; evolved with both noise and variation of silences: all except number 4), (ii) over-recognizers (TPR stays high, but FDR increases; evolved only with noise: 1, 3, 4, 8, 12, 14; evolved with both: number 4), (iii) wrong-recognizers (low TPR, high FDR; evolved only with noise: number 0, 7, 10, 11), (iv) mute networks (champion 9 evolved only with noise), for which long intervals of silence between signals result in only noise driven activity (negligible) of the output neuron. To illustrate what allows for both recognition and memory, we first analyse one memory-keeper evolved with both noise and variation of silences (champion 6; Fig. 2), one over-recognizer (champion 4; Fig. 3), one wrong-recognizer (champion 7; Fig. 4), and the mute network (champion 9; Fig. 5). The champions 4, 7 and 9 fail when silences are 50 ms long for the same reasons they fail with 100 ms silences; we use 50 ms in the figures to keep them compact. While the activities of the pruned networks that fail are slightly different from the activities of the evolved networks, they fail for the same reasons; we will present only the analysis of the pruned networks for simplicity.

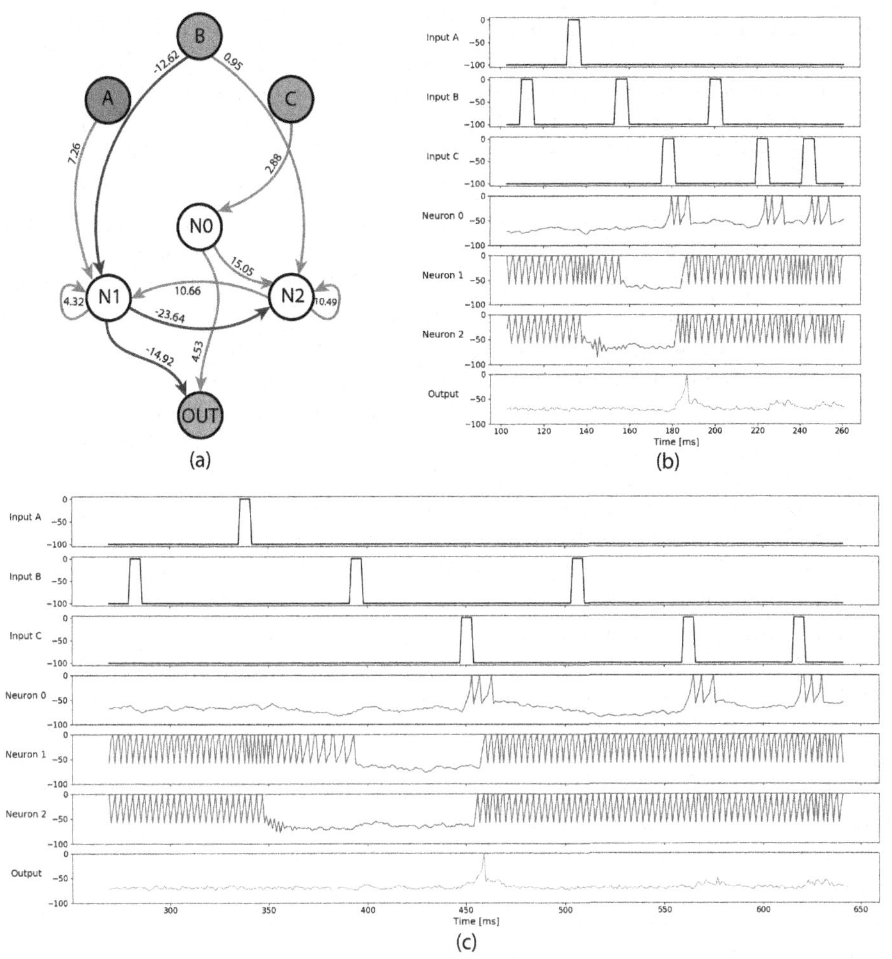

Fig. 2. Champion 6 evolved with both noise and variation of silences. The activity of the pruned network (a) is shown for short (16 ms; b), and long (50 ms; c) silences, which indicates that this champion is a memory-keeper.

In order to analyse the transitions of the network, we will use the paradigm we proposed previously, based on mapping the network states onto the states of a finite state transducer (FST) [38–40]. A FST, a formal computational model [28], is frequently used for analysing computations on time series performed in an online manner (that is, constantly producing an output for a continuous input). The minimal FST for recognizing a pattern with three symbols has four states (Fig. 1).

In the case of our memory-keeper (Fig. 2), the activity of input A, because of its excitatory connection to N1, makes N1 spike; this spiking continues thanks to the excitatory self-loop, while N0, N2, and output remain silent. Thus, we can denote the state hA (for 'had A', Fig. 1) as LHL, where L (H) means low (high) activity for interneurons in the order (N0, N1, N2). The state hAB (when the network receives B after A, for 'had AB') can be denoted as LLL, and the state hABC ('had ABC') as LHH. The only difference between the start state (S) and hABC is the intermittent activity of the output. Thus, the state of the network while waiting for the last signal in the pattern (state hAB) is maintained passively (all interneurons are silent), while the other states, hA and hABC/S, are maintained by the self-excitatory loops on N1 and N2. In hA, only N1 is continuously active; in hABC/S, both N0 and N1 are. The inhibitory connection from N1 to the output ensures that receiving a signal C will cause the output to spike (after N0 spikes) only when N1—and N2, which activates N1—are silent. The inhibitory connection from input B to N1 is necessary for N1 to cease its activity in hAB, but this does not happen when N2 is active (so when network is in the state hABC or S, it goes to S after receiving B). The inhibitory connection from N1 to N2 is necessary for the transition from hABC/S to hA (higher frequency of N1 shuts down N2). Finally, the weak excitatory connection from B to N2 is necessary to ensure that when N2 is silent (hAB), receiving a B would not silence both N1 and N2; indeed, when this connection is removed, the output wrongly spikes after receiving ABBC, ABBBC, etc. (the network recognizes the regular expression $AB^{+}C$, not just ABC).

While we only describe one memory-keeper here, in all such networks analysed so far, the state hAB is represented by LLL (and thus the networks will spike when they are initiated with no activity and receive just a C), and the networks maintain two states stably: hA and hABC/S (which differ only by the short-term activity of the output, triggered by the transition from hAB to hABC). Since the over-recognizer we have chosen for analysis (Fig. 3) shares its topology with the memory-keeper (Fig. 2), both recognize ABC correctly in the same fashion when the silence intervals are short—when the network receives A, it goes to the state LHL, when B follows, to LLL, and when C follows, to LHH. However, when the silences are long, the activity of N2 in LHH dies out (because the N2 self-excitatory loop is weak), and the network goes to LHL—the same as hA. When B is received in this state, all activity ceases (state LLL). If the next signal is C, the output neuron spikes, wrongly. This leads to a high FDR—the network recognizes the pattern BC when the intervals are long.

The analysis of the network activity of the wrong-recognizer (Fig. 4) reveals that the recognition when the intervals of silence are short depends on transitions from one unstable state to another. We can see that when the intervals are long, the S state (HHH) is stable, and maintained by the strong self-excitatory loop on N1. When A is received, N0 speeds up, and inhibits N1 (the networks goes to the state HLH). If the silence continues, the network goes to the state LLH (N0 does not have any self-loop), and then LLL (the self-loop of N2 is too weak to maintain its activity for long). If C is received at this point, N1 spikes, and without inhibition from N2, the output spikes, leading to the recognition of AC. When the intervals are short, the network transitions along the same trajectory when it recognizes ABC, but much quicker—when it is still in the state HLH after receiving A, the arrival of a B pushes it to LLH, which can relax to LLL

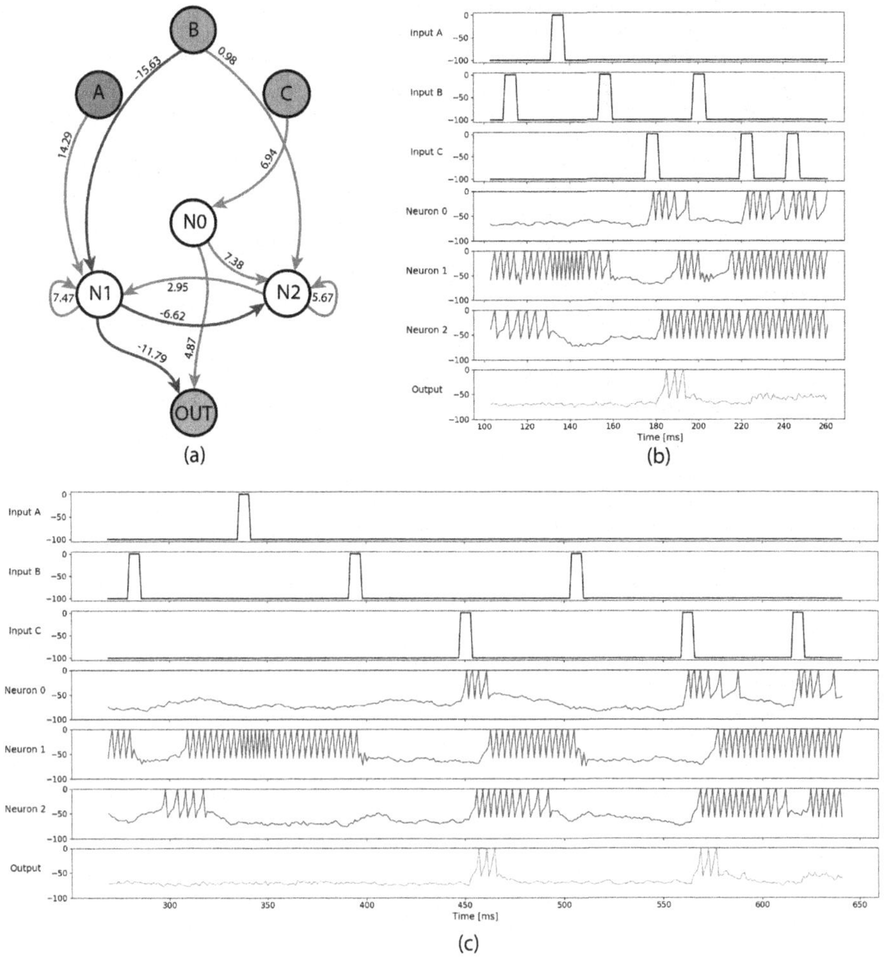

Fig. 3. Champion 4 evolved with noise and constant silences. The activity of the pruned network (a) is shown for short (16 ms; b), and long (50 ms; c) silences, for which this champion behaves as an over-recognizer.

in time to release the output from the inhibition from N2 when the spike of N1, induced by receiving a C, arrives. Any Bs that do not follow an A after a short interval of silence, and any Cs, cause the network to go the stable state HHH.

Finally, in champion 9 evolved with constant short intervals of silence, the recognition of ABC crucially depends on the network being in a particular unstable state when the network receives a C after having received the pattern AB—to activate the output, N2 (active after C is received) needs to spike fast; and for N2 to spike fast, N2 needs to receive also the activation of N1. However, N1 cannot spike too frequently because it inhibits the output. In addition, N0 (which also inhibits the output) needs to be inactive. This particular state can only be

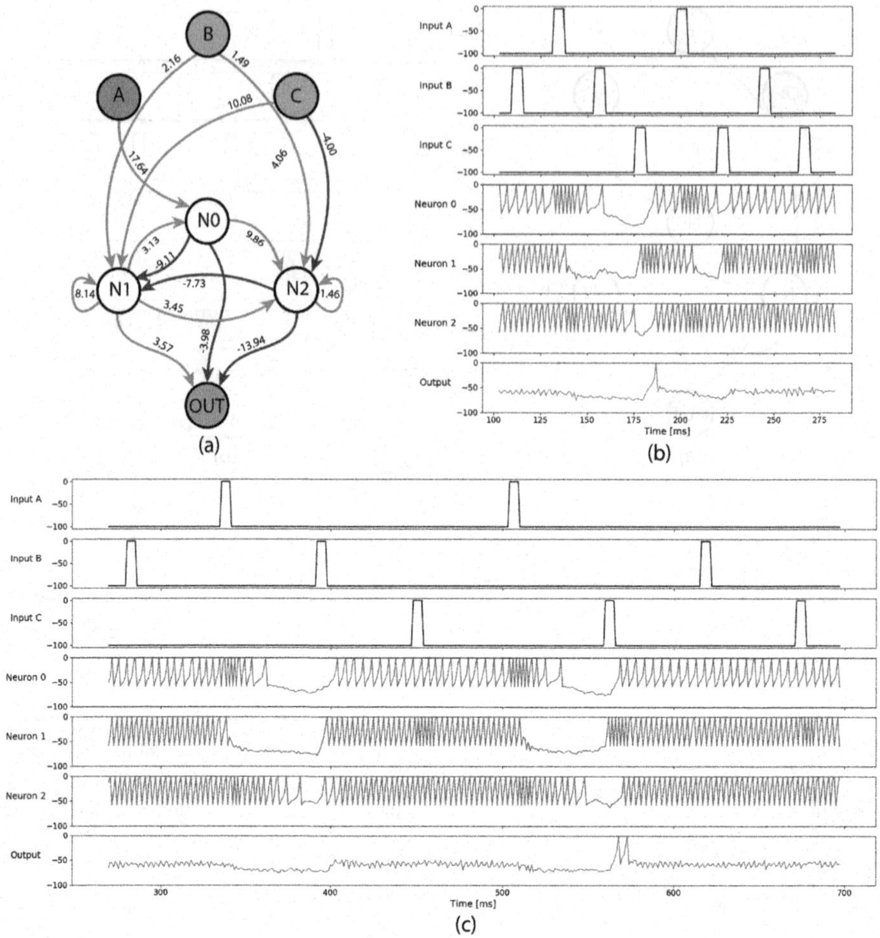

Fig. 4. Champion 7 evolved with noise and constant silences. The activity of the pruned network (a) is shown for short (16 ms; b), and long (50 ms; c) silences, for which this champion behaves as a wrong-recognizer.

achieved if the network first reaches the state HLL (which is stable thanks to the self-excitatory loop on N0). With short silences, this state is reached after receiving an A. When the silence is long, the right conditions for the output to spike never occur—even though there are times when N1 spikes slowly with N0 inactive, N2 never spikes frequently enough at that time to drive the output to spike. Moreover, even though N1 also has a self-excitatory loop, its activity cannot be sustained for long when N0 (which inhibits N1) is active, and because N1 activates N2, which in turn activates N0, N1 can only spike slowly.

Our experimental setup did not impose the Dale's rule [4] on the evolved networks. This is because our preliminary experiments showed that imposing the rule would require permitting more (roughly double) interneurons during

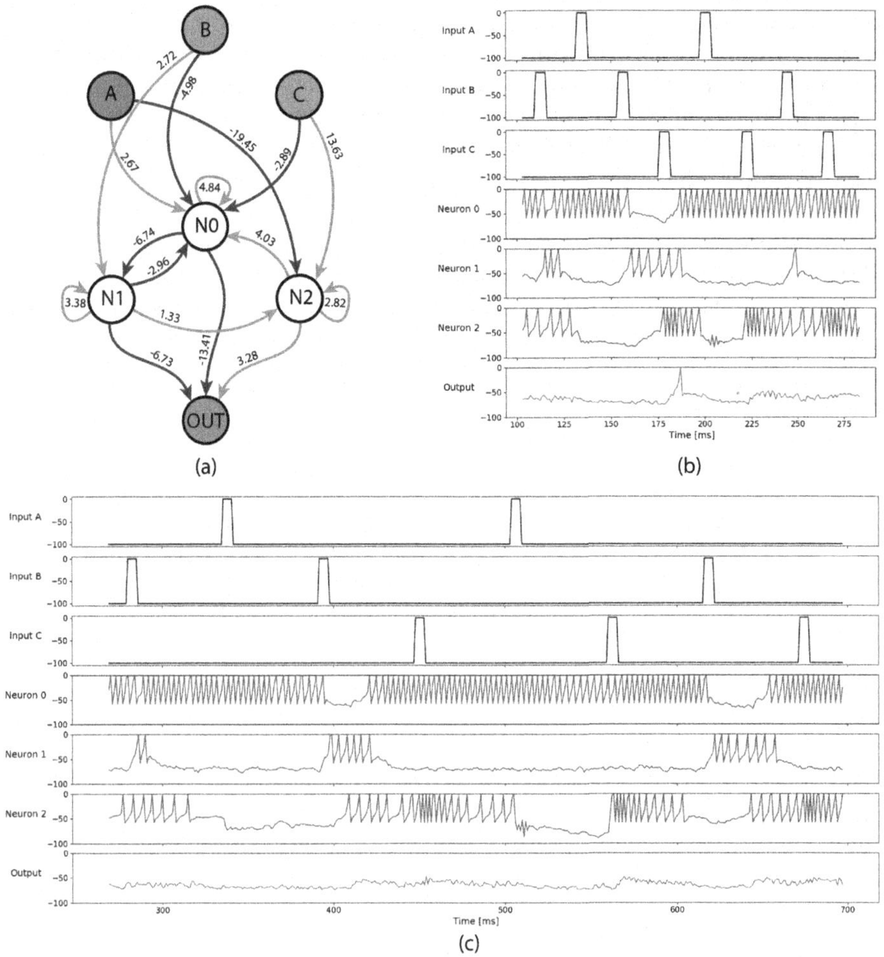

Fig. 5. Champion 9 evolved with noise and constant silences. The activity of the pruned network (a) is shown for short (16 ms; b), and long (50 ms; c) silences, for which this champion behaves as a mute network.

evolution, increasing the search space. All of the networks we analysed had at least one interneuron which had both excitatory and inhibitory connections to other neurons in the network, even after pruning the superfluous connections. However, once a network is evolved, it is straightforward to transform it to a network that conforms to the Dale's rule. This can be done by splitting a neuron that violates the rule into two new neurons, one excitatory and one inhibitory (Fig. 6). Pruning superfluous connections from the network leads to fewer neurons for which such splitting is necessary. Both new neurons receive the same inputs (with the same weights) as the original neuron. The weights of the outgoing connections are also maintained. If an excitatory self-loop is present, it is maintained with the same weight for the new excitatory neuron, and a new excitatory connection with the same weight is created from the new excitatory to the new inhibitory neuron (an analogous operation can be made for an inhibitory self-loop, should one exist). The formation of this new connection could, in principle, affect the functionality of the network, as it creates an additional synaptic delay. However, the networks evolved with noise can be expected to be robust to such a perturbation. On the other hand, creating two noisy neurons instead of one creates, in principle, a more noisy network. The performance of the networks analysed in this paper was not affected by the transformation detailed here. This applies, in particular, to champion 6, the memory-keeper, who has only one neuron (N1) that violates the rule (Figs. 2 and 6).

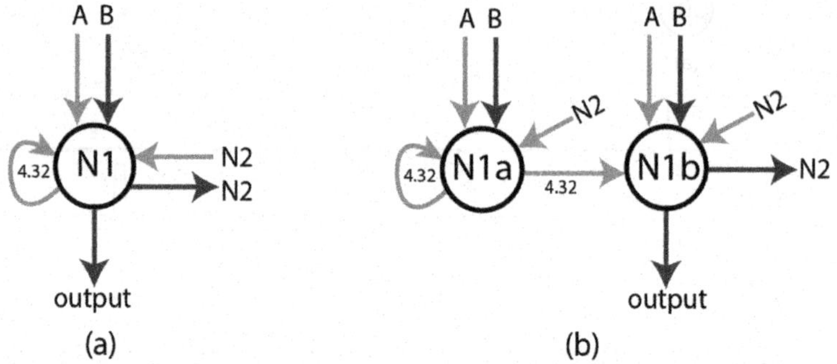

Fig. 6. Splitting a neuron that violates the Dale's rule in order to create the network that conforms to the rule. The single interneuron, N1, that violates the rule in champion 6 (Fig. 2), with two inhibitory outputs and one excitatory self-loop (a), can be split into two new neurons, one excitatory and one inhibitory (b).

4 Conclusions and Future Work

Our analysis of very small networks evolved to recognize simple temporal patters reveals that many connections in these networks can be removed without impairing the performance of the network. Such pruning allows for a much easier understanding of the mechanisms in which the networks accomplish this minimally cognitive task.

For the networks analysed in this paper, these mechanisms depend crucially on the presence of strong self-excitatory loops, necessary for both the pattern recognition and maintenance of network state—a form of memory. Our results indicate that to recognize a pattern consisting of three symbols with state maintenance, the networks need to consist of at least three interneurons (with one output), and need to have two self-excitatory loops with the weights sufficient to maintain the network states. Our analysis of the activity of the networks that keep memory, by mapping the network states on the states of an FST, shows that all the perfect recognizers that maintain the states of the network represent the state before the arrival of the final symbol by inactivity of the network (a state that does not need to be maintained actively). In all these networks, the accepting state differs from the start state only by the intermittent activity of the output (triggered on the transition to this state from the state of inactivity). This state is maintained actively, and so is the state reached after receiving the first symbol in the pattern.

Our analysis of the networks that fail to maintain the memory correctly reveals the following preliminary insights. With long intervals of silence between the signals, over-recognition happens when the network does not maintain the start state or the state after the correct pattern is recognized (which may be the same), but instead over the long interval of silence transitions to the same state as the one reached after receiving the first symbol in the pattern. With long silences, such networks continue to recognize the correct pattern but start to recognize wrong patterns. On the other hand, the networks that cannot maintain the other states with long silences can either stop recognizing the correct pattern while recognizing wrong ones, or become completely mute.

We show that the perfect recognizers that keep memory function essentially follow the paradigm of an FST. Previous work on creating finite state machines based on recurrent spiking neural networks [19,24,35] considered large multilayer networks. Here we show, essentially, a method to obtain very small networks that work a finite automata using artificial evolution. In future work, we plan to investigate the limits of the length of the temporal patterns for which prefect recognizers that keep memory can be evolved, and how many self-excitatory loops are necessary in such recognizers, for both shorter and longer patterns.

In the work reported here and previously [38–40], we have allowed only for the topology to change. In principle, the neuronal parameters could also be evolved, but this would hugely increase the search space. However, other spiking behaviours (for example, bursting) of the neurons in the network could perhaps lead to different classes of solutions. We plan to explore this issue in our future work using two approaches: (i) allowing a discrete change of the behaviour of each neuron in the network during evolution (for example, from tonic spiking to bursting, a change of the values of several parameters in one step), (ii) by exploring if the solutions change when all the neurons in the network have the same behaviour (different than used here). We could also modify our model of artificial evolution to allow for a more efficient search for the solutions; a different evolutionary model might possibly also lead to different classes of solutions.

Furthermore, we plan to revisit the question of robustness of the evolved networks to changes of parameters and synaptic weights. We also plan to investigate if other models of noise (such as an Ornstein-Uhlenbeck process, commonly used in computational neuroscience), variation of silences or neuronal parameters during evolution will influence the types of solutions, their evolvability and robustness.

Acknowledgements. This work was supported by the Polish National Science Center (project EvoSN, UMO-2013/08/M/ST6/00922). MY acknowledges the support of the KNOW RNA Research Center in Poznan (No. 01/KNOW2/2014) and POWR.03.02.00-00-I006/17.

References

1. Ahissar, E., Arieli, A.: Figuring space by time. Neuron **32**, 185–201 (2001)
2. Anderson, J.S., Lampl, I., Gillespie, D.C., Ferster, D.: The contribution of noise to contrast invariance of orientation tuning in cat visual cortex. Science **290**, 1968–1972 (2000)
3. Bialek, W., Rieke, F., van Steveninck, R.R.d.R., Warland, D., et al.: Reading a neural code. In: Neural Information Processing Systems, pp. 36–43 (1989)
4. Burnstock, G.: Autonomic neurotransmission: 60 years since sir Henry Dale. Annu. Rev. Pharmacol. Toxicol. **49**, 1–30 (2009)
5. Decharms, R.C., Zador, A.: Neural representation and the cortical code. Annu. Rev. Neurosci. **23**, 613–647 (2000)
6. Destexhe, A., Rudolph, M., Fellous, J.M., Sejnowski, T.: Fluctuating synaptic conductances recreate in vivo-like activity in neocortical neurons. Neuroscience **107**, 13–24 (2001)
7. Destexhe, A., Paré, D.: Impact of network activity on the integrative properties of neocortical pyramidal neurons in vivo. J. Neurophysiol. **81**, 1531–1547 (1999)
8. Faisal, A.A., Selen, L.P., Wolpert, D.M.: Noise in the nervous system. Nat. Rev. Neurosci. **9**, 292–303 (2008)
9. Finn, I.M., Priebe, N.J., Ferster, D.: The emergence of contrast-invariant orientation tuning in simple cells of cat visual cortex. Neuron **54**, 137–152 (2007)
10. Florian, R.V.: Biologically inspired neural networks for the control of embodied agents. Center for Cognitive and Neural Studies (Cluj-Napoca, Romania), Tech. rep. Coneural-03-03 (2003)
11. Gerstner, W., Kempter, R., van Hemmen, J.L., Wagner, H.: A neuronal learning rule for sub-millisecond temporal coding. Nature **383**, 76–78 (1996)
12. Huxter, J., Burgess, N., Okeefe, J.: Independent rate and temporal coding in hippocampal pyramidal cells. Nature **425**, 828–832 (2003)
13. Jacobson, G., et al.: Subthreshold voltage noise of rat neocortical pyramidal neurones. J. Physiol. **564**, 145–60 (2005)
14. Joris, P., Yin, T.: A matter of time: internal delays in binaural processing. Trends Neurosci. **30**, 70–78 (2007)
15. Laurent, G.: Dynamical representation of odors by oscillating and evolving neural assemblies. Trends Neurosci. **19**, 489–496 (1996)
16. Maex, R., Steuber, V.: The first second: models of short-term memory traces in the brain. Neural Netw. **22**, 1105–1112 (2009)
17. Major, G., Tank, D.: Persistent neural activity: prevalence and mechanisms. Curr. Opin. Neurobiol. **14**, 675–684 (2004)
18. Marder, E.: Variability, compensation, and modulation in neurons and circuits. Proc. Nat. Acad. Sci. U.S.A. **108**, 15542–15548 (2011)
19. Natschläger, T., Maass, W.: Spiking neurons and the induction of finite state machines. Theoret. Comput. Sci. **287**, 251–265 (2002)
20. Naud, R., Marcille, N., Clopath, C., Gerstner, W.: Firing patterns in the adaptive exponential integrate-and-fire model. Biol. Cybern. **99**, 335–347 (2008)
21. Paré, D., Shink, E., Gaudreau, H., Destexhe, A., Lang, E.J.: Impact of spontaneous synaptic activity on the resting properties of cat neocortical pyramidal neurons in vivo. J. Neurophysiol. **79**, 1450–1460 (1998)
22. Prinz, A.A., Bucher, D., Marder, E.: Similar network activity from disparate circuit parameters. Nat. Neurosci. **7**, 1345–1352 (2004)

23. Rieke, F., Warland, D., de Ruyter van Steveninck, R., Bialek, W.: Spikes: Exploring the Neural Code. MIT Press, Cambridge (1999)
24. Rutishauser, U., Douglas, R.J.: State-dependent computation using coupled recurrent networks. Neural Comput. **21**, 478–509 (2009)
25. Isaacson, J.S.: Odor representations in mammalian cortical circuits. Curr. Opin. Neurobiol. **20**, 328–31 (2010)
26. Saada, R., Miller, N., Hurwitz, I., Susswein, A.J.: Autaptic excitation elicits persistent activity and a plateau potential in a neuron of known behavioral function. Curr. Biol. **19**, 479–84 (2009)
27. Seung, H.S., Lee, D.D., Reis, B.Y., Tank, D.W.: The autapse: a simple illustration of short-term analog memory storage by tuned synaptic feedback. J. Comput. Neurosci. **9**, 171–185 (2000)
28. Sipser, M.: Introduction to the Theory of Computation. International Thomson Publishing, Stamford (1996)
29. Stacey, W., Durand, D.: Stochastic resonance improves signal detection in hippocampal neurons. J. Neurophysiol. **83**, 1394–1402 (2000)
30. Steuber, V., De Schutter, E.: Rank order decoding of temporal parallel fibre input patterns in a complex Purkinje cell model. Neurocomputing **44–46**, 183–188 (2002)
31. Steuber, V., Willshaw, D.J.: Adaptive leaky integrator models of cerebellar Purkinje cells can learn the clustering of temporal patterns. Neurocomputing **26–27**, 271–276 (1999)
32. Steuber, V., Willshaw, D.: A biophysical model of synaptic delay learning and temporal pattern recognition in a cerebellar Purkinje cell. J. Comput. Neurosci. **17**, 149–164 (2004)
33. Steuber, V., Willshaw, D., Ooyen, A.V.: Generation of time delays: simplified models of intracellular signalling in cerebellar Purkinje cells. Netw. Comput. Neural Syst. **17**, 173–191 (2006)
34. Thorpe, S., Fize, D., Marlot, C.: Speed of processing in the human visual system. Nature **381**, 520–522 (1996)
35. Tino, P., Mills, A.J.S.: Learning beyond finite memory in recurrent networks of spiking neurons. Neural Comput. **18**, 591–613 (2005)
36. Wang, C., et al.: Formation of autapse connected to neuron and its biological function. Complexity **2017**, 1–9 (2017)
37. Wiesenfeld, K., Moss, F.: Stochastic resonance and the benefits of noise: from ice ages to crayfish and squids. Nature **373**, 33–36 (1995)
38. Yaqoob, M., Wróbel, B.: Robust very small spiking neural networks evolved with noise to recognize temporal patterns. In: ALIFE 2018: Proceedings of the 2018 Conference on Artificial Life - MIT Press, pp. 665–672 (2018)
39. Yaqoob, M., Wróbel, B.: Very small spiking neural networks evolved to recognize a pattern in a continuous input stream. In: 2017 IEEE Symposium Series on Computational Intelligence (SSCI) - IEEE, pp. 3496–3503 (2017)
40. Yaqoob, M., Wróbel, B.: Very small spiking neural networks evolved for temporal pattern recognition and robust to perturbed neuronal parameters. In: Artificial Neural Networks and Machine Learning - ICANN, pp. 322–331 (2018)

Theoretical Neural Computation

Estimating and Factoring the Dropout Induced Distribution with Gaussian Mixture Model

Jingo Adachi(✉)

DENSO IT Laboratory, Shibuya-ku, Tokyo, Japan
jingo_a@hotmail.com

Abstract. The analytical method to capture the dropout induced distribution of forwarding output in a neural network as Gaussian mixture model (GMM) was proposed. In dropout Bayesian DNN, if the network is dropout-trained and a test data is dropout-forwarded for inference, then its output, usually approximated as a single mode Gaussian, becomes a posterior whose variance tells uncertainty of its inference [1]. Here, the proposed method can capture the arbitrary distribution analytically with high accuracy without Monte Carlo (MC) method for any network equipped with dropout and fully connected (FC) layers. Therefore, it is applicable to the general non-Gaussian posterior case for a better uncertainty estimate. The proposed method also has the advantage to provide a multimodal analysis in distribution by factoring which can be tuned with a user defined expressibility parameter while a MC estimate provides only a "flat" image. This helps to understand how the FC layer tries to code a dropout injected highly multimodal data into a single mode Gaussian while the unknown data becomes a complicated distribution.

Keywords: Neural network · Bayesian DNN · Uncertainty

1 Introduction

The dropout, originally introduced to prevent overfitting [2], also performs variational inference implicitly at training and testing in Bayesian DNN [1]. After dropout trained with data D_{train}, the network at inference phase for test data x with dropout generates the output distribution y as a posterior $p(y|x, D_{train})$. If its variance is bigger, it tells its inference is more uncertain [1] as shown in Eq. (1).

$$p(y|x, D_{train}) = \int p(y|x,\omega)p(\omega|D_{train})d\omega \approx \int p(y|x,\omega)\cdot q_\theta(\omega)d\omega \approx \frac{1}{T_{MC}}\sum_{t=1}^{T_{MC}} p(y|x,\hat{\omega}_t) \tag{1}$$

Estimating the dropout induced distribution is done by Monte Carlo [1,3,4], running forward pass T_{MC} multiple times sampling $\hat{\omega}_t \sim q_\theta(\omega)$, and collecting outputs y to build a posterior distribution histogram. Since the posterior is usually approximated as a single mode Gaussian, it can be further improved with a multimode posterior and possibly performs better than the current evaluation [5], while the MC estimate doesn't

I. V. Tetko et al. (Eds.): ICANN 2019, LNCS 11727, pp. 775–792, 2019.
https://doi.org/10.1007/978-3-030-30487-4_60

tell directly underlying modes it might have. In the past, the analytical estimation of the dropout induced distribution was proposed using Central Limit Theorem (CLT) in [6] but only for a single mode Gaussian case without covariance, and it was never extended to the multimode Gaussian or non-Gaussian case. In view of such situation, this paper proposes for the first time an analytical method to capture the arbitrary dropout induced distribution with the multivariate GMM by factoring into individual Gaussians, which is called "Dropout Fully connected layer Distribution Estimate (DFDE)".

2 Methodology

The basic intuitive idea of DFDE capturing the distribution is as follows. In fully connected layer, each input vector element $x_{in\,j}$ gets multiplied by weight $W_{i,j}$ and the sum of these products $\sum_j^n W_{i,j} \cdot x_{in\,j}$ become the output vector element $x_{out\,i}$ as later shown in Eq. (2). As [6] suggested, the dropout turns on/off each product term $W_{i,j} \cdot x_{in\,j}$ independently, therefore their sum can be treated as a "sampling sum" from the population of $W_{i,j} \cdot x_{in\,j}$ terms with a sample size determined by a dropout rate, and the sum becomes Gaussian with CLT. But since it is not always the case, it is desirable to eliminate extremely deviated $W_{i,j} \cdot x_{in\,j}$ terms from others like too small or too big, which make an entire population distribution skewed causing CLT invalid due to a large ratio of third moment to cubed standard deviation in Berry-Esseen Theorem. We search these responsible deviated terms one by one and treat them as not random variables but constants by considering drop/undrop conditions for each of them so that we can apply CLT for the rest of $W_{i,j} \cdot x_{in\,j}$ population. Therefore output is a sum of drop/undrop probabilities multiplied by its conditional CLT distributions, which is a Gaussian mixture rather than a single Gaussian.

2.1 Dropout + Fully Connected (DF) Layer

Throughout this paper, Dropout and Fully connected layer is treated as a single layer notated as "*DF*" layer. First, the simplest layer notated as $DF1$ is explained where the input is a constant vector and the output is a dropout induced random variable vector, and then the more general layer notated as $DF2$ where both input and output is random variable vector is discussed.

2.2 DF1 Layer: Input Is Constant and Output Is Dropout Induced Random Variable

In $DF1$ layer, the parameters for a fully connected (FC) layer are defined with weight $W_{i,j}^{DF1}$ $(1 \leqq i \leqq {n_{\mathrm{out}}}^{DF1}, 1 \leqq j \leqq {n_{\mathrm{in}}}^{DF1})$ and bias b_i^{DF1} $(1 \leqq i \leqq {n_{out}}^{DF1})$, and the dropout layer with dropout rate $p_{dropout}^{DF1}$ and random variable $z_j \sim Bernoulli(p_{dropout}^{DF1})$. The i-th component of output ${x_{\mathrm{out}}^{DF1}}_i$ is described as a sum of ${n_{\mathrm{in}}}^{DF1}$ "Wx" terms multiplied by z_j plus bias b_i^{DF1} as shown below.

$$\begin{aligned} {x_{out}^{DF1}}_i = W_{i,1}^{DF1} \cdot {x_{\mathrm{in}}^{DF1}}_1 \cdot z_1 + \ldots + W_{i,j}^{DF1} \cdot {x_{\mathrm{in}}^{DF1}}_j \cdot z_j + \ldots \\ + W_{i,n_{\mathrm{in}}^{DF1}}^{DF1} \cdot {x_{\mathrm{in}}^{DF1}}_{n_{\mathrm{in}}^{DF1}} \cdot z_{n_{\mathrm{in}}^{DF1}} + b_i^{DF1} \quad (1 \leqq j \leqq {n_{\mathrm{in}}}^{DF1}) \end{aligned} \tag{2}$$

In Eq. (2), calculating the all possible outcomes of ${x_{out}}^{DF1}{}_{i}$ is difficult because each of "Wx" term is multiplied by drop/undrop independent Bernoulli random variable z_j , in other words ${n_{in}}^{DF1}$ Bernoulli bimodes, generating $2^{{n_{in}}^{DF1}}$ possible outcomes. But the paper [6] suggested that by using CLT, the distribution of output ${x_{out}}^{DF1}{}_{i}$ can be approximated as Gaussian whose mean and variance can be determined by variance of "Wx"s, bias, and dropout rate. This can be interpreted as "Sampling distribution of sampling sum", where the only portion of values from a total population is randomly sampled and its sum is recorded. This procedure is repeated picking up different sample sets and calculate sums. After all the histogram of recorded sums becomes a Gaussian distribution. Here as Fig. 1(a) shows, a dropout does sampling "Wx" terms with a fixed "undropped" sample size $\overline{M} = {n_{in}}^{DF1}(1 - p^{DF1}_{dropout})$ without replacement, and its sum is output ${x_{out}}^{DF1}{}_{i}$ in Eq. (2) whose distribution becomes Gaussian [7]. Since the work in [6] is limited to mean and variance, the method needs to extend to the multivariate Gaussian with mean ${\mu_{out}}^{DF1}$ and variance covariance ${\Sigma_{out}}^{DF1}$ as a DF layer output ${X_{out}}^{DF1}$ defined below.

$$ {X_{out}}^{DF1} \sim \mathcal{N}({\mu_{out}}^{DF1}, {\Sigma_{out}}^{DF1}(\mathrm{Var_{out}}, \mathrm{Cov_{out}})) $$

The i-th mean ($1 \leqq i \leqq {n_{out}}^{DF1}$) can be calculated as

$$ {\mu_{out}}^{DF1}{}_{i} = E\left[{x_{out}}^{DF1}{}_{i}\right] = (1 - p^{DF1}_{dropout}) \sum_{j=1}^{{n_{in}}^{DF1}} (W_{i,j} \cdot {x_{in}}^{DF1}{}_{j}) + b_i \tag{3} $$

The i-th variance can be calculated as

$$ \mathrm{Var_{out}}^{DF1}{}_{i} = \frac{\overline{M}\left({n_{in}}^{DF1} - \overline{M}\right)}{{n_{in}}^{DF1} - 1} Var(\mathrm{List}W{x_{in}}^{DF1}{}_{i}) \tag{4} $$

where $Var(\mathrm{List}W{x_{in}}^{DF1}{}_{i})$ in Eq. (4) is defined as the variance of $\mathrm{List}W{x_{in}}^{DF1}{}_{i}$, which is a list of "$W_{i,j}x_j$" inner product terms ($1 \leqq j \leqq {n_{in}}^{DF1}$) in Eq. (2) without z_j as below.

$$ \mathrm{List}W{x_{in}}^{DF1}{}_{i} = \left\{W_{i,1} \cdot {x_{in}}^{DF1}{}_{1}, \ldots, W_{i,j} \cdot {x_{in}}^{DF1}{}_{j}, \ldots, W_{i,{n_{in}}^{DF1}} \cdot {x_{in}}^{DF1}{}_{{n_{in}}^{DF1}}\right\} \tag{5} $$

The $i1$-th and $i2$-th covariance for output ${x_{out}}^{DF1}{}_{i1}$ and ${x_{out}}^{DF1}{}_{i2}$, ($1 \leqq i1, i2 \leqq {n_{out}}^{DF1}, i1 \neq i2$) needs to be calculated as below because there is a correlation between them due to the fact that dropout is done j-th "Wx" columnwise over i, generating a dependency between i-th and other row outputs.

$$ \mathrm{Cov}_{\mathrm{out}\,i1,i2,i1\neq i2}{}^{DF1} = \frac{\overline{M}\left({n_{in}}^{DF1} - \overline{M}\right)}{2\left({n_{in}}^{DF1} - 1\right)} \cdot (Var(\mathrm{List}W{x_{in}}^{DF1}{}_{i1} + \mathrm{List}W{x_{in}}^{DF1}{}_{i2}) - Var\left(\mathrm{List}W{x_{in}}^{DF1}{}_{i1}\right) - Var(\mathrm{List}W{x_{in}}^{DF1}{}_{i2})) \tag{6} $$

In this paper, the constant term $\frac{1}{1-p^{DF1}_{dropout}}$ filling a missing portion due to the dropout is omitted.

2.3 Gaussian Mixture Model(GMM) Case: Factoring

This section explains how to further extend the Gaussian case to the general non-Gaussian case as shown in Fig. 1(b). When one of Wx terms in Eq. (2) has an extremely deviated (big or small) value from the rest of Wx terms, we call it "extreme value" with its index $j = je$. Then the sum can change drastically depending on the extreme value dropped/undropped. In other words, the population distribution is skewed and sampling needs a bigger sample size for CLT, but since it is fixed by a dropout rate, CLT fails. But if we consider the condition when the extreme value is dropped/undropped, we can treat it under each condition as not a random variable but a constant, and can apply CLT safely for the rest of population with moderate Wx terms. It means, if we consider N_{ex} extreme values, Wx_{je_k}, $(k = 1...N_{ex})$, each of which has drop/undrop cases, we need to consider $Mix^{DF} = 2^{N_{ex}}$ component Gaussian mixture. Therefore the number of extreme value, N_{ex} is "expressibility" for DFDE distribution estimation to factor into multiple Gaussians. The more extreme terms we consider, the more accurate the estimation gets relying on CLT approximation less but requiring more computation. Generally, during optimization, the values of Wx terms are well regularized not to be extreme. However in the case the input data has an unlearned feature, more extreme values are needed to capture a dropout induced output distribution as shown in Fig. 6 in a later experiment.

As stated before, the dropout is done by not i-th and j-th $W_{i,j}x_j$ termwise in Eq. (2) but j-th W_jx_j columnwise over all i-th output $(1 \leqq i \leqq n_{\text{in}}{}^{DF1})$. Because of this, not the extreme "scalar" value $W_{i,j}x_j$ but the extreme column "vector" W_jx_j with most extreme terms $W_{i,j}x_j$ in it needs to be found. A simple Algorithm 1 is used, which automatically selects N_{ex} most extreme columns which give the biggest impact to the output when dropped/undropped, where N_{ex} is defined by user for the computation cost.

For the convenience, only a single extreme column case $N_{ex} = 1$ is considered where the extreme column index is defined as $j = je_{k=1}(1 \leqq k \leqq N_{ex})$ and its column is notated as $W_{i,j=je_{k=1}} \cdot x_{\text{in}}{}^{DF1}{}_{j=je_{k=1}}$. A single extreme column has two conditions, one for drop and the other for undrop generating $Mix^{DF1} = 2$ component GMM. Under both drop and undrop cases the extreme column can be removed out of a Wx list as random variables, and in case for drop the extreme column is gone for good, while in case for undropped extreme column is treated as a constant just like a bias term. The CLT is applied to the rest of Wx terms as a single mode Gaussian.

The i-th mean $\mu_{\text{out}}{}^{DF1}{}_i$ under the condition $(m = 1)$ for extreme column dropped $(z_{je_{k=1}} = 0)$ and the condition $(m = 2)$ for extreme column undropped $(z_{je_{k=1}} = 1)$ are shown below respectively.

$$\left(\mu_{\text{out}}{}^{DF1}{}_i{}^{(m=1)} \,\middle|\, z_{je_{k=1}} = 0\right) = (1 - p^{DF1}_{dropout}) \sum_{j=1, j \neq je_{k=1}}^{n_{\text{in}}{}^{DF1}} (W_{i,j} \cdot x_{\text{in}}{}^{DF1}{}_j{}^{(1)}) + b_i \tag{7}$$

$$\begin{aligned} &\left(\mu_{\text{out}}{}^{DF1}{}_i{}^{(m=2)} \,\middle|\, z_{je_{k=1}} = 1\right) \\ &= (1 - p^{DF1}_{dropout}) \sum_{j=1, j \neq je_{k=1}}^{n_{\text{in}}{}^{DF1}} (W_{i,j} \cdot x_{\text{in}}{}^{DF1}{}_j{}^{(1)}) + W_{i,je_{k=1}} \cdot x_{\text{in}}{}^{DF1}{}_{je_{k=1}}{}^{(1)} + b_i \end{aligned} \tag{8}$$

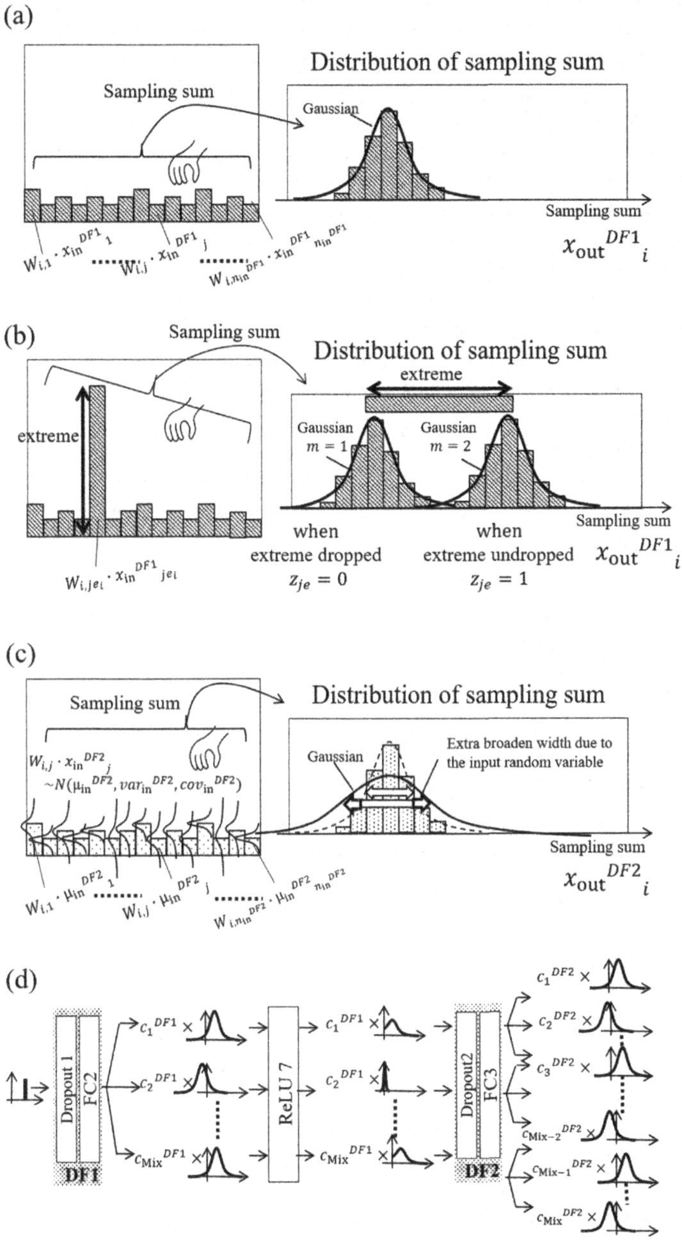

Fig. 1. Extension of sampling sum theory. (a) Sampling sum becomes a single Gaussian. (b) If the extreme values exist, a sampling sum splits into a mixture of conditional Gaussians. (c) If the input is not constant but a Gaussian random variable, the sampling sum becomes broaden by var and cov terms because of the input's extra randomness. (d) It shows how the data gets split into a mixture of Gaussians as going through multiple DF layers over the network.

Algorithm 1. Given a number of extreme columns (expressibility) N_{ex} ($N_{ex} \leqq n_{in}$) by user, this algorithm automatically determines which N_{ex} columns are most likely to give a significant change to output when dropped/undropped.

Input: weight W, input x, the number of extreme columns(expressibility) N_{ex}
Output: a list of N_{ex} indices of extreme columns

Initialize score boxes S_j for all j-th column ($1 \leqq j \leqq n_{in}$) with zero. The score means how much a column is deviated from other columns. We will accumulate scores in following loop and find out which N_{ex} columns have the biggest scores(deviation).

```
S_j=0 (1 ≦ j ≦ n_in)
LOOP each of i-th row and j-th column
for i = 1 to n_out do
    Get a list of Wx terms on i-th row.
    Calculate a mean of W_{i,j}x_j terms on i-th row and define as mean_i
    Then calculate how much each of j-th column has a deviated W_{i,j}x_j term in it from its
    corresponding i-th rows.
    for j = 1 to n_in do
        Calculate the difference between j-th W_{i,j}x_j and mean_i and define as |mean_i − W_{i,j}x_j|.
        Add the difference to score box S_j for j-th column to accumulate difference.
        S_j = S_j + |mean_i − W_{i,j}x_j|
    end for
end for
Sort score boxes S_j (1 ≦ j ≦ n_in) in descending order and choose top N_ex boxes.
return an index list of N_ex boxes
```

The conditional i-th variance and $i1$-th and $i2$-th covariance can be also calculated the same as before in Eqs. (4) and (6) except some modifications such as ${n_{\text{in}}}^{DF1} \rightarrow {n_{\text{in}}}^{DF1} - 1$, $\overline{M} \rightarrow \overline{M} = ({n_{\text{in}}}^{DF1} - 1)(1 - p^{DF1}_{dropout})$, and $\text{List}W{x_{\text{in}}}^{DF1}{}_{i}{}^{(m)} \rightarrow \text{List}W{x_{\text{in}}}^{DF1}{}_{i\ j \neq je_{k=1}}^{(m)}$ needed. It turns out that variance and covariance for two conditions are the same shown below.

$$\left({\text{Var}_{\text{out}}}^{DF1}{}_{i}{}^{(m=1)} \,\middle|\, z_{je_{k=1}} = 0\right) = \left({\text{Var}_{\text{out}}}^{DF1}{}_{i}{}^{(m=2)} \,\middle|\, z_{je_{k=1}} = 1\right) \tag{9}$$

$$\left({\text{Cov}_{\text{out}}}^{DF1}{}_{i1,i2}{}^{(m=1)} \,\middle|\, z_{je_{k=1}} = 0\right) = \left({\text{Cov}_{\text{out}}}^{DF1}{}_{i1,i2}{}^{(m=2)} \,\middle|\, z_{je_{k=1}} = 1\right) \tag{10}$$

Over all, each of two conditional output Gaussians is multiplied by its drop/undrop probability, and summed together as a two component mixture of Gaussian as below.

$$\begin{aligned}
{x_{\text{out}}}^{DF1}{}_{i} &\sim GMM \\
&= p\left(z_{je_{k=1}} = 0\right) \cdot \mathcal{N}\left({\mu_{\text{out}}}^{DF1}{}_{i}{}^{(m=1)}, {\text{Var}_{\text{out}}}^{DF1}{}_{i}{}^{(m=1)}, {\text{Cov}_{\text{out}}}^{DF1}{}_{i1,i2}{}^{(m=1)} \,\middle|\, z_{je_{k=1}} = 0\right) \\
&+ p\left(z_{je_{k=1}} = 1\right) \cdot \mathcal{N}\left({\mu_{\text{out}}}^{DF1}{}_{i}{}^{(m=2)}, {\text{Var}_{\text{out}}}^{DF1}{}_{i}{}^{(m=2)}, {\text{Cov}_{\text{out}}}^{DF1}{}_{i1,i2}{}^{(m=2)} \,\middle|\, z_{je_{k=1}} = 1\right) \\
&= {p_{\text{dropout}}}^{DF1} \cdot \mathcal{N}(m = 1) + \left(1 - {p_{\text{dropout}}}^{DF1}\right) \cdot \mathcal{N}(m = 2)
\end{aligned} \tag{11}$$

2.4 DF2 Layer: Both Input and Output Is Random Variable

This section explains the most general case where the input is also Gaussian mixture random variable. If there are Num_{DF} DF layers considering N^{DF}_{ex} extreme values over the network, each DF layer splits its input into $2^{N_{ex}^{DF}}$ Gaussians, which ends up with $Num_{DF} \cdot 2^{N_{ex}^{DF}}$ component GMM as shown in Fig. 1(d). For the second DF layer notated as "$DF2$", the input ${X_{\text{in}}}^{DF2}$ is no longer constant but Gaussian random variable generated from the previous $DF1$ layer whose parameters are assumed to be estimated by DFDE as $DF1$ layer case. Therefore as shown in Fig. 1(c), "sampling sum" theory needs to expand to "sampling Gaussian random variable sum", where each "Wx" term is Gaussian random variable multiplied by $z_j \sim Bernoulli(p^{DF2}_{dropout})$ due to the 2nd dropout layer.

The input ${X_{\text{in}}}^{DF2}$ and the output ${X_{\text{out}}}^{DF2}$ of $DF2$ layer are described as below.

$${X_{\text{in}}}^{DF2} \sim \mathcal{N}({\mu_{\text{in}}}^{DF2}, {\Sigma_{\text{in}}}^{DF2}\ ({\text{Var}_{\text{in}}}^{DF2}, {\text{Cov}_{\text{in}}}^{DF2}))$$

$${X_{\text{out}}}^{DF2} \sim \mathcal{N}({\mu_{\text{out}}}^{DF2}, {\Sigma_{\text{out}}}^{DF2}\ ({\text{Var}_{\text{out}}}^{DF2}, {\text{Cov}_{\text{out}}}^{DF2}))$$

Assuming that the input Gaussian parameters are known, we derive parameters of output Gaussian as follows.

The mean ${\mu_{\text{out}}}^{DF2}$ can be calculated with the almost same way as $DF1$ layer case in Eq. (3) except some modifications such as replacing a constant input with a mean of random variable input, ${X_{\text{in}}}^{DF2} \rightarrow {\mu_{\text{in}}}^{DF2}$, and changing a sample size $\overline{M} = {n_{\text{in}}}^{DF2}(1 - p^{DF2}_{dropout})$ for $DF2$ layer.
The i-th mean becomes as below.

$${\mu_{\text{out}}}^{DF2}{}_i = (1 - p^{DF2}_{dropout}) \sum_{j=1}^{{n_{\text{in}}}^{DF2}} (W_{i,j} \cdot {\mu_{\text{in}}}^{DF2}{}_j) + b_i \tag{12}$$

The i-th variance can be calculated as below. (The derivation is explained in Appendix 5.1.)

$$\begin{aligned} {\text{Var}_{\text{out}i}}^{DF2} &= \frac{\overline{M}\left({n_{\text{in}}}^{DF2} - \overline{M}\right)}{({n_{\text{in}}}^{DF2} - 1)} \cdot Var(\text{List}W{\mu_{\text{in}}}^{DF2}{}_i) \\ &+ \frac{\overline{M}}{{n_{\text{in}}}^{DF2}} \sum_{jj=1}^{{n_{\text{out}}}^{DF2}} \text{Var}W{x_{\text{in}}}^{DF2}{}_{jj} + \frac{2\overline{M}}{{n_{\text{in}}}^{DF2}} \frac{(\overline{M} - 1)}{({n_{\text{in}}}^{DF2} - 1)} \sum_{jj1<jj2}^{{n_{\text{out}}}^{DF2}} \text{Cov}W{x_{\text{in}\,jj1,jj2}}^{DF2} \end{aligned} \tag{13}$$

where $\text{List}W{\mu_{\text{in}}}^{DF2}{}_i$ is the same as $\text{List}W{x_{\text{in}}}^{DF2}{}_i$ in Eq. (5) except ${X_{\text{in}}}^{DF2} \rightarrow {\mu_{\text{in}}}^{DF2}$ and other two notations were defined as below.

$$\text{Var}W{x_{\text{in}}}^{DF2}{}_{jj} = W_{i,jj} \cdot W_{i,jj} \cdot {\text{Var}_{\text{in}\,jj}}^{DF2} \tag{14}$$

$$\text{Cov}W{x_{\text{in}\,jj1,jj2}}^{DF2} = W_{i,jj1} \cdot W_{i,jj2} \cdot {\text{Cov}_{\text{in}\,jj1,jj2}}^{DF2} \tag{15}$$

Interestingly, the variance ${\text{Var}_{\text{out}i}}^{DF2}$ in Eq. (13) can be interpreted as a broaden version of Eq. (4) by extra two terms, $\Sigma\text{Var}Wx$ and $\Sigma\text{Cov}Wx$, which is due to the fact that input ${x_{\text{in}}}^{DF2}$ is now random variable adding a secondary independent source of stochasticity. The $i1$-th and $i2$-th ($i1 \neq i2$) covariance can be calculated as follows.

$$\mathrm{Cov}_{\mathrm{out}\,i1,i2}{}^{DF2} = \frac{Var\left(x_{\mathrm{out}\,i1}{}^{DF2} + x_{\mathrm{out}\,i2}{}^{DF2}\right)}{2} - \frac{Var\left(x_{\mathrm{out}\,i1}{}^{DF2}\right)}{2} - \frac{Var\left(x_{\mathrm{out}\,i2}{}^{DF2}\right)}{2} \quad (16)$$

The last two terms, $Var\left(x_{\mathrm{out}\,i1}{}^{DF2}\right)$ and $Var\left(x_{\mathrm{out}\,i2}{}^{DF2}\right)$ can be calculated by (13), and first term $Var\left(x_{\mathrm{out}\,i1}{}^{DF2\,(m)} + x_{\mathrm{out}\,i2}{}^{DF2\,(m)}\right)$ can also be calculated as follows.

$$Var\left(x_{\mathrm{out}\,i1}{}^{DF2\,(m)} + x_{\mathrm{out}\,i2}{}^{DF2\,(m)}\right) = \frac{\overline{M}\left(n_{\mathrm{in}}{}^{DF2} - \overline{M}\right)}{\left(n_{\mathrm{in}}{}^{DF2} - 1\right)} \cdot Var(\mathrm{List}Wx_{\mathrm{in}}\,(i1 + i2)^{DF2}{}_{i1,i2}{}^{(m)})$$

$$+ \frac{\overline{M}}{n_{\mathrm{in}}{}^{DF2}} \sum_{jj=1}^{n_{\mathrm{in}}{}^{DF2}} \mathrm{Var}_{Wx_{\mathrm{in}\,i1,jj}+Wx_{\mathrm{in}\,i2,jj}}{}^{(m)} + \frac{2\overline{M}}{n_{\mathrm{in}}{}^{DF2}} \frac{\left(\overline{M} - 1\right)}{\left(n_{\mathrm{in}}{}^{DF2} - 1\right)} \cdot \sum_{jj1<jj2}^{n_{\mathrm{in}}{}^{DF2}} \mathrm{Cov}_{Wx_{\mathrm{in}\,i1,jj1,jj2}+Wx_{\mathrm{in}\,i2,jj1,jj2}}{}^{(m)} \quad (17)$$

where three notations are defined as below.

$$\begin{aligned}\mathrm{List}Wx_{\mathrm{in}}\,(i1 + i2)^{DF2}{}_{i1,i2}{}^{(m)} = &\Big\{(W_{i1,1} \cdot x_{\mathrm{in}}{}^{DF2}{}_{1}{}^{(m)} + W_{i2,1} \cdot x_{\mathrm{in}}{}^{DF2}{}_{1}{}^{(m)}), \ldots, \\ &\left(W_{i1,j} \cdot x_{\mathrm{in}}{}^{DF2}{}_{j}{}^{(m)} + W_{i2,j} \cdot x_{\mathrm{in}}{}^{DF2}{}_{j}{}^{(m)}\right), \ldots, \\ &(W_{i1,n_{\mathrm{in}}{}^{DF2}} \cdot x_{\mathrm{in}}{}^{DF2}{}_{n_{\mathrm{in}}{}^{DF2}}{}^{(m)} + W_{i2,n_{\mathrm{in}}{}^{DF2}} \cdot x_{\mathrm{in}}{}^{DF2}{}_{n_{\mathrm{in}}{}^{DF2}}{}^{(m)})\Big\} \\ &\left(1 \leqq j \leqq n_{\mathrm{in}}{}^{DF2}\right) \quad (18)\end{aligned}$$

$$\mathrm{Var}_{Wx_{\mathrm{in}\,i1,jj}+Wx_{\mathrm{in}\,i2,jj}}{}^{(m)} = (W_{i1,jj} + W_{i2,jj})^2 \cdot \mathrm{Var}_{\mathrm{in}\,jj}{}^{DF2\,(m)} \quad (19)$$

$$\mathrm{Cov}_{Wx_{\mathrm{in}\,i1,jj1,jj2}+Wx_{\mathrm{in}\,i2,jj1,jj2}}{}^{(m)} = (W_{i1,jj1} + W_{i2,jj1}) \cdot (W_{i1,jj2} + W_{i2,jj2}) \cdot \mathrm{Cov}_{\mathrm{in}\,jj1,jj2}{}^{DF2\,(m)} \quad (20)$$

2.5 ReLU Layer

Rectified Linear Unit (ReLU) layer as nonlinear was considered, whose operation is a max function $f(\mathrm{x}) = \max(x, 0)$. With a Gaussian input, the output becomes a rectified Gaussian distribution [8] $h\left(x; \mu, \sigma^2\right) = \Phi\left(-\frac{\mu}{\sigma}\right)\delta(x) + \frac{1}{\sqrt{2\pi\sigma^2}} e^{-\frac{(x-\mu)^2}{2\sigma^2}} U(x)$, featured by two terms, delta function and truncated Gaussian function [9]. $\Phi(x)$ is a cumulative distribution. This was approximated as a single multivariate Gaussian function as shown in experiment in Fig. 3(e). The detail is explained in Appendix 5.2.

3 Experiment

In following two experiments, MC estimates were calculated as a ground truth and plotted with a massive 100000 forward pass 2D dot cloud/1D histogram while analytical DFDE estimate is plotted as 2D contour/1D curve to see how they match visually as shown in Figs. 3, 5, 6, and 8. The DFDE uses 16 component GMM to estimate distribution.

3.1 Discriminator: AlexNet

In the first experiment, AlexNet [10] was used. More precisely, the only last two dropout layer portion for a stochastic propagation as shown in Fig. 2 which has $DF1$ layer (Dropout+FC2) - ReLU7 - $DF2$ layer (Dropout+FC3) - Softmax. Data from ImageNet [11] and the trained weight and bias parameters from [12] were used. For the last dropout portion of network, DFDE calculates analytically how a distribution propagates through layers and estimates FC3 output(right before softmax). The 100000 trial MC conventional forward pass was also calculated as a ground truth distribution. Then DFDE estimated GMM was evaluated with MC point cloud for DFDE accuracy by calculating log likelihood for a fitting error and BIC. For the comparison, the error and BIC of "EM direct fit" GMM to a MC distribution were also calculated where GMM is estimated by EM algorithm fitting to a MC final output distribution itself directly with the same number of mixture components used for DFDE but without any estimation of distribution propagation . This tells us how accurate DFDE propagation estimate is relative to direct EM fit under the same GMM condition.

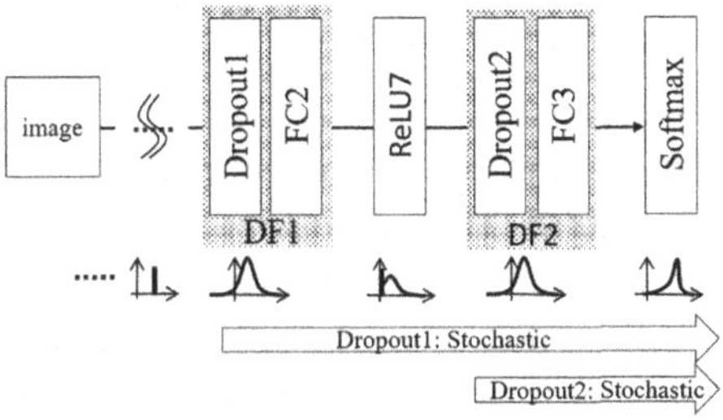

Fig. 2. Last layers of AlexNet with two DF layers.

The experiment result is shown in Fig. 3 and its corresponding BIC and average log likelihood per data as a fit score is shown in Table 1. AlexNet classifies 1000 categories, therefore the dropout induced output distribution is 1000 correlated dimensional GMM. The pairwise 2D distribution was plotted, which turns out almost a single mode Gaussian with 16 components GMM overlapped each other. When the input image is a cat in Fig. 3(a), it was observed the cat like classes positively correlated in Fig. 3(b) while dog and cat classes negatively correlated in Fig. 3(c). There is a slight discrepancy in DFDE to MC shown by black arrow in Fig. 3(b) and (c) due to the single Gaussian approximation at ReLU output in Fig. 3(e). Therefore, DFDE was also run to estimate FC3 with ReLU7 layer removed so that purely DFDE performance can be evaluated. Its result is shown in Fig. 3(f) and Table 1 bottom table with values close to the EM direct fit proving that DFDE alone works very accurately.

Table 2 shows how many mixture components are needed for fitting accuracy. For DFDE, the different combinations of components are evaluated since AlexNet has two DF layers as $DF1$ and $DF2$. For DFDE the $8 = 4 \times 2$ component GMM is the best and for EM the 8 component is the best with the smallest BIC. Both reach a saturation with a good fit since the distribution is close to a simple Gaussian, which is not the case for unlearned image as shown next.

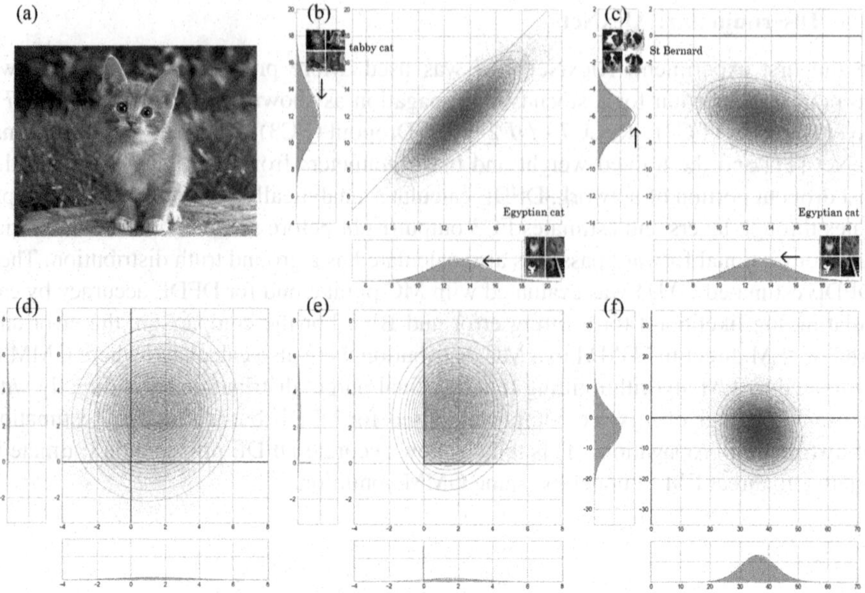

Fig. 3. Plots show how DFDE (2D contour/1D curve) captures the Monte Carlo (2D point cloud/1D histogram) distribution. The black arrow shows a discrepancy due to the single Gaussian approximation in ReLU shown in (e). (a) Input Image, (b)(c) FC3 2D output among pairwise classes, (d) Before ReLU7, (e) After ReLU7 approximating a rectified Gaussian as a single Gaussian. (f) FC3 with ReLU7 removed from a network showing no obvious discrepancy.

Table 1. 16 component GMM estimator comparison EM direct fit vs DFDE ($Mix^{DF1_{out}} = 4$) × ($Mix^{DF2_{out}} = 4$) = 16

	FC3 in Fig. 3(b)		FC3 in Fig. 3(c)		FC3 without ReLU in Fig. 3(f)	
Method	EM	DFDE	EM	DFDE	EM	DFDE
BIC	739515	744125	770901	772458	1292658	1291861
Log likelihood	−3.69210	−3.71516	−3.84903	−3.85682	−6.45782	−6.45383

Table 2. Fitting in Fig. 3(b) with a different number of mixture component $Mix^{DF} = 16, 8, 4$ In DFDE case, the total number of components is the multiplication of ones from $DF1$ and $DF2$ layers as $Mix^{DF1_{out}} \times Mix^{DF2_{out}} = Mix^{DF}$

Method Mix^{DF}	EM 16	DFDE 4×4	EM 8	DFDE $4 \times 2 = 8$	DFDE $2 \times 4 = 8$	EM 4	DFDE $2 \times 2 = 4$
BIC	739515	744125	738269	738959	739905	738691	739876
Log likelihood	-3.69210	-3.71516	-3.68864	-3.69209	-3.69682	-3.69213	-3.69805

3.2 Generative Model: Dropout + Standard Autoencoder

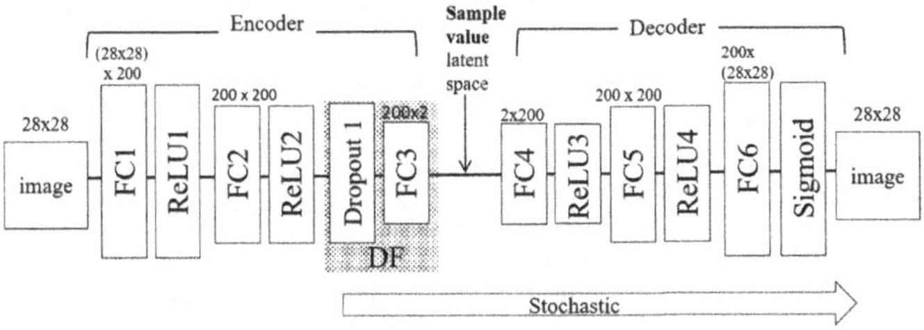

Fig. 4. Standard autoencoder with a dropout

The method DFDE can be used for any network with DF layer. In next experiment a standard autoencoder was built shown in Fig. 4, with in/out x at front and end, 2D latent variable z in the middle and network weight parameter θ. A single DF layer with dropout rate 0.6 for train/test was implemented in encoder so that its output z becomes a random variable drawn from unknown distribution $q_\theta(z|x)$, which can be estimated by DFDE. FC3 layer has no nonlinear layer so that DFDE can estimate the latent distribution precisely. Before training, z is a variable from a dropout induced "meaningless" distribution $q_{\theta_{initial}}(z|x)$ determined by initial parameter $\theta_{initial}$. But throughout training, z is sampled as $z \sim q_\theta(z|x)$, then at decoder it is used to optimize for the reconstruction condition $x_{in} = x_{out}$, updating $\theta_{initial} \rightarrow \theta_{optimized}$, which leads to a "meaningful" distribution $q_{\theta_{optimized}}(z|x)$, which a new z is sampled from. The training was done with MNIST [13] alone by minimizing the output reconstruction log likelihood error. The both MNIST as "known" and NotMNIST [14] as "unknown" were tested to see the distribution trend in latent space for the inference uncertainty measure.

Figure 5(a), (b), (c) and (d) shows that DFDE was able to capture a latent distribution $q_\theta(z|x)$ with $16 \sim 64$ component GMM matching the ground truth MC cloud. Interestingly, MNIST(red) latent distribution becomes a single Gaussian with mixture components overlapped each other in Fig. 5(a) and (b), while NotMNIST(blue) in Fig. 5(c) and (d) becomes non-Gaussian distribution and DFDE needed a bigger number of Gaussian components to express a complex distribution. The conceptual drawing in Fig. 5(e) shows the empirical geometrical "trend" in latent distribution for known and unknown input. It was observed in MNIST, 16 Gaussian components form a single Gaussian as a single factor with its major axis facing origin, while in NotMNIST the components get scattered not facing origin.

To quantify this trend, a provisional method was used to separate the known from the unknown by computing the average component angle α between a direction from a center of DFDE estimated Gaussian to the origin and a direction of Gaussian major axis as defined in inset in Fig. 5(f). The angle α for each GMM is a measure of how much Gaussians facing the origin along with its major axis, and overlapped with other Gaussians. The smaller the angle is, the more overlapping and facing the origin they are as a single factor. A histogram of these angles is plotted for 500 MNIST and 500

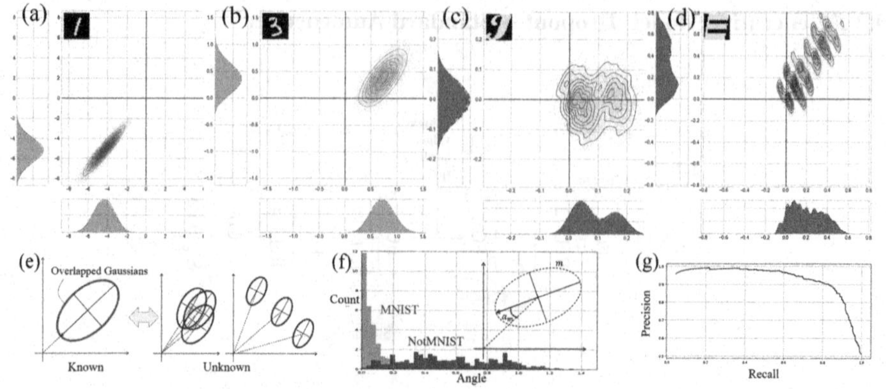

Fig. 5. (a)(b)The latent distribution for MNIST(known), (c)(d)The latent distribution for NotMNIST(unknown). (e)The typical $q_\theta(z|x)$ trend for known and unknown input. (f) Histogram shows a separation of MNIST from NotMNIST by the angle α defined as in inset.(g)Precision vs Recall curve for (f) (color figure online).

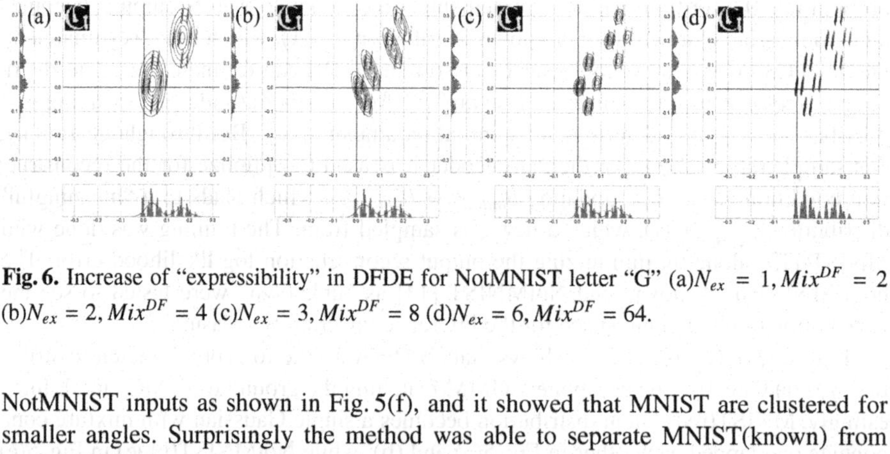

Fig. 6. Increase of "expressibility" in DFDE for NotMNIST letter "G" (a)$N_{ex} = 1, Mix^{DF} = 2$ (b)$N_{ex} = 2, Mix^{DF} = 4$ (c)$N_{ex} = 3, Mix^{DF} = 8$ (d)$N_{ex} = 6, Mix^{DF} = 64$.

NotMNIST inputs as shown in Fig. 5(f), and it showed that MNIST are clustered for smaller angles. Surprisingly the method was able to separate MNIST(known) from NotMNIST(unknown) with a good precision vs recall curve as in Fig. 5(g) only by a Gaussian angular geometry of a latent dropout induced distribution without decoder reconstructing images as in [4], which is impossible with a single Gaussian assumption or unfactored MC estimate. This trend of bundling a known data into a single Gaussian and a rare unknown data being a complicated mixture of Gaussians can be seen to have a similarity to Shannon–Fano coding where the frequently used data can be coded in a simple form while the rare data is coded into a long complicated form in compression.

Figures 6 and 7 shows the number of "extreme" values, N_{ex}, needed to express non-Gaussian distribution. The BIC and error values reached a saturation around 128 component mixture for both DFDE and EM direct fit in Fig. 7, and a baseline as [6] would be a single Gaussian approximation as $Mix^{DF} = 1$ in Fig. 7 if covariance had been given.

Lastly 1000 MNIST dropout induced distributions in latent space such as single Gaussian looking red ones in Fig. 5(a) and (b) were calculated and superimposed as

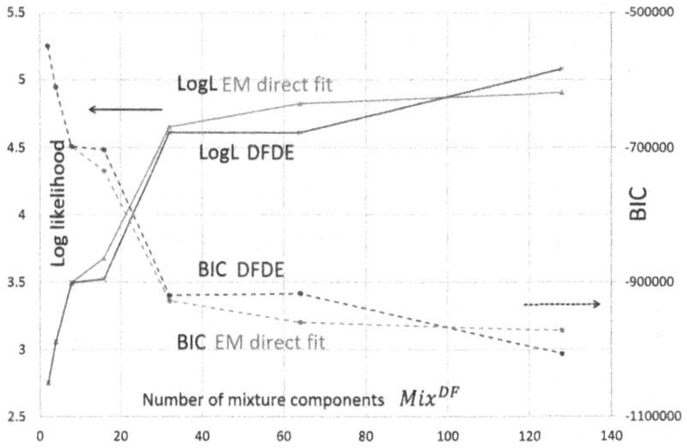

Fig. 7. BIC/Log likelihood vs Number of mixture component Mix^{DF} for latent space distributions

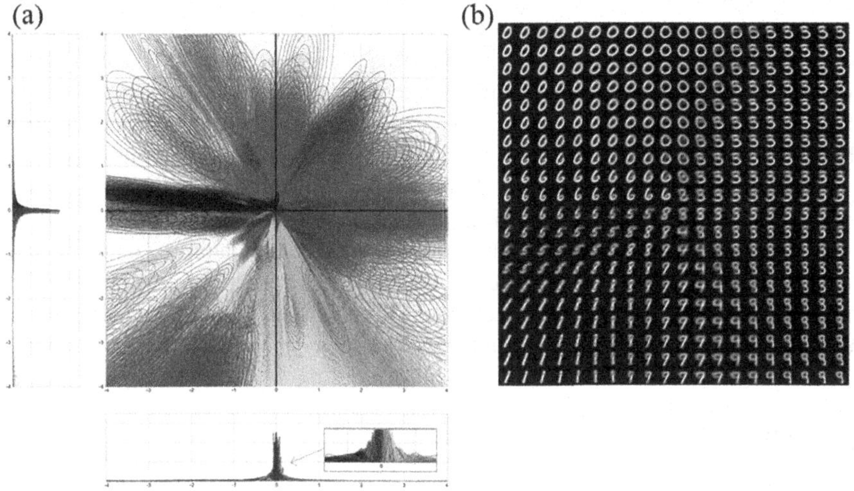

Fig. 8. (a) The superposition of DFDE latent dropout induced distributions $q_\theta(z|x)$ of MNIST colored by digit. (b) The reconstructed image from latent space.

shown in Fig. 8(a). From latent space, the latent variables were sampled with an equal spacing and decoded as reconstructed images as shown in Fig. 5(b). Note that Fig. 8(a) is not the just clustered "points" often seen in latent space in autoencoder as in [15] but the clustered dropout induced "distributions" $q_\theta(z|x)$ with each single Gaussian looking distribution composed of 16 component GMM. Remarkably, each distribution is positioned with its major axis facing the origin and well separated depending on its digit label indicating the reconstruction condition $\mathbb{E}_{z \sim q_{\theta(z|x)}}[\log p_\theta(x|z)]$, while as the two side view plots Fig. 8(a) show Gaussians near the origin tend to be sharp and those away from the origin get flat, forming the overall asymptotical distribution showing the regularization $D_{KL}\left(q_\theta(z|x) \parallel p_\theta(z)\right)$ following variational inference.

As an extension of this paper, the latent distribution $q_\theta(z|x)$ can be further regularized during optimization since we know what $q_\theta(z|x)$ looks like as GMM with DFDE during back propagation. Namely the KL distance between any desired GMM distribution as a prior and a DFDE estimated GMM latent distribution can be formulated with [16]. By taking the derivative of it with respect to weight, it can be plugged into a cost function. Without DFDE, MC estimates for optimization like that during back propagation would be difficult running many trials every training iteration.

4 Conclusion

The analytical method to estimate the dropout induced distribution as GMM forwarding through DNN was proposed and evaluated its performance to be highly accurate. The method shows how the output distribution of a dropout injected FC layer, which can be highly multimodal with multiple Bernoulli bimodes, becomes a single mode Gaussian through learning while the unknown data with the unlearned feature can be a complicated distribution requiring a more computation for the accurate estimate. Therefore the proposed algorithm has a flexibility with a user defined parameter, "expressibility", which tunes its estimation for a wide range of accuracy and mode analysis by factoring, while the conventional MC estimate provides only a "flat image" without factoring. In autoencoder, the method shows how dropout induced latent distributions follow variational inference condition and a possibility of a new uncertainty measure at latent space level. Since in dropout Bayesian DNN the distribution can be interpreted as a posterior, the method can help to improve Bayesian DNN algorithm from a single mode approximation to multimode for a better uncertainty estimate. This is still an ongoing research and hopefully the method can be used for various uses on stochastic DNN.

5 Appendix

5.1 Appendix 1: The Output of Gaussian Variance of DF Layer When Input Is Gaussian

As pointed out in this paper, a DF layer takes the input values and outputs the Gaussian distribution of a sampling sum of inputs. This appendix shows the derivation of the variance of output Gaussian when input is also Gaussian as in Eq. 13. Let us refer to the sampling mean/sum formula for a constant population case in Cornfield (1944) [7] with their notation. The population Y with N constant elements y is described as below.

$$Y = (y_1, \dots, y_i, \dots y_N) \qquad (1 \leq \mathrm{i} \leq N) \tag{21}$$

If we sample n elements from total N elements in Y, the sampling sum becomes as below.

$$variance_{sample\ sum} = \frac{n\,(N-n)}{(N-1)} \cdot Var(y) \tag{22}$$

where $Var(y)$ is the variance of the population Y in Eq. (21). We calculate the sampling sum rather than the sampling mean since we consider the fully connected layer output.

We extend this to the case where the input population Y is not constant but random variable drawn from N dimensional multivariate Gaussian distribution, with a N dimensional mean vector μy and a N times N variance-covariance matrix Σy as shown below.

$$Y = (y_1, \ldots, y_i, \ldots y_N) \sim \mathcal{N}(\mu y, \Sigma y) \qquad (1 \leq i \leq N) \tag{23}$$

The variance of a sampling sum can be written as below.

$$variance_{sample\ sum} = Var\left(\sum_{i=1}^{N} a_i y_i\right) = [\sum_{i=1}^{N} Var(a_i y_i) + 2\sum_{i<j}^{N} Cov\left(a_i y_i, a_j y_j\right)] \tag{24}$$

where $a_i \sim$ *Bernoulli* is a dropout random variable representing sampling or not sampling. Therefore in Eq. 24 there are two independent sources of stochasticity, a random variable a due to the DF layer dropout for sampling/not sampling and a random variable y from population Y which has the Gaussian distribution. By using

$$Var(a_i y_i) = E(y_i)^2 Var(a_i) + E(a_i)^2 Var(y_i) + Var(a_i)\, Var(y_i) \tag{25}$$

the first term in (24) becomes

$$\sum_{i=1}^{N} Var(a_i y_i) = -\left(\frac{n}{N}\right)^2 \sum_{i=1}^{N} E(y_i)^2 + \left(\frac{n}{N}\right) \sum_{i=1}^{N} E\left(y_i^2\right) \tag{26}$$

Also by using

$$Cov\left(a_i y_i, a_j y_j\right) = E\left(a_i y_i a_j y_j\right) - E(a_i y_i)\, E\left(a_j y_j\right) = E\left(a_i a_j\right) E\left(y_i y_j\right) - E(a_i)E(y_i)E(a_j)E(y_j) \tag{27}$$

the second term in (24) becomes

$$\sum_{i<j}^{N} Cov\left(a_i y_i, a_j y_j\right) = 2\frac{n}{N}\frac{(n-1)}{(N-1)} \sum_{i<j}^{N} E\left(y_i y_j\right) - \left(\frac{n}{N}\right)^2 2\sum_{i<j}^{N} E(y_i)\, E\left(y_j\right) \tag{28}$$

By using (24), (26), (28), the variance of sampling sum becomes

$$variance_{sample\ sum} = \left(\frac{n}{N}\right) \sum_{i=1}^{N} E\left(y_i^2\right) - n^2 \left(mean_{sampling\ mean}\right)^2 + 2\frac{n}{N}\frac{(n-1)}{(N-1)} \sum_{i<j}^{N} E\left(y_i y_j\right) \tag{29}$$

where $mean_{sampling\ mean}$ is a mean of sampling mean.

This equation Eq. (29) is hard to interpret, therefore we rewrite it by introducing a variance $Var(\mu y)$ and avoid using the expectation E as shown below.

$$variance_{sample\ sum} = \frac{n(N-n)}{(N-1)} \cdot Var(\mu y) + \frac{n}{N} \sum_{i=1}^{N} Var(y_i) + \frac{2n}{N}\frac{(n-1)}{(N-1)} \sum_{i<j}^{N} Cov\left(y_i, y_j\right) \tag{30}$$

where $Var(\mu y)$ is a variance of N dimensional Gaussian input mean μy defined in 23, and the variance $Var(y_i)$ in second term and the covariance $Cov\left(y_i, y_j\right)$ in third term are nothing but the variance and covariance of Gaussian input population $\Sigma y = (Var(y_i), Cov(y_i, y_j))$ in (23). As a result, Eq. (30), the variance of sampling sum when the population is also Gaussian, can be interpreted as following. The first term in Eq. (30) is the same as the variance of constant value y from population Y in Eq. (22) except the values being replaced by their "mean" μy since they are Gaussian random variables $y \sim \mathcal{N}(\mu y, \Sigma y)$. Furthermore two additional terms in Eq. (30), second and third terms, are added explaining the input stochasticity as Gaussian variance $\sum_{i=1}^{N} Var(y_i)$ and covariance $\sum_{i<j}^{N} Cov(y_i, y_j)$ respectively.

5.2 Appendix 2: A Single Gaussian Approximation for the Output of ReLU Layer

This appendix shows how to approximate the output of the Rectified Linear Unit layer (ReLU) as a single Gaussian when an input is a single Gaussian as shown in Fig. 9. When a Gaussian goes through ReLU layer, it becomes a rectified Gaussian $h(x; \mu, \sigma^2)$ as shown in Eq. (31), which is described as a combination of delta $\delta(x)$ function and the truncated Gaussian as shown in [8] and below.

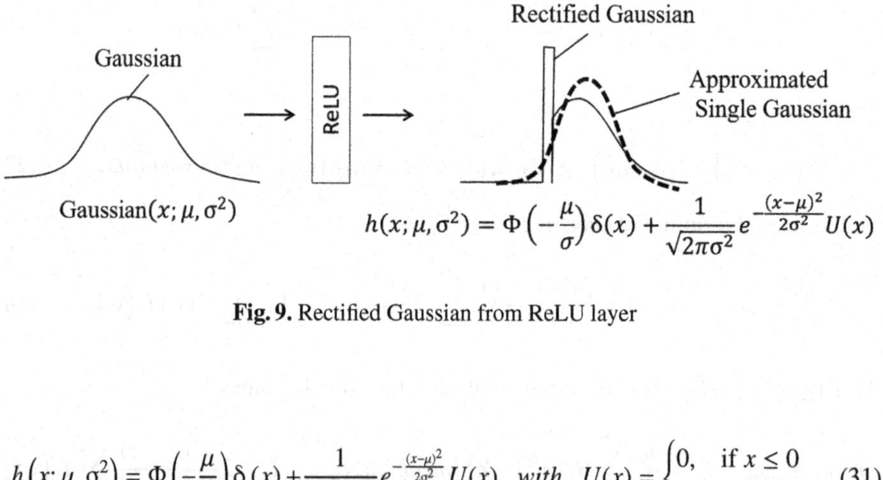

Fig. 9. Rectified Gaussian from ReLU layer

$$h(x;\mu,\sigma^2) = \Phi\left(-\frac{\mu}{\sigma}\right)\delta(x) + \frac{1}{\sqrt{2\pi\sigma^2}} e^{-\frac{(x-\mu)^2}{2\sigma^2}} U(x) \quad with \quad U(x) = \begin{cases} 0, & \text{if } x \le 0 \\ 1, & \text{otherwise} \end{cases} \tag{31}$$

This rectified Gaussian can be approximated as a single Gaussian with mean, variance, and covariance of (31) as follows.

The mean of a rectified Gaussian $h(x)$ is calculated by

$$E[h(x)] = \mu\Phi\left(\frac{\mu}{\sigma}\right) + \sigma\varphi\left(\frac{\mu}{\sigma}\right) \tag{32}$$

where the cumulative distribution is

$$\Phi(x) = \frac{1}{\sqrt{2\pi}} \int_{-\infty}^{x} e^{-\frac{t^2}{2}} dt \tag{33}$$

and the standard normal distribution is

$$\varphi(x) = \frac{1}{\sqrt{2\pi}} e^{-\frac{x^2}{2}}. \tag{34}$$

The variance of a rectified Gaussian $h(x)$ is given by

$$\mathrm{Var}[h(x)] = \mathrm{Var}[TG(x)]\,\Phi\left(\frac{\mu}{\sigma}\right) + E[TG(x)]^2\Phi\left(\frac{\mu}{\sigma}\right)(1 - \Phi\left(\frac{\mu}{\sigma}\right)) \tag{35}$$

where $TG(x) = Gaussian(x|x > 0)$ is a truncated Gaussian function with a truncated remaining range $0 \le x \le \infty$, whose mean, variance, and covariance can be calculated as in [9].

The covariance between i-th and j-th elements of a rectified Gaussian $h(x)$ is

$$\begin{aligned} \mathrm{Cov}\left[h_i(x_i), h_j(x_j)\right] &= E\left[h_i(x_i)\, h_j(x_j)\right] - E[h_i(x_i)]\, E\left[h_j(x_j)\right] \\ &= \left\{\mathrm{Cov}[TG_i(x_i), TG_j(x_j)] + E[TG_i(x_i)]E[TG_j(x_j)]\right\} \\ &\qquad \cdot \mathrm{MVNCDF} \\ &\qquad - E[TG_i(x_i)]\Phi\left(\frac{\mu_i}{\sigma_i}\right) \cdot E[TG_j(x_j)]\Phi\left(\frac{\mu_j}{\sigma_j}\right) \end{aligned} \tag{36}$$

where MVNCDF is a multivariate normal cumulative distribution function which is intractable but can be acquired by a table or matlab built-in function. We only need two dimension of MVNCDF as in Eq. (37), since a covariance matrix needs only pairwise values.

$$\mathrm{MVNCDF} = \mathrm{p}\left(x_i > 0, x_j > 0\right) \tag{37}$$

One way to speed up this calculation is to make a table with a normal Gaussian input, so that it can be used by normalizing a given Gaussian and refer to the table, and unnormalize values in table to get the estimated output.

Although it was not used in this paper, a single Gaussian approximation output for the other nonlinear layers such as Sigmoid and Softmax can be found in [17].

References

1. Gal, Y.: Uncertainty in Deep Learning. PhD thesis, University of Cambridge (2016)
2. Srivastava, N., Hinton, G., Krizhevsky, A., Sutskever, I., Salakhutdinov, R.: Dropout: a simple way to prevent neural networks from overfitting. J. Mach. Learn. Res. **15**(1), 1929–1958 (2014)
3. Gal, Y., Ghahramani, Z.: Dropout as a Bayesian approximation: Representing model uncertainty in deep learning. In: Balcan, M.F., Kilian Q.W. (eds), Proceedings of The 33rd International Conference on Machine Learning. Proceedings of Machine Learning Research, vol. 48, pp. 1050–1059, New York, USA, 20–22 Jun 2016. PMLR
4. Leibig, C., Allken, V., Berens, P., Wahl, S.: Leveraging uncertainty information from deep neural networks for disease detection. bioRxiv (2016)

5. Louizos, C., Welling, M.: Multiplicative normalizing flows for variational Bayesian neural networks. In: Proceedings of the 34th International Conference on Machine Learning, ICML 2017, vol. 70, pp. 2218–2227. JMLR.org (2017)
6. Wang, S.I., Manning, C.D.: Fast dropout training. In: Proceedings of the 30th International Conference on International Conference on Machine Learning, ICML 2013, vol. 28, pp. II-118-II-126. JMLR.org (2013)
7. Tahir, M.H., Ghazali, S.S.A., Gilani, G.M.: On the variance of the sample mean from finite population, approach iii (2005)
8. Wikipedia. Rectified Gaussian distribution – Wikipedia, the free encyclopedia. https://en.wikipedia.org/wiki/Rectified_Gaussian_distribution. Accessed 01 Jul 2019
9. Manjunath, B.G., Wilhelm, S.: Moments calculation for the double truncated multivariate normal density. SSRN Electron. J. (2009)
10. Krizhevsky, A., Sutskever, I., Hinton, G.E.: Imagenet classification with deep convolutional neural networks. In Proceedings of the 25th International Conference on Neural Information Processing Systems, NIPS 2012, vol. 1, pp. 1097–1105, USA. Curran Associates Inc. (2012)
11. ImageNet. http://www.image-net.org/
12. BVLC caffe AlexNet. https://github.com/BVLC/caffe/tree/master/models/bvlc_reference_caffenet
13. THE MNIST DATABASE. http://yann.lecun.com/exdb/mnist/
14. NotMNIST Dataset. https://www.kaggle.com/lubaroli/notmnist/
15. Hinton, G.E., Salakhutdinov, R.R.: Reducing the dimensionality of data with neural networks. Science **313**, 504–507 (2006)
16. Hershey, J.R., Olsen, P.A.: Approximating the kullback leibler divergence between Gaussian mixture models. In: 2007 IEEE International Conference on Acoustics, Speech and Signal Processing, April 2007, ICASSP 2007. IEEE (2007)
17. Daunizeau, J.: Semi-analytical approximations to statistical moments of sigmoid and softmax mappings of normal variables (2017)

Sequence Disambiguation with Synaptic Traces in Associative Neural Networks

Ramon H. Martinez[1(✉)], Oskar Kviman[1], Anders Lansner[1,2], and Pawel Herman[1]

[1] Computational Brain Science Lab, KTH Royal Institute of Technology, Stockholm, Sweden
{rhmm,okviman,paherman}@kth.se, ala@csc.kth.se
[2] Mathematics Department, Stockholm University, Stockholm, Sweden

Abstract. Among the abilities that a sequence processing network should possess sequence disambiguation, that is, the ability to let temporal context information influence the evolution of the network dynamics, is one of the most important. In this work we propose an instance of the Bayesian Confidence Propagation Neural Network (BCPNN) that learns sequences with probabilistic associative learning and is able to disambiguate sequences with the use of synaptic traces (low pass filtered versions of the activity). We describe first how the BCPNN achieves both sequence recall and sequence learning from temporal input. Our main result is that the BCPNN network equipped with dynamical memory in the form of synaptic traces is capable of solving the sequence disambiguation problem in a reliable way. We characterize the relationship between the sequence disambiguation capabilities of the network and its dynamical parameters. Furthermore, we show that the inclusion of an additional fast synaptic trace greatly increases the network disambiguation capabilities.

Keywords: Sequence learning · Attractor neural networks · Sequence disambiguation · Synaptic trace

1 Introduction

The ability to learn, process and predict sequences is a fundamental computational building block of the cognitive function of the human brain [1]. In particular, sequence disambiguation aimed at differentiating between overlapping sequences based on temporal context in domains such as language [1], motor production [2,3] and memory [4] is regarded as one of the most challenging tasks for networks delegated to process sequential information [5]. In this light, it is not surprising that many neural network based approaches ranging from supervised learning, context codes and attractor neural networks have been proposed. While supervised learning rules can modify recurrent neural networks of

I. V. Tetko et al. (Eds.): ICANN 2019, LNCS 11727, pp. 793–805, 2019.
https://doi.org/10.1007/978-3-030-30487-4_61

excitatory and inhibitory units to produce the desired response [6–8], the biological plausibility of the feedback error remains a matter of concern as supervised learning requires units to have access to a global representation of error. Another proposal is the use of context codes, where a particular subset of the network encodes either statistically or dynamically the history of the network activity and this information is subsequently used for prediction. This was initially proposed in the framework of dynamical reservoirs [9], which neither scales efficiently nor provides a transparent operational mechanism. While later iterations of this idea have reduced the number of units involved in the context code they rely on localized or idiosyncratic mechanism that do not generalize well outside of their area of application [10,11]. More recently there have been varied proposals for implementing varied sequence learning mechanisms such as changes in synaptic short-term dynamics in spiking and firing rate models [12,13], feedback coupling between neural field layers [14,15] and dendritic computation [16,17]. While such proposals are able to accomplish sequence learning in a variety of contexts we found that the problem of learning and recalling multiple sequences in the fashion needed to study disambiguation systematically was not properly addressed by them.

In this work we propose an attractor neural network model that is capable of solving the problem of learning sequences with overlapping elements and performing dynamical disambiguation in an unsupervised Hebbian fashion without the need for external units supplying contextual information. The network dynamics and connectivity intrinsically facilitate robust sequence processing. Although the mechanisms underlying sequence encoding and recall in attractor neural networks were proposed earlier [18,19], their reliance on non-local learning rules and a large number of parameters made them less appealing as a generic principle for sequence learning. Here, we apply the established Bayesian confidence propagation neural network (BCPNN) [20] learning rule to construct a recurrent neural network model, which implements associative probabilistic learning and approximates probabilistic inference [21]. We take inspiration from the "canonical circuit of the cortex" [22,23] to build a network where recurrent connectivity within the layer 2/3 of the cortex coupled with local competition implement attractor dynamics [24]. Our main contribution is to equip the proposed network with synaptic traces during the recall process and study the implications for the network's ability to disambiguate largely overlapping sequences under noise conditions. In particular, we demonstrate the facilitating role of the interplay between fast and slow currents mediating synaptic traces.

2 Results

2.1 Network Recall

Building upon our previous work [20,25–27] we developed an attractor neural network model with sequence learning capabilities where sequence transition is initiated by adaptation, guided by connectivity and resolved by competition. A schematic of the network topology is shown in Fig. 1A. Patterns are defined as activations of particular units (one hot encoding enforced by competition) and the connectivity of the network provides (*i*) a self-excitatory component w_{self} that fixes a pattern once activated, (*ii*) a priming component w_{next} that preferentially excites the unit coding for the next pattern in the sequence, and (*iii*) a strong inhibitory component w_{rest} that inhibits all the other units. We use asymmetric connectivity matrices to induce sequential dynamics (see Fig. 1B), and in Sect. 2.2 we show how such matrices are produced by associative learning.

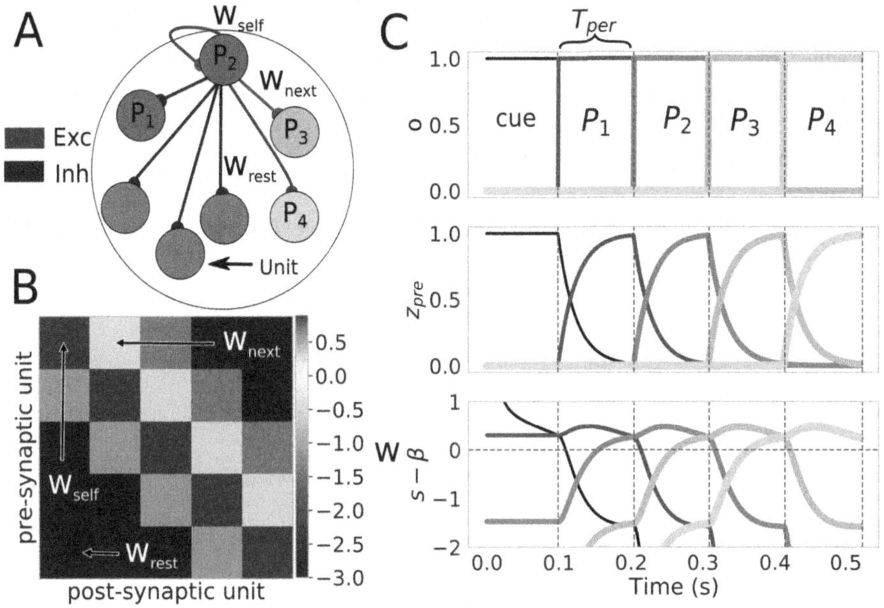

Fig. 1. Schematic of the network and a sequence recall example. (A) Schematic of network connectivity. (B) An example of a connectivity matrix. (C) Example of recall dynamics, from top to bottom: unit activations, o, z-traces and the current components (difference between s and β; cf. Eq. 1). Note that the transition occurs at the point at which the current $s - \beta$ for one unit becomes larger than the one the following unit is receiving. The time required for this to happen is the transition time, T_{per} here shown for the transition between P_1 and P_2.

In the model the currents evolve according to Eq. 1, where the currents $\boldsymbol{s}$ integrate the information provided by the rest of the network through $\mathbf{W}$ and the bias term $\boldsymbol{\beta}$ (accounting for so-called intrinsic excitability). Competition is implemented in Eq. 2, which at every time point activates the unit with the largest current and suppresses the rest. In the absence of additional mechanisms the dynamics of the network converge to the equilibrium values and stay there. In order to induce sequential transition we introduce an intrinsic adaptation mechanism (Eq. 3) whose role is to gradually counteract the self-excitatory currents. This process continues until the feed-forward current promoting the next pattern in the sequence is greater than the self-excitatory current, which initiates a transition (see Fig. 1C bottom). The persistence time, T_{per}, is the time a pattern remains activated in a sequential recall and it depends on the interplay between connectivity and adaptation [26]. To recall a sequence we cue the first element (we clamp the first unit for 10 ms) and let the network dynamics unfold, as shown in Fig. 1C. Note that units propagate current with a delay implemented with the variable $\mathbf{z}_{pre}$ in Eq. 1. The variable $\mathbf{z}_{pre}$ is a low-pass filtered version of the unit activation $\mathbf{o}$ and it is meant to represent the biochemical cascade of synaptic events at different time constants (here represented by different values of τ_z). In Sects. 2.3 and 2.4 we introduce an additional fast current $\mathbf{z}^{fast}$ to study the effect of synaptic traces with two different time constants. This is equivalent to using two connectivity matrices in Eq. 1, one for each of the $\mathbf{z}$ terms [21]. Finally, σ controls the level of noise in the current. Most representative values for the parameters are presented in Table 1.

$$\tau_s \frac{ds}{dt} = \boldsymbol{\beta} + \mathbf{W}^{\mathbf{T}} \cdot \mathbf{z}_{pre} - g_a \mathbf{a} + \sigma d\boldsymbol{\xi}(t) - \mathbf{s} \tag{1}$$

$$o_i = \begin{cases} 1, & s_i = \max(\mathbf{s}), \\ 0, & \text{otherwise} \end{cases} \tag{2}$$

$$\tau_a \frac{d\mathbf{a}}{dt} = \mathbf{o} - \mathbf{a} \tag{3}$$

$$\tau_{z_{pre}} \frac{d\mathbf{z}_{pre}}{dt} = \mathbf{o} - \mathbf{z}_{pre} \tag{4}$$

$$\tau_{z_{post}} \frac{d\mathbf{z}_{post}}{dt} = \mathbf{o} - \mathbf{z}_{post} \tag{5}$$

Table 1. Network parameters

Symbol	Name	Values
τ_s	Unit time constant	10 ms
τ_a	Adaptation time constant	250 ms
g_a	Adaptation gain	0–2.5 (units of **W**)
$\tau_{z_{pre}}$	Pre synaptic z-filter time constant	5–150 ms
$\tau_{z_{post}}$	Post synaptic z-filter time constant	5 ms
$\tau_{z_{pre}}^{fast}$	Fast pre synaptic z-filter time constant	5 ms
$\tau_{z_{post}}^{fast}$	Fast post synaptic z-filter time constant	5 ms
σ	Standard deviation of s values	0–2
T_{per}	Persistence time	50–3000 ms
T_p	Pulse time	100 ms

2.2 Network Learning

The network weights are trained by means of the BCPNN learning rule [20]. The BCPNN implements a probabilistic associative learning rule to build a connectivity matrix that reflects the statistical structure of the input. When equipped with the z-traces as temporal filters the BCPNN is able to learn the temporal structure by binding patterns that are contiguous in time, as shown in Fig. 2A. In particular, the BCPNN calculates probability traces that are used to estimate the probability of unit activation (Eqs. 6 and 7) as well as their co-activations (Eq. 8) over the training input. These estimates assign positive (excitatory) connections between units whose joint probability is larger than the product of their independent probabilities (Eq. 9) and negative (inhibitory) connections in the opposite case (note that statistically independent unit activations imply a corresponding weight of 0). Furthermore, the bias, $\boldsymbol{\beta}$, calculated in Eq. 10 penalizes units with low activation probabilities $\boldsymbol{p}_{post}$ independently of their co-activation statistics.

$$t\frac{d\mathbf{p}_{pre}}{dt} = \mathbf{z}_{pre} - \mathbf{p}_{pre} \tag{6}$$

$$t\frac{d\mathbf{p}_{joint}}{dt} = \mathbf{z}_{pre} \times \mathbf{z}_{post} - \mathbf{p}_{joint} \tag{7}$$

$$t\frac{d\mathbf{p}_{post}}{dt} = \mathbf{z}_{post} - \mathbf{p}_{post} \tag{8}$$

$$\mathbf{W} = \log\left(\frac{\mathbf{p}_{joint}}{\mathbf{p}_{pre} \times \mathbf{p}_{post}}\right) \tag{9}$$

$$\boldsymbol{\beta} = \log\left(\boldsymbol{p}_{post}\right) \tag{10}$$

In a typical training protocol each unit coding for a pattern in the sequence is clamped subsequently for a duration $T_p = 100\,\text{ms}$ (pulse time), as shown in Fig. 2B. The evolution of the connection weight between units corresponding to patterns 2 and 3, reflecting the process of learning, is illustrated in Fig. 2C. In general, the longer the $\tau_{z_{pre}}$ values the larger the connection between two units adjacent in time. Note that while the BCPNN rule traditionally uses an exponentially moving average to estimate the probability traces [27], here we rely on the differential equation corresponding to an accumulated average. This modification allows us to learn the steady state connectivity values of the traditional BCPNN with just one training epoch.

2.3 Noise Effects

The robustness of sequence processing can be reliably validated in the presence of noise. It becomes obvious that the Gaussian noise process, here characterized by the value of σ, diminishes the network's capability to correctly recall full sequences (see Fig. 3A). We define the success rate as the percentage of correct recalls in a given number of trials. The effect of noise in recall is modulated by the value of $\tau_{z_{pre}}$, where longer values of the time constant render the network

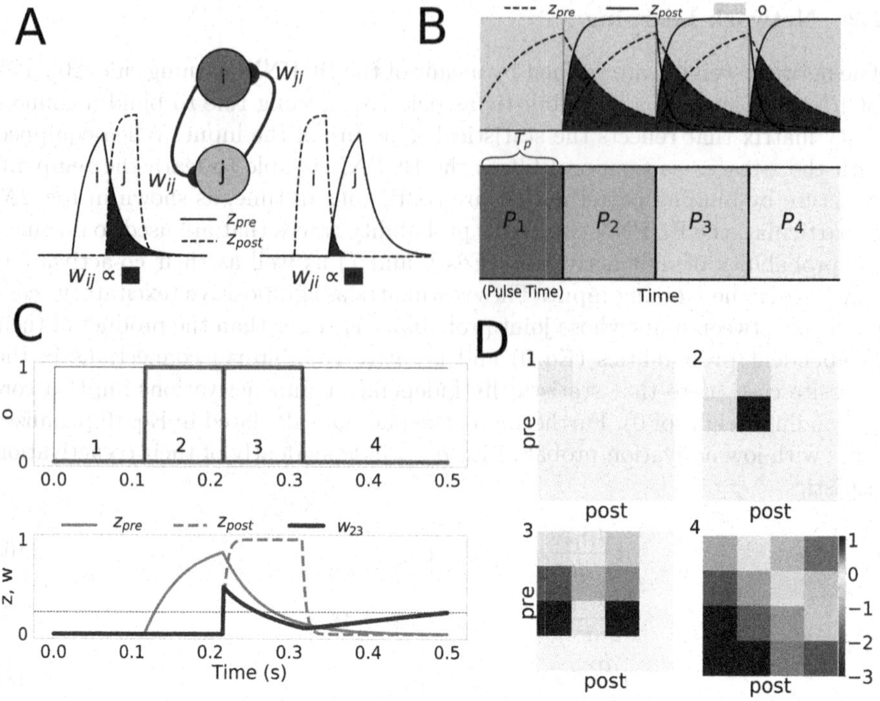

Fig. 2. Learning. (A) The weight between two units contiguous in time is proportional to the intersection between the z-traces. Note that an asymmetry between $\tau_{z_{pre}}$ and $\tau_{z_{post}}$ implies an asymmetry in the weights between the units leading to an asymmetry in the overall connectivity matrix. (B) The training protocol with four patterns. (C) The evolution of the weight between pattern 2 and 3 is described. (D) Evolution of the connectivity matrices at times denoted by 1, 2, 3 and 4 in the top C.

less robust to noise (see Fig. 3A, one trace). This can be explained by the fact that larger values of the $\tau_{z_{pre}}$ make the connectivity more homogeneous and, in consequence, the network becomes more prone to failure.

Robustness can be greatly improved, however, with the addition of another current inducing fast synaptic dynamics. As a result, the transition process gets stabilised by supplying an excitatory feed-forward current component to the unit corresponding to the next pattern in the sequence and a strong inhibitory current to the other units (see Fig. 3A, two traces). Moreover, the persistence time T_{per}, describing the pace of the recall process, also decays more quickly for larger values of $\tau_{z_{pre}}$ (see Fig. 3B). This effect can be explained by the fact that the noise fluctuations tend to induce the network state transition sooner than in noise-free conditions.

2.4 Disambiguation

The disambiguation task we propose for the network consists in both learning and recalling two overlapping sequences (see Fig. 4). We parameterised the difficulty of the task by the number of elements that the two sequences share, which we refer to as a disambiguation window. In order to handle this challenging case, the network has to be equipped with internal memory that keeps information about the previous states, especially those unique to the sequence, i.e. a non-ovelapping segment of the sequence. Moreover, the information should be maintained long enough to serve at the forking decision point at the end of the overlapping segment, i.e. following the disambiguation window. In our network this memory mechanism is implemented by the z-traces, which influence the currents until they completely decay (Fig. 4C).

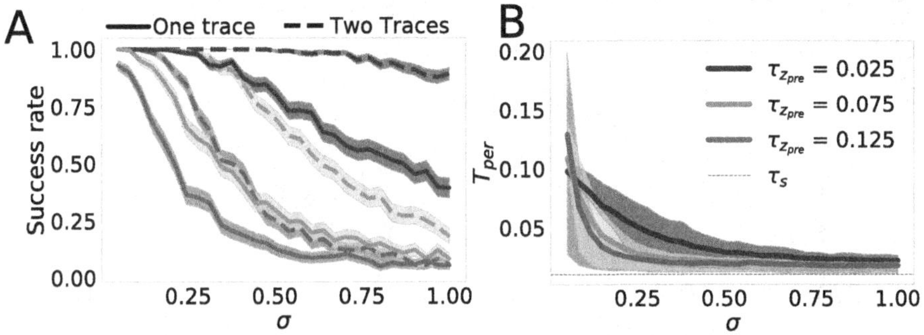

Fig. 3. Noise effects in sequence recall. (A) Solid line: The effect of noise on the success rate for different values of $\tau_{z_{pre}}$ in a network with only one current. The dashed line corresponds to the results obtained by simulating the same network (one trace) with the addition of a fast stabilizing current (two traces). Shaded area represents confidence intervals derived by assuming a Bernoulli distribution. (B) The effect of noise on T_{per} for different values of $\tau_{z_{pre}}$. Shaded area represents the area between the 25th and the 75th percentile to convey an idea of the distribution of T_{per} values. We utilized 500 trials to calculate the success rate in these simulations.

In general, our network's disambiguation capabilities are modulated by the following factors

1. The value of $\tau_{z_{pre}}$: longer values of the time constant allow the z-traces to keep the required information for longer times and therefore make the network more likely to recall the sequence correctly.
2. The size of the disambiguation window: longer windows are harder to disambiguate.
3. The persistence time of the patterns, T_{per}: longer values extending the overall time that the network spends in the disambiguation window, which in turns dilutes the z-traces even further thereby making it harder for the network to use that information.

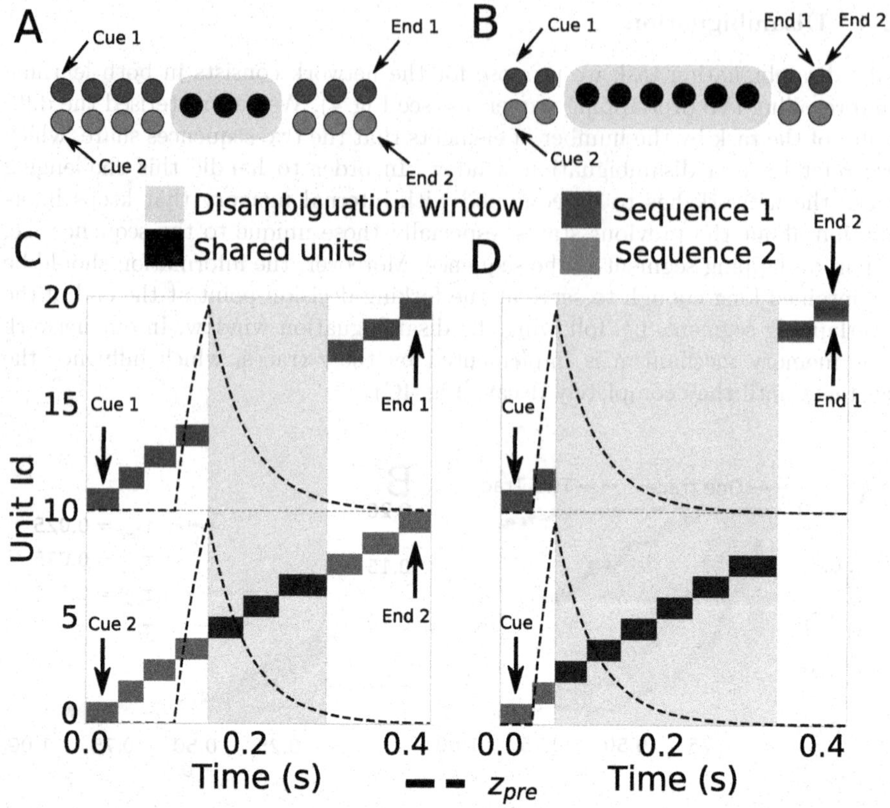

Fig. 4. Sequence disambiguation. (A) A disambiguation task with a short disambiguation of size 3. (B) A disambiguation task with a long disambiguation window of size 6. (C) Schematic of the disambiguation mechanism. A longer value of $\tau_{z_{pre}}$ implies that the z-traces of the units that are located just before the disambiguation window decay slower. Ultimately, this is the information that is used to bias the network sequential dynamics at the forking point and lead the network in the right direction. (D) When the disambiguation window is too long for the value of the z-trace to outlive it the recall fails.

4. The degree of noise in the system: the sequence recall is more likely to fail with larger values of σ (see Fig. 3A). In the proposed network the noise enacts two phenomena with opposite effects in the disambiguation capabilities of the network. First, larger values of σ bury the signal used for disambiguation (the value of $\mathbf{z_{pre}}$) under noise and, in consequence, the network is more prone to failure. However, as shown in Fig. 3B stronger noise results in the shortening of the overall recall time of the overlapping part, which in turn facilitates the disambiguation of the sequences as $\mathbf{z_{pre}}$ has less time to decay. We therefore control the persistence time indirectly (by means of g_a) during our recall process.

In order to systematically study the disambiguation capacities of the network in terms of the aforementioned parameters we employ the following framework. We define the so-called maximum disambiguation window as the longest window that the network could successfully disambiguate with over 80% success rate (see Fig. 5A). We then examine the effect of $\tau_{z_{pre}}$ on the aforementioned maximum disambiguation window under two noise regimes. We observe an inverted u-shape behavior with low disambiguation power for small and large values of $\tau_{z_{pre}}$, and an increased performance in the intermediate zone (Fig. 5C, squares, one trace). For small values of $\tau_{z_{pre}}$ the information in the network decays rather quickly and therefore the maximum disambiguation window is rather small. As $\tau_{z_{pre}}$ grows the network handles longer disambiguation windows until the network becomes too homogeneous to solve the task correctly for values around $\tau_{z_{pre}} \sim$ 90 ms mark, when it suddenly fails to disambiguate sequences at all. We can overcome such limitations by introducing another fast current inducing short-lasting synaptic traces, which helps in biasing the network transition to the next pattern (the inhibitory effect on the other units is worth emphasising here). As can be seen in Fig. 5B (dots, two traces), this additional synaptic trace allows the network to extend the maximum disambiguation window to the maximum possible size in this task (overlap of 8 units) for a wide range of time constants governing the dynamics of the original traces.

3 Discussion

We have shown that the BCPNN network equipped with synaptic traces is to disambiguate sequences robustly by using the traces as a dynamical memory. In our model the role of the fast synaptic trace is to stabilize the patterns while the slow synaptic trace primes the network in the desired direction by implementing a memory of the context. This separation of currents has been observed in cortical circuits, e.g. [28]. In particular, we propose that the biological substrate of the slow current corresponds to NMDA meditated synaptic transmission with kinetics distributed in the range that we explored systematically in this paper (25–150 ms) [29,30] and that the fast current corresponds to the fast activation of the synaptic AMPA receptor, which we have kept constant within the range observed empirically (2.5–10 ms) [31]. In our view, it is not unreasonable to model the biochemical cascades that implement synaptic plasticity with memory-like variables that track both the activations and co-activations of unit activity (Eqs. 6, 7 and 8). That said, the particular way in which we combine the p-traces to calculate the weights between our units (Eq. 9) is a strong assumption motivated by Bayesian inference in the brain [20,21]. The proposed model of fast synaptic plasticity still awaits convincing biological evidence but meanwhile we present here the computational consequences of such an arrangement with the hope of testing the possibilities of cortical-like computation. In short, we have demonstrated how a rather general computational mechanism can be implemented with a cortical-like circuit with biologically plausible components.

An undesirable consequence of using associative Hebbian learning is typically the development of pathological runaway dynamics [32]. A common solution to

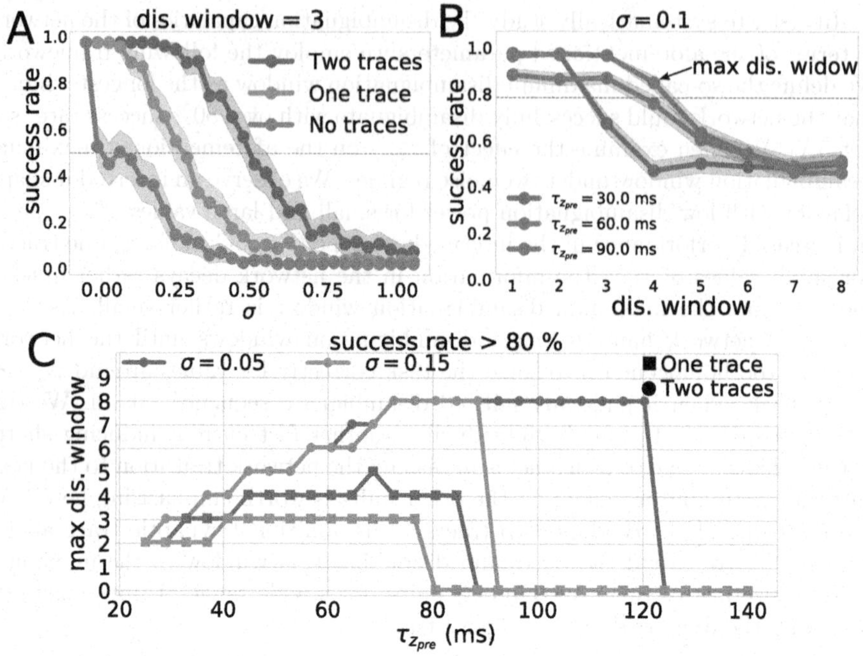

Fig. 5. Disambiguation characterization. (A) Success rate as a function of the noise, σ, for three different networks: (i) one that does not rely on any traces during recall (activity $\mathbf{o}$ is used to propagate the currents instead of $\mathbf{z_{pre}}$), (ii) a network with one trace ($\mathbf{z_{pre}}$ with $\tau_{z_{pre}}$), and (iii) with two traces ($\mathbf{z_{pre}}$ and $\mathbf{z}^{fast}_{\mathbf{pre}}$). We use $\tau_{z_{pre}} = 50\,\text{ms}$ for all the examples. (B) Success rate as function of the size of the disambiguation window for different values of $\tau_{z_{pre}}$. Notice that middle values of $\tau_{z_{pre}}$ lead to the better performance than the longer ones. We set a threshold of 80% success rate to define the maximum disambiguation window. (C) Characterization of the maximum disambiguation window as a function of $\tau_{z_{pre}}$ for two noise regimes. The squared marker represents the network with only one synaptic trace type (single time constant, $\tau_{z_{pre}}$). The dot marker corresponds to the same network with the addition of fast synaptic traces (two traces, with $\tau_{z_{pre}}$ and $\tau^{fast}_{z_{pre}}$ time constant, respectively). For all the points above, we ran 500 trials to calculate the success rate for each set of parameters.

this conundrum is to constrain the learning rule with the addition of compensatory processes (e.g. synaptic scaling). While most of the sequence learning networks require adding such compensatory mechanisms to the associative part of the learning rule [13,33] the probabilistic nature of the BCPNN learning rule accounts for this effect without any need for extra complexity [21]. This is of fundamental importance in the learning of forking points in the exit part of the disambiguation windows where a unit has to project equally to the subsequent sequences. To illustrate the problem, two representative cases of compensatory processes are worth mentioning. Firstly, learning rules with weight decay result in stronger connections for the sequences learnt most recently. In consequence, the decay time has to be adjusted so that the connections mediating out-of-fork transitions are not too different among themselves. Secondly, learning rules that adjust all the incoming or outgoing synapses to a unit require tight balance between this two forces to ensure equilibrium in the forks, which is difficult to achieve in practice [9]. The BCPNN learning rule, on the other hand, assures the equilibrium as long as the training process is well mixed in the number of examples from all the sequences involved.

On a more general note, we would like to point out that there is a long standing interest in building predictive algorithms that make use of context information [34–36]. We have shown that a simple cortical-like circuit endowed with synaptic traces can perform a basic context operation using the simplest form of unsupervised learning available to the brain: Hebbian associative learning. We think of it as a stepping zone in the general problem of explaining the capabilities of the brain to use contextual information over broad temporal scales in the range of the hundreds of milliseconds [37]. It is believed that receptive fields with longer temporal characteristics arise out of the hierarchical and modular anatomy of the brain [38]. In the future work, we aim to explore how to integrate the principles of temporal processing here outlined with biologically plausible hierarchical and modular structures [39] in order to shed light on both cortical function and the design of network models for processing temporal information at a range of temporal scales.

References

1. Lashley, K.: The problem of serial order in behavior. In: Cerebral Mechanisms in Behavior, pp. 112–136 (1951)
2. Koedijker, J.M., Oudejans, R.R., Beek, P.J.: Interference effects in learning similar sequences of discrete movements. J. Mot. Behav. **42**(4), 209–222 (2010)
3. Panzer, S., Wilde, H., Shea, C.H.: Learning of similar complex movement sequences: proactive and retroactive effects on learning. J. Mot. Behav. **38**(1), 60–70 (2006)
4. Agster, K.L., Fortin, N.J., Eichenbaum, H.: The hippocampus and disambiguation of overlapping sequences. J. Neurosci. **22**(13), 5760–5768 (2002)
5. Levy, W.B.: A sequence predicting ca3 is a flexible associator that learns and uses context to solve hippocampal-like tasks. Hippocampus **6**(6), 579–590 (1996)
6. Rajan, K., Harvey, C.D., Tank, D.W.: Recurrent network models of sequence generation and memory. Neuron **90**(1), 128–142 (2016)
7. Sussillo, D., Abbott, L.F.: Generating coherent patterns of activity from chaotic neural networks. Neuron **63**(4), 544–557 (2009)
8. Wang, Q., Rothkopf, C.A., Triesch, J.: A model of human motor sequence learning explains facilitation and interference effects based on spike-timing dependent plasticity. PLoS Comput. Biol. **13**(8), e1005632 (2017)
9. Minai, A.A., Barrows, G.L., Levy, W.B.: Disambiguation of pattern sequences with recurrent networks. In: Proceedings WCNN, San Diego, vol. 4, pp. 176–180 (1994)
10. Samura, T., Hattori, M., Ishizaki, S.: Sequence disambiguation and pattern completion by cooperation between autoassociative and heteroassociative memories of functionally divided hippocampal CA3. Neurocomputing **71**(16–18), 3176–3183 (2008)

11. Sohal, V.S., Hasselmo, M.E.: Gabab modulation improves sequence disambiguation in computational models of hippocampal region CA3. Hippocampus **8**(2), 171–193 (1998)
12. Deco, G., Rolls, E.T.: Sequential memory: a putative neural and synaptic dynamical mechanism. J. Cogn. Neurosci. **17**(2), 294–307 (2005)
13. Veliz-Cuba, A., Shouval, H.Z., Josić, K., Kilpatrick, Z.P.: Networks that learn the precise timing of event sequences. J. Comput. Neurosci. **39**(3), 235–254 (2015)
14. Amari, S.I.: Dynamics of pattern formation in lateral-inhibition type neural fields. Biol. Cybern. **27**(2), 77–87 (1977)
15. Sandamirskaya, Y., Schöner, G.: An embodied account of serial order: how instabilities drive sequence generation. Neural Netw. **23**(10), 1164–1179 (2010)
16. Bhalla, U.S.: Dendrites, deep learning, and sequences in the hippocampus. Hippocampus **29**(3), 239–251 (2019)
17. Branco, T., Clark, B.A., Häusser, M.: Dendritic discrimination of temporal input sequences in cortical neurons. Science **329**(5999), 1671–1675 (2010)
18. Fukushima, K.: A model of associative memory in the brain. Kybernetik **12**(2), 58–63 (1973)
19. Guyon, I., Personnaz, L., Nadal, J., Dreyfus, G.: Storage and retrieval of complex sequences in neural networks. Phys. Rev. A **38**(12), 6365 (1988)
20. Lansner, A., Ekeberg, Ö.: A one-layer feedback artificial neural network with a bayesian learning rule. Int. J. Neural Syst. **1**(01), 77–87 (1989)
21. Tully, P.J., Hennig, M.H., Lansner, A.: Synaptic and nonsynaptic plasticity approximating probabilistic inference. Frontiers Synaptic Neurosci. **6**, 8 (2014)
22. Douglas, R.J., Martin, K.A., Whitteridge, D.: A canonical microcircuit for neocortex. Neural Comput. **1**(4), 480–488 (1989)
23. Douglas, R.J., Martin, K.A.: Neuronal circuits of the neocortex. Annu. Rev. Neurosci. **27**, 419–451 (2004)
24. Lundqvist, M., Herman, P., Lansner, A.: Functional Brain Mapping and the Endeavor to Understand the Working Brain. IntechOpen (2013)
25. Lansner, A., Marklund, P., Sikström, S., Nilsson, L.G.: Reactivation in working memory: an attractor network model of free recall. PLoS ONE **8**(8), e73776 (2013)
26. Martinez, R.H., Herman, P., Lansner, A.: Probabilistic associative learning suffices for learning the temporal structure of multiple sequences. BioRxiv, p. 545871 (2019)
27. Tully, P., Lindén, H., Hennig, M., Lansner, A.: Spike-based bayesian-hebbian learning of temporal sequences. PLoS Comput. Biol. **12**(5), e1004954 (2016)
28. Self, M.W., Kooijmans, R.N., Supèr, H., Lamme, V.A., Roelfsema, P.R.: Different glutamate receptors convey feedforward and recurrent processing in macaque V1. Proc. Natl. Acad. Sci. **109**(27), 11031–11036 (2012)
29. Jensen, O., Lisman, J.E.: Theta/gamma networks with slow NMDA channels learn sequences and encode episodic memory: role of NMDA channels in recall. Learn. Mem. **3**(2–3), 264–278 (1996)
30. Wang, H., Stradtman, G.G., Wang, X.J., Gao, W.J.: A specialized NMDA receptor function in layer 5 recurrent microcircuitry of the adult rat prefrontal cortex. Proc. Natl. Acad. Sci. **105**(43), 16791–16796 (2008)
31. Holthoff, K., Zecevic, D., Konnerth, A.: Rapid time course of action potentials in spines and remote dendrites of mouse visual cortex neurons. J. Physiol. **588**(7), 1085–1096 (2010)
32. Zenke, F., Gerstner, W.: Hebbian plasticity requires compensatory processes on multiple timescales. Philos. Trans. Roy. Soc. B Biol. Sci. **372**(1715), 20160259 (2017)

33. Fiete, I.R., Senn, W., Wang, C.Z., Hahnloser, R.H.: Spike-time-dependent plasticity and heterosynaptic competition organize networks to produce long scale-free sequences of neural activity. Neuron **65**(4), 563–576 (2010)
34. Elman, J.L.: Finding structure in time. Cogn. Sci. **14**(2), 179–211 (1990)
35. Hochreiter, S., Schmidhuber, J.: Long short-term memory. Neural Comput. **9**(8), 1735–1780 (1997)
36. Vaswani, A., et al.: Attention is all you need. In: Advances in Neural Information Processing Systems, pp. 5998–6008 (2017)
37. Hasson, U., Yang, E., Vallines, I., Heeger, D.J., Rubin, N.: A hierarchy of temporal receptive windows in human cortex. J. Neurosci. **28**(10), 2539–2550 (2008)
38. Himberger, K.D., Chien, H.Y., Honey, C.J.: Principles of temporal processing across the cortical hierarchy. Neuroscience **389**, 161–174 (2018)
39. Lansner, A., Benjaminsson, S., Johansson, C.: From ANN to biomimetic information processing. In: Gutiérrez, A., Marco, S. (eds.) Biologically Inspired Signal Processing for Chemical Sensing, pp. 33–43. Springer, Heidelberg (2009). https://doi.org/10.1007/978-3-642-00176-5_2

Robust Optimal-Size Implementation of Finite State Automata with Synfire Ring-Based Neural Networks

Jérémie Cabessa[1,2(✉)] and Jiří Šíma[2]

[1] Laboratory of Mathematical Economics and Applied Microeconomics, University Paris 2 – Panthéon-Assas, 4, Rue Blaise Desgoffe, 75006 Paris, France
jeremie.cabessa@u-paris2.fr

[2] Institute of Computer Science, Czech Academy of Sciences, P. O. Box 5, 18207 Prague 8, Czech Republic
sima@cs.cas.cz

Abstract. Synfire rings are important neural circuits capable of conveying synchronous, temporally precise and self-sustained activities in a robust manner. We describe a robust and optimal-size implementation of finite state automata with neural networks composed of synfire rings. More precisely, given any finite automaton, we build a corresponding neural network partly composed of synfire rings and capable of simulating it. The synfire ring activities encode the successive states of the automaton throughout its computation. The robustness of the network results from its architecture, which involves synfire rings and duplicated core components. We finally show that the network's size is asymptotically optimal: for an automaton with n states, the network has $\Theta(\sqrt{n})$ cells.

Keywords: Recurrent neural networks · Threshold circuits · Finite state automata · Synfire rings

1 Introduction

In theoretical neural computation, the computational capabilities of various neural models has been shown to range from the finite automaton degree, up to the Turing, or even to the super-Turing levels (see the thorough survey [24]). In summary, Boolean recurrent neural networks are computationally equivalent to finite state automata [15,19]; sigmoidal rational-weighted neural networks are Turing complete [22]; and sigmoidal real-weighted and evolving neural networks are super-Turing powerful [5,21].

Supports from DARPA – Lifelong Learning Machines (L2M) program, cooperative agreement No. HR0011-18-2-0023, as well as from the ICS CAS RVO: 67985807 and the Czech Science Foundation, grant No. 19-05704S, are gratefully acknowledged.

I. V. Tetko et al. (Eds.): ICANN 2019, LNCS 11727, pp. 806–818, 2019.
https://doi.org/10.1007/978-3-030-30487-4_62

In the 90's, the equivalence between Boolean neural networks and finite state automata has been extensively studied, motivated by the possibility to implement abstract machines on parallel hardwares. In particular, it has been shown that any deterministic automaton with n states can be implemented by a neural network of optimal size containing $\Theta(\sqrt{n})$ neurons [11,13]. The energy complexity of this network construction can be minimized without changing its optimal size [23]. Furthermore, any regular language described by a regular expression of length ℓ can be recognized by an optimal-size neural network having $\Theta(\ell)$ units [25].

But the neural models involved in these studies fail to capture biological features that are so essential to brain information processing. For instance, the computational behaviors of those networks do certainly comply with the paradigms of computation of biological neural systems: the computational states are represented by discrete (spiking) configurations of the networks, rather than by sustained and temporally robust activities of cell assemblies. Also, the networks' dynamics is not robust to the possibility of architectural failures.

In biology, the concept of synfire chains and synfire rings have been demonstrated to play significant roles in the processing and coding of information in the brain. *Synfire chains* are feedforward neural circuits whose every layer is connected to the next by means of excitatory convergent/divergent synaptic patterns [1,2,7,12,18]. According to this architecture, the neurons of each layer tend to fire simultaneously, and the firing activity propagates through the successive layers in a synchronized manner. Hence, synfire chains are able to convey repeated complex spatiotemporal patterns of discharges in a robust and highly temporally precise way. *Synfire rings* are looping synfire chains [16,26]. As an additional dynamical feature, the ring shape gives rise to self-sustained activities, which correspond to attractor dynamics. Synfire chains and rings have been shown to spontaneously emerge in self-organizing networks subjected to various kinds of synaptic plasticity (see for instance [8,9,14,16,26]).

Based on these considerations, it has been shown that finite state automata can be simulated by Boolean recurrent neural networks composed of synfire rings [4]. The results have then been generalized to the more biological cases of networks of Izhikevich spiking neurons [3], and even to Hodgkin-Huxley neurons [6]. The obtained architecture is, to a certain extent, robust to synaptic pruning as well as to the introduction of synaptic noises.

Here, we extend these results by describing a robust optimal-size implementation of finite state automata with synfire ring-based neural networks. The paper is organized as follows. Section 2 introduces the concepts of Boolean neural networks and synfire rings. Section 3 recalls the definition of finite state automata, presents the simulation result of finite automata by optimal-size threshold circuits [17], and describes the generalization of this construction to the context of Boolean neural networks [11]. Section 4 contains our results. Given any finite automaton, we build a robust and optimal-size neural network partly composed of synfire rings capable of simulating it. The synfire ring activities encode the successive states of the automaton throughout its computation. The robustness of the network results from its architecture, which is composed of synfire rings and duplicated core components. Based on previous work [11,17], we show that the network's size is asymptotically optimal: for an automaton with n states, the network has $\Theta(\sqrt{n})$ cells. The implementation of this construction is deferred to an extended journal version of this paper. Finally, Sect. 5 offers a brief conclusion.

2 Neural Networks and Synfire Rings

Boolean Neural Networks. A *Boolean recurrent neural network (BRNN)* $\mathcal{N}$ consists of a synchronous network of Boolean cells related together in a general architecture. The network is composed of M input neurons $(u_i)_{i=1}^M$ and N internal neurons $(x_i)_{i=1}^N$. The dynamics of network is computed as follows: given the activation values of the input neurons $(u_j(t))_{j=1}^M$ and internal neurons $(x_j(t))_{j=1}^N$ at time step t, the activation values of the internal neurons $(x_i(t+1))_{i=1}^N$ at time step $t+1$ are given by the following equations:

$$x_i(t+1) = \theta\left(\sum_{j=1}^{N} a_{ij} \cdot x_j(t) + \sum_{j=1}^{M} b_{ij} \cdot u_j(t) + c_i\right), \text{ for } i = 1, \ldots, N \tag{1}$$

where $a_{ij} = w(x_j, x_i)$ and $b_{ij} = w(u_j, x_i)$ are the *weights* of the synaptic connections from x_j to x_i and from u_j to x_i, respectively, c_i is the *bias* of cell x_i, and θ is the *hard-threshold* activation function defined by

$$\theta(x) = \begin{cases} 0 & \text{if } x < 0 \\ 1 & \text{if } x \geq 0. \end{cases}$$

Neural networks can be exploited as acceptors of formal languages (here, we consider languages over the alphabet $\{0,1\}$) [20]. Towards this purpose, several input/output protocols have been proposed in the literature. Here, a so-called offline input/output is considered. The Boolean networks are provided with two input cells called `inp` and `val`, as well as with a specific internal cell called `out`. The neurons `inp` is used to transmit the input strings (words) to the network in a sequential way, i.e., bit by bit. The neuron `out` outputs the decisions of the network to accept or reject its inputs. The cell `val` is used to identify the time steps at which new input bits are received.

Formally, suppose that the input (string) $x = x_0 \cdots x_m \in \{0,1\}^*$ is to be processed by the BRNN $\mathcal{N}$. Assume further that the successive bits of x are presented to the network at successive time steps $0 < t_0 < t_1 < \cdots < t_m$ separated by at least $d \geq 4$ units of time, i.e., $t_{i+1} - t_i \geq d$ for every $i = 0, \ldots, m-1$. The processing of input x is implemented as follows. The activations values of `inp`, `val` are externally set to the following values

$$\mathtt{inp}(t) = \begin{cases} x_i & \text{if } t = t_i \\ 0 & \text{otherwise} \end{cases} \quad \text{and} \quad \mathtt{val}(t) = \begin{cases} 1 & \text{if } t = t_i \\ 0 & \text{otherwise} \end{cases}$$

for all $t \geq 0$. Now, let $t^* = t_m + d + 1$. We say that x is *accepted* (resp. *rejected*) by $\mathcal{N}$ iff $\texttt{out}(t^*) = 1$ (resp. $\texttt{out}(t^*) = 0$). The set of words accepted by $\mathcal{N}$ is the *language recognized by* $\mathcal{N}$, denoted by $L(\mathcal{N})$. A language L is *recognizable* by some BRNN if there exists some $\mathcal{N}$ such that $L = L(\mathcal{N})$.

Synfire Rings. A *synfire ring* R of width $w \geq 1$ and length $\ell \geq 2$ is a specific BRNN composed of $\ell \cdot w$ cells $(x_{ij})_{i=1,j=1}^{w,\ell}$. For every $j = 1, \dots, \ell$, the cells $x_{1j}, \dots, x_{wj}$ is the *j-th layer* of R, and for every $i = 1, \dots, w$, the cells $x_{i1}, \dots, x_{i\ell}$ form the *i-th level* of R. For every $i = 1, \dots, w-1$, each cell of the i-th layer is connected to all cells of the $(i+1)$-th layer with connections of weight 1. Also, each cell of the ℓ-th layer is connected to all cells of the 1-st layer with connections of weight 1.

3 Finite State Automata and Boolean Neural Networks

Finite State Automata. A *deterministic finite state automaton (DFSA)* is a tuple $\mathcal{A} = (Q, \Sigma, \delta, q_0, F)$, where $Q = \{q_0, \dots, q_{n-1}\}$ is a finite set of *states*, Σ is a finite alphabet of *input symbols* (here, $\Sigma = \{0,1\}$), $\delta \colon Q \times \Sigma \longrightarrow Q$ is the *transition function*, $q_0 \in Q$ is the *initial state* and $F \subseteq Q$ is the set of *final states.* Each relation of the form $\delta(q, x) = q'$ signifies that if the automaton is in state $q \in Q$ and reads input symbol $x \in \Sigma$, then it will move to state $q' \in Q$.

For any input (string) $x = x_0 x_1 \cdots x_m \in \Sigma^*$, the *computation* of $\mathcal{A}$ over x is the finite sequence $\mathcal{A}(x) = \big((q_{i_0}, x_0, q_{i_1}), (q_{i_1}, x_1, q_{i_2}), \dots, (q_{i_m}, x_m, q_{i_{m+1}})\big)$ such that $q_{i_0} = q_0$ and $\delta(q_{i_k}, x_k) = q_{i_{k+1}}$, for all $k = 0, \dots, m$. Such a computation is usually denoted as

$$\mathcal{A}(x) : q_0 \xrightarrow{x_0} q_{i_1} \xrightarrow{x_1} q_{i_2} \cdots q_{i_m} \xrightarrow{x_m} q_{i_{m+1}}.$$

The input x is said to be *accepted* by $\mathcal{A}$ iff $q_{i_{m+1}} \in F$. The set of all inputs accepted by $\mathcal{A}$ is the *language recognized by* $\mathcal{A}$. Finite state automata recognize the class of *regular languages.* A finite state automaton is generally represented as a directed graph: the nodes and labelled edges of the graph represent the states and transitions of the automaton [10].

Note that if $|Q| = n$, then each state $q \in Q$ can be encoded by a corresponding Boolean vector $\boldsymbol{q} = (\boldsymbol{q}_1, \dots, \boldsymbol{q}_p) \in \{0,1\}^p$, where $p = \lceil \log n \rceil + 1$. The first $p-1$ bits $\boldsymbol{q}_1, \dots, \boldsymbol{q}_{p-1}$ encode the "value" of q and the last bit $\boldsymbol{q}_p$ encodes the "F-membership" of q, i.e., $\boldsymbol{q}_p = 1$ iff $q \in F$. Accordingly, the transition function $\delta : Q \times \{0,1\} \longrightarrow Q$ can naturally be encoded by the *Boolean transition function* $\boldsymbol{f}_\delta : \{0,1\} \times \{0,1\}^p \longrightarrow \{0,1\}^p$ defined by $\boldsymbol{f}_\delta(x, \boldsymbol{q}) = \boldsymbol{q}'$ iff $\delta(q, x) = q'$ (for the sake of consistency with the notations used in [23], we suppose that the first argument of $\boldsymbol{f}_\delta$ represents an input bit of $\mathcal{A}$, while the p remaining ones represent the encoding of a state of $\mathcal{A}$). In the sequel, the space $\{0,1\} \times \{0,1\}^p$ will be naturally identified with $\{0,1\}^{p+1}$.

Simulation of DFSA by Threshold Circuits. Using the method of threshold circuit synthesis by Lupanov [17], any Boolean transition function $\boldsymbol{f}_\delta$ can be implemented by a four-layer *threshold circuit* $\mathcal{C}$ of asymptotically optimal size $\Theta(\sqrt{2^p}) = \Theta(\sqrt{n})$. The construction is fairly intricate and can be found in detail in [23] (in a slightly different context). We now describe, layer by layer, the threshold gates and connections of these circuit. The description of the weights is not provided (due to space constraint) but can be found in [23]. For the sake of consistency, we respect the notations used in [23]. This *Lupanov circuit* is illustrated in Fig. 1.

Layer 0 (Inputs). Recall that the first argument of $\boldsymbol{f}_\delta$ represents the next input bit $x \in \{0,1\}$ of $\mathcal{A}$, while the remaining p ones encode the current state $q \in Q$ of $\mathcal{A}$. The zeroth layer of $\mathcal{C}$, denoted by l_0, is composed of these $p+1$ arguments, partitioned into three groups as follows:

$$l_0 = \{u_1, \dots, u_{p_1}\} \cup \{v_1, \dots, v_{p_2}\} \cup \{z_1, \dots, z_{p_3}\}$$

where

$$\begin{aligned} p_3 &= \lfloor \log(p+1-\log p) - 2 \rfloor \\ p_1 &= \left\lfloor \frac{p+1-\log p - \log(p+1-\log p)}{2} \right\rfloor \\ p_2 &= p+1-p_3-p_1 \,. \end{aligned}$$

These parameters are chosen such that, for sufficiently large p, the number of units in $\mathcal{C}$ is asymptotically optimal.

Layer 1. The first layer l_1 consists of the following set of 2^{p_2} units:

$$l_1 = \{\mu_{\boldsymbol{b}} : \boldsymbol{b} \in \{0,1\}^{p_2}\}.$$

Each input of the second group $\{v_1, \dots, v_{p_2}\}$ is connected to all units of this layer.

Layer 2. The second layer l_2 consists of the following set of $p \cdot 2^{p_1+3}$ units:

$$l_2 = \left\{\gamma_{kj}^{\varphi a}, \lambda_{kj}^{\varphi a}, \gamma_{kj}^{\psi a}, \lambda_{kj}^{\psi a} : k \in \{1 \dots, p\}, j \in \{0, \dots, 2^{p_1}-1\}, a \in \{0,1\}\right\}.$$

These units are organized into p blocks of 2^{p_1+3} elements each parametrized by index $k \in \{1 \dots, p\}$, and denoted as $l_{21}, \dots, l_{2p}$. Each input from the first group $\{u_1, \dots, u_{p_1}\}$ (including the next input bit to $\mathcal{A}$) and each unit of the first layer l_1 are connected to all units of this layer.

Layer 3. The third layer l_3 consists of a set of $p \cdot 2^{p_3+1}$ units:

$$l_3 = \left\{\pi_{k,\boldsymbol{c}}, \varrho_{k,\boldsymbol{c}} : k \in \{1 \dots, p\}, \boldsymbol{c} \in \{0,1\}^{p_3}\right\}.$$

These units are also organized into p blocks of 2^{p_3+1} elements each parametrized by index $k \in \{1 \dots, p\}$, denoted by $l_{31}, \dots, l_{3p}$. For each $k = 1, \dots, p$, each unit of the group l_{2k} is connected to all units of the group l_{3k}. In addition, each input of the third group $\{z_1, \dots, z_{p_3}\}$ is connected to all units of this layer.

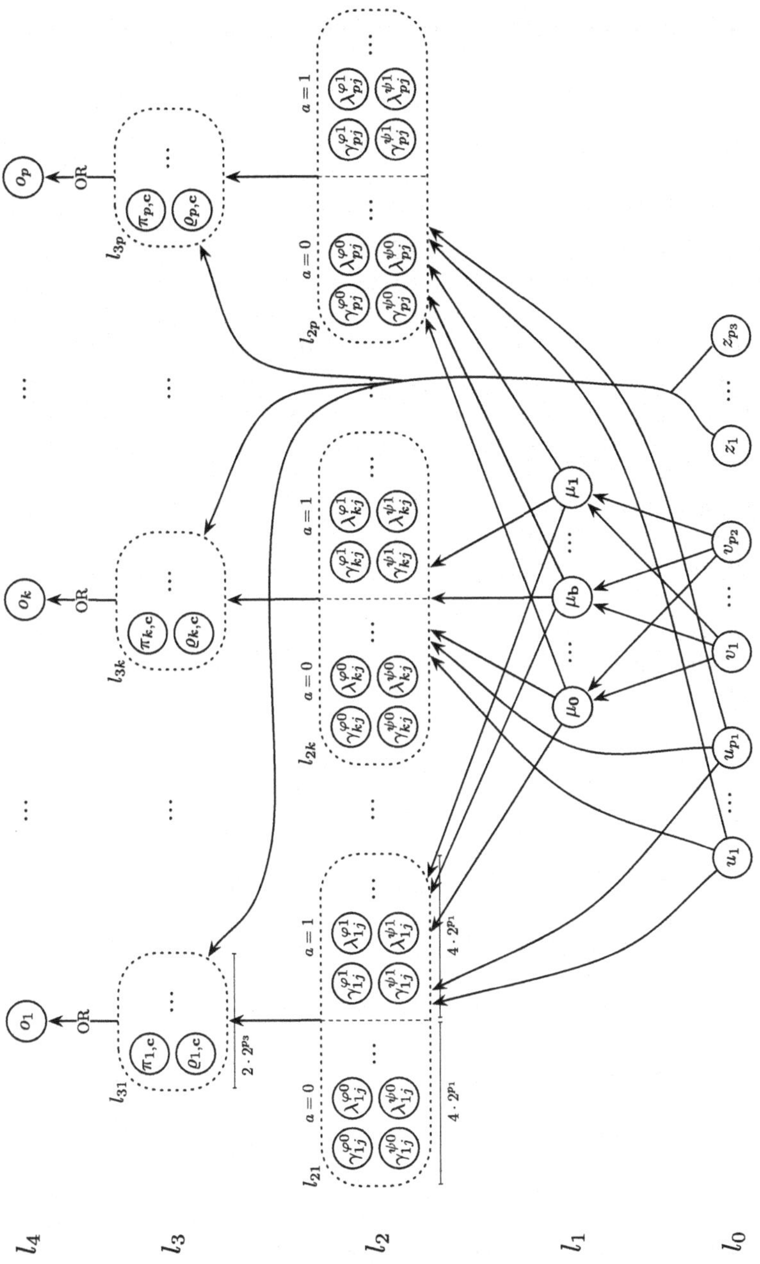

Fig. 1. Architecture of the threshold circuit $\mathcal{C}$ computing the Boolean transition function $\boldsymbol{f}_\delta$. The picture is rotated by 90°. The circuit is composed of an input layer l_0 and four layers l_1, l_2, l_3, l_4 of units (gates). An arrow connecting one unit to a block of units means that the former unit is connected to all units of the block (one-to-all connections). An arrow connecting one block of units to one unit means that all units of the block are connected to the latter unit (all-to-one connections). An arrow connecting one block of units to another means that all units of the former block are connected to all units of the latter (all-to-all connections).

Layer 4. The fourth layer l_4 is composed of the p following units:

$$l_4 = \{o_1, \ldots, o_p\}.$$

For each $k = 1, \ldots, p$, the unit o_k computes the logical disjunction (OR gate) of the outputs from the group l_{3k}. In order to implement these p OR gates, all weights associated to these units are equal to 1 whereas their biases equal -1.

Simulation of DFSA by Boolean Neural Networks. The Lupanov threshold circuit $\mathcal{C}$ computing $\boldsymbol{f}_\delta$ can easily be transformed into a recurrent neural network $\mathcal{N}$ simulating the automaton $\mathcal{A}$ [11]. This transformation is schematically illustrated and described in Fig. 2. According to this construction, the $p+1$ inputs forming the *input layer* of $\mathcal{C}$ correspond now to $p+3$ *input and state cells* in $\mathcal{N}$: one input cell `inp`, p state cells, and two additional validation and output cell `val` and `out` in order to comply with the input/output protocol. The activation values of these cells hold the consecutive encodings of the successive input symbols and computational states of $\mathcal{A}$. More specifically, if the input and state cells have activation values $(x, \boldsymbol{q}) \in \{0,1\}^{p+1}$ at time t, then the state cells will have activation values $\boldsymbol{q}' \in \{0,1\}^p$ at time $t+4$, where $\boldsymbol{q}'$ is such that $\delta(q, x) = q'$.

From these considerations, it follows that any finite state automaton with n states can be implemented by an optimal-size recurrent neural net with $\Theta(\sqrt{n})$ cells [11].

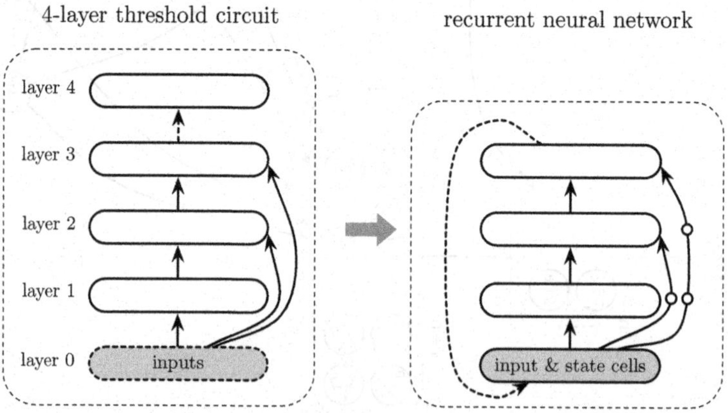

Fig. 2. Transformation of the 4-layer Lupanov threshold circuit $\mathcal{C}$ computing the Boolean function $\boldsymbol{f}_\delta$ into the recurrent neural network $\mathcal{N}$ simulating the automaton $\mathcal{A}$. The fourth layers of $\mathcal{C}$ is removed in $\mathcal{N}$; the connections from the third to the fourth layers in $\mathcal{C}$ (dashed arrow) are replaced by recurrent connections in $\mathcal{N}$ (dashed arrow); the connections from the input layer to the second and third layers in $\mathcal{C}$ are replaced by corresponding connections in $\mathcal{N}$ interspersed with delay cells (little circles), in order to ensure that the input propagation in the network is correctly timed.

4 Finite State Automata and Boolean Neural Networks Composed of Synfire Rings

Based on the results of Sect. 3, we show that any finite state automaton with n states can be implemented by a neural net composed of synfire rings containing $\Theta(\sqrt{n})$ cells. Compared to the construction of Sect. 3 and due to the addition of synfire rings, the proposed architecture has the advantage of being not only of asymptotic optimal-size, but also robust to possible failures of its constitutive cells. The general idea of this construction can be summarized as follows:

- the "state cells" of the network $\mathcal{N}$ of Sect. 3 are replaced by specific synfire rings: hence, the successive states of the automaton are now encoded by self-sustained activities of synfire rings instead of activations of "state cells";
- each *level* (not layer) of the synfire rings is connected to a copy of the network $\mathcal{N}$ of Sect. 3 (i.e., a modified copy of the Lupanov circuit).

Let $\mathcal{A} = (Q, \Sigma, \delta, q_0, F)$ be a finite state automaton and $\mathcal{C}$ be the Lupanov circuit computing $\boldsymbol{f}_\delta$ (Sect. 3). We provide the description of a synfire ring-based neural network $\mathcal{N}^{SR}$ simulating $\mathcal{A}$. The network is illustrated in Fig. 3.

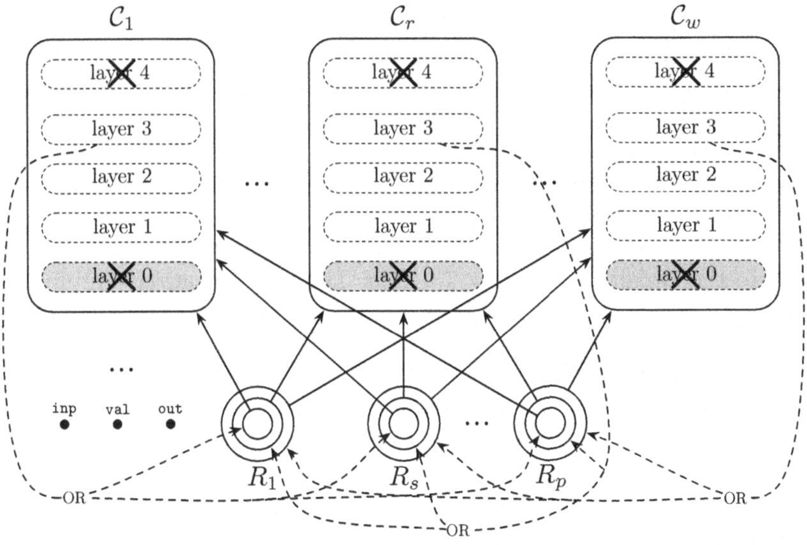

Fig. 3. Recurrent neural network composed of synfire rings $\mathcal{N}^{SR}$ simulating the automaton $\mathcal{A}$. The network is composed of an input, validation and output cell `inp`, `val` and `out`, respectively, of p synfire rings $R_1, \ldots, R_p$ of same widths w, and of w modified copies $\mathcal{C}_1, \ldots, \mathcal{C}_w$ of the Lupanov circuit $\mathcal{C}$. For each $r = 1, \ldots, w$, the r-th levels of the respective rings $R_1, \ldots, R_p$ are connected to the first, second and third layers of $\mathcal{C}_r$ (solid arrows) as described in the text. For each $r = 1, \ldots, w$ also, the third layer of $\mathcal{C}_r$ is recurrently connected to the r-th levels of all rings $R_1, \ldots, R_p$ (dashed arrows).

The network $\mathcal{N}^{SR}$ involves two input cells inp and val (as well as other cells of this kind described later), one output cell out, and p synfire rings $R_1, \ldots, R_p$ of respective lengths $\ell_1, \ldots, \ell_p \geq 2$ and of fixed widths $w \geq 1$. These rings will serve to encode the successive states of automaton $\mathcal{A}$. In addition, $\mathcal{N}^{SR}$ also involves of w copies of the circuit $\mathcal{C}$, denoted by $\mathcal{C}_1, \ldots, \mathcal{C}_w$. For each $r = 1, \ldots, w$, we let the p last inputs and p outputs of $\mathcal{C}_r$, i.e.,

$$u_2, \ldots, u_{p_1}, v_1, \ldots, v_{p_2}, z_1, \ldots, z_{p_3} \text{ and } o_1, \ldots, o_p$$

be denoted by $u'_{r1}, \ldots, u'_{rp}$ and $o_{r1}, \ldots, o_{rp}$, respectively.

As a first step, for each $r = 1, \ldots, w$, we remove the first layer of $\mathcal{C}_r$. Then, for every $r = 1, \ldots, w$ and $s = 1, \ldots, p$, we replace each connection from input u'_{rs} to some unit u in $\mathcal{C}_r$ by a corresponding fibre of connections from all cells of the r-th level of R_s to u. Furthermore, for each $r = 1, \ldots, w$, we remove the fourth layer (OR gates) of $\mathcal{C}_r$. Then, for every $r = 1, \ldots, w$ and $s = 1, \ldots, p$, we replace each connections from some unit u of the third layer of $\mathcal{C}_r$ to output o_{rs} by a recurrent connection from u to the first cell (only!) of the r-th level of R_s. In this way, each input u'_{rs} of $\mathcal{C}_r$ is represented by the r-th *level* of the ring R_s (ℓ_s cells). Recall that the dynamics of each ring R_s ensures that at most one cell is active within any of its level. Moreover, each output o_{rs} (OR gate) of $\mathcal{C}_r$ is implemented by recurrent connections from the third layer of $\mathcal{C}_r$ to the first cell (only) of the r-th level of the ring R_s.

The cells inp, val and out implement the input/output protocol of $\mathcal{N}^{SR}$. The connectivity related to these cells is described in Fig. 4. Recall that the activity of the last synfire ring R_p indicates whether the state currently encoded by the activities of the other rings $R_1, \ldots, R_{p-1}$ belongs to the set of final states F or not. This information is then transmitted from R_p to the output cell out via connections of weights 1 and a bias of -1 (OR gate implementation).

In order to complete the construction, further modifications need to be applied to the circuits $\mathcal{C}_r$, for $r = 1, \ldots, w$. These modifications are illustrated in Fig. 4 also. First of all, each unit of the first, second and third layer of $\mathcal{C}_r$ are provided with a sufficiently large negative bias $-W$ which prevents them from being activated. The validation cell val is connected to all units of the first layer of $\mathcal{C}_r$ with weights W. In this way, each time the cell val spikes, it cancels the negative biases of the first-layer units of $\mathcal{C}_r$, and therefore releases their activities. In addition, two new cells $\mathtt{inp}_{r1}$ and $\mathtt{val}_{r1}$ are added to the first layer of $\mathcal{C}_r$. These cells copy the current activities of inp and val via connections of weights $w(\mathtt{inp}, \mathtt{inp}_{r1}) = w(\mathtt{val}, \mathtt{val}_{r1}) = 1$. The cell $\mathtt{inp}_{r1}$ is connected to all units of the second layer of $\mathcal{C}_r$ with the weights given in [23], and the cell $\mathtt{val}_{r1}$ is also connected to all units of the second layer of $\mathcal{C}_r$ with weights W. Furthermore, a new cell $\mathtt{val}_{r2}$ is added to the second layer of $\mathcal{C}_r$, which just copies the current activity $\mathtt{val}_{r1}$ by a connection of weight $w(\mathtt{val}_{r1}, \mathtt{val}_{r2}) = 1$. The cell $\mathtt{val}_{r2}$ is connected to all units in the third layer of $\mathcal{C}_r$ via connections of weights W. Finally, connections with large negative weights $-W'$ connect $\mathtt{val}_{r2}$ to all cells of the r-th levels of $R_1, \ldots, R_p$. The weight $-W'$ is chosen such that it suffices to inhibit an activity propagating in a synfire ring.

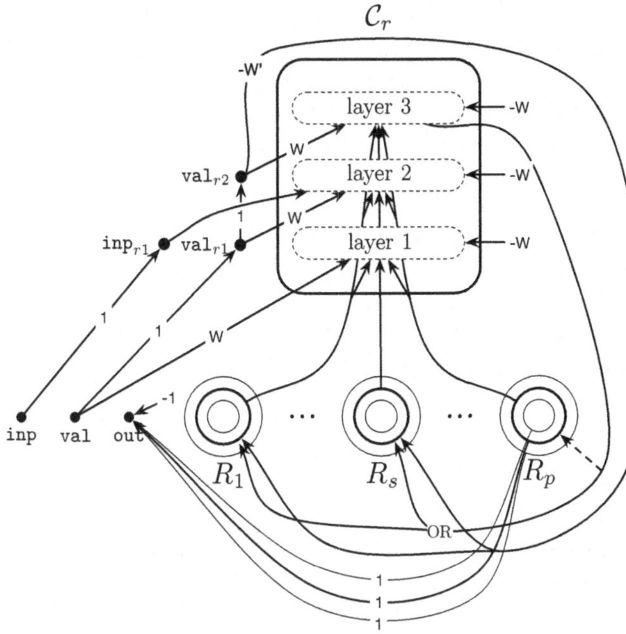

Fig. 4. Illustration of the r-th modified Lupanov circuits involved in the construction of the synfire ring-based network $\mathcal{N}^{SR}$. Biases of weights $-W$ are added to every cells of the first, second and third layers. Three cells $\texttt{inp}_{r1}$, $\texttt{val}_{r1}$, $\texttt{val}_{r2}$ are also added. The connection between those, and from those to the circuit's layers are described in the figure. In addition, recurrent connections of weights $-W'$ from $\texttt{val}_{r2}$ to the r-th levels of all rings $R_1, \ldots, R_p$ (in bold) serve to inhibit the rings (reinitialization), before the latter are reactivated by the recurrent connections from the third layer to their r-th levels (in bold). Finally, the cells `inp`, `val` and `out` implement the input/output protocol as described in the text.

Correctness of the Construction. We now sketch the proof that the synfire ring-based network $\mathcal{N}^{SR}$ simulates the finite state automaton $\mathcal{A}$ correctly. Suppose that the activities of the p synfire rings $R_1, \ldots, R_p$ are currently encoding the state $q \in Q$ of automaton $\mathcal{A}$. Suppose further that the input bit $x \in \{0, 1\}$ is received at time t. According to the input protocol, this means that $\texttt{inp}(t) = x$ and $\texttt{val}(t) = 1$. The network's architecture ensures that, for any $r = 1, \ldots, w$, the combined activities of the r-th levels of $R_1, \ldots, R_p$ together with the activation of `val` at time t will activate the first layer of $\mathcal{C}_r$ at time $t + 1$. The connections of $\mathcal{C}_r$ also ensure that $\texttt{inp}(t) = \texttt{inp}_{r1}(t+1)$ and $\texttt{val}(t) = \texttt{val}_{r1}(t+1) = 1$. Hence, the combined activities of the first layer of $\mathcal{C}_r$ together with the activation of $\texttt{val}_{r1}$ at time $t+1$ will activate the second layer of $\mathcal{C}_r$ at time $t+2$. The connections of $\mathcal{C}_r$ also ensure that $\texttt{val}_{r1}(t+1) = \texttt{val}_{r2}(t+2) = 1$. Consequently, the combined activities of the second layer of $\mathcal{C}_r$ together with the activation of $\texttt{val}_{r2}$ at time $t + 2$ will activate the third layer of $\mathcal{C}_r$ at time $t + 3$. But at time

$t+2$ also, $\mathtt{val}_{r2}$ sends strong inhibitions to the r-th levels of all rings $R_1, \ldots, R_p$. Since this happens for all $r \in \{1, \ldots, w\}$ simultaneously, the rings $R_1, \ldots, R_p$ are shut down at time $t+3$. Finally, the (special) recurrent activities from the third layers of all circuits $\mathcal{C}_1, \ldots, \mathcal{C}_w$ at time $t+3$ ensure that the activities of all rings $R_1, \ldots, R_p$ are correctly updated at time $t+4$. From the Lupanov's construction, it follows that, from time $t+4$ onwards, the activities of the rings $R_1, \ldots, R_p$ encode the state q' of $\mathcal{A}$ such that $\delta(q, x) = q'$. Finally, the unit out fires at the next time step $t+5$ iff q' is a final state. In this sense, each transition of $\mathcal{A}$ is correctly simulated by the network $\mathcal{N}^{SR}$.

If the automaton $\mathcal{A}$ contains n states, it has been shown that each Lupanov circuit $\mathcal{C}_r$ $(r = 1, \ldots, w)$ involved in the construction has an optimal-size of $\Theta(\sqrt{n})$. Therefore, the network $\mathcal{N}^{SR}$ has a size of $\Theta(w \cdot \sqrt{n}) = \Theta(\sqrt{n})$, which is also optimal.

5 Conclusion

We described a robust and optimal-size implementation of finite state automata by means of neural networks composed of synfire rings. The robustness of the network results from its architecture, which is composed of synfire rings and duplicated core components. For an automaton with n states, the corresponding network has an optimal size of $\Theta(\sqrt{n})$ cells.

This study makes one step forward in the implementation of finite state machines by biologically inspired neural networks. In an extended journal version of this paper, the construction is expected to be implemented, and examples of such synfire ring-based neural networks will be computationally simulated. Furthermore, the construction is expected to be generalized in such a way that only synfire rings are involved.

References

1. Abeles, M.: Corticonics: Neuronal Circuits of the Cerebral Cortex. Cambridge University Press, Cambridge (1991)
2. Abeles, M.: Time is precious. Science **304**(5670), 523–524 (2004). https://doi.org/10.1126/science.1097725
3. Cabessa, J., Horcholle-Bossavit, G., Quenet, B.: Neural computation with spiking neural networks composed of synfire rings. In: Lintas, A., Rovetta, S., Verschure, P.F.M.J., Villa, A.E.P. (eds.) ICANN 2017. LNCS, vol. 10613, pp. 245–253. Springer, Cham (2017). https://doi.org/10.1007/978-3-319-68600-4_29
4. Cabessa, J., Masulli, P.: Emulation of finite state automata with networks of synfire rings. In: 2017 International Joint Conference on Neural Networks, IJCNN 2017, Anchorage, AK, USA, May 14–19, 2017, pp. 4641–4648. IEEE (2017). https://doi.org/10.1109/IJCNN.2017.7966445
5. Cabessa, J., Siegelmann, H.T.: The super-turing computational power of plastic recurrent neural networks. Int. J. Neural Syst. **24**(8), 1450029 (2014). https://doi.org/10.1142/S0129065714500294

6. Cabessa, J., Tchaptchet, A.: Automata computation with Hodgkin-Huxley based neural networks composed of synfire rings. In: 2018 International Joint Conference on Neural Networks, IJCNN 2018, Rio de Janeiro, Brazil, July 8–13, 2018, pp. 1–8. IEEE (2018). https://doi.org/10.1109/IJCNN.2018.8489700
7. Diesmann, M., Gewaltig, M.O., Aertsen, A.: Stable propagation of synchronous spiking in cortical neural networks. Nature **402**, 529–533 (1999). https://doi.org/10.1038/990101
8. Hertz, J., Prügel-Bennett, A.: Learning synfire chains by self-organization. Netw.: Comput. Neural Syst. **7**(2), 357–363 (1996). https://doi.org/10.1088/0954-898X_7_2_017
9. Hertz, J., Prügel-Bennett, A.: Learning synfire chains: turning noise into signal. Int. J. Neural Syst. **7**(4), 445–450 (1996). https://doi.org/10.1142/S0129065796000427
10. Hopcroft, J.E., Motwani, R., Ullman, J.D.: Introduction to Automata Theory, Languages, and Computation, 3rd edn. Pearson international edition, Addison-Wesley, Boston (2007)
11. Horne, B.G., Hush, D.R.: Bounds on the complexity of recurrent neural network implementations of finite state machines. Neural Netw. **9**(2), 243–252 (1996). https://doi.org/10.1016/0893-6080(95)00095-X
12. Ikegaya, Y., et al.: Synfire chains and cortical songs: temporal modules of cortical activity. Science **304**(5670), 559–564 (2004). https://doi.org/10.1126/science.1093173
13. Indyk, P.: Optimal simulation of automata by neural nets. In: Mayr, E.W., Puech, C. (eds.) STACS 1995. LNCS, vol. 900, pp. 337–348. Springer, Heidelberg (1995). https://doi.org/10.1007/3-540-59042-0_85
14. Jun, J.K., Jin, D.Z.: Development of neural circuitry for precise temporal sequences through spontaneous activity, axon remodeling, and synaptic plasticity. PLOS One **2**(8), 1–17 (2007). https://doi.org/10.1371/journal.pone.0000723
15. Kleene, S.C.: Representation of events in nerve nets and finite automata. In: Shannon, C., McCarthy, J. (eds.) Automata Studies, vol. 34, pp. 3–42. Princeton University Press, Princeton (1956). https://doi.org/10.1515/9781400882618-002
16. Levy, N., Horn, D., Meilijson, I., Ruppin, E.: Distributed synchrony in a cell assembly of spiking neurons. Neural Netw. **14**(6–7), 815–824 (2001). https://doi.org/10.1016/S0893-6080(01)00044-2
17. Lupanov, O.B.: On the synthesis of threshold circuits. Probl. Kibernet. **26**, 109–140 (1973)
18. Mainen, Z., Sejnowski, T.: Reliability of spike timing in neocortical neurons. Science **268**(5216), 1503–1506 (1995). https://doi.org/10.1126/science.7770778
19. Minsky, M.L.: Computation: Finite and Infinite Machines. Prentice-Hall Inc., Englewood Cliffs (1967)
20. Siegelmann, H.T.: Neural Networks and Analog Computation: Beyond the Turing Limit. Birkhauser Boston Inc., Cambridge (1999)
21. Siegelmann, H.T., Sontag, E.D.: Analog computation via neural networks. Theor. Comput. Sci. **131**(2), 331–360 (1994). https://doi.org/10.1016/0304-3975(94)90178-3
22. Siegelmann, H.T., Sontag, E.D.: On the computational power of neural nets. J. Comput. Syst. Sci. **50**(1), 132–150 (1995). https://doi.org/10.1006/jcss.1995.1013
23. Šíma, J.: Energy complexity of recurrent neural networks. Neural Comput. **26**(5), 953–973 (2014). https://doi.org/10.1162/NECO_a_00579
24. Šíma, J., Orponen, P.: General-purpose computation with neural networks: a survey of complexity theoretic results. Neural Comput. **15**(12), 2727–2778 (2003). https://doi.org/10.1162/089976603322518731

25. Šíma, J., Wiedermann, J.: Theory of neuromata. J. ACM **45**(1), 155–178 (1998). https://doi.org/10.1145/273865.273914
26. Zheng, P., Triesch, J.: Robust development of synfire chains from multiple plasticity mechanisms. Front. Comput. Neurosci. **8**(66) (2014). https://doi.org/10.3389/fncom.2014.00066

A Neural Circuit Model of Adaptive Robust Tracking Control for Continuous-Time Nonlinear Systems

Pavlo Tymoshchuk[1,2(✉)]

[1] Silesian University of Technology, 44-100 Gliwice, Poland
pavlo.tymoshchuk@polsl.pl
[2] L'viv Polytechnic National University, L'viv 79000, Ukraine
pavlo.v.tymoshchuk@lpnu.ua

Abstract. A neural circuit model of adaptive robust tracking control for continuous-time unknown nonlinear dynamic systems is presented. A first-order differential equation with variable structure and an output equation are used to describe the circuit. A corresponding functional block-diagram of the circuit is given. There is discussed a possibility of software and hardware implementation of the circuit. Stability and convergence analysis of the circuit states is performed based on Lyapunov second method. An upper bound is estimated for the time required to reach a steady state by the circuit. The circuit operation with disturbances of its nonlinearity is discussed. The circuit has simple architecture, it can provide bounded tracking error and finite controlled convergence time to steady states and does not need off-line learning phase. Computer simulations of the circuit operation confirming the theoretical derivations and illustrating the performance of the circuit are provided.

Keywords: Neural circuit model · Nonlinear system · Tracking control

1 Introduction

A tracking control problem is to design such a system whose output approximately repeats the time-variable reference trajectory that is supposed to be predetermined. Tracking control systems are used in telecommunications, video, automobiles, ships, aircrafts, robotics, biomedical engineering, and in many other applications. For instance, problems such as the performance of a ship movement along a required route or fulfilling a manipulator arm movement are typical tracking control tasks. There are many approaches to tracking nonlinear dynamic systems which deal with an approximation, in particular, with linearization of the system nonlinearities. Moreover, these methods use assumptions concerning the structure of the tracker and PID-type control [1–3]. A linear feedback is used most often in order to track a given trajectory. Although the linearization method provides a good performance in many cases, there are many applications where more advanced tracking controllers are necessary. This problem is especially important if a high accuracy and speed tracking control of an essentially nonlinear system should be fulfilled in online mode.

I. V. Tetko et al. (Eds.): ICANN 2019, LNCS 11727, pp. 819–835, 2019.
https://doi.org/10.1007/978-3-030-30487-4_63

Different tracking controllers of nonlinear dynamic systems were proposed [4]. Most of such controllers have been designed for the nonlinear dynamic systems affine in the control. These methods of continuous-time and discrete-time tracking control of nonlinear systems unsure convergence of control inputs to steady states during theoretically infinite time [5], exponential stability and convergence to steady states [6], and uniform stability and convergence to steady states [7].

The second-order robust nonlinear dynamic system is used in [8] for designing a tracking control for multi-agent systems with the application for multi-robot systems that have input disturbances. The finite convergence time of the state variable trajectories to steady states is provided by using first-order terminal sliding variable. A robust continuous-time cooperative tracking control neural network (NN) for higher-order non-autonomous nonlinear systems with unknown but concise dynamics and with limited external unknown perturbations is presented in [9]. The network ensures finite convergence time to steady states. It is assumed that the system nonlinearities are locally Lipschitz continuous. The network is described by differential equations in the Brunovsky form with unknown nonlinearities. The nonlinearities are approximated by a set of basic functions.

In this paper, continuous-time neural circuit (NC) model of adaptive robust tracking control for unknown nonlinear dynamic systems is designed. The model is described by the first order differential equation with variable structure and by output equation. The circuit uses a difference between the output of the unknown nonlinear dynamic system and a reference in order to minimize the reference trajectory tracking error. A corresponding functional block-diagram of the circuit is presented. A possibility of the circuit implementation in software and analog hardware is discussed. Stability and convergence analysis of the circuit to steady states is fulfilled by using a second method of Lyapunov. A limit from above for convergence time of the circuit trajectories to the steady states is defined. The convergence time can be changed by varying the circuit single parameter. The tracking error of the circuit is bounded. The circuit operation in the conditions of disturbances of its nonlinearity is analyzed. Computer simulations confirming theoretical derivations and illustrating the circuit performance are given. In particular, the circuit is used to simulate the tracking of rotation angles of two-link planar elbow manipulator arm, to simulate change laws of rotation angles of stepping motors of two axis azimuth/elevation solar tracking system, and to tracking control of nonlinear dynamic system in 3D space.

The main contribution of the paper is that unlike other close analogs, the controller is described by using first order differential equation with variable structure and by output equation, it has simple architecture, provides bounded tracking error and finite controlled convergence time to steady states and does not need off-line learning phase. Moreover, it is promising for software and hardware implementation.

2 A Model of Continuous-Time Neural Circuit for the Tracking Control

2.1 The Problem Formulation

Continuous-time NNs compared to discrete-time versions are capable of providing a stable operation in broad change ranges of their parameters. Moreover, continuous-time circuits implemented in an analog hardware can reach a high operation speed, miniaturization level, and energy efficiency compared to their discrete-time counterparts [10]. Let us consider the continuous-time tracking control problem of an unknown non-affine in control nonlinear dynamic system that is defined as follows [1, 4]:

$$\dot{x}(t) = f(x(t), w(t)), \tag{1}$$

where $x(t) \in \Re^n$ is the continuous differentiable state vector of the system, $w(t) \in \Re^n$ is the control input, $f(x, w) \in \Re^n$ is the unknown nonlinear function, $\dot{x}(t)dx/dt$ is the time derivative of the system state vector, $x(0) = x_0 \in \Re^n$ is the initial condition.

The cost function associated with (1) is given by

$$J(x, d) = \int_0^\infty \varphi(x(t), d(t)), \tag{2}$$

where $d(t) \in \Re^n$ is the reference trajectory (i.e., the desired trajectory), $\varphi(x, d) \in \Re^n$ is the positive definite function.

The tracking control problem is to design a continuous-time tracking controller so that, starting from arbitrary finite initial state $-\infty < x_0 < \infty$, as t tends to infinity, (2) is minimized, i.e., optimal value function

$$V^*(x) = \min_d \int_0^\infty \varphi(x(t), d(t)) \tag{3}$$

for all possible initial values x_0. Equation (3) means that starting from any initial value, (2) should converge to its minimum, i.e., the circuit should be stable. In order to solve the tracking control problem of the continuous-time unknown non-affine nonlinear dynamic system formulated above it is necessary to design a controller such that *x(t)* tracks a given time-varying reference trajectory *d(t)*.

2.2 The Model of the Tracking Control Neural Circuit

Since the structure and parameters of the dynamic system described by (1) are unknown, one can approximate the function $f(x, w)$ of this system by using multilayer NN based on Stone-Weierstrass theorem [11]. The control input can be approximated in the same way. However, an error of such approximation goes to zero only if a number of the network layers and neurons approaches infinity. This can lead to an unrealistic increase of the circuit complexity. Therefore, we design a continuous-time tracking control NC for special case of (1) in the following way. Consider an unknown nonlinear dynamic system given by

$$\dot{y}(t) = g(y(t)), \tag{4}$$

where $y(t) \in \Re^n$ is the system continuous differentiable state vector, $g(y) \in \Re^n$ is the unknown nonlinear function, $\dot{y}(t) = dy/dt \in \Re^n$ is the time derivative of the system state vector, $y(0) = y_0 \in \Re^n$ is the initial condition. We define a controlled trajectory of the system as follows:

$$z(t) = y(t) + u(t), \tag{5}$$

where $u(t) \in \Re^n$ is the control input. Let us use the state Eq. (4) and output Eq. (5) to describe a nonlinear dynamic system with controlled output.

For derivation convenience, we define the augmented reference trajectory given by

$$v(t) = r(t) - y(t), \tag{6}$$

where $r(t) \in \Re^n$ is the reference continuous differentiable trajectory, i.e., the desired output. Taking into account (5) and (6), the tracking error can be presented as follows:

$$e(t) = z(t) - r(t) = u(t) - v(t). \tag{7}$$

Let us suppose that the desired output $r(t)$, the system state $y(t)$, and their time derivatives $\dot{r}(t)$ and $\dot{y}(t)$ are bounded and available for computation. This assumption can be satisfied by a tracking control task for real systems, where $r(t)$ and $y(t)$ are accessible at each time and $r(t)$, $y(t)$, $\dot{r}(t)$, $\dot{y}(t)$ are bounded. Therefore, the time derivatives of $r(t)$ and $y(t)$ can be obtained by using their numerical differentiation [1] and the time derivative of the augmented reference trajectory can be given by

$$\dot{v}(t) = \dot{r}(t) - \dot{y}(t). \tag{8}$$

We describe the NC model of continuous-time tracking control by using the following state equation with variable structure:

$$\dot{u} = \frac{du}{dt} = -(\alpha + |\dot{v}|) sgn(u - v) \tag{9}$$

where $u \in \Re^n$ is a state vector, $a \in \Re^n$ is a constant parameter,

$$sgn(u_k - v_k) = \begin{cases} 1, & if \quad u_k > v_k; \\ 0, & if \quad u_k = v_k; \\ -1, & if \quad u_k < v_k \end{cases} \tag{10}$$

is a signum activation function [12], $k = 1, \ldots, n$, $u(0) = u_0 \in \Re^n$ is an initial condition. It is proved below that the state Eq. (9) provides a convergence of the state variable u trajectory to the augmented reference v trajectory. Moreover, it is shown that (9) ensures finite time of this convergence. In addition, it is stated that the parameter α can be used to reduce a convergence time of the state variable u trajectories to the steady states that leads to reducing a tracking error of the circuit.

Consider the model described by the state Eq. (9) and by output Eq. (5). In these equations, $v \in \Re^n$ can be interpreted as the input signal, the function $sgn(u - v)$ is the signum activation function, the state vector $u \in \Re^n$ is the variable bias, and $z \in \Re^n$ is the output signal. However, the elements listed above are basic elements of nonlinear model of the artificial neuron [12]. Moreover, the state Eq. (9) can be interpreted as the equation of the supervised learning of the neuron with learning rate $\alpha + |\dot{v}|$. In addition, the model (9), (5) describes only one layer of neurons which do not have interconnections unlike multilayer interconnected NNs. Therefore, the model described by the state Eq. (9) and by output Eq. (5) is called here the NC model of continuous-time tracking control.

Note that in the case if $y(t) = 0$ and $\dot{y}(t) = 0$, equality $z(t) = u(t)$ follows from (5) and equalities $v(t) = r(t)$, $\dot{v}(t) = \dot{r}(t)$ are obtained from (6) and (8). Therefore, in order to use the model described by the state Eq. (9) and by output Eq. (5) for tracking control of unknown nonlinear dynamic systems in the case if $y(t)$ is purely noise or has chaotic dynamics, one can change values of $y(t)$, $\dot{y}(t)$ having set $y(t) = 0$ and $\dot{y}(t) = 0$ correspondingly.

2.3 A Functional Block-Diagram of the Circuit

A functional block-diagram of the tracking control NC described by (9) and (5) is shown in Fig. 1. It includes the system state y, desired reference r, augmented reference v, blocks of system S, summing $\sum$, variable structure function F, integration I, differentiation D, absolute value Abs, external sources of constant signals u_0 and α, and control input u. The block of variable structure function F computes the right-hand side of (9) by using $\alpha + |\dot{v}|$ and $u - v$ terms. The diagram presented in Fig. 1 can be implemented by four summers, two controlled switches, two inverters, an integrator, a differentiator, and two sources of constant signals. In particular, the Abs block and F block can be implemented using controlled switches and inverters.

This continuous-time tracking controller described by (9) and (5) has simple structure unlike other close analogs. For instance, the tracking controller of continuous-time systems based on reinforcement learning presented in [13] requires three NNs, in particular, the actor NN, the critic NN, and the disturber NN comparatively to one tracking control NC presented in Fig. 1. The NN approximations to the optimal value function and the optimal policy are necessary to track continuous-time nonlinear systems by using optimal controller based on adaptive dynamic programming approach presented in [14]. Actor NN and critic NN are required to tune for optimal tracking of nonlinear discrete-time systems in [15].

The circuit can be implemented in a parallel software on a PC or workstation with no special hardware. The computer software provides a realization simplicity of the circuit, its operation accuracy and flexibility of changing the application. For this

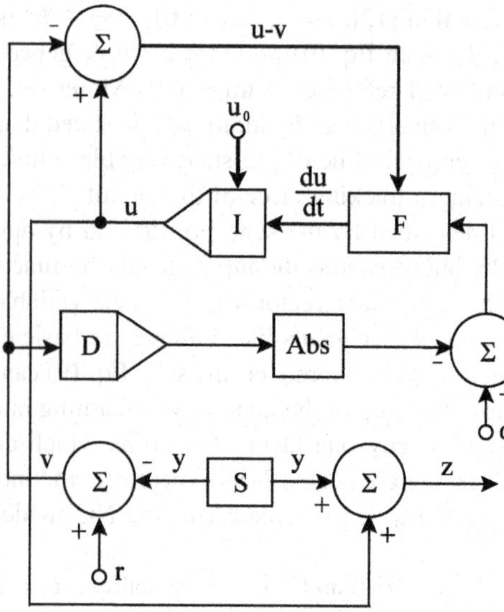

Fig. 1. The functional block-diagram of the tracking control NC described by (9) and (5).

purpose, one can use, for instance, a parallel computing toolbox of Matlab or Compute Unified Device Architecture (CUDA) [16]. Employing a power of modern Graphics Processing Units (GPUs) enables realization of the circuit using GPU code which significantly increases its operation speed. Practical operation accuracy and speed of the circuit is limited by its software implementation restrictions.

In the case of software realization of the circuit, its processing speed can be not high enough to meet the demands of real-time. Moreover, in this case, miniaturization level or/and energy efficiency of the circuit may be insufficient to satisfy the requirements of practical applications. Therefore, an analog hardware implementation of the circuit which is appropriate for real-time operation using VLSI technology and provides an increasing operation speed, miniaturization and energy efficiency can be designed. For the hardware implementation simulation of the circuit, Cadence, LabVIEW or other relevant code can be used [17, 18].

Practical operation accuracy of the circuit is also limited by its hardware implementation restrictions. In particular, the analog differentiator is capable of generating unstable outputs if noised outputs of real systems should be processed. This can require filtering of the differentiator inputs. Moreover, the most inertial element of the circuit hardware implementation is analog integrator which, however, is capable of operating in the frequency range up to MHz [10].

The circuit does not require a resetting if the inputs are changed, a suitable analog control circuit, and does not need spend extra processing time. This decreases its complexity and speeds up the circuit operation and makes it possible to use it in a real-time. Therefore, an analog hardware implementation of the circuit is expected to be fast, simple, compact, and energy efficient.

3 Stability and Convergence to the Circuit Steady States

It is required that state variable trajectory of (9) should be stable, i.e., that starting from the initial value u_0, after convergence, this trajectory accepts the steady-state $u(t*) = v(t)$. In order to ensure a stability of Eq. (9) solutions, let us investigate a convergence of these solutions to steady states having used a second method of Lyapunov [19]. We are going to obtain sufficient conditions for a stability and a convergence of the solutions of (9) to steady states.

Lemma 1. If the bounds $0 < \alpha < \infty$ are satisfied, then the solutions of (9) are Lyapunov stable and converge to steady states for any finite initial conditions $-\infty < u_0 < \infty$.

Proof. Using a shift of the origin to the equilibrium point $u = u* = v$, we write (9) in equivalent Persidskii type form [19]

$$\dot{s} = \frac{ds}{dt} = \begin{cases} -\alpha - |\dot{v}|, & if \quad s > 0; \\ 0, & if \quad s = 0; \\ \alpha + |\dot{v}|, & if \quad s < 0, \end{cases} \tag{11}$$

where $s := u - u* = u - v$.

Let us consider the following Lyapunov function candidate associated with the differential Eq. (11):

$$V(s) = \int_0^s \tau d\tau. \tag{12}$$

Observe that (12) is continuous, nonnegative function confined from below that accepts the smallest value equal to zero at $s = u - v = 0$. Further, $V(s) > 0$ for $s \neq 0$ and $V(s) = 0$ if and only if $s = 0$. From (12), the derivative $dV(s)/ds$ is given by

$$\frac{dV(s)}{ds} = s. \tag{13}$$

Therefore, the time derivative $\dot{V} = dV/dt$ along a solution $s(t)$ of (11) is defined as follows:

$$\dot{V} = \frac{dV}{dt} = \frac{dV}{ds}\frac{ds}{dt} = \begin{cases} (-\alpha - |\dot{v}|)s, & if \quad s > 0; \\ 0, & if \quad s = 0; \\ (\alpha + |\dot{v}|)s, & if \quad s < 0. \end{cases} \tag{14}$$

Let us analyze the Eq. (14). The right-hand side of (14) is less than zero if $s \neq 0$ and it is equal to zero if $s = 0$ for each $0 < \alpha < \infty$. Therefore, it follows here that if inequalities $0 < \alpha < \infty$ are met, then

$$\dot{V}\begin{cases} <0, & if \quad s \neq 0; \\ =0, & if \quad s = 0. \end{cases} \tag{15}$$

Thus, $\dot{V} \equiv 0$ if $s \equiv 0$. Derivative (15) is negative definite for each $s \neq 0$, i.e., $\dot{V} < 0$ if the condition $0 < \alpha < \infty$ holds excluding the points of steady-states in which the derivative disappears. Therefore, if inequalities $0 < \alpha < \infty$ are satisfied, (12) is a continuous-time function that decreases monotonously along the trajectory $s(t)$. Function $V(s)$ is limited from below, radially unbounded (i.e., $V \to +\infty$ if $|s| \to +\infty$), convex and accepts a zero minimal value. It follows that in accordance with the Lyapunov stability theory, this function and its derivative converge to zero. This ensures that $s = 0$ (or $u = v$) is a stable point, i.e., the dynamics of (11) is stable. Since the equality $s = 0$ holds at the point $u = v$, this point is a steady state solution of (11).

Hence, for $\dot{V} \leq 0$ with $\dot{V} = 0$ if $s = 0$, if a solution of (9) changes, the condition $0 < \alpha < \infty$ is sufficient for $u(t)$ to be stable in the sense of Lyapunov and convergent to the steady state. ■

Corrolary. Since (12) describes in fact the tracking error of the circuit, the tracking error converge to zero if inequalities $0 < \alpha < \infty$ are satisfied.

Let us analyze a convergence quality of Eq. (11) solutions to the steady states. Since the state Eq. (9) has a piecewise continuous right-hand side, define a certain set Ψ as follows:

$$\Psi := \{u : u - v = 0\}. \tag{16}$$

The right-hand side of Eq. (9) is discontinuous at each Ψ. Let a steady state solution of (9) be a scalar u such that $u \in \Psi$ and the set Ψ is referred to as a surface of discontinuity. We formulate the following lemma.

Lemma 2. If the inequalities $0 < \alpha < \infty$ are satisfied, then the solutions of (11) converge, from an arbitrary finite initial condition $-\infty < s_0 < \infty$, to the steady state set Ψ within a finite interval of time.

Proof. Consider (11), (12), (13), and the set Ψ (16). There exists such a scalar $\varepsilon > 0$ that $\dot{V} \leq -\varepsilon$ if $s \neq 0$. It follows from (14) and (15) that inequality $\dot{V} \leq -\alpha$ holds for each $s \neq 0$. Thus, $V(s)$ should decrease to zero in a finite period of time and the time required to overtake a surface of discontinuity $s = 0$

$$t^* \leq \frac{V_0}{\alpha}, \tag{17}$$

where V_0 is an initial value of $V(s)$. Since V_0 is finite for each $s \neq 0$ according to (12), therefore t^* is also finite for any $0 < \alpha < \infty$. Hence, one can claim that solution trajectories of (11) reach the set Ψ in a finite period of time. Since (11) has been derived by using (9), this is also valid for the solutions of (9). Thus, the solutions of (9, 8) converge to required values $u = v$ in finite time.

Let us show that the solutions of (9) remain in Ψ. If $s(t) \in \Psi$, then $V(s) = 0$ with $\dot{V} = 0$. If for a certain time $t = \chi$, the variable $s(\chi)$ leaves Ψ, then $\dot{V}(\chi) < 0$ and $V(\chi) > 0$, which is a collision since V is a decreasing or equal to zero function of the solution of (11). Hence, the solution of (11) reaches the set Ψ and stays in it. Since (9) and (11) are equivalent, this is also true for the solutions of (8). ■

Although V_0 in inequality (17) is unknown, the result is important. Since u_0 and v are finite, V_0 is also finite. Finite values of V_0 and α in (17) imply that the convergence time of the solutions of (9) to steady states t^* is finite. Moreover, since $V_0 = |u_0 - v|$, t^* in (17) is directly proportional to $|u_0 - v|$. This means that t^* decreases if $|u_0 - v|$ decreases. If bounds for $u(t)$ and for the augmented reference (6) are known, bound for maximal value of $t*$ can be defined as follows:

$$t^*_{max} = \frac{|u_b - r_b + y_b|_{max}}{\alpha}, \tag{18}$$

where $u_b = (u_{min}, u_{max})$, $r_b = (r_{min}, r_{max})$, $y_b = (y_{min}, y_{max})$ are bounds for u, r and y. In addition, t^* in (17) is inversely proportional to α, i.e., the convergence time t^* decreases if α increases and $t* \to 0$ if $\alpha \to \infty$.

If bounds for u and $v = r - y$ are known, bound for maximal value of the tracking error can be given by

$$V_{max} = |u_b - r_b + y_b|_{max}. \tag{19}$$

As it can be seen, the state Eq. (9) solution in fact approximates the augmented reference (6) by piecewise-constant time function. This function has transients t^* between its neighbor constant parts. An error of such approximation, i.e., the tracking error of the circuit $V = |u - v|$ decreases if the duration t^* of the transients decreases. This means that the tracking error of the circuit decreases if α increases.

The parameter α can be used for reducing the convergence time and tracking error of the circuit. A practical value of α can be chosen as a result of compromise between the convergence time, i.e., an accuracy of the tracking and software/hardware implementation restrictions of high value parameter/voltage source.

4 Disturbances of the Circuit Nonlinearity

The state Eq. (9) includes the nonlinear function of the time derivative of the augmented reference trajectory $\dot{v}$. This function can have disturbances which can cause changes in the nonlinearity from its nominal values. As a result, deviations of Eq. (9) solutions can take place. Therefore, conditions should be provided under which solutions of (9) will be stable to the disturbances of the nonlinearity.

Let us suppose that the function $\dot{v}$ is not perfect, but changes continuously within small ranges. The state Eq. (9) with the disturbed nonlinearity can be given by

$$\dot{w} = \begin{cases} -\beta - |\dot{v}|, & if \quad w > v; \\ 0, & if \quad w = v; \\ \beta + |\dot{v}|, & if \quad w < v, \end{cases} \tag{20}$$

where w is a deviated control input, $\dot{w} = dw/dt$ is a derivative of the disturbed control input, $\beta = \alpha + \delta$, $0 < \delta < \infty$ is a disturbance. In similar way as it was done above, the following result can be obtained. If the bounds $0 < \beta < \infty$ are satisfied, then the solutions of (20) are Lyapunov stable and converge to steady states for any finite initial conditions $-\infty < w_0 < \infty$.

The time of convergence can be given by

$$\rho^* \le \frac{E_0}{\beta}, \tag{21}$$

where

$$E(r) = \int_0^r \lambda d\lambda \tag{22}$$

is the Lyapunov function associated with the following differential equation:

$$\dot{q} = \frac{dr}{dt} = \begin{cases} -\beta - |\dot{v}|, & if \quad q > 0; \\ 0, & if \quad q = 0; \\ \beta + |\dot{v}|, & if \quad q < 0, \end{cases} \tag{23}$$

$q := w - w* = w - v$.

It follows from (20) that in order to ensure a correct operation of the state Eq. (9) in the presence of disturbances of the nonlinear function $\dot{v}$, value of parameter β should larger than that of the disturbance δ. Thus, in order to ensure a correct operation of the continuous-time tracking control NC described by the state Eq. (9) and output Eq. (5) in the presence of disturbances of the nonlinearity $\dot{v}$, the bound $\beta > \delta$ should be satisfied.

Let us define the set Ψ in the presence of disturbances of the nonlinearity $\dot{v}$ as follows:

$$\Omega := \{w : w - v = 0\}. \tag{24}$$

If a solution of the differential Eq. (20) is limited by the discontinuity surface Ω, the inequality $\beta > \delta$ is satisfied and conditions of sliding modes are met, a sliding motion can take place, i.e., the NC states can operate in a sliding mode [20, 21]. We suppose that the equation of the sliding mode is $q = w - v = 0$. Then, a sliding motion of solutions of the Eq. (20) in hyperplane q can occur if the conditions

$$\dot{q} \geq 0, \dot{q} \leq 0 \quad (25)$$
$$q \to -0 \quad q \to +0$$

are met [22]. Consider firstly the case if $q = w - v \to -0$. In this case, $\dot{q} = \begin{cases} \alpha + \delta + |\dot{v}| > 0, & if \quad q = w - v < 0; \\ = 0, & if \quad q = w - v = 0, \dot{v} = 0 \end{cases}$ according to (25). In the second case if $q = w - v \to +0$, it follows from (25) that $\dot{q} = \begin{cases} -\alpha - |\dot{v}| < 0, & if \quad q = w - v > 0; \\ = 0, & if \quad q = w - v = 0, \dot{v} = 0. \end{cases}$ Hence, since the conditions (25) of the existence of a sliding mode in solutions of the Eq. (9) can hold, the sliding motion in the NC can occur.

The border $\dot{q} = 0$ in (25) indicates the existence possibility of degenerative trajectories of Eq. (25) solutions and, therefore, the existence possibility of degenerative trajectories of Eq. (9) solutions. In this case, a solution of (9) is determined on the discontinuity surface Ψ from degenerative equation $\dot{u} = 0$ and the solution is $u = v$. If the deviations in (9) take place, the degenerative motion can be transformed to a sliding mode.

In practice, a speed of switching operations is finite. If the circuit described by the state Eq. (9) and by output Eq. (5) is implemented in a real software or hardware, then the errors in numerical calculations, e.g., numerical differentiation, operation inaccuracies and time delays can lead to a chattering of the Eq. (9) solution instead of sliding aboard the manifold Ψ. Therefore, the solution can present oscillations of finite frequency and amplitude [22].

5 Computer Simulations of the Circuit

Let us consider computer simulation examples of practical applications of continuous-time NC described by (9) and (5) for tracking control that illustrate its performance.

Example 1. For comparison with other close analogs, consider a simulation example of tracking rotation angles of two-link planar elbow manipulator arm with no friction term adopted from [23] and [24].The changes of the arm rotation angles are described by the joint variable $u = (u_1, u_2)^T$, where u_1 is an actual rotation angle of the first link and u_2 is an actual rotation angle of the second link. Since in this example $y = (y_1, y_2)^T = (0, 0)^T$, the equalities $z = (z_1, z_2)^T = u$ and $v = (v_1, v_2)^T = r = (r_1, r_2)^T$ are met, where r_1 and r_2 are desired rotation angles of the arm. The following laws are used for the desired rotation angles of the arms: $r_1(t) = sin(t)$ and $r_2(t) = cos(t)$. In order to solve (9) by numerical method, corresponding two difference equations are used with the time steps $r_2(t) = cos(t)\Delta t_1 = \Delta t_2 = 1.2 * 10^{-3}$. Elements of the function $|\dot{r}|$ in these difference equations are computed as first-order finite differences (Newton's difference quotients). In the difference equations, equality $u = r$ is replaced with inequality $|u - r| \leq 0.02v$.

Figure 2 shows the dynamics of the desired rotation angle r of the arm and the dynamics of the state *u(t)* of the continuous-time tracking control NC described by the difference equations, where $\alpha_k = 10, u_k(0) \in (-0.5, 0.5)$ are 100 uniformly distributed random numbers, k = *1, 2*. As one can see in Fig. 2, u_1 and u_2 converge to r_1 and r_2 correspondingly in finite time for different initial values $u_k(0)$, k = *1, 2*. The accuracy of tracking rotation angles of the arm is not lower than those in close analogs presented in [23] and [24]. However, standard adaptive controller described by second-order differential equations with fairly complicated matrix of robot functions that must be explicitly derived from the dynamics of each arm is used for the tracking in [23]. In [24], NN controller with 10 hidden-layer neurons is applied to track the rotation angles of the arms. The architecture of the continuous-time tracking control NC described by the state Eq. (9) and output Eq. (5) is simpler than those of standard adaptive controller described in [23] and multilayer NN controller presented in [24].

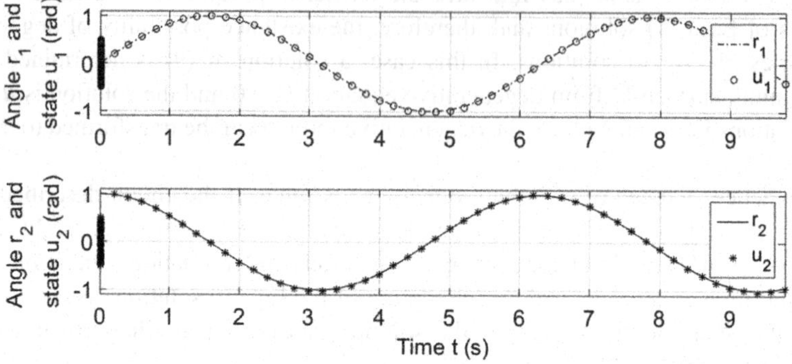

Fig. 2. The dynamics of the desired rotation angle $r(t) = (r_1(t), r_2(t))^T$ of the arm and the dynamics of the state $u(t) = (u_1(t), u_2(t))^T$ of continuous-time tracking NC described by a difference equation corresponding (9) with $\Delta t_1 = \Delta t_2 = 1.2 \times 10^{-3}$, $\alpha_k = 10$ where $u_k(0)$ are 100 uniformly distributed random numbers on the interval *(−0.5, 0.5)*, k = *1, 2* – Example 1.

Example 2. An important problem of transforming sunlight to the electrical energy by using solar cells is a decreasing cost of the obtained solar energy. A power of the solar concentrator rises if the solar tracking control technique is applied. Solar tracking controllers increase the efficiency of solar cells by keeping the cells in the sun beam direction. Using the solar tracking controller can essentially amplify the gathered energy in different time periods and climate conditions. Such a controller is capable of boosting the power output up to 100% depending on location and season [25]. An operation accuracy is very important in the solar tracking control system because the higher the accuracy of such a system is, the higher efficiency can be reached. This is due to the fact that if the solar tracking control system ensures an accurate sun tracking performance, the intensity of the solar energy reached at the receiver rises. In order to maintain the solar concentrator in the direction towards the sun beam, various approaches of solar tracking control were proposed [25, 26]. These methods require the use of computers or weather forecasts that should be updated in a real-time during the operation day. Moreover, such approaches can depend on expensive and sophisticated instruments and/or do not have formal guarantees for convergence to correct states.

Therefore, designing accurate and simple solar tracking control systems with guaranteed finite time convergence to correct states is an important and urgent problem to be solved.

Let us simulate change laws of rotation angles of stepping motors of two axis azimuth/elevation solar tracking system [27]. We suppose that desired references of sun position are defined by change laws of rotation angles of each stepping motor as follows:

$$v_1 = \begin{cases} q_1, & \textit{if} \quad t_{1min} < t < t_{1max}; \\ 90, & \textit{otherwise}, \end{cases} \tag{26}$$

$$v_2 = \begin{cases} q_2, & \textit{if} \quad t_{2min} < t < t_{2max}; \\ 0, & \textit{otherwise}, \end{cases} \tag{27}$$

where t is a time, $t_{1min} = \left(2 - \sqrt{0.99}\right)a_1$, $t_{1max} = \left(2 + \sqrt{0.99}\right)a_1$, $t_{2min} = (2 - \sqrt{0.99})a_2$, $t_{2max} = \left(2 + \sqrt{0.99}\right)a_2$, v_1 is a change law of required rotation angle of the altitude, v_2 is a change law of required rotation angle of the azimuth, $q_1 = \frac{b_1}{a_1}\sqrt{a_1^2 - (t - 2a_1)^2}$, $q_2 = \frac{0.45b_2}{\sqrt{0.99}a_2}\left(t - t_{2min}\right)$, a_1, a_2 and b_1, b_2 are constant parameters. As it can be seen, expression (26) for v_1 describes a positive part of an ellipse with radius a_1 on the t abscissa axis and with radius b_1 on the v_1 ordinate axis. The ellipse is shifted to the right by $2a_1$ on the abscissa axis and it is shifted down by $0.1b_1$ on the ordinate axis if $t_{1min} < t < t_{1max}$. Otherwise if $t \leq t_{1min}$, $t \geq t_{1max}$, v_1 is equal to 90. The expression (27) for v_2 describes a piecewise-linear function if $t_{2min} < t < t_{2max}$ and it is equal to zero otherwise.

Let us set $a = (6,\ 6)^{\ T}$ h, $b = (10^o, 180^o)^T$, $\alpha = (0.1, 0.1)^T$ and $u_1(0) = 0$, $u_2(0) = 0$, and, therefore, $T = (T_1, T_2)^T$, where $T_1 = t_{1max} - T_{1min} = T_1 = t_{1max} - T_{1min} = t_{1max} - T_{1min} = T_2 = t_{2max} - T_{2min} = 11.9$ h. We add to the right-hand side of the state Eq. (9) the random noise uniformly distributed on the interval $(-0.2,\ 0.2)$ for $k = 1$ and the random noise uniformly distributed on the interval $(-0.1,\ 0.1)$ for $k = 2$, i.e. we set $\delta_1 = 0.4$ and $\delta_2 = 0.2$. Moreover, like in previous example, in this equation equality $u_k = v_k$, $k = 1,\ 2$ is replaced with inequality $|u_k - v_k| \leq 0.01v_k$. In addition, in order to obtain solutions of the differential Eq. (9) by numerical integration, we scale the references v_1 and v_2 by dividing their values by *100* and *1000*, correspondingly, before solving it.

The dynamics of state $u(t) = (u_1(t),\ u_2(t))^T$ of continuous-time tracking control NN described by the noised differential Eq. (9) obtained by solving corresponding finite difference equation, where $\alpha_k = 0.1$, $k=1,2$, $u_1(0) = 90°$, $u_2(0) = 0°$ with the time steps $\Delta t_1\ \Delta t_2 = 0.05$ and the dynamics of the reference vector $v(t) = (v_1(t),\ v_2(t))^T$ described by expressions (26) and (27) are presented in Fig. 3. Elements of the function $\dot{v}$ in this difference equation are computed as first-order finite differences.

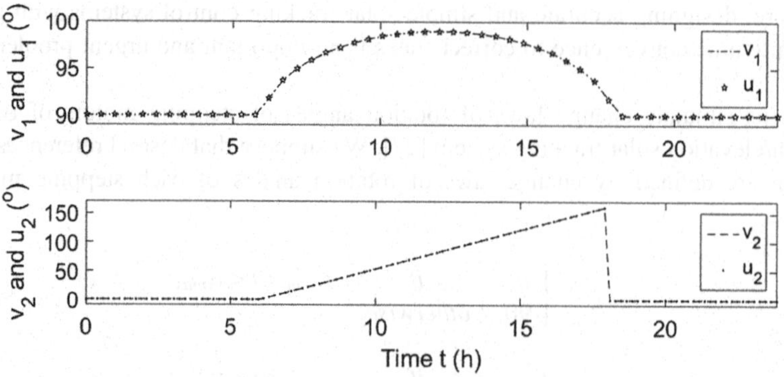

Fig. 3. Trajectories of the state $u(t) = (u_1(t), u_2(t))^T$ of the differential Eq. (9) with added to its right-hand side the random noise uniformly distributed on the interval $(-0.2, 0.2)$ for $k = 1$ and the random noise uniformly distributed on the interval $(-0.1, 0.1)$ for $k = 2$, the reference altitude $v_1(t)$ (26), and the reference azimuth $v_2(t)$ (27) – Example 2.

As it can be seen in Fig. 3, the state vector elements follow the altitude and the azimuth with high accuracy. In order to additionally increase an accuracy of tracking in the case of the noised Eq. (9), filtering of $\dot{u}_k$ (or u_k) can be applied, for instance, by using corresponding NN filters [28].

Example 3. Consider a simulation example of application the NC for system tracking control in 3D space. We describe a movement trajectory of the system (e.g., drone) as follows:

$$\dot{p} = -a(b+p), \tag{28}$$

where $p = (p_1, p_2, p_3)^T$, $b = (b_1, b_2, b_3)^T = (6, 7.2, 6.6)$, $a = (a_1, a_2, a_3)^T = (0.04, 0.05, 0.06)^T$, $\dot{p} = (\dot{p}_1, \dot{p}_2, \dot{p}_3)^T$, $p(0) = (0, 0, 0)^T$

$$\begin{aligned} \dot{q}_1 &= \omega\lfloor q_2 + q_1(1 - q_1^2 - q_2^2)\rfloor; \\ \dot{q}_2 &= \omega\lfloor q_1 + q_2(1 - q_1^2 - q_2^2)\rfloor; \\ \dot{q}_3 &= \omega\lfloor q_2^2 + q_1^2 + q_1 q_2 - q_3\rfloor \end{aligned} \tag{29}$$

is the autonomous periodic system adopted from [29], where $\omega = 3$ and $q(0) = (0, 1, 0)^T$,

$$y = p + q, \tag{30}$$

$y = (y_1, y_2, y_3)^T$.

The reference is given by

$$r = h_0 + h_1 t + h_2 t^2, \tag{31}$$

where $h_0 = (h_{01}, h_{02}, h_{03})^T = (2, 7, 6)^T$, $h_1 = (h_{11}, h_{12}, h_{13})^T = (0.3, 0.8, 0.7)^T$, $h_2 = (h_{21}, h_{22}, h_{23})^T = (0.004, 0.006, 0.005)^T$, $r = (r_1, r_2, r_3)^T$. The tracking control NC is described by (9), where $v_k = r_k - y_k$, $\dot{v}_k = \dot{r}_k - \dot{y}_k$, $k = 1, 2, 3$. The random noise uniformly distributed on the interval $(-0.2, 0.2)$ is added to the right-hand side of (9). In order to obtain solutions of (9), corresponding finite difference equations are used with parameters $\alpha = 2$, $k = 1, 2, 3$, initial values of control inputs $u_1(0) = \eta_1 + 2$, $u_2(0) = \eta_2 + 4$, $u_3(0) = \eta_3 + 3$, where $\eta = (\eta_1, \eta_2, \eta_3)T$ are 150 normally distributed random numbers with mean zero, variance one and standard deviation one, and time steps $\Delta t_k = 0.002$ $k = 1, 2, 3$, respectively. Elements $\dot{r}_k$ in these difference equations are computed as first-order finite differences. In the difference equations, equality $u_k = v_k$, $k = 1, 2, 3$ have been replaced with inequality $|u_k - v_k| \leq 0.001\ |v_k|$. The reference trajectory $r = (r_1, r_2, r_3)^T$ and different tracking trajectories $z = (z_1, z_2, z_3)^T$ in 3D space in normalized units are shown in Fig. 4. As it can be seen in Fig. 4, the tracking trajectories converge to the reference trajectory starting from each initial value $z(0) = (z_1(0), z_2(0), z_3(0))^T$.

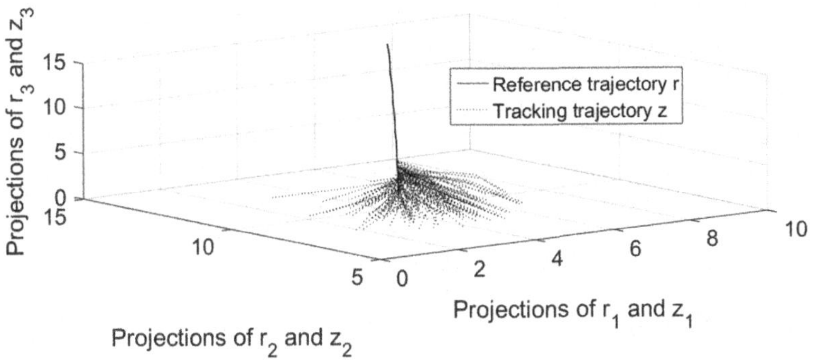

Fig. 4. The trajectory of the reference r and trajectories z of the tracking control NC in 3D space obtained by using difference equations corresponding (9), (28), (29), (30) and by (31) – Example 3.

6 Conclusions

The design and analysis of continuous-time NC model of adaptive robust tracking control for unknown nonlinear dynamic systems is presented. The circuit is described by the first-order differential equation with variable structure and by output equation. It provides finite convergence time to steady states and bounded tracking error, and does not need off-line learning phase. The convergence time can be controlled by given parameter of the circuit. For correct operation, the NC uses only the output of the system and the reference in order to minimize the trajectory tracking error. The circuit has simple architecture and can be used if the internal dynamics and parameters of the controlled system are unknown. This NC can be implemented in the parallel software and may be used in constructing accurate and flexible tracking controllers. Moreover, the circuit can be implemented in the parallel analog hardware if fast, compact and energy efficient tracking controller with a wide range of speed change is required. Computer simulations of the circuit application for tracking rotation angle optimal tracking of two-link planar elbow manipulator arm, for tracking control of changing laws of rotation angles of stepping motors of two axis azimuth/elevation solar tracking system, and for tracking control in 3D space confirm theoretical derivations and demonstrate its high operation performance. Thus, the presented continuous-time NC model can be used for designing efficient adaptive robust tracking controllers of unknown nonlinear dynamic systems.

References

1. Slotine, J.-J., Li, W.: Applied Nonlinear Control. Prentice-Hall, Englewood Cliffs (1991)
2. Sastry, S.: Nonlinear Systems Analysis, Stability, and Control. Springer, Heidelberg (1999). https://doi.org/10.1007/978-1-4757-3108-8
3. Naidu, D.: Optimal Control Systems. CRC Press, London (2003)
4. Lewis, F.L., Vrabie, D.L., Syrmos, V.L.: Optimal Control. Wiley, Hoboken (2012). https://doi.org/10.1002/9781118122631
5. Navabi, M., Mirzaei, H.: Robust optimal adaptive trajectory tracking control of quadrotor helicopter. Latin Am. J. Solids Struct. **14**, 1040–1063 (2017). https://doi.org/10.1590/1679-78253595
6. Perez-Cruz, J.H., Rubio, J.J., Ruiz-Velazquez, E., Solis-Perales, G.: Tracking control based on recurrent neural networks for nonlinear systems with multiple inputs and unknown dead zone. Abstract Appl. Anal. **2**, 1–18 (2012). https://doi.org/10.1155/2012/471281
7. Yen, H.-M., Li, T.-H.S., Chang, Y.-C.: Design of a robust neural network-based tracking controller for a class of electrically driven nonholonomic mechanical systems. Inf. Sci. **222**, 559–575 (2013). https://doi.org/10.1016/j.ins.2012.07.053
8. Khoo, S., Xie, L., Man, Z.: Robust finite-time consensus tracking algorithm for multirobot systems. IEEE/ASME Trans. Mechatron. **14**(2), 219–228 (2009). https://doi.org/10.1109/TMECH.2009.2014057
9. Zhand, H., Lewis, F.L.: Adaptive cooperative tracking control of higher-order nonlinear systems with unknown dynamics. Automatica **48**, 1432–1439 (2012). https://doi.org/10.1016/j.automatica.2012.05.008
10. Cichocki, A., Unbehauen, R.: Neural Networks for Optimization and Signal Processing. Wiley, New York (1993). https://doi.org/10.1002/acs.4480080309
11. Hornik, K., Stinchombe, M., White, H.: Multilayer feedforward networks are universal approximators. Neural Netw. **2**, 359–366 (1989). https://doi.org/10.1016/0893-6080(89)90020-8
12. Haykin, S.: Neural Networks and Learning Machines. Pearson, Ontario, Canada (2008)
13. Modares, H., Lewis, F.L., Jiang, Z.-P.: H_∞ tracking control of completely unknown continuous-time systems via off-policy reinforcement learning. IEEE Trans. Neural Netw. Learn. Syst. **26**(10), 2550–2562 (2015). https://doi.org/10.1109/tnnls.2015.2441749
14. Kamalapurkar, R., Dinh, H., Bhasin, S., Dixon, W.E.: Approximate optimal trajectory tracking for continuous-time nonlinear systems. Automatica **51**, 40–48 (2015). https://doi.org/10.1016/j.automatica.2014.10.103

15. Kiumarsi, B., Lewis, F.L.: Actor-critic based optimal tracking for partially unknown nonlinear discrete-time systems. IEEE Trans. Neural Netw. Learn. Syst. **26**(1), 140–151 (2015). https://doi.org/10.1109/tnnls.2014.2358227
16. Luo, Z. , Liu, H., Wu, X.: Artificial neural network computation on graphic process unit. In: IEEE International Joint Conference on Neural Networks, pp. 622–626. IEEE Press, Montreal (2005). https://doi.org/10.1109/ijcnn.2005.1555903
17. Prasanna, C.R., Pinjare, S.L.: Design and analog VLSI implementation of neural network architecture for signal processing. Eur. J. Sci. Res. **27**(2), 199–216 (2009)
18. Tymoshchuk, P., Shatnyi, S.: Hardware implementation design of analog neural rank-order filter. In: IEEE International Conference "Perspective Technologies and Methods in MEMS Design", pp. 88–91. IEEE Press, L'viv (2015)
19. Persidskii, S.K.: Problem of absolute stability. Autom. Remote Control **12**, 1889–1895 (1969)
20. Utkin, V.: Sliding modes in Control and Optimization. Springer-Verlag, Heidelberg (1992). https://doi.org/10.1007/978-3-642-84379-2
21. Edwards, C., Spurgeon, S.K.: Sliding mode Control: Theory and Applications. Taylor & Francis, New York (1998)
22. Coddington, E.A., Levinson, N.: Theory of Ordinary Differential Equations. McGraw- Hill, New York (1955)
23. Slotine, J.-J.E., Li, W.: Adaptive manipulator control: a case study. IEEE Trans. Autom. Control AC **33**(11), 995–1003 (1988). https://doi.org/10.1109/9.14411
24. Lewis, F.L., Yeşildirek, A., Liu, K.: Multilayer neural net robot controller with guaranteed tracking performance. IEEE Trans. Neural Netw. **7**(2), 388–399 (1996). https://doi.org/10.1109/72.485674
25. Eke, R., Senturk, A.: Performance comparison of a double-axis sun tracking versus fixed PV system. Sol. Energy **86**(9), 2665–2672 (2012). https://doi.org/10.1016/j.solener.2012.06.006
26. Panagopoulos, A.A., Chalkiadakis, G., Jennings, N.R.: Towards optimal solar tracking: a dynamic programming approach. In: IEEE International Conference on AAAI, pp. 695–701. IEEE Press, Austin (2015)
27. Alata, M., Al-Nimr, M.A., Qaroush, Y.: Developing a multipurpose sun tracking system using fuzzy control. Energy Convers. Manag. **46**, 1229–1245 (2005). https://doi.org/10.1016/j.enconman.2004.06.013
28. Tymoshchuk, P.V.: A fast analogue K-winners-take-all neural circuit. In: IEEE International Joint Conference on Neural Networks, pp. 882–889. IEEE Press, Dallas (2013). https://doi.org/10.1016/j.neunet.2013.01.013
29. Chua, L.O., Green, D.N.: Synthesis of nonlinear periodic systems. IEEE Trans. Circ. Syst. **21**(2), 286–294 (1974). https://doi.org/10.1109/TCS.1974.1083847

Author Index

Printed in the United States
By Bookmasters